FUNDAMENTAL ACCOUNTING PRINCIPLES

THIRTEENTH EDITION

KERMIT D. LARSON
University of Texas-Austin

PAUL B. W. MILLER
University of Colorado-Colorado Springs

IRWIN
Burr Ridge, Illinois
Boston, Massachusetts
Sydney, Australia

Part opening photos: Part I: © Mark Downey, Viesti Associates, Inc.
Part II: © Peter Bennett, Viesti Associates, Inc.
Part III: © Jay Maisel
Part IV: © Mark Weidman
Part VI: © Jay Maisel
Part VII: © Jay Maisel
Part VIII: © Jay Maisel
Part IX: © Jay Maisel

All chapter and appendix openers photographed by *Sharon Hoogstraten*. Styled by *Anne Dawson*.

Federal Express trademarks used by permission.
International Business Machines Corporation trademarks used by permission.
Lands' End, Inc. trademarks used by permission.
McDonald's Corporation trademarks used by permission.

Sponsoring editor:	Jeff Shelstad
Developmental editor:	Cheryl D. Wilson
Developmental editor, supplements:	Jackie Scruggs
Marketing manager:	Cindy L. Ledwith
Project editor:	Margaret Haywood
Production manager:	Irene H. Sotiroff
Designer:	Michael Warrell
Art manager:	Kim Meriwether
Photo research coordinator:	Patricia A. Seefelt
Compositor:	York Graphic Services
Typeface:	10/12 Times Roman
Printer:	Von Hoffmann Press

Library of Congress Cataloging-in-Publication Data

Larson, Kermit D.
Fundamental accounting principles/Kermit D. Larson, Paul B.W. Miller.—13th ed.
p. cm.
Includes bibliographical references.
ISBN 0-256-10128-0
1. Accounting. I. Miller, Paul B. W. II. Title.
HF5635.P975 1993
657—dc20 92–21073

Printed in the United States of America
3 4 5 6 7 8 9 0 VH 9 8 7 6 5 4

Dedicated to
Nancy, Julie, Tim, Cindy, Albrecht, and Megan
and to
Diana, David, and Greg

About the Authors

Kermit D. Larson is the Arthur Andersen & Co. Alumni Professor of Accounting at The University of Texas at Austin, where he has been a member of the faculty since 1966. He served as chairman of the U. T. Department of Accounting from 1971 to 1975 and was Visiting Associate Professor at Tulane University in 1970. His scholarly articles have been published in a variety of journals such as *The Accounting Review, Journal of Accountancy,* and *Abacus*. He is the author of several books, including *Financial Accounting,* published by Richard D. Irwin, Inc.

Professor Larson's professional activities range from service as chairman of the American Accounting Association's Committee on Concepts and Standards, vice president of the American Accounting Association, Southwest regional vice president of the AAA, and director of the AAA Doctoral Consortium, to member of the Constitutional Drafting Committee of the Federation of Schools of Accountancy and member of the Commission on Professional Accounting Education. He has served on the Accounting Accreditation Committee and on the Accounting Standards Committee of the AACSB and has been an expert witness on cases involving mergers, antitrust litigation, and expropriation of assets by foreign governments. Professor Larson has served on the board of directors and executive committee of Tekcon, Inc., the Strategic Planning Committee of the American Accounting Association, and the National Accountant's Advisory Board of Safeguard Business System, Inc. Presently he serves as president of the Richard D. Irwin Foundation.

Paul B. W. Miller is professor of accounting at The University of Colorado at Colorado Springs, where he has been a member of the faculty since 1988. After receiving his Ph.D. from The University of Texas at Austin, he joined the faculty of the University of Utah in 1972. His publications include articles in *The Journal of Accountancy, Accounting Horizons, Advances in Accounting, The Chartered Accountant in Australia, Research in Accounting Regulation,* and *Management Accounting*. He has written other books, including *Financial Accounting* and *The FASB: the People, the Process, and the Politics,* both published by Richard D. Irwin, Inc. In addition, he is the author of *Pension Accounting: A New Approach for Employers,* published by the American Institute of Certified Public Accountants. He received two Teaching Excellence Awards from the Beta Alpha Psi chapter of the University of Utah and, in 1991, received the first Outstanding Accounting Educator Award ever presented by the Colorado Society of CPAs.

In 1982–83, Professor Miller served as faculty fellow on the research and technical activities staff of the Financial Accounting Standards Board, where he worked on the conceptual framework and pension accounting projects. In 1987–88, he was the academic fellow in the office of the chief accountant of the Securities and Exchange Commission in Washington, D.C. He served three years as a member of the Technical Standards Subcommittee of the Ethics Executive Committee of the AICPA and has chaired and been a member of various committees of the American Accounting Association. He is licensed as a CPA by the state of Texas.

Preface

The tradition of *Fundamental Accounting Principles* includes clear explanations of accounting concepts and practices with closely related assignment material. Recent editions also reflect an educational philosophy we call *action learning*. We are firmly convinced that students learn most effectively when their study activities are designed to emphasize active behavior. The 13th edition continues this focus on the effective use of student study time.

By providing a wide variety of action-oriented items in the text and in support of the text, we hope to encourage student involvement within the classroom as well as during out-of-class study. Newly developed and thoroughly revised assignment materials provide an extensive basis for varied assignments that stimulate interest, promote a sense of accomplishment, show the real-world relevance of the subject matter, and sharpen the analytical and communications ability of each student. In addition, the study guides and the computerized tutorial give students a number of action-learning opportunities.

The *Fundamental Accounting Principles* package provides a fully integrated system for the first two-semester course at the college and university level. The system helps instructors and students meet the course objectives, which include providing a strong foundation for future courses in business and finance and initiating course work leading to a major and career in accounting. Both objectives are also served by the continuous development of the concepts that guide financial and managerial accounting practices.

Responses to the Accounting Education Change Commission

The 13th edition reflects many of the proposals of the AECC. A few examples include the integrated treatment of ethics, the revised overview of the accounting profession in Chapter 1, the expanded discussion of information systems in Chapter 6, and the analytical discussion of accounting concepts in Part V. Perhaps most notable is the inclusion of approximately 120 new problem assignments that require students to think analytically and to express their analyses in written essays. Many of the following features of the 13th edition respond to the AECC's objectives for the first accounting course.

Selected Features

Some of the key features of the 13th edition are listed in the following paragraphs.

"As a Matter of Fact" Articles. Several chapters contain newly selected excerpts from relevant articles that originally appeared in publications such as *Accounting Today, Forbes, Fortune,* and *The Wall Street Journal.*

"As a Matter of Ethics" Cases. Each chapter that contains a case entitled As a Matter of Ethics also includes a provocative problem requiring students to analyze and discuss the case. These problems are identified as As a Matter of Ethics: Essay. The AICPA's Code of Professional Conduct and the IMA's Standards of Ethical Conduct for Management Accountants are provided as resource material in Appendix L.

"As a Matter of Opinion" Interviews. A new feature in this edition, these inserts provide professional testimony about the relevance of the topical coverage to real-world decisions. Brief biographical sketches of the interviewees disclose the variety of career paths that relate to accounting.

Expanded Use of Visual Learning Aids. A significant number of new graphical illustrations have been created to appeal to today's students. These diagrams focus the readers' attention on relationships among concepts, actions, and financial measures.

Computer Systems and Assignments. Chapter 6 includes a new introduction to the computerized accounting systems used in today's businesses. In addition, a large number of homework assignments throughout the text are preloaded on the spreadsheet (SPATS) and general ledger (GLAS) software packages that are available with the text.

Excerpts and Assignments from Annual Reports. Most chapters contain a problem assignment related to the annual report of IBM in Appendix J. In addition, questions at the end of each chapter relate to the financial statements of McDonald's, Federal Express, and Lands' End contained in Appendix K.

Major Revision of Chapter 1. Essentially all of the sections in Chapter 1 have been thoroughly rewritten. We believe the revision is more interesting, more informative, and more effective in helping students prepare for the changing environment of accounting and business.

Part V. This separate learning unit describes the FASB's conceptual framework and now includes a presentation of the theoretical and practical dimensions of accounting measurement bases other than historical cost. The identification of this unit as Part V highlights its conceptual significance. Its placement between Chapters 13 and 14 facilitates its use as a capstone for the first semester or as a lead-in to the second semester.

Managerial Accounting

Perhaps the most significant revisions in this edition appear in the final eight chapters. During the last decade, many companies have begun to embrace a variety of new production management concepts that are affecting managerial accounting practices. These new concepts include customer orientation, total quality management, just-in-time manufacturing, the theory of constraints, and continuous improvement. As a result, many schools are putting more emphasis on managerial accounting in the principles course. We have responded to these developments with a major upgrade of the managerial accounting coverage in Chapters 20 through 27. The most important revisions are listed in the following paragraphs.

Introduction to Managerial Accounting. Chapter 20 opens with a thorough description of 10 differences between financial and managerial accounting, including their users, their purposes, their structures, and their reports. This discussion allows the course to make a clear transition from financial to managerial accounting.

Transparency Overlays. Following the very favorable response by adopters and students to the use of transparency overlays in Chapter 4 of the 12th edition, the 13th edition extends this form of presentation to Chapter 20. We use overlays to show the flows of materials, labor, and overhead information through the accounting system.

New Production Management Concepts. Chapter 21 begins with discussions of the new production management concepts listed earlier, with an emphasis on how they affect managers' needs for useful information. Subsequent chapters integrate these ideas in their presentations.

Separate Chapters on Job Order and Process Cost Accounting. To provide more thorough explanations of job order and process cost accounting systems, the 13th edition allocates a full chapter to each of these topics.

Parallel Examples. Chapters 20, 21, and 22 present parallel examples of production activities and the accounting records used to capture and report information about those events. The activities are represented in similar flowcharts and journal entries to clearly show how the same basic concepts are applied in increasingly complex situations.

Activity-Based Costing. Chapter 23 introduces the new topic of activity-based costing and contrasts it with traditional methods of cost allocation. The discussion focuses on the underlying concepts and advantages of the approach without undue attention to the mechanics.

Managerial Accounting for Service Oriented Businesses. Several of the managerial accounting chapters now include discussions showing the relevance of the topics to service businesses as well as manufacturing and merchandising businesses.

The Master Budget. Chapter 25 includes new flowcharts and illustrations that provide a clearer framework for understanding why and how the master budget is prepared. A new table ties together the sources of information used to develop the budgeted financial statements.

Management Decisions. Chapter 27 is now divided into two sections on capital budgeting and other management decisions. New discussions contrast alternative methods and new examples help the reader understand and apply the analytical tools described in the chapter.

Appendixes and End-of-Text Items

To provide instructors flexibility in planning course content, the 13th edition includes several appendixes. Those that clearly relate to a single chapter are placed at the end of the chapter. Others appear at the end of the book. Appendixes E, F, and I are new to this edition.

Appendix E. Located at the end of Chapter 12, this appendix explains accounting for deferred income taxes. It reflects the most basic requirements of FASB *Statement of Financial Accounting Standards No. 109,* which was issued in 1992.

Appendix F. Also at the end of Chapter 12, this appendix extends the chapter's discussion of payroll liabilities with a more detailed description of payroll records and procedures.

Appendix I. This appendix at the end of the book replaces the 12th edition's Chapter 28 with a concise discussion of federal income taxes.

Comprehensive List of Accounts Used in Exercises and Problems. This list exposes students to the large variety of accounts that companies use and that are needed to solve the exercises and problems provided in the text.

Professional Codes of Ethics. The AICPA's Code of Professional Conduct and the IMA's Standards of Ethical Conduct for Management Accountants are provided as a resource for students to use in preparing their answers to the ethics essay problems in the text.

Check Figures. In response to the request of adopters, the check figures are now listed at the end of the text.

New and Improved Supplements

Several new items have been added to the *Fundamental Accounting Principles* package and several others have been improved. New items include additional lecture enhancement videos, lecture review videos, additional practice sets, and a book of readings. Other significantly improved supplements include the General Ledger Applications Software (GLAS), the Solutions Manual, the Tutorial software, and Irwin's Computerized Testing Software. The test bank for the 13th edition has been substantially expanded. Also, the Working Papers now include forms for the exercises as well as the problems and alternate problems.

Acknowledgments

We are indebted to those adopters who maintained diaries as the basis for their thoughtful reviews and to several other reviewers who provided insight and extremely helpful criticisms. Many of the improvements in the 13th edition are based on the input from these reviewers. In addition, numerous adopters, students, and professional colleagues have made a variety of significant contributions and constructive suggestions. These individuals include:

Marilyn Allan, *Central Michigan University*
Sheila Ammons, *Austin Community College*
John Atella, *Harrisburg Area Community College*
Florence Atiase, *Austin Community College*
Sue Atkinson, *Tarleton State University*
Walter Bednar, *Luzerne County Community College*
Minta Berry, *Berry Publication Services*
Bruce Bridgman, *Community College of the Finger Lakes*
Alice P. Bursey, *Cedar Valley College of Dallas County Community College District*
Nora Coto Busby, *LeCroy Center of Ed. Telecommunications, Dallas County Community College District*
Pam Conrad, *Kirkwood Community College*
Alan Cronauer, *Herkimer County Community College*
Jim Crowther, *Kirkwood Community College*
J. Charles Cunningham, *Kirkwood Community College*
Doris deLespinasse, *Adrian College*
William J. Engel, Jr., *Longview Community College*
Anna Fowler, *The University of Texas at Austin*
Jessica Johnson Frazier, *Eastern Kentucky University*
Debra French, *Coopers & Lybrand*
Margie Hamilton, *Lewis and Clark Community College*
Betty S. Harper, *Middle Tennessee State University*
Phil Harper, *Middle Tennessee State University*
Linda Henderson, *University of South Carolina, Coastal Carolina*
Don Hester, *University of Alaska, Anchorage*
Norma Jean Hunting, *Heald Business College*
Christie W. Johnson, *Montana State University*
Ken Ketelhohn, *Milwaukee Area Technical College*
Frank Korman, *Mountain View College*
Terrie Kroshus, *Inver Hills Community College*
Cathy Xanthaky Larson, *Middlesex Community College*
Linda Lessing, *State University of New York, Farmingdale*

Terry Lindenberg, *Rock Valley College*
Leland E. Mansuetti, *Sierra College*
Kenneth Miller, *San Antonio College*
Timothy D. Miller, *El Camino College*
Laura Morgan, *Los Angeles Times*
Terri Niccum, *Los Angeles Times*
Sylvia Ong, *Maricopa Community College*
Anne M. Oppegard, *Augustana College, SD*
John F. Otto, *Grove City College*
L. J. Podsiadlik, *Oakland Community College*
Allan Reinstein, *Wayne State University*
George Ritchey, *Harrisburg Area Community College*
Tom Robinson, *University of Alaska, Fairbanks*
Fabiola Rubio, *El Paso Community College*
Stephen C. Schaefer, *Contra Costa College*
Joseph Schliep, *Normandale Community College*
Barbara A. Schnathorst, *University of Colorado, Colorado Springs*
Ed Schriefer, *Lewis and Clark Community College*
Eldon Shaefer, *Pacific Lutheran University*
Paul J. Shinal, *Cayuga County Community College*
Daniel P. Small, *J. Sargeant Reynolds Community College*
Dennis (Rocky) Spalazzi, *Bright Lights Productions, Inc.*
Linda Spalazzi, *Bright Lights Productions, Inc.*
John Spillner, *Pace University*
Charlene Spoede, *Baylor University*
Maurice Tassin, *Louisiana Tech University*
Jack E. Terry, *ComSource Associates, Inc.*
Mary Tharp, *Kirkwood Community College*
Leslie Thysell, *John Tyler Community College*
Frank Urbancic, *University of South Alabama*
Jacob Wambsganss, *Emporia State University*
Bill Wells, *Tulsa Junior College*
Kathleen A. Wessman, *Montgomery College*
Jeffrey R. Wright, *Johnson County Community College*
Carol Yacht, *Yavapai College*
Jack Zeller, *Kirkwood Community College*

We are especially indebted to our professional assistants, Betsey Jones, Sue Ann Meyer, and Barbara Schnathorst, for their unfailing and competent help in preparing the many manuscripts that make up this project.

Kermit D. Larson
Paul B. W. Miller

The Bridge

. . . to effective learning
. . . to full understanding
. . . to the language of business

Welcome to *Fundamental Accounting Principles*, your bridge to the world of business. This newest edition offers a wealth of special features to help you master accounting's basic principles and concepts. By listening to your instructor, participating in class, and actively studying the text, you will come away from the course with a solid understanding of accounting, the "language of business." Our hope is that the following learning tools will make your journey both exciting and educational.

CHAPTER 5

Accounting for a Merchandising Concern

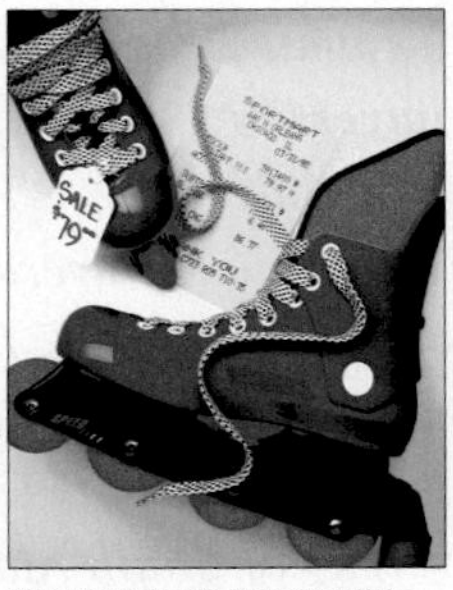

Whether they deal in roller blades or razor blades, many companies earn profits by buying merchandise and selling it to customers. Accounting helps managers determine the amount of income earned by these companies and the cost of the inventory they have on hand.

Topical Coverage

Chapter Opening Photo. A four-color photograph and its accompanying caption open every chapter. The collection of objects in the photo visually illustrate the chapter's key concepts.

Topical Coverage. An outline of the major topics provides a preview of the chapter's discussions.

248 *Part II Processing Accounting Data*

In previous chapters, we used illustrations of businesses that provided services to their customers, such as law firms, accounting firms, and real estate agencies. In this chapter, we shift our attention to merchandising businesses. These entities buy goods or products and then resell them to their customers. Your study of this chapter will focus on the problem of accounting for the goods that merchandising companies purchase for resale. You will learn to identify the elements of cost of goods sold and to complete the end-of-period accounting procedures used by merchandising companies, whether they are organized as corporations or proprietorships.

Learning Objectives

After studying Chapter 5, you should be able to:

1. Analyze and record transactions that involve the purchase and resale of merchandise.
2. Explain the nature of each item entering into the calculation of cost of goods sold and gross profit from sales.
3. Prepare a work sheet and the financial statements for a merchandising business that uses a periodic inventory system and that is organized as a corporation or as a single proprietorship.
4. Prepare adjusting and closing entries for a merchandising business organized as either a corporation or a single proprietorship.
5. Define or explain the words and phrases listed in the chapter glossary.

After studying Appendix C at the end of Chapter 5, you should be able to:

6. Explain the adjusting entry approach to accounting for inventories and prepare a work sheet, adjusting entries, and closing entries according to the adjusting entry approach.

The previous chapters have described the accounting records and financial statements of Jerry Dow, Attorney, which is a service enterprise. Other examples of service enterprises are laundries, taxi companies, airlines, financial planners, hair salons, theaters, and golf courses. Each provides a service to its customers for a commission, fare, or fee, and its net income is the difference between the revenues earned and the operating expenses incurred.

On the other hand, a merchandising company, whether a wholesaler or a retailer, earns revenue by buying and selling goods called merchandise. In such a company, net income results when revenue from sales exceeds the cost of the goods sold and the operating expenses, as follows:

Learning Objectives. Learning goals are listed after the chapter's introduction. Use them to give your studies direction and purpose. The learning objectives are repeated in the margin where relevant within the chapter. They are also tied to the summary and the end-of-chapter materials.

Illustrations. Charts, tables, sample forms, and diagrams clarify and summarize the textual discussion.

132 *Part II Processing Accounting Data*

ILLUSTRATION 3-1

Trial Balance Drawn from the Ledger of Jerry Dow, Attorney

JERRY DOW, ATTORNEY
Trial Balance
December 31, 1993

Cash	$ 650	
Office supplies	120	
Prepaid insurance	2,400	
Law library	2,880	
Office equipment	6,880	
Accounts payable		$ 760
Unearned legal fees		3,000
Jerry Dow, capital		9,000
Jerry Dow, withdrawals	1,100	
Legal fees earned		3,900
Salaries expense	1,400	
Rent expense	1,000	
Utilities expense	230	
Totals	$16,660	$16,660

The Adjustment Process

LO 2 Explain why adjustments are required by the revenue recognition and matching principles and why the accrual basis of accounting is preferred to a cash basis.

The adjustment process is based on two accounting principles, the *revenue recognition principle* and the matching principle. As explained in Chapter 1, the *revenue recognition principle* requires that revenue be reported in the income statement when it is earned, not before and not after. For most firms, revenue is earned at the time a service is rendered or a product is sold to the customer.

For example, if a lawyer renders legal services to a client during December, the legal fees are earned during December. According to the *revenue recognition principle*, the lawyer must report these legal fees as revenue on the December income statement, even though the cash receipt from the client may take place in November or January. In cases such as this, the adjustment process assigns the revenue to December, when it was earned.

The *matching principle* requires reporting expenses on the income statement in the same accounting period as the revenues that were earned as a result of the expenses. For example, assume that a business uses an office to earn revenues during December. According to the *revenue recognition principle*, the business must report the revenues on the December income statement. One expense the business incurred in the pursuit of those December revenues was the December office rent. Therefore, the *matching principle* requires reporting the rent for December on the December income statement. This must be done even if the December rent was paid in November (or in January). In such cases, the adjustment process is used to match the cost of December's rent with the revenues earned during December.

AS A MATTER OF
Opinion

Ms. Smith received her B.A. in accounting from the University of Colorado at Colorado Springs. She is the managing director of Strait Kushinsky and Company, a large public accounting firm in Colorado Springs. Among her partners is Marvin Strait, former chairman of the American Institute of CPAs. She is presently the chairperson of the Colorado Springs Chamber of Commerce, and serves on the governing boards of the American Group of CPAs and the Christian Management Association.

Brenda Smith, CPA

Successful business managers need information, and they need computers to get it for them. Yet, many people are still held back by a fear of computers. We need to learn to be as comfortable with computers as we are with our calculators.

The systems available to today's small businesses are great savers of time and effort. For example, many banks and businesses have linked their computers. This system instantly records deposits to a store's checking account and updates its sales and inventory records at the same time. A lot of paperwork is eliminated, and managers and employees can devote their skills to the business instead of bookkeeping.

Despite the abilities of these new systems, we have to know the appropriate accounting principles to avoid getting "garbage-in-garbage-out" results. While we don't need to understand how to program computers, we do need a basic understanding of their processes. And, we need to understand accounting so that we can make them work for us.

Computers and integrated software programs have dramatically reduced the bookkeeping tasks in accounting. However, do not think that computers have eliminated the need for accountants. Nor should you conclude that success in business no longer requires a knowledge of accounting. *The need for accountants and accounting knowledge is created by the need for information, not by the need for pencil and paper.* Accountants continue to be in demand because their expertise is necessary to determine ... information ... hat data should be us... ...nts

As a Matter of Opinion. New to this edition are interviews with individuals who use accounting information in the performance of their jobs. This feature clearly shows how information you learn in the classroom applies to the working world.

As a Matter of Fact. Excerpts of articles from publications such as *Fortune* and *The Wall Street Journal* show the relevance of accounting topics to contemporary business issues.

AS A MATTER OF
Fact

Cash: Once Trash, Now Treasure

Ex-billionaire Donald Trump knows a hot idea when he hears one. Several months ago, when he was trying to unload the Trump shuttle, he announced that cash was in, debt was out. Poor Donald—if only he had put his money where his mouth was, he wouldn't be in hock to banks and bondholders today.

In the decade of debt financing, cash was trash. It wasn't smart to sit with it when other assets were going to the moon. But in the past 12 months, everything except cash has come crashing down to earth. Mergers and acquisitions are off nearly 50% because few corporations can borrow the money to swing a deal. Reputable real estate developers are going bust, and heavily mortgaged homeowners cannot afford to sell at rock-bottom prices. Meanwhile, cash in the form of Treasury bills is returning a steady 7% to 8%.

The ascendancy of cash implies that credit will be tighter in the Nineties than in the Eighties. Lenders will discriminate against corporations with weak balance sheets, putting them at a competitive disadvantage. Compare Nordstrom, the well-financed Seattle-based department store chain that is steadily expanding, with R. H. Macy, which is selling equity and trying to shed assets to pay down debt.

For homeowners and commercial real estate developers, King Cash means that property prices will likely remain depressed. Why? Explains investment banker Lewis Ranieri, chairman of Ranieri Wilson & Co.: "In today's environment, where asset values are falling, tighter credit standards are being imposed." Take, for example, a $100 million office building. In the good old days of debt, you could finance its purchase by putting up only 5% cash—$5 million. Today, not only has the value of the property fallen to, say, $60 million, but a potential buyer must also come up with 25% cash—$15 million. That's a high enough hurdle to forestall any rapid recovery in real estate.

The implications of cash as an appreciating asset may not be pretty. James Grant, for one, thinks that deflation—that rare bird not seen on the American continent since the 1930s—is a distinct possibility. Says he: "If people decide that cash is a better store of value, then prices for houses and companies can only decline further. Potential buyers will demand that sellers capitulate on price before they will exchange the safety of cash for the illiquidity of other assets."

Source: Brett D. Fromson, *Fortune*, January 14, 1991, pp. 54 and 58.

responsibility for making all change. Alternatively, the business can use a register with separate cash drawers for each operator.

Maintain Adequate Records

... ...ening system ... ...mploy-

AS A MATTER OF
Ethics

Bill Pena is the accountant for Cryer Company. Just before Pena prepared the adjusting entries to record accrued expenses at the end of the company's first year of operations, he was called into the company president's office. The president asked about the accrued expenses and then told Pena not to make the adjustments. Although Pena expressed concern about these instructions, the president said that because the bills will not be received until January, they should not be reported as expenses until the next year.

In addition, the president asked how much this year's revenues will be increased by the purchase order recently received from Broker Company. Pena explained that there will be no effect on sales until January because Broker Company will not take delivery until after the first of the year. The president was exasperated and pointed out that the order had already been received and Cryer was ready to make the deliveries. Even though Broker Company's order indicated that the merchandise should not be delivered until late January, the president told Pena to record the sale in December.

Pena knows that the combination of recording the sale to Broker Company and not accruing the expenses will increase the reported income by a large amount and is not sure what to do. He also wonders what reaction the company's auditors will have when they review the adjustments. What should Pena do?

accounts payable also bear interest.) Interest expense is incurred with the passage of time. Therefore, unless the interest has been paid and recorded on the last day of the accounting period, some additional interest will have accrued since the last payment date. Record this accrued interest with an adjusting entry similar to the preceding entry to record accrued salaries.

Accrued Revenues

Many revenues are recorded when cash is received. Others are recorded at the time the goods or services are sold on credit and a bill is given to the customer.

As a Matter of Ethics. These brief scenarios illustrate the many ethical challenges faced by accounting professionals. End-of-chapter questions related to these cases are presented to help you understand the ramifications of various courses of action.

Recording invoices at their net amounts supplies management with useful information about the amount of discounts missed through oversight, carelessness, or some other reason. Thus, this practice gives management better control over the people responsible for paying bills on time so that cash discounts can be taken. When the accounts record the fact that discounts are missed, someone has to explain why. As a result, it is likely that fewer discounts are lost through carelessness.

Summary of the Chapter in Terms of Learning Objectives

LO 1. The liquidity of an asset refers to how easily the asset can be converted into other types of assets or used to buy services or satisfy obligations. Cash is the most liquid asset. To increase their return, companies may invest their idle cash balances in cash equivalents. These investments are readily convertible to a known amount of cash and are purchased so close to their maturity date that their market values are relatively insensitive to interest rate changes.

LO 2. Internal control systems are designed to encourage adherence to prescribed managerial policies. In doing so, they promote operational efficiencies, and protect assets against theft or misuse. They also help ensure that accurate and reliable accounting data are produced. Principles of good internal control include establishing clear responsibilities, maintaining adequate records, insuring assets and bonding employees, separating record-keeping and custody of assets, dividing responsibilities for related transactions, using mechanical devices whenever practicable, and performing regular independent reviews of internal control practices.

LO 3. To maintain control over cash, custody must be separated from record-keeping for cash. All cash receipts should be deposited intact in the bank on a daily basis, and all payments (except for minor petty cash payments) should be made by check. A voucher system helps maintain control over cash disbursements by ensuring that payments are made only after full documentation

Summary. A recap of the main ideas presented concludes every chapter. All summary points are keyed to the opening learning objectives. The list format makes it an excellent review tool.

Demonstration Problem with Solution. Each chapter includes an illustrative example that shows how the chapter's concepts are applied in problem-solving. *Planning the Solution* shows you the steps that should be taken to arrive at the correct answer. This is followed by the complete solution to the problem.

Demonstration Problem

The December 31, 1993, adjusted trial balance of Westside Appliance Repair, Inc., is as follows:

Cash	$ 83,300	
Accounts receivable	45,000	
Notes receivable	60,000	
Prepaid insurance	19,000	
Prepaid rent	5,000	
Equipment	165,000	
Accumulated depreciation, equipment		$ 52,000
Accounts payable		37,000
Income taxes payable		21,500
Long-term notes payable		58,000
Common stock		55,000
Retained earnings		99,000
Cash dividends declared	75,000	
Repair services revenue		420,000
Interest earned		6,500
Depreciation expense, equipment	26,000	
Wages expense	179,000	
Rent expense	47,000	
Insurance expense	7,000	
Interest expense	4,700	
Income taxes expense	33,000	
	$749,000	$749,000

Required

1. Prepare closing entries for Westside Appliance Repair, Inc.
2. Prepare a post-closing trial balance for the business.
3. Set up a Retained Earnings account, and post all necessary amounts to the account.

Solution to Demonstration Problem

Planning the Solution

- Examine the adjusted trial balance and identify all of the nominal accounts that must be closed.
- Prepare entries to close the revenue accounts to Income Summary, to close the expense accounts to Income Summary, to close Income Summary to Retained Earnings, and to close Cash Dividends Declared to Retained Earnings.
- List the permanent accounts with their balances on the post-closing trial balance, using the post-closing balance for the Retained Earnings account.

Glossary

LO 7 Define or explain the words and phrases listed in the chapter glossary.

Accounting cycle the recurring accounting steps performed each accounting period beginning with the recording of transactions and proceeding through posting the recorded amounts, preparing an unadjusted trial balance and completing a work sheet, journalizing and posting adjusting entries, preparing the financial statements, journalizing and posting closing entries, and preparing a post-closing trial balance. pp. 210–12

Cash Dividends Declared a temporary account that serves the same function for a corporation as does a withdrawals account for a proprietorship, and which is closed to Retained Earnings at the end of each accounting period. p. 207

Closing entries entries made at the end of each accounting period to establish zero balances in the temporary accounts and to transfer the temporary account balances to a capital account or accounts or to the Retained Earnings account. pp. 194–99

Date of declaration the date on which a dividend is declared by vote of a corporation's board of directors. p. 208

Date of payment the date on which a dividend liability of a corporation is satisfied by mailing checks to the stockholders. p. 208

Date of record the date on which the stockholders who are listed in a corporation's records are determined to be those who will receive a dividend. p. 208

Deficit a negative amount (debit balance) of retained earnings. pp. 209–10

Income Summary the account used in the closing process to summarize the amounts of revenues and expenses, and from which the amount of the net income or loss is transferred to the owner's capital account in a single proprietorship, or to the partners' capital accounts in a partnership, or to the Retained Earnings account in a corporation. p. 194

Nominal accounts another name for *temporary accounts*. p. 199

Permanent accounts accounts that remain open as long as the asset, liability, or owner's equity items recorded in the accounts continue in existence; therefore, accounts that appear on the balance sheet. p. 199

Post-closing trial balance a trial balance prepared after all adjusting and closing entries

Glossary. Key terms are briefly defined at the end of each chapter. Page references indicate where they are discussed. All glossary terms are highlighted in color in the index.

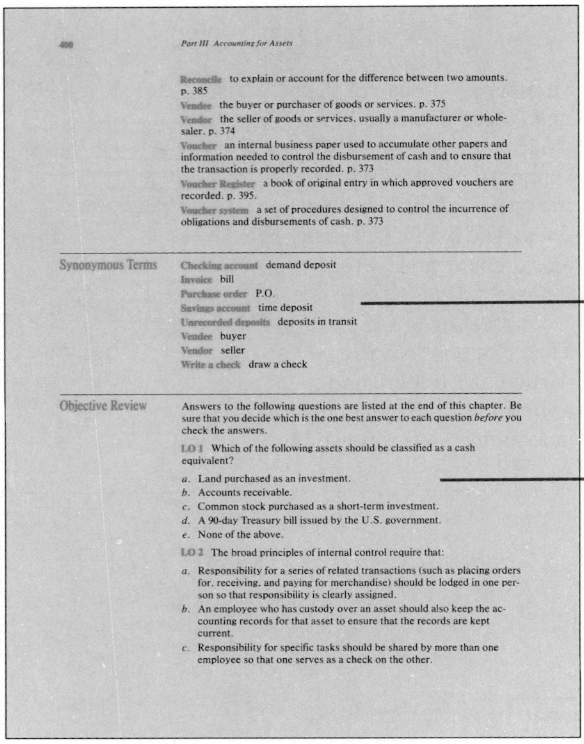

400 *Part III Accounting for Assets*

Reconcile to explain or account for the difference between two amounts. p. 385

Vendee the buyer or purchaser of goods or services. p. 375

Vendor the seller of goods or services, usually a manufacturer or wholesaler. p. 374

Voucher an internal business paper used to accumulate other papers and information needed to control the disbursement of cash and to ensure that the transaction is properly recorded. p. 373

Voucher Register a book of original entry in which approved vouchers are recorded. p. 395.

Voucher system a set of procedures designed to control the incurrence of obligations and disbursements of cash. p. 373

Synonymous Terms

Checking account demand deposit
Invoice bill
Purchase order P.O.
Savings account time deposit
Unrecorded deposits deposits in transit
Vendee buyer
Vendor seller
Write a check draw a check

Objective Review

Answers to the following questions are listed at the end of this chapter. Be sure that you decide which is the one best answer to each question *before* you check the answers.

LO 1 Which of the following assets should be classified as a cash equivalent?

a. Land purchased as an investment.
b. Accounts receivable.
c. Common stock purchased as a short-term investment.
d. A 90-day Treasury bill issued by the U.S. government.
e. None of the above.

LO 2 The broad principles of internal control require that:

a. Responsibility for a series of related transactions (such as placing orders for, receiving, and paying for merchandise) should be lodged in one person so that responsibility is clearly assigned.
b. An employee who has custody over an asset should also keep the accounting records for that asset to ensure that the records are kept current.
c. Responsibility for specific tasks should be shared by more than one employee so that one serves as a check on the other.

Synonymous Terms. A list of terms that are often used interchangeably follows the glossary.

Objective Review. See how well you understood the chapter's major concepts by taking the mini-quiz at its end. Since each question is tied to the learning objectives, you quickly see how well you accomplished the chapter goals.

Real-World Emphasis. Questions relating to the business operations of actual companies—Lands' End, Federal Express, IBM, and McDonald's—appear in nearly every chapter. For easy identification, the company logos appear in the margin opposite the questions.

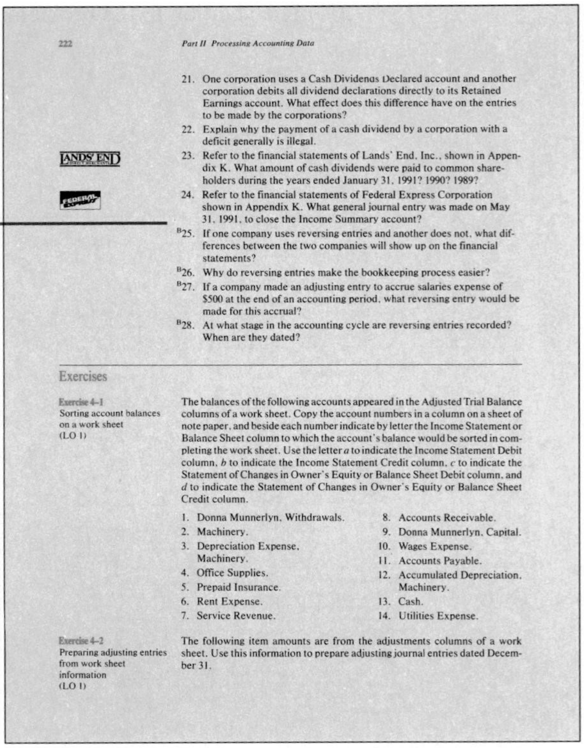

222 *Part II Processing Accounting Data*

21. One corporation uses a Cash Dividenas Declared account and another corporation debits all dividend declarations directly to its Retained Earnings account. What effect does this difference have on the entries to be made by the corporations?
22. Explain why the payment of a cash dividend by a corporation with a deficit generally is illegal.
23. Refer to the financial statements of Lands' End, Inc., shown in Appendix K. What amount of cash dividends were paid to common shareholders during the years ended January 31, 1991? 1990? 1989?
24. Refer to the financial statements of Federal Express Corporation shown in Appendix K. What general journal entry was made on May 31, 1991, to close the Income Summary account?

[B]25. If one company uses reversing entries and another does not, what differences between the two companies will show up on the financial statements?
[B]26. Why do reversing entries make the bookkeeping process easier?
[B]27. If a company made an adjusting entry to accrue salaries expense of $500 at the end of an accounting period, what reversing entry would be made for this accrual?
[B]28. At what stage in the accounting cycle are reversing entries recorded? When are they dated?

Exercises

Exercise 4–1
Sorting account balances on a work sheet
(LO 1)

The balances of the following accounts appeared in the Adjusted Trial Balance columns of a work sheet. Copy the account numbers in a column on a sheet of note paper, and beside each number indicate by letter the Income Statement or Balance Sheet column to which the account's balance would be sorted in completing the work sheet. Use the letter *a* to indicate the Income Statement Debit column, *b* to indicate the Income Statement Credit column, *c* to indicate the Statement of Changes in Owner's Equity or Balance Sheet Debit column, and *d* to indicate the Statement of Changes in Owner's Equity or Balance Sheet Credit column.

1. Donna Munnerlyn, Withdrawals.
2. Machinery.
3. Depreciation Expense, Machinery.
4. Office Supplies.
5. Prepaid Insurance.
6. Rent Expense.
7. Service Revenue.
8. Accounts Receivable.
9. Donna Munnerlyn, Capital.
10. Wages Expense.
11. Accounts Payable.
12. Accumulated Depreciation, Machinery.
13. Cash.
14. Utilities Expense.

Exercise 4–2
Preparing adjusting entries from work sheet information
(LO 1)

The following item amounts are from the adjustments columns of a work sheet. Use this information to prepare adjusting journal entries dated December 31.

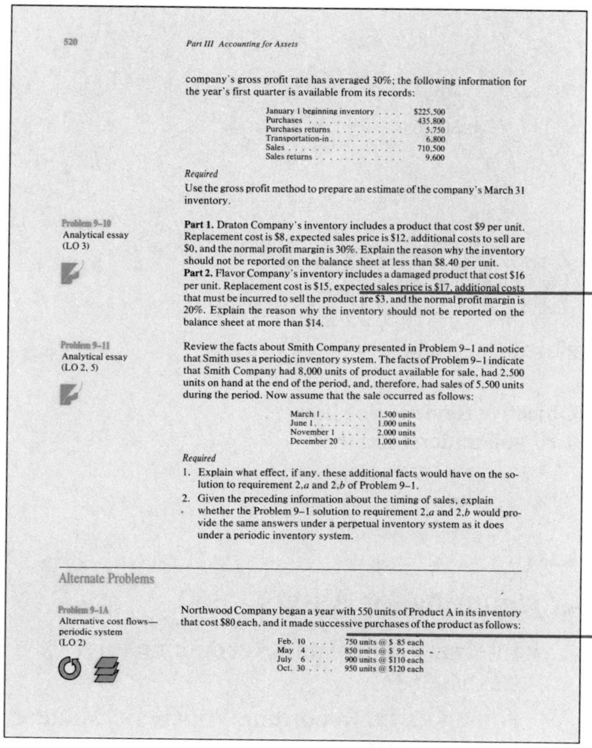

520 *Part III Accounting for Assets*

company's gross profit rate has averaged 30%; the following information for the year's first quarter is available from its records:

January 1 beginning inventory	$225,500
Purchases	435,800
Purchases returns	5,750
Transportation-in	6,800
Sales	710,500
Sales returns	9,600

Required

Use the gross profit method to prepare an estimate of the company's March 31 inventory.

Problem 9–10
Analytical essay
(LO 3)

Part 1. Draton Company's inventory includes a product that cost $9 per unit. Replacement cost is $8, expected sales price is $12, additional costs to sell are $0, and the normal profit margin is 30%. Explain the reason why the inventory should not be reported on the balance sheet at less than $8.40 per unit.
Part 2. Flavor Company's inventory includes a damaged product that cost $16 per unit. Replacement cost is $15, expected sales price is $17, additional costs that must be incurred to sell the product are $3, and the normal profit margin is 20%. Explain the reason why the inventory should not be reported on the balance sheet at more than $14.

Problem 9–11
Analytical essay
(LO 2, 5)

Review the facts about Smith Company presented in Problem 9–1 and notice that Smith uses a periodic inventory system. The facts of Problem 9–1 indicate that Smith Company had 8,000 units of product available for sale, had 2,500 units on hand at the end of the period, and, therefore, had sales of 5,500 units during the period. Now assume that the sale occurred as follows:

March 1	1,500 units
June 1	1,000 units
November 1	2,000 units
December 20	1,000 units

Required

1. Explain what effect, if any, these additional facts would have on the solution to requirement 2,*a* and 2,*b* of Problem 9–1.
2. Given the preceding information about the timing of sales, explain whether the Problem 9–1 solution to requirement 2,*a* and 2,*b* would provide the same answers under a perpetual inventory system as it does under a periodic inventory system.

Alternate Problems

Problem 9–1A
Alternative cost flows—periodic system
(LO 2)

Northwood Company began a year with 550 units of Product A in its inventory that cost $80 each, and it made successive purchases of the product as follows:

Feb. 10	750 units @ $ 85 each
May 4	850 units @ $ 95 each
July 6	900 units @ $110 each
Oct. 30	950 units @ $120 each

Analytical Essay. These questions give you the opportunity to develop both your communication and reasoning skills. They ask you to reflect on a particular situation and then to provide a written analysis in response to the questions posed.

Software Problems. End-of-chapter material solvable using *GLAS* (General Ledger Applications Software) or *SPATS* (Spreadsheet Applications Template Software) are identified by these symbols.

Provocative Problems. These are the most challenging of the end-of-chapter materials, requiring you to find solutions to more complex accounting problems. The majority of the chapters include a Provocative Problem tied to IBM's 1990 annual report. The IBM problems will allow you to apply what you've learned to an actual business situation.

As a Matter of Ethics: Essay. Accounting is far more than crunching numbers, as these questions illustrate. Directly related to the ethics cases in the chapters, they allow you to explore accounting's human factor. In a written essay you will explain how, in your opinion, the problems faced by the individuals in the scenarios should be handled and why.

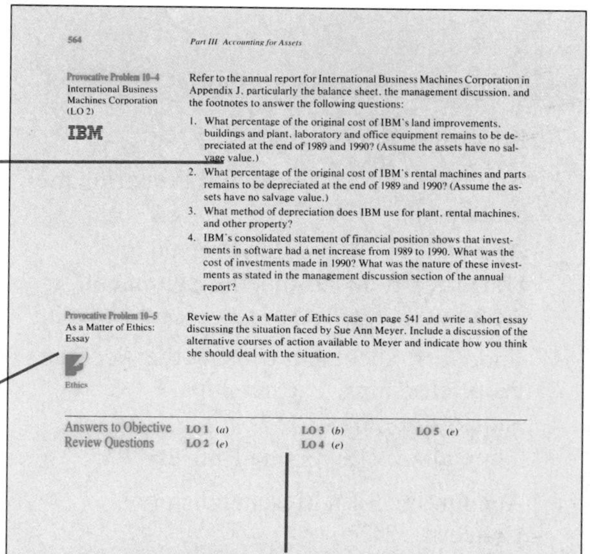

564 *Part III Accounting for Assets*

Provocative Problem 10–4
International Business Machines Corporation
(LO 2)
IBM

Refer to the annual report for International Business Machines Corporation in Appendix J, particularly the balance sheet, the management discussion, and the footnotes to answer the following questions:

1. What percentage of the original cost of IBM's land improvements, buildings and plant, laboratory and office equipment remains to be depreciated at the end of 1989 and 1990? (Assume the assets have no salvage value.)
2. What percentage of the original cost of IBM's rental machines and parts remains to be depreciated at the end of 1989 and 1990? (Assume the assets have no salvage value.)
3. What method of depreciation does IBM use for plant, rental machines, and other property?
4. IBM's consolidated statement of financial position shows that investments in software had a net increase from 1989 to 1990. What was the cost of investments made in 1990? What was the nature of these investments as stated in the management discussion section of the annual report?

Provocative Problem 10–5
As a Matter of Ethics: Essay
Ethics

Review the As a Matter of Ethics case on page 541 and write a short essay discussing the situation faced by Sue Ann Meyer. Include a discussion of the alternative courses of action available to Meyer and indicate how you think she should deal with the situation.

Answers to Objective Review Questions
LO 1 (*a*) LO 3 (*b*) LO 5 (*e*)
LO 2 (*e*) LO 4 (*e*)

Answers to Objective Review Questions. The answers to the chapter's mini-quiz appear here.

Contents in Brief

Contents

PART II

Processing Accounting Data 72

FUNDAMENTAL ACCOUNTING PRINCIPLES

PART

I

Introduction

In one form or another, accounting touches everyone's life. Young people add and subtract figures to decide how to spend their weekly allowances. Newspaper carriers keep records of payments by their customers. Students determine where the money for their education is coming from and how to spend it. Taxpayers account for their taxable income and deductions. And, businesses account for what they own and owe, and the profits they make from their operations. In fact, all of us use accounting information to make financial decisions of one kind or another.

As you study this text, a new world of understanding and knowledge will unfold for you. Because of what you learn about accounting, you will be better prepared to earn a living and to live on what you earn. You will also find more meaning in news stories about such things as a company that has achieved record high sales and profits or another that faces bankruptcy. In other words, what you learn will give you useful and productive skills that will help you understand much more about the business world and the role accounting information plays in our economy.

Part I of *Fundamental Accounting Principles* consists of:

To the Student Reader

Fundamental Accounting Principles is designed to get you actively involved in the learning process so that you will learn quickly and more thoroughly. The more time you spend expressing what you are learning, the more effectively you will learn. In accounting, you do this primarily by answering questions and solving problems. However, you can also express your ideas by using the wide margins for taking notes, summarizing a phrase, or writing down a question that remains unanswered in your mind. These notes will assist in your later review of the material, and the simple process of writing them will help you learn.

As you read the text, you will learn many important new terms. In addition to being defined and discussed in the chapter, these terms are defined in a glossary at the end of each chapter. You will find these terms printed in teal in the glossary and in the text where they are defined. The glossary is a good place to begin your review of important concepts. You can also find the key terms in the index at the back of the book.

To guide your study, learning objectives are listed at the beginning of each chapter, repeated in the margins next to the related topics throughout the chapter, and used as the basis for summarizing the chapter. The exercises and problems are also coded in terms of these objectives.

Other special features of the book include excerpts from news articles entitled "As a Matter of Fact." These relate real-world events to the material in the chapter. You also will find brief cases entitled "As a Matter of Ethics," which will help you think about the ethical aspects of accounting. In brief inserts called "As a Matter of Opinion," business and community leaders tell how they use accounting in their decisions.

The use of color in the book has been carefully planned to facilitate your learning. All of the textual headings are printed in teal as are important new terms where they are being defined. Teal also identifies the learning objectives. The colors in the illustrations have been selected to help you distinguish between different types of concepts and graphical entities. A cream background identifies the "As a Matter of Ethics," "As a Matter of Fact," and "As a Matter of Opinion" elements. The ethics cases are set off with a small blue box at the top, the fact cases with a green box, and the opinions with a purple. All financial reports, which are the output of the accounting process, are cream. A soft, noninterruptive teal color is used as a background in the illustrations and the end-of-chapter material. A light cream background identifies the comprehensive problems.

Each chapter contains a demonstration problem and related solution that illustrate many of the issues discussed in the chapter. There is also a short section entitled "Objective Review" that contains a series of multiple-choice questions related to the learning objectives. Answer them as a quick test of your learning. Then check your answers against the correct ones listed at the end of the chapter.

Ethics: The Most Fundamental Accounting Principle

"Each person capable of making moral decisions is responsible for making his own decisions. The ultimate locus of moral responsibility is in the individual."[1]

As college students, you no doubt realize that ethics and ethical behavior are important features of civilized society. Ethical considerations abound in daily life, both privately and professionally. The media often remind us of the importance of ethics to society. These reminders come in the form of news stories about such things as civil rights violations, fraudulent attempts to rip off the elderly, credit card scams, parents who fail to make child support payments, children who ignore or abuse their elderly parents, politicians who fail to disclose past instances of misconduct, the alleged bribery of government officials, and Wall Street moguls who use inside information for personal gain.

The Meaning of Ethics

As a discipline of study, ethics deals "with what is good and bad or right and wrong or with moral duty and obligation." In practice, ethics are "principles of conduct that govern an individual or a profession."[2] Some unethical actions are unlawful. Other actions may be within the law but, nevertheless, are widely recognized as being ethically wrong. In addition, some actions are not clearly right or wrong but are ethically questionable.

Many of the issues we face in school, in the workplace, and beyond have ethical dimensions; they are unavoidable aspects of life. How well we deal with ethical matters influences how we feel about ourselves, how we are perceived by others, and in the aggregate, the quality of our society. But why begin an accounting text with a prologue on ethics? How do ethics relate to business, and more specifically, to the discipline of accounting?

Ethics in Business

To answer the question of why we begin this text with a prologue on ethics, we must recognize that ethical standards in business and accounting are a matter of public concern. In recent years, many people have expressed concern about deteriorating ethical standards in business. For example, a recently conducted opinion survey on business ethics included over 1,100 business executives, deans of business schools, and members of Con-

[1] Harold H. Titus and Morris Keeton, *Ethics for Today,* 4th ed. (New York: American Book–Stratford Press, 1966), p. 131.

[2] *Webster's Third New International Dictionary of the English Language, Unabridged* (Springfield, Mass.: G & C Merriam Co., 1971), p. 780.

gress. Of those in the survey, 94% agreed that "the business community is troubled by ethical problems."[3] Ironically, those surveyed also believed that companies that are successful over the long run seem to have high ethical standards. You may infer from this that "ethics is good business." Ethical business practices can help create loyal customers and suppliers, trustworthy and productive employees, and a solid reputation.

Because of the widespread public interest in business ethics, many banks, insurance companies, and other businesses have recently revised or written new codes of ethics. Others are currently in the process of developing new codes of ethics. Companies generally use these codes as public statements of their commitment to ethical business practices and also as guides for employees to follow.

Ethics in Accounting

In accounting, many professional organizations such as the American Institute of Certified Public Accountants and the Institute of Management Accountants have had codes of ethics for years. Most of these codes have been reevaluated and revised in recent years. Ethics is important in accounting because accountants often are required to make decisions that have ethical implications. The activities performed by accountants have a profound impact on many individuals, businesses, and other institutions. An accountant's decisions can affect such things as the amount of money a corporation distributes to its stockholders; the price a buyer pays for a business enterprise; the compensation levels of managers and executives; the success or failure of specific products and divisions; and the amount of local, state, and federal taxes paid by an individual or a business.

To see how an accountant's decisions can have an ethical dimension, consider the following example. Assume that Smith and Jones agreed to be partners in a business venture that would last two years. Because the original idea for the business venture was Smith's, they agreed that Smith would receive 75% of the first year's profits and Jones would receive 25%. In the second year, however, their agreement was that Smith and Jones would split the profits evenly. At the end of the first year, their accountant discovers that there are two alternative methods for recording a recent transaction. If method A is used, a profit of $100,000 will be recognized in year 1. If method B is used, the profit of $100,000 will not be recognized until year 2. Clearly, the accountant's decision about which method should be used will affect each partner's compensation. If method A is used, Smith will receive $75,000 of the profit and Jones will receive $25,000. But if method B is used, each partner will receive $50,000.

In this example, more information is needed to help the accountant choose between methods A and B. As an ethical matter, however, the accountant's decision should not be influenced by the fact that method A is more favorable to Smith and method B is more favorable to Jones.

The preceding example is not unusual. Accountants are frequently called on to choose between alternative methods for recognizing profits. These decisions cannot be made lightly because, as the example shows, the decisions may shift wealth from one party to another.

Another aspect of accounting that illustrates the importance of ethical behavior involves the issue of confidentiality. Accountants, by the very nature of their duties, frequently work with private, confidential information. For example, accountants have access to individual salary records, future business plans and budgets, and a variety of information about the financial status of their clients or employers. As an ethical matter, accountants must respect and maintain the confidentiality of this information.

The Ethical Challenge

As you proceed in your study of accounting, you will encounter many other situations in which ethical considerations are important. We encourage you to seek out and explore any ethical issues that may arise. Accounting must be done ethically if it is to be an effective tool in the service of society. This is, perhaps, the most fundamental principle of accounting.

[3] Touche Ross & Co., *Ethics in American Business* (New York, 1988), pp. 1–2.

AS A MATTER OF

Opinion

Mr. Finkston received his B.A. in accounting from Brooklyn College and his J.D. from Brooklyn Law School. He is a member of the New York State Bar and was a public accountant early in his career. Since 1979, he has been the director of the Division of Professional Ethics of the American Institute of CPAs.

Herbert A. Finkston, CPA

The accounting profession has earned high regard because of its ethical standards. Our standards require ethical behavior in our relationships with our clients and our employers. They also require ethical behavior in our dealings with the public and its interests. And, our standards require us to render high-quality professional services. By adhering to the concepts of objectivity, integrity, and independence, and by continued striving for quality, the profession has won a respected place in the entire business community and among the other professions.

As a student of accounting, be aware of the ethical implications of all that you study. As a member of the accounting profession, or any other profession, practice ethics in all that you do. By doing so, you will bring honor to yourself and your profession.

Ethical decisions and the development of ethical standards are areas in your life where you are in control. Each one of us as an individual is free to shape our own moral positions. Adapting a phrase originally spoken by Supreme Court Justice Earl Warren in reference to the law: ''In civilized life, [accounting] floats on a sea of ethics.'' It is your choice how you elect to navigate this sea.

CHAPTER

1

Accounting: An Introduction to Its Concepts

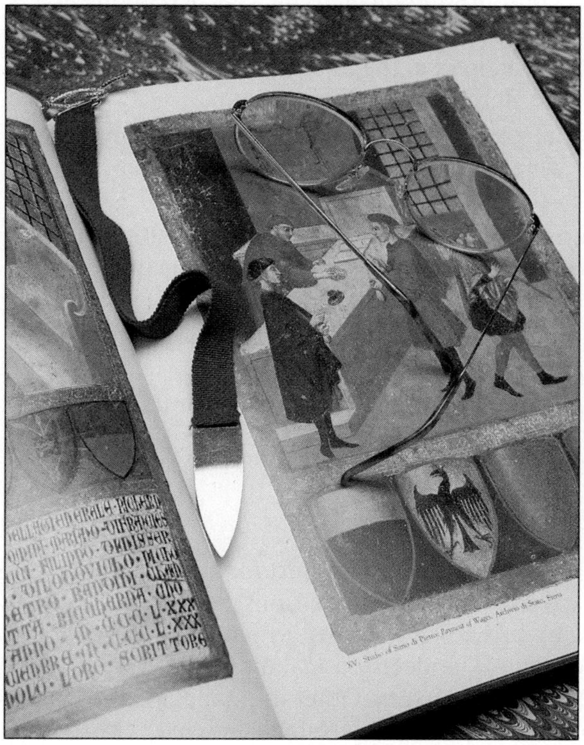

The factors that reshaped culture and art in the Renaissance also brought rapid advances to commerce and banking. Further progress was spurred when Luca Pacioli, an Italian cleric and mathematician, described double-entry accounting in the late 1400's. We still collect useful information with this system, despite five centuries of change.

Topical Coverage

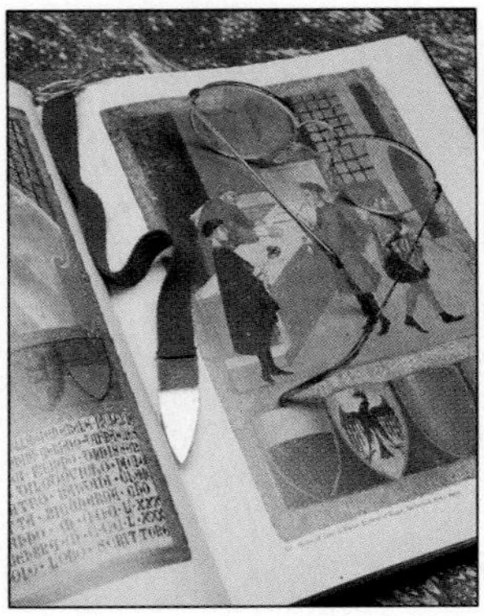

Your study of accounting begins in this chapter with the questions: What is accounting? and Why study accounting? Because many of you will either become accountants or work closely with them, this chapter also describes the accounting profession and the kinds of information that accountants provide in financial statements. We then discuss some general principles accountants follow in producing these statements and some of the organizations that govern or influence accounting practices. Next, we explain the different ways that businesses are organized. Finally, we introduce you to the way accountants analyze the effects of business transactions.

Learning Objectives

After studying Chapter 1, you should be able to:

1. Describe the function of accounting and the nature and purpose of the information it provides.
2. List the main fields of accounting and the activities carried on in each field.
3. Describe the information contained in the financial statements of a business and be able to prepare simple financial statements.
4. Briefly explain the accounting principles introduced in the chapter and describe the process by which generally accepted accounting principles are established.
5. Briefly explain the differences between a single proprietorship, a partnership, and a corporation, comparing the differing responsibilities of their owners for the debts of the business.
6. Recognize and be able to indicate the effects of transactions on the elements of the accounting equation.
7. Define or explain the words and phrases listed in the chapter glossary.

What Is Accounting?

LO 1 Describe the function of accounting and the nature and purpose of the information it provides.

The function of **accounting** is to provide useful information to people who make rational investment, credit, and similar decisions.[1] In effect, accountants *serve* decision makers by providing them with financial information to help them reach better decisions. The decision makers include present and potential investors, lenders, and other users. Other users include the managers of businesses and those who sell to or buy from businesses.

In addition to providing information about profit-oriented businesses, accountants also account for nonprofit organizations. Some examples of entities that are not operated for profit are churches, hospitals, museums, schools, and various government agencies. Accounting information about these enti-

[1] Financial Accounting Standards Board, *Statement of Financial Accounting Concepts Number 1,* "Objectives of Financial Reporting by Business Enterprises" (Norwalk, Conn., 1978), par. 34.

ties is used by people who manage them. The information is also used by people who donate to, pay taxes to, or use the services of these organizations.

In making decisions about an economic entity, people generally begin by asking questions about it. The answers are often found in accounting reports. For example, owners and managers of businesses look to accounting for help in answering questions like these:

- What resources does the business own?
- What debts does it owe?
- How much income is it earning?
- Are the expenses appropriate for the amount of sales?
- Is the right amount of merchandise being kept on hand?
- Are customers' accounts being collected promptly?
- Can the company's debts be paid on time?
- Should additional resources be acquired to expand operations?
- Should a new product be introduced?
- Should selling prices be increased?

Individual investors also use financial reports when they make decisions about buying, keeping, or selling their investments.

Banks and suppliers who loan money (grant credit) to a business use accounting information to answer questions like these:

- Should the company be granted additional credit now?
- Does it have good prospects for future earnings?
- Does it have the ability to pay its current debts?
- Has it promptly paid its debts in the past?

In addition, many government agencies use accounting information in carrying out their activities. These activities may include delivering public services, regulating businesses, or collecting taxes. Employees and labor unions also use accounting information when they negotiate contracts with businesses.

The Difference between Accounting and Bookkeeping

Some people mistakenly confuse accounting and bookkeeping by thinking that they are the same thing. While bookkeeping is critical to accounting, it is only the clerical part of the accounting process. That is, **bookkeeping** is the part of accounting that records transactions and other events, either manually or with computers. Accounting, on the other hand, is concerned with identifying how transactions and events should be described in financial reports. It is also concerned with designing bookkeeping systems that make it easy to produce useful reports and to control the operations of the business. Thus, the work of the accountant is much broader than bookkeeping. Accounting involves more professional expertise and judgment than bookkeeping because the accountant must analyze complex and unusual events. Also, the accountant must be able to interpret the information contained in accounting reports.

Initially, your study of accounting requires you to learn some basic bookkeeping practices. This knowledge of bookkeeping helps you understand how accountants gather financial data and use it to produce useful reports.

Accounting and Computers

Since computers became available in the 1950s, they have spread throughout our everyday lives and the business world. From the beginning, accounting and bookkeeping have been popular applications of computer technology. Computers are widely used in accounting because they are able to efficiently store, process, and summarize large quantities of financial data. Furthermore, computers perform these functions very rapidly and with little or no human intervention. Thus, using computers has reduced the time, effort, and cost of processing data. It has also improved clerical accuracy. As a result of these advantages, most accounting systems are now computerized. Even so, manual accounting systems are still used by a surprisingly large number of very small businesses.

To practice accounting in today's world, you should understand the important role computers now play in most accounting systems. Specifically, computers are important tools used by accountants to produce the information that users need. The coming of computers and the huge growth in their numbers has changed the way that accountants work. However, computers have not eliminated the need for people educated in accounting. A strong demand exists for individuals who can design accounting systems, supervise the operation of those systems, analyze complex transactions, and interpret the reports. While computers have taken over many routine accounting and bookkeeping tasks, they are not substitutes for qualified people.

Why Study Accounting?

Given the wide range of questions that you can answer with accounting information, you will almost certainly use accounting in your future career. To use it effectively, you need to understand the words and terms unique to accounting and the concepts that guide the preparation of accounting reports. You also should understand the procedures used to gather accounting information and to summarize it in financial reports.

Your study of accounting will also make you aware of its limitations. For example, you will learn that to a great extent much accounting information is not based on precise measurements. In fact, a lot of the information is based on estimates and predictions.

Another very good reason for studying accounting is to make it the basis for an interesting and highly rewarding career. The next sections of this chapter describe in more detail what accountants do. When you read these sections, you will learn more about the different kinds of accounting information. You will also learn about some of the career opportunities that exist for accountants.

AS A MATTER OF

Opinion

Mr. Garcia is a member of the City Council of Austin, Texas. He earned a BBA degree and has done additional graduate work at the University of Texas at Austin. He has been president of the Austin Chapter of CPAs, president of Austin's Hispanic Chamber of Commerce, and president and trustee of the Austin Independent School District and Austin Community College. He has served on the board of directors of the State Bar of Texas and the board of directors of the Greater Austin Chamber of Commerce.

Gustavo L. Garcia, CPA

My career in public service spans 20 years during which I have served both in appointed and elected positions. Currently, I am a member of the City Council of Austin, Texas. The Council oversees an annual budget of over $1 billion that includes the operation of an airport, an electric utility, a hospital, a general fund operation, and several other enterprises.

Having a good understanding of accounting has been like having an extra high-powered flashlight that helps me examine and understand the intricacies of this tremendously complex operation.

My accounting education is like a good friend that helps me effectively decipher the many difficult situations we face on a daily basis. My accounting experience allows me to quickly understand the full economic impact and effects of proposed transactions and activities. This gives me valuable insight in making decisions that hopefully protect and/or enhance the economic situation of our city and of its citizens.

The Types of Accountants

One way to classify different types of accountants is to identify the kinds of organizations for which they work. The three types are:

1. Accountants who work for a private company.
2. Accountants who offer their services to the public.
3. Accountants who work for a government agency.

Another way to classify accountants is to identify the kinds of work they do. In general, accountants work in three broad fields. These fields involve providing different kinds of information to various types of users. The fields of accounting are

1. Financial accounting.
2. Managerial accounting.
3. Tax accounting.

In the following paragraphs, we provide more information about the three types of accountants and their work within these fields.

Most accountants are **private accountants.** Private accountants work for a single employer, which is usually a business. A large business might employ a hundred or more private accountants, but most companies have fewer.

Many other accountants are **public accountants.** Public accountants provide their services to many different clients. They are called public accountants because they offer their services to the public. Some public accountants are self-employed. Many others work for public accounting firms. These firms may have only a few employees, or as many as several thousand employees.

Government accountants are employed by government agencies at local, state, and federal levels. Some government accountants perform accounting services for their employers. Other government accountants are involved with business regulation. Still others investigate violations of the law.

Accounting is considered to be a profession like law and medicine because accountants have special abilities and responsibilities. The professional status of an accountant is often indicated by one or more certificates.

The CPA Certificate

Each of the United States, the District of Columbia, Guam, Puerto Rico, and the Virgin Islands has an agency (called a *board*) that licenses Certified Public Accountants **(CPAs).** The licensing process helps ensure that a high standard of professional service is provided to the public. Individuals can legally identify themselves as CPAs only if they hold this license.

To be a licensed CPA, an individual must meet education and experience requirements and must pass the rigorous CPA examination. In general, most states require an applicant to be a citizen of the United States, to be at least 21 years of age, to have good ethical character, and to hold a college degree with a major in accounting.

The CPA examination covers topics in accounting theory, accounting practice, auditing, and business law. Each May and November, a uniform examination is administered in all states. After 1993, the exam will require two days instead of the previously required two and one-half days. Although the exam is administered by each state board, it is prepared and graded by the American Institute of Certified Public Accountants **(AICPA),** the leading national professional organization of CPAs.

In addition, many states require an applicant to have one or more years of work experience in the office of a CPA (or equivalent activity) before the certificate is granted. Nearly all states reduce the amount of experience if the applicant has completed a specified amount of coursework beyond the undergraduate degree. Some states do not require any work experience. A few states allow applicants to substitute work experience for part of the formal education requirements.

As early as 1969, the AICPA's governing council took the position that at least five years of college education (150 semester hours) are needed to obtain the knowledge needed to be a CPA. This position was supported in 1983 by the National Association of State Boards of Accountancy **(NASBA).**[2] In 1988, the members of the AICPA voted to require all CPAs admitted to the institute after 1999 to complete a year of education beyond the bachelor's degree. During the

---

[2] The Commission on Professional Accounting Education, *A Postbaccalaureate Education Requirement for the CPA Profession,* July 1983, pp. 8, 10.

1980s, and continuing into the 1990s, several states have changed their laws to require new CPAs to complete at least 150 semester hours of coursework. Many more are expected to adopt this requirement before 2000.

Because of the differences among states and the fact that changes are occurring, you should contact your state board to learn the requirements that may apply to you.

Other Professional Certificates

Many private accountants hold CPA certificates because they were public accountants earlier in their careers. Some private accountants hold other certificates in addition to or instead of the CPA license. For example, you may seek to obtain a Certificate in Management Accounting **(CMA)** or to become a Certified Internal Auditor **(CIA).** Holders of these certificates must meet professional examination, education, and experience requirements similar to those applied to CPAs. Unlike the CPA, the CMA and CIA certificates are not issued by the government and do not give their holders any legal authority. The CMA is awarded by the Institute of Management Accountants (IMA) and the CIA is granted by the Institute of Internal Auditors.

The Fields of Accounting

LO 2 List the main fields of accounting and the activities carried on in each field.

Accountants practice in three fields of accounting—financial accounting, managerial accounting, and tax accounting. The actual work done by an accountant depends on both the field and whether the person is a private, public, or government accountant. Illustration 1–1 identifies the specific activities of the three types of accountants within these fields.

Financial Accounting

Financial accounting provides information to decision makers who are not involved in the day-to-day operations of an organization. These decision makers include investors, lenders, and others. The information is distributed primarily through general purpose financial statements. Financial statements describe the condition of the organization and the events that happened during the year. The most common financial statements are described later in this chapter.

The Financial Accounting column of Illustration 1–1 shows that financial statements are prepared by a company's private accountants. However, many companies issue their financial statements only after they have been subjected to an **audit.** Audits are performed by independent CPAs who are in public practice.

The purpose of an audit is to add credibility to the financial statements. For example, banks require audits of the financial statements of companies applying for large loans. Also, the law requires companies to have audits before their securities (stocks and bonds) can be sold to the public. Thereafter, their financial statements must be audited as long as the securities are traded.

In performing an audit, the auditors examine the statements and the accounting records used to prepare them. During the audit, the auditors decide

ILLUSTRATION 1–1

Activities of Accountants

Types of Accountants	Fields of Accounting: Financial Accounting	Managerial Accounting	Tax Accounting
Private accountants	Preparing financial statements	General accounting Cost accounting Budgeting Internal auditing	Preparing tax returns Planning
Public accountants	Auditing financial statements	Providing management advisory services	Preparing tax returns Planning
Government accountants	Preparing financial statements Reviewing financial reports Writing regulations Assisting companies Investigating violations	General accounting Cost accounting Budgeting Internal auditing	Reviewing tax returns Assisting taxpayers Writing regulations Investigating violations

whether the statements reflect the company's financial position and operating results in agreement with **generally accepted accounting principles (GAAP).** These principles are the rules adopted by the accounting profession as guides in measuring, recording, and reporting the financial affairs and activities of a business. We discuss the purposes and origins of GAAP in a later section of this chapter. We also describe specific requirements of GAAP in many of the succeeding chapters.

When the audit is completed, the auditors prepare a report that states their professional opinion about the financial statements. The auditor's report must accompany the financial statements when they are distributed.

Some government accountants are also involved in financial accounting. In the bottom section of Illustration 1–1, the first column shows that some government accountants prepare financial statements. These statements describe the financial status of government agencies and results of events occurring during the year. The financial statements are published to allow voters to know more about the condition of the agencies and the performance of the elected or appointed officials who administer them. The statements are also distributed to lenders when state and local governments need to borrow money. Usually the financial statements of governmental bodies are audited by independent CPAs.

Other government accountants are involved with regulating the financial accounting activities of businesses. For example, many accountants work for the Securities and Exchange Commission **(SEC).** The SEC was created by Congress in 1934 to regulate securities markets, including the flow of information from companies to the public. SEC accountants review financial reports from companies before the reports are distributed to the public. The purpose of the review is to be sure the reports comply with the SEC's regulations.

Accountants who work for other regulatory agencies, such as the Interstate Commerce Commission, may review reports filed by businesses that are subject to the agencies' authority. Government accountants also help write regulations concerning financial accounting. Because the regulations can be complex, government accountants assist the companies in understanding and following the regulations.

Some government accountants investigate possible violations of laws and regulations. For example, accountants who work for the SEC investigate crimes related to securities. The Federal Bureau of Investigation employs accountants who assist in detecting financial frauds and other white-collar crimes.

Managerial Accounting

The field of managerial accounting involves providing information to the managers of organizations. Managerial accounting reports often include much of the same information provided through financial accounting. However, managerial accounting reports also include information not reported outside the company.

In Illustration 1–1, look at the first and third sections of the Managerial Accounting column. Note that private and government accountants have the same four major activities. The second section of the Managerial Accounting column shows that public accountants also perform activities related to managerial accounting. All of these managerial accounting activities are described next.

General Accounting. The task of recording transactions, processing the recorded data, and preparing reports for managers of businesses and government agencies is called **general accounting.** General accounting also includes preparing the financial statements presented to investors, lenders, and others. Accountants who work for an organization design the accounting information system, usually with help from a public accountant. The clerical and data processing staff work under the supervision of a chief accounting officer, who is often called the organization's **controller.** This title stems from the fact that a primary use of accounting data is to control the operations of an organization.

Cost Accounting. One managerial accounting activity is called **cost accounting** because it is designed to help managers identify, measure, and control operating costs. Cost accounting information is also useful for assessing the performance of managers who are responsible for controlling costs. Cost accounting may involve accounting for the costs of producing a given product or service or of performing some other specific activity. Good management requires knowledge of costs so that they can be controlled. Therefore, a large company may have a number of accountants engaged in cost accounting.

Budgeting. The process of developing formal plans for future business and government activities is called **budgeting.** A primary goal of budgeting is to provide managers with a clear understanding of the activities to be undertaken and completed to accomplish the company's objectives. Then, after the budget plan has been put into effect, it provides a basis for evaluating actual performance. Large companies and government agencies have many accountants who devote all their time to budgeting.

Internal Auditing. Just as independent auditing adds credibility to financial statements, **internal auditing** adds credibility to reports produced and used within an organization. Internal auditors not only evaluate the record-keeping processes but also assess whether managers throughout the organization are following established operating procedures. Internal auditors also evaluate the efficiency of the operating procedures. Almost all large companies and government agencies employ internal auditors.

Management Advisory Services. Public accountants participate in managerial accounting when they provide **management advisory services** to their clients. Independent auditors gain an intimate knowledge of a client's accounting and operating procedures. Thus, the auditors are in an excellent position to offer suggestions for improving the company's procedures. Clients often expect these suggestions as a useful by-product of the audit. Other advisory services may have nothing to do with the audit. For example, public accountants often help companies design and install new accounting systems. Many times, this effort includes offering advice on selecting new computer systems. Other advice might relate to budgeting or choosing employee benefit plans.

Tax Accounting

Many taxes raised by federal, state, and city governments are based on the income earned by taxpayers. These taxpayers include both individuals and corporate businesses. The amount of taxes is based on what the tax laws define to be income. Tax accountants help taxpayers comply with these laws by preparing their tax returns. Another **tax accounting** activity involves planning future transactions to minimize the amount of tax to be paid. The Tax Accounting column of Illustration 1–1 identifies the activities of tax accountants.

Large companies usually have their own private accountants who are responsible for preparing tax returns and doing tax planning. However, a large company may consult with a public accountant when special tax expertise is needed. Almost all smaller companies rely on public accountants for their tax work.

Many accountants are employed on the government side of the tax process. For example, the Internal Revenue Service **(IRS)** employs numerous tax accountants. The IRS has the duty of collecting federal income taxes and otherwise enforcing the income tax laws. Most IRS accountants review tax returns filed by taxpayers. Other IRS accountants offer assistance to taxpayers and help write tax regulations. Still other IRS accountants investigate possible violations of the tax laws.

Financial Statements

Financial statements communicate accounting information to managers and other decision makers. These statements are the primary product of the accounting process. Thus, financial statements are a good place to start your study of accounting. We begin by looking at two widely used financial statements: the income statement and the balance sheet.

ILLUSTRATION 1–2

Income Statement for Jerry Dow, Attorney

JERRY DOW, ATTORNEY
Income Statement
For Month Ended December 31, 1993

Revenues:		
Legal fees earned		$3,900
Operating expenses:		
Salaries expense	$ 700	
Rent expense	1,000	
Total operating expenses		1,700
Net income		$2,200

The Income Statement

LO 3 Describe the information contained in the financial statements of a business and be able to prepare simple financial statements.

An example of an **income statement** appears in Illustration 1–2. The income statement is considered by many people to be the most important financial statement. The income statement is important because it shows whether the business earned a profit (also called *net income*), which is one of its primary operating objectives. A **net income** is earned if the company's revenues exceed its expenses; a **net loss** is incurred if the expenses exceed the revenues. The example in Illustration 1–2 shows that the income statement does not simply report the amount of net income or net loss. Instead, it lists the types and amounts of the revenues and expenses. This detailed information is more useful for decisions than just a single number for the profit or loss.

Revenues are inflows of assets received in exchange for goods or services provided to customers as part of the major or central operations of the business. Instead of inflows of assets, revenues also may occur as decreases in liabilities.[3] (For now, you should think of an asset as a property or a property right. You can also think of a liability as a debt owed by a business. The words *asset* and *liability* are defined more completely on pages 20–21.)

The income statement in Illustration 1–2 shows that the business of Jerry Dow, Attorney, had $3,900 of revenues from providing legal services to clients during the month of December. Examples of revenues that other businesses might have include sales of products and amounts earned from rent, dividends, and interest.

Expenses are outflows or the using up of assets as a result of the major or central operations of a business. Instead of outflows or the using up of assets, expenses also may occur as increases in liabilities.[4] The income statement in Illustration 1–2 shows that the business, Jerry Dow, Attorney, used an employee's services. This cost is reported as salaries expense of $700. The busi-

[3] Financial Accounting Standards Board, *Statement of Financial Accounting Concepts No. 6,* "Elements of Financial Statements" (Norwalk, Conn., 1985), par. 78.

[4] Ibid., par. 80.

ness also used services in the form of office space rented to the business by the owner of a building. This cost is reported in Illustration 1–2 as rent expense of $1,000.

Note from Illustration 1–2 that the heading of an income statement begins with the name of the business. The heading also shows the time period covered by the statement. Knowledge of the time period is important for judging if the company's performance is satisfactory. For example, to evaluate the $3,900 of legal fees earned by Jerry Dow, you must know that they were earned during a one-month period.

The Balance Sheet

The purpose of the **balance sheet** is to provide information that helps users understand the financial *status* of the business. In fact, the balance sheet is often called the **statement of financial position.** The balance sheet describes financial position by listing the types and amounts of assets, liabilities, and equity of the business. (Equity is the difference between a company's assets and its liabilities.)

Illustration 1–3 presents the balance sheet for Jerry Dow, Attorney, as of December 31, 1993. The heading of the balance sheet begins with the company's name. The balance sheet describes conditions that exist at a point in time. Thus, the heading also shows the date on which the assets are identified and measured. The amounts in the balance sheet are understood to be stated as of the close of business on that date.

The balance sheet in Illustration 1–3 shows that the business owned three different assets at the close of business on December 31, 1993. The assets were cash, a law library, and office equipment. The total dollar amount for these assets was $10,860. The balance sheet also shows that there were liabilities of $760. Owner's equity was $10,100. This amount is the difference between the assets and the liabilities.

Observe that the total amounts on the two sides of the balance sheet are equal. This equality is the source of the name *balance sheet*. The name also reflects the fact that the statement reports the balances of the assets, liabilities, and equity on a given date.

Assets, Liabilities, and Owner's Equity

In general, the **assets** of a business are the properties or economic resources owned by the business. More precisely, assets are defined as "probable future economic benefits obtained or controlled by a particular entity as a result of past transactions or events."[5] One familiar asset is cash. Another asset consists of amounts owed to the business by its customers for goods and services sold to them on credit. This asset is called **accounts receivable.** In general, individuals who owe amounts to the business are called **debtors.** Other assets owned by businesses include merchandise held for sale, supplies, equipment,

[5] Financial Accounting Standards Board, *Statement of Financial Accounting Concepts No. 6,* "Elements of Financial Statements" (Norwalk, Conn., 1985), par. 25.

ILLUSTRATION 1–3

Balance Sheet for Jerry Dow, Attorney

JERRY DOW, ATTORNEY
Balance Sheet
December 31, 1993

Assets		**Liabilities**	
Cash	$ 1,100	Accounts payable	$ 760
Law library	2,880	**Owner's Equity**	
Office equipment	6,880	Jerry Dow, capital	10,100
Total assets	$10,860	Total liabilities and owner's equity	$10,860

buildings, and land. Assets also can be intangible rights, such as those granted by a patent or copyright.

The **liabilities** of a business are its debts. Liabilities are defined more precisely as "probable future sacrifices of economic benefits arising from present obligations of a particular entity to transfer assets or provide services to other entities in the future as a result of past transactions or events."[6] One common liability consists of amounts owed for goods and services bought on credit. This liability is called **accounts payable.** Other liabilities are salaries and wages owed to employees, taxes payable, notes payable, and interest payable.

A liability represents a claim against a business. In general, those who have the right to receive payments from a company are called its **creditors.** From the creditor's side, a liability is the right to be paid by a business. If a business fails to pay its debts, the law gives the creditors the right to force the sale of the business's assets to obtain the money to meet their claims. If the assets are sold under these conditions, the creditors are paid first, up to the full amount of their claims, with the remainder (the residual) going to the owner of the business.

Creditors often use a balance sheet to help them decide whether to loan money to a business. They use the balance sheet to compare the amounts of the existing liabilities and assets. A loan is less risky if the liabilities are small in comparison to the assets. There is less risk because there is a larger cushion if the assets cannot be sold at the amount shown on the balance sheet. On the other hand, a loan is more risky if the liabilities are large compared to the assets. The risk is greater because it is more likely that the assets cannot be sold for enough cash to pay all the debts.

Equity is defined as "the residual interest in the assets of an entity that remains after deducting its liabilities."[7] Equity is also called **net assets.**

---

[6] Ibid., par. 35.

[7] Ibid., par. 49.

If a business is owned by one person, the owner's equity is commonly shown on a balance sheet by listing that person's name, followed by the word *capital*. The amount of equity is then shown. This practice is used in Illustration 1–3 for Jerry Dow. The use of the word *capital* comes from the idea that the owner furnished the business with resources, or capital, equal to the amount of the equity. A later section in this chapter briefly describes the accounting practices used when the business has more than one owner.

With this background on the balance sheet and income statement in place, we can now go on to explain more about financial accounting. In the next sections of the chapter, you will learn about the principles that guide financial accounting.

Generally Accepted Accounting Principles (GAAP)

LO 4 Briefly explain the accounting principles introduced in the chapter and describe the process by which generally accepted accounting principles are established.

On page 16, you learned that financial accounting is governed by a set of rules called *generally accepted accounting principles,* or *GAAP*. Some knowledge of GAAP is essential for all who use or prepare financial statements.

The primary purpose of GAAP is to help accountants provide relevant and comparable information. In other words, financial accounting practices should produce information that is relevant to the decisions made by financial statement users. The information should also allow them to compare companies. These comparisons are more likely to be useful if all companies use the same practices. GAAP identify uniform practices that make financial statements more understandable and useful.

The Development of GAAP

From the earliest days of accounting up through the first third of the 20th century, GAAP were developed through common usage. In other words, a practice was considered good if it was acceptable to most accountants. This history is still reflected in the phrase, *generally accepted*. A principle became generally accepted as accountants came to agree that it would provide useful and dependable information. However, as the accounting profession grew and the world of business became more complex, many people were not satisfied with the rate of progress toward improved financial reporting.

Many professional accountants, managers, and the government wanted to bring more uniformity to practice. Thus, in the 1930s, they began to give authority for defining accepted principles to small groups of experienced people. Since then, there have been several authoritative bodies with different structures and procedures. The power to prescribe acceptable principles also has been greatly increased. Shortly, we describe the present arrangement for establishing GAAP.

Broad and Specific Accounting Principles

You should understand that GAAP consist of both broad and specific principles. *Broad* principles are rooted in long-used practices. More *specific* principles usually result from the work of authoritative bodies. These specific principles are described in the official pronouncements published by these bodies.

You will benefit from knowing about both broad and specific principles. Thus, we describe both kinds in this book. The broad principles are especially helpful for learning accounting. For this reason, they are emphasized in the beginning chapters of this book. The specific principles are also important. They are described throughout the book as we come to them. We use the following broad principles in this book.[8]

	First Introduced	
	Chapter	**Page**
Business entity principle	1	28
Objectivity principle	1	28
Cost principle.	1	29
Going-concern principle	1	29
Revenue recognition principle	1	35
Time-period principle.	3	130
Matching principle	3	132
Materiality principle	8	444
Full-disclosure principle	8	451
Consistency principle.	9	491
Conservatism principle	9	494

Accounting Principles, Auditing Standards, and Financial Accounting

Generally accepted accounting principles are not natural laws like the laws of physics or other sciences. GAAP are identified in response to needs of users and others affected by accounting. Thus, GAAP are subject to change as needs change. Current GAAP have developed through the experience and thinking of public, private, and government accountants, as well as accounting professors and others. In today's world, a formal system has been developed to allow these groups to get together to find a consensus.

This system reflects the fact that three groups are most affected by financial reporting. These groups are identified in Illustration 1–4 as *preparers, auditors,* and *users*. Private accountants prepare the financial statements. Auditors examine the statements and attach the audit report to the statements. The statements and the audit report are then distributed to the users.

Illustration 1–5 shows how accounting principles and auditing standards relate to the financial reporting process. First, Illustration 1–5 shows that GAAP are applied in preparing the financial statements. Preparers use GAAP in deciding which procedures to follow as they account for business transactions and put the statements together.

Second, Illustration 1–5 shows that audits are performed in accordance with **generally accepted auditing standards (GAAS).** GAAS are the rules adopted by the accounting profession as guides in conducting audits of financial statements. GAAS tell auditors what they must do in their audits.

[8] A problem arises in describing accounting principles because different writers have used different words to mean the same thing. For example, broad principles also have been called *concepts, theories, assumptions,* and *postulates*. For simplicity's sake, we have decided to call them *principles* in this book. Don't be confused if you see them called by other names in other books.

ILLUSTRATION 1–4

The Three Main Participant Groups in Fiancial Accounting

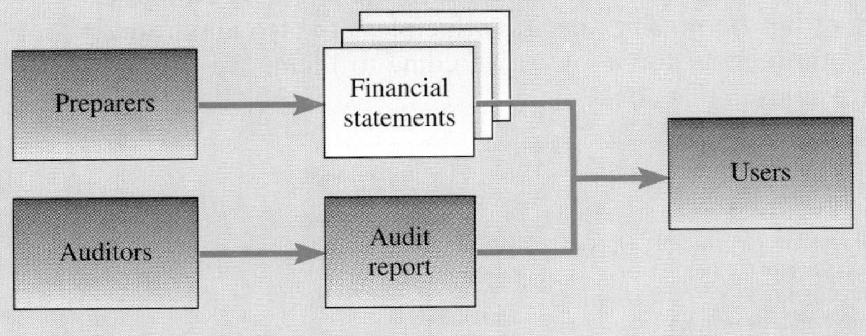

Third, Illustration 1–5 identifies two organizations as the primary sources of GAAP and GAAS.

How Accounting Principles Are Established

The primary source of GAAP is the Financial Accounting Standards Board **(FASB).** The FASB is a nonprofit organization. It has seven paid members who serve full time. (In 1992, their annual salaries were $300,000.) The FASB is located in Norwalk, Connecticut, approximately 50 miles from New York City. Board members use their collected knowledge and a 40-member research staff to identify problems in financial accounting and to find ways to solve them. They also seek advice and comments from groups affected by GAAP. The Board often holds public hearings for this purpose. In summary, the FASB's job is to improve financial reporting while balancing the interests of the affected groups.

The FASB announces its findings in several different publications. The most important publications are **Statements of Financial Accounting Standards (SFAS).** These statements *(SFAS*s) are understood to be pronouncements of GAAP.

The FASB gains its authority from a variety of sources. The most significant source is the Securities and Exchange Commission (SEC). The SEC was created by Congress in 1934 to regulate securities markets, including the flow of information from companies to the public. When the FASB began operating in 1973, the SEC designated it as the only authority for establishing GAAP. However, the SEC still retains oversight authority over the FASB. This oversight means that the SEC may overrule the FASB if the SEC thinks doing so will protect the public interest. To date, this authority has been exercised only one time.

The FASB also has authority because it has been endorsed by each of the state boards that license public accountants. If a CPA audits financial statements that do not comply with FASB pronouncements and does not note the exception in the audit report, an ethics violation occurs. As a result, the CPA may lose his or her license. The AICPA's Code of Ethics includes a similar

ILLUSTRATION 1–5

Generally Accepted Accounting Principles (GAAP), Generally Accepted Auditing Standards (GAAS), and the Participant Groups in Financial Accounting

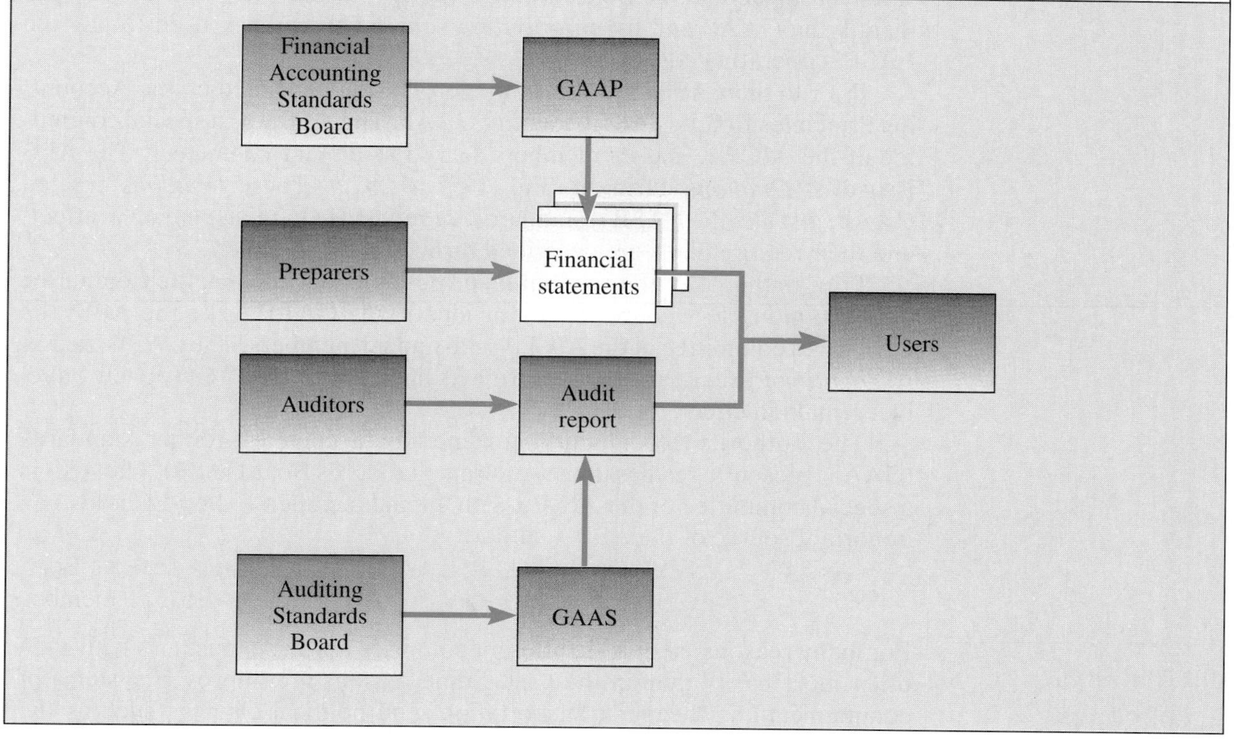

provision. A member of the AICPA may be expelled for not taking exception to noncompliance with FASB pronouncements.

A number of other professional organizations support the FASB's process by providing input and by giving financial support through the Financial Accounting Foundation.[9] They include:

- American Accounting Association **(AAA):** an association of people interested in accounting, most of whom are academic accountants.
- Financial Executives Institute **(FEI):** a professional association of private accountants.
- Institute of Management Accountants **(IMA):** A professional association of private accountants, formerly called the National Association of Accountants.
- Association for Investment Management and Research **(AIMR):** a professional association of persons who use financial statements in the process of evaluating the financial performance of businesses.

[9] Working alongside the FASB is the Governmental Accounting Standards Board (GASB), which identifies special accounting principles to be applied in preparing financial statements for state and local governments. Both the FASB and the GASB operate under the same parent organization, called the Financial Accounting Foundation.

- Securities Industry Association **(SIA):** an association of individuals involved with issuing and marketing securities.

These groups boost the Board's credibility by participating in its process for identifying GAAP and by contributing some of the money used to pay the FASB's operating costs.

Prior to the FASB, the accounting profession depended on the Accounting Principles Board **(APB)** to identify GAAP. The APB was a special committee of the AICPA, and its members served as unpaid volunteers. The APB issued 31 *Opinions* during its life (1959 to 1973). These *Opinions* created GAAP, just like the FASB's standards. Many APB *Opinions* remain in effect, and their requirements are described throughout this book.

Prior to the APB, the accounting profession depended on the Committee on Accounting Procedure **(CAP)** for identifying GAAP. Like the APB, the CAP was a committee of the AICPA with unpaid members. The CAP issued 51 *Accounting Research Bulletins* during its life (1936 to 1959). Only a few bulletins remain in effect.

The authority for identifying generally accepted auditing standards (GAAS) presently resides in the Auditing Standards Board **(ASB).** The ASB is a special committee of the AICPA with unpaid members. The SEC is also an important source of the ASB's authority.

International Accounting Standards

For many reasons, people in different countries engage in business with each other more easily than in the past. Some reasons are improved systems of communication, cheaper transportation, and political changes such as the breakup of the Soviet Union. These changes have opened up many international business opportunities. For example, a company in the United States might sell its products in countries all over the world. Another company in Singapore might raise cash by selling stock to American and Japanese investors. At the same time, it might borrow from creditors in Saudi Arabia and Germany.

The global nature of business creates a major accounting problem. The problem is that each country has its own unique accounting standards. Consider the impact of the problem on the Singapore company in the previous paragraph. Should it comply with Singapore accounting standards, or the standards used in the United States, Japan, Saudi Arabia, or Germany? Should it have to prepare five different sets of reports?

Accounting organizations from around the world responded to this problem by forming the International Accounting Standards Committee **(IASC)**. The IASC was created in 1973 and has its headquarters in London. The IASC identifies preferred accounting practices and encourages that they be adopted worldwide. By narrowing the range of alternatives, the IASC hopes to create more harmony among the accounting practices of different countries.

In many countries, the bodies that set accounting standards have encouraged the IASC. This includes the SEC in the United States. However, the IASC does not have the authority to impose its standards. Although some advances have occurred since 1987, progress has been slow. In the United

AS A MATTER OF

Fact

PW Chief Makes Pitch for Global Standards

Washington—In a speech before the Financial Executives Institute's Washington chapter, Shaun O'Malley [Price Waterhouse's chairman] said today's international business community needs a revamped financial reporting system that provides truly comparable financial statements and greater disclosure of risks and uncertainties. This new system, he said, would better protect investors and managers alike from the kind of unpleasant surprises associated with unforeseen business failures or financial setbacks.

"The advent of more intense foreign competition, plus today's more rapid pace of technology and more volatile economic and political conditions, all have added new complexities to judgments management must make."

* * *

To help users of financial statements better assess future adverse effects that might result from management's decisions, O'Malley proposed the adoption of internationally comparable financial statements that incorporate greater disclosure of risks and uncertainties. Such statements would better protect investors and would help companies in such activities as conducting competitive surveillance; extending credit to customers; evaluating alternative suppliers and potential partners for international alliances and joint ventures; raising capital abroad; and investing in foreign securities.

O'Malley emphasized that there are several courses of action to take in his proposed solution. For one, he suggested that the national standard-setting bodies of the world, such as FASB, could take the initiative in reaching agreement on accounting treatments.

Another possibility, he said, would be for the securities regulators of the world to agree to acknowledge the authority of a transnational organization in international standard setting, which would most likely be the International Accounting Standards Committee. Finally, he called on financial executives to develop solutions of their own.

The ultimate standards developed, said O'Malley, must be broad. They must provide the harmonization without constraint of local standard-setters and must find a way to assign priorities, perhaps giving top priorities to those principles that currently receive the most diverse treatment on an international basis, such as accounting for pensions, leases and business combinations, he said.

States, there is a growing interest in moving toward the IASC's preferred practices. The authority to make such changes continues to rest with the FASB and the SEC.

Understanding Generally Accepted Accounting Principles

Recall the first sentence of this chapter. It states that the function of accounting is to provide useful information to people who make rational investment, credit, and similar decisions. In fact, this description of the function of accounting comes from a FASB project called the *conceptual framework.* This framework also defines a number of terms used by accountants. For example, we relied on the conceptual framework when we defined revenue, expense, asset, liability, and equity.

LO 4 Briefly explain the accounting principles introduced in the chapter and describe the process by which generally accepted accounting principles are established.

Another purpose of the conceptual framework was to describe the characteristics that make accounting information useful. In particular, the conceptual framework expresses the commonsense ideas that information is useful only if it has both *relevance* and *reliability*. Information is relevant if it is capable of making a difference in a decision. For example, the amount of cash reported on the balance sheet is relevant to statement users who make decisions that depend on knowing whether the company can pay its bills within a short time period.

However, relevant information is useful only if users can rely on it to be what it is supposed to be. If they cannot trust the amount of cash reported on the balance sheet, that information is not useful. The need for reliability is also reflected in the requirement that financial statements be audited. The statements would not be as useful without the reliability provided by the audit.

Now that you have some understanding of how accounting principles are developed, we can begin to describe the broad principles listed on page 23.

Business Entity Principle

The **business entity principle** requires every business to be accounted for separately and distinctly from its owner or owners. This principle also requires us to account separately for other entities that might be controlled by the same owner. The reason behind this principle is that separate information for each business is relevant to decisions that its users will make.

To illustrate, suppose that an owner of a business wants to see how well the business is doing. To be useful, the financial statements for the business should not mix the owner's personal transactions with the business transactions. For example, since the owner's personal expenses do not contribute to the success of the business, they should not be subtracted from the revenues of the business on its income statement. Thus, the business's statements should not report such things as the owner's personal entertainment expenses. Otherwise, the net income of the business would be understated and the business would appear less profitable than is really the case.

To conclude, the records and reports of a business should not include either the transactions, assets, and liabilities of another business or the personal transactions, assets, and liabilities of its owner or owners. If this principle were not followed carefully, the reported financial position and net income of the business would be distorted.

Objectivity Principle

The **objectivity principle** requires the information in financial statements to be supported by evidence other than someone's imagination or opinion. The reason behind this principle is that information is not reliable if it is based only on what the statement preparer thinks might be true. This information may not be reliable because the preparer may be too optimistic or too pessimistic. In the worst case, an unethical preparer might try to mislead users of the financial statements by deliberately misrepresenting the truth. The objectivity principle is intended to make financial statements useful by ensuring that they present reliable information.

Cost Principle

The **cost principle** requires the information in financial statements to be based on costs incurred in business transactions. Sales and purchases are examples of **business transactions.** Business transactions are completed exchanges of economic consideration between two parties. The consideration may be such things as goods, services, money, or rights to collect money. In applying the cost principle, cost is measured on a cash or cash equivalent basis. If the consideration given for an asset or service is cash, the cost of the asset or service is measured as the entire cash outlay. If the consideration is something other than cash, cost is measured as the cash equivalent value of what was given up or of the item received, whichever is more clearly evident.[10]

The cost principle is acceptable because it puts relevant information in the financial statements. Cost is the amount initially sacrificed to purchase an asset or service. Cost also represents the market value at the time of purchase of what was received. Information about the amount sacrificed and the initial market value of what was received is generally assumed to be relevant to decision makers. The cost principle provides this information.

The cost principle also is generally accepted because it is consistent with the objectivity principle. Most accountants believe that information based on actual costs is more likely to be objective than information based on estimates of value. For example, reporting purchases of assets and services at cost is more objective than reporting the manager's estimate of their value. Thus, financial statements based on costs are more reliable because the information is more objective.

To illustrate, assume that a business pays $50,000 for land to be used in carrying on its operations. The cost principle tells us to record the purchase at $50,000. It would make no difference if the buyer and several independent appraisers think that the land is worth at least $60,000. The cost principle requires the acquisition to be recorded at the cost of $50,000.

Going-Concern Principle

The **going-concern principle** (also called the **continuing-concern principle**) requires accountants to prepare financial statements under the assumption that the business will continue operating instead of being put up for sale or closed. Thus, a business's operating assets to be held for the long term are not reported in the balance sheet at their liquidation values. Instead, the amounts reported for these assets are based on their cost. Usually, most decisions made about a business are made with the expectation that it will continue to exist in the future. Therefore, accountants generally conclude that the going-concern principle leads to reporting relevant information.

However, the going-concern principle must be ignored if the company is expected to fail or be liquidated. In these cases, the going-concern principle and the cost principle do not apply to the financial statements. Instead, estimated market values are thought to be more relevant than costs.

---

[10] FASB, *Accounting Standards—Current Text* (Norwalk, Conn., 1990), sec. N35.105. First published as *APB Opinion No. 29,* par. 18.

Applying the cost and going-concern principles means that a company's balance sheet seldom describes what the company is worth. Thus, if a company is to be bought or sold, the buyer and seller are well advised to obtain additional information from other sources.

Legal Forms of Business Organizations

LO 5 Briefly explain the differences between a single proprietorship, a partnership, and a corporation, comparing the differing responsibilities of their owners for the debts of the business.

This section of the chapter continues your introduction to accounting by describing three legal forms for business organizations. Some differences occur in financial statements depending on the form the company takes. The three forms are *single* (or *sole*) *proprietorships, partnerships,* and *corporations.*

Single Proprietorships

A **single proprietorship** (or **sole proprietorship**) is owned by one person and is not organized under state or federal laws as a corporation, which we discuss shortly. Small retail stores and service enterprises are commonly operated as single proprietorships. No special legal requirements must be met to start this kind of business. As a result, single proprietorships are the most numerous of all types of businesses.

Legally, a single proprietorship does not have a separate existence apart from its owner. Thus, for example, a court can order the owner's personal assets to be sold to pay the proprietorship's debts. Also, a court can force the proprietorship's assets to be sold to pay the owner's personal debts. Nevertheless, the *business entity principle* applies in accounting for a single proprietorship. That is, the business is treated as separate and distinct from its owner.

Partnerships

A **partnership** is owned by two or more people, called *partners,* and is not organized as a corporation. Like a single proprietorship, no special legal requirements must be met in starting a partnership. All that is required is for the partners to agree to operate a business together. The agreement can be either oral or written. However, a written partnership agreement is better because it helps the partners avoid later disagreements.

For accounting, a partnership is treated under the *business entity principle* as separate and distinct from its partners. However, just as with a single proprietorship, no *legal* distinction is made between the partnership and its owners with respect to its debts. That is, a court may order the personal assets of the partners to be sold to pay the business's debts. In fact, the personal assets of a partner may be ordered sold by a court to satisfy *all* the debts of the partnership, even if this amount exceeds his or her equity in the partnership. This unlimited liability aspect of partnerships can be an important disadvantage of organizing a business with this form.

Corporations

A **corporation** is a separate legal entity formed, or incorporated, under the laws of a state or the federal government. Unlike a single proprietorship or partnership, a corporation is legally separate and distinct from its owners.

The corporation's equity is divided into units called shares of **stock.** Therefore, the owners of a corporation are called **stockholders** or **shareholders.** For example, a corporation that has issued 1,000 shares of stock has divided its equity into 1,000 units. A stockholder who owns 500 shares owns 50% of the equity.

Perhaps the most important characteristic of a corporation is its status as a separate legal entity. This characteristic means that the corporation is responsible for its own acts and its own debts. This arrangement relieves the stockholders of liability for these acts and debts. This limited liability is a major advantage of corporations over proprietorships and partnerships.

The separate legal status of a corporation means that it can enter into contracts for which it is solely responsible. For example, a corporation can buy, own, and sell property in its own name. It also can sue and be sued in its own name. In short, the separate legal status enables a corporation to conduct its business affairs with all the rights, duties, and responsibilities of a person. Of course, a corporation lacks a physical body, and must act through its managers, who are its legal agents.

The separate legal status of a corporation also means that its life is not limited by its owners' lives or by a need for them to remain owners. Thus, a stockholder can sell or transfer shares to another person without affecting the operations of the corporation.

Even though there are fewer corporations than proprietorships in the United States, corporations dominate in the sense that they control more economic wealth than proprietorships. This is because the corporation offers greater advantages for accumulating and managing capital resources.

Accounting Differences

Despite the legal differences among the three forms of businesses, there are only a few accounting differences. One difference is found in the equity section of the balance sheet. A proprietorship usually lists the capital balance of the single owner beside his or her name. Partnerships do the same, unless there are too many owners for their names to fit in the allotted space. The names of a corporation's stockholders are not listed in the balance sheet. Instead, the total stockholders' equity is divided into contributed capital and retained earnings. Contributed capital is the equity created through investments by the stockholders. A corporation's retained earnings is the equity that has resulted from its profitable activities.

Another difference occurs in accounting for the amounts paid to the managers of the business. If the owner of a single proprietorship is also its manager, no salary expense is reported on the income statement. Instead, the owner achieves income only if the proprietorship earns a profit. The same is true for a partnership. However, salaries paid to managers of a corporation are reported as expenses on the income statement.

To keep things simple while you are beginning to learn accounting, the early examples in this book are based on single proprietorships. More is said about partnerships in Chapters 4 and 13, and details about corporate accounting are found in Chapters 4, 14, 15, and 18.

The Balance Sheet Equation

LO 6 Recognize and be able to indicate the effects of transactions on the elements of the accounting equation.

Recall that *owner's equity* is defined as the difference between a business entity's assets and liabilities. The definition of equity can be stated as the following equation:

Assets − Liabilities = Owner's Equity

Like any equation, this one can be modified by moving the terms. The following form of the equation is called the **balance sheet equation:**

Assets = Liabilities + Owner's Equity

The balance sheet equation is also known as the **accounting equation.** The following section shows you how this equation can be used to keep track of changes in the amounts of assets, liabilities, and owner's equity.

Effects of Transactions on the Accounting Equation

A *business transaction* was defined earlier as a completed exchange of economic consideration, such as goods, services, money, or rights to collect money. Because these exchanged items are assets and liabilities, business transactions affect the components of the accounting equation. It is important for you to see that every transaction always leaves the equation in balance. In other words, the total assets always equal the sum of the liabilities and the equity.

To demonstrate how this equality is maintained, we use the transactions of Jerry Dow's law practice as examples. Dow's business is organized as a single proprietorship.

Transaction 1. On December 1, 1993, Jerry Dow began a new law practice by investing $9,000 of his personal cash in the business. The money was then deposited in a bank account opened in the name of the business: "Jerry Dow, Attorney." After this investment, the cash (an asset) and the owner's equity each equal $9,000. Thus, the accounting equation is in balance:

Assets	=	Owner's Equity
Cash, $9,000		Jerry Dow, Capital, $9,000

The equation shows that the business has one asset, cash, equal to $9,000. It has no liabilities, and Dow's equity in the business is $9,000.

Transactions 2 and 3. Dow's second business transaction was to use $2,500 of the business cash to purchase books for a law library. Next, in transaction 3, he spent $5,600 of the business cash to buy office equipment. Transactions 2 and 3 are both exchanges of cash for other assets. Note that they did not produce expenses because no value was lost. Instead, the purchases merely changed the form of the assets from cash to books and equipment.

The effects of these transactions are shown in color in Illustration 1–6. Observe that the decreases in cash were exactly equalled by the increases in the law library and the equipment. Therefore, the equation remains in balance after each transaction.

ILLUSTRATION 1–6

The Effect on the Balance Sheet Equation of Asset Purchases for Cash

	Assets			=	Owner's Equity	
	Cash +	Law Library +	Office Equipment	=	Jerry Dow, Capital	Explanation of Change
(1)	$9,000				$9,000	Investment
(2)	−2,500	+$2,500				
Bal.	$6,500	$2,500			$9,000	
(3)	−5,600		+$5,600			
Bal.	$ 900 +	$2,500 +	$5,600	=	$9,000	

ILLUSTRATION 1–7

The Effect on the Balance Sheet Equation of Asset Purchases on Credit

	Assets			=	Liabilities +	Owner's Equity	
	Cash +	Law Library +	Office Equipment	=	Accounts Payable +	Jerry Dow, Capital	Explanation of Change
Bal.	$900	$2,500	$5,600			$9,000	
(4)		+ 380	+1,280		+$1,660		
Bal.	$900 +	$2,880 +	$6,880	=	$1,660 +	$9,000	

Transaction 4. Dow decided that he needed additional equipment and more library items for the office. The items to be purchased would have a total cost of $1,660. However, as shown on the last line of the first column in Illustration 1–6, the business had only $900 in cash. Because there was not enough cash on hand to make these purchases, Dow arranged to purchase them on credit from Equip-it Company. That is, he agreed to take delivery of the items and promised to pay for them later. The books cost $380, the equipment cost $1,280, and the total liability to Equip-it is $1,660.

The effects of this purchase are reflected in Illustration 1–7 as transaction 4. Notice that the purchase increased total assets by $1,660 and liabilities (called *accounts payable*) increased by the same amount. Also note that the transaction did not involve an expense since the amount of equity remains unchanged from the original $9,000 balance.

Transaction 5. A primary objective of a business is to increase the wealth of its owner. This goal is met when the business produces a profit (also called *net income*). A net income increases the owner's equity in the business. Dow's law practice seeks to produce net income by providing legal services to its clients for fees. The business will produce a net income only if these fees are greater than the expenses incurred in earning them. The acts of earning legal fees and incurring expenses change the accounting equation.

ILLUSTRATION 1–8

The Effect on the Balance Sheet Equation of Revenues Received in Cash and Expenses Paid in Cash

	Assets			= Liabilities +	Owner's Equity	
	Cash +	Law + Library	Office Equipment	= Accounts + Payable	Jerry Dow, Capital	Explanation of Change
Bal.	$ 900	$2,880	$6,880	$1,660	$ 9,000	
(5)	+2,200				+ 2,200	Revenue
Bal.	$3,100	$2,880	$6,880	$1,660	$11,200	
(6)	−1,000				−1,000	Expense
Bal.	$2,100	$2,880	$6,880	$1,660	$10,200	
(7)	− 700				− 700	Expense
Bal.	$1,400 +	$2,880 +	$6,880	= $1,660 +	$ 9,500	

Watch how the accounting equation is affected by transaction 5. In transaction 5, Jerry Dow provided legal assistance to a client on December 10 and immediately collected $2,200 cash for his services. Illustration 1–8 shows that this event increased cash by $2,200 and increased equity by $2,200. This event is identified in the last column as a revenue because it increased the business's assets and the owner's equity as a result of providing services. This information is used later in preparing the income statement.

Transactions 6 and 7. Also on December 10, Jerry Dow paid $1,000 rent for his office to the owner of the building. Paying this amount allowed Dow to occupy the space for the entire month of December. The effects of this event are shown in Illustration 1–8 as transaction 6. On December 12, Dow paid the $700 salary of the office secretary. This event is reflected in Illustration 1–8 as transaction 7.

Both transactions 6 and 7 produced expenses for the business. That is, they used up cash for the purpose of providing services to clients. Unlike the asset purchases in transactions 2 and 3, the cash payments in transactions 6 and 7 acquired services. The benefits of these services did not last beyond the end of the month. The equations in Illustration 1–8 show that both transactions reduced cash and owner's equity. Thus, the equation remains in balance after each event. The last column in Illustration 1–8 notes that these decreases were expenses. This information is useful when the income statement is prepared.

Summary. We said before that a business produces a net income when its revenues exceed its expenses. Net income is reflected as an increase in owner's equity. If expenses had exceeded the revenues, the company's equity would have been decreased, and a net loss would have resulted. You should understand that the amount of net income or loss is not affected by transactions completed between the business and its owners. Thus, Jerry Dow's initial investment of $9,000 is not income to the business, even though it increased the equity.

To keep things simple, and to emphasize the concept that revenues and expenses produce changes in equity, the illustrations in this first chapter add the revenues directly to Dow's equity and subtract the expenses from the equity. In actual practice, however, the revenues and expenses are accumulated separately and then added to or subtracted from equity. We discuss this process further in Chapters 2, 3, and 4.

Because of the importance of revenue for achieving net income, we are going to briefly interrupt the description of Jerry Dow's transactions to describe the revenue recognition principle that accountants follow in determining when to record a company's revenue.

Revenue Recognition Principle

LO 4 Briefly explain the accounting principles introduced in the chapter and describe the process by which generally accepted accounting principles are established.

History shows that managers and auditors need guidance to know when to recognize revenue. (*Recognize* means to record an event for the purpose of reporting its effects in the financial statements.) For example, if revenue is recognized too early, the income statement reports income sooner than it should and the business looks more profitable than it really is. On the other hand, if the revenue is not recognized on time, the income statement shows lower amounts of revenue and net income than it should and the business looks less profitable than it really is.

The question of when revenue should be recognized on the income statement is answered by the **revenue recognition principle** (also called the **realization principle**). This principle includes three important guidelines:

1. *Revenue should be recognized at the time, but not before, it is earned.* Theoretically, revenue is earned throughout the entire performance of a service or throughout the whole process of securing goods for sale, taking a customer's order, and delivering the goods. However, the amount of revenue to be recognized usually cannot be determined reliably until all these steps are completed and the business obtains the right to collect the sales price. Therefore, in most cases, revenue should not be recognized until the earnings process is essentially complete. For most businesses, this occurs at the time services are rendered or at the time the seller transfers title of goods sold to the buyer. Thus, no revenue has been earned if a customer pays in advance of taking delivery of a good or service. The seller must actually perform a revenue-earning act before recognizing the revenue.[11] This approach is known as the *sales basis of revenue recognition.*

2. *The inflow of assets associated with revenue does not have to be in the form of cash.* The most common noncash asset received in a revenue transaction is an account receivable from the customer. These transactions, called *credit sales,* occur because it is convenient for the customer to get the goods or services now and pay for them later.[12] As long as there is objective evidence that the seller has the right to collect the account receiva-

---

[11] FASB, *Accounting Standards—Current Text* (Norwalk, Conn., 1990), sec. R75.101. First published as *APB Opinion No. 10,* par. 12.

[12] Remember that Jerry Dow took advantage of this convenience in transaction 4 when he bought books and equipment on credit.

ble, the seller should recognize the revenue. When the cash is collected later, no additional revenue is recognized. Instead, collecting the cash simply changes the form of the asset from a receivable to cash.

3. *The amount of revenue recognized should be measured as the cash received plus the cash equivalent value (fair market value) of any other asset or assets received.* For example, if the transaction creates an account receivable, the seller should recognize revenue equal to the value of the receivable, which is usually the amount of cash to be collected.

Understanding the Effects of Transactions

To show how the revenue recognition principle works, we now return to the example of Jerry Dow, Attorney.

Transactions 8 and 9. Assume that Jerry Dow completed legal work and billed the client $1,700 for the services. This event is identified in Illustration 1–9 as transaction 8. Ten days later, in transaction 9, the client paid Dow the full $1,700.

In Illustration 1–9, observe that transaction 8 created a new asset, the account receivable from the client. The $1,700 increase in assets was accompanied by an equal increase in owner's equity. Notice that the increase in equity is labeled in the last column of Illustration 1–9 as a revenue.

Transaction 9 changed the receivable into cash. Because transaction 9 did not increase the total amount of assets, there was no change in equity. Thus, this transaction did not involve revenue. The revenue was generated when Dow rendered the services, not when the cash was collected. This emphasis on the earning process instead of collection is the goal of the revenue recognition principle.

Transaction 10. To demonstrate another effect on the accounting equation, assume that Jerry Dow paid $900 to Equip-it Company on December 24 as partial repayment of the account payable. Illustration 1–10 identifies this event as transaction 10. The illustration shows that this transaction decreased the law practice's cash by $900 and its liability to Equip-it by the same amount. Notice that there was no reduction in equity. This event is not an expense, even though cash flowed out of the company.

Transaction 11. Another type of event, the owner's withdrawal of assets from the business, is identified in Illustration 1–10 as transaction 11. In this case, Jerry Dow took $1,100 out of the business checking account for his own use. In accordance with the *business entity principle,* this transaction was not an expense of the business, even though its assets were decreased. As we said earlier, the owner of a single proprietorship does not earn a salary but receives income only if the business achieves a net profit. Thus, the last column in the illustration labels transaction 11 as a withdrawal instead of an expense.[13]

[13] For corporations, payments to the owners are called *dividends*. Dividends are not a factor in determining the corporation's net income.

ILLUSTRATION 1–9

The Effect on the Balance Sheet Equation of Noncash Revenues and the Later Receipt of Cash

	Assets				= Liabilities +	Owner's Equity	
	Cash +	Accounts + Receivable	Law + Library	Office Equipment	= Accounts + Payable	Jerry Dow, Capital	Explanation of Change
Bal.	$1,400		$2,880	$6,880	$1,660	$ 9,500	
(8)		+$1,700				+ 1,700	Revenue
Bal.	$1,400	$1,700	$2,880	$6,880	$1,660	$11,200	
(9)	+1,700	−1,700					
Bal.	$3,100 +	$ -0- +	$2,880 +	$6,880 =	$1,660 +	$11,200	

ILLUSTRATION 1–10

The Effect on the Balance Sheet Equation of Debt Repayments and Withdrawals by the Owner

	Assets				= Liabilities +	Owner's Equity	
	Cash +	Accounts + Receivable	Law + Library	Office Equipment	= Accounts + Payable	Jerry Dow, Capital	Explanation of Change
Bal.	$3,100	$ -0-	$2,880	$6,880	$1,660	$11,200	
(10)	− 900				− 900		
Bal.	$2,200	$ -0-	$2,880	$6,880	$ 760	$11,200	
(11)	−1,100					− 1,100	Withdrawal
Bal.	$1,100 +	$ -0- +	$2,880 +	$6,880 =	$ 760 +	$10,100	

Illustration 1–11 presents the effects of the entire series of 11 transactions for Jerry Dow's law practice. Take time now to see that the equation remained in balance after each transaction. This result occurred because the effects of each transaction are always in balance. Transactions 1, 5, and 8 increased total assets and equity by the same amount. Transactions 2, 3, and 9 increased one asset while decreasing another by the same amount. Transaction 4 increased total assets and a liability by the same amount. Transactions 6, 7, and 11 decreased assets and equity by the same amount. Finally, transaction 10 decreased total assets and a liability by the same amount. The equality of these effects is central to the working of double-entry accounting. You will learn more about double- entry accounting in the next chapter.

Illustration 1–12 shows how owner's equity is affected by different types of transactions. Recall that equity is the residual that remains after subtracting the company's liabilities from its assets. Equity is also a residual in the sense that it is what is left over from the owner's investments and net income after deducting the owner's withdrawals. Illustration 1–12 shows these changes in equity. It shows that equity was increased by the $9,000 investment from Jerry Dow and the $2,200 net income. It also shows that the $2,200 net income is the difference between the revenues of $3,900 and the expenses of $1,700. Finally, Illustration 1–12 shows that the $1,100 withdrawal reduced equity. These events leave a residual balance of $10,100 in equity at the end of the month.

ILLUSTRATION 1–11

The Effect on the Balance Sheet Equation of All Transactions

	Assets				= Liabilities +	Owner's Equity	
	Cash +	Accounts + Receivable	Law + Library	Office Equipment	= Accounts + Payable	Jerry Dow, Capital	Explanation of Change
(1)	$9,000					$ 9,000	Investment
(2)	−2,500		+$2,500				
Bal.	$6,500		$2,500			$ 9,000	
(3)	−5,600			+$5,600			
Bal.	$ 900		$2,500	$5,600		$ 9,000	
(4)			+380	+1,280	+$1,660		
Bal.	$ 900		$2,880	$6,880	$1,660	$ 9,000	
(5)	+2,200					+2,200	Revenue
Bal.	$3,100		$2,880	$6,880	$1,660	$11,200	
(6)	−1,000					−1,000	Expense
Bal.	$2,100		$2,880	$6,880	$1,660	$10,200	
(7)	− 700					− 700	Expense
Bal.	$1,400		$2,880	$6,880	$1,660	$ 9,500	
(8)		+$1,700				+1,700	Revenue
Bal.	$1,400	$1,700	$2,880	$6,880	$1,660	$11,200	
(9)	+1,700	−1,700					
Bal.	$3,100	$ -0-	$2,880	$6,880	$1,660	$11,200	
(10)	−900				−900		
Bal.	$2,200	$ -0-	$2,880	$6,880	$ 760	$11,200	
(11)	−1,100					−1,100	Withdrawal
Bal.	$1,100 +	$ -0- +	$2,880 +	$6,880 =	$ 760 +	$10,100	

Preparing the Financial Statements

LO 3 Describe the information contained in the financial statements of a business and be able to prepare simple financial statements.

The function of accounting is to provide useful information to people who make rational investment, credit, and similar decisions. This information is communicated to its users through the financial statements. Accountants prepare the financial statements from data gathered about transactions and other events. Although the record-keeping system described in this chapter is simpler than what is really used in practice, it is adequate for preparing the financial statements of Jerry Dow, Attorney.

Up to this point, you have learned about only two financial statements: the income statement and the balance sheet. GAAP also require that two other statements be reported. They are the statement of changes in owner's equity and the statement of cash flows.

The Income Statement

The top section of Illustration 1–13 shows the income statement for Jerry Dow. It is based on the information about revenues and expenses recorded in the Owner's Equity column of Illustration 1–11.

Notice that the heading of the income statement identifies the time period as December 1993. Next, note that the income statement lists total revenues of $3,900. This amount is the result of transactions 5 and 8. The revenues are

ILLUSTRATION 1–12

Transactions that Affect Owner's Equity

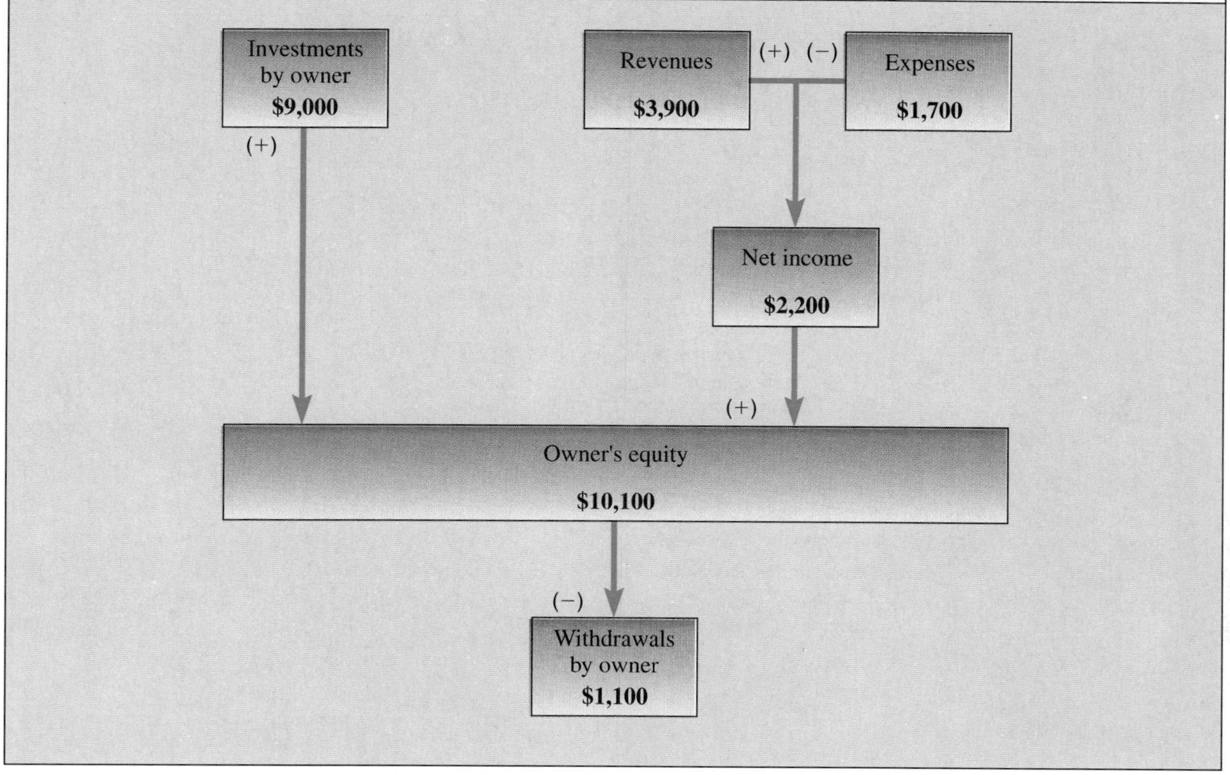

identified as legal fees earned. If the business had earned other kinds of revenues, they would have been listed separately. The income statement then lists the salaries and rent expenses incurred in transactions 7 and 6. The types of expenses are usually identified to help users form a more complete picture of the events of the time period. Finally, the income statement presents the amount of net income earned during the month.

The Statement of Changes in Owner's Equity

The **statement of changes in owner's equity** presents information about what happened to equity during a time period. The statement shows the beginning amount of equity, the events that increased it (new investments and net income), and the events that decreased it (net loss, if any, and withdrawals).

The middle section of Illustration 1–13 shows the statement of changes in owner's equity for Jerry Dow. The heading refers to December 1993 because the statement describes events that happened during that time period. The beginning balance of equity is zero because the business did not exist before December 1. The statement shows that $9,000 of equity came from Dow's initial investment. It also shows $2,200 of net income for the month. This item links the income statement and the statement of changes in owner's equity.

ILLUSTRATION 1–13

Financial Statements for Jerry Dow, Attorney

JERRY DOW, ATTORNEY
Income Statement
For Month Ended December 31, 1993

Revenues:		
Legal fees earned		$3,900
Operating expenses:		
Salaries expense	$ 700	
Rent expense	1,000	
Total operating expenses		1,700
Net income		$2,200

JERRY DOW, ATTORNEY
Statement of Changes in Owner's Equity
For Month Ended December 31, 1993

Jerry Dow, capital, November 30, 1993		$ -0-
Plus: Investments by owner	$9,000	
Net income	2,200	11,200
Total		$11,200
Less withdrawals by owner		1,100
Jerry Dow, capital, December 31, 1993		$10,100

JERRY DOW, ATTORNEY
Balance Sheet
December 31, 1993

Assets		**Liabilities**	
Cash	$ 1,100	Accounts payable	$ 760
Law library	2,880	**Owner's Equity**	
Office equipment	6,880	Jerry Dow, capital	10,100
Total assets	$10,860	Total liabilities and owner's equity	$10,860

The statement also reports Jerry Dow's withdrawal of $1,100 from the business and his $10,100 equity at the end of the month.

The Balance Sheet

The bottom section of Illustration 1–13 presents the balance sheet for Jerry Dow's law practice. The heading shows that the statement describes the company's financial condition at the close of business on December 31, 1993.

The left side of the balance sheet lists the assets of the business. In this case, they are cash, law library, and office equipment. It shows the balance of cash and the costs of the other two assets. The right side of the balance sheet shows that $760 is owed on accounts payable. If any other liabilities had existed (such as bank loans), they would have been listed in this section. Because the business is a single proprietorship, the equity section identifies only one item, Jerry Dow's capital. The $10,100 balance is the difference between the

ILLUSTRATION 1–14

A Statement of Cash Flows for Jerry Dow, Attorney

JERRY DOW, ATTORNEY
Statement of Cash Flows
For Month Ended December 31, 1993

Cash flows from operations:		
Cash received from customers	$ 3,900	
Cash paid to employee	(700)	
Cash paid for rent	(1,000)	
Net cash provided by operating activities		$ 2,200
Cash flows from investing activities:		
Purchase of office equipment	$(5,600)	
Purchase of law library	(2,500)	
Net cash used by investing activities		(8,100)
Cash flows from financing activities:		
Investments by owner	$ 9,000	
Withdrawals by owner	(1,100)	
Repayment of debt	(900)	
Net cash provided by financing activities		7,000
Net increase in cash		$ 1,100
Cash balance, November 30, 1993		-0-
Cash balance, December 31, 1993		$ 1,100

assets and liabilities. Notice that this amount equals the last line of the statement of changes in owner's equity. Thus, it links these two statements.

The Statement of Cash Flows

The fourth financial statement is the **statement of cash flows,** which describes where cash came from and where it went during the period. The statement also shows how much cash was on hand at the beginning of the period, and how much was left at the end. This information is important because good cash management is essential if a business is to prosper or even survive.

Illustration 1–14 shows the statement of cash flows for Jerry Dow's law practice. The information reported in the statement was taken fro[illegible] first column (labeled Cash) of Illustration 1–11. The heading identifies [illegible] as the time period covered by the statement.

The first section of the statement of cash flows shows the amount of cash provided by the *operating activities* of the business. This amount includes $3,900 of cash that was received from customers in transactions 5 and 9. This amount equals the total revenues only because Dow collected all fees in cash. If some revenues had not been received in cash, or if Dow had collected cash for work done in a prior month, the amount of cash received would not equal the revenues.

This first section also lists cash payments of $700 and $1,000 for salaries and rent expenses. These amounts occurred in transactions 7 and 6. Note that these amounts are shown in parentheses to indicate they are to be subtracted. The amount of cash paid out equaled the expenses only because Dow paid all expenses with cash. If there were noncash expenses, they would not appear in the statement of cash flows. The net inflow from operations was $2,200. The net amount of cash from operations equals net income only because all the revenues and expenses involved cash flows.

The second section of the statement of cash flows displays the amount of cash paid out for *investing activities*. Investing activities are the events that turn cash into some other asset or that turn some asset into cash. In this case, the only investing activities were the purchases of assets in transactions 2 and 3. Notice that no cash flows are reported for transaction 4, which was a purchase of assets on credit. The investing activities section shows that a total of $8,100 of cash was spent.

The third section of the statement shows the cash flows caused by *financing activities*. Financing activities involve borrowing cash from creditors and investments of cash by the owner. Financing activities also involve repayments of loans and withdrawals by owners. The statement of cash flows shows that the law practice obtained $9,000 from the initial investment by Jerry Dow in transaction 1. If the business had borrowed cash, the amount would appear here as an increase in cash.

The financing activities section of Illustration 1–14 also shows the $1,100 withdrawn by the owner in transaction 11 and the $900 that was paid to Equip-it in transaction 10. Note that the net effect of financing activities was a $7,000 inflow of cash. This section explains how the business was able to continue even though the cash spent on its investing activities greatly exceeded the cash provided by operations.

The last section of the statement of cash flows shows that the company increased its cash by $1,100. Because the company started out with no cash, the ending balance is also $1,100. This final amount links the statement of cash flows to the balance sheet. We present a more detailed explanation of the statement of cash flows in Chapter 17.

Summary of the Chapter in Terms of Learning Objectives

LO 1. The function of accounting is to provide useful information to people who make rational investment, credit, and similar decisions. In effect, accountants serve decision makers by providing them with financial information to help them reach better decisions. The decision makers include the owners and creditors of a business. Other users include business managers and those who sell to or buy from businesses. Financial reports are used to describe the activities and financial status of many different organizations in addition to businesses.

LO 2. Accountants work as private accountants, public accountants, and government accountants. All three groups have members who work in the fields of financial accounting, managerial accounting, and tax accounting. Financial accounting involves preparing and auditing financial statements that are distributed to people who are not involved in day-to-day management. Managerial accounting provides information to those who are involved in day-to-day management. Activities related to this field include general accounting, cost accounting, budgeting, internal auditing, and management advisory services. Tax accounting is concerned with determining the proper amount of income taxes to be paid, preparing tax returns, and tax planning.

LO 3. The income statement shows a business's revenues, expenses, and net income or loss. The balance sheet lists a business's assets, liabilities, and owner's equity. The statement of changes in owner's equity shows the increase in owner's equity from investments by the owner, the decrease from withdrawals, and the increase from net income or the decrease from a net loss. The statement of cash flows shows the events that caused cash to change; it classifies the cash flows as coming from operating, investing, and financing activities.

LO 4. Accounting principles are intended to help accountants produce relevant and reliable information. Broad accounting principles include the business entity principle, the objectivity principle, the cost principle, the going-concern principle, and the revenue recognition principle. Specific accounting principles for financial accounting are established in the United States primarily by the Financial Accounting Standards Board (FASB), which operates under the oversight of the Securities and Exchange Commission (SEC). Auditing standards are established by the Auditing Standards Board (ASB) which is a committee of the American Institute of CPAs (AICPA). The International Accounting Standards Committee (IASC) identifies preferred practices and encourages their adoption throughout the world. However, the IASC does not have the authority to impose its standards.

LO 5. A single (or sole) proprietorship is an unincorporated business owned by one individual. A partnership differs from a single proprietorship in that it has more than one owner. Proprietors and partners are personally responsible for the debts of their businesses. A corporation is a separate legal entity. As such, its owners (called *stockholders*) are not personally responsible for its debts.

LO 6. The accounting equation states that Assets = Liabilities + Owner's Equity. Business transactions always have at least two effects on the elements in the accounting equation. The accounting equation is always in balance when business transactions are properly recorded.

Demonstration Problem

After planning for several months, Barbara Schmidt decided to start her own haircutting business, called The Cutlery. During its first month of operation, The Cutlery completed the following transactions:

a. On August 1, 1993, Schmidt put $2,000 of her savings into a checking account in the name of The Cutlery.

b. On August 2, she bought store supplies for $600 cash.

c. On August 3, she paid $500 rent for the month of August for a small store.

d. On August 5, she furnished the store, installing new fixtures sold to her on credit by the supplier for $1,200. This amount is to be repaid in three equal payments at the end of August, September, and October.

e. The Cutlery opened August 12, and in the first week of business ended August 16, receipts from cash sales amounted to $825.

f. On August 17, Schmidt paid $125 to an assistant for working during the business's grand opening.

g. Receipts from cash sales during the two-week period ended August 30 amounted to $1,930.

h. On August 31, Schmidt paid the first installment on the fixtures.

i. On August 31, she withdrew $900 cash for her personal expenses.

Required

1. Arrange the following asset, liability, and owner's equity titles in an equation like the one in Illustration 1–11: Cash, Store Supplies, Store Equipment (for the fixtures), Accounts Payable, and Barbara Schmidt, Capital. Show by additions and subtractions the effects of each of the preceding transactions on the equation.
2. Prepare an income statement for The Cutlery for August 1993.
3. Prepare a statement of changes in owner's equity for August 1993.
4. Prepare a statement of cash flows for August 1993.
5. Prepare an August 31, 1993, balance sheet for the business.

Solution to Demonstration Problem

Planning the Solution

- Set up a table with the appropriate columns, including a final column in which to describe the events that involve revenues and expenses.
- Analyze each transaction and show its effects as increases or decreases in the appropriate columns of the table, being sure that the accounting equation remains in balance after each event.
- To prepare the income statement, find the revenues and expenses in the last column. Then list those items on the statement, calculate the difference, and label the result as *net income* or *net loss*.
- Prepare the statement of changes in owner's equity using the information shown in the owner's equity column.
- In preparing the statement of cash flows, include all the events listed in the Cash column of the table. Classify each cash flow as an operating, investing, or financing activity following the example presented in Illustration 1–14.
- Finally, use the information on the last row of the table to prepare the balance sheet.

1.

	Assets			= Liabilities +	Owner's Equity	
	Cash +	**Store Supplies +**	**Store Equip. =**	**Accounts Payable +**	**Barbara Schmidt, Capital**	**Explanation of Change**
a.	$2,000				$2,000	Investment
b.	− 600	+$600				
Bal.	$1,400	$600			$2,000	
c.	− 500				− 500	Expense
Bal.	$ 900	$600			$1,500	
d.			+$1,200	+$1,200		
Bal.	$ 900	$600	$1,200	$1,200	$1,500	
e.	+ 825				+ 825	Revenue
Bal.	$1,725	$600	$1,200	$1,200	$2,325	
f.	− 125				− 125	Expense
Bal.	$1,600	$600	$1,200	$1,200	$2,200	
g.	+1,930				+1,930	Revenue
Bal.	$3,530	$600	$1,200	$1,200	$4,130	
h.	− 400			− 400		
Bal.	$3,130	$600	$1,200	$ 800	$4,130	
i.	− 900				− 900	Withdrawal
Bal.	$2,230 +	$600 +	$1,200 =	$ 800 +	$3,230	

2.

THE CUTLERY
Income Statement
For Month Ended August 31, 1993

Revenues:		
Sales		$2,755
Operating expenses:		
Rent expense	$500	
Wages expense	125	
Total operating expenses		625
Net income		$2,130

3.

THE CUTLERY
Statement of Changes in Owner's Equity
For Month Ended August 31, 1993

Barbara Schmidt, capital, July 31, 1993		$ -0-
Plus: Investments by owner	$2,000	
Net income	2,130	4,130
Total		$4,130
Less withdrawals by owner		(900)
Barbara Schmidt, capital, August 31, 1993		$3,230

4.

THE CUTLERY
Statement of Cash Flows
For Month Ended August 31, 1993

Cash flows from operations:		
Cash received from customers	$2,755	
Cash paid for rent	(500)	
Cash paid for wages	(125)	
Net cash provided by operating activities		$2,130
Cash flows from investing activities:		
Purchase of store supplies		(600)
Cash flows from financing activities:		
Investments by owner	$2,000	
Withdrawals by owner	(900)	
Repayment of debt	(400)	
Net cash provided by financing activities		700
Net increase in cash		$2,230
Cash balance, July 31, 1993		–0–
Cash balance, August 31, 1993		$2,230

5.

THE CUTLERY
Balance Sheet
August 31, 1993

Assets		**Liabilities**	
Cash	$2,230	Accounts payable	$ 800
Store supplies	600	**Owner's Equity**	
Store equipment	1,200	Barbara Schmidt, capital	3,230
Total assets	$4,030	Total liabilities and owner's equity	$4,030

Glossary

LO 7 Define or explain the words or phrases listed in the chapter glossary

AAA the American Accounting Association, the professional association of people who teach accounting. p. 25

Accounting a service-oriented activity that provides useful information to people who make rational investment, credit, and similar decisions to help them reach better decisions. pp. 10–12

Accounting equation an expression in dollar amounts of the relationship between the assets and the liabilities and equity of an enterprise; stated as Assets = Liabilities + Owner's Equity; also called the *balance sheet equation*. pp. 32–35

Accounts payable liabilities resulting from the purchase of goods or services on credit. p. 21

Accounts receivable amounts owed to a business by its customers for goods or services sold to them on credit. p. 20

AICPA American Institute of Certified Public Accountants, the leading national professional organization of certified public accountants in the United States. p. 14

AIMR Association for Investment Management and Research; a professional association of persons who use financial statements in the process of evaluating the financial performance of businesses. p. 25

APB Accounting Principles Board, a former authoritative committee of the AICPA that was responsible for identifying generally accepted accounting principles prior to the FASB. p. 26

ASB the Auditing Standards Board; the authority for identifying generally accepted auditing standards. p. 26

Assets the properties or economic resources owned by the business; more precisely, they are probable future economic benefits obtained or controlled by a particular entity as a result of past transactions or events. p. 20

Audit an examination of an entity's accounting records and statements designed to determine whether the statements fairly reflect the company's financial position and operating results in accordance with generally accepted accounting principles; an audit is designed to add credibility to the information in the financial statements. p. 15

Balance sheet a financial statement providing information that helps users understand the financial status of the business; it lists the types and amounts of assets, liabilities, and equity as of a specific date. Also called the *statement of financial position*. pp. 20–21

Balance sheet equation another name for the *accounting equation*. pp. 32–35

Bookkeeping the part of accounting that records transactions and other events, either manually or with computers. p. 11

Budgeting the process of developing formal plans for future business and government activities, which then serve as a basis for evaluating actual accomplishments. pp. 17–18

Business entity principle the principle that requires every business to be accounted for separately and distinctly from its owner or owners; based on the goal of providing relevant information about the business. p. 28

Business transaction a completed exchange between two parties of economic consideration, such as goods, services, money, or rights to collect money. p. 29

CAP the Committee on Accounting Procedure; the authoritative body for identifying generally accepted accounting principles from 1936 to 1959. p. 26

CIA Certified Internal Auditor; a certification of an individual's professional level of competence in the field of internal auditing; granted by the Institute of Internal Auditors. p. 15

CMA Certificate in Management Accounting; a certification of an individual's professional level of competence in management accounting, granted by the Institute of Management Accountants. p. 15

Continuing-concern principle another name for the *going-concern principle*. p. 29

Controller the chief accounting officer of a business. p. 17

Corporation a business established as a separate legal entity *(incorporated)* under the laws of a state or the federal government. pp. 30–31

Cost accounting a type of accounting designed to help managers identify, measure, and control operating costs. p. 17

Cost principle the accounting principle that requires the financial statements to present information based on costs incurred in a transaction; it requires assets, services, and liabilities to be recorded initially at the cash or cash-equivalent amount given in exchange. p. 29

CPA Certified Public Accountant; an accountant who has passed a rigorous examination of accounting and related knowledge and has met education and experience requirements; CPAs are licensed by states to practice public accounting. pp. 14–15

Creditors individuals or organizations entitled to receive payments from a company. p. 21

Debtors individuals or organizations that owe an amount to a business. p. 20

Equity the difference between a company's assets and its liabilities; more precisely, it is the residual interest in the assets of an entity that remains after deducting its liabilities; also called *net assets*. pp. 21–22

Expenses outflows or the using up of assets as a result of the major or central operations of a business; also, liabilities may be incurred as an alternative to outflows of assets. p. 19

FASB Financial Accounting Standards Board; the seven-member private board that currently has the authority to issue pronouncements of generally accepted accounting principles. p. 24

FEI Financial Executives Institute; a professional association of private accountants. p. 25

GAAP the abbreviation for *generally accepted accounting principles*. pp. 16, 22–30

GAAS the abbreviation for *generally accepted auditing standards*. pp. 23–25

General accounting the field of accounting that deals primarily with recording transactions, processing the recorded data, and preparing financial reports for management, investors, creditors, and others. p. 17

Generally accepted accounting principles rules adopted by the accounting profession as guides in measuring, recording, and reporting the financial affairs and activities of a business; GAAP include both broad and specific principles. pp. 16, 22–30

Generally accepted auditing standards rules adopted by the accounting profession as guides in conducting audits of financial statements. pp. 23–25

Going-concern principle the rule that requires accountants to prepare financial statements under the assumption that the business will continue operating instead of being put up for sale or closed, unless evidence shows that it will not continue. p. 29

Government accountants accountants who are employed by government agencies at local, state, and federal levels. p. 14

IASC International Accounting Standards Committee; a committee that attempts to create harmony among the accounting practices of different countries by identifying preferred practices and encouraging their adoption throughout the world. pp. 26–27

IMA Institute of Management Accountants; a professional association of accountants, formerly called the National Association of Accountants. pp. 15, 25

Income statement the financial statement that shows whether the business earned a profit; it also lists the types and amounts of the revenues and expenses. p. 19

Internal auditing an activity that adds credibility to reports produced and used within an organization; internal auditors not only evaluate the recordkeeping processes but also assess whether managers throughout the organization are following established operating procedures; internal auditors also evaluate the efficiency of the operating procedures. p. 18

IRS Internal Revenue Service; the federal agency that has the duty of collecting federal income taxes and otherwise enforcing the income tax laws. p. 18

Liabilities debts owed by a business or organization; probable future sacrifices of economic benefits arising from present obligations of a particular entity to transfer assets or provide services to other entities in the future as a result of past transactions or events. p. 21

Management advisory services the activity in which public accountants provide advice to managers; the services may include designing and installing an accounting system, advice on selecting a new computer system, or help with budgeting or selecting employee benefit plans. p. 18

NASBA National Association of State Boards of Accountancy. p. 14

Net assets another name for *equity*. pp. 21–22

Net income the excess of revenues over expenses. p. 19

Net loss the excess of expenses over revenues. p. 19

Objectivity principle the accounting guideline that requires the information in financial statements to be supported by evidence other than someone's imagination or opinion; objectivity adds to the reliability of accounting information. p. 28

Partnership a business that is owned by two or more people and is not organized as a corporation. p. 30

Private accountants accountants who work for a single employer, usually a business. p. 13

Public accountants accountants who offer their services to the public. p. 14

Realization principle another name for the *revenue recognition principle*. pp. 35–36

Revenues inflows of assets received in exchange for goods or services provided to customers as part of the major or central operations of the business; may occur as decreases in liabilities as well as inflows of assets. p. 19

Revenue recognition principle the rule that states: (1) revenue should be reported when it is earned and not before, (2) the inflow of assets associated with revenue does not have to be in the form of cash, and (3) the amount of revenue should be measured as the cash received plus the cash equivalent value of any noncash assets received from customers in exchange for goods or services. pp. 35–36

SEC Securities and Exchange Commission; a federal agency created by Congress in 1934 to regulate securities markets, including the flow of information from companies to the public; the SEC granted authority to the FASB for creating generally accepted accounting principles. p. 16

Shareholders another name for *stockholders*. p. 31

SIA Securities Industry Association; an association of individuals involved with issuing and marketing securities. p. 26

Single proprietorship a business owned by one individual, not organized as a corporation. p. 30

Sole proprietorship another name for a single proprietorship. p. 30

Statement of cash flows a financial statement that describes where the business's cash came from and where it went during the period; the cash flows are classified as being associated with operations, investing activities, and financing activities. pp. 41–42

Statement of changes in owner's equity a financial statement that presents information about what happened to equity during a time period; it shows the beginning amount of equity, the events that increased it (new investments and net income), and the events that decreased it (net loss, if any, and withdrawals). pp. 39–40

Statement of financial position another name for the *balance sheet*. p. 20

Statements of Financial Accounting Standards (SFAS) the publications of the FASB that establish generally accepted accounting standards. p. 24

Stock equity of a corporation divided into units or shares. p. 31

Stockholders the owners of a corporation; also called *shareholders*. p. 31

Tax accounting the field of accounting that includes preparing tax returns and planning future transactions to minimize the amount of tax that has to be paid; involves private, public, and government accountants. p. 18

Synonymous Terms

Accounting equation balance sheet equation.

Balance sheet statement of financial position; position statement.

Equity net assets; owner's equity.

Going-concern principle continuing-concern principle.

Revenue recognition principle realization principle.

Stockholders shareholders.

Single proprietorship sole proprietorship.

Objective Review

Answers to the following questions are listed at the end of this chapter. Be sure that you decide which is the one best answer to each question *before* you check the answers.

LO 1. The primary function of accounting is:

a. To provide the information that the managers of an economic entity need to control its operations.

b. To provide information that the creditors of an economic entity can use in deciding whether to make additional loans to the entity.

c. To measure the periodic net income of economic entities.

d. To provide financial information that is useful in making rational investment, credit, and similar decisions.

e. To measure the resources owned by economic entities and the financial obligations of economic entities.

LO 2. Accountants who are employed in public accounting generally work in one or more of the following fields:

a. Tax services, management advisory services, and auditing.

b. Internal auditing, income tax services, and management advisory services.

c. General accounting, auditing, and budgeting.

d. Government accounting, private accounting, and auditing.

e. Income tax services, cost accounting, and budgeting.

LO 3. The financial statements usually presented to the owner of a business and to other outside parties are the:

a. Revenues, expenses, assets, liabilities, and owner's equity.

b. Income statement, balance sheet, and statement of cash flows.

c. Income statement and balance sheet.

d. Income statement, statement of changes in owner's equity, and balance sheet.

e. Balance sheet, statement of cash flows, income statement, and statement of changes in owner's equity.

LO 4. At the present, generally accepted accounting principles in the United States usually are established by:

a. The SEC, subject to the legal authority of the U.S. Congress.
b. CPA firms, subject to the auditing standards established by the AICPA.
c. The U.S. Congress, subject to the review of the SEC.
d. The FASB, subject to the oversight of the SEC.
e. The AICPA, subject to the oversight of the FASB.

LO 5. Compared to a partnership or corporation, the nature of a single proprietorship is such that:

a. Its owner holds all the shares of stock issued by the business.
b. It is not a separate legal entity but is owned by more than one person.
c. It is a separate legal entity.
d. The debts of the business are the responsibility of the business but not of the owner.
e. It is not a separate legal entity and it has only one owner who is personally responsible for its debts.

LO 6. A new business has the following transactions: (1) the owner invested $3,600; (2) $2,600 of supplies were purchased for cash; (3) $2,300 was received in payment for services rendered by the business; (4) a salary of $1,000 was paid to an employee; and (5) $3,000 was borrowed from the bank. After these transactions are completed, the total assets, total liabilities, and total owner's equity of the business are:

a. $ 7,900; $5,300; $2,600
b. $ 7,900; $3,000; $4,900
c. $10,500; $5,600; $4,900
d. $ 7,900; $ -0- ; $7,900
e. $ 7,900; $4,300; $3,600

LO 7. The rule that helps accounting information be reliable is called:

a. The objectivity principle.
b. The going-concern principle.
c. Accounting.
d. Budgeting.
e. Equity.

Questions for Class Discussion

1. What is the function of accounting?
2. What are three or four examples of questions that a business owner or manager might try to answer by looking to accounting information?
3. What is the difference between accounting and bookkeeping?
4. Why is the study of accounting necessary for someone who uses a computer to process accounting data?
5. Why do the states license certified public accountants?
6. According to the AICPA, how much education should a person have to enter the accounting profession in the future?
7. What are three fields of accounting?

8. What three types of services are typically offered by certified public accountants?
9. What is the purpose of an audit? What do certified public accountants do when they perform an audit?
10. Why is the head accountant of a company called the controller?
11. What are some examples of management advisory services typically provided by public accountants?
12. What four activities of managerial accounting are performed by private and government accountants?
13. Accountants who work for the government do many different types of work. Give some examples.
14. What do tax accountants do in addition to preparing tax returns?
15. What information is presented in an income statement?
16. What is a revenue? An expense?
17. Why does the user of an income statement need to know the period of time that it covers?
18. What information is presented in a balance sheet?
19. Where does a balance sheet get its name?
20. Define *(a)* assets, *(b)* liabilities, *(c)* equity, and *(d)* net assets.
21. What is the primary purpose of generally accepted accounting principles?
22. What are two categories of generally accepted accounting principles?
23. What are the titles of two kinds of pronouncements that identify authoritative accounting principles? What body issues or issued them?
24. Give the names and meanings of two qualities of useful information identified by the FASB's conceptual framework.
25. Why is a business treated as a separate entity for accounting purposes?
26. Why is there a need for objectivity in accounting?
27. What is required by the cost principle? Why is this principle needed?
28. Why are the balance sheet amounts for assets held for use in a business originally recorded at cost?
29. A business shows office stationery on its balance sheet at its $430 cost, although the stationery cannot be sold for more than $10 as scrap paper. What accounting principles require this treatment?
30. How does a corporation's status as a separate legal entity affect the responsibility of its stockholders for the debts of the corporation? Does this responsibility or lack of responsibility for the debts of the business apply to the owner of a single proprietorship or owners of a partnership?
31. How is accounting for a business affected by its legal form?
32. State the accounting equation. How does it relate to the definition of equity? Why is it important to accounting?
33. Is it possible for a transaction to increase or decrease one liability without affecting any other asset, liability, or owner's equity item? Explain.
34. Why is there a need for the revenue recognition principle? What does it require?

35. What events or activities change owner's equity?
36. Name four financial statements that businesses present to their owners and other users.
37. In the financial statements of Lands' End, Inc., in Appendix K, the dollar amounts are rounded to what level of significance? What time period is covered by the income statement?
38. Review the financial statements of Federal Express Corporation shown in Appendix K. What is the amount of total assets reported at the end of the 1991 year? What was the net cash provided by operating activities during the 1991 year?

Exercises

Exercise 1–1
Balance sheet for a single proprietorship
(LO 3, 5, 6)

On April 30, 1993, the accounting equation for Sue's Shoes, a single proprietorship, showed the following:

Cash	$ 4,000
Other assets	75,000
Accounts payable	40,000
Sue Hahn, Capital	39,000

On that date, Sue Hahn sold the "other assets" for $50,000 cash in preparation for ending and liquidating the business of Sue's Shoes.

Required

1. Prepare a balance sheet for the shop as it would appear immediately after the sale of the assets.
2. Tell how the shop's cash should be distributed in ending the business and why.

Exercise 1–2
The accounting equation
(LO 6)

Determine the missing amount on each of the following lines:

	Assets	= Liabilities	+ Owner's Equity
a.	$57,600	$10,500	?
b.	$47,700	?	$29,700
c.	?	$ 9,800	$36,900

Exercise 1–3
Effects of transactions on the accounting equation
(LO 6)

The effects of five transactions on the assets, liabilities, and owner's equity of Mike Levin in his medical practice are shown in the following equation with each transaction identified by a letter. Write a short sentence or phrase describing the probable nature of each transaction.

	Assets				= Liabilities +	Owner's Equity
	Cash +	Accounts Receivable +	Office Supplies +	Land	= Accounts Payable +	Mike Levin, Capital
	$12,300		$6,360	$ 3,200		$21,860
a.	−11,000			+11,000		
	$ 1,300		$6,360	$14,200		$21,860
b.			+ 560		+$560	
	$ 1,300		$6,920	$14,200	$560	$21,860
c.		+$860				+860
	$ 1,300	$860	$6,920	$14,200	$560	$22,720
d.	− 560				− 560	
	$ 740	$860	$6,920	$14,200	$-0-	$22,720
e.	+ 860	− 860				
	$ 1,600 +	$-0- +	$6,920 +	$14,200 =	$-0- +	$22,720

Exercise 1–4
Use of the accounting equation
(LO 6)

Determine:

a. The equity of the owner in a business having $156,300 of assets and owing $23,900 of liabilities.

b. The liabilities of a business having $110,300 of assets and in which the owner has a $79,300 equity.

c. The assets of a business with $10,500 of liabilities and in which the owner has a $48,600 equity.

Exercise 1–5
Analyzing the accounting equation
(LO 6)

On October 1, Roy Devon began operating a new travel agency. After each of the agency's first five transactions, the accounting equation for the agency showed the following balances. Analyze the equations and describe the probable nature of the five transactions with their amounts.

Balances after Transaction	Cash	+ Accounts Receivable	+ Office Supplies	+ Office Furniture	= Accounts Payable	+ Roy Devon, Capital
1	$25,000	$ –0–	$ –0–	$ –0–	$–0–	$25,000
2	23,800	–0–	2,000	–0–	800	25,000
3	13,800	–0–	2,000	10,000	800	25,000
4	13,800	2,300	2,000	10,000	800	27,300
5	12,100	2,300	2,800	10,900	800	27,300

Exercise 1–6
Determination of net income
(LO 3, 6)

A business had the following assets and liabilities at the beginning and at the end of a year:

	Assets	Liabilities
Beginning of the year	$ 86,000	$34,000
End of the year	100,000	23,000

Determine the net income or net loss of the business during the year under each of the following unrelated assumptions:

a. The owner of the business made no additional investments in the business and no withdrawals of assets from the business during the year.

b. The owner made no additional investments in the business during the year but withdrew $2,900 per month to pay personal living expenses.

c. During the year, the owner made no withdrawals but made a $40,000 additional investment in the business.

d. The owner withdrew $3,500 from the business each month to pay personal living expenses and near the year-end invested an additional $15,000 in the business.

Exercise 1–7
Effects of transactions on the accounting equation
(LO 6)

Irina Orman began the practice of pediatrics on November 1 and will prepare financial statements at the end of each month. During November, Dr. Orman completed these transactions:

a. Invested $15,700 in cash and medical equipment having a $3,500 fair market (cash equivalent) value.

b. Paid the rent on the office space for November, $2,500.

c. Purchased additional medical equipment on credit, $7,600.

d. Completed medical work for a patient and immediately collected $260 cash for the work.

e. Completed medical work for a patient on credit, $2,800.

f. Purchased additional medical equipment for cash, $590.

g. Paid the medical assistant's wages for November, $1,900.

h. Collected $2,000 of the amount owed by the patient of transaction *e*.

i. Paid for the equipment purchased in transaction *c*.

Required

Arrange the following asset, liability, and equity titles in an equation form like Illustration 1–11: Cash; Accounts Receivable; Medical Equipment; Accounts Payable; and Irina Orman, Capital. Then, show by additions and subtractions the effects of the transactions on the elements of the equation. Show new totals after each transaction.

Exercise 1–8
Analysis of transaction effects on the accounting equation
(LO 6)

For each of the following five pairs of changes in components of the accounting equation, provide an example of a transaction that will produce the described effects:

a. Increase an asset and decrease an asset.

b. Increase an asset and increase a liability.

c. Decrease an asset and decrease a liability.

d. Decrease a liability and increase a liability.

e. Increase an asset and increase equity.

f. Decrease an asset and decrease equity.

Exercise 1–9
An income statement for a single proprietorship
(LO 3)

On March 1, 1993, Lynn Lyonne began the practice of tax accounting under the name of Lynn Lyonne, CPA. On March 31, her record showed the following assets, liabilities, owner's investments, owner's withdrawals, revenues, and expenses:

Cash	$ 600	Owner's withdrawals	$3,000
Accounts receivable	400	Tax fees earned	4,900
Office supplies	800	Miscellaneous expense	75
Professional library	4,000	Rent expense	700
Office equipment	2,600	Salaries expense	1,000
Accounts payable	2,775	Telephone expense	500
Owner's investments	6,000		

From the preceding information, prepare a March 1993 income statement for the business.

Exercise 1–10
A statement of changes in owner's equity for a single proprietorship
(LO 3)

Based on the facts provided in Exercise 1–9, prepare a March 1993 statement of changes in owner's equity for the business of Lynn Lyonne, CPA.

Exercise 1–11
A balance sheet for a single proprietorship
(LO 3)

Based on the facts provided in Exercise 1–9, prepare a March 31, 1993, balance sheet for the business of Lynn Lyonne, CPA.

Exercise 1–12
Identifying the information in each financial statement
(LO 3)

Linda Tomas is in the business of managing commercial real estate. Examine each of the following items related to the business and state with the appropriate letter (*a, b, c,* or *d*) whether the item should appear on *(a)* an income statement, *(b)* a statement of changes in owner's equity, *(c)* a balance sheet, or *(d)* a statement of cash flows. If an item should appear on two statements, list both letters.

1. Management fees earned.
2. Accounts receivable.
3. Investments of cash by owner.
4. Cash received from customers.
5. Rent expense paid in cash.
6. Cash withdrawals by owner.
7. Office supplies.
8. Accounts payable.

Exercise 1–13
Calculating missing information
(LO 6)

Calculate the missing item in each of the following independent cases:

	a	b	c	d
Owner's equity, January 1, 1993	$ –0–	$ –0–	$ –0–	$ –0–
Owner's investments during 1993. . . .	25,000	32,000	47,000	?
Owner's withdrawals during 1993 . . .	4,000	?	13,000	6,000
Net income (loss) in 1993.	?	16,000	(22,000)	25,000
Owner's equity, December 31, 1993 . .	36,000	40,000	?	53,000

Problems

Problem 1–1
Effects of transactions on the accounting equation
(LO 6)

Daisy Pell secured her broker's license and opened a real estate office. During a short period, she completed these transactions:

a. Sold a personal investment in IBM stock for $52,640, and deposited $50,000 of the proceeds in a bank account opened in the name of the business, Daisy Pell, Realtor.
b. Purchased for $125,000 a small building to be used as an office. Paid $45,000 in cash and signed a note payable promising to pay the balance over a period of years.
c. Took office equipment from home for use in the business. The equipment had a $900 fair value.
d. Purchased office supplies for cash, $425.
e. Purchased office equipment on credit, $7,000.
f. Completed a real estate appraisal on credit and billed the client $720 for the work done.
g. Paid a local newspaper $150 for a notice of the opening of the agency.
h. Sold a house for a client and collected a $12,000 cash commission on completion of the sale.

i. Made a $700 installment payment on the equipment purchased in transaction *e*.

j. The client of transaction *f* paid $500 of the amount he owed.

k. Paid the office secretary's wages, $850.

l. Daisy Pell withdrew $400 from the bank account of the business to pay personal living expenses.

Required

1. Arrange the following asset, liability, and owner's equity titles in an equation like Illustration 1–11: Cash; Accounts Receivable; Office Supplies; Office Equipment; Building; Accounts Payable; Notes Payable; and Daisy Pell, Capital. Leave space for an Explanation column to the right of Daisy Pell, Capital.
2. Show by additions and subtractions the effects of each transaction on the elements of the equation. Show new totals after each addition or subtraction. Next to each change in Daisy Pell, Capital, state whether it was caused by an investment, a revenue, an expense, or a withdrawal.

Problem 1–2
Preparation of balance sheet and income statement
(LO 3, 6)

Isaac Trou graduated from college in May 1993 with a degree in architecture. On July 1, he invested $5,600 in a new business under the name Isaac Trou, Architect. Financial statements for the business will be prepared at the end of each month. The following transactions occurred during July:

July 1 Rented the furnished office and equipment of an architect who was retiring, paying $1,000 cash for July's rent.

1 Purchased drafting supplies for cash, $120.

3 Paid $175 for July's janitorial expense.

6 Completed architectural work for a client and immediately collected $450 cash.

9 Completed architectural work for Jacks Realty on credit, $1,275.

16 Paid the draftsman's salary for the first half of July, $825.

19 Received payment in full for the work completed for Jacks Realty on July 9.

21 Completed architectural work for Western Contractors on credit, $1,750.

22 Purchased additional drafting supplies on credit, $200.

24 Completed architectural work for Bob Urick on credit, $1,200.

28 Purchased on credit the service of copying blueprints; the copies were delivered to clients. The cost was $220.

29 Received payment in full from Western Contractors for the work completed on July 21.

30 Paid for the drafting supplies purchased on July 22.

31 Paid the July telephone bill, $150.

31 Paid the July utilities expense, $125.

31 Paid the draftsman's salary for the second half of July, $825.

July 31 Purchased insurance protection for the next 12 months (beginning August 1) by paying a $2,100 premium. Since none of this insurance protection had been used up on July 31, it was at that time an asset called Prepaid Insurance.

31 Trou withdrew $1,000 from the business for his personal use.

Required

1. Arrange the following asset, liability, and owner's equity titles in an equation like Illustration 1–11: Cash; Accounts Receivable; Prepaid Insurance; Drafting Supplies; Accounts Payable; and Isaac Trou, Capital. Include an Explanation column for changes in owner's equity.
2. Show the effects of the transactions on the elements of the equation by recording increases and decreases in the appropriate columns. Indicate an increase with a + and a decrease with a − before the amount. Do not determine new totals for the items of the equation after each transaction. Next to each change in Isaac Trou, Capital, state whether it was caused by an investment, a revenue, an expense, or a withdrawal.
3. After recording the final transaction, calculate and insert on the next line the ending total for each item of the equation and determine if the equation is in balance.
4. Analyze (classify) the items in the last column of the equation and prepare a July income statement for the practice.
5. Prepare a July statement of changes in owner's equity.
6. Prepare a July 31 balance sheet.

Problem 1–3
Preparation of balance sheet; calculation of net income
(LO 3, 6)

The accounting records of Caren Cox's medical practice show the following assets and liabilities as of the end of 1992 and 1993:

	December 31	
	1992	**1993**
Cash	$10,700	$ 2,200
Accounts receivable	6,800	8,000
Office supplies	1,200	900
Automobiles	7,500	7,500
Office equipment	20,100	24,150
Land		85,000
Building		127,500
Accounts payable	1,500	2,000
Notes payable		152,500

Late in December 1993 (just before the amounts in the second column were calculated), Dr. Cox purchased a small office building in the name of the practice, Caren Cox, M.D., and moved the practice from rented quarters to the new building. The building and the land it occupies cost $212,500. The practice paid $60,000 in cash and a note payable was signed for the balance. Dr. Cox had to invest an additional $50,000 in the practice to enable it to pay the $60,000. The practice earned a satisfactory net income during 1993, which enabled Dr. Cox to withdraw $5,000 per month from the practice to pay personal living expenses.

Required

1. Prepare two balance sheets for the business, as of the end of 1992 and the end of 1993. (Remember that the owner's equity equals assets less liabilities.)
2. By comparing the owner's equity amounts from the balance sheets, and using the additional information just presented, prepare a calculation to show the net income earned by the business during 1993.

Problem 1–4
Analyzing transactions and preparing financial statements
(LO 3, 6)

Harry Moss began a new law practice and completed these transactions during June 1993:

June 1 Transferred $7,000 from his personal savings account to a checking account opened in the name of the law practice, Harry Moss, Attorney.
1 Rented the furnished office of a lawyer who was retiring, and paid cash for June's rent, $2,000.
1 Purchased the law library of the retiring lawyer for $5,000, paying $3,000 in cash and agreeing to pay the balance in six months.
2 Purchased office supplies for cash, $300.
7 Completed legal work for a client and immediately collected $750 in cash for the work done.
10 Purchased office equipment on credit, $500.
13 Completed legal work for Central Bank on credit, $2,765.
17 Purchased office supplies on credit, $50.
20 Paid for the office equipment purchased on June 10.
23 Completed legal work for Orr Realty on credit, $1,300.
25 Received $2,765 from Central Bank for the work completed on June 13.
30 Paid the office secretary's salary, $1,500.
30 Paid the monthly utility bills, $140.
30 Harry Moss took $2,100 out of the business for his personal use.

Required

1. Arrange the following asset, liability, and owner's equity titles in an equation like Illustration 1–11: Cash; Accounts Receivable; Office Supplies; Professional Library; Office Equipment; Accounts Payable; and Harry Moss, Capital. Leave space for an Explanation column to the right of Harry Moss, Capital.
2. Show by additions and subtractions the effects of each transaction on the items of the equation. Show new totals after each transaction. Next to each change in Harry Moss, Capital, state whether it was caused by an investment, a revenue, an expense, or a withdrawal.
3. Analyze (classify) the increases and decreases in the last column of the equation and prepare a June income statement for the practice.

4. Prepare a June statement of changes in owner's equity.
5. Prepare a June 30 balance sheet.

Problem 1–5
Calculating financial statement amounts (LO 3)

The following financial statement information is known about five unrelated companies:

	Company 1	Company 2	Company 3	Company 4	Company 5
December 31, 1992:					
Assets	$35,000	$39,000	$46,000	$29,000	$63,000
Liabilities	27,000	30,000	30,000	20,000	?
December 31, 1993:					
Assets	37,000	48,000	75,000	?	88,000
Liabilities	23,800	?	36,000	27,000	40,000
During 1993:					
Owner investments	4,600	7,000	?	23,000	–0–
Net income	?	6,000	20,000	10,000	23,000
Owner withdrawals	2,000	2,600	4,000	5,000	7,000

Required

1. Answer the following questions about Company 1:
   a. What was the owner's equity on December 31, 1992?
   b. What was the owner's equity on December 31, 1993?
   c. What was the net income for 1993?
2. Answer the following questions about Company 2:
   a. What was the owner's equity on December 31, 1992?
   b. What was the owner's equity on December 31, 1993?
   c. What was the amount of liabilities owed on December 31, 1993?
3. For Company 3, calculate the amount of owner investments during 1993.
4. For Company 4, calculate the amount of assets on December 31, 1993.
5. For Company 5, calculate the amount of liabilities owed on December 31, 1992.

Problem 1–6
Identifying effects of transactions on the financial statements (LO 3, 6)

For each of the 14 transactions on page 62, identify how it affects the company's financial statements. For the balance sheet, identify how each transaction affects total assets, total liabilities, and owner's equity. For the income statement, identify how each transaction affects net income. For the statement of cash flows, identify how each transaction affects cash flows from operations, cash flows from financing activities, and cash flows from investing activities. If there is an increase, place a + in the column or columns. If there is a decrease, place a – in the column or columns. If there is both an increase and a decrease, place +/– in the column or columns.

The lines for the first two transactions are completed as examples.

Transaction		Balance Sheet			Income Statement	Statement of Cash Flows		
		Total Assets	Total Liabilities	Equity	Net Income	Operating	Financing	Investing
1	Owner invests cash	+		+			+	
2	Purchases supplies on credit	+	+					
3	Owner invests equipment							
4	Pays wages with cash							
5	Sells services on credit							
6	Sells services for cash							
7	Buys office equipment for cash							
8	Acquires services on credit							
9	Owner withdraws cash							
10	Sells extra equipment for cash (at cost)							
11	Buys land with note payable							
12	Borrows cash with note payable							
13	Pays rent with cash							
14	Collects receivable from (5)							

Problem 1–7
Analytical essay
(LO 3, 4)

Review the facts presented in Problem 1–1, and focus on transactions *f* and *j*. Indicate which of these transactions involves a revenue and explain why that transaction is a revenue and why the other transaction is not. Also review transactions *d* and *k*. Indicate which one of these transactions involves an expense and explain why that transaction is an expense and why the other is not.

Problem 1–8
Analytical essay
(LO 2, 6)

Review the facts presented in Problem 1–4. Now assume that all of the business's revenue transactions had been for cash and none had been for credit. Also assume that all of the expense transactions had been paid in cash and none were on credit. Describe the differences, if any, these assumptions would make in the appearance of the income statement, the statement of changes in owner's equity, and the balance sheet. Describe the differences in general terms without calculating actual dollar amounts of difference. Also explain why each statement is affected or not affected by the preceding assumptions.

Alternate Problems

Problem 1–1A
Effects of transactions on the accounting equation
(LO 6)

Patsy Dane opened a medical practice and during a short period completed these transactions:

a. Sold a personal investment in Chrysler Corporation stock for $90,000 and deposited $85,000 of the proceeds in a bank account opened in the name of the practice, Patsy Dane, M.D.

b. Purchased for $140,000 a small building to be used as an office. Paid $50,000 in cash and signed a note payable promising to pay the balance over a period of years.

c. Purchased office equipment for cash, $13,300.

d. Took office equipment from home for use in the practice. The equipment had a $620 fair value.

e. Purchased on credit office supplies for $300 and office equipment for $7,000.

f. Paid the local paper $150 for a notice announcing the opening of the practice.

g. Completed medical work and billed the patient $550, which is to be paid later.

h. Performed medical services and received $250 cash.

i. Patsy Dane withdrew $3,000 from the business to pay personal expenses.

j. The patient paid for the services of transaction *g*.

k. Made a $4,500 installment payment on the amount owed from transaction *e*.

l. Paid the medical assistant's wages, $1,400.

Required

1. Arrange the following asset, liability, and owner's equity titles in an equation like Illustration 1–11: Cash; Accounts Receivable; Office Supplies; Office Equipment; Building; Accounts Payable; Notes Payable; and Patsy Dane, Capital. Leave space for an Explanation column to the right of Patsy Dane, Capital.
2. Show by additions and subtractions the effects of each transaction on the elements of the equation. Show new totals after each transaction. Next to each change in Patsy Dane, Capital, state whether it was caused by an investment, a revenue, an expense, or a withdrawal.

Problem 1–2A
Preparation of balance sheet and income statement
(LO 3, 6)

Sam Henry graduated from college, completed his internship, and on September 1, 1993, began an engineering practice by investing $9,000 in the practice. Financial statements for the business will be prepared at the end of each month. The following transactions occurred during September:

Sept. 1 Rented the office and equipment of an engineer who was retiring, paying $2,100 cash for September's rent.

1 Paid $225 for janitorial expense during September.

2 Purchased engineering supplies for cash, $75.

4 Completed an engineering engagement for a client and immediately collected $3,200 cash.

7 Purchased additional engineering supplies on credit, $175.

9 Completed engineering work for Berk Contractors on credit, $2,600.

15 Paid the assistant's salary for September 1–15, $1,200.

16 Paid for the engineering supplies purchased on September 7.

19 Received payment in full from Berk Contractors for the work completed on September 9.

21 Completed engineering work for Younger Realtors on credit, $2,100.

25 Purchased additional engineering supplies on credit, $150.

29 Completed additional architectural work for Berk Contractors on credit, $1,350.

30 Paid the assistant's salary for September 16–30, $1,200.

30 Paid the September telephone bill, $65.

30 Paid the September electric bill, $210.

30 Purchased liability insurance protection for the next year (beginning October 1) by paying a premium of $3,000. Since none of this insurance protection had been used up on September 30, it was at that time an asset called prepaid insurance.

30 Henry withdrew $2,800 from the business's checking account to pay for some personal items.

Required

1. Arrange the following asset, liability, and owner's equity titles in an

equation like Illustration 1–11: Cash; Accounts Receivable; Prepaid Insurance; Engineering Supplies; Accounts Payable; and Sam Henry, Capital. Include an Explanation column for changes in owner's equity.

2. Show the effects of the transactions on the elements of the equation by recording increases and decreases in the appropriate columns. Indicate an increase with a + and a decrease with a − before the amount. Do not determine new totals for the items of the equation after each transaction. Next to each change in Sam Henry, Capital, state whether it was caused by an investment, a revenue, an expense, or a withdrawal.
3. After recording the final transaction, determine and enter on the next line the ending total for each item and determine if the equation is in balance.
4. Analyze the items in the last column of the equation and prepare a September income statement for the practice.
5. Prepare a September statement of changes in owner's equity.
6. Prepare a September 30 balance sheet.

Problem 1–3A
Preparation of balance sheet; calculation of net income
(LO 3, 6)

The accounting records of Wendy Stone's real estate office show the following assets and liabilities as of the end of 1992 and 1993:

	December 31	
	1992	**1993**
Cash	$10,700	$ 2,700
Accounts receivable	6,800	8,000
Office supplies	2,000	900
Automobiles	5,900	5,900
Office equipment	19,600	24,300
Land		80,000
Building		130,000
Accounts payable	2,500	2,700
Notes payable		150,000

During the last week of December 1993 (just before the amounts in the second column were calculated), Stone purchased a small building in the name of the realty office, Stone Realtors, and moved her business from rented quarters to the new building. The building and the land it occupies cost $210,000; the business paid $60,000 in cash and signed a note payable for the balance. Stone had to invest an additional $50,000 in the business to enable it to pay the $60,000. The business earned a satisfactory net income during 1993, which enabled Stone to withdraw $4,100 per month from the business to pay personal living expenses.

Required

1. Prepare two balance sheets for the business, as of the end of 1992 and the end of 1993. (Remember that the owner's equity equals assets less liabilities.)
2. Using the information just presented and by comparing the owner's equity amount from the balance sheets, prepare a calculation to show the net income earned by the business during 1993.

Problem 1–4A
Analyzing transactions and preparing financial statements
(LO 3, 6)

James Bell completed graduate school in May 1993, and on June 1 began private practice as a CPA by investing $6,000 in cash in the practice. He also transferred to the business some office equipment having a cash value of $9,600. Then, he completed these additional transactions during June:

June	1	Rented the office of a CPA who was retiring and paid the rent for June, $900.
	1	Moved accounting books required in college from home to the office. (In other words, invested the books in the practice.) The books had a $500 fair value.
	2	Purchased office supplies for cash, $130.
	4	Purchased additional accounting books costing $1,500. Paid $500 in cash and promised to pay the balance within 90 days.
	5	Completed accounting work for a client and immediately collected $600.
	10	Completed accounting work for Village Store on credit, $1,600.
	15	Purchased additional office supplies on credit, $70.
	20	Received $1,600 from Village Store for the work completed on June 10.
	25	Completed accounting work for Olson Realty on credit, $1,400.
	30	Made a $400 installment payment on the accounting books purchased on June 4.
	30	Paid the June telephone bill, $80.
	30	Paid the office secretary's wages, $1,300.
	30	James Bell took $1,500 out of the business for his personal use.

Required

1. Arrange the following asset, liability, and owner's equity titles in an equation like Illustration 1–11: Cash; Accounts Receivable; Office Supplies; Professional Library; Office Equipment; Accounts Payable; and James Bell, Capital. Leave space for an Explanation column to the right of James Bell, Capital.
2. Show by additions and subtractions the effects of each transaction on the elements of the equation. Show new totals after each transaction. Next to each change in James Bell, Capital, state whether it was caused by an investment, a revenue, an expense, or a withdrawal.
3. Analyze the items in the last column of the equation and prepare a June income statement for the practice.
4. Prepare a June statement of changes in owner's equity.
5. Prepare a June 30 balance sheet.

Problem 1–5A
Calculating financial statement amounts
(LO 3)

The following financial statement information is known about five unrelated companies:

	Company A	Company B	Company C	Company D	Company E
December 31, 1992:					
Assets	$73,000	$69,000	$30,000	$67,000	$83,000
Liabilities	57,000	52,000	25,000	49,000	?
December 31, 1993:					
Assets	80,000	97,000	?	83,000	96,000
Liabilities	?	60,000	29,000	43,000	50,000
During 1993:					
Owner investments	8,000	19,000	21,000	?	10,000
Net income	24,000	?	8,600	17,500	17,000
Owner withdrawals	3,000	5,000	3,600	-0-	6,000

Required

1. Answer the following questions about Company A:
   a. What was the owner's equity on December 31, 1992?
   b. What was the owner's equity on December 31, 1993?
   c. What was the amount of liabilities owed on December 31, 1993?
2. Answer the following questions about Company B:
   a. What was the owner's equity on December 31, 1992?
   b. What was the owner's equity on December 31, 1993?
   c. What was the net income for 1993?
3. For Company C, calculate the amount of assets on December 31, 1993.
4. For Company D, calculate the amount of owner investments during 1993.
5. For Company E, calculate the amount of liabilities owed on December 31, 1992.

Problem 1–6A
Identifying effects of transactions on the financial statements
(LO 3, 6)

For each of the 14 transactions on page 68, identify how it affects the company's financial statements. For the balance sheet, identify how each transaction affects total assets, total liabilities, and owner's equity. For the income statement, identify how each transaction affects net income. For the statement of cash flows, identify how each transaction affects cash flows from operations, cash flows from financing activities, and cash flows from investing activities. If there is an increase, place a + in the column or columns. If there is a decrease, place a − in the column or columns. If there is both an increase and a decrease, place +/− in the column or columns. The lines for the first two transactions are completed as examples.

Problem 1–7A
Analytical essay
(LO 3, 4)

Review the facts presented in Problem 1–1A, and focus on transactions *g* and *j*. Indicate which of these transactions involves a revenue and explain why that transaction is a revenue and why the other transaction is not. Also review transactions *f* and *k*. Indicate which of these transactions involves an expense and explain why that transaction is an expense and why the other transaction is not.

Problem 1–8A
Analytical essay
(LO 2, 6)

Review the facts presented in Problem 1–4A. Now assume that all of the business's revenue transactions had been on credit and none had been for cash. Also assume that the expense transactions had been on credit and the resulting

		Balance Sheet			Income Statement	Statement of Cash Flows		
Transaction		Total Assets	Total Liabilities	Equity	Net Income	Operating	Financing	Investing
1	Owner invests cash	+		+			+	
2	Pays wages with cash	−		−	−	−		
3	Buys store equipment for cash							
4	Purchases supplies on credit							
5	Owner invests supplies							
6	Owner withdraws cash							
7	Sells services on credit							
8	Sells extra equipment for cash (at cost)							
9	Acquires services on credit							
10	Sells services for cash							
11	Borrows cash with note payable							
12	Pays rent with cash							
13	Collects receivable from (7)							
14	Buys land with note payable							

accounts payable were not paid prior to the end of the period. Describe the differences, if any, these assumptions would make in the appearance of the income statement, the statement of changes in owner's equity, and the balance sheet. Describe the differences in general terms without calculating actual dollar amounts of difference. Also explain why each statement is affected or not affected by the preceding assumptions.

Provocative Problems

Provocative Problem 1–1
Weekend Farmers' Market
(LO 3, 6)

On September 5, 1993, Norma Clay invested $500 cash in a short-term enterprise that participated in a local Farmers' Market set up in her rural community especially for the Labor Day weekend. She paid $200 for a spot in the market to sell homegrown vegetables and homemade jams and jellies. She bought paper sacks (supplies) at a cost of $55. She also paid a neighbor $85 for materials to construct a stand, which would not have any value at the end of the weekend. Norma purchased her vegetables and jams from several neighbors at a total cost of $450; because she had only $160 in cash, she could not pay in full for everything. However, her neighbors knew Norma's credit was good, and agreed to accept $150 in cash and the promise that she would pay the $300 balance the day after the market closed. During the weekend, she collected $1,120 in cash from sales and paid a young person $60 for helping her with the sales. Norma estimated a $25 value for her unsold goods, which she thought could be sold in the future. None of the sacks were left.

She wanted to decide whether she should look for similar opportunities elsewhere and continue her enterprise, which she called Norma Clay's Homegrown Goods. Assemble the information and prepare an income statement for the three-day market period, which ended on September 7. Then prepare a statement of changes in owner's equity for the same period and a balance sheet dated September 7. Finally, prepare a statement of cash flows for the three days.

Provocative Problem 1–2
Joe's Rock Band
(LO 3)

Joe Sterling ran out of money at the end of the first semester of his sophomore year in college. He looked for work but could not find a satisfactory job. Since he had a set of drums, Joe decided to hire himself out to bands. Consequently, billing himself as Joe Rockhead, he began his enterprise with no assets other than the drums, which had a fair market value of $1,500. He kept no accounting records. Now, at the year-end, he has engaged you to determine the net income that he earned during the year. You find that Joe's business has a $650 year-end bank balance plus $25 of undeposited cash. A local band owes Joe $125 for his last job. In the last week of the year, Joe sold his drums for $950 and used some of the cash proceeds to help buy a new set of drums that cost $4,200. Joe still owes a finance company $3,000 as a result of the purchase. Joe also borrowed $650 from his father to help make the down payment. This loan made to Joe's business was interest-free and has not been repaid. Finally, since Joe's enterprise has been profitable from the beginning, Joe has withdrawn $150 of its earnings each week for the 52 weeks of its existence to pay personal living expenses. Determine the amount of net income earned by the business during the first year of its operations. Show your calculation in a form that will be understandable by others.

Provocative Problem 1–3
OMI Corp.
(LO 4)

OMI Corp. is a major U.S. bulk shipping company engaged in the ocean transport of liquid and dry bulk cargoes for both the international and U.S. domestic markets. The company's headquarters are in New York City. In a recent annual report, the company reported revenues for the year as $192,986,000. Net income was $27,484,000. The notes to the financial statements included the following comments:

> **Related-Party Transactions:** OMI has entered into management service agreements with certain of its joint ventures, wherein, the Company acts as technical and/or commercial managers for certain of the ventures' vessels. During the year, OMI received a $1,000,000 dividend from a 49% owned foreign subsidiary. During the year, OMI entered into a joint venture agreement with members of a group of established shipping companies controlled by members of the non-immediate family of an outside director of OMI. OMI contributed a vessel to this joint venture at an estimated fair value of $20,500,000. OMI recognized a gain of approximately $11,004,000. On January 1, two of OMI's foreign flag carriers were bareboat chartered to a 49.9% owned foreign subsidiary. The charter agreements are for $2,400,000 per year, per vessel. The charter periods may be extended for a period of three years and an additional option of three years. OMI has extended the option to purchase these vessels at the end of any of the option periods.
>
> *(Courtesy of OMI Corp.)*

Why do you think OMI Corp. included the preceding comments in its annual report? What accounting principle might be compromised by related-party transactions?

Provocative Problem 1–4
International Business Machines Corporation
(LO 3)

IBM

IBM is in the business of applying advanced information technology to help solve the problems of business, government, science, space exploration, defense, education, medicine, and other areas of human activity. The financial statements and related financial information disclosed in IBM's 1990 annual report are shown in Appendix J. From your inspection of IBM's 1990 financial statements, answer the following questions:

1. What is the closing date of IBM's annual accounting period?
2. What amount of net earnings (net income) was earned by IBM during 1990?
3. How much cash (plus cash equivalents) was held by the company on December 31, 1990?
4. What was the net amount of cash provided from operating activities during 1990?
5. Did the company's investing activities during 1990 result in a net cash inflow or outflow? By what amount?
6. In IBM's consolidated statement of financial position, the dollar amounts are rounded to what amount?
7. Comparing 1989 to 1990, did the company's total revenues increase or decrease? By what amount?

8. What amount was reported as total assets at the end of the 1990 accounting period?
9. Comparing 1989 to 1990, what was the change in net earnings?

Answers to Objective Review Questions

LO 1 (*d*)
LO 2 (*a*)
LO 3 (*e*)
LO 4 (*d*)
LO 5 (*e*)
LO 6 (*b*)
LO 7 (*a*)

PART

II

Processing Accounting Data

In the next five chapters, we describe the accounting process that starts with an analysis of a business's transactions and ends with the periodic preparation of financial statements. Your careful study of these chapters will pay great dividends. It will make the later parts of the book much easier to understand.

Part II consists of the following chapters:

CHAPTER

2

Recording Transactions

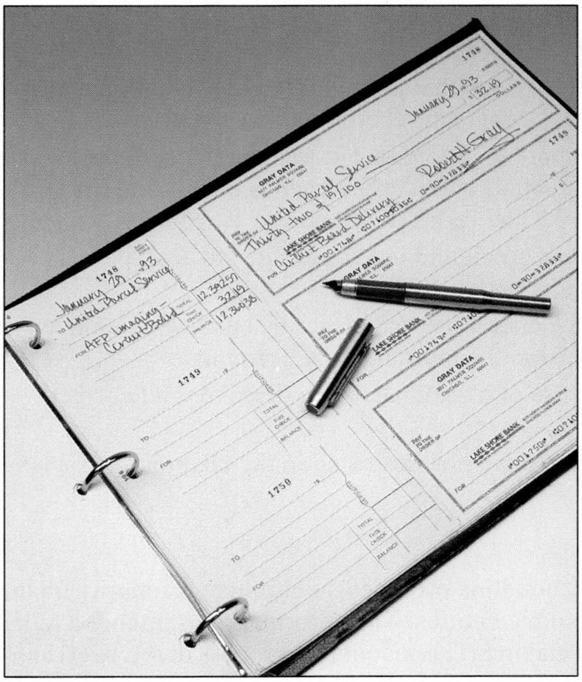

Whether an organization is small or large, an important key to gathering useful information is a system that records the effects of transactions as soon as they occur. Double-entry accounting serves this purpose very well.

Topical Coverage

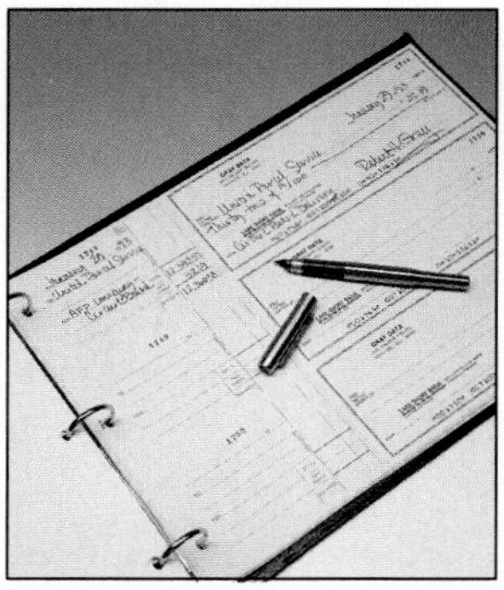

In Chapter 1, you were introduced to the accounting equation (Assets = Liabilities + Owner's Equity) and the effect of business transactions on the accounting equation. Now you will learn how the effects of business transactions are recorded and stored in the accounting records. You can use the procedures you learn in this chapter to record the effects of any type of business transactions you may encounter. No matter how unique or complex the business is, you can use these procedures to successfully record its transactions.

We begin this chapter with a discussion of business papers that provide evidence of transactions. Then, we explain how accounts are used to store information and describe several commonly used accounts. Next, we describe the rules of debit and credit and illustrate how a variety of transactions affect the accounts. With this background in place, we then describe the actual process of recording transactions.

Learning Objectives

After studying Chapter 2, you should be able to:

1. Describe the nature of the events that are recorded in accounting and the importance of business papers in recording those events.
2. Describe the use of accounts to record and store the effects of business transactions, the use of a number to identify each account, and the meaning of the words *debit* and *credit* in relation to T-accounts.
3. State the rules of debit and credit and use those rules to analyze transactions and show their effects on the accounts.
4. Record transactions in a General Journal, describe balance column accounts, and post entries from the journal to the accounts.
5. Prepare and explain the use of a trial balance to discover and correct errors.
6. Define or explain the words and phrases listed in the chapter glossary.

The Accounting Process Starts by Analyzing Economic Events

LO 1 Describe the nature of the events that are recorded in accounting and the importance of business papers in recording those events.

In Chapter 1, we said that accounting provides quantitative (primarily financial) information about economic entities. This information is intended to be useful in economic decision making. The accounting process involves (1) analyzing the economic events of an entity and recording the effects of those events; and (2) classifying and summarizing the recorded effects in reports or financial statements that individuals find useful in making economic decisions about the entity. This process is presented graphically in Illustration 2–1.

Business Transactions

In Illustration 2–1, note that economic events consist of business transactions and other (internal) events. Remember from Chapter 1 that business transactions are completed exchanges of economic consideration between two or more parties. Whenever an entity engages in a business transaction, the trans-

ILLUSTRATION 2–1

The Accounting Process

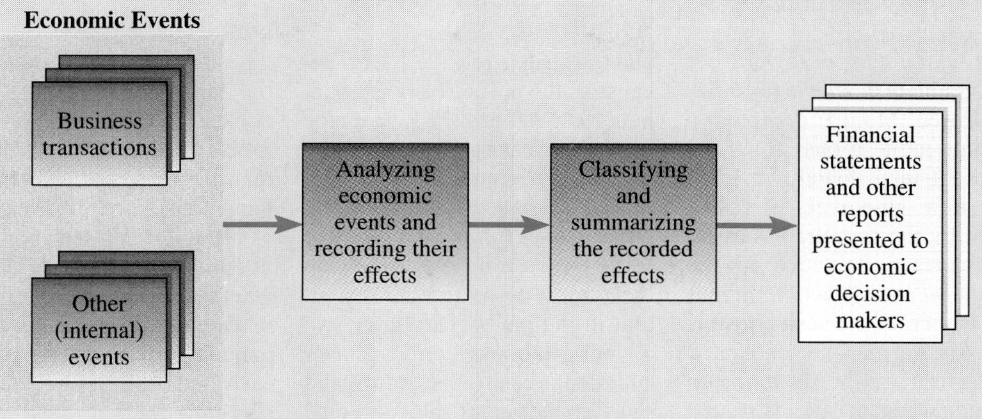

action affects the entity's accounting equation. The accounting process begins by analyzing an entity's transactions to determine their effects on the accounting equation. Then, those effects are recorded in the accounting records, which are sometimes referred to as *the books*. Because business transactions are between the entity and some other (outside) party, they are sometimes called **external transactions.**

Other (Internal) Events

Some economic events affect an entity's accounting equation even though they are not transactions with outside parties. For example, a business uses a machine in its operations. As a result, the remaining usefulness of the machine is decreased. That is, the economic benefit of the machine is partially used up. The using up of the machine's economic benefit is an economic event that decreases the assets and decreases the owner's equity in the business. Internal economic events of this sort are not transactions between two or more parties. Nevertheless, because they affect the accounting equation, they are sometimes called **internal transactions.** The analysis and recording of internal economic events is the central topic of Chapter 3.

Many years ago, most companies used pen and ink to manually record and process the data resulting from transactions. Today, only very small companies use this method. Now, large and small companies use computers in recording transactions and in processing the recorded data. A few companies still use electric bookkeeping machines. These machines were developed years ago as an early step in the path of progress from manual to computerized systems.

Nevertheless, you will begin your study of accounting by learning to process accounting data manually. By manually processing the data, you can

AS A MATTER OF

Ethics

While taking classes toward her undergraduate degree in accounting, Karen Muñoz accepted a part-time job at a busy fast-food restaurant in a downtown mall. As a new employee, she was trained by the restaurant's assistant manager. Included in the training were instructions about how to operate the cash register. The assistant manager explained that the formal policy is to ring up each sale when an order is placed and the cash is received. But, because of the pressure of the noon-hour rush, it is easier to accept the cash and make change without ringing up the sales.

The assistant manager explained that it is more important to serve the customers promptly so they won't go to another restaurant in the mall. Then, after two o'clock, the assistant manager adds up the cash in the drawer and rings up sufficient sales to equal the amount collected. In this way, the tape in the register always comes out right and there are no problems to explain when the manager arrives at four o'clock to handle the dinner traffic.

Muñoz sees the advantages in this shortcut but wonders whether something is wrong with it. She also wonders what will happen if the manager comes in early and observes her taking this shortcut.

more readily understand the importance of each step in the accounting process. Also, the general concepts you learn through manual methods apply equally well to computerized accounting systems.

Business Papers

The printed documents that businesses use in the process of completing transactions are called **business papers.** They include such things as sales slips or invoices, checks, purchase orders, customer billings, employee earnings records, and bank statements. Because they provide evidence of business transactions and are the basis for accounting entries, business papers are also called **source documents.**

For example, if you buy a pocket calculator on credit, two or more copies of an invoice or sales ticket are prepared. One copy is given to you. The other is sent to the store's accounting department and becomes the basis for an entry to record the sale. On the other hand, if you pay cash for the calculator and do not buy it on credit, the sale typically is rung up on a cash register that records and stores the amount of each sale. Some cash registers print the amount of each sale on a paper tape locked inside the register and some store the data electronically. In either case, the proper keyboard commands at the end of the day cause the cash register to calculate and print the total cash sales for that day. This printed total becomes the basis for an entry to record the sales.

Business papers such as sales invoices often are used by both the seller and the buyer as a basis for recording the transaction in their accounting records. For example, if you bought the calculator for use in your business, your copy of the invoice or sales ticket would provide the information you would need to record the transaction in the accounting records of your business.

To summarize, business papers are the starting point in the accounting process. Furthermore, verifiable business papers, especially those that originate outside the business, provide objective evidence of completed transactions and the amounts at which they should be recorded. As you learned in Chapter 1, this type of evidence is important because of the *objectivity principle*.

Storing Information in Accounts

LO 2 Describe the use of accounts to record and store the effects of business transactions, the use of a number to identify each account, and the meaning of the words *debit* and *credit* in relation to T-accounts.

In accounting for an entity, the different effects of its business transactions must be recorded and stored in separate locations so that they can be sorted and combined when financial reports are prepared. These locations in the accounting system are called **accounts.** A number of accounts are normally required. A separate account summarizes the increases and decreases in each asset, liability, and owner's equity item that appears on the balance sheet. Further, a separate account is used for each revenue and expense item that appears on the income statement.

The specific accounts a business uses depend on the assets owned, the debts owed, and the information it needs to obtain from the accounting records. While different businesses use a variety of accounts, the following accounts are widely used:

Asset Accounts

If the accounting system is to provide useful information about the different assets of a company, you must keep a separate account for each kind of asset owned. Generally, accounts are maintained for the following common assets:

Cash. Increases and decreases in cash are recorded in a Cash account. The cash of a business consists of money or any medium of exchange that a bank accepts at face value for deposit. Cash includes coins, currency, checks, and postal and bank money orders. The balance of the Cash account shows both the cash on hand in the store or office and the cash on deposit in the bank.

Accounts Receivable. Goods and services are commonly sold to customers on the basis of oral or implied promises of future payment. Such sales are called *credit sales* or *sales on account;* and the oral or implied promises to pay are called *accounts receivable*. Accounts receivable are increased by credit sales and are decreased by customer payments. Since a company must know the amount currently owed by each customer, a separate record must be kept of each customer's purchases and payments. We discuss this separate record in a later chapter. For the present, however, all increases and decreases in accounts receivable are recorded in a single Accounts Receivable account.

Notes Receivable. A **promissory note** is an unconditional written promise to pay a definite sum of money on demand or on a defined future date (or dates). When amounts due from others are evidenced by promissory notes, the notes are known as notes receivable and recorded in a Notes Receivable account.

Prepaid Insurance. Insurance contracts normally require payment in advance for protection against fire, liability, or other losses. The amount paid is called a premium and the protection lasts for a period of time such as one year or even as much as three years. As a result, a large portion of the premium may be an asset for a considerable time after payment.

When an insurance premium is paid in advance, the payment normally is recorded in an asset account called Prepaid Insurance. Thereafter, whenever financial statements are prepared, the cost of the insurance that has expired is calculated and recorded as an expense, and the balance of the Prepaid Insurance account is reduced accordingly.

Office Supplies. Stamps, stationery, paper, pencils, and similar items are called *office supplies*. They are assets when purchased and continue to be assets until used up. As the supplies are used up, their cost becomes an expense. Increases and decreases in the asset are commonly recorded in an Office Supplies account.

Store Supplies. Wrapping paper, cartons, bags, tape, and similar items used by a store are called *store supplies*. Increases and decreases in such items are recorded in a Store Supplies account.

Other Prepaid Expenses. When payments are made for economic benefits that do not expire until later, the payments create assets called **prepaid expenses.** Then, as the economic benefits are used up or expire, the assets become expenses. As a practical matter, if a purchased benefit will fully expire before the next income statement is prepared, the payment usually is recorded as an expense. When purchased benefits will not be used up or will not fully expire in the current time period, the payments are recorded in asset accounts as prepaid expenses. Examples of prepaid expenses include prepaid insurance, office supplies, and store supplies. Rent that is paid for more than one period in advance is another example. Others include legal fees and management fees paid in advance of receiving the legal or management services. Each type of prepaid expense is accounted for in a separate asset account.

Equipment. Increases and decreases in physical assets such as typewriters, desks, chairs, and office machines are commonly recorded in an Office Equipment account. In a similar manner, physical assets used in the selling operations of a store—for example, counters, showcases, and cash registers—are recorded in a Store Equipment account.

Buildings. A building used by a business in carrying on its operations may be a store, garage, warehouse, or factory. Such assets are commonly recorded in a Buildings account. If several buildings are owned, a separate account may be kept for each building.

Land. An account called Land is commonly used to record increases and decreases in the land owned by a business. However, land does not include buildings located on the land. Although the land and the buildings may be physically inseparable, the buildings wear out, or depreciate, while the land on which they are placed does not. Therefore, the land and the buildings must be recorded in separate accounts.

Liability Accounts

Recall from Chapter 1 that liabilities are present obligations to transfer assets or provide services to other entities in the future. A business may have several different liabilities, each of which requires a separate account. The following are common:

Accounts Payable. When purchases are made on the basis of oral or implied promises to pay, the amounts owed are called *accounts payable*. The items purchased on credit may be merchandise, supplies, equipment, or services. Since a business must know the amount owed to each creditor, a separate record must be kept of the purchases from and the payments to each creditor. We discuss this individual record in a later chapter. For the present, however, all increases and decreases in accounts payable are recorded in a single Accounts Payable account.

Notes Payable. When an entity makes a formal written promise to pay a definite sum of money on a defined future date (or dates), the liability is called a *note payable*. Depending on how soon the liability must be repaid, it is recorded in a Short-Term Notes Payable account or in a Long-Term Notes Payable account.

Unearned Revenues. As you learned in Chapter 1, the revenue recognition principle states that you should not report revenues on the income statement until the revenues are earned. This rule raises the question of how you should record a cash receipt from a customer for products or services to be delivered at some future date. Because receipts such as this are received in advance of being earned, they are called **unearned revenues.**

An unearned revenue is a liability that will be satisfied by delivering the product or service that was paid for in advance. Examples are subscriptions collected in advance by a magazine publisher, rent collected in advance by a building owner, and legal fees collected in advance by a lawyer. On receipt, the amounts collected are recorded in liability accounts such as Unearned Subscriptions, Unearned Rent, and Unearned Legal Fees. When the products or services are delivered, the amounts earned are transferred to the revenue accounts: Subscriptions Earned, Rent Earned, and Legal Fees Earned.

Other Short-Term Payables. Other examples of short-term payables include wages payable, taxes payable, and interest payable. Each of these items must be recorded in a separate account.

Owner's Equity, Withdrawals, Revenue, and Expense Accounts

In Chapter 1, we illustrated four different types of transactions that affected the owner's equity in a proprietorship. They are (1) investments by the owner, (2) withdrawals of cash or other assets by the owner, (3) revenues, and (4) expenses. Recall that in the illustrations of Chapter 1, all such transactions were entered in a column under the name of the owner. This procedure was used to show the effect of transactions on the accounting equation. However, when we prepared an income statement and a statement of changes in owner's equity in Chapter 1, we had to analyze the items entered in the owner's column. Now you can see that such an analysis is not necessary. All that you need is a separate account for the owner's capital, for the owner's withdrawals, and for each revenue and each expense. Then, as each transaction affecting owner's equity is completed, it is recorded in the proper account. We describe these accounts in the following paragraphs.

Capital Account. When a person invests in his or her own proprietorship, the investment is recorded in an account that carries the owner's name and the word *Capital*. For example, an account called Jerry Dow, Capital, is used to record the investment of Jerry Dow in his law practice. In addition to the original investment, the **capital account** is used for any additional increases or decreases in owner's equity that are expected to be relatively permanent.

Withdrawals Account. Perhaps the most obvious reason why a person might invest in a business is to earn an income. If the business earns an income, the net assets of the business increase. The owner may choose to leave the additional assets invested in the business or may, from time to time, withdraw assets from the business. As the owner withdraws assets, perhaps to pay living expenses or for other personal uses, both the assets and the owner's equity of the business are reduced.

To record the withdrawal of assets by an owner, use an account that has the name of the owner and the word *Withdrawals*. For example, an account called Jerry Dow, Withdrawals, is used to record the withdrawals of cash by Jerry Dow from his law practice. The **withdrawals account** is also known as the **personal account** or **drawing account.**

In many cases, the owner of an unincorporated business plans to withdraw a fixed amount each week or month to pay personal living expenses. The owner may even think of these withdrawals as a salary. However, in a legal sense, they are not a salary because an unincorporated business is not legally separate from its owner and one cannot contract with oneself. In other words, one cannot hire oneself or pay oneself a salary. Therefore, according to law, such withdrawals are neither a salary nor an expense of the business. They are simply the opposite of investments by the owner.

Revenue and Expense Accounts. When you prepare an income statement for an entity, you need to know the amount of each kind of revenue earned and each kind of expense incurred during the period covered by the statement. To accumulate this information, a business may need to use a wide variety of revenue and expense accounts. Furthermore, various businesses may have very different kinds of revenues and expenses. As a result, we cannot possibly list all of the possible revenue and expense accounts that are used. Nevertheless, common examples of revenue accounts are Commissions Earned, Legal Fees Earned, Rent Earned, and Interest Earned. Common examples of expense accounts are Advertising Expense, Store Supplies Expense, Office Salaries Expense, Office Supplies Expense, Rent Expense, Utilities Expense, and Insurance Expense. Note that the title of each account generally indicates the kind of revenue or expense that should be recorded in the account.

To get an idea for the variety of accounts that may be used, you will find a long list of accounts at the back of this text. It is a comprehensive list of all the accounts we have used in writing the exercises and problems in this book.

The Ledger and the Chart of Accounts

The size of a business generally affects the number of accounts that it uses to record its transactions. A small company may get by with as few as two dozen accounts, while a large company may use several thousand accounts. Depending on the accounting system, the accounts may take different forms. In a computerized system, each account is stored on a disk or on a tape. In a manual system, each account is placed on a separate page in a bound or loose-leaf book, or on a separate card in a tray of cards.

Regardless of the physical form the accounts of a business may take, the collection of accounts is called the **ledger.** If the accounts are kept in a book, the book is the ledger. If they are kept on cards in a file tray, the tray of cards is the ledger. In other words, a ledger is simply a group of accounts.

All companies should follow a systematic method of assigning identifying numbers to their accounts. A list of all the accounts used by a company, showing the identifying number assigned to each account, is called a **chart of accounts.** One example of a system that service businesses might use in developing a chart of accounts is to assign numbers as follows:

Asset accounts, 101 through 199.
Liability accounts, 201 through 299.
Owner's equity accounts, 301 through 399.
Revenue accounts, 401 through 499.
Operating expense accounts, 501 through 699.

Observe that the first (or hundreds) digit of the numbers assigned to asset accounts is 1. The first (or hundreds) digit of the numbers assigned to liability accounts is 2, and so on. In each case, the first digit of an account's number tells its balance sheet or income statement classification. The second and third digits further identify the account. We describe this type of account numbering system more completely in the next chapter.

Using T-Accounts

In its simplest form, an account looks like the letter **T**, as follows:

(Place for the Name of the Item Recorded in This Account)	
(Left side)	(Right side)

Given its shape, this simple form of account is called a *T-account*. Note that the **T** format gives the account a left side, a right side, and a place for the name of the account. The name indicates the type of items or effects to be stored in this particular account. For example, the *Cash* account is the location where all cash increases and decreases are recorded and stored.

When a **T-account** is used to record increases and decreases in an item, the increases are placed on one side of the account and the decreases on the other. For example, recall the transactions of Jerry Dow's law practice discussed in Chapter 1. Many of those transactions affected cash. When the increases and decreases in the cash of Jerry Dow's law practice are recorded in a T-account, they appear as follows:

Cash

Investment	9,000	Purchase of law books	2,500
Legal fees earned	2,200	Purchase of office equipment	5,600
Collection of account receivable	1,700	Rent payment	1,000
		Payment of salary	700
		Payment of account payable	900
		Withdrawal by owner	1,100

Calculating the Balance of an Account

Putting the increases on one side and the decreases on the other makes it easy to determine the balance of an account. To do so, you simply add the increases shown on one side, separately add the decreases on the other side, and then subtract the sum of the decreases from the sum of the increases. Regardless of the type of account, the **account balance** is the difference between its increases and decreases. Thus, the balance of an asset account is the amount of that asset owned by the entity on the date the balance is calculated. The balance of a liability account is the amount owed by the entity on the date of the balance.

In the Cash account for Jerry Dow's law practice, the total increases were $12,900, the total decreases were $11,800, and the account balance is $1,100, as follows:

Cash

Investment	9,000	Purchase of law books	2,500
Legal fee earned	2,200	Purchase of office equipment	5,600
Collection of account receivable	1,700	Rent payment	1,000
		Payment of salary	700
		Payment of account payable	900
		Withdrawal by owner	1,100
Total increases	12,900	Total decreases	11,800
Less decreases	−11,800		
Balance	1,100		

Debits and Credits

Note again that a T-account has a left side and a right side. In accounting, the left side is called the **debit** side, abbreviated "Dr."; and the right side is called the **credit** side, abbreviated "Cr."[1] When amounts are entered on the left side of an account, they are called *debits,* and the account is said to be *debited.*

[1] These abbreviations are remnants of 18th-century English practices, when the terms used were *Debitor* and *Creditor*. The abbreviations take the first and last letters from the words, just as is done for *Mister* (Mr.) and *Doctor* (Dr.).

When amounts are entered on the right side, they are called *credits,* and the account is said to be *credited.* The difference between the total debits and the total credits recorded in an account is the *account balance.* The balance may be either a *debit balance* or a *credit balance.* It is a debit balance when the sum of the debits exceeds the sum of the credits. It is a credit balance when the sum of the credits exceeds the sum of the debits.

The words *to debit* and *to credit* should not be confused with *to increase* and *to decrease.* To debit means to enter an amount on the left side of an account. To credit means to enter an amount on the right side. Whether a debit (or credit) is an increase or a decrease depends on the type of account. For example, notice the way in which the investment of Jerry Dow is recorded in the Cash and capital accounts:

Cash			
Investment	9,000		

Jerry Dow, Capital			
		Investment	9,000

When Dow invested $9,000 in his law practice, both the cash of the business and Dow's equity increased. Observe in the accounts that the increase in cash is recorded on the left or debit side of the Cash account, while the increase in owner's equity is recorded on the right or credit side. The transaction is recorded in this manner because of the mechanics of **double-entry accounting,** which we explain in the next section.

The Rules of Debit and Credit in Double-Entry Accounting

LO 3 State the rules of debit and credit and use those rules to analyze transactions and show their effects on the accounts.

In double-entry accounting, every transaction affects and is recorded in two or more accounts. Also, in *recording each transaction, the total amount debited must equal the total amount credited.* Since every transaction is recorded with total debits equal to total credits, the sum of the debit account balances in the ledger should equal the sum of the credit balances. If the sum of the debit balances does not equal the sum of the credit balances, an error has been made. Thus, one by-product of having equal debits and credits is that many errors are easy to detect.

In double-entry accounting, increases in assets are recorded on the debit side of asset accounts. Why do assets have debit balances? There is no specific reason; it is simply a matter of convention. However, since assets have debit balances, we can reason that increases in liabilities and owner's equity must be recorded as credits. This results from the accounting equation, $A = L + OE$, and from the requirement that debits equal credits. In other words, if assets have debit balances, equal debits and credits are possible only if increases in liabilities and owner's equity are recorded on the opposite or credit side. Therefore, increases and decreases in all balance sheet accounts have to be recorded as follows:

Assets		=	Liabilities		+	Owner's Equity	
Debit for increases	Credit for decreases		Debit for decreases	Credit for increases		Debit for decreases	Credit for increases

As pictured in these T-accounts, the rules for recording transactions under a double-entry system may be expressed as follows:

1. Increases in assets are debited to asset accounts; therefore, decreases in assets must be credited.
2. Increases in liability and owner's equity items are credited to liability and owner's equity accounts; therefore, decreases in liabilities and owner's equity must be debited.

Recall from Chapter 1 that owner's equity is increased by the owner's investment and by revenues. Owner's equity is decreased by expenses and by withdrawals. Because of these facts, we offer these additional rules:

3. Investments by the owner of a business are credited to the owner's capital account.
4. Since the owner's withdrawals of assets decrease owner's equity, they are debited to the owner's withdrawals account.
5. Since revenues increase owner's equity, they are credited in each case to a revenue account that shows the kind of revenue earned.
6. Since expenses decrease owner's equity, they are debited in each case to an expense account that shows the kind of expense incurred.

At this stage, you will find it helpful to memorize these rules. You will apply them over and over in the course of your study. Eventually, the rules will become second nature to you.

Transactions Illustrating the Rules of Debit and Credit

The following transactions for Jerry Dow's law practice illustrate how to apply the rules of debit and credit while recording transactions in the accounts. The number before each transaction is used throughout the illustration so that you can identify the transaction in the accounts. Note that the first 11 transactions were used in Chapter 1 to illustrate the effects of transactions on the accounting equation. Five additional transactions (12 through 16) are presented in this chapter.

To record a transaction, first analyze it to determine which items were increased or decreased. The rules of debit and credit are then applied to determine the debit and credit effects of the increases or decreases. An analysis of each of the following transactions is given to demonstrate the process.

1. On December 1, Jerry Dow invested $9,000 in a new law practice.

Cash

(1)	9,000		

Jerry Dow, Capital

		(1)	9,000

Analysis of the transaction: The transaction increased the cash of the practice. At the same time, it increased Dow's equity in the business. Increases in assets are debited, and increases in owner's equity are credited. Therefore, to record the transaction, Cash should be debited and Jerry Dow, Capital, should be credited for $9,000.

2. Purchased books for a law library, paying cash of $2,500.

Cash

(1)	9,000	(2)	2,500

Law Library

(2)	2,500		

Analysis of the transaction: The law library is an asset that is increased by the purchase of books; and cash is an asset that is decreased. Increases in assets are debited, and decreases are credited. Therefore, to record the transaction, debit Law Library and credit Cash for $2,500.

3. Purchased office equipment for cash, $5,600.

Cash

(1)	9,000	(2)	2,500
		(3)	5,600

Office Equipment

(3)	5,600		

Analysis of the transaction: The asset office equipment is increased, and the asset cash is decreased. Debit Office Equipment and credit Cash for $5,600.

4. Purchased on credit from Equip-it Company law library items, $380, and office equipment, $1,280.

Law Library

(2)	2,500		
(4)	380		

Office Equipment

(3)	5,600		
(4)	1,280		

Accounts Payable

		(4)	1,660

Analysis of the transaction: This transaction increased the assets, law library and office equipment, but it also created a liability. Increases in assets are debits, and increases in liabilities are credits. Therefore, debit Law Library for $380 and Office Equipment for $1,280, and credit Accounts Payable for $1,660.

5. Completed legal work for a client and immediately collected a $2,200 fee.

Cash

(1)	9,000	(2)	2,500
(5)	2,200	(3)	5,600

Legal Fees Earned

		(5)	2,200

Analysis of the transaction: This revenue transaction increased both assets and owner's equity. Increases in assets are debits, and increases in owner's equity are credits. Since revenues increase owner's equity, revenue accounts are increased with credits. Therefore, debit Cash to record the increase in assets. Credit Legal Fees Earned to increase owner's equity and accumulate information for the income statement.

6. Paid the office rent for December, $1,000.

Cash

(1)	9,000	(2)	2,500
(5)	2,200	(3)	5,600
		(6)	1,000

Rent Expense

(6)	1,000		

Analysis of the transaction: The cost of renting the office during December is an expense, the effect of which is to decrease owner's equity. Since decreases in owner's equity are debits, expenses are recorded as debits. Therefore, debit Rent Expense to decrease owner's equity and to accumulate information for the income statement. Also, credit Cash to record the decrease in assets.

7. Paid the secretary's salary for the two weeks ended December 12, $700.

Cash

(1)	9,000	(2)	2,500
(5)	2,200	(3)	5,600
		(6)	1,000
		(7)	700

Salaries Expense

(7)	700		

Analysis of the transaction: The secretary's salary is an expense that decreased owner's equity. Debit Salaries Expense to have the effect of decreasing owner's equity and to accumulate information for the income statement. Also, credit Cash to record the decrease in assets.

8. Completed legal work for a client on credit and billed the client $1,700 for the services rendered.

Accounts Receivable

(8)	1,700		

Legal Fees Earned

		(5)	2,200
		(8)	1,700

Analysis of the transaction: This revenue transaction gave the law practice the right to collect $1,700 from the client, and thus increased assets and owner's equity. Therefore, debit Accounts Receivable for the increase in assets and credit Legal Fees Earned to increase owner's equity and at the same time accumulate information for the income statement.

9. The client paid the $1,700 legal fee billed in transaction 8.

Cash

(1)	9,000	(2)	2,500
(5)	2,200	(3)	5,600
(9)	1,700	(6)	1,000
		(7)	700

Accounts Receivable

(8)	1,700	(9)	1,700

Analysis of the transaction: One asset was increased, and the other decreased. Debit Cash to record the increase in cash, and credit Accounts Receivable to record the decrease in the account receivable, or the decrease in the right to collect from the client.

10. Paid Equip-it Company $900 of the $1,660 owed for the items purchased on credit in transaction 4.

Cash

(1)	9,000	(2)	2,500
(5)	2,200	(3)	5,600
(9)	1,700	(6)	1,000
		(7)	700
		(10)	**900**

Accounts Payble

(10)	**900**	(4)	1,660

Analysis of the transaction: Payments to creditors decrease in equal amounts both assets and liabilities. Decreases in liabilities are debited, and decreases in assets are credited. Debit Accounts Payable and credit Cash.

11. Jerry Dow withdrew $1,100 from the law practice for personal use.

Cash

(1)	9,000	(2)	2,500
(5)	2,200	(3)	5,600
(9)	1,700	(6)	1,000
		(7)	700
		(10)	900
		(11)	**1,100**

Jerry Dow, Withdrawals

(11)	**1,100**		

Analysis of the transaction: This transaction reduced in equal amounts both assets and owner's equity. Cash is credited to record the asset reduction; and the Jerry Dow, Withdrawals, account is debited to decrease owner's equity and to accumulate information for the statement of changes in owner's equity.

12. Signed a contract with Chemical Supply to do its legal work on a fixed-fee basis for $500 per month. Received the fee for the first six months in advance, $3,000.

Cash

(1)	9,000	(2)	2,500
(5)	2,200	(3)	5,600
(9)	1,700	(6)	1,000
(12)	**3,000**	(7)	700
		(10)	900
		(11)	1,100

Unearned Legal Fees

		(12)	**3,000**

Analysis of the transaction: The $3,000 receipt of cash increased assets but is not a revenue until earned. Receipt of cash before it is earned creates a liability that will be satisfied by doing the client's legal work over the next six months. Record the asset increase by debiting Cash. Record the liability increase by crediting Unearned Legal Fees.

13. Paid a $2,400 premium for liability insurance protection that lasts two years.

Cash

(1)	9,000	(2)	2,500
(5)	2,200	(3)	5,600
(9)	1,700	(6)	1,000
(12)	3,000	(7)	700
		(10)	900
		(11)	1,100
		(13)	**2,400**

Prepaid Insurance

(13)	**2,400**		

Analysis of the transaction: The advance payment of an insurance premium creates an asset by decreasing another asset. The new asset is recorded with a debit to Prepaid Insurance, and the payment is recorded with a credit to Cash.

14. Purchased office supplies for cash, $120.
15. Paid the December utilities bill for electricity and water, $230.
16. Paid the secretary's salary for the two weeks ended December 26, $700.

Cash

(1)	9,000	(2)	2,500
(5)	2,200	(3)	5,600
(9)	1,700	(6)	1,000
(12)	3,000	(7)	700
		(10)	900
		(11)	1,100
		(13)	2,400
		(14)	120
		(15)	230
		(16)	700

Analysis of the transactions: These transactions are alike because each decreased cash; but they differ in that office supplies are assets while the utilities and secretary's services have been used up and are expenses. The cost of the supplies should be debited to an asset account, while the utilities and the salary should be debited to separate expense accounts. Each transaction involves a credit to Cash.

Office Supplies

(14)	120		

Utilities Expense

(15)	230		

Salaries Expense

(16)	700		

The Accounts and the Equation

Illustration 2–2 shows the accounts of the Dow law practice after the transactions have been recorded in them. The accounts are classified according to the elements of the accounting equation.

Transactions Should First Be Recorded in a Journal

LO 4 Record transactions in a General Journal, describe balance column accounts, and post entries from the journal to the accounts.

In the previous pages, we used the rules of debit and credit to show how a variety of transactions affected the accounts. As a learning exercise, this process of analyzing transactions and recording their effects directly in the accounts is helpful. However, if you use a manual accounting system in the real world, you should not record transactions directly in the accounts. If you attempt to record the effects directly in the accounts and you make errors, the errors will be very difficult to locate. Even with a transaction that has only one debit and one credit, the debit is entered on one ledger page or card and the credit on another, and there is nothing to link the two together.

Therefore, *before transactions are recorded in the accounts, they are first entered in a* **journal.** This practice links together the debits and credits of each transaction and provides in one place a complete record of each transaction. Remember this rule: all transactions should be recorded first in a journal. Then, after the transactions are entered in a journal, the debit and credit information about each transaction is copied from the journal to the ledger accounts. These procedures reduce the likelihood of errors. And, if errors are

ILLUSTRATION 2–2

The Ledger for Jerry Dow, Attorney

Assets = Liabilities + Owner's Equity

Assets

Cash

(1)	9,000	(2)	2,500
(5)	2,200	(3)	5,600
(9)	1,700	(6)	1,000
(12)	3,000	(7)	700
		(10)	900
		(11)	1,100
		(13)	2,400
		(14)	120
		(15)	230
		(16)	700
Total	15,900	Total	15,250
	−15,250		
Balance	650		

Accounts Receivable

(8)	1,700	(9)	1,700

Office Supplies

(14)	120		

Prepaid Insurance

(13)	2,400		

Law Library

(2)	2,500		
(4)	380		
Balance	2,880		

Office Equipment

(3)	5,600		
(4)	1,280		
Balance	6,880		

Liabilities

Accounts Payable

(10)	900	(4)	1,660
Total	900	Total	1,660
			−900
		Balance	760

Unearned Legal Fees

		(12)	3,000

Owner's Equity

Jerry Dow, Capital

		(1)	9,000

Jerry Dow, Withdrawals

(11)	1,100		

Legal Fees Earned

		(5)	2,200
		(8)	1,700
		Balance	3,900

Salaries Expense

(7)	700		
(16)	700		
Balance	1,400		

Rent Expense

(6)	1,000		

Utilities Expense

(15)	230		

The accounts in this box involve increases and decreases in owner's equity and are reported on the income statement or the statement of changes in owner's equity.

made, the journal record makes it possible to trace the debits and credits into the accounts for the purpose of locating the errors.

The process of recording transactions in a journal is called *journalizing transactions*. The process of copying journal entry information from a journal to a ledger is called **posting**. Remember the sequence of these steps, as shown in Illustration 2–3. Since transactions are first journalized and then posted to the ledger, a journal is called a **book of original entry** and a ledger a **book of final entry**.

ILLUSTRATION 2–3

The Sequence of Steps in Recording Transactions

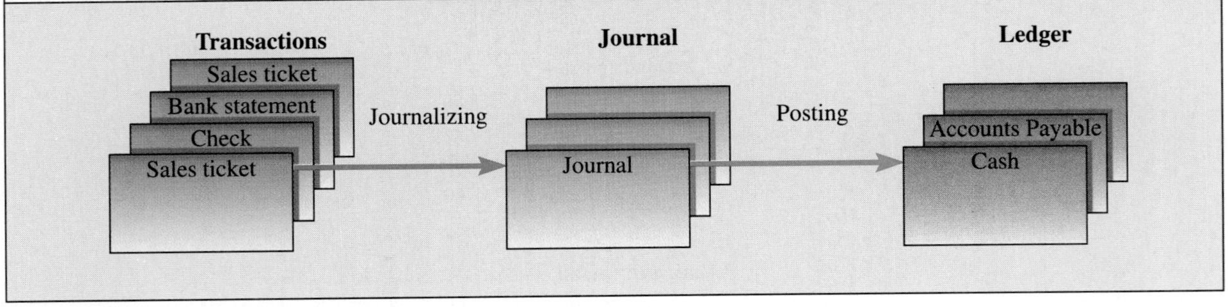

The General Journal

The simplest and most flexible type of journal is a **General Journal.** The General Journal is designed so that it can be used to record any kind of transaction. For each transaction, it provides places for recording:

1. The transaction date.
2. The names of the accounts involved.
3. The amount of each debit and credit.
4. An explanation of the transaction.

And, when the amounts are copied from the journal to the accounts in the ledger, the General Journal provides

5. A column in which to mark the identifying numbers of the accounts to which the debit(s) and credit(s) were copied.

Illustration 2–4 shows a typical general journal page on which the first four transactions of the Dow law practice have been recorded.

The last entry in Illustration 2–4 records the credit purchase of law books and office equipment. Note that three accounts are involved in this transaction. When a transaction involves three or more accounts, it is recorded in the General Journal with a **compound journal entry.** That is, a compound journal entry involves three or more accounts.

Recording Transactions in a General Journal

Use the following procedures to record transactions in a General Journal:

1. Write the year in small figures at the top of the first column.
2. Write the month on the first line in the first column. The year and the month are not repeated except at the top of a new page or at the beginning of a new month or year.
3. Write the day of each transaction in the second column on the first line of the transaction.
4. Write the names of the accounts to be debited and credited and an explanation of the transaction in the Account Titles and Explanation column. *The names of the accounts debited are written first, beginning at*

ILLUSTRATION 2–4

A General Journal Showing Transactions of Jerry Dow, Attorney

GENERAL JOURNAL Page 1

Date		Account Titles and Explanation	PR	Debit	Credit
1993 Dec.	1	Cash		9,000 00	
		Jerry Dow, Capital			9,000 00
		Investment by owner.			
	2	Law Library		2,500 00	
		Cash			2,500 00
		Purchased law books for cash.			
	3	Office Equipment		5,600 00	
		Cash			5,600 00
		Purchased office equipment for cash.			
	6	Law Library		380 00	
		Office Equipment		1,280 00	
		Accounts Payable			1,660 00
		Purchased supplies and equipment on credit.			

the left margin of the column. The names of the accounts credited are written on the following lines, indented about one inch. The explanation is placed on the next line, indented about a half inch from the left margin. The explanation should be short but sufficient to explain the transaction and set it apart from other transactions.

5. Write the debit amount in the Debit column on the same line as the name of the account to be debited. Write the credit amount in the Credit column on the same line as the account to be credited.
6. Skip a single line between each journal entry to keep the entries separate.

When transactions are first recorded in the General Journal, nothing is entered in the **Posting Reference (PR) column.** However, when the debits and credits are copied from the journal to the ledger, the account numbers of the ledger accounts to which the debits and credits are copied are entered in this column. The Posting Reference column is sometimes called the **Folio column.**

Balance Column Accounts

T-accounts like the ones shown so far are used only in textbook illustrations and in accounting classes for demonstrations. In both cases, their use eliminates details and lets you concentrate on ideas. In real-world accounting systems, however, T-accounts are not used. Instead, accounts like the one in Illustration 2–5 are generally used.

The account in Illustration 2–5 is called a **balance column account.** It differs from a T-account because it has columns for specific information about each debit and credit entered in the account. Also, its Debit and Credit columns are placed side by side, and it has a third Balance column. In this Balance column, the account's new balance is entered each time the account is debited or credited. As a result, the last amount in the column is the account's current balance. For example, on December 1, the illustrated Cash account was debited for the $9,000 investment of Jerry Dow, which caused it to have a $9,000 debit balance. It was then credited for $2,500, and its new $6,500 balance was entered. On December 3, it was credited again for $5,600, which reduced its balance to $900. Then, on December 10, it was debited for $2,200, and its balance was increased to $3,100.

When a balance column account like that of Illustration 2–5 is used, the heading of the Balance column does not tell whether the balance is a debit balance or a credit balance. However, this should not create a problem. You should be able to determine the normal balance of any account by reading the account title and recognizing what type of account it is. The following normal balances result from the rules of debit and credit:

Account Classification	Since Increases Are Recorded as:	The Normal Balance Is:
Asset	Debits	Debit
Liability	Credits	Credit
Owner's equity:		
Capital	Credits	Credit
Withdrawals	Debits.	Debit
Revenue	Credits	Credit
Expense	Debits.	Debit

When an unusual transaction causes an account to have a balance opposite from its normal kind of balance, this abnormal balance is indicated in the account by circling the amount or by entering it in red. Also, a –0– or 0.00 is written in the Balance column when a debit or credit entered in an account causes the account to have no balance.

Posting Transaction Information

The process of posting journal entry information from the journal to the ledger may be done daily, weekly, or as time permits. In any case, posting should be done without undue delay and all transactions must be posted before financial statements can be prepared at the end of each accounting period.

In the posting procedure, journal debits are copied and become ledger account debits and journal credits are copied and become ledger account credits. Illustration 2–6 shows the posting procedures for a journal entry. As shown in the illustration, the procedures to post a journal entry are as follows:

ILLUSTRATION 2–5

A Cash Account Formatted as a Balance Column Account

Cash — **Account No.** 101

Date		Explanation	PR	Debit	Credit	Balance
1993 Dec.	1		G1	9,000 00		9,000 00
	2		G1		2,500 00	6,500 00
	3		G1		5,600 00	900 00
	10		G1	2,200 00		3,100 00

For the debit:

1. In the ledger, find the account named in the debit of the journal entry.
2. Enter in the account the date of the entry as shown in the journal.
3. In the Debit column of the account, write the debit amount shown in the journal.
4. Enter the letter *G* and the journal page number from which the entry is being posted in the Posting Reference column of the account. The letter *G* indicates that the amount was posted from the General Journal. We discuss other journals later in the text, and each is identified by its own letter.
5. Determine the effect of the debit on the account balance and enter the new balance.
6. Enter in the Posting Reference column of the journal the account number of the account to which the amount was posted.

For the credit:

Repeat the preceding steps. However, the credit amount is entered in the Credit column and has a credit effect on the account balance.

Observe that the last step (step 6) in the posting procedure for either the debit or the credit of an entry is to insert the account number in the Posting Reference column of the journal. Inserting the account number in this column serves two purposes: (1) The account number in the journal and the journal page number in the account act as a cross-reference when you want to trace an amount from one record to the other. (2) Writing the account number in the journal as a last step in posting indicates that posting is completed. If posting is interrupted, the bookkeeper can examine the journal's Posting Reference column to see where posting stopped.

ILLUSTRATION 2–6

Procedures to Follow in Posting a General Journal Entry

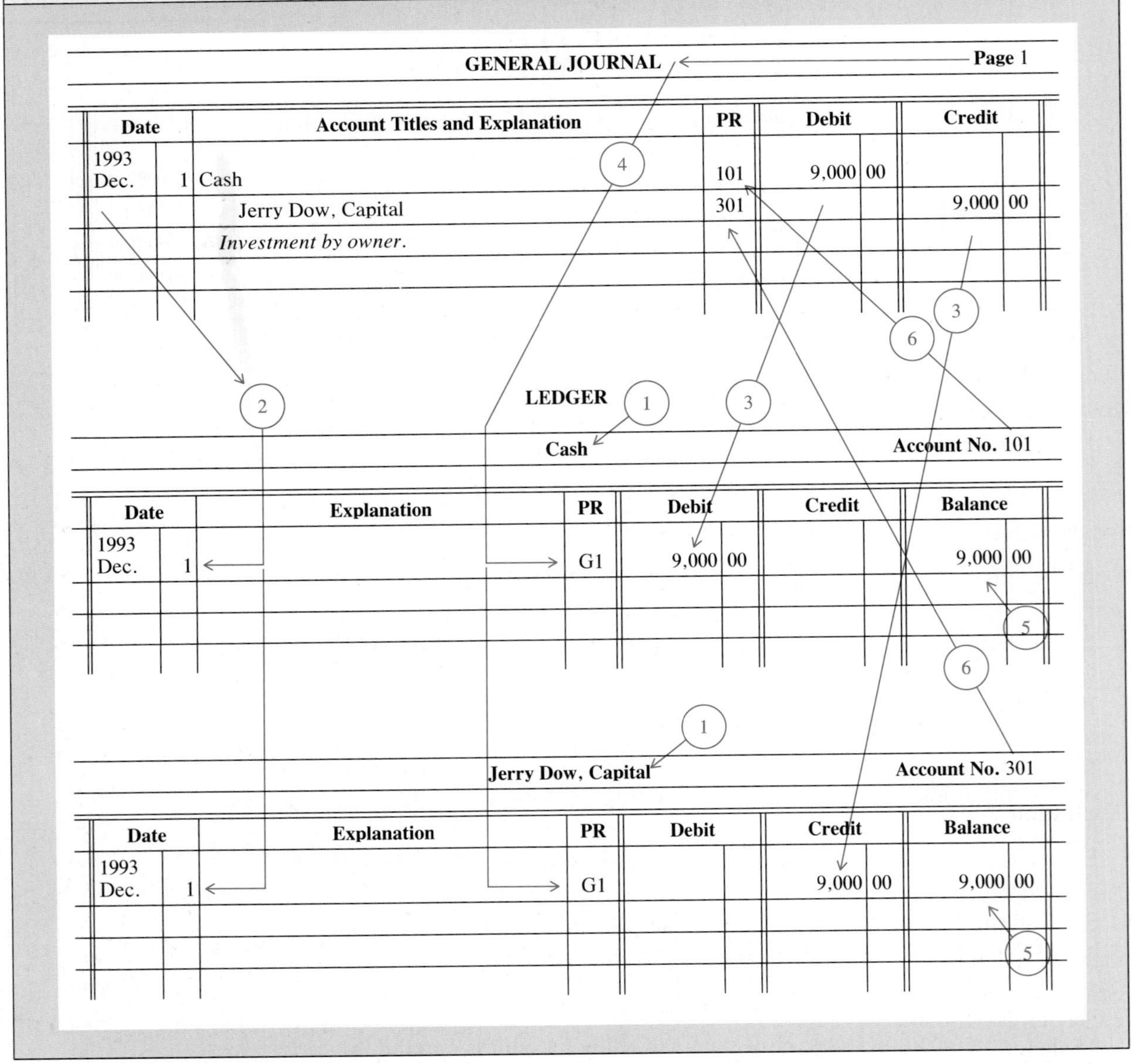

Preparing a Trial Balance

LO 5 Prepare and explain the use of a trial balance to discover and correct errors.

Recall that in a double-entry accounting system, every transaction is recorded with equal debits and credits. As a result, you know that an error has been made if the total of the debits in the ledger does not equal the total of the credits. Also, when the balances of the accounts are determined, the sum of the debit balances must equal the sum of the credit balances; otherwise, you know an error has been made. This equality is tested by preparing a **trial balance.** Preparing a trial balance requires five steps:

ILLUSTRATION 2–7

Trial Balance Drawn from the Ledger of Jerry Dow, Attorney

JERRY DOW, ATTORNEY
Trial Balance
December 31, 1993

Cash	$ 650	
Office supplies	120	
Prepaid insurance	2,400	
Law library	2,880	
Office equipment	6,880	
Accounts payable		$ 760
Unearned legal fees		3,000
Jerry Dow, capital		9,000
Jerry Dow, withdrawals	1,100	
Legal fees earned		3,900
Salaries expense	1,400	
Rent expense	1,000	
Utilities expense	230	
Totals	$16,660	$16,660

1. Determine the balance of each account in the ledger.
2. List the accounts with balances other than zero, with the debit balances in one column and the credit balances in another (see Illustration 2–7).
3. Add the debit balances.
4. Add the credit balances.
5. Compare the sum of the debit balances with the sum of the credit balances.

The trial balance in Illustration 2–7 was prepared from the accounts in Illustration 2–2 on page 91. Note that its column totals are equal; in other words, the trial balance is in balance. Therefore, debits equal credits in the ledger.

The Evidence of Accuracy Offered by a Trial Balance

When a trial balance does not balance, one or more errors have been made. The error(s) may have been in journalizing the transactions, in posting to the ledger, in determining the account balances, in copying the balances to the trial balance, or in adding the columns of the trial balance. On the other hand, if the trial balance balances, the accounts are probably free of those errors that cause an inequality in debits and credits.

However, a trial balance that balances is not proof of complete accuracy. Some errors do not affect the equality of the trial balance columns. For example, you may record a correct debit amount to the wrong account. This error will not cause a trial balance to be out of balance. Another example would be to record a wrong amount with an equal debit and credit. Because errors of this sort do not affect the equality of debits and credits, a trial balance that balances does not prove recording accuracy. It does, however, provide evidence that several types of errors have not been made.

Locating Errors

When a trial balance does not balance, one or more errors have been made. To locate the error or errors, check the journalizing, posting, and trial balance preparation steps in their reverse order. First check the addition of the columns in the trial balance to see that no addition errors were made. Then check to see that the account balances were correctly copied from the ledger. Note that if a debit (or credit) balance was incorrectly listed in the trial balance as a credit (or debit), the difference between total debits and total credits would be twice the amount of the incorrectly listed amount.

Next, recalculate the account balances. If the error or errors are not found at this stage, check the posting and then the original journalizing of the transactions. A common error to look for involves transposing numbers. For example, a $691 debit may have been posted as $619. As a result, total debits would be larger than total credits by $72. That is, $691 − $619 = $72. To test for a transposing error, note that all transposing errors are divisible evenly by nine. Note that 72 is divisible by 9, or 72/9 = 8.

Correcting Errors

When an error is discovered in either the journal or the ledger, it must be corrected. The method of correction depends on the nature of the error and the stage in the accounting procedures at which it is discovered.

If an error is discovered in a journal entry before the error is posted, it may be corrected by ruling a single line through the incorrect amount or account name and writing the correct amount or account name above. Likewise, if a correctly journalized amount was posted incorrectly as a different (wrong) amount, you may correct it in the same manner. However, if a journal entry to the wrong account has been posted to that account, you should correct the error with a new journal entry. The correcting journal entry should transfer the change from the wrong account to the proper account. For example, the following journal entry to record the purchase of office supplies was made and posted:

Oct.	14	Office Equipment	160.00	
		Cash		160.00
		To record the purchase of office supplies.		

Obviously, the debit of the entry is to the wrong account; therefore, the following entry is needed to correct the error:

Oct.	17	Office Supplies	160.00	
		Office Equipment		160.00
		To correct the entry of October 14 in which the Office Equipment account was debited in error for the purchase of office supplies.		

The debit of the second entry correctly records the purchase of supplies, and the credit cancels the error of the first entry. Note the full explanation of the correcting entry. Such an explanation should always be full and complete so that anyone can see exactly what occurred.

Bookkeeping Techniques

When amounts are entered in a journal or a ledger, it is not necessary to use commas indicating thousands of dollars or decimal points to separate dollars and cents. The ruled lines accomplish this. However, when statements are prepared on unruled paper, you should use decimal points and commas.

Dollar signs are not used in journals or ledgers; however, you should use them on financial reports prepared on unruled paper. On such reports, place a dollar sign (1) before the first amount in each column of figures and (2) before the first amount appearing after a ruled line that indicates an addition or a subtraction. Examine Illustration 3–6, page 146, for examples of the use of dollar signs on a financial report.

When an amount to be entered in a ledger or a journal is an amount of dollars and no cents, some bookkeepers save time by using a dash in the cents column in the place of two zeros to indicate that there are no cents. On financial reports, however, two zeros are preferred.

To save space and simplify some of the illustrations, we often use exact dollar amounts in this text. In such cases, neither zeros nor dashes are used.

Summary of the Chapter in Terms of Learning Objectives

LO 1. The economic events recorded in accounting include business transactions and other (internal) events that have an effect on the assets and liabilities of the entity. Business papers provide evidence of completed transactions and the amounts that should be used to record the transactions.

LO 2. In an accounting system, the different effects of business transactions are stored in separate locations called accounts. Commonly used asset accounts include Cash, Notes Receivable, Accounts Receivable, Prepaid Insurance, Office Supplies, Store Supplies, Equipment, Buildings, and Land. Commonly used liability accounts include Notes Payable and Accounts Payable, as well as other unearned revenue accounts. The owner's investments in a proprietorship and other relatively permanent changes in the owner's equity are recorded in the owner's capital account. Revenue, expense, and withdrawal accounts are used to accumulate changes in owner's equity.

The collection of accounts used by a business is called a ledger. Each account in the ledger is assigned a unique number to identify the account. The chart of accounts for a business lists all the account titles (and the account numbers) that are used in recording the transactions of the business.

In the accounts, debits record increases in assets, withdrawals, and expenses. Decreases in liabilities, the owner's capital account, and revenues are also recorded with debits. Credits record increases in liabilities, the owner's capital account, and revenues. Credits are also used to record decreases in assets, withdrawals, and expenses.

LO 3. To understand the effects of a transaction on a business, first analyze the transaction to determine what accounts were increased or decreased. Every transaction affects two or more accounts and the sum of the debits always equals the sum of the credits. As a result, the effects of business transactions never violate the accounting equation, Assets = Liabilities + Owner's Equity.

LO 4. A transaction is first recorded in a journal so that all of the transaction's effects on the accounts are shown in one place. Then, each effect is posted (copied) to the appropriate account in the ledger so that the accounts classify and summarize the effects of all transactions. After each amount is posted, the account number is recorded in the journal and the journal page number is recorded in the account as a cross-reference to assist in the discovery of errors.

LO 5. To prepare a trial balance, list the ledger accounts that have balances, showing the debit and credit balances in separate columns. The columns are totaled to show that the sum of all debit account balances in the ledger equals the sum of all credit account balances. If the totals are not equal, search for the errors that were made and then make appropriate corrections.

Demonstration Problem

This demonstration problem is based on the same facts as the demonstration problem presented at the end of Chapter 1. During its first month of operation, Barbara Schmidt's haircutting business (The Cutlery) completed the following transactions:

a. On August 1, 1993, Schmidt put $2,000 of her savings into a checking account in the name of The Cutlery.

b. On August 2, she bought $600 of supplies for the shop.

c. On August 3, she paid $500 rent for the month of August for a small store.

d. On August 5, she furnished the store, installing new fixtures that the supplier sold to her for $1,200. This amount was to be repaid in three equal payments at the end of August, September, and October.

e. The Cutlery opened August 12, and in the first week of business ended August 16, receipts from cash sales amounted to $825.

f. On August 17, Schmidt paid $125 to an assistant for working during the business's grand opening.

g. Receipts from cash sales during the two-week period ended August 30 amounted to $1,930.

h. On August 31, Schmidt paid the first installment on the fixtures.

i. On August 31, she withdrew $900 cash for her personal expenses.

Required

1. Prepare general journal entries to record the preceding transactions.
2. Open the following accounts: Cash, 101; Store Supplies, 125; Store Equipment, 165; Accounts Payable, 201; Barbara Schmidt, Capital, 301; Barbara Schmidt, Withdrawals, 302; Haircutting Services Revenue, 403; Wages Expense, 623; and Rent Expense, 640.

3. Post the journal entries to the proper ledger accounts.
4. Prepare a trial balance for The Cutlery.

Solution to Demonstration Problem

Planning the Solution

- Analyze each transaction to determine which accounts are affected by the transaction and the amount of each effect.
- Use the rules of debit and credit to prepare a journal entry for each transaction.
- Transfer each debit and each credit in the journal to the appropriate ledger accounts and cross-reference each posted amount in the Posting Reference columns of the journal and the account.
- Calculate each account balance and list the accounts with their balances on a trial balance.
- As evidence of error-free work, observe that total debits equal total credits on the trial balance.

1.

Page 1

	Date		Account Titles and Explanations	PR	Debit	Credit
	1993					
a.	Aug.	1	Cash	101	2,000.00	
			Barbara Schmidt, Capital	301		2,000.00
			Invested $2,000 in business.			
b.		2	Store Supplies	125	600.00	
			Cash	101		600.00
			Purchased store supplies.			
c.		3	Rent Expense	640	500.00	
			Cash	101		500.00
			Paid rent for August.			
d.		5	Store Equipment	165	1,200.00	
			Accounts Payable	201		1,200.00
			Purchased fixtures on credit.			
e.		16	Cash	101	825.00	
			Haircutting Services Revenue	403		825.00
			Cash sales to customers.			
f.		17	Wages Expense	623	125.00	
			Cash	101		125.00
			Paid wages to assistant.			
g.		30	Cash	101	1,930.00	
			Haircutting Services Revenue	403		1,930.00
			Two weeks' sales to customers.			
h.		31	Accounts Payable	201	400.00	
			Cash	101		400.00
			Paid first payment on store equipment purchase of August 5.			
i.		31	Barbara Schmidt, Withdrawals	302	900.00	
			Cash	101		900.00
			Withdrew cash for personal use.			

2, 3.

Cash — **Account No.** 101

Date		Explanation	PR	Debit	Credit	Balance
1993						
Aug.	1		G1	2,000		2,000
	2		G1		600	1,400
	3		G1		500	900
	16		G1	825		1,725
	17		G1		125	1,600
	30		G1	1,930		3,530
	31		G1		400	3,130
	31		G1		900	2,230

Store Supplies — **Account No.** 125

Date		Explanation	PR	Debit	Credit	Balance
1993						
Aug.	2		G1	600		600

Store Equipment — **Account No.** 165

Date		Explanation	PR	Debit	Credit	Balance
1993						
Aug.	5		G1	1,200		1,200

Accounts Payable — **Account No.** 201

Date		Explanation	PR	Debit	Credit	Balance
1993						
Aug.	5		G1		1,200	1,200
	31		G1	400		800

Barbara Schmidt, Capital — **Account No.** 301

Date		Explanation	PR	Debit	Credit	Balance
1993						
Aug.	1		G1		2,000	2,000

Barbara Schmidt, Withdrawals — **Account No.** 302

Date		Explanation	PR	Debit	Credit	Balance
1993						
Aug.	31		G1	900		900

Haircutting Services Revenue — **Account No.** 403

Date		Explanation	PR	Debit	Credit	Balance
1993						
Aug.	16		G1		825	825
	30		G1		1,930	2,755

Wages Expense **Account No.** 623

Date		Explanation	PR	Debit	Credit	Balance
1993						
Aug.	17		G1	125		125

Rent Expense **Account No.** 640

Date		Explanation	PR	Debit	Credit	Balance
1993						
Aug.	3		G1	500		500

4.

THE CUTLERY
Trial Balance
August 31, 1993

Cash	$2,230	
Store supplies	600	
Store equipment	1,200	
Accounts payable		$ 800
Barbara Schmidt, capital		2,000
Barbara Schmidt, withdrawals	900	
Haircutting services revenue		2,755
Wages expense	125	
Rent expense	500	
Totals	$5,555	$5,555

Glossary

LO 6 Define or explain the words and phrases listed in the chapter glossary.

Account balance the difference between the increases and decreases recorded in an account. p. 84

Accounts separate locations in an accounting system each one of which is used to store the increases and decreases in a different type of revenue, expense, asset, liability, or owner's equity item. pp. 79–83

Balance column account an account that has debit and credit columns for entering changes in the account and a third column for entering the new account balance after each debit or credit is posted to the account. pp. 94–95

Book of final entry a ledger in which amounts are posted from a journal. p. 91

Book of original entry a journal in which transactions are first recorded. p. 91

Business papers printed documents that businesses use in the process of completing business transactions and that provide evidence of the transactions; sometimes called *source documents*. p. 78

Capital account an account used to record the owner's investments in the business plus any more or less permanent changes in the owner's equity. p. 82

Chart of accounts a list of all the accounts used by a company, showing the identifying number assigned to each account. p. 83

Compound journal entry a journal entry that has more than one debit and/or more than one credit. pp. 92–93

Credit the right side of a T-account, or entries that decrease asset and expense accounts, or increase liability, owner's equity, and revenue accounts. pp. 84–86

Debit the left side of a T-account, or entries that increase asset and expense accounts, or decrease liability, owner's equity, and revenue accounts. pp. 84–86

Double-entry accounting a system of accounting in which each transaction affects and is recorded in two or more accounts with total debits equal to total credits. p. 85

Drawing account another name for the *withdrawals account*. p. 82

External transactions completed exchanges of economic consideration between the entity being accounted for and some other outside parties. p. 77

Folio column another name for the *Posting Reference column*. p. 93

General Journal a book of original entry designed flexibly so that it can be used to record any type of transaction. pp. 92–93

Internal transactions a name sometimes given to economic events that have an effect on an entity's accounting equation but that do not involve transactions with outside parties. p. 77

Journal a book of original entry in which a complete record of transactions is first recorded and from which transaction amounts are posted to the ledger accounts. pp. 90–92

Ledger a group of accounts used by a business in recording its transactions. p. 83

Personal account another name for the *withdrawals account*. p. 82

Posting transcribing the debit and credit amounts from a journal to the ledger accounts. p. 91

Posting Reference (PR) column a column in a journal and in each account that is used for cross-referencing amounts that have been posted from a journal to the account. Also called a *folio column*. p. 93

Prepaid expenses assets created by payments for economic benefits that do not expire until some later time; then, as the benefits expire or are used up, the assets become expenses. p. 80

Promissory note a formal written promise to pay a definite sum of money on demand or at a fixed or determinable future date. p. 79

Source documents another name for *business papers*. p. 78

T-account a simple form of account that is widely used in accounting education to illustrate the debits and credits required in recording a transaction. pp. 83–84

Trial balance a list of the accounts that have balances in the ledger, the debit or credit balance of each account, the total of the debit balances, and the total of the credit balances. pp. 96–97

Unearned revenues liabilities created by the receipt of cash from customers in payment for products or services that have not yet been delivered to the customers; the liabilities will be satisfied by delivering the product or service. p. 81

Withdrawals account the account used to record the transfers of assets from a business to its owner; also known as *personal account* or *drawing account*. p. 82

Synonymous Terms

Journal book of original entry.

Ledger book of final entry.

Business papers source documents.

Withdrawals account drawing account; personal account.

Posting reference column folio column.

Objective Review

Answers to the following questions are listed at the end of this chapter. Be sure that you decide which is the one best answer to each question *before* you check the answers.

LO 1. Examples of the source documents used in accounting are

a. Journals and ledgers.

b. Income statements and balance sheets.

c. External transactions and internal transactions.

d. Bank statements and sales slips.

e. All of the above.

LO 2 The following are commonly used accounts: (1) Prepaid Rent, (2) Unearned Legal Fees, (3) Buildings, (4) Owner, Capital, (5) Wages Payable, (6) Owner, Withdrawals, (7) Office Supplies. These accounts should be classified as assets, liabilities, or owner's equity as follows:

	Assets	Liabilities	Owner's Equity
a.	1,3,7	2,5	4,6
b.	1,3,7	2,5,6	4
c.	1,3,7	5,6	2,4
d.	1,7	5,6	2,3,4
e.	1,7	2,5	3,4,6

LO 3 The requirements of double-entry accounting are such that:

a. All transactions that involve debits to asset accounts must also involve credits to liability or owner's equity accounts.
b. Each transaction is recorded with total debits equal to total credits.
c. The total debits of all recorded transactions equal the total credits of all recorded transactions.
d. The effects on the balance sheet equation of external transactions can be recorded but the effects of other economic events, sometimes called internal transactions, cannot be recorded.
e. Both *(b)* and *(c)* are correct.

LO 4 When David Shipman started his business, he invested $15,000 cash plus some land that had a fair market value of $23,000. Also, the business assumed responsibility for a note payable of $18,000 that was issued to finance the purchase of the land. In recording Shipman's investment:

a. The entry will consist of one debit and one credit.
b. The entry will consist of two debits and one credit.
c. The entry will consist of two debits and two credits.
d. The entry will consist of debits that total $38,000 and credits that total $33,000.
e. None of the above answers is correct.

LO 5 A trial balance shows total debits of $14,000 and total credits of $17,000. Which of the following errors would explain this situation?

a. A journal entry that debited Wages Expense for $1,500 was incorrectly posted to the ledger account as a credit.
b. A journal entry that debited Wages Expense for $3,000 was incorrectly posted to the ledger account as a credit.
c. A journal entry that credited Services Fees Earned for $1,500 was incorrectly posted to the ledger account as a debit.
d. A journal entry that credited Services Fees Earned for $3,000 was incorrectly posted to the ledger account as a debit.
e. None of the above is correct.

LO 6 A list of all the accounts used by a company, showing the identifying number assigned to each account, is called:

a. A journal.
b. A ledger.
c. A trial balance.
d. A source document.
e. A chart of accounts.

Questions for Class Discussion

1. What two types of economic events affect an entity's accounting equation?
2. What are the two fundamental steps in the accounting process?
3. Why are business papers called source documents?
4. Why is the evidence provided by business papers important to accounting?
5. What is an account? What is a ledger?
6. What determines the number and type of accounts a business will use?
7. What is the difference between a note receivable and an account receivable?
8. What types of transactions increase the owner's equity in a business? What types decrease owner's equity?
9. What is the meaning of each of the following: (*a*) debit, (*b*) to debit, (*c*) credit, and (*d*) to credit?
10. Does debit always mean increase and credit always mean decrease?
11. If a transaction has the effect of decreasing an asset, is the decrease recorded as a debit or as a credit? If the transaction has the effect of decreasing a liability, is the decrease recorded as a debit or as a credit?
12. Why are some accounting systems called *double-entry* accounting systems?
13. Given that assets have economic value and that they have debit balances, why do expenses also have debit balances?
14. What entry (debit or credit) would you make to (*a*) increase a revenue, (*b*) decrease an expense, (*c*) record an owner's withdrawals, and (*d*) record an owner's investment?
15. Why are the rules of debit and credit the same for both liability and owner's equity accounts?
16. List the steps in the preparation of a trial balance.
17. Why is a trial balance prepared?
18. What kinds of errors would cause the column totals of a trial balance to be unequal? What are some examples of errors that would not be revealed by a trial balance?
19. Should transactions be recorded first in a journal or first in the ledger? Why?
20. In recording transactions manually in a General Journal, which is written first, the debit or the credit? Which is indented?
21. What is a compound entry?

22. What kind of transactions can be recorded in a General Journal?
23. What is the purpose of posting reference numbers that are entered in the journal at the time entries are posted to the accounts?
24. What is a chart of accounts?
25. If a wrong amount was journalized and posted to the accounts, how should it be corrected?
26. When are dollar signs used in accounting reports?
27. Define or describe each of the following:
    a. Journal.
    b. Ledger.
    c. Folio column.
    d. Posting.
    e. Posting Reference column.
28. Review the 1990 consolidated statement of cash flows for McDonald's Corporation presented in Appendix K. When McDonald's recorded its 1990 transactions involving the sales of restaurant businesses, what was the total effect of these transactions on Cash? Were these effects on Cash recorded with debits or credits to Cash?
29. Review the 1991 statement of cash flows for Lands' End, Inc., presented in Appendix K. When Lands' End recorded purchases of property, plant, and equipment during the year ended January 31, 1991, what was the total effect of these transactions on Cash? Were these effects on Cash recorded with debits or credits to Cash?

Exercises

Exercise 2–1
Increases, decreases, and normal balances of accounts
(LO 2, 3)

Prepare the following columnar form. Then enter the word *debit* or *credit* in each of the last three columns to indicate the action necessary to increase the account, to indicate the action necessary to decrease the account, and to show the normal balance of the account.

Kind of Account	Increases	Decreases	Normal Balance
Asset			
Liability			
Owner's capital			
Owner's withdrawals			
Revenue			
Expense			

Exercise 2–2
Actions to increase or decrease different accounts
(LO 2, 3)

Indicate the necessary action (debit or credit) to increase or decrease each of the following accounts:

a. To decrease Cash.
b. To increase owner's withdrawals account.

c. To decrease Rent Expense.
d. To increase Accounts Payable.
e. To decrease the owner's capital account.
f. To decrease Prepaid Insurance.
g. To decrease Unearned Legal Fees.
h. To increase Rent Earned.
i. To increase Office Equipment.

Exercise 2–3
Analyzing the effect of a transaction on the accounts
(LO 3)

On March 12, Karen Tucker billed a client $40,000 for construction consulting services. The client did not have enough cash to pay the bill and asked Ms. Tucker to accept ownership of a building valued at $75,000 and to assume responsibility for a $35,000 note payable. Ms. Tucker agreed. The effects of the March 12 transaction on Ms. Tucker's accounts would include which of the following:

a. A $40,000 increase in an asset account.
b. A $75,000 increase in Ms. Tucker's capital account.
c. A $35,000 increase in a revenue account.
d. A $75,000 increase in a revenue account.
e. A $35,000 increase in a liability account.

Exercise 2–4
Showing the effect of transactions on T-accounts
(LO 3)

Place the following T-accounts on a sheet of notebook paper: Cash; Accounts Receivable; Office Supplies; Office Equipment; Accounts Payable; J. J. Wright, Capital; Services Revenue; and Utilities Expense. Then record these transactions by entering debits and credits directly in the accounts. Use the transaction letters to identify amounts entered in the accounts.

a. J. J. Wright began a service business, called N.E. Time, by investing $3,500 in the business.
b. Purchased office supplies for cash, $90.
c. Purchased office equipment on credit, $2,800.
d. Received $500 cash for services provided to a customer.
e. Paid for the office equipment purchased in transaction *c*.
f. Billed a customer $400 for services provided to the customer.
g. Paid the monthly utility bills, $60.
h. Collected $200 of the amount owed by the customer of transaction *f*.

Exercise 2–5
Preparing a trial balance
(LO 5)

After recording the transactions of Exercise 2–4, prepare a trial balance for N.E. Time. Use the current date.

Exercise 2–6
Trial balance errors
(LO 5)

Prepare a form with the following three column headings: (1) Error, (2) Amount Out of Balance, and (3) Column Having Larger Total. Then for each of the following errors: (1) in the first column list the error by letter, (2) in the second column show the difference in the trial balance column totals that will result from the error, and (3) in the third column indicate which trial balance column (debit or credit) will have the larger total as a result of the error. If the error does not affect the trial balance, write *none* in each of the last two columns.

a. A $500 debit to Prepaid Rent was debited to Rent Expense.
b. A $230 debit to Automobiles was debited to Accounts Payable.
c. A $90 credit to Cash was credited to the Cash account twice.
d. A $128 debit to Utilities Expense was posted as a $120 debit.
e. A $25 debit to Office Supplies was not posted.
f. A $440 credit to Fees Earned was posted as a $400 credit.

Exercise 2–7
Analyzing a trial balance error
(LO 5)

A trial balance does not balance. In looking for the error, you notice that Office Equipment has a debit balance of $15,600. However, you discover that a transaction for the purchase of a computer for $1,100 had been recorded with a $1,100 credit to Office Equipment and a $1,100 credit to Accounts Payable. Answer each of the following questions, giving the dollar amount of the misstatement, if any.

a. Was the balance of the Office Equipment account overstated, understated, or correctly stated in the trial balance?
b. Was the balance of the Accounts Payable account overstated, understated, or correctly stated in the trial balance?
c. Was the debit column total of the trial balance overstated, understated, or correctly stated?
d. Was the credit column total of the trial balance overstated, understated, or correctly stated?
e. If the debit column total of the trial balance was $142,000 before the error was corrected, what was the total of the credit column?

Exercise 2–8
Preparing a corrected trial balance
(LO 5)

A careless bookkeeper prepared the following trial balance, which does not balance, and you have been asked to prepare a corrected trial balance. In examining the records of the concern you discover the following: (1) The debits to the Cash account total $62,850, and the credits total $57,120. (2) A $280 receipt of cash from a customer in payment of the customer's account was not posted to Accounts Receivable. (3) A $70 purchase of shop supplies on credit was entered in the journal but was posted only to Accounts Payable. (4) The bookkeeper made a transposition error in copying the balance of the Services Revenue account in the trial balance. The correct amount was $40,270.

WANDA'S WELDING SHOP
Trial Balance
December 31, 1993

Cash	$ 5,930	
Accounts receivable		$ 6,660
Shop supplies	2,800	
Shop equipment	11,200	
Accounts payable	1,800	
Wanda Wong, capital	12,930	
Wanda Wong, withdrawals	19,800	
Services revenue		42,070
Rent expense		7,800
Advertising expense	1,220	
Totals	$55,680	$56,530

Exercise 2–9
Analyzing account entries and balances
(LO 2, 3)

1. During the month of February, Sun Company had cash receipts of $37,000 and cash disbursements of $36,500. The February 28 cash balance was $8,400. Calculate the beginning (January 31) cash balance.
2. On January 31, Sun Company had an Accounts Receivable balance of $16,000. During the month of February, total credits to Accounts Receivable were $20,000, which resulted from customer payments. The February 28 Accounts Receivable balance was $24,000. Calculate the amount of credit sales during February.
3. Fred Dukes, the owner of Sun Company, had a capital account balance of $40,000 on January 31 and $34,000 on February 28. Net income for the month of February was $11,000. Calculate the owner's withdrawals during February.

Exercise 2–10
Analyzing transactions from T-accounts
(LO 2, 3)

The following accounts contain seven transactions keyed together with letters. Write a short explanation of each transaction with the amount or amounts involved.

Cash

(*a*)	3,500	(*b*)	1,800
(*e*)	1,250	(*c*)	300
		(*f*)	1,200
		(*g*)	350

Camera Equipment

(*a*)	2,800		
(*d*)	4,700		

Carol Reed, Capital

		(*a*)	11,800

Photography Supplies

(*c*)	300		
(*d*)	100		

Darkroom Equipment

(*a*)	5,500		

Photography Fees Earned

		(*e*)	1,250

Prepaid Rent

(*b*)	1,800		

Accounts Payable

(*f*)	1,200	(*d*)	4,800

Advertising Expense

(*g*)	350		

Exercise 2–11
General journal entries
(LO 4)

Prepare a form like Illustration 2–4 and then prepare general journal entries to record the following transactions. Omit the year in the journal date column.

Mar.	1	Tom Waits invested $5,000 in cash and an automobile having a $35,000 fair value in a limousine service he called Star Limousines.
	1	Rented furnished office space and paid for six months in advance, $1,200.
	2	Purchased a cellular phone for the limo for cash, $900.
	15	Chauffeured clients for two weeks and collected $2,500 in fees.
	31	Paid for gas and oil used in the limousine during March, $260.

Exercise 2–12
T-accounts and the trial balance
(LO 3, 5)

1. Open T-accounts for each of the following items: Cash; Prepaid Rent; Automobiles; Equipment; Tom Waits, Capital; Fees Earned; and Gas and Oil Expense.
2. Post the transactions of Exercise 2–11 to the T-accounts. Omit posting reference numbers.
3. Prepare a trial balance of the T-accounts.

Exercise 2–13
Analyzing and journalizing revenue transactions
(LO 5)

Examine each of the following transactions and prepare general journal entries to record only the revenue transactions. Explain why the remaining transactions are not revenue transactions.

a. Received $1,500 cash for orthodontic services provided to customer.
b. Received $2,500 cash from Robin Walker, the owner of the business.
c. Received $300 from a customer in partial payment of his account receivable.
d. Rendered orthodontic services to a customer on credit, $600.
e. Borrowed $10,000 from the bank by signing a promissory note.
f. Received $1,600 from a customer in payment for services to be rendered next year.

Exercise 2–14
Analyzing and journalizing expense transactions
(LO 4)

Examine each of the following transactions and prepare general journal entries to record only the expense transactions. Explain why the remaining transactions are not expense transactions.

a. Paid $1,500 cash for shop equipment.
b. Paid $2,400 in partial payment for supplies purchased 30 days previously.
c. Paid utility bill of $310.
d. Paid $900 to owner of the business for his personal use.
e. Paid $750 wages of shop employee.

Problems

Problem 2–1
Recording transactions in T-accounts; preparing a trial balance
(LO 2, 3, 5)

April Stewart opened an advertising business and during a short period as an agent completed these business transactions:

a. Invested $50,000 in cash and office equipment with a $20,000 fair value in an advertising agency she called Stewart Advertising.
b. Purchased land valued at $60,000 and a small office building valued at $230,000, paying $43,500 cash and signing a long-term note payable to pay the balance over a period of years.
c. Purchased office supplies on credit, $480.
d. Stewart contributed her personal automobile, which had a $17,200 fair value, for exclusive use in the business.
e. Purchased additional office equipment on credit, $2,500.
f. Paid the office secretary's salary, $800.
g. Sold an advertisement and collected a $3,500 cash fee on the sale.
h. Paid $450 for a magazine advertisement that had already appeared.
i. Paid for the supplies purchased on credit in transaction *c*.
j. Purchased a new typewriter for the business, paying $1,000 cash plus an old typewriter carried in the accounting records at $200.

k. Completed a marketing research assignment on credit and billed the client $1,300.

l. Paid the secretary's salary, $800.

m. Received payment in full for the marketing research of transaction *k*.

n. Stewart withdrew $1,800 from the business to pay personal expenses.

Required

1. Open the following T-accounts: Cash; Accounts Receivable; Office Supplies; Automobiles; Office Equipment; Building; Land; Accounts Payable; Long-Term Notes Payable; April Stewart, Capital; April Stewart, Withdrawals; Advertising Fees Earned; Marketing Research Fees Earned; Office Salaries Expense; and Advertising Expense.
2. Show the effects of the transactions on the accounts by entering debits and credits directly in the accounts. Use the transaction letters to identify each debit and credit amount.
3. Determine the balance of each account in the ledger and prepare a trial balance using the current date.

Problem 2–2
Recording transactions in T-accounts; preparing a trial balance
(LO 2, 3, 5)

Alan Meaken began business as a surveyor and during a short period completed these transactions:

a. Began business by investing cash, $20,000; office equipment, $3,000; and surveying equipment, $45,000.

b. Purchased land for an office site, $19,000. Paid $3,800 in cash and signed a long-term note payable for the balance.

c. Purchased for cash a used prefabricated building and moved it onto the land for use as an office, $8,000.

d. Prepaid the annual premium on two insurance policies, $4,800.

e. Completed a surveying job and collected $800 cash in full payment.

f. Purchased additional equipment costing $3,700. Gave $700 in cash and signed a long-term note payable for the balance.

g. Completed a surveying job on credit for Kilmer Contractors, $2,100.

h. Purchased additional office equipment on credit, $250.

i. Completed a surveying job for Valley Hospital on credit, $3,150.

j. Received and recorded as an account payable a bill for rent on special machinery used on the Valley Hospital job, $150.

k. Received $2,100 from Kilmer Contractors for the work of transaction *g*.

l. Paid the wages of the surveying assistant, $840.

m. Paid for the office equipment purchased in transaction *h*.

n. Paid $350 cash for repairs to a piece of surveying equipment.

o. Alan Meaken wrote a $260 check on the bank account of the business to pay for repairs to his personal automobile. (The car is not used for business purposes.)

p. Paid the wages of the surveying assistant, $880.

q. Paid fee to county for surveying permits, $150.

Required

1. Open the following T-accounts: Cash; Accounts Receivable; Prepaid Insurance; Office Equipment; Surveying Equipment; Building; Land; Accounts Payable; Long-Term Notes Payable; Alan Meaken, Capital; Alan Meaken, Withdrawals; Surveying Fees Earned; Wages Expense; Machinery Rental Expense; Permits Expense; and Repairs Expense, Surveying Equipment.
2. Record the transactions by entering debits and credits directly in the accounts. Use the transaction letters to identify each debit and credit. Prepare a trial balance using the current date and titled Alan Meaken, Surveyor.

Problem 2–3
Posting from general journal entries; preparing a trial balance
(LO 4, 5)

Kay Martinez, CPA, completed these transactions during June of the current year:

June 1 Began a public accounting practice by investing $5,700 in cash and office equipment having an $8,100 fair value.

1 Prepaid three months' rent in advance on suitable office space, $2,250.

2 Purchased on credit office equipment, $800, and office supplies, $300.

4 Completed accounting work for a client and immediately received payment of $350 cash.

8 Completed accounting work on credit for Bank One, $1,700.

10 Paid for the items purchased on credit on June 2.

14 Paid the annual $2,400 premium on an insurance policy.

18 Received payment in full from Bank One for the work completed on June 8.

24 Completed accounting work on credit for Turner Construction, $400.

28 Martinez withdrew $1,000 cash from the practice to pay personal expenses.

29 Purchased additional office supplies on credit, $120.

30 Paid the June utility bills, $210.

Required

1. Open the following accounts: Cash; Accounts Receivable; Office Supplies; Prepaid Insurance; Prepaid Rent; Office Equipment; Accounts Payable; Kay Martinez, Capital; Kay Martinez, Withdrawals; Accounting Fees Earned; and Utilities Expense.
2. Prepare general journal entries to record the transactions.
3. Post to the accounts.
4. Prepare a trial balance. Title the trial balance Kay Martinez, CPA.

Problem 2–4
Journalizing, posting, and preparing a trial balance
(LO 4, 5)

Mike Leaman completed these transactions during April of the current year:

Apr. 1 Began an engineering firm by investing cash, $25,000; drafting supplies, $700; and office and drafting equipment, $18,500.
1 Prepaid two months' rent in advance on suitable office space, $3,100.
3 Paid the annual premium on an insurance policy taken out in the name of the business, $2,400.
4 Purchased drafting equipment, $680, and drafting supplies, $90, on credit.
9 Delivered a set of plans to a contractor and collected $4,000 cash in full payment.
15 Paid the draftsman's salary, $960.
16 Completed and delivered a set of plans to the City of Camden on credit, $7,800.
18 Purchased drafting supplies on credit, $40.
19 Paid for the equipment and supplies purchased on Apr. 4.
26 Received $7,800 from the city of Camden for the plans delivered on Apr. 16.
27 Mike Leaman withdrew $2,000 from the business for personal use.
28 Paid for the supplies purchased on Apr. 18.
29 Completed engineering work for Acme Construction on credit, $1,400.
30 Paid the draftsman's salary, $960.
30 Paid the April utility bill, $170.
30 Paid the blueprinting expenses incurred in April, $110.

Required

1. Open the following accounts: Cash; Accounts Receivable; Drafting Supplies; Prepaid Insurance; Prepaid Rent; Office and Drafting Equipment; Accounts Payable; Mike Leaman, Capital; Mike Leaman, Withdrawals; Engineering Fees Earned; Salaries Expense; Blueprinting Expense; and Utilities Expense.
2. Prepare and post general journal entries to record the transactions. Prepare a trial balance, titling it Mike Leaman, Engineer.

Problem 2–5
Journalizing, posting, and preparing financial statements
(LO 4, 5)

Jay Ball completed these transactions during November of the current year:

Nov. 1 Began a new chiropractic practice by investing $27,000 in cash and medical equipment having a $20,500 fair value.
1 Rented the furnished office of a chiropractor who was retiring because of illness, and paid the rent (expense) for November, $1,600.
1 Took out a malpractice insurance policy giving one year's protection and paid the premium (expense) for the month of November, $1,500.

Nov. 3 Purchased medical supplies on credit, $580.

9 Completed chiropractic work and immediately collected $2,400 cash for the work.

13 Paid for the medical supplies purchased on November 3.

16 Completed chiropractic work for Ed Albe on credit, $700.

23 Completed chiropractic work for Pat Gillespie on credit, $200.

26 Received $700 from Ed Albe for the work completed on Nov. 16.

28 Jay Ball wrote a $70 check on the bank account of the chiropractic practice to pay his home telephone bill.

29 Purchased additional medical supplies on credit, $340.

30 Paid the November telephone bill of the office, $80.

30 Paid the salaries of the receptionist and assistant, $2,350.

30 Prepaid the rent on the office for December and January, $3,200.

30 Prepaid the malpractice insurance premium for the next three months, $4,500.

Required

1. Open the following accounts: Cash; Accounts Receivable; Medical Supplies; Prepaid Insurance; Prepaid Rent; Medical Equipment; Accounts Payable; Jay Ball, Capital; Jay Ball, Withdrawals; Chiropractic Fees Earned; Salaries Expense; Insurance Expense; Rent Expense; and Telephone Expense.
2. Prepare general journal entries to record the transactions, post to the accounts, and prepare a trial balance titled Jay Ball, Chiropractor.
3. Prepare an income statement for the month ended November 30.
4. Prepare a statement of changes in owner's equity for the month ended November 30.
5. Prepare a balance sheet dated November 30.

Problem 2–6
Analytical essay
(LO 3)

Review the facts provided in Problem 2–2 and focus on transactions *h* and *o*. Explain how the effects of transaction *h* on the balance sheet, income statement, and statement of changes in owner's equity differ from the effects of transaction *o*. Also discuss how your explanation would be changed if Meaken had used the $260 from transaction *o* to pay for renting a machine that was used in the business.

Problem 2–7
Analytical essay
(LO 3, 5)

Review the facts provided in Problem 2–3 and assume that certain mistakes had been made in journalizing and posting the transactions. Explain the effects of each of the following errors on the account balances listed in the trial balance and on the trial balance column totals:

a. The June 1 investment by Martinez was journalized correctly but the debit to Cash was posted to the Cash account as $7,500.

b. The June 4 transaction was incorrectly recorded as a receipt of cash for work that was to be done the next year.

c. In journalizing the June 14 transaction, the account that should have been debited was credited and the account that should have been credited was debited.

d. In posting the June 29 transaction, the debit was correctly posted but the credit was not posted.

e. The $210 payment on June 30 was incorrectly journalized as a $120 payment.

Alternate Problems

Problem 2–1A
Recording transactions in T-accounts; preparing a trial balance
(LO 2, 3, 5)

April Stewart completed these transactions during a short period:

a. Opened an advertising agency by investing the following assets at their fair values: cash, $15,000; office equipment, $5,500; automobile, $9,000; land, $27,500; and building, $120,000. The business should also assume responsibility for a $100,000 long-term promissory note that was given to the bank to finance the purchase of the land and building.

b. Purchased office supplies, $100, and additional office equipment, $700, on credit.

c. Collected a $6,500 fee for an advertising campaign for a client.

d. Purchased additional office equipment on credit, $1,100.

e. Paid for advertising that had appeared in a national magazine, $1,800.

f. Traded the agency's automobile and $10,000 in cash for a new automobile.

g. Paid the office secretary's salary, $850.

h. Paid for the supplies and equipment purchased in transaction *b*.

i. Completed a marketing research assignment for a client on credit, $800.

j. Collected a $2,950 fee from the sale of an advertisement for a client.

k. The client of transaction *i* paid $400 of the amount owed.

l. Paid the secretary's salary, $850.

m. Paid $475 for a magazine advertisement that had already appeared.

n. Stewart withdrew $1,500 from the business for personal use.

Required

1. Open the following T-accounts: Cash; Accounts Receivable; Office Supplies; Automobiles; Office Equipment; Building; Land; Accounts Payable; Long-Term Notes Payable; April Stewart, Capital; April Stewart, Withdrawals; Advertising Fees Earned; Marketing Research Fees Earned; Office Salaries Expense; and Advertising Expense.
2. Record the transactions by entering debits and credits directly in the accounts. Use the transaction letters to identify the amounts in the accounts.
3. Determine the balance of each account in the ledger and prepare a trial balance under the name Stewart Advertising and using the current date.

Problem 2–2A
Recording transactions in T-accounts; preparing a trial balance
(LO 2, 3, 5)

Alan Meaken completed these transactions during a short period:

a. Began business as a surveyor by investing cash, $18,000; office equipment, $2,800; and surveying equipment, $19,200.

b. Purchased for $24,000 land to be used as an office site. Paid $4,800 in cash and signed a long-term promissory note for the balance.

c. Purchased additional surveying equipment costing $13,950. Paid $4,650 in cash and signed a long-term promissory note for the balance.

d. Paid $5,400 cash for a used prefabricated building and moved it on the land for use as an office.

e. Completed a surveying job and immediately collected $2,300 in cash for the work.

f. Prepaid the premium on an insurance policy giving one year's protection, $660.

g. Completed a $1,650 surveying job for Ace Contractors on credit.

h. Paid the wages of the surveying assistant, $890.

i. Paid $190 cash for repairs to surveying equipment.

j. Received $1,650 from Ace Contractors for the work of transaction *g*.

k. Completed a $750 surveying job for Benton Real Estate Company on credit.

l. Received and recorded as an account payable a $130 bill for the rental of special machinery used on the Ace Contractors job.

m. Purchased additional office equipment on credit, $500.

n. Alan Meaken withdrew $350 from the business for personal use.

o. Paid the wages of the surveying assistant, $740.

p. Paid the $130 account payable resulting from renting the machine of transaction *l*.

q. Paid for surveying permits acquired from the county, $260.

Required

1. Open the following T-accounts: Cash; Accounts Receivable; Prepaid Insurance; Office Equipment; Surveying Equipment; Building; Land; Accounts Payable; Long-Term Notes Payable; Alan Meaken, Capital; Alan Meaken, Withdrawals; Surveying Fees Earned; Wages Expense; Machinery Rental Expense; Permits Expense; and Repairs Expense, Surveying Equipment.
2. Record the transactions by entering debits and credits directly in the accounts. Use the transaction letters to identify each debit and credit. Prepare a trial balance using the current date and headed Alan Meaken, Surveyor.

Problem 2–3A
Posting from general journal entries; preparing a trial balance
(LO 4, 5)

Kay Martinez began a public accounting practice and completed these transactions during September of the current year:

Sept. 1 Invested $5,000 in a public accounting practice begun this day.

1 Rented suitable office space and prepaid two months' rent in advance, $1,600.

Sept. 2 Purchased office supplies, $140, and office equipment, $4,750, on credit.

4 Paid the annual premium on a liability insurance policy, $900.

6 Completed accounting work for a client and immediately collected $580 in cash for the work done.

12 Completed accounting work for Toronto Savings on credit, $1,400.

16 Purchased additional office supplies on credit, $35.

22 Received $1,400 from Toronto Savings for the work completed on September 12.

25 Kay Martinez withdrew $600 from the accounting practice to pay personal expenses.

29 Completed accounting work for Alice's Restaurant on credit, $700.

30 Made an installment payment of $1,000 on the equipment and supplies purchased on September 2.

30 Paid the September utility bills of the accounting practice, $180.

Required

1. Open the following accounts: Cash; Accounts Receivable; Office Supplies; Prepaid Insurance; Prepaid Rent; Office Equipment; Accounts Payable; Kay Martinez, Capital; Kay Martinez, Withdrawals; Accounting Fees Earned; and Utilities Expense.
2. Prepare general journal entries to record the transactions.
3. Post to the accounts.
4. Prepare a trial balance titled Kay Martinez, CPA.

Problem 2–4A
Journalizing, posting, and preparing a trial balance (LO 4, 5)

Mike Leaman completed these transactions during July of the current year:

July 1 Began an engineering firm by opening a bank account in the name of the business, Mike Leaman, Engineer, and deposited $14,700 therein.

1 Rented suitable office space and prepaid six months' rent in advance, $4,800.

2 Purchased for $6,500 office and drafting equipment under an agreement calling for a $1,500 down payment and the balance in monthly installments. Paid the down payment and recorded the account payable.

4 Purchased drafting supplies for cash, $270.

8 Completed and delivered a set of plans to a contractor and immediately received $2,900 cash in full payment.

12 Paid the annual premium on a liability insurance policy, $1,500.

14 Purchased on credit additional drafting supplies, $60, and drafting equipment, $230.

15 Paid the salary of the draftsman, $750.

July 17 Completed and delivered a set of plans to Ridgemont School District on credit, $2,000.

21 Paid in full for the supplies and equipment purchased on July 14.

25 Completed additional engineering work for Ridgemont School District on credit, $900.

27 Received $2,000 from Ridgemont School District for the plans delivered on July 17.

28 Mike Leaman withdrew $1,300 cash from the business to pay personal expenses.

31 Paid the salary of the draftsman, $750.

31 Paid the July utility bills, $90.

31 Paid $80 cash for blueprinting expense.

Required

1. Open the following accounts: Cash; Accounts Receivable; Drafting Supplies; Prepaid Insurance; Prepaid Rent; Office and Drafting Equipment; Accounts Payable; Mike Leaman, Capital; Mike Leaman, Withdrawals; Engineering Fees Earned; Salaries Expense; Blueprinting Expense; and Utilities Expense.
2. Prepare general journal entries to record the transactions, post to the accounts, and prepare a trial balance.

Problem 2–5A
Journalizing, posting, and preparing financial statements
(LO 4, 5)

Jay Ball completed these transactions in August of the current year:

Aug. 1 Began a chiropractic practice by investing $10,000 in cash and medical equipment having a $4,200 fair value.

1 Rented the furnished office of a chiropractor who was retiring and paid the rent (expense) for August, $1,000.

2 Purchased medical equipment costing $6,600 under an agreement calling for a $2,000 down payment and the balance in monthly installments. Paid the down payment and recorded the remaining $4,600 as an account payable.

5 Purchased medical supplies on credit, $1,760.

6 Took out a malpractice insurance policy giving one year's protection and paid the premium (expense) for the month of August, $900.

8 Completed chiropractic work for clients and immediately collected $1,350 for the work done.

12 Paid for the medical supplies purchased on credit on August 5.

16 Completed chiropractic work for Richard Tuck on credit, $550.

22 Jay Ball wrote a $300 check on the bank account of the chiropractic practice to pay for plumbing repairs of his personal residence.

24 Received $550 from Richard Tuck for the work completed July 16.

Aug. 26 Completed chiropractic work for clients on credit, $3,440.
30 Paid the telephone bill of the chiropractic practice, $210.
31 Paid the salary of the office receptionist, $1,200.
31 Prepaid the rent on the office for September and October, $2,000.
31 Prepaid the malpractice insurance premium for the next two months, $1,800.

Required

1. Open the following accounts: Cash; Accounts Receivable; Medical Supplies; Prepaid Insurance; Prepaid Rent; Medical Equipment; Accounts Payable; Jay Ball, Capital; Jay Ball, Withdrawals; Chiropractic Fees Earned; Salaries Expense; Insurance Expense; Rent Expense; and Telephone Expense.
2. Prepare general journal entries to record the transactions, post to the accounts, and prepare a trial balance titled Jay Ball, Chiropractor.
3. Prepare an income statement for the month ended August 31.
4. Prepare a statement of changes in owner's equity for the month ended August 31.
5. Prepare a balance sheet dated August 31.

Problem 2–6A
Analytical essay
(LO 3)

Review the facts provided in Problem 2–2A and focus on transactions *n* and *o*. Explain how the effects of transaction *n* on the balance sheet, income statement, and statement of changes in owner's equity differ from the effects of transaction *o*. Also discuss how your explanation would be changed if Meaken had used the $350 from transaction *n* to purchase equipment for use in the office.

Problem 2–7A
Analytical essay
(LO 3, 5)

Review the facts provided in Problem 2–3A and assume that certain mistakes had been made in journalizing and posting the transactions. Explain the effects of each of the following errors on the account balances listed in the trial balance and on the trial balance column totals:

a. The September 1 investment of $5,000 by Martinez was incorrectly recorded as a $3,000 investment.
b. The September 6 transaction was incorrectly recorded as work done on credit.
c. In journalizing the September 16 transaction, the account that should have been debited was credited and the account that should have been credited was debited.
d. In posting the September 29 transaction, the debit was correctly posted but the credit was not posted.
e. The $180 payment on September 30 was incorrectly journalized as an $18 payment.

Serial Problem

Precision Computer Services

(This problem is continued in Chapters 3, 4, and 5. Do not assign this problem unless the Working Papers are being used.)

On October 1, 1993, John Conard started a computer service company named Precision Computer Services. Precision is organized as a single proprietorship, with Conard doing consulting services, computer system installations, and computer program development to meet specific customer needs. Conard expects to prepare financial statements for the first time on December 31, 1993. To begin accounting for the business, Conard opened the following general ledger accounts.

Accounts	Number
Cash	101
Accounts receivable	106
Computer supplies	126
Prepaid insurance	128
Prepaid rent	131
Office equipment	163
Computer equipment	167
Accounts payable	201
John Conard, capital	301
John Conard, withdrawals	302
Computer services revenue	403
Wages expense	623
Advertising expense	655
Mileage expense	676
Miscellaneous expenses	677
Repairs expense, computer	684
Telephone expense	688
Utilities expense	690

Required

Journalize and post the following transactions completed by Precision Computer Services during October and November.

Oct. 1 John Conard invested $5,000 personal cash in the business, along with a $3,000 computer and $340 of office equipment.

2 Rented office space in the Town Hall Shopping Center for $225 per month and paid four months' rent in advance.

3 Purchased computer supplies on credit for $50 from Ajax Supply Company.

4 Paid one year's premium on a fire/theft and liability insurance policy, $195.

5 Billed Ball Company $500 for work this week installing a new computer.

8 Paid for the computer supplies purchased from Ajax Supply.

10 Hired an assistant, Ann White, for $70 a day, as needed. She will start on October 15 and will be paid every other Friday.

12 Withdrew $600 for personal expenses.

12 Worked this week again at Ball Company and billed them for $750.

Oct. 15 Received $500 from Ball Company for work performed the first week of October.

17 Purchased $25 of parts to repair Precision's computer, which was damaged in the move to the new office.

18 Billed AB Company for computer services performed this week, $1,000.

19 Paid $15 for an advertisement in the Shopper Newspaper announcing Precision's grand opening.

22 Received the $750 billed to Ball Company on October 12.

23 Received $250 cash from Dog Enterprise for computer services.

24 Completed work for Ear Hearing and billed them $425.

25 Paid Ann White for six days' work.

25 Purchased on credit from Ajax Supply additional computer supplies for $55.

28 Billed Call Company for computer services, $725.

30 Paid the electric bill for the month, $47; and the telephone bill, $115.

30 Paid $600 to John Conard for personal use.

Nov. 1 Reimbursed Ann White's business car mileage, 150 miles at $0.24 per mile.

1 Reimbursed John Conard's business car mileage, 450 miles at $0.24 per mile.

4 Received $425 from Ear Hearing for work done on October 24.

5 Received $300 cash from Dog Enterprise for computer services.

6 Received $1,000 from AB Company, billed on October 18.

7 Purchased an additional $45 of computer supplies from Ajax Supply. Paid for both this purchase and the one on October 25.

8 Billed Farm Research for services, $895.

8 Paid Ann White for five days' work.

11 Notified by AB Company that Precision's bid of $1,500 was accepted and began work this day.

13 Received a notice from Republic Bank that a $4 service charge had been deducted from Precision's checking account.

15 Paid John Conard $600 as a withdrawal.

18 Paid John Conard's home water bill, $35.

20 Received $500 from Call Company against the bill dated October 28.

22 Gave a $10 donation to the American Cancer Society on behalf of Precision.

22 Paid Ann White for six days' work.

25 Completed work begun on November 11 for AB Company and billed them for the amount due.

27 Sent another bill to Call Company for the past due amount of $225 related to billing on October 28.

Nov. 28 Paid the electric bill for the month, $49; and the telephone bill, $118.

28 Paid $650 to John Conard as a withdrawal.

29 Reimbursed Ann White's business car mileage, 200 miles at $0.24 per mile.

29 Reimbursed John Conard's business car mileage, 500 miles at $0.24 per mile.

Provocative Problems

Provocative Problem 2–1
Sheila Lyon, Landscape Architect
(LO 2)

Sheila Lyon operates a landscape architecture business. Through the month of October, the accounting records for the business had been maintained by a CPA. Those records showed that Lyon's October 31 capital balance was $25,000. However, Lyon believed that the CPA had overcharged for her work in the past. As a result, Lyon decided to keep her own records. At the end of November, she prepared the following statements. She was shocked to discover how unprofitable her business had become, and asked you to review the statements. You should prepare new financial statements including a statement of changes in owner's equity.

SHEILA LYON, LANDSCAPE ARCHITECT
Income Statement
For Month Ended November 30, 19--

Revenue:		
Unearned landscape architecture fees		$ 2,000
Investments by owner		1,000
Total		$ 3,000
Operating expenses:		
Rent expense	$ 700	
Telephone expense	200	
Professional library	1,800	
Utilities expense	100	
Withdrawals by owner	2,000	
Travel and entertainment expense	1,400	
Insurance expense	300	
Total operating expenses		6,500
Net income (loss)		$(3,500)

SHEILA LYON, LANDSCAPE ARCHITECT
Balance Sheet
November 30, 19--

Assets		**Liabilities**	
Cash	$ 1,300	Accounts payable	$ 800
Accounts receivable	900	Landscape architecture fees earned	6,000
Prepaid insurance	600	Short-term notes payable	16,000
Prepaid rent	1,400	Total liabilities	$22,800
Office supplies	100		
Buildings	27,000	**Owner's Equity**	
Land	12,000		
Salaries expense	1,000	Sheila Lyon, capital	21,500
Total assets	$44,300	Total liabilities and owner's equity	$44,300

Provocative Problem 2–2
Jensen's Computer Classes
(LO 2, 4)

Paul Jensen opened a new business as a computer instructor and completed a number of transactions during April, the first month of operation. He recorded all transactions with double entries in just two accounts, Cash and Income Summary. At the end of the first month, he asks you to review his records and improve his ledger. Based on the following information, you should present a compound general journal entry dated April 30 to show your corrections and improvements.

Cash Acct. No. 101

Date		Explanation	PR	Debit	Credit	Balance
Apr.	1	Investment by owner.	G1	6,000		6,000
	1	Purchased computer equipment.	G1		4,200	1,800
	1	Purchased office equipment.	G1		1,000	800
	5	Signed short-term note payable to bank.	G1	2,000		2,800
	11	Paid for April office rental.	G1		400	2,400
	14	Received cash for lessons given.	G1	600		3,000
	14	Paid wages of assistant.	G1		270	2,730
	27	Received cash for May lessons.	G1	1,200		3,930
	28	Purchased computer supplies.	G1		200	3,730
	29	Received cash for lessons given.	G1	800		4,530
	29	Paid wages of assistant.	G1		230	4,300
	30	Withdrew cash for personal use.	G1		800	3,500

Income Summary Acct. No. 901

Date		Explanation	PR	Debit	Credit	Balance
Apr.	1		G1		6,000	6,000
	1		G1	4,200		1,800
	1		G1	1,000		800
	5		G1		2,000	2,800
	11		G1	400		2,400
	14		G1		600	3,000
	14		G1	270		2,730
	27		G1		1,200	3,930
	28		G1	200		3,730
	29		G1		800	4,530
	29		G1	230		4,300
	30		G1	800		3,500

Provocative Problem 2–3
Wind Jammin'
(LO 4, 5)

Barry Young, a graduate student, has just completed the first summer's operation of a concession on Paradise Lake, where he rents sailboats and sells T-shirts, caps, and sunglasses. He began the summer's operation with $7,000 in cash and a five-year lease on a boat dock and a small concession building on the lake. The lease requires a $1,800 annual rental, although the concession is open only from June 1 through August 31. On opening day, Barry paid the first year's rent and purchased three sailboats at $900 each, paying cash.

During the summer, he purchased T-shirts, caps, and sunglasses costing $5,750, all of which was paid for by summer's end, except for T-shirts purchased for $180 during the last week's operation. By summer's end, he had paid utility bills, $220, and wages of a part-time helper, $1,000. He had also withdrawn $160 of earnings of the concession each week for 12 weeks for personal expenses.

He took in $5,460 in sailboat rentals during the summer and sold $8,340 worth of T-shirts, caps, and sunglasses. All of this was collected in cash, except $200 owed by The Captain's Club for T-shirts for its members.

On August 31, when he closed for the summer, Barry was able to return to the sunglasses company several pairs of sunglasses for which he received a $150 cash refund. However, he had to take home for personal consumption a number of T-shirts and caps that cost $90 and that could have been sold for $135. He then sold the three sailboats to a used sporting goods dealer for $300 each.

Prepare an income statement showing the results of the summer's operations, a statement of changes in owner's equity, and an August 31 balance sheet. Head the statements Wind Jammin'. (T-accounts may be helpful in organizing the data.)

Provocative Problem 2–4
Cliff's Clean Up Service
(LO 4, 5)

On graduation from high school last summer, Cliff Sands needed a job to earn a portion of his first-year college expenses. He was unable to find anything satisfactory and decided to go into the construction clean up business. He had $160 in a savings account that he used to buy a wheelbarrow, tools, and supplies. However, to haul the debris from the construction site to a dump, he needed a truck. Consequently, he borrowed $2,400 from a bank by signing a short-term promissory note that had an interest rate of 1% per month in exchange for a secondhand truck.

From the beginning, he had as much work as he could do, and after two months, he repaid the bank loan plus two months' interest. On August 28, he ended the business after exactly three months' operations. Throughout the summer, he followed the practice of depositing in the bank all cash received from customers. An examination of his checkbook record showed he had deposited $4,050. He had written checks to pay $180 for gas, oil, and lubricants used in the truck, and a $90 check for dumping fees. A notebook in the truck contained copies of credit card tickets that showed the business owed $40 for additional gas and oil used in the truck. The notebook also showed that customers owed Cliff $150 for services. He decided to give his equipment and tools to his parents, and estimated they had a fair value of $100. He received a good offer on the truck and sold it for $2,500. Under the assumption that Cliff had withdrawn $300 from the business during the summer for spending money and to buy clothes, prepare an income statement showing the results of the summer's operations. Also prepare a statement of changes in owner's equity and an August 28 balance sheet. Head the statements Cliff's Clean Up Service. (T-accounts should be helpful in organizing the data.)

Provocative Problem 2–5
Widmark Real Estate Agency
(LO 2, 5)

Debra Widmark began a real estate agency, and completed seven transactions. The transactions included a cash investment by Widmark, a purchase on credit, and other cash transactions. After completing these transactions, she prepared the trial balance that follows. Analyze the trial balance and prepare a list describing each transaction and its amount. (Hint: T-accounts may help.)

DEBRA WIDMARK, REALTOR
Trial Balance
November 7, 1993

Cash	$ 4,620	
Office supplies	230	
Prepaid insurance	1,400	
Office equipment	5,000	
Accounts payable		$ 5,000
Debra Widmark, capital		6,110
Debra Widmark, withdrawals	13,000	
Commissions earned		15,890
Advertising expense	2,750	
Totals	$27,000	$27,000

Provocative Problem 2–6
International Business Machines Corporation
(LO 2)

The financial statements and related financial information disclosed in IBM's 1990 annual report are shown in Appendix J. Based on your examination of those statements, answer the following questions:

1. IBM reported four different types of revenue. What were they?
2. IBM's current asset account balances were reported as seven different items. What were they?
3. The current liability account balances were reported as six different items. What were they?
4. How much provision for income tax expense was recorded by IBM in 1990? In 1989?
5. Did IBM purchase any plant, rental machines, and other property during 1990? Assuming no plant, rental machines, or other property items were sold during 1990, what total amount was purchased during 1990?

Provocative Problem 2–7
As a Matter of Ethics: Essay

Ethics

Review the As a Matter of Ethics case on page 78. Discuss the nature of the problem faced by Karen Muñoz and evaluate the alternative courses of action she should consider.

Answers to Objective Review Questions

LO 1 (*d*) LO 3 (*e*) LO 5 (*a*)
LO 2 (*a*) LO 4 (*c*) LO 6 (*e*)

CHAPTER

3

Adjusting the Accounts and Preparing the Statements

Although most economic events that affect an organization occur as external transactions, other kinds of events also change its assets, liabilities, and net income. The adjusting process records these events so that the financial statements present more useful information.

Topical Coverage

At the beginning of Chapter 2, we recognized that an entity's accounting equation is affected by business transactions and by other (internal) economic events. The primary focus of Chapter 2 was to teach the double-entry process of recording the effects of business transactions. This process involves journalizing the transactions in a book of original entry and then posting to the accounts. In studying Chapter 3, you will learn that some of the account balances that result from recording business transactions must be adjusted. These adjustments are recorded so that the entity's internal economic events will be reflected in the account balances.

Learning Objectives

After studying Chapter 3, you should be able to:

1. Explain why the life of a business is divided into accounting periods of equal length and why unrecorded economic events require adjustments at the end of each period.
2. Explain why adjustments are required by the revenue recognition and matching principles and why the accrual basis of accounting is preferred to a cash basis.
3. Prepare adjusting entries for prepaid expenses, depreciation, unearned revenues, accrued expenses, and accrued revenues.
4. Show the effects of making adjustments by preparing a schedule that reconciles the unadjusted and adjusted trial balances and by preparing financial statements from the adjusted trial balance.
5. Prepare entries to record cash receipts and cash disbursements of items that were recorded at the end of the previous period as accrued expenses and accrued revenues.
6. Define each asset and liability classification appearing on a balance sheet, classify balance sheet items, and prepare a classified balance sheet.
7. Define or explain the words and phrases listed in the chapter glossary.

After studying Appendix A at the end of Chapter 3, you should be able to:

8. Explain why some companies record prepaid and unearned items in income statement accounts and prepare adjusting entries when this procedure is used.

LO 1 Explain why the life of a business is divided into accounting periods of equal length and why unrecorded economic events require adjustments at the end of each period.

The life of a business often spans many years, during which its activities go on without interruption. However, decision makers such as managers and investors cannot wait for the business to conclude its operations before they evaluate its financial progress. Instead, they expect a business to provide financial reports periodically. To accomplish this, the accounting process is based on a **time period principle.** In other words, the activities of a business are identified as occurring during specific time periods such as months or three-month periods or years. Then, financial reports that show the results of operations are prepared for each period. Since this division of the life of a business into time periods is done for accounting purposes, the time periods are called **accounting periods.** The primary accounting period used by most businesses is one year, for which they prepare annual financial statements. However, businesses also prepare **interim financial reports** based on one-month or three-month accounting periods.

Businesses do not always adopt the calendar year ending December 31 as the annual accounting period. They may adopt a period of any 12 consecutive months. The specific 12-month period that a business adopts as its annual accounting period is called the **fiscal year.** In choosing a fiscal year, businesses that do not have much seasonal fluctuation in their sales volume often choose the calendar year. Those that have wide fluctuations in volume tend to choose their **natural business year,** which ends when business activities are at their lowest ebb. For example, in department stores, the natural business year begins on February 1, after the Christmas and January sales, and ends the following January 31. Therefore, the annual accounting periods of department stores commonly begin on February 1 and end the following January 31.

Need for Adjustments at the End of an Accounting Period

At the end of an accounting period, after all transactions are recorded, several of the accounts in a company's ledger typically do not show proper end-of-period balances for presentation in the financial statements. This occurs even though all transactions were recorded correctly. The balances must be updated for statement purposes, not because errors have been made but because internal economic events have occurred and have not yet been recorded.

One event of this type involves costs that expire with the passage of time. For example, the third item on the trial balance of Dow's law practice, as prepared in Chapter 2 and reproduced again as Illustration 3–1, is "Prepaid insurance, $2,400." This $2,400 represents the insurance premium for two years. The insurance protection began on December 1. However, by December 31, $2,400 is not the correct balance sheet amount for this asset. During December, one month's insurance ($2,400/24 = $100) expired and became an expense. Only $2,300, or ($2,400 − $100), remains as an asset. Likewise, the $120 balance in Office Supplies includes the cost of some supplies that have been used up and become an expense during December. Also, the items in the law library have a limited useful life and part of their usefulness expired during December. Therefore, part of the $2,880 cost of the law library should be reported as expense during December. Likewise, the office equipment has begun to wear out and some of its cost should be charged to December. Because of these events, the balances of the Prepaid Insurance, Office Supplies, Law Library, and Office Equipment accounts are not the proper amounts to appear on the December 31 balance sheet. These items must be *adjusted* before financial statements are prepared.

Some of the other accounts in the trial balance of Dow's law practice also must be adjusted before financial statements are prepared. They include Office Salaries Expense, Unearned Legal Fees, and Legal Fees Earned.

ILLUSTRATION 3-1

Trial Balance Drawn from the Ledger of Jerry Dow, Attorney

JERRY DOW, ATTORNEY
Trial Balance
December 31, 1993

Cash	$ 650	
Office supplies	120	
Prepaid insurance	2,400	
Law library	2,880	
Office equipment	6,880	
Accounts payable		$ 760
Unearned legal fees		3,000
Jerry Dow, capital		9,000
Jerry Dow, withdrawals	1,100	
Legal fees earned		3,900
Salaries expense	1,400	
Rent expense	1,000	
Utilities expense	230	
Totals	$16,660	$16,660

The Adjustment Process

LO 2 Explain why adjustments are required by the revenue recognition and matching principles and why the accrual basis of accounting is preferred to a cash basis.

The adjustment process is based on two accounting principles, the *revenue recognition principle* and the **matching principle.** As explained in Chapter 1, the *revenue recognition principle* requires that revenue be reported in the income statement when it is earned, not before and not after. For most firms, revenue is earned at the time a service is rendered or a product is sold to the customer.

For example, if a lawyer renders legal services to a client during December, the legal fees are earned during December. According to the *revenue recognition principle,* the lawyer must report these legal fees as revenue on the December income statement, even though the cash receipt from the client may take place in November or January. In cases such as this, the adjustment process assigns the revenue to December, when it was earned.

The *matching principle* requires reporting expenses on the income statement in the same accounting period as the revenues that were earned as a result of the expenses. For example, assume that a business uses an office to earn revenues during December. According to the *revenue recognition principle,* the business must report the revenues on the December income statement. One expense the business incurred in the pursuit of those December revenues was the December office rent. Therefore, the *matching principle* requires reporting the rent for December on the December income statement. This must be done even if the December rent was paid in November (or in January). In such cases, the adjustment process is used to match the cost of December's rent with the revenues earned during December.

Accrual Basis Accounting versus Cash Basis Accounting

When the adjustment process is used to assign revenues to the periods in which they are earned and to match expenses with revenues, the accounting system is described as **accrual basis accounting.** The accrual basis reflects the understanding that the economic effect of a revenue generally occurs when it is earned, not when cash is received.

Expenses involve the expiration or using up of assets and generally are assumed to produce revenues during the period in which the assets expire. Thus, to match expenses with revenues, the accrual basis reports expenses in the period the assets expire, not when cash is paid.

An alternative to accrual basis accounting is the **cash basis of accounting.** Under the cash basis, revenues are reported when cash is received and expenses are reported when cash is paid. For example, if revenue is earned in December but cash from the customer is not received until January, an adjustment is *not* made to report the revenue in December. Instead, the revenue is reported in January. Because revenues are reported when cash is received and expenses are deducted when cash is paid, net income is calculated as the difference between revenue receipts and expense disbursements.

In discussing the objectives of financial reporting, the FASB concluded that "information about enterprise earnings and its components measured by accrual accounting generally provides a better indication of enterprise performance than information about current cash receipts and payments."[1] Some concerns use a cash basis, but it is acceptable only if the difference between earned revenues and cash receipts from customers is so small that it is not important. Also, the difference between incurred expenses and cash payments must not be important.

One important benefit of accrual accounting is that it makes the information on accounting statements comparable from period to period. For example, in December 1993, the Dow law practice paid $2,400 for two years of insurance coverage beginning December 1. Under accrual accounting, insurance expense of $100 is reported on the December 1993 income statement. Twelve hundred dollars will be reported as expense during 1994 ($100 each month if monthly income statements are prepared), and $1,100 will be reported as expense during 1995 ($100 each month for the first 11 months). This allocation of the insurance cost is shown graphically in Illustration 3–2.

In contrast, a cash basis income statement for December 1993 would show insurance expense of $2,400; and the income statements related to the next 23 months would show $–0– expense. If you compare monthly income statements for the 24 months of insurance coverage, the accrual basis correctly shows that all 24 months incurred the expense of insurance coverage. The cash basis would suggest that December 1993 was much less profitable than the following 23 months.

[1] *Statement of Financial Accounting Concepts No. 1,* "Objectives of Financial Reporting by Business Enterprises" (Norwalk, Conn., 1978), par. 44.

ILLUSTRATION 3–2

Allocating the $2,400 Cost of Insurance Protection for 24 Months beginning December 1, 1993

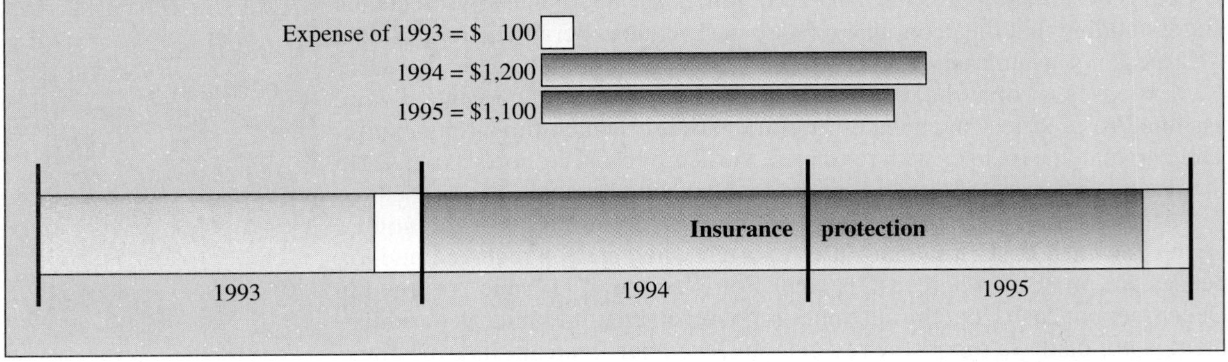

Adjusting the Accounts

LO 3 Prepare adjusting entries for prepaid expenses, depreciation, unearned revenues, accrued expenses, and accrued revenues.

The process of adjusting the accounts is essentially the same as the process of analyzing and recording business transactions. Each account balance and the economic events that affect that account are analyzed to determine whether an adjustment is needed. If an adjustment is required, an **adjusting entry** is prepared to bring the asset or liability account balance up to date. This process also brings the related expense or revenue account balance up to date. After the adjusting entries are journalized, they are posted to the accounts. In the following paragraphs, we explain why adjusting entries are needed to account for prepaid expenses, depreciation, unearned revenues, accrued expenses, and accrued revenues.

Prepaid expenses, depreciation, and unearned revenues involve previously recorded assets and liabilities. However, since they were first recorded, economic events or simply the passage of time have affected these assets and liabilities and adjusting entries must be made to record the effects. Accrued expenses and accrued revenues, on the other hand, involve assets and liabilities that have not yet been recorded. Adjusting entries are used to record these assets and liabilities as well as the related expenses and revenues.

Prepaid Expenses

As the name implies, a prepaid expense is an economic benefit that has been paid for in advance of its use. At the time of payment, an asset is acquired that will expire or be used up. As it is used up, it becomes an expense.

For example, recall Jerry Dow's December prepayment of $2,400 for two years' insurance protection. Although the payment was made on December 26, the policy went into effect on December 1. The allocation of this cost to 1993, 1994, and 1995 is shown in Illustration 3–2. As each day of December went by, the benefit of insurance protection expired, and a portion of the prepaid insurance became an expense. On December 31, one month's insurance, valued at 1/24 of $2,400, or $100, had expired. Therefore, the following adjusting entry is required so that the accounts reflect proper asset and expense amounts on December 31:

		Adjustment (a)		
Dec.	31	Insurance Expense	100.00	
		Prepaid Insurance		100.00
		To record the expired insurance.		

Posting the adjusting entry has the following effect on the accounts:

Prepaid Insurance			
Dec. 26	2,400	Dec. 31	100

Insurance Expense			
Dec. 31	100		

After the entry is posted, the $2,300 balance in Prepaid Insurance and the $100 balance in Insurance Expense are proper statement amounts.

In looking at Illustration 3–2, you should recognize that adjusting entries will be required to allocate $1,200, or ($2,400/24) × 12, to 1994, and to allocate $1,100, or ($2,400/24) × 11, to 1995.

Another prepaid expense item that requires an adjustment is office supplies. For example, during December, the Dow law practice purchased some office supplies and placed them in the office for use. In the following days, the secretary used some of the supplies. The amount used was an expense that reduced the supplies on hand. However, the daily reductions were not recognized in the accounts because day-by-day information about amounts used and remaining was not needed. Also, labor is saved by making only one entry to record the total cost of all supplies used during the month.

Therefore, for the accounts to reflect proper statement amounts on December 31, the dollar amount of office supplies used during the month must be determined and recorded. To learn the amount used, you must count, or take an inventory of, the remaining supplies. Then, deduct the cost of the remaining supplies from the cost of the supplies purchased. If, for example, $75 of supplies remain, $45 ($120 − $75 = $45) of supplies were used and became an expense. The following adjusting entry records the using up of the supplies:

		Adjustment (b)		
Dec.	31	Office Supplies Expense	45.00	
		Office Supplies		45.00
		To record the supplies used.		

The effect of the adjusting entry on the accounts is:

Office Supplies			
Dec. 26	120	Dec. 31	45

Office Supplies Expense			
Dec. 31	45		

Unlike the two previous examples, some items that are prepaid expenses at the time of purchase are both bought and fully used up within a single accounting period. For example, a company might pay its rent in advance on the first day of each month. Each month, the amount paid results in a prepaid expense that fully expires before the month's end and before the end of the accounting period. In such cases, you should ignore the fact that an asset results from each prepayment because an adjustment can be avoided if each prepayment is originally recorded as an expense.

Depreciation

Tangible, long-lived assets held for use in the production or sale of other assets or services are called **plant and equipment.** They include assets such as land, buildings, machines, professional libraries, and automobiles. All items of plant and equipment, except for land, eventually wear out or lose their usefulness. Therefore, the cost of these assets must be charged to expense over their useful lives. This process of allocating the cost of these items to expense is called **depreciation.** Depreciation is recorded with adjusting entries similar to those used for prepaid expenses.

For example, the Dow law practice owns a law library that cost \$2,880. Dow estimates that beginning December 1, 1993, the items in this library will be useful for three years, after which they will have to be discarded and replaced. Based on this estimate, the depreciation expense for December is calculated as \$2,880/36 months = \$80. You record this expense with the following adjusting entry:

		Adjustment (c)		
Dec.	31	Depreciation Expense, Law Library	80.00	
		Accumulated Depreciation, Law Library.		80.00
		To record depreciation for December.		

The effect of the entry on the accounts is:

Law Library

Debit		Credit
Dec. 2	2,500	
6	380	

Depreciation Expense, Law Library

Debit		Credit
Dec. 31	80	

Accumulated Depreciation, Law Library

Debit	Credit	
	Dec. 31	80

After the entry is posted, the Law Library account and its related Accumulated Depreciation, Law Library account together show the December 31 balance sheet amounts for this asset. The Depreciation Expense, Law Library account shows the amount of depreciation expense that should appear on the December income statement.

In most cases, a decrease in an asset is recorded with a credit to the account in which the asset is recorded. However, note in the illustrated accounts that this procedure is not followed in recording depreciation. Rather, depreciation is recorded in a **contra account.** (A contra account's balance is subtracted from the balance of an associated account to show a more proper amount for the item recorded in the associated account.) In the present case, the contra account is Accumulated Depreciation, Law Library.

Why are contra accounts used to record depreciation? Contra accounts allow balance sheet readers to observe both the original cost of the asset and the estimated amount of depreciation that has been charged to expense. Knowing both the original cost and the accumulated depreciation, readers are better able to evaluate the productive capacity and the potential need to replace the company's assets. For example, if the balance sheet for Jerry Dow's law practice shows both the $2,880 original cost of the law library and the $80 balance in the accumulated depreciation contra account, readers can better judge the size of the library and can see that it is almost new.

Note the words **accumulated depreciation** in the title of the contra account. This emphasizes the fact that depreciation taken in all prior periods is recorded in this account. For example, if monthly financial statements are prepared for Dow's law practice, the Law Library account and its related accumulated depreciation account at the end of February 1994 appear as follows:

Law Library

Dec. 2	2,500		
6	380		

Accumulated Depreciation, Law Library

		Dec. 31	80
		Jan. 31	80
		Feb. 28	80

And the law library's cost and three months' accumulated depreciation are shown on its February 28 balance sheet thus:

Law library	$2,880	
Less accumulated depreciation	240	$2,640

The office equipment of Dow's law practice is another type of plant and equipment that must be depreciated. Early in December, Dow made two purchases of office equipment for $5,600 and $1,280. For convenience, assume that all of the items purchased are estimated to have a four-year useful life. Also, Dow estimates that at the end of the four-year useful life, the business will receive $880 for the equipment as a trade-in allowance on new equipment. Therefore, the cost that will expire over the 48-month life is $6,880 − $880, or $6,000. Depreciation expense for each month is $6,000/48 = $125 and the entry to record depreciation for December is

		Adjustment (d)		
Dec.	31	Depreciation Expense, Office Equipment.	125.00	
		Accumulated Depreciation, Office Equipment		125.00
		To record depreciation for December.		

The effects of posting this entry to the accounts appear as follows:

Office Equipment

Dec. 3	5,600		
6	1,280		

Depreciation Expense, Office Equipment

Dec. 31	125		

Accumulated Depreciation, Office Equipment

		Dec. 31	125

Accumulated depreciation accounts are sometimes titled *Allowance for Depreciation*. However, the word *accumulated* better describes the depreciation procedure than does *allowance*.

Unearned Revenues

An unearned revenue results when payment for goods or services is received in advance of delivering the goods. For instance, Jerry Dow entered into an agreement with Chemical Supply to do its legal work on a fixed-fee basis of $500 per month, beginning December 15. On December 26, Dow received $3,000 in payment for providing legal services for the six-month period beginning December 15. This entry records the fee:

Dec.	26	Cash	3,000.00	
		Unearned Legal Fees		3,000.00
		Received a legal fee in advance.		

Receiving the fee in advance increased the cash of the law practice and created a liability, the obligation to do Chemical Supply's legal work for the next six months. However, by December 31, the law practice has discharged $250 of the liability and earned that much revenue. According to the *revenue recognition principle,* the $250 that has been earned should appear on the December income statement. Therefore, on December 31, the following adjusting entry is required:

		Adjustment (e)		
Dec.	31	Unearned Legal Fees	250.00	
		Legal Fees Earned ($500 × ½)		250.00
		Earned legal fees that had been received in advance.		

Posting the entry has this effect on the accounts:

Unearned Legal Fees

Dec. 31	250	Dec. 26	3,000

Legal Fees Earned

		Dec. 10	2,200
		12	1,700
		31	250

The effect of the entry is to transfer the $250 earned portion of the fee from the liability account to the revenue account. It reduces the liability and records as a revenue the $250 that has been earned.

Accrued Expenses

Most expenses are recorded at the time they are paid. That is because when the cash payment is recorded, the credit to Cash is balanced by a debit to the expense account. However, at the end of an accounting period, some expenses incurred during the period may remain unrecorded because payment is not due. Incurred expenses that are unpaid and therefore unrecorded are called **accrued expenses.** One common example is unpaid wages to employees for work that has already been done.

For example, the Dow law practice has a secretary who earns $70 per day or $350 for a week that begins on Monday and ends on Friday. The secretary's wages are due and payable every two weeks on Friday. During December, these wages were paid on the 12th and 26th and were recorded as follows:

Cash			
		Dec. 12	700
		26	700

Salaries Expense			
Dec. 12	700		
26	700		

December						
S	M	T	W	T	F	S
	1	2	3	4	5	6
7	8	9	10	11	12	13
14	15	16	17	18	19	20
21	22	23	24	25	26	27
28	29	30	31			

Notice on the calendar shown in the margin that December included three workdays after the December 26 payment of wages. As a result, at the close of business on Wednesday, December 31, the secretary has earned three days' wages for which payment is not yet due. Because payment has not been made, the wages have not yet been recorded. However, this $210 of earned but unpaid wages is as much a part of the December expenses as the $1,400 of wages that have been paid. Also, on December 31, the unpaid wages are a liability. Therefore, for the accounts to show the correct salary expense for December and all liabilities owed on December 31, you must make the following adjusting entry:

		Adjustment (f)		
Dec.	31	Salaries Expense	210.00	
		Salaries Payable		210.00
		To record accrued wages.		

The effect of the entry on the accounts is:

Salaries Expense			
Dec. 12	700		
26	700		
31	210		

Salaries Payable			
		Dec. 31	210

Another typical accrued expense that requires an adjusting entry at the end of the period is interest incurred on outstanding notes payable. (Some

AS A MATTER OF

Ethics

Bill Pena is the accountant for Cryer Company. Just before Pena prepared the adjusting entries to record accrued expenses at the end of the company's first year of operations, he was called into the company president's office. The president asked about the accrued expenses and then told Pena not to make the adjustments. Although Pena expressed concern about these instructions, the president said that because the bills will not be received until January, they should not be reported as expenses until the next year.

In addition, the president asked how much this year's revenues will be increased by the purchase order recently received from Broker Company. Pena explained that there will be no effect on sales until January because Broker Company will not take delivery until after the first of the year. The president was exasperated and pointed out that the order had already been received and Cryer was ready to make the deliveries. Even though Broker Company's order indicated that the merchandise should not be delivered until late January, the president told Pena to record the sale in December.

Pena knows that the combination of recording the sale to Broker Company and not accruing the expenses will increase the reported income by a large amount and is not sure what to do. He also wonders what reaction the company's auditors will have when they review the adjustments. What should Pena do?

accounts payable also bear interest.) Interest expense is incurred with the passage of time. Therefore, unless the interest has been paid and recorded on the last day of the accounting period, some additional interest will have accrued since the last payment date. Record this accrued interest with an adjusting entry similar to the preceding entry to record accrued salaries.

Accrued Revenues

Many revenues are recorded when cash is received. Others are recorded at the time the goods or services are sold on credit and a bill is given to the customer. However, at the end of an accounting period, some revenues may remain unrecorded even though they have been earned. Earned revenues that are unrecorded because payment has not been received are called **accrued revenues.** For example, on December 20, Jerry Dow agreed to do Guaranty Bank's legal work for a fixed fee of $600 per month. The fee was to be paid on the 20th of each month for work completed in the preceding 30 days. Therefore, by December 31, the law practice has earned one third of a month's fee, or $200. According to the *revenue recognition principle,* this revenue should be reported on the December income statement. To record the amount that has been earned, make the following adjusting entry:

		Adjustment (g)		
Dec.	31	Accounts Receivable	200.00	
		Legal Fees Earned		200.00
		To record accrued legal fees.		

Posting the entry has this effect on the accounts:

ILLUSTRATION 3–3

The December 31, 1993, Unadjusted and Adjusted Trial Balances for Jerry Dow, Attorney

	Unadjusted Trial Balance		Adjustments		Adjusted Trial Balance	
	Dr.	**Cr.**	**Dr.**	**Cr.**	**Dr.**	**Cr.**
Cash	650				650	
Office supplies	120			(*b*) 45	75	
Prepaid insurance	2,400			(*a*) 100	2,300	
Law library	2,880				2,880	
Office equipment	6,880				6,880	
Accounts payable		760				760
Unearned legal fees		3,000	(*e*) 250			2,750
Jerry Dow, capital		9,000				9,000
Jerry Dow, withdrawals	1,100				1,100	
Legal fees earned		3,900		(*e*) 250		4,350
				(*g*) 200		
Salaries expense	1,400		(*f*) 210		1,610	
Rent expense	1,000				1,000	
Utilities expense	230				230	
Totals	16,660	16,660				
Insurance expense			(*a*) 100		100	
Office supplies expense			(*b*) 45		45	
Depreciation expense, law library			(*c*) 80		80	
Accumulated depreciation, law library				(*c*) 80		80
Depreciation expense, office equipment			(*d*) 125		125	
Accumulated depreciation, office equipment				(*d*) 125		125
Salaries payable				(*f*) 210		210
Accounts receivable			(*g*) 200		200	
Totals			1,010	1,010	17,275	17,275

Accounts Receivable

Dec. 12	1,700	Dec. 22	1,700
31	200		

Legal Fees Earned

		Dec. 10	2,200
		12	1,700
		31	250
		31	200

We mentioned earlier that interest was a typical example of an accrued expense that requires an adjusting entry. Interest is also a typical example of an accrued revenue. If a company has outstanding notes receivable or accounts receivable that bear interest, you must make an adjusting entry to record any accrued interest earned since the last cash receipt.

The Adjusted Trial Balance

A trial balance prepared before adjustments have been recorded is called an **unadjusted trial balance.** By comparison, an **adjusted trial balance** shows the account balances after the adjusting entries have been posted. Illustration 3–3

LO 4 Show the effects of making adjustments by preparing a schedule that reconciles the unadjusted and adjusted trial balances and by preparing financial statements from the adjusted trial balance.

shows the December 31, 1993, unadjusted trial balance, the adjustments, and the adjusted trial balance for the law practice of Jerry Dow. Note that in the adjustments columns, letters identify debits and credits with the adjusting entries explained earlier in the chapter.

Preparing Statements from the Adjusted Trial Balance

An adjusted trial balance shows proper balance sheet and income statement amounts. Therefore, you can use it to prepare the financial statements. When this is done, the income statement is prepared first because the net income, as calculated on the income statement, is needed to complete the statement of changes in owner's equity.

Illustration 3–4 shows how the revenues and expenses of Dow's law practice are arranged into an income statement and a statement of changes in owner's equity. In preparing the statement of changes in owner's equity, refer back to the ledger to determine how much of the owner's capital account balance existed at the beginning of the period and how much resulted from the owner's investments during the current period.

Illustration 3–5 shows how the asset, liability, and owner's equity items are drawn from the adjusted trial balance and arranged into a balance sheet. The balance sheet is prepared last because the owner's equity is calculated in the statement of changes in owner's equity.

Disposing of Accrued Items

LO 5 Prepare entries to record cash receipts and cash disbursements of items that were recorded at the end of the previous period as accrued expenses and accrued revenues.

Accrued Expenses

Earlier in this chapter, we recorded the December 29, 30, and 31 accrued wages of the secretary as follows:

Dec.	31	Salaries Expense	210.00	
		Salaries Payable		210.00
		To record accrued wages.		

When these wages are paid on Friday, January 9, you must make the following entry:

Jan.	9	Salaries Payable	210.00	
		Salaries Expense	490.00	
		Cash		700.00
		Paid two weeks' wages.		

The first debit in the January 9 entry cancels the liability for the three days' wages accrued on December 31. The second debit records the wages of January's first seven working days as an expense of the January accounting period. The credit records the total amount paid to the secretary.

Accrued Revenues

On December 20, Jerry Dow agreed to do Guaranty Bank's legal work on a fixed-fee basis for $600 per month. On December 31, the following adjusting entry was made to record one third of a month's revenue earned under this contract:

ILLUSTRATION 3–4

Preparing the Income Statement and Statement of Changes in Owner's Equity from the Adjusted Trial Balance

JERRY DOW, ATTORNEY
Adjusted Trial Balance
December 31, 1993

Cash	$ 650	
Office supplies	75	
Prepaid insurance	2,300	
Law library	2,880	
Office equipment	6,880	
Accounts payable		$ 760
Unearned legal fees		2,750
Jerry Dow, capital		9,000
Jerry Dow, withdrawals	1,100	
Legal fees earned		4,350
Salaries expense	1,610	
Rent expense	1,000	
Utilities expense	230	
Insurance expense	100	
Office supplies expense	45	
Depreciation expense, law library	80	
Accumulated depreciation, law library		80
Depreciation expense, office equipment	125	
Accumulated depreciation, office equipment		125
Salaries payable		210
Accounts receivable	200	
Totals	$17,275	$17,275

JERRY DOW, ATTORNEY
Income Statement
For the Month Ended December 31, 1993

Revenues:		
Legal fees earned		$4,350
Operating expenses:		
Salaries expense	$1,610	
Rent expense	1,000	
Utilities expense	230	
Insurance expense	100	
Office supplies expense	45	
Depreciation expense, law library	80	
Depreciation expense, office equipment	125	
Total operating expenses		3,190
Net income		$1,160

JERRY DOW, ATTORNEY
Statement of Changes in Owner's Equity
For the Month Ended December 31, 1993

Jerry Dow, capital, November 30, 1993		$ -0-
Plus:		
Investments by owner	$9,000	
Net income	1,160	10,160
Total		$10,160
Less:		
Withdrawals by owner		1,100
Jerry Dow, capital, December 31, 1993		$ 9,060

ILLUSTRATION 3–5

Preparing the Balance Sheet from the Adjusted Trial Balance

JERRY DOW, ATTORNEY
Adjusted Trial Balance
December 31, 1993

Cash	$ 650	
Office supplies	75	
Prepaid insurance	2,300	
Law library	2,880	
Office equipment	6,880	
Accounts payable		$ 760
Unearned legal fees		2,750
Jerry Dow, capital		9,000
Jerry Dow, withdrawals	1,100	
Legal fees earned		4,350
Salaries expense	1,610	
Rent expense	1,000	
Utilities expense	230	
Insurance expense	100	
Office supplies expense	45	
Depreciation expense, law library	80	
Accumulated depreciation, law library		80
Depreciation expense, office equipment	125	
Accumulated depreciation, office equipment		125
Salaries payable		210
Accounts receivable	200	
Totals	$17,275	$17,275

JERRY DOW, ATTORNEY
Balance Sheet
December 31, 1993

Assets

Cash		$ 650
Accounts receivable		200
Office supplies		75
Prepaid insurance		2,300
Law library	$2,880	
Less accumulated depreciation	80	2,800
Office equipment	$6,880	
Less accumulated depreciation	125	6,755
Total assets		$12,780
Liabilities		
Accounts payable	$ 760	
Unearned legal fees	2,750	
Salaries payable	210	
Total liabilities		$ 3,720
Owner's Equity		
Jerry Dow, capital, December 31, 1993		9,060
Total liabilities and owner's equity		$12,780

From statement of changes in owner's equity

Dec.	31	Accounts Receivable	200.00	
		Legal Fees Earned		200.00
		To record accrued legal fees.		

When payment of the first month's fee is received on January 20, you should make the following entry:

Jan.	20	Cash	600.00	
		Accounts Receivable		200.00
		Legal Fees Earned		400.00
		Received cash for accrued and earned legal fees.		

The first credit in the January 20 entry records the collection of the fee accrued at the end of December. The second credit records as revenue the fee earned during the first 20 days of January.

Classification of Balance Sheet Items

LO 6 Define each asset and liability classification appearing on a balance sheet, classify balance sheet items, and prepare a classified balance sheet.

The balance sheets that we have presented up to this point (for example, see Illustration 3–5) are **unclassified balance sheets.** This means that we did not attempt to divide the assets or liabilities into classes. However, a balance sheet becomes more useful when its assets and liabilities are classified into meaningful groups. Readers of such **classified balance sheets** can better judge the adequacy of the different assets used in the business. Also, they can better estimate the probable availability of funds to meet the various liabilities as they become due.

Businesses do not all use the same system of classifying assets and liabilities on their balance sheets. However, most businesses classify them as shown in Illustration 3–6. Assets are classified as (1) current assets, (2) investments, (3) plant and equipment, and (4) intangible assets. Liabilities are either (1) current liabilities or (2) long-term liabilities. We explain the nature of these classes next.

Current Assets

Current assets are cash and other assets that are reasonably expected to be realized in cash or to be sold or consumed within one year or within the normal **operating cycle of the business,** whichever is longer.[2] In addition to cash, current assets typically include short-term investments in marketable securities, accounts receivable, notes receivable, products held for resale (merchandise inventory), and prepaid expenses.

The operating cycle of a business depends on the nature of its activities. For a business that sells services, the operating cycle is the average time between the payment of salaries to the employees who perform the services and

[2] FASB, *Accounting Standards—Current Text* (Stamford, Conn., 1990), sec. B05.105. First published as *Accounting Research Bulletin No. 43,* ch3A, par. 4.

ILLUSTRATION 3–6

A Classified Balance Sheet

NATIONAL ELECTRICAL SUPPLY
Balance Sheet
December 31, 1993

Assets			
Current assets:			
Cash		$ 1,050	
Short-term investments		2,145	
Accounts receivable		3,961	
Notes receivable		600	
Merchandise inventory		10,248	
Prepaid expenses		405	
Total current assets			$ 18,409
Investments:			
Chrysler Corporation common stock		$ 2,400	
Land held for future expansion		8,000	
Total investments			10,400
Plant and equipment:			
Store equipment	$ 3,200		
Less accumulated depreciation	800	$ 2,400	
Buildings	$70,000		
Less accumulated depreciation	18,400	51,600	
Land		24,200	
Total plant and equipment			78,200
Intangible assets:			
Franchise			10,000
Total assets			$117,009
Liabilities			
Current liabilities:			
Accounts payable	$ 2,715		
Wages payable	480		
Notes payable	3,000		
Current portion of long-term liabilities	1,200		
Total current liabilities		$ 7,395	
Long-term liabilities:			
Notes payable		48,800	
Total liabilities			$ 56,195
Owner's Equity			
Bruce Brown, capital			60,814
Total liabilities and owner's equity			$117,009

the receipt of cash from customers in payment for those services. For a business that sells merchandise, the operating cycle is the average time between the payment of cash to purchase merchandise and the receipt of cash from customers in payment for the merchandise. Illustration 3–7 shows typical operating cycles for service businesses and merchandising businesses.

ILLUSTRATION 3–7

The Operating Cycle of a Business

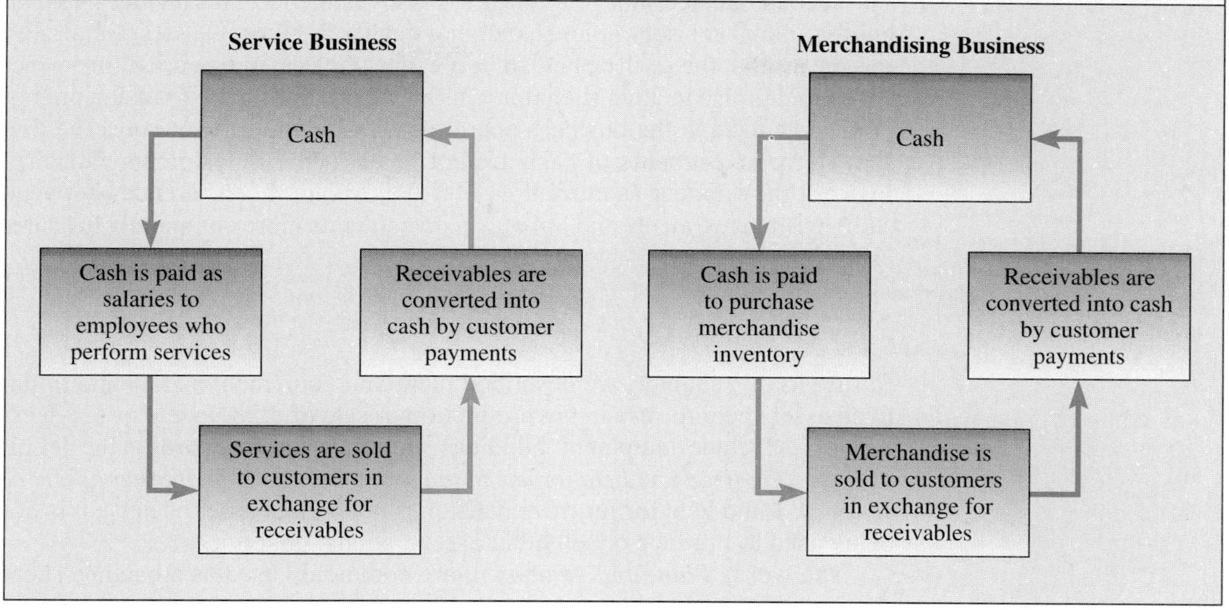

Most companies have an operating cycle that is less than one year. As a result, these companies use a one-year period to decide whether assets should be reported as current assets. Some companies, however, have an operating cycle that is longer than one year. For example, wine distributors may age some products for several years before the products are ready for sale. In such companies, the average length of the operating cycle should be used to decide whether assets satisfy the current asset definition.

Return to Illustration 3–6 and note that current assets are listed first. This is because they are more easily converted into cash than are other types of assets. In other words, current assets are said to be more *liquid* than other assets. Also, within the current asset category, the items are listed in the order of their liquidity, the most liquid first and the least liquid last. Note that prepaid expenses are listed last among the current assets. Unlike other current assets, prepaid expenses will not be converted into cash. Nevertheless, prepaid expenses substitute for future cash payments that would be required if the expenses had not been prepaid. Therefore, prepaid expenses are listed as current assets until their benefits expire or they are used up.

The prepaid expenses of a business, as a total, are seldom a major item on its balance sheet. As a result, instead of listing them individually, they often are totaled and shown as a single item called Prepaid expenses. Therefore, the "Prepaid expenses" in Illustration 3–6 may include several items such as prepaid insurance, office supplies, and store supplies.

Investments

The second balance sheet classification is investments. This includes stocks, bonds, and promissory notes that do not qualify as current assets. Generally, this means that they will be held for more than one year or one operating cycle. Investments also include such things as land held for future expansion but not now being used in the business operations. In Illustration 3–6, observe that short-term investments of cash are not listed in the Investments category. Instead, they appear as current assets. We explain the differences between short-term investments and long-term investments more completely in a later chapter.

Plant and Equipment

Earlier in this chapter, we described plant and equipment as tangible, long-lived assets held for use in the production or sale of other assets or services. Examples include equipment, buildings, and land. The key words in the definition are *long-lived* and *held for use in the production or sale of other assets or services*. Land held for future expansion is not a plant asset because it is not being used to produce or sell other assets, goods, or services.

The words *Plant and equipment* are commonly used as a balance sheet caption. Alternative captions are *Property, plant, and equipment,* or *Land, buildings, and equipment,* or simply *Plant assets*. The order in which plant assets are listed within the balance sheet classification varies from one business to another.

Intangible Assets

Economic benefits or resources that do not have a physical substance are called **intangible assets.** Their value stems from the privileges or rights that accrue to their owner. Examples of intangible assets are goodwill, patents, trademarks, copyrights, and franchises.

Current Liabilities

Obligations that are due to be paid or liquidated within one year or one operating cycle of the business, whichever is longer, are classified as **current liabilities.** Current liabilities usually are satisfied by paying current assets or by incurring new current liabilities. Common current liabilities are accounts payable, notes payable, wages payable, taxes payable, interest payable, and unearned revenues. Also, since long-term liabilities often require periodic payments, the portion of long-term liabilities that is due to be paid within one year or one operating cycle must be classified as a current liability. Illustration 3–6 shows how this item usually is described. The order in which current liability items are listed is not uniform.

Unearned revenues are classified as current liabilities because current assets normally are required in their liquidation. For example, advance receipts for future delivery of merchandise will be earned and the liability liquidated by delivering merchandise, which is a current asset.

Long-Term Liabilities

The second liability classification is **long-term liabilities.** Liabilities that are not due to be paid within one year or the current operating cycle are listed under this classification. Common long-term liability items are notes payable and bonds payable. Because businesses may owe both long-term notes payable and notes payable that are current liabilities, they often use two different accounts, one called Short-Term Notes Payable and the other Long-Term Notes Payable.

Owner's Equity on the Balance Sheet

The equity section of a balance sheet differs depending on whether the business is organized as a single proprietorship, a partnership, or a corporation.

Single Proprietorships and Partnerships

When a business is organized as a single proprietorship, the equity section of the balance sheet is presented as a single line that reports the owner's equity as of the date of the balance sheet. Thus, Illustration 3–5 shows "Jerry Dow, capital, December 31, 1993 . . . 9,060." In the unusual case where total liabilities exceed total assets, the negative (or debit) equity amount is shown in parentheses and subtracted from total liabilities.

When a business is organized as a partnership, separate capital accounts and withdrawals accounts are maintained for each partner. Changes in the partners' equities are reported in a statement of changes in partners' equities similar to the statement of changes in owner's equity. In the equity section of the balance sheet, the equity of each partner is listed as follows:

Partners' Equities

Shirley Tucker, capital	$17,300	
Mark Jackman, capital	24,800	
Total equities of the partners		$42,100

Corporations

Corporations are established under the laws of a state or under federal laws. These laws generally distinguish between the amounts a corporation receives from its stockholders through investments, and the increase or decrease in stockholders' equity due to net incomes, net losses, and **dividends.** (A dividend is a distribution, generally of cash, made by a corporation to its stockholders. A cash dividend reduces the assets and the equity of a corporation in the same way a withdrawal reduces the assets and equity of a proprietorship.)

The amounts stockholders have invested are classified as **contributed capital** or **paid-in capital.** The equity that represents the corporation's cumulative net incomes less net losses and dividends is called **retained earnings.** Therefore, stockholders' equity is shown on a corporation balance sheet as follows:

Stockholders' Equity		
Contributed capital:		
Common stock	$400,000	
Retained earnings	124,400	
Total stockholders' equity		$524,400

If a corporation issues only one kind of stock (others are discussed later), it is called **common stock** or sometimes *capital stock*. The $400,000 amount of common stock shown is the amount originally contributed to the corporation by its stockholders through the purchase of the corporation's stock. The $124,400 of retained earnings represents the increase in the stockholder's equity resulting from cumulative net incomes that exceeded any net losses and any dividends paid to the stockholders.

Alternative Balance Sheet Arrangements

The balance sheet in Illustration 1–3 (p. 21), with the liabilities and owner's equity placed to the right of the assets, is called an **account form balance sheet.** Such an arrangement emphasizes that assets equal liabilities plus owner's equity. Alternatively, when balance sheet items are arranged vertically, such as in Illustration 3–5, the format is called a **report form balance sheet.** Both forms are commonly used, and neither is preferred over the other.

Identifying Accounts by Number

We introduced a typical three-digit account numbering system in Chapter 2. In such a system, the number assigned to an account usually identifies the account and also identifies the balance sheet or income statement classification of the account. For example, in the following system, the first digit in an account's number tells its primary balance sheet or income statement classification. Account numbers with first digits of 1 are assigned to asset accounts. Liability accounts are assigned numbers with first digits of 2. The accounts in each balance sheet and income statement classification of a concern selling merchandise are numbered as follows:

101 to 199 are assigned to asset accounts.

201 to 299 are assigned to liability accounts.

301 to 399 are assigned to owner's equity accounts.

401 to 499 are assigned to sales or revenue accounts.

501 to 599 are assigned to cost of goods sold accounts.

601 to 699 are assigned to operating expense accounts.

701 to 799 are assigned to accounts that reflect unusual and/or infrequent gains.

801 to 899 are assigned to accounts that reflect unusual and/or infrequent losses.

In a system like this, the second digit of each account number can be used to identify the subclassification of the account, as follows:

101 to 199. Asset accounts
- 101 to 139. Current asset accounts (second digits of 0, 1, 2, or 3)
- 141 to 149. Long-term investment accounts (second digit is 4)
- 151 to 179. Plant asset accounts (second digits of 5, 6, or 7)
- 181 to 189. Natural resources (second digit is 8)
- 191 to 199. Intangible asset accounts (second digit is 9)

201 to 299. Liability accounts
- 201 to 249. Current liability accounts (second digits of 0, 1, 2, 3, or 4)
- 251 to 269. Long-term liability accounts (second digits of 5 or 6)

Finally, a third digit is assigned so that each account is uniquely identified by its number. For example, specific current asset accounts might be assigned numbers as follows:

101 to 199. Asset accounts
- 101 to 139. Current asset accounts
  - 101. Cash
  - 106. Accounts Receivable
  - 110. Rent Receivable
  - 128. Prepaid Insurance

The preceding three-digit account numbering system would be adequate for many simple businesses. For more complex businesses, however, the account numbering system may use four, five, or more digits. Chapter 5 discusses the sales and cost of goods sold accounts listed in the previous account numbering system.

Summary of the Chapter in Terms of Learning Objectives

LO 1. The life of a business is divided into accounting periods so that periodic financial reports can be prepared and used to evaluate the financial progress of the business. Adjustments at the end of each period are necessary to update some of the asset, liability, expense, and revenue accounts and to show the effects of previously unrecorded internal economic events of the business.

LO 2. When revenues are earned and the related cash is received in different periods, the revenue recognition principle requires that adjusting entries be made as necessary to report the revenues in the period they are earned. And when assets expire or are used up in one period but are paid for in another period, the matching principle requires that adjusting entries be made to report expenses in the period the assets expire.

These principles are the essence of accrual accounting, which is preferred because it reports revenues and expenses when they have an economic impact on the entity. In contrast to accrual basis accounting, cash basis accounting reports revenues when cash is received and reports expenses when cash is paid. Hence, the cash basis of accounting does not require adjustments.

LO 3. Adjusting entries are used: (*a*) to charge the expired portion of prepaid expenses to expense; (*b*) to charge the expired portion of plant and equipment cost to depreciation expense; (*c*) to recognize as revenues the earned portion of unearned revenue liabilities; (*d*) to accrue expenses and record the related liabilities; and (*e*) to accrue revenues and record the related assets.

LO 4. A six-column schedule can show the effects of the adjustments on the accounts by listing the unadjusted trial balance in the first two columns, the debits and credits of the adjusting entries in the next two columns, and the adjusted trial balance in the last two columns. The adjusted trial balance shows all of the ledger accounts with balances, including revenues, expenses, withdrawals, assets, liabilities, and owner's equity. Hence, it contains all of the account balance information needed to prepare the income statement, then the statement of changes in owner's equity, and finally the balance sheet.

LO 5. When accrued expenses are paid early in a new accounting period, the entry to record the payment includes a debit to the previously recorded liability and a debit to expense for the portion incurred during the new period. When payment of accrued revenues is received, the entry includes a credit to the previously recorded asset and a credit to revenue for the portion earned during the new period.

LO 6. Classified balance sheets usually report four classes of assets: current assets, investments, plant and equipment, and intangible assets. Liabilities are either current liabilities or long-term liabilities. The equity of a single proprietorship is reported on one line, while a separate capital account is reported for each partner in a partnership. Corporations report the investments of its stockholders as contributed capital; the equity from net incomes less net losses and dividends is reported as retained earnings.

Demonstration Problem

The following information relates to Best Plumbing Company on December 31, 1993. The company prepares financial statements annually on a calendar-year basis.

a. Best Plumbing Company's weekly payroll is $2,800, paid every Friday for a five-day workweek. At the 1993 year-end, the employees have worked Monday through Wednesday.

b. On December 1, 1993, the company borrowed $45,000 from a local bank for 90 days at 12% interest.

c. During December, the company advertised in the local paper at a cost of $600, which remains unpaid and unrecorded.

d. Equipment that cost $10,000 and has no salvage value was purchased on July 1, 1992. It has a five-year useful life.

e. At the beginning of the year, office supplies amounted to $210. During the year, $650 of supplies were purchased and charged to the asset account. At year-end, there were $280 of supplies on hand.

f. On October 1, 1993, Best Plumbing Company contracted to install plumbing for a new housing project. The contract was for $144,000 to install plumbing in 24 new houses. The $144,000 was received on October 1, 1993, and credited to Unearned Plumbing Revenue. As of December 31, 1993, 18 houses have been completed.

g. On September 1, 1993, a one-year insurance policy was purchased for $1,200 and was debited to Prepaid Insurance.

h. The previous year, on December 1, 1992, the company had purchased a one-year policy for $900. The portion of the cost that relates to 1993 exists in the Prepaid Insurance account.

Required

1. Prepare the necessary adjusting journal entries on December 31, 1993.
2. Complete the following schedule:

Entry	Account	Amount of Adjustment	Amount that Will Appear on Balance Sheet	Classification of Account on Balance Sheet*
a	Wages payable	$	$	
b	Interest payable			
c	Accounts payable			
d	Accumulated depreciation			
e	Office supplies			
f	Unearned plumbing revenue			
g and *h*	Prepaid insurance			

* Indicate whether the account is a current asset, plant and equipment, current liability, or long-term liability.

3. State whether the effect of each adjustment was to increase, or decrease, or leave unchanged each of the following: net income, total assets, total liabilities.

Solution to Demonstration Problem

Planning the Solution

- Analyze the information related to each potential adjustment to determine which accounts need to be updated.
- Calculate the amount of adjustment required for each item and prepare the necessary journal entries.
- Enter the amount of each adjustment in the table, calculate the resulting account balance that will appear on the balance sheet, and determine the balance sheet classification of the account.
- Review the debit and credit of each adjusting entry to determine the entry's overall effect on net income, and total assets or total liabilities.

1. Adjusting journal entries:

a.	Dec.	31	Wages Expense	1,680.00	
			Wages Payable		1,680.00
			To accrue wages for the last three days of the year (3/5 × $2,800).		
b.		31	Interest Expense	450.00	
			Interest Payable		450.00
			To accrue interest for one month ($45,000 × .12 × 1/12).		
c.		31	Advertising Expense	600.00	
			Accounts Payable		600.00
			To record advertising expense.		
d.		31	Depreciation Expense, Equipment	2,000.00	
			Accumulated Depreciation, Equipment		2,000.00
			To record depreciation expense for the year ($10,000/5 = $2,000).		
e.		31	Office Supplies Expense	580.00	
			Office Supplies		580.00
			To record office supplies used ($210 + $650 − $280).		
f.		31	Unearned Plumbing Revenue	108,000.00	
			Plumbing Services Revenue		108,000.00
			To recognize plumbing revenues earned ($144,000 × 18/24).		
g.		31	Insurance Expense	400.00	
			Prepaid Insurance		400.00
			To adjust for the expired portion of insurance ($1,200 × 4/12).		
h.		31	Insurance Expense	825.00	
			Prepaid Insurance		825.00
			To record the expiration of insurance ($900 × 11/12).		

2.

Entry	Account	Amount of Adjustment	Amount that Will Appear on Balance Sheet	Classification of Account on Balance Sheet
a	Wages payable	$ 1,680	$ 1,680	Current liability
b	Interest payable	450	450	Current liability
c	Accounts payable	600	600	Current liability
d	Accumulated depreciation	2,000	3,000	Plant and equipment
e	Office supplies	(580)	280	Current asset
f	Unearned plumbing revenue	(108,000)	36,000	Current liability
g and *h*	Prepaid insurance	(1,225)	800*	Current asset

*$825 + $1,200 − $825 − $400 = $800.

3.

Entry	Net Income Increase (Decrease)	Total Assets Increase (Decrease)	Total Liabilities Increase (Decrease)
a	$ (1,680)	$ –0–	$ 1,680
b	(450)	–0–	450
c	(600)	–0–	600
d	(2,000)	(2,000)	–0–
e	(580)	(580)	–0–
f	108,000	–0–	(108,000)
g	(400)	(400)	–0–
h	(825)	(825)	–0–

APPENDIX

A

Recording Prepaid and Unearned Items in Income Statement Accounts

Prepaid Expenses

LO 8 Explain why some companies record prepaid and unearned items in income statement accounts and prepare adjusting entries when this procedure is used.

The discussion in Chapter 3 emphasized the fact that prepaid expenses are assets at the time they are purchased. Therefore, at the time of purchase, we recorded prepaid expenses with debits to asset accounts. Then, at the end of the accounting period, adjusting entries transferred the cost that had expired to expense accounts. In the chapter, we also recognized that some prepaid expenses are purchased and will fully expire before the end of the accounting period. When this is expected, it is easier to charge prepaid expenses to expense accounts at the time of purchase. Then, no adjusting entry is necessary.

Some companies follow a practice of recording all prepaid expenses with debits to expense accounts. Then, at the end of the accounting period, if any amounts remain unused or unexpired, adjusting entries are made to transfer the cost of the unused portions from the expense accounts to prepaid expense (asset) accounts. This practice is perfectly acceptable. The reported financial statements are exactly the same under either procedure.

To illustrate the differences between the two procedures, recall that on December 26, the Dow law practice purchased office supplies for $120. We recorded that purchase with a debit to an asset account but could have recorded a debit to an expense account. The alternatives are as follows:

		Purchase Recorded as Asset		Purchase Recorded as Expense	
Dec. 26	Office Supplies	120.00			
	Cash		120.00		
26	Office Supplies Expense			120.00	
	Cash				120.00

At the end of the accounting period (December 31), an inventory of the office supplies on hand revealed unused supplies that cost $75. That means $120 − $75 = $45 of office supplies were used and became an expense of December.

The required adjusting entry depends on how the original purchase was recorded. The alternative adjusting entries are as follows:

		Purchase Recorded as Asset		Purchase Recorded as Expense	
Adjusting entries:					
Dec. 31	Office Supplies Expense	45.00			
	Office Supplies		45.00		
31	Office Supplies			75.00	
	Office Supplies Expense				75.00

When these entries are posted to the accounts, you can see that the two alternative procedures give the same results. Regardless of which procedure is followed, the December 31 adjusted account balances show office supplies of $75 and office supplies expense of $45.

Purchase Recorded as Asset

Office Supplies

Dec. 26	120 −45	Dec. 31	45
Bal.	75		

Office Supplies Expense

Dec. 31	45		

Purchase Recorded as Expense

Office Supplies

Dec. 31	75		

Office Supplies Expense

Dec. 26	120 −75	Dec. 31	75
Bal.	45		

To continue the example for another month, assume that during January Dow's law practice purchased $150 of supplies. On January 31, an inventory showed $100 of supplies on hand. As you can see in the preceding accounts, the December 31 balance in the Office Supplies account was $75, regardless of which procedure is used. Therefore, the total supplies available for use during January was $75 + $150 = $225. Since $100 of supplies remain unused on January 31, the adjusting entry on January 31 must be designed to report a supplies asset of $100 and a supplies expense of $225 − $100 = $125. Depending on how the purchases were recorded, the alternative adjusting entries are

		Purchase Recorded as Asset		Purchase Recorded as Expense	
Adjusting entries:					
Jan. 31	Office Supplies Expense.	125.00			
	Office Supplies		125.00		
31	Office Supplies			25.00	
	Office Supplies Expense				25.00

Note that if the purchases of supplies are debited to an expense account, the required adjusting entry increases the Office Supplies account balance $25, from $75 to $100. The credit in the entry reduces the Office Supplies Expense account debit balance from $150 to $125.

Unearned Revenues

The procedures for recording unearned revenues are similar to those used to record prepaid expenses. Receipts of unearned revenues may be recorded with credits to liability accounts (as described in Chapter 3) or they may be recorded with credits to revenue accounts. The adjusting entries at the end of the period are different, depending on which procedure is followed. Nevertheless, either procedure is acceptable. The amounts reported in the financial statements are exactly the same, regardless of which procedure is used.

To illustrate the alternative procedures of recording unearned revenues, recall that on December 26, the Dow law practice received $3,000 in payment for legal services to be provided over the six-month period beginning December 15. In Chapter 3, that receipt was recorded with a credit to a liability account. The alternative would be to record it with a credit to a revenue account. Both alternatives follow:

		Receipt Recorded as a Liability		Receipt Recorded as a Revenue	
Dec. 26	Cash	3,000.00			
	Unearned Legal Fees		3,000.00		
26	Cash			3,000.00	
	Legal Fees Earned				3,000.00

By the end of the accounting period (December 31), the Dow law practice had earned $250 of these legal fees. That means $250 of the liability had been satisfied. Depending on how the original receipt was recorded, the required adjusting entry is as follows:

		Receipt Recorded as a Liability		Receipt Recorded as a Revenue	
Adjusting entries:					
Dec. 31	Unearned Legal Fees	250.00			
	Legal Fees Earned		250.00		
31	Legal Fees Earned			2,750.00	
	Unearned Legal fees				2,750.00

Posting these entries shows that the two alternative procedures give the same results. Regardless of which procedure is followed, the December 31 adjusted account balances show unearned legal fees of $2,750 and legal fees earned of $250.

Receipt Recorded as a Liability

Unearned Legal Fees

Dec. 31	250	Dec. 26	3,000 −250
		Bal.	2,750

Legal Fees Earned

		Dec. 31	250

Receipt Recorded as a Revenue

Unearned Legal Fees

		Dec. 31	2,750

Legal Fees Earned

Dec. 31	2,750	Dec. 26	3,000 −2,750
		Bal.	250

Summary of Appendix A in Terms of Learning Objective

LO 8. Because many prepaid expenses expire during the same period they are purchased, some companies choose to charge all prepaid expenses to expense accounts at the time they are purchased. When this is done, end-of-period adjusting entries are required to transfer any unexpired amounts from the expense accounts to appropriate asset accounts. Also, unearned revenues may be credited to revenue accounts at the time cash is received. If so, end-of-period adjusting entries are required to transfer any unearned amounts from the revenue accounts to appropriate unearned revenue accounts.

Glossary

LO 7 Define or explain the words and phrases listed in the chapter glossary.

Account form balance sheet a balance sheet that is arranged so that the assets are listed on the left and the liability and owner's equity items are listed on the right. p. 150

Accounting period the length of time into which the life of a business is divided for the purpose of preparing periodic financial statements. p. 131

Accrual basis of accounting a system of accounting in which the adjustment process is used to assign revenues to the periods in which they are earned and to match expenses with revenues. pp. 133–34

Accrued expenses expenses incurred during an accounting period but that, prior to end-of-period adjustments, remain unrecorded because payment is not due. pp. 139–40, 41

Accrued revenues revenues earned during an accounting period but that, prior to end-of-period adjustments, remain unrecorded because payment has not been received. pp. 140–41, 42

Accumulated depreciation the total amount of depreciation recorded against an asset or group of assets during the entire time the asset or assets have been owned. pp. 136–37

Adjusted trial balance a trial balance that shows the account balances after they have been revised to reflect the effects of end-of-period adjustments. pp. 140–41

Adjusting entry a journal entry made at the end of an accounting period for the purpose of assigning revenues to the period in which they are earned, assigning expenses to the period in which the expiration of benefit is incurred, and to update related liability and asset accounts. p. 134

Cash basis of accounting an accounting system in which revenues are reported in the income statement when cash is received and expenses are reported when cash is paid. p. 133

Classified balance sheet a balance sheet that shows assets and liabilities grouped in meaningful subclasses. pp. 145–46

Common stock the name given to a corporation's stock when it issues only one kind or class of stock. p. 150

Contra account an account the balance of which is subtracted from the balance of an associated account to show a more proper amount for the item recorded in the associated account. pp. 136–37

Contributed capital the portion of a corporation's equity that represents investments in the corporation by its stockholders; also called paid-in capital. pp. 149–50

Current assets cash or other assets that are reasonably expected to be realized in cash or to be sold or consumed within one year or one operating cycle of the business, whichever is longer. pp. 145–47

Current liabilities obligations due to be paid or liquidated within one year or one operating cycle of the business, whichever is longer. p. 148

Depreciation the expiration of the usefulness of plant and equipment, and the related process of allocating the cost of such assets to expense of the periods during which the assets are used. pp. 136–38

Dividends a distribution, generally of assets, made by a corporation to its stockholders. p. 149

Fiscal year any 12 consecutive months used by a business as its annual accounting period. p. 131

Intangible assets economic benefits or resources without physical substance, the value of which stems from the privileges or rights that accrue to their owner. p. 148

Interim financial reports financial reports of a business that are based on one-month or three-month accounting periods. p. 131

Long-term liabilities obligations not due to be paid within one year or the current operating cycle of the business. p. 149

Matching principle the accounting requirement that expenses be reported in the same accounting period as the revenues that were earned as a result of the expenses. p. 132

Natural business year the 12-month period that ends when the activities of a business are at their lowest point. p. 131

Operating cycle of a business the average time a business takes to pay cash for salaries of employees who perform services or to pay for merchandise and then to receive cash from customers in exchange for the sale of the services or merchandise. pp. 145–47

Paid-in-capital another name for contributed capital. pp. 149–50

Plant and equipment tangible, long-lived assets held for use in the production or sale of other assets or services. p. 136

Report form balance sheet a balance sheet with a vertical format that shows the assets above the liabilities and the liabilities above the owner's equity. p. 150

Retained earnings the portion of a corporation's equity that represents its cumulative net income, less net losses and dividends. p. 150

Time period principle identifying the activities of a business as occurring during specific time periods such as months, or three-month periods, or years so that periodic financial reports of the business can be prepared. pp. 130–31

Unadjusted trial balance a trial balance prepared before any adjustments have been recorded. p. 140

Unclassified balance sheet a balance sheet that presents a single list of assets and a single list of liabilities with no attempt to divide them into classes. p. 145

Synonymous Terms

Accumulated depreciation allowance for depreciation

Common stock capital stock

Contributed capital paid-in capital

Plant and equipment property, plant, and equipment; land, buildings, and equipment; plant assets; fixed assets

Objective Review

Answers to the following questions are listed at the end of this chapter. Be sure that you decide which is the one best answer to each question *before* you check the answers.

LO 1 For purposes of preparing financial statements, the act of dividing the life of a business into equal time periods:

a. Results in an annual accounting period called the fiscal year.
b. Always is done so that the annual accounting period ends at the close of the natural business year.
c. Results in annual financial reports called interim financial reports.
d. Always is done so that the annual accounting period ends at the close of the calendar year.
e. None of the above is correct.

LO 2 On April 1, 1993, Collier Company paid $2,400 for two years' insurance coverage. In accounting for this item:

a. Under the cash basis of accounting, 1994 insurance expense will be $-0-.
b. Under the accrual basis of accounting, 1993 insurance expense will be $2,400.
c. Under the cash basis of accounting, 1995 insurance expense will be $300.
d. Under the accrual basis of accounting, an adjusting entry for insurance will not be required at the end of 1994.
e. Under the cash basis of accounting, 1993 insurance expense will be $900.

LO 3 On December 31, 1993, Colony Company failed to make an adjustment for $200 of accrued service revenues earned and also failed to record the expiration of $700 of insurance premiums that had been debited to Prepaid Insurance. As a result of these errors, on the 1993 income statement:

a. Net income will be understated by $200.
b. Revenues will be overstated $200 and expenses will be understated $700.
c. Revenues will be overstated $200 and expenses will be overstated $700.
d. Revenues will be understated $200 and expenses will be overstated $700.
e. Revenues will be understated $200 and expenses will be understated $700.

LO 4 Selected information from B. Jones Company's unadjusted and adjusted trial balances follows:

	Unadjusted Trial Balance		Adjusted Trial Balance	
	Debit	**Credit**	**Debit**	**Credit**
Prepaid insurance	6,200		5,900	
Salaries payable				1,400
Office supplies	900		800	

The adjusting entries included which of the following:

a. A $300 debit to Prepaid Insurance, a $1,400 credit to Salaries Payable, and a $100 credit to Office Supplies.

b. A $300 credit to Prepaid Insurance, a $1,400 debit to Salaries Payable, and a $100 credit to Office Supplies.

c. A $300 credit to Insurance Expense, a $1,400 debit to Salaries Expense, and a $100 debit to Office Supplies Expense.

d. A $300 debit to Insurance Expense, a $1,400 credit to Salaries Payable, and a $100 debit to Office Supplies.

e. A $300 debit to Insurance Expense, a $1,400 debit to Salaries Expense, and a $100 debit to Office Supplies Expense.

LO 5. On December 31, 1993, Holland Photo Company made an entry to record $1,600 of accrued salaries. The next payment of salaries, on January 5, was $8,000. Related to these transactions only:

a. You can be sure that Holland Photo Company is using the cash basis of accounting.

b. The entry on January 5 will include a $6,400 credit to Cash.

c. The salaries expense charged to 1994 will be $8,000.

d. The salaries expense charged to 1994 will be $6,400.

e. The salaries expense charged to 1993 will be $6,400.

LO 6. A company owns the following items:

1. Land used in the operations of the business.
2. Office supplies.
3. Receivables from customers due in 10 months.
4. A three-year note receivable from the purchaser of land previously owned by the company.
5. The right to receive insurance protection for the next nine months.
6. Land held in case expanded operations require it.
7. Trucks used in servicing customers.
8. Trademarks used in selling the company's services.

These items should be classified as follows:

	Current Assets	Investments	Plant and Equipment	Intangible Assets
a.	2	4,6	1,7	3,5,8
b.	2,3,4	6	1,7	5,8
c.	2,3	4,6	1,7	5,8
d.	2,3,5	4	1,6,7	8
e.	2,3,5	4,6	1,7	8

LO 7. A distribution, generally of assets, made by a corporation to its stockholders is called:

a. A dividend.

b. Paid-out capital.

c. Retained earnings.
d. An intangible asset.
e. A withdrawal.

LO 8 Blalock Consulting Company records prepaid and unearned items in income statement accounts. In preparing adjusting entries at the end of the company's first operating period:

a. The accrual of unpaid salaries will require a debit to Prepaid Salaries and a credit to Salaries Expense.
b. The entry to recognize the existence of unused office supplies will require a debit to Supplies Expense and a credit to Office Supplies.
c. The entry to record the fact that some cash receipts for services remain unearned will require a debit to Consulting Fees Earned and a credit to Unearned Consulting Fees.
d. The accrual of earned but unbilled consulting fees will require a debit to Unearned Consulting Fees and a credit to Consulting Fees Earned.
e. None of the above is correct.

A letter ^{A} identifies the questions, exercises, and problems based on Appendix A at the end of the chapter.

Questions for Class Discussion

1. Why is the life of a business divided into time periods of equal length?
2. If a business adopts the calendar year as its annual accounting period, how would you describe financial reports of the business that are based on one-month or three-month accounting periods?
3. Which month would most likely end the natural business year of a business that operates outdoor tennis camps in Minnesota: June or September?
4. In selecting a fiscal year, what type of businesses are most apt to select their natural business year instead of the calendar year?
5. Why would you expect some account balances of a concern to require updating at the end of an accounting period even though all transactions were correctly recorded?
6. What purposes are served by making end-of-period adjustments?
7. A prepaid expense is an asset at the time of its purchase or prepayment. When is it best to ignore this and record the prepayment as an expense? Why?
8. What kind of assets require adjusting entries for depreciation?
9. What is a contra account? Give an example.
10. What contra account is used to record depreciation? Why is such an account used?
11. If a building is purchased for $100,000 and depreciation of $2,500 is taken each year, what amount of accumulated depreciation will appear in the balance sheet at the end of five years?
12. What is an accrued expense? Give an example.

13. How does an unearned revenue arise? Give an example of an unearned revenue.
14. What is the balance sheet classification of an unearned revenue?
15. What is an accrued revenue? Give an example.
16. When financial statements are prepared from an adjusted trial balance, why should the income statement be prepared first? What statement is prepared next?
17. Which accounting principles provide the basis for the adjustment process?
18. What is meant by the matching principle?
19. Is the cash basis of accounting consistent with the matching principle?
20. What is the difference between the cash and accrual bases of accounting?
21. What are the typical classes of assets and liabilities shown on a classified balance sheet?
22. What are the characteristics of a current asset?
23. What is meant by the operating cycle of a business?
24. What are some examples of assets shown in the investment category of the balance sheet?
25. What are the characteristics of assets classified as plant and equipment?
26. A local fast-food restaurant paid $20,000 for a franchise that identifies the restaurant as belonging to a nationally recognized chain of restaurants. How should this asset be classified on the local restaurant's balance sheet?
27. What are current liabilities? Long-term liabilities?
28. What are the two classes of equity on the balance sheet of a corporation?
29. Review the consolidated balance sheets of Federal Express Corporation in Appendix K. Assume that all accrued expenses at the end of each year are paid the following year. In making the adjusting entries at the end of the 1991 year, what total amount of accrued expenses was recorded?
30. Review the consolidated balance sheet of McDonald's Corporation presented in Appendix K. Assuming the company did not sell any property and equipment during 1990, what total amount of depreciation (and amortization) was recorded in making the adjusting entries at the end of 1990?

[A]31. If a company records its prepaid expenses with debits to expense accounts, what type of account does it debit in making end-of-period adjustments for prepaid expenses?

[A]32. Bee Company records revenues received in advance with credits to liability accounts, while Cee Company records revenues received in advance with credits to revenue accounts. Will these companies have differences in their financial statements as a result of this difference in their procedures? Why or why not?

Exercises

Exercise 3–1
Adjusting entries for accrued expenses
(LO 3)

Ora Company's two employees each earn $90 per day for a four-day week that begins on Monday and ends on Thursday. They were paid for the week ended Thursday, December 27, and both worked a full day on Monday, December 31. January 1 of the next year was an unpaid holiday, but the employees all worked on Wednesday and Thursday, January 2 and 3. Journalize the year-end adjusting entry to record the accrued wages and the entry to pay the employees on January 3.

Exercise 3–2
Adjusting entries for expenses (LO 3)

Prepare adjusting journal entries on December 31, 1993, prior to the preparation of annual financial statements, for the following independent situations:

a. The Supplies account had a $470 debit balance on January 1, 1993; $330 of supplies were purchased during the year; and a year-end inventory showed $100 of supplies on hand.

b. The Prepaid Insurance account had a $1,700 debit balance at the end of the accounting period before adjustment for expired insurance. An examination of insurance policies showed $1,360 of insurance had expired.

c. The Prepaid Insurance account had a $640 debit balance at the end of the accounting period before adjustment for expired insurance. An examination of insurance policies showed $440 of unexpired insurance.

d. Depreciation on equipment was estimated at $3,470 for the accounting period.

e. Six months' property taxes, estimated at $1,260, have accrued but are unrecorded and unpaid at the accounting period end.

Exercise 3–3
Omission of adjusting entries
(LO 1, 4)

Assume that the required adjustments of Exercise 3–2 were not made at the end of the accounting period. For each adjustment, tell the effect of its omission on the income statement and balance sheet prepared at that time.

Exercise 3–4
Missing data in calculations of supplies
(LO 3)

Determine the amounts indicated by the question marks in the following columns. The amounts in each column constitute a separate problem.

	(a)	(b)	(c)	(d)
Supplies on hand on January 1	$180	$410	$745	$?
Supplies purchased during the year	230	390	?	645
Supplies remaining at the year-end	80	?	115	560
Supplies expense for the year	?	320	850	425

Exercise 3–5
Adjustments and payments of accrued items
(LO 3, 5)

Prepare adjusting journal entries dated March 31 for the following items. Then prepare journal entries to record the April payments.

a. Employees are paid total salaries of $2,400 each Friday after they complete a five-day workweek. As of March 31, the employees had worked three days since the last payment. The next payment date is April 2.

b. The company owes a $90,000 note payable, which requires that 1% interest be paid each month on the 10th of the month. The interest was paid March 10 and the next payment is due April 10.

c. On March 1, the company retained a lawyer at a monthly fee of $300 payable on the 15th of the following month.

Exercise 3–6
Cash basis versus accrual basis expense amounts
(LO 2, 4)

Tote Company paid the $4,860 premium on a three-year insurance policy on September 1, 1993. The policy gave protection beginning on that date.

a. Assuming the accrual basis of accounting, how many dollars of the premium will appear as an expense on the annual income statement for 1993? for 1994? for 1995? for 1996?

b. Assuming the accrual basis, how many dollars of the premium will appear as an asset on each December 31 balance sheet for 1993? for 1994? for 1995? for 1996?

c. Assuming the cash basis of accounting, how many dollars of the premium will appear as an expense on the annual income statement for 1993? for 1994? for 1995? for 1996?

d. Assuming the cash basis, how many dollars of the premium will appear as an asset on each December 31 balance sheet for 1993? for 1994? for 1995? for 1996?

Exercise 3–7
Unearned and accrued revenues
(LO 2, 4)

The owner of an office building prepares annual financial statements based on a calendar-year accounting period.

a. A tenant rented space in the building on September 1 at $1,600 per month, paying six months' rent in advance. The receipt was credited to Unearned Rent. Give the December 31 adjusting entry of the building owner, prior to the preparation of annual financial statements.

b. Another tenant rented space in the building at $760 per month on November 1. The tenant paid the November rent on the first day of November, but by December 31 the December rent had not yet been paid. Give the December 31 adjusting entry of the building owner.

c. Assume the tenant in (*b*) paid the rent for December and January on January 3 of the new year. Give the entry to record the receipt of the $1,520.

Exercise 3–8
Classified balance sheet
(LO 6)

The adjusted trial balance that follows was taken from the ledger of Anthony Joseph, Photographer. Calculate the amount of owner's equity on December 31, 1993, and prepare a classified balance sheet for the business.

ANTHONY JOSEPH, PHOTOGRAPHER
Adjusted Trial Balance
December 31, 1993

Cash	$ 6,700	
Accounts receivable	4,100	
Photography supplies	1,950	
Prepaid insurance	2,050	
Investment in Geffen Corporation common stock	2,200	
Photography equipment	42,400	
Accumulated depreciation, photography equipment		$ 20,750
Building	85,000	
Accumulated depreciation, building		31,600
Land	70,000	
Salaries Payable		400
Unearned photography fees		2,800
Long-term notes payable		108,500
Anthony Joseph, capital		56,350
Anthony Joseph, withdrawals	47,000	
Photography fees earned		80,300
Operating expenses (combined)	39,300	
Totals	$300,700	$300,700

Exercise 3–9
Analyzing statements for adjusting entries
(LO 3, 4)

An inexperienced bookkeeper prepared the income statement shown below in columns 1 and 2, but he forgot to adjust the accounts before its preparation. The accountant discovered the oversight and prepared the statement shown in columns 3 and 4. Analyze the statements and prepare the adjusting journal entries made between the preparation of the two statements. Assume that one fourth of the additional property management fees resulted from recognizing accrued fees and three fourths resulted from previously recorded unearned fees earned by the date of the statements.

SAMSON REALTY
Income Statements
For Year Ended December 31, 1993

	Prepared without Adjustments		Prepared after Adjustments	
Revenues:				
Property management fees earned		$ 6,400		$ 7,800
Commissions earned		89,050		89,050
Total revenues		$95,450		$96,850
Operating expenses:				
Depreciation expense, automobiles			$ 4,000	
Depreciation expense, office equipment			1,400	
Salaries expense	$16,500		17,700	
Insurance expense			1,800	
Rent expense	13,500		13,500	
Office supplies expense			200	
Advertising expense	3,750		3,750	
Utilities expense	1,900		1,900	
Total operating expenses		35,650		44,250
Net income		$59,800		$52,600

Exercise 3–10
Balance sheet equity section for a corporation
(LO 6)

A corporation had $3 million of common stock issued and outstanding during all of 1993. It began the year with $650,000 of retained earnings, and it declared and paid $255,000 of cash dividends to its stockholders. It also earned a

$640,000 1993 net income. Prepare the equity section of the corporation's year-end balance sheet.

Exercise 3–11
Calculating elements of change in owner's equity (Review exercise)

Calculate the missing item in each of the following cases:

	Case 1	Case 2	Case 3	Case 4	Case 5
The Owner, capital, January 1, 1993	$45,000	$72,000	$ (*c*)	$89,300	$56,000
Total revenues during 1993	29,200	(*b*)	26,500	47,700	38,300
Total expenses during 1993	31,700	43,400	19,900	(*d*)	29,600
Withdrawals during the year	18,500	24,000	7,800	15,000	(*e*)
The Owner, capital, December 31, 1993	(*a*)	65,900	21,300	52,100	44,500

Exercise 3–12
Calculating statement of changes in owner's equity amounts (Review exercise)

Calculate the missing item in each of the following cases:

	Case 1	Case 2	Case 3	Case 4
The Owner, capital, January 1, 1993	$37,000	$53,800	$ (*c*)	$66,600
Owner's investments during the year	12,500	(*b*)	26,500	17,700
Net income (loss) during 1993	14,000	32,500	(9,400)	(*d*)
Owner's withdrawals during the year	(*a*)	20,000	11,000	14,500
The Owner, capital, December 31, 1993	22,000	66,300	84,200	47,300

[A]Exercise 3–13
Adjustments for prepaid items recorded in expense and revenue accounts (LO 8)

Alderan Consulting was organized on December 1 and follows the procedure of debiting expense accounts when it records prepayments of expenses; also, revenue accounts are credited when unearned revenues are received. Prepare adjusting journal entries on December 31 for the following items:

a. Shop Supplies were purchased during December for $840. A December 31 inventory showed that $505 of supplies were on hand.

b. The company paid insurance premiums of $660 during December. On December 31, an examination of the insurance policies showed that $110 of insurance had expired.

c. During December, the business received $3,500 from one client for two consulting projects. As of December 31, only one project, for which the client was charged $2,700, had been completed.

d. Late in December, the business received $800 from a second client for consulting services to be performed in January.

[A]Exercise 3–14
Adjustments for supplies when purchases were recorded as expenses (LO 8)

Ritz-Carlton Company prepares monthly financial statements. On September 30, the balance in the Office Supplies account was $350. During October, $490 of supplies were purchased and debited to Office Supplies Expense.

a. Prepare an adjusting journal entry on October 31 to account for the supplies, assuming an October 31 inventory of supplies showed that $120 of supplies were on hand.

b. Prepare an adjusting journal entry on October 31 to account for the supplies, assuming an October 31 inventory of supplies showed that $510 of supplies were on hand.

Problems

Problem 3–1
Adjusting journal entries
(LO 3, 5)

The following information for adjustments was available on December 31, 1993, the end of Ming Company's annual accounting period.

a. The Office Supplies account had an $80 debit balance at the beginning of the year, $490 of supplies were purchased during the year, and the inventory of supplies at year-end totaled $140.

b. An examination of insurance policies showed three policies, as follows:

Policy	Date of Purchase	Life of Policy	Cost
1	September 1, 1992	3 years	$2,700
2	March 1, 1993	2 years	3,480
3	July 1, 1993	1 year	540

Prepaid Insurance was debited for the cost of each policy at the time of its purchase. Expired insurance was correctly recorded at the end of 1992.

c. The company's three employees earn $60 per day, $70 per day, and $120 per day, respectively. They are paid each Friday for a five-day workweek that begins on Monday. This year, December 31 fell on Thursday, and the employees all worked on Monday, Tuesday, Wednesday and Thursday. The next payment for five days' work will be on January 1.

d. The company purchased a building on June 1, 1993. The building cost $396,000, has an estimated 30-year life, and is not expected to have any salvage value at the end of that time.

e. The company occupies most of the space in its building, and it also rents space. One tenant rented a small amount of space on October 1 at $540 per month. The tenant paid the rent on the first day of October and November, and the amounts paid were credited to Rent Earned. However, the tenant did not pay the December rent until January 15, 1994, at which time he also paid the rent for January.

f. Another tenant agreed on November 1 to rent a small amount of space at $750 per month, and on that date paid three months' rent in advance. The receipt was credited to Unearned Rent.

Required

1. Given the preceding information, journalize adjusting entries dated December 31, 1993, prior to the preparation of annual financial statements.
2. Prepare journal entries to record the January payments and receipts that involve amounts accrued on December 31.

Problem 3–2
Adjusting entries and the adjusted trial balance (LO 3, 4, 6)

Community Technical School's unadjusted trial balance on December 31, 1993, the end of its annual accounting period, is as follows:

COMMUNITY TECHNICAL SCHOOL
Trial Balance
December 31, 1993

Cash	$ 7,200	
Office supplies	4,300	
Prepaid insurance	8,100	
Professional library	19,800	
Accumulated depreciation, professional library		$ 8,490
Equipment	43,300	
Accumulated depreciation, equipment		14,900
Accounts payable		860
Unearned extension fees		2,400
Kay Perry, capital		55,950
Kay Perry, withdrawals	15,000	
Enrollment fees earned		43,400
Salaries expense	16,800	
Rent expense	9,600	
Advertising expense	500	
Utilities expense	1,400	
Totals	$126,000	$126,000

Required

1. Set up accounts for the items in the trial balance plus these additional accounts: Accounts Receivable; Salaries Payable; Extension Fees Earned; Depreciation Expense, Equipment; Depreciation Expense, Professional Library; Insurance Expense; and Office Supplies Expense. Enter the trial balance amounts in the accounts.
2. Use the following information to prepare and post adjusting entries:
   a. An examination of insurance policies shows $900 of expired insurance.
   b. An inventory shows $1,670 of office supplies on hand.
   c. Estimated annual depreciation on the equipment is $3,300.
   d. Estimated annual depreciation on the professional library is $1,320.
   e. Community Technical School offers extended services to those in need of training beyond the campus. On November 1, the company agreed to in-home tutoring for a client. The contract calls for a $600 monthly fee, and the client paid the first four months' fees in advance at the time the contract was signed. The amount paid was credited to the Unearned Extension Fees account.
   f. On October 15, the school agreed to teach a three-month computer class for a local business for $1,080 per month payable at the end of the class. Extension fees for two and one half months have accrued.
   g. The one employee is paid weekly; and on December 31, three days' wages at $70 per day have accrued.
3. After posting the adjusting entries, prepare an adjusted trial balance, an income statement, a statement of changes in owner's equity, and a classified balance sheet. Perry did not make additional investments in the business during the year.

Problem 3–3
Adjusting entries and the adjusted trial balance
(LO 3, 4, 6)

The unadjusted trial balance of Eden's Garden follows:

EDEN'S GARDEN
Trial Balance
December 31, 1993

Cash	$ 3,000	
Accounts receivable	1,400	
Landscaping supplies	1,680	
Prepaid insurance	3,200	
Investment in Sierra, Inc., common stock (long-term)	6,000	
Trucks	42,000	
Accumulated depreciation, trucks		$ 17,000
Landscaping equipment	5,700	
Accumulated depreciation, landscaping equipment		1,900
Building	68,000	
Accumulated depreciation, building		19,800
Land	16,000	
Franchise	30,000	
Unearned landscape architecture fees		1,050
Long-term notes payable		75,600
Eve Adams, capital		49,270
Eve Adams, withdrawals	27,000	
Landscape architecture fees earned		12,250
Landscaping services revenue		84,000
Office salaries expense	14,200	
Landscape wages expense	31,950	
Interest expense	6,800	
Gas, oil, and repairs expense	3,940	
Totals	$260,870	$260,870

Required

1. Set up accounts for the items in the trial balance plus these additional accounts: Wages Payable; Depreciation Expense, Building; Depreciation Expense, Trucks; Depreciation Expense, Landscaping Equipment; Insurance Expense; and Landscaping Supplies Expense. Enter the trial balance amounts in the accounts. Journalize and post adjusting entries given the following information:
   a. Insurance premiums of $2,220 expired during the year.
   b. An inventory showed $410 of unused landscaping supplies on hand.
   c. Estimated depreciation on the landscaping equipment, $820.
   d. Estimated depreciation on the trucks, $6,600.
   e. Estimated depreciation on the building, $3,020.
   f. Of the $1,050 credit balance in Unearned Landscape Architecture Fees, $750 was earned by the year-end.
   g. Accrued landscape architecture fees earned but unrecorded at year-end totaled $480.
   h. There were $630 of earned but unrecorded landscape wages at the year-end.
2. Prepare an adjusted trial balance, an income statement for the year, a statement of changes in owner's equity, and a classified year-end balance sheet. Adams's capital account balance reflects the December 31, 1992, balance plus a January 1, 1993, investment of $12,000. A $9,000 installment on the note payable is due within one year.

Problem 3–4
Adjusting entries and the adjusted trial balance
(LO 3, 4, 6)

Cherokee Campground's unadjusted trial balance is as follows:

CHEROKEE CAMPGROUND
Trial Balance
December 31, 1993

Cash	$ 2,850	
Office supplies	180	
Prepaid insurance	1,470	
Office equipment	3,400	
Accumulated depreciation, office equipment		$ 2,300
Buildings	174,500	
Accumulated depreciation, buildings		28,750
Land	48,000	
Unearned fees		1,300
Long-term notes payable		155,750
John Eagle, capital		30,260
John Eagle, withdrawals	12,000	
Fees earned		51,640
Wages expense	8,700	
Interest expense	13,470	
Property taxes expense	3,100	
Utilities expense	2,330	
Totals	$270,000	$270,000

Required

1. Set up accounts for the items in the trial balance plus these additional accounts: Accounts Receivable; Interest Payable; Wages Payable; Estimated Property Taxes Payable; Depreciation Expense, Buildings; Depreciation Expense, Office Equipment; Insurance Expense; and Office Supplies Expense. Enter the trial balance amounts in the accounts.
2. Use the following information to prepare adjusting journal entries:
   a. An insurance policy examination showed $1,100 of expired insurance.
   b. An inventory showed $60 of office supplies on hand.
   c. Estimated depreciation expense on office equipment, $680.
   d. Estimated depreciation on buildings, $7,200.
   e. By year-end, $840 of the Unearned Fees account balance was earned.
   f. A camper is in arrears on fee payments, and this $90 of accrued revenue was unrecorded at the time the trial balance was prepared.
   g. The one employee of the campground works a five-day workweek at $40 per day. The employee was paid last week but has worked three days this week for which he has not been paid.
   h. Three months' property taxes, totaling $780, have accrued. This additional amount of property tax expense has not been recorded.
   i. One month's interest on the note payable, $1,120, has accrued but is unrecorded.
3. Post the adjusting entries and prepare an adjusted trial balance, an income statement for the year, a statement of changes in owner's equity, and a classified balance sheet. Eagle's capital account balance has not been increased by investments during 1993. A $9,000 installment on the note payable is due within one year.

Problem 3–5
Comparing the unadjusted and adjusted trial balances
(LO 3, 4)

Foster Company's unadjusted trial balance and adjusted trial balance on December 31, 1993, the end of its annual accounting period, appear as follows:

	Unadjusted Trial Balance		Adjusted Trial Balance	
Cash	$ 15,450		$ 15,450	
Accounts receivable			3,050	
Office supplies	1,320		480	
Prepaid insurance	2,400		1,200	
Office equipment	8,700		8,700	
Accumulated depreciation, office equipment		$ 1,600		$ 2,400
Accounts payable		720		1,130
Interest payable				1,230
Salaries payable				1,500
Unearned consulting fees		6,750		3,670
Long-term notes payable		7,300		7,300
Frank Foster, capital		8,470		8,470
Frank Foster, withdrawals	44,040		44,040	
Consulting fees earned		93,130		99,260
Depreciation expense, office equipment			800	
Salaries expense	28,100		29,600	
Interest expense			1,230	
Insurance expense			1,200	
Rent expense	13,500		13,500	
Office supplies expense			840	
Advertising expense	4,460		4,870	
Totals	$117,970	$117,970	$124,960	$124,960

Required

Examine Foster Company's unadjusted and adjusted trial balances and prepare the year-end adjusting journal entries that Foster must have made. Your adjusting entries should explain the differences between the two trial balances.

Problem 3–6
Accrual basis income statement
(LO 2, 3, 5)

Andrea Perkins purchased Four Seasons, an eight-unit apartment building, last September 1, and she has operated it four months without keeping formal accounting records. However, she has deposited all receipts in the bank and has kept an accurate checkbook record of payments. An analysis of the cash receipts and payments follows:

	Receipts	Payments
Investment	$114,000	
Purchased Four Seasons:		
Office equipment		$ 2,620
Buildings		156,000
Land		89,000
Total		$247,620
Less long-term note payable signed		148,500
Cash paid		$ 99,120
Wages paid		7,380
Insurance premium paid		4,200
Office supplies purchased		500
Property taxes paid		2,100
Utilities paid		800
Owner's withdrawals of cash		3,200
Apartment rentals collected	16,000	
Totals	$130,000	$117,300
Cash balance, December 31		12,700
Totals	$130,000	$130,000

Perkins wants you to prepare an accrual basis income statement for the apartment for the four-month period she has operated the business, a statement of changes in owner's equity, and a December 31 classified balance sheet. You ascertain the following (T-accounts may be helpful in organizing the data):

The building was estimated to have a 20-year remaining life when purchased and at the end of that time will be wrecked. It is estimated that the sale of salvaged materials will just pay the wrecking costs and the cost of clearing the site. The office equipment is in good condition. At the time of purchase, Perkins estimated she would use the equipment for three years and would then trade it in on new equipment of like kind. She thought $100 was a fair estimate of what she would receive for the old equipment when she traded it in at the end of three years.

The $4,200 payment for insurance was for a policy taken out on September 1. The policy's protection was for one year beginning on that date. Perkins estimates that one half of the office supplies purchased have been used. She also says that the one employee of the apartment earns $50 per day for a five-day week that ends on Friday. The employee was paid last week but has worked three days, December 29 through 31, for which he has not been paid.

Included in the $16,000 of apartment rentals collected is $1,500 received from a tenant for three months' rent beginning on December 1. Also, a tenant has not paid his $500 rent for the month of December.

The long-term note payable requires an annual payment of 10 percent interest on the beginning principal balance plus a $7,500 annual payment on the principal. The first payment is due next September 1. The property tax payment was for one year's taxes that were paid on October 1 for the tax year beginning on September 1, the day Perkins purchased the business.

[A]Problem 3–7
Recording prepayments and unearned items in income statement accounts
(LO 2, 8)

Masquerade Company debits expense accounts when recording prepaid expenses; it credits revenue accounts when recording unearned receipts. The following information was available on December 31, 1993, the end of the company's annual accounting period.

a. The Store Supplies account had a $740 debit balance at the beginning of the year, $1,600 of supplies were purchased during the year, and an inventory of unused supplies at the year-end totaled $520.

b. An examination of insurance policies showed two policies, as follows:

Policy	Date of Purchase	Life of Policy	Cost
1	April 1, 1991	3 years	$3,240
2	August 1, 1993	2 years	960

Insurance Expense was debited for the cost of each policy at the time of its purchase. However, the correct amount of Prepaid Insurance was recorded during the adjustment processes at the end of 1991 and 1992.

c. On November 15, 1993, Masquerade Company agreed to provide consulting services to a client and received an advance payment of $4,200. At year-end, the client agreed that two thirds of the services had been provided.

d. The company occupies most of the space in its building but it also rents space to one tenant. The tenant agreed on November 1 to rent a small amount of space at $400 per month, and on that date paid three months' rent in advance.

e. The Office Supplies account had a $320 debit balance at the beginning of the year and $650 of supplies were purchased during the year. A year-end inventory of office supplies indicated that supplies amounting to $710 had been used during the year.

Required

Prepare adjusting journal entries dated December 31, 1993, prior to the preparation of annual financial statements. For item *(b)*, prepare a separate adjusting entry for each insurance policy.

Problem 3–8
Analytical essay
(LO 3, 4, 5)

Review the information presented in Problem 3–3 and focus on the adjustment information described in requirement 1. Then describe the effects of each of the following assumptions on the 1993 income statement; the December 31, 1993, balance sheet; the 1994 income statement; and the December 31, 1994, balance sheet.

1. Assume that the company failed to record the estimated 1993 depreciation of $6,600 on the trucks. This error was not discovered during 1993 or 1994.
2. Assume that the company failed to record the $480 of accrued landscape architecture fees at the end of 1993. Instead, these fees were recorded as earned when the cash was received during 1994.
3. Assume that the December 31, 1993, adjusting entry to record the $630 of accrued landscape wages was incorrectly made for $360. Then, when the correct amount of wages was paid in 1994, $360 was removed from Wages Payable and the rest of the payment was charged to Landscape Wages Expense.

[A]Problem 3–9
Analytical essay
(LO 3, 4, 8)

On October 1, 1993, Able Company and Bravo Company each paid $3,600 for two-year insurance policies. Able recorded its payment with a debit to Prepaid Insurance and Bravo recorded its payment with a debit to Insurance Expense. Explain the differences between the adjusting entries the two companies should make on December 31, 1993, the end of their annual accounting periods. Also explain how the difference in the two companies' procedures affect the financial statements.

Alternate Problems

Problem 3–1A
Adjusting journal entries
(LO 3, 5)

The following information for preparing adjusting entries was available on December 31, 1993, the end of Sherwood Company's annual accounting period:

a. The Office Supplies account had a $240 debit balance at the beginning of the year, $760 of supplies were purchased during the year, and the inventory of supplies at year-end totaled $190.

b. An examination of insurance policies showed three policies, as follows:

Policy	Protection Began on	Life of Policy	Cost
1	April 14, 1991	3 years	$1,440
2	July 1, 1991	2 years	1,800
3	October 1, 1993	1 year	420

Prepaid Insurance was debited for the cost of each policy at the time of purchase. Expired insurance was correctly recorded at the end of 1991 and 1992.

c. The company's two employees earn $45 per day and $80 per day, respectively. They are paid each Friday for a five-day workweek that begins on Monday. December 31 fell on Tuesday, and the employees both worked on Monday and Tuesday but have not been paid. The next payment for five days' work will be on January 3.

d. The company purchased a building on May 1, 1993. The building cost $472,500, has an estimated 25-year life, and is not expected to have any salvage value at the end of its life.

e. The company occupies most of the space in its building, and it also rents space. One tenant rented a small amount of space on September 1 at $650 per month. The tenant paid the rent on the first day of each month, September through November, and the amounts paid were credited to Rent Earned. However, the tenant did not pay the December rent until January 12, at which time she also paid the rent for January.

f. Another tenant agreed on November 1 to rent a small amount of space at $490 per month and on that date paid three months' rent in advance. The amount paid was credited to Unearned Rent.

Required

1. Given the preceding information, journalize adjusting entries dated December 31, 1993, prior to the preparation of annual financial statements.
2. Prepare journal entries to record the January payments and receipts that involve amounts accrued on December 31.

Problem 3–2A

Adjusting entries and the adjusted trial balance (LO 3, 4, 6)

Landscape Design School's unadjusted trial balance on December 31, 1993, the end of its annual accounting period, is as follows:

LANDSCAPE DESIGN SCHOOL
Trial Balance
December 31, 1993

Cash	$ 7,200	
Office supplies	4,300	
Prepaid insurance	8,100	
Professional library	19,800	
Accumulated depreciation, professional library . .		$ 8,490
Equipment	43,300	
Accumulated depreciation, equipment		14,900
Accounts payable		860
Unearned extension fees		2,400
Kay Perry, capital		55,950
Kay Perry, withdrawals	15,000	
Enrollment fees earned		43,400
Salaries expense	16,800	
Rent expense	9,600	
Advertising expense	500	
Utilities expense	1,400	
Totals	$126,000	$126,000

Required

1. Set up accounts for the items in the trial balance plus these additional accounts: Accounts Receivable; Salaries Payable; Extension Fees Earned; Depreciation Expense, Equipment; Depreciation Expense, Professional Library; Insurance Expense; and Office Supplies Expense. Enter the trial balance amounts in the accounts.
2. Use the information that follows to prepare and post adjusting entries:
   a. An examination of insurance policies shows $2,025 of expired insurance.
   b. An inventory shows $1,075 of supplies on hand.
   c. Estimated annual depreciation on the equipment is $3,830.
   d. Estimated annual depreciation on the library is $2,800.
   e. The December utilities bill arrived after the trial balance was prepared, and its $420 amount was not included in the trial balance amounts. Also, a $120 bill for newspaper advertising that had appeared in December was not included in the trial balance amounts.
   f. A client who was landscaping his office building signed a contract with Landscape Design School for consulting assistance through the extension services offered. The contract calls for a $150 monthly fee and services began on December 1. The client paid three months' fees in advance, and the amount paid was credited to the Unearned Extension Fees account.
   g. Landscape Design School agreed to hold a seminar, through the extension services, on xeriscape design for the City Environmental Services Department for $400 per month payable at the end of three months. The contract was signed on November 15, and one and one half months' fees have accrued.
   h. The one employee is paid weekly; and on December 31, four days' wages at $80 per day have accrued.
3. After posting the adjusting entries, prepare an adjusted trial balance, an income statement, a statement of changes in owner's equity, and a classified balance sheet. Perry's capital account balance of $55,950 consists of a $48,950 balance on December 31, 1992, plus a $7,000 investment during 1993.

The unadjusted trial balance of Tejas Landscape follows:

Problem 3–3A
Adjusting entries and the adjusted trial balance
(LO 3, 4, 6)

TEJAS LANDSCAPE
Trial Balance
December 31, 1993

Cash	$ 3,000	
Accounts receivable	1,400	
Landscaping supplies	1,680	
Prepaid insurance	3,200	
Investment in Sierra, Inc., common stock (long-term)	6,000	
Trucks	42,000	
Accumulated depreciation, trucks		$ 17,000
Landscaping equipment	5,700	
Accumulated depreciation, landscaping equipment		1,900
Building	68,000	
Accumulated depreciation, building		19,800
Land	16,000	
Franchise	30,000	
Unearned landscape architecture fees		1,050
Long-term notes payable		75,600
Eve Adams, capital		49,270
Eve Adams, withdrawals	27,000	
Landscape architecture fees earned		12,250
Landscaping services revenue		84,000
Office salaries expense	14,200	
Landscape wages expense	31,950	
Interest expense	6,800	
Gas, oil, and repairs expense	3,940	
Totals	$260,870	$260,870

Required

1. Set up accounts for the items in the trial balance plus these additional accounts: Wages Payable; Depreciation Expense, Building; Depreciation Expense, Trucks; Depreciation Expense, Landscaping Equipment; Insurance Expense; and Landscaping Supplies Expense. Enter the trial balance amounts in the accounts.
2. Use the information that follows to prepare and post adjusting entries:
   a. Insurance premiums of $960 expired during the year.
   b. An inventory shows $990 of unused landscaping supplies on hand.
   c. Depreciation on the landscaping equipment, $1,400.
   d. Depreciation on the trucks, $8,300.
   e. Depreciation on the building, $3,800.
   f. Of the $1,050 balance in the Unearned Landscape Architecture Fees account, $350 was earned by the year-end.
   g. Accrued landscape architecture fees earned but unrecorded at year-end totaled $1,000.
   h. There were $720 of earned but unrecorded landscape wages at the year-end.
3. Prepare an adjusted trial balance, an income statement for the year, a statement of changes in owner's equity, and a classified year-end balance sheet. Adams's $49,270 capital balance reflects the December 31, 1992, balance plus a January 15, 1993, investment of $15,000. A $9,450 installment on the long-term note payable is due within one year.

Problem 3–4A
Adjusting entries and the adjusted trial balance
(LO 3, 4, 6)

Great Outdoors' unadjusted trial balance, at the end of its annual accounting period, follows:

GREAT OUTDOORS
Trial Balance
December 31, 1993

Cash	$ 2,850	
Office supplies	180	
Prepaid insurance	1,470	
Office equipment	3,400	
Accumulated depreciation, office equipment		$ 2,300
Buildings	174,500	
Accumulated depreciation, buildings		28,750
Land	48,000	
Unearned fees		1,300
Long-term notes payable		155,750
John Eagle, capital		30,260
John Eagle, withdrawals	12,000	
Fees earned		51,640
Wages expense	8,700	
Interest expense	13,470	
Property taxes expense	3,100	
Utilities expense	2,330	
Totals	$270,000	$270,000

Required

1. Set up accounts for the items in the trial balance plus these additional accounts: Accounts Receivable; Interest Payable; Wages Payable; Estimated Property Taxes Payable; Depreciation Expense, Buildings; Depreciation Expense, Office Equipment; Insurance Expense; and Office Supplies Expense. Enter the trial balance amounts in the accounts.
2. Use the information that follows to prepare adjusting journal entries:
   a. An insurance policy examination shows $490 of expired insurance.
   b. An inventory shows $50 of office supplies on hand.
   c. Estimated depreciation of office equipment, $600.
   d. Depreciation of buildings, $8,100.
   e. An examination reveals that $550 of the Unearned Fees balance was earned by the year-end.
   f. One camper is in arrears on fee payments, and this $150 of accrued revenue was unrecorded at the time the trial balance was prepared.
   g. Four months' property tax expense, estimated at $1,040, has accrued but was not recorded at the time the trial balance was prepared.
   h. The one employee of the campground works a five-day week at $50 per day. He was paid last week but has worked four days this week for which he has not been paid.
   i. Three months' interest on the note payable, $3,900, has accrued but is unpaid on the trial balance date.
3. Post the adjusting entries and prepare an adjusted trial balance, an income statement for the year, a statement of changes in owner's equity, and a classified balance sheet. Eagle's capital account balance has not been increased by investments during 1993. A $7,800 payment on the long-term note payable is due within one year.

Problem 3–5A
Comparing the unadjusted and adjusted trial balances
(LO 3, 4)

Northside Management's unadjusted trial balance and adjusted trial balance on December 31, the end of its annual accounting period, appear as follows:

	Unadjusted Trial Balance		Adjusted Trial Balance	
Cash	$ 23,515		$ 23,515	
Accounts receivable			2,220	
Office supplies	960		320	
Prepaid insurance	12,000		8,000	
Office equipment	13,220		13,220	
Accumulated depreciation, office equipment		$ 4,250		$ 6,120
Building	195,000		195,000	
Accumulated depreciation, building		45,600		58,400
Land	65,000		65,000	
Accounts payable		1,750		3,790
Interest payable				8,560
Estimated property taxes payable				6,400
Unearned management fees		15,270		7,190
Long-term notes payable		92,700		92,700
Susan Rain, capital		22,775		22,775
Susan Rain, withdrawals	52,200		52,200	
Management fees earned		261,750		272,050
Depreciation expense, building			12,800	
Depreciation expense, office equipment			1,870	
Wages expense	54,800		54,800	
Interest expense			8,560	
Insurance expense			4,000	
Office supplies expense			640	
Advertising expense	21,660		23,700	
Property taxes expense			6,400	
Utilities expense	5,740		5,740	
Totals	$444,095	$444,095	$477,985	$477,985

Required

Examine Northside Management's unadjusted and adjusted trial balances and prepare the year-end adjusting journal entries that must have been entered. Your entries should explain the differences between the two trial balances.

Problem 3–6A
Accrual basis income statement
(LO 2, 3, 5)

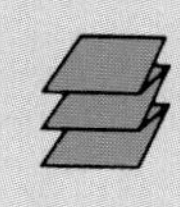

David Pittard, a lawyer, has always kept his records on a cash basis; at the end of 1993, he prepared the following cash basis income statement:

DAVID PITTARD, ATTORNEY
Income Statement
For Year Ended December 31, 1993

Revenues	$256,000
Expenses	80,450
Net income	$175,550

In preparing the statement, the following amounts of prepaid, unearned, and accrued items were ignored at the end of 1992 and 1993:

	End of	
	1992	1993
Prepaid expenses	$12,600	$14,200
Accrued expenses	6,120	5,800
Unearned revenues	10,400	7,500
Accrued revenues	12,000	14,900

Required

Under the assumptions that the 1992 prepaid expenses were consumed or expired in 1993, the 1992 unearned revenues were earned in 1993, and the 1992 accrued items were either paid or received in cash in 1993, prepare a 1993 accrual basis income statement for David Pittard's law practice. Attach to your statement calculations showing how you arrived at each 1993 income statement amount.

[A]Problem 3–7A
Recording prepayments and unearned items in income statement accounts
(LO 2, 8)

In recording prepaid expenses and unearned revenues, Major League Company debits the disbursements to expense accounts and credits the receipts to revenue accounts. The following information was available on December 31, 1993, the end of Major League Company's annual accounting period:

a. The Store Supplies account had a $400 debit balance at the beginning of the year, $1,150 of supplies were purchased during the year, and an inventory of unused supplies at the year-end totaled $1,250.

b. An examination of insurance policies showed two policies, as follows:

Policy	Date of Purchase	Life of Policy	Cost
1	July 1, 1991	3 years	$3,420
2	October 1, 1993	2 years	8,640

Insurance Expense was debited for the cost of each policy at the time of its purchase. However, the correct amount of Prepaid Insurance was recorded during the adjustment processes at the end of 1991 and 1992.

c. On September 17, 1993, Major League Company agreed to provide consulting services to a client and received an advance payment of $9,450. At year-end, the client agreed that two thirds of the services had been provided.

d. The company occupies most of the space in its building, and it also rents space to one tenant. The tenant agreed on October 1 to rent a small amount of space at $750 per month, and on that date paid six months' rent in advance.

e. The Office Supplies account had a $220 debit balance at the beginning of the year and $540 of supplies were purchased during the year. A year-end inventory of office supplies indicated that supplies amounting to $400 had been used during the year.

Required

Prepare adjusting journal entries dated December 31, 1993, prior to the preparation of annual financial statements. For item *b*, prepare a separate adjusting entry for each insurance policy.

Problem 3–8A
Analytical essay
(LO 3, 4, 5)

Review the information presented in Problem 3–3A and focus on the adjustment information described in requirement 2. Then describe the effects of each of the following assumptions on the 1993 income statement; the December 31, 1993, balance sheet; the 1994 income statement; and the December 31, 1994, balance sheet.

1. Assume that the company incorrectly recorded the $8,300 estimated 1993 depreciation on the trucks as $3,800. This error was not discovered during 1993 or 1994.
2. Assume that the company failed to record the fact that $350 of the $1,050 balance in the Unearned Landscape Architecture Fees account had been earned by the end of the 1993 year. Instead, when the adjusting entries were made on December 31, 1994, these fees were recorded as earned during 1994.
3. Assume that the company failed to record the $720 of accrued landscape wages on December 31, 1993. Then, when the correct amount of wages was paid in 1994, the entire payment was recorded as wages expense.

[A]Problem 3–9A
Analytical essay
(LO 3, 4, 8)

On September 1, 1993, Delta Company and Echo Company each received $5,400 for consulting services to be provided over the next several months. Delta recorded its receipt with a credit to Unearned Consulting Services Revenue and Echo recorded its receipt with a credit to Consulting Services Revenue. As of December 31, 1993, each company had earned $1,200 of the amount received in advance. Explain the differences between the adjusting entries the two companies should make on December 31, 1993, the end of their annual accounting periods. Also explain how the difference in the two companies' procedures affect the financial statements.

Serial Problem

Precision Computer Services

(This problem should not be assigned unless the Working Papers are being used. This is the second segment of a serial problem that started in Chapter 2 and continues in Chapters 4 and 5. If you did not complete the solution in Chapter 2, you can begin the problem at this point. However, you may need to review some of the facts presented in the Chapter 2 segment of the problem. See page 122).

Precision Computer Services has had a successful two months of business since it started on October 1, 1993. At the request of John Conard, the owner, you already recorded the transactions that occurred during October and November. (This was done in Chapter 2.) Now, before making the December entries, several additional accounts have been added to the General Ledger, as follows:

Accounts	Number
Accumulated Depreciation, Office Equipment	164
Accumulated Depreciation, Computer Equipment . .	168
Wages Payable	210
Unearned Computer Fees	233
Depreciation Expense, Office Equipment	612
Depreciation Expense, Computer Equipment	613
Insurance Expense	637
Rent Expense	640
Computer Supplies Expense	652

Required

1. Journalize and post the following December transactions and end-of-period adjusting entries:

Dec. 2 Paid $300 to the Town Hall Shopping Center for Precision's share of advertising that benefited all businesses in the center.

3 Paid $76 to repair the company's computer.

5 Received total amount due from AB Company as a result of the transaction on November 25.

6 Paid Ann White for four days' work at her regular daily rate of $70.

9 Received notice from AB Company that Precision's bid of $1,850 for computer services was accepted. An advance of $450 was received.

11 Purchased on credit from Ajax Supply additional computer supplies, $85.

12 Sent a second bill to Farm Research for services originally recorded on November 8.

13 Received notice that Republic had deducted a $4 service charge from the checking account.

16 Paid Shopper Newspaper $15 for newspaper advertisement.

18 Completed work for Dog Enterprise and received $495.

20 Paid John Conard $675 for personal use.

20 Ann White did not work during the last two weeks.

22–26 Took the week off for Christmas holiday.

29 Received a $450 payment from Farm Research on their outstanding account balance that resulted from a November 8 transaction.

30 Paid electric bill of $51 and telephone bill of $110.

31 Reimbursed Ann White's business car mileage, 50 miles at $0.24 per mile.

31 Reimbursed John Conard's business car mileage, 300 miles at $0.24 per mile.

31 In anticipation of preparing financial statements for the three-month period since the business started, gathered the following information related to adjusting entries:

a) Computer supplies ending inventory, $17.

b) Three months' insurance has expired.

c) December 31 falls on Wednesday, and Ann White has worked three days, but will not be paid until Friday, January 2.

d) The computer is expected to have a three-year useful life with no salvage value.

e) The office equipment is expected to have a four-year useful life with no salvage value.

f) Recalled that four months' rent had been paid in advance early in October.

2. After you have journalized and posted these transactions and adjusting entries, prepare an adjusted trial balance; an income statement for the

last three months of 1993; a statement of changes in owner's equity for the last three months of 1993; and a December 31, 1993, balance sheet.

Provocative Problems

Provocative Problem 3–1
Landmark Property Services
(LO 3, 4)

The 1992 and 1993 balance sheets of Landmark Property Services show the following assets and liabilities at the end of each of the years:

	December 31	
	1992	**1993**
Accounts receivable	$ 4,450	$ 3,180
Prepaid insurance	5,720	2,600
Interest payable	14,625	11,700
Unearned property management fees	5,200	6,460

The company's records show the following amounts of cash disbursed and received for these items during 1993:

Cash disbursed to pay insurance premiums . .	$ 4,470
Cash disbursed to pay interest	18,750
Cash received for managing property	76,200

Present calculations to show the amounts to be reported on Landmark Property Services' 1993 income statement for *(a)* insurance expense, *(b)* interest expense, and *(c)* property management fees earned.

Provocative Problem 3–2
AAA Appliance Repair
(LO 2, 3, 4, 6)

Arthur McNair began AAA Appliance Repair, a new business, on January 2, 1993. After one year's operation, McNair believes the business has done a lot of work during its first year. However, the bank has begun to dishonor AAA's checks. Creditors are billing the company for amounts it is unable to pay, and McNair is concerned that the business has not been profitable. He would like to determine whether or not to continue operations. Consequently, he has asked your help in evaluating the first year's operations.

You find that the service's accounting records, such as they are, have been kept by McNair's son, who has no formal training in record-keeping. However, he has prepared for your inspection the following statement of cash receipts and disbursements:

AAA APPLIANCE REPAIR
Cash Receipts and Disbursements
For Year Ended December 31, 1993

Receipts:		
Owner's investment	$25,000	
Received from customers for services	45,900	$70,900
Disbursements:		
Rent expense	$ 5,590	
Repair equipment purchased	22,750	
Service truck expense	13,100	
Wages expense	17,500	
Insurance expense	3,000	
Repair parts and supplies	9,290	71,230
Bank overdraft		$ (330)

There were no errors in the statement, and you learn these additional facts:

1. The lease contract for the shop space runs for five years and requires rent payments of $430 per month, with the first and last month's rent to be paid in advance. All required payments were made on time.
2. The repair equipment has an estimated five-year life, after which it will be valueless. It has been used a full year.
3. The service truck expense consists of $11,500 paid for the truck on January 2, plus $1,600 paid for gas, oil, and repairs. McNair expects to use the truck five years, after which he expects to get $2,000 for it as a trade-in on a new truck.
4. The wages expense consists of $4,000 paid the repair service's one employee who was hired on September 1, plus $13,500 of personal withdrawals by McNair. Also, the one employee is owed $190 of earned but unpaid wages.
5. The $3,000 of insurance expense resulted from paying premiums on two insurance policies on January 2. One policy cost $840 and gave protection for one year. The other policy cost $2,160 for two years' protection.
6. In addition to the $9,290 of repair parts and supplies paid for during the year, creditors have billed the business $430 for parts and supplies purchased and delivered but not paid for. Also, an inventory shows $1,660 of parts and supplies on hand.
7. McNair reports that the business does most of its work for cash, but customers owe $620 for repair work done on credit.

Prepare an accrual basis income statement for the year, a statement of changes in owner's equity, and a classified balance sheet showing its year-end financial position. (The bank overdraft represents a current obligation of the service business to the bank.)

Provocative Problem 3–3
Benchmark Design and Goldsmith
(LO 2, 3, 4, 6)

During the first week of January 1993, Sheila Lyon began a jewelry design and repair business she calls Benchmark Design and Goldsmith. She has kept no accounting records, but she does keep any unpaid invoices in a box near her workbench. She has kept a good record of the year's receipts and payments, which follows:

	Receipts	Payments
Investment	$18,000	
Shop equipment		$ 8,200
Repair parts and supplies		10,600
Rent payments		5,850
Insurance premiums paid		720
Newspaper advertising paid		1,470
Utility bills paid		1,020
Part-time helper's wages paid		5,200
Sheila Lyon for personal use		16,500
Revenue from repairs	34,150	
Subtotals	$52,150	$49,560
Cash balance, December 31, 1993		2,590
Totals	$52,150	$52,150

Lyon would like to know how much the business actually earned during its first year. Therefore, she would like you to prepare an accrual basis income statement, a statement of changes in owner's equity, and a year-end classified balance sheet for the shop.

The shop equipment has an estimated eight-year life, after which it will be worthless. There is a $980 unpaid invoice in the box near Lyon's workbench for supplies received, and an inventory shows $1,740 of supplies on hand. The shop space rents for $450 per month on a five-year lease. The lease contract requires payment of the first and last months' rents in advance, which were paid. The insurance premiums were for two policies taken out on January 2. The first is a one-year policy that cost $300. The second is a two-year policy that cost $420. There are $120 of earned but unpaid wages owed the helper, and customers owe the shop $1,650 for services they have received.

Provocative Problem 3–4
International Business Machines Corporation
(LO 6)

The financial statements and related financial information disclosed in IBM's 1990 annual report are shown in Appendix J. From your inspection of IBM's 1990 financial statements, including the Notes that follow the statements, answer the following questions:

1. Is the Consolidated Statement of Financial Position a classified balance sheet?
2. How many classifications of assets are presented on the Consolidated Statement of Financial Position? What are they?
3. What is the total amount of accumulated depreciation on December 31, 1990?
4. On December 31, 1990, what amount of accumulated depreciation relates to land improvements, buildings, and plant, laboratory, and office equipment? What amount relates to rental machines and parts?
5. How many shares of capital stock did IBM have issued as of December 31, 1990?
6. What amount of IBM's long-term debt on December 31, 1990, was payable in U.S. dollars? What amount was payable in currencies other than U.S. dollars? (Note: Ignore net unamortized discount and current maturities.)

Provocative Problem 3–5
As a Matter of Ethics: Essay

Ethics

Review the As a Matter of Ethics case on page 140. Discuss the problem faced by Pena and evaluate the alternative courses of action Pena might take. Also explain how your answer would differ given the following assumptions: (*a*) Pena knows that the company's financial statements are not going to be audited; (*b*) Pena knows that the president's bonus depends on the amount of income reported in the first year; (*c*) Pena's job depends on complying with the president's wishes.

Answers to Objective Review Questions

LO 1. (*a*)
LO 2. (*a*)
LO 3. (*e*)
LO 4. (*e*)
LO 5. (*d*)
LO 6. (*e*)
LO 7. (*a*)
LO 8. (*c*)

CHAPTER

4

The Work Sheet and Closing the Accounts of Proprietorships, Partnerships, and Corporations

A systematic approach is essential for efficient and accurate processing of large amounts of information. Whether work sheets are on paper or computerized, they help provide this structure. Proprietorships, partnerships, and corporations all use similar work sheets.

Topical Coverage

Your study of Chapter 4 will focus on some of the procedures performed at the end of each accounting period. You will learn to use a work sheet to show the effects of the adjustments and to organize the data prior to preparing financial statements. Also, you will learn the necessary steps to get the accounts ready for use in the following accounting period.

Learning Objectives

After studying Chapter 4, you should be able to:

1. Explain why a work sheet is prepared and be able to prepare a work sheet for a service business.
2. Prepare closing entries for a service business and explain why it is necessary to close the temporary accounts at the end of each accounting period.
3. Prepare a post-closing trial balance and explain its purpose.
4. Explain the nature of a corporation's retained earnings and its relationship to the declaration of dividends.
5. Prepare entries to record the declaration and payment of a dividend and to close the temporary accounts of a corporation.
6. List the steps in the accounting cycle in the order they are completed and perform each step.
7. Define or explain the words and phrases listed in the chapter glossary.

After studying Appendix B at the end of Chapter 4, you should be able to:

8. Prepare reversing entries and explain when and why they are used.

Using a Work Sheet at the End of Each Accounting Period

LO 1 Explain why a work sheet is prepared and be able to prepare a work sheet for a service business.

In the process of organizing the data that go into the formal financial reports given to managers and other interested parties, accountants prepare numerous memoranda, analyses, and informal papers. These analyses and memoranda are called **working papers** and are invaluable tools of the accountant. One important example of such working papers is the **work sheet** described in this chapter. The work sheet for a business is not given to the business owner or manager. It is prepared solely for the accountant's use and is kept by the accountant.

Recall the end-of-period procedures discussed in Chapter 3. After all transactions were recorded, an unadjusted trial balance was prepared and adjusting entries were entered in the journal and posted to the accounts. Then, an adjusted trial balance was prepared and used as a basis for preparing the financial statements.

For a very small business, these procedures are satisfactory. However, if a company has more than a few accounts and adjustments, you will make fewer errors by inserting an additional step into the procedures. The additional step is to prepare a work sheet. A work sheet is prepared before the adjusting entries are journalized or posted to the accounts.

On the work sheet, the accountant (1) shows the unadjusted trial balance; (2) shows the effects of the adjustments on the account balances; (3) shows the adjusted trial balance; and (4) sorts the adjusted amounts into columns according to whether the accounts are used in preparing the income statement or the statement of changes in owner's equity or balance sheet. Also, the amount of net income is calculated on the work sheet. After the work sheet is completed, the work sheet information is used to prepare the financial statements and to journalize the adjusting entries and the closing entries. (We discuss closing entries later in this chapter.)

Preparing a Work Sheet

Illustration 4–1 shows the multicolumn form used to prepare a work sheet. Note that this form provides two columns each for the unadjusted trial balance, the adjustments, the adjusted trial balance, the income statement, and the statement of changes in owner's equity or balance sheet. A work sheet could contain two separate columns for the statement of changes in owner's equity and two separate columns for the balance sheet. However, because the statement of changes in owner's equity includes only a few items, this usually is not done. Instead, most work sheets provide only two columns for both statements, as Illustration 4–1 shows.

When you use a work sheet, do not prepare the unadjusted trial balance on a separate form. Instead, the first step in preparing the work sheet is to prepare the unadjusted trial balance in the first two money columns of the work sheet form. Turn the first transparency overlay to see Illustration 4–2, which shows this first step in preparing the work sheet for Jerry Dow, Attorney. This is the same example that we used in Chapters 1 through 3.

Remember that Dow's law practice completed a number of transactions during December 1993. The unadjusted trial balance in Illustration 4–2 reflects the account balances after these December transactions were recorded but *before any adjusting entries were journalized or posted*.

In Illustration 4–2, a blank line was left after the Legal Fees Earned account. Based on past experience, the accountant may realize that more than one line will be needed to show the adjustments to a particular account. When you turn the second transparency overlay, you will see in Illustration 4–3 that Legal Fees Earned is an example. Another alternative is to squeeze two adjustments on one line or to combine the effects of two or more adjustments in one amount.

The next step in preparing a work sheet is to enter the adjustments in the columns labeled Adjustments, as shown in Illustration 4–3. The adjustments shown in Illustration 4–3 are the same ones that we discussed in Chapter 3. Notice that an identifying letter relates the debit and credit of each adjustment. After preparing a work sheet, you still have to enter the adjusting entries in the journal and post them to the ledger. At that time, the identifying letters help you to match correctly the debit and credit of each adjusting entry.

Explanations of the adjustments on the illustrated work sheet are as follows:

Adjustment (*a*): To adjust for expired insurance.

Adjustment (*b*): To adjust for the office supplies used.

Adjustment (*c*): To adjust for depreciation of the law library.

Adjustment (*d*): To adjust for depreciation of the office equipment.

Adjustment (*e*): To adjust for unearned revenue.

Adjustment (*f*): To adjust for accrued salaries.

Adjustment (*g*): To adjust for accrued revenue.

Most of the adjustments on the illustrated work sheet required one or two additional accounts to be written in below the original trial balance. These accounts did not have balances when the trial balance was prepared. Therefore, they were not listed in the trial balance. If you anticipate that additional accounts will be required, however, you may list them in the process of preparing the unadjusted trial balance.

After the adjustments are entered in the Adjustments columns, the columns are totaled to prove the equality of the debit and credit adjustments. Then, proceed to prepare the adjusted trial balance. To do so, each amount in the Unadjusted Trial Balance columns is combined with its adjustments in the Adjustments columns, if any, and is entered in the Adjusted Trial Balance columns.

For example, in Illustration 4–3, the Prepaid Insurance account has a $2,400 debit balance in the Unadjusted Trial Balance columns. This $2,400 debit is combined with the $100 credit in the Adjustments columns to give Prepaid Insurance a $2,300 debit in the Adjusted Trial Balance columns. Insurance Expense has no balance in the Unadjusted Trial Balance columns, but it has a $100 debit in the Adjustments columns. Therefore, no balance combined with a $100 debit gives Insurance Expense a $100 debit in the Adjusted Trial Balance columns. Cash, Office Equipment, and several other accounts have trial balance amounts that were not adjusted. As a result, their unadjusted trial balance amounts are carried unchanged into the Adjusted Trial Balance columns.

After carrying the combined amounts to the Adjusted Trial Balance columns, add the Adjusted Trial Balance columns to prove their equality. Then, sort the amounts in these columns to the proper financial statement columns, as shown in Illustration 4–4. (Turn the next transparency overlay.) Sort expense items to the Income Statement Debit column, and revenues to the Income Statement Credit column. Then sort assets and the owner's withdrawals to the Statement of Changes in Owner's Equity or Balance Sheet Debit column. Liability items and the owner's capital account are sorted to the Statement of Changes in Owner's Equity or Balance Sheet Credit column. This easy task requires answers to only two questions: (1) Is the item to be sorted a debit or a credit? and (2) On which statement does it appear?

After sorting the amounts to the proper columns, total the columns as shown in Illustration 4–5. (Turn the last transparency overlay.) At this point, the difference between the totals of the Income Statement columns is the net income or loss. The difference is the net income or loss because revenues are entered in the Credit column and expenses in the Debit column. If the Credit column total exceeds the Debit column total, the difference is a net income. If the Debit column total exceeds the Credit column total, the difference is a net loss. In the illustrated work sheet, the Credit column total exceeds the Debit column total, and the result is a $1,160 net income.

After calculating the net income in the Income Statement columns, add it to the Statement of Changes in Owner's Equity or Balance Sheet Credit column. In that final column, the $9,000 balance of the capital account does not yet reflect the increase in capital that resulted from net income. Therefore, adding the net income to this column has the effect of adding it to the capital account.

Had there been a loss, it would have been necessary to add the loss to the Debit column. This is because losses decrease owner's equity, and adding the loss to the Debit column has the effect of subtracting it from the capital account.

When the net income or net loss is added to the appropriate Statement of Changes in Owner's Equity or Balance Sheet column, the totals of the last two columns should balance. If they do not balance, one or more errors were made in constructing the work sheet. The error or errors may have been mathematical or an amount may have been sorted to a wrong column.

Although balancing the last two columns is done in an effort to discover errors, the fact that they balance is not proof that the work sheet is free from error. These columns balance even when certain types of errors have been made. For example, if you incorrectly carry an asset amount into the Income Statement Debit column, the columns still balance. Or, if you carry a liability amount into the Income Statement Credit column, the columns still balance. Either error causes the net income amount to be incorrect. But, the columns are in balance. Therefore, exercise care in sorting the adjusted trial balance amounts into the correct financial statement columns.

Preparing Adjusting Entries from the Work Sheet

Entering the adjustments in the Adjustments columns of a work sheet does not get these adjustments into the ledger accounts. Therefore, after completing the work sheet, you must prepare adjusting journal entries like the ones described in Chapter 3. The adjusting entries must be entered in the General Journal and posted to the accounts in the ledger. The work sheet makes this easy, because its Adjustments columns provide the information for these entries. All that is needed is an entry for each adjustment that appears in the columns. If you prepare adjusting entries from the information in Illustration 4–5, you will see that they are the same adjusting entries we discussed in the last chapter.

Preparing Financial Statements from the Work Sheet

A work sheet is not a substitute for the financial statements. The work sheet is nothing more than a supporting tool that the accountant uses at the end of an accounting period to help organize the data. However, as soon as it is completed, the accountant uses the work sheet to prepare the financial statements. The items in the Income Statement columns provide the information necessary to prepare the formal income statement. Next, information is taken from the last two columns to prepare the statement of changes in owner's equity and the balance sheet. The financial statements prepared from the information in Illustration 4–5 are shown in Illustration 4–6.

ILLUSTRATION 4–1

Preparing a Work Sheet at the End of the Accounting Period

The heading should identify the entity, the nature of the document, and the time period

JERRY DOW, ATTORNEY
Work Sheet for Month Ended December 31, 1993

	Unadjusted Trial Balance		Adjustments		Adjusted Trial Balance		Income Statement		Statement of Changes in Owner's Equity or Balance Sheet	
Account Titles	**Dr.**	**Cr.**	**Dr.**	**Cr.**	**Dr.**	**Cr.**	**Dr.**	**Cr.**	**Dr.**	**Cr.**

The multicolumn work sheet can be prepared manually or with a computer spreadsheet program

The work sheet collects and summarizes the information used to prepare financial statements and to journalize adjusting and closing entries

ILLUSTRATION 4–6

Financial Statements Prepared from the Work Sheet

JERRY DOW, ATTORNEY
Income Statement
For Month Ended December 31, 1993

Revenues:		
Legal fees earned		$4,350
Operating expenses:		
Salaries expense	$1,610	
Rent expense	1,000	
Utilities expense	230	
Insurance expense	100	
Office supplies expense	45	
Depreciation expense, law library	80	
Depreciation expense, office equipment	125	
Total operating expenses		3,190
Net Income		$1,160

JERRY DOW, ATTORNEY
Statement of Changes in Owner's Equity
For Month Ended December 31, 1993

Jerry Dow, capital, November 30, 1993		$ –0–
Plus:		
Investments by owner	$9,000	
Net income	1,160	10,160
Total		$10,160
Less withdrawals by owner		1,100
Jerry Dow, capital, December 31, 1993		$ 9,060

JERRY DOW, ATTORNEY
Balance Sheet
December 31, 1993

Assets			Liabilities		
Cash		$ 650	Accounts payable	$ 760	
Accounts		200	Unearned legal fees	2,750	
Prepaid insurance		2,300	Salaries payable	210	
Office supplies		75	Total liabilities		$ 3,720
Law library	$2,880				
Less accumulated depreciation	80	2,800			
Office equipment	$6,880		**Owner's Equity**		
Less accumulated depreciation	125	6,755	Jerry Dow, Capital		9,060
Total assets		$12,780	Total liabilities and owner's equity		$12,780

Closing Entries—What They Involve and Why They Are Made

LO 2 Prepare closing entries for a service business and explain why it is necessary to close the temporary accounts at the end of each accounting period.

After the work sheet and statements are completed and the adjusting entries are recorded, you must journalize and post **closing entries.** As shown in Illustration 4–7, closing entries are designed to transfer the end-of-period balances in the revenue accounts, the expense accounts, and the withdrawals account to a balance sheet equity account. To close the revenue and expense accounts, transfer their balances first to a summary account called **Income Summary.** Then, for a single proprietorship, transfer the Income Summary account balance (the net income or loss) to the owner's capital account. Finally, transfer the owner's withdrawals account to the owner's capital account. After the closing entries are posted, the revenue, expense, and withdrawals accounts have zero balances. Thus, these accounts are said to be closed or cleared.

One reason why closing entries are prepared at the end of each accounting period is to update the owner's capital account. The transfers of the revenue, expense, and withdrawals account balances to the owner's capital account are necessary because

1. Revenues increase owner's equity, while expenses and withdrawals decrease owner's equity.
2. During an accounting period these increases and decreases are temporarily accumulated in revenue, expense, and withdrawals accounts rather than in the owner's capital account.
3. By transferring the effects of revenues, expenses, and withdrawals from the revenue, expense, and withdrawals accounts to the owner's capital account, closing entries install the correct, end-of-period balance in the owner's capital account.

Also, closing entries cause the revenue, expense, and withdrawals accounts to begin each new accounting period with zero balances. This is necessary because

1. An income statement reports the revenues earned and expenses incurred during one accounting period and is prepared from information recorded in the revenue and expense accounts.
2. The revenue and expense accounts are not discarded at the end of each accounting period but are used to record the revenues and expenses of succeeding periods.
3. Because these accounts should reflect only one period's revenues and expenses, the accounts must begin each period with zero balances.
4. Since the statement of changes in owner's equity reports the owner's withdrawals during only one period, the withdrawals account also must begin each period with a zero balance.

Closing Entries Illustrated

At the end of December, after its adjusting entries were posted but before its accounts were closed, the revenue, expense, withdrawals, and capital accounts of Dow's law practice had the balances shown in Illustration 4–8. (As a rule, an account's Balance column heading does not tell whether the balance is debit or credit. However, in Illustration 4–8, and in the illustrations that immediately follow, the nature of each account's balance is shown as a study aid.)

In Illustration 4–8, notice that Dow's Capital account shows only the $9,000 investment by Dow made on December 1. This is not the amount of Dow's equity on December 31. Closing entries are required to make this account show the December 31 equity.

ILLUSTRATION 4–7

Closing Entries

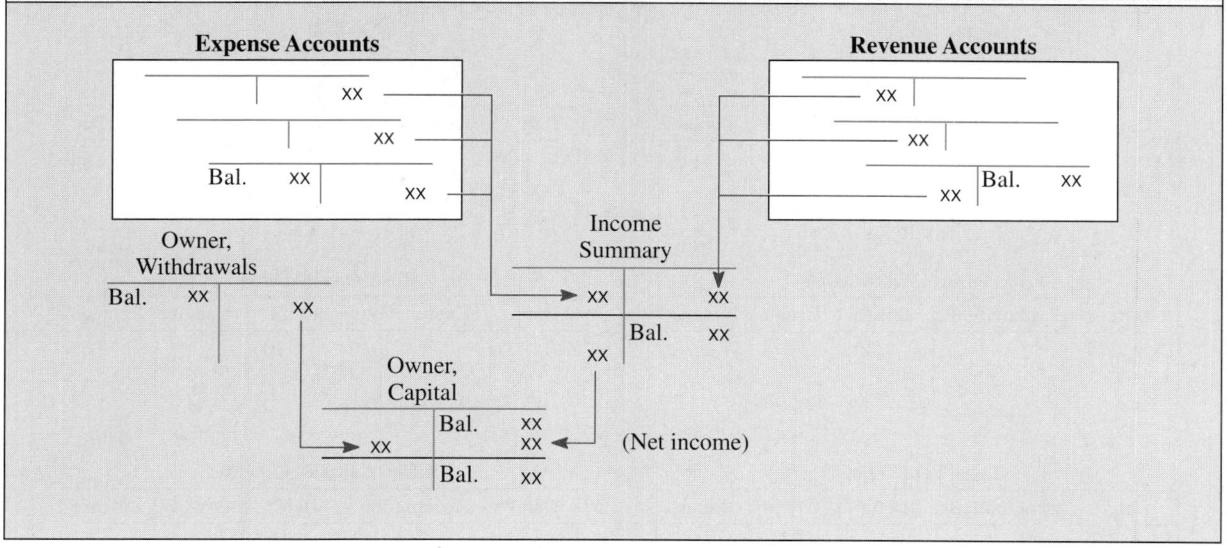

Notice also the last account in Illustration 4–8, the Income Summary account. This account is used only at the end of the accounting period to summarize and clear the revenue and expense accounts.

Closing Revenue Accounts

Before closing entries are posted, revenue accounts have credit balances. Therefore, to close revenue accounts, you must debit each revenue account and credit Income Summary.

The Dow law practice has only one revenue account, and the entry to close it is:

Dec.	31	Legal Fees Earned	4,350.00	
		Income Summary		4,350.00
		To close the revenue account.		

Posting this entry has the following effect on the accounts:

Legal Fees Earned

Date		Explanation	Debit	Credit	Balance
Dec.	10			2,200	2,200
	12			1,700	3,900
	31			250	4,150
	31			200	4,350
	31		4,350		–0–

Income Summary

Date		Explanation	Debit	Credit	Balance
Dec.	31			4,350	4,350

ILLUSTRATION 4–8

Revenue, Expense, Withdrawals, and Capital Accounts of Jerry Dow, Attorney

Jerry Dow, Capital (Credit balance)

Date		Explanation	Debit	Credit	Balance
Dec.	1			9,000	9,000

Jerry Dow, Withdrawals (Debit balance)

Date		Explanation	Debit	Credit	Balance
Dec.	24		1,100		1,100

Legal Fees Earned (Credit balance)

Date		Explanation	Debit	Credit	Balance
Dec.	10			2,200	2,200
	12			1,700	3,900
	31			250	4,150
	31			200	4,350

Salaries Expense (Debit balance)

Date		Explanation	Debit	Credit	Balance
Dec.	12		700		700
	26		700		1,400
	31		210		1,610

Rent Expense (Debit balance)

Date		Explanation	Debit	Credit	Balance
Dec.	10		1,000		1,000

Utilities Expense (Debit balance)

Date		Explanation	Debit	Credit	Balance
Dec.	26		230		230

Insurance Expense (Debit balance)

Date		Explanation	Debit	Credit	Balance
Dec.	31		100		100

Office Supplies Expense (Debit balance)

Date		Explanation	Debit	Credit	Balance
Dec.	31		45		45

Depreciation Expense, Law Library (Debit balance)

Date		Explanation	Debit	Credit	Balance
Dec.	31		80		80

Depreciation Expense, Office Equipment (Debit balance)

Date		Explanation	Debit	Credit	Balance
Dec.	31		125		125

Income Summary

Date		Explanation	Debit	Credit	Balance

Note that the entry clears the revenue account by transferring its balance as a credit to the Income Summary account. It also causes the revenue account to begin the new accounting period with a zero balance.

Closing Expense Accounts

Before closing entries are posted, expense accounts have debit balances. Therefore, to close a concern's expense accounts, debit the Income Summary account and credit each individual expense account. The Dow law practice has seven expense accounts, and the compound entry to close them is:

Dec.	31	Income Summary	3,190.00	
		Salaries Expense		1,610.00
		Rent Expense		1,000.00
		Utilities Expense		230.00
		Insurance Expense		100.00
		Office Supplies Expense		45.00
		Depreciation Expense, Law Library		80.00
		Depreciation Expense, Office Equipment		125.00
		To close the expense accounts.		

Posting the entry has the effect shown in Illustration 4–9. In that illustration, notice that the entry clears the expense accounts of their balances by transferring the balances as a debit to the Income Summary account. Also, the entry causes the expense accounts to begin the new period with zero balances.

Closing the Income Summary Account

After a business's revenue and expense accounts are closed to Income Summary, the balance of the Income Summary account is equal to the net income or loss. When revenues exceed expenses, there is a net income and the Income Summary account has a credit balance. On the other hand, when expenses exceed revenues, there is a loss and the account has a debit balance. Regardless of the nature of its balance, the Income Summary account must be closed by transferring its balance to the capital account. The Dow law practice earned $1,160 during December. Therefore, after its revenue and expense accounts are closed, its Income Summary account has a $1,160 credit balance. Transfer this balance to the Jerry Dow, Capital account with this entry:

Dec.	31	Income Summary	1,160.00	
		Jerry Dow, Capital		1,160.00
		To close the Income Summary account.		

Posting this entry has the following effect on the accounts:

Income Summary (Credit balance)

Date		Explanation	Debit	Credit	Balance
Dec.	31			4,350	4,350
	31		3,190		1,160
	31		1,160		–0–

Jerry Dow, Capital (Credit balance)

Date		Explanation	Debit	Credit	Balance
Dec.	1			9,000	9,000
	31			1,160	10,160

Notice that the entry clears the Income Summary account, transferring its balance, the amount of the net income in this case, to the capital account.

ILLUSTRATION 4–9

The Entry to Close the Expense Accounts

Salaries Expense

Date		Explanation	Debit	Credit	Balance
Dec.	12		700		700
	26		700		1,400
	31		210		1,610
	31			1,610	–0–

Rent Expense

Date		Explanation	Debit	Credit	Balance
Dec.	10		1,000		1,000
	31			1,000	–0–

Utilities Expense

Date		Explanation	Debit	Credit	Balance
Dec.	26		230		230
	31			230	–0–

Insurance Expense

Date		Explanation	Debit	Credit	Balance
Dec.	31		100		100
	31			100	–0–

Office Supplies Expense

Date		Explanation	Debit	Credit	Balance
Dec.	31		45		45
	31			45	–0–

Depreciation Expense, Law Library

Date		Explanation	Debit	Credit	Balance
Dec.	31		80		80
	31			80	–0–

Depreciation Expense, Office Equipment

Date		Explanation	Debit	Credit	Balance
Dec.	31		125		125
	31			125	–0–

$1,610
1,000
230
100
45
80
125
$3,190

Income Summary

Date		Explanation	Debit	Credit	Balance
Dec.	31			4,350	4,350
	31		3,190		1,160

Closing the Withdrawals Account

At the end of an accounting period, the withdrawals account shows the decrease in the owner's equity due to the owner's withdrawals. To close the account, transfer its debit balance to the capital account with this entry:

Dec.	31	Jerry Dow, Capital	1,100.00	
		Jerry Dow, Withdrawals		1,100.00
		To close the withdrawals account.		

Posting the entry has this effect on the accounts:

Jerry Dow, Withdrawals

Date		Explanation	Debit	Credit	Balance
Dec.	24		1,100		1,100
	31			1,100	-0-

Jerry Dow, Capital

Date		Explanation	Debit	Credit	Balance
Dec.	1			9,000	9,000
	31			1,160	10,160
	31		1,100		9,060

After you post the entry to close the withdrawals account, notice that the two reasons for making closing entries are accomplished: (1) all revenue, expense, and withdrawals accounts have zero balances; (2) the net effect of the period's revenue, expense, and withdrawals transactions on the owner's equity is shown in the capital account.

Temporary (Nominal) Accounts and Permanent (Real) Accounts

Revenue accounts, expense accounts, withdrawals accounts, and the Income Summary account are often called **temporary accounts** or **nominal accounts.** We use these terms because amounts are stored in these accounts only temporarily. Such accounts are closed at the end of each accounting period. By contrast, accounts that appear in the balance sheet are often called **permanent accounts** or **real accounts,** because they remain open as long as the asset, liability, or owner's equity items recorded in the accounts continue in existence.

Sources of Closing Entry Information

Information for closing entries may be taken from the individual revenue and expense accounts. However, the work sheet provides this information in a more convenient form. Look at the work sheet in Illustration 4–5. Every account that has a balance in the Income Statement columns must be closed. In addition, the withdrawals account must be closed.

The Accounts after Closing

After both adjusting and closing entries are posted, the Dow law practice accounts appear as in Illustration 4–10. Observe that the asset, liability, and owner's capital accounts show their end-of-period balances. Also, note that the revenue and expense accounts have zero balances and are ready to be used when revenues and expenses are recorded in the next accounting period.

The Post-Closing Trial Balance

LO 3 Prepare a post-closing trial balance and explain its purpose.

Because errors may have been introduced in the process of adjusting and closing the accounts, a new trial balance is prepared after all adjusting and closing entries have been posted. This **post-closing trial balance** is prepared to retest the equality of the accounts. The post-closing trial balance for Dow's law practice appears in Illustration 4–11.

Compare Illustration 4–11 with the accounts that have balances in Illustration 4–10. Note that only asset, liability, and the owner's capital accounts have balances in Illustration 4–10. Note also that these are the only accounts that appear on the post-closing trial balance. The revenue and expense accounts have been cleared and have zero balances at this stage.

Accounting for Partnerships and Corporations

Partnership Accounting

Accounting for a partnership is like accounting for a single proprietorship except for transactions that directly affect the partners' capital and withdrawals accounts. These transactions require a capital account and a withdrawals account for each partner. To close the Income Summary account, make a compound entry that allocates to each partner his or her share of the net income or loss such as the following:

Dec.	31	Income Summary	7,000.00	
		Julie Ehlers, Capital		3,000.00
		Megan Brinkoeter, Capital		4,000.00
		To close the Income Summary account.		

Corporate Accounting

LO 4 Explain the nature of a corporation's retained earnings and its relationship to the declaration of dividends.

Accounting for a corporation also differs from that of a single proprietorship for transactions that affect the equity accounts of the corporation. The accounts of a corporation are designed to distinguish between equity resulting from amounts invested in the corporation by its stockholders and equity resulting from earnings. This distinction is important because a corporation generally cannot pay a legal dividend unless it has stockholders' equity resulting from earnings. In making the distinction, two kinds of stockholders' equity accounts are kept: (1) *contributed capital accounts* and (2) *retained earnings accounts*. Amounts invested in a corporation (contributed) by its stockholders are shown in contributed capital accounts such as the Common Stock account. Stockholders' equity resulting from earnings is shown in a retained earnings account.

ILLUSTRATION 4–10

The General Ledger for Jerry Dow, Attorney

Cash — **Acct. No. 101**

Date		Explanation	PR	Debit	Credit	Balance
1993 Dec.	1		G1	9,000 00		9,000 00
	2		G1		2,500 00	6,500 00
	3		G1		5,600 00	900 00
	10		G1	2,200 00		3,100 00
	10		G1		1,000 00	2,100 00
	12		G1		700 00	1,400 00
	22		G1	1,700 00		3,100 00
	24		G2		900 00	2,200 00
	24		G2		1,100 00	1,100 00
	26		G2	3,000 00		4,100 00
	26		G2		2,400 00	1,700 00
	26		G2		120 00	1,580 00
	26		G2		230 00	1,350 00
	26		G2		700 00	650 00

Accounts Receivable — **Acct. No. 106**

Date		Explanation	PR	Debit	Credit	Balance
1993 Dec.	12		G1	1,700 00		1,700 00
	22		G2		1,700 00	–0–
	31		G3	200 00		200 00

Office Supplies — **Acct. No. 124**

Date		Explanation	PR	Debit	Credit	Balance
1993 Dec.	26		G2	120 00		120 00
	31		G3		45 00	75 00

ILLUSTRATION 4–10

(continued)

Prepaid Insurance — **Acct. No.** 128

Date		Explanation	PR	Debit		Credit		Balance	
1993 Dec.	26		G2	2,400	00			2,400	00
	31		G3			100	00	2,300	00

Law Library — **Acct. No.** 159

Date		Explanation	PR	Debit		Credit		Balance	
1993 Dec.	2		G1	2,500	00			2,500	00
	6		G1	380	00			2,880	00

Accumulated Depreciation, Law Library — **Acct. No.** 160

Date		Explanation	PR	Debit		Credit		Balance	
1993 Dec.	31		G3			80	00	80	00

Office Equipment — **Acct. No.** 163

Date		Explanation	PR	Debit		Credit		Balance	
1993 Dec.	3		G1	5,600	00			5,600	00
	6		G1	1,280	00			6,880	00

Accumulated Depreciation, Office Equipment — **Acct. No.** 164

Date		Explanation	PR	Debit		Credit		Balance	
1993 Dec.	31		G3			125	00	125	00

ILLUSTRATION 4–10

(continued)

Accounts Payable — **Acct. No.** 201

Date		Explanation	PR	Debit	Credit	Balance
1993 Dec.	6		G1		1,660 00	1,660 00
	24		G2	900 00		760 00

Salaries Payable — **Acct. No.** 209

Date		Explanation	PR	Debit	Credit	Balance
1993 Dec.	31		G3		210 00	210 00

Unearned Legal Fees — **Acct. No.** 231

Date		Explanation	PR	Debit	Credit	Balance
1993 Dec.	26		G2		3,000 00	3,000 00
	31		G3	250 00		2,750 00

Jerry Dow, Capital — **Acct. No.** 301

Date		Explanation	PR	Debit	Credit	Balance
1993 Dec.	1		G1		9,000 00	9,000 00
	31		G3		1,160 00	10,160 00
	31		G3	1,100 00		9,060 00

Jerry Dow, Withdrawals — **Acct. No.** 302

Date		Explanation	PR	Debit	Credit	Balance
1993 Dec.	24		G2	1,100 00		1,100 00
	31		G3		1,100 00	–0–

ILLUSTRATION 4–10

(continued)

Legal Fees Earned						Acct. No. 401
Date		**Explanation**	**PR**	**Debit**	**Credit**	**Balance**
1993 Dec.	10		G1		2,200 00	2,200 00
	12		G1		1,700 00	3,900 00
	31		G3		250 00	4,150 00
	31		G3		200 00	4,350 00
	31		G3	4,350 00		–0–

Depreciation Expense, Law Library						Acct. No. 610
Date		**Explanation**	**PR**	**Debit**	**Credit**	**Balance**
1993 Dec.	31		G3	80 00		80 00
	31		G3		80 00	–0–

Depreciation Expense, Office Equipment						Acct. No. 612
Date		**Explanation**	**PR**	**Debit**	**Credit**	**Balance**
1993 Dec.	31		G3	125 00		125 00
	31		G3		125 00	–0–

Salaries Expense						Acct. No. 622
Date		**Explanation**	**PR**	**Debit**	**Credit**	**Balance**
1993 Dec.	12		G1	700 00		700 00
	26		G2	700 00		1,400 00
	31		G3	210 00		1,610 00
	31		G3		1,610 00	–0–

ILLUSTRATION 4–10

(concluded)

Insurance Expense **Acct. No.** 637

Date		Explanation	PR	Debit		Credit		Balance	
1993 Dec.	31		G3	100	00			100	00
	31		G3			100	00	–0–	

Rent Expense **Acct. No.** 640

Date		Explanation	PR	Debit		Credit		Balance	
1993 Dec.	10		G1	1,000	00			1,000	00
	31		G3			1,000	00	–0–	

Office Supplies Expense **Acct. No.** 650

Date		Explanation	PR	Debit		Credit		Balance	
1993 Dec.	31		G3	45	00			45	00
	31		G3			45	00	–0–	

Utilities Expense **Acct. No.** 690

Date		Explanation	PR	Debit		Credit		Balance	
1993 Dec.	26		G2	230	00			230	00
	31		G3			230	00	–0–	

Income Summary **Acct. No.** 901

Date		Explanation	PR	Debit		Credit		Balance	
1993 Dec.	31		G3			4,350	00	4,350	00
	31		G3	3,190	00			1,160	00
	31		G3	1,160	00			–0–	

ILLUSTRATION 4–11

The Post-Closing Trial Balance

JERRY DOW, ATTORNEY
Post-Closing Trial Balance
December 31, 1993

Cash	$ 650	
Accounts receivable	200	
Office supplies	75	
Prepaid insurance	2,300	
Office equipment	6,880	
Accumulated depreciation, office equipment		$ 125
Law library	2,880	
Accumulated depreciation, law library		80
Accounts payable		760
Salaries payable		210
Unearned legal fees		2,750
Jerry Dow, capital		9,060
Totals	$12,985	$12,985

To demonstrate corporate accounting, assume that five persons secured a charter for a new corporation. Each invested $10,000 in the corporation by buying 1,000 shares of its $10 par value common stock. The corporation's entry to record their investments is

Jan.	5	Cash	50,000.00	
		Common Stock		50,000.00
		Issued 5,000 shares of $10 par value common stock for cash.		

In this case, note that the stock was issued at its $10 *par value,* which is an arbitrary amount established in the corporation's charter. You will learn more about par values in Chapter 14.

If during its first year the corporation earned $20,000, the entry to close its Income Summary account is

Dec.	31	Income Summary	20,000.00	
		Retained Earnings		20,000.00
		To close the Income Summary account.		

If these are the only entries that affected the Common Stock and Retained Earnings accounts during the first year, the corporation's year-end balance sheet will show the stockholders' equity as follows:

Stockholders' Equity		
Common stock, $10 par value, 5,000 shares authorized and outstanding	$50,000	
Retained earnings	20,000	
Total stockholders' equity		$70,000

Because a corporation is a separate legal entity, the names of its stockholders usually are of little interest to a balance sheet reader and are not shown in the equity section. However, in this case, the section does show that the net assets or equity of the corporation is $70,000. Of this amount, $50,000 resulted from the issuance of stock to the stockholders and $20,000 was the result of net income that has not been paid out as dividends.

Perhaps the concept of retained earnings would be clearer if the balance sheet item were labeled "Stockholders' equity resulting from earnings." However, the retained earnings caption is commonly used; it does not represent a specific amount of cash or any other asset. These are shown in the asset section of the balance sheet. Retained earnings represents the stockholders' equity resulting from earnings.

LO 5 Prepare entries to record the declaration and payment of a dividend and to close the temporary accounts of a corporation.

To continue, assume that on January 10 of the corporation's second year, its board of directors met and by vote declared a $1 per share dividend payable on February 1 to the January 25 **stockholders of record** (stockholders according to the corporation's records). The entry to record the declaration of the dividend is as follows:

Jan.	10	Cash Dividends Declared	5,000.00	
		Common Dividend Payable		5,000.00
		Declared a $1 per share dividend.		

The **Cash Dividends Declared** account is a temporary account that serves the same function for a corporation as does a withdrawals account for a proprietorship. At the end of each period, the Cash Dividends Declared account is closed to Retained Earnings. The entry to record the payment of the dividend is as follows:

Feb.	1	Common Dividend Payable	5,000.00	
		Cash		5,000.00
		Paid the dividend declared on January 10.		

Note from the two entries that the dividend declaration reduces stockholders' equity and increases liabilities, while the payment of the dividend reduces the corporation's assets and liabilities. The net result is to reduce assets and stockholders' equity just as a withdrawal of cash by the owner of a single proprietorship reduces assets and the owner's equity.

A cash dividend is normally paid by mailing checks to the stockholders. Also, as in this case, three dates are normally involved in a dividend declaration and payment. They are (1) the **date of declaration,** (2) the **date of record,** and (3) the **date of payment.** On the date of declaration, the dividend becomes a liability of the corporation. However, if some stockholders sell their stock to new investors in time for the new stockholders to be listed in the corporation's records on the date of record, the new stockholders will receive the dividend on the date of payment. Otherwise, the dividend will be paid to the old stockholders.

A dividend must be formally voted by a corporation's board of directors. Also, courts have generally held that the board is the final judge of when a dividend should be paid. Therefore, stockholders have no right to a dividend until it is declared. However, as soon as a cash dividend is declared, it becomes a liability of the corporation, normally a current liability, and must be paid. Furthermore, stockholders have the right to sue and force payment of a cash dividend once it is declared.

If during its second year (1994) the corporation suffered a $7,000 net loss, the entries to close its Income Summary and Dividends Declared accounts are

1994				
Dec.	31	Retained Earnings	7,000.00	
		Income Summary		7,000.00
		To close the Income Summary account.		
	31	Retained Earnings	5,000.00	
		Cash Dividends Declared		5,000.00
		To close the Cash Dividends Declared account.		

Now assume that during 1995, the corporation paid no dividends but suffered a net loss of $14,000. The entry to close the Income Summary account at the end of 1995 is

1995				
Dec.	31	Retained Earnings	14,000.00	
		Income Summary		14,000.00
		To close the Income Summary account.		

Posting these entries has the following effects on the Retained Earnings account:

Retained Earnings **Acct. No.** 318

Date		Explanation	PR	Debit	Credit	Balance
1993						
Dec.	31	Net income	G4		20,000.00	20,000.00
1994						
Dec.	31	Net loss	G5	7,000.00		13,000.00
	31	Cash dividends declared	G7	5,000.00		8,000.00
1995						
Dec.	31	Net loss	G9	14,000.00		(6,000.00)

AS A MATTER OF
Fact

Corporate Dividend News: *Dividend Increases Rose in December from Year Earlier*

By Neal Lipschutz

New York—More U.S. companies raised dividends in December than in the year-earlier month.

It was the second consecutive month of such positive dividend news and the third time in the final four months of 1991 that there were more dividend increases than in the year-earlier month, according to data from Standard & Poor's Corp. Until September, there had been 22 consecutive months of negative year-to-year dividend comparisons.

"December was perhaps a little better than we thought, but the comparison was pretty easy" because in December 1990 the economy was in recession and the U.S. was headed toward war in the Persian Gulf, said Arnold Kaufman, editor of S&P's Outlook newsletter.

S&P said 102 companies raised their dividends in December, compared with 88 in the year-earlier month and 137 in December 1989.

Despite the better trend near the end of the year, 1991 was a dismal one for dividends. S&P said 1,086 companies raised their dividends in 1991, down from 1,263 in 1990 and 1,656 in 1989.

The 1991 dividend increase total was the lowest since 1971, when 885 companies raised dividends. But because dividends were subject to federal wage and price controls in 1970 and 1971, Mr. Kaufman said, a more valid comparison would go all the way back to 1962, which also saw 1,086 companies raising dividends.

Sixteen companies cut their dividends last month, compared with 15 a year earlier. For all of 1991, 187 companies cut dividends, compared with 143 in 1990. Mr. Kaufman said the 1991 total was the highest since 258 dividends were cut in 1982, which also was a recession year.

Eighteen companies omitted dividends in December, compared with 32 a year earlier. In all of 1991, there were 250 omissions, compared with 266 in 1990.

* * *

Dividends Reported January 2

Company	Period	Amt.	Payable date	Record date
REGULAR				
AmerWaterWrks 5%pf.	.Q	.31¼	3– 1–92	2– 7
AmerWaterWks5%pref	.Q	.31¼	3– 1–92	2– 7
Elm Finl Services	.Q	.12½	1–24–92	1–10
Lubys Cafeterias. . . .	.Q	.12½	3–30–92	3–13
McGrath RentCorp. . .	.Q	.08	1–31–92	1–16
National City Corp. . .	.Q	.47	2– 1–92	1–13
Rogers Corp	.Q	.03	2–12–92	1–15
Sun Co.	.Q	.45	3–10–92	2–10
Winn-Dixie Stores . . .	.M	.10	2– 3–92	1–15
Winn-Dixie Stores . . .	.M	.10	3– 2–92	2–14
Winn-Dixie Stores . . .	.M	.10	4– 1–92	3–16
X-Rite Inc	.Q	.04	2–12–92	1–15
IRREGULAR				
Natl City depshrs	.–	1.00	2– 1–92	1–13
FUNDS · REITS · INVESTMENT COS · LPS				
ACM Govt Inco	.M	h.06	1–24–92	1–13
ACM Managed Inco . .	.M	h.039	1–24–92	1–13
AmerCap Fedl Mfg . .	.M	h.076	1–31–92	1–31
AmerCap TxEx HiYid.	.M	h.07	1–31–92	1–31
AmerCap TxExInsMun	.M	h.057	1–31–92	1–31
Blackstone Income. . .	.M	h.0509	1–31–92	1–15

INCREASED

Company	Period	–Amounts– New	Old	Payable date	Record date
Amer Water Works	.Q	.23⅛	.21½	2–15–92	1–24
Mobile America . .	.A	1.20	1.00	1–24–92	1–15
Pulitzer Publishing.	.Q	.13½	.13	2– 3–92	1–15

FOREIGN

Company	Period	Amt.	Payable date	Record date
Banco Bilbao Viz	.–	t.36	2– 3–92	1–10

SPECIAL

Company	Period	Amt.	Payable date	Record date
Kinnard Invest	.–	.10	1–21–92	1–10

A-Annual; b-Payable in Canadian funds; h-From income; k-From capital gains; M-Monthly; Q-Quarterly; S-Semiannual; t-Approximate U.S. dollar amount per American Depositary Receipt/Share.

* * *

Stocks Ex-Dividend January 6

Company	Amount	Company	Amount
Air Express Intl	.04	IllinoisPwr4.08%pf	.51
AllstateMunlincoOp	.06	IllinoisPwr4.20%pf	.52½
Banco Bilbao Viz	t.36	DeanWitterGovtinco	.06½
Bell Atlantic	.63	Disney (Walt) Co	.17½
BellSouth Corp	.69	Du Pont $3.50pf	.87½
Boston Edison Co.	.41	Du Pont $4.50pf	1.12½
Boston Ed 8.88%pf	2.22	Enserch adj pfD	1.02½
Carolina Pwr & Lt	.79	Enserch dep pfE	1.77½
Central Hudson G&E	.48	Friedman Indus	.03

Source: *The Wall Street Journal*, January 3, 1992. p. C9. Reprinted by permission of *The Wall Street Journal*.

Due to the dividend and the net losses, the Retained Earnings account has a $6,000 debit balance. A debit balance in a Retained Earnings account indicates a negative amount of retained earnings. A corporation with a negative amount of retained earnings is said to have a **deficit.** A deficit may be shown on a corporation's balance sheet as follows:

Stockholders' Equity		
Common stock, $10 par value, 5,000 shares authorized and outstanding	$50,000	
Deduct retained earnings deficit	(6,000)	
Total stockholders' equity		$44,000

In most states, a corporation with a deficit is not allowed to pay a cash dividend. This legal requirement is intended to protect the creditors of the corporation. Because a corporation is a separate legal entity, it is responsible for its own debts. However, the corporation's stockholders normally are not responsible for the corporation's debts. Therefore, if a corporation's creditors are to be paid, they must be paid from the corporation's assets. By making dividends illegal when there is a deficit, a corporation in financial difficulty is prevented from paying its assets in dividends and leaving nothing for payment of its creditors.

The Accounting Cycle

LO 6 List the steps in the accounting cycle in the order they are completed and perform each step.

In Chapters 2, 3, and 4, we have discussed all of the accounting procedures that must be completed during each accounting period, beginning with the recording of transactions in a journal and ending with a post-closing trial balance. Since these steps are repeated each period, they are called the **accounting cycle.** Illustration 4–12 shows the steps in the order of their occurrence. Review this illustration to be sure that you understand and know how to perform each step in the proper sequence. To assist your review, we briefly describe each step as follows:

1. **Journalizing** . . . . Analyzing and recording transactions in a journal.
2. **Posting** . . . . Copying the debits and credits of the journal entries into the ledger accounts.
3. **Preparing an unadjusted trial balance** . . Summarizing the ledger accounts and testing the recording accuracy.
4. **Completing the work sheet** . . . . Gaining the effects of the adjustments before entering the adjustments in the accounts. Then sorting the account balances into the proper financial statement columns and calculating the net income or net loss.
5. **Adjusting the ledger accounts** . . . . Preparing adjusting journal entries from information in the Adjustments columns of the work sheet and posting the entries to bring the account balances up to date.

ILLUSTRATION 4–12

The Accounting Cycle

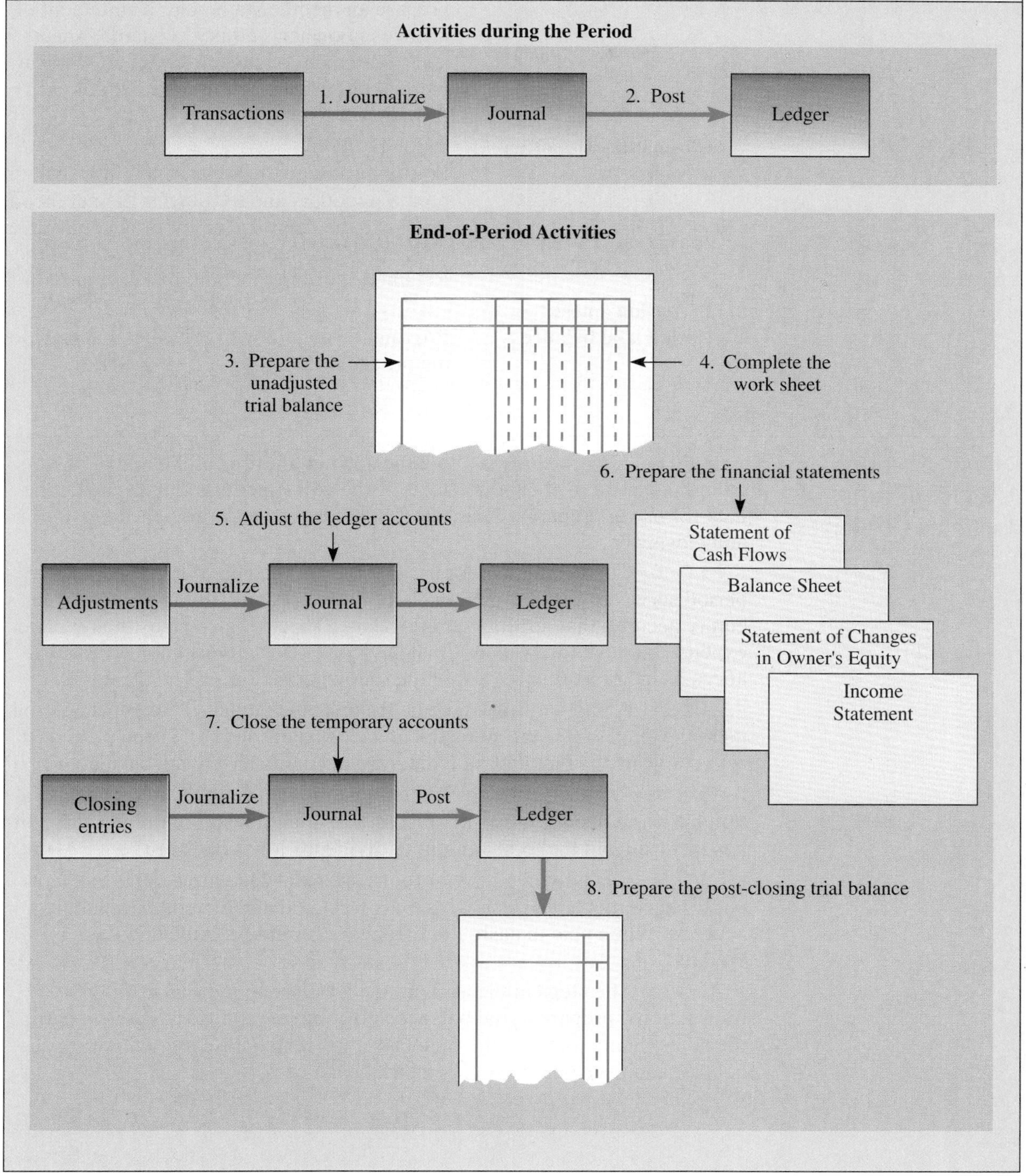

6. **Preparing the statements** . . . . Using the information on the work sheet to prepare an income statement, a statement of changes in owner's equity, a balance sheet, and a statement of cash flows. (You will learn more about preparing the statement of cash flows in Chapter 17.)
7. **Closing the temporary accounts** . . . . Preparing and posting entries to close the temporary accounts and to transfer the net income or loss to the capital account or accounts in a single proprietorship or partnership or to the Retained Earnings account in a corporation.
8. **Preparing a post-closing trial balance** . . . Proving the accuracy of the adjusting and closing procedures.

Summary of the Chapter in Terms of Learning Objectives

LO 1. A work sheet is a tool the accountant uses at the end of an accounting period to show the effects of the adjustments and to organize the data for use in preparing financial statements and recording the adjusting and closing entries.

LO 2. Closing the temporary accounts at the end of each accounting period serves to transfer the effects of these accounts to the proper owner's equity account that appears on the balance sheet. It also gives the revenue, expense, and withdrawals or Cash Dividends Declared accounts zero balances, preparing them for use in the following period.

LO 3. A post-closing trial balance tests the equality of debits and credits in the ledger after the adjusting and closing entries have been posted. It also confirms the fact that all temporary accounts have been closed.

LO 4. Retained earnings is the total amount of net incomes a corporation has earned since it was organized, less the total amount of net losses it has incurred and the total amount of dividends it has declared.

LO 5. Cash dividend declarations are recorded with a debit to a temporary account called Cash Dividends Declared and a credit to a liability account. When paid in cash, the liability account is debited and Cash is credited.

LO 6. The steps in the accounting cycle are to journalize and post transactions, prepare a trial balance and complete the work sheet, record the adjustments, prepare the financial statements, close the temporary accounts, and prepare a post-closing trial balance.

Demonstration Problem

The December 31, 1993, adjusted trial balance of Westside Appliance Repair, Inc., is as follows:

Cash	$ 83,300	
Accounts receivable	45,000	
Notes receivable	60,000	
Prepaid insurance	19,000	
Prepaid rent	5,000	
Equipment	165,000	
Accumulated depreciation, equipment		$ 52,000
Accounts payable		37,000
Income taxes payable		21,500
Long-term notes payable		58,000
Common stock		55,000
Retained earnings		99,000
Cash dividends declared	75,000	
Repair services revenue		420,000
Interest earned		6,500
Depreciation expense, equipment	26,000	
Wages expense	179,000	
Rent expense	47,000	
Insurance expense	7,000	
Interest expense	4,700	
Income taxes expense	33,000	
	$749,000	$749,000

Required

1. Prepare closing entries for Westside Appliance Repair, Inc.
2. Prepare a post-closing trial balance for the business.
3. Set up a Retained Earnings account, and post all necessary amounts to the account.

Solution to Demonstration Problem

Planning the Solution

- Examine the adjusted trial balance and identify all of the nominal accounts that must be closed.
- Prepare entries to close the revenue accounts to Income Summary, to close the expense accounts to Income Summary, to close Income Summary to Retained Earnings, and to close Cash Dividends Declared to Retained Earnings.
- List the permanent accounts with their balances on the post-closing trial balance, using the post-closing balance for the Retained Earnings account.
- In the Retained Earnings account, enter the balance shown on the adjusted trial balance and post the closing entries to the account.

1.

Closing entries:

1993				
Dec.	31	Repair Services Revenue	420,000.00	
		Interest Earned	6,500.00	
		Income Summary		426,500.00
	31	Income Summary	296,700.00	
		Depreciation Expense, Equipment		26,000.00
		Wages Expense		179,000.00
		Interest Expense		4,700.00
		Insurance Expense		7,000.00
		Rent Expense		47,000.00
		Income Taxes Expense		33,000.00
	31	Income Summary	129,800.00	
		Retained Earnings		129,800.00
	31	Retained Earnings	75,000.00	
		Cash Dividends Declared		75,000.00

2.

WESTSIDE APPLIANCE REPAIR, INC.
Post-Closing Trial Balance
December 31, 1993

Cash	$ 83,300	
Accounts receivable	45,000	
Notes receivable	60,000	
Prepaid insurance	19,000	
Prepaid rent	5,000	
Equipment	165,000	
Accumulated depreciation, equipment		$ 52,000
Accounts payable		37,000
Income taxes payable		21,500
Long-term notes payable		58,000
Common stock		55,000
Retained earnings		153,800
Totals	$377,300	$377,300

3.

Retained Earnings

Date		Explanation	PR	Debit	Credit	Balance
1993						
Jan.	1	Beginning balance			99,000	99,000
Dec.	31	Close Income Summary			129,800	228,800
	31	Close Cash Dividends Declared		75,000		153,800

APPENDIX

B

Reversing Entries

LO 8 Prepare reversing entries and explain when and why they are used.

In this appendix, we explain some optional entries accountants may use in accounting for accrued items. These optional entries, called **reversing entries**, make the bookkeeping process easier.

In accounting for Jerry Dow's law practice, the December 31, 1993, adjusting entries included an accrual of the secretary's salary. This entry was as follows:

1993 Dec.	31	Salaries Expense	210.00	
		Salaries Payable		210.00
		To record accrued wages.		

Then, on December 31, the Salaries Expense account was closed to Income Summary.

Since the secretary is paid every two weeks, the next payment is on January 9, and is recorded as follows:

Jan.	9	Salaries Payable	210.00	
		Salaries Expense	490.00	
		Cash		700.00
		Paid wages for two weeks.		

To make the January 9 entry correctly, the bookkeeper must remember that part of the cash payment is of accrued salaries and part is expense of the current period. Since the accrual is easy to forget, you can avoid the need to remember by preparing and posting entries to reverse any end-of-period adjustments of accrued items. These reversing entries are made after the adjusting and closing entries are posted and are normally dated the first day of the new accounting period.

Also, Appendix A at the end of Chapter 3 explained that some companies follow the practice of recording prepaid and unearned items in income statement accounts. When that is the practice, the end-of-period adjusting entries transfer the unused or unearned portions to asset and liability accounts. Thereafter, reversing entries may be used to transfer the prepaid asset and unearned liability account balances back into the expense and revenue accounts.

To reverse the accrual of wages, make the following entry:

Jan.	1	Salaries Payable	210.00	
		Salaries Expense		210.00
		To reverse the accrual of salaries.		

Observe that the reversing entry is the exact opposite of the original, December 31 adjusting entry. After the adjusting, closing, and reversing entries are posted, the Salaries Expense and Salaries Payable accounts appear as follows:

Salaries Expense

Date		Explanation	Debit	Credit	Balance
Dec.	12	Paid wages	700		700
	26	Paid wages	700		1,400
	31	Accrued wages	210		1,610
	31	Closing		1,610	–0–
1994					
Jan.	1	Reversal		210	(210)

Salaries Payable

Date		Explanation	Debit	Credit	Balance
Dec.	31	Accrued wages		210	210
1994					
Jan.	1	Reversal	210		–0–

Notice that the reversing entry cancels the $210 of salaries that appeared in the Salaries Payable account. It also causes the accrued salaries to appear in the Salaries Expense account as a $210 credit. (Remember that a circled balance means a balance opposite from normal.) Therefore, due to the reversing entry, when the salaries are paid on January 9, you can record the transaction with this entry:

Jan.	9	Salaries Expense	700.00	
		Cash		700.00
		Paid wages for two weeks.		

The entry's $700 debit to Salaries Expense includes both the $210 salary incurred during 1993 and the $490 salary expense incurred during 1994. However, when the entry is posted, because of the previously posted reversing entry, the balance of the Salaries Expense account shows only the $490 expense of the current period, as follows:

Salaries Expense

Date		Explanation	Debit	Credit	Balance
Dec.	12	Paid wages	700		700
	26	Paid wages	700		1,400
	31	Accrued wages	210		1,610
	31	Closing		1,610	-0-
1994					
Jan.	1	Reversal		210	(210)
	9	Paid wages	700		490

Summary of Appendix B in Terms of Learning Objective

LO 8. Reversing entries may be applied to all accrued items, such as accrued interest earned, accrued interest expense, accrued taxes, and accrued salaries and wages. Reversing entries also may be used for prepaid and unearned items if (and only if) the business records prepaid expenses with debits to expense accounts, and records unearned revenues with credits to revenue accounts (as explained in Appendix A at the end of Chapter 3). In any case, reversing entries are not required. The financial statements appear exactly the same whether or not reversing entries are used. Reversing entries are used as a convenience in bookkeeping.

Glossary

LO 7 Define or explain the words and phrases listed in the chapter glossary.

Accounting cycle the recurring accounting steps performed each accounting period beginning with the recording of transactions and proceeding through posting the recorded amounts, preparing an unadjusted trial balance and completing a work sheet, journalizing and posting adjusting entries, preparing the financial statements, journalizing and posting closing entries, and preparing a post-closing trial balance. pp. 210–12

Cash Dividends Declared a temporary account that serves the same function for a corporation as does a withdrawals account for a proprietorship, and which is closed to Retained Earnings at the end of each accounting period. p. 207

Closing entries entries made at the end of each accounting period to establish zero balances in the temporary accounts and to transfer the temporary account balances to a capital account or accounts or to the Retained Earnings account. pp. 194–99

Date of declaration the date on which a dividend is declared by vote of a corporation's board of directors. p. 208

Date of payment the date on which a dividend liability of a corporation is satisfied by mailing checks to the stockholders. p. 208

Date of record the date on which the stockholders who are listed in a corporation's records are determined to be those who will receive a dividend. p. 208

Deficit a negative amount (debit balance) of retained earnings. pp. 209–10

Income Summary the account used in the closing process to summarize the amounts of revenues and expenses, and from which the amount of the net income or loss is transferred to the owner's capital account in a single proprietorship, or to the partners' capital accounts in a partnership, or to the Retained Earnings account in a corporation. p. 194

Nominal accounts another name for *temporary accounts*. p. 199

Permanent accounts accounts that remain open as long as the asset, liability, or owner's equity items recorded in the accounts continue in existence; therefore, accounts that appear on the balance sheet. p. 199

Post-closing trial balance a trial balance prepared after all adjusting and closing entries have been posted. p. 200

Real accounts another name for *permanent accounts*. p. 199

Reversing entries optional entries that transfer the balances in balance sheet accounts which arose as a result of certain adjusting entries (usually accruals) to income statement accounts. pp. 215–17

Stockholders of record the stockholders of a corporation as reflected in the records of the corporation. p. 207

Temporary accounts accounts that are closed at the end of each accounting period; therefore, the revenue, expense, Income Summary, and withdrawals accounts. p. 199

Working papers the memoranda, analyses, and other informal papers prepared by accountants in the process of organizing the data that go into the formal financial reports given to managers and other interested parties. p. 190

Work sheet a working paper on which the accountant shows the unadjusted trial balance, shows the effects of the adjustments on the account balances, calculates the net income or loss, and sorts the adjusted amounts according to the financial statements on which the amounts appear. pp. 190–93

Synonymous Terms

Permanent accounts real accounts; balance sheet accounts.
Temporary accounts nominal accounts.

Objective Review

Answers to the following questions are listed at the end of this chapter. Be sure that you decide which is the one best answer to each question *before* you check the answers.

LO 1 In preparing a work sheet at the end of the annual accounting period, Ritz Company's accountant incorrectly extended a $9,400 salaries expense amount from the adjusted trial balance to the Statement of Changes in Owner's Equity or Balance Sheet Debit column. As a result of this error:

a. The adjusted trial balance columns will not balance.
b. The net income calculated on the work sheet will be understated.
c. The net income calculated on the work sheet will be overstated.
d. On the bottom row of the work sheet, the totals of the last two columns will not be equal.
e. Both (*b*) and (*d*) are correct.

LO 2 Related to the process of preparing closing entries:

a. Expenses, revenues, and the withdrawals account are closed to Income Summary.
b. All expense accounts are first closed to the revenue accounts, which are then closed to Income Summary.
c. After the process is completed, the Income Summary account balance equals net income or net loss for the period.
d. After the process is completed, all temporary accounts have zero balances.
e. None of the above is correct.

LO 3 A post-closing trial balance:

a. Includes the balances of all accounts that appear on the financial statements.
b. Is one of the important financial statements presented to the owner of a business and other outside parties.
c. Must be prepared as the first step in the end-of-period procedures that lead to the preparation of financial statements.
d. Should include the balances of accounts that appear on the income statement and on the balance sheet.
e. Should include only balances of accounts that appear on the balance sheet.

LO 4. The retained earnings of a corporation:

a. Will be reported as a deficit if the sum of all prior net losses plus all dividend declarations exceeds the sum of all prior net incomes.
b. Less any contributed capital amounts equals the total stockholders' equity of the corporation.
c. Represent cash balances the corporation has available to pay dividends.
d. Will be reported as a positive amount if net income for the current period exceeds dividend declarations during the period.
e. Include the sum of all past net incomes (less net losses) of the corporation plus any dividends that have been declared but not paid.

LO 5. In accounting for cash dividends that a corporation declares and pays:

a. The Cash Dividends Declared account is reported on the balance sheet as a liability.
b. No entry is required on the date of record.
c. A dividend declaration is debited to Retained Earnings and credited to Cash Dividends Declared.
d. The Cash Dividends Declared account is closed to Income Summary.
e. A payment of a previously recorded dividend declaration is debited to Cash Dividends Declared and credited to Cash.

LO 6. The steps in the accounting cycle:

a. Are the eight procedures followed in preparing a work sheet.
b. Begin with the preparation of an unadjusted trial balance.
c. Are completed once during the life of each business.
d. Are concluded with the preparation of a post-closing trial balance.
e. All of the above are correct.

LO 7. The date on which the stockholders listed in a corporation's records are determined to be those who will receive dividends is the:

a. Date of transfer.
b. Date of declaration.
c. Date of record.
d. Date of payment.
e. Closing date.

LO 8. Reversing entries:

a. Must be used by all companies that have an accrual accounting system.
b. Are journalized and posted at the end of the accounting period after the adjusting entries are posted and prior to posting the closing entries.
c. Have the effect of deferring the reporting of accrued expenses from one period to the next.
d. Have no effect on the amounts reported on the financial statements.
e. None of the above is correct.

A letter [B] identifies the questions, exercises, and problems based on Appendix B at the end of the chapter.

Questions for Class Discussion

1. What is the difference between working papers and a work sheet?
2. What tasks are performed on a work sheet?
3. Is it possible to complete the statements and adjust and close the accounts without preparing a work sheet? What is gained by preparing a work sheet?
4. At what stage in the accounting process is a work sheet prepared?
5. Where do you obtain the amounts that are entered in the Unadjusted Trial Balance columns of a work sheet?
6. Why are the adjustments in the Adjustments columns of a work sheet keyed together with letters?
7. What is the result of combining the amounts in the Unadjusted Trial Balance columns with the amounts in the Adjustments columns of a work sheet?
8. Why must you exercise care in sorting the items in the Adjusted Trial Balance columns to the proper Income Statement or Balance Sheet columns?
9. In extending the items in the Adjusted Trial Balance columns of a work sheet, what would be the effect on the net income of extending (*a*) an expense to the Statement of Changes in Owner's Equity or Balance Sheet Debit column; (*b*) a liability to the Income Statement Credit column; and (*c*) a revenue to the Statement of Changes in Owner's Equity or Balance Sheet Debit column? Which, if any, of these errors would be detected automatically on the work sheet? Why would they be detected?
10. Why are revenue and expense accounts called temporary accounts? Are there any other temporary accounts?
11. What two purposes are accomplished by recording closing entries?
12. What accounts are affected by closing entries? What accounts are not affected?
13. Explain the difference between adjusting and closing entries.
14. What is the purpose of the Income Summary account?
15. Why is a post-closing trial balance prepared?
16. An accounting student listed the item, "Depreciation expense, building, $1,800," on a post-closing trial balance. What did this indicate?
17. What two kinds of accounts are shown in the stockholders' equity section of a corporation's balance sheet?
18. Explain how the retained earnings item found on a corporate balance sheet arises.
19. What three dates are normally involved in the declaration and payment of a cash dividend?
20. What is the purpose of using a Cash Dividends Declared account?

21. One corporation uses a Cash Dividends Declared account and another corporation debits all dividend declarations directly to its Retained Earnings account. What effect does this difference have on the entries to be made by the corporations?
22. Explain why the payment of a cash dividend by a corporation with a deficit generally is illegal.
23. Refer to the financial statements of Lands' End, Inc., shown in Appendix K. What amount of cash dividends were paid to common shareholders during the years ended January 31, 1991? 1990? 1989?
24. Refer to the financial statements of Federal Express Corporation shown in Appendix K. What general journal entry was made on May 31, 1991, to close the Income Summary account?
[B]25. If one company uses reversing entries and another does not, what differences between the two companies will show up on the financial statements?
[B]26. Why do reversing entries make the bookkeeping process easier?
[B]27. If a company made an adjusting entry to accrue salaries expense of $500 at the end of an accounting period, what reversing entry would be made for this accrual?
[B]28. At what stage in the accounting cycle are reversing entries recorded? When are they dated?

Exercises

Exercise 4–1
Sorting account balances on a work sheet
(LO 1)

The balances of the following accounts appeared in the Adjusted Trial Balance columns of a work sheet. Copy the account numbers in a column on a sheet of note paper, and beside each number indicate by letter the Income Statement or Balance Sheet column to which the account's balance would be sorted in completing the work sheet. Use the letter *a* to indicate the Income Statement Debit column, *b* to indicate the Income Statement Credit column, *c* to indicate the Statement of Changes in Owner's Equity or Balance Sheet Debit column, and *d* to indicate the Statement of Changes in Owner's Equity or Balance Sheet Credit column.

1. Donna Munnerlyn, Withdrawals.
2. Machinery.
3. Depreciation Expense, Machinery.
4. Office Supplies.
5. Prepaid Insurance.
6. Rent Expense.
7. Service Revenue.
8. Accounts Receivable.
9. Donna Munnerlyn, Capital.
10. Wages Expense.
11. Accounts Payable.
12. Accumulated Depreciation, Machinery.
13. Cash.
14. Utilities Expense.

Exercise 4–2
Preparing adjusting entries from work sheet information
(LO 1)

The following item amounts are from the adjustments columns of a work sheet. Use this information to prepare adjusting journal entries dated December 31.

	Adjustments			
	Debit		Credit	
Prepaid insurance			(*a*)	2,475
Office supplies			(*b*)	360
Accumulated depreciation, office equipment			(*c*)	1,670
Accumulated depreciation, plant equipment			(*d*)	8,200
Office salaries expense	(*e*)	780		
Insurance expense, office equipment	(*a*)	625		
Insurance expense, plant equipment	(*a*)	1,850		
Office supplies expense	(*b*)	360		
Depreciation expense, office equipment	(*c*)	1,670		
Depreciation expense, plant equipment	(*d*)	8,200		
Salaries payable			(*e*)	780
Totals		13,485		13,485

Exercise 4–3
Using T-account information to prepare closing entries
(LO 2)

On a sheet of paper, copy the following T-accounts and their end-of-period balances. Below the accounts, prepare entries to close the accounts. Post to the T-accounts.

Rita Ivy, Capital

		Dec. 31	19,700

Rent Expense

Dec. 31	5,400		

Rita Ivy, Withdrawals

Dec. 31	22,500		

Salaries Expense

Dec. 31	4,200		

Income Summary

Supplies Expense

Dec. 31	9,775		

Fees Earned

		Dec. 31	38,100

Depreciation Expense, Equipment

Dec. 31	3,600		

Exercise 4–4
Using work sheet information to prepare closing entries
(LO 2)

The following items appeared in the Income Statement columns of a December 31 work sheet prepared for Alfred Dole, an accountant. Assume that Dole withdrew $32,000 from his accounting practice during the year and prepare entries to close the accounts.

	Income Statement	
	Debit	Credit
Accounting fees earned		71,000
Office salaries expense	18,000	
Rent expense	9,600	
Insurance expense	3,360	
Office supplies expense	580	
Depreciation expense, office equipment	2,300	
	33,840	71,000
Net income	37,160	
	71,000	71,000

Exercise 4–5
Preparing and posting closing entries for a corporation
(LO 2, 5)

Open the following T-accounts on notepaper for a corporation that does word processing for other companies. Below the T-accounts prepare entries to close the accounts. Post to the T-accounts.

Common Stock

		Dec. 31	50,000

Rent Expense

Dec. 31	7,800		

Retained Earnings

		Dec. 31	6,800

Salaries Expense

Dec. 31	33,280		

Income Summary

Insurance Expense

Dec. 31	1,500		

Services Revenue

		Dec. 31	62,400

Depreciation Expense, Equipment

Dec. 31	7,600		

Cash Dividends Declared

Nov. 15	8,750		

Exercise 4–6
Closing entries for a corporation
(LO 2)

A corporation debited Cash Dividends Declared for $50,000 during the year ended December 31. The items that follow appeared in the Income Statement columns of the work sheet prepared at year-end. Prepare closing journal entries for the corporation.

	Income Statement	
	Debit	Credit
Services revenue		285,700
Office salaries expense	187,000	
Rent expense	18,000	
Insurance expense	4,400	
Office supplies expense	400	
Depreciation expense, office equipment . .	5,100	
	214,900	285,700
Net income	70,800	
	285,700	285,700

Exercise 4–7
Recording corporate transactions in T-accounts
(LO 4, 5)

1. On a sheet of notepaper, open the following T-accounts: Cash, Accounts Receivable, Equipment, Notes Payable, Common Dividend Payable, Common Stock, Retained Earnings, Income Summary, Cash Dividends Declared, Services Revenue, and Operating Expenses.
2. Record directly in the T-accounts these transactions of a new corporation:
   a. Issued common stock for $150,000 cash.
   b. Purchased equipment for $146,500 cash.
   c. Sold and delivered $30,000 of services on credit.
   d. Collected $27,000 of accounts receivable.
   e. Paid $18,000 of operating expenses.
   f. Declared cash dividends of $7,500.
   g. Paid the dividends declared in *(f)*.

h. Purchased $12,000 of additional equipment, giving $5,000 in cash and a $7,000 promissory note.
i. Closed the revenue accounts, (*j*) the expense accounts, (*k*) Income Summary, and (*l*) Cash Dividends Declared.

3. Answer these questions:
   a. Does the corporation have retained earnings?
   b. Does it have any cash?
   c. If the corporation has retained earnings, why does it not also have cash?
   d. Can the corporation legally declare additional cash dividends?
   e. Can it pay additional cash dividends?
   f. What does the balance of the Notes Payable account tell the financial statement reader about the makeup of the corporation's assets?
   g. Explain what the balance of the Common Stock account represents.
   h. Explain what the balance of the Retained Earnings account represents.

Exercise 4–8
Preparing a work sheet
(LO 1)

Following is an alphabetical list of Ware Printing Company's accounts and their unadjusted balances. All are normal balances. To save you time, the balances are in one- and two-digit numbers.

Trial Balance Accounts and Balances

Accounts payable	$ 2	Rent expense	$ 7
Accounts receivable	5	Printing services revenue	24
Accumulated depreciation, printing equipment	12	Uby Ware, capital	30
Cash	4	Uby Ware, withdrawals	8
Notes payable	3	Printing equipment	30
Prepaid insurance	2	Printing supplies	6
		Wages expense	9

Required

1. Prepare a work sheet form and enter the trial balance accounts and amounts on the work sheet.
2. Complete the work sheet using the following information:
   a. Estimated depreciation of printing equipment, $4.
   b. Expired insurance, $1.
   c. Unused printing supplies per inventory, $3.
   d. Earned but unpaid wages, $1.

Exercise 4–9
Preparing a work sheet
(LO 1)

The unadjusted trial balance of Frame Factory, Inc., as of December 31, 1993 (the end of its annual accounting period) follows:

Cash	$ 15,500	
Prepaid insurance	1,400	
Framing supplies	24,300	
Framing equipment	28,000	
Accumulated depreciation, framing equipment		$ 6,500
Common stock		30,000
Retained earnings		7,000
Cash dividends declared	5,000	
Services revenue		82,900
Salaries expense	42,000	
Rent expense	10,200	
Totals	$126,400	$126,400

Required

1. Prepare a work sheet form on note paper and enter the trial balance.
2. Complete the work sheet using the information that follows:
   a. Expired insurance, $800.
   b. Unused framing supplies per inventory, $5,100.
   c. Estimated depreciation of framing equipment, $1,300.
   d. Earned but unpaid salaries, $500.

Exercise 4–10
Adjusting and closing entries
(LO 5)

Prepare adjusting and closing journal entries for the corporation of Exercise 4–9.

Exercise 4–11
The steps in the accounting cycle
(LO 6)

List the letters identifying the following steps in the accounting cycle in the order the steps are performed:

a. Preparing a post-closing trial balance.
b. Journalizing and posting adjusting entries.
c. Completing the work sheet.
d. Preparing an unadjusted trial balance.
e. Journalizing and posting closing entries.
f. Journalizing transactions.
g. Posting the entries to record transactions.
h. Preparing the financial statements.

[B]Exercise 4–12
Reversing entries
(LO 8)

On December 31, adjusting entry information for Laredo Company is as follows:

a. Depreciation on office equipment, $3,400.
b. Eight hundred dollars of the Prepaid Insurance balance has expired.
c. Employees have earned salaries of $1,700 that have not been paid.
d. The Unearned Service Fees account balance includes $2,100 that has been earned.
e. The company has earned $4,900 of service fees that have not been collected or recorded.

Required

List the letters that identify adjustments for which reversing entries should be made. Assuming the appropriate adjusting entries have been recorded, prepare the reversing entries.

[B]Exercise 4–13
Reversing entries
(LO 8)

The following information relates to Lomas Company on December 31, 1993, the end of its annual accounting period:

a. Lomas rents office space for $6,200 per month. The company failed to pay the rent for December until January 6, at which time it paid the rent for December and January.

b. Because Lomas does not use all of its office space, it subleases space to a tenant for $800 per month. The tenant failed to pay the December rent until January 8, at which time it paid the rent for December and January.

Required

1. Assuming that Lomas does not use reversing entries, prepare adjusting journal entries dated December 31. Also prepare entries to record Lomas's payment of rent in January and the receipt of rent in January from Lomas's tenant.
2. Assuming that Lomas uses reversing entries, prepare adjusting journal entries dated December 31 and reversing entries dated January 1. Also prepare entries to record Lomas's payment of rent in January and the receipt of rent in January from Lomas's tenant.

Problems

Problem 4–1
The work sheet; financial statements and closing entries
(LO 1, 2)

At the end of its annual accounting period, a trial balance from the ledger of Dunhill Employment Services appeared as follows:

DUNHILL EMPLOYMENT SERVICES
Unadjusted Trial Balance
December 31, 1993

Cash	$ 4,850	
Office supplies	1,100	
Prepaid insurance	2,120	
Office equipment	27,860	
Accumulated depreciation, office equipment		$11,630
Accounts payable		890
B. K. Dunhill, capital		16,380
B. K. Dunhill, withdrawals	22,500	
Employment fees earned		56,400
Wages expense	18,220	
Rent expense	7,500	
Utilities expense	1,150	
Totals	$85,300	$85,300

Required

1. Enter the trial balance on a work sheet form and complete the work sheet using the information that follows:
   a. Expired insurance, $1,410.
   b. An office supplies inventory showed $460 of supplies on hand.
   c. Estimated depreciation on office equipment, $2,800.
   d. Wages earned by the one employee but unpaid and unrecorded, $220.
2. Journalize the adjusting entries and the closing entries.
3. From the work sheet prepare an income statement, a statement of changes in owner's equity, and a classified balance sheet. Dunhill did not make additional investments in the business during 1993.

Problem 4–2
End-of-period accounting procedures
(LO 1, 2, 3)

The accounts of Mesa Surveying Company, showing balances as of the end of its annual accounting period, appear in the booklet of working papers that accompanies this text, and a trial balance of its ledger is reproduced on a work sheet form provided there. The trial balance has the items that follow:

MESA SURVEYING COMPANY
Unadjusted Trial Balance
December 31, 1993

Cash	$ 2,740	
Surveying supplies	1,930	
Prepaid insurance	3,500	
Surveying equipment	85,365	
Accumulated depreciation, surveying equipment		$ 35,460
Accounts payable		900
Long-term notes payable		12,000
Lisa Garza, capital		34,680
Lisa Garza, withdrawals	21,000	
Surveying fees earned		58,400
Wages expense	16,820	
Interest expense	720	
Rent expense	5,400	
Property taxes expense	2,470	
Repairs expense, equipment	535	
Utilities expense	960	
Totals	$141,440	$141,440

Required

1. Enter the unadjusted trial balance on a work sheet form and complete the work sheet using the information that follows:
   a. Surveying supplies inventory, $840.
   b. Expired insurance, $1,600.
   c. Estimated depreciation on surveying equipment, $6,300.
   d. The December electric bill for the office arrived in the mail after the trial balance was prepared. Its $85 amount was unrecorded.
   e. Wages earned but unpaid and unrecorded, $210.
   f. The lease contract on the office calls for total annual rent equal to 10% of the annual revenue, with $450 payable each month on the first day of the month. The $450 was paid each month and debited to the Rent Expense account.
   g. Personal property taxes on the surveying equipment amounting to $620 have accrued but are unrecorded and unpaid.
   h. The long-term note payable was signed on September 1, and interest on the debt is at a 12% annual rate or $120 per month. The note calls for payment in advance of $360 interest every three months. Payments are recorded in the Interest Expense account. Interest payments were made on September 1 and December 1. A $1,200 payment on the note principal is due next September 1.
2. Journalize and post the adjusting entries. (Omit posting if you are not using the working papers.)
3. Prepare an income statement, a statement of changes in owner's equity, and a classified balance sheet. Garza did not make additional investments in the business during 1993.
4. Journalize and post the closing entries and prepare a post-closing trial balance. (Omit this requirement if you are not using the working papers.)

Problem 4–3
End-of-period accounting procedures
(LO 1, 2, 3)

The unadjusted trial balance of Tower Window Cleaning is as follows:

TOWER WINDOW CLEANING
Unadjusted Trial Balance
December 31, 1993

Cash	$ 890	
Accounts receivable	1,400	
Cleaning supplies	470	
Prepaid insurance	2,100	
Prepaid rent	350	
Trucks	18,235	
Accumulated depreciation, trucks		$ 7,295
Cleaning equipment	4,930	
Accumulated depreciation, cleaning equipment		1,970
Accounts payable		985
Unearned cleaning services revenue		800
Marian Stone, capital		10,115
Marian Stone, withdrawals	15,000	
Cleaning services revenue		52,850
Office salaries expense	9,600	
Cleaning wages expense	15,840	
Rent expense	3,500	
Gas, oil, and repairs expense	1,220	
Telephone expense	480	
Totals	$74,015	$74,015

Required

1. Enter the unadjusted trial balance on a work sheet form and complete the work sheet using the information that follows:
   a. Insurance expired on the cleaning equipment, $130, and on the truck, $1,450.
   b. An inventory showed $265 of cleaning supplies on hand.
   c. Estimated depreciation on the cleaning equipment, $495.
   d. Estimated depreciation on the truck, $3,650.
   e. In December 1992, the company had prepaid the January 1993 rent for garage and office space occupied by the window cleaning service. This amount appears as the balance of the Prepaid Rent account. Rents for February through November were paid each month and debited to the Rent Expense account. As of the trial balance date, the December 1993 rent had not been paid.
   f. Three office buildings signed contracts with Tower, agreeing to pay a fixed fee for the cleaning services. Two of the office buildings made advance payments on their contracts, and the amounts received were credited to the Unearned Cleaning Services Revenue account. An examination of the contracts shows $600 of the $800 received was earned by the end of the accounting period. The third building's contract provides for a $250 monthly fee to be paid at the end of each month's service. It was signed on December 15, and one half of a month's revenue has accrued but is unrecorded.
   g. A $45 December telephone bill and a $190 bill for repairs to the truck used in the business arrived in the mail on December 31. Neither bill was paid or recorded before the trial balance was prepared.
   h. Office salaries, $145, and cleaning wages, $255, have accrued but are unpaid and unrecorded.

2. Journalize and post the adjusting entries. (Omit posting if you are not using the working papers.)
3. Prepare an income statement, a statement of changes in owner's equity, and a classified balance sheet. Stone did not make additional investments in the business during 1993.
4. Journalize and post the closing entries and prepare a post-closing trial balance. (Omit this requirement if you are not using the working papers.)

[B]Problem 4–4
Reversing entries
(LO 2, 8)

Melton Realty Company's unadjusted trial balance on December 31, 1993, (the end of its annual accounting period) is as follows:

MELTON REALTY COMPANY
Unadjusted Trial Balance
December 31, 1993

Cash	$ 12,450	
Notes receivable	63,000	
Office supplies	1,100	
Building	480,000	
Unearned commissions		$ 15,000
Notes payable		290,000
J. Melton, capital		150,820
J. Melton, withdrawals	180,000	
Commissions earned		288,000
Rent earned		57,600
Interest earned		6,930
Salaries expense	38,000	
Interest expense	26,100	
Insurance expense	7,700	
Totals	$808,350	$808,350

Information necessary to prepare adjusting entries is as follows:

a. Employees, who are paid $3,270 every two weeks, have earned $1,960 since the last payment. The next payment of $3,270 will be on January 4.

b. Melton rents office space to several tenants one of whom has paid only $500 of the $1,000 rent for December. On January 10, the tenant will pay the remainder along with the rent for January.

c. An inventory of office supplies discloses $550 of supplies on hand.

d. Premiums for medical insurance for employees are paid monthly. The $700 premium for December will be paid January 12.

e. Melton owes $290,000 on a note payable that requires quarterly payments of accrued interest. The quarterly payments of $8,700 each are made on the 15th of January, April, July, and October.

f. An analysis of Melton's sales contracts with customers shows that $5,200 of the amount customers have prepaid remains unearned.

g. Melton has a $63,000 note receivable on which interest of $315 has accrued. On January 15, the note and the total accrued interest of $630 will be repaid to Melton.

h. Melton has earned but not yet recorded revenue of $9,000 for commissions from a customer who will pay for the work on January 25. At that time, the customer will also pay $1,800 for sales services Melton will perform in early January.

Required

1. Prepare adjusting journal entries.
2. Prepare closing journal entries.
3. Prepare reversing entries.
4. Prepare journal entries to record the January 1994 cash receipts and cash payments identified in the preceding information.

Problem 4–5
Closing entries for partnerships and corporations
(LO 2, 4, 5)

Carol Boyce, Sarah Reed, and John Hudson started a business on January 7, 1992, and each invested $75,000 in the business. During 1992, the business lost $30,240; and during 1993, it earned $83,550. On January 5, 1994, the three owners agreed to pay out to themselves $36,000 of the accumulated earnings of the business. On January 9, 1994, the $36,000 was paid out.

Required

1. Assume that the business is a partnership and the partners share net incomes and net losses equally. Give the entries to record the investments and to close the Income Summary account at the end of 1992 and again at the end of 1993. Also assume that the partners shared equally in the $36,000 of earnings paid out. Give the entry to record the withdrawals.
2. Assume that the business is organized as a corporation and that each owner invested $75,000 in it by buying 7,500 shares of its $10 par value common stock. Give the entry to record the investments. Also, give the entries to close the Income Summary account at the end of 1992 and again at the end of 1993 and to record the declaration and payment of the $1.60 per share dividend. (Ignore corporate income taxes and assume that the three owners are the corporation's board of directors.)

Problem 4–6
All steps in the accounting cycle (covers two accounting cycles)
(LO 1, 2, 3, 4, 6)

Ted Dey opened a financial consulting business called Dey Financial Services. During June, he completed these transactions:

June	3	Invested in the business $70,000 in cash and an automobile having an $18,000 fair value.
	3	Rented furnished office space and paid one month's rent, $1,250.
	4	Purchased office supplies for cash, $680.
	8	Paid the premium on a one-year insurance policy, $1,080.
	14	Paid the salary of the office secretary for two weeks, $750.
	16	Provided consulting services and collected a $2,700 fee.
	28	Paid the salary of the office secretary for two weeks, $750.
	30	Paid the June telephone bill, $320.
	30	Paid for gas and oil used in the automobile during June, $90.

Required Work for June

1. Open these accounts: Cash; Office Supplies; Prepaid Insurance; Automobiles; Accumulated Depreciation, Automobiles; Salaries Payable; Ted Dey, Capital; Ted Dey, Withdrawals; Consulting Fees Earned; De-

preciation Expense, Automobiles; Salaries Expense; Insurance Expense; Rent Expense; Office Supplies Expense; Gas, Oil, and Repairs Expense; Telephone Expense; and Income Summary.

2. Prepare and post journal entries to record the transactions.
3. Prepare an unadjusted trial balance on a work sheet form and complete the work sheet using the following information:
   a. Two thirds of a month's insurance has expired.
   b. An inventory shows $640 of office supplies remaining.
   c. Estimated depreciation on the automobile, $375.
   d. Earned but unpaid salary of the office secretary, $150.
4. Journalize and post the adjusting entries.
5. Prepare an income statement and a statement of changes in owner's equity for June, and prepare a June 30 classified balance sheet.
6. Journalize and post the closing entries.
7. Prepare a post-closing trial balance.

During July, Ted Dey completed these transactions:

July	1	Paid the July rent on the office space, $1,250.
	3	Purchased additional office supplies for cash, $35.
	11	Paid the salary of the office secretary for two weeks, $750.
	15	Withdrew $2,000 cash from the business for personal use.
	18	Provided consultation and collected a $4,200 fee.
	25	Paid the salary of the office secretary for two weeks, $750.
	31	Paid for gas and oil used in the automobile during July, $70.
	31	Paid the July telephone bill, $190.

Required Work for July

1. Prepare and post journal entries to record the transactions.
2. Prepare an unadjusted trial balance on a work sheet form and complete the work sheet using the following information:
   a. One month's insurance has expired.
   b. An office supplies inventory shows $580 of supplies on hand.
   c. Estimated depreciation on the automobile, $375.
   d. Earned but unpaid secretary's salary, $300.
3. Journalize and post the adjusting entries.
4. Prepare an income statement and a statement of changes in owner's equity for July and prepare a July 31 classified balance sheet.
5. Journalize and post the closing entries.
6. Prepare a post-closing trial balance.

Problem 4–7
Analytical essay
(LO 1)

Refer to the information presented in Problem 4–2 and describe the incorrect amounts that would appear on the work sheet as a result of each of the following assumptions:

1. In adjusting the surveying supplies inventory, $840 was debited to Surveying Supplies Expense and credited to Surveying Supplies.

2. In making the adjustment for the accrual of personal property taxes, $620 was debited to Surveying Equipment and credited to Estimated Property Taxes Payable.
3. In extending the combined unadjusted trial balance amounts and the adjustment amounts, the Cash balance was extended to the Credit column of the adjusted trial balance.
4. In extending the adjusted trial balance amounts to the financial statement columns, the Prepaid Insurance was extended to the Income Statement Debit column.

[B]Problem 4–8
Analytical essay
(LO 8)

In preparing adjusting entries on December 31, 1993, Castillo Company and Barnum Company each recorded a $5,000 accrual of wages payable and a $2,400 accrual of interest earned. The next date on which both companies pay wages is January 4, at which time both will pay wages of $14,000. The accrued interest will be received in cash on February 24, as part of a total receipt of $3,700.

Describe the differences in the entries Castillo Company and Barnum Company will make when the wages are paid and when the interest is received if Barnum follows a practice of making reversing entries and Castillo Company does not make reversing entries. Explain why these differences exist and also describe any differences in the two companies' financial statements that result from the differences in the procedures used by the two companies.

Alternate Problems

Problem 4–1A
The work sheet; financial statements and closing entries
(LO 1, 2)

A trial balance of the ledger of Bass Fisherman's Guided Tours at the end of its annual accounting period appeared as follows:

BASS FISHERMAN'S GUIDED TOURS
Unadjusted Trial Balance
December 31, 1993

Cash	$ 3,680	
Accounts receivable	1,700	
Fishing supplies	2,100	
Prepaid insurance	4,920	
Prepaid rent	1,200	
Boats	82,900	
Accumulated depreciation, boats		$ 24,870
Fishing equipment	24,400	
Accumulated depreciation, fishing equipment		7,320
Accounts payable		2,550
Unearned tour fees		3,500
Bill Mayes, capital		62,210
Bill Mayes, withdrawals	27,000	
Tour fees earned		68,800
Wages expense	11,400	
Rent expense	5,400	
Gas, oil, and repairs expense	4,550	
Totals	$169,250	$169,250

Required

1. Enter the trial balance on a work sheet form and complete the work sheet using the information that follows:
   a. Expired insurance, $3,640.
   b. An inventory of fishing supplies showed $1,100 of supplies on hand.
   c. The fishing guide service rents equipment storage and garage space. At the beginning of the year, two months' rent was prepaid as shown by the debit balance of the Prepaid Rent account. Rents for March through November were paid on the first day of each month and debited to the Rent Expense account. The December 1993 rent was unpaid on the trial balance date.
   d. Estimated depreciation on the fishing equipment, $2,440.
   e. Estimated depreciation on the boats, $13,800.
   f. On November 15, Bass Fisherman's Guided Tours contracted and began guided tours for the Galvan Resort for $1,750 per month. The resort company paid for two months' service in advance, and the amount paid was credited to the Unearned Tour Fees account. Bass also entered into a contract and conducted tours for Traveler's International on December 15. By the month's end, a half month's revenue, $500, had been earned on this contract but was unrecorded.
   g. Employee's wages amounting to $175 had accrued but were unrecorded on the trial balance date.
2. Journalize the adjusting entries and the closing entries.
3. Prepare an income statement, a statement of changes in owner's equity, and a classified balance sheet for the business. Mayes did not make additional investments in the business during 1993.

Problem 4–2A
End-of-period accounting procedures
(LO 1, 2, 3)

The accounts of Mesa Surveying Company, showing balances as of the end of its annual accounting period, appear in the booklet of working papers that accompanies this text, and a trial balance of its ledger is reproduced on a work sheet form provided there. The trial balance has the items that follow:

MESA SURVEYING COMPANY
Unadjusted Trial Balance
December 31, 1993

Cash	$ 2,740	
Surveying supplies	1,930	
Prepaid insurance	3,500	
Surveying equipment	85,365	
Accumulated depreciation, surveying equipment		$ 35,460
Accounts payable		900
Long-term notes payable		12,000
Lisa Garza, capital		34,680
Lisa Garza, withdrawals	21,000	
Surveying fees earned		58,400
Wages expense	16,820	
Interest expense	720	
Rent expense	5,400	
Property taxes expense	2,470	
Repairs expense, equipment	535	
Utilities expense	960	
Totals	$141,440	$141,440

Required

1. Enter the unadjusted trial balance on a work sheet form and complete the work sheet using the information that follows:
   a. Surveying supplies inventory, $630.
   b. Expired insurance, $2,400.
   c. Estimated depreciation on surveying equipment, $7,100.
   d. The December electric bill for the office arrived in the mail after the trial balance was prepared. Its $140 amount was unrecorded.
   e. Wages earned but unpaid and unrecorded, $330.
   f. The lease contract on the office calls for total annual rent equal to 10% of the annual revenue, with $450 payable each month on the first day of the month. The $450 was paid each month and debited to the Rent Expense account.
   g. Personal property taxes on the surveying equipment amounting to $460 have accrued but are unrecorded and unpaid.
   h. The long-term note payable was signed on September 1, and interest on the debt is at a 12% annual rate or $120 per month. The note calls for payment in advance of $360 interest every three months. Payments are recorded in the Interest Expense account. Interest payments were made on September 1 and December 1. A $3,000 payment on the note principal is due next September 1.
2. Journalize and post adjusting entries. (Omit the posting if you are not using the working papers.)
3. Prepare an income statement, a statement of changes in owner's equity, and a classified balance sheet. Garza did not make additional investments in the business during 1993.
4. Journalize and post closing entries and prepare a post-closing trial balance. (Omit this requirement if you are not using the working papers.)

Problem 4–3A
End-of-period accounting procedures
(LO 1, 2, 3)

The unadjusted trial balance of Tower Window Cleaning is as follows:

TOWER WINDOW CLEANING
Unadjusted Trial Balance
December 31, 1993

Cash	$ 890	
Accounts receivable	1,400	
Cleaning supplies	470	
Prepaid insurance	2,100	
Prepaid rent	350	
Trucks	18,235	
Accumulated depreciation, trucks		$ 7,295
Cleaning equipment	4,930	
Accumulated depreciation, cleaning equipment		1,970
Accounts payable		985
Unearned cleaning services revenue		800
Marian Stone, capital		10,115
Marian Stone, withdrawals	15,000	
Cleaning services revenue		52,850
Office salaries expense	9,600	
Cleaning wages expense	15,840	
Rent expense	3,500	
Gas, oil, and repairs expense	1,220	
Telephone expense	480	
Totals	$74,015	$74,015

Required

1. Enter the unadjusted trial balance on a work sheet form and complete the work sheet using the information that follows:
   a. Insurance expired on the cleaning equipment, $150, and on the truck, $1,200.
   b. An inventory showed $160 of cleaning supplies on hand.
   c. Estimated depreciation on the cleaning equipment, $1,020.
   d. Estimated depreciation on the truck, $2,850.
   e. In December 1992, the company had prepaid the January 1993 rent for garage and office space occupied by the window cleaning service. This amount appears as the balance of the Prepaid Rent account. Rents for February through November were paid each month and debited to the Rent Expense account. As of the trial balance date, the December 1993 rent had not been paid.
   f. Three office buildings signed contracts with Tower, agreeing to pay a fixed fee for the cleaning services. Two of the office buildings made advance payments on their contracts, and the amounts received were credited to the Unearned Cleaning Services Revenue account. An examination of the contracts shows $400 of the $800 received was earned by the end of the accounting period. The third building's contract provides for a $400 monthly fee to be paid at the end of each month's service. It was signed on December 15, and one half of a month's revenue has accrued but is unrecorded.
   g. A $50 December telephone bill and a $320 bill for repairs to the truck used in the business arrived in the mail on December 31. Neither bill was paid or recorded before the trial balance was prepared.
   h. Office salaries, $200, and cleaning wages, $280, have accrued but are unpaid and unrecorded.
2. Journalize and post adjusting entries. (Omit posting if you are not using the working papers.)
3. Prepare an income statement, a statement of changes in owner's equity, and a classified balance sheet. Stone did not make additional investments in the business during 1993.
4. Journalize and post closing entries and prepare a post-closing trial balance. (Omit this requirement if you are not using the working papers.)

[B]**Problem 4–4A**
Reversing entries
(LO 2, 8)

Ogletree Design Associates' unadjusted trial balance on December 31, 1993 (the end of its annual accounting period), is as follows:

OGLETREE DESIGN ASSOCIATES
Unadjusted Trial Balance
December 31, 1993

Cash	$ 14,120	
Notes receivable	17,500	
Office supplies	1,700	
Building	290,000	
Land	375,000	
Unearned design fees		$ 7,800
Notes payable		471,100
M. Ogletree, capital		67,950
M. Ogletree, withdrawals	120,000	
Design fees earned		367,400
Rent earned		17,250
Interest earned		1,500
Salaries expense	77,600	
Interest expense	31,800	
Insurance expense	5,280	
Totals	$933,000	$933,000

Information necessary to prepare adjusting entries is as follows:

a. Employees, who are paid $3,040 every two weeks, have earned $1,440 since the last payment. The next payment of $3,040 will be on January 6.

b. Ogletree rents office space to a tenant who has paid only $750 of the $1,500 rent for December. On January 10, the tenant will pay the remainder along with the rent for January.

c. An inventory of supplies discloses $650 of supplies on hand.

d. Premiums for employees' medical insurance are paid monthly. The $480 premium for December will be paid January 12.

e. Ogletree owes $471,100 on a note payable that requires quarterly payments of accrued interest. The quarterly payments of $10,600 each are made on the 15th of January, April, July, and October.

f. An analysis of Ogletree's service contracts with customers shows that $4,300 of the amount customers have prepaid remains unearned.

g. Ogletree has a $17,500 note receivable on which interest of $50 has accrued. On January 22, the note and the total accrued interest of $125 will be repaid to Ogletree.

h. Ogletree has earned but unrecorded fees of $20,000 for design work provided to a customer who will pay for the work on January 24. At that time, the customer will also pay $3,500 for design work Ogletree will perform in early January.

Required

1. Prepare adjusting journal entries.
2. Prepare closing journal entries.
3. Prepare reversing entries.
4. Prepare journal entries to record the January 1994 cash receipts and cash payments identified in the preceding information.

Problem 4–5A
Closing entries for partnerships and corporations
(LO 2, 4, 5)

On January 7, 1992, John Aspen, Sarah Khan, and Paul Glen started a business in which John Aspen invested $10,000, Sarah Khan invested $20,000, and Paul Glen invested $40,000. During 1992, the business lost $7,000; and during 1993, it earned $24,500. On January 5, 1994, the three business owners agreed to pay out to themselves $14,000 of the accumulated earnings of the business; and on January 10, the $14,000 was paid out.

Required

1. Assume that the business is a partnership and that the partners share net incomes and net losses in proportion to their investments. Give the entries to record the investments and to close the Income Summary account at the end of 1992 and again at the end of 1993. Also assume that the partners paid out the accumulated earnings in proportion to their investments. Give the entry to record the withdrawals.
2. Assume that the business is organized as a corporation and that the owners invested in the corporation by buying its $5 par value common stock, with John Aspen buying 2,000 shares, Sarah Khan buying 4,000 shares, and Paul Glen buying 8,000 shares. Give the entry to record the investments. Also, give the entries to close the Income Summary account at the end of 1992 and again at the end of 1993. Then give the entries to record the declaration and payment of the $1 per share dividend. (Ignore corporation income taxes and assume the investors are the corporation's board of directors.)

Problem 4–6A
All steps in the accounting cycle (covers two accounting cycles)
(LO 1, 2, 3, 4, 6)

Ted Dey opened a financial consulting business called Dey Financial Services. During June, he completed these transactions:

June	3	Invested in the business $40,000 in cash and an automobile having a $16,000 fair value.
	3	Rented furnished office space and paid one month's rent, $900.
	4	Purchased office supplies for cash, $750.
	7	Provided consulting services and collected a $3,200 fee.
	14	Paid the premium on a one-year insurance policy, $840.
	14	Paid the salary of the office secretary for two weeks, $700.
	16	Provided consulting services and collected a $1,800 fee.
	28	Paid the salary of the office secretary for two weeks, $700.
	30	Paid the June telephone bill, $240.
	30	Paid for gas and oil used in the business car during June, $80.

Required Work for June

1. Open these accounts: Cash; Office Supplies; Prepaid Insurance; Automobiles; Accumulated Depreciation, Automobiles; Salaries Payable; Ted Dey, Capital; Ted Dey, Withdrawals; Consulting Fees Earned; Depreciation Expense, Automobiles; Salaries Expense; Insurance Expense; Rent Expense; Office Supplies Expense; Gas, Oil, and Repairs Expense; Telephone Expense; and Income Summary.
2. Prepare and post journal entries to record the transactions.

3. Prepare an unadjusted trial balance on a work sheet form and complete the work sheet using the following information:
   a. One half of a month's insurance has expired.
   b. An inventory shows $670 of office supplies remaining.
   c. Estimated depreciation on the automobile, $200.
   d. Earned but unpaid salary of the office secretary, $70.
4. Journalize and post the adjusting entries.
5. Prepare an income statement and a statement of changes in owner's equity for June, and prepare a June 30 classified balance sheet.
6. Journalize and post the closing entries.
7. Prepare a post-closing trial balance.

During July, Ted Dey completed these transactions:

July	1	Paid the July rent on the office space, $900.
	3	Purchased additional office supplies for cash, $30.
	12	Paid the salary of the office secretary for two weeks, $700.
	15	Ted Dey withdrew $2,000 cash from the business for personal use.
	18	Provided consultation and collected a $2,400 fee.
	26	Paid the salary of the office secretary for two weeks, $700.
	31	Paid for gas and oil used in the business car during July, $100.
	31	Paid the July telephone bill, $170.

Required Work for July

1. Prepare and post journal entries to record the transactions.
2. Prepare an unadjusted trial balance on a work sheet form and complete the work sheet using the following information:
   a. One month's insurance has expired.
   b. An office supplies inventory shows $610 of supplies on hand.
   c. Estimated depreciation on the automobile, $200.
   d. Earned but unpaid secretary's salary, $210.
3. Journalize and post the adjusting entries.
4. Prepare an income statement and a statement of changes in owner's equity for July and prepare a July 31 classified balance sheet.
5. Journalize and post the closing entries.
6. Prepare a post-closing trial balance.

Problem 4–7A
Analytical essay
(LO 1)

Refer to the information in Problem 4–2A and describe the incorrect amounts that would appear on the work sheet as a result of each of the following assumptions:

1. In adjusting the Prepaid Insurance account, $1,100 was debited to Insurance Expense and credited to Prepaid Insurance.
2. In making the adjustment for rent expense, $440 was debited to Rent Expense and credited to Surveying Fees Earned.
3. On the work sheet, the company failed to record the adjustment for personal property taxes on the surveying equipment.

4. In extending the adjusted trial balance amounts to the financial statement columns, the Utilities Expense balance was extended to the Statement of Changes in Owner's Equity or Balance Sheet Debit column.

[B]Problem 4–8A
Analytical essay
(LO 8)

In preparing adjusting entries on December 31, 1993, Craven Company and Luong Company each recorded an $8,500 accrual of interest payable and a $4,600 accrual of consulting services revenue. The next date on which both companies pay interest is March 1, at which time both will pay interest of $27,000. The accrued consulting services revenue will be received in cash on January 30, as part of a total receipt of $52,600.

Describe the differences in the entries Craven Company and Luong Company will make when the interest is paid and when the consulting services revenue is received if Luong follows a practice of making reversing entries and Craven Company does not make reversing entries. Explain why these differences exist and also describe any differences in the two companies' financial statements that will result from the differences in the procedures used by the two companies.

Serial Problem

Precision Computer Services

(This problem should not be assigned unless the Working Papers are being used. This is the third segment of a serial problem that started in Chapter 2, was continued in Chapter 3, and will be continued in Chapter 5. If you did not complete the solutions in Chapters 2 and 3, you can begin the problem at this point. However, you may need to review some of the facts presented in the Chapter 2 and Chapter 3 segments of the problem on pages 122 and 183.)

After being in business for the last three months of 1993, John Conard, the owner of Precision Computer Services, is preparing to begin the new year. In fulfilling the requirements of the problem in Chapters 2 and 3, all transactions that occurred during October, November, and December 1993 have been journalized and posted, as have been the December 31 adjusting entries. Also, financial statements for the three-month period ended December 31 have been prepared.

In anticipation of closing the books, an Income Summary account (Acct. No. 901) has been added to the General Ledger. To complete the accounting cycle, you should journalize and post the closing entries. Also, prepare a post-closing trial balance.

Provocative Problems

Provocative Problem 4–1
Galaxy Cleaners
(Review problem)

During his second year in college, Daniel Rusk inherited Galaxy Cleaners when his father died. He immediately dropped out of school and took over management of the business. At the time he took over, Rusk recognized he knew little about accounting. However, he reasoned that since the business performed its services strictly for cash, if the cash of the business increased, the business was doing all right. Therefore, he was pleased as he watched the cash balance grow from $3,700 when he took over to $24,780 at year-end. Furthermore, since he had withdrawn $25,000 from the business to buy a new car and to pay personal expenses, he reasoned that the business must have earned $46,080 during the year. He arrived at the $46,080 by adding the $21,080 increase in cash to the $25,000 he had withdrawn from the business. Daniel was shocked when he received the following income statement and learned that the business had earned only slightly more than the amount withdrawn.

GALAXY CLEANERS
Income Statement
For Year Ended December 31, 1993

Cleaning services revenue		$73,750
Operating expenses:		
Depreciation expense, building	$ 5,750	
Depreciation expense, trucks	6,000	
Depreciation expense, cleaning equipment	7,400	
Wages expense	12,100	
Insurance expense	1,310	
Cleaning supplies expense	6,040	
Gas, oil, and repairs expense	1,745	
Property taxes expense	4,235	
Utilities expense	2,760	
Total operating expenses		47,340
Net income		$26,410

After thinking about the statement for several days, Rusk asked you to explain how, in a year in which the cash increased $21,080 and he withdrew $25,000, the business earned only $26,410. In examining the accounts of the business, you note that accrued wages payable at the beginning of the year were $235 but increased to $475 at year's end. Also, the accrued property taxes payable were $860 at the beginning of the year but had increased to $950 at year-end. Also, the balance of the Prepaid Insurance account was $180 more and the balance of the Cleaning Supplies account was $370 less at the end of the year than at the beginning. However, except for the changes in these accounts, the change in cash, and the changes in the balances of the accumulated depreciation accounts, there were no other changes in the balances of the concern's asset and liability accounts between the beginning of the year and the end. Back your explanation with a calculation that accounts for the increase in the business's cash.

Provocative Problem 4–2
Louise O'Connor, Attorney
(LO 2)

During the first year-end closing of the accounts of Louise O'Connor's law practice, the office bookkeeper became seriously ill and entered the hospital, unable to have visitors. O'Connor is certain the bookkeeper prepared a work sheet and complete financial statements, but she has only the income statement and cannot find the work sheet or remaining statements. She does have the unadjusted trial balance. She has asked you to take the information she has and prepare adjusting and closing entries. She also wants you to prepare a statement of changes in owner's equity and a classified balance sheet. She says the $5,000 of unearned legal fees on the trial balance represents a retainer fee paid by First City Bank. The bank retained Louise O'Connor on November 1 to do its legal work, and agreed to pay her $1,250 per month for her services. She says she has also agreed with Goodwin Realty to do its legal work on a fixed-fee basis. The agreement calls for a $750 monthly fee payable at the end of each three months. The agreement was signed on December 1, and one month's fee has accrued but has not been recorded. O'Connor did not make any additional investments in the business during the year.

LOUISE O'CONNOR, ATTORNEY
Unadjusted Trial Balance
December 31, 1993

Cash	$ 8,320	
Legal fees receivable	3,500	
Office supplies	300	
Prepaid insurance	4,450	
Office equipment	27,900	
Accounts payable		$ 1,810
Unearned legal fees		5,000
Short-term notes payable		6,000
Louise O'Connor, capital		19,220
Louise O'Connor, withdrawals	38,000	
Legal fees earned		83,400
Salaries expense	22,400	
Rent expense	9,000	
Telephone expense	1,560	
Totals	$115,430	$115,430

LOUISE O'CONNOR, ATTORNEY
Income Statement
For Year Ended December 31, 1993

Revenue:		
Legal fees earned		$86,650
Operating expenses:		
Depreciation expense, office equipment	$ 2,790	
Salaries expense	22,560	
Interest expense	720	
Insurance expense	3,900	
Rent expense	9,000	
Office supplies expense	200	
Telephone expense	1,560	
Total operating expenses		40,730
Net income		$45,920

Provocative Problem 4–3
Mark Mitchell Graphic Design
(LO 1)

The balance sheet that follows was prepared for Mark Mitchell Graphic Design at the end of its annual accounting period:

MARK MITCHELL GRAPHIC DESIGN
Balance Sheet
December 31, 1993

Assets

Current assets:			
Cash		$ 4,845	
Office supplies		530	
Prepaid insurance		670	
Total current assets			$ 6,045
Plant and equipment:			
Automobiles	$24,500		
Less accumulated depreciation	14,700	$ 9,800	
Office equipment	$52,700		
Less accumulated depreciation	29,860	22,840	
Total plant and equipment			32,640
Total assets			$38,685

Liabilities

Current liabilities:		
Accounts payable	$1,090	
Salaries payable	335	
Unearned illustration fees	500	
Total liabilities		$1,925

Owner's Equity

Mark Mitchell, capital, December 31, 1993 . .		36,760
Total liabilities and owner's equity		$38,685

After completing the balance sheet, Mark Mitchell Graphic Design's accountant prepared and posted the following adjusting and closing entries for the concern:

Dec.	31	Insurance Expense	1,100.00	
		Prepaid Insurance		1,100.00
	31	Office Supplies Expense	740.00	
		Office Supplies		740.00
	31	Depreciation Expense, Office Equipment	5,400.00	
		Accumulated Depreciation, Office Equipment		5,400.00
	31	Depreciation Expense, Automobiles	5,880.00	
		Accumulated Depreciation, Automobiles		5,880.00
	31	Unearned Illustration Fees	1,000.00	
		Illustration Fees Earned		1,000.00
	31	Salaries Expense	335.00	
		Salaries Payable		335.00
	31	Graphic Design Fees Earned	58,850.00	
		Illustration Fees Earned	7,200.00	
		Income Summary		66,050.00
	31	Income Summary	37,720.00	
		Depreciation Expense, Automobiles		5,880.00
		Depreciation Expense, Office Equipment		5,400.00
		Salaries Expense		15,000.00
		Insurance Expense		1,100.00
		Rent Expense		7,500.00
		Office Supplies Expense		740.00
		Gas, Oil, and Repairs Expense		1,270.00
		Telephone Expense		830.00
	31	Income Summary	28,330.00	
		Mark Mitchell, Capital		28,330.00
	31	Mark Mitchell, Capital	24,000.00	
		Mark Mitchell, Withdrawals		24,000.00

Enter the relevant information from the balance sheet and the adjusting and closing entries on a work sheet form and complete the work sheet by working backward to the items that appeared in its Unadjusted Trial Balance columns.

Provocative Problem 4–4
International Business Machines Corporation
(LO 3)

IBM's December 31, 1990, consolidated statement of financial position is presented in Appendix J. Assuming that a ledger account exists for each item in that statement, prepare a December 31, 1990, post-closing trial balance for IBM. (Express amounts in millions of dollars.)

IBM

Comprehensive Problem

Paramount Moving and Storage
(Review of Chapters 1–4)

Following is the November 30, 1993, unadjusted trial balance of Paramount Moving and Storage, which is owned by George Sanders. The temporary account balances represent the results of entries recorded during the first 11 months of 1993; the balance in George Sanders's capital account has not changed since December 31, 1992.

PARAMOUNT MOVING AND STORAGE
Unadjusted Trial Balance
November 30, 1993

	Acct. No.	Debits	Credits
Cash	101	$ 51,610	
Office supplies	124	450	
Moving supplies	126	8,700	
Prepaid insurance	128	7,475	
Trucks	153	350,000	
Accumulated depreciation, trucks	154		$200,000
Building	173	185,000	
Accumulated depreciation, building	174		29,120
Accounts payable	201		2,350
Interest payable	203		–0–
Wages payable	210		–0–
Unearned storage fees	233		700
Long-term notes payable	251		245,000
George Sanders, capital	301		42,205
George Sanders, withdrawals	302	26,500	
Moving fees earned	401		179,600
Storage fees earned	402		26,750
Depreciation expense, building	606	–0–	
Depreciation expense, trucks	611	–0–	
Wages expense	623	41,700	
Interest expense	633	–0–	
Insurance expense	637	–0–	
Office supplies expense	650	–0–	
Moving supplies expense	652	–0–	
Advertising expense	655	5,900	
Gas, oil, and repairs expense	669	31,510	
General and administrative expenses	672	16,880	
Income summary	901		–0–
		$725,725	$725,725

The following transactions occurred during the month of December 1993:

Dec. 2 Received $180 as advance payments on storage rental.
5 Paid accounts payable of $720.
6 Paid insurance premiums of $8,100 in advance.
7 Deposited $8,700 of moving fee receipts.
10 Purchased $1,560 of moving supplies on credit.
12 Acquired additional truck worth $56,000 by paying $6,000 cash and giving a long-term note payable for the balance.
14 Paid wages of $2,700 for the period December 1–14.
17 Purchased $130 of office supplies on credit.

Dec. 21 Deposited $6,260 from moving fee receipts and $1,600 from storage fee receipts.

24 Paid $860 for repairs to truck for damages sustained in an accident.

28 Paid wages of $2,850 for the period December 15–28.

30 Paid $900 to a magazine for advertisements that appeared in December.

31 Deposited $4,700 from moving fee receipts and $800 from storage fee receipts.

Required

1. Set up accounts for the items listed in the November 30 trial balance and enter the November 30 balances in them.
2. Prepare and post journal entries to record the December transactions previously listed.
3. Prepare a 10-column work sheet and enter the December 31 unadjusted balances from the accounts. Also enter adjusting entries for the following items, and complete the work sheet:
   a. Unpaid wages were $610 as of December 31.
   b. The December 31 office supplies inventory was $180.
   c. The moving supplies inventory was $4,530 on December 31.
   d. The unexpired portion of the prepaid insurance was $9,475 as of December 31.
   e. Depreciation for the year on the trucks was $50,350.
   f. Depreciation for the year on the building was $7,400.
   g. Unearned storage fees balance at December 31 was $650.
   h. Sanders had withdrawn $1,600 cash on December 30, but he had not taken the time to record it.
   i. Interest expense on the notes payable for 1993 was $24,700.
4. Journalize and post the adjusting entries.
5. Prepare an income statement and a statement of changes in owner's equity for the year ended December 31, 1993, and a December 31, 1993, classified balance sheet.
6. Journalize and post the closing entries.
7. Prepare a post-closing trial balance.

Answers to Objective Review Questions

LO 1. (*c*)
LO 2. (*d*)
LO 3. (*e*)
LO 4. (*a*)
LO 5. (*b*)
LO 6. (*d*)
LO 7. (*c*)
LO 8. (*d*)

CHAPTER

5

Accounting for a Merchandising Concern

Whether they deal in roller blades or razor blades, many companies earn profits by buying merchandise and selling it to customers. Accounting helps managers determine the amount of income earned by these companies and the cost of the inventory they have on hand.

Topical Coverage

In previous chapters, we used illustrations of businesses that provided services to their customers, such as law firms, accounting firms, and real estate agencies. In this chapter, we shift our attention to merchandising businesses. These entities buy goods or products and then resell them to their customers. Your study of this chapter will focus on the problem of accounting for the goods that merchandising companies purchase for resale. You will learn to identify the elements of cost of goods sold and to complete the end-of-period accounting procedures used by merchandising companies, whether they are organized as corporations or proprietorships.

Learning Objectives

After studying Chapter 5, you should be able to:

1. Analyze and record transactions that involve the purchase and resale of merchandise.
2. Explain the nature of each item entering into the calculation of cost of goods sold and gross profit from sales.
3. Prepare a work sheet and the financial statements for a merchandising business that uses a periodic inventory system and that is organized as a corporation or as a single proprietorship.
4. Prepare adjusting and closing entries for a merchandising business organized as either a corporation or a single proprietorship.
5. Define or explain the words and phrases listed in the chapter glossary.

After studying Appendix C at the end of Chapter 5, you should be able to:

6. Explain the adjusting entry approach to accounting for inventories and prepare a work sheet, adjusting entries, and closing entries according to the adjusting entry approach.

The previous chapters have described the accounting records and financial statements of Jerry Dow, Attorney, which is a service enterprise. Other examples of service enterprises are laundries, taxi companies, airlines, financial planners, hair salons, theaters, and golf courses. Each provides a service to its customers for a commission, fare, or fee, and its net income is the difference between the revenues earned and the operating expenses incurred.

On the other hand, a merchandising company, whether a wholesaler or a retailer, earns revenue by buying and selling goods called **merchandise.** In such a company, net income results when revenue from sales exceeds the cost of the goods sold and the operating expenses, as follows:

EASTSIDE HARDWARE STORE
Condensed Income Statement
For Month Ended July 31, 1993

Revenue from sales	$100,000
Less cost of goods sold	60,000
Gross profit from sales	$ 40,000
Less operating expenses	25,000
Net income	$ 15,000

This income statement shows that Eastside Hardware Store sold goods to customers for $100,000. Eastside acquired the goods that were sold at a cost of $60,000. As a result, the company earned a $40,000 **gross profit,** which is the difference between the revenue and the cost of goods sold. Also, note that the company incurred operating expenses of $25,000 and achieved a $15,000 net income for the month.

The elements of this calculation are what make accounting for a merchandising company different from accounting for a service company. To account for a merchandising company, you must understand how to account for the two components of gross profit: revenue from sales and cost of goods sold.

Revenue from Sales

LO 1 Analyze and record transactions that involve the purchase and resale of merchandise.

Revenue from sales consists of the gross proceeds from merchandise sales less returns, allowances, and discounts. It may be reported on an income statement as follows:

IOWA SALES, INCORPORATED
Income Statement
For Year Ended December 31, 1993

Revenue from sales:		
Gross sales		$306,200
Less: Sales returns and allowances	$1,900	
Sales discounts	4,300	6,200
Net sales		$300,000

Gross Sales

On this partial income statement, the gross sales item is the total cash and credit sales made by the company during the year. Cash sales were rung up on the cash register as each sale was completed. At the end of each day, the register total showed the amount of that day's cash sales, which was recorded with an entry such as this:

Nov.	3	Cash	1,205.00	
		Sales		1,205.00
		To record the day's cash sales.		

Also, an entry such as the following was used to record credit sales:

Nov.	3	Accounts Receivable	45.00	
		Sales		45.00
		Sold merchandise on credit.		

Sales Returns and Allowances

Most stores allow customers to return any unsatisfactory merchandise that they bought. Sometimes, customers are allowed to keep the unsatisfactory goods and are given an *allowance,* which is an amount off the sales price. Either way, returns and allowances involve dissatisfied customers. Therefore, management must know the amount of returns and allowances and their size in relation to sales. The Sales Returns and Allowances account supplies this information because each return or allowance is recorded as follows:

Nov.	4	Sales Returns and Allowances	20.00	
		Accounts Receivable (or Cash)		20.00
		Customer returned unsatisfactory merchandise.		

The Sales Returns and Allowances account is contra to the Sales account.

Sales Discounts

When goods are sold on credit, the terms of payment must be stated clearly to avoid any misunderstanding about the amount and time of the future payment or payments. These **credit terms** specify the amounts and timing of payments that a buyer agrees to make in return for being granted credit to purchase goods or services. The credit terms normally appear on the invoice or sales ticket and are part of the sales agreement. Exact terms usually depend on the custom of the trade. In some areas of business, it is customary for invoices to become due and payable 10 days after the end of the month **(EOM)** in which the sale occurred. These credit terms are stated on the sales invoices as "n/10 EOM." In other lines of business, invoices become due and payable 30 days after the invoice date. These invoices are said to carry terms of "n/30."

When credit periods are long, creditors often grant a **cash discount** for early payment. Early payments bring the cash into the selling company more quickly, and thus make it easier for the firm's managers to carry on their activities. When cash discounts for early payment are granted, they are made part of the credit terms and appear on the invoice as, for example, "Terms: 2/10, n/60." Terms of 2/10, n/60 mean that there is a 60-day **credit period,** which is the agreed period of time for which credit is granted. Although the payment is not due for 60 days, the debtor may deduct 2% from the invoice amount if payment is made within 10 days after the invoice date. The 10-day period is known as the **discount period.**

At the time of a sale, the merchandiser does not know if the customer will pay within the discount period and take advantage of a cash discount. As a result, a sales discount usually is not recorded until the customer pays. For example, on November 12, Iowa Sales, Incorporated, sold merchandise to a customer at a gross sales price of $100, subject to credit terms of 2/10, n/60. The sale was recorded as follows:

Nov.	12	Accounts Receivable	100.00	
		Sales		100.00
		Sold merchandise, terms 2/10, n/60.		

The customer has two alternative ways to satisfy this $100 obligation. One option is to pay $98 any time on or before November 22. Or, the customer can wait up to 60 days, until January 11, and pay the full $100. If the customer elects to pay by November 22 and take advantage of the cash discount, Iowa Sales, Incorporated, records the receipt of the $98 as follows:

Nov.	22	Cash	98.00	
		Sales Discounts	2.00	
		Accounts Receivable		100.00
		Received payment for the November 12 sale less the discount.		

Cash discounts granted to customers are called **sales discounts,** and are accumulated in the Sales Discounts account until the end of an accounting period. This account is contra to the Sales account. In other words, the total discounts are deducted from gross sales in calculating net revenue from sales. Deducting discounts from sales makes sense because a sales discount is an amount off the regular price of goods that is granted for early payment. As a result, it reduces revenue from sales.

Periodic and Perpetual Inventory Systems

Some businesses, such as automobile dealers or major appliance stores, make a limited number of sales each day. Therefore, they can easily refer to their records at the time of each sale and determine the cost of the car or appliance sold. On the other hand, a drugstore or a hardware store may find this task to be more difficult. For instance, if a drugstore clerk sells a customer a tube of toothpaste, a box of aspirin, and a magazine, the cash register can easily be used to record the sale of these items at their marked selling prices. However, with large-volume, low-priced items, it would be quite difficult to determine quickly the cost of each item so that the cost of goods sold could be recorded at the time of sale. Some computerized systems allow this task to be done. Many stores that sell a large volume of low-priced items, however, make no effort to record the cost of goods sold at the time of each sale. Rather, they wait until the end of an accounting period to make the calculation. At that time, they count their **inventory**, which is the collection of goods on hand waiting to be sold. This counting process is called *taking a physical inventory*. This information plus data from the accounting records is then used to determine the cost of all goods sold during the period.

Drug, hardware, grocery, or similar stores often use **periodic inventory systems** to learn the cost of their inventories and the cost of goods sold. We describe and explain these periodic inventory systems in this chapter. An alternative approach to accounting for inventories and cost of goods sold involves recording the cost of goods sold each time a sale is made and keeping an up-to-date record of the goods on hand. These systems are called **perpetual inventory systems.** You will learn more about them when you study Chapter 9.

Cost of Goods Sold, Periodic Inventory System

LO 2 Explain the nature of each item entering into the calculation of cost of goods sold and gross profit from sales.

As we mentioned earlier, a store that uses a periodic inventory system does not record the cost of items sold at the time they are sold. Rather, it waits until the end of an accounting period and determines the cost of all the goods sold during the period. To do this, it must have information about (1) the cost of the merchandise on hand at the beginning of the period; (2) the cost of merchandise purchased during the period; and (3) the cost of unsold goods on hand at the end of the period. With this information, a store can calculate the cost of goods sold during a period by applying the flows represented in Illustration 5–1.

Illustration 5–1 shows that the company had $251,000 of goods available for sale during the period. This included $19,000 of goods on hand when the period started and $232,000 of goods newly purchased during the period. Some of the available goods were sold during the period and the rest remained on hand at the end of the period. Because $21,000 were on hand at the end, $230,000 must have been sold. To summarize, calculate the cost of goods sold as follows:

Cost of goods on hand at beginning of the period . .	$ 19,000
Cost of goods purchased during the period	232,000
Goods available for sale during the period.	$251,000
Less unsold goods on hand at the period end	21,000
Cost of goods sold during the period	$230,000

The following paragraphs explain how to accumulate the information that you need to perform this calculation.

Merchandise Inventories

The merchandise on hand at the beginning of an accounting period is called the beginning inventory. The merchandise on hand at the end is called the ending inventory. Because a new accounting period starts as soon as the old period ends, the ending inventory of one period is automatically the beginning inventory of the next.

When a periodic inventory system is used, the dollar amount of the ending inventory is determined by (1) counting the unsold items on the shelves in the

ILLUSTRATION 5–1

The Flow of Goods through Inventory

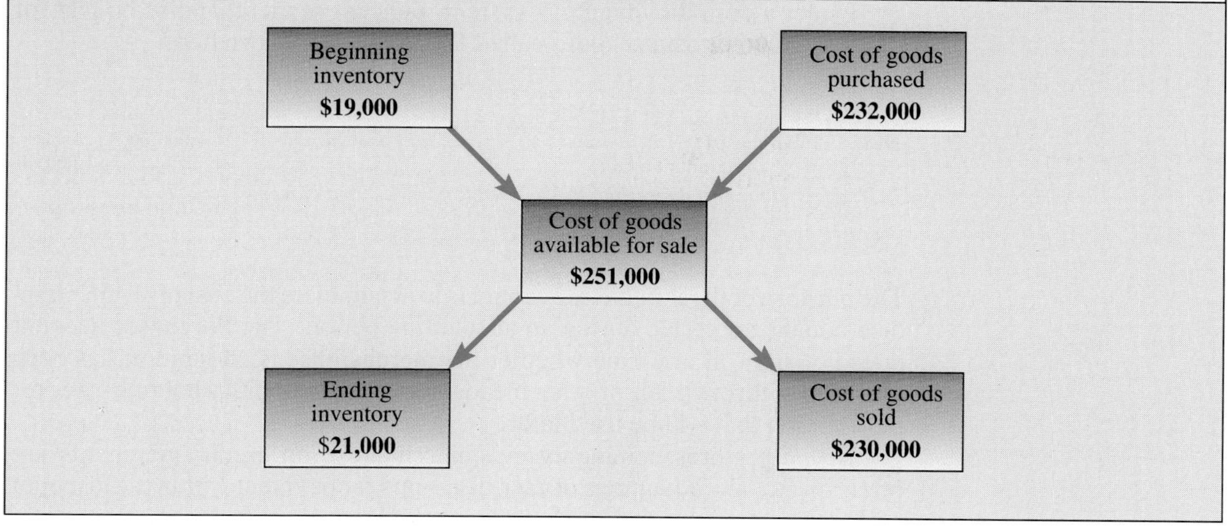

store and in the stockroom, (2) multiplying the counted quantity of each type of good by its cost, and (3) adding all the costs of the different types of goods.

After the cost of the ending inventory is determined in this manner, it is subtracted from the cost of the goods available for sale to arrive at cost of goods sold. Then, a journal entry is made to record the ending inventory amount in an asset account called *Merchandise Inventory*. This ending inventory amount remains as the balance in the Merchandise Inventory account during the next accounting period. Thus, throughout the new accounting period, the balance of the Merchandise Inventory account represents the cost of the inventory on hand at the end of the previous period, which is also the beginning inventory of the current period.

Other than to correct errors, entries are made in the Merchandise Inventory account *only* at the end of each accounting period. As time passes during an accounting period and merchandise is both purchased and sold, neither the purchases nor the cost of goods sold amounts are entered in the Merchandise Inventory account. Therefore, as soon as any goods are purchased or sold in the current period, the Merchandise Inventory account does not show the dollar amount of merchandise on hand. Rather, the account's balance reflects the beginning inventory of the period. Later in this chapter, we explain how the appropriate entry is made at the end of the period to update the account.

Cost of Merchandise Purchased

To determine the cost of purchased merchandise, you must record the invoice price of goods purchased and subtract any cash discounts that were taken. You also need to record all returns and allowances for any unsatisfactory goods purchased. Then, add any freight or other transportation costs incurred by the purchaser to ship the goods from the supplier to the purchaser's place of

LO 1 Analyze and record transactions that involve the purchase and resale of merchandise.

business. The following paragraphs explain how these amounts are accumulated in the accounts.

Under a periodic inventory system, the cost of merchandise bought for resale is debited to an account called Purchases, as shown here:

Nov.	5	Purchases	1,000.00	
		Accounts Payable		1,000.00
		Purchased merchandise on credit, invoice dated November 2, terms 2/10, n/30.		

The purpose of the Purchases account is to accumulate the cost of all merchandise bought for resale during an accounting period. The Purchases account does not show at any time whether the merchandise is on hand or has been disposed of through sale or other means. It is just a temporary holding place for information that will be used later.

Because stores commonly buy merchandise on credit, merchants are often able to take advantage of cash discounts for payment within the discount period. The discounts on purchases are called **purchases discounts.** When payment is made within the discount period, the accounting system records a credit to the contra account called Purchases Discounts, as shown in the following entry:

Nov.	12	Accounts Payable	1,000.00	
		Purchases Discounts		20.00
		Cash		980.00
		Paid for the purchase of November 5 less the discount.		

When suppliers offer cash discounts, the total amount to be saved by the buyer is usually significant. The information in the Purchases Discounts account helps managers know whether the discounts are being taken.

To ensure that discounts are not missed, a company should set up a system to pay all invoices within any discount period described in the credit terms. On the other hand, good cash management requires that no invoice be paid until the *last* day of its discount period. To accomplish both objectives, a helpful system files every invoice in such a way that it automatically comes to the attention of the person responsible for its payment on the last day of its discount period. A simple manual system uses a file with 31 folders, one for each day in a month. After an invoice is recorded, it is placed in the file folder of the last day of its discount period. For example, if the last day of an invoice's discount period is November 12, it is filed in folder number 12. Then, on November 12, the invoice and any other invoices in the same folder are removed and paid. Computerized systems accomplish the same result by having the operator enter a code that identifies the last date in the discount period. When that date is reached, the computer provides a reminder that the account should be paid.

Sometimes, merchandise received from suppliers is not acceptable and must be returned. Or, the purchaser may keep defective merchandise because the supplier grants an allowance or reduction in its price. When merchandise is returned, the purchaser gets a refund, or a reduction in the amount owed to the supplier. Even though there is no charge for the returned goods, the process of receiving, inspecting, evaluating, and returning defective merchandise creates costs that should be minimized. As a result, the amount of purchase returns or allowances must be controlled and a purchaser may look for another supplier if purchased merchandise is frequently defective.

An important key to controlling the problem of defective merchandise purchases is information about the amount of returns and allowances. To get this information, returns and allowances on purchases are commonly recorded in a contra account called Purchases Returns and Allowances. This account is used to record a return of merchandise as follows:

Nov.	14	Accounts Payable	65.00	
		Purchases Returns and Allowances		65.00
		Returned defective merchandise.		

When an invoice for purchased goods is subject to a cash discount and a portion of the goods is returned before the invoice is paid, the discount applies only to the goods kept. For example, assume that you buy merchandise for $500, subject to a 2% cash discount. Then, you return $100 of the goods before the invoice is paid. When you pay the amount due before the discount period expires, the discount of 2% applies only to the remaining $400. In other words, you pay $392, which is the gross cost of $400 minus the discount of $8, or 2% of $400.

Sometimes a supplier assumes responsibility for the costs of transporting the sold goods to the merchandiser's place of business. In this case, the total cost of the goods to the purchaser is the amount the purchaser must pay to the supplier. In other situations, the purchaser must pay the transportation costs called **transportation-in.** When these costs are incurred, they are properly added to the cost of the purchased goods and may be recorded with an additional debit to the Purchases account. However, more complete information is obtained if such costs are debited to a special account called Transportation-In. The balance of this account is eventually added to the Purchases account balance to get the total cost. The use of this account is shown in the following entry, which records a $22 charge for freight on incoming merchandise:

Nov.	24	Transportation-In	22.00	
		Cash		22.00
		Paid express charges on merchandise purchased.		

Note that freight paid on purchased goods coming from suppliers must be accounted for separately from freight paid on sold goods being sent to customers. The shipping cost of incoming goods should be included in the cost of goods sold, while the cost of shipping outgoing goods should be an expense of making sales.

When a purchase or sale involves transportation charges, the buyer and seller must understand which party is responsible for paying them. Because costs are involved, the responsibility for shipping should be part of the negotiations. Under one arrangement, called *free on board factory,* the seller transfers ownership of the goods to the buyer at the seller's place of business, and the buyer must pay the shipping charges. This arrangement is usually abbreviated as **FOB** *factory*. Alternatively, the terms of the purchase may be *FOB destination,* which means that ownership of the goods passes at the buyer's place of business. In this case, the seller is responsible for the shipping charges. As an example, a seller may quote a price of $300, FOB factory. A buyer who wants the seller to pay the freight (and assume the risk of loss in transit) tries to get terms of $300, FOB destination.

Even though the terms are FOB factory, a seller may agree to prepay the transportation costs as a service to the buyer. Of course, these charges are then added to the amount the buyer must pay. If the credit terms include a cash discount, the discount does not apply to the transportation charges. In other words, the purchaser must reimburse the seller for 100% of the transportation charges, even if the bill is paid within the discount period.

At the end of the period, the cost of the merchandise purchased during the period is determined by combining the balances of the Purchases, Purchases Returns and Allowances, Purchases Discounts, and Transportation-In accounts. This calculation may appear on the income statement of a merchandising company in the following form:

Purchases		$235,800	
Less: Purchases returns and allowances	$1,200		
Purchases discounts	4,100	5,300	
Net purchases		$230,500	
Add transportation-in		1,500	
Cost of goods purchased			$232,000

Cost of Goods Sold

The last item in the preceding calculation is the cost of the merchandise purchased during the accounting period. To calculate the cost of goods sold, you must combine this amount with the beginning and ending inventories, as follows:

Cost of goods sold:				
Merchandise inventory, December 31, 1992			$ 19,000	
Purchases		$235,800		
Less: Purchases returns and allowances	$1,200			
Purchases discounts	4,100	5,300		
Net purchases		$230,500		
Add transportation-in		1,500		
Cost of goods purchased			232,000	
Goods available for sale			$251,000	
Merchandise inventory, December 31, 1993			21,000	
Cost of goods sold				$230,000

AS A MATTER OF

Ethics

Renee Fleck was recently hired as an accountant for Printers, Inc., a medium-sized company that purchases most of its supplies on credit. Fleck's duties include managing cash and accounts payable. She overlapped for several days on the job with Martin Hull, the outgoing accountant, so that they could spend time together to help Fleck learn the ropes.

One of Fleck's responsibilities is to ensure that the accounts are paid promptly to maintain the company's credit standing with its suppliers and to take advantage of all cash discounts. Hull told Fleck that the system in place has accomplished both goals easily, and has also made another contribution to the company's profits. Hull explained that when credit purchases are made on terms that include a discount for early payment, the system has been to prepare checks for the "net-of-discount" amounts. Then, the checks are not mailed until *after* the end of the discount period. The checks are dated the last day of the discount period, but are not mailed until four or five days later. Because the accounts are always paid, Printers, Inc., has had little difficulty with its creditors. "It's simple," Hull said, "we get the free use of the cash for an extra five days, and who's going to complain? Even if someone gripes, we can always blame the computer or the mail room."

Only a few days later, on April 18, Hull has departed and Fleck recognizes that the discount period on a $10,000 payable is about to lapse. The purchase was made on April 9, subject to terms of 2/10, n/30. Fleck is trying to decide whether she should pay the bill on the 19th or wait until April 23.

Notice that the sum of the beginning inventory and purchases is calculated and identified as the cost of *goods available for sale*.

Inventory Losses

Merchandising companies lose merchandise in a variety of ways, such as spoilage or shoplifting. When merchandise is lost, it is called *shrinkage*. A periodic inventory system automatically includes the cost of shrinkage in cost of goods sold. For example, assume that during a year shoplifters stole merchandise that cost $500 from a store. Because the stolen goods were not on hand at the end of the year when the inventory was counted, these thefts caused the store's year-end inventory to be $500 less than it otherwise would have been. And, since the year-end inventory was $500 smaller as a result of the loss, the number assigned to the cost of the goods sold was $500 larger.

Many merchandisers are troubled with shoplifting or other inventory losses. Unfortunately, a disadvantage of the periodic inventory system is its inability to provide clear information about the amount of such losses. Instead, the amount of the losses is hidden in the cost of goods sold figure. The perpetual inventory systems described in Chapter 9 provide more complete information about merchandise losses. Chapter 9 also discusses a method of estimating inventory losses when using a periodic inventory system.

Income Statement of a Merchandising Company

A classified income statement for a merchandising company has (1) a revenue section, (2) a cost of goods sold section, and (3) an operating expenses section. Note in Illustration 5–2 how the first two sections are brought together to show gross profit from sales. (This example includes many details of the calculations not often found in statements presented to users outside the company.)

Also notice in Illustration 5–2 how operating expenses are classified as either selling expenses or general and administrative expenses. **Selling expenses** include expenses of storing and preparing goods for sale, promoting sales, actually making sales, and delivering goods to customers. **General and administrative expenses** support the overall management and operations of a business. Examples are the central office, accounting, personnel, and credit and collection expenses.

Sometimes an expenditure should be divided or prorated between selling expenses and general and administrative expenses. For example, as you can see in Illustration 5–2, Iowa Sales, Incorporated divided the $9,000 rent on its store building between these categories. Ninety percent ($8,100) was selling expense, and the remaining 10% ($900) was general and administrative expense.[1] This division should be made on a logical basis such as the relationship between the rental values of space occupied for selling and for administration.

In Illustration 5–2, the last item subtracted is income taxes expense. This income statement was prepared for Iowa Sales, Incorporated, which is a corporation. Of the three kinds of business organizations, only corporations pay state and federal income taxes. Notice in Illustration 5–2 that the result of subtracting operating expenses from gross profit is called *Income from operations*. Income taxes expense is determined to be $1,700, and then subtracted from income from operations to obtain net income.

Work Sheet of a Merchandising Company

LO 3 Prepare a work sheet and the financial statements for a merchandising business that uses a periodic inventory system and that is organized as a corporation or as a single proprietorship.

In organizing the end-of-period accounting procedures, the work sheet for a merchandising company is like the work sheet for a service company. In both cases, the work sheet serves as a tool to help bring together the information needed at the end of the period to prepare the financial statements and prepare the adjusting and closing entries. Illustration 5–3 shows the work sheet for Iowa Sales, Incorporated.

Illustration 5–3 differs from the Chapter 4 work sheet in several places. Most notably, Illustration 5–3 does not have Adjusted Trial Balance columns. Experienced accountants frequently omit these columns from a work sheet to reduce the time and effort required for its preparation. They first enter the adjustments in the Adjustments columns. Then, in a single operation, they combine the adjustments with the unadjusted trial balance amounts and sort the combined amounts directly to the proper financial statement columns. In summary, omitting the Adjusted Trial Balance columns in preparing a work sheet is a suitable shortcut.

[1] These expenses can be recorded in separate accounts in the ledger. Alternatively, they can be recorded in one account, and the classification can be done by the accountant before preparing the financial statements.

ILLUSTRATION 5–2

A Classified Income Statement for a Merchandising Company

IOWA SALES, INCORPORATED
Income Statement
For Year Ended December 31, 1993

Revenue from sales:				
Gross sales				$306,200
Less: Sales returns and allowances			$ 1,900	
Sales discounts			4,300	6,200
Net sales				$300,000
Cost of goods sold:				
Merchandise inventory, December 31, 1992			$ 19,000	
Purchases		$235,800		
Less: Purchases returns and allowances	$1,200			
Purchases discounts	4,100	5,300		
Net purchases		$230,500		
Add transportation-in		1,500		
Cost of goods purchased			232,000	
Goods available for sale			$251,000	
Merchandise inventory, December 31, 1993			21,000	
Cost of goods sold				230,000
Gross profit from sales				$ 70,000
Operating expenses:				
Selling expenses:				
Depreciation expense, store equipment		$ 3,000		
Sales salaries expense		18,500		
Rent expense, selling space		8,100		
Store supplies expense		400		
Advertising expense		700		
Total selling expenses			$ 30,700	
General and administrative expenses:				
Depreciation expense, office equipment		$ 700		
Office salaries expense		25,800		
Insurance expense		600		
Rent expense, office space		900		
Office supplies expense		200		
Total general and administrative expenses			28,200	
Total operating expenses				58,900
Income from operations				$ 11,100
Less income taxes expense				1,700
Net income				$ 9,400

The next three differences all relate to the fact that Illustration 5–3 was prepared for a corporation instead of a proprietorship. The first one is minor—it is simply the presence of the word *Incorporated* in the company's name. Second, notice that the heading of the last two columns is Retained Earnings Statement or Balance Sheet. Later in this chapter, we explain how the **retained earnings statement** reports the changes in a corporation's retained earnings that occurred during an accounting period.

ILLUSTRATION 5–3

A Work Sheet for a Merchandising Company

IOWA SALES, INCORPORATED
Work Sheet
For Year Ended December 31, 1993

	Account Titles	**Unadjusted Trial Balance**		**Adjustments**		**Income Statement**		**Retained Earnings Statement or Balance Sheet**	
		Dr.	**Cr.**	**Dr.**	**Cr.**	**Dr.**	**Cr.**	**Dr.**	**Cr.**
1	Cash	8,200						8,200	
2	Accounts receivable	11,200						11,200	
3	Merchandise inventory	19,000				19,000	21,000	21,000	
4	Prepaid insurance	900			(*a*) 600			300	
5	Office supplies	300			(*b*) 200			100	
6	Store supplies	600			(*c*) 400			200	
7	Office equipment	4,400						4,400	
8	Accum. depr., office equipment		600		(*d*) 700				1,300
9	Store equipment	29,100						29,100	
10	Accum. depr., store equipment		2,500		(*e*) 3,000				5,500
11	Accounts payable		3,600						3,600
12	Income taxes payable				(*f*) 100				100
13	Common stock		50,000						50,000
14	Retained earnings		8,600						8,600
15	Cash dividends declared	4,000						4,000	
16	Sales		306,200				306,200		
17	Sales returns and allowances	1,900				1,900			
18	Sales discounts	4,300				4,300			
19	Purchases	235,800				235,800			
20	Purch. returns and allowances		1,200				1,200		
21	Purchases discounts		4,100				4,100		
22	Transportation-in	1,500				1,500			
23	Depr. expense, store equipment			(*e*) 3,000		3,000			
24	Sales salaries expense	18,500				18,500			
25	Rent expense, selling space	8,100				8,100			
26	Store supplies expense			(*c*) 400		400			
27	Advertising expense	700				700			
28	Depr. expense, office equipment			(*d*) 700		700			
29	Office salaries expense	25,800				25,800			
30	Insurance expense			(*a*) 600		600			
31	Rent expense, office space	900				900			
32	Office supplies expense			(*b*) 200		200			
33	Income taxes expense	1,600		(*f*) 100		1,700			
34		376,800	376,800	5,000	5,000	323,100	332,500	78,500	69,100
35	Net income					9,400			9,400
36						332,500	332,500	78,500	78,500

The third difference is on lines 13 and 14 in Illustration 5–3. Specifically, the corporation work sheet includes Common Stock and Retained Earnings accounts instead of the owner's capital item that would appear on a proprietorship work sheet. Notice that the balances of these two corporation accounts are carried unchanged from the Unadjusted Trial Balance Credit column into the Retained Earnings Statement or Balance Sheet Credit column. The remaining similarities and differences of Illustration 5–3 are best described column by column.

Account Titles Column

The Account Titles column of the work sheet in Illustration 5–3 lists several accounts that do not have unadjusted trial balance amounts. (For example, see Store supplies expense on line 26.) These accounts are needed in the financial statements and are listed in the order of their appearance on the statements. They are debited and credited in making the adjustments. Entering their names on the work sheet in financial statement order at the time the work sheet is begun makes it easier to prepare the statements later. Of course, any accounts that were not listed may be entered below the unadjusted trial balance totals as was done in Chapter 4.

Unadjusted Trial Balance Columns

In Illustration 5–3, the amounts in the Unadjusted Trial Balance columns are the account balances as of December 31, 1993, the end of Iowa Sales, Incorporated's annual accounting period. They were taken from the company's ledger after all transactions were recorded but before any end-of-period adjustments were made.

Note the $19,000 inventory amount that appears in the Unadjusted Trial Balance Debit column on line 3. This amount is the cost of inventory the company had on hand as of December 31, 1992. (As the ending inventory for 1992, this amount is also the beginning inventory for 1993.) Because the company uses the periodic system, the $19,000 was debited to the Merchandise Inventory account at the end of 1992 and remained in the account as its balance throughout 1993.

Adjustments Columns

Six adjustments appear on the illustrated work sheet. The first five are similar to those discussed in Chapter 4:

a. The Prepaid Insurance account included $600 of insurance expense.
b. A count of the office supplies showed that $100 was on hand.
c. A count of the store supplies showed that $200 was on hand.
d. Annual depreciation expense on the office equipment was $700.
e. Annual depreciation expense on the store equipment was $3,000.

The sixth adjustment for income taxes is new and deserves explanation.

A business organized as a corporation is subject to the payment of federal (and perhaps state) income taxes. Near the beginning of each year, a corporation must estimate the amount of income it expects to earn during the year. Then, it estimates the amount of income tax the firm will have to pay. This estimated tax must be paid in a series of installment payments during the year. Each payment is debited to Income Taxes Expense and credited to Cash.

Therefore, a corporation that expects to earn a profit reaches the end of the year with a debit balance in its Income Taxes Expense account. However, because the balance is an estimate (and usually less than the full amount of the tax), an adjustment must be made to get the proper amount of expense and liability recorded. Thus, adjusting entry (*f*) on lines 12 and 33 accrues the additional tax expense of $100 and the taxes payable of the same amount.

Combining and Sorting the Items

After all adjustments are entered and totaled on the work sheet, the amounts in the Unadjusted Trial Balance and Adjustments columns are combined and sorted to the proper financial statement columns. Revenue, cost of goods sold, and expense items are sorted to the Income Statement columns. Asset, liability, and stockholders' equity accounts (including Cash Dividends Declared) are sorted to the Retained Earnings Statement or Balance Sheet columns.

Income Statement Columns

Observe in Illustration 5–3 that revenue, cost of goods sold, and expense items maintain their debit and credit positions when sorted to the Income Statement columns. Because sales returns and sales discounts are contra to sales, they are entered in the Debit column. The effect is to subtract them from sales when the columns are totaled and the net income is determined.

The Beginning Inventory Amount. Look at the beginning inventory amount on line 3. Note that the $19,000 unadjusted trial balance amount is sorted to the Income Statement Debit column. It is put in this column simply because it has a debit balance. This placement also helps us calculate the cost of goods sold. That is, the cost of goods available for sale is calculated by adding the beginning inventory to net purchases (another debit remainder, consisting of purchases, minus purchases returns and allowances, minus purchases discounts, plus transportation-in).

The Ending Inventory Amount. Recall that when using the periodic inventory system, you must take a physical inventory of merchandise on hand at the end of each accounting period. The December 31, 1993, physical inventory of Iowa Sales, Incorporated, showed that it had a $21,000 ending inventory. This amount was determined by counting the items of unsold merchandise and multiplying the quantities by the cost of each item.

After all adjusted account balances are sorted to the proper work sheet columns, the next step in preparing a work sheet is to simply insert the ending inventory amount in the Income Statement *Credit* column. The ending inventory amount is placed in the Income Statement Credit column because it must be subtracted from cost of goods available for sale (beginning inventory plus net purchases) when cost of goods sold is calculated for the income statement. Next, the ending inventory amount is put in the Retained Earnings Statement or Balance Sheet *Debit* column. Thus, the ending balance of $21,000 will appear on the balance sheet as the cost of the merchandise owned on the balance sheet date. In Illustration 5–3, note that the $21,000 ending inventory was inserted in these columns on line 3 of the work sheet. (Later in this chapter, we describe how to make the journal entry to record the ending inventory in the accounts.)

Cost of Goods Sold on the Work Sheet

The amounts used in the calculation of cost of goods sold are in color in the Income Statement columns of Illustration 5–3. The beginning inventory, purchases, and transportation-in amounts appear in the Debit column. The amounts of the ending inventory, purchases returns and allowances, and purchases discounts appear in the Credit column. Note in the following calculations that the sum of the three debit items minus the sum of the three credit items equals the $230,000 cost of goods sold shown in the income statement of Illustration 5–2.

Debits:	
Beginning inventory	$ 19,000
Purchases	235,800
Transportation-in	1,500
Total debits	$256,300
Credits:	
Ending inventory	$ (21,000)
Purchases returns and allowances	(1,200)
Purchases discounts	(4,100)
Total credits	(26,300)
Cost of goods sold	$230,000

Therefore, the combined effect of entering the six components of the cost of goods sold calculation in the Income Statement columns is a net $230,000 debit.

Completing the Work Sheet and Preparing Financial Statements

LO 3 Prepare a work sheet and the financial statements for a merchandising business that uses a periodic inventory system and that is organized as a corporation or as a single proprietorship.

After all items are sorted to the proper columns and the ending inventory amount is entered, you complete a work sheet such as Illustration 5–3 by adding the columns and then determining and adding in the net income or loss. When the work sheet for a corporation is completed, it is used to prepare an income statement, a retained earnings statement, and a balance sheet.

Preparing the Income Statement

After the work sheet is completed, the items in the Income Statement columns are used to prepare an income statement. The classified income statement prepared from information in the Income Statement columns of Illustration 5–3 is shown in Illustration 5–2 on page 259.

Preparing the Retained Earnings Statement

The retained earnings statement reports the changes in the corporation's retained earnings during the period. Therefore, the statement describes the events that changed the amounts of retained earnings reported on two successive end-of-period balance sheets.

The last two columns of the work sheet contain the information you need to prepare the retained earnings statement. The beginning retained earnings balance appears on the line showing the Retained Earnings account. The net income (or net loss) appears on a line near the bottom of the work sheet and the amount of cash dividends declared also appears on a separate line.

Illustration 5–4 shows the retained earnings statement of Iowa Sales, Incorporated. The statement shows that the company began the year with $8,600 of retained earnings, which is also the amount of retained earnings reported on its previous year-end balance sheet. Its retained earnings balance was increased by the $9,400 net income and reduced by the declaration of $4,000 of cash dividends. The result is the final balance of $14,000, which is also reported on the December 31, 1993, balance sheet.

Preparing the Balance Sheet

The classified balance sheet for Iowa Sales, Incorporated, appears in Illustration 5–5. As a matter of convenience, all of the prepaid expense items (prepaid insurance, store supplies, and office supplies) have been combined and presented as a single item on the balance sheet. This shortcut is justified by the fact that each of them has a small balance. It might also be possible to combine the $100 of taxes payable with the accounts payable, but those two debts are not as similar as the prepaid expense items. Also note that the $14,000 retained earnings amount on the balance sheet is the same amount calculated on the retained earnings statement shown in Illustration 5–4.

Adjusting and Closing Entries

LO 4 Prepare adjusting and closing entries for a merchandising business organized as either a corporation or a single proprietorship.

After the work sheet and statements are completed, you must prepare and post adjusting and closing entries. Illustration 5–6 on page 266 shows the entries for Iowa Sales, Incorporated. Notice that they differ from previously illustrated adjusting and closing entries because an explanation for each entry is not given. Individual explanations may be given but are not necessary. The words *Adjusting Entries* before the first adjusting entry and *Closing Entries* before the first closing entry are sufficient to explain why they were recorded.

As you learned in Chapter 4, the Adjustments columns of a work sheet provide the information needed to prepare a company's adjusting entries. Each adjustment in the Adjustments columns must be recorded in the journal and posted to the ledger. Thus, the adjusting entries in Illustration 5–6 are the same as the adjustments on the work sheet of Illustration 5–3.

The work sheet in Illustration 5–3 also contains the information you need to prepare closing entries. Look at the first closing entry of Illustration 5–6 and compare it with the items in the Income Statement Debit column of Illustration 5–3. Note that Income Summary is debited for the $323,100 column total and that each account with an amount in the column is credited. This entry removes the $19,000 beginning inventory amount from the Merchandise Inventory account. It also closes all the contra revenue, cost of goods sold, and expense accounts that have debit balances.

Now compare the second closing entry with the items in the Income Statement Credit column of Illustration 5–3. Note that each account with an amount in the credit column is debited and the Income Summary account is

ILLUSTRATION 5–4

A Corporation's Retained Earnings Statement

IOWA SALES, INCORPORATED
Retained Earnings Statement
For Year Ended December 31, 1993

Retained earnings, December 31, 1992	$ 8,600
Add 1993 net income	9,400
Total	$18,000
Deduct cash dividends declared	4,000
Retained earnings, December 31, 1993	$14,000

ILLUSTRATION 5–5

A Corporation's Classified Balance Sheet

IOWA SALES, INCORPORATED
Balance Sheet
December 31, 1993

Assets

Current assets:			
Cash		$ 8,200	
Accounts receivable		11,200	
Merchandise inventory		21,000	
Prepaid expenses		600	
Total current assets			$41,000
Plant and equipment:			
Office equipment	$ 4,400		
Less accumulated depreciation	1,300	$ 3,100	
Store equipment	$29,100		
Less accumulated depreciation	5,500	23,600	
Total plant and equipment			26,700
Total assets			$67,700

Liabilities

Current liabilities:		
Accounts payable	$ 3,600	
Income taxes payable	100	
Total liabilities		$ 3,700

Stockholders' Equity

Common stock, $5 par value, 10,000 shares authorized and outstanding	$50,000	
Retained earnings	14,000	
Total stockholders' equity		64,000
Total liabilities and stockholders' equity		$67,700

ILLUSTRATION 5–6

Adjusting and Closing Entries for a Merchandising Corporation

Date		Account Titles and Explanation	PR	Debit	Credit
1993		Adjusting Entries			
Dec.	31	Insurance Expense		600.00	
		Prepaid Insurance			600.00
	31	Office Supplies Expense		200.00	
		Office Supplies			200.00
	31	Store Supplies Expense		400.00	
		Store Supplies			400.00
	31	Depreciation Expense, Office Equipment		700.00	
		Accumulated Depreciation, Office Equipment			700.00
	31	Depreciation Expense, Store Equipment		3,000.00	
		Accumulated Depreciation, Store Equipment			3,000.00
	31	Income Taxes Expense		100.00	
		Income Taxes Payable			100.00
		Closing Entries			
	31	Income Summary		323,100.00	
		Merchandise Inventory			19,000.00
		Sales Returns and Allowances			1,900.00
		Sales Discounts			4,300.00
		Purchases			235,800.00
		Transportation-In			1,500.00
		Depreciation Expense, Store Equipment			3,000.00
		Sales Salaries Expense			18,500.00
		Rent Expense, Selling Space			8,100.00
		Store Supplies Expense			400.00
		Advertising Expense			700.00
		Depreciation Expense, Office Equipment			700.00
		Office Salaries Expense			25,800.00
		Insurance Expense			600.00
		Rent Expense, Office Space			900.00
		Office Supplies Expense			200.00
		Income Taxes Expense			1,700.00
	31	Merchandise Inventory		21,000.00	
		Sales		306,200.00	
		Purchases Returns and Allowances		1,200.00	
		Purchases Discounts		4,100.00	
		Income Summary			332,500.00
	31	Income Summary		9,400.00	
		Retained Earnings			9,400.00
	31	Retained Earnings		4,000.00	
		Cash Dividends Declared			4,000.00

credited for the $332,500 column total. This entry closes the revenue and cost of goods sold accounts that have credit balances. It also enters the $21,000 ending inventory amount in the Merchandise Inventory account.

The third closing entry transfers the $9,400 net income from Income Summary to Retained Earnings. Finally, the fourth closing entry closes the Cash Dividends Declared account and reduces the balance of Retained Earnings.

Closing Entries and the Inventories

There is nothing new about the closing entries of a merchandising company except for the beginning and ending inventories. However, you should understand how the closing entries affect the Merchandise Inventory account.

Before closing entries for 1993 are posted, the Merchandise Inventory account of Iowa Sales, Incorporated, shows the $19,000 beginning inventory balance:

Merchandise Inventory **Acct. No. 119**

Date		Explanation	PR	Debit	Credit	Balance
1992						
Dec.	31		G10	19,000		19,000

Then, when the first closing entry for 1993 is posted, its $19,000 credit to Merchandise Inventory clears the beginning inventory amount from the inventory account:

Merchandise Inventory **Acct. No. 119**

Date		Explanation	PR	Debit	Credit	Balance
1992						
Dec.	31		G10	19,000		19,000
1993						
Dec.	31		G20		19,000	-0-

When the second closing entry is posted, its $21,000 debit to Merchandise Inventory puts the amount of the ending inventory into the account:

Merchandise Inventory **Acct. No. 119**

Date		Explanation	PR	Debit	Credit	Balance
1992						
Dec.	31		G10	19,000		19,000
1993						
Dec.	31		G20		19,000	-0-
	31		G20	21,000		21,000

The $21,000 debit balance of the inventory account remains throughout 1994 as a historical record of the amount of inventory at the end of 1993 and the beginning of 1994.

Other Inventory Methods

There are several ways to handle the inventories in the end-of-period accounting procedures. However, all have the same objectives of (1) removing the beginning inventory balance from the inventory account and charging (debiting) it to Income Summary; and (2) entering the ending inventory amount in the inventory account and crediting it to Income Summary. As we have just shown, these objectives can be achieved with closing entries. Alternatively, adjusting entries may be used to accomplish the same results. Either method is satisfactory. The adjusting entry method is explained in Appendix C at the end of this chapter.

Multiple-Step and Single-Step Income Statements

The income statement in Illustration 5–2 on page 259 is called a *classified* income statement because its items are classified in significant groups. (Note that selling expenses are separated from general and administrative expenses.) It is also a **multiple-step income statement** because cost of goods sold and the expenses are subtracted in steps to get net income.

Illustration 5–7 shows another statement format, the **single-step income statement.** Note how cost of goods sold and the expenses are added together in the illustration and are then subtracted from net sales in one step to get net income. This format is commonly used in published statements. Also, note that the information in the income statement is condensed. For example, it does not show the various components of net sales and cost of goods sold. Published statements often condense data in this manner.

Combined Income and Retained Earnings Statement

Many corporations present their income and retained earnings statements as a single, combined statement. Such a statement may be prepared in either single-step or multiple-step form. Illustration 5–8 shows a combined single-step income and retained earnings statement.

Debit and Credit Memoranda

When they do business together, buyers and sellers sometimes find that they need to adjust the amount that is owed by one to the other. For example, merchandise purchased may not meet specifications, goods may be received that were not ordered, fewer goods may be received than were ordered and billed, and errors may occur in preparing billings.

In many cases, the adjustment can be accomplished by the buyer without a negotiation. An example is an error on an invoice. If the buying company makes the adjustment, it notifies the seller of its action by sending a **debit memorandum** or a **credit memorandum.** A debit memorandum is a business form that has spaces for the name and address of the recipient and words such as, "We debit your account," followed by space for typing in the reason for the debit. A credit memorandum, on the other hand, would say, "We credit your account." Illustration 5–9 shows the use of these documents.

To explain the use of a debit memorandum, assume that a buyer discovers an error that overstated the total bill by $10. The buyer notifies the seller of the mistake with a debit memorandum reading: "We have debited your account to correct a $10 error on your November 17 invoice." A *debit* memorandum is sent because the correction reduces an account payable on the books of the buyer, and a debit is required to reduce an account payable. If the error is discovered before the purchase is recorded, the buyer should mark the correction on the bill and attach a copy of the debit memorandum to show that the seller was notified. Then, the buyer should record an entry that debits Purchases and credits Accounts Payable for the correct amount. If the purchase has already been recorded in the accounts before the error is discovered, the buyer would make another entry debiting Accounts Payable for $10 and crediting Purchases for $10.

Other adjustments require negotiations between the buyer and the seller before they can be recorded. For example, a buyer's claim that merchandise does not meet specifications normally requires discussion with the seller. In this case, the buyer should debit Purchases and credit Accounts Payable for

ILLUSTRATION 5–7

A Single-Step Income Statement

IOWA SALES, INCORPORATED
Income Statement
For Year Ended December 31, 1993

Revenue from sales		$300,000
Expenses:		
Cost of goods sold	$230,000	
Selling expenses	30,700	
General and administrative expenses	28,200	
Income taxes expense	1,700	
Total expenses		290,600
Net income		$ 9,400

ILLUSTRATION 5–8

Combining the Income Statement and the Retained Earnings Statement

IOWA SALES, INCORPORATED
Statement of Income and Retained Earnings
For Year Ended December 31, 1993

Revenue from sales		$300,000
Expenses:		
Cost of goods sold	$230,000	
Selling expenses	30,700	
General and administrative expenses	28,200	
Income taxes expense	1,700	
Total expenses		290,600
Net income		$ 9,400
Add retained earnings, December 31, 1992		8,600
Total		$ 18,000
Deduct cash dividends declared		4,000
Retained earnings, December 31, 1993		$ 14,000

the full amount and then negotiate with the seller for a return or a price adjustment. If the seller agrees, it formally notifies the buyer with a credit memorandum. A *credit* memorandum is used because the return or adjustment reduces an account receivable on the books of the seller, and a credit is required to reduce an account receivable. When the credit memorandum is received, the buyer records it by debiting Accounts Payable and crediting Purchases Returns and Allowances because the purchase was originally recorded at the full invoice price.

As this discussion shows, a debit or a credit memorandum may originate with either party to a transaction. The memorandum gets its name from the action of the originator. If the originator debits an account receivable or payable, it issues a debit memorandum. If the originator credits an account receivable or payable, it issues a credit memorandum.

ILLUSTRATION 5-9

Debit and Credit Memoranda

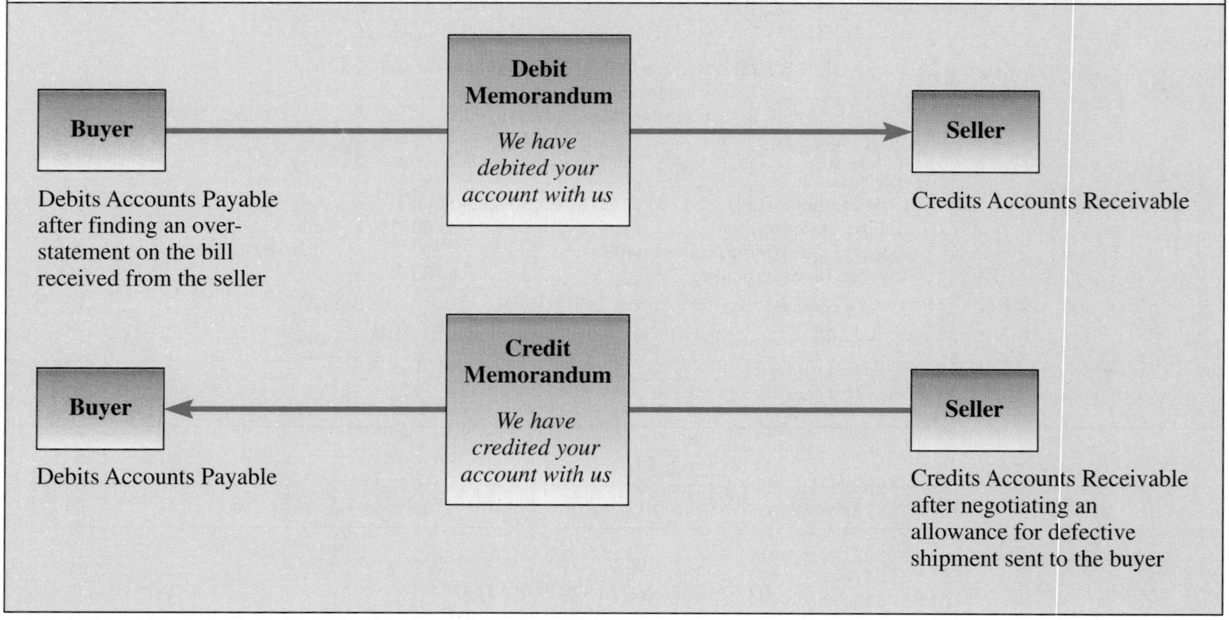

Trade Discounts

LO 1 Analyze and record transactions that involve the purchase and resale of merchandise.

When a manufacturer or wholesaler prepares a catalog of items for sale, each item is given a **list price**, which is also called a *catalog price*. This amount is the *nominal* selling price of the item. A **trade discount** is a reduction (perhaps as much as 40% or more) in a list price that is applied to determine the actual sales price of the goods sold to a customer. Trade discounts are commonly used by manufacturers and wholesalers to change selling prices without republishing their catalogs. When the seller wants to change the selling prices, it can notify its customers merely by sending them a new set of trade discounts to apply to the catalog prices.

Trade discounts are accounted for differently from the cash discounts discussed earlier in this chapter. Specifically, *trade discounts offered or taken are not entered in the accounts by either party to a sale*. Instead, they are used only to calculate the sales price. For example, if a manufacturer deducts a 40% trade discount on an item listed in its catalog at $100, the selling price is $60, which is computed as [$100 − (40% × $100)]. The seller records the credit sale as follows:

Dec.	10	Accounts Receivable	60.00	
		Sales		60.00
		Sold merchandise on credit.		

The buyer also records the purchase in its journal at $60. And, if a cash discount is allowed, it applies only to the amount of the purchase, $60.

Summary of the Chapter in Terms of Learning Objectives

LO 1. In determining the amount to record as a purchase (or sale), trade discounts are subtracted from list prices to calculate the invoice price, which is debited to Purchases (or credited to Sales). Purchases discounts, purchases returns and allowances, transportation-in, sales discounts, and sales returns and allowances are recorded in separate accounts.

LO 2. Sales discounts and sales returns and allowances are subtracted from sales to get net sales. The beginning inventory plus net purchases equals the cost of goods available for sale. The ending inventory is subtracted from the cost of goods available for sale to get cost of goods sold. The cost of goods sold is subtracted from net sales to get gross profit.

LO 3. When using the closing entry approach on the work sheet, the beginning inventory is sorted to the Income Statement Debit column and the ending inventory is inserted in the Income Statement Credit column and the Statement of Retained Earnings or Balance Sheet Debit column. This treatment of the inventory is used whether the company is a corporation or single proprietorship.

LO 4. With the closing entry approach, the beginning inventory is transferred from Merchandise Inventory to Income Summary in the closing process. Also, the ending inventory is debited to Merchandise Inventory and credited to Income Summary as part of a closing entry.

Demonstration Problem

The following partially completed work sheet was prepared for Continental Sales, Inc., as of December 31, 1993, the end of its annual accounting period.

CONTINENTAL SALES, INC.
Work Sheet
For Year Ended December 31, 1993

Account Titles	Unadjusted Trial Balance Dr.	Unadjusted Trial Balance Cr.	Adjustments Dr.	Adjustments Cr.
Cash	19,000			
Merchandise inventory	52,000			
Store supplies	7,000			(*a*) 6,000
Equipment	40,000			
Accumulated depreciation, equipment		11,000		(*b*) 5,500
Accounts payable		3,000		
Income taxes payable		6,000		(*c*) 1,000
Common stock		50,000		
Retained earnings		19,000		
Cash dividends declared	8,000			
Sales		320,000		
Sales discounts	20,000			
Purchases	147,000			
Purchases discounts		12,000		
Transportation-in	11,000			
Depreciation expense			(*b*) 5,500	
Salaries expense	43,000			
Insurance expense	12,000			
Rent expense	24,000			
Store supplies expense			(*a*) 6,000	
Advertising expense	21,000			
Income taxes expense	17,000		(*c*) 1,000	
	421,000	421,000	12,500	12,500

Required

1. Complete the work sheet. (Ending inventory is $50,000.)
2. Prepare the 1993 income statement.
3. Prepare the 1993 retained earnings statement.
4. Prepare a balance sheet as of December 31, 1993.
5. Prepare closing entries.

Solution to Demonstration Problem

Planning the Solution

- For all accounts, combine the unadjusted balances with any adjustments and sort to the appropriate columns in the work sheet. Enter the ending inventory in the Income Statement Credit column and the Balance Sheet Debit column. Take the totals of the Income Statement columns, find the net income for the year, and enter it in the Income Statement Debit column and the Balance Sheet Credit column.
- To prepare the income statement, first find the net sales by combining the sales accounts, and then find the cost of goods sold by combining the inventory related accounts. After computing gross profit, deduct the rest of the expenses.
- To prepare the retained earnings statement, list the beginning balance, net income, and cash dividends declared, and then find the ending balance.
- To prepare the balance sheet, use the amounts in the last two columns, being sure to substitute the ending balance of retained earnings from the statement of retained earnings.
- The first closing entry credits all accounts with debit balances in the income statement columns. The second closing entry debits all accounts with credit balances in the income statement columns. The third entry closes Income Summary to Retained Earnings. The fourth closing entry closes the Cash Dividends Declared account to Retained Earnings.

1.

CONTINENTAL SALES, INC.
Work Sheet
For Year Ended December 31, 1993

	Unadjusted Trial Balance		Adjustments		Income Statement		Retained Earnings Statement or Balance Sheet	
Account Titles	**Dr.**	**Cr.**	**Dr.**	**Cr.**	**Dr.**	**Cr.**	**Dr.**	**Cr.**
Cash	19,000						19,000	
Merchandise inventory	52,000				52,000	50,000	50,000	
Store supplies	7,000			(*a*) 6,000			1,000	
Equipment	40,000						40,000	
Accumulated depreciation, equipment		11,000		(*b*) 5,500				16,500
Accounts payable		3,000						3,000
Income taxes payable		6,000		(*c*) 1,000				7,000
Common stock		50,000						50,000
Retained earnings		19,000						19,000
Cash dividends declared	8,000						8,000	
Sales		320,000				320,000		
Sales discounts	20,000				20,000			
Purchases	147,000				147,000			
Purchases discounts		12,000				12,000		
Transportation-in	11,000				11,000			
Depreciation expense			(*b*) 5,500		5,500			
Salaries expense	43,000				43,000			
Insurance expense	12,000				12,000			
Rent expense	24,000				24,000			
Store supplies expense			(*a*) 6,000		6,000			
Advertising expense	21,000				21,000			
Income taxes expense	17,000		(*c*) 1,000		18,000			
	421,000	421,000	12,500	12,500	359,500	382,000	118,000	95,500
Net income					22,500			22,500
					382,000	382,000	118,000	118,000

2.

CONTINENTAL SALES, INC.
Income Statement
For Year Ended December 31, 1993

Revenue from sales:			
Gross sales			$320,000
Less sales discounts			20,000
Net sales			$300,000
Cost of goods sold:			
Merchandise inventory, December 31, 1992		$ 52,000	
Purchases	$147,000		
Less purchases discounts	12,000		
Net purchases	$135,000		
Plus transportation-in	11,000		
Cost of goods purchased		146,000	
Cost of goods available for sale		$198,000	
Merchandise inventory, December 31, 1993		50,000	
Cost of goods sold			148,000
Gross profit from sales			$152,000
Operating expenses:			
Depreciation expense		$ 5,500	
Salaries expense		43,000	
Insurance expense		12,000	
Rent expense		24,000	
Store supplies expense		6,000	
Advertising expense		21,000	
Total operating expenses			111,500
Income from operations			$ 40,500
Less income taxes expense			18,000
Net income			$ 22,500

3.

CONTINENTAL SALES, INC.
Retained Earnings Statement
For Year Ended December 31, 1993

Retained earnings, December 31, 1992	$19,000
Add 1993 net income	22,500
Total	$41,500
Deduct cash dividends declared	8,000
Retained earnings, December 31, 1993	$33,500

4.

CONTINENTAL SALES, INC.
Balance Sheet
December 31, 1993

Assets		
Current assets:		
Cash		$19,000
Merchandise inventory		50,000
Store supplies		1,000
Total current assets		$70,000
Equipment	$40,000	
Less accumulated depreciation	16,500	
Total equipment		23,500
Total assets		$93,500
Liabilities		
Current liabilities:		
Accounts payable	$ 3,000	
Income taxes payable	7,000	
Total liabilities		$10,000
Stockholders' Equity		
Common stock	$50,000	
Retained earnings	33,500	
Total stockholders' equity		83,500
Total liabilities and stockholders' equity		$93,500

5.

1993				
Dec.	31	Income Summary	359,500.00	
		Merchandise Inventory		52,000.00
		Sales Discounts		20,000.00
		Purchases		147,000.00
		Transportation-In		11,000.00
		Depreciation Expense		5,500.00
		Salaries Expense		43,000.00
		Insurance Expense		12,000.00
		Rent Expense		24,000.00
		Store Supplies Expense		6,000.00
		Advertising Expense		21,000.00
		Income Taxes Expense		18,000.00
	31	Merchandise Inventory	50,000.00	
		Sales	320,000.00	
		Purchases Discounts	12,000.00	
		Income Summary		382,000.00
	31	Income Summary	22,500.00	
		Retained Earnings		22,500.00
	31	Retained Earnings	8,000.00	
		Cash Dividends Declared		8,000.00

APPENDIX

C

The Adjusting Entry Approach to Accounting for Merchandise Inventories

LO 6 Explain the adjusting entry approach to accounting for inventories and prepare a work sheet, adjusting entries, and closing entries according to the adjusting entry approach.

In the closing entries described in Chapter 5, we first transferred the amount of the beginning merchandise inventory to the Income Summary account. Then we recorded the ending inventory in the Merchandise Inventory account as part of a second closing entry. An alternative approach accomplishes these two transfers as adjustments on the work sheet; then they are recorded in the journal as adjusting entries.

Some accountants prefer the closing entry approach and others prefer the adjusting entry approach. Either accomplishes the same result, and the choice creates absolutely no difference in the financial statements. Some computerized accounting systems, however, prepare closing entries automatically. That is, the person who uses a computer system does not manually prepare closing entries. On receiving a single command of ''close the accounts,'' the computer automatically closes all of the temporary accounts—but only the temporary accounts. Because the inventory account is not temporary, its balance is left unchanged by the automatic closing process. Thus, when using a system like this, you have to apply the adjusting entry approach to bring the Merchandise Inventory account balance up to date.

To illustrate the difference between the closing and adjusting entry approaches, we return to the example of Iowa Sales, Incorporated. In the closing entry approach used in Chapter 5, we removed the $19,000 beginning inventory balance from the Merchandise Inventory account and transferred it to the Income Summary account in the first closing entry. We recorded the $21,000 ending inventory in the Income Summary account in the second closing entry. This entry also put the $21,000 ending inventory balance in the Merchandise Inventory account.

In the adjusting entry approach, the first adjusting entry is prepared to transfer the beginning inventory out of the Merchandise Inventory account and into the Income Summary. A second adjusting entry records the ending inventory as a debit balance in the Merchandise Inventory account and as a credit to Income Summary. The adjusting and closing entries under both approaches are shown side by side in Illustration C–1. The entries to the inventory account are in color.

ILLUSTRATION C–1

Adjusting and Closing Entries for a Merchandising Corporation

		Closing Entry Approach		Adjusting Entry Approach	
1993	Adjusting Entries				
Dec. 31	Insurance Expense	600.00		600.00	
	Prepaid Insurance		600.00		600.00
31	Office Supplies Expense	200.00		200.00	
	Office Supplies		200.00		200.00
31	Store Supplies Expense	400.00		400.00	
	Store Supplies		400.00		400.00
31	Depreciation Expense, Office Equipment	700.00		700.00	
	Accumulated Depreciation, Office Equipment		700.00		700.00
31	Depreciation Expense, Store Equipment	3,000.00		3,000.00	
	Accumulated Depreciation, Store Equipment		3,000.00		3,000.00
31	Income Taxes Expense	100.00		100.00	
	Income Taxes Payable		100.00		100 00
31	**Income Summary**	—		**19,000.00**	
	Merchandise Inventory		—		**19,000.00**
31	**Merchandise Inventory**	—		**21,000.00**	
	Income Summary		—		**21,000.00**
	Closing Entries				
31	Income Summary	323,100.00		304,100.00	
	Merchandise Inventory		**19,000.00**		—
	Sales Returns and Allowances		1,900.00		1,900.00
	Sales Discounts		4,300.00		4,300.00
	Purchases		235,800.00		235,800.00
	Transportation-In		1,500.00		1,500.00
	Depreciation Expense, Store Equipment		3,000.00		3,000.00
	Sales Salaries Expense		18,500.00		18,500.00
	Rent Expense, Selling Space		8,100.00		8,100.00
	Store Supplies Expense		400.00		400.00
	Advertising Expense		700.00		700.00
	Depreciation Expense, Office Equipment		700.00		700.00
	Office Salaries Expense		25,800.00		25,800.00
	Insurance Expense		600.00		600.00
	Rent Expense, Office Space		900.00		900.00
	Office Supplies Expense		200.00		200.00
	Income Taxes Expense		1,700.00		1,700.00
31	**Merchandise Inventory**	**21,000.00**		—	
	Sales	306,200.00		306,200.00	
	Purchases Returns and Allowances	1,200.00		1,200.00	
	Purchases Discounts	4,100.00		4,100.00	
	Income Summary		332,500.00		311,500.00
31	Income Summary	9,400.00		9,400.00	
	Retained Earnings		9,400.00		9,400.00
31	Retained Earnings	4,000.00		4,000.00	
	Cash Dividends Declared		4,000.00		4,000.00

Illustration C–1 shows that both approaches accomplish exactly the same changes in the Merchandise Inventory account. The beginning inventory of $19,000 was removed from the account with a credit and the $21,000 ending inventory was added to the account with a debit. The only difference between the two approaches was whether the changes were made in a closing entry or an adjusting entry.

Also, both approaches produce exactly the same credit balance of $9,400 in the Income Summary account. Under the adjusting entry approach, the effects of the beginning and ending inventories on Income Summary are recorded with adjusting entries. And under the closing entry approach, these effects are recorded with closing entries.

The Work Sheet under the Adjusting Entry Approach

The effect of the adjusting entry approach on the work sheet is depicted in Illustration C–2, which shows the work sheet for Iowa Sales, Incorporated. The transfer of the $19,000 beginning inventory from Merchandise Inventory to Income Summary is entered in the Adjustments columns of the work sheet as entry (*g*) on lines 3 and 15. The $21,000 ending inventory amount is debited to Merchandise Inventory and credited to Income Summary in the Adjustments columns as entry (*h*) on lines 3 and 15.

On line 3 of Illustration C–2, note that adjustment (*g*) removes the beginning inventory balance from the Merchandise Inventory account.

Adjustment (*h*) establishes the ending inventory amount in the account. Because the ending balance is an asset on December 31, 1993, it is carried directly to the Statement of Retained Earnings or Balance Sheet Debit column. Illustration C–2 also shows that the Income Summary account (line 15) was listed at the time the work sheet was first prepared. Note as well that the debit and credit adjustments (*g*) and (*h*) to this account are each carried into the Income Statement columns. Then, both these amounts are used to prepare the income statement. Therefore, you should *not* subtract one from the other and carry only the net amount over to the Income Statement columns. Rather, the $19,000 beginning inventory is extended to the Income Statement Debit column and the $21,000 ending inventory is extended to the Income Statement Credit column. Thus, the Income Statement columns end up being identical under the closing and adjusting entry approaches.

The remaining steps for completing the work sheet are exactly the same under either the adjusting entry approach or the closing entry approach, with one major exception. Specifically, the closing entries do not have a debit or credit for inventory. To see the work sheet differences between the two methods, compare Illustration C–2 (the adjusting entry approach) with Illustration 5–3 on p. 260 (the closing entry approach).

Summary of Appendix C in Terms of Learning Objective

LO 6. With the adjusting entry approach, adjusting entries update the Merchandise Inventory account and record the beginning and ending inventory elements of cost of goods sold in the Income Summary account. On the work sheet, these adjustments are entered in the Adjustments columns. Then, the ending inventory is extended to the Retained Earnings Statement or Balance Sheet Debit column. Both the debit and credit adjustments to Income Summary are individually extended to the Income Statement columns.

ILLUSTRATION C-2

The Work Sheet when the Adjusting Entry Approach Is Used

IOWA SALES, INCORPORATED
Work Sheet
For Year Ended December 31, 1993

		Unadjusted Trial Balance		Adjustments		Income Statement		Retained Earnings Statement or Balance Sheet	
	Account Titles	Dr.	Cr.	Dr.	Cr.	Dr.	Cr.	Dr.	Cr.
1	Cash	8,200						8,200	
2	Accounts receivable	11,200						11,200	
3	Merchandise inventory	19,000		(*h*) 21,000	(*g*) 19,000			21,000	
4	Prepaid insurance	900			(*a*) 600			300	
5	Office supplies	300			(*b*) 200			100	
6	Store supplies	600			(*c*) 400			200	
7	Office equipment	4,400						4,400	
8	Accum. depr., office equipment		600		(*d*) 700				1,300
9	Store equipment	29,100						29,100	
10	Accum. depr., store equipment		2,500		(*e*) 3,000				5,500
11	Accounts payable		3,600						3,600
12	Income taxes payable				(*f*) 100				100
13	Common stock		50,000						50,000
14	Retained earnings		8,600						8,600
15	Income summary			(*g*) 19,000	(*h*) 21,000	19,000	21,000		
16	Cash dividends declared	4,000						4,000	
17	Sales		306,200				306,200		
18	Sales returns and allowances	1,900				1,900			
19	Sales discounts	4,300				4,300			
20	Purchases	235,800				235,800			
21	Purchases returns and allowances		1,200				1,200		
22	Purchases discounts		4,100				4,100		
23	Transportation-in	1,500				1,500			
24	Depr. expense, store equipment			(*e*) 3,000		3,000			
25	Sales salaries expense	18,500				18,500			
26	Rent expense, selling space	8,100				8,100			
27	Store supplies expense			(*c*) 400		400			
28	Advertising expense	700				700			
29	Depr. expense, office equipment			(*d*) 700		700			
30	Office salaries expense	25,800				25,800			
31	Insurance expense			(*a*) 600		600			
32	Rent expense, office space	900				900			
33	Office supplies expense			(*b*) 200		200			
34	Income taxes expense	1,600		(*f*) 100		1,700			
35		376,800	376,800	45,000	45,000	323,100	332,500	78,500	69,100
36	Net income					9,400			9,400
37						332,500	332,500	78,500	78,500

Glossary

LO 5 Define or explain the words and phrases listed in the chapter glossary.

Cash discount a deduction from the invoice price of goods that is granted if payment is made within a specified period of time. p. 250

Credit memorandum a memorandum sent to notify its recipient that the sender has credited the recipient's account in its records. p. 268–69

Credit period the agreed period of time for which credit is granted and at the end of which payment is expected. p. 250

Credit terms the specified amounts and timing of payments that a buyer agrees to make in return for being granted credit to purchase goods or services. p. 250

Debit memorandum a memorandum sent to notify its recipient that the sender has debited the recipient's account in its records. p. 268–69

Discount period the period of time during which, if payment is made, a cash discount may be deducted from the invoice price. p. 250

EOM an abbreviation for the words *end-of-month* that is sometimes used in expressing the credit terms of a sales agreement. p. 250

FOB the abbreviation for *free on board,* which is the legal arrangement for identifying the location (shipping point or destination) at which the seller transfers ownership of purchased goods to the buyer; if the terms are FOB factory (or shipping point), the buyer must pay the shipping costs; if the terms are FOB destination, the seller must pay the shipping costs. p. 256

General and administrative expenses expenses that support the overall management and operations of a business, such as central office, accounting, personnel, and credit and collection expenses. p. 258

Gross profit the difference between revenue and the cost of goods sold. p. 249

Inventory the collection of goods on hand waiting to be sold to customers. p. 252

List price the nominal price of an item from which any trade discount is deducted to determine the actual sales price; also known as the catalog price. p. 270

Merchandise goods bought and sold to others. p. 248

Multiple-step income statement an income statement on which cost of goods sold and the expenses are subtracted in steps to get net income. p. 268

Periodic inventory system a method of accounting for inventories in which the inventory account is brought up to date once each period; requires the business to count the items on hand at the end of the period. p. 252

Perpetual inventory system a method of accounting for inventories in which cost of goods sold is recorded each time a sale is made and an up-to-date record of goods on hand is maintained. p. 252

Purchases discounts deductions from the invoice price of purchased items granted by suppliers in return for early payment; that is, cash discounts from suppliers. p. 254

Retained earnings statement a financial statement that reports the changes in a corporation's retained earnings that occurred during an accounting period. p. 259, 263–64

Sales discount a deduction from the invoice price granted to customers in return for early payment; that is, cash discounts to customers. p. 251

Selling expenses the expenses of preparing and storing merchandise for sale, promoting sales, actually making sales, and delivering goods to customers. p. 258

Single-step income statement an income statement on which cost of goods sold and operating expenses are added together and subtracted from net sales in one step to get net income. p. 268

Trade discount a deduction from a list or catalog price that is used to determine the actual sales price of goods. p. 270

Transportation-in costs incurred by a purchaser for transporting purchased merchandise to its place of business. p. 255

Synonymous Terms

Actual sales price invoice price

FOB factory FOB shipping point

Gross profit gross margin

List price catalog price

Merchandise goods

Objective Review

Answers to the following questions are listed at the end of this chapter. Be sure that you decide which is the one best answer to each question *before* you check the answers.

LO 1. A deduction from the sales price of goods that is granted if payment is made within a specified period of time is a:

a. Trade discount.
b. Favored customer.
c. Credit discount.
d. Cash discount.
e. Merchandise discount.

LO 2. On the work sheet for a merchandising company that uses the closing entry approach to account for inventories:

a. The beginning inventory is extended from the trial balance to the Income Statement Credit column.
b. The ending inventory is inserted in the Income Statement Debit column and then extended to the Retained Earnings Statement or Balance Sheet Debit column.
c. The amount of cost of goods sold is calculated in the Adjustments columns.
d. The beginning inventory and ending inventory amounts appear in the Income Statement Debit and Income Statement Credit columns, respectively.

e. The components of the cost of purchases are extended to the Retained Earnings Statement or Balance Sheet Debit column.

LO 3 With a periodic inventory system, cost of goods sold:

a. Is subtracted from the cost of goods available for sale to determine gross profit from sales.
b. Plus the net cost of purchases equals the cost of goods available for sale.
c. Is calculated as the cost of the beginning inventory plus the cost of purchases less the cost of the ending inventory.
d. Is subtracted from gross sales to determine net sales.
e. Includes all operating expenses related to merchandising operations.

LO 4 In recording transactions that involve the purchase and resale of merchandise when a periodic inventory system is used:

a. The sales price of merchandise returned by customers is credited to Sales Returns and Allowances.
b. The purchase price of merchandise returned to a supplier is debited to Purchases Returns and Allowances.
c. The Sales account is credited for the cost of merchandise sold to customers.
d. The amount of any sales discounts taken by customers is debited to a Sales Discounts account.
e. The amount of any purchases discounts is debited to a Purchases Discounts account.

LO 5 When closing entries are used to account for merchandise inventories:

a. The closing entries include a credit to Merchandise Inventory for the cost of the beginning inventory.
b. The closing entries include a debit to Merchandise Inventory for the cost of the ending inventory.
c. The cost of goods sold is recorded in a separate Cost of Goods Sold account that is closed to Income Summary.
d. Cost of goods sold is calculated as the difference between the beginning and ending merchandise inventory amounts.
e. Both *(a)* and *(b)* are correct.

LO 6 When adjusting entries are used to account for merchandise inventories:

a. The adjusting entries include a debit to Merchandise Inventory for the cost of the beginning inventory.
b. The adjusting entries include a debit to Merchandise Inventory for the cost of the ending inventory.
c. The cost of goods sold is recorded in a separate Cost of Goods Sold account that is closed to Income Summary.

d. Cost of goods sold is calculated as the difference between the beginning and ending merchandise inventory amounts.

e. Both (*a*) and (*b*) are correct.

A letter [C] *identifies the questions, exercises, and problems that are based on Appendix C at the end of the chapter.*

Questions for Class Discussion

1. What is gross profit?
2. Can a business earn a gross profit on its sales and still suffer a net loss? How?
3. Why should the manager of a business be interested in the amount of its sales returns and allowances?
4. Since sales returns and allowances are subtracted from sales on the income statement, why not save the effort of this subtraction by debiting all such returns and allowances directly to the Sales account?
5. What is a cash discount?
6. What is the difference between cash discounts offered as sales discounts and purchases discounts?
7. If terms are 2/10, n/60, what is the length of the credit period? What is the length of the discount period?
8. How and when is cost of goods sold determined in a store that uses a periodic inventory system?
9. Which of the following transactions would be debited to the Purchases account of a grocery store: (*a*) the purchase of a cash register; (*b*) the purchase of a refrigerated display case; (*c*) the purchase of advertising space in a newspaper; and (*d*) the purchase of a case of chicken soup?
10. If a business is allowed to return all unsatisfactory merchandise purchased and receive full credit for the purchase price, why should it be interested in controlling the amount of its returns?
11. What do the letters FOB mean? What does the term *FOB destination* mean?
12. At the end of an accounting period, does the beginning or ending inventory appear on the unadjusted trial balance of a company that uses a periodic inventory system?
13. What information appears on a retained earnings statement?
14. What relationship does a retained earnings statement have to the balance sheets at the end of the prior period and at the end of the current period?
15. How does a single-step income statement differ from a multiple-step income statement?
16. During the year, a company purchased merchandise that cost $165,000. What was the company's cost of goods sold if there were: (*a*) no beginning or ending inventories? (*b*) a beginning inventory of $35,000 and no ending inventory? (*c*) a $30,000 beginning inventory and a $42,000 end-

ing inventory? and (*d*) no beginning inventory and a $21,000 ending inventory?

17. In counting the merchandise on hand at the end of an accounting period, a clerk failed to count and consequently omitted from the inventory all the merchandise on one shelf. If the cost of the merchandise on that shelf was $150, what was the effect of the omission on (*a*) the balance sheet and (*b*) the income statement?
18. Suppose that the omission of the $150 from the inventory in the previous question was not discovered. What would be the effect on the balance sheet and income statement prepared at the end of the next accounting period?
19. Distinguish between cash discounts and trade discounts. Is the amount of a trade discount on purchased merchandise credited to the Purchases Discounts account?
20. When a debit memorandum is issued, who records the described debit, the originator of the memorandum or the company receiving it?
21. Refer to the consolidated statement of income of McDonald's Corporation shown in Appendix K. What item appears to represent the company's cost of goods sold?
22. Refer to the balance sheets of Lands' End, Inc., shown in Appendix K. What percentage of total assets was represented by inventory on January 31, 1991? On January 31, 1990?
23. [C] What are the procedural differences between the adjusting entry and closing entry approaches to accounting for inventories?
24. [C] Where is the ending inventory entered on the work sheet when a company uses the adjusting entry approach to accounting for inventories?
25. [C] In comparing the adjusting entry and closing entry approaches to accounting for inventories, what effect does the adjusting entry approach have on the reported amount of the ending inventory? What effect does it have on the net income or net loss?

Exercises

Exercise 5–1
Analyzing and recording purchases and purchases discounts
(LO 1)

Village Store purchased merchandise having a $7,000 invoice price, terms 2/10, n/60, from a manufacturer and paid for the merchandise within the discount period. (*a*) Give (without dates) the journal entries made by the store to record the purchase and payment. (*b*) Give (without dates) the entries made by the manufacturer to record the sale and collection. (*c*) If Village Store borrowed sufficient money at a 12% annual rate of interest on the last day of the discount period to pay the invoice, how much did the store save by borrowing to take advantage of the discount?

Exercise 5–2
Journalizing merchandise transactions
(LO 1)

Prepare journal entries to record the following transactions of Harris General Store:

July 5 Purchased merchandise from Eastern Company subject to the following terms: $600 invoice price, 2/15, n/60, FOB factory.

7 Paid Martin Trucking $65 for shipping charges on the purchase of July 5.

9 Returned to Eastern Company unacceptable merchandise with a list price of $200.

19 Sent Eastern Company a check to pay for the July 5 purchase, net of discount and return.

20 Purchased merchandise from Southern Company subject to the following terms: $900 list price, 2/10, n/30, FOB Southern Company factory. The invoice showed that Southern Company had paid the trucking company $70 to ship the merchandise to Harris.

24 After advising Southern Company that some merchandise was damaged, received a credit memorandum granting Harris a $300 allowance on the July 20 purchase.

30 Paid Southern Company for the July 20 purchase, net of the allowance, and the shipping charges prepaid by Southern.

Exercise 5–3
Journal entries for purchases and sales and returns
(LO 1)

On July 6, 1993, F Company received $7,000 of merchandise and an invoice dated July 5, terms of 2/10, n/30, FOB G Company's factory. On the day the goods were received, F Company paid Fast Freight Company $270 for shipping charges on the purchased merchandise. The next day, F Company returned to G Company $600 of defective goods and, on July 15, mailed G Company a check for the amount owed. Prepare general journal entries to record these transactions (*a*) on the books of F Company and (*b*) on the books of G Company. Assume that G Company recorded the return and the check the day after each was sent.

Exercise 5–4
Calculating expenses and income
(LO 2)

Copy the following tabulation and fill in the missing amounts. Indicate a loss by placing parentheses around the amount. Each horizontal row of figures is a separate situation.

Sales	Beginning Inventory	Purchases	Ending Inventory	Cost of Goods Sold	Gross Profit	Expenses	Net Income or Loss
$198,000	$144,000	$126,000	$?	$171,000	$?	$ 90,000	$?
333,000	117,000	?	135,000	144,000	?	99,000	90,000
270,000	90,000	?	54,000	?	153,000	81,000	72,000
?	135,000	198,000	108,000	?	180,000	72,000	?
288,000	108,000	171,000	?	189,000	?	126,000	?
90,000	27,000	?	45,000	54,000	?	?	9,000
?	207,000	396,000	234,000	?	252,000	?	90,000
144,000	?	90,000	63,000	?	54,000	?	18,000

Exercise 5–5
Multiple-step income statement for a proprietorship
(LO 3)

The Cottage is a single proprietorship business that ends its annual accounting period on December 31. The Income Statement columns of The Cottage's December 31, 1993, work sheet are on the next page. Use the information in these columns to prepare a 1993 multiple-step income statement for The Cottage.

	Income Statement	
	Debit	Credit
Merchandise inventory	64,500	72,000
Sales		360,000
Sales returns and allowances	2,250	
Sales discounts	2,700	
Purchases	216,000	
Purchases returns and allowances		1,500
Purchases discounts		4,500
Transportation-in	1,050	
Selling expenses	54,000	
General and administrative expenses	37,500	
	378,000	438,000
Net income	60,000	
	438,000	438,000

Exercise 5–6
Preparing and posting proprietorship closing entries
(LO 4)

Part 1. Assume that The Cottage of Exercise 5–5 is owned by Carrie Black and prepare entries to close the temporary accounts of the business.

Part 2. Construct a Merchandise Inventory account in the form of a balance column account and enter the $64,500 beginning inventory of Exercise 5–5 as its balance on December 31, 1992. Then post to the account the portions of the closing entries that affect this account.

Exercise 5–7
Preparing an income statement from closing entries
(LO 3, 4)

The following two closing entries for Western Sales were made at the end of its 1993 annual accounting period. (Note that the individual expense accounts are combined to shorten the exercise.)

Dec.	31	Income Summary	475,200.00	
		Merchandise Inventory		63,000.00
		Sales Returns and Allowances		3,600.00
		Sales Discounts		5,400.00
		Purchases		270,000.00
		Transportation-In		7,200.00
		Selling Expenses		72,000.00
		General and Administrative Expenses		54,000.00
	31	Merchandise Inventory	82,500.00	
		Sales	450,000.00	
		Purchases Returns and Allowances	1,800.00	
		Purchases Discounts	3,600.00	
		Income Summary		537,900.00

Required

Use the information in the closing entries to prepare an income statement for Western Sales.

Exercise 5–8
Multiple-step income statement and retained earnings statement
(LO 3)

The following items (with expenses condensed to conserve space) appeared in the last four columns of a work sheet prepared for Little Store, Incorporated, as of December 31, 1993, the end of its annual accounting period. Use this information to prepare a 1993 multiple-step income statement and a retained earnings statement for the corporation.

	Income Statement		Retained Earnings Statement or Balance Sheet	
	Debit	**Credit**	**Debit**	**Credit**
Merchandise inventory	71,000	90,000	90,000	
Other assets			225,000	
Common stock				111,500
Retained earnings				160,500
Cash dividends declared			30,000	
Sales		540,000		
Sales returns and allowances	2,700			
Sales discounts	5,400			
Purchases	324,000			
Purchases returns and allowances		1,800		
Purchases discounts		4,500		
Transportation-in	900			
Selling expenses	81,000			
General and administrative expenses	63,900			
Income taxes expense	14,400			
	563,300	636,300	345,000	272,000
Net income	73,000			73,000
	636,300	636,300	345,000	345,000

Exercise 5–9
Preparing and posting closing entries
(LO 4)

Part 1. Prepare entries to close the temporary accounts of Little Store, Incorporated (Exercise 5–8).

Part 2. Construct a Merchandise Inventory account in the form of a balance column account and enter the $71,000 beginning inventory of Exercise 5–8 as its December 31, 1992, balance. Then post to the account those portions of the store's closing entries that affect its balance.

Exercise 5–10
Calculating operating expenses and cost of goods sold
(LO 2, 3)

The following information was taken from a single proprietorship's income statement:

Sales	$270,000	Purchases returns and allowances	$ 900
Sales returns	1,800	Purchases discounts	2,700
Sales discounts	3,600	Transportation-in	5,400
Beginning inventory	72,000	Gross profit from sales	84,600
Purchases	171,000	Net loss	7,200

Required

Prepare calculations to determine (*a*) total operating expenses, (*b*) cost of goods sold, and (*c*) ending inventory.

Exercise 5–11
Preparing a work sheet for a merchandising corporation
(LO 3)

The following trial balance was taken from the ledger of Crown, Incorporated, at the end of its annual accounting period. (To simplify the exercise and save time, the account balances are in one- and two-digit numbers.)

CROWN, INCORPORATED
Unadjusted Trial Balance
December 31, 1993

Cash	$ 3	
Accounts receivable	11	
Merchandise inventory	9	
Store supplies	6	
Store equipment	15	
Accumulated depreciation, store equipment		$ 4
Accounts payable		6
Salaries payable	—	—
Common stock, $1 par value		18
Retained earnings		15
Cash dividends declared	2	
Sales		63
Sales returns and allowances	3	
Purchases	28	
Purchases discounts		5
Transportation-in	3	
Depreciation expense, store equipment	—	—
Salaries expense	17	
Rent expense	10	
Store supplies expense	—	—
Advertising expense	4	
Totals	$111	$111

Required

Prepare a work sheet for Crown, Incorporated (do not include columns for an adjusted trial balance). Copy the unadjusted trial balance onto the work sheet and complete the work sheet using the following information:

a. Ending store supplies inventory, $2.
b. Estimated depreciation on the store equipment, $6.
c. Accrued salaries payable, $3.
d. Ending merchandise inventory, $10.

ᶜExercise 5–12
Work sheet for a merchandising corporation; adjusting entry approach
(LO 6)

Use the information in Exercise 5–11 to prepare a work sheet according to the adjusting entry approach to accounting for merchandise inventories.

ᶜExercise 5–13
Updating the Merchandise Inventory account; adjusting entry approach
(LO 6)

Use the adjusting entry approach to accounting for merchandise inventories and prepare adjusting journal entries and closing journal entries for Crown, Incorporated, the company described in Exercise 5–11.

Exercise 5–14
Preparing a work sheet for a merchandising proprietorship
(LO 3)

The following trial balance was taken from the ledger of Martin Sales at the end of its annual accounting period. Jim Martin, owner of Martin Sales, did not make additional investments in the business during 1993. (To simplify the exercise and save time, the account balances are in one- and two-digit numbers.)

MARTIN SALES
Unadjusted Trial Balance
December 31, 1993

Cash	$ 12	
Accounts receivable	16	
Merchandise inventory	24	
Store supplies	14	
Accounts payable		$ 28
Salaries payable	—	—
Jim Martin, capital		39
Jim Martin, withdrawals	9	
Sales		93
Sales returns and allowances	8	
Purchases	37	
Purchases discounts		6
Transportation-in	7	
Salaries expense	28	
Rent expense	11	
Store supplies expense	—	—
Totals	$166	$166

Required

Prepare a work sheet form (do not include columns for an adjusted trial balance). Copy the unadjusted trial balance onto the work sheet and complete the work sheet using the following information:

a. Ending store supplies inventory, $7.
b. Accrued salaries payable, $5.
c. Ending merchandise inventory, $32.

CExercise 5–15
Work sheet for a merchandising proprietorship; adjusting entry approach (LO 6)

Use the information in Exercise 5–14 to prepare a work sheet according to the adjusting entry approach to accounting for merchandise inventories.

CExercise 5–16
Updating the Merchandise Inventory account; adjusting entry approach (LO 6)

Use the adjusting entry approach to accounting for merchandise inventories and prepare adjusting journal entries and closing journal entries for Martin Sales, the company described in Exercise 5–14.

Problems

Problem 5–1
Journal entries for merchandising transactions (LO 1)

Prepare general journal entries to record the following transactions of Ibis Sales Company:

Sept. 2 Purchased merchandise priced at $4,700 on credit, terms 1/15, n/30, FOB the seller's factory.
3 Purchased a new computer for office use on credit for $10,000.
3 Sold merchandise on credit; terms 2/10, 1/30, n/60; $2,900.

Sept. 4 Paid $225 cash for freight charges on the shipment of merchandise purchased on September 2.

8 Sold merchandise for cash, $470.

10 Purchased merchandise on credit; terms 2/15, n/30; $2,600.

12 Received a $400 credit memorandum for merchandise purchased on September 10 and returned for credit.

19 Sold merchandise on credit; terms 2/10, n/30; $2,460.

22 Issued a $335 credit memorandum to customer who had returned a portion of the merchandise purchased on September 19.

23 Purchased office supplies on credit, $295.

24 Received a credit memorandum of $70 for unsatisfactory office supplies purchased on September 23 and returned for credit.

25 Paid for the merchandise purchased on September 10, less the return and the discount.

29 The customer who purchased merchandise on September 3 paid for the purchase of that date less the applicable discount.

29 Received payment for the merchandise sold on September 19, less the return and applicable discount.

Oct. 1 Paid for the merchandise purchased on September 2.

Problem 5–2
Corporate income and retained earnings statements, and closing entries
(LO 3)

On December 31, 1993, the end of Helgeson Sales, Inc.'s annual accounting period, the financial statement columns of the company's work sheet were as follows:

	Income Statement		Retained Earnings Statement or Balance Sheet	
	Debit	Credit	Debit	Credit
Merchandise inventory	40,518	42,948	42,948	
Other assets			312,000	
Common stock				120,000
Retained earnings				223,284
Cash dividends declared			30,000	
Sales		396,612		
Sales returns and allowances	2,364			
Purchases	260,118			
Purchases returns and allowances		936		
Purchases discounts		3,906		
Transportation-in	1,686			
Depreciation expense, store equipment	3,810			
Sales salaries expense	39,312			
Rent expense, selling space	19,440			
Store supplies expense	990			
Advertising expense	1,422			
Depreciation expense, office equipment	954			
Office salaries expense	19,170			
Insurance expense	2,592			
Rent expense, office space	2,160			
Office supplies expense	390			
Telephone expense	1,026			
Income taxes expense	6,786			
	402,738	444,402	384,948	343,284
Net income	41,664			41,664
	444,402	444,402	384,948	384,948

Required

1. Prepare a 1993 classified, multiple-step income statement for the corporation, showing in detail the expenses and the items that make up cost of goods sold.
2. Prepare a 1993 retained earnings statement.
3. Prepare closing entries for the corporation.
4. Open a Merchandise Inventory account and enter a December 31, 1992, balance of $40,518. Then, post the portions of the closing entries that affect this account.
5. Prepare a combined, single-step income and retained earnings statement. Condense each revenue and expense category into a single item.

Problem 5–3
Proprietorship work sheet and closing entries (LO 3)

A December 31, 1993, year-end, unadjusted trial balance from the ledger of The Window Store, a single proprietorship, is as follows:

THE WINDOW STORE
Unadjusted Trial Balance
December 31, 1993

Cash	$ 2,400	
Merchandise inventory	61,152	
Office supplies	438	
Store supplies	1,410	
Prepaid insurance	3,276	
Office equipment	10,644	
Accumulated depreciation, office equipment		$ 3,840
Store equipment	38,178	
Accumulated depreciation, store equipment		15,372
Accounts payable		8,766
Ed Walker, capital		72,540
Ed Walker, withdrawals	32,400	
Sales		342,774
Sales returns and allowances	2,094	
Sales discounts	3,816	
Purchases	205,650	
Purchases returns and allowances		1,332
Purchases discounts		5,292
Transportation-in	1,158	
Depreciation expense, store equipment	–0–	
Sales salaries expense	38,304	
Rent expense, selling space	23,220	
Store supplies expense	–0–	
Advertising expense	684	
Depreciation expense, office equipment	–0–	
Office salaries expense	22,356	
Insurance expense	–0–	
Rent expense, office space	2,736	
Office supplies expense	–0–	
Totals	$449,916	$449,916

Required

1. Copy the unadjusted trial balance on a work sheet and complete the work sheet using the following information:
   a. Ending store supplies inventory, $240.
   b. Ending office supplies inventory, $150.
   c. Expired insurance, $2,682.
   d. Estimated depreciation of store equipment, $3,816.

e. Estimated depreciation of office equipment, $690.
f. Ending merchandise inventory, $62,784.

2. Prepare closing entries for the store.
3. Open a balance column Merchandise Inventory account and enter a December 31, 1992, balance of $61,152. Then post the portions of the closing entries that affect this account.

CProblem 5–4
Adjusting entry approach to proprietorship work sheet, adjusting and closing entries
(LO 6)

Solve this problem using the information presented in Problem 5–3 for The Window Store. However, in satisfying the following requirements, use the adjusting entry approach to account for merchandise inventory.

Required

1. Copy the unadjusted trial balance on a work sheet and complete the work sheet. (Use the information presented in (1) of Problem 5–3.)
2. Prepare adjusting and closing entries for the store.
3. Open a balance column Merchandise Inventory account and enter a December 31, 1992, balance of $61,152. Then post those portions of the adjusting and closing entries that affect this account.

Problem 5–5
Corporate work sheet, income and retained earnings statements, and closing entries
(LO 3)

Following is the unadjusted trial balance of Honcho Shop, Incorporated, on December 31, 1993, the end of the annual accounting period:

HONCHO SHOP, INCORPORATED
Unadjusted Trial Balance
December 31, 1993

Cash	$ 6,570	
Merchandise inventory	62,778	
Office supplies	570	
Store supplies	1,104	
Prepaid insurance	3,798	
Office equipment	15,192	
Accumulated depreciation, office equipment		$ 1,662
Store equipment	66,954	
Accumulated depreciation, store equipment		6,372
Accounts payable		1,434
Salaries payable		–0–
Income taxes payable		–0–
Common stock, $10 par value		72,000
Retained earnings		26,190
Cash dividends declared	18,000	
Sales		494,676
Sales returns and allowances	3,348	
Purchases	302,058	
Purchases returns and allowances		1,344
Purchases discounts		5,262
Transportation-in	3,930	
Depreciation expense, store equipment	–0–	
Sales salaries expense	44,370	
Rent expense, selling space	18,900	
Store supplies expense	–0–	
Advertising expense	6,180	
Depreciation expense, office equipment	–0–	
Office salaries expense	45,288	
Insurance expense	–0–	
Rent expense, office space	2,700	
Office supplies expense	–0–	
Income taxes expense	7,200	
Totals	$608,940	$608,940

Required

1. Copy the unadjusted trial balance on a work sheet and complete the work sheet using the information that follows:
   a. Ending store supplies inventory, $294.
   b. Ending office supplies inventory, $222.
   c. Expired insurance, $2,958.
   d. Depreciation on the store equipment, $6,498.
   e. Depreciation on the office equipment, $1,782.
   f. Accrued sales salaries payable, $402, and accrued office salaries payable, $288.
   g. Additional income taxes expense, $762.
   h. Ending merchandise inventory, $59,688.
2. Prepare a multiple-step classified income statement that shows in detail the expenses and the items that make up cost of goods sold.
3. Prepare a retained earnings statement.
4. Prepare closing entries for the corporation.
5. In addition to the preceding, prepare a single-step statement of income and retained earnings with the items condensed as they would be likely to appear in published statements.

[C]Problem 5–6
Adjusting entry approach to corporate work sheet, income and retained earnings statements, adjusting and closing entries
(LO 6)

Use the information presented in Problem 5–5 for Honcho Shop, Incorporated, in solving this problem. However, in satisfying the following requirements, use the adjusting entry approach to accounting for merchandise inventories.

Required

1. Copy the unadjusted trial balance on a work sheet and complete the work sheet. (Use the adjustments information presented in requirement 1 of Problem 5–5.)
2. Prepare a multiple-step classified income statement that shows in detail the expenses and the items that make up cost of goods sold.
3. Prepare a retained earnings statement.
4. Prepare adjusting and closing entries for the corporation.
5. In addition to the preceding, prepare a single-step statement of income and retained earnings with the items condensed as they would be likely to appear in published statements.

Problem 5–7
Proprietorship work sheet, financial statements, and closing entries
(LO 4)

Following is the unadjusted trial balance of Comfort Clothes on December 31, 1993, the end of the annual accounting period:

COMFORT CLOTHES
Unadjusted Trial Balance
December 31, 1993

Cash	$ 12,330	
Accounts receivable	27,198	
Merchandise inventory	62,214	
Office supplies	930	
Store supplies	2,898	
Prepaid insurance	3,906	
Office equipment	15,012	
Accumulated depreciation, office equipment		$ 3,390
Store equipment	74,376	
Accumulated depreciation, store equipment		12,996
Accounts payable		9,972
Salaries payable		–0–
Trudy Geller, capital		127,218
Trudy Geller, withdrawals	18,000	
Sales		674,568
Sales returns and allowances	6,084	
Purchases	462,102	
Purchases returns and allowances		2,184
Purchases discounts		5,652
Transportation-in	6,150	
Depreciation expense, store equipment	–0–	
Sales salaries expense	51,864	
Rent expense, selling space	24,300	
Store supplies expense	–0–	
Depreciation expense, office equipment	–0–	
Office salaries expense	57,996	
Insurance expense	–0–	
Rent expense, office space	10,620	
Office supplies expense	–0–	
Totals	$835,980	$835,980

Required

1. Copy the unadjusted trial balance on a work sheet form and complete the work sheet using the information that follows:
   a. Ending store supplies inventory, $534.
   b. Ending office supplies inventory, $270.
   c. Expired insurance, $3,366.
   d. Depreciation on the store equipment, $6,498.
   e. Depreciation on the office equipment, $1,782.
   f. Accrued sales salaries payable, $533, and accrued office salaries payable, $252.
   g. Ending merchandise inventory, $65,238.
2. Prepare a multiple-step income statement that shows in detail the expenses and the items that make up cost of goods sold.
3. Prepare a statement of changes in owner's equity. On December 31, 1992, the Trudy Geller, Capital account had a balance of $43,218. Early in 1993, Geller invested an additional $84,000 in the business.
4. Prepare a year-end classified balance sheet with the supplies and prepaid insurance combined and shown as a single item.
5. Prepare adjusting and closing entries.

Problem 5–8
Analytical essay
(LO 3, 4)

In Problem 5–2, the first row of the work sheet shows the merchandise inventory amounts to be reported on the financial statements. Explain why merchandise inventory amounts are shown in both Income Statement columns and explain the work sheet procedures that resulted in the merchandise inventory amounts appearing as they do in the financial statement columns of the work sheet. Also describe the end-of-period journal entries that involve the merchandise inventory amounts shown on the work sheet.

CProblem 5–9
Analytical essay
(LO 3, 6)

In Problem 5–2, the first row of the work sheet shows the merchandise inventory amounts to be reported on the financial statements. Explain how the presentation of these amounts in the work sheet would be different if Helgeson Sales, Inc. had used the adjusting entry approach to accounting for merchandise inventories. Include in your answer an explanation of the work sheet procedures and the end-of-period journal entries when the adjusting entry approach is used.

Alternate Problems

Problem 5–1A
Journal entries for merchandising transactions
(LO 1)

Prepare general journal entries to record the following transactions of Taylor Merchandising:

Nov. 1 Purchased merchandise on credit; terms 2/10, n/30; $8,640.
3 Sold merchandise for cash, $900.
8 Purchased merchandise on credit; terms 2/10, n/30; $6,300, FOB the seller's factory.
8 Paid $270 cash for freight charges on the merchandise shipment of the previous transaction.
9 Purchased delivery equipment on credit, $14,400.
13 Sold merchandise on credit, terms 2/15, 1/30, n/60; $3,600.
14 Received a $900 credit memorandum for merchandise purchased on November 8 and returned for credit.
14 Purchased office supplies on credit, $288, n/30.
16 Sold merchandise on credit, terms 2/10, 1/30, n/60; $2,520.
16 Paid for the merchandise purchased on November 8, less the return and the discount.
17 Received a credit memorandum for unsatisfactory office supplies purchased on November 14 and returned, $72.
20 Issued a $252 credit memorandum to the customer who purchased merchandise on November 16 and returned a portion for credit.
26 Received payment for the merchandise sold on November 16, less the return and applicable discount.
28 The customer of November 13 paid for the purchase of that date, less the applicable discount.

Dec. 1 Paid for the merchandise purchased on November 1.

Problem 5–2A
Corporate income and retained earnings statements, and closing entries
(LO 3)

On December 31, 1993, the end of Pacific Sales, Inc.'s annual accounting period, the financial statement columns of its work sheet appeared as follows:

	Income Statement		Retained Earnings Statement or Balance Sheet	
	Debit	Credit	Debit	Credit
Merchandise inventory	83,196	79,854	79,854	
Other assets			585,342	
Common stock				240,000
Retained earnings				374,844
Cash dividends declared			60,000	
Sales		1,156,464		
Sales returns and allowances	6,858			
Sales discounts	17,496			
Purchases	782,082			
Purchases returns and allowances		3,276		
Purchases discounts		10,764		
Transportation-in	11,046			
Depreciation expense, store equipment	10,692			
Sales salaries expense	84,096			
Rent expense, selling space	39,600			
Store supplies expense	1,944			
Depreciation expense, office equipment	3,312			
Office salaries expense	68,184			
Insurance expense	4,068			
Rent expense, office space	3,600			
Office supplies expense	882			
Income taxes expense	22,950			
	1,140,006	1,250,358	725,196	614,844
Net income	110,352			110,352
	1,250,358	1,250,358	725,196	725,196

Required

1. Prepare a 1993 classified, multiple-step income statement for the corporation, showing in detail the expenses and the items that make up cost of goods sold.
2. Prepare a 1993 retained earnings statement.
3. Prepare closing entries for the corporation.
4. Open a Merchandise Inventory account and enter a December 31, 1992, balance of $83,196. Then, post those portions of the closing entries that affect this account.
5. Prepare a combined, single-step income and retained earnings statement. Condense each revenue and expense category into a single item.

Problem 5–3A
Proprietorship work sheet and closing entries
(LO 3)

The December 31, 1993, year-end, unadjusted trial balance of the ledger of Ocean Store, a single proprietorship, follows:

OCEAN STORE
Unadjusted Trial Balance
December 31, 1993

Cash	$ 8,766	
Merchandise inventory	56,400	
Office supplies	774	
Store supplies	2,058	
Prepaid insurance	4,608	
Office equipment	16,956	
Accumulated depreciation, office equipment		$ 4,404
Store equipment	69,282	
Accumulated depreciation, store equipment		11,490
Accounts payable		5,616
B. J. Ocean, capital		112,302
B. J. Ocean, withdrawals	37,800	
Sales		574,620
Sales returns and allowances	3,822	
Sales discounts	6,228	
Purchases	397,578	
Purchases returns and allowances		2,214
Purchases discounts		5,670
Transportation-in	3,372	
Depreciation expense, store equipment	–0–	
Sales salaries expense	41,652	
Rent expense, selling space	28,800	
Store supplies expense	–0–	
Advertising expense	1,464	
Depreciation expense, office equipment	–0–	
Office salaries expense	33,156	
Insurance expense	–0–	
Rent expense, office space	3,600	
Office supplies expense	–0–	
Totals	$716,316	$716,316

Required

1. Copy the unadjusted trial balance on a work sheet form and complete the work sheet using the following information:
   a. Ending store supplies inventory, $462.
   b. Ending office supplies inventory, $216.
   c. Expired insurance, $3,318.
   d. Depreciation on the store equipment, $7,038.
   e. Depreciation on the office equipment, $2,106.
   f. Ending merchandise inventory, $58,776.
2. Prepare closing entries for the store.
3. Open a balance column Merchandise Inventory account and enter a December 31, 1992, balance of $56,400. Then, post those portions of the closing entries that affect this account.

[C]**Problem 5–4A**
Adjusting entry approach to proprietorship work sheet, adjusting and closing entries
(LO 6)

Solve this problem using the information presented in Problem 5–3A for the Ocean Store. However, in satisfying the following requirements, use the adjusting entry approach to account for the merchandise inventory.

Required

1. Copy the unadjusted trial balance on a work sheet and complete the work sheet. (Use the adjustments information presented in requirement 1 of Problem 5–3A.)

2. Prepare adjusting and closing entries for the store.
3. Open a balance column Merchandise Inventory account and enter a December 31, 1992, balance of $56,400. Then post those portions of the adjusting and closing entries that affect this account.

Problem 5–5A
Corporate work sheet, income and retained earnings statements, and closing entries
(LO 3, 4)

The unadjusted trial balance of Hilger Sales, Inc., on December 31, 1993, the end of the annual accounting period, follows:

HILGER SALES, INC.
Unadjusted Trial Balance
December 31, 1993

Cash	$ 10,602	
Merchandise inventory	80,172	
Office supplies	792	
Store supplies	1,752	
Prepaid insurance	5,208	
Office equipment	17,406	
Accumulated depreciation, office equipment		$ 2,742
Store equipment	78,084	
Accumulated depreciation, store equipment		11,220
Accounts payable		4,050
Salaries payable		–0–
Income taxes payable		–0–
Common stock, $10 par value		90,000
Retained earnings		16,746
Cash dividends declared	9,000	
Sales		641,772
Sales returns and allowances	3,816	
Purchases	422,814	
Purchases returns and allowances		2,598
Purchases discounts		5,916
Transportation-in	3,990	
Depreciation expense, store equipment	–0–	
Sales salaries expense	50,574	
Rent expense, selling space	23,400	
Store supplies expense	–0–	
Advertising expense	6,594	
Depreciation expense, office equipment	–0–	
Office salaries expense	47,160	
Insurance expense	–0–	
Rent expense, office space	3,600	
Office supplies expense	–0–	
Income taxes expense	10,080	
Totals	$775,044	$775,044

Required

1. Copy the unadjusted trial balance on a work sheet and complete the work sheet using the information that follows:
   a. Ending store supplies inventory, $474.
   b. Ending office supplies inventory, $222.
   c. Expired insurance, $4,458.
   d. Depreciation on the store equipment, $7,668.
   e. Depreciation on the office equipment, $2,058.
   f. Accrued sales salaries payable, $618, and accrued office salaries payable, $150.
   g. Additional income taxes expense, $942.
   h. Ending merchandise inventory, $77,166.
2. Prepare a multiple-step classified income statement that shows in detail the expenses and the items that make up cost of goods sold.

3. Prepare a retained earnings statement.
4. Prepare closing entries for the corporation.
5. In addition to the preceding, prepare a single-step statement of income and retained earnings with the items condensed as they would be likely to appear in published statements.

[C]Problem 5–6A
Adjusting entry approach to corporate work sheet, income and retained earnings statements, adjusting and closing entries
(LO 6)

Solve this problem using the information presented in Problem 5–5A for Hilger Sales, Inc. However, in satisfying the following requirements, use the adjusting entry approach to accounting for the merchandise inventory.

Required

1. Copy the unadjusted trial balance on a work sheet and complete the work sheet. (Use the adjustments information presented in requirement 1 of Problem 5–5A.)
2. Prepare a multiple-step classified income statement that shows in detail the expenses and the items that make up cost of goods sold.
3. Prepare a retained earnings statement.
4. Prepare adjusting and closing entries for the corporation.
5. In addition to the preceding, prepare a single-step statement of income and retained earnings with the items condensed as they would be likely to appear in published statements.

Problem 5–7A
Proprietorship work sheet, financial statements, and closing entries
(LO 4)

The unadjusted trial balance of Ingram's Designs on December 31, 1993, the end of the annual accounting period, follows:

INGRAM'S DESIGNS
Unadjusted Trial Balance
December 31, 1993

Cash	$ 12,204	
Accounts receivable	28,698	
Merchandise inventory	62,226	
Office supplies	1,008	
Store supplies	2,670	
Prepaid insurance	4,284	
Office equipment	14,262	
Accumulated depreciation, office equipment		$ 3,300
Store equipment	67,536	
Accumulated depreciation, store equipment		11,004
Accounts payable		4,608
Salaries payable		-0-
Sally Ingram, capital		135,408
Sally Ingram, withdrawals	30,000	
Sales		662,112
Sales returns and allowances	5,382	
Purchases	458,424	
Purchases returns and allowances		2,304
Purchases discounts		5,178
Transportation-in	5,310	
Depreciation expense, store equipment	-0-	
Sales salaries expense	47,430	
Rent expense, selling space	24,300	
Store supplies expense	-0-	
Depreciation expense, office equipment	-0-	
Office salaries expense	50,280	
Insurance expense	-0-	
Rent expense, office space	9,900	
Office supplies expense	-0-	
Totals	$823,914	$823,914

Required

1. Copy the unadjusted trial balance on a work sheet and complete the work sheet using the following information:
   a. Ending store supplies inventory, $618.
   b. Ending office supplies inventory, $330.
   c. Expired insurance, $3,546.
   d. Depreciation on the store equipment, $5,958.
   e. Depreciation on the office equipment, $1,698.
   f. Accrued sales salaries payable, $582, and accrued office salaries payable, $330.
   g. Ending merchandise inventory, $64,602.
2. Prepare a multiple-step classified income statement that shows in detail the expenses and the items that make up cost of goods sold.
3. Prepare a statement of changes in owner's equity. On December 31, 1992, the Sally Ingram, Capital account had a balance of $45,408. Early in the year, Ingram invested an additional $90,000 in the business.
4. Prepare a year-end classified balance sheet with the supplies and prepaid insurance combined and shown as a single item.
5. Prepare adjusting and closing entries.

Problem 5–8A
Analytical essay
(LO 3, 4)

In Problem 5–2A, the first row of the work sheet shows the merchandise inventory amounts to be reported on the financial statements. Since merchandise inventory is an asset, explain why merchandise inventory amounts are shown in the Income Statement columns. Also explain the work sheet procedures that resulted in the merchandise inventory amounts appearing as they do in the financial statement columns of the work sheet.

The fifth row of the work sheet shows $60,000 of cash dividends declared in the next to last column. Explain what this item represents and whether the $60,000 is likely to have been extended from the Unadjusted Trial Balance or from the Adjustments columns of the work sheet.

CProblem 5–9A
Analytical essay
(LO 3, 6)

In Problem 5–2A, the first row of the work sheet shows the merchandise inventory amounts to be reported on the financial statements. Explain how the presentation of these amounts in the work sheet would be different if Pacific Sales, Inc., had used the adjusting entry approach to accounting for merchandise inventories. Although the Adjustments columns of the work sheet are not shown in Problem 5–2A, describe the difference in the totals of the Adjustments columns that would have resulted if Pacific Sales, Inc., had used the adjusting entry approach to accounting for merchandise inventories.

Serial Problem

Precision Computer Services

(This problem should not be assigned unless the Working Papers are being used. This is the last segment of a serial problem that started in Chapter 2 and was continued in Chapters 3 and 4. If you did not complete the solutions in those chapters, you can begin the problem at this point. However, as you solve the problem in this chapter, you may need to review some of the facts pre-

sented in the Chapter 2, 3, and 4 segments of the problem. *See pages 122, 183, and 240.)*

John Conard started Precision Computer Services on October 1, 1993. Because the business had only a few credit customers during its first three months, the General Ledger included only one Accounts Receivable account. However, as business operations expanded, Conard decided that the General Ledger should be expanded to contain a separate Account Receivable for each credit customer. Although each general ledger account was originally assigned a three-digit number, Conard decided to add a fourth digit to the separate Account Receivable accounts. The Account Receivable accounts are as follows:

Account	Number
Account Receivable—AB Company	1060
Account Receivable—Ball Company	1061
Account Receivable—Call Company	1062
Account Receivable—Dog Enterprise . . .	1063
Account Receivable—Ear Hearing	1064
Account Receivable—Farm Research . . .	1065
Account Receivable—Goodall Limited . . .	1066
Account Receivable—Iceman, Inc.	1067
Account Receivable—Jackets and More . .	1068

Ever since Precision has been in business, there have been repeated inquiries from its customers as to whether or not the company sold computer software and hardware. Conard has analyzed the market potential and decided to carry a limited inventory of some software programs and peripheral equipment. Precision's credit terms to all of its customers who purchase merchandise on credit is 1/10, n/30.

To account for Precision's expanded operations, several additional accounts have been added to the General Ledger. They are:

Account	Number
Merchandise Inventory	119
Sales	413
Sales Returns and Allowances	414
Sales Discounts	415
Purchases	505
Purchases Returns and Allowances	506
Purchases Discounts	507
Transportation-In	508

Precision does not use reversing entries. Journalize and post the following transactions for January, February, and March 1994:

Jan. 2 Paid Ann White for four days, three days last year and one day this year, at her normal rate of $70 per day.

5 Conard invested an additional $3,000 in the business to purchase merchandise inventory.

6 Purchased from DataMax merchandise inventory priced at $5,750 on credit terms of 1/10, n/30, FOB seller's warehouse.

7 Received $445 from Farm Research as final payment on its account. See transactions on November 8 (Chapter 2) and December 29 (Chapter 3).

Jan. 9 Completed a $1,850 job for AB Company and billed $1,400, which is $1,850 less $450 previously received in advance. See transaction on December 9 (Chapter 3).

12 Sold merchandise on credit to Dog Enterprise for $945.

13 Paid $138 for freight charges on the merchandise purchased on January 6.

14 Received notice that Republic Bank had deducted a $9 service charge from the checking account balance.

15 Received $420 from Goodall Limited for computer services.

16 Paid DataMax for the January 6 purchase, net of the discount.

20 Dog Enterprise returned $125 of defective merchandise it had originally purchased on January 12.

21 Notified by Iceman, Inc., of acceptance of Precision's bid of $1,925 for computer services. Received a $500 advance payment.

22 Received balance due from Dog Enterprise as a result of the January 12 sale, net of the discount and the merchandise returned on January 20.

26 Returned defective merchandise to DataMax and accepted credit to apply against future purchases. Cost, less discount, was $95.

27 Sold $2,740 of merchandise on credit to Jackets and More.

28 Purchased an additional $895 of merchandise inventory on credit from DataMax, terms 1/10, n/30, FOB seller's warehouse.

29 Received a $95 credit memo from DataMax acknowledging the return of merchandise on January 26.

30 Paid electric bill of $62 and telephone bill of $105.

30 Paid Ann White for seven days' work.

Feb. 2 Paid $675 to Town Hall Shopping Center for an additional three months' rent.

2 Completed job for Iceman, Inc., for which they had made a partial payment in advance on January 21. Billed them for the balance due.

5 Paid DataMax for merchandise purchased on January 28, less the credit that resulted from the merchandise return on January 26, and less the discount.

9 Paid Shopper Newspaper $25 for advertisement.

10 Received amount due from AB Company as a result of the billing on January 9.

11 Completed work for Ball Company and billed them for $950.

14 Received notice that Republic Bank had deducted a $12 service charge from the checking account balance.

14 Conard withdrew $650.

19 Received $520 from Ball Company in response to our February 11 billing.

20 Notified by AB Company of acceptance of Precision's bid of $2,125 for computer services. Received $600 in advance.

Feb. 24 Sold merchandise, $1,285, on credit to Goodall Limited.
26 Paid telephone bill, $108, and electric bill, $58.
27 Paid Ann White for six days' work.
27 Reimbursed Ann White for business car mileage, 200 miles at $0.24 per mile.
27 Reimbursed Conard for business car mileage, 300 miles at $0.24 per mile.
Mar. 3 Received balance due from Ball Company (see transactions on February 11 and 19).
5 Completed job for AB Company and billed the balance due (see transaction on February 20).
8 Purchased $190 of computer supplies from Ajax Supply on credit.
9 Received balance due from Goodall Limited as a result of the February 24 sale.
15 Replaced damaged parts on Precision's computer. Cost was $120.
16 Notified by Jackets and More of acceptance of Precision's bid of $2,450 for computer services and received $600 in advance.
19 Paid Ajax Supply balance due. See transactions on December 11 (Chapter 3) and on March 8.
24 Completed $850 worth of service work for Ball Company and billed them.
25 Sold $1,780 worth of merchandise on credit to Dog Enterprise.
30 Sold $290 worth of merchandise on credit to Call Company.
30 Paid the electric bill, $62, and the telephone bill, $110.
31 Paid Ann White's business car mileage, 100 miles at $0.24 per mile, and Conard's business car mileage, 200 miles at $0.24 per mile.

At the end of the first quarter of 1994, John Conard is interested in knowing how Precision is doing. Therefore, you need to prepare interim financial statements. Information necessary to prepare the work sheet, adjustments, and interim statements is as follows:

a. Computer supplies ending inventory, $19.
b. Three additional months of insurance has expired (a one-year policy was purchased on October 4 for $195).
c. Ann White has worked four days for which she has not been paid.
d. Three months of prepaid rent has expired.
e. Depreciation on the office equipment for January through March is $21.25.
f. Depreciation on the computer for January through March is $250.
g. Ending merchandise inventory, $2,167.

Do not prepare closing entries.

Provocative Problems

Provocative Problem 5–1
Jane's Workout Wear
(LO 3)

Jeff Frey and Jane Grey were partners in a store specializing in workout clothes. They had a major disagreement and decided to close the business and end their partnership. In settlement for her partnership interest, Jane Grey received an inventory of clothes having a $33,750 wholesale value. Because there was nothing practical she could do with the inventory except to open a new store, she did so by investing it and $27,000 in cash. She used $22,500 of the cash to buy store equipment and opened for business on June 1. During the succeeding seven months, she paid out $75,200 to creditors for additional inventory and $31,500 for operating expenses. She also withdrew $22,000 cash for personal expenses. At year-end, she prepared the following balance sheet:

JANE'S WORKOUT WEAR
Balance Sheet
December 31, 1993

Cash		$13,325	Accounts payable (all for merchandise)	$ 4,950
Merchandise inventory		39,975	Jane Grey, capital	69,050
Equipment	$22,500			
Less accum. depr.	1,800	20,700		
Total assets		$74,000	Total liabilities and owner's equity	$74,000

Based on the given information, calculate (*a*) the net income earned by the business, (*b*) the cost of goods sold, and (*c*) the amount of sales. Then, prepare an income statement that shows the results of the store's operations during its first seven months (June 1, 1993, to December 31, 1993).

Provocative Problem 5–2
Westworld Store
(LO 3)

Wally West, the owner of Westworld Store, has not maintained an adequate accounting system and has asked you to help him prepare an income statement for 1993. Based on data that he has provided, the following balance sheet information is available:

	December 31	
	1992	1993
Cash	$ 4,500	$ 14,580
Accounts receivable	11,160	13,140
Merchandise inventory	54,720	51,300
Equipment (net after depreciation)	44,640	37,080
Total assets	$115,020	$116,100
Accounts payable	$ 16,740	$ 14,760
Wages payable	540	900
Wally West, capital	97,740	100,440
Total liabilities and owner's equity	$115,020	$116,100

Also, the store's records of cash receipts and disbursements provide the following information:

Collection of accounts receivable	$483,120
Payments for:	
Accounts payable	299,160
Employees' wages	86,580
Other operating expenses	33,300
Wally West, withdrawals	54,000

Assuming that the store makes all merchandise purchases and sales on credit, calculate the amounts of its sales, purchases, and wages expense for 1993. Then, prepare an accrual basis income statement for 1993.

Provocative Problem 5–3
Larry's Lights Fantastic
(LO 3)

Larry Lowe worked in the Mountain Valley Store for 20 years, until his father died, leaving him a sizable estate. After sitting around long enough to get bored and see his bank balance start to dwindle, Lowe decided to open a lighting store. When he started the business on May 1, 1993, there were no other lighting stores in the town of Mountain Valley, and Lowe thought that the business would have a good chance to succeed.

On May 1, Lowe deposited $64,200 in a bank account under the name of Larry's Lights Fantastic. He then paid $14,400 cash for store equipment, which he expected to last 10 years before it became worthless. He also bought merchandise for $45,000 cash and paid $4,320 in advance for eight months' rent for the shop.

Lowe estimated that most lighting stores sold their lamps at prices averaging 40% above cost. For example, a lamp that cost $10 was sold for $14. To attract customers from other towns, Lowe decided to mark his merchandise for sale at only 35% above cost. Because his other operating costs would be low, he thought that this pricing strategy would leave a net income equal to at least a suitable 10% of sales.

On December 31, 1993, eight months after opening his store, Lowe has come to you for advice. He thinks business has been good. However, he doesn't quite understand why his cash balance has fallen to $4,000. He has not withdrawn any cash from the business.

In talking with Lowe and examining his records, you determine that the inventory was replaced three times during the eight months, each time at a cost of $45,000. All merchandise purchases have been paid in cash, except for one bill of $13,020, which is not yet due. A full stock of merchandise (cost of $45,000) is on hand and customers owe Lowe $39,110. In addition to the rent paid in advance, Lowe paid $17,640 for other expenses. There are no outstanding bills for expenses.

Prepare (*a*) an income statement for the business covering the eight-month period ended December 31, (*b*) a statement of changes in owner's equity, (*c*) a December 31, 1993, balance sheet, and (*d*) a schedule of cash flows that explains where the $4,000 cash balance came from by showing the cash receipts and cash disbursements during the eight months ended December 31.

Provocative Problem 5–4
International Business Machines Corporation
(LO 2)

For this problem, turn to the financial statements of International Business Machines Corporation shown in Appendix J. Use the information presented in the consolidated statements of earnings and financial position to provide answers to these questions:

1. For each of the four types of revenue and cost (of goods sold) reported (sales, support services, software, and rentals and financing), calculate the amount of gross profit for 1989 and 1990. Identify which area had the greatest and which area had the least amount of growth between the two years.

2. For each of the four types of revenue and cost (of goods sold) reported (sales, support services, software, and rentals and financing), calculate gross profit as a percentage of revenue for 1989 and 1990. In which area did the gross profit percentage increase the most from 1989 to 1990?
3. Although IBM manufactures most of the items it sells, assume that the amounts reported for inventories and cost (of goods sold) were purchased ready for resale. Based on this assumption, calculate the total cost of purchases during 1990.

Provocative Problem 5–5
As a Matter of Ethics: Essay

Ethics

Review the As a Matter of Ethics case on page 257. Discuss the nature of the problem faced by Renee Fleck and evaluate her alternative courses of action.

Answers to Objective Review Questions

LO 1. (*d*)	**LO 3.** (*c*)	**LO 5.** (*e*)
LO 2. (*d*)	**LO 4.** (*d*)	**LO 6.** (*b*)

CHAPTER

6

Accounting Systems

As businesses grow, the number of their transactions becomes very large. To handle this load, companies use special accounting methods and records. Today, most companies use the powerful capabilities of computers to achieve accurate and fast information processing.

Topical Coverage

Even in a small business, a large amount of information must be processed through the accounting system. Thus, the accounting system should be designed to process the information efficiently. As you study this chapter, you will learn some general concepts to follow in designing an efficient accounting system. The chapter begins by explaining the basic components of an accounting system, whether it is a manual or computer-based system. After considering some of the special characteristics of computer-based systems, the chapter then explains some of the labor-saving procedures employed in manual systems. These include efficient ways of processing routine transactions such as credit sales, cash receipts, credit purchases, and cash disbursements.

Learning Objectives

After studying Chapter 6, you should be able to:

1. Describe the five basic components of an accounting system.
2. Describe the types of computers used in large and small accounting systems, the role of software in those systems, and the different approaches to inputting and processing data, including the use of networking.
3. Explain how special journals save labor and journalize and post transactions when special journals are used.
4. Explain how a controlling account and its subsidiary ledger are related and how a subsidiary ledger is used to maintain a separate account for each credit customer or each account payable.
5. Explain how to test the posting of entries to the Accounts Receivable and Accounts Payable subsidiary ledgers and prepare schedules of accounts in those subsidiary ledgers.
6. Explain how sales taxes are recorded in special journals, how sales invoices can serve as a Sales Journal, and how sales returns and allowances are recorded.
7. Define or explain the words and phrases listed in the chapter glossary.

The Components of an Accounting System

LO 1 Describe the five basic components of an accounting system.

Accounting systems consist of people, forms, procedures, and equipment. These systems must be designed to capture data about the transactions of the entity and to generate from that data a variety of financial, managerial, and tax accounting reports. Because all accounting systems must accomplish these same objectives, both manual and computerized accounting systems include the same basic components. However, computer-based systems provide more accuracy, speed, efficiency, and convenience.

The five common components of manual and computerized accounting systems are

ILLUSTRATION 6–1

The Components of an Accounting System

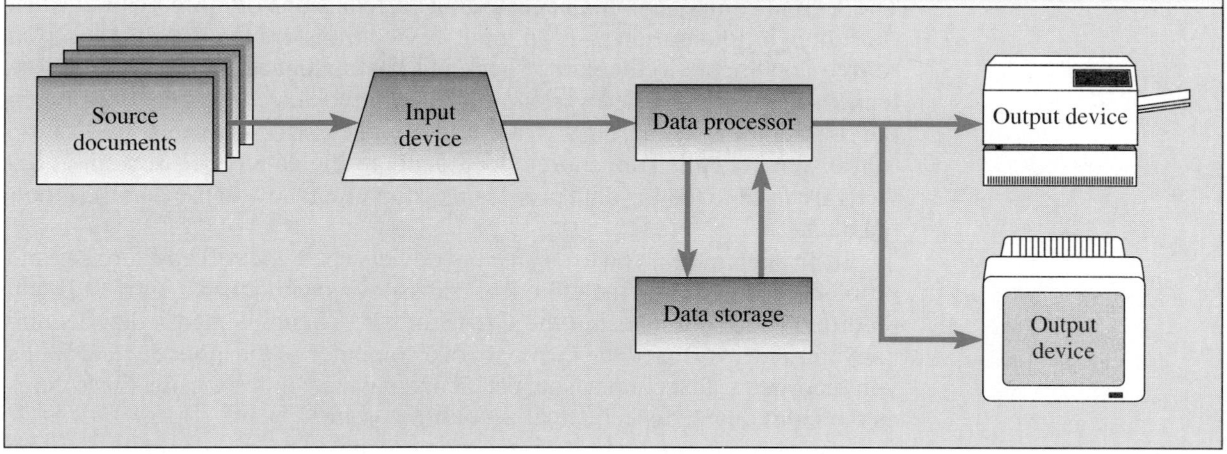

- Source documents.
- Input devices.
- Data processor.
- Data storage.
- Output devices.

Illustration 6–1 shows the relationships between these five components.

Source Documents

Chapter 2 described some of the business papers that companies use in the process of completing transactions. These business papers are called *source documents* because they provide a basis for making accounting entries. In other words, they provide the data that are entered in and processed by the accounting system. From your personal experience, you are no doubt familiar with some kinds of source documents such as bank statements and checks received from other parties. Other examples of source documents include invoices from suppliers, billings to customers, and employee earnings records.

In manual accounting systems, source documents always consist of paper documents. Paper documents are also very important for computerized systems, but newer technologies allow some source documents to take other forms. For example, some companies send invoices directly from their own computers to their customers' computers.

Accurate source documents are important for the proper functioning of an accounting system. If the information going into the system is faulty and incomplete, the information coming out of the system will also be faulty and incomplete. (In computer jargon, the results of defective input are sometimes described as "garbage in, garbage out.")

Input Devices

The second component of an accounting system is one or more **input devices.** As shown in Illustration 6–1, an input device transfers the information from source documents to the data processing component of the accounting system. In a computer-based system, this often involves converting the data on the source documents from a written form into electronic signals. In addition to transferring data from source documents to the data processor, input devices are used to tell the data processing component how to process the inputted data.

In prior chapters, you used an input device when you solved exercises and problems by recording the effects of transactions with journal entries. If you recorded transactions using the GLAS or SPATS supplements that accompany this text, you used the keyboard of a computer as the input device. When you recorded transactions using pencil and paper, you were using these items as the input device for a manual accounting system.

The most common input device for a computer-based accounting system is a keyboard. System operators use keyboards to transfer data from the source documents into the computer. Another input device is a *bar code reader* like those used in grocery and other retail stores. With a bar code reader, the clerk merely moves purchased items over the reader, which picks up their code numbers and sends the data to the computer. Other input devices include *scanners* that read words and numbers directly from source documents.

In both manual systems and computer systems, companies promote clerical accuracy by using routine procedures for inputting data. Also, controls should be in place to ensure that only authorized individuals can input data to the accounting system. Such controls help to protect the integrity of the system and also allow incorrect input to be traced back to its source.

Data Processor

The third component of an accounting system is the **data processor** which interprets, manipulates, and summarizes recorded information so it can be used in analyses and reports. In manual systems, the primary data processor is the accountant's brain. However, the manual processing of data is not entirely a mental process. That is, the accountant uses the journal, the ledger, the working papers, and such procedures as posting to convert the journal entry data into more useful information. Of course, few if any accounting systems are completely manual. For example, calculators are considered essential equipment for manual systems.

As a result of technological developments over the last two decades, many manual accounting systems have been replaced by computer-based systems. The data processor in a computer-based system includes both hardware and software. Hardware is the machinery that performs the steps called for by the software. The software consists of computer programs that specify the opera-

needed data, organizes it in the form of a report, and sends the information to an output device.

Depending on the output device, the information may be displayed on a screen, printed on paper, or expressed as a voice over the telephone. For example, a bank customer may call to find out the balance in his or her checking account. If a touch-tone telephone serves as an input/output device, a recording may ask the customer to enter appropriate identifying information including the number of the account. With this input, the computer searches the database for the information and sends it back over the telephone. If the telephone is not used as an input/output device, the bank employee who answers the phone inputs the information request using a keyboard. The employee then reads the output on a video screen and relays it over the phone to the customer.

Another kind of output involves paying employees without writing paychecks. Instead, the company's computer system may send the payroll data directly to the computer system of the company's bank. Thus, the output of the company's system is an electronic fund transfer (EFT) from the company's bank account to the employees' bank accounts. The output device in this instance is the connection or interface between the computer systems of the company and the bank. Large companies are increasingly using EFTs. In other situations, the company's computer outputs the payroll data on a magnetic tape or disk. The tape or disk is then used by the bank to transfer the funds to the employees' bank accounts.

In addition to the preceding forms of output, many situations require printed output that computer systems produce on laser, impact, or ink-jet printers.

For companies using manual accounting systems, production of output involves physically searching the records to find the needed data and then organizing it in a written report.

Small and Large Computer-Based Systems

LO 2 Describe the types of computers used in large and small accounting systems, the role of software in those systems, and the different approaches to inputting and processing data, including the use of networking.

The world has seen radical changes in the use of computers since the first Apple computer was sold in 1980. Everyone reading this book has at least seen and probably operated a small computer. In fact, many of you are already proficient users of personal computers (PC) such as those produced by International Business Machines (IBM) or by Apple Computer Company. If not, you probably will be by the time you finish your formal education. These computers (often called *microcomputers*) are physically small, easy to operate, and increasingly inexpensive.

Although the use of microcomputers in business has greatly expanded in recent years, many companies also use larger computers called *mainframes*. These machines are able to process huge quantities of accounting data quickly. In addition, they help businesses perform other important tasks such as analyzing the results of market research, compiling stockholder information, and doing engineering design work for products and production lines. These computers include the AS series of machines produced by IBM and the VAX family manufactured by Digital Equipment Company (DEC).

Custom Designed and Off-the-Shelf Programs

Regardless of its size and speed, every computer does nothing more than execute instructions organized as programs. A program consists of a series of very specific instructions for obtaining data from input or storage, processing it, returning it to storage for later use, and sending it to an output device to produce a report.

Illustration 6–2 presents a flowchart of the steps that a computer program might use to process a stack of customer orders for merchandise. When this program is executed in a normal situation, the system creates a shipping order that identifies the products to be sent to customers. If a shipment causes the quantity on hand to fall below the minimum level, the system generates a purchase order to be approved by a manager. If the quantity on hand is less than the customer ordered, the system produces a partial shipping order, as well as a report to the customer that the remainder is on back order. Then, if replacements have not already been ordered, the system produces a purchase order. If no units of the desired product are on hand, the system notifies the customer of the back order and issues a purchase order, unless one already exists. The system follows this process for each item ordered by each customer until the stack of orders is exhausted.

Despite the apparent complexity of the instructions in Illustration 6–2, this routine is actually incomplete. For example, it does not update the accounting records for sales and accounts receivable. Nor does it deal with cash and trade discounts that might be offered to customers.

In the early days of computer systems, each program had to be custom designed using a programming language such as COBOL or FORTRAN. Since then, programmers have developed more flexible and easier-to-use languages. However, programming is a skill that only a limited number of people need to master. Instead, today's markets are rich with two kinds of off-the-shelf programs that are ready to be used.

Some off-the-shelf programs are general, multipurpose applications that accomplish a variety of different tasks. These programs include familiar word processor programs (such as Microsoft Word® and WordPerfect®), spreadsheet programs (such as Microsoft Excel® and Lotus® 1–2–3®), and database management programs (such as dBase®).

Other off-the-shelf programs are designed to meet very specific needs of users. These programs include a large number of accounting programs such as DacEasy Accounting®, Peachtree Complete III®, and Great Plains Accounting Series®. Off-the-shelf programs are user-friendly programs that guide users through the input steps and then ask which reports are desired.

Many of the off-the-shelf accounting programs save time and minimize errors because they operate as *integrated* systems. In an integrated system, actions taken in one part of the system also produce results in related parts.

For example, when a credit sale is recorded in an integrated system, several parts of the system are updated with one or two simple commands. First, the system stores the transaction data (as in a journal) so that you can review the entire entry at a later time. Second, it updates the Cash and Accounts Receivable accounts. Third, it updates a detailed record of the amount owed by the customer. Fourth, it might update a detailed record of the products held for sale to show the number of units sold and the number that remain on hand.

ILLUSTRATION 6–2

Flowchart for an Order-Processing Program

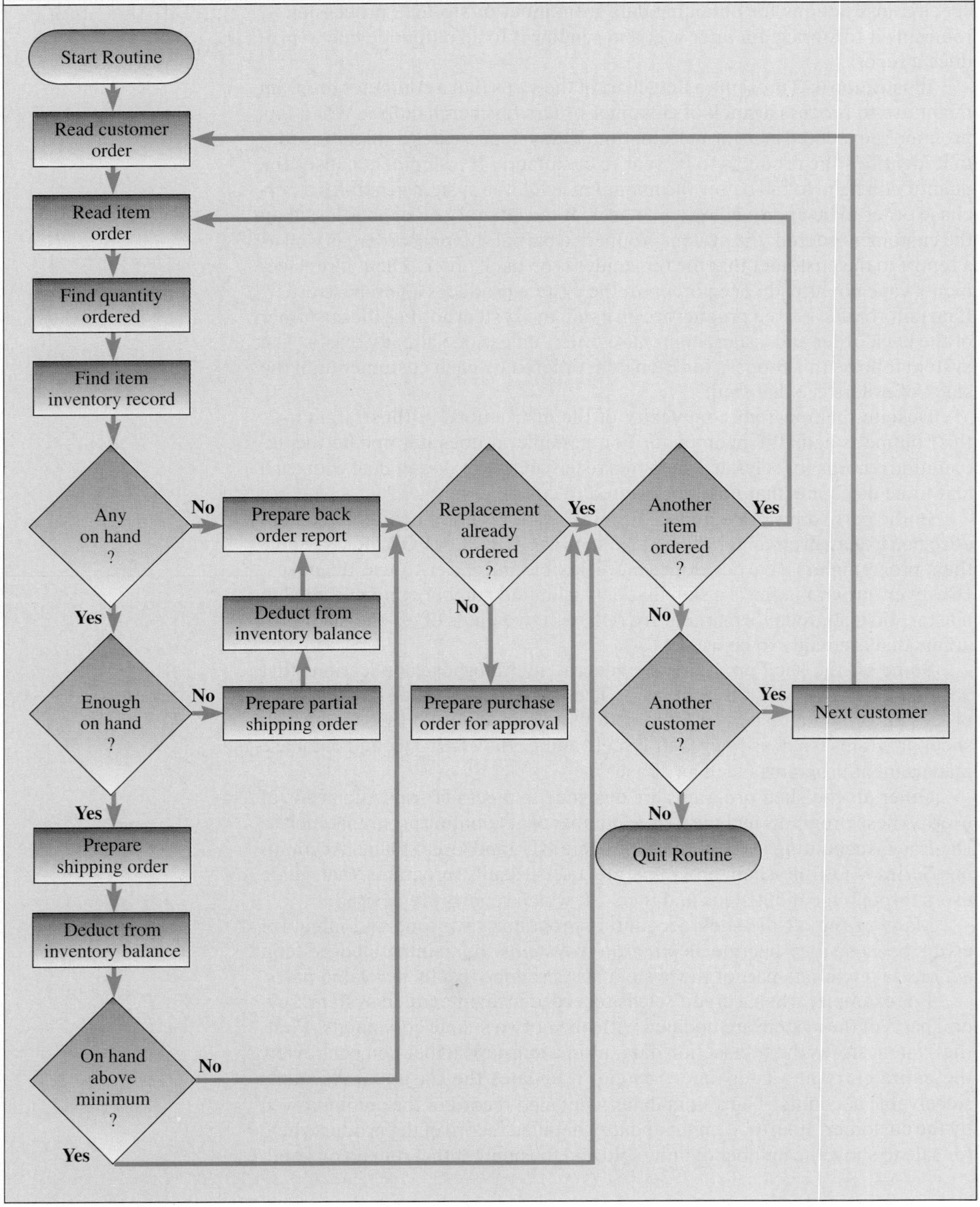

AS A MATTER OF

Opinion

Brenda Smith, CPA

Ms. Smith received her B.A. in accounting from the University of Colorado at Colorado Springs. She is the managing director of Strait Kushinsky and Company, a large public accounting firm in Colorado Springs. Among her partners is Marvin Strait, former chairman of the American Institute of CPAs. She is presently the chairperson of the Colorado Springs Chamber of Commerce, and serves on the governing boards of the American Group of CPAs and the Christian Management Association.

Successful business managers need information, and they need computers to get it for them. Yet, many people are still held back by a fear of computers. We need to learn to be as comfortable with computers as we are with our calculators.

The systems available to today's small businesses are great savers of time and effort. For example, many banks and businesses have linked their computers. This system instantly records deposits to a store's checking account and updates its sales and inventory records at the same time. A lot of paperwork is eliminated, and managers and employees can devote their skills to the business instead of bookkeeping.

Despite the abilities of these new systems, we have to know the appropriate accounting principles to avoid getting "garbage-in-garbage-out" results. While we don't need to understand how to program computers, we do need a basic understanding of their processes. And, we need to understand accounting so that we can make them work for us.

Computers and integrated software programs have dramatically reduced the bookkeeping tasks in accounting. However, do not think that computers have eliminated the need for accountants. Nor should you conclude that success in business no longer requires a knowledge of accounting. *The need for accountants and accounting knowledge is created by the need for information, not by the need for pencil and paper.* Accountants continue to be in demand because their expertise is necessary to determine what information ought to be produced and what data should be used to produce it. Accountants are also needed to analyze and explain the output. Furthermore, writing new, improved programs requires a knowledge of accounting.

In short, the value of accounting knowledge does not disappear just because mechanical steps are done with a computer. You still need to understand the effects of events on the company and how they are reflected in financial statements and management reports.

Batch and On-Line Systems

Accounting systems also differ in terms of how the input is entered and processed. With **batch processing,** the source documents are accumulated for a period of time and then processed all at the same time, such as once a day, week, or month. By comparison, with **on-line processing,** data is entered and processed as soon as source documents are available. As a result, the database is immediately updated.

The disadvantage of batch processing is that the database is not kept up to date during the times that source documents are being accumulated. In many situations, however, companies use batch processing because the database requires only periodic updating. For example, records used in sending bills to customers may require updating only once each month.

On-line processing has the advantage of keeping the database always up to date. However, it is more expensive because the software is more complicated and because it usually requires a much larger investment in hardware. On-line processing applications include airline reservations, credit card records, and rapid response mail-order processing.

Computer Networks

In many circumstances, firms create advantages by linking or networking computers with each other. **Computer networks** allow different users to share access to the same data and the same programs. A relatively small computer network is called a *local area network (LAN)*. This type of network links the machines within an office by special *hard-wire* hookups. For example, many universities have networks in their computer labs. Larger computer networks that are spread over long distances communicate over telephone lines by using *modems*.

In some circumstances, the need for information requires very large networks. Examples include the system used by Federal Express for tracking its packages and billing its customers and the system used by WalMart for monitoring inventory levels in each of its stores. These networks involve many computers (desktops and mainframes) and satellite communications to gather information and to provide ready access to the database from all locations.

We now turn to a discussion of some of the labor-saving procedures used to process transactions in manual systems. However, remember that accounting systems have similar purposes whether they are computer-based or manual in operation. Thus, your understanding of computer-based systems will be improved when you understand manual procedures.

Special Journals

LO 3 Explain how special journals save labor and journalize and post transactions when special journals are used.

The General Journal is a flexible journal in which you can record any transaction. However, each debit and credit entered in a General Journal must be individually posted. As a result, a firm that uses a General Journal to record all the transactions of its business requires much time and labor to post the individual debits and credits.

One way to reduce the writing and the posting labor is to divide the transactions of a business into groups of similar transactions and to provide a separate **special journal** for recording the transactions in each group. For example, most of the transactions of a merchandising business fall into four groups: sales on credit, purchases on credit, cash receipts, and cash disbursements. When a special journal is provided for each group, the journals are

1. A Sales Journal for recording credit sales.

AS A MATTER OF

Ethics

A CPA has a client whose business has grown significantly over the last couple of years and has reached the point where its accounting system has become inadequate for handling both the volume of transactions and management's needs for financial information. The client asks the CPA for advice on which software system would work best for the company.

The CPA has been offered a 10% commission by a software company for each purchase of its system by one of the CPA's clients. The price of one of these systems falls within the range specified by the client. Do you think that the CPA's evaluation of the alternative systems could be affected by this commission arrangement? Should it be? Should the CPA feel compelled to tell the client about the commission arrangement before making a recommendation?

2. A Purchases Journal for recording credit purchases.
3. A Cash Receipts Journal for recording cash receipts.
4. A Cash Disbursements Journal for recording cash payments.
5. A General Journal for all the miscellaneous transactions not recorded in the special journals and also for adjusting, closing, and correcting entries.

The following illustrations show how special journals save time in journalizing and posting transactions. They do this by providing special columns for accumulating the debits and credits of similar transactions. These journals allow you to post the amounts entered in the special columns as column totals rather than as individual amounts. For example, you can save posting labor if you record credit sales for a month in a Sales Journal like the one at the top of Illustration 6–3. As the illustration shows, you do not post the credit sales to the general ledger accounts until the end of the month. Then, you calculate the total sales for the month and post the total as one debit to Accounts Receivable and as one credit to Sales. Only seven sales are recorded in the illustrated journal. However, if you assume the 7 sales represent 700 sales, you can better appreciate the posting labor saved by making only one debit to Accounts Receivable and one credit to Sales.

The special journal in Illustration 6–3 is also called a **columnar journal** because it has columns for recording the date, the customer's name, the invoice number, and the amount of each credit sale. Only credit sales are recorded in it, and they are recorded daily, with the information about each sale placed on a separate line. Normally, the information is taken from a copy of the sales ticket or invoice prepared at the time of the sale. However, before discussing the journal further, you need to understand the role played by subsidiary ledgers.

ILLUSTRATION 6–3

Sales Journal — Page 3

Date		Account Debited	Invoice Number	PR	Amount
Feb.	2	James Henry	307	√	450.00
	7	Albert Smith	308	√	500.00
	13	Sam Moore	309	√	350.00
	15	Paul Roth	310	√	200.00
	22	James Henry	311	√	225.00
	25	Frank Booth	312	√	175.00
	28	Albert Smith	313	√	250.00
	28	Total—Accounts Receivable, Dr.; Sales, Cr.			2,150.00
					(106/413)

Individual amounts are posted daily to the subsidiary ledger.

Total is posted at the end of the month to the general ledger accounts.

Accounts Receivable Ledger

Frank Booth

Date		PR	Debit	Credit	Balance
Feb.	25	S3	175.00		175.00

James Henry

Date		PR	Debit	Credit	Balance
Feb.	2	S3	450.00		450.00
	22	S3	225.00		675.00

Sam Moore

Date		PR	Debit	Credit	Balance
Feb.	13	S3	350.00		350.00

Paul Roth

Date		PR	Debit	Credit	Balance
Feb.	15	S3	200.00		200.00

Albert Smith

Date		PR	Debit	Credit	Balance
Feb.	7	S3	500.00		500.00
	28	S3	250.00		750.00

General Ledger

Accounts Receivable — No. 106

Date		PR	Debit	Credit	Balance
Feb.	28	S3	2,150.00		2,150.00

Sales — No. 413

Date		PR	Debit	Credit	Balance
Feb.	28	S3		2,150.00	2,150.00

Note that the customer accounts are in a subsidiary ledger and the financial statement accounts are in the **General Ledger.**

Explanation columns are omitted from the accounts due to a lack of space.

Keeping a Separate Account for Each Credit Customer

LO 4 Explain how a controlling account and its subsidiary ledger are related and how a subsidiary ledger is used to maintain a separate account for each credit customer or each account payable.

In previous chapters, when we recorded credit sales, we debited a single account called Accounts Receivable. However, when a business has more than one credit customer, the accounts must show how much each customer has purchased, how much each customer has paid, and how much remains to be collected from each customer. To provide this information, businesses with credit customers must maintain a separate Account Receivable for each customer.

One possible way of keeping a separate account for each customer would be to keep all of these accounts in the same ledger that contains the financial statement accounts. However, this usually is not done. Instead, the ledger that contains the financial statement accounts, now called the **General Ledger**, continues to hold a single Accounts Receivable account. Then, a supplementary record is established in which a separate account is maintained for each customer. This supplementary record is called the **Accounts Receivable Ledger**. This subsidiary ledger may exist on tape or disk storage in a computerized system. In a manual system, the Accounts Receivable Ledger may take the form of a book or tray that contains the customer accounts. In either case, the customer accounts in the subsidiary ledger are kept separate from the Accounts Receivable account in the General Ledger.

Understand that when debits (or credits) to Accounts Receivable are posted twice (once to Accounts Receivable and once to the customer's account), this does not violate the requirement that debits equal credits. The equality of debits and credits is maintained in the General Ledger. The Accounts Receivable Ledger is simply a supplementary record that provides detailed information concerning each customer.

Illustration 6–4 shows the relationship between the Accounts Receivable controlling account and the accounts in the subsidiary ledger. Note that after all items are posted, the balance in the Accounts Receivable account should equal the sum of the balances in the customers' accounts. As a result, the Accounts Receivable account controls the Accounts Receivable Ledger and is called a **controlling account**. Since the Accounts Receivable Ledger is a supplementary record controlled by an account in the General Ledger, it is called a **subsidiary ledger**. After posting is completed, if the Accounts Receivable balance does not equal the sum of the customer account balances, you know an error has been made.

Maintaining a Separate Record for Each Account Payable

The Accounts Receivable account and the Accounts Receivable Ledger are not the only examples of controlling accounts and subsidiary ledgers. Most companies buy on credit from several suppliers. As a result, a company must keep a separate account for each creditor. To accomplish this, the firm maintains an Accounts Payable controlling account in the General Ledger and a separate account for each creditor in a subsidiary **Accounts Payable Ledger**. The controlling account, subsidiary ledger, and columnar journal techniques demonstrated thus far with accounts receivable also apply to the creditor accounts. The only difference is that a Purchases Journal and a Cash Disbursements Journal are used to record most of the transactions that affect these accounts. You will learn about these journals later in the chapter.

ILLUSTRATION 6–4

The Accounts Receivable Controlling Account and Subsidiary Ledger

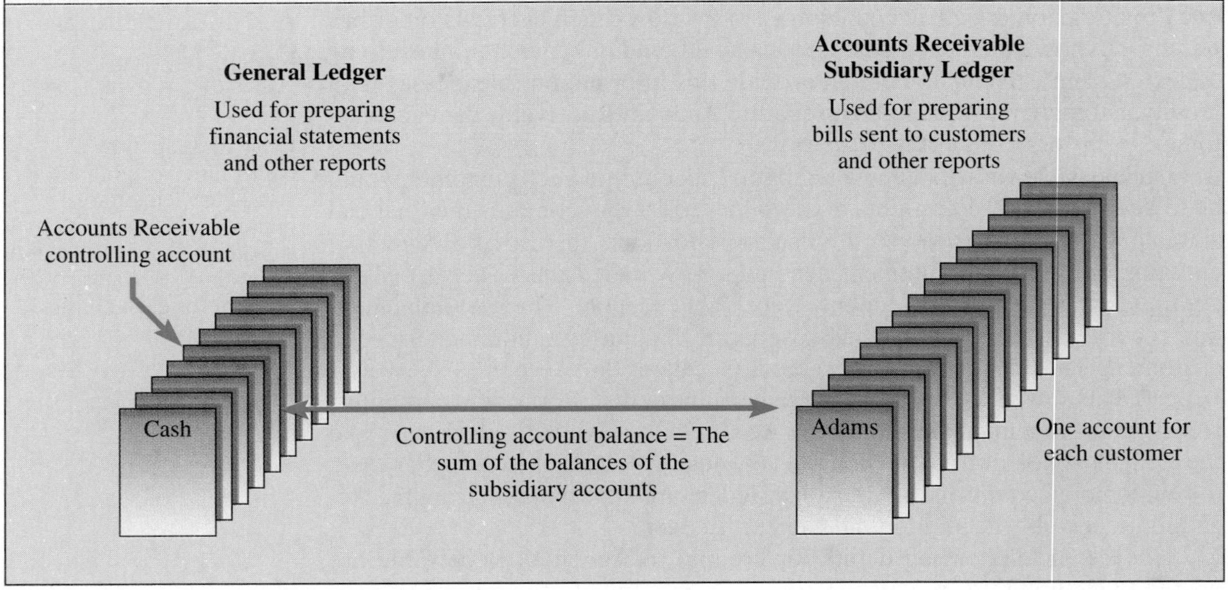

Another situation in which a subsidiary ledger often is used involves equipment. For example, a company with many items of office equipment might keep only one Office Equipment account in its General Ledger. This account would control a subsidiary ledger in which each item of equipment is recorded in a separate account.

Posting the Sales Journal

LO 3 Explain how special journals save labor and journalize and post transactions when special journals are used.

When customer accounts are maintained in a subsidiary ledger, a Sales Journal is posted as shown in Illustration 6–3. The individual sales recorded in the Sales Journal are posted each day to the proper customer accounts in the Accounts Receivable Ledger. These daily postings keep the customer accounts up-to-date. This is important in granting credit because the person responsible for granting credit should know the amount the credit-seeking customer currently owes. The source of this information is the customer's account, and if the account is not up-to-date, an incorrect decision may be made.

Note the check marks in the Sales Journal's Posting Reference column. They indicate that the sales recorded in the journal were individually posted to the customer accounts in the Accounts Receivable Ledger. Check marks rather than account numbers are used because customer accounts may not be numbered. When the accounts are not numbered, they are arranged alphabetically in the Accounts Receivable Ledger so they can be located easily.

In addition to the daily postings to customer accounts, the Sales Journal's Amount column is totaled at the end of the month. Then, the total is debited to Accounts Receivable and credited to Sales. The credit records the month's revenue from charge sales. The debit records the resulting increase in accounts receivable.

Identifying Posted Amounts

When posting several journals to ledger accounts, you should indicate in the Posting Reference column before each posted amount the journal and the page number of the journal from which the amount was posted. Indicate the journal by using its initial. Thus, items posted from the Cash Disbursements Journal carry the initial *D* before their journal page numbers in the Posting Reference columns. Likewise, items from the Cash Receipts Journal carry the letter *R*. Those from the Sales Journal carry the initial *S*. Items from the Purchases Journal carry the initial *P*, and from the General Journal, the letter *G*.

Cash Receipts Journal

A Cash Receipts Journal that is designed to save labor through posting column totals must be a multicolumn journal. A multicolumn journal is necessary because different accounts are credited when cash is received from different sources. For example, the cash receipts of a store normally fall into three groups: (1) cash from credit customers in payment of their accounts, (2) cash from cash sales, and (3) cash from miscellaneous sources. Note in Illustration 6–5 that a special column is provided for the credits that result when cash is received from each of these sources.

Cash from Credit Customers

When a Cash Receipts Journal similar to Illustration 6–5 is used to record cash received in payment of a customer's account, the customer's name is entered in the Journal's Account Credited column. The amount credited to the customer's account is entered in the Accounts Receivable Credit column, and the debits to Sales Discounts and Cash are entered in the journal's last two columns.

Look at the Accounts Receivable Credit column. First, observe that this column contains only credits to customer accounts. Second, the individual credits are posted daily to the customer accounts in the subsidiary Accounts Receivable Ledger. Third, the column total is posted at the end of the month as a credit to the Accounts Receivable controlling account. This is the normal recording and posting procedure when using special journals and controlling accounts with subsidiary ledgers. Transactions are normally entered in a special journal column and the individual amounts are then posted to the subsidiary ledger accounts and the column totals are posted to the general ledger accounts.

Cash Sales

After cash sales are entered on one or more cash registers and totaled at the end of each day, the daily total is recorded with a debit to Cash and a credit to Sales. When using a Cash Receipts Journal like Illustration 6–5, enter the debits to Cash in the Cash Debit column, and the credits in a special column headed Sales Credit. By using a separate Sales Credit column, you can post the total cash sales for a month as a single amount, the column total. (Although cash sales are normally journalized daily based on the cash register reading, cash sales are journalized only once each week in Illustration 6–5 to shorten the illustration.)

ILLUSTRATION 6–5

Cash Receipts Journal

Cash Receipts Journal — Page 2

Date		Account Credited	Explanation	PR	Other Accounts Credit	Accts. Rec. Credit	Sales Credit	Sales Discounts Debit	Cash Debit
Feb.	7	Sales	Cash sales	√			4,450.00		4,450.00
	12	James Henry	Invoice, 2/2	√		450.00		9.00	441.00
	14	Sales	Cash sales	√			3,925.00		3,925.00
	17	Albert Smith	Invoice, 2/7	√		500.00		10.00	490.00
	20	Notes Payable	Note to bank	245	1,000.00				1,000.00
	21	Sales	Cash sales	√			4,700.00		4,700.00
	23	Sam Moore	Invoice, 2/13	√		350.00		7.00	343.00
	25	Paul Roth	Invoice, 2/15	√		200.00		4.00	196.00
	28	Sales	Cash sales	√			4,225.00		4,225.00
	28	Totals			1,000.00	1,500.00	17,300.00	30.00	19,770.00
					(√)	(106)	(413)	(415)	(101)

Individual amounts in the Other Accounts Credit and Accounts Receivable Credit columns are posted daily.

Total is not posted.

Totals posted at the end of the month.

Accounts Receivable Ledger

Frank Booth

Date		PR	Debit	Credit	Balance
Feb.	25	S3	175.00		175.00

James Henry

Date		PR	Debit	Credit	Balance
Feb.	2	S3	450.00		450.00
	12	R2		450.00	–0–
	22	S3	225.00		225.00

Sam Moore

Date		PR	Debit	Credit	Balance
Feb.	13	S3	350.00		350.00
	23	R2		350.00	–0–

Paul Roth

Date		PR	Debit	Credit	Balance
Feb.	15	S3	200.00		200.00
	25	R2		200.00	–0–

Albert Smith

Date		PR	Debit	Credit	Balance
Feb.	7	S3	500.00		500.00
	17	R2		500.00	–0–
	28	S3	250.00		250.00

General Ledger

Cash — No. 101

Date		PR	Debit	Credit	Balance
Feb.	28	R2	19,770.00		19,770.00

Accounts Receivable — No. 106

Date		PR	Debit	Credit	Balance
Feb.	28	S3	2,150.00		2,150.00
	28	R2		1,500.00	650.00

Notes Payable — No. 245

Date		PR	Debit	Credit	Balance
Feb.	20	R2		1,000.00	1,000.00

Sales — No. 413

Date		PR	Debit	Credit	Balance
Feb.	28	S3		2,150.00	2,150.00
	28	R2		17,300.00	19,450.00

Sales Discounts — No. 415

Date		PR	Debit	Credit	Balance
Feb.	28	R2	30.00		30.00

At the time they record daily cash sales in the Cash Receipts Journal, some bookkeepers, as in Illustration 6–5, place a check mark in the Posting Reference (PR) column to indicate that no amount is individually posted from that line of the journal. Other bookkeepers use a double check (√√) to distinguish amounts that are not posted to customer accounts from amounts that are posted.

Miscellaneous Receipts of Cash

Most cash receipts are from collections of accounts receivable and from cash sales. However, other sources of cash include borrowing money from a bank or selling unneeded assets. The Other Accounts Credit column is for receipts that do not occur often enough to warrant a separate column. In most companies, the items entered in this column are few and are posted to a variety of general ledger accounts. As a result, postings are less apt to be omitted if these items are posted daily.

The Cash Receipts Journal's Posting Reference column is used only for daily postings from the Other Accounts and Accounts Receivable columns. The account numbers in the Posting Reference column indicate items that were posted to general ledger accounts. The check marks indicate either that an item (like a day's cash sales) was not posted or that an item was posted to the subsidiary Accounts Receivable Ledger.

Month-End Postings

At the end of the month, the amounts in the Accounts Receivable, Sales, Sales Discounts, and Cash columns of the Cash Receipts Journal are posted as column totals. However, the transactions recorded in any journal must result in equal debits and credits to general ledger accounts. Therefore, to be sure that the total debits and credits in a columnar journal are equal, you must *crossfoot* the column totals before posting them. To *foot* a column of numbers is to add it. To crossfoot, add the debit column totals and add the credit column totals; then compare the two sums for equality. For Illustration 6–5, the two sums appear as follows:

Debit Columns		**Credit Columns**	
Sales discounts debit	$ 30	Other accounts credit	$ 1,000
Cash debit	19,770	Accounts receivable credit	1,500
		Sales credit	17,300
Total	$19,800	Total	$19,800

Because the sums are equal, you may assume that the debits in the journal equal the credits.

After crossfooting the journal to confirm that debits equal credits, post the totals of the last four columns as indicated in each column heading. As for the Other Accounts column, do not post the column total because the individual items in this column are posted daily. Note in Illustration 6–5 the check mark below the Other Accounts column. The check mark indicates that the column total was not posted. The account numbers of the accounts to which the remaining column totals were posted are in parentheses below each column.

Posting items daily from the Other Accounts column with a delayed posting of the offsetting items in the Cash column (total) causes the General Ledger to be out of balance during the month. However, this does not matter because posting the Cash column total causes the offsetting amounts to reach the General Ledger before the trial balance is prepared.

Posting Rule

Now that we have explained the procedures for posting from two different journals to a subsidiary ledger and its controlling account, the rule that governs all such postings should be clear. The rule for posting to a subsidiary ledger and its controlling account is: *The controlling account must be debited periodically for an amount or amounts equal to the sum of the debits to the subsidiary ledger, and it must be credited periodically for an amount or amounts equal to the sum of the credits to the subsidiary ledger.*

Purchases Journal

You can use a Purchases Journal with one money column to record purchases of merchandise on credit. However, a Purchases Journal usually is more useful if it is a multicolumn journal in which all credit purchases on account are recorded. Such a journal may have columns similar to those in Illustration 6–6. In the illustrated journal, the invoice date and terms together indicate the date on which payment for each purchase is due. The Accounts Payable Credit column is used to record the amounts credited to each creditor's account. These amounts are posted daily to the individual creditor accounts in a subsidiary Accounts Payable Ledger.

In Illustration 6–6, note that each line of the Account column shows the subsidiary ledger account that should be posted for the amount in the Accounts Payable Credit column. The Account column also shows the general ledger account to be debited when a purchase involves an amount recorded in the Other Accounts Debit column.

In this illustration, note the separate column for purchases of office supplies on credit. A separate column such as this is useful whenever several transactions involve debits to a particular account. The Other Accounts Debit column in Illustration 6–6 allows the Purchases Journal to be used for all purchase transactions involving credits to Accounts Payable. The individual amounts in the Other Accounts Debit column typically are posted daily to the indicated general ledger accounts.

At the end of the month, all of the column totals except the Other Accounts Debit column are posted to the appropriate general ledger accounts. After this is done, the balance in the Accounts Payable controlling account should equal the sum of the account balances in the subsidiary Accounts Payable Ledger.

The Cash Disbursements Journal or Check Register

The Cash Disbursements Journal, like the Cash Receipts Journal, has columns so that you can post repetitive debits and credits in column totals. The repetitive cash payments involve debits to the Accounts Payable controlling account and credits to both Purchases Discounts and Cash. Most companies usually purchase merchandise on credit. Therefore, a Purchases column is not

ILLUSTRATION 6–6

Purchases Journal

Purchases Journal — **Page 1**

Date		Account	Date of Invoice	Terms	PR	Purchases Debit	Office Supplies Debit	Other Accounts Debit	Accounts Payable Credit
Feb.	3	Horn Supply Co.	2/2	n/30	√	275.00	75.00		350.00
	5	Acme Mfg. Co..	2/5	2/10, n/30	√	200.00			200.00
	13	Wycoff & Co.	2/10	2/10, n/30	√	150.00			150.00
	20	Smith & Co.	2/18	2/10, n/30	√	300.00			300.00
	25	Acme Mfg. Co..	2/24	2/10, n/30	√	100.00			100.00
	28	Store Supplies/HAG Co.. . . .	2/28	n/30	125/√	125.00	25.00	75.00	225.00
	28	Totals				1,150.00	100.00	75.00	1,325.00
						(505)	(124)	(√)	(201)

These totals are posted at the end of the month.

Individual amounts in the Other Accounts Debit and Accounts Payable Credit columns are posted daily.

General Ledger

Office Supplies — **No. 124**

Date		PR	Debit	Credit	Balance
Feb.	28	P1	100.00		100.00

Store Supplies — **No. 125**

Date		PR	Debit	Credit	Balance
Feb.	28	P1	75.00		75.00

Accounts Payable — **No. 201**

Date		PR	Debit	Credit	Balance
Feb.	28	P1		1,325.00	1,325.00

Purchases — **No. 505**

Date		PR	Debit	Credit	Balance
Feb.	28	P1	1,150.00		1,150.00

Accounts Payable Ledger

Acme Mfg. Company

Date		PR	Debit	Credit	Balance
Feb.	5	P1		200.00	200.00
	25	P1		100.00	300.00

HAG Company

Date		PR	Debit	Credit	Balance
Feb.	28	P1		225.00	225.00

Horn Supply Company

Date		PR	Debit	Credit	Balance
Feb.	3	P1		350.00	350.00

Smith & Company

Date		PR	Debit	Credit	Balance
Feb.	20	P1		300.00	300.00

Wycoff & Company

Date		PR	Debit	Credit	Balance
Feb.	13	P1		150.00	150.00

ILLUSTRATION 6–7

Cash Disbursements Journal

Cash Disbursements Journal — Page 2

Date		Ch. No.	Payee	Account Debited	PR	Other Accounts Debit	Accounts Payable Debit	Purchases Discounts Credit	Cash Credit
Feb.	3	105	L. & N. Railroad . . .	Transportation-In . . .	508	15.00			15.00
	12	106	East Sales Co.	Purchases	505	25.00			25.00
	15	107	Acme Mfg. Co.	Acme Mfg. Co.	√		200.00	4.00	196.00
	15	108	Jerry Hale	Salaries Expense . . .	622	250.00			250.00
	20	109	Wycoff & Co.	Wycoff & Co.	√		150.00	3.00	147.00
	28	110	Smith & Co.	Smith & Co.	√		300.00	6.00	294.00
	28		Totals			290.00	650.00	13.00	927.00
						(√)	(201)	(507)	(101)

Individual amounts in the Other Accounts Debit column and Accounts Payable Debit column are posted daily.

Totals posted at the end of the month.

Accounts Payable Ledger

Acme Mfg. Company

Date		PR	Debit	Credit	Balance
Feb.	5	P1		200.00	200.00
	15	D2	200.00		-0-
	25	P1		100.00	100.00

HAG Company

Date		PR	Debit	Credit	Balance
Feb.	28	P1		225.00	225.00

Horn Supply Company

Date		PR	Debit	Credit	Balance
Feb.	3	P1		350.00	350.00

Smith & Company

Date		PR	Debit	Credit	Balance
Feb.	20	P1		300.00	300.00
	28	D2	300.00		-0-

Wycoff & Company

Date		PR	Debit	Credit	Balance
Feb.	13	P1		150.00	150.00
	20	D2	150.00		-0-

General Ledger

Cash — No. 101

Date		PR	Debit	Credit	Balance
Feb.	28	R2	19,770.00		19,770.00
	28	D2		927.00	18,843.00

Accounts Payable — No. 201

Date		PR	Debit	Credit	Balance
Feb.	28	P1		1,325.00	1,325.00
	28	D2	650.00		675.00

Purchases — No. 505

Date		PR	Debit	Credit	Balance
Feb.	12	D2	25.00		25.00
	28	P1	1,150.00		1,175.00

Purchases Discounts — No. 507

Date		PR	Debit	Credit	Balance
Feb.	28	D2		13.00	13.00

Transportation-In — No. 508

Date		PR	Debit	Credit	Balance
Feb.	3	D2	15.00		15.00

Salaries Expense — No. 622

Date		PR	Debit	Credit	Balance
Feb.	15	D2	250.00		250.00

needed. Instead, the occasional cash purchase is recorded as shown on line 2 of Illustration 6–7.

Observe that the illustrated journal has a column headed Check Number (Ck. No.). To gain control over cash disbursements, all payments except for very small amounts should be made by check.[1] The checks should be prenumbered by the printer and should be entered in the journal in numerical order with each check's number in the column headed Ck. No. This makes it possible to scan the numbers in the column for omitted checks. When a Cash Disbursements Journal has a column for check numbers, it is often called a **Check Register.**

To post a Cash Disbursements Journal or Check Register similar to Illustration 6–7, do the following. Each day, post the individual amounts in the Other Accounts Debit column to the appropriate general ledger accounts. Also on a daily basis, post the individual amounts in the Accounts Payable Debit column to the named creditors' accounts in the subsidiary Accounts Payable Ledger. At the end of the month, after you crossfoot the column totals, post the Accounts Payable Debit column total to the Accounts Payable controlling account. Then, post the Purchases Discounts Credit column total to the Purchases Discounts account and post the Cash Credit column total to the Cash account. Because the items in the Other Accounts column are posted individually, do not post the column total.

Testing the Accuracy of the Ledgers

LO 5 Explain how to test the posting of entries to the Accounts Receivable and Accounts Payable subsidiary ledgers and prepare schedules of accounts in those subsidiary ledgers.

Periodically, after all posting is completed, the account balances in the General Ledger and the subsidiary ledgers should be tested for accuracy. To do this, first prepare a trial balance of the General Ledger to confirm that debits equal credits. If the trial balance balances, the accounts in the General Ledger, including the controlling accounts, are assumed to be correct. Then test the subsidiary ledgers by preparing schedules of accounts receivable and accounts payable.

To prepare a **schedule of accounts payable,** for example, list the accounts in the Accounts Payable Ledger with their balances and calculate the sum of the balances. If the total is equal to the balance of the Accounts Payable controlling account, you can assume the accounts in the Accounts Payable Ledger are correct. Illustration 6–8 shows a schedule of accounts payable drawn from the Accounts Payable Ledger of Illustration 6–7.

You prepare a **schedule of accounts receivable** in the same way as a schedule of accounts payable. Also, if its total equals the balance of the Accounts Receivable controlling account, you can assume the accounts in the Accounts Receivable Ledger are correct.

[1] In Chapter 7, we discuss a system that controls small payments made with currency and coins.

ILLUSTRATION 6–8

Schedule of Accounts Payable, December 31, 19—

Acme Mfg. Company	$100
HAG Company	225
Horn Supply Company	350
Total accounts payable	$675

Sales Taxes

LO 6 Explain how sales taxes are recorded in special journals, how sales invoices can serve as a Sales Journal, and how sales returns and allowances are recorded.

Many cities and states require retailers to collect sales taxes from their customers and to periodically remit these taxes to the city or state treasurer. When using a columnar Sales Journal, you can have a record of the taxes collected by adding special columns in the journal as shown in Illustration 6–9.

As we described earlier in the chapter, the column totals of a Sales Journal are typically posted at the end of each month. This, of course, includes crediting the Sales Taxes Payable account for the total of the Sales Taxes Payable column. The individual amounts in the Accounts Receivable column are posted daily to the customer accounts in the Accounts Receivable Ledger. The individual amounts in the Sales Taxes Payable and Sales columns are not posted.

A business that collects sales taxes on its cash sales may use a special Sales Taxes Payable column in its Cash Receipts Journal.

Sales Invoices as a Sales Journal

To save labor, some retailers avoid using Sales Journals for credit sales. Instead, they post each sales invoice total directly to the customer's account in the subsidiary Accounts Receivable Ledger. Then, they place copies of the invoices in numerical order in a binder. At the end of the month, they total all the invoices of that month, and make a general journal entry to debit Accounts Receivable and credit Sales for the total. In effect, the bound invoice copies act as a Sales Journal. Such a procedure is known as direct posting of sales invoices.

Sales Returns

A business that has only a few sales returns may record them in a General Journal with an entry like the following:

Oct.	17	Sales Returns and Allowances.	414	17.50	
		Accounts Receivable—George Ball	106/√		17.50
		Customer returned merchandise.			

The debit of the entry is posted to the Sales Returns and Allowances account. The credit is posted to both the Accounts Receivable controlling account and the customer's account. Note the account number and the check mark, 106/√, in the PR column on the credit line. This indicates that both the

tions to be performed on the data. Software actually controls the whole system, including input, file management, processing, and output.

Data Storage

Data storage is an essential component of both manual and computer-based systems. As data is inputted and processed, it must be saved so it can be used as output or processed further. This stockpile of data (database) stored in the accounting system should be readily accessible so periodic financial reports can be compiled quickly. In addition, data storage should support the preparation of special purpose reports that managers may request. The accounting database also serves as the primary source of information auditors use when they audit the financial statements. Companies also maintain files of source documents for use by auditors and to clear up errors or disputes.

In manual systems, data storage consists of files of paper documents. You learned about several of these documents, such as journals and ledgers, in prior chapters.

With a computer-based system, some of the data is stored in the form of paper documents. However, most of the data is stored on floppy diskettes, hard disks, or magnetic tapes. As a result of recent improvements, these devices can store very large amounts of data. For example, floppy diskettes can hold up to two megabytes of information (one megabyte is roughly equivalent to 500 double-spaced typed pages). Small digital-audio-tape (DAT) cassettes can hold hundreds of megabytes of information. Some hard disks can hold thousands of megabytes (one thousand megabytes is a gigabyte). Because of the recent improvements in data storage, accounting systems now store much more detailed and extensive databases than was possible in the past. As a result, managers have much more information available to help them plan and control business activities.

In a computer-based system, data storage can be on-line (usually on a hard disk), which means that the data can be accessed whenever it is needed by the software. In contrast, when data is stored off-line, the data cannot be accessed until the computer operator inserts a disk or a magnetic tape into a drive.

Generally, we do not use the concepts of *on-line* and *off-line* storage in reference to manual accounting systems. However, one might argue that in a manual system only the data stored in the accountant's brain is on-line; everything else is off-line.

Output Devices

The fifth component of an accounting system is the **output devices.** These allow information to be taken out of the system and placed in the hands of users. Examples of output include bills to customers, checks payable to suppliers and employees, financial statements, and a variety of other internal reports.

For computer-based systems, the most common output devices are video screens and printers. Other output devices include telephones or direct phone line connections to the computer system of a supplier or customer. When requests for output are entered, the data processor searches the database for the

ILLUSTRATION 6–9

A Sales Journal with a Column for Sales Taxes Payable

Sales Journal

Date		Account Debited	Invoice Number	PR	Accounts Receivable Debit	Sales Taxes Payable Credit	Sales Credit
Dec.	1	D. R. Horn	7–1698		103.00	3.00	100.00

ILLUSTRATION 6–10

Sales Returns and Allowances Journal

Date		Account Credited	Explanation	Credit Memo No.	PR	Amount
Oct.	7	Robert Moore	Defective merchandise	203	√	10.00
	14	James Warren	Defective merchandise	204	√	12.00
	18	T. M. Jones	Not ordered	205	√	6.00
	23	Sam Smith	Defective merchandise	206	√	18.00
	31	Sales Returns and Allowances, Dr.; Accts. Receivable, Cr.				46.00
						(414/106)

Accounts Receivable controlling account in the General Ledger and the George Ball account in the Accounts Receivable Ledger were credited for $17.50. Both were credited because the balance of the controlling account in the General Ledger will not equal the sum of the customer account balances in the subsidiary ledger unless both are credited.

A company with a large number of sales returns can save posting labor by recording them in a special Sales Returns and Allowances Journal similar to Illustration 6–10. Note that this is in keeping with the idea that a company can design and use a special journal for any group of similar transactions if there are enough transactions to warrant the journal. When using a Sales Returns and Allowances Journal to record returns, the amounts in the journal are posted daily to the customers' accounts. Then, at the end of the month, the journal total is posted as a debit to Sales Returns and Allowances and as a credit to Accounts Receivable.

General Journal Entries

When special journals are used, a General Journal is always necessary for adjusting, closing, and correcting entries and for a few transactions that cannot be recorded in the special journals. If a Sales Returns and Allowances Journal is not provided, some of these transactions are sales returns, purchases returns, and purchases of plant assets.

Summary of the Chapter in Terms of Learning Objectives

LO 1. The five components of accounting systems are source documents, input devices, the data processor, data storage, and output devices. Both manual and computerized systems must have all five components.

LO 2. There are many different ways to set up computer systems, including small and large systems, self-developed and off-the-shelf programming, batch and on-line processing, and computer networks.

LO 3. Columnar journals are designed so that repetitive debits to a specific account are entered in a separate column. The same is done for repetitive credits. As a result, the column totals can be posted as single amounts, thereby eliminating the need to post individually each debit and credit.

Companies that use special journals enter all credit sales in a Sales Journal. Purchases on credit are entered in a Purchases Journal. All cash receipts are entered in the Cash Receipts Journal and all cash payments by check are entered in the Cash Disbursements Journal (or Check Register). Any transactions that cannot be entered in the special journals are entered in the General Journal.

When posting transactions from special journals to the accounts, post individual debits and credits to subsidiary Accounts Receivable and Accounts Payable Ledgers daily. Other amounts that must be posted individually also may be posted daily. Normally, the columns of each special journal are totaled and crossfooted at the end of each month. Then, the column totals are posted to the appropriate General Ledger accounts.

LO 4. When many accounts of the same type are required, such as an account receivable for each credit customer, they usually are kept in a separate subsidiary ledger. Then, a single controlling account is maintained in the General Ledger. After all transactions are posted to the accounts in the subsidiary ledger and to the controlling account, the controlling account balance should equal the sum of the account balances in the subsidiary ledger.

LO 5. To test the accuracy of a subsidiary ledger after all posting is completed, you should prepare a schedule of the accounts in the ledger and compare the total of the account balances with the balance in the related controlling account. If they are not equal, you know an error has been made. If they are equal, you assume the balances are correct.

LO 6. To record sales taxes, the Sales Journal and the Cash Receipts Journal should include a separate Sales Taxes Payable column. When sales invoices substitute for a Sales Journal, the customer accounts in the Accounts Receivable Ledger are posted directly from the sales invoices. Copies of the invoices for each month are then bound and totaled as a basis for recording the sales in the General Ledger. Sales returns and allowances may be recorded in the General Journal, or a special journal for sales returns and allowances may be used.

Glossary

LO 7 Define or explain the words and phrases listed in the chapter glossary.

Accounting system the people, forms, procedures, and equipment that are used to capture data about the transactions of an entity and to generate from that data a variety of financial, managerial, and tax accounting reports. pp. 308–309.

Accounts Payable Ledger a subsidiary ledger that contains a separate account for each party that grants credit on account to the entity. p. 319.

Accounts Receivable Ledger a subsidiary ledger that contains an account for each credit customer. pp. 319–20.

Batch processing an approach to inputting data that accumulates source documents for a period of time such as a day, week, or month and inputs all of them at the same time. pp. 315–16.

Check Register a book of original entry for recording cash payments by check. p. 327.

Columnar journal a book of original entry having columns, each of which is designated as the place for entering specific data about each transaction of a group of similar transactions. p. 317.

Controlling account a general ledger account the balance of which (after posting) equals the sum of the balances of the accounts in a related subsidiary ledger. p. 319.

Computer network a system in which computers are linked with each other so that different users on different computers can share access to the same data and the same programs. p. 316.

Data processor the component of an accounting system that interprets, manipulates, and summarizes the recorded information so that it can be used in analyses and reports. p. 310.

Data storage the component of an accounting system that keeps the inputted data in a readily accessible manner so that financial reports can be drawn from it efficiently. p. 311.

General Ledger the ledger that contains the financial statement accounts of a business. p. 319.

Input device a means of transferring information from source documents to the data processing component of an accounting system. pp. 309–10.

On-line processing an approach to inputting data whereby the data on each source document is inputted as soon as the document is available. pp. 315–16.

Output devices the means by which information is taken out of the accounting system and made available for use. pp. 311–12.

Schedule of accounts payable a list of the balances of all the accounts in the Accounts Payable Ledger that is summed to show the total amount of accounts payable outstanding. pp. 327–28.

Schedule of accounts receivable a list of the balances of all the accounts in the Accounts Receivable Ledger that is summed to show the total amount of accounts receivable outstanding. p. 327.

Special journal a book of original entry that is designed and used for recording only a specified type of transaction. pp. 316–18.

Subsidiary ledger a group of accounts that show the details underlying the balance of a controlling account in the General Ledger. p. 319.

Objective Review

Answers to the following questions are listed at the end of this chapter. Be sure that you decide which is the one best answer to each question *before* you check the answers.

LO 1 In a computer-based accounting system, which basic component of the system is likely to include a hard disk located in the computer?

a. Source documents.
b. Input device.
c. Data processor.
d. Data storage.
e. Output devices.

LO 2 In a computer-based accounting system:

a. The accounting software is more efficient if it operates as an integrated system.
b. Bookkeeping tasks take somewhat more time than they do with a manual system.
c. Data about transactions must be entered with on-line processing.
d. The accountant must have the ability to program the computer.
e. None of the above is correct.

LO 3 When special journals are used:

a. A General Journal is not used.
b. All cash payments by check are recorded in the Cash Disbursements Journal.
c. All purchase transactions are recorded in the Purchases Journal.
d. All sales transactions are recorded in the Sales Journal.
e. All cash receipts except from cash sales of merchandise are recorded in the Cash Receipts Journal.

LO 4 If an accounting system includes an Accounts Receivable controlling account and an Accounts Receivable Ledger:

a. Two accounts are debited when posting sales on credit.
b. The rule that debits must equal credits is not maintained.
c. Two accounts are debited when posting cash sales.
d. Two accounts are credited when posting cash receipts from credit customers.
e. Both (*a*) and (*d*) are correct.

LO 5 A schedule of accounts receivable:

a. Serves as the means of data storage with respect to the amounts customers owe to the entity.
b. May be prepared at any point during an accounting period for the purpose of testing the equality of the general ledger Accounts Receivable account balance and the sum of the account balances in the subsidiary ledger.

c. Should, if all transactions have been correctly posted, disclose a total amount equal to the total amount of credit sales made during the period.
d. Should, if all transactions have been correctly posted, disclose a total amount equal to the balance of the general ledger Accounts Receivable account.
e. None of the above is correct.

LO 6 If sales taxes must be recorded and special journals are used:

a. The sales taxes must be recorded in the General Journal.
b. A separate column for sales taxes should be included in the Cash Disbursements Journal.
c. A separate column for sales taxes should be included in the Purchases Journal.
d. A special Sales Taxes Journal should be used.
e. None of the above is correct.

Questions for Class Discussion

1. What advantages do computer systems offer over manual systems?
2. What are the five basic components of an accounting system?
3. What are source documents? Give some examples.
4. What is the purpose of an input device? Give some examples of input devices for computer systems.
5. What does the data processor component of a system accomplish?
6. The data processor of a computer system consists of two subcomponents. What are they?
7. What uses are made of the data that is stockpiled in the data storage of an accounting system?
8. What is the difference between data that is stored off-line and data that is stored on-line?
9. What purpose is served by the output devices of an accounting system?
10. Identify two categories of computers according to their size and complexity.
11. What is a computer program?
12. What is the difference between batch and on-line processing?
13. How does a columnar journal save posting labor?
14. When special journals are used, separate special journals normally are used to record each of four different types of transactions. What are these four types of transactions?
15. Why should sales to and receipts of cash from credit customers be recorded and posted daily?
16. Both credits to customer accounts and credits to miscellaneous accounts are individually posted from a Cash Receipts Journal similar to the one in Illustration 6–5. Why not put both kinds of credits in the same column and thus save journal space?

17. What procedures allow copies of a company's sales invoices to be used as a Sales Journal?
18. When a general journal entry is used to record a returned credit sale, the credit of the entry must be posted twice. Does this cause the trial balance to be out of balance? Why or why not?
19. How does one tell from which journal a particular amount in a ledger account was posted?
20. In Appendix J containing IBM's annual 1990 financial statements and related disclosures, review the ''Results of Operations'' portion of the ''Management Discussion.'' By what percentage did software revenue in 1990 increase over 1989? What was the percentage change in revenue from processors from 1989 to 1990?

Exercises

Exercise 6–1
Special journals
(LO 3)

A company uses a Sales Journal, a Purchases Journal, a Cash Receipts Journal, a Cash Disbursements Journal, and a General Journal like the ones described in the chapter. The company recently completed the following transactions. List the transactions by letter and opposite each letter give the name of the journal in which the transaction would be recorded.

a. Purchased merchandise on credit.
b. Gave a customer credit for merchandise purchased on credit and returned.
c. Purchased office equipment and signed a promissory note for the purchase price.
d. Sold merchandise for cash.
e. A customer paid for merchandise previously purchased on credit.
f. Sold merchandise on credit.
g. Recorded adjusting and closing entries.
h. Returned merchandise purchased on credit.
i. Purchased office supplies on credit.
j. Paid a creditor.
k. A customer returned merchandise sold for cash; a check was issued.

Exercise 6–2
The Sales Journal
(LO 3)

A company uses a Sales Journal, a Purchases Journal, a Cash Receipts Journal, a Cash Disbursements Journal, and a General Journal. The following transactions occurred during April:

Apr. 1 Purchased merchandise for $460 on credit from Trader Company.
3 Sold merchandise to O. Neville for $280 cash, Invoice No. 1511.
6 Sold merchandise to R. Davis for $1,200; terms 2/10, n/60; Invoice No. 1512.
7 Borrowed $2,500 from the bank by giving a note to the bank.

Apr. 9 Sold merchandise to G. Hoffman for $810, terms n/30, Invoice No. 1513.
15 Received $1,176 from R. Davis to pay for the purchase of April 6.
26 Sold used store equipment to Barker Company for $620.
29 Sold merchandise to M. Rogers for $280, terms n/30, Invoice No. 1514.

Required

On a sheet of notebook paper, draw a Sales Journal like the one that appears in Illustration 6–3. Journalize the April transactions that should be recorded in the Sales Journal.

Exercise 6–3
The Cash Receipts Journal
(LO 3)

A company uses a Sales Journal, a Purchases Journal, a Cash Receipts Journal, a Cash Disbursements Journal, and a General Journal. The following transactions occurred during October:

Oct. 2 F. Ray, the owner of the business, invested $7,000 in the business.
5 Purchased merchandise for $4,300 on credit from TQ Company.
11 Sold merchandise on credit to D. Parker for $3,750, subject to a $75 sales discount if paid by the end of the month.
14 Borrowed $1,500 from the bank by giving a note to the bank.
15 Sold merchandise to T. Sharpe for $240 cash.
19 Paid TQ Company $4,300 for the merchandise purchased on October 5.
28 Received $3,675 from D. Parker to pay for the purchase of October 11.
31 Paid salaries of $900.

Required

1. On a sheet of notebook paper, draw a multicolumn Cash Receipts Journal like the one that appears in Illustration 6–5.
2. Journalize the October transactions that should be recorded in the Cash Receipts Journal.

Exercise 6–4
The Purchases Journal
(LO 3)

A company uses a Sales Journal, a Purchases Journal, a Cash Receipts Journal, a Cash Disbursements Journal, and a General Journal. The following transactions occurred during May:

May 2 B. Wolfe, the owner of the business, invested $8,000 in the business.
4 Purchased merchandise for $4,400 on credit from Isle Company, terms n/30.
7 Purchased store supplies from Best Company for $60 cash.
9 Sold merchandise on credit to H. Sawyer for $900, subject to a $27 sales discount if paid by the end of the month.

May 12 Purchased on credit from P Company office supplies for $90 and store supplies for $175, terms n/30.

19 Sold merchandise to Z. Bennett for $650 cash.

31 Paid Isle Company $4,400 for the merchandise purchased on May 4.

Required

1. On a sheet of notebook paper, draw a multicolumn Purchases Journal like the one that appears in Illustration 6–6.
2. Journalize the May transactions that should be recorded in the Purchases Journal.

Exercise 6–5
The Cash Disbursements Journal
(LO 3)

A company uses a Sales Journal, a Purchases Journal, a Cash Receipts Journal, a Cash Disbursements Journal, and a General Journal. The following transactions occurred during August:

Aug. 2 Purchased merchandise for $1,100 on credit from Zap Company; terms 2/10, n/30.

4 Purchased merchandise for $3,300 on credit from B&B Company; terms 2/15, n/60.

7 Issued check number 57 to T Company to buy store supplies for $88.

17 Sold merchandise on credit to F. Hoyt for $390, terms n/30.

18 Issued check number 58 for $270 to repay a note payable to State Bank.

19 Issued check number 59 to B&B Company to pay the amount due for the purchase of August 4, less the discount.

31 Issued check number 60 to Zap Company to pay the amount due for the purchase of August 2.

31 Paid salary of $1,000 to S. Capra by issuing check number 61.

Required

1. On a sheet of notebook paper, draw a multicolumn Cash Disbursements Journal like the one that appears in Illustration 6–7.
2. Journalize the August transactions that should be recorded in the Cash Disbursements Journal.

Exercise 6–6
General Journal transactions
(LO 3)

A company uses a Sales Journal, a Purchases Journal, a Cash Receipts Journal, a Cash Disbursements Journal, and a General Journal. The following transactions occurred during January:

Jan. 1 P. Lewis, the owner of the business, invested $12,000 in the business.

4 Purchased merchandise for $7,600 on credit from Bay Company; terms 2/10, n/30.

9 P. Lewis, the owner of the business, contributed an automobile worth $16,000 to the business.

Jan. 11 Issued check number 141 to V&J Company to buy store supplies for $157.

14 Sold merchandise on credit to K. Whalem for $840, terms n/30.

16 Returned $250 of defective merchandise to Bay Company from the purchase on January 4.

22 Issued check number 142 to Madd Company to pay the $905 due for a purchase of December 20.

25 K. Whalem returned $85 of merchandise originally purchased on August 14.

31 Accrued salaries payable were $750.

Required

Journalize the January transactions that should be recorded in the General Journal.

Exercise 6–7
Special journal transactions
(LO 3)

A company uses the following journals: Sales Journal, Purchases Journal, Cash Receipts Journal, Cash Disbursements Journal, and General Journal. On February 10, the company purchased merchandise priced at $22,700, subject to credit terms of 2/10, n/30. On February 20, the company paid the net amount due. However, in journalizing the payment, the bookkeeper debited Accounts Payable for $22,700 and failed to record the cash discount. Cash was credited for the actual amount paid. In what journals would the February 10 and the February 20 transactions have been recorded? What procedure is likely to discover the error in journalizing the February 20 transaction?

Exercise 6–8
Posting to subsidiary ledger accounts
(LO 3, 4, 5)

As of the end of June, the Sales Journal of Abilene Company appeared as follows:

Sales Journal

Date		Account Debited	Invoice Number	PR	Amount
June	3	Sheila Lee	604		845.00
	12	Barbara Lyon	605		630.00
	18	Tomas Cantu	606		1,280.00
	23	Tomas Cantu	607		460.00
	30	Total			3,215.00

The company had also recorded the return of merchandise with the following entry:

June	15	Sales Returns and Allowances	140.00	
		Accounts Receivable—Barbara Lyon		140.00
		Customer returned merchandise.		

Required

1. On a sheet of notebook paper, open a subsidiary Accounts Receivable Ledger that has a T-account for each customer listed in the Sales Journal. Post to the customer accounts the entries of the Sales Journal and also the portion of the general journal entry that affects a customer's account.
2. Open a General Ledger that has T-accounts for Accounts Receivable, Sales, and Sales Returns and Allowances. Post the Sales Journal and the portions of the general journal entry that affect these accounts.
3. Prepare a list or schedule of the accounts in the subsidiary Accounts Receivable Ledger and add their balances to show that the total equals the balance in the Accounts Receivable controlling account.

Exercise 6–9
Accounts Receivable Ledger
(LO 4, 5, 6)

Robon Company posts its sales invoices directly and then binds the invoices into a Sales Journal. Robon had the following sales during November:

Nov. 7	Teresa Katz	$ 4,900
9	Arnold Swartz	8,100
13	Sam Smith	17,900
21	Milton Gibbs	27,300
26	Sam Smith	15,000
30	Teresa Katz	9,800
	Total	$83,000

Required

1. On a sheet of notebook paper, open a subsidiary Accounts Receivable Ledger having a T-account for each customer. Post the invoices to the subsidiary ledger.
2. Give the general journal entry to record the end-of-month total of the Sales Journal.
3. Open an Accounts Receivable controlling account and a Sales account and post the general journal entry.
4. Prepare a list or schedule of the accounts in the subsidiary Accounts Receivable Ledger and add their balances to show that the total equals the balance in the Accounts Receivable controlling account.

Exercise 6–10
Posting from special journals to T-accounts
(LO 3)

Following are the condensed journals of a merchandising concern. The journal column headings are incomplete in that they do not indicate whether the columns are debit or credit columns.

Required

1. Prepare T-accounts on notebook paper for the following general ledger and subsidiary ledger accounts. Separate the accounts of each ledger group as follows:

General Ledger Accounts	Accounts Receivable Ledger Accounts
Cash	Customer A
Accounts Receivable	Customer B
Prepaid Insurance	Customer C
Store Equipment	
Accounts Payable	
Notes Payable	
Sales	**Accounts Payable Ledger Accounts**
Sales Returns and Allowances	Company One
Sales Discounts	Company Two
Purchases	Company Three
Purchases Returns and Allowances	
Purchases Discounts	

2. Without referring to any of the illustrations in the chapter that show complete column headings for the journals, post the following journals to the proper T-accounts.

Sales Journal

Account	Amount
Customer A	7,650
Customer B	2,050
Customer C	11,200
Total	20,900

Purchases Journal

Account	Amount
Company One	4,200
Company Two	9,600
Company Three . . .	3,990
Total	17,790

General Journal

. . . .	. .	Sales Returns and Allowances	250.00	
	. .	Accounts Receivable—Customer B		250.00
	. .	Accounts Payable—Company Two	1,200.00	
	. .	Purchases Returns and Allowances		1,200.00

Cash Receipts Journal

Account	Other Accounts	Accounts Receivable	Sales	Sales Discounts	Cash
Customer B		1,800		36	1,764
Cash sales			8,080		8,080
Notes payable	8,000				8,000
Cash sales			9,475		9,475
Customer C		11,200		224	10,976
Store Equipment	990				990
Totals	8,990	13,000	17,555	260	39,285

Cash Disbursements Journal

Accounts	Other Accounts	Accounts Payable	Purchases Discounts	Cash
Prepaid insurance . . .	720			720
Company One		4,200	126	4,074
Company Two		8,400	168	8,232
Store equipment	3,850			3,850
Totals	4,570	12,600	294	16,876

Exercise 6–11
Errors related to the Purchases Journal
(LO 3, 4, 5)

A company that records credit purchases in a Purchases Journal and records purchases returns in its General Journal made the following errors. List each error by letter, and opposite each letter tell when the error should be discovered:

a. Made an addition error in totaling the Accounts Payable column of the Purchases Journal.

b. Posted a purchases return to the Accounts Payable account and to the creditor's account but did not post to the Purchases Returns and Allowances account.

c. Posted a purchases return to the Purchases Returns and Allowances account and to the Accounts Payable account but did not post to the creditor's account.

d. Correctly recorded a $2,500 purchase in the Purchases Journal but posted it to the creditor's account as a $250 purchase.

e. Made an addition error in determining the balance of a creditor's account.

Problems

Problem 6–1
Special journals and subsidiary ledgers
(LO 3, 4, 5)

Semnar Company completed these transactions during November of the current year:

Nov. 1 Purchased merchandise on credit from Fiore Company, invoice dated November 1; terms 2/10, n/60; $10,700.

2 Issued Check No. 237 to *The U.S. Journal* for advertising expense, $650.

3 Sold merchandise on credit to Frank Mendoza, Invoice No. 530, $1,600. (The terms of all credit sales are 2/10, n/30.)

3 Purchased on credit from Weisman Company office supplies, $1,110. Invoice dated November 2, terms n/10 EOM.

5 Received a $680 credit memorandum from Weisman Company for unsatisfactory merchandise received on November 3 and returned for credit.

5 Sold merchandise on credit to Janet Dalton, Invoice No. 531, $4,850.

7 Purchased store equipment on credit from Century Company, invoice dated November 7, terms n/10 EOM, $8,900.

11 Issued Check No. 238 to Fiore Company in payment of its November 1 invoice, less the discount.

11 Sold merchandise on credit to Cynthia Montgomery, Invoice No. 532, $7,600.

13 Received payment from Frank Mendoza for the November 3 sale, less the discount.

15 Sold merchandise on credit to Frank Mendoza, Invoice No. 533, $3,250.

Nov. 15 Issued Check No. 239, payable to Payroll, in payment of the sales salaries for the first half of the month, $7,800. Cashed the check and paid the employees.

15 Cash sales for the first half of the month were $40,670. (Cash sales are usually recorded daily from the cash register readings. However, they are recorded only twice in this problem to reduce the repetitive transactions.)

15 Received payment from Janet Dalton for the November 5 sale, less the discount.

17 Purchased merchandise on credit from Kramer Company, invoice dated November 16; terms 2/10, n/30; $10,200.

18 Borrowed $32,000 from First National Bank by giving a long-term note payable.

21 Received payment from Cynthia Montgomery for the November 11 sale, less the discount.

21 Purchased on credit from Century Company store supplies, $585. Invoice dated November 20, terms n/10 EOM.

25 Received payment from Frank Mendoza for the November 15 sale, less the discount.

25 Purchased merchandise on credit from Fiore Company, invoice dated November 24; terms 2/10, n/60; $8,300.

25 Received a $350 credit memorandum from Kramer Company for defective merchandise received on November 17 and returned.

26 Issued Check No. 240 to Kramer Company in payment of its November 16 invoice, less the return and the discount.

27 Sold merchandise on credit to Janet Dalton, Invoice No. 534, $2,460.

28 Sold merchandise on credit to Cynthia Montgomery, Invoice No. 535, $4,620.

30 Issued Check No. 241, payable to Payroll, in payment of the sales salaries for the last half of the month, $7,800.

30 Cash sales for the last half of the month were $56,780.

Required

1. Open the following general ledger accounts: Cash, Accounts Receivable, Long-Term Notes Payable, Sales, and Sales Discounts. Also open subsidiary accounts receivable ledger accounts for Janet Dalton, Frank Mendoza, and Cynthia Montgomery.
2. Prepare a Sales Journal and a Cash Receipts Journal like the ones illustrated in this chapter.
3. Review the transactions of Semnar Company and enter those transactions that should be journalized in the Sales Journal and those that should be journalized in the Cash Receipts Journal. Ignore any transactions that should be journalized in a Purchases Journal, a Cash Disbursements Journal, or a General Journal.
4. Post the items that should be posted as individual amounts from the

journals. (Normally, such items are posted daily; but since they are few in number in this problem you are asked to post them only once.)

5. Foot and crossfoot the journals and make the month-end postings.
6. Prepare a trial balance of the General Ledger and test the accuracy of the subsidiary ledger by preparing a schedule of accounts receivable.

Problem 6–2
Special journals, subsidiary ledgers, schedule of accounts payable
(LO 3, 4, 5)

On October 31, Semnar Company had a cash balance of $134,000 and a Long-Term Notes Payable balance of $134,000. The November transactions of Semnar Company included those listed in Problem 6–1.

Required

1. Open the following general ledger accounts: Cash, Office Supplies, Store Supplies, Store Equipment, Accounts Payable, Long-Term Notes Payable, Purchases, Purchases Returns and Allowances, Purchases Discounts, Sales Salaries Expense, and Advertising Expense. Enter the October 31 balances of Cash and Long-Term Notes Payable ($134,000 each).
2. Open subsidiary accounts payable ledger accounts for Century Company, Fiore Company, Kramer Company, and Weisman Company.
3. Prepare a General Journal and a Cash Disbursements Journal like the ones illustrated in this chapter. Prepare a Purchases Journal with a debit column for purchases, a debit column for other accounts, and a credit column for accounts payable.
4. Review the November transactions of Semnar Company and enter those transactions that should be journalized in the General Journal, the Purchases Journal, or the Cash Disbursements Journal. Ignore any transactions that should be journalized in a Sales Journal or Cash Receipts Journal.
5. Post the items that should be posted as individual amounts from the journals. (Normally, such items are posted daily; but since they are few in number in this problem you are asked to post them only once.)
6. Foot and crossfoot the journals and make the month-end postings.
7. Prepare a trial balance and a schedule of accounts payable.

Problem 6–3
Special journals, subsidiary ledgers, and a trial balance
(LO 3, 4, 5)

(If the Working Papers that accompany this text are not being used, omit this problem.)

It is December 16 and you have just taken over the accounting work of Custom Design Company, whose annual accounting periods end each December 31. The company's previous accountant journalized its transactions through December 15 and posted all items that required posting as individual amounts, as an examination of the journals and ledgers in the Working Papers will show.

The company completed these transactions beginning on December 16:

Dec. 16 Purchased on credit from Southwest Supply Company office supplies, $685. Invoice dated December 15, terms n/10 EOM.

17 Received a $1,135 credit memorandum from Walker Company for merchandise received on December 15 and returned for credit.

Dec. 18 Received a $45 credit memorandum from Southwest Supply Company for office supplies received on December 16 and returned for credit.

19 Sold merchandise on credit to Katherine Hoffer, Invoice No. 306, $8,600. (Terms of all credit sales are 2/10, n/30.)

20 Issued a credit memorandum to Kevin Oliver for defective merchandise sold on December 15 and returned for credit, $545.

21 Purchased store equipment on credit from Southwest Supply Company, invoice dated December 21, terms n/10 EOM, $7,500.

22 Issued Check No. 543 to Walker Company in payment of its December 15 invoice less the return and the discount.

22 Received payment from Katherine Hoffer for the December 12 sale less the discount.

23 Issued Check No. 544 to Starbrite Company in payment of its December 15 invoice less a 2% discount.

24 Sold merchandise on credit to Maria Perez, Invoice No. 307, $1,400.

24 Sold a neighboring merchant five boxes of file folders (office supplies) for cash at cost, $56.

25 Received payment from Kevin Oliver for the December 15 sale less the return and the discount.

26 Received merchandise and an invoice dated December 25; terms 2/10, n/60; from Starbrite Company, $8,900.

30 Carol Morgan, the owner of Custom Design Company, used Check No. 545 to withdraw $2,800 cash from the business for personal use.

31 Issued Check No. 546 to Mark Arlos, the company's only sales employee, in payment of his salary for the last half of December, $1,800.

31 Issued Check No. 547 to City Electric Company in payment of the December electric bill, $565.

31 Cash sales for the last half of the month were $32,890. (Cash sales are usually recorded daily but are recorded only twice in this problem to reduce the repetitive transactions.)

Required

1. Record the transactions in the journals provided.
2. Post to the customer and creditor accounts and also post any amounts that should be posted as individual amounts to the general ledger accounts. (Normally, these amounts are posted daily, but they are posted only once by you in this problem because they are few in number.)
3. Foot and crossfoot the journals and make the month-end postings.
4. Prepare a December 31 trial balance and test the accuracy of the subsidiary ledgers by preparing schedules of accounts receivable and payable.

Problem 6–4
Special journals, preparing and proving the trial balance
(LO 3, 4, 5)

Xanox Company completed these transactions during July of the current year:

July 1 Received merchandise and an invoice dated June 30; terms 2/10, n/30; from Farnswood Company, $21,300.

2 Sold merchandise on credit to John Nelson, Invoice No. 324, $7,900. (Terms of all credit sales are 2/10, n/30.)

3 Purchased on credit from Corsair Company office supplies, $560. Invoice dated July 3, terms n/10 EOM.

3 Sold merchandise on credit to Thomas Zak, Invoice No. 325, $4,600.

6 Borrowed $18,000 by giving First State Bank a long-term promissory note payable.

9 Purchased office equipment on credit from McKay Company, invoice dated July 9, terms n/10 EOM, $10,400.

10 Sent Farnswood Company Check No. 876 in payment of its June 30 invoice less the discount.

10 Sold merchandise on credit to Margo Edwards, Invoice No. 326, $2,300.

12 Received payment from John Nelson for the July 2 sale less the discount.

13 Received payment from Thomas Zak for the July 3 sale less the discount.

14 Received merchandise and an invoice dated July 13; terms 2/10, n/30; from Wellsbranch Company, $15,825.

15 Issued Check No. 877, payable to Payroll, in payment of sales salaries for the first half of the month, $7,950. Cashed the check and paid the employees.

15 Cash sales for the first half of the month were $67,340. (Normally, cash sales are recorded daily; however, they are recorded only twice in this problem to reduce the repetitive entries.)

15 *Post to the customer and creditor accounts and also post any amounts that should be posted as individual amounts to the general ledger accounts. (Normally, such items are posted daily; but you are asked to post them on only two occasions in this problem because they are few in number.)*

16 Purchased on credit from Corsair Company store supplies, $840. Invoice dated July 16, terms n/10 EOM.

17 Received a credit memorandum from Wellsbranch Company for unsatisfactory merchandise received on July 14 and returned for credit, $1,225.

19 Received a credit memorandum from McKay Company for office equipment received on July 9 and returned for credit, $300.

20 Received payment from Margo Edwards for the sale of July 10 less the discount.

23 Issued Check No. 878 to Wellsbranch Company in payment of its invoice of July 13 less the return and the discount.

July 27 Sold merchandise on credit to Margo Edwards, Invoice No. 327, $6,540.

28 Sold merchandise on credit to Thomas Zak, Invoice No. 328, $2,650.

31 Issued Check No. 879, payable to Payroll, in payment of sales salaries for the last half of the month, $7,950. Cashed the check and paid the employees.

31 Cash sales for the last half of the month were $72,345.

31 *Post to the customer and creditor accounts and post any amounts that should be posted as individual amounts to the general ledger accounts.*

31 *Foot and crossfoot the journals and make the month-end postings.*

Required

1. Open the following general ledger accounts: Cash, Accounts Receivable, Office Supplies, Store Supplies, Office Equipment, Accounts Payable, Long-Term Notes Payable, Sales, Sales Discounts, Purchases, Purchases Returns and Allowances, Purchases Discounts, and Sales Salaries Expense.
2. Open the following accounts receivable ledger accounts: Margo Edwards, John Nelson, and Thomas Zak.
3. Open the following accounts payable ledger accounts: Corsair Company, Farnswood Company, McKay Company, and Wellsbranch Company. Enter the transactions in a Sales Journal, a Purchases Journal, a Cash Receipts Journal, a Cash Disbursements Journal, and a General Journal similar to the ones illustrated in this chapter. Post when instructed to do so.
4. Prepare a trial balance and test the accuracy of the subsidiary ledgers by preparing schedules of accounts receivable and payable.

Problem 6–5
Special journals, subsidiary ledgers, and the trial balance
(LO 3, 4, 5)

Crawford Company completed these transactions during June of the current year:

June 1 Received merchandise and an invoice dated May 31; terms 2/10, n/60; from Hollingsworth Company, $47,800.

2 Purchased office equipment on credit from Dunlap Company, invoice dated June 2, terms n/10 EOM, $14,625.

3 Sold merchandise on credit to Tamara Smith, Invoice No. 902, $22,300. (Terms of all credit sales are 2/10, n/30.)

5 Sold merchandise on credit to Dean Grammer, Invoice No. 903, $31,700.

8 Cash sales for the week ended June 8 were $38,950.

8 *Post to the customer and creditor accounts and also post any amounts that should be posted as individual items to the general ledger accounts. (Normally, such items are posted daily; but to simplify the problem, you are asked to post them only once each week.)*

June 8 Issued Check No. 548 to *The Monthly News* for advertising, $275.

9 Sold merchandise on credit to Mary Cortez, Invoice No. 904, $12,400.

10 Issued Check No. 549 to Hollingsworth Company in payment of its May 31 invoice less the discount.

10 Purchased on credit from The Store Depot merchandise, $5,870 and office supplies, $570. Invoice dated June 10, terms n/10 EOM.

11 Sold unneeded office equipment at cost for cash, $940.

13 Received payment from Tamara Smith for the sale of June 3 less the discount.

15 Cash sales for the week ended June 15 were $23,620.

15 Issued Check No. 550, payable to Payroll, in payment of the sales salaries for the first half of the month, $16,280. Cashed the check and paid the employees.

15 *Post to the customer and creditor accounts and also post any amounts that should be posted as individual items to the general ledger accounts.*

15 Received payment from Dean Grammer for the sale of June 5 less the discount.

16 Sold merchandise on credit to Mary Cortez, Invoice No. 905, $9,735.

19 Sold merchandise on credit to Tamara Smith, Invoice No. 906, $6,430.

19 Received payment from Mary Cortez for the sale of June 9 less the discount.

20 Received merchandise and an invoice dated June 18; terms 2/10, n/60; from Riteway Company, $17,500.

21 Issued a credit memorandum to Mary Cortez for defective merchandise sold on June 16 and returned for credit, $1,835.

22 Cash sales for the week ended June 22 were $28,150.

22 *Post to the customer and creditor accounts and also post any amounts that should be posted as individual items to the general ledger accounts.*

24 Received a $1,700 credit memorandum from Riteway Company for defective merchandise received on June 18 and returned for credit.

25 Purchased on credit from The Store Depot merchandise, $22,390, and store supplies, $2,825. Invoice dated June 25, terms n/10 EOM.

25 Received merchandise and an invoice dated June 24; terms 2/10, n/60; from Hollingsworth Company, $35,860.

26 Received payment from Mary Cortez for the June 16 sale less the return and the discount.

26 Sold merchandise on credit to Dean Grammer, Invoice No. 907, $22,540.

June 28 Issued Check No. 551 to Riteway Company in payment of its June 18 invoice, less the return and the discount.

30 Issued Check No. 552, payable to Payroll, in payment of the sales salaries for the last half of the month, $16,280.

30 Cash sales for the week ended June 30 were $31,230.

30 *Post to the customer and creditor accounts and also post any amounts that should be posted to the general ledger accounts as individual items.*

30 *Foot and crossfoot the journals and make the month-end postings.*

Required

1. Open the following general ledger accounts: Cash, Accounts Receivable, Office Supplies, Store Supplies, Office Equipment, Accounts Payable, Sales, Sales Returns and Allowances, Sales Discounts, Purchases, Purchases Returns and Allowances, Purchases Discounts, Sales Salaries Expense, and Advertising Expense.
2. Open the following subsidiary accounts receivable ledger accounts: Mary Cortez, Dean Grammer, and Tamara Smith.
3. Open the following subsidiary accounts payable ledger accounts: Dunlap Company, Hollingsworth Company, Riteway Company, and The Store Depot.
4. Prepare a Sales Journal, a Cash Receipts Journal, a Cash Disbursements Journal, and a General Journal like the ones illustrated in this chapter. Prepare a Purchases Journal with a debit column for purchases, a debit column for other accounts, and a credit column for accounts payable. Enter the transactions in the journals and post when instructed to do so.
5. Prepare a trial balance and test the accuracy of the subsidiary ledgers with schedules of accounts receivable and payable.

Problem 6–6
Analytical essay
(LO 3)

Lynn's Products uses a Cash Receipts Journal similar to the one in Illustration 6–5. In the process of crossfooting the journal at the end of a month, the company's bookkeeper found that the sum of the debits did not equal the sum of the credits.

Required

Describe the procedures you would follow in an effort to discover the reason why the journal does not crossfoot correctly.

Problem 6–7
Analytical essay
(LO 5)

Tucker's Tidbits is a merchandising company that uses the special journals described in Chapter 6. At the end of the accounting period, the bookkeeper for the company prepared a trial balance and a schedule of accounts receivable. The trial balance is in balance but the sum of the account balances on the schedule of accounts receivable does not equal the balance in the controlling account.

Required

Describe the procedures you would follow to discover the reason for the imbalance between the controlling account and the total shown on the schedule of accounts receivable.

Alternate Problems

Problem 6–1A
Special journals and subsidiary ledgers
(LO 3, 4, 5)

Stanford Equipment Company completed these transactions during October of the current year:

Oct. 1 Issued Check No. 640 to *Pacific Monthly* for advertising expense, $980.

1 Purchased merchandise on credit from Fiore Company, invoice dated September 30; terms 2/10, n/30; $3,500.

5 Sold merchandise on credit to Frank Mendoza, Invoice No. 768, $10,200. (The terms of all credit sales are 2/10, n/30.)

5 Purchased on credit from Weisman Company store supplies, $750. Invoice dated October 5, terms n/10 EOM.

6 Sold merchandise on credit to Janet Dalton, Invoice No. 769, $4,700.

8 Received an $80 credit memorandum from Weisman Company for unsatisfactory merchandise received on October 5 and returned for credit.

9 Purchased store equipment on credit from Century Company, invoice dated October 8, terms n/10 EOM, $20,950.

10 Issued Check No. 641 to Fiore Company in payment of its September 30 invoice, less the discount.

13 Sold merchandise on credit to Cynthia Montgomery, Invoice No. 770, $4,650.

15 Received payment from Frank Mendoza for the October 5 sale, less the discount.

15 Issued Check No. 642, payable to Payroll, in payment of the sales salaries for the first half of the month, $15,900. Cashed the check and paid the employees.

15 Sold merchandise on credit to Frank Mendoza, Invoice No. 771, $2,300.

15 Cash sales for the first half of the month were $56,320. (Cash sales are usually recorded daily from the cash register readings. However, they are recorded only twice in this problem to reduce the repetitive transactions.)

16 Received payment from Janet Dalton for the October 6 sale, less the discount.

17 Purchased merchandise on credit from Kramer Company, invoice dated October 17; terms 2/10, n/30; $4,600.

Oct. 21 Borrowed $8,500 from City Bank by giving a long-term note payable.

23 Received payment from Cynthia Montgomery for the October 13 sale, less the discount.

24 Received a $1,300 credit memorandum from Kramer Company for defective merchandise received on October 17 and returned.

25 Purchased on credit from Century Company office supplies, $420. Invoice dated October 24, terms n/10 EOM.

25 Received payment from Frank Mendoza for the October 15 sale, less the discount.

26 Purchased merchandise on credit from Fiore Company, invoice dated October 26; terms 2/10, n/30; $5,430.

27 Issued Check No. 643 to Kramer Company in payment of its October 17 invoice, less the return and the discount.

29 Sold merchandise on credit to Janet Dalton, Invoice No. 772, $15,600.

30 Sold merchandise on credit to Cynthia Montgomery, Invoice No. 773, $8,750.

31 Issued Check No. 644, payable to Payroll, in payment of the sales salaries for the last half of the month, $15,900.

31 Cash sales for the last half of the month were $43,900.

Required

1. Open the following general ledger accounts: Cash, Accounts Receivable, Long-Term Notes Payable, Sales, and Sales Discounts. Also open subsidiary accounts receivable ledger accounts for Janet Dalton, Frank Mendoza, and Cynthia Montgomery.
2. Prepare a Sales Journal and a Cash Receipts Journal similar to the ones illustrated in this chapter.
3. Review the transactions of Stanford Equipment Company and enter those transactions that should be journalized in the Sales Journal and those that should be journalized in the Cash Receipts Journal. Ignore any transactions that should be journalized in a Purchases Journal, a Cash Disbursements Journal, or a General Journal.
4. Post the items that should be posted as individual amounts from the journals. (Normally, such items are posted daily; but since they are few in number in this problem you are asked to post them only once.)
5. Foot and crossfoot the journals and make the month-end postings.
6. Prepare a trial balance of the General Ledger and test the accuracy of the subsidiary ledger by preparing a schedule of accounts receivable.

Problem 6–2A
Special journals, subsidiary ledgers, schedule of accounts payable
(LO 3, 4, 5)

On September 30, Stanford Equipment Company had a cash balance of $92,000 and a Long-Term Notes Payable balance of $92,000. The October transactions of Stanford Equipment Company included those listed in Problem 6–1A.

Required

1. Open the following general ledger accounts: Cash, Office Supplies, Store Supplies, Store Equipment, Accounts Payable, Long-Term Notes Payable, Purchases, Purchases Returns and Allowances, Purchases Discounts, Sales Salaries Expense, and Advertising Expense. Enter the September 30 balances of Cash and Long-Term Notes Payable ($92,000 each).
2. Open subsidiary accounts payable ledger accounts for Century Company, Fiore Company, Kramer Company, and Weisman Company.
3. Prepare a General Journal and a Cash Disbursements Journal like the ones illustrated in this chapter. Prepare a Purchases Journal with a debit column for purchases, a debit column for other accounts, and a credit column for accounts payable.
4. Review the October transactions of Stanford Equipment Company and enter those transactions that should be journalized in the General Journal, the Purchases Journal, or the Cash Disbursements Journal. Ignore any transactions that should be journalized in a Sales Journal or Cash Receipts Journal.
5. Post the items that should be posted as individual amounts from the journals. (Normally, such items are posted daily; but since they are few in number in this problem you are asked to post them only once.)
6. Foot and crossfoot the journals and make the month-end postings.
7. Prepare a trial balance and a schedule of accounts payable.

Problem 6–3A
Special journals, subsidiary ledgers, and a trial balance
(LO 3, 4, 5)

(If the Working Papers that accompany this text are not being used, omit this problem.)

It is December 16 and you have just taken over the accounting work of Sierra Company, whose annual accounting periods end each December 31. The company's previous accountant journalized its transactions through December 15 and posted all items that required posting as individual amounts, as an examination of the journals and ledgers in the booklet of working papers will show.

The company completed these transactions beginning on December 16:

Dec. 16 Sold merchandise on credit to Katherine Hoffer, Invoice No. 306, $3,500. (Terms of all credit sales are 2/10, n/30.)

17 Received a $435 credit memorandum from Walker Company for merchandise received on December 15 and returned for credit.

17 Purchased on credit from Southwest Supply Company office supplies, $850. Invoice dated December 17, terms n/10 EOM.

19 Issued a credit memorandum to Kevin Oliver for defective merchandise sold on December 15 and returned for credit, $145.

20 Received a $270 credit memorandum from Southwest Supply Company for office supplies received on December 17 and returned for credit.

20 Purchased store equipment on credit from Southwest Supply Company, invoice dated December 19, terms n/10 EOM, $8,300.

Dec. 21 Sold merchandise on credit to Maria Perez, Invoice No. 307, $4,600.

22 Received payment from Katherine Hoffer for the December 12 sale less the discount.

24 Received payment from Kevin Oliver for the December 15 sale less the return and the discount.

25 Issued Check No. 543 to Walker Company in payment of its December 15 invoice less the return and the discount.

25 Issued Check No. 544 to Starbrite Company in payment of its December 15 invoice less a 2% discount.

28 Received merchandise and an invoice dated December 28; terms 2/10, n/60; from Starbrite Company, $6,700.

28 Sold a neighboring merchant a carton of calculator tape (store supplies) for cash at cost, $60.

29 Carol Morgan, the owner of Sierra Company, used Check No. 545 to withdraw $6,900 cash from the business for personal use.

31 Issued Check No. 546 to City Power Company in payment of the December electric bill, $980.

31 Issued Check No. 547 to Mark Arlos, the company's only sales employee, in payment of his salary for the last half of December, $1,800.

31 Cash sales for the last half of the month were $46,750. (Cash sales are usually recorded daily but are recorded only twice in this problem to reduce the repetitive entries.)

Required

1. Record the transactions in the journals provided.
2. Post to the customer and creditor accounts and also post any amounts that should be posted as individual amounts to the general ledger accounts. (Normally, these amounts are posted daily, but they are posted only once by you in this problem because they are few in number.)
3. Foot and crossfoot the journals and make the month-end postings.
4. Prepare a December 31 trial balance and test the accuracy of the subsidiary ledgers by preparing schedules of accounts receivable and payable.

Problem 6–4A
Special journals, preparing and proving the trial balance
(LO 3, 4, 5)

Safelite Company completed these transactions during August of the current year:

Aug. 1 Borrowed $75,000 by giving City National Bank a long-term promissory note payable.

4 Received merchandise and an invoice dated August 3; terms 2/10, n/30; from Farnswood Company, $15,200.

5 Purchased on credit from Corsair Company store supplies, $1,360. Invoice dated August 5, terms n/10 EOM.

6 Sold merchandise on credit to John Nelson, Invoice No. 789, $8,500. (Terms of all credit sales are 2/10, n/30.)

Aug. 7 Purchased office equipment on credit from McKay Company, invoice dated August 6, terms n/10 EOM, $6,750.

10 Sold merchandise on credit to Thomas Zak, Invoice No. 790, $16,700.

13 Sent Farnswood Company Check No. 423 in payment of its August 3 invoice less the discount.

13 Received merchandise and an invoice dated August 13; terms 2/10, n/30; from Wellsbranch Company, $3,850.

15 Issued Check No. 424, payable to Payroll, in payment of sales salaries for the first half of the month, $11,250. Cashed the check and paid the employees.

15 Cash sales for the first half of the month were $22,760. (Normally, cash sales are recorded daily; however, they are recorded only twice in this problem to reduce the repetitive entries.)

15 *Post to the customer and creditor accounts and also post any amounts that should be posted as individual amounts to the general ledger accounts. (Normally, such items are posted daily; but you are asked to post them on only two occasions in this problem because they are few in number.)*

15 Sold merchandise on credit to Margo Edwards, Invoice No. 791, $5,700.

16 Received payment from John Nelson for the August 6 sale less the discount.

16 Purchased on credit from Corsair Company office supplies, $745. Invoice dated August 16, terms n/10 EOM.

20 Received payment from Thomas Zak for the August 10 sale less the discount.

20 Received a credit memorandum from Wellsbranch Company for unsatisfactory merchandise received on August 13 and returned for credit, $650.

23 Issued Check No. 425 to Wellsbranch Company in payment of its invoice of August 13 less the return and the discount.

24 Sold merchandise on credit to Margo Edwards, Invoice No. 792, $4,330.

25 Received payment from Margo Edwards for the sale of August 15 less the discount.

26 Received a credit memorandum from McKay Company for office equipment received on August 7 and returned for credit, $1,230.

27 Sold merchandise on credit to Thomas Zak, Invoice No. 793, $3,460.

31 Issued Check No. 426, payable to Payroll, in payment of sales salaries for the last half of the month, $11,250. Cashed the check and paid the employees.

31 Cash sales for the last half of the month were $34,270.

Aug. 31 *Post to the customer and creditor accounts and post any amounts that should be posted as individual amounts to the general ledger accounts.*

31 *Foot and crossfoot the journals and make the month-end postings.*

Required

1. Open the following general ledger accounts: Cash, Accounts Receivable, Office Supplies, Store Supplies, Office Equipment, Accounts Payable, Long-Term Notes Payable, Sales, Sales Discounts, Purchases, Purchases Returns and Allowances, Purchases Discounts, and Sales Salaries Expense.
2. Open the following accounts receivable ledger accounts: Margo Edwards, John Nelson, and Thomas Zak.
3. Open the following accounts payable ledger accounts: Corsair Company, Farnswood Company, McKay Company, and Wellsbranch Company. Enter the transactions in a Sales Journal, a Purchases Journal, a Cash Receipts Journal, a Cash Disbursements Journal, and a General Journal similar to the ones illustrated in this chapter. Post when instructed to do so.
4. Prepare a trial balance and test the accuracy of the subsidiary ledgers by preparing schedules of accounts receivable and payable.

Problem 6–5A
Special journals, subsidiary ledgers, and the trial balance
(LO 3, 4, 5)

Wolfe Company completed these transactions during April of the current year:

Apr. 1 Received merchandise and an invoice dated April 1; terms 2/10, n/30; from Hollingsworth Company, $5,400.

1 Sold merchandise on credit to Tamara Smith, Invoice No. 234, $1,600. (Terms of all credit sales are 2/10, n/30.)

3 Issued Check No. 722 to *Northern Living* for advertising, $545.

3 Purchased office equipment on credit from Dunlap Company, invoice dated April 2, terms n/10 EOM, $3,790.

5 Sold merchandise on credit to Dean Grammer, Invoice No. 235, $4,300.

8 Cash sales for the week ended April 8 were $15,870.

8 *Post to the customer and creditor accounts and also post any amounts that should be posted as individual items to the general ledger accounts. (Normally, such items are posted daily; but to simplify the problem, you are asked to post them only once each week.)*

8 Sold merchandise on credit to Mary Cortez, Invoice No. 236, $2,400.

9 Received a credit memorandum from Dunlap Company for the return of defective equipment originally purchased on April 3, $390.

Apr. 11 Issued Check No. 723 to Hollingsworth Company in payment of its April 1 invoice less the discount.

11 Sold unneeded office equipment at cost for cash, $550.

11 Received payment from Tamara Smith for the sale of April 1 less the discount.

15 Cash sales for the week ended April 15 were $12,340.

15 Issued Check No. 724, payable to Payroll, in payment of the sales salaries for the first half of the month, $3,860. Cashed the check and paid the employees.

15 *Post to the customer and creditor accounts and also post any amounts that should be posted as individual items to the general ledger accounts.*

15 Received payment from Dean Grammer for the sale of April 5 less the discount.

17 Purchased on credit from The Store Depot merchandise, $6,820, and store supplies, $540. Invoice dated April 16, terms n/10 EOM.

18 Received merchandise and an invoice dated April 18; terms 2/10, n/60; from Riteway Company, $4,740.

18 Sold merchandise on credit to Mary Cortez, Invoice No. 237, $3,630.

18 Sold merchandise on credit to Tamara Smith, Invoice No. 238, $5,700.

18 Received payment from Mary Cortez for the sale of April 8 less the discount.

22 Issued a credit memorandum to Mary Cortez for defective merchandise sold on April 18 and returned for credit, $230.

22 Cash sales for the week ended April 22 were $17,220.

22 *Post to the customer and creditor accounts and also post any amounts that should be posted as individual items to the general ledger accounts.*

23 Received a $1,140 credit memorandum from Riteway Company for defective merchandise received on April 18 and returned for credit.

24 Purchased on credit from The Store Depot merchandise, $9,780, and office supplies, $965. Invoice dated April 23, terms n/10 EOM.

25 Received merchandise and an invoice dated April 25; terms 2/10, n/30; from Hollingsworth Company, $7,540.

28 Received payment from Mary Cortez for the April 18 sale less the return and the discount.

28 Issued Check No. 725 to Riteway Company in payment of its April 18 invoice, less the return and the discount.

29 Sold merchandise on credit to Dean Grammer, Invoice No. 239, $2,970.

Apr. 30 Issued Check No. 726, payable to Payroll, in payment of the sales salaries for the last half of the month, $3,860.

30 Cash sales for the week ended April 30 were $9,520.

30 *Post to the customer and creditor accounts and also post any amounts that should be posted to the general ledger accounts as individual items.*

30 *Foot and crossfoot the journals and make the month-end postings.*

Required

1. Open the following general ledger accounts: Cash, Accounts Receivable, Office Supplies, Store Supplies, Office Equipment, Accounts Payable, Sales, Sales Returns and Allowances, Sales Discounts, Purchases, Purchases Returns and Allowances, Purchases Discounts, Sales Salaries Expense, and Advertising Expense.
2. Open the following subsidiary accounts receivable ledger accounts: Mary Cortez, Dean Grammer, and Tamara Smith.
3. Open the following subsidiary accounts payable ledger accounts: Dunlap Company, Hollingsworth Company, Riteway Company, and The Store Depot.
4. Prepare a Sales Journal, a Cash Receipts Journal, a Cash Disbursements Journal, and a General Journal like the ones illustrated in this chapter. Prepare a Purchases Journal with a debit column for purchases, a debit column for other accounts, and a credit column for accounts payable. Enter the transactions in the journals and post when instructed to do so.
5. Prepare a trial balance and test the accuracy of the subsidiary ledgers with schedules of accounts receivable and payable.

Problem 6–6A
Analytical essay
(LO 3)

Russell's Novelties uses a Cash Disbursements Journal similar to the one in Illustration 6–7. In the process of crossfooting the journal at the end of a month, the company's bookkeeper found that the sum of the debits did not equal the sum of the credits.

Required

Describe the procedures you would follow in an effort to discover the reason why the journal does not crossfoot correctly.

Problem 6–7A
Analytical essay
(LO 5)

Michael's Autoparts is a merchandising company that uses the special journals described in Chapter 6. At the end of the accounting period, the bookkeeper for the company prepared a trial balance and a schedule of accounts payable. The trial balance is in balance but the sum of the account balances on the schedule of accounts payable does not equal the balance in the controlling account.

Required

Describe the procedures you would follow to discover the reason for the imbalance between the controlling account and the total shown on the schedule of accounts payable.

Provocative Problem

Provocative Problem 6–1
As a Matter of Ethics: Essay

Ethics

Review the As a Matter of Ethics case presented on page 317. Discuss the problem faced by the CPA and the factors the CPA should consider in deciding on a course of action.

Answers to Objective Review Questions

LO1 (*d*)	LO3 (*b*)	LO5 (*d*)
LO2 (*a*)	LO4 (*e*)	LO6 (*e*)

Comprehensive Problem

Draper Company
(Review of chapters 1–6)

(If the Working Papers that accompany this text are not available, omit this comprehensive problem.)

Assume it is Monday, May 1, the first business day of the month, and you have just been hired as the accountant for Draper Company, which operates with monthly accounting periods. All of the company's accounting work has been completed through the end of April and its ledgers show April 30 balances. During your first month on the job, you record the following transactions:

May 3 Purchased on credit from Flintrock Suppliers merchandise, $19,650; store supplies, $340; and office supplies, $80. Invoice dated May 3, terms n/10 EOM.

4 Sold merchandise on credit to Arcam Company, Invoice No. 622, $6,500. (The terms of all credit sales are 2/10, n/30.)

5 Issued Check No. 817 to Ross Realty in payment of the May rent, $4,150. (Use two lines to record the transaction. Charge 80% of the rent to Rent Expense, Selling Space and the balance to Rent Expense, Office Space.)

6 Received a $390 credit memorandum from Natural Products for merchandise received on April 28 and returned for credit.

6 Issued a $350 credit memorandum to Legacy Company for defective merchandise sold on April 30 and returned for credit. The total selling price (gross) was $2,750.

7 Purchased office equipment on credit from Flintrock Suppliers, invoice dated May 5, terms n/10 EOM, $4,740.

8 Sold store supplies to the merchant next door at cost for cash, $30.

9 Issued Check No. 818 to Natural Products to pay for the $2,790 of merchandise received on April 28 less the return and a 2% discount.

10 Received payment from Legacy Company for the remaining balance from the sale of April 30 less the return and the discount.

13 Received merchandise and an invoice dated May 11; terms 2/10, n/30; from Carousel, Inc., $8,000.

13 Received a $180 credit memorandum from Flintrock Suppliers for defective office equipment received on May 7 and returned for credit.

14 Received payment from Arcam Company for the May 4 sale less the discount.

15 Issued Check No. 819, payable to Payroll, in payment of sales salaries, $2,200, and office salaries, $1,340. Cashed the check and paid the employees.

May 15 Cash sales for the first half of the month, $28,285. (Such sales are normally recorded daily. They are recorded only twice in this problem to reduce the repetitive entries.)

15 *Post to the customer and creditor accounts. Also, post individual items that are not included in column totals at the end of the month to the general ledger accounts. (Such items are normally posted daily, but you are asked to post them only twice each month because they are few in number.)*

17 Received merchandise and an invoice dated May 16; terms 2/10, n/60; from Sante Fe Designs, $12,950.

19 Sold merchandise on credit to Seaside Clinic, Invoice No. 623, $7,400.

20 Issued Check No. 820 to Carousel, Inc. in payment of its May 11 invoice less the discount.

21 Sold merchandise on credit to Legacy Company, Invoice No. 624, $1,900.

22 Purchased on credit from Flintrock Suppliers merchandise, $3,060; store supplies, $140; and office supplies, $100. Invoice dated May 22, terms n/10 EOM.

25 Sold merchandise on credit to Applause Interiors, Invoice No. 625, $11,100.

25 Issued Check No. 821 to Sante Fe Designs in payment of its May 16 invoice less the discount.

27 Received merchandise and an invoice dated May 26; terms 2/10, n/30; from Carousel, Inc., $1,900.

28 Received payment from Seaside Clinic for the May 19 sale less the discount.

28 Frank Holcomb, the owner of Draper Company, used Check No. 822 to withdraw $3,000 from the business for personal use.

30 Issued Check No. 823, payable to Payroll, in payment of sales salaries, $2,200, and office salaries, $1,340. Cashed the check and paid the employees.

30 Issued Check No. 824 to City Utility in payment of the May electric bill, $1,180.

31 Cash sales for the last half of the month were $21,960.

31 *Post to the customer and creditor accounts. Also, post individual items that are not included in column totals at the end of the month to the general ledger accounts.*

31 Foot and crossfoot the journals and make the month-end postings.

Required

1. Enter the transactions in the appropriate journals and post when instructed to do so.
2. Prepare a trial balance in the Trial Balance columns of the provided work sheet form and complete the work sheet using the following information:

a. Ending merchandise inventory, $189,430.
b. Expired insurance, $280.
c. Ending store supplies inventory, $730; and office supplies inventory, $270.
d. Estimated depreciation of store equipment, $550; and of office equipment, $170.

3. Prepare a multiple-step classified May income statement, a May statement of changes in owner's equity, and a May 31 classified balance sheet.
4. Prepare and post adjusting and closing entries.
5. Prepare a post-closing trial balance. Also prepare a list of the Accounts Receivable Ledger accounts and a list of the Accounts Payable Ledger accounts. Total the balances of each to confirm that the totals equal the balances in the controlling accounts.

PART

III

Accounting for Assets

Businesses use many different kinds of assets in carrying on their operations. These include such things as cash, receivables, merchandise inventories, land, buildings, equipment, natural resources, and intangible assets. As you study the next five chapters, you will learn the basic principles of accounting for all these different assets. You will see how transactions that involve assets are recorded. You will also learn how the assets and events concerning them are reported in the financial statements. In addition, you will learn several accounting procedures that help management safeguard and control the assets of the business.

Part III consists of the following chapters:

CHAPTER

7

Internal Control and Accounting for Cash

Because almost all business activities involve cash, it must be carefully controlled. Internal control systems are designed to make accounting information dependable and to help companies avoid misplacing or misusing their assets.

Topical Coverage

Cash is an asset that every business owns and uses. Cash includes such specific items as currency, coins, checking accounts (also called *demand deposits*), and perhaps savings accounts (also called *time deposits*). Most organizations also own at least some assets known as *cash equivalents*, which are very similar to cash. In studying this chapter, you will learn the principles of internal control that guide businesses in managing and accounting for cash. The chapter shows how to establish and use a petty cash fund and how to reconcile a checking account. Also, you will learn a method of accounting for purchases that helps management determine whether cash discounts on purchases are being lost and, if so, how much has been lost.

Learning Objectives

After studying Chapter 7, you should be able to:

1. Explain the concept of liquidity and the difference between cash and cash equivalents.
2. Explain why internal control procedures are needed in a large organization and state the broad principles of internal control.
3. Describe internal control procedures used to protect cash received from cash sales, cash received through the mail, and cash disbursements.
4. Explain the operation of a petty cash fund and be able to prepare journal entries to record petty cash fund transactions.
5. Explain why the bank balance and the book balance of cash should be reconciled and be able to prepare a reconciliation.
6. Tell how recording invoices at net amounts helps gain control over cash discounts taken and be able to account for invoices recorded at net amounts.
7. Define or explain the words and phrases listed in the chapter glossary.

After studying Appendix D at the end of Chapter 7, you should be able to:

8. Explain the use of a Voucher Register and Check Register and prepare entries to record and pay liabilities when these registers are used in a manual accounting system.

Cash, Cash Equivalents, and the Concept of Liquidity

LO 1 Explain the concept of liquidity and the difference between cash and cash equivalents.

In previous chapters, you have learned that a company can own many different kinds of assets, including accounts receivable, merchandise inventory, and various kinds of equipment. You have also learned that the value invested in these assets is not lost when they are acquired. For example, if cash of $10,000 is spent on equipment, the equipment is recorded at a cost of $10,000. The transaction does not involve an expense; owner's equity is not reduced.

Although value is not lost when equipment is purchased for cash, the equipment is not as easily used as cash when buying other assets, acquiring services, or paying off liabilities. Another way to state this is to say that cash is more *liquid* than equipment. Thus, although value is not lost when equipment is purchased for cash, the investment in equipment is less liquid than was the investment in cash.

In more general terms, the **liquidity** of an asset refers to how easily the asset can be converted into other types of assets or be used to buy services or satisfy obligations. All assets can be evaluated in terms of their relative liquidity. Assets such as cash are said to be **liquid assets** because they can be easily converted into other types of assets or used to buy services or pay liabilities.

You should realize that a company needs more than valuable assets to stay in business. That is, the company must own some liquid assets so that bills will be paid on time and purchases can be made for cash when that is necessary.

For financial accounting, the asset *cash* includes not only currency and coins but also amounts on deposit in bank accounts, including checking accounts (sometimes called demand deposits) and some savings accounts (also called time deposits). Cash also includes items that are acceptable for deposit in those accounts, especially customers' checks made payable to the company.

To increase their return, many companies invest their idle cash balances in assets called **cash equivalents.** These assets are short-term, highly liquid investments that satisfy two criteria:

1. The investment must be readily convertible to a known amount of cash.
2. The investment must be sufficiently close to its maturity date so that its market value is relatively insensitive to interest rate changes.

In general, only investments that are purchased within three months of their maturity dates satisfy these criteria.[1] Examples of cash equivalents include short-term investments in U.S. treasury bills, commercial paper (short-term corporate notes payable), and money market funds.

Because cash equivalents are so similar to cash, many companies combine them with cash on the balance sheet. Others show them separately. For example, IBM Corporation shows these items on its published balance sheet:

(in millions)	**December 31**	
	1990	**1989**
Cash	$1,189	$ 741
Cash equivalents	2,664	2,959

Note that IBM had two to four times as much invested in cash equivalents as it did in cash.

As you would expect, cash is an important asset for every business. Because cash is so important, companies need to be careful about keeping track of it. They also need to carefully control access to cash by employees and others who might want to take it for their own use. A good accounting system provides for both goals. It can keep track of how much cash is on hand, and it can control who has access to the cash. Because of the special importance of

[1] FASB, *Accounting Standards—Current Text* (Norwalk, Conn. 1990), sec. C25.106. First published in *Statement of Financial Accounting Standards No. 95*, par. 8.

cash, this chapter describes the practices companies follow to account for and protect cash.

Internal Control

LO 2 Explain why internal control procedures are needed in a large organization and state the broad principles of internal control.

In a small business, the owner-manager often controls the entire operation through personal supervision and direct participation in all its activities. For example, he or she commonly buys all the assets and services used in the business. The manager also hires and supervises all employees, negotiates all contracts, and signs all checks. As a result, the manager knows from personal contact and observation whether the business actually received the assets and services for which the checks were written. However, as a business grows, it becomes increasingly difficult to maintain this close personal contact. Therefore, at some point the manager must delegate responsibilities and rely on formal procedures rather than personal contact in controlling the operations of the business.

The procedures that control the operations of a business make up its **internal control system.** A properly designed internal control system encourages adherence to prescribed managerial policies. In doing so, it also promotes operational efficiencies and protects the business assets from waste, fraud, and theft. The system also helps ensure that accurate and reliable accounting data are produced.

Specific internal control procedures vary from company to company and depend on such factors as the nature of the business and its size. However, the same broad principles of internal control apply to all companies. These broad principles are:

1. Clearly establish responsibilities.
2. Maintain adequate records.
3. Insure assets and bond employees.
4. Separate record-keeping and custody over assets.
5. Divide responsibilities for related transactions.
6. Use mechanical devices whenever practicable.
7. Perform regular and independent reviews.

We discuss these seven principles in the following paragraphs. Throughout, we describe various internal control procedures in terms of their ability to prevent fraud and theft. Remember, however, that these procedures are needed to ensure that the accounting records are complete and accurate.

Clearly Establish Responsibilities

To have good internal control, responsibility for each task must be clearly established and one person made accountable for its fulfillment. When responsibility is not clearly spelled out, it is difficult to determine who is at fault when something goes wrong. For example, when two sales clerks share access to the same cash register and there is a shortage, it may not be possible to tell which clerk is at fault. Each tends to blame the other. Neither can prove that he or she did not cause the shortage. To prevent this problem, one clerk should be given

AS A MATTER OF
Fact

Cash; Once Trash, Now Treasure

Ex-billionaire Donald Trump knows a hot idea when he hears one. Several months ago, when he was trying to unload the Trump shuttle, he announced that cash was in, debt was out. Poor Donald—if only he had put his money where his mouth was, he wouldn't be in hock to banks and bondholders today.

In the decade of debt financing, cash was trash. It wasn't smart to sit with it when other assets were going to the moon. But in the past 12 months, everything except cash has come crashing down to earth. Mergers and acquisitions are off nearly 50% because few corporations can borrow the money to swing a deal. Reputable real estate developers are going bust, and heavily mortgaged homeowners cannot afford to sell at rock-bottom prices. Meanwhile, cash in the form of Treasury bills is returning a steady 7% to 8%.

The ascendancy of cash implies that credit will be tighter in the Nineties than in the Eighties. Lenders will discriminate against corporations with weak balance sheets, putting them at a competitive disadvantage. Compare Nordstrom, the well-financed Seattle-based department store chain that is steadily expanding, with R. H. Macy, which is selling equity and trying to shed assets to pay down debt.

For homeowners and commercial real estate developers, King Cash means that property prices will likely remain depressed. Why? Explains investment banker Lewis Ranieri, chairman of Ranieri Wilson & Co.: "In today's environment, where asset values are falling, tighter credit standards are being imposed." Take, for example, a $100 million office building. In the good old days of debt, you could finance its purchase by putting up only 5% cash—$5 million. Today, not only has the value of the property fallen to, say, $60 million, but a potential buyer must also come up with 25% cash—$15 million. That's a high enough hurdle to forestall any rapid recovery in real estate.

The implications of cash as an appreciating asset may not be pretty. James Grant, for one, thinks that deflation—that rare bird not seen on the American continent since the 1930s—is a distinct possibility. Says he: "If people decide that cash is a better store of value, then prices for houses and companies can only decline further. Potential buyers will demand that sellers capitulate on price before they will exchange the safety of cash for the illiquidity of other assets."

Source: Brett D. Fromson, *Fortune*, January 14, 1991, pp. 54 and 58,

responsibility for making all change. Alternatively, the business can use a register with separate cash drawers for each operator.

Maintain Adequate Records

A good record-keeping system helps protect assets and ensures that employees follow prescribed procedures. Reliable records are also a source of information that management uses to monitor the operations of the business. For example, if detailed records of manufacturing equipment and tools are maintained, items are unlikely to be lost or otherwise disappear without any discrepancy being noticed. As another example, expenses and other expenditures are less likely to be debited to the wrong accounts if a comprehensive chart of accounts is established and followed carefully. If the chart is not in place or is not used correctly, management may never discover that some expenses are excessive.

Numerous preprinted forms and internal business papers should be designed and properly used to maintain good internal control. For example, if sales slips are properly designed, sales personnel can record the needed information efficiently without errors or delays to customers. And, if all sales slips are prenumbered and controlled, each salesperson can be held responsible for the sales slips issued to him or her. As a result, a salesperson is not able to pocket cash by making a sale and destroying the sales slip. Computerized point-of-sale systems can be designed to achieve the same control results.

Insure Assets and Bond Key Employees

Assets should be covered by adequate casualty insurance, ahd employees who handle cash and negotiable assets should be bonded. An employee is said to be *bonded* when the company purchases an insurance policy, or bond, against losses from theft by that employee. Bonding clearly reduces the loss suffered by a theft. It also tends to discourage theft because bonded employees know that an impersonal bonding company must be dealt with when a theft is discovered.

Separate Record-Keeping and Custody over Assets

A fundamental principle of internal control is that the person who has access to or is otherwise responsible for an asset should not maintain the accounting record for that asset. When this principle is followed, the custodian of an asset, knowing that a record of the asset is being kept by another person, is not as likely to misplace, misappropriate, or waste the asset. And, the record-keeper, who does not have access to the asset, has no reason to falsify the record. As a result, two people would have to agree to commit a fraud (called *collusion*) if the asset were to be misappropriated and the theft concealed in the records. Because collusion is necessary to commit the fraud, it is far less likely to happen.

Divide Responsibility for Related Transactions

Responsibility for a transaction or a series of related transactions should be divided between individuals or departments so that the work of one acts as a check on the other. However, this principle does not call for duplication of work. Each employee or department should perform an unduplicated portion.

For example, responsibility for placing orders, receiving the merchandise, and paying the vendors should not be given to one individual or department. Doing so creates a situation in which mistakes and perhaps fraud are more likely to occur. Having a different person check incoming goods for quality and quantity may encourage more care and attention to detail than having it done by the person who placed the order. And, designating a third person to approve the payment of the invoice offers additional protection against error and fraud. Finally, giving a fourth person the authority to actually write checks adds another measure of protection.

Use Mechanical Devices Whenever Practicable

Cash registers, check protectors, time clocks, and mechanical counters are examples of control devices that should be used whenever practicable. A cash register with a locked-in tape makes a record of each cash sale. A check protector perforates the amount of a check into its face, and makes it difficult to change the amount. A time clock registers the exact time an employee arrives on the job and the exact time the employee departs. Using mechanical change and currency counters is faster and more accurate than counting by hand and reduces the possibility of loss.

Perform Regular and Independent Reviews

Even a well-designed internal control system has a tendency to deteriorate as time passes. Changes in personnel and computer equipment present opportunities for shortcuts and other omissions. The stress of time pressures tends to bring about the same results. Thus, regular reviews of internal control systems are needed to be sure that the standard procedures are being followed. Where possible, these reviews should be performed by internal auditors who are not directly involved in operations. From their independent perspective, internal auditors can evaluate the overall efficiency of operations as well as the effectiveness of the internal control system.

Many companies also have audits by independent auditors who are CPAs. After testing the company's financial records, the CPAs give an opinion as to whether the company's financial statements are presented fairly in accordance with generally accepted accounting principles. However, before CPAs decide on how much testing they must do, they first evaluate the effectiveness of the internal control system. When making their evaluation, they can find areas for improvement and offer suggestions.

Computers and Internal Control

LO 2 Explain why internal control procedures are needed in a large organization and state the broad principles of internal control.

The broad principles of internal control should be followed for both manual and computerized accounting systems. However, computers have several important effects on internal control. Perhaps the most obvious is that computers provide rapid access to large quantities of information. As a result, management's ability to monitor and control business operations can be greatly improved.

Computers Reduce Processing Errors

Computers reduce the number of errors in processing information. Once the data are entered correctly, the possibility of mechanical and mathematical errors is largely eliminated. On the other hand, data entry errors may occur because the process of entering data may be more complex in a computerized system. Also, the lack of human involvement in later processing may cause data entry errors to go undiscovered.

Computers Allow More Extensive Testing of Records

The regular review and audit of computerized records can include more extensive testing because information can be accessed so rapidly. When manual methods are used, managers may select only small samples of data to test in order to reduce costs. But, when computers are used, large samples or even complete data files can be reviewed and analyzed.

Computerized Systems May Limit Hard Evidence of Processing Steps

Because many data processing steps are performed by the computer, fewer items of documentary evidence may be available for review. However, computer systems can actually create additional evidence by recording more information about who made entries and even when they were made. And, the computer can be programmed to require the use of passwords before making entries so that access to the system is limited. Therefore, internal control may depend more on reviews of the design and operation of the computerized processing system and less on reviews of the documents left behind by the system.

Separation of Duties Must Be Maintained

Because computerized systems are so efficient, it is common to find that fewer employees are needed. This savings carries the risk that the separation of critical responsibilities may not be maintained. In addition, companies that use computers need employees with special skills to program and operate them. The duties of such employees must be controlled to minimize undetected errors and the risk of fraud. For example, better control is maintained if the person who designs and programs the system does not also serve as the operator. Similarly, control over programs and files related to cash receipts and disbursements should be separated. To prevent fraud, check-writing activities should not be controlled by the computer operator. However, achieving a suitable separation of duties can be especially difficult in small companies that have only a few employees.

Internal Control for Cash

LO 3 Describe internal control procedures used to protect cash received from cash sales, cash received through the mail, and cash disbursements.

Now that we have covered the principles of good internal control in general, it will be helpful to see how they are applied to cash, the most liquid of all assets.

A good system of internal control for cash should provide adequate procedures for protecting both cash receipts and cash disbursements. In designing the procedures, three basic guidelines should always be observed:

1. Duties should be separated so that people responsible for actually handling cash are not also responsible for keeping the cash records.
2. All cash receipts should be deposited in the bank, intact, each day.
3. All cash payments should be made by check.

The reason for the first principle is that a division of duties helps avoid errors. It also requires two or more people to collude if cash is to be embezzled (stolen) and the theft concealed in the accounting records. One reason for the second guideline is that the daily deposit of all receipts produces a timely independent test of the accuracy of the count of the cash received and the deposit. It also helps prevent loss or theft and keeps an employee from personally using the money for a few days before depositing it.

Finally, if all payments are made by check, the bank records provide an independent description of cash disbursements. This arrangement also tends to prevent thefts of cash. (One exception to this principle allows small disbursements of currency and coins to be made from a petty cash fund. Petty cash funds are discussed later in this chapter.) Note especially that the daily intact depositing of receipts and making disbursements by check allow you to use the bank records as a separate and external record of essentially all cash transactions. Later in the chapter, you will learn how the bank records are used to confirm the accuracy of your own records.

The exact procedures used to achieve control over cash vary from company to company. They depend on such factors as company size, number of employees, the volume of cash transactions, and the sources of cash. Therefore, the procedures described in the following paragraphs illustrate many but not all situations.

Cash from Cash Sales

Cash sales should be recorded on a cash register at the time of each sale. To help ensure that correct amounts are entered, each register should be placed so that customers can read the amounts when they are displayed. Also, clerks should be required to ring up each sale before wrapping the merchandise and should give the customer a receipt. Finally, each cash register should be designed to provide a permanent, locked-in record of each transaction. In some systems, the register is directly connected to a computer. The computer is programmed to accept cash register transactions and enter them in the accounting records. In other cases, the register simply prints a record of each transaction on a paper tape that is locked inside the register.

We stated earlier that custody over cash should be separated from recordkeeping for cash. For cash sales, this separation begins with the cash register. The salesclerk who has access to the cash in the register should not have access to its locked-in record. At the end of each day, the salesclerk should count the cash in the register, record the result, and turn the cash and this record of the count over to an employee in the cashier's office. The employee in the cashier's office, like the salesclerk, has access to the cash and should not have access to the computerized accounting records (or the register tape). A third employee, preferably from the accounting department, examines the computerized record of register transactions (or the register tape) and compares its total with the cash receipts reported by the cashier's office. The computer record (or register tape) becomes the basis for the journal entry to record cash sales. Note that the accounting department employee has access to the records for cash but does not have access to the actual cash. The salesclerk and the employee from the cashier's office have access to the cash but not to the accounting records. Thus, their accuracy is automatically checked, and none of them can make a mistake or divert any cash without the difference being revealed.

Cash Received through the Mail

Control of cash that comes in through the mail begins with the person who opens the mail. Preferably, two people should be present when the mail is opened. One should make a list (in triplicate) of the money received. The list should record each sender's name, the amount, and the purpose for which the money was sent. One copy is sent to the cashier with the money. The second copy goes to the accounting department. The third copy is kept by the clerk who opened the mail. The cashier deposits the money in the bank, and the bookkeeper records the amounts received in the accounting records. Then, when the bank balance is reconciled (this process is discussed later in the chapter) by a fourth person, errors or fraud by the clerk, the cashier, or the bookkeeper will be detected. They will be detected because the bank's record of the amount of cash deposited and the records of three people must agree. Note how this arrangement makes errors and fraud nearly impossible, unless the employees enter into collusion. If the clerk does not report all receipts accurately, the customers will question their account balances. If the cashier does not deposit all receipts intact, the bank balance will not agree with the bookkeeper's cash balance. The bookkeeper and the fourth person who reconciles the bank balance do not have access to cash and, therefore, have no opportunity to divert any to themselves. Thus, undetected errors and fraud are made highly unlikely.

Cash Disbursements

The previous discussions clearly show the importance of gaining control over cash from sales and cash received through the mail. Most large embezzlements, however, are actually accomplished through payments of fictitious invoices. Therefore, controlling cash disbursements is perhaps even more critical than controlling cash receipts.

As described earlier, the key to controlling cash disbursements is to require all expenditures to be made by check, except very small payments from petty cash. And, if authority to sign checks is assigned to some person other than the business owner, that person should not have access to the accounting records. This separation of duties helps prevent an employee from concealing fraudulent disbursements in the accounting records.

In a small business, the owner-manager usually signs checks and normally knows from personal contact that the items being paid for were actually received. However, this arrangement is impossible in a medium-sized or large business. In these settings, internal control procedures must be substituted for personal contact. The procedures are designed to assure the check signer that the obligations to be paid were properly incurred and should be paid. Often these controls are achieved through a voucher system.

The Voucher System and Control

LO 3 Describe internal control procedures used to protect cash received from cash sales, cash received through the mail, and cash disbursements.

A **voucher system** is a set of procedures designed to control the incurrence of obligations and disbursements of cash. This kind of system:

1. Establishes procedures for incurring obligations that result in cash disbursements, such as permitting only authorized individuals to make purchase commitments.
2. Provides established procedures for verifying, approving, and recording these obligations.
3. Permits checks to be issued only in payment of properly verified, approved, and recorded obligations.
4. Requires that every obligation be recorded at the time it is incurred and that every purchase be treated as an independent transaction, complete in itself.

A good voucher system produces these results for every transaction, even if several purchases are made from the same company during a month or other billing period.

When a voucher system is used, control over cash disbursements begins as soon as the company incurs an obligation that will result in cash being paid out. A key factor in making the system work is that only specified departments and individuals are authorized to incur such obligations. Managers should also limit the kind of obligations that each department or individual can incur. For example, in a large retail store, only a specially created purchasing department should be authorized to incur obligations through merchandise purchases. In addition, the procedures for purchasing, receiving, and paying for merchandise should be divided among several departments. These departments include the one that originally requested the purchase, the purchasing department, the receiving department, and the accounting department. To coordinate and control the responsibilities of these departments, several different business papers are used. Illustration 7–1 shows how these papers are accumulated in a **voucher.** A voucher is an internal business paper used to accumulate other papers and information needed to control the disbursement of cash and to ensure that the transaction is properly recorded. The following explanation of each paper going into the voucher shows how companies use this system to gain control over cash disbursements for merchandise purchases.

Purchase Requisition

In a large retail store, department managers generally are not allowed to place orders directly with suppliers. If each manager could deal directly with suppliers, the amount of merchandise purchased and the resulting liabilities would not be well controlled. Therefore, to gain control over purchases and the resulting liabilities, department managers are usually required to place all orders through the purchasing department. When merchandise is needed, the department managers inform the purchasing department of their needs. Each manager performs this function by preparing and signing a business paper called a **purchase requisition.** On the requisition, the manager lists the merchandise needed by the department and requests that it be purchased. The original and

ILLUSTRATION 7–1

The Accumulation of Documents in the Voucher

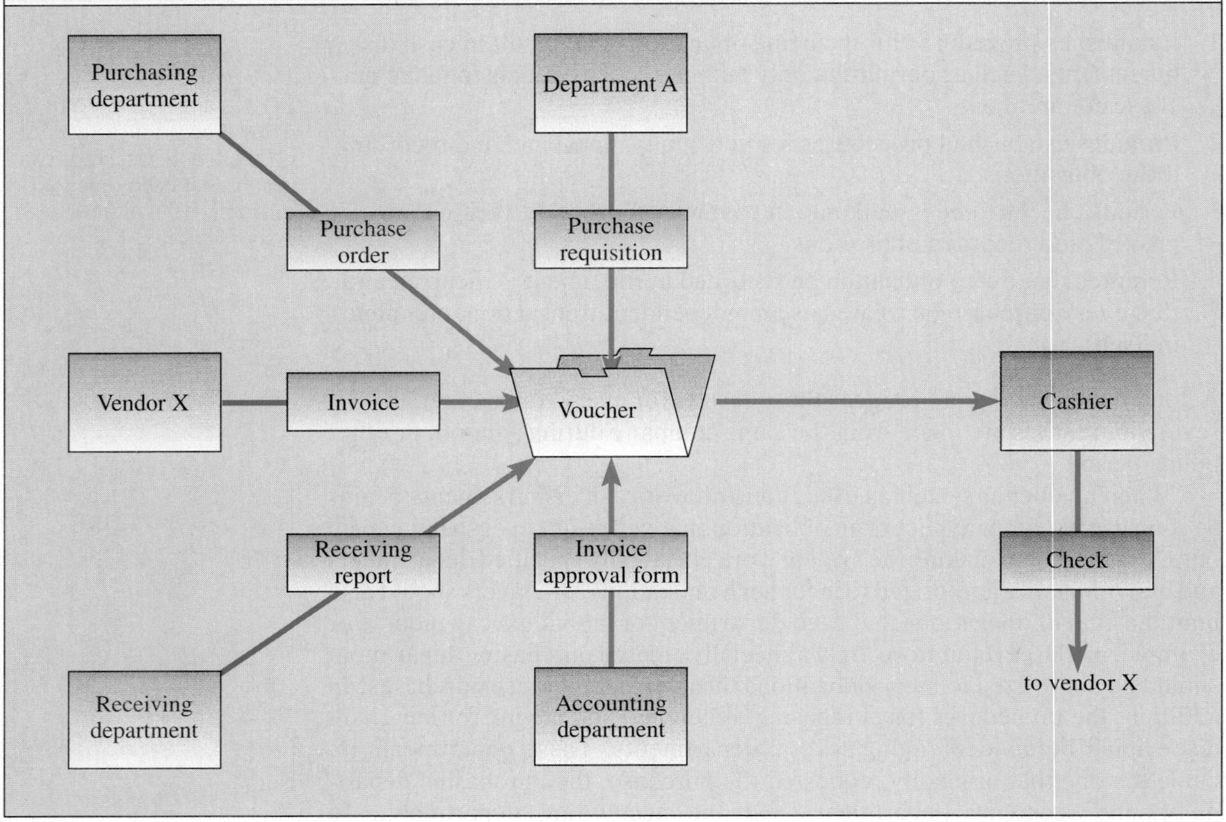

one copy of the purchase requisition are sent to the purchasing department. The manager of the requisitioning department (identified in Illustration 7–1 as department A) keeps the third copy as a back up. The purchasing department sends the second copy to the accounting department. When it is received, the accounting department creates a new voucher.

Purchase Order

A **purchase order** is a business paper used by the purchasing department to place an order with the seller or **vendor**, which usually is a manufacturer or wholesaler. The purchase order (often abbreviated P.O.) authorizes the vendor to ship the ordered merchandise at the stated price and terms.

When a purchase requisition is received by the purchasing department, it prepares at least four copies of a purchase order. The copies are distributed as follows:

Copy 1, the original, is sent to the vendor as a request to purchase and as authority to ship the merchandise.

Copy 2, with a copy of the purchase requisition attached, is sent to the accounting department, where it is used in approving the payment of the invoice for the purchase; this copy is shown in Illustration 7–1.

Copy 3 is sent to the department originally issuing the requisition to inform its manager that the action has been taken.

Copy 4 is retained on file by the purchasing department.

Invoice

An **invoice** is an itemized statement prepared by the vendor that lists the customer's name, the items sold, the sales prices, and the terms of sale. In effect, the invoice is the bill sent to the buyer by the seller. (From the vendor's point of view, it is a *sales invoice*.) The vendor sends the invoice to the buyer or **vendee**, who treats it as a *purchase invoice*. On receiving a purchase order, the vendor ships the ordered merchandise to the buyer and mails a copy of the invoice that covers the shipment. The goods are delivered to the buyer's receiving department and the invoice is sent directly to the buyer's accounting department, where it is placed in the voucher. Illustration 7–1 also presents this document flow.

Receiving Report

Most large companies maintain a special department that receives all merchandise or other purchased assets. When each shipment arrives, this receiving department counts the goods and checks them for damage and agreement with the purchase order. Then, it prepares four or more copies of a **receiving report.** This report is a form used within the business to notify the appropriate persons that ordered goods were received and to describe the quantities and condition of the goods. As shown in Illustration 7–1, one copy is sent to the accounting department and placed in the voucher. Copies are also sent to the original requisitioning department and the purchasing department to notify them that the goods have arrived. The receiving department retains a copy in its files.

Invoice Approval Form

After the receiving report arrives, the accounting department should have copies of these papers on file in the voucher:

1. The *purchase requisition* listing the items to be ordered.
2. The *purchase order* listing the merchandise that was actually ordered.
3. The *invoice* showing the quantity, description, price, and total cost of the goods shipped by the seller.
4. The *receiving report* listing the quantity and condition of the items actually received by the buyer.

With the information on these papers, the accounting department is in a position to make an entry recording the purchase and to approve its eventual pay-

ILLUSTRATION 7–2

An Invoice Approval Form

	By	Date
Purchase order number	______	______
Requisition check	______	______
Purchase order check	______	______
Receiving report check	______	______
Invoice check:		
Price approval	______	______
Calculations	______	______
Terms	______	______
Approved for payment	______	______

ment before the end of the discount period. In approving the invoice for payment, the accounting department checks and compares the information on all the papers. To facilitate the checking procedure and to ensure that no step is omitted, the department commonly uses an **invoice approval form.** (See Illustration 7–2.) This form is a document on which the accounting department notes that it has performed each step in the process of checking an invoice and approving it for recording and payment. An invoice approval form may be a separate business paper that is filed in the voucher or it may be preprinted on the voucher. It may also be stamped on the invoice. For clarity, the flowchart in Illustration 7–1 shows the form as a separate document.

As each of the steps in the checking procedure is finished, the clerk initials the invoice approval form and records the current date. Initials in each space on the form indicate that the following administrative actions have been taken:

1. **Requisition check** . . . . The items on the invoice were actually requisitioned, as shown on the copy of the purchase requisition.
2. **Purchase order check** . . . . . The items on the invoice were actually ordered, as shown on the copy of the purchase order.
3. **Receiving report check** . . . . The items on the invoice were actually received, as shown on the copy of the receiving report.
4. **Invoice check:**
   Price approval . . . . The invoice prices are stated as agreed with the vendor.
   Calculations . . . . The invoice has no mathematical errors.
   Terms . . . . The terms are stated as agreed with the vendor.

ILLUSTRATION 7–3

Inside of a Voucher

VALLEY SUPPLY COMPANY Voucher No. *93–767*
Eugene, Oregon

Date *Oct. 1, 1993*
Pay to *A. B. Seay Wholesale Company*
City *Salem* State *Oregon*

For the following: (attach all invoices and supporting papers)

Date of Invoice	Terms	Invoice Number and Other Details	Amount
Sept. 30, 1993	*2/10, n/60*	*Invoice No. C-11756*	*800.00*
		Less discount	*16.00*
		Net amount payable	*784.00*

Payment approved
N. O. Neal
Auditor

The Voucher

After an invoice is checked and approved, the voucher is complete. At this point, the voucher is a record that summarizes the transaction. The voucher shows that the transaction has been certified as correct and authorizes its recording as an obligation of the buyer. The voucher also contains approval for paying the obligation on the appropriate date. Of course, the actual physical form used for vouchers varies substantially from company to company. In general, they are designed so that the invoice and other documents from which they are prepared are placed inside the voucher, which is often a folder. The information printed on the inside of a typical voucher is shown in Illustration 7–3, and the information on the outside is shown in Illustration 7–4.

The preparation of a voucher requires a clerk to enter the specified information in the proper blanks. The information is taken from the invoice and all the supporting documents, filed inside the voucher. Once the steps are completed, the voucher is sent to the appropriate authorized individual (sometimes called the *auditor*), who completes one final review of the information, approves the accounts and amounts to be debited (called the *accounting distribution*), and approves the voucher for recording.

After a voucher is approved and recorded, it is filed until its due date, when it is sent to the cashier's office for payment. Here, the person responsi-

ILLUSTRATION 7-4

Outside of a Voucher

Voucher No. 93–767

ACCOUNTING DISTRIBUTION

Account Debited	Amount
Purchases	800.00
Transportation-In	
Store Supplies	
Office Supplies	
Sales Salaries	
Other	
Total Vouch. Pay. Cr.	800.00

Due date October 6, 1993

Pay to A. B. Seay Wholesale Company
City Salem
State Oregon

Summary of charges:
Total charges 800.00
Discount 16.00
Net payment 784.00

Record of payment:
Paid ______
Check No ______

ble for issuing checks relies on the approved voucher and its signed supporting documents as proof that the obligation was properly incurred and should be paid. As described earlier, the purchase requisition and purchase order attached to the voucher confirm that the purchase was authorized. The receiving report shows that the items were received, and the invoice approval form verifies that the invoice was checked for errors. As a result, there is little chance for error. There is even less chance for fraud without collusion, unless all the documents and signatures are forged.

The Voucher System and Expenses

LO 3 Describe internal control procedures used to protect cash received from cash sales, cash received through the mail, and cash disbursements.

Under a voucher system, obligations should be approved for payment and recorded as liabilities as soon as possible after they are incurred. As shown in the example, this practice should be followed for all purchases. It should also be followed for all expenses. For example, when a company receives a monthly telephone bill, the charges (especially long-distance calls) should be examined for accuracy. A voucher should be prepared, and the telephone bill should be filed inside the voucher. The voucher is then recorded with a journal entry. If the amount is due at once, a check should be issued. Otherwise, the voucher should be filed for payment on the due date.

The requirement that expenses be recorded in a voucher when they are incurred helps ensure that every expense payment is approved only when adequate information is available. However, invoices or bills for such things as equipment repairs are sometimes not received until weeks after the work is done. If no record of the repairs exists, it may be difficult to determine whether the invoice or bill correctly states the amount owed. Also, if no records exist, it may be possible for a dishonest employee to arrange with an outsider for more than one payment of an obligation, or for payment of excessive amounts, or for payment for goods and services not received. A properly functioning voucher system helps prevent all of these undesirable results.

Recording Vouchers

Normally, a company large enough to use a voucher system uses a computer in recording its transactions. For this reason and also because the primary purpose of this discussion is to describe the control techniques of a voucher system, we do not describe a manual system of recording vouchers here. However, Appendix D at the end of this chapter describes such a system.

The Petty Cash Fund

LO 4 Explain the operation of a petty cash fund and be able to prepare journal entries to record petty cash fund transactions.

A basic principle for controlling cash disbursements requires that all disbursements be made by check. However, an exception to this rule is made for *petty cash disbursements*. Every business must make many small payments for items such as postage, express charges, repairs, and small items of supplies. If firms made such payments by check, they would end up writing many checks for small amounts. This arrangement would be both time consuming and expensive. Therefore, to avoid writing checks for small amounts, a business establishes a petty cash fund and uses the money in this fund to make payments such as those listed above.

The first step in establishing a petty cash fund requires estimating the total amount of small payments likely to be made during a short period, such as a month. Then, a check is drawn by the company cashier's office for an amount slightly in excess of this estimate. This check is recorded with a debit to the Petty Cash account (an asset) and a credit to Cash. The check is cashed, and the currency is turned over to a member of the office staff designated as the *petty cashier*. This person is responsible for the safekeeping of the cash, for making payments from this fund, and for keeping accurate records.

The petty cashier should keep the petty cash in a locked box in a safe place. As each disbursement is made, the person receiving payment signs a *petty cash receipt* (see Illustration 7–5). The receipt is then placed in the petty cashbox with the remaining money. Under this system, the cashbox should always contain petty cash receipts and cash equal to the amount of the fund. The total should remain constant. For example, a $100 petty cash fund could have *(a)* $100 in cash, *(b)* $80 in cash and $20 in receipts, or *(c)* $10 in cash and $90 in receipts. Notice that each disbursement reduces the cash and increases the sum of the receipts in the petty cashbox. When the cash is nearly gone, the fund should be reimbursed.

To reimburse the fund, the petty cashier presents the receipts to the company cashier. The company cashier stamps all receipts *paid* so that they cannot be reused, retains them, and gives the petty cashier a check for their sum. When this check is cashed and the proceeds returned to the cashbox, the money in the box is restored to its original amount, and the fund is ready to begin a new cycle of operations.

ILLUSTRATION 7–5

A Petty Cash Receipt

No. - 1 - $ $10.00

RECEIVED OF PETTY CASH

Date Nov. 2 19 93

For Washing windows

Charge to Miscellaneous expenses

Approved by CAB

Received by Bob Jones

TOPS-Form 3008

At the time a check is written to reimburse the petty cash fund, the petty cashier should sort the paid receipts according to the type of expense or other accounts to be debited in recording payments from the fund. Each group is then totaled and used in making the entry to record the reimbursement.

Illustration of a Petty Cash Fund

To avoid writing numerous checks for small amounts, a company established a petty cash fund on November 1, designating one of its office clerks, Carl Burns, as petty cashier. A $75 check was drawn, cashed, and the proceeds turned over to Burns. The following entry recorded the check:

Nov.	1	Petty Cash	75.00	
		Cash		75.00
		Established a petty cash fund.		

Notice that this entry transfers $75 from the regular Cash account to the Petty Cash account. After the petty cash fund is established, the Petty Cash account is not debited or credited again unless the size of the total fund is changed. For example, the fund should be increased if it is being exhausted and reimbursed too frequently. Another entry like the preceding one would be made to record an increase in the size of the fund. That is, there would be a debit to Petty Cash

ILLUSTRATION 7–6

Summary of Petty Cash Payments

Miscellaneous expenses:		
Nov. 2, washing windows	$10.00	
Nov. 17, washing windows	10.00	
Nov. 27, computer repairs	26.50	$46.50
Transportation-in:		
Nov. 5, delivery of merchandise purchased	$ 6.75	
Nov. 20, delivery of merchandise purchased	8.30	15.05
Delivery expense:		
Nov. 18, customer's package delivered		5.00
Office supplies:		
Nov. 15, purchased office supplies		4.75
Total.		$71.30

and credit to Cash for the amount of the increase. If the fund is too large, some of the money in the fund should be redeposited in the checking account. Such a reduction in the fund is recorded with a debit to Cash and a credit to Petty Cash.

During November, Carl Burns, the petty cashier, made several payments from the cash fund. Each time, he asked the person who received payment to sign a receipt. On November 27, after making a $26.50 payment for repairs to an office computer, Burns decided there might not be enough cash in the fund for another payment. Therefore, he summarized and totaled the petty cash receipts as shown in Illustration 7–6. Then, the summary and the petty cash receipts were given to the company cashier in exchange for a $71.30 check to reimburse the fund. Burns cashed the check, put the $71.30 proceeds in the petty cashbox, and was then ready to make additional payments from the fund.

The reimbursing check is recorded with the following journal entry:

Nov.	27	Miscellaneous Expenses	46.50	
		Transportation-In	15.05	
		Delivery Expense	5.00	
		Office Supplies	4.75	
		Cash		71.30
		Reimbursed petty cash.		

Information for this entry came from the petty cashier's summary of payments. Note that the debits in the entry record the petty cash payments. Even if the petty cash fund is not low on funds at the end of an accounting period, it may be reimbursed at that time to record the expenses in the proper period. Otherwise, the financial statements will show an overstated petty cash asset and understated expenses or assets that were paid for out of petty cash. (Of course, the amounts involved are seldom if ever significant to users of the financial statements.)

Cash Over and Short

Sometimes, a petty cashier fails to get a receipt for a payment. Then, when the fund is reimbursed, he or she may forget the purpose of the expenditure. This mistake causes the fund to be short. If, for whatever reason, the petty cash fund is short at reimbursement time, the shortage is recorded as an expense in the reimbursing entry with a debit to the **Cash Over and Short account.** This account is an income statement account that records the income effects of cash overages and cash shortages arising from omitted petty cash receipts and from errors in making change.

Errors in making change are discovered when there are differences between the cash in a cash register and the record of the amount of cash sales. Even though a cashier is careful, some customers may be given too much or too little change. As a result, at the end of a day, the actual cash from a cash register may not equal the cash sales rung up. For example, assume that a cash register shows cash sales of $550 but the actual count of cash in the register is $555. The entry to record the cash sales and the overage would be:

Nov.	23	Cash	555.00	
		Cash Over and Short		5.00
		Sales		550.00
		Day's cash sales and overage.		

On the other hand, if there were a shortage of cash in the register on the next day, the entry to record cash sales and the shortage would look like the following:

Nov.	24	Cash	621.00	
		Cash Over and Short	4.00	
		Sales		625.00
		Day's cash sales and shortage.		

Because customers are more likely to dispute being shortchanged, the Cash Over and Short account usually has a debit balance by the end of the accounting period. Because it is a debit, this balance represents an expense. This expense can be shown on the income statement as a separate item in the general and administrative expense section. Or, because the amount is usually small, you can combine it with other small expenses and report them as a single item called *miscellaneous expenses*. If Cash Over and Short has a credit balance at the end of the period, it usually is shown on the income statement as part of *miscellaneous revenues*.

Reconciling the Bank Balance

At least once every month, banks send depositors a bank statement that shows the activity in their accounts during the month. Different banks use a variety of formats for their bank statements. However, all of them include the following items of information in one place or another:

AS A MATTER OF

Ethics

Nancy Tucker is an internal auditor for a large corporation and is in the process of making surprise counts of three $200 petty cash funds in various offices in the headquarters building. She arrived at the office of one of the fund custodians shortly before lunch while he was on the telephone. Tucker explained the purpose of her visit, and the custodian asked politely that she come back after lunch so that he could finish the business he was conducting by long distance. She agreed and returned around 1:30. The custodian opened the petty cashbox and showed her nine new $20 bills with consecutive serial numbers plus receipts that totaled $20. Would you suggest that the auditor take any further action or comment on these events in her report to management?

LO 5 Explain why the bank balance and the book balance of cash should be reconciled and be able to prepare a reconciliation.

1. The balance of the depositor's account at the beginning of the month.
2. Deposits and any other amounts added to the account during the month.
3. Checks and any other amounts deducted from the account during the month.
4. The account balance at the end of the month.

Of course, all this information is presented as it appears in the bank's records. Illustration 7–7 presents an example of a typical bank statement. Examine it now to find the four items just listed.

Note that section A of Illustration 7–7 summarizes the changes in the account. Section B lists specific debits and credits to the account (other than canceled checks). Section C lists all paid checks in numerical order and section D shows the daily account balances.

Enclosed with the monthly statement are the depositor's **canceled checks** and any debit or credit memoranda that have affected the account. Canceled checks are checks that the bank has paid and deducted from the customer's account during the month. They are called canceled checks because they have been stamped to show that they were paid. Other deductions that may appear on the bank statement for an individual include withdrawals through automatic teller machines (ATM withdrawals) and periodic payments arranged in advance by the depositor.[2] Other deductions from the depositor's account may include service charges and fees assessed by the bank, customer checks deposited that prove to be uncollectible, and corrections of previous errors. Except for the service charges, the bank notifies the depositor of the deduction in each case with a debit memorandum at the time that the bank reduces the

[2] Because of the need to make all disbursements by check, it is unusual to find a business checking account that allows ATM withdrawals.

ILLUSTRATION 7–7

A Typical Bank Statement

First City National Bank of Austin P.O. BOX 1727 AUSTIN, TEXAS 78767 512/473-4343

	ACCOUNT NUMBER	DATE OF THIS STATEMENT	DATE OF LAST STATEMENT	PAGE NO.
01	494 504 2	10/31/93	9/30/93	1

FIRSTCITY™

First City
National Bank
of Austin
Member FDIC

VALLEY COMPANY
1300 FALCON LEDGE
AUSTIN, TEXAS 78746

A

BALANCE OF PREVIOUS STATEMENT ON 9/30/93	1,609.58
5 DEPOSITS AND OTHER CREDITS TOTALING	1,155.00
10 CHECKS AND OTHER DEBITS TOTALING	723.00
SERVICE CHARGE AMOUNT	.00
INTEREST AMOUNT AT 5.2500%	8.42
CURRENT BALANCE AS OF THIS STATEMENT	2,050.00
AVERAGE BALANCE AS OF THIS STATEMENT	1,924.95
TOTAL INTEREST PAID TO DATE	124.00

B

CHECKING ACCOUNT TRANSACTIONS

DATE	AMOUNT	TRANSACTION DESCRIPTION
10/02	240.00+	DEPOSIT
10/09	180.00+	DEPOSIT
10/12	23.00−	CHARGE FOR PRINTING NEW CHECKS
10/15	100.00+	DEPOSIT
10/16	150.00+	DEPOSIT
10/23	485.00+	NOTE COLLECTION LESS FEE
10/25	30.00−	NSF CHECK AND NSF CHARGE
10/31	8.42+	INTEREST PAID

C

DATE	CHECK NO	AMOUNT	DATE	CHECK NO	AMOUNT
10/03	119	55.00	10/16	123	25.00
10/19	120	200.00	10/23	125*	10.00
10/10	121	120.00	10/26	127*	50.00
10/14	122	75.00	10/29	128	135.00

*INDICATES A SKIP IN CHECK NUMBER SEQUENCE

D

DAILY BALANCE SUMMARY

DATE	BALANCE	DATE	BALANCE	DATE	BALANCE
10/01	1,609.58	10/12	1,831.58	10/23	2,256.58
10/02	1,849.58	10/14	1,756.58	10/25	2,226.58
10/03	1,794.58	10/15	1,856.58	10/26	2,176.58
10/09	1,974.58	10/16	1,981.58	10/29	2,041.58
10/10	1,854.58	10/19	1,781.58	10/31	2,050.00

FOR QUESTIONS ON DIRECT DEPOSITS, PLEASE CALL 473-4522, BETWEEN 9:00–4:00 MONDAY-FRIDAY OR WRITE P. O. BOX 1727, AUSTIN, TEXAS 78767.

balance. For completeness, a copy of each debit memorandum is usually sent with the monthly statement.[3]

In addition to deposits made by the depositor, the bank may add amounts to the depositor's account. Examples of additions would be amounts the bank has collected on behalf of the depositor and corrections of previous errors. Credit memoranda notify the depositor of all additions when they are first recorded. For completeness, a copy of each credit memorandum may be sent with the monthly statement.

Another item commonly added to the bank balance on the statement is interest earned by the depositor. Many checking accounts pay the depositor interest based on the average cash balance maintained in the account. The bank calculates the amount of interest earned and credits it to the depositor's account each month. In Illustration 7–7, note that the bank credited $8.42 of interest to the account of Valley Company. (The methods used to calculate interest are discussed in the next chapter.)

When the business deposits all receipts intact and when all payments (other than petty cash payments) are drawn from the checking account, the bank statement is a device for proving the accuracy of the depositor's cash records. The test of the accuracy begins by preparing a **bank reconciliation**, which is an analysis that explains the difference between the balance of a checking account shown in the depositor's records and the balance shown on the bank statement.

Need for Reconciling the Bank Balance

For virtually all checking accounts, the balance shown on the bank statement does not agree with the balance in the depositor's accounting records. Therefore, to prove the accuracy of both the depositor's records and those of the bank, you must **reconcile** the two balances. In other words, you must explain or account for the differences between them.

Numerous factors cause the bank statement balance to differ from the depositor's book balance. Some are:

1. **Outstanding checks.** These checks were written (or drawn) by the depositor, deducted on the depositor's records, and sent to the payees. However, they are called **outstanding checks** because they had not reached the bank for payment and deduction before the statement date.
2. **Unrecorded deposits.** Companies often make deposits at the end of each business day, after the bank is closed. These deposits are made in the bank's night depository and are not recorded by the bank until the next business day. Therefore, if a deposit is placed in the night depository on the last day of the month, it will not appear on the bank statement for that month. In addition, deposits mailed to the bank toward the end of

[3] As a matter of clarification, the depositor's account is a liability on the bank's records. Thus, a deposit increases the account balance, and the bank records it with a *credit* to the account. The depositor, on the other hand, considers the deposit to be an increase in an asset, and records it with a *debit* to the Cash account. Checks reduce the account balance, and the bank records them as a *debit* while the depositor records them with a *credit*. Debit memos from the bank produce *credits* on the depositor's books, and credit memos lead to *debits*.

the month may be in transit and unrecorded when the statement is prepared.

3. **Charges for uncollectible items and for service.** Occasionally, a company deposits a customer's check that bounces, or turns out to be uncollectible. Usually, the problem is nonsufficient funds in the customer's account to cover the check. In these cases, the check is called a nonsufficient funds (NSF) check. In other situations, the customer's account has been closed. In processing deposited checks, the bank first credits the depositor's account for the full amount. Later, when the bank learns that the check is uncollectible, it debits (reduces) the depositor's account for the amount of the check. Also, the bank may charge the depositor a fee for processing the uncollectible check. At the same time, the bank notifies the depositor of each deduction by mailing a debit memorandum. Although each deduction should be recorded by the depositor on the day the debit memorandum is received, sometimes an entry is not made until the bank reconciliation is prepared.

   Other charges to a depositor's account that a bank might report on the bank statement include the printing of new checks. Also, the bank may assess a monthly service charge for maintaining the account. Notification of these charges is not provided until the statement is mailed.

4. **Credits for collections and for interest.** Banks occasionally act as collection agents for their depositors by collecting promissory notes and other items. When the bank collects an item, it deducts a fee and adds the net proceeds to the depositor's account. At the same time, it sends a credit memorandum to notify the depositor of the transaction. As soon as the memorandum is received, it should be recorded by the depositor. However, these items may remain unrecorded until the time of the bank reconciliation.

   Many bank accounts earn interest on the average cash balance in the account during the month. If an account earns interest, the bank statement includes a credit for the amount earned during the past month. Notification of earned interest is provided only by the bank statement.

5. **Errors.** Regardless of care and systems of internal control for automatic error detection, both banks and depositors make errors. Errors by the bank may not be discovered until the depositor completes the bank reconciliation. Also, the depositor's errors often are not discovered until the balance is reconciled.

Steps in Reconciling the Bank Balance

To obtain the benefits of separated duties, an employee who does not handle cash receipts, process checks, or maintain cash records should prepare the bank reconciliation. In preparing to reconcile the balance, this employee must gather information from the bank statement and from other sources in the records. The person who performs the reconciliation must do the following:

- Compare the deposits listed on the bank statement with the deposits shown in the accounting records. Identify any discrepancies and determine which is correct. Make a list of any errors or unrecorded deposits.

- Examine all other credits shown on the bank statement and determine whether each was recorded in the books. These items include collections by the bank, correction of previous bank statement errors, and interest earned by the depositor. List any unrecorded items.
- Compare the canceled checks listed on the bank statement with the actual checks returned with the statement. For each check, make sure that the correct amount was deducted by the bank and that the returned check was properly charged to the company's account. List any discrepancies or errors.
- Compare the canceled checks listed on the bank statement with the checks recorded in the books. (To make this process easier, the bank statement normally lists canceled checks in numerical order.) Prepare a list of any outstanding checks.

  Although an individual may occasionally write a check and fail to record it in the books, companies with reasonable internal controls would rarely, if ever, write a check without recording it. Nevertheless, prepare a list of any canceled checks unrecorded in the books.
- Determine whether any outstanding checks listed on the previous month's bank reconciliation are not included in the canceled checks listed on the bank statement. Prepare a list of any of these checks that remain outstanding at the end of the current month. Send this list to the cashier's office for follow-up with the payees to see if the checks were actually received.
- Examine all other debits to the account shown on the bank statement and determine whether each one was recorded in the books. These include bank charges for newly printed checks, NSF checks, and monthly service charges. List those not yet recorded.

When this information has been gathered, the employee can complete the reconciliation like the one in Illustration 7–8 by using these steps:

1. Start with the bank balance of the cash account.
2. Identify and list any unrecorded deposits and any bank errors that understated the bank balance. Add them to the bank balance.
3. Identify and list any outstanding checks and any bank errors that overstated the bank balance. Subtract them from the bank balance.
4. Compute the adjusted balance. This amount is also called the *correct* or *reconciled* balance.
5. Start with the book balance of the cash account.
6. Identify and list any unrecorded credit memoranda from the bank (perhaps for the proceeds of a collected note), interest earned, and any errors that understated the book balance. Add them to the book balance.
7. Identify and list any unrecorded debit memoranda from the bank (perhaps for a NSF check from a customer), service charges, and any errors that overstated the book balance. Subtract them from the book balance.
8. Compute the reconciled balance. This is also the correct balance.
9. Verify that the two adjusted balances from steps 4 and 8 are equal. If so, they are reconciled. If not, check for mathematical accuracy and for any missing data.

ILLUSTRATION 7–8

A Typical Bank Reconciliation

VALLEY COMPANY
Bank Reconciliation
October 31, 1993

① Bank statement balance	$2,050.00	⑤ Book balance	$1,404.58
② Add:		⑥ Add:	
Deposit of 10/31	145.00	Proceeds of note less collection fee	$ 485.00
		Interest earned	8.42
		Total	$ 493.42
Total	$2,195.00	Total	$1,898.00
③ Deduct:		⑦ Deduct:	
Outstanding checks:		NSF check plus service charge	$ 30.00
No. 124	$ 150.00	Check printing charge	23.00
No. 126	200.00		
Total	$ 350.00	Total	$ 53.00
③ Reconciled balance	$1,845.00	⑧ Reconciled balance	$1,845.00

⑨ The two balances both equal $1,845.00

When the reconciliation is complete, the employee should send a copy to the accounting department so that any needed journal entries can be recorded. For example, entries are needed to record any unrecorded debit and credit memoranda and any of the company's mistakes. Another copy should go to the cashier's office, especially if the bank has made an error that needs to be corrected.

Illustration of a Bank Reconciliation

We can illustrate a bank reconciliation by preparing one for Valley Company as of October 31. In preparing to reconcile the bank account, the Valley Company employee gathered the following facts:

- The bank balance shown on the bank statement was $2,050.
- The cash balance according to the accounting records was $1,404.58.
- A $145 deposit was placed in the bank's night depository on October 31 and was unrecorded by the bank when the bank statement was mailed.
- Enclosed with the bank statement was a copy of a credit memorandum showing that the bank had collected a note receivable for the company on October 23. The note's proceeds of $500 (less a $15 collection fee) were credited to the company's account. This credit memorandum had not been recorded by the company.
- The bank statement also showed a credit of $8.42 for interest earned on the average cash balance in the account. Because there had been no prior

notification of this item, it had not been recorded on the company's books.

- A comparison of canceled checks with the company's books showed that two checks were outstanding—No. 124 for $150 and No. 126 for $200.
- Other debits on the bank statement that had not been previously recorded on the books included (*a*) a $23 charge for checks printed by the bank; and (*b*) an NSF (nonsufficient funds) check for $20 plus the related processing fee of $10. The NSF check had been received from a customer, Frank Green, on October 16 and had been included in that day's deposit.

Illustration 7–8 shows the bank reconciliation that reflects these items. The numbers in the circles beside the various parts of the reconciliation correspond to the numbers of the steps listed earlier.

Preparing a bank reconciliation helps locate any errors made by either the bank or the depositor. It also identifies unrecorded items that should be recorded on the company's books. For example, in Valley Company's reconciliation, the adjusted balance of $1,845.00 is the correct balance as of October 31, 1993. However, at that date, Valley Company's accounting records show a $1,404.58 balance. Therefore, journal entries must be made to increase the book balance to the correct balance. This process requires four entries. The first is

Nov.	2	Cash	485.00	
		Collection Expense	15.00	
		Notes Receivable		500.00
		To record the collection fee and proceeds of a note collected by the bank.		

This entry records the net proceeds of Valley Company's note receivable that had been collected by the bank, the expense of having the bank perform that service, and the reduction in the Notes Receivable account.

The second entry records the interest credited to Valley Company's account by the bank:

Nov.	2	Cash	8.42	
		Interest Earned		8.42
		To record interest earned on the average cash balance maintained in the checking account.		

Interest earned is a revenue, and the entry recognizes both the revenue and the related increase in Cash.

The third entry records the NSF check that was returned as uncollectible. The $20 check was received from Green in payment of his account and deposited. The bank charged $10 for handling the NSF check and deducted $30 from Valley Company's account. Therefore, the company must reverse the entry made when the check was received and also record the $10 processing fee:

Nov.	2	Accounts Receivable—Frank Green	30.00	
		Cash		30.00
		To charge Frank Green's account for his NSF check and for the bank's fee.		

This entry reflects the fact that Valley Company followed customary business practice and added the NSF $10 fee to Green's account. Thus, it will try to collect the entire $30 from Green.

The fourth entry debits Miscellaneous General Expenses for the check printing charge. The entry is

Nov.	2	Miscellaneous Expenses	23.00	
		Cash		23.00
		Check printing charge.		

After these entries are recorded, the balance of cash is increased to the correct amount of $1,845.00 ($1,404.58 + $485.00 + 8.42 − $30.00 − $23.00).

Other Internal Control Procedures

LO 6 Tell how recording invoices at net amounts helps gain control over cash discounts taken and be able to account for invoices recorded at net amounts.

Internal control principles apply to every phase of a company's operations including merchandise purchases, sales, cash receipts, cash disbursements, and owning and operating plant assets. Many of these procedures are discussed in later chapters. At this point, we consider a way that a company can gain more control over *purchases discounts*.

Recall that entries such as the following have been used to record the receipt and payment of an invoice for a purchase of merchandise:

Oct.	2	Purchases	1,000.00	
		Accounts Payable		1,000.00
		Purchased merchandise, terms 2/10, n/60.		
	12	Accounts Payable	1,000.00	
		Purchases Discounts		20.00
		Cash		980.00
		Paid the invoice of October 2.		

These entries reflect the **gross method of recording purchases.** That is, the invoice was recorded at its gross amount of $1,000 before considering the cash discount. Many companies record invoices in this way. However, the **net method of recording purchases** records invoices at their *net* amounts (after cash discounts). This method is widely thought to provide more useful information to management.

To illustrate the net method, assume that a company purchases merchandise with a $1,000 invoice price and terms of 2/10, n/60. On receiving the goods, the purchasing company deducted the offered $20 discount from the gross amount and recorded the purchase at the $980 net amount:

ILLUSTRATION 7–9

Reporting Discounts Lost When the Net Method of Recording Purchases Is Used

XYZ COMPANY
Income Statement
For Year Ended December 31, 1993

Sales	$100,000
Cost of goods sold	60,000
Gross profit from sales	$ 40,000
Operating expenses	28,000
Income from operations	$ 12,000
Other expenses:	
Discounts lost	150
Net income.	$ 11,850

Oct.	2	Purchases	980.00	
		Accounts Payable		980.00
		Purchased merchandise on credit.		

If the invoice for this purchase is paid within the discount period, the entry to record the payment debits Accounts Payable and credits Cash for $980. However, if payment is not made within the discount period and the discount is *lost*, an entry such as the following must be made either before or when the invoice is paid:

Dec.	1	Discounts Lost	20.00	
		Accounts Payable		20.00
		To record the discount lost.		

A check for the full $1,000 invoice amount is then written, recorded, and mailed to the creditor.[4]

Advantage of the Net Method

When invoices are recorded at *gross* amounts, the amount of discounts taken is deducted from the balance of the Purchases account on the income statement to arrive at the cost of merchandise purchased. However, the amount of any lost discounts does not appear in any account or on the income statement. Therefore, lost discounts may not come to the attention of management.

On the other hand, when purchases are recorded at *net* amounts, the amount of discounts taken does not appear on the income statement. Instead, an expense for **discounts lost** is brought to management's attention through its appearance on the income statement. This practice is shown in the condensed income statement of Illustration 7–9. Its balance equals the cost resulting from the failure to take advantage of cash discounts on purchases.

[4] Alternatively, the lost discount can be recorded with the late payment in a single entry.

Recording invoices at their net amounts supplies management with useful information about the amount of discounts missed through oversight, carelessness, or some other reason. Thus, this practice gives management better control over the people responsible for paying bills on time so that cash discounts can be taken. When the accounts record the fact that discounts are missed, someone has to explain why. As a result, it is likely that fewer discounts are lost through carelessness.

Summary of the Chapter in Terms of Learning Objectives

LO 1. The liquidity of an asset refers to how easily the asset can be converted into other types of assets or used to buy services or satisfy obligations. Cash is the most liquid asset. To increase their return, companies may invest their idle cash balances in cash equivalents. These investments are readily convertible to a known amount of cash and are purchased so close to their maturity date that their market values are relatively insensitive to interest rate changes.

LO 2. Internal control systems are designed to encourage adherence to prescribed managerial policies. In doing so, they promote operational efficiencies, and protect assets against theft or misuse. They also help ensure that accurate and reliable accounting data are produced. Principles of good internal control include establishing clear responsibilities, maintaining adequate records, insuring assets and bonding employees, separating record-keeping and custody of assets, dividing responsibilities for related transactions, using mechanical devices whenever practicable, and performing regular independent reviews of internal control practices.

LO 3. To maintain control over cash, custody must be separated from record-keeping for cash. All cash receipts should be deposited intact in the bank on a daily basis, and all payments (except for minor petty cash payments) should be made by check. A voucher system helps maintain control over cash disbursements by ensuring that payments are made only after full documentation and approval.

LO 4. The petty cashier, who should be a responsible employee, makes small payments from the petty cash fund and obtains signed receipts for the payments. The Petty Cash account is debited when the fund is established or increased in size. Petty cash disbursements are recorded with a credit to cash whenever the fund is replenished.

LO 5. A bank reconciliation is produced to prove the accuracy of the depositor's and the bank's records. In completing the reconciliation, the bank statement balance is adjusted for such items as outstanding checks and unrecorded deposits made on or before the bank statement date but received by the bank after. The depositor's cash account balance is adjusted to the correct balance. The difference arises from such items as service charges, collections the bank has made for the depositor, and interest earned on the average checking account balance.

LO 6. When the net method of recording invoices is used, missed cash discounts are reported as an expense. In contrast, when the gross method is used, discounts taken are reported as reductions in the cost of the purchased goods. Therefore, the net method directs management's attention to instances where the company failed to take advantage of discounts.

Demonstration Problem

Complete the following table for a bank reconciliation as of September 30. Place an *x* in the appropriate columns to indicate whether the item should be added to or deducted from the book or bank balance, or whether it should not appear on the reconciliation. If the book balance is to be adjusted, place a *Dr.* or *Cr.* in the Must Adjust column to indicate whether the cash balance should be debited or credited.

	Bank Balance		Book Balance			Not Shown on the Reconciliation
	Add	Deduct	Add	Deduct	Must Adjust	
1. Interest earned on the account.						
2. Deposit made on September 30 after the bank was closed.						
3. Checks outstanding on August 31 that cleared the bank in September.						
4. NSF check from customer returned on September 15 but not recorded by the company.						
5. Checks written and mailed to payees on September 30.						
6. Deposit made on September 5 that was processed on September 8.						
7. Unrecorded withdrawal by owner using Automatic Teller Machine.						
8. Bank service charge.						
9. Checks written and mailed to payees on October 5.						
10. Check written by another depositor but charged against the company's account.						
11. Principal and interest collected by the bank but not recorded by the company.						
12. Special charge for collection of note in No. 11 on company's behalf.						
13. Check written against the account and cleared by the bank; erroneously omitted by the bookkeeper.						

Solution to Demonstration Problem

Planning the Solution

- Examine each item to determine whether it affects the book balance or the bank balance.
- If it acts to increase the balance, place an *x* in the Add column. If it acts to decrease the balance, place an *x* in the Deduct column.
- If the item increases or decreases the book balance, enter a *Dr.* or *Cr.* in the adjustment column.
- If the item does not affect either balance, place an *x* in the Not Shown on the Reconciliation column.

	Bank Balance		Book Balance			Not Shown on the Reconcil-iation
	Add	Deduct	Add	Deduct	Must Adjust	
1. Interest earned on the account.			x		Dr.	
2. Deposit made on September 30 after the bank was closed.	x					
3. Checks outstanding on August 31 that cleared the bank in September.						x
4. NSF check from customer returned on September 15 but not recorded by the company.				x	Cr.	
5. Checks written and mailed to payees on September 30.		x				
6. Deposit made on September 5 that was processed on September 8.						x
7. Unrecorded withdrawal by owner using Automatic Teller Machine.				x	Cr.	
8. Bank service charge.				x	Cr.	
9. Checks written and mailed to payees on October 5.						x
10. Check written by another depositor but charged against the company's account.	x					
11. Principal and interest collected by the bank but not recorded by the company.			x		Dr.	
12. Special charge for collection of note in No. 11 on company's behalf.				x	Cr.	
13. Check written against the account and cleared by the bank; erroneously omitted by the bookkeeper.				x	Cr.	

APPENDIX

D

Recording Vouchers: Manual System

LO 8 Explain the use of a Voucher Register and Check Register and prepare entries to record and pay liabilities when these registers are used in a manual accounting system.

When a voucher system is in use, an account called Vouchers Payable replaces the Accounts Payable account described in previous chapters. And for every transaction that will result in a cash disbursement, a voucher is prepared and credited to this account. For example, when merchandise is purchased, the voucher covering the transaction is recorded with a debit to Purchases and a credit to Vouchers Payable. Likewise, when a plant asset is purchased or an expense is incurred, the voucher of the transaction is recorded with a debit to the proper plant asset or expense account and a credit to Vouchers Payable.

In a manual system, vouchers are recorded in a **Voucher Register** similar to Illustration D–1. Such a register has a Vouchers Payable Credit column and a number of debit columns. The exact debit columns vary from company to company, but merchandising concerns always provide a Purchases Debit column. Also, as long as space is available, special debit columns are provided for transactions that occur frequently. In addition, an Other Accounts Debit column is provided for transactions that do not occur often.

In recording vouchers in a register like that of Illustration D–1, all information about each voucher, other than information about its payment, is entered as soon as the voucher is approved for recording. The information as to payment date and the number of the paying check is entered later as each voucher is paid.

In posting a Voucher Register like that in Illustration D–1, the columns are first totaled and crossfooted to prove their equality. The Vouchers Payable column total is then credited to the Vouchers Payable account. The totals of the Purchases, Transportation-In, Sales Salaries Expense, Advertising Expense, Delivery Expense, and Office Salaries Expense columns are debited to these accounts. None of the individual amounts in these columns are posted. However, the individual amounts in the Other Accounts column are posted as individual amounts, and the column total is not posted.

ILLUSTRATION D-1

A Voucher Register

Page 32									**Voucher**
				When and How Paid					
Date 19—		**Voucher No.**	**Payee**	**Date**	**Check No.**	**Vouchers Payable Credit**	**Purchases Debit**	**Transportation-In Debit**	
Oct.	1	767	A. B. Seay Co.	10/6	733	800.00	800.00		1
	1	768	Daily Sentinel	10/9	744	53.00			2
	2	769	Seaboard Supply Co.	10/12	747	235.00	155.00	10.00	3
	6	770	George Smith	10/6	734	85.00			4
	6	771	Frank Jones	10/6	735	95.00			5
	6	772	George Roth	10/6	736	95.00			6
	30	998	First National Bank	10/30	972	505.00			33
									34
	30	999	Pacific Telephone Co.	10/30	973	18.00			35
	31	1000	Tarbell Wholesale Co.			235.00	235.00		36
	31	1001	Office Equipment Co.	10/31	974	195.00			37
	31		Totals			5,079.00	2,435.00	156.00	38
						(226)	(505)	(508)	39
									40
									41

The Unpaid Vouchers File

When a voucher system is in use, some vouchers are paid as soon as they are recorded. Others must be filed until payment is due. As an aid in taking cash discounts, vouchers for which payment is not due are generally filed in an unpaid vouchers file under the dates on which they are to be paid.

The file of unpaid vouchers takes the place of a subsidiary Accounts Payable Ledger. Actually, the file is a subsidiary ledger of amounts owed creditors. Likewise, the Vouchers Payable account is in effect a controlling account controlling the unpaid vouchers file. Therefore, after posting is completed at the end of a month, the balance of the Vouchers Payable account should equal the sum of the unpaid vouchers in the unpaid vouchers file. This is verified each month by preparing a schedule or an adding machine list of the unpaid vouchers in the file and comparing its total with the balance of the Vouchers Payable account. In addition, the unpaid vouchers in the file are compared with the unpaid vouchers shown in the Voucher Register's record of payments column. The number of each paying check and the payment date are entered in the Voucher Register's payments column as each voucher is paid. Therefore, the vouchers in the register without check numbers and payment dates should be the same as those in the unpaid vouchers file.

ILLUSTRATION D–1

(Continued)

Register **Page 32**

	Sales Salaries Expense Debit	Adver-tising Expense Debit	Delivery Expense Debit	Office Salaries Expense Debit	Other Accounts Debit		
					Account Name	PR	Amount Debit
1							
2		53.00					
3					Store Supplies	125	70.00
4				85.00			
5	95.00						
6	95.00						
33					Notes Payable	245	500.00
34					Interest Expense.	633	5.00
35					Telephone Expense	688	18.00
36							
37					Office Equipment	163	195.00
38	740.00	115.00	358.00	340.00			935.00
39	(621)	(655)	(663)	(620)			(√)
40							
41							

The Voucher System Check Register

In a voucher system, the Cash Disbursements Journal is replaced by a simpler *Check Register*. All checks drawn in payment of vouchers are recorded in the Check Register. No obligation is paid until a voucher covering the payment is prepared and recorded in the Voucher Register. Likewise, no check is drawn except in payment of a specific voucher. Therefore, all checks drawn result in debits to Vouchers Payable and credits to Cash, unless a discount must be recorded. Then, there are credits to both Purchases Discounts and to Cash. A Check Register is shown in Illustration D–2. Note that it has columns for debits to Vouchers Payable and credits to Purchases Discounts and to Cash. In posting, all amounts entered in these columns are posted in the column totals.

Purchases Returns

Occasionally, an item must be returned after the voucher recording its purchase has been prepared and entered in the Voucher Register. In such cases, the return is recorded with a general journal entry like the one on the following page.

ILLUSTRATION D-2

A Check Register

Check Register

Date 19—		Payee	Voucher No.	Check No.	Vouchers Payable Debit	Purchases Discounts Credit	Cash Credit
Oct.	1	C. B. & Y. RR Co.	765	728	14.00		14.00
	3	Frank Mills	766	729	73.00		73.00
	3	Ajax Wholesale Co.	753	730	250.00	5.00	245.00
	4	Normal Supply Co.	747	731	100.00	2.00	98.00
	5	Office Supply Co.	763	732	43.00		43.00
	6	A. B. Seay Co.	767	733	800.00	16.00	784.00
	6	George Smith	770	734	85.00		85.00
	6	Frank Jones	771	735	95.00		95.00
	30	First National Bank	998	972	505.00		505.00
	30	Pacific Telephone Co.	999	973	18.00		18.00
	31	Office Equipment Co.	1001	974	195.00		195.00
	31	Totals			6,468.00	28.00	6,440.00
					(226)	(507)	(101)

Nov.	5	Vouchers Payable	15.00	
		Purchases Returns and Allowances		15.00
		Returned defective merchandise.		

In addition to the entry, the amount of the return is deducted on the voucher, and the credit memorandum and other documents verifying the return are attached to the voucher. Then, when the voucher is paid, a check is drawn for its corrected amount.

Summary of Appendix D in Terms of Learning Objective

LO 8. When a voucher system is used, all transactions that will require payments by check are recorded in a Voucher Register, which serves as a book of original entry. A Purchases Journal is not used. Then, checks drawn in payment of vouchers are recorded in the Check Register, which replaces the Cash Disbursements Journal. The file of unpaid vouchers takes the place of a subsidiary Accounts Payable Ledger.

Glossary

LO 7 Define or explain the words and phrases listed in the chapter glossary.

Bank reconciliation an analysis that explains the difference between the balance of a checking account shown in the depositor's records and the balance shown on the bank statement. p. 385

Canceled checks checks that the bank has paid and deducted from the customer's account during the month; they are called *canceled checks* because they have been stamped to show that they were paid. p. 383

Cash equivalents temporary liquid investments that can be easily and quickly converted to cash. p. 365

Cash Over and Short account an income statement account used to record cash overages and cash shortages arising from omitted petty cash receipts and from errors in making change. p. 382

Discounts lost an expense resulting from failing to take advantage of cash discounts on purchases. p. 391

Gross method of recording purchases a method of recording purchases at the full invoice price without deducting any cash discounts. p. 390

Internal control system procedures adopted by a business to encourage adherence to prescribed managerial policies; in doing so, the system also promotes operational efficiencies and protects the business assets from waste, fraud, and theft, and helps ensure that accurate and reliable accounting data are produced. p. 366

Invoice an itemized statement prepared by the vendor that lists the customer's name, the items sold, the sales prices, and the terms of sale. p. 375

Invoice approval form a document on which the accounting department notes that it has performed each step in the process of checking an invoice and approving it for recording and payment. p. 376

Liquid asset an asset, such as cash, that is easily converted into other types of assets or used to buy services or pay liabilities. p. 365

Liquidity a characteristic of an asset that refers to how easily the asset can be converted into another type of asset or used to buy services or to satisfy obligations. p. 365

Net method of recording purchases a method of recording purchases at the full invoice price less any cash discounts. p. 390

Outstanding checks checks that were written (or drawn) by the depositor, deducted on the depositor's records, and sent to the payees; however, they had not reached the bank for payment and deduction before the statement date. p. 385

Purchase order a business paper used by the purchasing department to place an order with the vendor; authorizes the vendor to ship the ordered merchandise at the stated price and terms; often abbreviated P.O. p. 374

Purchase requisition a business paper used to request that the purchasing department buy the needed merchandise or other items. pp. 373–74

Receiving report a form used within the business to notify the appropriate persons that ordered goods were received and to describe the quantities and condition of the goods. p. 375

Reconcile to explain or account for the difference between two amounts. p. 385

Vendee the buyer or purchaser of goods or services. p. 375

Vendor the seller of goods or services, usually a manufacturer or wholesaler. p. 374

Voucher an internal business paper used to accumulate other papers and information needed to control the disbursement of cash and to ensure that the transaction is properly recorded. p. 373

Voucher Register a book of original entry in which approved vouchers are recorded. p. 395.

Voucher system a set of procedures designed to control the incurrence of obligations and disbursements of cash. p. 373

Synonymous Terms

Checking account demand deposit

Invoice bill

Purchase order P.O.

Savings account time deposit

Unrecorded deposits deposits in transit

Vendee buyer

Vendor seller

Write a check draw a check

Objective Review

Answers to the following questions are listed at the end of this chapter. Be sure that you decide which is the one best answer to each question *before* you check the answers.

LO 1 Which of the following assets should be classified as a cash equivalent?

a. Land purchased as an investment.
b. Accounts receivable.
c. Common stock purchased as a short-term investment.
d. A 90-day Treasury bill issued by the U.S. government.
e. None of the above.

LO 2 The broad principles of internal control require that:

a. Responsibility for a series of related transactions (such as placing orders for, receiving, and paying for merchandise) should be lodged in one person so that responsibility is clearly assigned.
b. An employee who has custody over an asset should also keep the accounting records for that asset to ensure that the records are kept current.
c. Responsibility for specific tasks should be shared by more than one employee so that one serves as a check on the other.

d. Employees who handle cash and negotiable assets should be bonded.
e. All of the above are correct.

LO 3 Regarding internal control procedures for cash receipts:

a. All cash disbursements, other than from petty cash, should be made by check.
b. At the end of each day, each salesclerk who receives cash should analyze and correct any errors in the cash register's record of receipts before the records are submitted to the accounting department.
c. An accounting department employee should count the cash received from sales and promptly deposit the cash receipts in the bank.
d. Mail containing cash receipts should be opened by an accounting department employee who is responsible for recording the amount of the receipts and for depositing the receipts in the bank.
e. All of the above are correct.

LO 4 When a petty cash fund is used:

a. The balance in the Petty Cash account should be reported in the balance sheet as a long-term investment since this amount is kept in the fund on a long-term basis.
b. The petty cashier's summary of petty cash payments serves as a journal entry that is posted to the appropriate General Ledger accounts.
c. At the time that they are made, payments from the petty cash fund should be recorded with entries that include a credit to the Cash account.
d. At the time that they are made, payments from the petty cash fund should be recorded with entries that include a credit to the Petty Cash account.
e. Reimbursements of the petty cash fund should be credited to the Cash account.

LO 5 In the process of preparing a bank reconciliation:

a. Outstanding checks should be added to the bank balance of cash.
b. Outstanding checks should be subtracted from the book balance of cash.
c. All of the reconciling items shown on a bank reconciliation must be entered in the accounting records after the reconciliation is completed.
d. Items that appear on the reconciliation as corrections to the book balance of cash should be entered in the accounting records.
e. Items that appear on the reconciliation as corrections to the bank statement balance should be entered in the accounting records.

LO 6 When invoices are recorded at net amounts:

a. The Purchases account is debited for the amount of any purchases discounts offered plus the amount to be paid if a purchase discount is taken.

b. The amount of purchases discounts lost is not recorded in a separate account.
c. The amount of purchases discounts taken is not recorded in a separate account.
d. Purchases discounts taken are recorded in a Purchases Discounts account.
e. The cash expenditures for purchases will always be less than if the invoices are recorded at gross amounts.

LO 7 A form used within a business to notify the appropriate persons that ordered goods were received and to describe the quantities and condition of the goods is called a (an):

a. Invoice.
b. Invoice approval form.
c. Purchase order.
d. Receiving report.
e. Voucher.

LO 8 When a voucher system is in use, a Voucher Register:

a. Is used in place of a Cash Disbursements Journal.
b. Is used in place of a Cash Receipts Journal.
c. Serves as the journal in which purchases returns and allowances are recorded.
d. Is used in place of a Check Register.
e. Is used in place of a Purchases Journal.

A letter [D] identifies the questions, exercises, and problems based on Appendix D at the end of the chapter.

Questions for Class Discussion

1. Why does a company need to own liquid assets?
2. Why does a company own cash equivalent assets in addition to cash?
3. List the seven broad principles of internal control.
4. Why should the person who keeps the record of an asset not be the person responsible for custody of the asset?
5. Internal control procedures are important in every business, but at what stage in the development of a business do they become critical?
6. Why should responsibility for a sequence of related transactions be divided among different departments or individuals?
7. In a small business, it may be impossible to separate the functions of record-keeping and asset custody, and it is sometimes impossible to divide responsibilities for related transactions. What should be substituted for these control procedures?
8. Are the principles of internal control for computerized accounting systems different from the principles of internal control for manual accounting systems?

9. What are some of the effects of computers on internal control?
10. What is meant by the phrase *all receipts should be deposited intact?* Why should all receipts be deposited intact on the day of receipt?
11. Why should a company's bookkeeper not be given responsibility for receiving cash for the company nor the responsibility for signing checks or making cash disbursements in any other way?
12. When merchandise is purchased for a large store, why are department managers not permitted to deal directly with suppliers?
13. What is the role of the selling department managers in the purchasing procedures of a large store?
14. Tell (*a*) who prepares, (*b*) who receives, and (*c*) the purpose of each of the following business papers:

Purchase requisition	Receiving report
Purchase order	Invoice approval form
Invoice	Voucher

15. Do all companies need a voucher system? At what approximate point in a company's growth would you recommend installing a voucher system?
16. When a disbursing officer issues a check for a large business, he or she usually cannot know from personal contact that the assets, goods, or services being paid for were received by the business or that the purchase was properly authorized. However, if the company has an internal control system, the officer can depend on it. Exactly which documents does the officer depend on to tell that the purchase was authorized and that the goods were actually received?
17. Why are some cash payments made from a petty cash fund?
18. What is a petty cash receipt? When a petty cash receipt is prepared, who signs it?
19. Explain how a petty cash fund operates.
20. Why would it be helpful to reimburse a petty cash fund at the end of an accounting period?
21. What are two results of reimbursing the petty cash fund?
22. What is a bank statement? What kind of information appears on a bank statement?
23. What is the meaning of the phrase *to reconcile a bank balance?*
24. Why should you reconcile the bank statement balance of cash and the depositor's book balance of cash?
25. The following items were identified in the process of preparing a bank reconciliation. Which item or items require entries on the books of the depositor?
    a. Outstanding checks.
    b. Service charges.
    c. Deposits left in the night depository of the bank on the date the bank statement was prepared.
    d. Collection by the bank of the depositor's note receivable.
26. What valuable information becomes readily available to management

when invoices are recorded at net amounts? Is this information as readily available when invoices are recorded at gross amounts?

27. Refer to the Lands' End, Inc., balance sheets shown in Appendix K. Comparing cash and cash equivalents as a percentage of total current assets, is the mixture of current assets on January 31, 1991, more or less liquid than it was on January 31, 1990?
28. McDonald's Corporation's consolidated statement of cash flows (see Appendix K) describes the changes in cash and cash equivalents that occurred during 1990. What amount was provided (or used) by investing activities and what amount was provided (or used) by financing activities?

D29. What kind of transactions are entered in a Voucher Register?

D30. What kind of transactions are entered in a Check Register?

Exercises

Exercise 7–1
Analyzing internal control
(LO 2, 3)

Gladstone Company is a young business that has grown rapidly. The company's bookkeeper, who was hired two years ago, left town suddenly after the owner discovered that a great deal of money had disappeared over the past 18 months. An audit disclosed that the bookkeeper had written and signed checks made payable to the bookkeeper's cousin, and then recorded the checks as salaries expense. The cousin, who cashed the checks but had never worked for the company, left town with the bookkeeper. As a result, the company incurred an uninsured loss of $81,000.

Evaluate Gladstone Company's internal control system and indicate which principles of internal control appear to have been ignored in this situation.

Exercise 7–2
Recommending internal control procedures
(LO 2, 3)

What internal control procedures would you recommend in each of the following situations?

a. Campus T's has one employee who sells T-shirts at a stand next to a college campus. Each day, the employee is given enough T-shirts to last through the day and enough cash to make change. The money is kept in a box at the stand.

b. A used goods variety store has one employee who is given cash and sent to garage sales each weekend. The employee pays cash for merchandise to be resold at the variety store.

Exercise 7–3
Petty cash fund
(LO 4)

A company established a $200 petty cash fund on October 1. Two weeks later, on October 15, there was $37.25 in cash in the fund and receipts for these expenditures: postage, $36.50; transportation-in, $19.00; miscellaneous expenses, $61; and office supplies, $46.25.

Prepare the journal entries to (*a*) establish the fund and (*b*) reimburse it on October 15.

(*c*) Now assume that the fund was not only reimbursed on October 15 but also increased to $300 because it was exhausted so quickly. Give the entry to reimburse and increase the fund to $300.

Exercise 7–4
Petty cash fund
(LO 4)

A company established a $100 petty cash fund on February 5. On February 28, there was $30.80 in cash in the fund and receipts for these expenditures: transportation-in, $6.05; miscellaneous expenses, $18.70; and office supplies, $42.45. The petty cashier could not account for the $2 shortage in the fund. Prepare (*a*) the February 5 entry to establish the fund and (*b*) the February 28 entry to reimburse the fund and reduce it to $75.

Exercise 7–5
Internal control over cash receipts
(LO 2, 3)

Some of APL Company's cash receipts from customers are sent to the company in the mail. APL Company's bookkeeper opens the letters and deposits the cash received each day. What internal control problem is inherent in this arrangement? What changes would you recommend?

Exercise 7–6
Bank reconciliation
(LO 5)

Quantum Company deposits all receipts intact on the day received and makes all payments by check. On November 30, 1993, after all posting was completed, its Cash account showed a $3,180 debit balance. However, its November 30 bank statement showed only $2,627 on deposit in the bank on that day. Prepare a bank reconciliation for the store, using the following information:

a. Outstanding checks, $482.
b. Included with the November canceled checks returned by the bank was a $10 debit memorandum for bank services.
c. Check No. 977, returned with the canceled checks, was correctly drawn for $124 in payment of the telephone bill and was paid by the bank on November 9. However, it had been recorded with a debit to Telephone Expense and a credit to Cash as though it were for $142.
d. The November 30 cash receipts, $1,043, were placed in the bank's night depository after banking hours on that date and were unrecorded by the bank at the time the November bank statement was prepared.

Exercise 7–7
Adjusting entries resulting from bank reconciliation
(LO 5)

Give the journal entries that Quantum Company should make as a result of having prepared the bank reconciliation in the previous exercise.

Exercise 7–8
Recording invoices at gross or net amounts
(LO 6)

Shoney, Inc., incurred $147,000 of operating expenses in April 1993, a month in which its sales were $302,000. The company began April with a $175,000 merchandise inventory and ended the month with a $306,200 inventory. During the month, it purchased merchandise having a $252,000 invoice price, all of which was subject to a 2% discount for prompt payment. The company took advantage of the discounts on $228,000 of the purchases. However, a filing error caused it to miss taking the discount on a $24,000 invoice paid on April 30.

Required

1. Prepare an April income statement for the company under the assumption that it records invoices at gross amounts.
2. Prepare an April income statement for the company under the assumption that it records invoices at net amounts.

Exercise 7–9
Completion of bank reconciliation
(LO 5)

Complete the following bank reconciliation by filling in the missing amounts:

CAMBRIDGE COMPANY
Bank Reconciliation
March 31, 1993

Bank statement balance	$6,420	Book balance of cash	$?
Add: Deposit of March 31	?	Add: Collection of note	5,000
Bank error	30	Interest earned	150
	$?		$7,880
Deduct: Outstanding checks	1,635	Deduct: Service charge	?
		NSF check	200
Reconciled balance	$7,670	Reconciled balance	$?

Problems

Problem 7–1
Establishing and reimbursing petty cash fund
(LO 4)

A concern completed the following petty cash transactions during September of the current year:

Sept. 1 Drew a $100 check, cashed it, and gave the proceeds and the petty cashbox to Joy Reed, the petty cashier.

5 Purchased computer paper, $14.80.

7 Paid $7.55 COD delivery charges on merchandise purchased for resale.

10 Paid $4.50 parcel post charges on merchandise sold to a customer and delivered by mail.

12 Gave June Donners, wife of the business owner, $10 from petty cash for cab fare and other personal expenses.

19 Paid $6.50 COD delivery charges on merchandise purchased for resale.

23 Paid a service station attendant $7.50 for washing the personal car of Phil Donners, the business owner.

24 Paid Zippy Delivery Service $15.00 from petty cash to deliver merchandise sold to a customer.

26 Paid $32.00 for minor repairs to an office computer.

29 Joy Reed sorted the petty cash receipts by accounts affected and exchanged them for a check to reimburse the fund for expenditures. However, there was only $1.15 in cash in the fund, and she could not account for the shortage.

Required

1. Prepare a general journal entry to record establishing the petty cash fund.
2. Prepare a summary of petty cash payments that has these categories: Office supplies, Transportation-in, Delivery expense, Withdrawals, and Miscellaneous expenses. Sort the payments into the appropriate categories and total the expenses in each category.
3. Prepare the general journal entry to record the reimbursement of the fund.

Problem 7–2
Establishing, reimbursing, and increasing petty cash fund
(LO 4)

A business completed these transactions:

Mar. 8 Drew a $150 check to establish a petty cash fund, cashed it, and delivered the proceeds and the petty cashbox to Jay Yi, an office secretary who was to act as petty cashier.

12 Paid Town's Delivery Service $25 to deliver merchandise sold to a customer.

21 Purchased office supplies with petty cash, $37.50.

22 Paid $45 from petty cash to have the office windows washed.

29 Rita Moore, the owner of the business, signed a petty cash receipt and took $10 from petty cash for lunch.

Apr. 3 Paid $11.25 COD delivery charges on merchandise purchased for resale.

5 Jay Yi noted that there was only $21.25 cash remaining in the fund. Thus, he sorted the paid petty cash receipts by accounts affected and exchanged them for a check to reimburse the fund. Because the fund was so quickly used up, the check was made for an amount large enough to increase the size of the fund to $200.

9 Paid Town's Delivery Service $15.00 to deliver merchandise to a customer.

12 Paid the American Cleaner's delivery person $40.80 on the delivery to the office of clothes Moore had dropped off for dry cleaning.

13 Paid $35.50 COD delivery charges on merchandise purchased for resale.

16 Gave Tom Moore, the husband of the business owner, $20 from petty cash for cab fare and other personal expenditures.

20 Paid $30.85 for maintenance on an office copier.

26 Purchased office supplies with petty cash, $23.90.

27 Paid $9.45 COD delivery charges on merchandise purchased for resale.

30 Since there was $21.20 in cash in the fund, Jay Yi sorted the petty cash receipts by accounts affected and exchanged them for a check to reimburse the fund. There was also a small shortage that he could not explain.

Required

1. Prepare a journal entry to record the check establishing the petty cash fund.
2. Prepare a summary of petty cash payments for March 8 to April 5 that has these categories: Office supplies, Transportation-in, Delivery expense, Withdrawals, and Miscellaneous expenses. Sort the payments into the appropriate categories and total each category. Prepare a similar summary of petty cash payments after April 5.
3. Prepare entries to reimburse the fund and increase its size on April 5 and to reimburse the fund on April 30.

Problem 7–3
Petty cash fund; reimbursement and analysis of errors (LO 4)

The Faxton Company has only a General Journal in its accounting system and uses it to record all transactions. However, the company recently set up a petty cash fund to facilitate payments of small items. The following petty cash transactions were noted by the petty cashier as occurring during June (the last month of the company's fiscal year):

June 4 Received a company check for $125 to establish the petty cash fund.

20 Received a company check to replenish the fund for the following expenditures made since June 4 and to increase the fund to $175:
- *a.* Payment of $20.50 to Atlas Trucking for freight on merchandise sold and delivered to Atkins Company.
- *b.* Purchased postage stamps for $25.
- *c.* Gave Shara Kahn, owner of the business, $35 for personal use.
- *d.* Paid $38.50 to AAA Company for repairs of office equipment.
- *e.* Discovered that only $4.00 remained in the petty cashbox.

30 Having decided that the June 20 increase in the fund was too large, received a company check to replenish the fund for the following expenditures made since June 20 but causing the fund to be reduced in size to $150.
- *f.* Payment of $22.75 for emergency repairs to the company's office computer printer.
- *g.* Payment of $40 for janitorial service.
- *h.* Purchased office supplies for $16.30.
- *i.* Payment of $33.20 to *The Gazette-Telegraph* for an advertisement in the newspaper.

Required

1. Prepare general journal entries to record the establishment of the fund on June 4 and its replenishments on June 20 and on June 30.
2. Explain how the company's financial statements would be affected if the petty cash fund is not replenished and no entry is made on June 30. (Hint: The amount of Office Supplies that appears on a balance sheet is determined by a physical count of the supplies on hand.)

Problem 7–4
Preparation of bank reconciliation and recording adjustments (LO 5)

The following information was available to reconcile Repcon Company's book cash balance with its bank statement balance as of December 31, 1993:

a. The December 31 cash balance according to the accounting records was $8,263, and the bank statement balance for that date was $11,562.

b. Check No. 1976 for $278 and Check No. 1979 for $100, both written and entered in the accounting records in December, were not among the canceled checks returned. Two checks, No. 1843 for $587 and No. 1902 for $95, were outstanding on November 30 when the bank and book statement balances were last reconciled. Check No. 1902 was returned with the December canceled checks but Check No. 1843 was not.

c. When the December checks were compared with entries in the accounting records, it was found that Check No. 1954 had been correctly drawn for $654 in payment for store supplies but was erroneously entered in the accounting records as though it were drawn for $645.

d. Two debit memoranda and a credit memorandum were included with the returned checks and were unrecorded at the time of the reconciliation. The credit memorandum indicated that the bank had collected a $5,000 note receivable for the company, deducted a $25 collection fee, and credited the balance to the company's account. One of the debit memoranda was for $215 and dealt with an NSF check for $205 that had been received from a customer, Ralph Crumley, in payment of his account. It also assessed a $10 fee for processing. The second debit memorandum covered check printing and was for $72.

e. The December 31 cash receipts, $2,345, had been placed in the bank's night depository after banking hours on that date and did not appear on the bank statement.

Required

1. Prepare a bank reconciliation for the company as of December 31.
2. Prepare the general journal entries necessary to bring the company's book balance of cash into conformity with the reconciled balance.

Problem 7–5
Preparation of bank reconciliation and recording adjustments (LO 5)

Pneumo Company reconciled its bank and book statement balances of cash on March 31 and showed two checks outstanding at that time, No. 3762 for $500 and No. 3776 for $1,240. The following information was available for the April 30, 1993, reconciliation:

From the April 30 bank statement:

BALANCE OF PREVIOUS STATEMENT ON 3/31/93	10,265.00
5 DEPOSITS AND OTHER CREDITS TOTALING	6,404.00
INTEREST AT 4.75%	30.00
9 CHECKS AND OTHER DEBITS TOTALING	8,117.00
CURRENT BALANCE AS OF 4/30/93	8,582.00

CHECKING ACCOUNT TRANSACTIONS

DATE	AMOUNT	TRANSACTION DESCRIPTION
4/6	1,980.00+	Deposit
4/13	852.00+	Deposit
4/20	1,113.00+	Deposit
4/27	857.00+	Deposit
4/28	85.00−	NSF check
4/30	30.00+	Interest
4/30	1,572.00+	Credit memorandum

DATE	CHECK NO.	AMOUNT	DATE	CHECK NO.	AMOUNT
4/2	3776	1,240.00	4/14	3782	672.00
4/6	3779*	95.00	4/19	3783	32.00
4/7	3780	5,078.00	4/22	3785*	143.00
4/11	3781	271.00	4/28	3786	501.00

*Indicates a skip in check sequence.

From Pneumo Company's accounting records:

Cash Receipts Deposited

Date		Cash Debit
Apr.	6	1,980.00
	13	852.00
	20	1,113.00
	27	857.00
	30	690.00
		5,492.00

Cash Disbursements

Check No.	Cash Credit
3779	95.00
3780	5,078.00
3781	271.00
3782	692.00
3783	32.00
3784	750.00
3785	143.00
3786	501.00
3787	76.00
	7,638.00

Cash — Acct. No. 101

Date		Explanation	PR	Debit	Credit	Balance
Mar.	31	Balance				8,555.00
Apr.	30	Total receipts	R8	5,492.00		14,047.00
	30	Total disbursements	D9		7,638.00	6,409.00

Check No. 3782 was correctly drawn for $672 in payment for office equipment; however, the bookkeeper misread the amount and entered it in the accounting records with a debit to Office Equipment and a credit to Cash as though it were for $692.

The NSF check was originally received from a customer, Pat Carriker, in payment of her account. Its return was not recorded when the bank first notified the company. The credit memorandum resulted from the collection of a $1,600 note for Pneumo Company by the bank. The bank had deducted a $28 collection fee. The collection has not been recorded.

Required

1. Prepare an April 30 bank reconciliation for the company.
2. Prepare the general journal entries needed to adjust the book balance of cash to the reconciled balance.

Problem 7–6
Recording invoices at gross or net amounts (LO 6)

The July 31, 1993, credit balance in the Sales account of Cardina Company showed it had sold merchandise for $147,000 during the month. The concern began July with a $280,700 merchandise inventory and ended the month with a $237,000 inventory. It had incurred $34,300 of operating expenses during the month, and it had also recorded the following transactions:

July 2 Received merchandise purchased at a $6,300 invoice price; invoice dated June 27; terms 2/10, n/30.

July 5 Received a $1,300 credit memorandum (invoice price) for merchandise received on July 2 and returned for credit.

10 Received merchandise purchased at a $14,000 invoice price; invoice dated July 8; terms 2/10, n/30.

14 Received merchandise purchased at a $7,800 invoice price, invoice dated July 12; terms 2/10, n/30.

17 Paid for the merchandise received on July 10, less the discount.

21 Paid for the merchandise received on July 14, less the discount.

27 Paid for the merchandise received on July 2. Payment was delayed because the invoice was mistakenly filed for payment today. This error caused the discount to be lost. The filing error occurred after the credit memorandum received on July 5 was attached to the invoice dated June 27.

Required

1. Assume that Cardina Company records invoices at gross amounts.
   a. Prepare general journal entries to record the transactions.
   b. Prepare a July income statement.
2. Assume that Cardina Company records invoices at net amounts.
   a. Prepare general journal entries to record the transactions.
   b. Prepare a July income statement.

Problem 7–7
Analytical essay
(LO 4)

In Problem 7–1, several of the transactions involved payments of cash from a petty cash fund. Nevertheless, the entry to record these payments does not include a credit to Petty Cash. Explain why this is true. Under what circumstances would the entry to record payments from the petty cash fund include a credit to Petty Cash?

Problem 7–8
Analytical essay
(LO 5)

The bank statement in Problem 7–5 discloses two places where the canceled checks returned with the bank statement are not numbered sequentially. In other words, some of the prenumbered checks in the sequence are missing. There are several possible situations that would explain why the canceled checks returned with a bank statement might not be numbered sequentially. Describe three situations, each of which is a possible explanation of why the canceled checks returned with a bank statement are not numbered sequentially.

DProblem 7–9
Using a voucher system
(LO 8)

Coltrain Company completed these transactions involving vouchers payable:

July 3 Recorded Voucher No. 281 payable to Zachary Company for merchandise having a $1,600 invoice price; invoice dated June 30; terms FOB factory, 2/10, n/30. The vendor had prepaid the freight, $65, adding the amount to the invoice and bringing its total to $1,665.

5 Recorded Voucher No. 282 payable to *The Herald* for advertising expense, $175. Issued Check No. 424 in payment of the voucher.

July 6 Received a credit memorandum for merchandise having a $133 invoice price. The merchandise had been received from Zachary Company on July 3, recorded on Voucher No. 281, and later returned for credit.

7 Recorded Voucher No. 283 payable to Global Realty for one month's rent on the space occupied by the store, $1,100. Issued Check No. 425 in payment of the voucher.

10 Recorded Voucher No. 284 payable to Carroll Supply Company for store supplies, $147, terms n/10 EOM.

11 Recorded Voucher No. 285 payable to Penn Company for merchandise having a $3,800 invoice price; invoice dated July 9; terms FOB factory, 2/10, n/60. The vendor had prepaid the freight charges, $141, adding the amount to the invoice and bringing its total to $3,941.

14 Recorded Voucher No. 286 payable to Payroll for sales salaries, $1,500, and office salaries, $1,200. Issued Check No. 426 in payment of the voucher. Cashed the check and paid the employees.

17 Recorded Voucher No. 287 payable to Northwood Company for merchandise having a $798 invoice price; invoice dated July 14; terms 2/10, n/60, FOB factory. The vendor had prepaid the freight charges, $39, adding the amount to the invoice and bringing its total to $837.

19 Issued Check No. 427 in payment of Voucher No. 285.

21 Recorded Voucher No. 288 payable to Penn Company for merchandise having a $4,663 invoice price; invoice dated July 18; terms FOB factory, 2/10, n/60. The vendor had prepaid the freight charges, $186, adding the amount to the invoice and bringing its total to $4,849.

24 Discovered that Voucher No. 281 had been filed in error for payment on the last day of its credit period rather than on the last day of its discount period, causing the discount to be lost. Issued Check No. 428 in payment of the voucher, less the return.

28 Recorded Voucher No. 289 payable to Payroll for sales salaries, $1,500, and office salaries, $1,200. Issued Check No. 429 in payment of the voucher. Cashed the check and paid the employees.

Required

1. Assume that Coltrain Company records vouchers at gross amounts. Prepare a Voucher Register, a Check Register, and a General Journal, and record the transactions.
2. Prepare a Vouchers Payable account and post those entry portions that affect the account.
3. Prove the balance of the Vouchers Payable account by preparing a schedule of vouchers payable.

Alternate Problems

Problem 7–1A
Establishing and reimbursing petty cash fund
(LO 4)

A concern completed the following petty cash transactions during May of the current year:

May 1 Drew a $100 check, cashed it, and turned the proceeds and the petty cashbox over to Walter Cleaver, the petty cashier.
4 Paid $4.35 parcel post charges on merchandise sold to a customer and delivered by mail.
6 Purchased office supplies, $11.75.
10 Paid $21.20 for repairs to an office copier.
12 Paid $7 COD delivery charges on merchandise purchased for resale.
16 Paid Hatley Delivery Service $8.50 to deliver merchandise sold to a customer.
21 Gave Russell Johnson, the owner of the business, $10 from petty cash for personal use.
24 Paid $23.55 COD delivery charges on merchandise purchased for resale.
27 Russell Johnson, owner of the business, signed a petty cash receipt and took $10 from petty cash for lunch.
31 Walter Cleaver exchanged his paid petty cash receipts for a check reimbursing the fund for expenditures and a shortage of cash in the fund that he could not account for. He reported a cash balance of $2.55 in the fund.

Required

1. Prepare a general journal entry to record establishing the petty cash fund.
2. Prepare a summary of petty cash payments that has these categories: Office supplies, Transportation-in, Delivery expense, Withdrawals, and Miscellaneous expenses. Sort the payments into the appropriate categories and total the expenses in each category.
3. Prepare the general journal entry to record the reimbursement of the fund.

Problem 7–2A
Establishing, reimbursing, and increasing petty cash fund
(LO 4)

A company completed these petty cash transactions:

July 6 Drew an $85 check to establish a petty cash fund, cashed it, and turned the proceeds and the petty cashbox over to Jean Fisher, the petty cashier.
8 Paid $6.30 parcel post charges on merchandise sold to a customer and delivered by mail.
9 Paid $35 to have the office windows washed.
13 Purchased office supplies with petty cash, $12.25.

July	15	Marilyn Morgan, owner of the business, signed a petty cash receipt and took $7 from petty cash for coffee money.
	18	Paid $21.70 COD delivery charges on merchandise purchased for resale.
	20	Jean Fisher noted that only $2.75 remained in the petty cashbox. Thus, she sorted the petty cash receipts into the accounts affected and exchanged the receipts for a check to reimburse the fund. Because the fund was so quickly used up, the check was made for an amount large enough to increase the size of the fund to $150.
	22	Paid $41 from petty cash for minor repairs to an office machine.
	25	Paid $18 COD delivery charges on merchandise purchased for resale.
	26	Paid Express Courier $10.85 to deliver merchandise sold to a customer.
	27	Purchased office supplies with petty cash, $16.30.
	29	Marilyn Morgan, owner of the business, signed a petty cash receipt and took $20 from petty cash for lunch.
Aug.	1	Paid $15 COD delivery charges on merchandise purchased for resale.
	4	Purchased paper clips and pencils with petty cash, $7.45.
	11	Paid $18.50 COD delivery charges on merchandise purchased for resale.
	15	Jean Fisher sorted the petty cash receipts by accounts affected and exchanged them for a check to reimburse the fund. There was also a small shortage that she could not explain. There was only $2.50 cash left in the fund.

Required

1. Prepare a journal entry to record the check establishing the petty cash fund.
2. Prepare a summary of petty cash payments for July 6 to July 20 that has these categories: Delivery expense, Office supplies, Miscellaneous expenses, Withdrawals, and Transportation-in. Sort the payments into the appropriate categories and total the expenses in each category. Prepare a similar summary of petty cash payments after July 20.
3. Prepare entries to reimburse the fund and increase its size on July 20 and to reimburse the fund on August 15.

Problem 7–3A
Petty cash fund; reimbursement and analysis of errors (LO 4)

The accounting system used by the York Dental Laboratory requires that all entries be journalized in a General Journal. To facilitate payments for small items, York established a petty cash fund. The following transactions involving the petty cash fund occurred during December (the last month of the company's fiscal year).

Dec. 1 A company check for $150 was drawn and made payable to the petty cashier to establish the petty cash fund.

14 A company check was drawn to replenish the fund for the following expenditures made since December 1 and to increase the fund to $200.

a. Purchased postage stamps for $25.

b. Payment of $32.90 to Action Delivery Service for delivery of merchandise to customers.

c. Gave Larry Tyson, owner of the business, $40 for personal use.

d. Paid $44.50 to Acme Repairs for repairs of office equipment.

e. Discovered that only $7.10 remained in the petty cashbox.

31 The petty cashier noted that $7.60 remained in the fund. Having decided that the December 14 increase in the fund was not large enough, a company check was drawn to replenish the fund for the following expenditures made since December 14 and to increase it to $250.

f. Payment of $33.05 for office supplies to support the company's computer.

g. Payment of $39.35 for items classified as miscellaneous expenses.

h. Payment of $75 for janitorial service.

i. Payment of $45 to Regional Publications Company for an advertisement in a weekly newsletter.

Required

1. Prepare general journal entries to record the establishment of the fund on December 1 and its replenishments on December 14 and on December 31.
2. Explain how the company's financial statements would be affected if the petty cash fund is not replenished and no entry is made on December 31. (Hint: The amount of Office Supplies that appears on a balance sheet is determined by a physical count of the supplies on hand.)

Problem 7–4A
Preparation of bank reconciliation and recording adjustments (LO 5)

The following information was available to reconcile Advance Company's book balance of cash with its bank statement balance as of April 30, 1993:

a. After all posting was completed on April 30, the company's Cash account had a $1,699 debit balance, but its bank statement showed a $4,006 balance.

b. Checks No. 617 for $78 and No. 622 for $457 were outstanding on the March 31 bank reconciliation. Check No. 622 was returned with the April canceled checks, but Check No. 617 was not. It was also found that Check No. 631 for $383 and Check No. 633 for $17, both drawn in April, were not among the canceled checks returned with the statement.

c. In comparing the canceled checks returned with the bank statement with the entries in the accounting records, it was found that Check No. 697 for the purchase of office equipment was correctly drawn for $1,477 but was erroneously entered in the accounting records as though it were for $1,747.

d. A credit memorandum enclosed with the bank statement indicated that the bank had collected a $2,700 noninterest-bearing note for Advance Company, deducted a $27 collection fee, and had credited the remainder to the account. This event was not recorded by Advance Company before receiving the statement.

e. A debit memorandum for $315 listed a $300 NSF check plus a $15 NSF charge. The check had been received from a customer, Walter Bellows. Advance Company had not recorded this bounced check before receiving the statement.

f. Also enclosed with the statement was a $10 debit memorandum for bank services. It had not been recorded because no previous notification had been received.

g. The April 30 cash receipts, $789, were placed in the bank's night depository after banking hours on that date and this amount did not appear on the bank statement.

Required

1. Prepare a bank reconciliation for the company as of April 30, 1993.
2. Prepare the general journal entries necessary to bring the company's book balance of cash into conformity with the reconciled balance.

Problem 7–5A
Preparation of bank reconciliation and recording adjustments
(LO 5)

Lange Company reconciled its bank balance on September 30 and showed two checks outstanding at that time, No. 1408 for $67 and No. 1409 for $124. The following information is available for the October 31, 1993, reconciliation:

From the October 31 bank statement:

BALANCE OF PREVIOUS STATEMENT ON 09/30/93	1,256.00
5 DEPOSITS AND OTHER CREDITS TOTALING	2,443.00
8 CHECKS AND OTHER DEBITS TOTALING	1,897.00
SERVICE CHARGE AMOUNT	7.00
CURRENT BALANCE AS OF THIS STATEMENT	1,795.00

CHECKING ACCOUNT TRANSACTIONS

DATE	AMOUNT	TRANSACTION DESCRIPTION
10/6	387.00+	Deposit
10/13	460.00+	Deposit
10/20	286.00+	Deposit
10/27	330.00+	Deposit
10/30	59.00−	NSF check
10/31	7.00−	Service charge
10/31	980.00+	Credit memorandum

DATE	CHECK NO.	AMOUNT	DATE	CHECK NO.	AMOUNT
10/26	1409	124.00	10/17	1413	25.00
10/4	1410	65.00	10/14	1414	1,275.00
10/2	1411	31.00	10/28	1416*	88.00
10/7	1412	230.00			

*Indicates a skip in check sequence.

From Lange Company's accounting records:

Cash Receipts Deposited

Date			Cash Debit
Oct.	6		387.00
	13		460.00
	20		286.00
	27		330.00
	31		401.00
			1,864.00

Cash Disbursements

Check No.		Cash Credit
1410		65.00
1411		31.00
1412		230.00
1413		25.00
1414		1,275.00
1415		107.00
1416		80.00
1417		194.00
		2,007.00

Cash — Acct. No. 101

Date		Explanation	PR	Debit	Credit	Balance
Sept.	30	Balance				1,065.00
Oct.	31	Total receipts	R8	1,864.00		2,929.00
	31	Total disbursements	D9		2,007.00	922.00

Check No. 1416 was correctly drawn for $88 in payment for store supplies; however, the bookkeeper misread the amount and entered it in the accounting records with a debit to Store Supplies and a credit to Cash as though it were for $80. The bank paid and deducted the correct amount.

The NSF check was originally received from a customer, Wilma Stone, in payment of her account. Its return was unrecorded. The credit memorandum resulted from a $1,000 note that the bank had collected for the company. The bank had deducted a $20 collection fee and deposited the remainder in the company's account. The collection has not been recorded.

Required

1. Prepare a bank reconciliation for Lange Company.
2. Prepare the general journal entries needed to adjust the book balance of cash to the reconciled balance.

Problem 7–6A
Recording invoices at gross or net amounts
(LO 6)

The June 30, 1993, credit balance in the Sales account of Clipper Company showed it had sold merchandise for $288,000 during the month. The concern began June with a $227,000 merchandise inventory and ended the month with a $185,000 inventory. It had incurred $74,000 of operating expenses during the month, and it had also recorded the following transactions:

June 2 Received merchandise purchased at a $54,000 invoice price; invoice dated May 30; terms 2/10, n/30.

7 Received a $5,000 credit memorandum (invoice price) for merchandise received on June 2 and returned for credit.

12 Received merchandise purchased at a $42,000 invoice price; invoice dated June 11; terms 2/10, n/30.

15 Received merchandise purchased at a $137,750 invoice price; invoice dated June 13; terms 2/10, n/30.

June 20 Paid for the merchandise received on June 12, less the discount.

22 Paid for the merchandise received on June 15, less the discount.

29 Paid for the merchandise received on June 2. Payment was delayed because the invoice was mistakenly filed for payment today. This error caused the discount to be lost. The filing error occurred after the credit memorandum received on June 7 was attached to the invoice dated May 30.

Required

1. Assume that Clipper Company records invoices at gross amounts.
   a. Prepare general journal entries to record the transactions.
   b. Prepare a June income statement.
2. Assume that Clipper Company records invoices at net amounts.
   a. Prepare general journal entries to record the transactions.
   b. Prepare a June income statement.

Problem 7–7A
Analytical essay
(LO 4)

In Problem 7–1A, several of the transactions involved payments of cash from a petty cash fund. Assume that when the petty cash fund was reimbursed, the company's bookkeeper made an entry of the following general form:

May	31	xxxxxxxxxxxx (Expense)	xxx	
		xxxxxxxxxxxx (Expense)	xxx	
		xxxxxxxxxxxx (Asset)	xxx	
		Petty Cash		xxx

Explain why this entry is not correct. Also explain the effects of the error on the General Ledger and on the balance sheet.

Problem 7–8A
Analytical essay
(LO 5)

Review the facts about Advance Company presented in Problem 7–4A. Assume that an April 30, 1993, bank reconciliation for the company has already been prepared and some of the items were treated incorrectly in preparing the reconciliation. For each of the following errors, explain the effect of the error on: (1) the final balance that was calculated by adjusting the bank statement balance, and (2) the final balance that was calculated by adjusting the Cash account balance.

a. The company's Cash account balance of $1,699 was listed on the reconciliation as $1,996.

b. Check No. 622 for $457 was deducted from the bank statement balance as an outstanding check.

c. The correction for Check No. 697 was subtracted from the bank statement balance.

d. The bank's collection of a $2,700 note less the deduction of a $27 collection fee was added to the bank statement balance.

[D]Problem 7–9A
Using a voucher system
(LO 8)

Garth Company completed these transactions involving vouchers payable:

Oct. 2 Recorded Voucher No. 827 payable to Blackmon Company for merchandise having a $4,300 invoice price; invoice dated September 29; terms FOB destination, 2/10, n/30.

4 Recorded Voucher No. 828 payable to Swann Company for merchandise having a $2,400 invoice price; invoice dated October 2; terms FOB factory, 2/10, n/60. The vendor had prepaid the freight charges, $110, adding the amount to the invoice and bringing its total to $2,510.

6 Received a credit memorandum for merchandise having a $550 invoice price. The merchandise was received on October 2, Voucher No. 827, and returned for credit.

11 Issued Check No. 630 in payment of Voucher No. 828.

15 Recorded Voucher No. 829 payable to Payroll for sales salaries, $2,100, and office salaries, $1,100. Issued Check No. 631 in payment of the voucher. Cashed the check and paid the employees.

17 Recorded Voucher No. 830 payable to Miaki Company for the purchase of office equipment having a $1,250 invoice price, terms n/10 EOM.

20 Recorded Voucher No. 831 payable to *The Daily Echo* for advertising expense, $479. Issued Check No. 632 in payment of the voucher.

24 Recorded Voucher No. 832 payable to Plaza Industries for merchandise having a $1,730 invoice price; invoice dated October 22; terms FOB factory, 2/10, n/60. The vendor had prepaid the freight charges, $86, adding the amount to the invoice and bringing its total to $1,816.

27 Discovered that Voucher No. 827 had been filed in error for payment on the last day of its credit period rather than on the last day of its discount period, causing the discount to be lost. Issued Check No. 633 in payment of the voucher, less the return.

31 Recorded Voucher No. 833 payable to Payroll for sales salaries, $2,100, and office salaries, $1,100. Issued Check No. 634 in payment of the voucher. Cashed the check and paid the employees.

Required

1. Assume that Garth Company records vouchers at gross amounts. Prepare a Voucher Register, a Check Register, and a General Journal and record the transactions.
2. Prepare a Vouchers Payable account and post those portions of the journal and register entries that affect the account.
3. Prove the balance of the Vouchers Payable account by preparing a schedule of unpaid vouchers.

Provocative Problems

Provocative Problem 7–1
Ridgefield Company
(LO 2, 3)

The bookkeeper at Ridgefield Company will retire next week. Originally hired more than 30 years ago by the father of the store's present owner, he has always been very dependable. As a result, the bookkeeper has been given more and more responsibilities over the years. Actually, for the past 15 years, he has run the company's office, keeping the books, verifying invoices, and issuing checks in their payment. Whenever the store's owner, L. F. Winfield, was not around, the bookkeeper even signed the checks. In addition, at the end of each day, the store's salesclerks turned over their daily cash receipts to the bookkeeper. After counting the money and comparing the amounts with the cash register tapes—which he was responsible for removing from the cash registers—he made the journal entry to record cash sales and then deposited the money in the bank. He also reconciled the bank balance with the book balance of cash each month.

Winfield realizes he cannot expect a new bookkeeper to do as much as the old bookkeeper. And, because the store is not large enough to warrant more than one office employee, he knows that he will probably have to take over some of the duties after the bookkeeper retires. Winfield already places all orders for merchandise and supplies and closely supervises all employees and does not want to add more to his duties than necessary.

Identify the internal control principle that has been violated and select the bookkeeper's tasks that should be taken over by Winfield to improve the store's internal control over cash.

Provocative Problem 7–2
Tom Mix Company
(LO 2, 3)

The Tom Mix Company has enjoyed rapid growth since it was created several years ago. Last year, for example, its sales exceeded $8 million. However, its purchasing procedures have not kept pace with its growth. When a plant supervisor or department head needs raw materials, plant assets, or supplies, he or she telephones a request to the purchasing department manager. The purchasing department manager then prepares a purchase order in duplicate, sends one copy to the company selling the goods, and keeps the other copy in the files. When the seller's invoice is received, it is sent directly to the purchasing department. When the goods arrive, receiving department personnel count and inspect the items and prepare only one copy of a receiving report, which is then sent to the purchasing department. The purchasing department manager attaches the receiving report and the file copy of the purchase order to the invoice. If all is in order, the invoice is stamped *approved for payment* and signed by the purchasing department manager. The invoice and its supporting documents are then sent to the accounting department to be recorded and filed until due. On its due date, the invoice and its supporting documents are sent to the office of the company treasurer, and a check is prepared and mailed. The number of the check is entered on the invoice and the invoice is sent to the accounting department for an entry to record its payment.

Do the procedures of Tom Mix Company make it fairly easy for someone in the company to initiate the payment of fictitious invoices by the company? If so, who is most likely to commit the fraud and what would that person have to do to receive payment of a fictitious invoice? What changes should be made in the company's purchasing procedures, and why should each change be made?

Provocative Problem 7–3
International Business Machines Corporation (LO 1)

For this problem, turn to the financial statements of International Business Machines Corporation in Appendix J. Use the information presented in the financial statements to answer these questions:

1. Suppose that the company can earn 7% interest on cash equivalents balances and only 4% on cash balances. Calculate the additional income (before income taxes) that would have been earned in 1990 if the average cash balance had been invested entirely in cash equivalents. (Calculate the average cash balance as the average of the beginning and ending balances.)
2. For both 1990 and 1989, determine the total amount of cash and cash equivalents that IBM held at the end of the year. Determine the percentage that this amount represents of total current assets, total current liabilities, total equity, and total assets.
3. For both 1990 and 1989, determine the total amount of cash, cash equivalents, and investments in marketable securities that IBM held at the end of the year. Determine the percentage that this amount represents of total current assets, total current liabilities, total equity, and total assets.
4. For 1990, use the information in the statement of cash flows to determine the percentage change between the beginning of the year and end of the year holding of cash and cash equivalents.

Provocative Problem 7–4
As a Matter of Ethics: Essay

Ethics

Review the As a Matter of Ethics case on page 383. Discuss the nature of the problem faced by Nancy Tucker and evaluate the alternative courses of action she should consider.

Answers to Objective Review Questions

LO 1 (*d*)	LO 4 (*e*)	LO 7 (*d*)
LO 2 (*d*)	LO 5 (*d*)	LO 8 (*e*)
LO 3 (*a*)	LO 6 (*c*)	

CHAPTER

8

Short-Term Investments and Receivables

Companies rarely operate in today's economy without extending credit to customers. By being careful in granting credit, a business can increase sales without incurring high costs. Accounting information helps managers assess the risk and the success of their credit decisions.

Topical Coverage

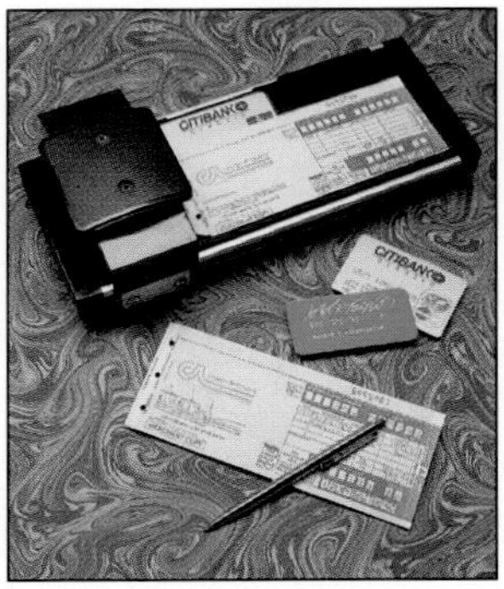

The focus of the prior chapter was on accounting for cash, which is the most liquid of all assets. This chapter continues the discussion of liquid assets by focusing on short-term investments, accounts receivable, and short-term notes receivable.

Learning Objectives

After studying Chapter 8, you should be able to:

1. Prepare journal entries to account for short-term investments and calculate, record, and report the lower of cost or market of short-term investments in marketable equity securities.
2. Prepare entries to account for credit card sales.
3. Prepare entries to account for transactions with credit customers, including accounting for bad debts under the allowance method and the direct write-off method.
4. Calculate the interest on promissory notes and prepare entries to record the receipt of promissory notes and their payment or dishonor.
5. Calculate the discount and proceeds on discounted notes receivable and prepare entries to record the discounting of notes receivable and their dishonoring, if necessary.
6. Define or explain the words and phrases listed in the chapter glossary.

Because cash is used by companies to acquire assets and to pay expenses and obligations, good management generally requires that companies have an adequate amount available, including a surplus over the minimum amount that might be needed. Also, surplus cash may be available during some months of each year because of seasonal variations in sales volume. Rather than leave this unneeded cash in checking accounts that pay low rates of interest at best, most concerns invest their surplus where it can earn higher returns.

Short-Term Investments

LO 1 Prepare journal entries to account for short-term investments and calculate, record, and report the lower of cost or market of short-term investments in marketable equity securities.

Recall from Chapter 7 that cash equivalents are investments that are readily convertible into a known amount of cash; generally, they mature not more than three months after purchase. Some investments of idle cash balances do not meet these criteria of cash equivalents but, nevertheless, are classified as current assets. Although these **short-term investments** or **temporary investments** do not qualify as cash equivalents, they serve a similar purpose. Like cash equivalents, short-term investments can be converted into cash easily and are held as a source of cash to satisfy the needs of current operations. Management usually expects to convert them into cash within one year or the current operating cycle of the business, whichever is longer.[1]

[1] FASB, *Accounting Standards—Current Text* (Norwalk, Conn., 1990), sec. B05.105. First published as *Accounting Research Bulletin No. 43,* chap. 3A, par. 4.

Short-term investments may be made in the form of government or corporate debt obligations (called *debt securities*) or in the form of stock (called *equity securities*). Some investments in debt securities are classified as current assets because they mature within one year or the current operating cycle of the business. Investments in other securities that do not mature in a short time can be classified as current assets only if they are marketable. In other words, such securities must be sellable without excessive delays. For example, stocks that are actively traded on a stock exchange qualify as marketable.

When short-term investments are purchased, you should record them at cost. For example, assume that Alpha Company purchased Ford Motor Company's short-term notes payable for $40,000. Alpha's entry to record the transaction is:

Jan.	10	Short-Term Investments	40,000.00	
		Cash		40,000.00
		Bought $40,000 of Ford Motor Company notes due March 31.		

Assume that these notes mature, and that the cash proceeds are $40,000 plus $800 interest. When the receipt is recorded, you must credit the interest to a revenue account, as follows:

Mar.	31	Cash	40,800.00	
		Short-Term Investments		40,000.00
		Interest Earned		800.00
		Received cash proceeds from matured notes.		

To determine the cost of an investment, you must include any commissions paid. For example, assume that on April 15, 1993, Bailey Company purchased 1,000 shares of Xerox Corporation common stock as a short-term investment. The purchase price was 70⅛ ($70.125 per share) plus a $625 broker's commission. The entry to record the transaction is:[2]

Apr.	15	Short-Term Investments	70,750.00	
		Cash		70,750.00
		Bought 1,000 shares of Xerox stock at 70⅛ plus $625 broker's commission.		

Notice that the commission is not recorded in a separate account.

When cash dividends are received on stock held as a short-term investment, they are credited to a revenue account as follows:

---

[2] Stock prices are quoted on stock exchanges on the basis of dollars and ⅛ dollars per share. For example, a stock quoted at 23⅛ sold for $23.125 per share and one quoted at 36½ sold for $36.50 per share.

Dec.	12	Cash	1,000.00	
		Dividends Earned		1,000.00
		Received dividend of $1 per share on 1,000 shares of Xerox stock.		

When a company sells a short-term investment, it records the difference between its cost and the cash proceeds from the sale as a gain or loss. For example, assume that on December 20, 1993, Bailey Company sells 500 shares of Xerox for 69¼ per share less a $350 commission. Bailey receives cash proceeds from the sale of $34,275, or [(500 × $69.25) − $350]. Bailey's cost of the sold shares is $35,375, or one half of the $70,750 original cost of the 1,000 shares. The following entry records the sale:

Dec.	20	Cash	34,275.00	
		Loss on Sale of Short-Term Investments	1,100.00	
		Short-Term Investments		35,375.00
		Sold 500 shares of Xerox stock at 69¼ less $350 broker's commission.		

Investments in debt obligations are usually carried in the accounts at cost until they are sold or mature. However, short-term investments in marketable equity securities must be reported on the balance sheet at the **lower of cost or market (LCM)**.[3] To calculate the lower of cost or market, the *total* cost of all marketable equity securities held as short-term investments (called the *portfolio*) is compared with the *total* market value of the portfolio.

For example, assume that Bailey Company did not have any short-term investments prior to its purchase of the Xerox stock on April 15, 1993. Later during 1993, Bailey Company purchased two other short-term investments in marketable equity securities. On December 31, 1993, the lower of cost or market is determined by comparing the total cost and total market value of the entire portfolio, as follows:

Short-Term Investments	Cost	Market	LCM
Johnson & Johnson common stock	$ 42,600	$ 43,500	
Polaroid Corporation common stock	30,500	28,200	
Xerox Corporation common stock	35,375	34,000	
Total	$108,475	$105,700	$105,700

The difference between the $108,475 cost and the $105,700 market value amounts to a $2,775 loss of market value.

Since all of the short-term investments were purchased during 1993, this $2,775 market value decline occurred entirely during 1993. The following adjusting entry on December 31, 1993, records the loss:

[3] FASB, *Accounting Standards—Current Text* (Norwalk, Conn., 1990), sec. I89.102–103. First published as *FASB Statement of Financial Accounting Standards No. 12,* par. 8–9.

1993 Dec.	31	Loss on Market Decline of Short-Term Investments	2,775.00	
		Allowance to Reduce Short-Term Investments to Market		2,775.00
		To record the decline in value of the investments below their original cost.		

The Loss on Market Decline of Short-Term Investments account is closed to Income Summary and is reported on the income statement. The Allowance to Reduce Short-Term Investments to Market account is a contra asset account. Its balance is subtracted from the total cost of the short-term investments so that on the balance sheet they are reported at the lower of cost or market. For example, the Bailey Company would report its short-term investments as follows:

Current assets:	
Cash and cash equivalents	$ xx,xxx
Short-term investments, at lower of cost or market (cost is $108,475) . .	105,700

In this example, notice that the $2,775 loss recorded during 1993 is equal to the December 31, 1993, balance in the allowance account. This occurs because we have assumed that no investments were owned prior to 1993. Therefore, the allowance account had a zero balance on December 31, 1992.

If an additional loss occurs in a future year, the allowance account balance after recording that loss probably will not equal the amount of that loss. To see why this is true, assume that on December 31, 1994, the total cost of Bailey Company's short-term investments portfolio is $108,475 and the total market value is $104,700. In other words, market value is $3,775 less than cost. Because the allowance account already has a credit balance of $2,775 as a result of the adjusting entry made on December 31, 1993, the adjusting entry to record the 1994 loss is:

1994 Dec.	31	Loss on Market Decline of Short-Term Investments	1,000.00	
		Allowance to Reduce Short-Term Investments to Market		1,000.00
		To record the market value decline during 1994.		

Thus, the loss recorded in 1994 is $1,000 and the December 31, 1994, balance in the allowance account is $3,775.

Because short-term investments in marketable equity securities must be reported at the *lower* of cost or market, market value increases above cost are not recorded as gains until the investments are sold. However, if a portfolio of short-term investments has been written down to a market value below cost, later increases in market value up to the original cost are reported on the income statement.

For example, assume that on December 31, 1995, the market value of Bailey Company's short-term investments is $500 less than cost. Since the allowance account had a credit balance of $3,775 at the end of 1994, the December 31, 1995, adjusting entry is:

1995				
Dec.	31	Allowance to Reduce Short-Term Investments to Market .	3,275.00	
		Recovery of Market Value Decline, Short-Term Investments		3,275.00
		To adjust the allowance account from $3,775 to $500.		

Notice that the only entries that change the allowance (contra asset) account balance are the end-of-period adjusting entries. The entries to record purchases and sales of investments during a period do not affect the allowance account.

If cost and market are about the same, a company can just report the investments at cost. For example, the 1990 balance sheet for IBM Corporation shows this information:

Current assets:	
Marketable securities, at cost, which approximates market	$698,000,000

Some people criticize the lower of cost or market method because it is a departure from the *cost principle*. In recent years, however, an increasing number of people have criticized LCM because it does not record all changes in value, including increases above the original cost. In fact, accounting principles may soon require reporting all investments at market value, whether higher or lower than cost. (See the As a Matter of Fact article on page 429.)

In addition to cash, cash equivalents, and short-term investments, the liquid assets of a business include receivables that result from credit sales to customers. In the following sections, we first discuss the procedures to account for sales when customers use credit cards issued by banks or credit card companies. Then, we focus on accounting for credit sales when a business grants credit directly to its customers. This situation requires the company (1) to maintain a separate account receivable for each customer and (2) to account for bad debts that result from credit sales. In addition, we discuss how to account for notes receivable, many of which arise from extending credit to customers.

Credit Card Sales

LO 2 Prepare entries to account for credit card sales.

Many customers use credit cards such as VISA, MasterCard, or American Express to charge purchases from various businesses. This practice gives the customers the ability to make purchases without carrying cash or writing checks. It also allows them to defer their payments to the credit card company. Furthermore, once credit is established with the credit card company, the customer does not have to open an account with each store. Finally,

AS A MATTER OF

Fact

WASHINGTON—The new chief accountant for the Securities and Exchange Commission is stepping up pressure on accounting groups to force banks and thrifts to use more up-to-date figures on their books.

In his first speech since accepting the post last week, Walter Schuetze, who officially becomes chief accountant in two weeks, bluntly said that industry standard-setters have examined the issue long enough. "Some of these issues have been studied enough in the laboratories of academic journals and need to be tested in the crucible of American business," he told the American Institute of Certified Public Accountants.

While Mr. Schuetze, a longtime KPMG Peat Marwick partner, has in the past argued in favor of market-value accounting, his statements added a sense of urgency to the debate by showing the agency's impatience with the rule-making process. This pressure to change is causing banks to worry about the impact on their balance sheets.

* * *

For the past two years, the SEC has prodded the accounting industry to adopt what the agency sees as more relevant accounting standards. In particular, the agency wants to force banks and thrifts to reflect on their books current values of such financial instruments as stocks and bonds, rather than the value of those investments when they were bought. Chairman Breeden calls such historical values "once upon a time" accounting rules that don't reflect changes in the markets.

Under federal law, the SEC has authority over accounting rules but cedes day-to-day responsibility for the standards to such industry groups as the Financial Accounting Standards Board. Last month, after months of study and pressure from the SEC, the FASB issued a statement requiring all companies to disclose in footnotes to their balance sheets the fair market value of all financial instruments.

But the mandate, which goes into effect for the 1992 reports, didn't go as far as the SEC wanted, as it doesn't change the balance sheets themselves. Balance-sheet changes would be far more pertinent for the vast majority of investors, who often overlook the footnotes, the SEC argues.

While praising the FASB's action, Mr. Schuetze indicated he doesn't feel the guideline is enough. "I eagerly look forward to other uses of fair-value accounting," he told the accountants group.

The SEC's push on the subject is spooking banks, which have complained that the move would be too costly, too time-consuming and too confusing to investors. Bankers also have said they can't get an accurate reading of the loans that make up about 60% of their balance-sheet assets. The FASB received 204 comment letters on the issue, about three-quarters of which opposed market-value accounting.

* * *

Current-value accounting "is woefully bad because of the inexactness of the presented numbers," said Bob Muth, president and chief executive officer of Andover Bank in Andover, Ohio, and chairman of the Independent Bankers Association of America's Bank Operations Committee. Small banks, which often lend to small businesses, would have an especially tough time valuing loans, he added.

"With historical-cost accounting, you at least have solid numbers," Mr. Muth said. If banks are forced to use only current values, "it would depend on which CPA you use. The numbers would be so inexact as to be incomparable."

Source: Kevin G. Salwen, "SEC Renews Call for Pressure on Banks and S&Ls to Update Accounting Rules," *The Wall Street Journal,* January 8, 1992, p. A3. Reprinted by permission of *The Wall Street Journal,*

customers who use credit cards can make single monthly payments instead of several to different creditors.

There are good reasons why businesses allow customers to use credit cards instead of maintaining their own accounts receivable. First, the business does not have to evaluate the credit standing of each customer or make decisions about who should get credit and how much. Second, the business avoids the risk of extending credit to customers who cannot or do not pay. Instead, this risk is faced by the credit card company. Third, the business typically receives cash from the credit card company sooner than it would if it granted credit directly to its customers.

In dealing with some credit cards, usually those issued by banks, the business deposits a copy of each credit card sales receipt in its bank account just like it deposits a customer's check. Thus, the business receives a credit to its checking account immediately on deposit. With other credit cards, the business sends the appropriate copy of each receipt to the credit card company and is paid shortly thereafter. Until payment is received, the business has an account receivable from the credit card company. In return for the services provided by the credit card company, a business will pay a fee ranging from 2% to 5% of credit card sales. This charge is deducted from the credit to the checking account or the cash payment to the business.

The procedures used in accounting for credit card sales depend on whether cash is received immediately on deposit or is delayed until paid by the credit card company. If cash is received immediately, the entry to record $100 of credit card sales with a 4% fee would be:

Jan.	25	Cash	96.00	
		Credit Card Expense	4.00	
		Sales		100.00
		To record credit card sales less a 4% credit card expense.		

If the business must send the receipts to the credit card company and wait for payment, this entry on the date of the sale records them:

Jan.	25	Accounts Receivable, Credit Card Company	100.00	
		Sales		100.00
		To record credit card sales.		

When cash is received from the credit card company, the entry to record the receipt and the deduction of the fee is:

Feb.	10	Cash	96.00	
		Credit Card Expense	4.00	
		Accounts Receivable, Credit Card Company		100.00
		To record cash receipt less 4% credit card expense.		

In the last two entries, notice that the credit card expense was not recorded until cash was received from the credit card company. This practice is used merely as a matter of convenience. By following this procedure, the business avoids having to calculate and record the credit card expense each time sales are recorded. Instead, the expense related to many sales can be calculated once and recorded when cash is received. However, the *matching principle* requires reporting credit card expense in the same period as the sale. Therefore, if the sale and the cash receipt occur in different periods, you must accrue and report the credit card expense in the period of the sale by using an adjusting entry at the end of the year. For example, this year-end adjustment accrues $24 of credit card expense on a $600 receivable that the Credit Card Company has not yet paid.

Dec.	31	Credit Card Expense	24.00	
		Accounts Receivable, Credit Card Company.		24.00
		To accrue credit card expense that is unrecorded at the end of the year.		

Then, when the account is collected in January, the following entry is made:

Jan.	5	Cash	576.00	
		Accounts Receivable, Credit Card Company.		576.00
		To record collection of the amount due from Credit Card Company.		

Some firms report credit card expense in the income statement as a type of discount that is deducted from sales to get net sales. Other companies classify it as a selling expense or even as an administrative expense. Arguments can be made for all three alternatives but there is little practical difference in the result.

Maintaining a Separate Account for Each Customer

LO 3 Prepare entries to account for transactions with credit customers, including accounting for bad debts under the allowance method and the direct write-off method.

In previous chapters, we recorded credit sales by debiting a single Accounts Receivable account. However, a business with more than one credit customer must design its accounting system to show how much each customer has purchased, how much each customer has paid, and how much remains to be collected from each customer. This information provides the basis for sending bills to the customers. To have this information on hand, businesses that extend credit directly to their customers must maintain a separate account receivable for each of them.

One possible way of keeping a separate account for each customer would be to include all of these accounts in the same ledger that contains the financial statement accounts. However, this approach is usually not used because there are too many customers. Instead, the **General Ledger**, which is the ledger that contains the financial statement accounts, has only a single Accounts Receivable account. In addition, a supplementary record is established in which a separate account is maintained for each customer. This supplementary record is the **Accounts Receivable Ledger.**

Illustration 8–1 shows the relationship between the Accounts Receivable account in the General Ledger and the individual customer accounts in the Accounts Receivable Ledger. In Part A of Illustration 8–1, notice that the $3,000 sum of the three balances in the Accounts Receivable Ledger is equal to the balance of the Accounts Receivable account in the General Ledger as of February 1. To maintain this relationship, each time that credit sales are posted with a debit to the Accounts Receivable account in the General Ledger, they are also posted with debits to the appropriate customer accounts in the Accounts Receivable Ledger. Also, cash receipts from credit customers must be posted with credits to both the Accounts Receivable account in the General Ledger and to the appropriate customer accounts.

Part B shows the general journal entry that would be made to record two credit sales on February 5 and February 14 to customers V. F. Zeller and Karen Johnson. It also shows the entry to record the collection of $720 from James Harrison.

Part C presents the general ledger account and the Accounts Receivable Ledger as of February 28. Notice how the General Ledger account shows the effects of the sales and the collection, and that it has a $5,030 balance. The same events are reflected in the accounts for the three customers: Harrison now has a balance of only $280, Johnson owes $2,950, and Zeller has a balance of $1,800. The $5,030 sum of their accounts equals the debit balance of the General Ledger account.

Note that posting debits or credits to Accounts Receivable twice does not violate the requirement that debits equal credits. The equality of debits and credits is maintained *in the General Ledger*. The Accounts Receivable Ledger is simply a supplementary record that provides detailed information concerning each customer.

Because the balance in the Accounts Receivable account is always equal to the sum of the balances in the customers' accounts, the Accounts Receivable account is said to control the Accounts Receivable Ledger and is an example of a **controlling account.** Also, the Accounts Receivable Ledger is an example of a supplementary record that is controlled by an account in the General Ledger; this kind of supplementary record is called a **subsidiary ledger.**

The Accounts Receivable account and the Accounts Receivable Ledger are not the only examples of controlling accounts and subsidiary ledgers. Most companies buy on credit from several suppliers and must use a controlling account and subsidiary ledger for accounts payable. Another example might be an Office Equipment account that would control a subsidiary ledger in which the cost of each item of equipment is recorded in a separate account.

Bad Debts

When a company grants credit to its customers, there usually are a few who do not pay what they promised. The accounts of such customers are called **bad debts.** These bad debt amounts that cannot be collected are an expense of selling on credit.

ILLUSTRATION 8–1

The Accounts Receivable Account and the Accounts Receivable Ledger

Part A—Beginning situation: February 1

GENERAL LEDGER

Accounts Receivable

Balance	3,000	

PROOF

$1,000
2,000
0
$3,000

ACCOUNTS RECEIVABLE LEDGER

James Harrison

Balance	1,000	

Karen Johnson

Balance	2,000	

V. F. Zeller

Balance	0	

Part B—Entries to record $1,800 sale to V. F. Zeller and $950 sale to Karen Johnson, and $720 collection from James Harrison

GENERAL JOURNAL

Feb.	5	Accounts Receivable—V. F. Zeller	1,800.00	
		Sales		1,800.00
	14	Accounts Receivable—Karen Johnson	950.00	
		Sales		950.00
	23	Cash	720.00	
		Accounts Receivable—James Harrison		720.00

Part C—Ending situation: February 28

GENERAL LEDGER

Accounts Receivable

Balance	3,000	
	1,800	
	950	
		720
Balance	5,030	

PROOF

$ 280
2,950
1,800
$5,030

ACCOUNTS RECEIVABLE LEDGER

James Harrison

Balance	1,000	
		720
Balance	280	

Karen Johnson

Balance	2,000	
	950	
Balance	2,950	

V. F. Zeller

Balance	1,800	

You might ask why merchants sell on credit if it is likely that some of the accounts will prove to be uncollectible. The answer is that they believe granting credit increases revenues and profits. They are willing to take a reasonable loss from bad debts if the results are greater sales and profits than would have been achieved if all customers had to pay cash. Therefore, bad debt losses are an expense of selling on credit that is incurred to increase sales.

The reporting of bad debts expense on the income statement is governed by the *matching principle*. This principle requires that the expense from bad debts be reported in the same accounting period as the revenues they helped produce.

Matching Bad Debt Expenses with Sales

When credit sales are made, management usually realizes that some portion of those sales will result in bad debts. However, the fact that a specific credit sale will not be collected does not become apparent until later. If a customer fails to pay within the credit period, most businesses send out several repeat billings and make other efforts to collect. Usually, they do not accept the fact that a customer is not going to pay until every reasonable means of collection has been exhausted. In many cases, this point may not be reached until one or more accounting periods after the period in which the sale was made. Thus, matching this expense with the revenue it produced requires the company to estimate its unknown amount at the end of the year. The **allowance method of accounting for bad debts** is used to accomplish this matching of bad debts expense with revenues.

Allowance Method of Accounting for Bad Debts

At the end of each accounting period, the allowance method of accounting for bad debts requires estimating the total bad debts expected to result from the period's sales. An allowance is then provided for the loss. This method has two advantages: (1) the estimated expense is charged to the period in which the revenue is recognized; and (2) the accounts receivable are reported on the balance sheet at the amount of cash proceeds that is expected from their collection.

Recording the Estimated Bad Debts Expense

Under the allowance method of accounting for bad debts, you calculate the estimated bad debts expense at the end of each accounting period. Then, you enter it as an adjustment on the work sheet and record it with an adjusting journal entry. For example, assume that Fritz Company had credit sales of $300,000 during the first year of its operations. At the end of the year, $20,000 remains uncollected in accounts receivable. Based on the experience of similar businesses, Fritz Company estimates that $1,500 of accounts receivable will be uncollectible. This estimated expense is recorded with the following adjusting entry:

Dec.	31	Bad Debts Expense . . . . Allowance for Doubtful Accounts . . . . *To record the estimated bad debts.*	1,500.00	 1,500.00

The debit part of this entry causes the estimated bad debts expense to appear on the income statement of the year in which the sales were made. As a result, the estimated $1,500 expense of selling on credit is matched with the $300,000 of revenue it helped produce.

Note that the credit of the entry is to a contra account called the **Allowance for Doubtful Accounts.** A contra account must be used because at the time of the adjusting entry, you do not know for certain which customers will not pay. In fact, you will not know exactly which customers will not pay until every means of collection is exhausted. Therefore, because specific bad accounts are not identifiable at the time of the adjusting entry, they cannot be removed from the subsidiary Accounts Receivable Ledger. Because the customer accounts are left in the subsidiary ledger, the controlling account for Accounts Receivable cannot be reduced. Instead, the Allowance for Doubtful Accounts account *must* be credited.

Observe that if the controlling account had been credited directly, its balance would be less than the sum of the balances in the subsidiary ledger. This result would not be consistent with the purpose served by the subsidiary ledger system.

Bad Debts in the Accounts and in the Financial Statements

The process of evaluating customers and approving them for credit usually is not assigned to the selling department of a business. Otherwise, given the primary objective of increasing sales, the selling department might not use good judgment in approving customers for credit. Because the sales department is not responsible for granting credit, it should not be held responsible for bad debts expense. Therefore, bad debts expense normally appears on the income statement as an administrative expense rather than a selling expense.

Recall from the previous example that Fritz Company has $20,000 of outstanding accounts receivable at the end of its first year of operations. Thus, after the bad debts adjusting entry is posted, the company's Accounts Receivable and Allowance for Doubtful Accounts accounts show these balances:

Accounts Receivable			
Dec. 31	20,000		

Allowance for Doubtful Accounts			
		Dec. 31	1,500

The Allowance for Doubtful Accounts credit balance of $1,500 has the effect of reducing accounts receivable (net of the allowance) to their estimated **realizable value.** This term *realizable value* means the expected proceeds from converting the assets into cash. Although $20,000 is legally owed to Fritz Company by all of its customers, only $18,500 is likely to be realized in cash collections from customers.

When the balance sheet is prepared, the allowance for doubtful accounts is subtracted from the accounts receivable to show the amount that is expected to be realized from the accounts. For example, this information could be reported as follows:

Current assets:		
Cash and cash equivalents		$11,300
Short-term investments, at lower of cost or market (cost is $16,200)		14,500
Accounts receivable	$20,000	
Less allowance for doubtful accounts	(1,500)	18,500
Merchandise inventory		52,700
Prepaid expenses		1,100
Total current assets		$98,100

In this example, compare the presentations of short-term investments and accounts receivable, and note that contra accounts are subtracted in both cases. Even though the contra account to the Short-Term Investments account is not shown on the statement, you can easily determine that its balance is $1,700 by comparing the $16,200 cost with the $14,500 net amount. Sometimes, the contra account to Accounts Receivable is presented in a similar fashion, as follows:

Accounts receivable (net of $1,500 estimated uncollectible accounts)	$18,500

Writing Off a Bad Debt

When specific accounts are identified as uncollectible, they are written off against the Allowance for Doubtful Accounts. For example, after spending a year trying to collect from Jack Vale, the Fritz Company finally decided that his $100 account was uncollectible and made the following entry to write it off:

Jan.	23	Allowance for Doubtful Accounts.	100.00	
		Accounts Receivable—Jack Vale		100.00
		To write off an uncollectible account.		

Posting the credit of the entry to the Accounts Receivable account removes the amount of the bad debt from the controlling account. Posting it to the Jack Vale account removes the amount of the bad debt from the subsidiary ledger. And, removing it from the subsidiary ledger ensures that Fritz Company will no longer send bills to Vale. After the entry is posted, the general ledger accounts appear as follows:

Accounts Receivable

Dec. 31	20,000		
		Jan. 23	100

Allowance for Doubtful Accounts

		Dec. 31	1,500
Jan. 23	100		

Notice two aspects of the entry and the accounts. First, although bad debts are an expense of selling on credit, the allowance account is debited in the write-off. The expense account is *not* debited. The expense account is not debited because the estimated expense was previously recorded at the end of the period in which the sale occurred. At that time, the expense was estimated and recorded with an adjusting entry.

Second, although the write-off removed the amount of the account receivable from the ledgers, it did not affect the estimated realizable value of Fritz Company's net accounts receivable, as the following tabulation shows:

	Before	After
Accounts receivable	$20,000	$19,900
Less allowance for doubtful accounts . . .	1,500	1,400
Estimated realizable accounts receivable . .	$18,500	$18,500

Thus, neither total assets nor net income are affected by the decision to write off a specific account. However, both total assets and net income are affected by the recognition of the year's bad debts expense in the adjusting entry. Again, a primary purpose of writing off a specific account is to avoid the cost of additional collection efforts.

Bad Debt Recoveries

When a customer fails to pay and the account is written off, his or her credit standing is jeopardized. Therefore, the customer may choose to voluntarily pay all or part of the amount owed after the account is written off as uncollectible. This payment helps restore the credit standing. Thus, when this event happens, it should be recorded in the customer's subsidiary account where the information will be retained for use in future credit evaluations.

When a company collects an account that was previously written off, it makes two journal entries. The first reverses the original write-off and has the effect of reinstating the customer's account. The second entry merely records the collection of the reinstated account. For example, assume that on August 15 Jack Vale pays in full the account that Fritz Company had previously written off. The entries to record the bad debt recovery are

Aug.	15	Accounts Receivable—Jack Vale	100.00	
		Allowance for Doubtful Accounts		100.00
		To reinstate the account of Jack Vale written off on January 23.		
	15	Cash	100.00	
		Accounts Receivable—Jack Vale		100.00
		Received full payment of account.		

In this case, Jack Vale paid the entire amount previously written off. In other situations, the customer may pay only a portion of the amount owed. The question then arises of whether the entire balance of the account should be returned to accounts receivable or just the amount paid. The answer is a matter of judgment. If you believe the customer will later pay in full, the entire amount owed should be returned. However, only the amount paid should be returned if you believe that no more will be collected.

Estimating the Amount of Bad Debts Expense

As you already learned, the allowance method of accounting for bad debts requires an adjusting entry at the end of each accounting period to record management's estimate of the bad debts expense for the period. That entry takes the following form:

Dec.	31	Bad Debts Expense	????	
		Allowance for Doubtful Accounts		????
		To record the estimated bad debts.		

What process does a business use to predict the amount to record in this entry? There are actually two broad alternatives. One focuses on the income statement relationship between bad debts expense and sales. The other focuses on the balance sheet relationship between accounts receivable and the allowance for doubtful accounts. Both alternatives require a careful analysis of past experience.

Estimating Bad Debts by Focusing on the Income Statement

The income statement approach to estimating bad debts is based on the idea that some particular percentage of a company's credit sales for the period will become uncollectible.[4] Hence, in the income statement, the amount of bad debts expense should equal that amount.

For example, suppose that Baker Company had credit sales of $400,000 in 1993. Based on past experience and the experience of similar companies, Baker Company estimates that 0.6% of credit sales will be uncollectible. Using this prediction, Baker Company can expect $2,400 of bad debts expense to result from the year's sales ($400,000 × 0.006 = $2,400). The adjusting entry to record this estimated expense is:

Dec.	31	Bad Debts Expense	2,400.00	
		Allowance for Doubtful Accounts		2,400.00
		To record the estimated bad debts.		

This entry does not mean the December 31, 1993, balance in Allowance for Doubtful Accounts will be $2,400. A $2,400 balance would occur only if the

[4] Note that the factor to be considered is *credit* sales. Naturally, cash sales do not produce bad debts, and they generally should not be used in the calculation. However, if cash sales are relatively small compared to credit sales, there will be no practical difference in the result.

account had a zero balance immediately prior to posting the adjusting entry. For several reasons, however, the unadjusted balance of Allowance for Doubtful Accounts is not likely to be zero.

First, unless the Baker Company was created during the current year, the Allowance for Doubtful Accounts would have had a credit balance at the beginning of the year. The beginning-of-year credit balance would have resulted from entries made in past years to record estimated bad debts expense and to write off uncollectible accounts. The cumulative effect of these entries would show up as a credit balance at the beginning of the current year.

Second, because bad debts expense must be estimated each year, the total amount of expense recorded in past years is not likely to equal the amounts that were written off as uncollectible. Although annual expense estimates are based on past experience, some residual difference between recorded expenses and amounts written off should be expected to show up in the unadjusted Allowance for Doubtful Accounts balance.

Third, some of the amounts written off as uncollectible during the current year probably relate to credit sales made during the current year. These debits affect the unadjusted Allowance for Doubtful Accounts balance. In fact, they may cause the account to have a debit balance prior to posting the adjusting entry for bad debts expense.

For these reasons, you should not expect the Allowance for Doubtful Accounts to have an unadjusted balance of zero at the end of the year. As we stated earlier, this means that the adjusted balance reported on the balance sheet normally will not equal the amount of expense reported on the income statement.

Remember that expressing bad debts expense as a percentage of sales is an estimate based on past experience. As new experience is gained over time, the percentage used may appear to have been too large or too small. When this happens, a different rate should be used in future periods.

Estimating Bad Debts by Focusing on the Balance Sheet

The balance sheet approach to estimating bad debts is based on the idea that information about the realizable value of accounts receivable is useful to investors, creditors, and managers. From this point of view, the goal of the bad debts adjusting entry is to make the Allowance for Doubtful Accounts balance equal to the portion of outstanding accounts receivable estimated to be uncollectible. To obtain this required balance in the Allowance for Doubtful Accounts account, simply compare its balance before the adjustment with the required balance. The difference between the two is debited to Bad Debts Expense and credited to Allowance for Doubtful Accounts. Estimating the required balance of the Allowance account can be done in two ways: (1) by the simplified approach and (2) by aging the accounts receivable.

The Simplified Balance Sheet Approach. Using the simplified balance sheet approach, a company estimates that a certain percentage of its outstanding receivables will prove to be uncollectible. This estimated percentage is based on past experience and the experience of similar companies. It also may include taking into consideration current conditions such as recent prosperity or economic difficulties faced by the firm's customers. Then, the total dollar amount of all outstanding receivables is multiplied by the estimated percentage to determine the estimated dollar amount of uncollectible accounts. This amount must appear in the balance sheet as the balance of the Allowance for Doubtful Accounts. To put this balance in the account, you must prepare an adjusting entry that debits Bad Debts Expense and credits Allowance for Doubtful Accounts. The amount of the adjustment is the amount necessary to provide the required balance in Allowance for Doubtful Accounts.

For example, assume that Baker Company (of the previous illustration) has $50,000 of outstanding accounts receivable on December 31, 1993. Past experience suggests that 5% of the outstanding receivables are uncollectible. Thus, after the adjusting entry is posted, the Allowance for Doubtful Accounts should have a $2,500 credit balance (5% of $50,000). Assume that the account appears as follows before any adjustment:

Allowance for Doubtful Accounts

		Dec. 31, 1992, balance	2,000
Feb. 6	800		
July 10	600		
Nov. 20	400		
		Unadjusted balance	200

The $2,000 beginning balance appeared on the December 31, 1992, balance sheet. During 1993, accounts of specific customers were written off on February 6, July 10, and November 20. As a result, the account has a $200 credit balance prior to the December 31, 1993, adjustment. The adjusting entry to give the Allowance the required $2,500 balance is

Dec.	31	Bad Debts Expense	2,300.00	
		Allowance for Doubtful Accounts		2,300.00
		To record the estimated bad debts.		

After this entry is posted, the Allowance has a $2,500 credit balance, as shown here:

Allowance for Doubtful Accounts

		Dec. 31, 1992, balance	2,000
Feb. 6	800		
July 10	600		
Nov. 20	400		
		Unadjusted balance	200
		Dec. 31	2,300
		Dec. 31, 1993, balance	2,500

Aging Accounts Receivable. Both the income statement approach and the simplified balance sheet approach use knowledge gained from past experience to estimate the amount of bad debts expense. Another balance sheet centered method produces a more refined estimate based on information about current conditions.

ILLUSTRATION 8–2

Estimating Bad Debts by Aging the Accounts

BAKER COMPANY
Schedule of Accounts Receivable by Age
December 31, 1993

Customer's Name	Total	Not Due	1 to 30 Days Past Due	31 to 60 Days Past Due	61 to 90 Days Past Due	Over 90 Days Past Due
Charles Abbot	$ 450.00	$ 450.00				
Frank Allen	710.00			$ 710.00		
George Arden	500.00	300.00	$ 200.00			
Paul Baum	740.00				$ 100.00	$ 640.00
ZZ Services	1,000.00	810.00	190.00			
Totals	$49,900.00	$37,000.00	$6,500.00	$3,500.00	$1,900.00	$1,000.00
Rate		×2%	×5%	×10%	×25%	×40%
Estimated uncollectible accounts	$ 2,290.00	$ 740.00	$ 325.00	$ 350.00	$ 475.00	$ 400.00

This method involves **aging of accounts receivable.** Under this method, each account receivable is examined in the process of estimating the amount that is uncollectible. Specifically, the receivables are classified in terms of how long they have been outstanding. Then, estimates of uncollectible amounts are made under the assumption that the longer an amount is outstanding, the more likely it will be uncollectible.

To age the accounts receivable outstanding at the end of the period, you must examine each account and classify the outstanding amounts in terms of how much time has passed since they were created. The selection of the classes to be used depends on the judgment of each company's management. It is typical, however, for them to be based on 30-day (or one month) periods. After the outstanding amounts have been classified (or aged), past experience is used to estimate a percentage of each class that will become uncollectible. These percentages are applied to the amounts in the classes to determine the required balance of the Allowance for Doubtful Accounts. The calculation is completed by setting up a schedule like the one in Illustration 8–2 for Baker Company.

In Illustration 8–2, notice that each customer's account is listed with its total balance. Then, each balance is allocated to five categories based on the age of the unpaid charges that make up the balance. (In computerized systems, this allocation is done automatically.) When all accounts have been aged, the amounts in each category are totaled and multiplied by the estimated percentage of uncollectible accounts for each category.

For example, Illustration 8–2 shows that Baker Company is owed $3,500 that is 31 to 60 days past due. Baker's management estimates that 10% of the amounts in this age category will not be collected. Thus, the dollar amount of uncollectible accounts in this category is \$350 (\$3,500 × 10%). The total in the first column tells us that the adjusted balance in Baker Company's Allowance for Doubtful Accounts should be \$2,290 (\$740 + \$325 + \$350 + \$475 + \$400). Because the Allowance has an unadjusted credit balance of \$200, the aging of accounts receivable approach requires the following change in its balance:

Unadjusted balance.	\$ 200 credit
Required balance	2,290 credit
Required adjustment	\$2,090 credit

As a result, Baker should record the following adjusting entry:

Dec.	31	Bad Debts Expense	2,090.00	
		Allowance for Doubtful Accounts		2,090.00
		To record the estimated bad debts.		

For instructional purposes, suppose that Baker's Allowance had an unadjusted *debit* balance of \$500. In this case, the calculation of the adjustment amount and the entry would be:

Unadjusted balance.	\$ 500 debit
Required balance	2,290 credit
Required adjustment	\$2,790 credit

Dec.	31	Bad Debts Expense	2,790.00	
		Allowance for Doubtful Accounts		2,790.00
		To record the estimated bad debts.		

Recall from page 438 that when the income statement approach was used, Baker's bad debts expense for 1993 was estimated to be \$2,400. When the simplified balance sheet approach was used (see page 440), the estimate was \$2,300. And when aging of accounts receivable was used the first time, the estimate was \$2,090. Do not be surprised that the amounts are different; after all, each approach is only an estimate of what will prove to be true. However, the aging of accounts receivable is based on a more detailed examination of specific outstanding accounts and is usually the most reliable.[5]

[5] In many cases, the aging analysis is supplemented with information about specific customers that allows management to decide whether those accounts should be classified as uncollectible. This information often is supplied by the sales and credit department managers.

Direct Write-Off Method of Accounting for Bad Debts

The allowance method of accounting for bad debts is designed to satisfy the requirements of the *matching principle*. Therefore, it is the method that should be used in most cases. However, another method may be suitable under certain limited circumstances. Under this method, the **direct write-off method of accounting for bad debts**, no attempt is made to estimate uncollectible accounts or bad debts expense at the end of each period. In fact, no adjusting entry is made. Instead, when you decide an account is uncollectible, you write it off directly to Bad Debts Expense with an entry such as this one, which removes a receivable with a $52 balance:

Nov.	23	Bad Debts Expense	52.00	
		Accounts Receivable—Dale Hall		52.00
		To write off the uncollectible account under the direct write-off method.		

The debit of the entry charges the uncollectible amount directly to the current year's Bad Debts Expense account. The credit removes the balance of the account from the subsidiary ledger and from the controlling account.

If an account previously written off directly to Bad Debts Expense is later collected in full, the following entries record the recovery:

Mar.	11	Accounts Receivable—Dale Hall	52.00	
		Bad Debts Expense		52.00
		To reinstate the account of Dale Hall previously written off.		
	11	Cash	52.00	
		Accounts Receivable—Dale Hall		52.00
		In full payment of account.		

Sometimes an amount previously written off directly to Bad Debts Expense is recovered in the year following the write-off. If there is no balance in the Bad Debts Expense account from previous write-offs and no other write-offs are expected, the credit portion of the entry recording the recovery can be made to a Bad Debt Recoveries revenue account.

As discussed next, the direct write-off method should be used only in limited situations.

Direct Write-Off Mismatches Revenues and Expenses

The direct write-off method usually mismatches revenues and expenses. The mismatch occurs because bad debts expense is not recorded until an account becomes uncollectible, which often does not occur during the same period as the credit sale. Despite this weakness, the direct write-off method may be used when a company's bad debts expenses are very small in relation to other financial statement items such as total sales and net income. In such cases, the direct write-off method is justified by the materiality principle, which is explained next.

The Materiality Principle

The basic idea of the **materiality principle** is that the requirements of accounting principles may be ignored if the effect on the financial statements is unimportant to their users. In other words, failure to follow the requirements of an accounting principle is acceptable when the failure does not produce an error or misstatement large enough to influence a financial statement reader's judgment of a given situation.

Installment Accounts and Notes Receivable

Many companies allow their credit customers to make periodic payments over several months. When this is done, the selling company's assets may be in the form of **installment accounts receivable** or notes receivable. As is true for other accounts receivable, the evidence behind installment accounts receivable includes sales slips or invoices that describe the sales transactions. A note receivable, on the other hand, is a written document that promises payment and is signed by the customer. In either case, when payments will be made over several months or if the credit period is long, the customer is usually charged interest. Although the credit period of installment accounts and notes receivable is often more than one year, they should be classified as current assets if the company regularly offers customers such terms.

Generally, creditors prefer notes receivable over accounts receivable when the credit period is long and the receivable relates to a single sale for a fairly large amount. Notes are also used to replace accounts receivable when customers ask for additional time to pay their past-due accounts. In these situations, creditors prefer notes to accounts receivable because the notes can be more easily converted into cash before becoming due by discounting (or selling) them to a bank. (However, accounts receivable also may be sold at a discount.) Notes are also preferred for legal reasons. If a lawsuit is needed to collect from a customer, a note represents a clear written acknowledgment by the debtor of the debt, its amount, and its terms.

Promissory Notes

LO 4 Calculate the interest on promissory notes and prepare entries to record the receipt of promissory notes and their payment or dishonor.

A **promissory note** is an unconditional written promise to pay a definite sum of money on demand or at a fixed or determinable future date. In the promissory note shown in Illustration 8–3, Hugo Brown promises to pay Frank Tomlinson or to his order (that is, according to Tomlinson's instructions) a definite sum of money ($1,000), called the **principal of the note**, at a fixed future date (April 8, 1993). As the one who signed the note and promised to pay it at maturity, Hugo Brown is the **maker of the note.** As the person to whom the note is payable, Frank Tomlinson is the **payee of the note.** To Hugo Brown, the illustrated note is a liability called a *note payable*. To Frank Tomlinson, the same note is an asset called a *note receivable*.

The Hugo Brown note bears **interest** at 12%. Interest is the charge assessed for the use of money. To a borrower, interest is an expense. To a lender, it is a revenue. The rate of interest that a note bears is stated on the note. (In Chapter 12, we discuss notes with no stated interest rate that are called *noninterest-bearing notes*.)

ILLUSTRATION 8-3

A Promissory Note

$1,000.00 *Eugene, Oregon* *March 9, 1993*

Thirty days after date *I* promise to pay to

the order of *Frank Tomlinson*

One thousand and no / 100 -- dollars

for value received with interest at *12%*

payable at *First National Bank of Eugene, Oregon*

Hugo Brown

Calculating Interest

Unless otherwise stated, the rate of interest on a note is the rate charged for the use of the principal for one year. The formula for calculating interest is

$$\text{Principal of the note} \times \text{Annual rate of interest} \times \text{Time of the note expressed in years} = \text{Interest}$$

For example, interest on a $1,000, 12%, six-month note is calculated as:

$$\$1{,}000 \times 12\% \times \frac{6}{12} = \$60$$

The **maturity date of a note** is the day on which the note (principal and interest) must be repaid. Many notes mature in less than a full year, and the period covered by them is often expressed in days. When the time of a note is expressed in days, the maturity date is the specified number of days after the day the note is dated. As a simple example, a one-day note dated June 15 matures and is due on June 16. Also, a 90-day note dated July 10 matures on October 8. This October 8 due date is calculated as follows:

Number of days in July	31
Minus the date of the note	10
Gives the number of days the note runs in July	21
Add the number of days in August	31
Add the number of days in September	30
Total through September 30	82
Days in October needed to equal the 90-day time of the note, also the maturity date of the note—October	8
Total time the note runs in days	90

In other situations, the period of a note is expressed in months. In these cases, the note matures and is payable in the month of its maturity on the same day of the month as its original date. For example, a three-month note dated July 10 is payable on October 10.

To simplify interest calculations for notes that have periods expressed in days, a common practice has been to treat a year as having just 360 days. Although this practice is not applied as frequently as it used to be, we use it in this book to make it easier for you to work the exercises and problems assigned by your instructor. We also assume a 360-day year in the following discussion. Suppose, for example, that there is a 90-day, 12%, $1,000 note. The amount of interest is calculated as follows:

$$\text{Interest} = \text{Principal} \times \text{Rate} \times \frac{\text{Exact days}}{360}$$

or

$$\text{Interest} = \$1{,}000 \times 12\% \times \frac{90}{360} = \$30$$

Recording the Receipt of a Note

To simplify record-keeping, notes receivable are usually recorded in a single Notes Receivable account. When a balance column account is used, each note may be identified by writing the name of the maker in the Explanation column on the line of the entry to record its receipt or payment. Only one account is needed because the individual original notes are on hand. Therefore, the maker, rate of interest, due date, and other information may be learned by examining each note.[6]

When a company receives a note at the time of a sale, an entry such as this one is recorded:

Dec.	5	Notes Receivable	650.00	
		Sales		650.00
		Sold merchandise, terms six-month, 9% note.		

A business also may accept a note from an overdue customer as a way of granting a time extension on the past-due account receivable. When this happens, the business usually collects part of the past-due balance in cash. This partial payment forces a concession from the customer, reduces the customer's debt (and the seller's risk), and produces a note for a smaller amount. For example, Symplex Company agrees to accept $232 in cash and a $600, 60-day, 15% note from Joseph Cook to settle his $832 past-due account. When Symplex receives the cash and note, the following entry is made:

[6] If the company holds a large number of notes, it may be more efficient to set up a controlling account and a subsidiary ledger.

Oct.	5	Cash	232.00	
		Notes Receivable	600.00	
		Accounts Receivable—Joseph Cook		832.00
		Received cash and a note in settlement of an account.		

When Cook pays the note on the due date, this entry records the receipt:

Dec.	4	Cash	615.00	
		Notes Receivable		600.00
		Interest Earned		15.00
		Collected the Joseph Cook note.		

The \$15.00 of interest is computed as \$600 × 15% × 60/360.

Dishonored Notes Receivable

Occasionally, the maker of a note either cannot or will not pay the note at maturity. When a note's maker is unable or refuses to pay at maturity, the note is said to be dishonored. This act of **dishonoring a note** does not relieve the maker of the obligation to pay. Furthermore, the payee should use every legitimate means to collect. However, collection may require lengthy legal proceedings.

The usual practice is to have the balance of the Notes Receivable account show only the amount of notes that have not matured. Therefore, when a note is dishonored, you should remove the amount of the note from the Notes Receivable account and charge it back to an account receivable from its maker. To illustrate, Symplex Company holds an \$800, 12%, 60-day note of George Hart. At maturity, Hart dishonors the note. To remove the dishonored note from the Notes Receivable account, the company makes the following entry:

Oct.	14	Accounts Receivable—George Hart	816.00	
		Interest Earned		16.00
		Notes Receivable		800.00
		To charge the account of George Hart for his dishonored note.		

The \$16.00 of interest is computed as \$800 × 12% × 60/360.

Charging a dishonored note back to the account of its maker serves two purposes. First, it removes the amount of the note from the Notes Receivable account, leaving in the account only notes that have not matured. It also records the dishonored note in the maker's account. The second purpose is important. If the maker of the dishonored note again applies for credit in the future, his or her account will show all past dealings, including the dishonored note. Restoring the account also reminds the business to continue collection efforts.

Note that Hart owes both the principal and the interest. Therefore, the entry records the full amount owed in Hart's account and credits the interest to Interest Earned. This procedure assures that the interest will be included in future efforts to collect from Hart.

Discounting Notes Receivable

LO 5 Calculate the discount and proceeds on discounted notes receivable and prepare entries to record the discounting of notes receivable and their dishonoring, if necessary.

As previously stated, a note receivable often is preferred to an account receivable. One reason is that a note may be more easily converted into cash before the due date. This conversion might be done for a number of reasons; perhaps the most common is to allow the holder to avoid having to borrow money by signing its own note. One frequently used way of obtaining cash early is by **discounting the note receivable.** In essence, this step involves selling the note to a bank or to some other buyer. When a note receivable is discounted, the owner endorses and delivers the note to the bank in exchange for cash. The bank holds the note to maturity and then collects its maturity value from the original maker.

To illustrate, assume that on May 28, Symplex Company received a $1,200, 60-day, 12% note dated May 27 from John Owen. It held the note until June 2 and then discounted it at the bank at 14%. Since the maturity date of this note is July 26, the bank must wait 54 days after discounting the note to collect from Owen. These 54 days are called the **discount period,** which is the number of days between the date on which a note is discounted at the bank and its maturity date. The discount period is calculated for this note as follows:

Original period of the note in days		60
Less time held by Symplex Company:		
Number of days in May	31	
Less the date of the note	27	
Days held in May	4	
Days held in June	2	
Total days held by Symplex		6
Discount period in days		54

At the end of the discount period, the bank expects to collect the maturity value of this note from Owen. The **maturity value of a note** is its principal plus any interest due on its maturity date. The maturity value of the Owen note is

Principal of the note	$1,200
Interest on $1,200 for 60 days at 12%	24
Maturity value	$1,224

In calculating the interest or discount to be charged, banks traditionally base their discount on the maturity value of the note. In this case, we assume the bank has a 14% **discount rate,** which is the rate of interest it charges for lending money by discounting a note. Therefore, in discounting this note, the bank deducts 54 days' interest at 14% from the note's maturity value and gives Symplex Company the remainder. The amount of interest deducted in advance is called the **bank discount**, and the remainder is called the **proceeds of the discounted note.** The bank discount and the proceeds are calculated as follows:

Maturity value of the note	$1,224.00
Less discount on $1,224 for 54 days at 14%	25.70*
Proceeds	$1,198.30

* $1,224 × .14 × (54/360) = $25.70

In this case, the proceeds, $1,198.30, are $1.70 less than the $1,200 principal amount of the note. Therefore, Symplex makes this entry to record the discount transaction:

June.	2	Cash	1,198.30	
		Interest Expense	1.70	
		Notes Receivable		1,200.00
		Discounted the John Owen note for 54 days at 14%.		

In this entry, note that the $24 of interest Symplex would have earned by holding the note to maturity is offset against the $25.70 discount charged by the bank. The $1.70 difference is debited to Interest Expense.

In the situation just described, the principal of the discounted note exceeded the proceeds. However, in other cases, the proceeds can exceed the principal. When this happens, the difference is credited to Interest Earned. For example, suppose that instead of discounting the John Owen note on June 2, Symplex discounted it on June 26 at 14%. Therefore, the discount period is 30 days, the discount is $14.28, and the proceeds of the note are $1,209.72, calculated as follows:

Maturity value of the note	$1,224.00
Less discount on $1,224 for 30 days at 14%	14.28*
Proceeds	$1,209.72

* $1,224 × .14 × (30/360) = $14.28

Because the proceeds exceed the principal, the transaction is recorded as follows:

June	26	Cash	1,209.72	
		Interest Earned		9.72
		Notes Receivable		1,200.00
		Discounted the John Owen note for 30 days at 14%.		

Contingent Liability

A person or company that discounts a note receivable is ordinarily required to endorse the note. This endorsement, unless it is qualified, makes the endorser contingently liable for payment of the note.[7] This endorsement creates a **contingent liability**, which is a potential liability that will become an actual liability only if certain events occur. The event that would turn a discounted note from a contingent liability to an actual liability would be the dishonoring of the note by its maker. If the maker pays as agreed, the endorser has no liability. However, if the maker defaults, the endorser's contingent liability becomes an *actual* liability, and the endorser must pay the maturity value of the note to the bank. The endorser then has the legal right to collect that amount from the maker.

Because a contingent liability can become an actual liability, it may affect the credit standing of the person who is contingently liable. Therefore, the existence of a material contingent liability should be disclosed in the financial statements. To help the accountant know that the contingency exists, a discounted note should be identified in the Explanation column of the Notes Receivable account. For example, assume that Symplex Company holds $500 of notes receivable in addition to the John Owen note. After the entry to record the discounting of John Owen's note is posted, the Notes Receivable account appears as follows:

Notes Receivable **Account No. 111**

Date		Explanation	PR	Debit	Credit	Balance
May	28	John Owen note	G6	1,200.00		1,200.00
June	7	Earl Hill note	G6	500.00		1,700.00
	26	Discounted the John Owen note	G7		1,200.00	500.00

Alternatively, it is possible to reflect the contingent liability by crediting a contra account for Notes Receivable Discounted instead of crediting the Notes Receivable account.

Contingent liabilities resulting from discounting notes receivable are commonly disclosed in a footnote to the balance sheet. If Symplex Company follows this practice, the company's June 30 balance sheet will show the $500 of notes it has not discounted and the contingent liability that resulted from discounting the John Owen note as follows:

[7] A qualified endorsement is one in which the endorser states in writing that he or she will not be liable for payment. Such an endorsement is also said to be "without recourse."

Current assets:	
Cash	$ 5,315
Accounts receivable	21,275
Notes receivable (See note 2.)	500

Note 2: Symplex Company is contingently liable for $1,200 of discounted notes receivable.

Full-Disclosure Principle

The balance sheet disclosure of contingent liabilities is required by the **full-disclosure principle.** This principle requires a concern's financial statements (including the footnotes) to contain all relevant information about the operations and financial position of the entity. Any data that are important enough to affect a statement reader's evaluation of the concern's operations and financial position should be reported. This principle does not mean that the concern should report excessive amounts of detail. It simply means that no significant information should be withheld and that enough information should be provided to make the reports understandable. Examples of items that need to be reported to satisfy the full-disclosure principle include the following:

Contingent Liabilities. In addition to discounted notes, a company should disclose in its financial reports any items for which the company is contingently liable. Examples of such items are possible additional tax assessments, debts of other parties that the company has guaranteed, and pending lawsuits against the company.

Long-Term Commitments under Contracts. A company should disclose that it has signed a long-term lease requiring material annual payments, even though the obligation does not appear in the accounts. Also, the company should reveal that it has pledged certain of its assets as security for a loan.

Accounting Methods Used. Whenever several acceptable accounting methods may be followed, a company should report the method it uses, especially when the choice of methods can materially affect reported net income.[8] For example, a company should report by means of financial statement footnotes such items as the inventory method or methods used, depreciation methods used, and the method of recognizing revenue under long-term construction contracts. (These methods are all described in future chapters.)

[8] FASB, *Accounting Standards—Current Text* (Norwalk, Conn., 1990), sec. A10.105. First published as *APB Opinion No. 22*, pars. 12, 13.

Dishonor of a Discounted Note

A bank always tries to collect a discounted note directly from the maker. If it is able to do so, the endorser (the one who discounted the note) does not hear from the bank and needs to do nothing more in regard to the note. However, if a discounted note is dishonored the bank promptly notifies the endorser of the note in order to hold that person liable for its payment. (In fact, there may be more than one endorser if the note is discounted more than once.) The process of notifying an endorser that a note has been dishonored is called *protesting the note*. To protest a note, the bank prepares and mails a **notice of protest** to each endorser. A notice of protest is a statement, usually witnessed by a notary public, that says the note was duly presented to the maker for payment and that payment was refused. The fee charged for preparing and issuing a notice of protest is called a **protest fee.** The bank tries to collect both the note's maturity value and the protest fee from the one who discounted the note.

For example, suppose that John Owen dishonored the $1,200 note previously discussed. In this case, the bank would immediately notify Symplex Company of the dishonoring by mailing a notice of protest and a letter asking payment for the note's maturity value plus the protest fee. If the protest fee is $25, Symplex must pay the bank $1,249. To record the payment, Symplex charges the $1,249 to the account of John Owen, as follows:

July	27	Accounts Receivable—John Owen	1,249.00	
		Cash		1,249.00
		To charge the account of Owen for the maturity value of his dishonored note ($1,200 + $24) plus the protest fee ($25).		

On receipt of the $1,249, the bank delivers the dishonored note to Symplex Company. Symplex then makes every reasonable effort to make Owen pay not only the maturity value of the note and the protest fee but also additional interest on the total of those two amounts from the maturity date (the date of dishonor) until the date of final settlement. However, after exhausting every reasonable means to collect, it may have to write off the account as a bad debt. For example, if Symplex Company concludes on August 24 that John Owen will not be able to pay, the account should be written off as follows:

Aug.	24	Allowance for Doubtful Accounts	1,249.00	
		Accounts Receivable—John Owen		1,249.00
		To write off uncollectible account.		

On the other hand, some dishonored notes are eventually paid by their makers. For example, assume that the entry on August 24 was not made. Instead, assume that 30 days beyond maturity, John Owen pays the maturity value of his dishonored note, plus the protest fee, plus interest at 12% on both for 30 days. The total amount is:

Problem 8–6
Journalizing notes receivable and bad debts transactions
(LO 4)

Prepare general journal entries to record these transactions and events experienced by Petrol Company:

Jan. 8 Accepted a $2,850, 60-day, 10% note dated this day in granting a time extension on the past-due account of Pat Wilkins.

Mar. 9 Pat Wilkins paid the maturity value of his $2,850 note.

11 Accepted a $3,300, 60-day, 11% note dated this day in granting a time extension on the past-due account of Paula Mathers.

May 10 Paula Mathers dishonored her note when presented for payment.

17 Accepted a $2,000, 90-day, 13% note dated May 15 in granting a time extension on the past-due account of Elmer Mayes.

25 Discounted the Elmer Mayes note at the bank at 15%.

Aug. 16 Because the company had not received a notice protesting the Elmer Mayes note, assumed that it had been paid.

17 Accepted a $1,500, 60-day, 11% note dated August 15 in granting a time extension on the past-due account of Steve Rollins.

Sept. 8 Discounted the Steve Rollins note at the bank at 13%.

Oct. 15 Received notice protesting the Steve Rollins note. Paid the bank the maturity value of the note plus a $20 protest fee.

16 Received a $4,100, 60-day, 12% note dated this day from Martha Watson in granting a time extension on her past-due account.

Nov. 15 Discounted the Martha Watson note at the bank at 15%.

Dec. 16 Received notice protesting the Martha Watson note. Paid the bank the maturity value of the note plus a $20 protest fee.

27 Received payment from Martha Watson of the maturity value of her dishonored note, the protest fee, and interest on both for 12 days beyond maturity at 12%.

31 Wrote off the accounts of Paula Mathers and Steve Rollins against Allowance for Doubtful Accounts.

Problem 8–7
Analysis and journalizing of notes receivable transactions
(LO 5)

Prepare general journal entries to record the following transactions of Ute City Company:

1992

Dec. 11 Accepted a $5,000, 60-day, 12% note dated this day in granting Fred Calhoun a time extension on his past-due account.

31 Made an adjusting entry to record the accrued interest on the Fred Calhoun note.

31 Closed the Interest Earned account.

1993

Jan. 10 Discounted the Fred Calhoun note at the bank at 14%.

Feb. 10 Received notice protesting the Fred Calhoun note. Paid the bank the maturity value of the note plus a $20 protest fee.

Mar. 5 Accepted a $1,500, 11%, 60-day note dated this day in granting a time extension on the past-due account of Donna Reed.

29 Discounted the Donna Reed note at the bank at 15%.

May 7 Because no notice protesting the Donna Reed note had been received, assumed that it had been paid.

June 9 Accepted a $2,250, 60-day, 10% note dated this day in granting a time extension on the past-due account of Jack Miller.

Aug. 8 Received payment of the maturity value of the Jack Miller note.

11 Accepted a $2,700, 60-day, 10% note dated this day in granting Roger Addison a time extension on his past-due account.

31 Discounted the Roger Addison note at the bank at 13%.

Oct. 12 Received notice protesting the Roger Addison note. Paid the bank the maturity value of the note plus a $20 protest fee.

Nov. 19 Received payment from Roger Addison of the maturity value of his dishonored note, the protest fee, and interest on both for 40 days beyond maturity at 10%.

Dec. 23 Wrote off the Fred Calhoun account against Allowance for Doubtful Accounts.

Problem 8–8
Entries and LCM application for short-term investments
(LO 1)

The David Gregory Company had some surplus cash balances on hand and projected that excess cash would continue to be available over the next few years. Gregory decided to invest company funds in the stock market, and obtained professional advice in putting together the company's portfolio.

Following is a series of events and other facts relevant to the short-term investment activity of the company:

1993

May 8 Purchased 1,000 shares of Apple Computer at $50.50 plus $1,515 commission.

July 14 Purchased 2,000 shares of Beatrice/Hunt-Wesson at $40.50 plus $2,430 commission.

Sept. 29 Purchased 3,000 shares of Consolidated Edison (ConEd) at $24.00 plus $2,160 commission.

Dec. 31 These per share market values were known for the stocks in the portfolio: Apple $62.50; Beatrice $36.25; ConEd $18.00.

1994

Feb. 4 Sold 2,000 shares of Beatrice at $25.25 less $1,515 commission.

July 12 Sold 3,000 shares of ConEd at $21.50 less $1,935 commission.

Aug. 17 Purchased 4,000 shares of Delta Airlines at $17.00 plus $2,040 commission.

Dec. 15 Purchased 2,400 shares of Exxon at $50.75 plus $3,654 commission.

Dec. 31 These per share market values were known for the stocks in the portfolio: Apple $75.75; Delta $10.25; Exxon $43.50.

1995

Jan.	2	Purchased 4,000 shares of Fairchild Industries at $9.00 plus $1,080 commission.
Feb.	5	Sold 4,000 shares of Delta at $24.75 less $2,970 commission.
May	18	Sold 1,000 shares of Apple at $90.50 less $2,715 commission.
Nov.	28	Purchased 1,000 shares of General Electric (GE) at $32.00 plus $960 commission.
Nov.	30	Sold 2,400 shares of Exxon at $38.00 less $2,736 commission.
Dec.	31	These per share market values were known for the stocks in the portfolio: Fairchild $14.25; GE $22.50.

Required

1. Prepare journal entries to record the events and any year-end adjustments needed to record the application of the lower of cost or market method of accounting for short-term investments.
2. Prepare a schedule that shows how the short-term investment portfolio would be described on the balance sheet at the end of each of the three years.
3. Prepare a schedule that shows the components of income (gains and losses, including LCM effects) from these investment activities, and their total effect, for each of the three years. Ignore dividends.

Problem 8–9
Analytical essay
(LO 1)

Blalock Company did not own any short-term investments prior to 1993. After purchasing some short-term investments in 1993, the company's accountant made the following December 31, 1993, adjusting entry:

Dec.	31	Loss on Market Decline of Short-Term Investments	1,100.00	
		Allowance to Reduce Short-Term Investments to Market		1,100.00
		To adjust short-term investments portfolio to the LCM amount.		

When Blalock Company's accountant reviewed the year-end adjustments with an office manager of the company, the accountant commented that the previous adjustment might have been different if the company had owned short-term investments on December 31, 1992. The office manager thought the accountant must be confused. The manager said that since the December 31, 1993, adjustment was supposed to record a loss that occurred during 1993, it should not be affected by any events that occurred during 1992.

Required

Explain why the accountant's comment is correct.

Problem 8–10
Analytical essay
(LO 1)

Review the facts about Pittsburgh Company presented in Problem 8–3.

Required

1. Recall that Allowance for Doubtful Accounts is a contra asset account. Nevertheless, Pittsburgh Company's unadjusted trial balance shows that this account has a $2,100 debit balance. Explain how this contra asset account could have a debit balance.
2. In Problem 8–3, requirement 1, *c* indicates that 7% of the outstanding accounts receivable ($142,700 × 7% = $9,989) will become uncollectible. Given this conclusion, explain why the adjusting entry should not include a $9,989 credit to Accounts Receivable.

Alternate Problems

Problem 8–1A
Accounting for short-term investments
(LO 1)

Columbia Company had no short-term investments on December 31, 1992, but had these transactions involving short-term investments during 1993:

Jan.	11	Paid $20,000 to buy six-month, U.S. Treasury bills, $20,000 principal amount, 8%, dated January 11.
Feb.	2	Purchased 600 shares of Coca Cola common stock at 38½ plus a $230 brokerage fee.
	15	Purchased 2,000 shares of Chrysler common stock at 9¾ plus a $200 brokerage fee.
Mar.	5	Paid $25,000 for U.S. Treasury notes, $25,000 principal amount, 9%, dated March 2, 1993, due March 2, 1994.
	16	Purchased 1,200 shares of Clorox common stock at 34⅝ plus a $350 brokerage fee.
June	8	Received a $0.35 per share cash dividend on the Coca Cola common shares.
	16	Sold 400 shares of Coca Cola common stock at 40 less a $160 brokerage fee.
July	13	Received a check for the principal and accrued interest on the U.S. Treasury bills that matured on July 11.
Aug.	15	Received a $0.10 per share cash dividend on the Chrysler common shares.
Sept.	5	Received a check for six-months' interest on the U.S. Treasury notes purchased on March 5.
	8	Received a $0.35 per share cash dividend on the remaining Coca Cola common shares owned by Columbia Company.
Nov.	15	Received a $0.10 per share cash dividend on the Chrysler common shares.

On December 31, 1993, the market prices of the equity securities held by Columbia Company were: Coca Cola, 40⅛; Chrysler, 8½; and Clorox, 34.

Required

1. Prepare general journal entries to record the preceding transactions.

2. Prepare a schedule to calculate the lower of cost or market of Columbia's short-term investments in marketable equity securities.
3. Prepare adjusting entries, if necessary, to record accrued interest on Columbia Company's investments in debt obligations and to reduce the marketable equity securities to the lower of cost or market.

Problem 8–2A
Credit sales and credit card sales
(LO 2)

Carr Company allows a few customers to make purchases on credit. Other customers may use either of two credit cards. The Tower Bank deducts a 2% service charge for sales on its credit card but immediately credits the checking account of its commercial customers when credit card receipts are deposited. Carr deposits the Tower Bank credit card receipts at the close of each business day.

When customers use the Pacific credit card, Carr Company accumulates the receipts for several days and then submits them to the Pacific Credit Company for payment. Pacific deducts a 3% service charge and usually pays within one week of being billed.

Carr Company completed the following transactions:

June 3 Sold merchandise on credit to Jan Burr for $980. (Terms of all credit sales are 2/15, n/60; all sales are recorded at the gross price.)

4 Sold merchandise for $4,990 to customers who used their Tower Bank credit cards. Sold merchandise for $7,230 to customers who used their Pacific credit cards.

7 Sold merchandise for $1,700 to customers who used their Pacific credit cards.

9 Wrote off the account of R. Carne against Allowance for Doubtful Accounts. The $650 balance in Carne's account stemmed from a credit sale in August of last year.

14 The Pacific credit card receipts accumulated since June 2 were submitted to the credit card company for payment.

17 Received Jan Burr's check paying for the purchase of June 3.

20 Received the amount due from Pacific Credit Company.

Required

Prepare general journal entries to record the preceding transactions.

Problem 8–3A
Estimating bad debts expense
(LO 3)

On December 31, 1993, Eagle Corporation's records showed the following results for the year:

Cash sales	$537,000
Credit sales	731,000

In addition, the unadjusted trial balance included the following items:

Accounts receivable	$345,000 debit
Allowance for doubtful accounts	1,300 credit

Required

1. Prepare the adjusting entry on the books of Eagle Corporation to estimate bad debts under each of the following independent assumptions:
   a. Bad debts are estimated to be 2% of total sales.
   b. Bad debts are estimated to be 3.5% of credit sales.
   c. An analysis suggests that 7.5% of outstanding accounts receivable on December 31, 1993, will become uncollectible.
2. Show how Accounts Receivable and the Allowance for Doubtful Accounts would appear on the December 31, 1993, balance sheet given the facts in requirement 1, *b*.
3. Show how Accounts Receivable and the Allowance for Doubtful Accounts would appear on the December 31, 1993, balance sheet given the facts in requirement 1, *c*.

Problem 8–4A
Aging accounts receivable (LO 3)

Cosmic Corporation had credit sales of $3.4 million in 1993. On December 31, 1993, the company's Allowance for Doubtful Accounts had a debit balance of $2,800. The accountant for Cosmic Corporation has prepared a schedule of the December 31, 1993, accounts receivable by age, and on the basis of past experience has estimated the percentage of the receivables in each age category that will become uncollectible. This information is summarized as follows:

December 31, 1993 Accounts Receivable	Age of Accounts Receivable	Expected Percentage Uncollectible
$470,000	Not due (under 30 days)	2%
265,000	1 to 30 days past due	3
30,000	31 to 60 days past due	15
18,000	61 to 90 days past due	40
9,000	over 90 days past due	75

Required

1. Calculate the amount that should appear in the December 31, 1993, balance sheet as the Allowance for Doubtful Accounts.
2. Prepare the general journal entry to record bad debts expense for 1993.
3. On July 31, 1994, Cosmic Corporation concluded that a customer's $3,900 receivable (created in 1993) was uncollectible and that the account should be written off. What effect will this action have on Cosmic Corporation's 1994 net income? Explain your answer.

Problem 8–5A
Recording accounts receivable transactions and bad debts adjustments (LO 3)

After beginning operations on January 1, 1992, Cyborg Corporation completed a number of transactions during 1992 and 1993 that involved credit sales, accounts receivable collections, and bad debts. These transactions are summarized as follows:

1992

a. Sold merchandise on credit for $277,400, terms n/30.

b. Received cash of $228,000 in payment of outstanding accounts receivable.

c. Wrote off uncollectible accounts receivable in the amount of $800.

d. In adjusting the accounts on December 31, concluded that 1.5% of the outstanding accounts receivable would become uncollectible.

1993

e. Sold merchandise on credit for $375,300, terms n/30.

f. Received cash of $390,600 in payment of outstanding accounts receivable.

g. Wrote off uncollectible accounts receivable in the amount of $1,200.

h. In adjusting the accounts on December 31, concluded that 1.5% of the outstanding accounts receivable would become uncollectible.

Required

Prepare general journal entries to record the 1992 and 1993 summarized transactions of Cyborg Corporation and the adjusting entries to record bad debts expense at the end of each year.

Problem 8–6A
Journalizing notes receivable and bad debts transactions
(LO 4)

Prepare general journal entries to record these transactions by Tom Mix Company:

Jan. 9 Accepted a $1,000, 30-day, 10% note dated this day in granting a time extension on the past-due account of Daniel Ford.

Feb. 8 Daniel Ford dishonored his note when presented for payment.

Mar. 14 Accepted a $3,600, 90-day, 12% note dated this day in granting a time extension on the past-due account of Rhonda Jackson.

20 Discounted the Rhonda Jackson note at the bank at 16%.

June 20 Because the company had not received a notice protesting the Rhonda Jackson note, assumed the note had been paid.

26 Accepted $500 in cash and a $1,500, 60-day, 11% note dated this day in granting a time extension on the past-due account of Paula Walker.

July 20 Discounted the Paula Walker note at the bank at 14%.

Aug. 27 Received notice protesting the Paula Walker note. Paid the bank the maturity value of the note plus a $20 protest fee.

Sept. 4 Accepted a $1,800, 60-day, 11% note dated this day in granting a time extension on the past-due account of Jean Tyne.

Oct. 10 Discounted the Jean Tyne note at the bank at 15%.

Nov. 6 Received notice protesting the Jean Tyne note. Paid the bank the maturity value of the note plus a $20 protest fee.

Dec. 3 Received payment from Jean Tyne of the maturity value of her dishonored note, the protest fee, and interest at 11% on both for 30 days beyond maturity.

Dec. 28 Decided the accounts of Daniel Ford and Paula Walker were uncollectible and wrote them off against Allowance for Doubtful Accounts.

Problem 8–7A
Analysis and journalizing of notes receivable transactions
(LO 5)

Prepare general journal entries to record the following transactions of Global Company:

1992

Dec. 6 Accepted a $4,500, 60-day, 12% note dated this day in granting a time extension on the past-due account of Joe Garza.

31 Made an adjusting entry to record the accrued interest on the Joe Garza note.

31 Closed the Interest Earned account.

1993

Jan. 5 Discounted the Joe Garza note at the bank at 14%.

Feb. 8 Because no notice protesting the Joe Garza note had been received, assumed that it had been paid.

Mar. 1 Accepted a $3,000, 90-day, 13% note dated this day in granting a time extension on the past-due account of David Pittard.

11 Discounted the David Pittard note at the bank at 15%.

June 1 Received notice protesting the David Pittard note. Paid the bank the maturity value of the note plus a $30 protest fee.

30 Received payment from David Pittard of the maturity value of his dishonored note, the protest fee, and interest on both for 30 days beyond maturity at 13%.

July 2 Accepted a $1,500, 60-day, 10% note dated July 1 in granting a time extension on the past-due account of Janet Evans.

Aug. 30 Janet Evans dishonored her note when presented for payment.

Sept. 5 Accepted $1,200 in cash and a $2,400, 60-day, 12% note dated this day in granting a time extension on the past-due account of T. J. Fields.

Oct. 10 Discounted the T. J. Fields note at the bank at 14%.

Nov. 5 Received notice protesting the T. J. Fields note. Paid the bank its maturity value plus a $25 protest fee.

Dec. 29 Decided the Janet Evans and T. J. Fields accounts were uncollectible and wrote them off against Allowance for Doubtful Accounts.

Problem 8–8A
Entries and LCM application for short-term investments
(LO 1)

The Laser Printer Company had some surplus cash balances on hand and projected that excess cash would continue to be available over the next few years. Sandy Thomas, the president, decided to invest company funds in the stock market, and obtained professional advice in putting together the company's portfolio.

Following is a series of events and other facts relevant to the short-term investment activity of the company:

1993

Jan. 2 Purchased 2,000 shares of Hershey Foods at $22.50 plus $1,350 commission.

Aug. 17 Purchased 3,000 shares of IBM at $15.25 plus $1,373 commission.

Dec.	15	Purchased 1,000 shares of Kmart at $30.00 plus $900 commission.
	31	These per share market values were known for the stocks in the portfolio: Hershey $27.50; IBM $12.50; Kmart $18.00.
1994		
Feb.	9	Sold 3,000 shares of IBM at $11.75 less $1,058 commission.
June	12	Sold 1,000 shares of Kmart at $36.00 less $1,080 commission.
July	14	Purchased 3,500 shares of Logitech at $11.75 plus $1,234 commission.
Sept.	29	Purchased 4,000 shares of MCI at $33.25 plus $3,990 commission.
Dec.	31	These per share market values were known for the stocks in the portfolio: Hershey $35.00; Logitech $15.50; MCI $19.00.
1995		
Feb.	5	Purchased 5,000 shares of Novell at $16.50 plus $2,475 commission.
May	8	Sold 3,500 shares of Logitech at $24.00 less $2,520 commission.
June	18	Sold 2,000 shares of Hershey at $45.50 less $2,730 commission.
Nov.	29	Purchased 1,500 shares of PepsiCo at $60.50 plus $2,723 commission.
Dec.	1	Sold 4,000 shares of MCI at $21.50 less $2,580 commission.
	31	These per share market values were known for the stocks in the portfolio: Novell $25.00; PepsiCo $54.00.

Required

1. Prepare journal entries to record the events and any year-end adjustments needed to record the application of the lower of cost or market method of accounting for short-term investments.
2. Prepare a schedule that shows how the short-term investment portfolio would be described on the balance sheet at the end of each of the three years.
3. Prepare a schedule that shows the components of income (gains and losses, including LCM effects) from these investment activities, and their total effect, for each of the three years. Ignore dividends.

Problem 8–9A
Analytical essay
(LO 1)

On December 31, 1992, Jones-Meyer Company's balance sheet included the following items:

Short-term investments	$50,000	
Allowance to reduce short-term investments to market	4,500	$45,500

On December 31, 1993, an analysis of the short-term investments portfolio showed a total cost of $75,000 and a total market value of $67,000. As a result of this analysis, the company recorded the following adjusting entry:

Dec.	31	Loss on Market Decline of Short-Term Investments	8,000.00	
		Short-Term Investments		8,000.00
		To adjust short-term investments portfolio to the LCM amount.		

Required

Explain why the 1993 adjusting entry is not correct.

Problem 8–10A
Analytical essay
(LO 1)

Review the facts about Eagle Corporation presented in Problem 8–3A.

Required

1. Prior to making the December 31, 1993, adjustments, Eagle Corporation's Allowance for Doubtful Accounts has a $1,300 credit balance. Explain how this account balance affects the bad debts expense adjusting entry, assuming the company estimates bad debts by aging its accounts receivable.
2. Requirement 1, *c* of Problem 8–3A indicates that 7.5% of the outstanding accounts receivable ($345,000 × 7.5% = $25,875) will become uncollectible. Given this conclusion, explain why the adjusting entry should not include a $25,875 credit to Accounts Receivable.

Provocative Problems

Provocative Problem 8–1
Prism Place
(Review problem)

When the auditor arrived early in January to begin the annual audit, Sandra Grey, the owner of Prism Place, asked that careful attention be given to accounts receivable. Two things caused this request. First, during the previous week, Grey had met Greg Box, a former customer, and had asked him about his account that had recently been written off as uncollectible. Box was surprised, and explained that he had returned $90 of merchandise and paid the remaining $580 account balance. Later, he provided copies of his canceled check endorsed by Prism Place to prove that the balance had been paid. Second, the income statement prepared for the quarter ended the previous July 31 showed an unusually large volume of sales returns. The bookkeeper who had prepared the statement was a new employee, having begun work on May 1, after being hired on the basis of out-of-town letters of reference. In addition to doing all the record-keeping, the bookkeeper also acted as the cashier, depositing the cash from sales and from mail receipts.

In the process of performing the audit, the auditor used the company's records to prepare the following analysis of all the accounts receivable activity for the period from May 1 through July 31:

	Able	Box	Cole	Dunn	Ellis	Friar	Gold	Total
Balance, May 1	$ 390	$ 100	$ 210	$ 400	$ 860	$1,850	$ 370	$ 4,180
Sales	2,440	570	1,455		6,300	420	1,450	12,635
Total	$2,830	$ 670	$1,665	$ 400	$7,160	$2,270	$1,820	$16,815
Collections	(2,080)		(985)		(6,040)	(1,475)	(1,300)	(11,880)
Returns	(450)	(90)	(130)		(290)	(250)	(70)	(1,280)
Bad debts written off		(580)		(400)				(980)
Balance, July 31	$ 300	$-0-	$ 550	$-0-	$ 830	$ 545	$ 450	$ 2,675

The auditor contacted all charge customers and learned that although their account balances as of July 31 agreed with the amounts shown in the company's records, the individual transactions did not. The customers provided information that allowed the auditor to determine that credit sales actually totaled $14,050 during the three-month period. Also, there were actual sales returns of $395 on credit sales to these customers. Correspondence with Perry Dunn, a customer whose $400 account had been written off, revealed that he had become bankrupt and his creditor's claims had been settled by his receiver in bankruptcy at $0.25 on the dollar. The checks had been mailed by his receiver on May 30, and all had been paid and returned by the bank, properly endorsed by the recipients.

Under the assumption that the bookkeeper has embezzled cash from the company, determine the total amount he has taken and attempted to conceal with false entries to Accounts Receivable. Explain the deficiency by listing the concealment methods used and the amount he attempted to conceal with each method. Also, outline an internal control system that would help protect the company's cash from future embezzlements. Assume the company will hire a new bookkeeper, but will continue to have only one office employee who must do all the bookkeeping.

Provocative Problem 8-2
FootGear
(LO 3)

John Holcomb has operated FootGear for five years. Three years ago, he liberalized the store's credit policy in an effort to increase credit sales. Credit sales have increased, but now Holcomb is concerned with the effects of the more liberalized credit policy. Bad debts written off (the store uses the direct write-off method) have increased materially in the last three years, and now Holcomb wonders if the increase justifies the substantial bad debt losses that he is certain have resulted from the new credit policy.

An examination of the store's credit sales records, bad debt losses, and accounts receivable for the five years' operations reveal:

	1st Year	2d Year	3d Year	4th Year	5th Year
Credit sales	$84,000	$92,400	$126,000	$151,200	$167,500
Cost of goods sold	50,400	55,440	75,600	90,720	100,500
Gross profit from credit sales	$33,600	$36,960	$ 50,400	$ 60,480	$ 67,000
Expenses other than bad debts	25,200	27,680	37,700	45,170	49,980
Income before bad debts	$ 8,400	$ 9,280	$ 12,700	$ 15,310	$ 17,020
Bad debts written off	85	370	630	1,980	2,020
Income from credit sales	$ 8,315	$ 8,910	$ 12,070	$ 13,330	$ 15,000
Bad debts by year of sale	$ 335	$ 280	$ 1,640	$ 1,820	$ 2,340

The last line in the tabulation results from reclassifying bad debt losses so that the losses appear in the same years as the sales that produced them. Because some of the fifth-year sales had not been collected at year-end, the $2,340 of fifth-year losses includes $1,320 of estimated bad debts that are still in the accounts receivable.

Prepare a schedule showing by years: income from credit sales before bad debt losses, bad debts incurred, and the resulting income from credit sales. Then, below the income figures, show for each year bad debts written off as a percentage of sales followed on the next line by estimated bad debts expense incurred as a percentage of sales. Also prepare a report for Holcomb in which you answer his concern about the new credit policy and recommend any changes you consider desirable in his accounting for bad debts.

Provocative Problem 8–3
International Business Machines Corporation
(LO 1)

IBM

The financial statements and related disclosures from IBM's 1990 annual report are presented in Appendix J. Based on your examination of this information, answer the following:

1. IBM's most liquid assets include cash, cash equivalents, marketable securities, and receivables. What total amount of those assets did IBM have on December 31, 1990?
2. What description did IBM provide of the types of items that it included as cash equivalents?
3. The marketable securities IBM listed as current assets included three different types of investments. What were they? As of December 31, 1990, what was the cost of each type of investment?
4. On December 31, 1989, the market value of IBM's marketable securities was higher than cost. How much higher? Which amount was reported on the balance sheet?
5. The December 31, 1990, balance sheet states that marketable securities are at cost, which approximates market. However, a footnote discloses that the market value of the marketable securities at December 31, 1989, exceeded cost by $2,000,000. Explain why IBM was justified in stating that cost approximates market value when the difference was $2,000,000.

Answers to Objective Review Questions

LO 1 (*c*)	LO 3 (*a*)	LO 5 (*c*)
LO 2 (*d*)	LO 4 (*b*)	LO 6 (*d*)

CHAPTER

9

Inventories and Cost of Goods Sold

Merchandising companies buy and sell large quantities and varieties of goods. These activities lead to complex accounting problems in measuring profits. Companies use several different methods to develop information about their inventories and cost of goods sold.

Topical Coverage

The operations of merchandising businesses involve the purchase and resale of tangible commodities. In Chapter 5, when we first introduced the topic of accounting for merchandising businesses, we left several important matters for later consideration. In this chapter, we return to the topic and examine the methods businesses use at the end of each period to assign dollar amounts to merchandise inventory and to cost of goods sold. The principles and procedures that we explain in this chapter are used in department stores, grocery stores, automobile dealerships, and any other businesses that purchase goods for resale.

Learning Objectives

After studying Chapter 9, you should be able to:

1. Describe (*a*) how the matching principle relates to accounting for merchandise; (*b*) the types of items that should be included in merchandise inventory; and (*c*) the elements that make up the cost of merchandise.
2. Calculate the cost of an inventory based on (*a*) specific invoice prices, (*b*) weighted-average cost, (*c*) FIFO, and (*d*) LIFO, and explain the financial statement effects of choosing one method over the others.
3. Calculate the lower-of-cost-or-market amount of an inventory.
4. Explain the effect of an inventory error on the income statements of the current and succeeding years.
5. Describe perpetual inventory systems and prepare entries to record merchandise transactions and maintain subsidiary inventory records under a perpetual inventory system.
6. Estimate an inventory by the retail method and by the gross profit method.
7. Define or explain the words and phrases listed in the chapter glossary.

The assets that a business buys and holds for resale are called *merchandise inventory*. As a rule, the items held as merchandise inventory are sold within one year or one operating cycle. Therefore, merchandise inventory is a current asset, usually the largest current asset on the balance sheet of a merchandiser.

Matching Merchandise Costs with Revenues

Accounting for inventories affects both the balance sheet and the income statement. However, "the major objective in accounting for the goods in the inventory is the matching of appropriate costs against revenues in order that there may be a proper determination of the realized income."[1] The matching process is already a familiar topic. For inventories, it consists of deciding how

[1] FASB, *Accounting Standards—Current Text* (Norwalk, Conn., 1990), sec. I78.104. First published as *Accounting Research Bulletin No. 43*, Ch. 4, par. 4.

much of the cost of the goods available for sale during a period should be deducted from the period's revenue and how much should be carried forward as inventory to be matched against a future period's revenue.

In a periodic inventory system, when the cost of goods available for sale is allocated between cost of goods sold and ending inventory, the key problem is assigning a cost to the ending inventory. Remember, however, that by assigning a cost to the ending inventory, you are also determining cost of goods sold. This is true because the ending inventory is subtracted from the cost of goods available for sale to determine cost of goods sold.

LO 1 Describe (*a*) how the matching principle relates to accounting for merchandise; (*b*) the types of items that should be included in merchandise inventory; and (*c*) the elements that make up the cost of merchandise.

Items to Include in Merchandise Inventory

The merchandise inventory of a business includes all goods owned by the business and held for sale, regardless of where the goods may be located at the time inventory is counted. In applying this rule, most items present no problem. All that is required is to see that all items are counted, that nothing is omitted, and that nothing is counted more than once. However, goods in transit, goods sold but not delivered, goods on consignment, and obsolete and damaged goods require special attention.

Should merchandise be included in the inventory of a business if the goods are in transit from a supplier to a business on the date the business takes an inventory? The answer to this question depends on whether the rights and risks of ownership have passed from the supplier to the purchasing business. If ownership has passed to the purchaser, they should be included in the purchaser's inventory. Usually, if the buyer is responsible for paying the freight charges, ownership passes as soon as the goods are loaded on the means of transportation. (As mentioned in Chapter 5, the terms would be FOB the seller's factory or warehouse.) On the other hand, if the seller is to pay the freight charges, ownership passes when the goods arrive at their destination (FOB destination).

Goods on consignment are goods shipped by their owner (known as the **consignor**) to another person or firm (called the **consignee**) who is to sell the goods for the owner. Consigned goods belong to the consignor and should appear on the consignor's inventory.

Damaged goods and deteriorated or obsolete goods should not be counted in the inventory if they are not salable. If such goods are salable at a reduced price, they should be included in the inventory at a conservative estimate of their **net realizable value** (sales price less the cost of making the sale). Thus, the accounting period in which the goods deteriorated, were damaged, or became obsolete suffers the resultant loss.

Elements of Merchandise Cost

As applied to merchandise, cost means the sum of the expenditures and charges directly or indirectly incurred in bringing an article to its existing condition and location.[2] Therefore, the cost of an inventory item includes the invoice price, less the discount, plus any additional or incidental costs necessary to put the item into place and condition for sale. The additional costs may

[2] Ibid., sec. I78.402. First published as *Accounting Research Bulletin No. 43*, ch. 4, par. 5.

include import duties, transportation-in, storage, insurance, and any other related costs such as those incurred during an aging process (for example, the aging of wine).

All of these costs should be included in the cost of merchandise. When calculating the cost of a merchandise inventory, however, some concerns do not include the incidental costs of acquiring merchandise. They price the inventory on the basis of invoice prices only. As a result, the incidental costs are allocated to cost of goods sold during the period in which they are incurred.

In theory, a share of each incidental cost should be assigned to every unit purchased. This causes a portion of each to be carried forward in the inventory to be matched against the revenue of the period in which the inventory is sold. However, the effort of computing costs on such a precise basis may outweigh the benefit from the extra accuracy. Therefore, many businesses take advantage of the *materiality principle* and charge such costs to cost of goods sold.

Taking an Ending Inventory

As you learned in Chapter 5, when a *periodic inventory system* is used, the dollar amount of the ending inventory is determined as follows: count the units of each product on hand, multiply the count for each product by its cost, and add the costs for all products. In making the count, items are less likely to be counted twice or omitted from the count if you use prenumbered **inventory tickets** like the one in Illustration 9–1.

Before beginning the inventory count, a sufficient number of the tickets, at least one for each product on hand, is issued to each department in the store. Next, a clerk counts the quantity of each product. From the count and the price tag attached to the merchandise, the clerk fills in the information on the inventory ticket and attaches it to the counted items. After the count is completed, clerks check each department for uncounted items. At this stage, because inventory tickets should be attached to all counted items, any products without tickets attached are uncounted. After all the items are counted, the tickets are removed and sent to the accounting department for completion of the inventory. To ensure that no ticket is lost or left attached to merchandise, the accounting department verifies that all the prenumbered tickets issued have been returned.

In the accounting department, the unit and cost data on the tickets are aggregated by multiplying the number of units of each product by its unit cost. This gives the dollar amount of each product in the inventory and the total for all the products is the dollar total of the inventory.

Assigning Costs to Inventory Items

One of the major issues in accounting for merchandise involves determining the unit cost amounts that will be assigned to items in the inventory. When all units are purchased at the same unit cost, this process is easy. However, when identical items were purchased at different costs, a problem arises as to which costs apply to the ending inventory and which apply to the goods sold. There are four commonly used methods of assigning costs to goods in the ending

ILLUSTRATION 9–1

Inventory Tickets Used to Tag Inventory Items as They Are Counted

INVENTORY
TICKET No. *786*

Item ____________

Quantity counted [ ]
Sales price $ [ ]
Cost price $ [ ]
Purchase date [ ]

Counted by ____________
Checked by ____________

inventory and to goods sold. They are (1) specific invoice prices; (2) weighted-average cost; (3) first-in, first-out; and (4) last-in, first-out. All four methods fall within generally accepted accounting principles.

> **LO 2** Calculate the cost of an inventory based on (*a*) specific invoice prices, (*b*) weighted-average cost, (*c*) FIFO, and (*d*) LIFO, and explain the financial statement effects of choosing one method over the others.

To illustrate the four methods, assume that a company has 12 units of Product X on hand at the end of its annual accounting period. Also, assume that the inventory at the beginning of the year and the purchases during the year were as follows:

Jan. 1	Beginning inventory	10 units @ $100 =	$1,000
Mar. 13	Purchased	15 units @ $108 =	1,620
Aug. 17	Purchased	20 units @ $120 =	2,400
Nov. 10	Purchased	10 units @ $125 =	1,250
Total		55 units	$6,270

Specific Invoice Prices

When each item in an inventory can be clearly related to a specific purchase and its invoice, **specific invoice inventory pricing** may be used to assign costs. For example, assume that 6 of the 12 unsold units of Product X were from the November purchase and 6 were from the August purchase. With this information, specific invoice prices can be used to assign cost to the ending inventory and to the goods sold as follows:

Total cost of 55 units available for sale		$6,270
Less ending inventory priced by means of specific invoices:		
6 units from the November purchase at $125 each	$750	
6 units from the August purchase at $120 each	720	
12 units in the ending inventory		1,470
Cost of goods sold		$4,800

Weighted Average

When using **weighted-average inventory pricing,** multiply the per unit costs of the beginning inventory and of each purchase by the number of units in the beginning inventory and in each purchase. Then, divide the total of these amounts by the total number of units available for sale to find the weighted-average cost per unit as follows:

10 units @ $100 =	$1,000
15 units @ $108 =	1,620
20 units @ $120 =	2,400
10 units @ $125 =	1,250
55	$6,270

$6,270/55 = $114 weighted-average cost per unit

After determining the weighted-average cost per unit, use this average to assign costs to the inventory and to the units sold as follows:

Total cost of 55 units available for sale	$6,270
Less ending inventory priced on a weighted-average cost basis: 12 units at $114 each	1,368
Cost of goods sold	$4,902

First-In, First-Out

When using **first-in, first-out inventory pricing (FIFO),** assume the items in the beginning inventory are to be sold first. Additional sales are assumed to come in the order in which they were purchased. Thus, the costs of the last items received are assigned to the ending inventory, and the remaining costs are assigned to goods sold. For example, when first-in, first-out is used, the costs of Product X are assigned to the inventory and goods sold as follows:

Total cost of 55 units available for sale		$6,270
Less ending inventory priced on a basis of FIFO:		
10 units from the November purchase at $125 each . .	$1,250	
2 units from the August purchase at $120 each	240	
12 units in the ending inventory		1,490
Cost of goods sold		$4,780

You need to understand that the use of FIFO is acceptable whether or not the physical flow of goods actually follows a first-in, first-out pattern. The physical flow of products depends on the nature of the product and the way the products are stored. If a product is perishable (for example, fresh tomatoes), the business attempts to sell it in a first-in, first-out pattern. Other products, for example, bolts or screws kept in a large bin, may tend to be sold on a last-in, first-out basis. In either case, the FIFO method of allocating cost may be used.

Last-In, First-Out

Under the **last-in, first-out inventory pricing (LIFO)** method, the cost of the last goods received are charged to cost of goods sold and matched with revenue from sales. Again, this method is acceptable even though the physical flow of goods may not be on a last-in, first-out basis.

One argument for the use of LIFO is based on the fact that a going concern must replace the inventory items it sells. When goods are sold, replacements are purchased. Thus, a sale causes the replacement of goods. According to this point of view, a correct matching of costs with revenues requires matching replacement costs with the sales that made replacements necessary. Although the costs of the most recent purchases are not quite the same as replacement costs, they usually are close approximations of replacement costs. Because LIFO assigns the most recent purchase costs to the income statement, LIFO (compared to FIFO or weighted average) comes closest to matching replacement costs with revenues.

Under LIFO, costs are assigned to the 12 remaining units of Product X and to the goods sold as follows:

Total cost of 55 units available for sale		$6,270
Less ending inventory priced on a basis of LIFO:		
10 units in the beginning inventory at $100 each	$1,000	
2 units from the March purchase at $108 each	216	
12 units in the ending inventory		1,216
Cost of goods sold		$5,054

Notice that when LIFO is used to match costs and revenues, the ending inventory cost is the cost of the oldest 12 units.

Comparison of Methods

In a stable market where prices remain unchanged, the choice of an inventory pricing method has little importance. When prices are unchanged over a period of time, all methods give the same cost figures. However, in a changing market where prices are rising or falling, each method may give a different result. These differences are shown in Illustration 9–2, where we assume that Product X sales were $6,000 and operating expenses were $500. In Illustration 9–2, note the differences that resulted from the choice of an inventory pricing method.

ILLUSTRATION 9–2

The Income Statement Effects of Alternative Inventory Pricing Methods

	Specific Invoice Prices	**Weighted Average**	**FIFO**	**LIFO**
Sales	$6,000	$6,000	$6,000	$6,000
Cost of goods sold:				
Merchandise inventory, January 1	$1,000	$1,000	$1,000	$1,000
Purchases	5,270	5,270	5,270	5,270
Cost of goods available for sale	$6,270	$6,270	$6,270	$6,270
Merchandise inventory, December 31	1,470	1,368	1,490	1,216
Cost of goods sold	$4,800	$4,902	$4,780	$5,054
Gross profit	$1,200	$1,098	$1,220	$ 946
Operating expenses	500	500	500	500
Income before taxes	$ 700	$ 598	$ 720	$ 446
Income taxes expense (30%)	210	179	216	134
Net income	$ 490	$ 419	$ 504	$ 312

Because purchase prices were rising throughout the period, FIFO resulted in the lowest cost of goods sold, the highest gross profit, and the highest net income. On the other hand, LIFO resulted in the highest cost of goods sold, the lowest gross profit, and the lowest net income. As you would expect, the results of using the weighted-average method fall between FIFO and LIFO. The results of using specific invoice prices depend entirely on which units were actually sold.

Each of the four pricing methods is generally accepted, and arguments can be made for using each. In one sense, one might argue that specific invoice prices exactly match costs and revenues. However, this method is practical only for relatively high-priced items when just a few units are kept in stock and sold. Weighted-average costs tend to smooth out price fluctuations. FIFO provides an inventory valuation on the balance sheet that most closely approximates current replacement cost. LIFO causes the last costs incurred to be assigned to cost of goods sold. Therefore, it results in a better matching of current costs with revenues on the income statement.

Because the choice of an inventory pricing method often has material effects on the financial statements, the choice of a method should be disclosed in the footnotes to the statements. This information is important to an understanding of the statements and is required by the *full-disclosure principle*.[3]

[3] Ibid., sec. A10.105, 106. First published as *APB Opinion No. 22*, pars. 12, 13.

AS A MATTER OF

Fact

Inventory Costing Methods Used by 600 Companies

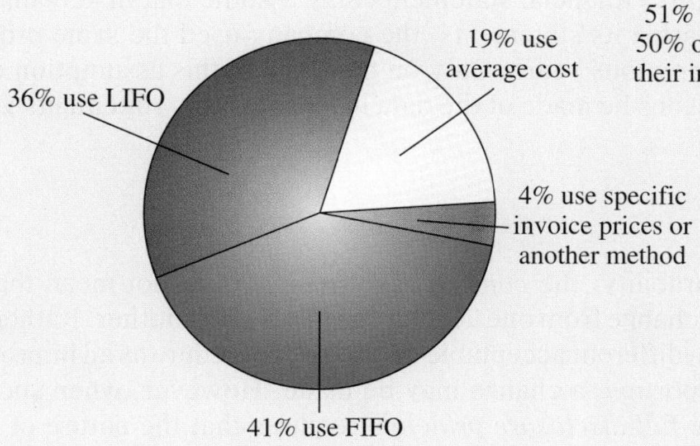

Of Those Companies that Use LIFO

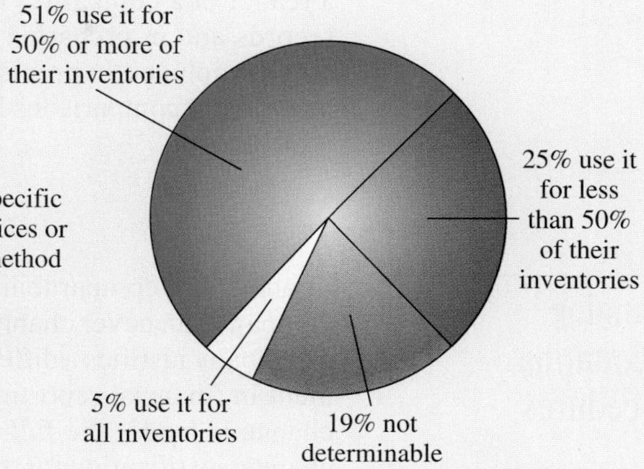

Source of data: American Institute of Certified Public Accountants, *Accounting Trends and Techniques*, New York, 1991, p. 144.

Tax Effect of LIFO

The income statements in Illustration 9–2 are assumed to be those of a corporation. Therefore, the income statements include income taxes expense (at an assumed rate of 30%). Note that because purchase prices were rising, a tax advantage was gained by using LIFO. This advantage arises because LIFO assigns the largest dollar amounts to cost of goods sold when purchase prices are increasing. As a result, the smallest income is reported when LIFO is used. This in turn results in the smallest income tax expense.

The Consistency Principle

Because the choice of an inventory pricing method can have a material effect on the financial statements, some companies might be inclined to make a new choice each year. Their objective would be to select whichever method would result in the most favorable financial statements. If this were allowed, however, readers of financial statements would find it extremely difficult to compare the company's financial statements from one year to the next. If income increased, the reader would have difficulty deciding whether the increase resulted from more successful operations or from the change in the accounting method. The **consistency principle** is used to avoid this problem.

The *consistency principle* requires that a company use the same accounting methods period after period, so that the financial statements of succeeding periods will be comparable.[4] The *consistency principle* is not limited just to inventory pricing methods. Whenever a company must choose between alternative generally accepted accounting methods, consistency requires that the company continue to use the selected method period after period. As a result, a reader of a company's financial statements may assume that in keeping its records and in preparing its statements, the company used the same procedures employed in previous years. Only on the basis of this assumption can meaningful comparisons be made of the data in a company's statements year after year.

Changing Accounting Procedures

In achieving comparability, the *consistency principle* does not mean that a company can never change from one accounting method to another. Rather, if a company justifies a different acceptable method or procedure as an improvement in financial reporting, a change may be made. However, when such a change is made, the *full-disclosure principle* requires that the nature of the change, justification for the change, and the effect of the change on net income be disclosed in footnotes to the statements.[5]

Lower of Cost or Market

LO 3 Calculate the lower-of-cost-or-market amount of an inventory.

As we have discussed, the cost of the ending inventory is determined by using one of the four pricing methods (FIFO, LIFO, weighted average, or specific invoice prices). However, the cost of the inventory is not necessarily the amount reported on the balance sheet. Generally accepted accounting principles require that the inventory be reported at market value whenever market is lower than cost. Thus, merchandise inventory is shown on the balance sheet at the *lower of cost or market*.

Market Normally Means Replacement Cost

In applying lower of cost or market to merchandise inventories, what do accountants mean by the term *market?* For the purpose of assigning a value to merchandise inventory, market normally means *replacement cost*. That means the price a company would pay if it bought new items to replace those in its inventory. When the cost to replace merchandise drops below original cost, the sales price of the merchandise is also likely to fall. Therefore, the merchandise is worth less to the company and should be written down to replacement cost (or market).

[4] FASB, *Statement of Financial Accounting Concepts No. 2,* "Qualitative Characteristics of Accounting Information" (Norwalk, Conn., 1980), par. 120.

[5] FASB, *Accounting Standards—Current Text* (Norwalk, Conn., 1990), sec. A06.113. First published as *APB Opinion No. 20,* par. 17.

Lower of cost or market may be applied to merchandise inventory in either of two ways: First, it may be applied to the inventory as a whole. Alternatively, it may be applied separately to each product in the inventory. To illustrate, assume that a company's year-end inventory contains three products (X, Y, and Z) with the following costs and replacement costs:

Product	Units on Hand	Per Unit Cost	Per Unit Market	Total Cost	Total Market	Lower of Cost or Market (by Product)
X	20	$8	$7	$160	$140	$140
Y	10	5	6	50	60	50
Z	5	9	7	45	35	35
				$255		$225
Replacement cost (market) of whole inventory . . .					$235	

Note that when the whole inventory is priced at market, the total is $235, which is $20 lower than the $255 cost. Alternatively, when the lower of cost or market is applied separately to each product, the sum is only $225. A company may use either approach to calculate the lower of cost or market of merchandise inventory.

Recall from Chapter 8 that lower of cost or market is also used to value a company's short-term investments in marketable equity securities. However, in that case, only one approach is allowed. The total cost and total market value of the entire portfolio of investments is compared to determine the lower of cost or market. Thus, while the lower-of-cost-or-market calculation for merchandise inventory may be done two different ways, the calculation for short-term investments is restricted to one way.

Inventory Should Never Be Valued at More than Its Net Realizable Value

The idea that *market* is defined as replacement cost is subject to two important exceptions. One exception is that inventory should never be valued at more than its net realizable value, which is the expected sales price less additional costs to sell. Understand that merchandise is written down to market because the value of the merchandise to the company has declined. Sometimes, the net realizable value is even less than replacement cost. In that case, the merchandise is worth no more than net realizable value and should be written down to that amount.

For example, assume that merchandise was purchased for $100 and was originally priced to sell for $125. By year-end, a general decline in prices resulted in a replacement cost of $90. However, assume that the merchandise in question has been damaged. Management expects that the merchandise can be sold for $95 if it is first cleaned at a cost of $10. Therefore, net realizable value is $95 − $10, or $85. Since net realizable value ($85) is less than replacement cost ($90), the merchandise should be written down to net realizable value.

Inventory Should Never Be Valued at Less than Net Realizable Value minus a Normal Profit Margin

A second exception to defining market as replacement cost is that merchandise should never be written down to an amount that is less than net realizable value minus a normal profit margin. To illustrate, suppose that a company normally buys merchandise for $80 and sells it for $100. The gross profit of $20 is 20% of the selling price. Now suppose the selling price falls from $100 to $90. A normal gross profit margin would be $90 × 20% = $18. Therefore, the inventory should not be written down below $90 − $18 = $72, even if replacement cost is less than $72. If the inventory were written down below $72, the income statement of the current period would show an abnormally low gross profit margin. And when the merchandise is sold for $90 the next period, the income statement of that period would show an abnormally high gross profit margin.

The Conservatism Principle

Generally accepted accounting principles require writing inventory down to market when market is less than cost. On the other hand, inventory generally cannot be written up to market when market exceeds cost. If writing inventory down to market is justified, why not also write inventory up to market? What is the reason for this apparent inconsistency?

The reason inventory is not written up above cost to a higher market value is that the gain from a market value increase is not realized until a sales transaction provides verifiable evidence of the amount of the gain. But why, then, are inventories written down when market is below cost?

Accountants often justify the lower of cost or market rule by citing the **conservatism principle.** This principle is sometimes expressed simplistically as "recognize all losses but anticipate no profits." More realistically, the principle of conservatism attempts to guide the accountant in uncertain situations where amounts must be estimated. In general terms, it implies that when "two estimates of amounts to be received or paid in the future are about equally likely, . . . the less optimistic" should be used.[6] Because the value of inventory is uncertain, writing the inventory down when its market value falls is clearly the less optimistic estimate of the inventory's value to the company.

Inventory Errors—Periodic System

LO 4 Explain the effect of an inventory error on the income statements of the current and succeeding years.

When the *periodic inventory system* is used, you must be especially careful in taking the end-of-period inventory. If an error is made, it will cause misstatements in cost of goods sold, gross profit, net income, current assets, and owner's equity. Also, the ending inventory of one period is the beginning inventory of the next. Therefore, the error will carry forward and cause misstatements in the succeeding period's cost of goods sold, gross profit, and net income. Fur-

[6] FASB, *Statement of Financial Accounting Concepts No. 2* (Norwalk, Conn., 1980), par. 95.

ILLUSTRATION 9-3

Effects of Inventory Errors—Periodic Inventory System

	1992		1993		1994	
Sales		$100,000		$100,000		$100,000
Cost of goods sold:						
Beginning inventory	$20,000		$18,000*		$20,000	
Purchases	60,000		60,000		60,000	
Goods for sale	$80,000		$78,000		$80,000	
Ending inventory	18,000*		20,000		20,000	
Cost of goods sold		62,000		58,000		60,000
Gross profit		$38,000		$ 42,000		$ 40,000

* Should have been $20,000.

thermore, since the amount involved in an inventory often is large, the misstatements can materially reduce the usefulness of the financial statements.

To illustrate the effects of an inventory error, assume that in each of the years 1992, 1993, and 1994, a company had $100,000 in sales. If the company maintained a $20,000 inventory throughout the period and made $60,000 in purchases in each of the years, its cost of goods sold each year was $60,000 and its annual gross profit was $40,000. However, assume the company incorrectly calculated its December 31, 1992, inventory at $18,000 rather than $20,000. Illustration 9–3 shows the effects of the error.

Observe in Illustration 9–3 that the $2,000 understatement of the December 31, 1992, inventory caused a $2,000 overstatement in 1992 cost of goods sold and a $2,000 understatement in gross profit and net income. Also, because the ending inventory of 1992 became the beginning inventory of 1993, the error caused an understatement in the 1993 cost of goods sold and a $2,000 overstatement in gross profit and net income. However, by 1994 the error had no effect.

In Illustration 9–3, the December 31, 1992, inventory is understated. Had it been overstated, it would have caused opposite results—the 1992 net income would have been overstated and the 1993 income understated.

Because inventory errors correct themselves by causing offsetting errors in the next period, you might be inclined to think that they are not serious. Do not make this mistake. Management, creditors, and owners base many important decisions on fluctuations in reported net income. Therefore, inventory errors must be avoided.

Perpetual Inventory Systems

The previous discussion of inventories focused on the periodic inventory system. Under the periodic system, the Merchandise Inventory account is updated only once each accounting period, at the end of the period. Then, the Merchandise Inventory account reflects the current balance of inventory only until the first purchase or sale in the following period. Thereafter, the Merchandise Inventory account no longer reflects the current balance.

AS A MATTER OF

Opinion

Mr. Brown is vice president and director of auditing for JCPenney Company, a $16 billion national retail and catalog chain that includes 1,300 JCPenney stores, 450 Thrift Drug stores, the JCPenney Life Insurance Company, and 180,000 employees.

Mr. Brown began his career with Peat, Marwick, Mitchell & Co., and was director of auditing for Mohasco Industries before joining JCPenney. He is a Certified Internal Auditor, a Certified Public Accountant, and a graduate of the University of Kansas with a B.S. in Business Administration and Accounting.

Mr. Brown has been chairman of the Institute of Internal Auditors, an international professional organization recognized worldwide as the leading authority on internal auditing. He has also served as chairman of the Internal Audit Group of the National Retail Foundation, the international association of retailers.

Charles L. Brown

To maximize customer satisfaction and return to stockholders, the goal of any retailer is to consistently have the right merchandise at the right time and at a price customers are willing to pay. In addition to knowing our customers, a fully integrated and automated perpetual inventory system is the *heart* of a successful department store operation. It provides information on how fast customers are buying, by store and by item (including sizes and colors). As a result, we can anticipate future buying patterns.

Our perpetual inventory system also provides the basis for Electronic Data Interchange (EDI). This automates replenishment to stores from suppliers and reduces the cycle time from ordering to selling. In addition to providing financial information, the perpetual system automates invoice matching with payments to suppliers and allows us to determine shrinkage (inventory losses) by store and by time.

Accounting truly becomes the language of business when the accounting system is integrated into an active, day-to-day, management decision-making process. Perpetual inventory systems are an important example of this integration.

LO 5 Describe perpetual inventory systems and prepare entries to record merchandise transactions and maintain subsidiary inventory records under a perpetual inventory system.

By contrast, a *perpetual inventory system* updates the Merchandise Inventory account after each purchase and after each sale. As long as all entries have been posted, the account shows the current amount of inventory on hand. The system takes its name from the fact that the Merchandise Inventory account is perpetually up to date. When a perpetual inventory system is used, management is able to monitor the inventory on hand on a regular basis. This aids in planning future purchases.

Before the widespread use of computers in accounting, only companies that sold a limited number of products of relatively high value used perpetual inventory systems. The cost and effort of maintaining perpetual inventory records were simply too great for other types of companies. However, since computers have made the record-keeping chore much easier, an increasing number of firms are switching from periodic to perpetual systems.

ILLUSTRATION 9–4

A Comparison of Entries under Periodic and Perpetual Inventory Systems

X Company purchases merchandise for $15 per unit and sells it for $25. The company begins the current period with five units of product on hand, which cost a total of $75.

Periodic			Perpetual		
1. *Purchased on credit 10 units of merchandise for $15 per unit.*					
Purchases	150		Merchandise Inventory	150	
Accounts Payable		150	Accounts Payable		150
2. *Returned three units of merchandise purchased in (1).*					
Accounts Payable	45		Accounts Payable	45	
Purchases Ret. and Allow.		45	Merchandise Inventory		45
3. *Sold eight units for $200 cash.*					
Cash	200		Cash	200	
Sales		200	Sales		200
			Cost of Goods Sold	120	
			Merchandise Inventory		120
4. *Closing entries:*					
Merchandise Inventory (Ending)	60		Income Summary	120	
Sales	200		Cost of Goods Sold		120
Purchases Ret. and Allow.	45				
Income Summary		305	Sales	200	
			Income Summary		200
Income Summary	225				
Merchandise Inv. (Beginning)		75			
Purchases		150			

	Units	Cost
Beginning inventory	5	$ 75
Purchases	10	150
Purchase returns	(3)	(45)
Goods available	12	$180
Goods sold	(8)	(120)
Ending inventory	4	$ 60

Comparing Journal Entries under Periodic and Perpetual Inventory Systems

Using parallel columns, Illustration 9–4 shows the typical journal entries made under periodic and perpetual inventory systems. In Illustration 9–4, observe the entries for the purchase of transaction 1. The perpetual system does not use a Purchases account. Instead, the cost of the items purchased is debited directly to Merchandise Inventory. Also, in transaction 2, the perpetual system credits the cost of purchase returns directly to the Merchandise Inventory account instead of using a Purchases Returns and Allowances account.

Transaction 3 involves the sale of merchandise. Note that the perpetual system requires two entries to record the sale, one to record the revenue and

ILLUSTRATION 9–5

First-In, First-Out Cost Flow

Item Product Z Location in stockroom Bin 8

Maximum 25 Minimum 5

	Purchased			Sold			Balance		
Date	Units	Cost	Total	Units	Cost	Total	Units	Cost	Total
1/1							10	10.00	100.00
1/5				5	10.00	50.00	5	10.00	50.00
1/8	20	10.50	210.00				5	10.00	
							20	10.50	260.00
1/10				3	10.00	30.00	2	10.00	
							20	10.50	230.00

another to record cost of goods sold. Thus, the perpetual system uses a Cost of Goods Sold account. In the periodic system the elements of cost of goods sold are not transferred to such an account. Instead, they are transferred to Income Summary in the process of recording the closing entries.

The closing entries under the two systems are shown as item 4 in Illustration 9–4. Under the periodic system, all of the cost elements related to inventories are transferred to Income Summary. By comparison, under the perpetual system, those cost elements were already recorded in a Cost of Goods Sold account. Thus, the closing entries simply transfer the balance in the Cost of Goods Sold account to Income Summary. Of course, Sales must be closed under both inventory systems. In Illustration 9–4, both inventory systems result in the same amounts of sales, cost of goods sold, and end-of-period merchandise inventory.

Subsidiary Inventory Records—Perpetual System

When a company sells more than one product and uses the perpetual inventory system, the Merchandise Inventory account serves as a controlling account to a subsidiary Merchandise Inventory Ledger. This ledger contains a separate record for each product in stock. This ledger may be computerized or kept on a manual basis. In either case, the record for each product shows the number of units and cost of each purchase, the number of units and cost of each sale, and the resulting balance of product on hand.

Illustration 9–5 shows an example of a subsidiary merchandise inventory record. This particular record is for Product Z, which is stored in Bin 8 of the stockroom. In this case, the record also shows the company's policy of maintaining no more than 25 or no less than 5 units of Product Z on hand.

First-In, First-Out—Perpetual Inventory System

In Illustration 9–5, note that the beginning inventory consisted of 10 units that cost $10 each. The first transaction occurred on January 5 and was a sale of 5 units at $17. Next, 20 units were purchased on January 8 at a cost of $10.50 per unit. And on January 10, 3 units were sold. Observe that these 3 units were costed out at $10 per unit. This indicates that a first-in, first-out basis is being assumed for this product.

The entries to record the sale in the General Journal are the following:

Jan.	10	Cash (or Accounts Receivable)	85.00	
		Sales		85.00
	10	Cost of Goods Sold	30.00	
		Merchandise Inventory		30.00
		3 × $10.00 = $30.00		

Last-In, First-Out—Perpetual Inventory System

Firms may also keep perpetual inventories on a last-in, first-out basis. When they do this, each sale is recorded as being from the last units received. As these are exhausted, sales are from the next to last, and so on. For example, if LIFO was used for Product Z, the subsidiary merchandise inventory record would appear as in Illustration 9–6.

Compare Illustration 9–6 (LIFO) with Illustration 9–5 (FIFO). In both illustrations, the sale of 5 units on January 5 is recorded the same way. The cost of these units came from the 10 units in the beginning inventory. However, the sale of 3 units on January 10 is recorded differently under LIFO than it is under FIFO. Assuming LIFO, as in Illustration 9–6, the January 10 sale is costed out at $10.50 per unit. This results in a balance of $228.50, which includes 5 units at $10.00 plus 17 units at $10.50.

The general journal entries to record the January 10 sale, assuming LIFO, are as follows:

Jan.	10	Cash (or Accounts Receivable)	85.00	
		Sales		85.00
	10	Cost of Goods Sold	31.50	
		Merchandise Inventory		31.50
		3 × $10.50 = $31.50		

The Difference between LIFO (Perpetual) and LIFO (Periodic)

Look again at Illustration 9–6 (LIFO). Note the costs that were assigned to Cost of Goods Sold for the January 5 and January 10 sales. In each case, the costs were taken from the most recent purchase. Thus, the cost of the January 5 sale came from the units in the beginning inventory; they were the only units available on January 5. This means that using LIFO, a perpetual inventory system and a periodic inventory system result in different amounts of cost of

ILLUSTRATION 9–6

Last-In, First-Out Cost Flow

Item Product Z   Location in stockroom Bin 8

Maximum 25   Minimum 5

	Purchased			Sold			Balance		
Date	Units	Cost	Total	Units	Cost	Total	Units	Cost	Total
1/1							10	10.00	100.00
1/5				5	10.00	50.00	5	10.00	50.00
1/8	20	10.50	210.00				5	10.00	
							20	10.50	260.00
1/10				3	10.50	31.50	5	10.00	
							17	10.50	228.50

goods sold (and ending inventory). With a periodic inventory system, the eight units sold during the period would come from the last units purchased during the period. In the case of Product Z, the difference between LIFO (perpetual) and LIFO (periodic) is summarized as follows:

	LIFO (perpetual)	LIFO (periodic)
Cost of goods sold:		
January 5 sale	5 × $10.00 = $ 50.00	
January 10 sale	3 × 10.50 = 31.50	
Total	$ 81.50	8 × $10.50 = $ 84.00
Ending inventory:		
From beginning inventory	5 × $10.00 = $ 50.00	10 × $10.00 = $100.00
From January 8 purchase	17 × 10.50 = 178.50	12 × 10.50 = 126.00
Total	$228.50	$226.00
Total goods available for sale	$310.00	$310.00

In addition to FIFO and LIFO, perpetual inventory systems can be designed to accommodate an average cost flow assumption. However, illustration of this alternative is deferred to a later course.

The Retail Method of Estimating Inventories

Good management requires that income statements be prepared more often than once each year, and inventory information is necessary each time an income statement is prepared. However, taking a physical inventory in a retail store is both time-consuming and expensive. Therefore, some retailers use the so-called **retail inventory method** to estimate inventories without stopping to take a physical count of inventory. Many companies use the retail inventory method to estimate inventory for their monthly or quarterly statements. Then, they take a physical inventory at the end of each year. The monthly or quarterly statements are called **interim statements** because they are prepared between the regular year-end statements. Other companies also use the retail inventory method to prepare the year-end statements. However, all companies must take a physical inventory at least once each year to correct any errors or shortages.

LO 6 Estimate an inventory by the retail method and by the gross profit method.

Estimating an Ending Inventory by the Retail Method

When the retail method is used to estimate an inventory, the company's records must show the amount of inventory it had at the beginning of the period both at *cost* and at *retail*. You already know what is meant by the cost of an inventory. The retail amount of an inventory simply means the dollar amount of the inventory at the marked selling prices of the inventory items.

In addition to the beginning inventory, the accounting records must also show the amount of goods purchased during the period both at cost and at retail. Also, the records must show the amount of net sales at retail. This is the balance of the Sales account less returns and discounts. With this information, you estimate the ending inventory as follows:

Step 1: Compute the amount of goods available for sale during the period both at cost and at retail.

Step 2: Divide the goods available at cost by the goods available at retail to obtain a **retail method cost ratio.**

Step 3: Deduct sales (at retail) from goods available for sale (at retail) to determine the ending inventory at retail.

Step 4: Multiply the ending inventory at retail by the cost ratio to reduce the inventory to a cost basis.

Illustration 9–7 shows these calculations.

This is the essence of Illustration 9–7: (1) The company had $100,000 of goods (at marked selling prices) for sale during the period. (2) These goods cost 60% of the $100,000 total amount at which they were marked for sale. (3) The company's records (its Sales account) showed that $70,000 of these goods were sold, leaving $30,000 (retail value) of merchandise unsold and presumably in the ending inventory. (4) Since cost in this store is 60% of retail, the estimated cost of this ending inventory is $18,000.

An ending inventory calculated as in Illustration 9–7 is an estimate arrived at by deducting sales (goods sold) from goods available for sale. As we said before, this method may be used for interim statements or even for year-end statements. Nonetheless, a store must take a physical count of the inventory at least once each year to correct any errors or shortages.

Using the Retail Method to Reduce a Physical Inventory to Cost

In retail stores, items for sale normally have price tags that show selling prices. So, when a store takes a physical inventory, it commonly takes the inventory at the marked selling prices of the items on hand. It then reduces the dollar total of this inventory to a cost basis by applying its cost ratio. It does this because the selling prices are readily available and the application of the cost ratio eliminates the need to look up the invoice price of each item on hand.

ILLUSTRATION 9–7

Calculating the Ending Inventory Cost by the Retail Method

		At Cost	At Retail
(Step 1)	Goods available for sale:		
	Beginning inventory	$20,500	$ 34,500
	Net purchases	39,500	65,500
	Goods available for sale	$60,000	$100,000
(Step 2)	Cost ratio: ($60,000/$100,000) × 100 = 60%		
(Step 3)	Deduct sales at retail		70,000
	Ending inventory at retail		$ 30,000
(Step 4)	Ending inventory at cost ($30,000 × 60%) . .	$18,000	

For example, assume that the company in Illustration 9–7 estimates its inventory by the retail method and takes a physical inventory at the marked selling prices of the inventoried goods. Assume further that the total retail amount of this physical inventory is $29,600. Under these assumptions, the company may calculate the cost for this inventory, without having to look up the cost of each item on hand, simply by applying its cost ratio to the $29,600 inventory total as follows:

$$\$29{,}600 \times 60\% = \$17{,}760$$

The $17,760 cost figure for this company's ending physical inventory is a satisfactory figure for year-end statement purposes. It is also acceptable to the Internal Revenue Service for tax purposes.

Inventory Shortage

An inventory determined as in Illustration 9–7 is an estimate of the amount of goods on hand. Since it is arrived at by deducting sales from goods for sale, it does not reveal any shortages due to breakage, loss, or theft. However, you can estimate the amount of such shortages by comparing the inventory as calculated in Illustration 9–7 with the amount that results from taking a physical inventory.

For example, in Illustration 9–7, we estimated that the ending inventory at retail was $30,000. Then, we assumed that this same company took a physical inventory and counted only $29,600 of merchandise on hand (at retail). Therefore, the company must have had an inventory shortage at retail of $30,000 − $29,600 = $400. Stated in terms of cost, the shortage is $400 × 60% = $240.

Markups and Markdowns

The calculation of a cost ratio is often not as simple as that shown in Illustration 9–7. It is not simple because, after merchandise is purchased and marked at retail prices, a store may decide to change the retail prices by marking the goods up or down. When goods are first purchased and marked at selling price, the amount or percentage by which the marked selling prices exceed cost is

ILLUSTRATION 9–8

The Effect of Markups and Markdowns on the Retail Method

	At Cost	At Retail
Goods available for sale:		
Beginning inventory	$18,000	$27,800
Net purchases	34,000	50,700
Additional markups		1,500
Goods available for sale	$52,000	$80,000
Cost ratio: ($52,000/$80,000) × 100 = 65%		
Sales at retail		$54,000
Markdowns		2,000
Total sales and markdowns		$56,000
Ending inventory at retail ($80,000 less $56,000)		$24,000
Ending inventory at cost ($24,000 × 65%)	$15,600	

called a **normal markup.** It is also called a **markon.** For example, if a store's normal markup is 50% on cost and it applies this markup to an item that cost $10, it will mark the item for sale at $15. Normal markups appear in the calculation of a store's cost ratio as the difference between net purchases at cost and at retail.

After goods are first priced to sell at the normal markup, if the prices are increased, the amount of the additional price increases are called **markups.** And if selling prices are decreased, the amounts of the decreases are called **markdowns.** Stores may add markups to the price of goods because the quality or style of the goods make them especially attractive to customers. Goods often are marked down for a clearance sale or whenever the goods are moving slowly.

When using the retail inventory method, the store must keep a record of additional markups and markdowns. This information is used to calculate the ending inventory as shown in Illustration 9–8.

In Illustration 9–8, notice that the store's $80,000 of goods available for sale at retail were reduced $54,000 by sales and $2,000 by markdowns, a total of $56,000. To understand the markdowns, visualize this effect of a markdown. The store had an item for sale during the period at $25. The item did not sell, so the manager marked its price down from $25 to $20. By this act, the retail amount of goods for sale in the store was reduced by $5. The total of such markdowns during the year amounted to $2,000.

In the calculations of Illustration 9–8, note that the estimated ending inventory at retail is $24,000. Therefore, since cost is 65% of retail, the ending inventory at cost is $15,600.

Observe in Illustration 9–8 that markups enter into the calculation of the cost ratio but markdowns do not. Why are markdowns excluded from the cost ratio calculation? The reason for this is that a more conservative figure for the ending inventory results, a figure that approaches "the lower of cost or market." Further discussion of this version of the retail inventory method is reserved for a more advanced accounting course.

ILLUSTRATION 9–9

The Gross Profit Method of Estimating Inventory

Goods available for sale:		
Inventory, January 1, 1993		$ 12,000
Net purchases	$20,000	
Add transportation-in	500	20,500
Goods available for sale		$ 32,500
Less estimated cost of goods sold:		
Sales	$31,500	
Less sales returns	(1,500)	
Net sales	$30,000	
Estimated cost of goods sold (70% × $30,000)		(21,000)
Estimated March 27 inventory and inventory loss		$ 11,500

Gross Profit Method of Estimating Inventories

Sometimes, a business that does not use a perpetual inventory system or the retail method may need to estimate the cost of its inventory. For example, if a fire destroys the inventory or a burglary results in the theft of the inventory, the business must estimate the inventory so that it can file a claim with its insurance company. In cases such as this, the cost of the inventory can be estimated by the **gross profit method.** With this method, a business's historical relationship between cost of goods sold and sales is applied to sales of the current period as a way of estimating cost of goods sold during the current period. Then, cost of goods sold is subtracted from the cost of goods available for sale to get the estimated cost of the ending inventory.

To use the gross profit method, several items of accounting information must be available. This includes information about the normal gross profit margin or rate, the cost of the beginning inventory, the cost of net purchases, transportation-in, and the amount of sales and sales returns.

For example, assume that the inventory of a company was totally destroyed by a fire on March 27, 1993. The company's average gross profit rate during the past five years has been 30% of net sales. On the date of the fire, the company's accounts showed the following balances:

Sales	$31,500
Sales returns	1,500
Inventory, January 1, 1993	12,000
Net purchases	20,000
Transportation-in	500

With this information, the gross profit method may be used to estimate the company's inventory loss. To apply the gross profit method, the first step is to recognize that whatever portion of each dollar of net sales was gross profit, the remaining portion was cost of goods sold. Thus, if the company's gross profit rate averages 30%, then 30% of each net sales dollar was gross profit, and 70% was cost of goods sold. Illustration 9–9 shows how the 70% is used to estimate the inventory that was lost.

To understand Illustration 9–9, recall that an ending inventory is normally subtracted from goods available for sale to determine the cost of goods sold. Then observe in Illustration 9–9 that the opposite subtraction is made. Estimated cost of goods sold is subtracted from goods available for sale to determine the estimated ending inventory.

As we mentioned, the gross profit method is often used to estimate the amount of an insurance claim. The method is also used by accountants to see if an inventory amount determined by management's physical count of the items on hand is reasonable.

Summary of the Chapter in Terms of Learning Objectives

LO 1. The allocation of the cost of goods available for sale between cost of goods sold and ending inventory is an accounting application of the *matching principle*. Merchandise inventory should include all goods that are owned by the business and held for resale. This includes items the business has placed on consignment with other parties but excludes items that the business has taken on consignment from other parties. The cost of merchandise includes not only the invoice price less any discounts but also any additional or incidental costs that were incurred to put the merchandise into place and condition for sale.

LO 2. When specific invoice prices are used to price an inventory, each item in the inventory is identified and the cost of the item is determined by referring to the item's purchase invoice. With weighted-average cost, the total cost of the beginning inventory and of purchases is divided by the total number of units available to determine the weighted-average cost per unit. Multiplying this cost by the number of units in the ending inventory yields the cost of the inventory. FIFO prices the ending inventory based on the assumption that the first units purchased are the first units sold. LIFO is based on the assumption that the last units purchased are the first units sold. All of these methods are acceptable.

LO 3. When lower of cost or market is applied to merchandise inventory, market usually means replacement cost. But market is never higher than net realizable value and never lower than net realizable value minus a normal profit. Lower of cost or market may be applied separately to each product or to the merchandise inventory as a whole.

LO 4. When the periodic inventory system is used, an error in counting the ending inventory affects assets (inventory), net income (cost of goods sold), and owner's equity. Since the ending inventory is the beginning inventory of the next period, an error at the end of one period affects the cost of goods sold and the net income of the next period. These next period effects offset the financial statement effects in the previous period.

LO 5. Under a perpetual inventory system, purchases and purchases returns are recorded in the Merchandise Inventory account. At the time sales are recorded, the cost of goods sold is credited to Merchandise Inventory. As a result, the Merchandise Inventory is kept up to date throughout the accounting period.

LO 6. When the retail method is used, sales are subtracted from the retail amount of goods available for sale to determine the ending inventory at retail. This is multiplied by the cost ratio to reduce the inventory amount to cost. To calculate the cost ratio, divide the cost of goods available by the retail value of goods available (including markups but excluding markdowns).

With the gross profit method, multiply sales by (1 − the gross profit rate) to estimate cost of goods sold. Then, subtract the answer from the cost of goods available for sale to estimate the cost of the ending inventory.

Demonstration Problem

Tale Company uses a periodic inventory system and had the following beginning inventory and purchases during 1993:

		Item X		Item Y	
Date		**Units**	**Unit Cost**	**Units**	**Unit Cost**
1/1	inventory	400	$14	200	$11
3/10	Purchase	200	15	300	12
5/9	Purchase	300	16		
6/17	Purchase			450	18
9/22	Purchase	250	20		
11/28	Purchase	100	21	110	17

At December 31, 1993, there were 550 units of X and 320 units of Y on hand.

Required

1. Using the preceding information, apply FIFO inventory pricing and calculate the cost of goods available for sale in 1993, the ending inventory, and the cost of goods sold for each item and for both items combined.
2. In preparing the financial statements for 1993, the bookkeeper was instructed to use FIFO but failed to do so and computed the cost of goods sold according to LIFO. Determine the size of the misstatement of 1993's income from this error. Also determine the effect of the error on the 1994 income. Assume no income taxes.
3. Assume the following additional facts, and use the retail method to estimate the lower of cost or market of the ending inventory:

Retail value of the beginning inventory	$13,051
Retail value of purchases	41,381
Additional markups (at retail)	3,600
Sales	33,600
Markdowns	4,432

Solution to Demonstration Problem

Planning the Solution

- For each product, multiply the units of each purchase and the beginning inventory by the appropriate unit costs to determine the total costs. Then, calculate the cost of goods available for sale.
- For FIFO, calculate the ending inventory by multiplying the units on hand by the unit costs of the latest purchases. Then, subtract the total ending inventory from the cost of goods available for sale.

- For LIFO, calculate the ending inventory by multiplying the units on hand by the unit costs of the beginning inventory and the earliest purchases. Then, subtract the total ending inventory from the cost of goods available for sale.
- Compare the ending 1993 inventory amounts under FIFO and LIFO to determine the misstatement of 1993 income that resulted from using LIFO. The 1994 and 1993 errors are equal in amount but have opposite effects.
- Calculate the retail amount of goods available for sale including markups but excluding markdowns. Then, compare the cost of goods available with the retail amount to determine the cost ratio.
- Subtract sales and markdowns from the retail amount of goods available for sale to determine the ending inventory at retail. Then, determine the lower of cost or market of ending inventory by applying the cost ratio to the ending inventory at retail.

1. FIFO basis:

Item X		
1/1 inventory (400 @ $14)		$ 5,600
Purchases:		
3/10 purchase (200 @ $15)	$3,000	
5/9 purchase (300 @ $16)	4,800	
9/22 purchase (250 @ $20)	5,000	
11/28 purchase (100 @ $21)	2,100	14,900
Cost of goods available for sale		$20,500
Ending inventory at FIFO cost:		
11/28 purchase (100 @ $21)	$2,100	
9/22 purchase (250 @ $20)	5,000	
5/9 purchase (200 @ $16)	3,200	
Ending inventory		10,300
Cost of goods sold		$10,200
Item Y		
1/1 inventory (200 @ $11)		$ 2,200
Purchases:		
3/10 purchase (300 @ $12)	$3,600	
6/17 purchase (450 @ $18)	8,100	
11/28 purchase (110 @ $17)	1,870	13,570
Cost of goods available for sale		$15,770
Ending inventory at FIFO cost:		
11/28 purchase (110 @ $17)	$1,870	
6/17 purchase (210 @ $18)	3,780	
Ending inventory		5,650
Cost of goods sold		$10,120
Combined		
Cost of goods available ($20,500 + $15,770)		$36,270
Cost of ending inventory ($10,300 + $5,650)		15,950
Cost of goods sold ($10,200 + $10,120)		$20,320

2. LIFO basis:

Item X

Cost of goods available for sale		$20,500
Ending inventory at LIFO cost:		
1/1 inventory (400 @ $14)	$5,600	
3/10 purchase (150 @ $15)	2,250	
LIFO cost of ending inventory		7,850
Cost of goods sold		$12,650

Item Y

Cost of goods available for sale		$15,770
Ending inventory at LIFO cost:		
1/1 inventory (200 @ $11)	$2,200	
3/10 purchase (120 @ $12)	1,440	
LIFO cost of ending inventory		3,640
Cost of goods sold		$12,130

Combined

Cost of goods available ($20,500 + $15,770)	$36,270
Cost of ending inventory ($7,850 + $3,640)	11,490
Cost of goods sold	$24,780

If LIFO is mistakenly used when FIFO should have been used, cost of goods sold in 1993 would be overstated by $4,460, which is the difference between the FIFO and LIFO amounts of ending inventory. Income would be understated in 1993 by $4,460. In 1994, income would be overstated by $4,460 because of the understatement of the beginning inventory.

3. Retail method of estimating inventory:

	At Cost	At Retail
Goods available for sale:		
Beginning inventory ($5,600 + $2,200 = $7,800)	$ 7,800	$13,051
Purchases ($14,900 + $13,570 = $28,470)	28,470	41,381
Markups		3,600
Goods available for sale	$36,270	$58,032
Cost ratio: ($36,270/$58,032) × 100 = 62.5%		
Sales at retail		$33,600
Markdowns		4,432
Total sales and markdowns		$38,032
Ending inventory at retail ($58,032 − $38,032)		$20,000
Ending inventory at cost ($20,000 × 62.5%)	$12,500	

Glossary

LO 7 Define or explain the words and phrases listed in the chapter glossary.

Conservatism principle the accounting principle that guides accountants to select the less optimistic estimate when two estimates of amounts to be received or paid are about equally likely. p. 494

Consignee one who receives and holds goods owned by another party for the purpose of selling the goods for the owner. p. 485

Consignor an owner of goods who ships them to another party who will then sell the goods for the owner. p. 485

Consistency principle the accounting requirement that a company use the same accounting methods period after period so that the financial statements of succeeding periods will be comparable. pp. 491–92

First-in, first-out inventory pricing (FIFO) the pricing of an inventory under the assumption that the first items received were the first items sold. p. 488

Gross profit inventory method a procedure for estimating an ending inventory in which the past gross profit rate is used to estimate cost of goods sold, which is then subtracted from the cost of goods available for sale to determine the estimated ending inventory. pp. 504–505

Interim statements monthly or quarterly financial statements prepared in between the regular year-end statements. p. 501

Inventory ticket a form attached to the counted items in the process of taking a physical inventory. p. 486

Last-in, first-out inventory pricing (LIFO) the pricing of an inventory under the assumption that the last items received were the first items sold. p. 489

Markdown a reduction in the marked selling price of merchandise. p. 503

Markon the normal amount or percentage of cost that is added to the cost of merchandise to arrive at its selling price. p. 503

Markup an increase in the sales price of merchandise above the normal markon given to the goods. p. 503

Net realizable value the expected sales price of an item less any additional costs to sell. p. 485

Normal markup another name for *markon*. pp. 502–503

Retail inventory method a method for estimating an ending inventory based on the ratio of the amount of goods for sale at cost to the amount of goods for sale at marked selling prices. pp. 500–503

Retail method cost ratio the ratio of goods available for sale at cost to goods available for sale at retail prices. p. 501

Specific invoice inventory pricing the pricing of an inventory where the purchase invoice of each item in the ending inventory is identified and used to determine the cost assigned to the inventory. pp. 487–88

Weighted-average inventory pricing an inventory pricing system in which the unit prices of the beginning inventory and of each purchase are weighted by the number of units in the beginning inventory and each purchase. The total of these amounts is then divided by the total number of units available for sale to find the unit cost of the ending inventory and of the units that were sold. p. 488

Synonymous Terms

Markon normal markup.

Specific invoice inventory pricing specific identification method.

Objective Review

Answers to the following questions are listed at the end of this chapter. Be sure that you decide which is the one best answer to each question *before* you check the answers.

LO 1 Kramer Gallery purchased an original painting for $11,400. Additional costs incurred in obtaining and selling the artwork included $130 for transportation-in, $150 for import duties, $100 for insurance during shipment, $180 for advertising costs, $400 for framing, and $800 for sales commissions. In calculating the cost of inventory, what total cost should be assigned to the painting?

a. $11,400.
b. $11,530.
c. $11,780.
d. $12,180.
e. $13,160.

LO 2 The following data relate to a single inventory item for Montgomery Company:

Date		Units	Unit Cost
May 1	Beginning inventory	110	$5
2	Purchase	30	6
17	Sale	40	
19	Purchase	25	4
26	Sale	20	

Using a perpetual inventory system and costing inventory by LIFO, the ending inventory is

a. $260.
b. $520.
c. $525.
d. $530.
e. $830.

LO 3 A company's ending inventory includes the following items:

Product	Units on Hand	Unit Cost	Market Value per Unit
A	20	$ 6	$ 5
B	40	9	8
C	10	12	15

Applied separately to each product, the inventory's lower of cost or market amount is

a. $520.
b. $540.

c. \$570.

d. \$600.

e. None of the above.

LO 4 Falk Company maintains its inventory records on a periodic basis. In making the physical count of inventory at 1992 year-end, an error was made that overstated the 1992 ending inventory by \$10,000. What impact, if any, will this error have on cost of goods sold in 1992 and 1993?

a. 1992 overstated by \$10,000; 1993 understated by \$10,000.

b. 1992 understated by \$10,000; 1993 overstated by \$10,000.

c. 1992 overstated by \$10,000; no impact on 1993.

d. 1992 understated by \$10,000; no impact on 1993.

e. 1992 understated by \$10,000; no impact on 1993 cost of goods sold, but 1993 ending inventory will be overstated by \$10,000.

LO 5 With a perpetual inventory system:

a. The Merchandise Inventory account balance shows the amount of merchandise on hand.

b. Subsidiary inventory records are maintained for each type of product.

c. A sale of merchandise requires two entries, one to record the revenue and one to record the cost of goods sold.

d. A separate Cost of Goods Sold account is used.

e. All of the above are correct.

LO 6 The following data relates to Taylor Company's inventory during the year:

	Cost	Retail
Beginning inventory	\$324,000	\$530,000
Purchases	204,000	343,000
Purchases returns	3,600	8,000
Markups		9,000
Markdowns		75,000
Sales		320,000

Using the retail method, the estimated cost of the ending inventory is

a. \$129,400.

b. \$287,400.

c. \$290,370.

d. \$314,368.

e. \$479,000.

LO 7 The normal amount or percentage of cost that is added to the cost of merchandise to arrive at its selling price is a:

a. Markdown.

b. Profit.

c. Markup.

d. Markon.

e. Net markup.

Questions for Class Discussion

1. With respect to periodic inventory systems, it has been said that cost of goods sold and ending inventory are opposite sides of the same coin. What is meant by this?
2. Where is merchandise inventory disclosed in the financial statements?
3. If Fanshawe Company is the consignee and Johnson Company is the consignor with respect to goods being offered for sale, the goods should be included in the inventory of which company?
4. If Campbell sells goods to Thompson, FOB Campbell's factory, and the goods are still in transit from Campbell to Thompson, which company should include the goods in its inventory?
5. Of what does the cost of an inventory item consist?
6. Why are incidental costs often ignored in pricing an inventory? Under what accounting principle is this permitted?
7. Give the meanings of the following when applied to inventory: (*a*) FIFO; (*b*) LIFO; (*c*) cost; and (*d*) perpetual inventory.
8. If prices are rising, will the LIFO or the FIFO method of inventory valuation result in the higher gross profit?
9. If prices are falling, will the LIFO or the FIFO method of inventory valuation result in the higher ending inventory?
10. If prices are falling, will the LIFO or the FIFO method of inventory valuation result in the lower cost of goods sold?
11. May a company change its inventory pricing method each accounting period?
12. Does the accounting principle of consistency preclude any changes from one accounting method to another?
13. What effect does the full-disclosure principle have if a company changes from one acceptable accounting method to another?
14. What is meant when it is said that under a periodic inventory system, inventory errors correct themselves?
15. If inventory errors under a periodic inventory system correct themselves, why be concerned when such errors are made?
16. What guidance for accountants is provided by the principle of conservatism?
17. What accounts are used in a periodic inventory system but not in a perpetual inventory system?
18. What account is used in a perpetual inventory system but not in a periodic inventory system?
19. Assuming a last-in, first-out cost flow, why do perpetual inventory systems and periodic inventory systems result in different amounts of cost of goods sold and ending inventory?
20. What is the usual meaning of the word *market* as it is used in determining the lower of cost or market for merchandise inventory?
21. In what way is the use of lower of cost or market with merchandise inventory less restrictive than when it is used with temporary investments in marketable equity securities?

22. In deciding whether to reduce an item of merchandise to the lower of cost or market, what is the importance of the item's net realizable value?
23. Give the meanings of the following when applied in the retail method of estimating an inventory: (*a*) pricing inventory at retail, (*b*) cost ratio, (*c*) normal markup, (*d*) markon, (*e*) additional markup, and (*f*) markdown.
24. A company uses a periodic inventory system, records its merchandise purchases at cost, and assumes a FIFO cost flow. If a fire results in the loss of the company's inventory, what method might the company use to estimate the amount of inventory lost?
25. Refer to the financial statements of Lands' End, Inc., in Appendix K. The footnotes to those financial statements state that the inventory amounts on the balance sheets were determined using LIFO. If FIFO had been used, the inventory would have been approximately $14,200,000 and $12,987,000 higher than reported at January 31, 1991, and 1990. If FIFO had been used, what amount would have been reported as income before income taxes for the year ended January 31, 1991?
26. Refer to IBM's financial statements in Appendix J and Lands' End, Inc.'s financial statements in Appendix K. On December 31, 1990, what percentage of IBM's current assets was represented by inventories? On January 31, 1991, what percentage of Lands' End, Inc.'s current assets was represented by inventory?

Exercises

Exercise 9–1
Alternative cost flow assumptions, periodic inventory system
(LO 2)

Barnes Company began a year and purchased merchandise as follows:

Jan. 1	Beginning inventory	40 units @ $30.00 =	$ 1,200
Mar. 5	Purchased	200 units @ $28.00 =	5,600
July 10	Purchased	80 units @ $25.00 =	2,000
Oct. 2	Purchased	160 units @ $23.00 =	3,680
Dec. 22	Purchased	120 units @ $20.00 =	2,400
	Total	600 units	$14,880

Required

The company uses a periodic inventory system, and the ending inventory consists of 150 units, 50 from each of the last three purchases. Determine the share of the $14,880 cost of the units for sale that should be assigned to the ending inventory and to goods sold under each of the following: (*a*) costs are assigned on the basis of specific invoice prices, (*b*) costs are assigned on a weighted-average cost basis, (*c*) costs are assigned on the basis of FIFO, and (*d*) costs are assigned on the basis of LIFO. Assuming the company has enough income to require that it pay income taxes, which method provides a current tax advantage?

Exercise 9–2
Alternative cost flow assumptions, periodic inventory system
(LO 2)

Holt Company began a year and purchased merchandise as follows:

Jan. 1	Beginning inventory	40 units @ $20.00 =	$	800
Mar. 5	Purchased	200 units @ $23.00 =		4,600
July 10	Purchased	80 units @ $25.00 =		2,000
Oct. 2	Purchased	160 units @ $28.00 =		4,480
Dec. 22	Purchased	120 units @ $30.00 =		3,600
	Total	600 units		$15,480

Required

The company uses a periodic inventory system, and the ending inventory consists of 150 units, 50 from each of the last three purchases. Determine the share of the $15,480 cost of the units for sale that should be assigned to the ending inventory and to goods sold under each of the following: (*a*) costs are assigned on the basis of specific invoice prices, (*b*) costs are assigned on a weighted-average cost basis, (*c*) costs are assigned on the basis of FIFO, and (*d*) costs are assigned on the basis of LIFO. Assuming the company has enough income to require that it pay income taxes, which method provides a current tax advantage?

Exercise 9–3
Lower of cost or market
(LO 3)

Tucker Company's ending inventory includes the following items:

Product	Units on Hand	Unit Cost	Replacement Cost per Unit
A	20	$15	$17
B	25	24	20
C	30	13	12
D	22	10	10

After evaluating each product's selling price and normal profit margin, replacement cost is found to be the best measure of market. Calculate lower of cost or market for the inventory (*a*) as a whole, and (*b*) applied separately to each product.

Exercise 9–4
Lower of cost or market
(LO 3)

Calculate the lower of cost or market for the inventory in each of the following independent cases:

1. Horn Company's inventory consists of 50 units of Product Y, all of which have been damaged. The company bought the inventory for $19 per unit. Replacement cost is $18 per unit. Expected sales price is $22 per unit, but this can be realized only if $5 additional cost per unit is paid.
2. Post Company's inventory consists of 100 units of Product Z which were purchased for $35 per unit. Replacement cost is $22 per unit. Expected sales price is $39 per unit, and a normal profit margin based on this price is $12.

Exercise 9–5
Analysis of inventory errors
(LO 4)

Reynolds Company had $145,000 of sales during each of three consecutive years, and it purchased merchandise costing $100,000 during each of the years. It also maintained a $35,000 inventory from the beginning to the end of the three-year period. However, in accounting under a periodic inventory system, it made an error at the end of year 1 that caused its ending year 1 inventory to appear on its statements at $30,000, rather than the correct $35,000.

Required

1. State the actual amount of the company's gross profit in each of the years.
2. Prepare a comparative income statement like Illustration 9–3 to show the effect of this error on the company's cost of goods sold and gross profit in year 1, year 2, and year 3.

Exercise 9–6
Perpetual inventory system—FIFO cost flow
(LO 5)

In its beginning inventory on January 1, 1993, Z Company had 40 units of merchandise that had cost $4 per unit. Prepare general journal entries for Z Company to record the following transactions during 1993, assuming a perpetual inventory system and a first-in, first-out cost flow.

June 5 Purchased on credit 150 units of merchandise at $5.00 per unit.
12 Returned 30 defective units from the June 5 purchase to the supplier.
Oct. 2 Purchased for cash 90 units of merchandise at $4.25 per unit.
Nov. 10 Sold 100 units of merchandise for cash at a price of $6.25 per unit.
Dec. 31 Prepare entries to close the revenue and expense accounts to Income Summary.

Exercise 9–7
Perpetual inventory system—LIFO cost flow
(LO 5)

In its January 1, 1993, inventory, S Company had 45 units of merchandise that had cost $3 per unit. Prepare general journal entries for S Company to record the following transactions during 1993, assuming a perpetual inventory system and a last-in, first-out cost flow.

Feb. 15 Purchased on credit 70 units of merchandise at $3.50 per unit.
Apr. 4 Sold 55 units of merchandise for cash at $6.00 per unit.
July 12 Purchased for cash 50 units of merchandise at $4.00 per unit.
Oct. 23 Sold 60 units of merchandise for cash at a price of $6.25 per unit.
Dec. 31 Prepare entries to close the revenue and expense accounts to Income Summary.

Exercise 9–8
Estimating ending inventory—retail inventory method
(LO 6)

During an accounting period, Baker sold $340,000 of merchandise at marked retail prices. At the period end, the following information was available from its records:

	At Cost	At Retail
Beginning inventory	$ 70,000	$125,000
Net purchases	195,100	345,000
Additional markups		12,000
Markdowns		9,800

Use the retail method to estimate the store's ending inventory at cost.

Exercise 9–9
Reducing physical inventory to cost—retail method
(LO 6)

Assume that in addition to estimating its ending inventory by the retail method, Baker Company of Exercise 9–8 also took a physical inventory at the marked selling prices of the inventory items. Assume further that the total of this physical inventory at marked selling prices was $127,600. Then (*a*) determine the amount of this inventory at cost and (*b*) determine the store's inventory shrinkage from breakage, theft, or other cause at retail and at cost.

Exercise 9–10
Estimating ending inventory—gross profit method
(LO 6)

On January 1, a store had a $72,000 inventory at cost. During the first quarter of the year, it purchased $245,000 of merchandise, returned $3,500, and paid freight charges on purchased merchandise totaling $8,500. During the past several years, the store's gross profit on sales has averaged 30%. Under the assumption the company had $305,000 of sales during the first quarter of the year, use the gross profit method to estimate its inventory at the end of the first quarter.

Problems

Problem 9–1
Alternative cost flows—periodic system
(LO 2)

Smith Company began a year with 1,000 units of Product X in its inventory that cost $60 each, and it made successive purchases of the product as follows:

Feb. 11	1,750 units @ $65 each
May 25	2,000 units @ $70 each
Oct. 4	1,500 units @ $75 each
Dec. 9	1,750 units @ $70 each

The company uses a periodic inventory system. On December 31, a physical count disclosed that 2,500 units of Product X remained in inventory.

Required

1. Prepare a calculation showing the number and total cost of the units available for sale during the year.
2. Prepare calculations showing the amounts that should be assigned to the ending inventory and to cost of goods sold assuming (*a*) a FIFO basis, (*b*) a LIFO basis, and (*c*) a weighted-average cost basis. Round your calculation of the weighted-average cost per unit to three decimal places.

Problem 9–2
Income statement comparisons and cost flow assumptions
(LO 2)

Tyler Company sold 3,000 units of its product at $75 per unit during 1993. Incurring operating expenses of $12 per unit in selling the units, it began the year and made successive purchases of the product as follows:

January 1 beginning inventory	300 units costing $45.00 per unit
Purchases:	
February 20	500 units costing $48.00 per unit
May 14	900 units costing $48.50 per unit
August 29	1,500 units costing $50.50 per unit
November 20	250 units costing $52.00 per unit

Required

Prepare a comparative income statement for the company showing in adjacent columns the net incomes earned from the sale of the product assuming the company uses a periodic inventory system and prices its ending inventory on the basis of: (*a*) FIFO, (*b*) LIFO, and (*c*) weighted-average cost. Round your calculation of the weighted-average cost per unit to three decimal places.

Problem 9–3
Lower of cost or market
(LO 3)

Case 1: In this case, an evaluation of the expected selling price and normal profit margin for each product shows that replacement cost is the best measure of market. The inventory includes:

Product	Units on Hand	Cost	Replacement Cost
A	550	$12	$10
B	900	20	17
C	975	25	30

Case 2: In this case, the inventories of Products D and E have been damaged. If $7 additional cost per unit is paid to repackage the Product D units, they can be sold for $75 per unit. The Product E units can be sold for $60 per unit after paying additional cleaning costs of $6 per unit. The inventory includes:

Product	Units on Hand	Cost	Replacement Cost
D	150	$72	$70
E	400	58	64

Case 3: In this case, Product F normally is sold for $30 per unit and has a profit margin of 30%. However, the expected selling price has fallen to $20 per unit. Product G normally is sold for $65 per unit and has a profit margin of 25%. However, the expected selling price of Product G has fallen to $60 per unit. The inventory includes:

Product	Units on Hand	Cost	Replacement Cost
F	300	$19	$17
G	150	48	41

Required

In each of these independent cases, calculate the lower of cost or market (*a*) for the inventory as a whole and (*b*) for the inventory applied separately to each product.

Problem 9–4
Analysis of inventory errors
(LO 4)

Mitchell Company keeps its inventory records on a periodic basis. The company's financial statements reported the following amounts:

	Financial Statements for Year Ended December 31, 1992	1993	1994
(*a*) Cost of goods sold	$ 65,000	$ 77,000	$ 70,000
(*b*) Net income	20,000	25,000	21,000
(*c*) Total current assets	105,000	115,000	100,000
(*d*) Owners' equity	117,000	130,000	112,000

In making the physical counts of inventory the following errors were made:

Inventory on December 31, 1992	Understated $6,000
Inventory on December 31, 1993	Overstated 3,000

Required

1. For each of the preceding financial statement items—(*a*), (*b*), (*c*), and (*d*)—prepare a schedule similar to the following and show the adjustments that would have been necessary to correct the reported amounts.

	1992	1993	1994
Cost of goods sold:			
Reported	____	____	____
Adjustments: 12/31/92 error	____	____	____
12/31/93 error	____	____	____
Corrected	====	====	====

2. What is the error in the aggregate net income for the three-year period that resulted from the inventory errors?

Problem 9–5
Inventory records under FIFO and LIFO—perpetual systems
(LO 5)

The Kramer Company sells a product called Speedcleaner and uses a perpetual inventory system to account for its merchandise. The beginning balance of Speedcleaner and transactions during April of this year were as follows:

Apr.	1	Balance: 35 units costing $4 each.
	3	Purchased 60 units costing $5 each.
	9	Sold 27 units.
	15	Sold 32 units.
	18	Purchased 55 units costing $6 each.
	22	Sold 19 units.
	30	Sold 37 units.

Required

1. Under the assumption the business keeps its records on a FIFO basis, enter the beginning balance and the transactions on a subsidiary inventory record like the one in Illustration 9–5.
2. Under the assumption the business keeps its inventory records on a LIFO basis, enter the beginning inventory and the transactions on a second subsidiary inventory record like the one in Illustration 9–6.
3. Assume the 37 units sold on April 30 were sold on credit to Russell Sayer at $11 each and prepare general journal entries to record the sale on a LIFO basis.

Problem 9–6
Retail inventory method
(LO 6)

Hammond Company takes a year-end physical inventory at marked selling prices and uses the retail method to reduce the inventory total to a cost basis for statement purposes. It also uses the retail method to estimate the amount of inventory it should have at the end of a year, and by comparison, estimates any inventory shortage due to shoplifting or other causes. At the end of the year, its physical inventory at marked selling prices totaled $80,600, and the following information was available from its records:

	At Cost	At Retail
Beginning inventory	$ 40,400	$ 60,400
Purchases	287,560	435,700
Purchases returns	2,700	4,300
Additional markups		8,600
Markdowns		3,700
Sales		416,570
Sales returns		3,980

Required

1. Use the retail method to estimate the store's year-end inventory at cost.
2. Use the retail method to reduce the store's year-end physical inventory to a cost basis.
3. Prepare a schedule showing the inventory shortage at cost and at retail.

Problem 9–7
Retail inventory method
(LO 6)

The records of Westwood Company provided the following information for the year ended December 31:

	At Cost	At Retail
January 1 beginning inventory	$ 52,150	$ 88,300
Purchases	369,740	609,400
Purchases returns	6,200	11,320
Additional markups		6,420
Markdowns		3,400
Sales		523,400
Sales returns		5,200

Required

1. Prepare an estimate of the company's year-end inventory by the retail method.
2. Under the assumption the company took a year-end physical inventory at marked selling prices that totaled $159,600, prepare a schedule showing the store's loss from theft or other cause at cost and at retail.

Problem 9–8
Gross profit method
(LO 6)

While opening the Stereo Store for business on the morning of June 15, the owner discovered that thieves had broken in and stolen the store's entire inventory. The following information for the period January 1 through June 14 was available:

January 1 merchandise inventory at cost	$210,500
Purchases	454,725
Purchases returns	3,775
Transportation-in	3,940
Sales	700,500
Sales returns	5,450

Required

Under the assumption the store had earned an average 28% gross profit on sales during the past five years, prepare a statement showing the estimated loss.

Problem 9–9
Gross profit method
(LO 6)

Brown Supply wants to prepare interim financial statements for the first quarter of 1993. The company uses a periodic inventory system but would like to avoid making a physical count of inventory. During the last five years, the company's gross profit rate has averaged 30%; the following information for the year's first quarter is available from its records:

January 1 beginning inventory	$225,500
Purchases	435,800
Purchases returns	5,750
Transportation-in	6,800
Sales	710,500
Sales returns	9,600

Required

Use the gross profit method to prepare an estimate of the company's March 31 inventory.

Problem 9–10
Analytical essay
(LO 3)

Part 1. Draton Company's inventory includes a product that cost $9 per unit. Replacement cost is $8, expected sales price is $12, additional costs to sell are $0, and the normal profit margin is 30%. Explain the reason why the inventory should not be reported on the balance sheet at less than $8.40 per unit.

Part 2. Flavor Company's inventory includes a damaged product that cost $16 per unit. Replacement cost is $15, expected sales price is $17, additional costs that must be incurred to sell the product are $3, and the normal profit margin is 20%. Explain the reason why the inventory should not be reported on the balance sheet at more than $14.

Problem 9–11
Analytical essay
(LO 2, 5)

Review the facts about Smith Company presented in Problem 9–1 and notice that Smith uses a periodic inventory system. The facts of Problem 9–1 indicate that Smith Company had 8,000 units of product available for sale, had 2,500 units on hand at the end of the period, and, therefore, had sales of 5,500 units during the period. Now assume that the sale occurred as follows:

March 1.	1,500 units
June 1.	1,000 units
November 1	2,000 units
December 20	1,000 units

Required

1. Explain what effect, if any, these additional facts would have on the solution to requirement 2,*a* and 2,*b* of Problem 9–1.
2. Given the preceding information about the timing of sales, explain whether the Problem 9–1 solution to requirement 2,*a* and 2,*b* would provide the same answers under a perpetual inventory system as it does under a periodic inventory system.

Alternate Problems

Problem 9–1A
Alternative cost flows—periodic system
(LO 2)

Northwood Company began a year with 550 units of Product A in its inventory that cost $80 each, and it made successive purchases of the product as follows:

Feb. 10	750 units @ $ 85 each
May 4	850 units @ $ 95 each
July 6	900 units @ $110 each
Oct. 30	950 units @ $120 each

The company uses a periodic inventory system. On December 31, a physical count disclosed that 1,000 units of Product A remained in inventory.

Required

1. Prepare a calculation showing the number and total cost of the units available for sale during the year.
2. Prepare calculations showing the amounts that should be assigned to the ending inventory and to cost of goods sold assuming (*a*) a FIFO basis, (*b*) a LIFO basis, and (*c*) a weighted-average cost basis. Round your calculation of the weighted-average cost per unit to three decimal places.

Problem 9–2A
Income statement comparisons and cost flow assumptions
(LO 2)

Fairfield Company sold 3,800 units of its product at $75 per unit during 1993. Incurring operating expenses of $20 per unit in selling the units, it began the year and made successive purchases of the product as follows:

January 1 beginning inventory	950 units costing $30.00 per unit
Purchases:	
February 10	700 units costing $33.00 per unit
May 15	1,100 units costing $35.00 per unit
August 4	1,600 units costing $40.00 per unit
October 23	850 units costing $42.00 per unit

Required

Prepare a comparative income statement for the company showing in adjacent columns the net incomes earned from the sale of the product assuming the company uses a periodic inventory system and prices its ending inventory on the basis of: (*a*) FIFO, (*b*) LIFO, and (*c*) weighted-average cost. Round your calculation of the weighted-average cost per unit to three decimal places.

Problem 9–3A
Lower of cost or market
(LO 3)

Case 1: In this case, an evaluation of the expected selling price and normal profit margin for each product shows that replacement cost is the best measure of market. The inventory includes:

Product	Units on Hand	Cost	Replacement Cost
X	550	$70	$75
Y	420	65	60
Z	300	43	41

Case 2: In this case, the inventories of Products V and W have been damaged. If $10 additional cost per unit is paid to repackage the Product V units, they can be sold for $28 per unit. The Product W units can be sold for $45 per unit after paying additional cleaning costs of $7 per unit. The inventory includes:

Product	Units on Hand	Cost	Replacement Cost
V	620	$19	$20
W	1,100	47	40

Case 3: In this case, Product T normally is sold for $75 per unit and has a profit margin of 15%. However, the expected selling price has fallen to $60 per unit. Product U normally is sold for $25 per unit and has a profit margin of 20%. However, the expected selling price of Product T has fallen to $18 per unit. The inventory includes:

Product	Units on Hand	Cost	Replacement Cost
T	650	$52	$45
U	400	15	16

Required

In each of these independent cases, calculate the lower of cost or market (*a*) for the inventory as a whole and (*b*) for the inventory applied separately to each product.

Problem 9–4A
Analysis of inventory errors
(LO 4)

Kerwood Company keeps its inventory records on a periodic basis. The following amounts were reported in the company's financial statements:

	Financial Statements for Year Ended December 31,		
	1992	**1993**	**1994**
Cost of goods sold	$135,000	$140,000	$129,000
Net income	115,000	139,000	121,000
Total current assets . . .	175,000	182,000	173,000
Owners' equity	200,000	208,000	221,000

In making the physical counts of inventory, the following errors were made:

Inventory on December 31, 1992	Overstated	$14,000
Inventory on December 31, 1993	Understated	17,000

Required

1. For each of the preceding financial statement items, prepare a schedule similar to the following and show the adjustments that would have been necessary to correct the reported amounts.

	1992	1993	1994
Cost of goods sold:			
Reported	_____	_____	_____
Adjustments: 12/31/92 error	_____	_____	_____
12/31/93 error	_____	_____	_____
Corrected	=====	=====	=====

2. What is the error in the aggregate net income for the three-year period that resulted from the inventory errors?

Problem 9–5A
Inventory records under FIFO and LIFO—perpetual systems
(LO 5)

The Romero Company sells a product called GlueIt and uses a perpetual inventory system to account for its merchandise. The beginning balance of GlueIt and transactions during March of this year were as follows:

Mar. 1 Balance: 65 units costing $15 each.
5 Purchased 120 units costing $18 each.
11 Sold 55 units.
19 Sold 45 units.
23 Purchased 75 units costing $20 each.
25 Sold 45 units.
31 Sold 58 units.

Required

1. Under the assumption the concern keeps its records on a FIFO basis, enter the beginning balance and the transactions on a subsidiary inventory record like the one in Illustration 9–5.
2. Under the assumption the concern keeps its inventory records on a LIFO basis, enter the beginning inventory and the transactions on a second subsidiary inventory record like the one in Illustration 9–6.
3. Assume the 58 units sold on March 31 were sold on credit to Mark Gibson at $40 each and prepare general journal entries to record the sale on a LIFO basis.

Problem 9–6A
Retail inventory method
(LO 6)

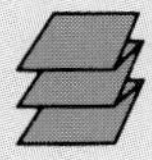

Worldwide Products takes a year-end physical inventory at marked selling prices and uses the retail method to reduce the inventory total to a cost basis for statement purposes. It uses the retail method to estimate the amount of inventory it should have at the end of a year, and by comparison, determines any inventory shortage due to shoplifting or other causes. At the end of the year, its physical inventory at marked selling prices totaled $192,400, and the following information was available from its records:

	At Cost	At Retail
Beginning inventory	$105,250	$153,570
Purchases	519,270	769,800
Purchases returns	2,760	4,200
Additional markups		8,830
Markdowns.		10,500
Sales		725,000
Sales returns		8,600

Required

1. Use the retail method to estimate the store's year-end inventory at cost.
2. Use the retail method to reduce the company's year-end physical inventory to a cost basis.
3. Prepare a schedule showing the inventory shortage at cost and at retail.

Problem 9–7A
Retail inventory method
(LO 6)

The records of McCoy Company provided the following information for the year ended December 31:

	At Cost	At Retail
January 1 beginning inventory	$ 60,200	$100,660
Purchases	318,560	524,200
Purchases returns.	2,470	4,200
Additional markups		6,490
Markdowns.		4,700
Sales		376,290
Sales returns		3,800

Required

1. Prepare an estimate of the company's year-end inventory by the retail method.
2. Under the assumption the company took a year-end physical inventory at marked selling prices that totaled $227,300, prepare a schedule showing the store's loss from theft or other cause at cost and at retail.

Problem 9–8A
Gross profit method
(LO 6)

While opening the Appliance Store for business on the morning of August 5, the manager discovered that thieves had broken in and stolen the store's entire inventory. The following information for the period January 1 through August 4 was available:

January 1 merchandise inventory at cost	$276,500
Purchases	824,000
Purchases returns	15,350
Transportation-in	27,450
Sales	945,600
Sales returns	19,700

Required

Under the assumption the store had earned an average 33% gross profit on sales during the past five years, prepare a statement showing the estimated loss.

Problem 9–9A
Gross profit method
(LO 6)

The Sanford Company wants to prepare interim financial statements for the first quarter of 1993. The company uses a periodic inventory system but would like to avoid making a physical count of inventory. During the last five years, the company's gross profit rate has averaged 35%; the following information for the year's first quarter is available from its records:

January 1 beginning inventory	$135,480
Purchases	345,350
Purchases returns	5,800
Transportation-in	11,100
Sales	624,500
Sales returns	10,200

Required

Use the gross profit method to prepare an estimate of the company's March 31 inventory.

Problem 9–10A
Analytical essay
(LO 3)

Part 1. Graftex Company's inventory includes a damaged product that cost $35 per unit. Replacement cost is $32, expected sales price is $40, additional costs that must be incurred to sell the product are $12, and the normal profit margin is 15%. Explain the reason why the inventory should not be reported on the balance sheet at more than $28.

Part 2. Monton Company's inventory includes a product that cost $32 per unit. Replacement cost is $28, expected sales price is $40, additional costs to sell are $0, and the normal profit margin is 25%. Explain the reason why the inventory should not be reported on the balance sheet at less than $30 per unit.

Problem 9–11A
Analytical essay
(LO 2, 5)

Review the facts about Northwood Company presented in Problem 9–1A and notice that Northwood uses a periodic inventory system. The facts of Problem 9–1A indicate that Northwood Company had 4,000 units of product available for sale, had 1,000 units on hand at the end of the period, and, therefore, had sales of 3,000 units during the period. Now assume that the sales occurred as follows:

April 7	1,000 units
June 14	400 units
September 17	700 units
December 3	900 units

Required

1. Explain what effect, if any, these additional facts would have on the solution to requirement 2,*a* and 2,*b* of Problem 9–1A.
2. Given the preceding information about the timing of sales, explain whether the Problem 9–1A solution to requirement 2,*a* and 2,*b* would provide the same answers under a perpetual inventory system as it does under a periodic inventory system.

Provocative Problems

Provocative Problem 9–1
The LTV Corporation
(LO 2)

The LTV Corporation manufactures and markets products in four principal categories: steel, aircraft products, missiles and electronics, and energy products. The company's headquarters is in Dallas, Texas. In the 1989 annual report of the company, the footnotes to the financial statements included the following:

Inventories

Liquidations of LIFO inventory quantities carried as though acquired at lower costs which prevailed in earlier years reduced cost of products sold by $6 million, $10 million and $6 million in 1989, 1988 and 1987, respectively.

(Courtesy of The LTV Corporation.)

Discuss the financial statement effects of experiencing a reduction in inventory when LIFO is used and explain how this applies to The LTV Corporation.

Provocative Problem 9–2
Johnson & Johnson
(LO 2)

Johnson & Johnson manufactures and markets a wide range of products related to medical care. Its headquarters is in New Brunswick, New Jersey. The 1989 annual report of Johnson & Johnson included the following footnote to its financial statements:

Note 3

Inventories At the end of 1989 and 1988, inventories comprised:

(Dollars in Millions)	1989	1988
Raw materials and supplies	$ 435	$ 388
Goods in process	259	238
Finished goods	659	647
	$1,353	$1,273

Inventories valued on the LIFO basis were approximately 19% and 22% of total inventories at the end of 1989 and 1988, respectively. If all inventories were valued on the FIFO basis, total inventories would have been $1,482 million and $1,385 million at December 31, 1989, and January 1, 1989, respectively.

(Courtesy of Johnson & Johnson.)

Johnson & Johnson reported a net income of $1,082 million in 1989. Retained earnings on December 31, 1989, was $5,260 million. If Johnson & Johnson had used FIFO for all of its inventories, how much larger would the total inventories reported on December 31, 1989, and January 1, 1989, have been? Assuming the average income tax rate applicable to the company was 30% in all past years, what would have been reported as 1989 net income? What would have been the balance of retained earnings on December 31, 1989? Comment on Johnson & Johnson's policy of using FIFO for some inventories and LIFO for other inventories. Is this practice acceptable in light of the consistency principle?

Provocative Problem 9–3
Samson's Sporting Goods
(LO 6)

The retail outlet of Samson's Sporting Goods suffered extensive smoke and water damage and a small amount of fire damage on October 5. The company carried adequate insurance, and the insurance company's claims adjuster appeared the same day to inspect the damage. After completing his survey, the adjuster agreed with Sam Corbin, the store's owner, that the inventory could be sold to a company specializing in fire sales for about one third of its cost. The adjuster offered Corbin $235,400 in full settlement for the damage to the inventory. He suggested that the offer be accepted and said he had authority to deliver at once a check for that amount. He also pointed out that a prompt settlement would provide funds to replace the inventory in time for the store to participate in the Christmas shopping season.

Corbin felt the loss might exceed $235,400, but he recognized that a time-consuming count and inspection of each item in the inventory would be required to establish the loss more precisely. He was anxious to get back into business before the Christmas rush, the season making the largest contribution to annual net income, and was reluctant to take the time for the inventory count. Yet, he was also unwilling to take a substantial loss on the insurance settlement.

Corbin asked for and received one day in which to consider the insurance company's offer and immediately went to his records for the following information:

		At Cost	At Retail
a.	January 1 inventory	$ 387,700	$ 640,315
	Purchases, Jan. 1 through Oct. 5	1,347,200	2,250,450
	Net sales, Jan. 1 through Oct. 5		2,261,400

b. On March 1, the remaining inventory of winter sportswear and equipment was marked down from $110,400 to $87,000 and placed on sale in the annual end-of-the-winter-season sale. Two thirds of the merchandise was sold. The markdown on the remainder was canceled, thereby returning the prices to regular retail amounts. (A markdown cancellation is subtracted from a markdown, and a markup cancellation is subtracted from a markup.)

c. In May, a special line of swimwear proved popular, and 110 suits were marked up from their normal $42.00 retail price to $52.50 per suit. Seventy suits were sold at the higher price; and on August 5, the markup on the remaining 40 suits was canceled and they were returned to their regular $42.00 price.

d. Between January 1 and October 5, markdowns totaling $11,300 were taken on several odd lots of sportswear. Recommend whether or not you think Corbin should accept the insurance company's offer. Back your recommendation with figures.

Provocative Problem 9–4
International Business Machines Corporation (Analysis and review problem)

The financial statements and related disclosures from IBM's 1990 annual report are presented in Appendix J. Based on your examination of this information, answer the following:

1. What was the total amount of inventories held as current assets by IBM at the end of 1990? At the end of 1989?
2. Inventories represented what percentage of total assets at the end of 1990? At the end of 1989?
3. Inventories at the end of 1990 represented what percentage of cost (of goods sold) during the year? Calculate a similar percentage for 1989.
4. Inventories at the end of 1990 represented what percentage of total revenue for the year? Calculate a similar percentage for 1989.
5. Based on your answers to questions 2, 3, and 4, would you say that IBM was more or less efficient in its use of inventories during 1990 compared to 1989?
6. What method did IBM use to determine the inventory amounts reported on its balance sheet?

Answers to Objective Review Questions

LO 1 (*d*)
LO 2 (*b*)
LO 3 (*b*)
LO 4 (*b*)
LO 5 (*e*)
LO 6 (*b*)
LO 7 (*d*)

CHAPTER

10

Plant and Equipment

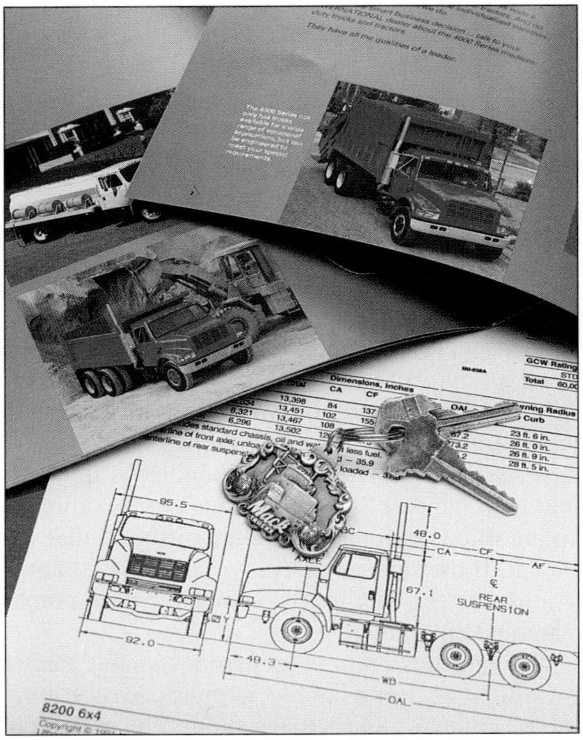

Companies invest large amounts in plant assets, such as trucks and equipment, that are used to produce and distribute goods and provide services to customers. Accounting provides information about the costs of obtaining, maintaining, and using these assets.

Topical Coverage

The focus of this chapter is long-term, tangible assets used in the operations of a business. In studying the chapter, you will learn what distinguishes them from other types of assets, how to determine their cost, and how companies allocate their cost to the periods that benefit from their use.

Learning Objectives

After studying Chapter 10, you should be able to:

1. Describe the differences between plant assets and other kinds of assets, calculate the cost of a plant asset, and prepare entries to record plant asset purchases.
2. Explain depreciation accounting (including the reasons for depreciation), calculate depreciation by the straight-line and units-of-production methods, and calculate depreciation after revising the estimated useful life of an asset.
3. Describe the use of accelerated depreciation for financial accounting purposes and calculate accelerated depreciation under (*a*) the declining-balance method, and (*b*) the sum-of-the-years'-digits method.
4. Describe the depreciation methods used for tax accounting and calculate depreciation using the Modified Accelerated Cost Recovery System.
5. Define or explain the words and phrases listed in the chapter glossary.

Plant Assets Compared to Other Types of Assets

LO 1 Describe the differences between plant assets and other kinds of assets, calculate the cost of a plant asset, and prepare entries to record plant asset purchases.

Tangible assets that are used in the production or sale of other assets or services and that have a useful life longer than one accounting period are called *plant assets*. In the past, such assets were often described as *fixed assets*. However, more descriptive terms such as *plant and equipment* or perhaps *property, plant, and equipment* are now used more frequently.

The main difference between plant assets and merchandise is that plant assets are held for *use* while merchandise is held for *sale*. For example, a computer is merchandise to an office equipment retailing business that purchases it with the intent to sell it. If the same retailer owns another computer that is used in business operations to account for the business and to prepare reports, it is classified as plant and equipment.

The characteristic that distinguishes plant assets from tangible current assets is the length of their useful lives. For example, supplies are consumed within a very short time after the company starts to use them. Thus, their cost is assigned to the single period in which they are used. By comparison, plant assets have longer useful lives that often extend over many accounting periods. As the usefulness of plant assets expires over these periods, their cost must be allocated among them. This allocation should be accomplished in a systematic and rational manner.[1]

[1] See FASB, *Statement of Financial Accounting Concepts No. 6,* "Elements of Financial Statements of Business Enterprises" (Norwalk, Conn., 1985), par. 149.

Plant assets are not the same as long-term investments. Although both are held for more than one accounting period, investments are not used in the primary operations of the business. For example, land that is held for future expansion is classified as a long-term investment. On the other hand, land on which the company's factory is located is a plant asset. In addition, standby equipment held for use in case of a breakdown or during peak periods of production is a plant asset. However, when equipment is removed from service and held for sale, it is no longer considered a plant asset.

Cost of a Plant Asset

The purchase of a plant asset should be recorded at cost. This cost includes all normal and reasonable expenditures necessary to get the asset in place and ready to use. For example, the cost of a factory machine includes its invoice price, less any cash discount for early payment, plus freight, unpacking, and assembling costs. The cost of an asset also includes the costs of installing a machine before placing it in service. Examples are the costs to build a concrete base or foundation for a machine, to provide electrical connections, and to adjust the machine before using it in operations.

A cost must be normal and reasonable as well as necessary if it is to be properly included in the cost of a plant asset. For example, if a machine is damaged by being dropped during unpacking, the repairs should not be added to its cost. Instead, they should be charged to an expense account. Also, a fine paid for moving a heavy machine on city streets without proper permits is not part of the cost of the machine. However, if proper permits are obtained, their cost is included in the cost of the asset. Sometimes, additional costs to modify or customize a new plant asset must be incurred before the asset meets the purchaser's needs. In this case, the expenditures should be charged to the asset's cost.

When a plant asset is constructed by a business for its own use, cost includes material and labor costs plus a reasonable amount of indirect overhead costs such as heat, lights, power, and depreciation on the machinery used to construct the asset. Cost also includes design fees, building permits, and insurance during construction. However, insurance costs for coverage after the asset has been placed in service are an operating expense.

When land is purchased for a building site, its cost includes the total amount paid for the land, including any real estate commissions. It also includes fees for insuring the title, legal fees, and any accrued property taxes paid by the purchaser. Payments for surveying, clearing, grading, draining, and landscaping also are included in the cost of land. Furthermore, any assessments by the local government, whether incurred at the time of purchase or later, for such things as installing streets, sewers, and sidewalks should be debited to the Land account because they add a more or less permanent value to the land.

Land purchased as a building site may have an old building that must be removed. In such cases, the entire purchase price, including the amount paid for the building, should be charged to the Land account. Also, the cost of removing the old building, less any amounts recovered through the sale of salvaged materials, should be charged to the Land account.

Because land has an unlimited life and is not consumed when it is used, it is not subject to depreciation. However, **land improvements**, such as parking lot surfaces, fences, and lighting systems have limited useful lives. Although these costs increase the usefulness of the land, they must be first charged to separate Land Improvement accounts so that they can be depreciated. Of course, a separate Building account must be charged for the costs of purchasing or constructing a building that will be used as a plant asset.

Land, land improvements, and buildings often are purchased in a single transaction for a lump-sum price. When this occurs, you must allocate the cost of the purchase among the different types of assets based on their relative market values. These market values may be estimated by appraisal or by using the tax-assessed valuations of the assets.

For example, assume that a company pays $90,000 cash to acquire land appraised at $30,000, land improvements appraised at $10,000, and a building appraised at $60,000. The $90,000 cost is allocated on the basis of appraised values as follows:

	Appraised Value	Percentage of Total	Apportioned Cost
Land	$ 30,000	30%	$27,000
Land improvements	10,000	10	9,000
Building	60,000	60	54,000
Totals	$100,000	100%	$90,000

This allocation is necessary for the proper determination of depreciation expense in the future.

Nature of Depreciation

LO 2 Explain depreciation accounting (including the reasons for depreciation), calculate depreciation by the straight-line and units-of-production methods, and calculate depreciation after revising the estimated useful life of an asset.

Because plant assets are purchased for use, you can think of a plant asset as a quantity of usefulness that will contribute to the operations of the business throughout the service life of the asset. And, because the life of any plant asset (other than land) is limited, this quantity of usefulness expires as the asset is used. This expiration of a plant asset's quantity of usefulness is generally described as *depreciation*. In accounting, this term describes the process of allocating and charging the cost of the usefulness to the accounting periods that benefit from the asset's use.

For example, when a company buys an automobile for use as a plant asset, it acquires a quantity of usefulness in the sense that it obtains a quantity of transportation. The cost of that transportation will expire during the useful life of the car. The total cost of the transportation is the cost of the car less the proceeds that will be received when the car is sold or traded in at the end of its service life. This net cost that will expire over the useful life of the car must be allocated to the accounting periods that benefit from the car's use. In other words, the asset's cost must be depreciated. Note that the depreciation process does not measure the decline in the car's market value each period. Furthermore, depreciation does not measure the physical deterioration of the car each period. Under generally accepted accounting principles, depreciation is a process of allocating a plant asset's cost to income statements of the years in which it is used.

Because depreciation represents the cost of using a plant asset, you should not begin recording depreciation charges until the asset is actually put to use providing services or producing products.

Service (Useful) Life of a Plant Asset

The **service life** of a plant asset is the length of time it will be used in the operations of the business. This service life (or useful life) may not be as long as the asset's potential life. For example, although computers have a potential life of six to eight years, a company may plan to trade in its old computers for new ones every three years. In this case, the computers have a three-year service life. Therefore, this company should charge the cost of the computers (less their expected trade-in value) to depreciation expense over this three-year period.

The service life of a plant asset often is difficult to predict because of several factors. Wear and tear from use determine the service life of many assets. However, two additional factors, **inadequacy** and **obsolescence,** often need to be considered. Usually, when a business acquires plant assets, it attempts to anticipate how much the business will grow and then acquires assets of a size and capacity to take care of its foreseeable needs. However, if a business grows more rapidly than anticipated, the capacity of the assets may become too small for the productive demands of the business. When this happens, the assets become inadequate. Obsolescence, like inadequacy, is difficult to anticipate because the exact occurrence of new inventions and improvements normally cannot be predicted. Yet, new inventions and improvements often cause an asset to become obsolete and the company may simply discard it long before it wears out.

Many times, a company is able to predict the service life of a new asset based on past experience with similar assets. In other cases, lacking experience with a particular type of asset, a company must depend on the experience of others or on engineering studies and judgment.

Salvage Value

The total amount of depreciation that should be taken over an asset's service life is the asset's cost minus its estimated **salvage value.** The salvage value of a plant asset is the amount you expect to receive from selling the asset at the end of its life. If you expect an asset to be traded in on a new asset, the salvage value is the expected trade-in value.

When the disposal of a plant asset involves additional costs, as in the wrecking of a building, the salvage value is the *net* amount you expect to realize from the sale of the asset at the end of its service life. This net amount is the amount you expect to receive for the asset less the disposal costs.

Allocating Depreciation

Many depreciation methods for allocating a plant asset's total cost among the several accounting periods in its service life have been suggested and used in the past. However, at present, most companies use the *straight-line method* of depreciation in their financial accounting records for presentation in their financial statements. Some types of assets are depreciated according to the *units-of-production method*. After explaining these two methods next, we discuss some other methods, called *accelerated depreciation*.

Straight-Line Method

When **straight-line depreciation** is used, each year in the asset's life receives the same amount of expense. The amount of depreciation to be taken each period is calculated by first finding the cost of the asset minus its estimated salvage value. Then, this amount is divided by the estimated number of accounting periods in the asset's service life.

For example, if a machine costs \$700, has an estimated service life of five years, and has an estimated \$200 salvage value, its depreciation per year by the straight-line method is \$100. This amount is calculated as follows:

$$\frac{\text{Cost} - \text{Salvage}}{\text{Service life in years}} = \frac{\$700 - \$200}{5 \text{ years}} = \$100 \text{ per year}$$

If this asset is purchased on December 31, 1992, and used throughout its predicted service life of five years, the straight-line method will allocate an equal amount of depreciation to each of those years (1993 through 1997). The left graph in Illustration 10–1 shows that this \$100 per year amount will be reported each year as an expense. The right graph shows the amount that will be reported on the six balance sheets that will be produced while the company actually owns the asset. This **book value** of the asset is its original cost less accumulated depreciation. The book value goes down by \$100 each year. Both graphs show why this method is called *straight line*.

Units-of-Production Method

The purpose of recording depreciation is to provide relevant information about the cost of consuming an asset's usefulness. Basically, depreciation accounting charges each accounting period in which an asset is used with a fair share of its cost. The straight-line method charges an equal share to each period. If plant assets are used about the same amount in each accounting period, this method produces a reasonable result. However, in some lines of business, the use of certain plant assets varies greatly from one accounting period to another. For example, a contractor may use a particular piece of construction equipment for a month and then not use it again for many months.

Because the use of such equipment changes from period to period, **units-of-production depreciation** may provide a better matching of expenses with revenues than straight-line depreciation. The units-of-production method allocates depreciation for a plant asset based on the relationship between the units of product produced by the asset during a given period to the total units the asset is expected to produce during its entire life. In effect, this method computes the amount of depreciation per unit of service provided by the asset.

ILLUSTRATION 10–1

The Financial Statement Effects of Straight-Line Depreciation

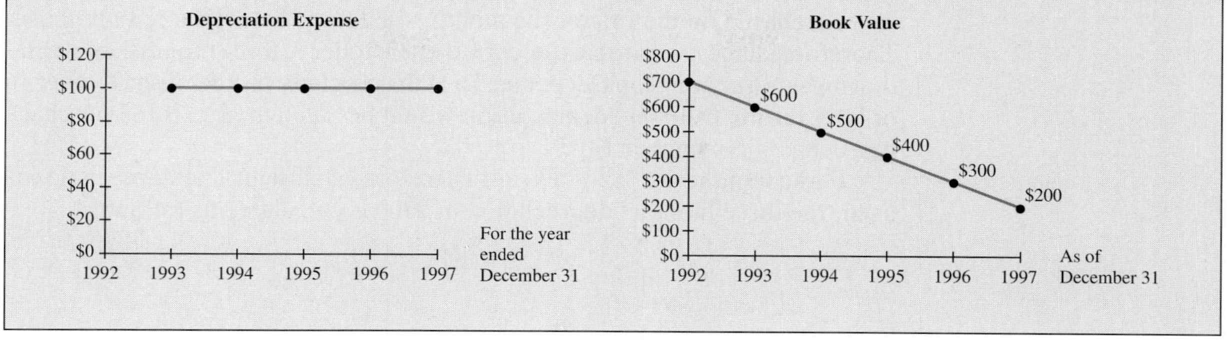

Then, the amount of depreciation taken in an accounting period is determined by multiplying the units produced in that period by the depreciation per unit.

When the units-of-production method is used, the cost of an asset minus its estimated salvage value is divided by the units that management predicts it will produce during its entire service life. Units of production may be expressed as units of product or in any other unit of measure such as hours of use or miles driven.

For example, a truck that cost $24,000 has a predicted salvage value of $4,000. Also, the truck's service life in miles is estimated to be 125,000 miles. The depreciation per mile, or the depreciation per unit of production, is $0.16, which is calculated as follows:

$$\text{Depreciation per unit of production} = \frac{\text{Cost} - \text{Salvage value}}{\text{Predicted units of production}}$$

$$= \frac{\$24{,}000 - \$4{,}000}{125{,}000 \text{ miles}}$$

$$= \$0.16 \text{ per mile}$$

If these estimates are used and the truck is driven 20,000 miles during its first year, depreciation for the first year is $3,200 (20,000 miles at $0.16 per mile). If the truck is driven 15,000 miles in the second year, depreciation for the second year is 15,000 miles times $0.16 per mile, or $2,400.

Depreciation for Partial Years

Of course, plant assets may be purchased or disposed of at any time during the year. When an asset is purchased (or disposed of) at some time other than the beginning or end of an accounting period, depreciation must be recorded for part of a year. Otherwise, the year of purchase or the year of disposal is not charged with its share of the asset's depreciation.

For example, assume that a machine was purchased and placed in service on October 8, 1993, and the annual accounting period ends on December 31. The machine cost $4,600, and has an estimated service life of five years and an estimated salvage value of $600. Because the machine was purchased and used nearly three months during 1993, the annual income statement should reflect depreciation expense on the machine for that part of the year. The amount of depreciation to be reported is often based on the assumption that the machine was purchased on the first of the month nearest the actual date of purchase. Therefore, since the purchase occurred on October 8, three months' depreciation must be recorded on December 31. If the purchase had been on October 16 or later during October, depreciation would be calculated as if the purchase had been on November 1.

Three months are 3/12 of a year. Therefore, if straight-line depreciation is used, the three months' depreciation of $200 is calculated as follows:

$$\frac{\$4{,}600 - \$600}{5} \times \frac{3}{12} = \$200$$

This entry records depreciation for 1993 on the machine purchased on October 8, 1993:

Dec.	31	Depreciation Expense, Machinery	200.00	
		Accumulated Depreciation, Machinery		200.00
		To record depreciation for three months.		

On December 31, 1994, and at the end of each of the following three years, the following journal entry records a full year's depreciation on this machine:

Dec.	31	Depreciation Expense, Machinery	800.00	
		Accumulated Depreciation, Machinery		800.00
		To record depreciation for one year.		

After the December 31, 1997, depreciation entry is recorded, the accounts show the history of this machine as follows:

Machinery

Oct. 8, 1993	4,600		

Accumulated Depreciation, Machinery

		Dec. 31, 1993	200
		Dec. 31, 1994	800
		Dec. 31, 1995	800
		Dec. 31, 1996	800
		Dec. 31, 1997	800

The disposal of an asset during a year also requires that depreciation be recognized for the portion of the year it was actually used. For example, suppose that the preceding asset is sold for $800 on June 24, 1998. To record the disposal, depreciation for six months (depreciation to the nearest full month) must first be recorded. The entry for this is:

June	24	Depreciation Expense, Machinery	400.00	
		Accumulated Depreciation, Machinery		400.00
		To record depreciation for one-half year.		

After making the entry to record depreciation to the date of sale, a second entry to record the actual sale is needed:

June	24	Cash	800.00	
		Accumulated Depreciation, Machinery	3,800.00	
		Machinery		4,600.00
		To record sale of machine at book value.		

The company sold the machine in this example for its book value. In the next chapter, we discuss more typical situations in which plant assets are sold for more or less than book value.

When depreciation must be recorded for part of a year, it is often calculated to the nearest whole month as in the preceding example. However, other conventions are sometimes used. For example, some companies take one half year's depreciation in the year of purchase and one half in the year of disposal, regardless of the dates on which the asset was purchased or sold.

Depreciation on the Balance Sheet

In presenting information about the plant assets of a business, both the cost and accumulated depreciation of plant assets should be reported. For example, Apple Computer, Inc.'s balance sheet at the close of its 1991 fiscal year included the following:

(Dollars in thousands)	1991	1990
Property, plant, and equipment:		
Land and buildings	$ 198,107	$117,350
Machinery and equipment	485,872	402,168
Office furniture and equipment	146,433	137,485
Leasehold improvements	205,602	187,868
	1,036,014	844,871
Accumulated depreciation and amortization	(588,036)	(446,706)
Net property, plant, and equipment	447,978	398,165

Notice that Apple reported only the total amount of accumulated depreciation and amortization. This is the usual practice in published financial statements. In fact, the balance sheets of many companies show plant and equipment on one line with the net amount of cost less accumulated depreciation. When this is done, however, the amount of accumulated depreciation is disclosed in a footnote. To satisfy the *full-disclosure principle,* companies also must provide a general description of the depreciation method or methods used.[2] Usually, they present this in a footnote.

Reporting both the cost and the accumulated depreciation of plant assets may help balance sheet readers compare the status of different companies. For

[2] FASB, *Accounting Standards—Current Text* (Norwalk, Conn., 1990), sec. D40.101. First published as *APB Opinion No. 12,* par. 5.

example, a company that holds assets with $50,000 original cost and $40,000 of accumulated depreciation may be in a quite different situation than another company with new assets that cost $10,000. Although the net undepreciated cost is the same in both cases, the first company may have more productive capacity available but probably is facing the need to replace its older assets. These differences are not conveyed if the balance sheets report only the $10,000 book values.

From the discussion so far, you should recognize that depreciation is a process of cost allocation rather than valuation. Plant assets are reported on balance sheets at their remaining undepreciated costs (book value), not at market values.

Some people involved in accounting have suggested that additional useful information would be provided if financial statements reported the market value of plant assets. However, this practice has not gained general acceptance. Instead, most accountants believe that financial statements should be based on the *continuing-concern* or *going-concern principle* described in Chapter 1. This principle dictates that, unless there is adequate evidence to the contrary, the accountant should assume the company will continue in business. As applied to depreciation, this principle leads to the assumption that plant assets will not be sold but will be held and used long enough to recover their original costs through the sale of products and services. Therefore, plant assets are carried on the balance sheet at cost less accumulated depreciation. This is the remaining portion of the original cost that is expected to be recovered in future periods. The ultimate outcome is that the book values of assets reported on the balance sheet rarely equal their market values.

Recovering the Cost of Plant Assets

Inexperienced financial statement readers may make the mistake of thinking that the accumulated depreciation shown on a balance sheet represents funds accumulated to buy new assets when the presently owned assets must be replaced. However, you know that accumulated depreciation is a contra account with a credit balance that cannot be used to buy anything. If a business has funds available to buy assets, the funds are shown on the balance sheet as liquid assets such as *cash,* not as accumulated depreciation.

A company that earns a profit or *breaks even* (a term that means the company neither earns a profit nor suffers a loss) recovers the original cost of its plant assets through the sale of its products and services. This result is demonstrated with a condensed income statement in Illustration 10–2, which shows that Even Steven Company broke even during 1993.

In Illustration 10–2, notice that the company broke even only after deducting $5,000 of the cost of its plant assets from its sales. As a result, we can say that the company recovered $5,000 of the cost of plant assets. This happened because $100,000 of cash and receivables flowed into the company from sales and only $95,000 of liability increases and cash and inventory outflows occurred for sold goods, rent, and salaries. No funds flowed out for depreciation expense. In this sense, the company recovered this $5,000 portion of the cost of its plant assets through the sale of its products. If the company remains in business for the life of its plant assets, it will recover the entire cost of the

ILLUSTRATION 10-2

Recovering the Cost of Plant Assets while Breaking Even

EVEN STEVEN COMPANY
Income Statement
For Year Ended December 31, 1993

Sales		$100,000
Cost of goods sold	$60,000	
Rent expense	10,000	
Salaries expense	25,000	
Depreciation expense	5,000	
Total		100,000
Net income		$ -0-

assets as long as it breaks even or earns a profit. In other words, depreciation is an expense like any other expense, except that it does not require cash to be paid out each year.

Revising Depreciation Rates

Because the calculation of depreciation must be based on an asset's *predicted* useful life, depreciation expense is an estimate. Therefore, you should be alert to the possibility that during the life of an asset, new information may show that the original prediction of useful life was inaccurate. Thus, if your estimate of an asset's useful life changes, what should be done? The answer is to use a new estimate of the remaining useful life to calculate depreciation in the future. In other words, revise the estimate of annual depreciation expense in the future by spreading the residual cost to be depreciated over the revised remaining useful life.

For example, assume that a machine was purchased seven years ago at a cost of $10,500. At that time, the machine was predicted to have a 10-year life with a $500 salvage value. Therefore, it was depreciated by the straight-line method at the rate of $1,000 per year [($10,500 − $500)/10 = $1,000]. At the beginning of the asset's eighth year, its book value is $3,500, calculated as follows:

Cost	$10,500
Less seven years' accumulated depreciation	7,000
Book value	$ 3,500

At the beginning of its eighth year, the prediction of the number of years remaining in the useful life is changed from three years to five years. The salvage value is also changed to be $300. Depreciation for each of the machine's five remaining years should be calculated as follows:

$$\frac{\text{Book value} - \text{Revised salvage value}}{\text{Revised remaining useful life}} = \frac{\$3{,}500 - \$300}{5\text{ years}} = \$640\text{ per year}$$

Thus, $640 of depreciation should be recorded for the machine at the end of the eighth and each succeeding year in its life.

Because this asset was depreciated at the rate of $1,000 per year for the first seven years, you might contend that depreciation expense was overstated during the first seven years. While that view may have merit, accountants have concluded that depreciation is an estimate based on the best information available at the time it is recorded. They have also concluded that past years' financial statements generally should not be restated to reflect facts that were *not* known when the statements were originally prepared.

A revision of the predicted useful life of a plant asset is an example of a **change in an accounting estimate.** Such changes result "from new information or subsequent developments and accordingly from better insight or improved judgment." Generally accepted accounting principles require that changes in accounting estimates, such as a change in estimated useful life or salvage value, be reflected only in future financial statements, not by modifying past statements.[3]

Accelerated Depreciation Methods

LO 3 Describe the use of accelerated depreciation for financial accounting purposes and calculate accelerated depreciation under (*a*) the declining-balance method, and (*b*) the sum-of-the-years'-digits method.

In contrast to straight line, other depreciation methods produce larger depreciation charges during the early years of an asset's life and smaller charges in the later years. These techniques are called **accelerated depreciation** methods. They are considered acceptable when more of the asset's usefulness is consumed in the early years of its life than in later years. In the past, many businesses prepared their income tax returns using two of these methods, called *declining-balance depreciation* and *sum-of-the-years'-digits depreciation*. The United States federal tax laws, as codified in the **Internal Revenue Code,** used to allow these two methods to be applied in a variety of situations. And, because they were used for tax purposes, many businesses also used them in their financial statements to reduce their record-keeping effort.

Since December 31, 1980, the tax laws have not allowed the declining-balance or sum-of-the-years'-digits methods to be used on tax returns for newly purchased assets. As a result, most companies do not use either declining-balance or sum-of-the-years'-digits in their financial statements to depreciate assets purchased after 1980. Of course, some long-lived plant assets acquired prior to 1981 are still being depreciated under one of these methods. Also, because these methods are still generally accepted accounting principles, a few companies have continued to use them for financial accounting purposes.

Declining-Balance Method

Under the **declining-balance depreciation** method, a depreciation rate of up to twice the straight-line rate is applied each year to the book value of the asset at the beginning of the year. Because the book value *declines* each year, the amount of depreciation gets smaller each year.

---

[3] FASB, *Accounting Standards—Current Text* (Norwalk, Conn., 1990), sec. A35.104 and sec. A06.130. First published as *APB Opinion No. 20*, par. 13 and par. 31.

AS A MATTER OF

Ethics

Fascar Company has struggled financially for more than two years. The economic situation surrounding the company has been depressed and there are no signs of improvement for at least two more years. As a result, net income has been almost zero, and the future seems bleak.

The operations of Fascar require major investments in equipment. As a result, depreciation is a large factor in the calculation of income. Because competition in Fascar's industry normally has required frequent replacements of equipment, the equipment has been depreciated over only three years. However, Fascar's president has recently instructed Sue Ann Meyer, the company's accountant, to revise the estimated useful lives of existing equipment to six years and to use a six-year life on new equipment.

Meyer suspects that the president's instruction is motivated by a desire to improve the reported income of the company. In trying to determine whether to follow the president's instructions, Meyer is torn between her loyalty to her employer and her responsibility to the public, the stockholders, and others who use the company's financial statements. Meyer also wonders what the independent CPA who audits the financial statements will think about the change.

When the depreciation rate used is twice the straight-line rate, the method is called the *double-declining-balance method*. To use the double-declining-balance method: (1) calculate the straight-line depreciation rate for the asset; (2) double it; and (3) at the end of each year in the asset's life, apply this rate to the asset's book value at the beginning of the year. Note that the salvage value is *not* used in the annual calculation.

For example, assume that the double-declining-balance method is used to calculate depreciation on a new $10,000 asset for which you have predicted a five-year life and a salvage value of $750. The steps to follow are:

1. Divide 100% by five years to determine the straight-line annual depreciation rate of 20% per year.
2. Double this 20% rate to get a declining-balance rate of 40% per year.
3. Calculate the annual depreciation charges as shown in the following table:

Year	Beginning Book Value	Annual Depreciation (40% of Book Value)	Accumulated Depreciation at Year-End	Ending Book Value ($10,000 Cost Less Accumulated Depreciation)
First	$10,000.00	$4,000.00	$4,000.00	$6,000.00
Second	6,000.00	2,400.00	6,400.00	3,600.00
Third	3,600.00	1,440.00	7,840.00	2,160.00
Fourth	2,160.00	864.00	8,704.00	1,296.00
Fifth	1,296.00	518.40	9,222.40	777.60
Total		$9,222.40		

Notice that the book value of a plant asset would never quite reach zero no matter how many years of declining-balance depreciation were taken. However, generally accepted accounting principles do not allow an asset to be depreciated below its salvage value. Thus, if the asset in the previous example had an estimated salvage value of $1,000 instead of $750, depreciation for its fifth year would be limited to $296. This would reduce the asset's book value to the $1,000 salvage value at the end of the fifth year, as follows:

Year	Beginning Book Value	Annual Depreciation (40% of Book Value)	Accumulated Depreciation at Year-End	Ending Book Value ($10,000 Cost Less Accumulated Depreciation)
First	$10,000.00	$4,000.00	$4,000.00	$6,000.00
Second	6,000.00	2,400.00	6,400.00	3,600.00
Third	3,600.00	1,440.00	7,840.00	2,160.00
Fourth	2,160.00	864.00	8,704.00	1,296.00
Fifth	1,296.00	296.00	9,000.00	1,000.00
Total		$9,000.00		

Sum-of-the-Years'-Digits Method

Under the **sum-of-the-years'-digits depreciation** method, the accountant multiplies the asset's depreciable cost (total cost less salvage value) by a series of decreasing fractions over its useful life. Thus, the amount of depreciation gets smaller each year. The total of the series of the fractions equals one, which means that the entire depreciable cost is charged to depreciation over the asset's life. The denominator of all the fractions is the sum of the digits from 1 up to the years in the asset's service life. The numerators of the fractions are these same digits in reverse order.

For example, assume that a machine has a predicted service life of five years. The denominator of the fractions is the sum of the digits from 1 to 5, which the following calculation shows to be 15:

$$\text{Denominator} = 1 + 2 + 3 + 4 + 5 = 15$$

Then, the numerators of the fractions run from the largest digit (5) down to 1. The fractions are:

$$\frac{5}{15} \quad \frac{4}{15} \quad \frac{3}{15} \quad \frac{2}{15} \quad \frac{1}{15}$$

Notice that the sum of these fractions is one.

Now, assume that the asset has a cost of $7,000 and an estimated salvage value of $1,000. The annual depreciation charges are calculated as follows:

Year	Fraction	Annual Depreciation (Fraction × $6,000)	Accumulated Depreciation at Year-End	Ending Book Value ($7,000 Cost Less Accumulated Depreciation)
First	5/15	$2,000.00	$2,000.00	$5,000.00
Second	4/15	1,600.00	3,600.00	3,400.00
Third	3/15	1,200.00	4,800.00	2,200.00
Fourth	2/15	800.00	5,600.00	1,400.00
Fifth	1/15	400.00	6,000.00	1,000.00
Total	15/15	$6,000.00		

When a plant asset has a long life, the denominator of the fractions (the sum-of-the-years' digits, or SYD) can be more easily calculated by using this formula, where n = the number of years in the asset's life:

$$SYD = n[(n + 1)/2]$$

For example, the sum-of-the-years' digits for an asset with a five-year life can be found this way:

$$5\frac{(5 + 1)}{2} = 15$$

And, for an asset with a 20-year life, the denominator can be found with the formula as follows:

$$20\frac{(20 + 1)}{2} = 210$$

Thus, the fraction for the first year's depreciation is $^{20}/_{210}$.

Apportioning Accelerated Depreciation between Accounting Periods

When accelerated depreciation methods are used and accounting periods do not coincide with the years in an asset's life, depreciation must be apportioned between accounting periods. For example, consider the previous case where we used the sum-of-the-years'-digits method to calculate depreciation on a machine. Annual depreciation on the machine is $2,000 during its first year of service, $1,600 during its second year, and so on for its five-year life. Assume that this machine is placed in service on April 1, 1993, and the annual accounting period ends on December 31. As a result, the machine will be in use for three fourths of a year during 1993. Therefore, this period should be charged with $1,500 depreciation ($2,000 × ¾ = $1,500). Then, 1994 should be charged with $1,700 depreciation [(¼ × $2,000) + (¾ × $1,600) = $1,700]. Similar calculations should be used for the remaining periods in the asset's life. The following table illustrates the apportioning process:

Part of Year		Calculation	Total
1/1/93– 3/31/93	. . . .	none	$ –0–
4/1/93–12/31/93	. . . .	¾ × $2,000	1,500
			$1,500
1/1/94– 3/31/94	. . . .	¼ × $2,000	$ 500
4/1/94–12/31/94	. . . .	¾ × $1,600	1,200
			$1,700
1/1/95– 3/31/95	. . . .	¼ × $1,600	$ 400
4/1/95–12/31/95	. . . .	¾ × $1,200	900
			$1,300
1/1/96– 3/31/96	. . . .	¼ × $1,200	$ 300
4/1/96–12/31/96	. . . .	¾ × $ 800	600
			$ 900
1/1/97– 3/31/97	. . . .	¼ × $ 800	$ 200
4/1/97–12/31/97	. . . .	¾ × $ 400	300
			$ 500
1/1/98– 3/31/98	. . . .	¼ × $ 400	$ 100
4/1/98–12/31/98	. . . .	none	–0–
			$ 100

Accelerated Depreciation for Tax Purposes

LO 4 Describe the depreciation methods used for tax accounting and calculate depreciation using the Modified Accelerated Cost Recovery System.

As we stated earlier, U.S. tax laws allow declining-balance and sum-of-the-years'-digits depreciation methods to be used for assets purchased prior to 1981. For assets purchased after 1980 and before 1987, the tax laws allow a different method of accelerated depreciation, called the **Accelerated Cost Recovery System (ACRS).** For assets purchased after 1986, taxpayers can use a revised version of ACRS called the **Modified Accelerated Cost Recovery System (MACRS).**

The Tax Reform Act of 1986 groups different types of depreciable property purchased after December 31, 1986, in a series of classes. For personal property (property other than real estate), these classes range from a 3-year class to a 20-year class. For example, computer equipment is in the 5-year class while office furniture is in the 7-year class. Real property is grouped in two classes: a 27.5-year class for residential rental property and a 31.5-year class for all other real estate. Both classes of real property must be depreciated on a straight-line basis. Personal property may be depreciated on a straight-line basis, but MACRS also is acceptable.

MACRS depreciation is accelerated in two ways. First, the expected service lives of the assets in any given class are usually longer than the number of years assigned to the class. For example, the five-year class includes such assets as computer equipment, office machinery, and general-purpose heavy trucks. Normally, assets such as these would be expected to have useful lives longer than five years. Thus, even when straight-line depreciation is used for tax purposes, acceleration occurs because the length of life assumed for tax purposes is shorter than the expected service life of the asset.

ILLUSTRATION 10–3

Modified Accelerated Cost Recovery System for Assets Placed in Service after December 31, 1986

Class Life	
3-year	200% declining balance, switching to straight line
5-year	200% declining balance, switching to straight line
7-year	200% declining balance, switching to straight line
10-year	200% declining balance, switching to straight line
15-year	150% declining balance, switching to straight line
20-year	150% declining balance, switching to straight line
27½-year	straight line
31½-year	straight line

Second, MACRS depreciation is also accelerated because it uses the declining-balance method with a switch to straight line at the point where straight line actually produces a larger expense. Illustration 10–3 shows the depreciation rates allowed for each class.

When calculating depreciation for tax purposes, you must ignore the salvage values of assets purchased after 1980. Also, depreciation methods for personal property are based on the assumption that the asset was purchased half-way through the year. This *half-year convention* is required regardless of when the asset was actually purchased.[4]

To illustrate the MACRS method, assume an asset in the five-year class (for example, a used general-purpose heavy truck) is purchased in 1993 at a cost of $10,000. The initial depreciation rate is 200% of the straight-line rate, which is 40%. Under the half-year convention, 1993's depreciation is one half of 40%, or 20%. The following table presents the calculations for the first four years' tax returns (the term *tax basis* in several of the columns is similar to book value):

MACRS—declining balance phase

Year	Beginning Tax Basis	Rate	Annual Tax Depreciation (Rate × Tax Basis)	Ending Tax Basis ($10,000 Cost − Accumulated Tax Depreciation
1993	$10,000.00	20%	$2,000.00	$8,000.00
1994	8,000.00	40	3,200.00	4,800.00
1995	4,800.00	40	1,920.00	2,880.00
1996	2,880.00	40	1,152.00	1,728.00

After December 31, 1996, the MACRS depreciation method switches from a declining-balance approach to straight line. This switch is made because after December 31, 1996, straight-line depreciation is more accelerated than declining-balance depreciation.

[4] Under certain conditions, a half-quarter convention must be used. Depreciation methods for real property are based on a half-month convention.

To see why this is true, note that as of December 31, 1996, 3.5 years of depreciation have been taken and 1.5 years remain. If the 40% declining-balance rate were to be applied to the $1,728 remaining tax basis, the tax depreciation for 1997 would be $691.20. By comparison, when the remaining tax basis of $1,728 is spread over the next 1.5 years using straight line, the tax depreciation for 1997 is $1,152. This amount is $1,728 × (1.0/1.5). Thus, straight line provides depreciation of $1,152 while declining balance would have provided only $691.20. Then, depreciation in the final year (1998) is $1,728 × (0.5/1.5), or $576. Thus, the next two lines of the table are as follows:

MACRS—straight-line phase

Year	Beginning Tax Basis	Remaining Life	Annual Tax Depreciation	Ending Tax Basis ($10,000 Cost − Accumulated Tax Depreciation)
1997	$1,728.00	1.5 yrs.	$1,152.00	$576.00
1998	576.00	0.5 yrs.	576.00	0.00

To simplify MACRS calculations, the Internal Revenue Service provides tables for each class of assets. The tables show the percentage of original cost to be reported as depreciation on each year's tax return. For example, the table for assets in the five-year class shows the following percentages:

First year	20.00%
Second year	32.00
Third year	19.20
Fourth year	11.52
Fifth year	11.52
Sixth year	5.76
Total	100.00%

A close look at the preceding example shows that these percentages produce the same results as did the previous calculations. For example, the 1997 tax depreciation of $1,152 equals 11.52% of the asset's original cost of $10,000.

Remember that MACRS depreciation is not suitable for financial statements prepared in compliance with generally accepted accounting principles. MACRS is not acceptable because it allocates depreciation over a shorter period than the estimated service life of the asset.

However, using MACRS depreciation for tax purposes may have an important cash flow advantage. Specifically, MACRS offers the advantage of deferring the payment of income taxes from early in a plant asset's life until later. Taxes are said to be deferred because they are postponed. They are postponed because the accelerated calculation causes larger amounts of depreciation to be charged to the early years. This results in smaller amounts of taxable income and income taxes paid in the early years. However, the taxes are only deferred; they are not avoided. The larger depreciation charges in earlier years are offset by smaller depreciation charges in later years. Thus, larger amounts of taxable income are reported and larger amounts of income taxes are paid in the later years of a plant asset's life.

Summary of the Chapter in Terms of Learning Objectives

LO 1. Plant assets are tangible items that have a useful life longer than one accounting period. Plant assets are not held for sale but are used in the production or sale of other assets or services. The cost of plant assets includes all normal and reasonable expenditures necessary to get the assets in place and ready to use. The cost of a lump-sum purchase should be allocated among the individual assets based on their relative market values.

LO 2. The cost of plant assets that have limited service lives must be allocated to the accounting periods that benefit from their use. When this depreciation is accomplished according to the straight-line method, divide the cost minus salvage value by the number of periods in the service life of the asset to determine the depreciation expense of each period. Under the units-of-production method, divide the cost minus salvage value by the estimated number of units the asset will produce to determine the depreciation per unit. If the estimated useful life of a plant asset is changed, the remaining cost to be depreciated is spread over the remaining (revised) useful life of the asset.

LO 3. Accelerated depreciation methods such as declining balance and sum-of-the-years' digits are acceptable for financial accounting purposes if they are based on realistic estimates of useful life. However, they are not widely used at the present time. The Accelerated Cost Recovery System (ACRS) and the Modified Accelerated Cost Recovery System (MACRS) are not acceptable for financial accounting purposes because they are not based on realistic estimates of useful life.

LO 4. When accelerated depreciation is used for tax purposes, declining-balance and sum-of-the-years'-digits methods are used to depreciate assets purchased prior to 1981. For assets purchased from 1981 through 1986, ACRS is used; and MACRS is used for assets purchased after December 31, 1986.

Demonstration Problem

On July 14, 1993, Tulsa Company paid $600,000 to acquire a fully equipped factory. The purchase included the following:

Asset	Appraised Value	Estimated Salvage Value	Estimated Service Life	Depreciation Method
Land	$160,000			Not depreciated
Land improvements . .	80,000	$ -0-	10 years	Straight line
Building	320,000	100,000	10 years	Sum-of-the-years' digits
Machinery	176,000	16,000	10,000 units	Units of production*
Computers	64,000	4,000	4 years	Declining balance (at twice the straight-line rate)
Total	$800,000			

* The machinery was used to produce 700 units in 1993 and 1,800 units in 1994.

Required

1. Allocate the total $600,000 cost among the five separate assets.
2. Calculate the 1993 (half year) and 1994 depreciation expense for each type of asset and calculate the total each year for all assets.
3. Compute MACRS depreciation for the company's computers for all years from 1993 through 1998, assuming the computers are classified as five-year assets. Round all amounts to the nearest whole dollar and remember to change to straight-line depreciation when it further accelerates the depreciation. Remember to take one half year's depreciation in 1993 and in 1998. Also compute MACRS using the IRS percentages.

Solution to Demonstration Problem

Planning the Solution

- Complete a three-column work sheet showing these amounts for each asset: appraised value, percent of total value, and allocated cost.
- Using the allocated costs, compute the amount of depreciation for 1993 (only one half year) and 1994 for each asset. Then, summarize those calculations in a table showing the total depreciation for each year.
- Calculate MACRS depreciation for the computers, first by taking double-declining balance combined with straight line, and then by using the IRS percentage for five-year class assets.

1. Allocation of total cost among the assets:

Asset	Appraised Value	Percent of Total Value	Allocated Cost
Land	$160,000	20%	$120,000
Land improvements	80,000	10	60,000
Building	320,000	40	240,000
Machinery	176,000	22	132,000
Computers	64,000	8	48,000
Total	$800,000	100%	$600,000

2. Depreciation for each asset:

Land Improvements:		
Cost		$60,000
Salvage value		–0–
Net cost		$60,000
Service life		10 years
Annual expense	$60,000/10 =	$6,000
1993 depreciation	$6,000 × (½) =	$3,000
1994 depreciation		$6,000
Building:		
Cost		$240,000
Salvage value		100,000
Net cost		$140,000

Sum-of-the-years' digits = (10 × 11)/2 = 55

1993 depreciation:	$140,000 × (10/55) × (½) =	$12,727
1994 depreciation:	$140,000 × (10/55) × (½) =	$12,727
	$140,000 × (9/55) × (½) =	11,455
Total		$24,182

Machinery:	
Cost	$132,000
Salvage value	16,000
Net cost	$116,000
Total expected units	10,000
Expected cost per unit ($116,000/10,000)	$ 11.60

Year	Units × Unit Cost	Depreciation
1993	700 × $11.60	$ 8,120
1994	1,800 × $11.60	20,880

Computers:	
Cost	$ 48,000
Salvage value	4,000
Straight-line rate (100%/4 years)	25%
Twice the straight-line rate (25% × 2)	50%

Year	Rate	Beginning Book Value	Depreciation Expense	Accumulated Depreciation	Ending Book Value
1993	25%	$48,000	$12,000	$12,000	$36,000
1994	50	36,000	18,000	30,000	18,000

Note: The 25% rate for 1993 is one half of 50%; it is applied because the computers were used for only one-half year.

Total depreciation expense:

	1993	1994
Land improvements	$ 3,000	$ 6,000
Building	12,727	24,182
Machinery	8,120	20,880
Computers	12,000	18,000
Total	$35,847	$69,062

3. MACRS depreciation for the computers:

Year	Beginning Tax Basis	Depreciation Expense	Ending Accumulated Depreciation	Ending Tax Basis	Rate/ Method
1993	$48,000	$ 9,600	$ 9,600	$38,400	20%/DB
1994	38,400	15,360	24,960	23,040	40%/DB
1995	23,040	9,216	34,176	13,824	40%/DB
1996	13,824	5,530	39,706	8,294	40%/DB
1997	8,294	5,529*	45,235	2,765	1.5 yrs/SL
1998	2,765	2,765†	48,000	0	
Total		$48,000			

DB = declining balance
SL = straight line
* Beginning tax basis for 1997 divided by one and one half years of remaining life, or $8,294/1.5 years = $5,529 per year.
† The full beginning balance for 1998 is charged as expense.

MACRS depreciation for the computers (using the IRS percentages):

Year	Original Cost	IRS Percentage	Depreciation for Year
1993	$48,000	20.00%	$ 9,600
1994	48,000	32.00	15,360
1995	48,000	19.20	9,216
1996	48,000	11.52	5,530
1997	48,000	11.52	5,530
1998	48,000	5.76	2,764
Total			$48,000

Glossary

LO 5 Define or explain the words and phrases listed in the chapter glossary.

Accelerated Cost Recovery System (ACRS) an accelerated depreciation method allowed in tax returns for assets placed in service after 1980 and before 1987. p. 544

Accelerated depreciation depreciation methods that produce larger depreciation charges during the early years of an asset's life and smaller charges in the later years. p. 540

Book value the amount assigned to an item in the accounting records and in the financial statements; for a plant asset, book value is its original cost less accumulated depreciation. p. 534

Change in an accounting estimate a change in a calculated amount used in the financial statements that results from new information or subsequent developments and from better insight or improved judgment. p. 540

Declining-balance depreciation a depreciation method in which a plant asset's depreciation charge for the period is determined by applying a constant depreciation rate (up to twice the straight-line rate) each year to the asset's beginning book value. pp. 540–42

Inadequacy a condition in which the capacity of plant assets becomes too small for the productive demands of the business. p. 533

Internal Revenue Code the codification of the United States federal tax laws. p. 540

Land improvements assets that increase the usefulness of land but that have a limited useful life and are subject to depreciation. p. 532

Modified Accelerated Cost Recovery System (MACRS) an accelerated depreciation method allowed in tax returns for assets placed in service after 1986. pp. 544–47

Obsolescence a condition in which, because of new inventions and improvements, a plant asset can no longer be used to produce goods or services with a competitive advantage. p. 533

Salvage value the amount that management predicts will be recovered at the end of a plant asset's service life through a sale or as a trade-in allowance on the purchase of a new asset. p. 533

Service life the length of time in which a plant asset will be used in the operations of the business. p. 533

Straight-line depreciation a method that allocates an equal portion of the total depreciation for a plant asset (cost minus salvage) to each accounting period in its service life. pp. 534–35

Sum-of-the-years'-digits depreciation a depreciation method that allocates depreciation to each year in a plant asset's life by multiplying the asset's depreciable cost (total cost less salvage value) by a series of decreasing fractions over its useful life; the denominator of the fractions used is the sum of the digits from 1 up to the years in the asset's service life (sum-of-the-years' digits), and the numerators run from the largest digit down to 1. pp. 542–43

Units-of-production depreciation a method that allocates an equal portion of the total depreciation for a plant asset (cost minus salvage) to each unit of product or service that it produces, or on a similar basis, such as hours of use or miles driven. p. 534

Synonymous Terms

Plant assets property, plant, and equipment; fixed assets.
Service life useful life.

Objective Review

Answers to the following questions are listed at the end of this chapter. Be sure that you decide which is the one best answer to each question *before* you check the answers.

LO 1 The recent purchase of a new production machine by the Wallace Company involved the following dollar amounts:

Gross purchase price	$700,000
Sales tax	49,000
Freight to move machine to plant	3,500
Assembly costs	3,000
Cost of foundation for machine	2,500
Cost of spare parts to be used in maintaining the machine	4,200
Purchase discount taken	21,000

The amount to be recorded as the cost of the machine is

a. $737,000.
b. $733,500.
c. $728,000.
d. $679,000.
e. $741,200.

LO 2 Clandestine, Inc., purchased a new machine for $96,000 on January 1, 1993. Its predicted useful life is five years or 100,000 units of product, and salvage value is $8,000. During 1993, 10,000 units of product were produced. Assuming (1) straight-line depreciation and (2) units-of-production depreciation, respectively, the book value of the machine on December 31, 1993, would be:

	Straight Line	Units of Production
a.	$76,800	$86,400.
b.	$78,400	$79,200.
c.	$76,800	$86,400.
d.	$70,400	$78,400.
e.	$78,400	$87,200.

LO 3 Temperware Industries purchased a new machine for $108,000 on January 1, 1993. Its predicted useful life is five years, and salvage value is estimated to be $9,000. Depreciation expense for 1994 using (1) double-declining balance and (2) sum-of-the-years'-digits depreciation, respectively, is

	Straight Line	Units of Production
a.	$17,280	$17,600.
b.	$25,920	$26,400.
c.	$43,200	$33,000.

d.	$25,920	$28,800.
e.	$23,760	$26,400.

LO 4 Which method should be used for tax accounting purposes to depreciate a plant asset that was purchased and placed in service on September 4, 1992?

a. Accelerated Cost Recovery System.
b. Units-of-production.
c. Declining balance.
d. Sum-of-the-years' digits.
e. Modified Accelerated Cost Recovery System.

LO 5 A condition in which the capacity of plant assets has become too small for the productive demands of the business is called:

a. Obsolescence.
b. Depreciation.
c. Useful life.
d. Service life.
e. Inadequacy.

Questions for Class Discussion

1. What are the characteristics of a plant asset that make it different from other assets?
2. What is the balance sheet classification of land held for future expansion? Why is the land not classified as a plant asset?
3. In general, what is included in the cost of a plant asset?
4. What is the difference between land and land improvements?
5. Tack Company asked for bids from several machine manufacturers for the construction of a special machine. The lowest bid was $37,500. The company decided to build the machine itself and did so at a total cash outlay of $30,000. It then recorded the machine's construction with a debit to Machinery for $37,500, a credit to Cash for $30,000, and a credit to Gain on the Construction of Machinery for $7,500. Was this a proper entry? Discuss.
6. As used in accounting, what is the meaning of the term *depreciation?*
7. Is it possible to keep a plant asset in such an excellent state of repair that recording depreciation is unnecessary?
8. A machine that normally lasts 10 years is purchased even though management knows future growth of the company's operations will require that the machine be replaced in approximately 4 years. What factor in this situation tends to suggest that the machine should be depreciated over 4 years?
9. A company purchases a machine that normally has a service life of 12 years. However, the company's management believes that the development of a more efficient machine will make it necessary to replace

the machine in eight years. What useful life should be used in calculating depreciation on this machine, and why?

10. A building estimated to have a useful life of 30 years was completed at a cost of $120,000. It was estimated that it would be demolished at the end of its life at a cost of $13,000 and that materials salvaged from the demolition would be sold for $25,000. How much straight-line depreciation should be charged on the building each year?
11. Define the following terms used in accounting for plant assets:
    a. Trade-in value. *c*. Book value. *e*. Inadequacy.
    b. Market value. *d*. Salvage value. *f*. Obsolescence.
12. What is the sum-of-the-years'-digits in the life of a plant asset that will be used for 24 years?
13. Does the recording of depreciation cause a plant asset to appear on the balance sheet at market value? What is accomplished by recording depreciation?
14. Does the balance of the account, Accumulated Depreciation, Machinery, represent funds accumulated to replace the machinery when it wears out? Describe what the balance of Accumulated Depreciation represents.
15. It is discovered at the end of five years that a machine expected to have a six-year life will actually have an eight-year life. How is this new information reflected in the accounts?
16. Why is the Modified Accelerated Cost Recovery System not generally accepted for financial accounting purposes?
17. Explain how a business that breaks even recovers the cost of its plant assets through the sale of its products. In what manner are the funds thus recovered?
18. In IBM's consolidated statement of financial position as shown in Appendix J, what phrase does IBM use to describe its plant assets? On December 31, 1990, what percentage of total plant asset cost was represented by accumulated depreciation?
19. In McDonald's Corporation's consolidated balance sheet that appears in Appendix K, what phrase does McDonald's use to describe its plant assets? On December 31, 1990, what percentage of total plant asset cost was represented by accumulated depreciation?

Exercises

Exercise 10–1
Cost of a plant asset
(LO 1)

Isaacs Corporation purchased a machine for $57,000; terms 2/10, n/60, FOB shipping point. The seller prepaid the freight charges, $1,350, adding the amount to the invoice and bringing its total to $58,350. The machine required a special steel mounting and power connections costing $3,480, and another $1,225 was paid to assemble the machine and get it into operation. In moving the machine onto its steel mounting, it was dropped and damaged. The repairs cost $530. Later, $200 of raw materials were consumed in adjusting the machine so that it would produce a satisfactory product. The adjustments were normal for this type of machine and were not the result of the damage. However, the items produced while the adjustments were being made were not sellable. Prepare a calculation to show the cost of this machine for accounting purposes.

Exercise 10–2
Allocating cost between land, land improvements, and buildings
(LO 1)

RTF Company paid $245,500 for real estate plus $18,500 in closing costs. The real estate included: land appraised at $148,200, land improvements appraised at $22,800, and a building appraised at $114,000. The plan calls for using the building as a factory. Prepare a calculation showing the allocation of the total cost among the three purchased assets and present the journal entry that would be made to record the purchase.

Exercise 10–3
Lump-sum purchase of plant assets
(LO 1)

Atlantis Company bought two pickup trucks and a forklift from a financially distressed supplier and had them shipped to the company's plant. The purchase price was $32,000. Another $1,500 was paid for shipping. The shipping charge was based on the weights of the vehicles. Each truck weighed 3,200 pounds, and the forklift weighed 1,600 pounds. The appraised values of the trucks and forklift follow with the other costs of repairs incurred to get them ready for service. Determine the cost of each asset for accounting purposes.

	Truck 1	Truck 2	Forklift
Appraised values	$18,000	$6,750	$20,250
Repair costs.	850	700	250

Exercise 10–4
Recording the costs of real estate
(LO 1)

After planning to build a new manufacturing plant, Stage One Company purchased a large lot on which a small building was located. The negotiated purchase price for this real estate was $430,000 for the lot plus $120,000 for the building. The company paid $40,000 to have the old building torn down and $38,000 for landscaping the lot. Finally, it paid $2.9 million construction costs for a new building, which included $90,000 for lighting and paving a parking lot next to the building. Present a general journal entry to record the costs incurred by the company, all of which were paid in cash.

Exercise 10–5
Calculating depreciation; four alternative methods
(LO 2, 3)

Apex Company installed a machine in its factory at a cost of $104,000. The machine's useful life was estimated at five years or 65,000 units of product with a $6,500 trade-in value. During its second year, the machine produced 8,600 units of product. Determine the machine's second-year depreciation calculated in each of the following ways: (*a*) straight line; (*b*) units of production; (*c*) declining balance at twice the straight-line rate; and (*d*) sum-of-the-years' digits.

Exercise 10–6
Calculating depreciation; three alternative methods; partial year
(LO 2, 3)

On October 1, 1993, Tandem Company purchased a machine for $290,000. The machine was expected to last four years and have a salvage value of $15,000. Calculate depreciation expense for 1994, using (*a*) straight line, (*b*) sum-of-the-years' digits, and (*c*) declining balance at twice the straight-line rate. Tandem calculates depreciation for partial years to the nearest whole month of the date of purchase or disposal.

Exercise 10–7
Partial year's depreciation; disposal of plant asset (LO 2)

Winston Company purchased and installed a machine on January 2, 1990, at a total cost of $105,600. Straight-line depreciation was taken each year for four years, based on the assumption of an eight-year life and no salvage value. The machine is disposed of on May 20, 1994, during its fifth year of service. Present the entries that would be made to record the partial year's depreciation on May 20 and to record the disposal assuming the cash proceeds from the disposal equal the book value of the machine. Winston calculates depreciation for partial years to the nearest whole month of the date of purchase or disposal.

Exercise 10–8
Revising depreciation rates (LO 2)

Shipman Company used straight-line depreciation for a machine that cost $29,000, under the assumption it would have a five-year life and a $3,000 trade-in value. After three years, Shipman determined that the machine still had four more years of remaining useful life, after which it would have an estimated $2,000 trade-in value. (*a*) Calculate the machine's book value at the end of its third year. (*b*) Calculate the amount of depreciation to be charged during each of the remaining years in the machine's revised useful life.

Exercise 10–9
MACRS depreciation (LO 4)

In January 1993, Yeti Company purchased computer equipment for $50,000. The equipment will be used in research and development activities for six years and then sold at an estimated salvage value of $5,000. The equipment is in the five-year class for tax purposes. Prepare schedules showing each year's depreciation for the company's tax returns assuming (*a*) five-year straight-line depreciation and (*b*) MACRS depreciation.

Exercise 10–10
Declining-balance depreciation (LO 3)

Octet Company purchased and installed a plant asset that cost $55,000 and was estimated to have a five-year life and a $5,000 trade-in value. Use declining-balance depreciation at twice the straight-line rate to determine the amount of depreciation to be charged against the machine in each of the five years of its life.

Exercise 10–11
Income statement effects of alternative depreciation methods (LO 2, 3)

Throckmorton Company recently paid $112,000 for equipment that will last four years and have a salvage value of $25,000. By using the machine in its operations for four years, the company expects to earn $35,000 annually, after deducting all expenses except depreciation. Present a schedule showing income before depreciation, depreciation expense, and net income for each year and the total amounts for the four-year period assuming (*a*) straight-line depreciation, (*b*) sum-of-the-years'-digits depreciation, and (*c*) declining-balance depreciation at twice the straight-line rate.

Problems

Problem 10–1
Alternative depreciation methods; retirement of plant assets (LO 2, 3)

Part 1. A machine that cost $72,000 with a five-year life and an estimated $7,200 salvage value was installed in Lynch Company's factory. The factory manager estimated that the machine would produce 180,000 units of product during its life. It actually produced the following numbers of units: year 1, 30,000; year 2, 33,000; year 3, 36,000; year 4, 31,500; and year 5, 39,500.

Required

1. Prepare a calculation showing the number of dollars of this machine's cost that should be charged to depreciation over its five-year life.
2. Prepare a form with the following column headings:

Year	Straight Line	Units of Production	Declining Balance	Sum-of-the-Years' Digits

Then show the depreciation for each year and the total depreciation for the machine under each depreciation method. Use twice the straight-line rate for the declining-balance method.

Part 2. Canyon Company purchased a used machine for $52,700 on January 3. It was repaired the next day at a cost of $3,200 and installed on a new platform that cost $1,100. The company predicted that the machine would be used for four years and would then have a $6,000 salvage value. Depreciation was to be charged on a straight-line basis. A full year's depreciation was charged on December 31, at the end of the first year of the machine's use. On May 1 of its fourth year in service, it was retired from service.

Required

1. Prepare general journal entries to record the purchase of the machine, the cost of repairing it, and the installation. Assume that cash was paid.
2. Prepare entries to record depreciation on the machine on December 31 of its first year and on May 1 in the year of its disposal. Also record the retirement of the machine assuming it was sold for its book value.

Problem 10–2
Real estate costs and partial year's depreciation
(LO 1, 2, 3)

In 1993, Barcelona Company paid $2.7 million for a tract of land on which two buildings were located. The plan was to demolish Building One and build a new store in its place. Building Two was to be used as a company office and was appraised at a value of $862,500, with a useful life of 15 years and a $120,000 salvage value. A lighted parking lot near Building Two had improvements valued at $287,500 that were expected to last another 10 years and have no salvage value. Without considering the buildings or improvements, the tract of land was estimated to have a value of $1,725,000.

Barcelona Company incurred the following additional costs:

Cost to demolish Building One	$ 157,500
Cost of additional landscaping	53,000
Cost to construct new building (Building Three), having a useful life of 30 years and a $257,000 salvage value	1,754,000
Cost of new land improvements near Building Three, which have a 15-year useful life and no salvage value	243,000

Required

1. Prepare a form having the following column headings: Land, Building Two, Building Three, Land Improvements Two, and Land Improvements Three. Allocate the costs incurred by Barcelona Company to the appropriate columns and total each column.

2. Prepare a single journal entry dated June 1 to record all the incurred costs, assuming they were paid in cash on that date.
3. Prepare December 31 adjusting entries to record depreciation for the seven months of 1993 during which the assets were in use. Use sum-of-the-years'-digits depreciation for the newly constructed Building Three and Land Improvements Three and straight-line depreciation for Building Two and Land Improvements Two.

Problem 10–3
Plant asset costs and depreciation, including MACRS
(LO 1, 2, 3, 4)

Tabu Company recently negotiated a lump-sum purchase of several assets from a limousine company that was going out of business. The purchase was completed on August 31, 1993, at a total cash price of $930,000, and included a building, land, certain land improvements, and 14 vehicles. The estimated market value of each asset was: building, $345,600; land, $268,800; land improvements, $57,600; and vehicles, $288,000.

Required

1. Prepare a schedule to allocate the lump-sum purchase price to the separate assets that were purchased. Also present the general journal entry to record the purchase.
2. Calculate the 1994 depreciation expense on the building using the sum-of-the-years'-digits method and assuming a 12-year life and a $35,000 salvage value.
3. Calculate the 1993 depreciation expense on the land improvements assuming a 10-year life and declining-balance depreciation at twice the straightline rate.
4. The vehicles are in the five-year class for tax purposes but are expected to last six years and have a salvage value of $39,000. Prepare a schedule showing each year's depreciation on the automobiles for tax purposes, assuming (*a*) five-year straight line, and (*b*) MACRS depreciation.

Problem 10–4
Plant asset costs and revising depreciation rates
(LO 1, 2)

On July 29, 1992, Phoenix Corporation made a lump-sum purchase of two machines from a company that was going out of business. The machines cost $525,600 and were placed in use on August 2, 1992. This additional information about the machines is available:

Machine Number	Appraised Value	Salvage Value	Estimated Life	Installation Cost
One	$367,500	$13,500	5 years	$ 600
Two	122,500	10,000	5 years	1,600

Phoenix Corporation uses the straight-line method of depreciation and calculates depreciation to the nearest whole month of the date of purchase. Shortly before recording 1993's depreciation, Phoenix concluded that machine one's remaining useful life would be 2½ years. Before recording 1995's depreciation, Phoenix decided that machine two would have a $0 salvage value and that the remaining useful life would be 2 years.

Required

Prepare a form that has the following column headings:

Machine Number	Depreciation				
	1992	1993	1994	1995	1996

Calculate the amount of depreciation to be charged during each year of the useful lives of machines one and two.

Problem 10–5
Analytical essay
(LO 3)

Frite Company's operations require the use of several items of equipment, which have estimated useful lives that range from 6 to 10 years. None of the assets has any salvage value. The senior managers of the company have decided that the company should use the method of depreciation that generates the most depreciation in the first year.

Required

Prepare a table that shows the first year's depreciation assuming (*a*) the double-declining-balance method and (*b*) the sum-of-the-years'-digits method. Separate rows of the table should show the first year's depreciation for assets with estimated lives of 6, 7, 8, 9, and 10 years. For each estimated useful life, assume the company owns one asset that cost $10,000.

Describe what the table reveals about the two alternative methods and state whether the company should use the double-declining-balance method or the sum-of-the-years'-digits method. Also, discuss how the comparison of the two depreciation methods would change if each asset had an estimated salvage value.

Problem 10–6
Analytical essay
(LO 4)

Blanco Company has purchased an asset that is in the five-year class for tax purposes. Under the Modified Accelerated Cost Recovery System (MACRS), depreciation of the asset involves using the double-declining-balance method until a switch to straight line is more accelerated.

Note that the straight-line depreciation rate depends on when the switch is made. Since a half-year convention is required for tax purposes, only one-half-year's depreciation is deducted in the first year. Thus, at the beginning of the second year, 4½ years of depreciation remain to be taken during years 2 through 6. If a switch to the straight-line method is made at the beginning of the second year, the annual straight-line rate is 100%/4.5 = 22.2%.

At the beginning of year 3, only 3½ years of depreciation remain to be taken during years 3 through 6. Assuming the company continues with the declining-balance method during year 2 and then switches to straight line at the beginning of the third year, the annual straight-line rate is 100%/3.5 = 28.6%.

Required

Explain why depreciation of an asset in the five-year class is more accelerated if you switch to straight-line depreciation instead of continuing with the declining-balance method. As part of your explanation, determine when during the life of the asset the switch to straight line should be made.

Alternate Problems

Problem 10–1A
Alternative depreciation methods; retirement of plant assets
(LO 2, 3)

Part 1. Ironworks Company purchased and installed a new machine that cost $75,000; it had a four-year life and an estimated $15,000 salvage value. Management estimated that the machine would produce 80,000 units of product during its life. Actual production of units of product was as follows: year 1, 8,000; year 2, 21,600; year 3, 27,000; and year 4, 23,200.

Required

1. Prepare a calculation showing the number of dollars of this machine's cost that should be charged to depreciation over its four-year life.
2. Prepare a form with the following column headings:

Year	Straight Line	Units of Production	Declining Balance	Sum-of-the-Years' Digits

   Then show the depreciation for each year and the total depreciation for the machine under each depreciation method. Use twice the straight-line rate for the declining-balance method.

Part 2. On January 4, Culby Company purchased a used machine for $159,000. The next day, it was repaired at a cost of $6,100 and was mounted on a new cradle that cost $4,900. Management estimated that the machine would be used for five years and would then have a $26,000 salvage value. Depreciation was to be charged on a straight-line basis. A full year's depreciation was charged on December 31 of the first and the second years of the machine's use; and on May 30 of its third year of use, the machine was retired from service.

Required

1. Prepare general journal entries to record the purchase of the machine, the cost of repairing it, and the installation. Assume that cash was paid.
2. Prepare entries to record depreciation on the machine on December 31 of its first year and on May 30 in the year of its disposal. Also record the retirement of the machine assuming it was sold for its book value.

Problem 10–2A
Real estate costs and partial year's depreciation
(LO 1, 2, 3)

In 1993, Marathon Company paid $657,000 for a tract of land on which two buildings were located. The plan was to demolish Building A and build a new store in its place. Building B was to be used as a company office and was appraised at a value of $375,000, with a useful life of 20 years and a $59,700 salvage value. A lighted parking lot near Building B had improvements valued at $75,000 that were expected to last another five years and have no salvage value. Without considering the buildings or improvements, the tract of land was estimated to have a value of $300,000.

Marathon Company incurred the following additional costs:

Cost to demolish Building A	$ 64,500
Cost of additional landscaping	57,000
Cost to construct new building (Building C), having a useful life of 25 years and a $121,500 salvage value	1,350,000
Cost of new land improvements near Building C, which have an eight-year useful life and no salvage value	120,960

Required

1. Prepare a form having the following column headings: Land, Building B, Building C, Land Improvements B, and Land Improvements C. Allocate the costs incurred by Marathon Company to the appropriate columns and total each column.
2. Prepare a single journal entry dated June 1 to record all the incurred costs, assuming they were paid in cash on that date.
3. Prepare December 31 adjusting entries to record depreciation for the seven months of 1993 during which the assets were in use. Use sum-of-the-years'-digits depreciation for the newly constructed Building C and Land Improvements C and straight-line depreciation for Building B and Land Improvements B.

Problem 10–3A
Plant asset costs and depreciation, including MACRS
(LO 1, 2, 3, 4)

Segal Company recently negotiated a lump-sum purchase of several assets from a boat dealer who was planning to change locations. The purchase was completed on July 31, 1993, at a total cash price of $445,000, and included a building, land, certain land improvements, and a new general-purpose heavy truck. The estimated market value of each asset was: building, $252,450; land, $123,750; land improvements, $89,100; and truck, $29,700.

Required

1. Prepare a schedule to allocate the lump-sum purchase price to the separate assets that were purchased. Also present the general journal entry to record the purchase.
2. Calculate the 1994 depreciation expense on the building using the sum-of-the-years'-digits method and assuming a 15-year life and a $45,510 salvage value.
3. Calculate the 1993 depreciation expense on the land improvements assuming a 10-year life and declining-balance depreciation at twice the straightline rate.
4. The truck is in the five-year class for tax purposes but is expected to last six years and have a salvage value of $2,000. Prepare a schedule showing each year's depreciation on the truck for tax purposes, assuming (*a*) five-year straight line, and (*b*) MACRS depreciation.

Problem 10–4A
Plant asset costs and revising depreciation rates
(LO 1, 2)

On April 25, 1992, McNair Company made a lump-sum purchase of two machines. The machines cost $168,500 and were placed in use on May 2, 1992. This additional information about the machines is available:

Machine Number	Appraised Value	Salvage Value	Estimated Life	Installation Cost
One	$129,450	$23,000	5 years	$2,000
Two	86,300	2,100	5 years	3,400

McNair Company uses the straight-line method of depreciation and calculates depreciation to the nearest whole month of the date of purchase. Early in 1993, McNair decided that machine one's remaining useful life would be 2 years. In January 1994, McNair concluded that machine two would have a $200 salvage value and that the remaining useful life would be 1½ years.

Required

Prepare a form with the following column headings:

Machine Number	Depreciation				
	1992	1993	1994	1995	1996

Calculate the amount of depreciation to be charged during each year of the useful lives of machines one and two.

Problem 10–5A
Analytical essay
(LO 3)

The operations of J-Mark Company require the use of several different items of equipment that have estimated useful lives ranging from 8 to 12 years. None of the assets has any salvage value. Renee Glover, the president of J-Mark, has decided that the company should use either double-declining-balance or sum-of-the-years'-digits depreciation. However, to keep the reported net income from appearing too conservative, Glover has asked you to select whichever one of the two methods generates the least amount of depreciation in the first year.

Required

Prepare a table that shows the first year's depreciation assuming (*a*) the double-declining-balance method and (*b*) the sum-of-the-years'-digits method. Separate rows of the table should show the first year's depreciation for assets with estimated lives of 8, 9, 10, 11, and 12 years. For each estimated useful life, assume that the company owns one asset that cost $20,000.

Describe what the table reveals about the two alternative methods and state whether the company should use the double-declining-balance method or the sum-of-the-years'-digits method. Also, discuss how the comparison of the two depreciation methods would change if each asset had an estimated salvage value.

Problem 10–6A
Analytical essay
(LO 4)

The Ann Moore Company has purchased an asset that is in the seven-year class for tax purposes. Under the Modified Accelerated Cost Recovery System (MACRS), depreciation of the asset involves using the double-declining-balance method until a switch to straight line is more accelerated.

Note that the straight-line depreciation rate depends on when the switch is made. Since a half-year convention is required for tax purposes, one-half year's depreciation is deducted in the first year. Thus, at the beginning of the second year, 6½ years of depreciation remain to be taken during years 2 through 8. If a switch to the straight-line method is made at the beginning of the second year, the annual straight-line rate is 100%/6.5 = 15.4%.

At the beginning of year 3, only 5½ years of depreciation remain to be taken during years 3 through 8. Assuming the company continues with the declining-balance method during year 2 and then switches to straight line at the beginning of the third year, the annual straight-line rate is 100%/5.5 = 18.2%.

Required

Explain why depreciating the asset in the seven-year class is more accelerated if you switch to straight-line depreciation instead of continuing with the declining-balance method. As part of your explanation, determine when during the life of the asset the switch to straight line should be made.

Provocative Problems

Provocative Problem 10–1
Bell & Howell Company
(LO 2, 3)

A recent Bell & Howell Company annual report to its stockholders included an income statement for the year ended December 31, which showed that the corporation earned a $32,895,000 net income. The footnotes to the financial statements contained the following item:

> **Note A**
> **Significant Accounting Policies:**
>
> **Property and Depreciation.** Property, plant and equipment is recorded at cost. In general, the straight-line method of depreciation is used for asset additions since the beginning of 1981 and the double-declining-balance method is used for prior years' assets. Estimated lives range from 5 to 35 years for land improvements, 10 to 50 years for buildings, 2 to 15 years for machinery and equipment and 5 to 15 years for product masters.
> *(Courtesy of Bell & Howell Co.)*

What might have caused Bell & Howell to switch from declining-balance depreciation to straight-line depreciation for assets purchased in 1981 and subsequent years? Assuming that the company's total investments in property, plant, and equipment have increased gradually each year, what effect would this change have on comparisons of income earned before and after 1980?

Provocative Problem 10–2
Aerodyne Company
(LO 1, 2)

Aerodyne Company temporarily recorded the costs of a new plant in a single account called Land and Buildings. Management has now asked you to examine this account and prepare any necessary entries to correct the account balance. In doing so, you find the following debits and credits to the account:

Debits

Jan.	3	Cost of land and building acquired for new plant site	$201,500
	11	Attorney's fee for title search	930
	24	Cost of demolishing old building on plant site	23,400
Feb.	2	Six months' liability and fire insurance during construction	3,570
June	29	Payment to building contractor on completion	486,000
July	2	Architect's fee for new building	31,025
	6	City assessment for street improvements	12,850
	14	Cost of landscaping new plant site	8,900
			$768,175

Credits

Jan.	26	Proceeds from sale of salvaged materials from building	$2,650
July	2	Refund of one month's liability and fire insurance premium	595
Dec.	31	Depreciation at 2½% per year	15,000
			$ 18,245
Dec.	31	Debit balance	$749,930

An account called Depreciation Expense, Land and Buildings was debited in recording the $15,000 of depreciation. Your investigation suggests that 40 years is a reasonable life expectancy for a building of the type involved and that an assumption of zero salvage value is reasonable.

To summarize your analysis, set up a schedule with columns headed Date, Description, Total Amount, Land, Buildings, and Other Accounts. Next, enter the items found in the Land and Buildings account on the schedule, distributing the amounts to the proper columns. Show credits on the schedule by enclosing the amounts in parentheses. Also, draft any required correcting entry or entries, under the assumption that the accounts have not been closed.

Provocative Problem 10–3
Cantu and Havner Companies
(A review problem)

Cantu Company and Havner Company are almost identical. Each began operations on January 1 of this year with $324,000 of equipment with a six-year life and a $51,000 salvage value. Each purchased merchandise during the year as follows:

Jan. 4	650 units @ $500 per unit =	$ 325,000
Mar. 22	730 units @ $525 per unit =	383,250
July 6	460 units @ $550 per unit =	253,000
Dec. 10	500 units @ $600 per unit =	300,000
		$1,261,250

Now, on December 31 at the end of the first year, each has 950 units of merchandise in its ending inventory. However, Cantu Company will use straight-line depreciation in arriving at its net income for the year, while Havner Company will use sum-of-the-years'-digits depreciation. Also, Cantu Company will use FIFO in costing its ending inventory, and Havner Company will use LIFO. The December 31 trial balances of the two concerns carried these amounts:

	Cantu Company		Havner Company	
Cash	$ 37,600		$ 37,600	
Accounts receivable	58,900		58,900	
Equipment	324,000		324,000	
Accounts payable		$ 72,300		$ 72,300
A. Cantu, capital		663,500		
S. Havner, capital				663,500
Sales		1,200,700		1,200,700
Purchases	1,261,250		1,261,250	
Salaries expense	123,400		123,400	
Rent expense	32,750		32,750	
Other cash expenses	98,600		98,600	
Totals	$1,936,500	$1,936,500	$1,936,500	$1,936,500

Required

Prepare an income statement for each company and a schedule that explains the difference in their reported net incomes. Write a short answer to this question: Which, if either, of the companies is the more profitable and why?

Provocative Problem 10–4
International Business Machines Corporation
(LO 2)

Refer to the annual report for International Business Machines Corporation in Appendix J, particularly the balance sheet, the management discussion, and the footnotes to answer the following questions:

1. What percentage of the original cost of IBM's land improvements, buildings and plant, laboratory and office equipment remains to be depreciated at the end of 1989 and 1990? (Assume the assets have no salvage value.)
2. What percentage of the original cost of IBM's rental machines and parts remains to be depreciated at the end of 1989 and 1990? (Assume the assets have no salvage value.)
3. What method of depreciation does IBM use for plant, rental machines, and other property?
4. IBM's consolidated statement of financial position shows that investments in software had a net increase from 1989 to 1990. What was the cost of investments made in 1990? What was the nature of these investments as stated in the management discussion section of the annual report?

Provocative Problem 10–5
As a Matter of Ethics: Essay

Ethics

Review the As a Matter of Ethics case on page 541 and write a short essay discussing the situation faced by Sue Ann Meyer. Include a discussion of the alternative courses of action available to Meyer and indicate how you think she should deal with the situation.

Answers to Objective Review Questions

LO 1 (*a*)	LO 3 (*b*)	LO 5 (*e*)
LO 2 (*e*)	LO 4 (*e*)	

CHAPTER

11

Plant and Equipment, Natural Resources, and Intangible Assets

A company's assets include many things in addition to tangible equipment and buildings. Patents, natural resources, and outstanding employees all contribute to profits. However, they create unique accounting problems that must be solved.

Topical Coverage

In this chapter, we continue to examine the accounting issues related to property, plant, and equipment. In studying the chapter, you will learn how accounting records are used to maintain control over plant assets, how to account for the costs of maintaining or improving plant assets, and how to account for disposals of plant assets. The chapter also introduces you to the issues of accounting for natural resources and intangible assets.

Learning Objectives

After studying Chapter 11, you should be able to:

1. Explain how subsidiary ledgers and related controlling accounts are used to maintain control over plant assets.
2. Describe the difference between revenue and capital expenditures and account properly for costs such as repairs and betterments incurred after the original purchase of plant assets.
3. Prepare entries to record the disposal of plant assets and the exchange of plant assets under accounting principles and under income tax rules and tell which should be applied in any given exchange.
4. Prepare entries to account for natural resources and intangible assets, including entries to record depletion and amortization.
5. Define or explain the words and phrases listed in the chapter glossary.

Controlling Plant Assets

LO 1 Explain how subsidiary ledgers and related controlling accounts are used to maintain control over plant assets.

Good internal control requires that each plant asset be separately identified, usually with a unique identification number that is either engraved on the asset or attached with a permanent sticker or tag such as the following:

Avondale Company
163–002

Periodically, an inventory of plant assets should be taken to verify the existence, location, condition, and continued use of each asset. This count should be compared to the formal records of plant assets that every company should maintain. For good internal control, the custodians of the assets must not have access to the records.

In keeping these records, companies usually divide their plant assets into functional groups and provide each group with a separate asset account and accumulated depreciation account in the General Ledger. The asset account and the related accumulated depreciation account for each group serve as controlling accounts for detailed subsidiary records. For example, a store will create a Store Equipment account and a related Accumulated Depreciation, Store Equipment account. Together, they control the **Store Equipment Ledger,** which is a subsidiary ledger that contains a separate record for each

item of store equipment. Similarly, the accountant creates accounts for Office Equipment and Accumulated Depreciation, Office Equipment, which control the **Office Equipment Ledger.**

Plant asset records provide the same basic information whether they are computerized or handwritten. To illustrate a simple plant asset record system, assume that a concern's collection of office equipment consists of only one desk and a chair. The general ledger accounts for these assets are Office Equipment and Accumulated Depreciation, Office Equipment. Both are controlling accounts that control the subsidiary record for the desk and chair. The general ledger and subsidiary ledger records for these assets are shown in Illustration 11–1.

At the top of each subsidiary record, observe the plant asset numbers assigned to these two items of office equipment (163–001 and 163–002). In each case, the assigned number consists of the number of the Office Equipment general ledger account, 163, followed by the asset's unique identification number. The remaining information on the subsidiary records is more or less self-evident. Notice how the $940 balance of the general ledger account, Office Equipment, is equal to the sum of the $190 and $750 balances in the asset record section of the two subsidiary records. The general ledger account controls this section of the subsidiary ledger.

Also observe how the Accumulated Depreciation, Office Equipment account controls the depreciation record section of the subsidiary records. Specifically, the $375 balance at December 31, 1993, equals the sum of the $75 accumulated on the chair and the $300 accumulated on the desk.

The disposition section at the bottom of the subsidiary records is used to record facts about the final disposal of the asset. When the asset is discarded, sold, or exchanged, a notation describing this action is entered here. The record is then removed from the subsidiary ledger and filed for future reference. Again, good internal control requires that the records of the assets should not be kept by the person who is responsible for their safekeeping. Otherwise, the custodian of the assets can use the records to cover up an accident or a theft. Many larger companies require that all assets be turned over to a special salvage department for final disposal.

Revenue and Capital Expenditures

LO 2 Describe the difference between revenue and capital expenditures and account properly for costs such as repairs and betterments incurred after the original purchase of plant assets.

By this time, you have learned that a company's expenditures can be recorded as expenses right away or as assets, with expenses coming later. After a plant asset is acquired and put into service, additional expenditures are incurred to operate, maintain, repair, and perhaps improve it. In recording these additional expenditures, the accountant must decide whether they should be debited to expense accounts or asset accounts. The issue faced by the accountant is whether more useful information is provided in the financial statements if these expenditures are reported as expenses on the income statement in the current year or if they are added to the plant asset's cost and depreciated over future years.

In traditional terms, a **revenue expenditure** should be recorded as an expense and deducted from revenues on the current period's income statement. Revenue expenditures are reported on the income statement because they do

ILLUSTRATION 11–1

Subsidiary Records and Controlling Accounts for Plant Assets

Plant Asset
No. *163–001*

SUBSIDIARY PLANT ASSET AND DEPRECIATION RECORD

Item *Office chair* Account *Office Equipment*
Description *Padded, straight-back, wood*
Mfg. serial no. *4G81545* Purchased from *Chairco*
Where located *Office*
Person responsible for the asset *Office Manager*
Estimated life *6 years* Estimated salvage value *$10.00*
Depreciation per year *$30.00* per month *$2.50*

			Asset Record			Depreciation Record		
Date	Explanation	PR	Dr.	Cr.	Bal.	Dr.	Cr.	Bal.
July 2, 1991		G1	190.00		190.00			
Dec. 31, 1991		G23					15.00	15.00
Dec. 31, 1992		G42					30.00	45.00
Dec. 31, 1993		G65					30.00	75.00

Final disposition of the asset ______

Plant Asset
No. *163–002*

SUBSIDIARY PLANT ASSET AND DEPRECIATION RECORD

Item *Desk* Account *Office Equipment*
Description *Wood, left hand return*
Mfg. serial no. *4527439* Purchased from *Office Equipment Co.*
Where located *Office*
Person responsible for the asset *Office Manager*
Estimated life *6 years* Estimated salvage value *$30.00*
Depreciation per year *$120.00* per month *$10.00*

			Asset Record			Depreciation Record		
Date	Explanation	PR	Dr.	Cr.	Bal.	Dr.	Cr.	Bal.
July 2, 1991		G1	750.00		750.00			
Dec. 31, 1991		G23					60.00	60.00
Dec. 31, 1992		G42					120.00	180.00
Dec. 31, 1993		G65					120.00	300.00

Final disposition of the asset ______

ILLUSTRATION 11–1 (concluded)

Account No. 163

Office Equipment

Date		Explanation	PR	Debit		Credit		Balance	
1991 July	2	Desk and chair	G1	940	00			940	00

Account No. 164

Accumulated Depreciation, Office Equipment

Date		Explanation	PR	Debit		Credit		Balance	
1991 Dec.	31		G23			75	00	75	00
1992 Dec.	31		G42			150	00	225	00
1993 Dec.	31		G65			150	00	375	00

not provide material benefits in future periods. Examples of revenue expenditures that relate to plant assets are wages, supplies, fuel, lubricants, and electrical power.

On the other hand, expenditures producing economic benefits that do not fully expire before the end of the current period are called **capital expenditures.** Because they are debited to asset accounts and reported on the balance sheet, they are also called **balance sheet expenditures.** Capital expenditures significantly modify or improve the kind or amount of service that an asset provides.

Because the information in the financial statements is affected for several years by the choice between recording a cost as a revenue or capital expenditure, you must be careful in deciding how to classify it. Although judgment is always involved, accountants have developed several guidelines that help you know what to do. The following sections describe these practices for ordinary repairs, extraordinary repairs, betterments, and assets with low costs.

Ordinary and Extraordinary Repairs

Ordinary repairs are made to keep an asset in normal good operating condition. For example, keeping a wood-frame building in good condition requires that you periodically repaint it and maintain its roof. Similarly, machines must be cleaned, lubricated, and adjusted, and small parts must be replaced when they wear out. Such repairs and maintenance typically are made every year,

and accountants treat them as *revenue expenditures*. Thus, their costs should appear on the current income statement as expenses.

In contrast to ordinary repairs that keep a plant asset in its normal good operating condition, **extraordinary repairs** extend the asset's service life beyond original expectations. Reflecting this nature, the costs of extraordinary repairs are *capital expenditures*. They are usually debited to the repaired asset's accumulated depreciation account to show that they counteract the effects of past usage reflected as depreciation. Because extraordinary repairs add to an asset's useful life, they also benefit future periods. Thus, their cost appears in the income statements of future periods as depreciation.

For example, a machine was purchased for $8,000 and depreciated under the assumption it would last eight years and have no salvage value. As a result, the machine's book value is $2,000 at the end of its sixth year, calculated as follows:

Cost of machine	$8,000
Less six years' accumulated depreciation	6,000
Book value	$2,000

At the beginning of the machine's seventh year, it is given a major overhaul that extends its estimated useful life three years beyond the eight originally estimated. Thus, the company now predicts that it will be used for five more years. The $2,100 cost of the extraordinary repair should be recorded as follows:

Jan.	12	Accumulated Depreciation, Machinery	2,100.00	
		Cash		2,100.00
		To record extraordinary repairs.		

This entry increases the book value of the asset from $2,000 to $4,100. In the remaining five years of the asset's life, depreciation should be based on this new book value. The effects of the extraordinary repairs are as follows:

	Before	**After**
Original cost	$ 8,000	$ 8,000
Accumulated depreciation	(6,000)	(3,900)
Book value	$ 2,000	$ 4,100
Revised annual depreciation expense for remaining years ($4,100/5 years)		$ 820

If the machine remains in use for five years after the major overhaul, the five annual $820 depreciation charges will write off its $4,100 book value, which includes the cost of the extraordinary repairs.

Betterments

A **betterment** (or an improvement) occurs when a plant asset is modified to make it more efficient, usually by replacing one of its old components with an improved or superior component. The result of a betterment is more efficiency or more productivity. However, the expenditure does not necessarily increase the asset's useful life. For example, if the manual controls on a machine are replaced with automatic controls, future labor costs will be reduced. But, the machine still wears out just as fast as it would have with the manual controls.

When a betterment occurs, accountants agree that its cost should be debited to the improved asset's account. Then, the cost and accumulated depreciation attributable to the replaced asset component should be removed from the accounts. Finally, the new book value (less salvage) should be depreciated over the remaining service life of the asset.

For example, suppose that a company paid $80,000 for a machine with an eight-year service life and no salvage value. On January 6, after three years and $30,000 of depreciation, the owner removes the manual control system and replaces it with an automatic system at a cost of $18,000. This betterment does not increase the service life beyond the remaining five years of the original prediction. The owner estimates that the cost of the manual control system represented approximately 10% of the total cost, or $8,000. The same proportion (10%) would also apply to the accumulated depreciation, so that $3,000 would be attributed to the manual system. The old component was sold to another company for $2,700 cash. The entry to record the removal and sale of the manual system would be as follows:

Jan.	6	Cash	2,700.00	
		Accumulated Depreciation, Machinery	3,000.00	
		Loss on Sale of Machinery	2,300.00	
		Machinery		8,000.00
		To record the removal and sale of the manual control system.		

Then, the cost of the betterment would be added to the Machinery account with this entry:

Jan.	6	Machinery	18,000.00	
		Cash		18,000.00
		To record the installation of the automatic control system.		

At this point, the new cost of the machine is $90,000 ($80,000 − $8,000 + $18,000), the accumulated depreciation is $27,000 ($30,000 − $3,000), and the book value is $63,000 ($90,000 − $27,000). Because five years remain in the useful life, the annual depreciation expense hereafter will be $12,600 per year ($63,000/5 years).

Plant Assets with Low Costs

Even with the help of computers, keeping individual plant asset records can be expensive. Therefore, many companies do not keep detailed records for assets that cost less than some minimum amount such as $50 or $100. Instead, they treat the acquisition as a revenue expenditure, and charge the cost directly to an expense account at the time of purchase. As long as the amounts are small, this practice is acceptable under the *materiality principle*. That is, treating these capital expenditures as revenue expenditures is unlikely to mislead a user of the financial statements.

Plant Asset Disposals

LO 3 Prepare entries to record the disposal of plant assets and the exchange of plant assets under accounting principles and under income tax rules and tell which should be applied in any given exchange.

Sooner or later, plant assets wear out. They also may become obsolete or inadequate because of changes in the business. When these conditions arise, the assets are discarded, sold, or traded in on new assets. The journal entry to record the disposal of a plant asset depends on which action is taken.

Discarding a Plant Asset

When an asset's accumulated depreciation is equal to its cost, the asset is said to be fully depreciated. If a fully depreciated asset with a cost of $1,500 is discarded on January 7, this entry would be made to record the disposal:

Jan.	7	Accumulated Depreciation, Machinery	1,500.00	
		Machinery		1,500.00
		Discarded a fully depreciated machine.		

It is not unusual to find a fully depreciated asset remaining in use beyond the end of its predicted service life. In these situations, the asset's cost and accumulated depreciation should remain on the books until the asset is discarded, sold, or traded. Otherwise, the accounts and the financial statements do not show its continued existence. However, no additional depreciation expense can be recorded since there is no more cost to be charged. In other words, the total amount of depreciation expense for an asset cannot exceed its cost.

In other situations, an asset may be discarded before it is fully depreciated. For example, suppose that an asset does not last as long as predicted, and becomes worthless, even though only $800 of its $1,000 cost has been depreciated. If it is discarded, there is a loss equal to its book value, and the entry to record the disposal is:

Jan.	10	Loss on Disposal of Machinery	200.00	
		Accumulated Depreciation, Machinery	800.00	
		Machinery		1,000.00
		Discarded a worthless machine.		

Remember from the earlier discussion of partial year's depreciation that it may be necessary to allocate depreciation to the part of the year in which the dis-

carded asset is actually used. Because this particular asset was discarded early in January, nothing was recorded.

Discarding a Damaged Plant Asset

Occasionally, a plant asset may be wrecked or destroyed in an accident before the end of its service life. For example, a machine that had a cost of $900 and accumulated depreciation of $400 was totally destroyed in a fire. If the machine was uninsured, a loss equal to the machine's $500 book value would be recorded as follows:

Jan.	12	Loss on Fire	500.00	
		Accumulated Depreciation, Machinery	400.00	
		Machinery		900.00
		To record the destruction of machinery not covered by insurance.		

Or, if the loss was partially covered by insurance and the insurance company paid $350 to settle the loss claim, the entry to record the machine's destruction would be:

Jan.	12	Cash	350.00	
		Loss on Fire[1]	150.00	
		Accumulated Depreciation, Machinery	400.00	
		Machinery		900.00
		To record the destruction of machinery and the receipt of insurance compensation.		

Selling a Plant Asset

If a plant asset is sold and the selling price exceeds the asset's book value, a gain is recorded in the accounts and reported on the income statement. And, if the price is less than book value, there is a loss. For example, assume a machine that cost $5,000 and has a book value of $1,000 is sold for $1,200. This sale results in a $200 gain and is recorded as follows:

Jan.	4	Cash	1,200.00	
		Accumulated Depreciation, Machinery	4,000.00	
		Machinery		5,000.00
		Gain on Sale of Machinery		200.00
		Sold a machine at a price in excess of book value.		

[1] Note that the economic loss from the fire depends on the difference between the cost of replacing the asset and any insurance settlement. A difference between this economic loss and the reported loss arises from the fact that the accounting records do not attempt to reflect the value of plant assets.

However, if the machine is sold for only $750, there is a $250 loss and the entry to record the sale is:

Jan.	4	Cash	750.00	
		Loss on Sale of Machinery	250.00	
		Accumulated Depreciation, Machinery	4,000.00	
		Machinery		5,000.00
		Sold a machine at a price below book value.		

Exchanging Plant Assets

LO 3 Prepare entries to record the disposal of plant assets and the exchange of plant assets under accounting principles and under income tax rules and tell which should be applied in any given exchange.

Many plant assets retired from use are sold for cash. Others, such as machinery, automobiles, and office equipment, are commonly exchanged for new assets that are similar in purpose. In a typical exchange, a trade-in allowance is received on the old asset, and any balance is paid in cash.

When a plant asset is exchanged for a new asset that is similar in purpose, the exchange may involve a loss or a gain. A loss occurs when the trade-in allowance is less than the book value of the old asset. A gain occurs when the trade-in allowance is more than the book value of the old asset. However, according to generally accepted accounting principles, you must not recognize a gain on an exchange of similar assets if the exchange also involves a cash payment. The same rules apply to an exchange of similar assets when the exchange does not involve any cash payment or receipt. Gains must not be recognized and material losses must be recognized.

Accounting for an exchange of similar assets is more complex when the exchange involves a cash receipt. Such cases are explained in more advanced accounting texts.[2]

Recognition of a Material Loss

To illustrate the recognition of a material loss on an exchange of similar plant assets, assume that a machine with a cost of $18,000 and accumulated depreciation of $15,000 is traded in on a new machine. The new machine has a $21,000 cash price, and a $1,000 trade-in allowance is received. The $20,000 balance of the cost is paid in cash. Under these assumptions, the $3,000 book value of the old machine and the loss on the exchange are calculated as follows:

Cost of old machine	$18,000
Less accumulated depreciation	15,000
Book value	$ 3,000
Less trade-in allowance	1,000
Loss on exchange	$ 2,000

[2] See FASB, *Accounting Standards—Current Text* (Norwalk, Conn., 1990), sec. N35.109. First published as *APB Opinion No. 29,* par. 22.

The entry to record this exchange transaction is:

Jan.	5	Machinery	21,000.00	
		Loss on Exchange of Machinery	2,000.00	
		Accumulated Depreciation, Machinery	15,000.00	
		Machinery		18,000.00
		Cash		20,000.00
		Exchanged old machine and cash for a similar machine.		

The $21,000 debit to Machinery puts the new machine in the accounts at its cash price. The debit to Loss on Exchange of Machinery records the loss. The old machine is removed from the accounts with the $15,000 debit to Accumulated Depreciation and the $18,000 credit to Machinery. Note that in this case, the $21,000 debit to Machinery is equal to the cash price of the machine. In all cases, you must avoid recording a new asset at an amount that is larger than its cash price or fair value. Also, a catalog or list price may not represent an asset's cash price.

Nonrecognition of a Gain

When there is a gain on an exchange of similar plant assets and the balance, if any, involves a cash payment, generally accepted accounting principles require following the conservative practice of recording the new asset at the sum of the old asset's book value plus the cash paid. Thus, no gain is recognized.

For example, assume that the exchange for the $21,000 machine in the previous section involved a trade-in allowance of $4,500 instead of $1,000. As a result, the balance to be paid in cash is only $16,500. Since the $4,500 trade-in allowance exceeds the $3,000 book value of the old asset, the difference is a gain. However, when you record the trade, you cannot recognize the gain in the accounts. Rather, it is absorbed into the cost of the new machine, which is recorded at an amount equal to the sum of the book value of the old machine plus the cash paid. This amount is calculated as follows:

Cost of old machine	$ 18,000
Accumulated depreciation	(15,000)
Book value of old machine	$ 3,000
Cash given in the exchange	16,500
Cost recorded for the new machine	$ 19,500

The transaction should be recorded as follows:

Jan.	5	Machinery	19,500.00	
		Accumulated Depreciation, Machinery	15,000.00	
		Machinery		18,000.00
		Cash		16,500.00
		Exchanged old machine and cash for a new machine of like purpose.		

Observe that the $19,500 amount recorded for the new machine is equal to its cash price less the unrecognized $1,500 gain on the exchange ($21,000 − $1,500 = $19,500). In other words, the $1,500 gain was absorbed into the amount at which the new machine was recorded. The $19,500 is the *cost basis* of the new machine and is the amount used to calculate its depreciation or any gain or loss on its sale.

In summary, when similar plant assets are exchanged and there is a cash payment, losses are recognized but gains are not recognized. This rule is based on the opinion that "revenue [or a gain] should not be recognized merely because one productive asset is substituted for a similar productive asset but rather should be considered to flow from the production and sale of the goods or services to which the substituted productive asset is committed."[3] As a result, the effect of the gain is delayed and appears in future income statements as increased net income from smaller depreciation charges on the acquired asset. In this case, depreciation calculated on the recorded $19,500 cost basis of the new machine is smaller than it would be if it was based on the machine's $21,000 cash price.

Exchanges of Dissimilar Assets

If a company exchanges a plant asset for another asset that is *dissimilar* in use or purpose, the accounting treatment for a loss is exactly the same as already described for exchanges of similar assets. However, the company can recognize a gain on an exchange of dissimilar assets. Suppose that the previous transaction involved an exchange of machinery for merchandise inventory worth $21,000. This entry would record the exchange:

Jan.	5	Merchandise Inventory (or Purchases)	21,000.00	
		Accumulated Depreciation, Machinery	15,000.00	
		Machinery		18,000.00
		Cash		16,500.00
		Gain on Exchange of Machinery		1,500.00
		Exchanged old machine and cash for merchandise inventory.		

Tax Rules and Plant Asset Exchanges

Because depreciation methods used for financial statements are often different from those used for income tax returns, many companies keep two sets of depreciation records on each asset. One set is kept to determine depreciation expense for financial accounting purposes and the other is kept to determine the depreciation deduction for tax purposes. Two sets of records may be necessary even when the depreciation methods and estimated lives are the same for tax and accounting purposes. This situation is caused by the fact that income tax rules and generally accepted accounting principles do not always

[3] APB, "Accounting for Nonmonetary Transactions," *APB Opinion No. 29* (New York: AICPA, May 1973), par. 16.

agree on the treatment of losses on exchanges of similar plant assets. (In the case of a gain on similar asset exchanges, the tax rules and accounting principles both agree that none should be reported.)

According to the tax rules, when an old asset is traded in on a similar, new asset, both gains and losses must be absorbed into the cost of the new asset. For tax purposes, this cost basis must be used to calculate depreciation on the new asset. Therefore, for tax purposes, it makes no difference whether there is a gain or a loss on the exchange; the cost basis of an asset acquired in an exchange is the sum of the book value of the old asset plus the cash given.

Because accounting principles and tax rules differ in their treatment of losses on exchanges of similar assets, two sets of depreciation records must be kept for a new asset acquired in an exchange that involved a material loss. Keeping two sets of records is necessary because a material loss is recognized for financial accounting purposes but is not recognized for tax purposes. On the other hand, when an exchange results in a loss that is not material, you can appeal to the *materiality principle* and record the new asset on the books at the same cost basis used for tax purposes. By following this shortcut, you may avoid having to keep two sets of records for at least some assets.

For example, assume that a computer used in an office is traded in on a new computer with a cash price of $1,800. The purchaser is granted a trade-in allowance of $150 on the old computer and the $1,650 difference is paid in cash. The old computer had cost $1,500 and had been depreciated $1,260 for both tax and accounting purposes. In this case, the old computer's book value is $240, and the trade-in allowance of $150 results in a $90 loss on the exchange. However, if the $90 loss is immaterial, the exchange can be recorded using the income tax method as follows:

Jan.	7	Office Equipment	1,890.00	
		Accumulated Depreciation, Office Equipment	1,260.00	
		Office Equipment		1,500.00
		Cash		1,650.00
		Traded an old computer and cash for a new computer.		

The new computer is taken into the accounts at $1,890, which is also its cost basis for tax purposes. This amount is calculated as follows:

Cost of old computer	$ 1,500
Accumulated depreciation	(1,260)
Book value of old computer	$ 240
Cash paid ($1,800 less the $150 trade-in allowance)	1,650
Income tax cost basis for the new computer	$ 1,890

The income tax method takes the new computer into the accounts at its cost basis and does not record the loss. As a result, the method violates the financial reporting rule that a loss on a plant asset exchange should be recorded. However, when the loss is not material, the violation is permissible under the *materiality principle*. In this case, we are assuming that the failure to report the $90 loss does not produce a material effect on the financial statements.

Natural Resources

LO 4 Prepare entries to account for natural resources and intangible assets, including entries to record depletion and amortization.

Natural resources include such things as standing timber, mineral deposits, and oil reserves. Because they are physically consumed when they are used, they are known as *wasting assets*. In their natural state, they represent inventories of raw materials that will be converted into a product by cutting, mining, or pumping. However, until the conversion takes place, they are noncurrent assets and appear on a balance sheet under captions such as "Timberlands," "Mineral deposits," or "Oil reserves." Sometimes, this caption appears under the property, plant, and equipment category of assets and sometimes it is shown as a separate category.

Natural resources are accounted for at their original cost. Like the cost of plant assets, the cost of natural resources is allocated to the periods in which they are consumed. The cost created by consuming the usefulness of natural resources is called **depletion.** On the balance sheet, natural resources are shown at cost less *accumulated depletion*. The amount such assets are depleted each year by cutting, mining, or pumping is usually calculated on a "units-of-production" basis.

For example, if a mineral deposit has an estimated 500,000 tons of available ore and is purchased for $500,000, the depletion charge per ton of ore mined is $1. Thus, if 85,000 tons are mined during the first year, the depletion charge for the year is $85,000 and is recorded as follows:

Dec.	31	Depletion of Mineral Deposit	85,000.00	
		Accumulated Depletion, Mineral Deposit		85,000.00
		To record depletion of the mineral deposit.		

On the balance sheet prepared at the end of the first year, the mineral deposit should appear at its $500,000 cost less accumulated depletion of $85,000. If the 85,000 tons of ore are sold by the end of the first year, the entire $85,000 depletion charge reaches the income statement as the depletion cost of the ore mined and sold. However, if a portion remains unsold at year-end, the depletion cost of the unsold ore is carried forward on the balance sheet as part of the cost of the unsold ore inventory, which is a current asset.

The conversion of natural resources through mining, cutting, or pumping often requires the use of machinery and buildings. Because the usefulness of these assets is related to the depletion of the natural resource, their costs should be depreciated over the life of the natural resource in proportion to the annual depletion charges. For example, if a machine is installed in a mine and one eighth of the mine's ore is removed during a year, one eighth of the machine's cost (less salvage value) should be depreciated. Furthermore, because the depreciation is necessary for the mining operation, it should be recognized as an additional cost of the mined ore.

Intangible Assets

Some assets represent certain legal rights and economic relationships beneficial to the owner. Because they have no physical existence, they are called **intangible assets.** Patents, copyrights, leaseholds, leasehold improvements, goodwill, and trademarks are intangible assets. We discuss each of these items in more detail in following sections. Although notes and accounts receivable are also intangible in nature, they are not used to produce products or provide services. Therefore, they are not listed on the balance sheet as intangible assets; instead, they are classified as current assets or investments.

When an intangible asset is purchased, it is recorded at cost. Thereafter, its cost must be systematically written off to expense over its estimated useful life through the process of **amortization.** Generally accepted accounting principles require that the amortization period for an intangible asset be 40 years or less.[4]

Amortization of intangible assets is similar to depreciation of plant assets and depletion of natural resources in that all three are processes of cost allocation. However, only the straight-line method can be used for amortizing intangibles unless you can demonstrate that another method is more appropriate. Also, while the effects of depreciation and depletion on the assets are recorded in a contra account (Accumulated Depreciation or Accumulated Depletion), amortization usually is credited directly to the intangible asset account. As a result, intangible assets are reported in the balance sheet at that portion of cost not previously written off without reporting the full original cost. Normally, intangible assets are shown in a separate balance sheet section that follows immediately after the plant and equipment section.

However, all companies do not follow these traditions. For example, the IBM balance sheet in Appendix J does not identify any intangible assets. But, in a footnote labeled Investments and Sundry Assets, the company reported $383 million of goodwill at the end of 1990. Also, the amount of accumulated amortization was disclosed.

The following sections describe several specific types of intangible assets.

Patents

The federal government grants **patents** to encourage the invention of new machines, mechanical devices, and production processes. A patent gives its owner the exclusive right to manufacture and sell a patented machine or device, or to use a process, for 17 years. When patent rights are purchased, the cost of acquiring the rights is debited to an account called Patents. Also, if the owner engages in lawsuits to defend a patent, the cost of the lawsuits should be debited to the Patents account. However, the costs of research and development leading to a new patent are *not* debited to an asset account.[5]

Although a patent gives its owner exclusive rights to the patented device or process for 17 years, the cost of the patent should be amortized over its predicted useful life, which might be less than the full 17 years. For example, if a patent that cost $25,000 has an estimated useful life of 10 years, the following adjusting entry is made at the end of each of those years to write off 1/10 of its cost:

[4] FASB, *Accounting Standards—Current Text* (Norwalk, Conn., 1990), sec. I60.110. First published as *APB Opinion No. 17*, par. 29.

[5] FASB, *Accounting Standards—Current Text* (Norwalk, Conn., 1990), sec. R50.108. First published as *Statement of Financial Accounting Standards No. 2*, par. 12.

Dec.	31	Amortization of Patents	2,500.00	
		Patents		2,500.00
		To write off patent costs over the expected 10-year life.		

The entry's debit causes $2,500 of patent costs to appear on the annual income statement as one of the costs of the product manufactured under the protection of the patent. Note that we have followed the convention of crediting the amortization directly to the Patents account.

Copyrights

A **copyright** is granted by the federal government or by international agreement. In most cases, a copyright gives its owner the exclusive right to publish and sell a musical, literary, or artistic work during the life of the composer, author, or artist and for 50 years thereafter. Most copyrights have value for a much shorter time, and their costs should be amortized over the shorter period. Often, the only identifiable cost of a copyright is the fee paid to the Copyright Office. If this fee is not material, it may be charged directly to an expense account. Otherwise, the copyright costs should be capitalized (recorded as a capital expenditure), and the periodic amortization of a copyright should be charged to an account called Amortization Expense, Copyrights.

Leaseholds

Property is rented under a contract called a **lease.** The person or company that owns the property and grants the lease is called the **lessor.** The person or company that secures the right to possess and use the property is called the **lessee.** The rights granted to the lessee by the lessor under the lease are called a **leasehold.** A leasehold is an intangible asset for the lessee.

Some leases require no advance payment from the lessee but do require monthly rent payments. In such cases, a Leasehold account is not needed and the monthly payments are debited to a Rent Expense account. Sometimes, a long-term lease requires the lessee to pay the final year's rent in advance when the lease is signed. If so, the lessee records the advance payment with a debit to its Leasehold asset account. Because the usefulness of the advance payment is not consumed until the final year is reached, the Leasehold account balance remains intact until that year. At that time, the balance is transferred to Rent Expense.

Leasehold Improvements

Long-term leases often require the lessee to pay for any alterations or improvements to the leased property, such as new partitions and storefronts. Normally, the costs of these **leasehold improvements** are debited to an account called Leasehold Improvements. Also, since the improvements become part of the property and revert to the lessor at the end of the lease, the lessee must amortize the cost of the improvements over the life of the lease or the life of the improvements, whichever is shorter. The amortization entry commonly debits Rent Expense and credits Leasehold Improvements.

Goodwill

The term **goodwill** has a special meaning in accounting. In theory, a business has an intangible asset called goodwill when its rate of expected future earnings is greater than the rate of earnings normally realized in its industry. Above-average earnings and the existence of theoretical goodwill may be demonstrated with the following information about Companies A and B, both of which are in the same industry:

	Company A	Company B
Net assets (other than goodwill)	$100,000	$100,000
Normal rate of return in this industry	10%	10%
Normal return on net assets	$ 10,000	$ 10,000
Expected net income	10,000	15,000
Expected earnings above average	$ -0-	$ 5,000

Company B is expected to have an above-average earnings rate compared to its industry and, therefore, is said to have goodwill. This goodwill may be the result of excellent customer relations, the location of the business, the quality and uniqueness of its products, monopolistic market advantages, a superior management and work force, or a combination of these and other factors.[6] Consequently, a potential investor would be willing to pay more for Company B than for Company A. Thus, goodwill is theoretically an asset that has value.

To keep financial statement information from being too subjective, accountants have agreed that goodwill should not be recorded unless it is purchased. Normally, goodwill is purchased only when a business is acquired in its entirety.

When a business is to be purchased, the buyer and seller may estimate the amount of goodwill in several different ways. If the business is expected to have $5,000 each year in above-average earnings, its goodwill may be valued at, say, four times its above-average earnings, or $20,000. Or, if the $5,000 is expected to continue indefinitely, they may think of it as a return on an investment at a given rate of return, say, 10%. In this case, the estimated amount of goodwill is $5,000/10% = $50,000. However, in the final analysis, the value of goodwill is confirmed only by the price the seller is willing to accept and the buyer is willing to pay.

Trademarks and Trade Names

Companies often adopt unique symbols or select unique names that they use in marketing their products. Sometimes, the ownership and exclusive right to use such a **trademark** or **trade name** can be established simply by demonstrating that one company has used the trademark or trade name before other businesses. However, ownership generally can be established more definitely by registering the trademark or trade name at the U.S. Patent Office. The cost of

[6] Of course, the value of the location may be reflected in a higher cost for the land owned and used by the company.

AS A MATTER OF
Fact

Intangible assets amortized

	Number of Companies			
Assets Being Amortized	**1990**	**1989**	**1988**	**1987**
Goodwill recognized in a business combination	379	367	340	338
Patents, patent rights	62	62	67	59
Trademarks, brand names, copyrights	46	38	41	34
Licenses, franchises, memberships	16	19	22	26
Other—described	57	52	47	20

Amortization period used—1990

	Number of Companies			
Period	**Goodwill**	**Patent**	**Trademark**	**License**
40 years	195	1	7	—
"Not exceeding 40"	84	1	3	1
25–30.	12	—	1	1
20	15	—	—	1
10–15.	15	2	1	—
Legal/estimated life	27	45	23	8
Other.	60	12	10	4

Excerpted with permission from *Accounting Trends & Techniques*, Annual Survey of Accounting Practices Followed in 600 Stockholders' Reports, Forty-Fifth Edition, Copyright © 1991 by American Institute of Certified Public Accountants, Inc., Tables 2–17 and 2–18, p. 174.

developing, maintaining, or enhancing the value of a trademark or trade name, perhaps through advertising, should be charged to expense in the period or periods incurred. However, if a trademark or trade name is purchased, the purchase cost should be debited to an asset account and amortized over time.

Amortization of Intangibles

Some intangibles, such as patents, copyrights, and leaseholds, have limited useful lives that are determined by law, contract, or the nature of the asset. Other intangibles, such as goodwill, trademarks, and trade names, have indeterminable lives. In general, the cost of intangible assets should be amortized over the periods expected to be benefited by their use, which in no case is longer than their legal existence. However, as we stated earlier, generally accepted accounting principles require that the amortization period of intangible assets never be longer than 40 years. This limitation applies even if the life of the asset (for example, goodwill) may continue indefinitely into the future.

Summary of the Chapter in Terms of Learning Objectives

LO 1. To maintain control over plant assets, detailed records should be kept. These records usually require the use of subsidiary ledgers that are controlled by asset and accumulated depreciation accounts.

LO 2. All expenditures can be classified as revenue or capital expenditures. Revenue expenditures are debited to expense accounts and matched with current revenues. Capital expenditures are debited to asset accounts, and then charged to depreciation expense in later years. Examples of revenue expenditures related to plant assets are wages, supplies, fuel, lubricants, power, and ordinary repairs. Examples of capital expenditures for plant assets subsequent to their acquisition include extraordinary repairs and betterments. Amounts paid for assets with low costs are technically capital expenditures but they can be treated as revenue expenditures if they are not material.

LO 3. When a plant asset is discarded or sold, the cost and accumulated depreciation are removed from the accounts. Any cash proceeds are recorded and compared to the asset's book value to determine gain or loss. When an old asset is exchanged for a new asset that is similar in purpose, its book value is compared to its market value (as reflected in the trade-in allowance) to determine whether the exchange results in a gain or loss. A material loss must be recognized. However, a gain is not recognized. Instead, the new asset account is debited for the book value of the old asset plus any cash paid. When a plant asset and cash are given in exchange for a similar plant asset, neither gains nor losses are recognized for tax purposes. If the loss is not material in amount, this income tax method may also be used for financial accounting purposes. If the two assets are not similar, the new asset is recorded at its fair value, and either a gain or a loss on disposal is recognized.

LO 4. The cost of a natural resource is recorded in an asset account. Then, depletion of the natural resource is recorded by allocating the cost to expense according to a units-of-production basis. The depletion is credited to an accumulated depletion account. Intangible assets are recorded at the cost incurred to purchase the assets. The allocation of intangible asset cost to expense is done on a straight-line basis and is called amortization. Normally, amortization is recorded with credits made directly to the asset account instead of a contra account.

Demonstration Problem

On January 13, 1990, the Morgan Company purchased seven identical machines and paid $147,000 cash to the seller. The service life of each machine was predicted to be five years, and the salvage value of each was estimated at $1,000. All seven machines were placed in service at once. Depreciation is based on the assumption that machines are purchased and sold on the first of the month nearest the actual dates of purchase and sale. The straight-line method is used. Prepare entries to record each of the following transactions:

a. Machine No. 1 was used until July 7, 1995, when it was retired from service and sold for $1,000 cash. Record depreciation on Machine No. 1 for 1995 and record the sale of the machine.

b. Machine No. 2 was used until December 20, 1992, when it was stolen. On December 24, the insurance company paid Maxwell $4,800 cash, which equalled the estimate of the asset's fair value. Record depreciation on Machine No. 2 for 1992 and record the settlement with the insurance company.

c. Machine No. 3 was used until January 4, 1993, at which time it was sold for $13,000 cash. Record the sale of Machine No. 3.

d. Machine No. 4 was used until December 21, 1993, at which time it was traded in on Machine No. 8, with a cash payment of $20,000. Machine No. 8 had a cash price of $22,000. Record depreciation on Machine No. 4 for 1993 and record the exchange for Machine No. 8.

e. Machine No. 5 was used until December 23, 1993, when it was traded in on Machine No. 9, with a cash payment of $18,000. Machine No. 9 had a cash price of $25,500. Record depreciation on Machine No. 5 for 1993 and record the exchange for Machine No. 9.

f. Machine No. 6 was used until January 9, 1994, at which time it received a major overhaul that extended its useful life until the end of 1998 and left its expected salvage value at $1,000. The cost of the overhaul was $7,100, which was paid in cash. Record the overhaul, compute the machine's book value after the overhaul, and record depreciation for 1994.

g. Machine No. 7 was used only as a backup for the other six machines. Because the machines were more dependable than expected, Machine No. 7 did not deteriorate as quickly as the other machines. Therefore, during 1993, the company manager predicted that its useful life would probably extend until the end of 1997. The estimated salvage value was unchanged. Record depreciation expense on Machine No. 7 for 1993.

Solution to Demonstration Problem

Planning the Solution

- Calculate depreciation of each asset to the nearest whole month of the date of purchase or disposal, applying the straight-line method to cost less salvage value.
- Record any gain or loss on disposals of machines for cash, after bringing depreciation up to date.
- On trading an asset (plus cash) for a similar asset, compare the book value of the old asset with its trade-in value. If book value exceeds trade-in value, record a loss. If trade-in value exceeds book value, reduce the recorded cost of the new machine by the difference.
- Record the cost of the Machine No. 6 overhaul as a capital expenditure.
- When the estimated useful life of a machine changes, depreciate the remaining cost to be depreciated over the remaining life as revised.

For Machines No. 1 through 7, the initial cost of each is $147,000/7 = $21,000. Annual depreciation for each machine is ($21,000 − $1,000)/5 = $4,000.

	Date		Account	Debit	Credit
a.	1995				
	July	7	Cash	1,000.00	
			Accumulated Depreciation, Machine No. 1	20,000.00	
			Machine No. 1		21,000.00
			($21,000 − $20,000 = $1,000)		

Machine No. 1 was fully depreciated at the end of 1994, so depreciation is not recorded in 1995. The machine was sold for its salvage value, so there was no gain or loss on the disposal.

	Date		Account	Debit	Credit
b.	1992				
	Dec.	20	Depreciation Expense	4,000.00	
			Accumulated Depreciation, Machine No. 2		4,000.00
		24	Cash	4,800.00	
			Accumulated Depreciation, Machine No. 2	12,000.00	
			Loss on Theft	4,200.00	
			Machine No. 2		21,000.00
			$21,000 − $12,000 = $9,000		
			$9,000 − $4,800 = $4,200		
c.	1993				
	Jan.	4	Cash	13,000.00	
			Accumulated Depreciation, Machine No. 3	12,000.00	
			Gain on Disposal		4,000.00
			Machine No. 3		21,000.00
			$21,000 − $12,000 = $9,000		
			$13,000 − $9,000 = $4,000		
d.	1993				
	Dec.	21	Depreciation Expense	4,000.00	
			Accumulated Depreciation, Machine No. 4		4,000.00
		21	Machine No. 8	22,000.00	
			Accumulated Depreciation, Machine No. 4	16,000.00	
			Loss on Trade	3,000.00	
			Cash		20,000.00
			Machine No. 4		21,000.00
			$4,000 × 4 = $16,000		
e.	1993				
	Dec.	23	Depreciation Expense	4,000.00	
			Accumulated Depreciation, Machine No. 5		4,000.00
		23	Machine No. 9	23,000.00	
			Accumulated Depreciation, Machine No. 5	16,000.00	
			Cash		18,000.00
			Machine No. 5		21,000.00
			Machine No. 9 is recorded at less than its cash value to avoid reporting a gain on the trade-in.		

f.

1994				
Jan.	9	Accumulated Depreciation, Machine No. 6.	7,100.00	
		Cash		7,100.00

Book value before the overhaul: $21,000 − $16,000 = $5,000
Book value after the overhaul: $5,000 + $7,100 = $12,100

Dec.	31	Depreciation Expense	2,220.00	
		Accumulated Depreciation, Machine No. 6		2,220.00
		($12,100 − $1,000)/5 = $2,220		

g. Book value at 12/31/92: $21,000 − $12,000 = $9,000. Revised remaining useful life is from 1/1/93 to 12/31/97, or 5 years, and the revised annual depreciation charge is ($9,000 − $1,000)/5 = $1,600.

1993				
Dec.	31	Depreciation Expense	1,600.00	
		Accumulated Depreciation, Machine No. 7		1,600.00

Glossary

LO 5 Define or explain the words and phrases listed in the chapter glossary.

Amortization the process of systematically writing off the cost of an intangible asset to expense over its estimated useful life. p. 579

Balance sheet expenditure another name for *capital expenditure*. p. 569

Betterment a modification to an asset to make it more efficient, usually by replacing one of its components with an improved or superior component. p. 571

Capital expenditure an expenditure that produces economic benefits that do not fully expire before the end of the current period; because it creates or adds to existing assets, it should appear on the balance sheet as the cost of an asset. Also called a *balance sheet expenditure*. p. 569

Copyright an exclusive right granted by the federal government or by international agreement to publish and sell a musical, literary, or artistic work for a period of years. p. 580

Depletion the cost created by consuming the usefulness of natural resources. p. 578

Extraordinary repairs major repairs that extend the service life of a plant asset beyond original expectations; treated as a capital expenditure. p. 570

Goodwill an intangible asset of a business that creates future earnings greater than the average in its industry; recognized in the financial statements only when an entire business is acquired at a price in excess of the combined market values of its other assets. p. 581

Intangible asset an asset representing certain legal rights and economic relationships; it has no physical existence but is beneficial to the owner. pp. 578–82

Lease a contract under which the owner of property (the lessor) grants the right to the lessee to use the property. p. 580

Leasehold the rights granted to a lessee by the lessor under the terms of a lease contract. p. 580

Leasehold improvements improvements to leased property made and paid for by the lessee. p. 580

Lessee the individual or company that acquires the right to use property under the terms of a lease. p. 580

Lessor the individual or company that owns property to be used by a lessee under the terms of a lease. p. 580

Office Equipment Ledger a subsidiary ledger that contains a separate record for each individual item of office equipment. p. 567

Ordinary repairs repairs made to keep a plant asset in a normal good operating condition; treated as a revenue expenditure. pp. 569–70

Patent exclusive right granted by the federal government to manufacture and sell a patented machine or device, or to use a process, for 17 years. pp. 579–80

Revenue expenditure an expenditure that should appear on the current income statement as an expense and be deducted from the period's revenues because it does not provide a material benefit in future periods. pp. 567, 569

Store Equipment Ledger a subsidiary ledger that contains a separate record for each individual item of store equipment. pp. 566–67

Trademark a unique symbol used by a company in marketing its products or services. p. 581

Trade name a unique name used by a company in marketing its products or services. p. 581

Synonymous Terms

Betterment improvement.

Capital expenditure balance sheet expenditure.

Natural resources wasting assets.

Objective Review

Answers to the following questions are listed at the end of this chapter. Be sure that you decide which is the one best answer to each question *before* you check the answers.

LO 1 In keeping plant asset records:

a. Computerized records always provide more information than handwritten records.

b. To record a purchase of an office desk, separate general journal entries are made to Office Equipment and to the subsidiary account Office Desk.

c. The Office Equipment Ledger controls the Office Equipment account and the Accumulated Depreciation, Office Equipment account.

d. Detailed subsidiary records serve as controlling accounts for the related general ledger account.

e. The asset account and related accumulated depreciation account for each group of assets serve as controlling accounts for detailed subsidiary records.

LO 2 At the beginning of the fifth year of a machine's estimated six-year useful life, the machine was completely overhauled and its estimated useful life was extended to nine years in total. The machine originally cost $110,000, and the overhaul cost was $12,000. The cost of the overhaul should be recorded as follows:

a.	Depreciation Expense	12,000.00	
	Cash		12,000.00
b.	Machinery	12,000.00	
	Accumulated Depreciation, Machinery		12,000.00
c.	Repairs Expense	12,000.00	
	Cash		12,000.00
d.	Accumulated Depreciation, Machinery	12,000.00	
	Cash		12,000.00
e.	Accumulated Depreciation, Machinery	12,000.00	
	Machinery		12,000.00

LO 3 Standard Company traded an old truck for a new one. The original cost of the old truck was $30,000, and its accumulated depreciation at the time of the trade was $23,400. The new truck had a cash price of $45,000. However, Standard received a $3,000 trade-in allowance. Assuming that any book gain or loss is material, Standard should record the new truck at the cost of:

a. $48,600.
b. $45,000.
c. $42,000.
d. $41,400.
e. $ 6,600.

LO 4 Prospect Mining Company paid $650,000 for an ore deposit. The deposit had an estimated 325,000 tons of ore that would be fully mined during the next 10 years. During the current year, 91,000 tons were mined, processed, and sold. The amount of depletion for the year is:

a. $ 65,000.
b. $ 91,000.
c. $182,000.
d. $156,000.
e. $ -0-.

LO 5 An expenditure that affects future periods because the economic benefits obtained do not fully expire by the end of the current period is called a(n):

a. Betterment.
b. Extraordinary repair.
c. Intangible asset.
d. Capital expenditure.
e. Revenue expenditure.

Questions for Class Discussion

1. What is the purpose of periodically taking an inventory of plant assets?
2. Distinguish between revenue expenditures and capital expenditures and describe how they should be recorded.
3. What is the difference between balance sheet expenditures and capital expenditures?
4. Distinguish between ordinary repairs and extraordinary repairs.
5. How should ordinary repairs to a machine be recorded? How should extraordinary repairs be recorded?
6. What is a betterment? How should a betterment to a machine be recorded?
7. What accounting principle justifies charging the $75 cost of a plant asset immediately to an expense account?

8. What is the essential meaning of the accounting principle of materiality?
9. When should a loss on the exchange of a plant asset be recorded? When is it permissible to absorb a loss into the cost basis of the new plant asset? Should a gain on a plant asset exchange be recorded?
10. If an asset that has been depreciated is sold for cash and the remaining book value of the asset is more than the cash proceeds from the sale, should the difference be debited to depreciation expense? How should the difference be recorded?
11. When cash and a plant asset are exchanged for a similar asset, what is the cost basis of the newly acquired asset for federal income tax reporting purposes?
12. When the loss on an exchange of plant assets is immaterial, why would it be convenient to take the newly acquired asset into the accounting records at the cost basis used for tax reporting?
13. When an old plant asset is traded in for a new similar asset, any loss is not recognized for tax reporting purposes. In what sense does this treatment not reduce the total tax deductions available to the taxpayer?
14. What is the name for the process of allocating the cost of natural resources to expense as the natural resources are used?
15. What are the characteristics of an intangible asset?
16. Is the declining-balance method an acceptable means of calculating depletion of natural resources?
17. What general procedures are followed in accounting for intangible assets?
18. Define (*a*) lease, (*b*) lessor, (*c*) lessee, (*d*) leasehold, and (*e*) leasehold improvement.
19. When does a business have goodwill? Under what conditions can goodwill appear in a company's balance sheet?
20. X Company bought an established business and paid for goodwill. If X Company plans to incur substantial advertising and promotional costs each year to maintain the value of the goodwill, must the company also amortize the goodwill?
21. In McDonald's Corporation's consolidated balance sheet that appears in Appendix K, what was the net change in intangible assets from 1989 to 1990?
22. In Federal Express Corporation's consolidated balance sheets in Appendix K, what phrase does Federal Express use to describe goodwill? What percentage of total assets is represented by goodwill at May 31, 1991?

Exercises

Exercise 11–1
Ordinary repairs, extraordinary repairs, and betterments
(LO 2)

Baytown Company paid $49,500 for a machine that was expected to last five years and have a salvage value of $7,500. Present general journal entries to record the following costs related to the machine:

a. During the second year of the machine's life, $1,300 was paid for repairs necessary to keep the machine in good working order.

b. During the third year of the machine's life, $4,500 was paid for a new component that was expected to increase the machine's productivity by 15% each year. The new component was added to the machine without removing any old component.

c. During the fourth year of the machine's life, $6,400 was paid for repairs that were expected to increase the service life of the machine from five to seven years.

Exercise 11–2
Extraordinary repairs
(LO 2)

Topek Company owns a building that appeared on its balance sheet at the end of last year at its original $947,000 cost less $719,720 accumulated depreciation. The building has been depreciated on a straight-line basis under the assumption that it would have a 25-year life and no salvage value. During the first week in January of the current year, major structural repairs were completed on the building at a cost of $178,000. The repairs did not increase the building's capacity but they did extend its expected life for 10 years beyond the 25 years originally estimated.

a. Determine the building's age as of the end of last year.

b. Give the entry to record the repairs, which were paid with cash.

c. Determine the book value of the building after its repairs were recorded.

d. Give the entry to record the current year's depreciation.

Exercise 11–3
Recording sales of plant assets
(LO 3)

A machine with an expected service life of seven years and salvage value of $7,000 was purchased by Bedrock Company for $63,000. After taking straight-line depreciation for four years, the machine was sold. Present general journal entries dated December 31 to record the sale assuming the cash proceeds from the sale were: (*a*) $31,000; (*b*) $40,250; (*c*) $21,400.

Exercise 11–4
Recording plant asset disposal or trade-in
(LO 3)

On January 2, 1993, Revere Company disposed of a machine that cost $163,000 and that had been depreciated $91,500. Present the general journal entries to record the disposal under each of the following unrelated assumptions:

a. The machine was sold for $58,500 cash.

b. The machine was traded in on a new machine of like purpose having a $205,000 cash price. A $75,000 trade-in allowance was received, and the balance was paid in cash.

c. A $65,000 trade-in allowance was received for the machine on a new machine of like purpose having a $205,000 cash price. The balance was paid in cash, and the loss was considered material.

d. Transaction *c* was recorded by the income tax method because the loss was considered immaterial.

e. The machine was traded for vacant land adjacent to the company to be used as a parking lot. The land had a fair value of $150,000, and Revere paid $70,000 cash in addition to giving the seller the machine.

Exercise 11–5
Exchanging plant assets
(LO 3)

Anneal Company traded in its old truck on a new truck, receiving a $21,400 trade-in allowance and paying the remaining $53,400 in cash. The old truck cost $62,000, and straight-line depreciation of $36,000 had been recorded under the assumption that it would last six years and have an $8,000 salvage value. Answer the following questions:

a. What was the book value of the old truck?

b. What is the loss on the exchange?

c. Assuming the loss is deemed to be material, what amount should be debited to the new Truck account?

d. Assuming the loss is not material and the income tax method is used to record the exchange, what amount should be debited to the new Truck account?

Exercise 11–6
Mid-year disposal of asset
(LO 3)

Travis Company purchased and installed a machine on January 3, 1993, at a total cost of $120,000. Straight-line depreciation was taken each year for three years, based on the assumption of a five-year life and no salvage value. Travis disposed of the asset on April 30, 1996. Present the entries to record the partial year's depreciation on April 30 and to record the disposal under each of the following unrelated assumptions: (*a*) the machine was sold for $56,500; (*b*) it was sold for $34,600; and (*c*) the machine was totally destroyed in a fire, and the insurance company settled the insurance claim for $29,000.

Exercise 11–7
Depletion of natural resources
(LO 4)

On January 1, 1993, Redstone Company paid $812,000 for an ore deposit containing 2,030,000 tons of ore. The company also installed machinery in the mine that cost $91,350, had an estimated 12-year life and no salvage value, and was capable of removing all the ore in 6 years. The machine will be abandoned when the ore is completely mined. Redstone began operations on April 1, 1993, and mined 304,500 tons of ore during the remaining nine months of the year. Give the December 31, 1993, entries to record the depletion of the ore deposit and the depreciation of the mining machinery.

Exercise 11–8
Amortization of intangible assets
(LO 4)

Espy Company purchased the copyright to a trade manual for $72,500 on January 1, 1993. The copyright legally protects its owner for 25 more years. However, management believes the trade manual can be successfully published and sold for only five more years. Prepare journal entries to record (*a*) the purchase of the copyright and (*b*) the annual amortization of the copyright on December 31, 1993.

Exercise 11–9
Estimating goodwill
(LO 4)

R. Donovan has devoted years to developing a profitable business that earns an attractive return. Donovan is now considering the possibility of selling the business and is attempting to estimate the value of the goodwill in the business. The fair value of the net assets of the business (excluding goodwill) is $400,000, and in a typical year, net income is about $72,000. Most businesses of this type are expected to earn a return of about 15% on net assets. Estimate the value of the goodwill assuming (*a*) the value is equal to six times the excess earnings above average, and (*b*) the value can be found by capitalizing the excess earnings above average at a rate of 12%.

Problems

Problem 11–1
Plant asset records
(LO 1)

Barker Ready Mix Company completed the following transactions involving plant assets:

1992

Jan. 3 Purchased on credit an electronic scale priced at $18,875 from Weigh Systems, Inc. The serial number of the scale was W–66557, its service life was estimated at five years with a trade-in value of $4,000, and it was assigned plant asset number 167–2.

Mar. 1 Purchased on credit a Bulldog mixer priced at $12,200 from Cement Systems, Inc. The serial number of the mixer was M–10102, its service life was estimated at four years with a trade-in value of $2,000, and it was assigned plant asset number 167–3.

Dec. 31 Recorded straight-line depreciation on the plant equipment for 1992.

1993

Oct. 2 Sold the Bulldog mixer to Crider Cement for $7,300 cash.

4 Purchased on credit a new TopJob mixer from Stamford Equipment for $15,400. The serial number of the mixer was TJ–87651, its service life was estimated at six years with a trade-in value of $2,800, and it was assigned plant asset number 167–4.

Dec. 31 Recorded straight-line depreciation on the plant equipment for 1993.

Required

1. Open general ledger accounts for Plant Equipment and for Accumulated Depreciation, Plant Equipment. Prepare a subsidiary plant asset record card for each item of equipment purchased.
2. Prepare general journal entries to record the transactions and adjustments, and post them to the proper general ledger and subsidiary ledger accounts.
3. Prove that the December 31, 1993, balances of the Plant Equipment and Accumulated Depreciation, Plant Equipment accounts equal the totals of the balances shown on the subsidiary plant asset records. You should

accomplish this step by preparing a list showing the cost and accumulated depreciation on each item of plant equipment owned by Barker Ready Mix Company on that date.

Problem 11–2
Purchases, betterments, sales of plant assets, partial year's depreciation (LO 2, 3)

The Blackhawk Company completed these transactions involving the purchase and operation of delivery trucks:

1992

Mar. 29 Paid cash for a new truck, $26,600 plus $1,600 state and city sales taxes. The truck was estimated to have a five-year life and a $4,300 salvage value.

Apr. 2 Paid $1,400 for special racks and cleats installed in the truck. The racks and cleats did not increase the truck's estimated trade-in value.

Dec. 31 Recorded straight-line depreciation on the truck.

1993

July 7 Paid $1,825 to install an air-conditioning unit in the truck. The unit increased the truck's estimated trade-in value by $700.

Dec. 31 Recorded straight-line depreciation on the truck.

1994

Aug. 13 Paid $280 for repairs to the truck's fender, which was damaged when the driver backed into a loading dock.

Dec. 31 Recorded straight-line depreciation on the truck.

1995

July 2 Traded the old truck and paid $21,400 in cash for a new truck. The new truck was estimated to have a four-year life and an $8,000 trade-in value, and the invoice for the exchange showed these items:

Price of the new truck	$31,900
Trade-in allowance granted on the old truck	(12,500)
Balance of purchase price	$19,400
State and city sales taxes	2,000
Total paid in cash	$21,400

The loss on the exchange was considered to be material.

July 5 Paid $2,100 for special cleats and racks installed in the truck.

Dec. 31 Recorded straight-line depreciation on the new truck.

Required

Prepare general journal entries to record the transactions.

Problem 11–3
Depreciating and exchanging plant assets (LO 3)

A company completed the following transactions involving machinery:

Machine No. 106–12 was purchased for cash on February 1, 1989, at an installed cost of $29,400. Its useful life was estimated to be four years with a $3,000 trade-in value. Straight-line depreciation was recorded for the machine at the end of 1989 and 1990, and on October 3, 1991, it was traded for Machine

No. 106–13. A trade-in allowance of $12,800 was actually received, and the balance was paid in cash.

Machine No. 106–13 was purchased on October 3, 1991, at an installed cash price of $33,000, less the trade-in allowance received on Machine No. 106–12. The new machine's life was predicted to be five years with a $3,200 trade-in value. Sum-of-the-years'-digits depreciation was recorded on each December 31 of its life, and on January 4, 1996, it was sold for $5,200.

Machine No. 107–24 was purchased for cash on January 6, 1991, at an installed cost of $63,000. Its useful life was estimated to be five years, after which it would have an $8,400 trade-in value. Declining-balance depreciation at twice the straight-line rate was recorded for the machine at the end of 1991, 1992, and 1993; and, on January 3, 1994, it was traded in as part of the purchase of Machine No. 107–25. A $13,500 trade-in allowance was received, the balance was paid in cash, the loss was considered immaterial, and the income tax method was used to record the transaction.

Machine No. 107–25 was purchased on January 3, 1994, at an installed cash price of $75,900, less the trade-in allowance received on Machine No. 107–24. It was estimated that the new machine would produce 70,000 units of product during its useful life, after which it would have a $3,800 trade-in value. Units-of-production depreciation was recorded for the machine for 1994, a period in which it produced 7,000 units of product. Between January 1 and October 3, 1995, the machine produced 10,500 more units. On the latter date, it was sold for $50,000.

Required

Prepare general journal entries to record: (*a*) the purchase of each machine, (*b*) the depreciation recorded on the first December 31 of each machine's life, and (*c*) the disposal of each machine. (Only one entry is needed to record the exchange of one machine for another.)

Problem 11–4
Intangible assets and natural resources
(LO 4)

Part 1. Ten years ago, Aqua Products Company leased space in a building for 20 years. The lease contract calls for annual rental payments of $51,000 to be made on each January 1 throughout the life of the lease and also provides that the lessee must pay for all additions and improvements to the leased property. Because recent nearby construction has made the location more valuable, Aqua Products Company subleased the space to Oberon, Inc., on December 27 for the remaining 10 years of the lease, beginning the next January 1. Oberon paid $90,000 to Aqua Products for the right to sublease the property and agreed to assume the obligation to pay the $51,000 annual rental charges to the building owner. After taking possession of the leased space, Oberon, Inc., paid for improving the office portion of the leased space at a cost of $174,000. The improvement was paid for on January 7 and is estimated to have a life equal to the 20 years in the remaining life of the building.

Required

Prepare entries for Oberon, Inc., to record: (*a*) its payment to sublease the building space, (*b*) its payment of the next annual rental charge to the building owner, and (*c*) payment for the improvements. Also, prepare the adjusting entries required at the end of the first year of the sublease to amortize (*d*) a proper share of the $90,000 cost of the sublease and (*e*) a proper share of the office improvement.

Part 2. On May 4 of the current year, Seacort Company paid $3,990,000 for land estimated to contain 9.5 million tons of recoverable ore of a valuable mineral. It installed machinery costing $855,000, which had an 18-year life and no salvage value, and was capable of exhausting the ore deposit in 15 years. The machinery was paid for on July 28, three days before mining operations began. The company removed 356,250 tons of ore during the first five months' operations.

Required

Prepare entries to record (*a*) the purchase of the land, (*b*) the installation of the machinery, (*c*) the first five months' depletion under the assumption that the land will be valueless after the ore is mined, and (*d*) the first five months' depreciation on the machinery to be abandoned after the ore is fully mined.

Problem 11–5
Goodwill
(LO 4)

Lancelot Company's balance sheet on December 31, 1993, is as follows:

Cash	$ 81,750
Merchandise inventory	235,500
Buildings	422,000
Accumulated depreciation	(253,200)
Land	178,500
Total assets	$664,550
Accounts payable	$ 26,300
Long-term note payable	187,750
Common stock	304,600
Retained earnings	145,900
Total liabilities and stockholders' equity	$664,550

In this industry, earnings average 12% of common stockholders' equity. Lancelot Company, however, is expected to earn $66,000 annually. The owners believe that the balance sheet amounts are reasonable estimates of fair market values for all assets except goodwill, which does not appear on the financial statement. In discussing a plan to sell the company, they have suggested to the potential buyer that goodwill can be measured by capitalizing the amount of above-average earnings at a rate of 15%. On the other hand, the potential buyer thinks that goodwill should be valued at five times the amount of excess earnings above the average for the industry.

Required

1. Calculate the amount of goodwill claimed by Lancelot Company's owners.
2. Calculate the amount of goodwill according to the potential buyer.
3. Suppose that the buyer finally agrees to pay the full price requested by Lancelot Company's owners. If the amount of expected earnings (before amortization of goodwill) is obtained and the goodwill is amortized over the longest permissible time period, what amount of net income will be reported for the first year after the company is purchased?

4. If the buyer pays the full price requested by Lancelot Company's owners, what rate of return on the purchaser's investment will be earned as net income the first year?

Problem 11–6
Depreciation, repairs, and exchanges of plant assets
(LO 2, 4)

Part 1. On January 4, 1987, Meyer Company purchased for cash and placed in operation a machine estimated to have an eight-year life and no salvage value. The machine cost $288,000 and was depreciated on a straight-line basis. On January 5, 1990, a $24,500 device was added to the machine that increased its output by one third. The device did not change the machine's estimated life or its zero salvage value. During the first week of January 1992, the machine was completely overhauled at a $90,380 cost (paid for on January 7). The overhaul added four additional years to the machine's estimated life but did not change its zero salvage value. On June 30, 1994, the machine was destroyed in a fire and the insurance company settled the loss claim for $122,400.

Required

Prepare general journal entries to record: (*a*) the purchase of the machine, (*b*) the 1987 depreciation, (*c*) the addition of the new device, (*d*) the 1990 depreciation, (*e*) the machine's overhaul, (*f*) the 1992 depreciation, and (*g*) 1994 depreciation and the insurance settlement.

Part 2. On January 4, 1989, Weishaar Company paid $124,900 cash for Machine One. It was depreciated on a straight-line basis at the end of 1989, 1990, 1991, and 1992 under the assumption it would have an eight-year life and a $19,300 salvage value. Before recording 1993 depreciation, the company revised its estimate of the machine's remaining years downward from four years to three and revised the estimate of its salvage value downward to $6,100. On July 1, 1995, after recording 1993, 1994, and part of a year's depreciation for 1995, the company traded in Machine One on Machine Two, receiving a $24,600 trade-in allowance. The cash paid for Machine Two was $138,800 less the trade-in allowance. On December 31, 1995, Machine Two was depreciated on a straight-line basis under the assumption it would have a five-year life and a $31,300 salvage value.

Required

Prepare entries to record: (*a*) the purchase of Machine One, (*b*) its 1989 depreciation, (*c*) its 1993 depreciation, (*d*) the exchange of the machines, and (*e*) the 1995 depreciation on Machine Two.

Problem 11–7
Analytical essay
(LO 2)

It is January 15, 1994, and you have just been hired as an accountant for PetroServ Inc., an oil field service company. The previous accountant brought the accounting records up to date through December 31, the end of the fiscal year, including the year-end adjusting entries. In reviewing the entries made last year, you discover the following three items:

1. An expenditure for changing the oil on a truck was recorded as a debit to Accumulated Depreciation, Trucks.
2. An expenditure for upgrading the memory of the computer system was debited to Computer Equipment.

3. An expenditure to install a new engine in a fork lift was recorded as a debit to Repairs Expense, Machinery. As a result of the replacement, the fork lift is expected to last three years longer than originally estimated.

Required

For each of the three items, indicate whether it was classified by the previous accountant as a revenue expenditure, extraordinary repair, or betterment. Then state whether or not you agree with this classification and explain why. If you disagree, indicate what the proper classification should be.

Problem 11–8
Analytical essay
(LO 2)

Refer to the transactions of PetroServ Inc. discussed in Problem 11–7. Assume that you prepare the 1993 financial statements for PetroServ Inc. without correcting any errors that may have been made in recording the transactions. Explain the effects of any recording errors on the 1993 income statement and the December 31, 1993, balance sheet.

Alternate Problems

Problem 11–1A
Plant asset records
(LO 1)

Avalon Gravel Company completed the following transactions involving plant assets:

1992

Jan. 3 Purchased on credit an electric grinder priced at $19,140 from AAA Equipment. The serial number of the grinder was 0–9470–2, its service life was estimated at six years with a trade-in value of $1,500, and it was assigned plant asset number 167–1.

Apr. 30 Purchased on credit a Halburn conveyor priced at $40,000 from AAA Equipment. The serial number of the conveyor was 7–8496–8, its service life was estimated at five years with a trade-in value of $4,000, and it was assigned plant asset number 167–2.

Dec. 31 Recorded straight-line depreciation on the plant equipment for 1992.

1993

Nov. 2 Sold the Halburn conveyor to Colville Aggregate Products for $24,500 cash.

7 Purchased on credit a new Weston conveyor from Jones Construction Equipment for $47,200. The serial number of the conveyor was JC–45736, its service life was estimated at seven years with a trade-in value of $5,200, and it was assigned plant asset number 167–3.

Dec. 31 Recorded straight-line depreciation on the plant equipment for 1993.

Required

1. Open general ledger accounts for Plant Equipment and for Accumulated Depreciation, Plant Equipment. Prepare a subsidiary plant asset record card for each item of equipment purchased.
2. Prepare general journal entries to record the transactions and adjustments, and post them to the proper general ledger and subsidiary ledger accounts.
3. Prove that the December 31, 1993, balances of the Plant Equipment and Accumulated Depreciation, Plant Equipment accounts equal the totals of the balances shown on the subsidiary plant asset records. You should accomplish this step by preparing a list showing the cost and accumulated depreciation on each item of plant equipment owned by Avalon Gravel Company on that date.

Problem 11–2A
Purchases, betterments, and sales of plant assets
(LO 2, 3)

The Twins Company completed these transactions involving the purchase and operation of delivery trucks.

1992

July 2 Paid cash for a new delivery van, $42,450 plus $2,650 state and city sales taxes. The van was estimated to have a four-year life and a $7,100 salvage value.

July 6 Paid $2,400 for special racks and bins installed in the van. The racks and bins did not increase the van's estimated trade-in value.

Dec. 31 Recorded straight-line depreciation on the van.

1993

June 29 Paid $1,980 to install an air-conditioning unit in the van. The unit increased the van's estimated trade-in value by $240.

Dec. 31 Recorded straight-line depreciation on the van.

1994

Mar. 15 Paid $410 for repairs to the van's fender damaged when the driver backed into a tree.

Dec. 31 Recorded straight-line depreciation on the van.

1995

Sept. 29 Traded the old van and paid $30,590 in cash for a new van. The new van was estimated to have a four-year life and an $8,500 trade-in value, and the invoice for the exchange showed these items:

Price of the new van	$40,260
Trade-in allowance granted on the old van	(12,700)
Balance of purchase price	$27,560
State and city sales taxes	3,030
Total paid in cash	$30,590

The loss on the exchange was considered to be material.

Oct. 4 Paid $3,210 for special racks and bins installed in the new van.

Dec. 31 Recorded straight-line depreciation on the new van.

Required

Prepare general journal entries to record the transactions.

Problem 11–3A
Depreciation and exchanges of plant assets
(LO 3)

Bart Company completed the following transactions involving machinery:

Machine No. 10–232 was purchased for cash on July 2, 1989, at an installed cost of $99,120. Its useful life was predicted to be five years with a $12,000 trade-in value. Straight-line depreciation was recorded for the machine at the end of 1989 and 1990, and on October 4, 1991, it was traded for Machine No. 10–233. A trade-in allowance of $61,416 was actually received, and the balance was paid in cash.

Machine No. 10–233 was purchased on October 4, 1991, at an installed cash price of $110,800, less the trade-in allowance received on Machine No. 10–232. The new machine's life was estimated to be six years with a $19,000 trade-in value. Sum-of-the-years'-digits depreciation was recorded on each December 31 of its life, and on February 5, 1996, it was sold for $34,400.

Machine No. 11–008 was purchased for cash on January 10, 1991, at an installed cost of $36,000. Its useful life was estimated to be five years, after which it would have a $5,400 trade-in value. Declining-balance depreciation at twice the straight-line rate was recorded for the machine at the end of 1991, 1992, and 1993; and, on January 2, 1994, it was traded in as part of the purchase of Machine No. 11–009. A $7,590 trade-in allowance was received, the balance was paid in cash, the loss was considered immaterial, and the income tax method was used to record the transaction.

Machine No. 11–009 was purchased on January 2, 1994, at an installed cash price of $50,310, less the trade-in allowance received on Machine No. 11–008. It was estimated that the new machine would produce 65,000 units of product during its useful life, after which it would have a $9,000 trade-in value. Units-of-production depreciation was recorded for the machine for 1994, a period in which it produced 9,750 units of product. Between January 1 and October 2, 1995, the machine produced 13,000 more units. On the latter date, it was sold for $39,900.

Required

Prepare general journal entries to record: (*a*) the purchase of each machine, (*b*) the depreciation recorded on the first December 31 of each machine's life, and (*c*) the disposal of each machine. (Only one entry is needed to record the exchange of one machine for another.)

Problem 11–4A
Intangible assets and natural resources
(LO 4)

Part 1. Five years ago, Alba Corporation leased space in a building for 20 years. The lease contract calls for annual rental payments of $69,600 to be made on each January 1 throughout the life of the lease and also provides that the lessee must pay for all additions and improvements to the leased property. Because recent nearby construction has made the location more valuable, Alba Corporation subleased the space to Anson Company on December 30 for the remaining 15 years of the lease, beginning the next January 1. Anson paid

$252,000 to Alba for the right to sublease the space and agreed to assume the obligation to pay the $69,600 annual rental charges to the building owner. After taking possession of the leased space, Anson Company paid for improving the office portion of the leased space at a cost of $189,000. The improvement was paid for on January 8 and is estimated to have a life equal to the 25 years in the remaining life of the building.

Required

Prepare entries for Anson Company to record: (*a*) its payment to sublease the building space, (*b*) its payment of the next annual rental charge to the building owner, and (*c*) payment for the improvements. Also, prepare the adjusting entries required at the end of the first year of the sublease to amortize (*d*) a proper share of the $252,000 cost of the sublease and (*e*) a proper share of the office improvement.

Part 2. On June 4 of the current year, Standish Company paid $1,890,000 for land estimated to contain 7 million tons of recoverable ore of a valuable mineral. It installed machinery costing $231,000, which had an eight-year life and no salvage value, and was capable of exhausting the ore deposit in five years. The machinery was paid for on August 28, four days before mining operations began. The company removed 560,000 tons of ore during the first five months' operations.

Required

Prepare entries to record (*a*) the purchase of the land, (*b*) the installation of the machinery, (*c*) the first four months' depletion under the assumption that the land will be valueless after the ore is mined, and (*d*) the first four months' depreciation on the machinery to be abandoned after the ore is fully mined.

Problem 11–5A
Goodwill
(LO 4)

Trinity Company's balance sheet on December 31, 1993, is as follows:

Cash	$ 39,600
Merchandise inventory	198,300
Buildings	346,000
Accumulated depreciation	(216,250)
Land	125,850
Total assets	$493,500
Accounts payable	$ 49,900
Long-term note payable	153,800
Common stock	225,000
Retained earnings	64,800
Total liabilities and stockholders' equity	$493,500

In this industry, earnings average 10% of common stockholders' equity. Trinity Company, however, is expected to earn $36,000 annually. The owners believe that the balance sheet amounts are reasonable estimates of fair market values for all assets except goodwill, which does not appear on the financial statement. In discussing a plan to sell the company, they have suggested to the potential buyer that goodwill can be measured by capitalizing the amount of above-average earnings at a rate of 15%. On the other hand, the potential buyer thinks that goodwill should be valued at four times the amount of excess earnings above the average for the industry.

Required

1. Calculate the amount of goodwill claimed by Trinity Company's owners.
2. Calculate the amount of goodwill according to the potential buyer.
3. Suppose that the buyer finally agrees to pay the full price requested by Trinity Company's owners. If the amount of expected earnings (before amortization of goodwill) is obtained and the goodwill is amortized over the longest permissible time period, what amount of net income will be reported for the first year after the company is purchased?
4. If the buyer pays the full price requested by Trinity Company's owners, what rate of return on the purchaser's investment will be earned as net income the first year?

Problem 11–6A
Depreciation, repairs, and exchanges of plant assets
(LO 2, 4)

Part 1. On January 2, 1987, Baylor Company purchased for cash a machine estimated to have a 12-year life and no salvage value. The machine cost $98,520 and was depreciated on a straight-line basis. On January 6, 1992, a $14,280 improvement was added to the machine which had the effect of increasing its output by one third. The improvement did not change the machine's estimated life or its zero salvage value. During the first week of January 1994, the machine was completely overhauled at a $46,050 cost (paid for on January 4). The overhaul added two additional years to the machine's estimated life but did not change its zero salvage value. On October 1, 1996, the machine was destroyed in a fire and the insurance company settled the loss claim for $39,775.

Required

Prepare general journal entries to record: (*a*) the purchase of the machine, (*b*) the 1987 depreciation, (*c*) the addition of the new improvement, (*d*) the 1992 depreciation, (*e*) the machine's overhaul, (*f*) the 1994 depreciation, and (*g*) the 1996 depreciation and the insurance settlement.

Part 2. On January 9, 1990, Sierra Company purchased Machine One for a cash price of $267,000. It was depreciated on a straight-line basis at the end of 1990 and 1991 under the assumption it would have a six-year life and a $63,000 salvage value. Before recording 1992 depreciation, the company revised its estimate of the machine's remaining years downward from four years to three and revised the estimate of its salvage value downward to $43,000. On July 5, 1994, after recording 1992, 1993, and part of a year's depreciation for 1994, the company traded in Machine One on Machine Two, receiving a $42,500 trade-in allowance. The cash paid for Machine Two was $298,800 less the trade-in allowance. Machine Two was depreciated on a straight-line basis under the assumption it would have a nine-year life and a $75,600 salvage value.

Required

Prepare entries to record: (*a*) the purchase of Machine One, (*b*) its 1990 depreciation, (*c*) its 1992 depreciation, (*d*) the exchange of the machines, and (*e*) the 1994 depreciation on Machine Two.

Problem 11–7A
Analytical essay
(LO 2)

Early in 1994, Phonic Company hired a CPA to prepare its financial statements for the year ended December 31, 1993. The owner of the company had brought the accounting records up to date through December 31, except for the year-end adjusting entries. Prior to preparing the adjusting entries, the CPA becomes concerned that some expenditures may have been recorded incorrectly. For each of the following transactions, describe the correcting entry, if any, the CPA should make. Also, explain why you think a correction is or is not necessary.

1. An expenditure to have a factory machine reconditioned by the manufacturer so it would last three years longer than originally estimated was recorded as a debit to Repairs Expense, Machinery.
2. The lubrication of factory machinery was recorded as a debit to Machinery.
3. The installation of a security system for the building was recorded as a debit to Building Improvements. The new system allowed the company to reduce the number of security guards.

Problem 11–8A
Analytical essay
(LO 2)

Refer to the transactions of Phonic Company discussed in Problem 11–7A. Assume that the CPA prepares the financial statements for Phonic Company without making correcting entries for any errors made in recording the transactions. Explain the effects of any recording errors on the 1993 income statement and the December 31, 1993, balance sheet.

Provocative Problems

Provocative Problem 11–1
Distress Company
(LO 2, 3)

While examining the accounting records of Distress Company, you discover two 1993 entries that appear questionable. The first entry recorded the cash proceeds from an insurance settlement as follows:

Oct.	18	Cash	34,000.00	
		Loss on Fire	9,000.00	
		Accumulated Depreciation, Machinery	37,000.00	
		Machinery		80,000.00
		Received payment of fire loss claim.		

Your investigation shows that this entry was made to record the receipt of an insurance company's $34,000 check to settle a claim resulting from the destruction of a machine in a small fire on September 29, 1993. The machine originally cost $74,000 and was put in operation on January 4, 1990. It was depreciated on a straight-line basis for three years, under the assumptions that it would have a six-year life and no salvage value. During the first week of January 1993, the machine had been overhauled at a cost of $6,000. The overhaul did not increase the machine's capacity or its salvage value. However, it was expected that the overhaul would lengthen the machine's service life two years beyond the six originally expected.

The second entry that appears questionable was made to record the receipt of a check from selling a portion of a tract of land. The land was adjacent to the company's plant and had been purchased the year before. It cost

$88,000, and another $11,000 was paid for clearing and grading it. Both amounts had been debited to the Land account. The land was to be used for storing finished product but, sometime after the grading was completed, it became obvious the company did not need the entire tract. Distress Company received an offer from a purchaser to buy the east half for $54,000 or the west half for $66,000. The company decided to sell the west half, and recorded the receipt of the purchaser's check with the following entry:

Dec.	10	Cash	66,000.00	
		Land		66,000.00
		Sold unneeded land.		

Were any errors made in recording these transactions? If so, describe them, and, in each case, provide an entry or entries to correct the account balances under the assumption that the 1993 gain and loss accounts have not been closed.

Provocative Problem 11–2
Nickel and Dime Companies
(A review problem)

Nickel Company and Dime Company are similar businesses that sell competing products. Both companies acquired their equipment and began operating five years ago. Now, both of them are up for sale. The Dollar Company is considering the possibility of buying either Nickel or Dime.

In evaluating the two companies, the management of Dollar has observed that Nickel Company has reported an average annual net income of $98,920. Dime Company, on the other hand, has reported an average of $127,095. However, the companies have not used the same accounting procedures and Dollar Company management is concerned that the numbers are not comparable. The current balance sheets of the two companies show these items:

	Nickel Company	Dime Company
Cash	$ 65,750	$ 72,200
Accounts receivable	486,200	538,500
Allowance for doubtful accounts	(28,500)	-0-
Merchandise inventory	634,100	833,000
Store equipment	248,400	210,400
Accumulated depreciation, store equipment	(207,000)	(131,500)
Total assets	$1,198,950	$1,522,600
Current liabilities	$ 588,400	$ 704,300
Owners' equity	610,550	818,300
Total liabilities and owners' equity	$1,198,950	$1,522,600

Nickel Company has used the allowance method of accounting for bad debts and has added to its allowance each year an amount equal to 1% of sales. However, this amount is revealed to be excessive by an audit that shows that only $15,000 of its accounts are probably uncollectible. Dime Company has used the direct write-off method but has been slow to write off bad debts. An examination of its accounts shows $27,000 of accounts that are probably uncollectible.

During the past five years, Nickel Company has priced its inventories on a LIFO basis, with the result that its current inventory appears on its balance sheet at an amount that is $88,000 below replacement cost. Dime Company has used FIFO, and its ending inventory appears at its approximate replacement cost. Dollar Company management believes that FIFO produces the most useful measure of inventory and cost of goods sold.

Both companies have assumed eight-year lives and no salvage value in depreciating equipment. However, Nickel Company has used sum-of-the-years'-digits depreciation, while Dime Company has used straight line. The management of Dollar Company believes that straight-line depreciation has resulted in reporting Dime Company's equipment on the balance sheet at its approximate fair market value. They believe that straight line would have had the same result for Nickel Company.

Dollar Company is willing to pay what its management considers fair market value for the assets of either business. The management of Dollar believes that each company has goodwill equal to four times the average annual earnings in excess of 15% of the fair market value of the net tangible assets. Dollar Company's management defines net tangible assets as all assets (including accounts receivable) other than goodwill, minus liabilities. Dollar Company will also assume the liabilities of the purchased business, paying its owner the difference between total assets purchased (excluding cash) and the liabilities assumed.

Required

Prepare the following schedules: (*a*) the net tangible assets of each company at fair market values assessed by Dollar Company management; (*b*) the revised net incomes of the companies based on adjusted amounts of bad debts expense, FIFO inventories, and straight-line depreciation; (*c*) the calculation of each company's goodwill; and (*d*) the maximum amount Dollar Company would offer to pay for each business and the net cash cost for each one, after deducting the cash that it owns.

Provocative Problem 11–3
International Business Machines Corporation
(LO 4)

IBM®

Refer to the annual report for International Business Machines Corporation in Appendix J. Based on the information presented in the consolidated statement of financial position and in the accompanying footnotes, answer the following:

1. How is goodwill reported on IBM's consolidated statement of financial position?
2. What percentage of IBM's total assets is comprised of goodwill as of December 31, 1990?
3. What method does IBM use to amortize goodwill? What is the period of time over which goodwill is amortized?
4. Assume that in 1990, IBM did not sell or otherwise dispose of any business it owned as of December 31, 1989.
   a. What amount of goodwill amortization expense did IBM record for 1990?
   b. How much goodwill did IBM purchase in 1990?

Answers to Objective Review Questions

LO 1 (*e*)
LO 2 (*d*)
LO 3 (*b*)
LO 4 (*c*)
LO 5 (*d*)

PART

IV

Accounting for Liabilities and Partnerships

In this part of the book, you will learn about some of the liabilities incurred by businesses and about the special accounting issues that relate to partnerships. Businesses incur many different kinds of liabilities in the process of conducting their operations. Some of these liabilities are short-term obligations such as accounts payable, wages payable, notes payable, unearned revenues, property taxes payable, product warranties, and payroll liabilities. Business liabilities also include long-term obligations such as capital leases, notes payable, and deferred income tax liabilities.

Many small businesses and some large businesses are organized as partnerships. Accounting issues that are unique to partnerships include the allocation of net incomes and losses among the partners, the admission of a new partner to the business, the withdrawal of a partner from the business, and the liquidation of the business.

Part IV consists of the following:

CHAPTER

12

Current and Long-Term Liabilities

Despite the risks of being in debt, companies with liabilities enjoy many advantages. For example, sales can be increased if a company agrees to repair or replace defective products under a warranty obligation. Careful borrowing also allows companies to increase their income and assets.

Topical Coverage

As you already know, liabilities are one of the three elements in the accounting equation. Some of the liabilities we discussed in previous chapters include accounts payable, notes payable, wages payable, and unearned revenues. In this chapter, we examine liabilities such as property taxes payable, product warranty liabilities, single-payment notes payable, lease liabilities, payroll liabilities, and deferred income tax liabilities. We also introduce the important concept of present values and reconsider the topic of contingent liabilities. As you study this chapter, you will learn how to define, classify, and measure liabilities.

Learning Objectives

After studying Chapter 12, you should be able to:

1. Explain the difference between current and long-term liabilities.
2. Explain the difference between definite and estimated liabilities.
3. Record transactions that involve such liabilities as property taxes payable, product warranty liabilities, and short-term notes payable.
4. Explain the difference between liabilities and contingent liabilities.
5. Calculate the present value of a sum of money that will be received a number of periods in the future or that will be received periodically.
6. Prepare entries to account for long-term noninterest-bearing notes payable and for capital and operating leases.
7. Prepare entries to account for payroll liabilities.
8. Define or explain the words and phrases listed in the chapter glossary.

After studying Appendix E at the end of Chapter 12, you should be able to:

9. Explain and account for deferred income tax liabilities.

After studying Appendix F at the end of Chapter 12, you should be able to:

10. Describe an employer's payroll reports and records, and the procedures used to calculate tax withholdings and issue checks to employees.

The Definition and Classification of Liabilities

LO 1 Explain the difference between current and long-term liabilities.

Liabilities are present obligations that require the future payment of assets or performance of services. Not every expected future payment is a liability. To qualify as a liability, the future payment must be a present obligation of the debtor that resulted from a past transaction. Because liabilities result from past transactions, they normally are enforceable as legal claims against the enterprise. However, in some circumstances, an obligation should be recognized as a liability on the debtor's balance sheet, even if it is not legally enforceable as of that date. These important characteristics of liabilities were summarized by the FASB when it defined liabilities as "probable future sacrifices of economic benefits arising from present obligations of a particular entity to transfer assets or provide services to other entities in the future as a result of past transactions or events.''[1]

Current and Long-Term Liabilities

A business typically classifies its liabilities as either current or long-term liabilities. *Current liabilities* are debts or other obligations that are expected to be liquidated (paid) by using existing current assets or creating other current liabilities.[2] Current liabilities are due within one year of the balance sheet date or within the operating cycle of the business, whichever is longer. Examples of current liabilities are accounts payable, short-term notes payable, wages payable, dividends payable, product warranty liabilities, payroll and other taxes payable, and unearned revenues.

Obligations that do not mature within one year (or one operating cycle, whichever is longer) are classified as *long-term liabilities*. Examples of long-term liabilities include lease liabilities, long-term notes payable, product warranty liabilities, and bonds payable. However, any given liability—such as a note payable—may be either current or long term. The critical difference is the question of whether or not payment will be made within one year or the current operating cycle of the business, whichever is longer.

Some liabilities will be settled with installment payments occurring in the current year and future years. Such liabilities are classified on the balance sheet in part as current liabilities and in part as long-term liabilities. Other liabilities do not have a fixed due date but are payable on the creditor's demand. Since the creditor can demand payment at any time, such liabilities are classified as current liabilities.

Definite versus Estimated Liabilities

LO 2 Explain the difference between definite and estimated liabilities.

Three important questions concerning liabilities are: Who must be paid? When is payment due? How much is to be paid? In many situations, the answers to these three questions are determined at the time the liability is incurred. For example, assume that a company has an account payable for precisely $100, payable to R. L. Tucker, and due on August 15, 1994. This liability is definite with respect to all three points. Other types of liabilities may be indefinite with respect to one or more of the three questions.

When the Identity of the Creditor Is Uncertain. In some cases, financial statements are prepared when the debtor knows a future payment will be required but does not know who will be paid. For example, in the case of dividends payable, the amount that will be paid and the due date are definite. The question of who will be paid, however, is not answerable until after the *date of record*. Even though the identity of the creditor may be uncertain, there is no doubt that the debtor is obligated to pay and the liability should be recognized.

---

[1] Financial Accounting Standards Board, *Statement of Financial Accounting Concepts No. 6*, ''Elements of Financial Statements'' (Norwalk, Conn., 1985), par. 35.

[2] FASB, *Accounting Standards—Current Text* (Norwalk, Conn., 1990), sec. B05.402. First published as *Accounting Research Bulletin No. 43*, ch. 3A, par. 7.

When the Due Date Is Uncertain. An example of a liability with an uncertain due date is unearned legal fees revenue that a lawyer accepts in return for the obligation to provide services to a client on call. In this situation, the amount of the liability is known. The client for whom services will be provided is also known. However, the question of *when* the services will be performed is not definite. Usually, such arrangements are settled in the short term and are classified as current liabilities on the debtor's balance sheet.

When the Amount to Be Paid Is Uncertain. When an obligation definitely exists but the amount that will be paid is uncertain, the obligation is called an **estimated liability.** Two important examples of estimated liabilities involve property taxes and product warranties.

Property Taxes Payable

LO 3 Record transactions that involve such liabilities as property taxes payable, product warranty liabilities, and short-term notes payable.

Property taxes are levied annually by a variety of governmental authorities, such as counties, cities, and school districts. In many cases, the exact amount of tax to be paid is not known until the tax year is partially over. For example, suppose that the amount of property tax that will be paid for calendar year 1993 will not be fixed in amount until September 1993. Also assume that the tax payment is not due until October 1993. Thus, if monthly financial statements are prepared during 1993, the amount of property tax expense must be estimated when statements are prepared for January through August.

To illustrate, assume that a company owns property throughout 1993. The tax on the property for 1992 was $11,400. In preparing monthly financial statements during the first part of 1993, before the actual amount of tax is known, the company estimates that it has a monthly tax expense of $950 ($11,400/12). Until the amount of the 1993 tax becomes definite, the company will make monthly entries like this one:

1993				
Jan.	31	Property Taxes Expense	950.00	
		Estimated Property Taxes Payable		950.00
		To accrue property taxes for the month.		

In September 1993, the city announces that the tax levy for 1993 will be $3 per $100 of assessed value. The city also notifies the taxpayer that this property has an assessed valuation of $400,000 for property tax purposes. Now, the company can calculate the actual amount of property tax for 1993 as $12,000 [$400,000 × ($3/$100)], which is $1,000 per month. For the first eight months (January through August), the accumulated estimated tax expense was only $7,600 [8 × $950], which is $400 less than the actual tax. This entry should be recorded at the end of September to accrue September's $1,000 expense and to catch up for the $400 understatement of the expense and the liability:

Sept.	30	Property Taxes Expense	1,400.00	
		Estimated Property Taxes Payable		1,400.00
		To record property taxes for September and to correct the $400 estimated shortfall in prior months.		

When the annual tax is paid at the end of October 1993, the entry to record the payment is:

Oct.	31	Property Taxes Expense	1,000.00	
		Prepaid Property Taxes	2,000.00	
		Estimated Property Taxes Payable	9,000.00	
		Cash		12,000.00
		To pay property tax for 1993.		

At the end of November and December, two entries like the following one will be made to record the monthly expense. They also remove the Prepaid Property Taxes account balance from the books:

Nov.	30	Property Taxes Expense	1,000.00	
		Prepaid Property Taxes		1,000.00
		To record property tax expense for November.		

Note that the total expense recorded for 1993 is $12,000, which has been accumulated in the account as follows:

January–August	$ 7,600
September	1,400
October	1,000
November	1,000
December	1,000
Total	$12,000

Product Warranty Liabilities

LO 3 Record transactions that involve such liabilities as property taxes payable, product warranty liabilities, and short-term notes payable.

A product warranty liability is another estimated liability. Most companies incur this kind of liability because they provide warranties (or guarantees) for their products. A **product warranty** is a promise to the customer that obligates the seller or manufacturer for a limited time to pay for such things as replacement parts or other repair costs if the product breaks or otherwise fails to perform. For example, an automobile may be sold with a warranty that covers the mechanical parts for a period of one year or 12,000 miles, whichever comes first. The warranty also may include the cost of labor to install replacement parts.

The *matching principle* requires recording all expenses that help produce the sale in the same period as the sale. Therefore, when a product is sold with a warranty, the expense of fulfilling the warranty must be recognized at the time of the sale. Because the exact amount of expense is not known at the time of the sale, the expense and the related liability must be estimated based on past experience.

For example, assume that a used car is sold on September 1, 1993, with a one-year or 12,000-mile warranty. The warranty covers mechanical parts, but the customer must pay any labor charges. Also suppose that the car was sold at a price of $16,000. Past experience shows that warranty expense is about 2% of the sales price. In this case, the expense is $320 [$16,000 × 0.02]. The entry to record the expense and liability would be:

1993				
Sept.	1	Warranty Expense	320.00	
		Estimated Warranty Liability.		320.00
		To record warranty expense and liability at 2% of the selling price.		

Now suppose that the customer has a problem with the car and returns it for warranty repairs on January 9, 1994. The auto dealer performs the warranty work by replacing parts that cost $90 and charges the customer $110 for labor. The entry to record the warranty work and the customer's payment is as follows:

1994				
Jan.	9	Cash	110.00	
		Estimated Warranty Liability	90.00	
		Auto Parts Inventory		90.00
		Services Revenue		110.00
		To record warranty work and services revenue.		

Observe that no expense is recorded in 1994 for the cost of the parts. Instead, the warranty liability is reduced. This process includes the warranty expense in the income for 1993, when the car was sold.

What happens if the total warranty costs actually turn out to be different from the estimated $320 amount? In fact, some difference is likely on any particular sale. Over the longer term, management must monitor warranty costs to be sure that 2% is the best estimate. When continued experience shows that the rate of warranty costs has changed, the percentage should be modified.

Contingent Liabilities

LO 4 Explain the difference between liabilities and contingent liabilities.

We first discussed contingent liabilities in Chapter 8, where we presented discounted notes receivable as an example of contingent liabilities. Contingent liabilities are not existing obligations and, therefore, are not recorded in the books as liabilities. However, the *full-disclosure principle* requires disclosure of contingent liabilities in the financial statements or in the footnotes.

What Distinguishes Liabilities from Contingent Liabilities?

Contingent liabilities become definite obligations only if some previously uncertain event actually takes place. For example, a discounted note receivable is a contingent liability that becomes a definite obligation only if the original signer of the note fails to pay it at maturity.

Does a product warranty create a liability or a contingent liability? A product warranty requires service or payment only if the product fails and the

AS A MATTER OF

Opinion

Ms. Scott is a graduate of Wittenberg University. She worked for Price Waterhouse in its national office in New York before joining the FASB staff as a project manager in 1985. After leaving that position in 1991, she joined the management consulting firm of Towers Perrin in Chicago, where she is a consultant on postretirement benefit accounting and plan design.

Diana J. Scott, CPA

In recent years, accountants have begun to pay much more attention to the potential future payments businesses may be obligated to make as a result of current operations. A good example involves the promises of employers to pay postretirement health care benefits to employees. Prior to the FASB's new standard on this topic (*SFAS 106*), companies generally did not report this obligation except for recognizing payments they had already made. The new standard demands that they disclose these obligations and begin to recognize expenses related to probable future payments.

Are there other examples of obligations that we currently ignore but someday may recognize as liabilities? I would not be surprised. One that comes to mind is potential claims from injuries to product users. Some juries have given large awards many years after a product was sold. Another conceivable liability is the cost of cleaning up toxic wastes discarded before anyone was aware of the danger.

I cannot say whether these particular examples will eventually result in new accounting disclosures. But I have no doubt that accounting will continue to evolve in response to an increasing emphasis on the obligations of doing business.

customer returns it for service. These conditions make it appear to be like a contingent liability. However, the FASB ruled that *a contingent obligation should be recorded in the books as a liability if the occurrence of the future contingency is probable and if the amount of the liability can be reasonably estimated.*[3] Therefore, product warranties are usually recorded as liabilities because: (1) the failure of some percentage of the sold products is probable, and (2) past experience allows the seller to develop a reasonable estimate of the amount to be paid.

Other Examples of Contingent Liabilities

Potential Legal Claims. In today's legal environment, many companies find themselves being sued for damages for a variety of reasons. The accounting question to be asked is whether the defendant should recognize a liability on the balance sheet or disclose a contingent liability in the footnotes while a lawsuit is outstanding and not yet settled. The answer is that the potential

[3] FASB, *Accounting Standards—Current Text* (Norwalk, Conn., 1990), sec. C59.105. First published as *FASB Statement No. 5,* par. 8.

claim should be recorded as a liability only if a payment for damages is probable and the amount can be reasonably estimated. Otherwise, the potential claim is a contingent liability.

Debt Guarantees. Sometimes a company will guarantee the payment of a debt owed by a supplier, customer, or other company. This arrangement is usually created by cosigning a note payable of the other party. When this is done, the guarantor is contingently liable for the debt of the other company. The guarantor will not recognize the liability unless it is probable that the original debtor will default.

Short-Term Notes Payable

LO 3 Record transactions that involve such liabilities as property taxes payable, product warranty liabilities, and short-term notes payable.

Another category of current liabilities that requires careful study is short-term notes payable. When a business purchases merchandise on credit and then needs to gain an extension of the credit period, a short-term note payable may be substituted for the account payable. Also, short-term notes payable frequently arise when borrowing from a bank.

Note Given to Secure a Time Extension on an Account

A note payable may be given to secure an extension of time for paying an account payable. For example, assume that Brock Company cannot pay its past-due $600 account with Ajax Company. As an accommodation, Ajax Company agrees to accept Brock Company's 60-day, 12%, $600 note in granting an extension on the due date of the debt. Brock Company records the issuance of the note as follows:

Aug.	23	Accounts Payable—Ajax Company	600.00	
		Notes Payable		600.00
		Gave a 60-day, 12% note to extend the due date on the amount owed.		

Observe that the note does not pay off the debt. Rather, the form of the debt is merely changed from an account payable to a note payable. Ajax Company should prefer holding the note to the account because, in case of default, the note is very good written evidence of the debt's existence and its amount.

When the note becomes due, Brock Company will give Ajax Company a check for $612 and record the payment of the note and its interest with this entry:

Oct.	22	Notes Payable	600.00	
		Interest Expense	12.00	
		Cash		612.00
		Paid our note with interest.		

Borrowing from a Bank

When lending money, banks typically require that the borrower sign a promissory note. Sometimes, the note states that the signer of the note promises to pay the principal (the amount borrowed) plus interest. If the note is written in this way, the *face value* of the note is the principal and the lending transaction is called a *loan*. Alternatively, a note may say nothing about interest and simply state that the signer promises to pay a given amount. In this case, the face value of the note includes the amount borrowed plus the interest to be charged and the lending transaction involves discounting the note. The *discount* is the difference between the face value of the note and the amount of cash advanced by the bank to the borrower. In other words, the discount equals the amount of interest to be paid. To illustrate loans and discounts, assume that H. A. Green wishes to borrow approximately $2,000 for 60 days at the prevailing 15% rate of interest.

A Loan. In a loan transaction, the bank lends Green $2,000 in exchange for a signed promissory note that reads: "Sixty days after September 10, I promise to pay $2,000 plus interest at 15%." Thus, the face value of the note is $2,000, which is the amount borrowed by Green. This loan transaction is recorded by Green as follows:

Sept.	10	Cash	2,000.00	
		Notes Payable		2,000.00
		Gave the bank a 60-day, 15% note.		

When the note and interest are paid, Green makes this entry:

Nov.	9	Notes Payable	2,000.00	
		Interest Expense	50.00	
		Cash		2,050.00
		Paid our 60-day, 15% note.		

Observe that in this loan transaction, the interest was paid at maturity in addition to the principal amount of the debt.

A Discount. If Green's bank deducts interest at the time a loan is made, the bank is said to have *discounted* Green's note. If it discounts the $2,000 note at 15% for 60 days, it will loan Green only $1,950. This amount equals the face amount of the note less 60 days' interest at 15%, which is $50 [$2,000 × 15% × (60/360)]. The $50 of deducted interest is called the **bank discount.** The net amount received by Green, $1,950, is called the *proceeds* of the discounted note. Green records the transaction as follows:

Sept.	10	Cash	1,950.00	
		Discount on Notes Payable	50.00	
		Notes Payable		2,000.00
		Discounted our $2,000 note payable at 15%.		

The Discount on Notes Payable account is *contra* to the Notes Payable account. When the note matures, Green is required to pay the bank the full face amount of the note, $2,000. Green records the payment with this entry:

Nov.	9	Notes Payable	2,000.00	
		Cash		2,000.00
		Paid our discounted note payable.		

Also, Green must record the interest expense, as follows:

Nov.	9	Interest Expense	50.00	
		Discount on Notes Payable		50.00
		To record interest expense.		

In this example, note that this last entry could have been omitted if the $50 interest had been debited to Interest Expense in the original entry on September 10, as follows:

Sept.	10	Cash	1,950.00	
		Interest Expense	50.00	
		Notes Payable		2,000.00
		Discounted our $2,000 notes payable at 15%.		

Purely as a matter of convenience, many companies use this simpler bookkeeping procedure when a discounted note is signed and will be due within the same accounting period.

Because the interest is deducted from the principal at the time a debt is created in a discount transaction, the note states that only the principal amount is to be repaid at maturity. That is, the note does not call for any additional interest to be paid at maturity. For example, Green's note would read: "Sixty days after September 10, I promise to pay $2,000, with no interest." As a result, this type of note is commonly called a *noninterest-bearing note*. However, we all know that banks are not in business to lend money interest free. In a discount transaction, the interest is simply deducted in advance. Because the amount of the interest is not loaned when the debt is created, the note simply states that no additional interest will be collected at maturity beyond the face amount. In fact, the rate of interest in a discount situation is actually higher than in a loan situation at the same stated interest rate. For example, Green paid $50 for the use of $1,950 for 60 days, so the effective interest rate was a little in excess of 15% on the $1,950 received.[4]

End-of-Period Adjustments

Discount on Notes Payable

When a note payable is discounted at a bank, and the note will not become due until the next accounting period, the interest deducted in advance should be debited to a *contra liability* account called Discount on Notes Payable. In the same entry, Notes Payable is credited for the face amount of the note. As a result, the net liability equals the amount of cash borrowed. Then, at the end of the period, an adjusting entry records the accrued interest expense. This adjustment reduces the balance of the discount account and thereby increases the size of the net liability by the amount of accrued interest.

For example, suppose that on December 11, 1993, a company discounts at 15% its own $6,000, 60-day, noninterest-bearing note payable. The amount of the discount is $150 [$6,000 × 15% × (60/360)], and the company records the transaction as follows:

Dec.	11	Cash	5,850.00	
		Discount on Notes Payable	150.00	
		Notes Payable		6,000.00
		Discounted our noninterest-bearing, 60-day note at 15%.		

Thus, the net liability equals the $5,850 of cash borrowed [$6,000 − $150].

If this company's accounting period ends on December 31, it needs to recognize 20 days' interest on this note as an expense of the 1993 accounting period. This amount is $50 [$150 × (20/60)]. Therefore, the company must make the following adjusting entry on December 31, 1993:

Dec.	31	Interest Expense	50.00	
		Discount on Notes Payable		50.00
		To record 1993 interest expense.		

This adjusting entry records interest expense of $50 in 1993 and removes the same amount from the Discount on Notes Payable account. The $50 then appears on the 1993 income statement as an expense. The entry also leaves $100 in the discount account until it is reported as an expense of 1994.

On the December 31, 1993, balance sheet, the $100 is deducted from the $6,000 nominal balance of the note payable, so that the net liability is shown at

[4] Green pays $50 interest for the use of $1,950 for 60 days. This amount represents 2.564% for the 60 days, which is equivalent to 15.38% per year [($50/$1,950) × (360/60)].

the proper amount of $5,900. If this note is the only one the company has outstanding, the December 31, 1993, balance sheet is as follows:

Current liabilities:		
Notes payable	$6,000	
Less discount on notes payable	100	
Net liability		$5,900

Alternatively, the note may be presented this way:

Current liabilities:	
Notes payable (less discount of $100)	$5,900

Or, the note can be reported on the balance sheet at $5,900 with the amount of the discount mentioned in a footnote.

Accrued Interest Expense

The preceding section showed how interest is accrued on a noninterest-bearing note created in a discount transaction. Interest on an interest-bearing note also accrues as time passes, and must be recorded to produce a complete income statement and balance sheet. Therefore, if any interest-bearing notes payable are outstanding at the end of an accounting period, the accrued interest should be recorded.

For example, suppose that a company borrowed $4,000 on December 16, 1993, and gave its bank a $4,000, 60-day, 12% note. When the company's accounting period ends 15 days later on December 31, $20 of interest has accrued [$4,000 × 12% × (15/360)]. This adjusting entry records the interest:

1993				
Dec.		Interest Expense	20.00	
		Interest Payable		20.00
		To record accrued interest on a note payable.		

This adjusting entry causes the $20 accrued interest to appear on the income statement as an expense of the period that benefits from 15 days' use of the money. It also causes the interest payable to appear on the balance sheet, thereby causing the total debt of $4,020 to be reported as a current liability.

When the note matures in the next accounting period, its payment is recorded as follows:

1994				
Feb.		Notes Payable	4,000.00	
		Interest Payable	20.00	
		Interest Expense	60.00	
		Cash		4,080.00
		Paid a $4,000 note and its interest.		

Interest expense on this note for the 45 days during 1994 is $60 [$4,000 × 12% × (45/360)]. The two entries show that the total interest expense of $80 is allocated between the two accounting periods, with $20 assigned to 1993 and $60 assigned to 1994.

The Concept of Present Value

LO 5 Calculate the present value of a sum of money that will be received a number of periods in the future or that will be received periodically.

Information based on the concept of *present value* enters into many financing and investing decisions. It also enters into accounting for liabilities resulting from those decisions. Therefore, an understanding of present value is important for all business students. The concept is based on the idea that the right to receive, say, $1 a year from today (or at any other point in the future) is worth less than $1 today. That is, $1 to be received one year from now has a **present value** of less than $1. How much less depends on how much can be earned with invested funds. In general terms, present value is the amount of money that can be currently invested at a given interest rate to accumulate a total value equal to a given amount to be received (or paid) at some future date. This amount to be invested is the *value* in the *present* of the future amount.

For example, if an 8% annual return can be earned, the expectation of receiving $1 one year from now has a present value of $0.9259. This can be verified as follows: $0.9259 invested today to earn 8% annually will earn $0.0741 in one year. When the $0.0741 earned is added to the $0.9259 invested, the original investment plus the earnings equals $1.0000, as shown here:

Investment	$0.9259
Earnings	0.0741
Total	$1.0000

Likewise, the present value of $1 to be received two years from now is $0.8573 if an 8% compound annual return is expected. This amount can be verified as follows: $0.8573 invested to earn 8% compounded annually will earn $0.0686 the first year it is invested. When the original investment of $0.8573 is added to the return of $0.0686, the result is:

Investment	$0.8573
First year earnings	0.0686
End-of-year-1 amount	$0.9259

When this $0.9259 remains invested another year at 8%, it earns $0.0741, and the accumulated amount equals $1.0000:

End-of-year-1 amount	$0.9259
Second year earnings	0.0741
End-of-year-2 amount	$1.0000

Thus, you can see how the present value of $0.8573 accumulates to a future amount of $1.0000 in two years if it can be invested to return 8% compounded, which means that the income can also be invested to earn 8%.

Present Value Tables

The present value of $1 to be received any number of years in the future can be calculated by using the formula, $1/(1 + i)^n$. The i is the interest rate, and n is the number of years to the expected receipt. Fortunately, you do not need to use the formula because inexpensive electronic calculators are preprogrammed to find present values. As an alternative, you can use a **present value table** that shows present values computed with the formula at various interest rates for various time periods. In fact, you may find it to your advantage in learning this material to use the tables until you become comfortable with present value concepts.

The present value table presented in Table 12–1 shows the present value amounts rounded to four decimal places.[5] Notice that the first amount in the 8% column in Table 12–1 is the value of 0.9259 used in the previous section to introduce the concept of present value. The value of 0.9259 in the 8% column means that the expectation of receiving $1 one period from now has a present value of $0.9259 when discounted at 8%. Also note that the amount in the second row of the 8% column is the 0.8573 previously used. This number means that the expectation of receiving $1 two periods from now, discounted at 8%, has a present value of $0.8573.

Using a Present Value Table

To demonstrate the use of a present value table like Table 12–1, assume that a company has an opportunity to invest $55,000 in a project. The investment will return $20,000 at the end of the first year, $25,000 at the end of the second year, $30,000 at the end of the third year, and nothing thereafter. Also assume that the company believes the risks of the project justify a 12% return, compounded annually.

Will the project return the original investment plus the 12% demanded? The calculations shown in Illustration 12–1 indicate that it will do so, with an excess. Illustration 12–1 shows the expected returns in the second column, and then multiplies them by the present value table amounts in the third column to determine their present values in the fourth column. Note that the total of the present values exceeds the required investment. Thus, we can conclude that the project will return the $55,000 investment, plus a 12% return on the investment, plus an additional amount that has a present value of $4,142.

In Illustration 12–1, the present value of each year's return was calculated separately. Then, the present values of each expected return were totaled. When the periodic inflows of cash (called *returns*) are unequal, as in this exam-

[5] Four decimal places may not be sufficiently precise for some uses but they are certainly sufficient for the applications described in this book.

TABLE 12–1

Present Value of $1 at Compound Interest

Periods Hence	4½%	5%	6%	7%	8%	9%	10%	12%	14%	16%
1	0.9569	0.9524	0.9434	0.9346	0.9259	0.9174	0.9091	0.8929	0.8772	0.8621
2	0.9157	0.9070	0.8900	0.8734	0.8573	0.8417	0.8264	0.7972	0.7695	0.7432
3	0.8763	0.8638	0.8396	0.8163	0.7938	0.7722	0.7513	0.7118	0.6750	0.6407
4	0.8386	0.8227	0.7921	0.7629	0.7350	0.7084	0.6830	0.6355	0.5921	0.5523
5	0.8025	0.7835	0.7473	0.7130	0.6806	0.6499	0.6209	0.5674	0.5194	0.4761
6	0.7679	0.7462	0.7050	0.6663	0.6302	0.5963	0.5645	0.5066	0.4556	0.4104
7	0.7348	0.7107	0.6651	0.6228	0.5835	0.5470	0.5132	0.4523	0.3996	0.3538
8	0.7032	0.6768	0.6274	0.5820	0.5403	0.5019	0.4665	0.4039	0.3506	0.3050
9	0.6729	0.6446	0.5919	0.5439	0.5003	0.4604	0.4241	0.3606	0.3075	0.2630
10	0.6439	0.6139	0.5584	0.5084	0.4632	0.4224	0.3855	0.3220	0.2697	0.2267
11	0.6162	0.5847	0.5268	0.4751	0.4289	0.3875	0.3505	0.2875	0.2366	0.1954
12	0.5897	0.5568	0.4970	0.4440	0.3971	0.3555	0.3186	0.2567	0.2076	0.1685
13	0.5643	0.5303	0.4688	0.4150	0.3677	0.3262	0.2897	0.2292	0.1821	0.1452
14	0.5400	0.5051	0.4423	0.3878	0.3405	0.2993	0.2633	0.2046	0.1597	0.1252
15	0.5167	0.4810	0.4173	0.3625	0.3152	0.2745	0.2394	0.1827	0.1401	0.1079
16	0.4945	0.4581	0.3937	0.3387	0.2919	0.2519	0.2176	0.1631	0.1229	0.0930
17	0.4732	0.4363	0.3714	0.3166	0.2703	0.2311	0.1978	0.1456	0.1078	0.0802
18	0.4528	0.4155	0.3503	0.2959	0.2503	0.2120	0.1799	0.1300	0.0946	0.0691
19	0.4333	0.3957	0.3305	0.2765	0.2317	0.1945	0.1635	0.1161	0.0830	0.0596
20	0.4146	0.3769	0.3118	0.2584	0.2146	0.1784	0.1486	0.1037	0.0728	0.0514

ILLUSTRATION 12–1

Present Value of a Series of Unequal Amounts

Years from Now	Expected Returns	Present Value of $1 at 12%	Present Value of Expected Returns
1	$20,000	0.8929	$17,858
2	25,000	0.7972	19,930
3	30,000	0.7118	21,354
Total present value of the returns			$59,142
Less investment required			(55,000)
Excess present value over 12% demanded . .			$ 4,142

ple, you must separately calculate the present value of each one. However, when the periodic returns are equal, there is a simpler way to calculate the sum of their present values.

For instance, suppose that a $17,500 investment will return $5,000 at the end of each year in its five-year life and that an investor wants to know the present value of these returns, discounted at 12%. In this case, the present value can be calculated as shown in Illustration 12–2. But, because the periodic returns are equal, there is a shorter way to determine their total present value at 12%. To do so, add the present values of $1 at 12% for periods 1

ILLUSTRATION 12–2

Present Value of a Series of Equal Amounts

Years from Now	Expected Returns	Present Value of $1 at 12%	Present Value of Expected Returns
1	$5,000	0.8929	$ 4,465
2	5,000	0.7972	3,986
3	5,000	0.7118	3,559
4	5,000	0.6355	3,177
5	5,000	0.5674	2,837
		3.6048	
Total present value of the returns . . .			$18,024

through 5 (from Table 12–1) as shown in the third column of Illustration 12–2. Then, multiply the 3.6048 total by the $5,000 annual return to get the present value of $18,024. Although the result is the same either way, the method demonstrated in Illustration 12–2 requires four fewer multiplications.

Present Value of $1 Received Periodically for a Number of Periods

Table 12–2 is designed to help you work with situations like the one discussed in the preceding paragraphs. That is, the present value of a series of equal returns to be received at periodic intervals can be calculated by taking the sum of the present values of the individual returns.[6] Note the amount on the table's fifth line in the 12% column. This 3.6048 is the same amount that is calculated in Illustration 12–2 by adding the first five present values of $1 at 12% from Table 12–1. All the amounts shown in Table 12–2 can be determined by adding amounts found in Table 12–1. However, there might be some slight variations due to rounding.[7]

Table 12–2 can be used to determine the present value of a series of equal amounts to be received at periodic intervals. For example, what is the present value of a series of ten $1,000 amounts to be received at the end of each of 10 successive years, discounted at 8%? To determine the answer, look down the 8% column to the amount on the row for 10 periods (in this case, years). The table value is 6.7101, and $6.7101 is the present value of $1 to be received annually at the end of each of 10 years, discounted at 8%. Therefore, the present value of the ten $1,000 amounts is $6,710.10 [$1,000 × 6.7101].

---

[6] A common term used to describe a stream of equal returns occurring at equal time intervals is *annuity*. Notice the similarity between the words *annuity* and *annual*.

[7] The formula for finding these values is: $\dfrac{1 - \dfrac{1}{(1+i)^n}}{i}$

TABLE 12–2

Present Value of $1 Received Periodically for a Number of Periods

Payments	4½%	5%	6%	7%	8%	9%	10%	12%	14%	16%
1	0.9569	0.9524	0.9434	0.9346	0.9259	0.9174	0.9091	0.8929	0.8772	0.8621
2	1.8727	1.8594	1.8334	1.8080	1.7833	1.7591	1.7355	1.6901	1.6467	1.6052
3	2.7490	2.7232	2.6730	2.6243	2.5771	2.5313	2.4869	2.4018	2.3216	2.2459
4	3.5875	3.5460	3.4651	3.3872	3.3121	3.2397	3.1699	3.0373	2.9137	2.7982
5	4.3900	4.3295	4.2124	4.1002	3.9927	3.8897	3.7908	3.6048	3.4331	3.2743
6	5.1579	5.0757	4.9173	4.7665	4.6229	4.4859	4.3553	4.1114	3.8887	3.6847
7	5.8927	5.7864	5.5824	5.3893	5.2064	5.0330	4.8684	4.5638	4.2883	4.0386
8	6.5959	6.4632	6.2098	5.9713	5.7466	5.5348	5.3349	4.9676	4.6389	4.3436
9	7.2688	7.1078	6.8017	6.5152	6.2469	5.9953	5.7590	5.3282	4.9464	4.6065
10	7.9127	7.7217	7.3601	7.0236	6.7101	6.4177	6.1446	5.6502	5.2161	4.8332
11	8.5289	8.3064	7.8869	7.4987	7.1390	6.8052	6.4951	5.9377	5.4527	5.0286
12	9.1186	8.8633	8.3838	7.9427	7.5361	7.1607	6.8137	6.1944	5.6603	5.1971
13	9.6829	9.3936	8.8527	8.3577	7.9038	7.4869	7.1034	6.4235	5.8424	5.3423
14	10.2228	9.8986	9.2950	8.7455	8.2442	7.7862	7.3667	6.6282	6.0021	5.4675
15	10.7395	10.3797	9.7123	9.1079	8.5595	8.0607	7.6061	6.8109	6.1422	5.5755
16	11.2340	10.8378	10.1059	9.4467	8.8514	8.3126	7.8237	6.9740	6.2651	5.6685
17	11.7072	11.2741	10.4773	9.7632	9.1216	8.5436	8.0216	7.1196	6.3729	5.7487
18	12.1600	11.6896	10.8276	10.0591	9.3719	8.7556	8.2014	7.2497	6.4674	5.8179
19	12.5933	12.0853	11.1581	10.3356	9.6036	8.9501	8.3649	7.3658	6.5504	5.8775
20	13.0079	12.4622	11.4699	10.5940	9.8182	9.1286	8.5136	7.4694	6.6231	5.9288

Interest Periods Less than One Year in Length

In the examples presented so far, the interest rates have been applied to time periods that were one year in length. However, interest is often applied to time periods shorter than one year. For instance, the interest on corporate bonds is normally paid semiannually, although interest rates on such bonds are usually quoted on an annual basis. As a result, the present value of the interest payments to be received from these bonds must be based on interest periods that are six months long.

To illustrate a calculation based on six-month interest periods, assume an investor wants to know the present value of the interest that will be received over five years on some corporate bonds. The bonds have a $10,000 par value, and interest is paid on them every six months at a 14% annual rate. Although the interest rate is described as an annual rate of 14%, it is actually a rate of 7% per six-month interest period. Therefore, the investor receives $700 interest on these bonds at the end of each six-month interest period [$10,000 × 7%]. In five years, there are 10 six-month periods. Therefore, to determine the present value of these 10 receipts of $700 each, discounted at the 7% interest rate of the bonds, look down the 7% column of Table 12–2 to the amount on the row for 10 periods. The table value is 7.0236, and the present value of the ten $700 semiannual receipts is $4,916.52 [7.0236 × $700].

For a more complete discussion of discounting, turn to Appendix H at the end of the book. Appendix H expands the discussion of how present value tables are developed and explains the development of future value tables. More complete present value and future value tables are included in the appendix, which also has numerous exercises related to discounting.

Exchanging a Note for a Plant Asset

When purchasing a high-cost asset on credit, particularly if the credit period is long, the buyer often gives a note in exchange for the asset. For example, if the cash price of an asset is $4,500 and the stated interest rate on the note corresponds to the prevailing market rate, the amount of the note will probably be $4,500. The entry to record the transaction would be as follows:

Feb.	12	Store Equipment	4,500.00	
		Notes Payable		4,500.00
		Exchanged a $4,500, three-year, 12% note payable for a refrigerated display case.		

A note given in exchange for a plant asset has two elements, which may or may not be stated in the note. They are (1) a dollar amount equal to the bargained cash price of the asset, and (2) an interest factor to compensate the supplier for the use of the funds that would have been received in a cash sale. Therefore, when a note is exchanged for a plant asset, if the face amount of the note approximates the cash price of the asset and the note's interest rate approximates the prevailing market rate, the asset is recorded at the face amount of the note.

Notes that Have an Unreasonable or No Stated Interest Rate

LO 6 Prepare entries to account for long-term noninterest-bearing notes payable and for capital and operating leases.

In some cases, notes exchanged for assets do not have a stated interest rate. In others, the stated interest rate does not approximate the prevailing market rate. In both situations, the face amount of the note does *not* equal the cash price of the asset obtained in exchange for the note. Because the face amount of the note does not equal the asset's value in these cases, recording the asset at the note's face amount would initially misstate the asset and liability. Subsequently, these misstatements would lead to other misstatements of depreciation and interest expense. These misstatements may be material, especially for a long-term note of a large amount, so you must record the acquisition using the best information available. Therefore, the asset must be recorded at its cash price or at the fair value (present value) of the note, whichever is more clearly determinable.[8]

To illustrate a situation in which a note with no stated interest rate is exchanged for a plant asset, assume that a noninterest-bearing, five-year, $10,000 note payable is exchanged for a factory machine on January 2, 1993. Also assume that you cannot readily determine the cash price of the asset. If the prevailing market rate of interest on the day of the exchange is 14%, the present value of the note on that day is $5,194. This amount was calculated by multiplying the face amount of the note by the value on the fifth row in the 14% column of Table 12–1 [$10,000 × 0.5194 = $5,194]. Thus, the purchase should be recorded as follows:

[8] FASB, *Accounting Standards—Current Text* (Norwalk, Conn., 1990), sec. I69.105. First published as *APB Opinion No. 21*, par. 12.

1993				
Jan.	2	Machinery	5,194.00	
		Discount on Notes Payable	4,806.00	
		Long-Term Notes Payable		10,000.00
		Exchanged a five-year, noninterest-bearing note for a machine.		

The $5,194 amount debited to the Machinery account is the present value of the note on the day of the exchange. Since the buyer and seller have agreed to the terms of the transaction, the present value must approximate the cash price of the machinery. Therefore, the present value of the note is established as the cost of the machine and is the amount you must use to calculate depreciation.

The debit to Discount on Notes Payable and credit to Long-Term Notes Payable together measure the liability that resulted from the transaction. They would appear as follows on a balance sheet prepared immediately after the exchange:

Long-term liabilities:		
Long-term notes payable	$10,000	
Less unamortized discount based on the 14% interest rate prevailing on the date of issue	4,806	$5,194

As described before, alternative forms of presentation can be used. The main point to observe is that the net liability is reported at the present value of the note's future cash flows.

Amortizing the Discount on a Note Payable

As you have learned, the $4,806 discount on the preceding note is contra to the gross liability of $10,000. This amount is also the interest component of the purchase transaction in the sense that it is the difference between the value that the buyer received and the cash that the buyer will pay later. That is, the buyer essentially borrowed $5,194 and will have to pay back $10,000 in five years. The $4,806 difference is interest expense for the buyer.

In this discount situation, an important task faced by the accountant is to allocate the total interest among the five reporting years covered by the note. Illustration 12–3 shows one method of calculating the annual interest expense. This illustration presents the beginning net liability for each year in the second column, labeled (*a*). The next column, labeled (*b*), computes the interest expense for each year as 14% of the beginning balance. (Recall that 14% is the prevailing rate of interest at the date the note is signed.) This amount should appear on the buyer's income statement as an expense. The last column, labeled (*c*), shows the ending balance of the net liability, which equals the beginning balance plus the unpaid interest expense accrued for the year. The ending

ILLUSTRATION 12–3

Allocation of Interest for a Five-Year, $10,000 Note Payable, with an Initial Net Balance of $5,194

Year	(*a*) Beginning Net Liability	(*b*) 14% Interest Expense	(*c*) Ending Net Liability (*a*) + (*b*)
1993	$5,194	$ 727	$ 5,921
1994	5,921	829	6,750
1995	6,750	945	7,695
1996	7,695	1,077	8,772
1997	8,772	1,228	10,000
Total expense		$4,806	

balance is also equal to the present value of the future payment, discounted at the original interest rate.[9]

Note several points from the illustration: First, observe that the total interest expense for the five years equals the initial discount of $4,806. Second, notice that the ending net liability increases each year until it reaches the maturity amount of $10,000. Third, the amount of interest allocated to each year increases because the balance of the liability is increasing.

This process of allocating interest can also be described as a process of amortizing the discount on the note. In Illustration 12–4, an amortization schedule shows how the balance of the discount is reduced by amortization over the life of the note.

Look carefully at Illustration 12–4. Column (*a*) shows the $10,000 *gross* liability equal to the face amount of the note. Column (*b*) shows the remaining balance of the unamortized discount, which is deducted from the value in column (*a*) to show the *net* liability at the beginning of the year in column (*c*). For example, the $5,194 amount in column (*c*) for 1993 is the difference between the $10,000 face value of the note and the $4,806 discount. (This column is identical to column (*a*) of Illustration 12–3.) Column (*d*) shows the amount of interest expense allocated to each year, which is also the amount of discount to be amortized for the year. In each year, it equals 14% of the net liability in column (*c*). The amounts in this column are the same as those in column (*b*) of Illustration 12–3.

Using this information, the first year's amortization entry should be:

1993 Dec.	31	Interest Expense	727.00	
		Discount on Notes Payable.		727.00
		To recognize interest expense on our long-term note.		

[9] For example, the present value of the $10,000 maturity amount at December 31, 1995, is $7,695 [$10,000 × 0.7695].

ILLUSTRATION 12–4

Amortization Schedule for a Five-Year, $10,000 Note Payable, Discounted at 14%

Year	(a) Face Amount of Note	(b) Unamortized Discount at Beginning of Year	(c) Beginning Net Liability (a) − (b)	(d) Discount to Be Amortized (c) × 14%	(e) Unamortized Discount at Year-End (b) − (d)	(f) Ending Net Liability (a) − (e)
1993	$10,000	$4,806	$5,194	$ 727	$4,079	$ 5,921
1994	10,000	4,079	5,921	829	3,250	6,750
1995	10,000	3,250	6,750	945	2,305	7,695
1996	10,000	2,305	7,695	1,077	1,228	8,772
1997	10,000	1,228	8,772	1,228	-0-	10,000
Total				$4,806		

This entry accrues the expense that will appear on the income statement. It also reduces the balance of the discount account, which has the effect of increasing the net liability. Notice that the total amortization over the five years equals the initial $4,806 discount, and equals the total interest expense over those five years.

Column (*e*) of Illustration 12–4 shows the new balance of the discount account after the year-end adjusting entry. Notice that it grows smaller each year until it is eliminated completely at the end of 1997, when the note matures. Finally, column (*f*) shows the ending net liability, which is the difference between the note's face value in column (*a*) and the ending balance of the discount in column (*e*). For example, the $5,921 ending net liability for 1993 is the difference between the $10,000 face value and the remaining unamortized discount of $4,079. Also notice that the amounts presented in columns (*e*) and (*f*) become the amounts presented on the next year's columns (*b*) and (*c*).

Posting the December 31, 1993, amortization entry to the Discount on Notes Payable account causes the note to be presented on the buyer's balance sheet as follows:

Long-term liabilities:		
Long-term notes payable	$10,000	
Less unamortized discount based on the 14% interest rate prevailing on the date of issue	4,079	$5,921

Compare this $5,921 net amount at which the note is carried on the December 31, 1993, balance sheet with the $5,194 net amount presented for the note on the balance sheet prepared on its date of issue. Observe that the net liability, also called the **carrying amount of the note,** increased by $727 between the two dates. The $727 is the amount of discount amortized and charged to Interest Expense at the end of 1993.

At the end of 1993 and each succeeding year, the remaining amounts of discount shown in column (*d*) of Illustration 12–4 should be amortized and charged to Interest Expense. This process causes the carrying amount of the note to increase each year by the amount of discount amortized that year and to reach $10,000, the note's maturity value, at the end of the fifth year. Payment of the note will be recorded as follows:

1998				
Jan.	2	Long-Term Notes Payable	10,000.00	
		Cash		10,000.00
		Paid our long-term noninterest-bearing note.		

In this example, the note payable will be shown on each year-end balance sheet as a long-term liability until the balance sheet of December 31, 1997, where it will appear as a current liability. Other notes call for a series of installment payments, so that part of the principal is due within one year (or the current operating cycle, whichever is longer.) In these cases, generally accepted accounting principles require the carrying amount of a note payable to be divided into two parts for presentation on the balance sheet. The portion of the note to be paid during the next year (or operating cycle) must be shown as a current liability, with the remaining portion shown as a long-term liability.

Liabilities from Leasing

LO 6 Prepare entries to account for long-term noninterest-bearing notes payable and for capital and operating leases.

For a number of reasons, many businesses choose to lease plant assets instead of purchasing them. In most cases, the lease contract requires a series of payments to be made over the life of the lease. As a result, by leasing instead of purchasing, a business avoids the immediate cash outflow of the full purchase price that must be paid for the asset.

Although leases are contracts that require a series of future payments, all leases do not produce the same economic effect on the firm. Consequently, all leases are not accounted for the same way.

Categories of Leases

Some leases, called **capital leases** or **financing leases**, have essentially the same effect on the lessee and lessor as a purchase-sale transaction. That is, the outcome is just as if the lessee obtained a loan from the lessor and used the proceeds to purchase the leased asset. When an asset is leased under a capital lease, the lessee records the asset as if it has been purchased and also records a liability equal to the present value of the future lease payments. In most cases, this amount approximates the fair value of the leased asset.

In contrast to capital leases, other leases do not have the characteristics of a purchase-sale transaction. These **operating leases** merely give the lessee the right to use the leased asset for the time period covered by the contract. That is, the lessee does *not* acquire an ownership interest in the leased property, and the risks of ownership remain with the lessor.

When a lease is identified as an operating lease, the lessee's obligation to make payments is *not* recorded as a liability. Because these operating leases are not recorded as liabilities, they do not appear on the balance sheet. This kind of leasing activity is sometimes called *off-balance sheet financing*.

Whether a lease is classified as an operating lease or as a capital lease can have a significant effect on the financial statements. As a result, the financial statements of different lessees will not be comparable unless the companies use the same criteria to classify their leases. To make financial statements more comparable, the FASB has established rules or criteria that accountants use to decide how leases should be classified. According to the FASB's decision, a lease that meets any of the following criteria is a capital lease.

1. Ownership of the leased asset is automatically transferred to the lessee at the end of the lease period.
2. The lessee has the option to purchase the leased asset either during or at the end of the lease period at a bargain price. The price must be sufficiently less than the asset's expected fair value so that the option is likely to be exercised. (This arrangement is called a **bargain purchase option.**)
3. The period covered by the lease is 75% or more of the estimated service life of the leased asset.
4. The present value of the minimum payments under the lease is 90% or more of the fair value of the leased asset.[10]

A lease that does not meet any of these four criteria is classified by the lessee as an operating lease.

To illustrate accounting for leases, assume that Alpha Company plans to produce a product with a new machine that has a cash price of approximately $32,800 and an estimated 10-year life with no salvage value. Alpha Company does not have that much cash available and plans to lease the machine starting on December 31, 1993. Alpha Company will lease the machine under one of the following contracts, both of which require it to pay for maintenance, taxes, and insurance on the machine:

(*a*) Lease the machine for five years, with annual payments of $7,500 payable at the end of each of the five years. The machine will be returned to the lessor at the end of the lease period.

(*b*) Lease the machine for five years, with annual payments of $10,000 payable at the end of each of the five years. The machine will become the property of Alpha Company at the end of the lease period.

If Alpha had chosen to borrow sufficient cash to purchase the machine, it would have paid interest at an annual rate of 16%.

Accounting for an Operating Lease

The first lease contract does not pass ownership to the lessee, does not have a bargain purchase option, and covers only half of the asset's 10-year useful life. Therefore, it does not meet any of the first three criteria of a capital lease. Also, the present value of the lease payments, discounted at the 16% interest rate, is $24,557 [$7,500 × 3.2743]. This amount is less than 90% of $32,800, so

[10] FASB, *Accounting Standards—Current Text* (Norwalk, Conn., 1990), sec. L10.103. First published as *FASB Statement No. 13*, par. 7.

the lease also does not meet the fourth criterion of a capital lease. Therefore, the lease must be classified as an *operating lease*.

If Alpha Company chooses contract (*a*), no entry is made at the time the lease contract is signed. Later, each annual rental payment is recorded with an entry like the following one, which records the first payment at the end of 1994:

1994				
Dec.	31	Machinery Rental Expense	7,500.00	
		Cash		7,500.00
		Paid the annual rent on a leased machine.		

Alpha Company also must record any expenses it incurs for maintenance, taxes, and insurance on the machine. In addition, Alpha should add a footnote to its financial statements that gives a general description of the leasing arrangements. However, because the leased machine was not recorded as an asset, no entries are made for depreciation expense.

Accounting for a Capital Lease

The second lease contract, (*b*), meets the first capital lease criterion in that title to the asset is transferred to Alpha at the end of the lease. The contract also meets the fourth criterion because the present value of the five $10,000 payments is $32,743 [$10,000 × 3.2743], which is greater than 90% of the $32,800 cash price of the asset. Thus, it is a *capital lease*. In effect, this lease is a credit purchase transaction with the lessor providing financing to the lessee for acquiring the machine.

Recording the Lease Liability. If Alpha Company chooses the second lease contract, it should record the asset and the liability at the $32,743 present value of the five lease payments. Alpha makes this entry on the day the lease is signed:

1993				
Dec.	31	Machinery.	32,743.00	
		Discount on Lease Financing	17,257.00	
		Long-Term Lease Liability		50,000.00
		Purchased a machine through a long-term lease contract.		

In effect, the cost of the leased machine is $32,743. Like the cost of any other asset, this amount should be charged to depreciation expense over the machine's expected service life of 10 years. Sometimes, however, the terms of a lease are such that the expected service life of the leased asset is limited to the term of the lease. This condition exists if the lessee does not obtain ownership at the end of the lease and the lease period is shorter than the asset's expected life.

Reporting Long-Term Lease Liability on the Balance Sheet. As we showed for a noninterest-bearing note, the $17,257 discount on the lease liability is the interest component of the transaction. The net liability that results from the lease is the gross long-term lease liability less the amount of the discount. The two items should appear as follows on Alpha Company's December 31, 1993, balance sheet:

Long-term liabilities:		
Long-term lease liability[11]	$50,000	
Less unamortized discount based on the 16% interest rate available on the date of the contract	17,257	$32,743

Entries to Record Depreciation, Lease Payments, and Interest. If Alpha Company depreciates the machine on a straight-line basis over its 10-year life, it will make the following entries at the end of the first year in the life of the lease:

1994				
Dec.	31	Depreciation Expense, Machinery	3,274.30	
		Accumulated Depreciation, Machinery.		3,274.30
		To record depreciation on the machine. $32,743/10 years = $3,274.30		
	31	Long-Term Lease Liability	10,000.00	
		Cash		10,000.00
		Made the annual payment on the lease.		
	31	Interest Expense	5,239.00	
		Discount on Lease Financing		5,239.00
		Amortized a portion of the discount on the lease financing.		

The first entry records straight-line depreciation equal to the asset's cost of $32,743 divided by 10 years (there is no salvage value). The second entry records the first of the five $10,000 lease payments as a reduction in the gross lease liability. The third entry records $5,239 as interest expense on the net lease liability. To calculate this amount, apply the 16% interest rate to the $32,743 beginning carrying amount of the lease liability [$32,743 × 16% = $5,239].

Illustration 12–5 contains two schedules: The first is like Illustration 12–3, and shows the allocation of the total interest expense of $17,257 over the five years of the lease. This schedule differs from Illustration 12–3 by including an extra column that shows the decrease in the gross liability from the annual $10,000 payment.

The second schedule in Illustration 12–5 shows the amortization of the discount on the lease liability. To determine the amount of discount to be am-

[11] To simplify the illustration, we have disregarded the requirement that the lease liability be divided into its current and noncurrent portions. You should do the same thing when you work the exercises and problems at the end of the chapter.

ILLUSTRATION 12–5

Allocation of Interest for a 5-Year Lease Liability, $10,000 Payable per Year, with an Initial Net Balance of $32,743

Year	(a) Beginning Net Liability	(b) Interest Expense (a) × 16%	(c) Less Annual Payment	(d) Ending Net Liability (a) + (b) − (c)
1994	$32,743	$ 5,239	$10,000	$27,982
1995	27,982	4,477	10,000	22,459
1996	22,459	3,593	10,000	16,052
1997	16,052	2,568	10,000	8,620
1998	8,620	1,380*	10,000	–0–
Total expense		$17,257		

Amortization Schedule for a 5-Year Lease Liability, $10,000 Payable per Year, Discounted at 16%

Year	(a) Beginning Gross Lease Liability	(b) Unamortized Discount at Beginning of Year	(c) Beginning Net Liability (a) − (b)	(d) Discount to Be Amortized (c) × 16%	(e) Unamortized Discount at the End of Year (b) − (d)	(f) Ending Gross Lease Liability (a) − $10,000	(g) Ending Net Liability (f) − (e)
1994	$50,000	$17,257	$32,743	$ 5,239	$12,018	$40,000	$27,982
1995	40,000	12,018	27,982	4,477	7,541	30,000	22,459
1996	30,000	7,541	22,459	3,593	3,948	20,000	16,052
1997	20,000	3,948	16,052	2,568	1,380	10,000	8,620
1998	10,000	1,380	8,620	1,380*	–0–	–0–	–0–
Total				$17,257			

* Adjusted to compensate for rounding.

ortized each year, the net lease liability at the beginning of each year is multiplied by 16%. For example, the amount of discount to be amortized in 1995 is $4,477 [$27,982 × 16%]. Each ending net liability amount is found by subtracting the ending unamortized discount in column *(e)* from the ending gross liability in column *(f)*. For example, the December 31, 1995, carrying amount is $22,459 [$30,000 − $7,541]. Notice that the gross liability in column *(f)* gets smaller by $10,000 for each annual payment made on December 31. This process eventually reduces the gross and net liability measures to zero.

The **carrying amount of the lease** is the difference between the sum of the remaining rental payments less the unamortized discount. After posting the December 31, 1994, entries to record the $10,000 payment and the amortization of the discount, the carrying amount of the lease appears on the December 31, 1994, balance sheet as follows:

Long-term liabilities:		
Long-term lease liability.	$40,000	
Less unamortized discount based on the 16% interest rate available on the date of the contract	12,018	$27,982

Payroll Liabilities

LO 7 Prepare entries to account for payroll liabilities.

An employer's current liabilities typically include a number of different obligations that relate to the firm's payroll. These liabilities arise from amounts withheld from employees' wages, **payroll taxes** levied on the employer as percentages of the amount paid to employees, and employee (fringe) benefits provided by the employer. We discuss these withholdings, payroll taxes, employee (fringe) benefits, and the resulting liabilities in the following paragraphs.

FICA Taxes

The social security system provides a qualified worker who retires at age 62 with monthly payments from the federal government for the remainder of his or her life. The retiree also receives certain medical benefits (called *medicare benefits*) after reaching age 65. In addition, the system provides monthly payments to the surviving family of a qualified deceased worker. The funds to pay these benefits come from taxes levied under the Federal Insurance Contributions Act. These **FICA taxes** are also called *social security taxes*.

The Federal Insurance Contributions Act requires, among other things, that an employer withhold an amount of FICA tax from the wages of each employee each payday. Beginning in 1991, the two components of this tax, social security and medicare, must be calculated separately. In 1992, the amount withheld from each employee's pay for the social security (retirement) portion was equal to 6.2% of the first $55,500 of wages earned by the employee. The medicare portion was equal to 1.45% of the first $130,200 of earned wages.

Employers are also required to pay FICA taxes equal to the total FICA taxes withheld from the wages of all employees. The withheld taxes and the employer's tax must be remitted periodically to the Internal Revenue Service. Until they are paid, the employees' withheld FICA taxes and the employer's FICA tax are current liabilities of the employer.

Employees' Federal Income Taxes

With very few exceptions, employers must withhold federal income tax from each employee's paycheck. The amount withheld is determined from tax tables published by the Internal Revenue Service. In each case, the amount withheld depends on the employee's earnings and the number of exemptions (called *withholding allowances*) claimed by the employee. In 1992, each exemption, or allowance, exempted $2,300 of the employee's yearly earnings from withholding. (This amount is indexed each year so that it is increased for the effects of inflation.) The number of withholding allowances usually includes one for the employee, one for the employee's spouse, one for each dependent, and perhaps others depending on the circumstances. As in the case of FICA taxes, the income taxes withheld from employees must be paid to the IRS on a timely basis. Until they are paid, the withholdings must be reported as a current liability on the employer's balance sheet.

Other Deductions from Wages

In addition to these mandatory deductions for FICA and federal income taxes, employees may voluntarily authorize an employer to deduct other amounts from wages. These deductions may include amounts designated by the employee to pay for charitable contributions, medical and hospital insurance premiums, U.S. savings bonds, or union dues. (Of course, the last item is not voluntary if it is required by a union contract.) The amounts deducted are current liabilities of the employer until they are paid to the appropriate organizations.

Accruing the Payroll

At the end of each pay period, a general journal entry is required to accrue the payroll. Appendix F discusses the records an employer maintains to capture the information necessary to make the entry. The entry takes the following form:

Jan.	7	Sales Salaries Expense	1,500.00	
		Office Salaries Expense	500.00	
		FICA Taxes Payable		153.00
		Employees' Federal Income Taxes Payable		213.00
		Employees' Medical Insurance Payable		85.00
		Employees' Union Dues Payable		25.00
		Accrued Payroll Payable		1,524.00
		To record the payroll for the pay period ended January 7.		

In this example, the debits indicate that the sales employees earned $1,500 and that the office employees earned $500. However, the credit to Accrued Payroll Payable shows that they will receive only $1,524 of the $2,000 that they earned. The $476 remainder has been deducted from their pay, as recorded by the first four credits in the entry.

When the employees are paid, another entry (or series of entries) is required to record the checks actually written and distributed. To record the payments, Accrued Payroll Payable is debited and Cash is credited.

Employer's Payroll Taxes

Employer's FICA Tax

As you have already learned, an employer must pay FICA taxes equal in amount to the sum of the FICA taxes withheld from the wages of all the employees. The employer's tax is credited to the same FICA Taxes Payable account used to record the FICA taxes withheld from the employees. The debit is recorded in a Payroll Taxes Expense account.

Federal and State Unemployment Taxes

The federal government participates with the states in a joint federal-state unemployment insurance program. Under this joint program, each state administers its own program. These programs provide unemployment benefits to covered workers. The federal government approves the state programs and pays a portion of their administrative expenses.

The Federal Unemployment Tax (FUTA). In 1992, the Federal Unemployment Tax Act required employers of one or more employees to pay an excise tax (called the *FUTA* tax) equal to 6.2% of the first $7,000 in wages paid each employee, less a maximum credit of 5.4% for contributions to a state program. Because all states have unemployment tax programs, the net federal tax is normally 0.8%.

State Unemployment Taxes (SUTA). All states support their unemployment insurance programs by placing a payroll tax on employers. In many states, the basic rate is 5.4% of the first $7,000 paid each employee. However, the employer's experience in creating or avoiding unemployment is described in a **merit rating** assigned by the state. A good rating is based on high stability and allows the employer to pay less than the basic 5.4% rate. A history of high turnover or seasonal hirings and layoffs may cause the employer to pay more.

A favorable merit rating may offer important cash savings. For example, an employer with just 10 employees who each earn $7,000 or more per year would save $3,430 annually if it received a merit rating that reduced the rate from 5.4% to 0.5%. At the 5.4% rate, it would pay $3,780, but only $350 at the 0.5% rate.

Recording the Employer's Payroll Taxes

The payroll taxes of an employer are an expense. They are recorded each pay period with a general journal entry. For example, assume a payroll of $2,000 paid to employees who have not yet earned $7,000 for the year. Also assume a federal unemployment tax rate of 0.8% and a state unemployment tax rate of 5.4%. The entry to record the employer's taxes on the $2,000 payroll is:

Jan.	7	Payroll Taxes Expense	277.00	
		FICA Taxes Payable		153.00
		State Unemployment Taxes Payable		108.00
		Federal Unemployment Taxes Payable		16.00
		To record payroll taxes.		

The FICA taxes equal 7.65% of the $2,000 of gross pay. (This amount also equals the amount withheld from the employees.) The State Unemployment Taxes (SUTA) are shown at the full 5.4% of the $2,000 gross pay, and the Federal Unemployment Taxes (FUTA) are calculated at the 0.8% rate.

Employee (Fringe) Benefit Costs

In addition to the wages earned by employees and the related payroll taxes paid by the employer, many companies provide a variety of benefits for their employees. Because the costs of these benefits are paid by the employer, and the benefits are in addition to the amount of wages earned, they are often called **employee fringe benefits.** For example, an employer may pay for part (or all) of the premiums for the employees' medical insurance, life insurance, and disability insurance. Another common employee benefit involves employer contributions to a retirement income plan.

Employer Contributions to Employee Insurance and Retirement Plans

The entries for employee benefit costs are similar to those used for payroll taxes. For example, assume the employer with the previously described $2,000 payroll agreed to match the employees' contributions for medical insurance and also to contribute 10% of the employees' salaries to a retirement program. The entry to record these employee benefits is:

Jan.	7	Employees' Benefits Expense	285.00	
		Employees' Medical Insurance Payable		85.00
		Employees' Retirement Program Payable		200.00
		To record employees' benefits.		

Vacation Pay

Nearly all employers promise their employees paid vacation time as a benefit of employment. For example, many employees receive 2 weeks' vacation in return for working 50 weeks each year. The effect of a two-week vacation is to increase the employer's payroll expenses by 4% (2/50 = .04). However, new employees often do not begin to accrue vacation time until after they've worked for a period of time, perhaps as much as a year. The employment contract may say that no vacation is granted until the employee works one year; but if the first year is completed, the employee receives the full two weeks. In this situation, the expense associated with vacation pay depends on the employee turnover rate. If the turnover experience of the employer suggests that only 90% of employees actually will be granted vacation time, the additional expense of a two-week vacation benefit would be 90% of 4%, or 3.6%.

To account for vacation pay, an employer should estimate and record the additional expense during the weeks the employees are working and earning the vacation time. For example, assume that a company with a weekly payroll of $20,000 grants two weeks of vacation after one year's employment. Based on past turnover rates, the employer estimates that 90% of the employees actually will be granted vacation time. The entry to record the estimated vacation pay is:

Date	Employees' Benefits Expense	720.00	
	Estimated Vacation Pay Liability		720.00
	$20,000 × .04 × .9 = $720.		

As employees take their vacations and receive their vacation pay, the entries to record the vacation payroll take the following general form:

Date	Estimated Vacation Pay Liability	xxx	
	FICA Taxes Payable		xxx
	Employees' Income Taxes Payable		xxx
	Other withholding liability accounts such as Employees' Hospital Insurance Payable		xxx
	Accrued Payroll Payable		xxx

Payroll taxes and employee benefits costs are often a major category of expense incurred by a company. They may amount to more than 25% of the salaries earned by employees.

Summary of Chapter in Terms of Learning Objectives

LO 1. Current liabilities are due within one year of the balance sheet date or within one operating cycle, whichever is longer. The liquidation (payment) of current liabilities requires the use of existing current assets or the creation of other current liabilities. Long-term liabilities do not have to be paid within one year or one operating cycle.

LO 2. A liability is definite when you know the answer to all three of these questions: (*a*) Who will be paid? (*b*) When is payment due? (*c*) How much will be paid? When the amount to be paid is not precisely known, the obligation is called an estimated liability.

LO 3. Expenses for property taxes and product warranties often must be recorded before the amounts to be paid are known. Therefore, you must estimate the amounts of the liabilities based on the best information currently available. After more information becomes known, the liabilities should be corrected with corresponding adjustments to expense. Short-term notes payable are recorded at their face amounts when the stated interest rates of the notes are reasonable approximations of current market rates of interest. When the notes are not interest-bearing or the stated rates of interest do not reflect the current market rate, the notes are recorded at their present values or at the value of the assets received in exchange, whichever is more reliably known.

LO 4. Many obligations that qualify as liabilities do not depend on uncertain future events. In contrast, when an economic entity is obligated to make a future payment only if some future event takes place, the potential obligation is a contingent liability. However, if the future event that will confirm the existence of a present obligation is probable and the amount of the future payment can be reasonably estimated, the obligation is reported as a liability.

LO 5. The present value of an amount to be received or paid in the future is the amount that could be invested now at the given rate of interest to accumulate a total value equal to the amount to be received or paid. The present value of a series of equal payments is the sum of the present values of each payment.

LO 6. A long-term, noninterest-bearing note must be recorded at its present value calculated with the market interest rate. This amount should approximate the fair value of the assets received in exchange for the note. Each period during the life of the note, interest expense is calculated by multiplying the carrying value of the note at the beginning of the period by the interest rate that was used to discount the note. When an asset is acquired with a capital lease, the lessee records the leased asset and the lease liability at the present value of the lease payments calculated with the market interest rate. This amount should approximate the fair value of the asset. On the other hand, the periodic payments under an operating lease are debited to rent expense as they are incurred.

LO 7. Payroll liabilities include obligations to pay amounts deducted from the employees' wages as well as the amounts paid directly to the employees. Payroll liabilities also include obligations to pay certain taxes and fringe benefits that arise as a result of incurring wages and salaries expense.

Demonstration Problem

Prepare journal entries for the following 1993 transactions of Kearns Company:

a. Kearns accrued estimated property taxes during the first eight months of 1993 at the rate of $2,000 per month. On September 10, Kearns learned that the 1993 tax bill would be $21,720. The due date for these taxes is December 31. Show the property tax entries on September 30 and October 31.

b. During September, Kearns sold $140,000 of merchandise under a 180-day warranty. Prior experience shows that the costs of fulfilling the warranty will equal 5% of the selling price. Record the month's warranty expense and increase in the warranty liability as a September 30 adjusting entry. Also record an October 8 expenditure of $300 cash to service an item sold in September.

c. On October 10, Kearns arranged with a supplier to pay 25% of an overdue $10,000 account payable by Kearns to the supplier. The remaining balance was converted to a $7,500, 90-day note bearing 12% interest.

d. On October 15, Kearns borrowed $98,000 by discounting its $100,000, 60-day note to the bank. The discount rate charged by the bank was 12% per year.

e. On December 1, Kearns acquired a machine by giving a $60,000, noninterest-bearing note due in one year. The rate of interest available to Kearns for this type of debt was 12%.

f. On December 14, Kearns paid the note described in (*d*).

g. On December 31, Kearns accrued the interest on the notes described in (*c*) and (*e*). Show separate adjusting entries, assuming a 360-day year.

In addition to the preceding transactions, Kearns entered into a three-year lease of machinery on January 1, 1993, and agreed to make three payments of $30,158 on December 31, 1993, 1994, and 1995. The appropriate interest rate for this lease is 10%. Title to the machinery will pass to Kearns at the end of the lease, and the lease should be recorded as a capital lease.

h. Show the entry to record entering into the lease.

i. Prepare a table that shows the amount of interest expense to allocate to each year of the lease.

j. Show the entries to record the first payment on December 31, 1993; the interest expense for 1993; and the depreciation expense for 1993. The machine's useful life is predicted to be five years, with no salvage value, and straight-line depreciation is used.

k. Show how the leased asset and lease liability would appear on the balance sheet as of December 31, 1993.

Solution to Demonstration Problem

Planning the Solution

- Examine each situation to determine the required calculation and entry.
- For (*a*), determine the amount of liability that has been recorded and the balance that ought to be recorded as of September 30, and make an entry for the difference. Then, accrue the expense for October.
- For (*b*), compute and record the warranty expense for the month, and then show the expenditure in October as a reduction of the liability.
- For (*c*), eliminate the balance of the account payable, and create the note payable.
- For (*d*), record the discount deducted by the bank from the $100,000 face value of the note. Observe that the note will mature and be paid before the end of the year.
- For (*e*), estimate the cost of the asset by finding the present value of the cash that will be paid when the note payable matures.
- For (*f*), record the cash expenditure.
- For (*g*), calculate the interest expense on the note from (*c*) for 82 days, and on the note from (*e*) for 30 days, and record them. Pay close attention to the original entries to determine whether a discount should be involved in the adjusting entries.
- For (*h*), determine the present value of the lease payments, and record the effects of entering into the lease.
- For (*i*), prepare a table showing the calculation of interest expense by applying the rate to the net lease liability. (Two formats are possible.)
- For (*j*), prepare three entries to record the lease payment, the accrual of interest on the lease liability, and the depreciation on the asset, using its useful life.

- For (*k*), determine the gross liability, the unamortized discount, and the net liability for the lease as of the end of 1993.

a.	Sept.	30	Property Tax Expense	290.00	
			Estimated Property Taxes Payable		290.00

Actual liability on Sept. 30 ($21,720 × 9/12)	$16,290
Recorded liability as of Aug. 31 ($2,000 × 8)	16,000
Additional liability to record on Sept. 30	$ 290

	Oct.	31	Property Tax Expense	1,810.00	
			Estimated Property Taxes Payable		1,810.00
			$21,720/12 = $1,810 per month		
b.	Sept.	30	Warranty Expense	7,000.00	
			Estimated Warranty Liability		7,000.00
			$140,000 × 5% = $7,000		
	Oct.	8	Estimated Warranty Liability	300.00	
			Cash		300.00
c.	Oct.	10	Accounts Payable	10,000.00	
			Cash		2,500.00
			Notes Payable		7,500.00
d.	Oct.	15	Cash	98,000.00	
			Interest Expense	2,000.00	
			Notes Payable		100,000.00
			$100,000 × 12% × (60/360) = $2,000		
e.	Dec.	1	Machinery	53,574.00	
			Discount on Notes Payable	6,426.00	
			Notes Payable		60,000.00
			$60,000 × 0.8929 = $53,574		
f.	Dec.	14	Notes Payable	100,000.00	
			Cash		100,000.00
g.			*For the note in (c):*		
	Dec.	31	Interest Expense	205.00	
			Interest Payable		205.00
			Oct. 10 to Dec. 31 = 82 days		
			$7,500 × 12% × 82/360 = $205		
			For the note in (e):		
	Dec.	31	Interest Expense	535.74	
			Discount on Notes Payable		535.74
			Dec. 1 to Dec. 31 = 30 days		
			$53,574 × 12% × 30/360 = $535.74		
h.	Jan.	1	Machinery	75,000.00	
			Discount on Lease Financing	15,474.00	
			Long-Term Lease Liability		90,474.00
			$30,158 × 2.4869 = $75,000		
			$30,158 × 3 = $90,474		

i. Allocation of interest for a 3-year, $15,474 per year lease liability payable, with an initial balance of $75,000:

Year	(a) Beginning Net Liability	(b) 10% Interest Expense	(c) Less Annual Payment	(d) Ending Net Liability (a) + (b) − (c)
1993	$75,000	$ 7,500	$30,158	$52,342
1994	52,342	5,234	30,158	27,418
1995	27,418	2,740*	30,158	–0–
Total		$15,474		

* Adjusted for rounding.

Amortization schedule for a 3-year, $75,000 lease liability, discounted at 10%:

Year	(a) Beginning Gross Lease Liability	(b) Unamortized Discount at Beginning of Year	(c) Beginning Net Liability (a) − (b)	(d) Discount to Be Amortized (c) × 10%	(e) Unamortized Discount at Year-End (b) − (d)	(f) Ending Gross Lease Liability (a) − $30,158	(g) Ending Net Liability (a) − (e)
1993	$90,474	$15,474	$75,000	$ 7,500	$7,974	$60,316	$52,342
1994	60,316	7,974	52,342	5,234	2,740	30,158	27,418
1995	30,158	2,740	27,418	2,740*	–0–	–0–	–0–
Total				$15,474			

* Adjusted for rounding.

j.

Dec.	31	Long-Term Lease Liability	30,158.00	
		Cash		30,158.00
	31	Interest Expense	7,500.00	
		Discount on Lease Financing		7,500.00
	31	Depreciation Expense, Machinery	15,000.00	
		Accumulated Depreciation, Machinery		15,000.00
		$75,000/5 = $15,000		

k. Long-term liabilities:

Long-term lease liability	$60,316	
Less unamortized discount based on the 10% interest rate available on the date of the contract	7,974	$52,342

APPENDIX

E

FINANCIAL REPORTING OF INCOME TAX LIABILITIES AND EXPENSE

LO 9 Explain and account for deferred income tax liabilities.

Financial statements for a business should be prepared in accordance with generally accepted accounting principles. Income tax returns, on the other hand, must be prepared in accordance with income tax laws. As a result, a corporation's *income before taxes* measured in accordance with generally accepted accounting principles is not always the same as *taxable income* calculated on state or federal income tax returns. They may differ for the two reasons described in the next sections.

Permanent Differences between Financial Accounting and Income Tax Accounting

The first reason is that some items are included in the calculation of income according to generally accepted accounting principles but are permanently excluded from the calculation of taxable income according to the tax laws. Also, some items are included in the calculation of taxable income according to the tax laws but are permanently excluded from the calculation of income according to generally accepted accounting principles.

For example, interest received on state and municipal bonds must be recognized as revenue on the income statement of the company that owns them. In contrast, such interest usually is not subject to federal income tax and, therefore, is not included in taxable income. Another example is percentage depletion, a deduction that is allowed for tax purposes but that is not recorded as an expense under GAAP. These items are *permanent differences* between taxable income and income before taxes.

Temporary Differences between Financial Accounting and Income Tax Accounting

The second reason why taxable income on a corporation's tax return may not be the same as income before taxes on the financial statements involves *temporary differences* between the results of applying tax accounting procedures and financial accounting procedures. That is, a business may use one accounting procedure for tax purposes and another accounting procedure for financial statement purposes where the income effect of the difference between the procedures is temporary or a matter of timing.

For example, unearned revenue (such as rent collected in advance) is usually taxable in the year the cash is received. In the income statement, however, the revenue is recognized when it is earned, not when the cash is received. As another example, a corporation may apply straight-line depreciation over the estimated useful life of an asset for financial accounting purposes while using the Modified Accelerated Cost Recovery System for tax reporting purposes.

When a corporation uses revenue and expense recognition procedures that involve temporary differences between tax and financial accounting, a problem arises in measuring after-tax net income. The problem is to determine how much income tax expense should be shown on the income statement. If the tax due to be paid currently is shown as tax expense, the reported expense will not be consistent with the known tax rate applied to the pre-tax income on the income statement. Also, if the tax to be paid currently is the only amount of tax recorded, the balance sheet will fail to show the liability for taxes that will become due in future years as a result of transactions that have already taken place. (Remember that a liability is a *future* sacrifice for a *present* obligation arising from a *past* transaction.)

Therefore, generally accepted accounting principles have for many years required the use of special procedures to account for income taxes in the financial statements. These rules were significantly changed by the FASB in December 1987, when it issued *Statement of Financial Accounting Standards No. 96*. However, the requirements of *SFAS 96* were widely criticized and the FASB repeatedly postponed the effective date of the standard so that it could be reconsidered. Then, in February 1992, the FASB replaced *SFAS 96* with *SFAS 109*.[12] Portions of the new rules are complex and beyond the introductory scope of this text. However, the most basic concepts of accounting for income taxes are important to your understanding of financial statements. The following paragraphs will help you gain this basic understanding.

Accounting for Income Taxes in the Financial Statements—An Illustration

To illustrate accounting for income taxes, assume that Lott Company had no temporary differences between taxable income and income before taxes prior to 1993. Then, during 1993, Lott Company sold a tract of land with a cost of $7,000 in a transaction that calls for the entire selling price of $8,000 to be received in 1994. As a result, the gain on the sale is recognized for tax purposes in 1994 when the cash is received. For financial accounting purposes, the gain is recognized in 1993 and should be reported on the 1993 income statement. To

[12] FASB, *Statement of Financial Accounting Standards No. 109*, "Accounting for Income Taxes" (Norwalk, Conn., February 1992).

keep the example simple, assume that Lott Company's transactions during 1993 and 1994 were limited to the following:

	1993	1994
Service revenue	$2,700	$3,000
Operating expenses	500	600
Sales price of land sold in 1993 (cash to be received in 1994)	$8,000	$ -0-
Cost of land	(7,000)	-0-
Gain on sale of land	$1,000	$ -0-
Cash received from sale of land	$ -0-	$8,000

Observe that Lott has operating income of $2,200 in 1993 and $2,400 in 1994.

Assuming an income tax rate of 15%, Lott Company's tax returns for 1993 and 1994 would contain the calculations shown in the upper section of Illustration E–1. The company's income statements, except for income taxes expense, appear in the bottom half of the illustration.

In Illustration E–1, notice that the $1,000 difference between the $2,200 taxable income and the $3,200 income before income taxes in 1993 is only a temporary difference. It is temporary because the gain on the 1993 income statement shows up on the tax return for 1994. In other words, the temporary difference in 1993 reverses in 1994. Also notice that the sum of the pre-tax incomes for the two years is $5,600 under both systems.

In this example, the events of 1993 give rise to two different income tax liabilities. First, the $330 liability arises from the service income reported on the 1993 income tax return. Second, the $1,000 gain earned on the 1993 sale of land resulted in an additional future sacrifice (liability) of $150 in the form of 1994 taxes.

With this background in place, we can now deal with the accounting question of how to report income taxes on Lott Company's financial statements for 1993 and 1994. According to the FASB's rules, income tax expense must be calculated as the sum of the tax currently payable plus (or minus) the change in any **deferred income tax liability** from the beginning of the year to the end of the year. The deferred tax liability is the estimated amount of income taxes that will have to be paid in future years as a result of temporary differences created by transactions that have already occurred.

As shown in Illustration E–1, Lott Company's income tax return for 1993 produced a current tax liability of $330. Recall that Lott Company had no temporary differences between taxable income and income before taxes prior to 1993. Thus, at the beginning of 1993, there was no deferred tax liability because no tax was expected to become due in future years as a result of past transactions. However, because of the delayed reporting of the gain on the land sale, we can see that the 1993 events will eventually result in total tax payments greater than the $330 that is currently due.

At the end of 1993, we estimate that an additional $150 will be due next year because the $1,000 gain will be included on the 1994 tax return. The FASB says that this additional liability must be recorded, and the company must recognize it as an expense of 1993. Thus, Lott Company's entry to record

ILLUSTRATION E-1

Lott Company's Tax Returns and Income Statements for 1993 and 1994

	1993	1994
Tax returns:		
Service revenue	$2,700	$3,000
Deductions for expenses	(500)	(600)
Gain on sale of land	-0-	1,000
Taxable income	$2,200	$3,400 ←
Tax rate	× 15%	× 15%
Taxes payable	$ 330	$ 510
Income statements:		
Service revenue	$2,700	$3,000
Deductions for expenses	(500)	(600)
Gain on sale of land	1,000	-0-
Income before income taxes	$3,200	$2,400 ←
Income taxes expense	?	?
Net income	$?	$?

Notice the difference

income taxes at the end of 1993 must include the credit to the Deferred Income Tax Liability account, as follows:

1993				
Dec.	31	Income Taxes Expense	480.00	
		Income Taxes Payable		330.00
		Deferred Income Tax Liability		150.00
		To record 1993's tax expense and liabilities.		

Recall that $8,000 cash from the land sale is collected by Lott Company in 1994. Because the gain is taxable when the cash is collected, the 1994 tax return shows total taxable income of $3,400, consisting of $2,400 from the normal operations and $1,000 from the gain. Now, remember that income tax expense for 1994 is calculated as the sum of the amount currently due plus or minus the change in the deferred tax liability during the year. On December 31, 1993, the Deferred Income Tax Liability account had a credit balance of $150. But, on December 31, 1994, there are no future tax liabilities expected as a result of past transactions. Thus, the deferred liability must receive a debit of $150 to reduce its balance to zero. The entry to record the effects of income taxes for 1994 is:

1994				
Dec.	31	Income Taxes Expense	360.00	
		Deferred Income Tax Payable	150.00	
		Income Taxes Payable		510.00
		To record 1994's tax expense and liabilities.		

ILLUSTRATION E–2

Income Tax Information on Lott Company's Financial Statements

	1993	1994
Income statements:		
Service revenue	$2,700	$3,000
Expenses	(500)	(600)
Gain on sale of land	1,000	–0–
Income before income taxes	$3,200	$2,400
Income taxes expense	(480)	(360)
Net income	$2,720	$2,040
Balance sheets:		
Current Liabilities:		
Income taxes payable	$ 330	$ 510
Deferred income tax liability	150	–0–
Total	$ 480	$ 510

As this entry shows, income tax expense for 1994 equals the $510 taxes currently payable minus the $150 decrease in the deferred tax liability. This amount turns out to be $360, which is equal to 15% of the income from normal operations. This entry also gives the Deferred Income Tax Liability account a zero balance.

This treatment of the temporary difference causes the Lott Company's financial statements to appear as shown in Illustration E–2.

Before concluding this appendix on income taxes, we should mention the following additional features of the rules that govern accounting for income taxes.

1. In the Lott Company example, we assumed an income tax rate of 15% in both 1993 and 1994. If the laws existing at the end of 1993 state that tax rates in 1994 are going to be different, the deferred tax liability must be based on the 1994 rate. For example, if the 1993 tax laws state that the tax rate will increase to 20% in 1994, the deferred income tax liability at the end of 1993 will be calculated using the 1994 tax rate of 20%. As a result, the deferred tax liability at the end of 1993 will be $200 instead of $150, and the tax expense for 1993 will be $530 instead of $480.

2. In the Lott Company example, 1993 income before taxes was *greater than* taxable income because of a temporary difference that was expected to reverse in 1994. As a result, we recognized a deferred tax liability on the December 31, 1993, balance sheet. In other situations, just the opposite kind of temporary difference may occur. That is, a temporary difference that will reverse in the future may cause income before taxes to be *less than* taxable income. Under certain conditions, these situations may cause the company to recognize a deferred tax asset. However, to recognize a deferred tax asset on the balance sheet, the company's management must have sufficient evidence to believe that the future tax benefit or savings is more likely than not to be realized.

3. The balances of deferred tax liabilities (or assets) are reported on the balance sheet as current, noncurrent, or both, depending on the classification of the asset or liability that is associated with the temporary difference. For example, a deferred tax liability that results from a temporary difference in tax and financial accounting depreciation is classified as noncurrent because it is associated with noncurrent operating assets. If there is no connection between the temporary difference and an asset or liability, the deferred tax liability or asset is classified according to when it will be paid or realized. For example, a deferred tax liability that relates to a tax deferral for a gain on a sale of land is classified as current if the tax will be paid within the next year. If some of the tax will be paid within the next year and the rest after one year, the liability is part current and part long term. Otherwise, the liability will be reported as long term.

4. Federal tax laws generally require corporations to estimate their current year's tax liability and make advance payments of the estimated amount before the final tax return is filed. As a result, the end-of-year entries to record income taxes, such as those shown for Lott Company, often have to be altered to take into consideration any previously recorded prepayments.

Summary of Appendix E in Terms of Learning Objectives

LO 9. Generally accepted accounting principles are not the same as income tax rules. Therefore, the amount of net income before taxes reported on the income statement may differ from the taxable income on the tax return. When these differences are temporary (they occur as a matter of timing), the reported income tax expense is different from the amount of tax currently payable. For example, some current income statement transactions result in tax liabilities that are deferred in the sense that they will be paid in the future but are not yet due as a result of filing the current tax return. These liabilities must be recorded and added to the taxes currently payable to determine the total income taxes expense.

APPENDIX

F

Payroll Reports, Records, and Procedures

Payroll Reports

LO 10 Describe an employer's payroll reports and records, and the procedures used to calculate tax withholdings and issue checks to employees.

Payroll expenses involve liabilities to individual employees, to federal and state governments, and usually to other organizations such as insurance companies. In addition to paying these liabilities, employers are required to prepare and submit a variety of reports that explain how the payments were determined.

Reporting FICA Taxes and Income Tax Withholdings to the Federal Government

According to the Federal Insurance Contributions Act, each employer must file an Employer's Quarterly Federal Tax Return within one month after the end of each calendar quarter. (An example of this tax information return, known as Form 941, is shown in Illustration F–1.)

In Illustration F–1, notice that on line 2 of Form 941, an employer reports the total payments of wages subject to income tax withholding. The amount of income tax withheld is reported on lines 3 and 5. The combined amount of the employees' and employer's FICA (social security) taxes is reported on line 6a where it says, "Taxable social security wages" $34,370.50 × 12.4% = Tax, $4,261.94. The 12.4% is the sum of the (1992) 6.2% tax withheld from the employees' wages for the quarter plus the 6.2% tax levied on the employer. The combined amount of the employees' and employer's medicare wages is reported on line 7. Total FICA taxes (social security plus medicare) are reported on lines 8 and 10, and then are added to the total income taxes withheld. Finally, the total of the amounts deposited in a **federal depository bank** during the quarter is subtracted to determine if a balance remains to be paid. Federal depository banks are authorized to accept deposits of amounts payable to the federal government.

If the sum of the FICA taxes plus the employees' income taxes is less than $500 for a quarter, the taxes may be paid when the Form 941 is filed. If the taxes are $500 or more but less than $3,000 at the end of any month, payment must be made within 15 days after the end of the month. Companies with large payrolls may have to pay more often. Note in Illustration F–1 that each month is divided into eight periods. If the taxes are $3,000 or more but less than $100,000 at the end of any period, they must be paid within three banking days after the

ILLUSTRATION F–1

Employer's Quarterly Report of Federal Taxes Withheld

Form **941** (Rev. January 1991) Department of the Treasury Internal Revenue Service 4141

Employer's Quarterly Federal Tax Return

► See Circular E for more information concerning employment tax returns.

Please type or print.

OMB No. 1545-0029 Expires: 5-31-93

Your name, address, employer identification number, and calendar quarter of return. (If not correct, please change.)

Name (as distinguished from trade name)

Date quarter ended: Sept. 30, 1992

Trade name, if any: Graphic Planners, Inc.

Employer identification number: 74-1633163

Address and ZIP code: 907 Falcon Trail, Austin, Texas 78746

T / FF / FD / FP / I / T

If address is different from prior return, check here ► ☐

If you do not have to file returns in the future, check here . . . ► ☐ Date final wages paid . . . ►

If you are a seasonal employer, see **Seasonal employers** on page 2 and check here . ► ☐

1a	Number of employees (except household) employed in the pay period that includes March 12th . ►	1a	
b	If you are a subsidiary corporation AND your parent corporation files a consolidated Form 1120, enter parent corporation employer identification number (EIN) . . ► 1b –		
2	Total wages and tips subject to withholding, plus other compensation . . . . ►	2	34,370 50
3	Total income tax withheld from wages, tips, pensions, annuities, sick pay, gambling, etc. . . ►	3	3,820 20
4	Adjustment of withheld income tax for preceding quarters of calendar year (see instructions) . . ►	4	
5	Adjusted total of income tax withheld (line 3 as adjusted by line 4—see instructions)	5	3,820 20
6a	Taxable social security wages (Complete line 7) $ 34,370 50 × 12.4% (.124) =	6a	4,261 94
b	Taxable social security tips $ × 12.4% (.124) =	6b	
7	Taxable Medicare wages and tips . . . . . $ 34,370 50 × 2.9% (.029) =	7	996 74
8	Total social security and Medicare taxes (add lines 6a, 6b, and 7)	8	5,258 68
9	Adjustment of social security and Medicare taxes (see instructions for required explanation) . . .	9	
10	Adjusted total of social security and Medicare taxes (line 8 as adjusted by line 9—see instructions) ►	10	5,258 68
11	Backup withholding (see instructions)	11	
12	Adjustment of backup withholding tax for preceding quarters of calendar year. . . . ►	12	
13	Adjusted total of backup withholding (line 11 as adjusted by line 12)	13	
14	**Total taxes** (add lines 5, 10, and 13)	14	9,078 88
15	Advance earned income credit (EIC) payments made to employees, if any . . . ►	15	
16	Net taxes (subtract line 15 from line 14). **This should equal line IV below** (plus line IV of Schedule A (Form 941) if you have treated backup withholding as a separate liability)	16	9,078 88
17	**Total deposits for quarter,** including overpayment applied from a prior quarter, from your records. ►	17	9,078 88
18	**Balance due** (subtract line 17 from line 16). This should be less than $500. Pay to IRS . . . ►	18	-0-
19	**Overpayment,** if line 17 is more than line 16, enter here ► $ ______ and check if to be: ☐ Applied to next return **OR** ☐ Refunded.		

Record of Federal Tax Liability (You must complete if line 16 is $500 or more and Schedule B is not attached.) See instructions before checking these boxes.

Check only if you made deposits using the 95% rule ► ☐ Check only if you are a first time 3-banking-day depositor. . . ► ☐

Show tax liability here, **not deposits.** IRS gets deposit data from FTD coupons.

Do NOT Show Federal Tax Deposits Here

Date wages paid		First month of quarter		Second month of quarter		Third month of quarter
1st through 3rd	A		I		Q	
4th through 7th	B		J		R	
8th through 11th	C		K		S	
12th through 15th	D		L		T	
16th through 19th	E		M		U	
20th through 22nd	F		N		V	
23rd through 25th	G		O		W	
26th through the last	H		P		X	
Total liability for month	*I*	3,026.29	*II*	3,026.29	*III*	3,026.30

IV Total for quarter (add lines *I*, *II*, and *III*). **This should equal line 16 above** . . . . ►

Sign Here Under penalties of perjury, I declare that I have examined this return, including accompanying schedules and statements, and to the best of my knowledge and belief, it is true, correct, and complete.

Signature ► Gary De Shazo Print Your Name and Title ► President Date ► Oct. 25, 1992

For Paperwork Reduction Act Notice, see page 2.

end of that period. If the taxes are $100,000 or more at the end of any day, they must be paid by the end of the next banking day.

Reporting FUTA Taxes and SUTA Taxes

An employer's federal unemployment taxes are reported on an annual basis. The report is filed on an Annual Federal Unemployment Tax Return, Form 940. It must be mailed on or before January 31 following the end of each tax year. (Ten additional days are allowed for filing if all required tax deposits are made on a timely basis and the full amount of the tax is paid on or before January 31.) Payments of FUTA taxes are made quarterly to a federal depository bank if the total amount due exceeds $100. If $100 or less is due, the taxes are remitted annually with the Form 940.

Requirements for the payment and reporting of state unemployment taxes vary depending on the laws of the state. A requirement of quarterly payments and quarterly reports is typical.

Reporting Wages to Employees

Employers are required to provide each employee an annual report of the employee's wages subject to FICA and federal income taxes and the amounts of such taxes withheld. The report, a Wage and Tax Statement or Form W–2, must be given to the employee before January 31 following the year covered by the report. (Illustration F–2 shows an example of a Form W–2.)

Copies of the W–2 Forms must also be sent to the Social Security Administration, which posts to each employee's social security account the amount of the employee's wages subject to FICA tax and the FICA tax withheld. These posted amounts become the basis for determining the employee's retirement and survivor's benefits. The Social Security Administration also transmits to the Internal Revenue Service the amount of each employee's wages subject to federal income tax and the amount of such tax withheld.

Payroll Records Maintained by Employers

In addition to reports and payment of taxes, all employers must maintain certain payroll records. These generally include a **Payroll Register** for each pay period showing the pay period dates and the hours worked, gross pay, deductions, and net pay of each employee. An individual earnings record for each employee is also required.

The Payroll Register

Illustration F–3 shows a typical Payroll Register for a weekly pay period. Note that the columns under the heading Daily Time show the hours worked each day by each employee. If hours worked include overtime hours, these are entered in the column headed O.T. Hours.

ILLUSTRATION F-2

Reporting an Employee's Annual Wages and Taxes

1 Control number		OMB No. 1545-0008	
2 Employer's name, address, and ZIP code Graphic Planners, Inc. 907 Falcon Trail Austin, Texas 78746		6 Statutory employee ☐ Deceased ☐ Pension plan ☐ Legal rep. ☐ 942 emp. ☐ Subtotal ☐ Deferred compensation ☐ Void ☐	
		7 Allocated tips	8 Advance EIC payment
		9 Federal income tax withheld 2,460.00	10 Wages, tips, other compensation 24,560.60
3 Employer's identification number 74-1633163	4 Employer's state I.D. number 56-5678	11 Social security tax withheld 1,522.76	12 Social security wages 24,560.60
5 Employee's social security number 302-02-0222		13 Social security tips	14 Medicare wages and tips 24,560.60
19 Employee's name, address, and ZIP code Charles Robert Lusk 1310 East 5th Street Austin, Texas 78711		15 Medicare tax withheld 356.13	16 Nonqualified plans
		17 See Instrs. for Box 17	18 Other
20	21	22 Dependent care benefits	23 Benefits included in Box 10

24 State income tax	25 State wages, tips, etc.	26 Name of state	27 Local income tax	28 Local wages, tips, etc.	29 Name of locality

Copy B To Be Filed With Employee's FEDERAL Tax Return Department of the Treasury—Internal Revenue Service

Form **W-2 Wage and Tax Statement 1991**

This information is being furnished to the Internal Revenue Service.

The Regular Pay Rate column shows the hourly pay rate of each employee. Total hours worked multiplied by the regular pay rate equals regular pay. Overtime hours multiplied by the overtime premium rate equals overtime premium pay. Note that the overtime premium rate in this case is 50%. If employers are engaged in interstate commerce, federal law sets the minimum wage and overtime rate that must be paid to employees. In 1992, the minimum wage was $4.25 per hour. Also, the minimum overtime premium was 50% of the regular rate for hours worked in excess of 40 during any week. In other words, workers must earn at least 150% of their regular rate for hours in excess of 40 per week.

In Illustration F–3, notice the separate columns for each type of payroll deduction and for the expense accounts to which the payroll cost should be charged. As a result, the Payroll Register contains all of the data necessary to record the payroll in the General Journal.

ILLUSTRATION F–3

A Payroll Register

															Payroll Week ended
		Daily Time									**Earnings**				
Employees	**Clock Card No.**	**M**	**T**	**W**	**T**	**F**	**S**	**S**	**Total Hours**	**O.T. Hours**	**Reg-ular Pay Rate**	**Reg-ular Pay**	**O.T. Pre-mium Pay**	**Gross Pay**	
Robert Austin	114	8	8	8	8	8			40		10.00	400.00		400.00	
Judy Cross	102	8	8	8	8	8			40		15.00	600.00		600.00	
John Cruz	108	0	8	8	8	8	8		40		14.00	560.00		560.00	
Kay Keife	109	8	8	8	8	8	8		48	8	14.00	672.00	56.00	728.00	
Lee Miller	112	8	8	8	8	0			32		14.00	448.00		448.00	
Dale Sears	103	8	8	8	8	8	4		44	4	15.00	660.00	30.00	690.00	
Totals												3,340.00	86.00	3,426.00	

Employee's Individual Earnings Record

An **Employee's Individual Earnings Record,** as shown in Illustration F–4, provides a full year's summary of an employee's working time, gross earnings, deductions, and net pay. In addition, it accumulates information that indicates when an employee's earnings have reached the tax-exempt points for FICA and state and federal unemployment taxes. It also supplies the data the employer needs to prepare the Wage and Tax Statement, Form W–2. The payroll information on an Employee's Individual Earnings Record is taken from the Payroll Register.

Calculating Federal Income Tax Withholdings

The amount of tax to be withheld from each employee's wages is determined by the amount of the wages earned and the number of the employee's personal **withholding allowances.** Each employee indicates the number of withholding allowances claimed on a withholding allowance certificate (Form W–4) and gives it to the employer.

An employee's withholding allowances generally correspond to the personal exemptions that may be claimed on the employee's tax return. For example, in 1992, each personal exemption allowed the taxpayer to deduct $2,300 from yearly earnings in the process of calculating taxable income.

Most employers use a **wage bracket withholding table** similar to the one shown in Illustration F–5 to determine the federal income taxes to be withheld from each employee's gross pay. The illustrated table is for single employees who are paid weekly. Different tables are provided for married employees and for biweekly, semimonthly, and monthly pay periods.

When using the tables to determine the federal income tax to be withheld from an employee's gross wages, locate the employee's wage bracket in the

Register
March 23, 19—

Deductions						Payment		Distribution	
FICA TAXES									
Medicare	Social Security	Federal Income Taxes	Hosp. Ins.	Union Dues	Total Deductions	Net Pay	Check No.	Sales Salaries	Office Salaries
5.80	24.80	37.00	40.00		107.60	292.40	893		400.00
8.70	37.20	93.00	56.00	10.00	204.90	395.10	894	600.00	
8.12	34.72	82.00	56.00	10.00	190.84	369.16	895	560.00	
10.56	45.14	127.00	56.00	10.00	248.70	479.30	896	728.00	
6.50	27.78	53.00	56.00	10.00	153.28	294.72	897	448.00	
10.00	42.78	118.00	56.00		226.78	463.22	898		690.00
49.68	212.42	510.00	320.00	40.00	1,132.10	2,293.90		2,336.00	1,090.00

ILLUSTRATION F-4

Employee's Individual Earnings Record

Employee's Name Robert Austin S.S. Acct. No. 307-03-2195 Employee No. 114

Home Address 111 South Greenwood Notify in Case of Emergency Margaret Austin Phone No. 964-9834

Employed June 7, 1980 Date of Termination ____ Reason ____

Date of Birth June 6, 1962 Date Becomes 65 June 6, 2027 Male (X) Female ( ) Married (X) Single ( ) Number of Exemptions 1 Pay Rate $10.00

Occupation Clerk Place Office

Date		Time Lost		Time Worked					FICA Taxes							
Per. Ends	Paid	Hrs.	Reason	Total	O.T. Hours	Reg. Pay	O.T. Prem. Pay	Gross Pay	Medicare	Soc. Security	Fed. Income Taxes	Hosp. Ins.	Total Deductions	Net Pay	Check No.	Cumulative Pay
1/5	1/5			40		400.00		400.00	5.80	24.80	50.00	40.00	107.60	292.40	173	400.00
1/12	1/12			40		400.00		400.00	5.80	24.80	50.00	40.00	107.60	292.40	201	800.00
1/19	1/19			40		400.00		400.00	5.80	24.80	50.00	40.00	107.60	292.40	243	1,200.00
1/26	1/26	4	Sick	36		360.00		360.00	5.22	22.32	43.00	40.00	98.54	261.46	295	1,560.00
2/2	2/2			40		400.00		400.00	5.80	24.80	50.00	40.00	107.60	292.40	339	1,960.00
2/9	2/9			40		400.00		400.00	5.80	24.80	50.00	40.00	107.60	292.40	354	2,360.00
2/16	2/16			40		400.00		400.00	5.80	24.80	50.00	40.00	107.60	292.40	397	2,760.00
2/23	2/23			40		400.00		400.00	5.80	24.80	50.00	40.00	107.60	292.40	446	3,160.00
3/23	3/23			40		400.00		400.00	5.80	24.80	50.00	40.00	107.60	292.40	893	4,760.00

ILLUSTRATION F-5

A Wage Bracket Withholding Table

SINGLE Persons—WEEKLY Payroll Period
(For Wages Paid After February 1992)

And the wages are—		And the number of withholding allowances claimed is—										
At least	But less than	0	1	2	3	4	5	6	7	8	9	10
		The amount of income tax to be withheld shall be—										
$590	$600	$103	$90	$78	$66	$56	$49	$42	$36	$29	$22	$16
600	610	105	93	81	68	57	51	44	37	31	24	17
610	620	108	96	83	71	59	52	45	39	32	25	19
620	630	111	99	86	74	62	54	47	40	34	27	20
630	640	114	101	89	77	64	55	48	42	35	28	22
640	650	117	104	92	80	67	57	50	43	37	30	23
650	660	119	107	95	82	70	58	51	45	38	31	25
660	670	122	110	97	85	73	60	53	46	40	33	26
670	680	125	113	100	88	76	63	54	48	41	34	28
680	690	128	115	103	91	78	66	56	49	43	36	29
690	700	131	118	106	94	81	69	57	51	44	37	31
700	710	133	121	109	96	84	72	59	52	46	39	32
710	720	136	124	111	99	87	74	62	54	47	40	34
720	730	139	127	114	102	90	77	65	55	49	42	35
730	740	142	129	117	105	92	80	68	57	50	43	37
740	750	145	132	120	108	95	83	70	58	52	45	38
750	760	147	135	123	110	98	86	73	61	53	46	40
760	770	150	138	125	113	101	88	76	64	55	48	41
770	780	153	141	128	116	104	91	79	66	56	49	43
780	790	156	143	131	119	106	94	82	69	58	51	44
790	800	159	146	134	122	109	97	84	72	60	52	46
800	810	161	149	137	124	112	100	87	75	62	54	47
810	820	164	152	139	127	115	102	90	78	65	55	49
820	830	167	155	142	130	118	105	93	80	68	57	50
830	840	170	157	145	133	120	108	96	83	71	58	52
840	850	173	160	148	136	123	111	98	86	74	61	53
850	860	175	163	151	138	126	114	101	89	76	64	55
860	870	178	166	153	141	129	116	104	92	79	67	56
870	880	181	169	156	144	132	119	107	94	82	70	58
880	890	184	171	159	147	134	122	110	97	85	72	60

first two columns of the appropriate withholding table. Then, find the amount to be withheld by looking in the withholding allowance column appropriate for the employee.

Paying the Employees

In a company that has few employees, employees are paid with checks drawn on the regular bank account. A business with many employees normally uses a special **payroll bank account** to pay its employees. When such an account is used, one check for the total payroll is drawn on the regular bank account and deposited in the special payroll bank account. The entry to record this transaction is:

Mar.	23	Accrued Payroll Payable	2,293.90	
		Cash		2,293.90
		Transfer of cash to payroll bank account.		

Then, individual payroll checks are drawn on the payroll bank account. Because only one check for the payroll total is drawn on the regular bank account each payday, use of a special payroll bank account simplifies internal control, especially the reconciliation of the regular bank account. It may be reconciled without considering the payroll checks outstanding, and there may be many of these.

When companies use a payroll bank account, they often add a Check Number column to the Payroll Register. In this column, they enter the number of each employee's check. For example, look at Illustration F–3 and notice that check 893 was issued to Robert Austin. With this additional column, the payroll register serves as a permanent supplementary record of the wages earned by and paid to employees.

Summary of the Appendix in Terms of Learning Objective

LO 10. Employers report FICA taxes and federal income tax withholdings quarterly on Form 941. FUTA taxes are reported annually on Form 940. Annual earnings and deduction information are reported to each employee and to the federal government on Form W–2. An employer's payroll records include a Payroll Register for each pay period and an Employee's Individual Earnings Record for each employee.

Federal income tax withholdings depend on the employee's earnings and the number of withholding allowances claimed by the employee. Various wage bracket withholding tables are available for pay periods of different lengths and for several classes of employees such as single or married.

Employers with a large number of employees often use a separate payroll bank account. When this is done, the payment of employees is recorded with a single credit to Cash. This entry records the transfer of cash from the regular checking account to the payroll checking account.

Glossary

LO 8 Define or explain the words and phrases listed in the chapter glossary.

Bank discount interest deducted by a bank from the principal of the note when a debt is created. pp. 617–18

Bargain purchase option an option that allows the lessee to purchase the leased asset at the end of the lease period at a price sufficiently less than its expected fair value to make it likely that the option will be exercised. p. 631

Capital lease a lease that has essentially the same effect on the lessee and lessor as a purchase transaction in that the outcome is just as if the lessee obtained a loan and used the proceeds to purchase the leased asset; a lease is accounted for as a capital lease if it meets any of four criteria established by the FASB. pp. 630–34

Carrying amount of a lease the difference between the sum of the remaining rental payments less the unamortized discount. p. 634

Carrying amount of a note the face amount of a note minus the unamortized discount on the note. p. 629

Deferred income tax liability the estimated amount of income taxes that will have to be paid in future years as a result of temporary differences created by transactions that have already occurred. p. 646

Employee fringe benefits payments by an employer, in addition to wages and salaries, that are made to provide benefits for employees such as insurance coverage and retirement income programs. p. 638

Employee's individual earnings record a record of an employee's hours worked, gross pay, deductions, net pay, and certain personal information about the employee. pp. 654–55

Estimated liability an obligation that definitely exists but that has uncertainty about the amount that is to be paid. p. 612

Federal depository bank a bank authorized to accept deposits of amounts payable to the federal government. p. 650

FICA taxes taxes levied under the Federal Insurance Contributions Act, otherwise known as *social security* taxes; these taxes are paid by both employers and employees. p. 635

Financing lease another name for a capital lease. pp. 630–32

Merit rating an evaluation of an employer by a state, which reflects the employer's experience in maintaining steady employment for its employees or, alternatively, laying them off from time to time; a good rating reduces the employer's unemployment tax rate. p. 637

Operating lease a lease that merely gives the lessee the right to use the leased asset for the time period covered by the contract; an operating lease does not meet any of the criteria established by the FASB that would make it a capital lease. pp. 630–32

Payroll bank account a special bank account a company uses solely for the purpose of paying employees, by depositing in the account each pay period an amount equal to the total employees' net pay and drawing the employees' payroll checks on that account. pp. 656–57

Payroll Register a record for a pay period that shows the pay period dates and the hours worked, gross pay, deductions, and net pay of each employee. pp. 652, 654–55

Payroll tax a tax levied on employers and based on the amount of each employee's gross pay, including social security, medicare, and unemployment taxes. p. 635

Present value the amount of money that can be invested today at a given interest rate to accumulate a total value equal to a given amount to be received or paid at some future date or dates. pp. 621–25

Present value table a table that shows the present values of an amount to be received when discounted at various interest rates for various numbers of time periods, or that shows the present values of a series of equal payments to be received for a varying number of periods when discounted at various interest rates. pp. 622–23, 625

Product warranty a promise to a customer that obligates the seller or manufacturer for a limited period of time to pay for items such as replacement parts or repair costs if the product breaks or otherwise fails to perform. pp. 613–14

Wage bracket withholding table a table that shows the amounts of income tax to be withheld from employee's wage at various levels of earnings. pp. 654, 656

Withholding allowance a number used to reduce the amount of federal income tax withheld from an employee's pay, and corresponding to the personal exemptions the employee is allowed to subtract from annual earnings in calculating taxable income. p. 654

Synonymous Terms

Capital lease financing lease.

Carrying value of a note book value of a note.

FICA taxes social security taxes.

Warranty guarantee.

Objective Review

Answers to the following questions are listed at the end of this chapter. Be sure that you decide which is the one best answer to each question *before* you check the answers.

LO 1 Which of the following items would normally be classified as a current liability of a company that has a 14-month current operating cycle?

a. The portion of a long-term lease liability that is due within 14 months.
b. Salaries payable.
c. A note payable due in 10 months.
d. Accounts payable due in 12 months.
e. All of the above.

LO 2 Estimated liabilities include:

a. Obligations to pay an amount to an outside party if some uncertain future event occurs.
b. Obligations to pay a specific person on a specific date when the amount to be paid is uncertain but can be reasonably estimated.

c. Obligations to pay a specific amount to a specific person when the due date is not known.

d. Obligations to pay a specific amount on a specific date when the party to be paid is not known.

e. All of the above.

LO 3 An automobile was sold for $15,000 on June 1, 1993, with a one-year or 10,000-mile warranty. The warranty covers parts only. Based on past experience, warranty expense is estimated at 1.5% of the sales price. On March 1, 1994, the customer returned the car for warranty repairs. Replacement parts amounted to $75 and total labor charges were $60. The amount that should be recorded as warranty expense for the March 1 repair work performed is:

a. $ 0.

b. $ 60.

c. $ 75.

d. $135.

e. $225.

LO 4 A future payment should be reported on the balance sheet as a liability if:

a. The payment is contingent on a future event that is probable but the amount of the payment cannot be reasonably estimated.

b. The payment is contingent on a future event that is probable and the amount of the payment can be reasonably estimated.

c. The payment is contingent on a future event that is probable and the amount of the payment is certain.

d. The payment is contingent on a future event that is not probable but the amount of the payment can be reasonably estimated.

e. Both (*b*) and (*c*) are correct.

LO 5 A company enters into an agreement whereby it will make five semi-annual payments of $1,000 each, the first to be made in six months, plus an additional $15,000 payment to be made 30 months from now. If the annual rate of interest is 10%, the present value of these payments is

a. $ 9,934.40.

b. $12,536.00.

c. $13,104.30.

d. $13,643.00.

e. $16,082.00.

LO 6 On December 31, 1993, Fairview Paint Supply leased a building for 20 years. The building had a fair value of $400,000 and an estimated useful life of 30 years. Annual lease payments of $59,639.75 begin on December 31, 1994, and the prevailing interest rate available to Fairview Paint Supply was 14%. Which of the following expenses will be recognized on this lease during 1994?

a. Rental expense, $59,639.75.
b. Interest expense, $55,300.00.
c. Interest expense, $46,666.67.
d. Rental expense, $29,819.88.
e. Interest expense, $8,349.57.

LO 7 Midtown Repairs has one employee, who is paid $3,000 per month. Assume a federal unemployment tax rate of 0.8% and a state unemployment tax rate of 4.0% on the first $7,000 paid to each employee, and a FICA tax rate of 7.7%. The journal entry to record payroll taxes expense for March (the third month of the year) would include:

a. A $24 credit to Federal Unemployment Taxes Payable.
b. A $16 credit to Federal Unemployment Taxes Payable.
c. A $375 debit to Payroll Taxes Expense.
d. A $279 debit to Payroll Taxes Expense.
e. A $231 debit to FICA Taxes Payable.

LO 8 The interest deducted by a bank from the principal when a debt is created is called:

a. A bank discount.
b. A cash discount.
c. A debt guarantee.
d. A liability discount.
e. An interest deduction.

LO 9 In following the FASB's rules of accounting for income taxes:

a. Deferred tax liabilities are calculated as the amount shown to be due on the current year's tax return.
b. Income taxes expense is always more than the amount of income taxes currently payable.
c. A company may report a deferred income tax liability but would never report a deferred tax asset.
d. Income tax expense is calculated as the sum of the income taxes currently payable plus (or minus) the change in the deferred income tax liability that occurred during the year.
e. All of the above are correct.

LO 10 Which of the following steps must be completed when a company uses a special payroll bank account?

a. Record the information shown on the Payroll Register with a general journal entry.
b. Write a single check that is payable to Payroll Bank Account for the total amount of the payroll and record the payment with a debit to Accrued Payroll Payable and a credit to Cash.
c. Deposit a check for the total amount of the payroll in the payroll bank account.

d. Write individual payroll checks to be drawn on the payroll bank account.

e. All of the above.

A letter [E] or [F] identifies the questions, exercises, and problems that are based on Appendix E or Appendix F at the end of the chapter.

Questions for Class Discussion

1. What is a liability?
2. Are all expected future payments liabilities?
3. Define (*a*) a current liability and (*b*) a long-term liability.
4. If a liability is payable in 15 months, should it be classified as a current liability or as a long-term liability?
5. Three important factors about a liability may or may not be definite. What are those factors?
6. What is the nature of an estimated liability?
7. If a company has a definite obligation to pay a given amount of money to an outside party but the date the obligation must be paid is indefinite, should the obligation be reported as a liability on the balance sheet or disclosed as a contingent liability?
8. If a property tax liability is estimated at the end of year 1 and the actual payment of the liability in year 2 turns out to be more than the amount that was estimated, how is the excess accounted for in year 2?
9. What is the difference between a liability and a contingent liability?
10. Under what conditions should a contingency be reported on the balance sheet as a liability?
11. Why are product warranties often recorded as liabilities instead of being disclosed as contingent liabilities?
12. The legal position of a company may be strengthened by accepting a promissory note in exchange for granting a time extension on the due date of a customer's debt. Why?
13. What is the difference between a *loan* and a *discount* as those terms relate to borrowing money from a bank?
14. Which arrangement is more advantageous to a bank: (*a*) making a loan to a customer in exchange for the customer's $2,000, 90-day, 12% note or (*b*) making a loan to the customer by discounting the customer's $2,000 noninterest-bearing note for 90 days at 12%? Why?
15. Distinguish between bank discount and cash discount.
16. What determines the present value of $2,000 to be received at some future date?
17. Is $2,000 to be received in one year always worth less than a series of two $1,000 payments to be received semiannually for the next year?
18. If a $10,000 noninterest-bearing, five-year note is exchanged for a machine, the face amount of the note equals the sum of two different economic costs. What are these two costs?

19. If the Machinery account is debited for $10,000 and Notes Payable is credited for $10,000 in recording the acquisition of the machine described in Question 18, how will the buyer's financial statements be affected?
20. What is an advantage of leasing a plant asset over purchasing it outright?
21. Distinguish between an operating lease and a capital lease. Which causes an asset and a liability to appear on the balance sheet?
22. When a capital lease is to be recorded, how do you determine the amount to be debited to the asset account?
23. What are FICA taxes? Who pays these taxes and for what purposes are funds from FICA taxes used?
24. Who pays federal unemployment insurance taxes? What is the tax rate?
25. Who pays state unemployment insurance taxes?
26. What is an employer's unemployment merit rating? Why are such merit ratings assigned to employers?
27. What are employee fringe benefits? Identify some examples.

[E]28. Why does the taxable income of a business often differ from its net income?

[E]29. For financial accounting purposes, what is the importance of the distinction between permanent differences and temporary differences in income before taxes and taxable income?

30. In Lands' End, Inc.'s January 31, 1991, balance sheet that appears in Appendix K, what amount of the long-term debt was payable during the next year?

[E]31. The consolidated balance sheet of McDonald's Corporation appears in Appendix K. What amount of deferred income tax liability did the corporation report on December 31, 1990?

[F]32. What determines the amount that must be deducted from an employee's wages for federal income taxes?

[F]33. What is a wage bracket withholding table?

[F]34. What amount of income tax should be withheld from the salary of a single employee with three withholding allowances who earned $— in a week? What if the employee earned $— and had one withholding allowance? (Use the wage bracket withholding table in Illustration F–5 to find the answers.)

Exercises

Exercise 12–1
Property tax expense
(LO 3)

Throughout 1994, Rockland Supply Company owned property subject to county property taxes. The property's assessed valuation for tax purposes was $600,000. The 1993 tax levy was $1.10 per $100 of assessed valuation, and the company expected the 1994 rate to remain unchanged. In early August, the county announced that the 1994 tax levy would be $1.25 per $100 and that taxes would be due September 30, 1994. The annual taxes were paid on the due date. Prepare entries to record property tax expense for the months of July, August, and September.

Exercise 12–2
Product warranty expense
(LO 3)

Twin Oaks Electronics manufactures a product for $35 per unit and sells it for $52 per unit. In May, the company sold 60,000 units subject to a one-year warranty. According to the warranty, customers must pay a $5.75 service charge to return a defective unit and have it replaced by a new one. When a unit under warranty fails, the company simply discards the broken one and replaces it with a new unit. Past experience suggests a 1.5% failure rate of new products sold. In May, customers actually returned 750 defective units. Prepare summary entries as of the end of May to record product warranty expense and to record the replacement of the 750 units.

Exercise 12–3
Short-term notes payable
(LO 3)

On December 1, 1993, Rizutto Furniture Company borrowed $75,000 by giving a 60-day, 10% note payable. The company has a calendar-year accounting period and does not make reversing entries. Prepare general journal entries to record: (*a*) the issuance of the note, (*b*) the required year-end adjusting entry, and (*c*) the entry to pay the note on its due date.

Exercise 12–4
Discounted notes payable
(LO 3)

On December 1, 1993, Westwood Apparel discounted its own $75,000, 60-day note payable at the bank. The discount rate was 10%. Prepare general journal entries to record: (*a*) the issuance of the note; (*b*) the required December 31, 1993, adjusting entry; (*c*) the payment of the note on its due date; and (*d*) the interest expense on the note during 1994.

Exercise 12–5
Present value calculations
(LO 5)

Show calculations to produce the following:

(*a*) The present value of $50,000 to be received six years from now, discounted at 12%.

(*b*) The total present value of three payments consisting of $15,000 to be received two years from now, $20,000 to be received three years from now, and $45,000 to be received four years from now, all discounted at 8%.

(*c*) The present value of nine payments of $22,000 each, with a payment to be received at the end of each of the next nine years, discounted at 16%.

Exercise 12–6
Present value of investment
(LO 5)

AAA Service Company is offered an investment contract whereby it will be paid $6,000 every six months for the next five years. The first payment would be received six months from today. What will the company be willing to pay for this contract if it expects a 12% annual return on the investment? What if it expects an annual return of only 9%?

Exercise 12–7
Present value of investment
(LO 5)

Oakwood Corporation is offered an investment contract whereby it will be paid $8,000 annually for the next six years. The first payment would be received one year from today. What will the company be willing to pay for this contract if it expects a 16% annual return on the investment? What if it expects an annual return of only 12%?

Exercise 12–8
Choosing between payment patterns based on present values
(LO 5)

An individual has offered to sell equipment for $18,000. A potential buyer has agreed to purchase the equipment for the stated price but, as an alternative, has given the seller the option of receiving eight annual payments of $3,200 each, the first payment to be one year from now. Assuming the seller expects an annual return of at least 10%, which of the two alternatives should the seller accept?

Exercise 12–9
Exchanging a noninterest-bearing note for a plant asset
(LO 6)

Montvale Manufacturing Company purchased a machine on December 31, 1993. The terms of purchase included $8,000 cash plus a $20,000, noninterest-bearing, four-year note. The available interest rate on this date was 14%. (*a*) Prepare the entry to record the purchase of the machine. (*b*) Show how the liability will appear on a balance sheet prepared on the day of the purchase. (*c*) Prepare the entry to recognize interest expense and amortize a portion of the discount on the note at the end of 1994.

Exercise 12–10
Liabilities from leasing
(LO 6)

On December 31, 1993, a day when the available interest rate was 10%, North Point Printing Company leased equipment with an eight-year life under a contract calling for a $6,000 annual lease payment at the end of each of the next five years, with the equipment becoming the property of the lessee at the end of that period. Prepare entries to record: (*a*) the leasing of the equipment; (*b*) the recognition of interest expense on the lease liability at December 31, 1994; (*c*) depreciation expense for 1994; and (*d*) the December 31, 1994, payment under the lease.

Exercise 12–11
Journalizing payroll information
(LO 7)

On January 14, the end of its first pay period for the year, Fleming Company's January payroll record showed that its sales employees had earned $4,780 and its office employees had earned $2,400. The employees are to have the following items withheld from their paychecks: FICA taxes at 7.7%, $1,020 of federal income taxes, $210 of union dues, and $980 of hospitalization insurance premiums. Calculate the amount of FICA taxes to be withheld and give the general journal entry to record the payroll.

Exercise 12–12
Calculating payroll deductions and recording the payroll
(LO 7)

The following information about earnings and deductions for the pay period ended April 15 was taken from a company's payroll records:

Employees' Names	Gross Pay	Earnings to End of Previous Week	Federal Income Taxes	Medical Insurance Deductions
Chris Johnson	$1,100	$ 6,600	$150.00	$110.00
Amy Parker	1,850	11,100	234.00	65.00
Ed Gonzales	620	3,720	86.00	65.00
Jill Corbin	700	4,200	72.00	110.00
	$4,270		$542.00	$350.00

Required

Calculate the employees' FICA tax withholdings at the rate of 7.7% of wages paid to each employee (no employee has exceeded the base to which the rate is applied). Also calculate total FICA taxes withheld, total deductions, and net pay. Prepare a general journal entry to record the payroll. Assume all employees work in the office.

Exercise 12–13
Calculating and recording payroll taxes
(LO 7)

Use the information provided in Exercise 12–12 to complete the following requirements:

1. Prepare a general journal entry to record the employer's payroll taxes resulting from the payroll. Assume a state unemployment tax rate of 5.2% and a federal unemployment tax of 0.8% on the first $7,000 paid each employee.
2. Prepare a general journal entry to record the following employee benefits incurred by the company: (*a*) medical insurance costs to match the amounts contributed by each employee and (*b*) contributions equal to 15% of the gross pay for each employee's retirement income program.

Exercise 12–14
Analyzing total labor costs
(LO 7)

Kelley's Cosmetics employees earn a gross pay of $12 per hour and work 40 hours each week. The FICA tax rate is 7.7%, the federal unemployment tax rate is 0.8%, and the state unemployment tax rate is 4.4%. In addition, Kelley's Cosmetics contributes 15% of gross pay to a retirement program for employees and pays medical insurance premiums of $30 per week per employee. Assuming that all individuals' wages are less than the $7,000 unemployment tax limit, what is the average total cost of employing a person for one hour?

Exercise 12–15
Calculating the cost of payroll taxes and fringe benefits
(LO 7)

Paulsen Company's payroll taxes and fringe benefit expenses include unemployment taxes of 0.8% (federal) and 5.0% (state) on the first $7,000 of each employee's salary, FICA taxes of 6.2% on the first $56,000 plus 1.5% on the first $135,000 of each employee's salary, retirement fund contributions of 15% of total earnings, and medical insurance premiums of $90 per employee per month. Use the following list of employees' annual salaries to calculate the percentage of total gross salaries represented by payroll taxes and fringe benefits. (Round calculation results to the nearest dollar.)

Lozano	$140,000
Jones	50,000
Weissen	57,000
Keller	38,000

[E]Exercise 12–16
Recording corporate income tax expense
(LO 9)

Granger, Inc., began operations on January 1, 1993. During 1993, Granger, Inc.'s operations resulted in a current tax payable of $350,000. In addition, Granger sold land for $100,000 that had cost $20,000. The gain is subject to 34% income tax only when the cash is received on June 1, 1994. Present the December 31, 1993, entry to record Granger, Inc.'s income taxes.

[F]Exercise 12–17
Calculating gross and net pay
(LO 10)

Bonnie Morgan, an employee of a company subject to the Fair Labor Standards Act, worked 48 hours during the week ended January 12. Her pay rate is $14 per hour, and her wages are subject to no deductions other than FICA and federal income taxes. She claims two withholding allowances. Calculate her regular pay, overtime premium pay, gross pay, FICA tax deduction at an assumed 7.7% rate, income tax deduction (use the wage bracket withholding table of Illustration F–5), total deductions, and net pay.

Problems

Problem 12–1
Product warranty expense and property tax expense
(LO 2, 4)

Part 1. Faulkner Company buys and sells a single product subject to a six-month warranty that covers replacement parts but not labor. The company uses a periodic inventory system to account for merchandise. Prepare journal entries to record the following transactions completed by the company during the month of July. Cash was received or paid in each transaction.

July 6 Purchased 750 units of product for $40 per unit.

10 Purchased $2,300 of spare parts to be used in repairs to products that are expected to be returned for warranty work.

12 Sold 200 units of product for $75 per unit, receiving cash.

16 Repaired 12 units of product that customers returned under the warranty. Replacement parts cost $220, and the customers paid $180 for labor.

20 Sold 300 units of product for $80 per unit.

24 Repaired 18 units of product under the warranty. Replacement parts cost $310, and the customers paid $245 for labor.

31 Recorded warranty expense for July. Past experience shows that 3% of the units sold require warranty work, and the average cost of replacement parts is $17 per unit returned. Average labor charges are $13.95 per unit.

Part 2. Midland Flooring Company expects to accrue 1994 property taxes at the end of each month using the experience of 1993 to estimate the 1994 tax. In March 1993, Midland Flooring's property was assessed at $650,000. The 1993 tax levy was $1.50 per $100. In March 1994, Midland Flooring's property was reassessed at $720,000. (The reassessment was not expected to affect the tax levy of $1.50 per $100.) Early in August 1994, the annual tax levy was set at $1.80 per $100. On October 31, 1994, Midland Flooring paid the 1994 tax. Complete financial statements are prepared by the company every month.

Required

Prepare entries to be recorded at the end of January, March, August, October, and November 1994, to accrue property tax expense for each of those months and to record the annual tax payment.

Problem 12–2
Journalizing notes payable transactions
(LO 3)

Prepare general journal entries to record these transactions of Midtown Glass Company.

1993

Mar. 14 Purchased merchandise on credit from Precision Windows, invoice dated March 13, terms 2/10, n/30, $8,400.

Apr. 2 Borrowed money at American Security Bank by discounting Midtown's own $16,000 note payable for 90 days at 14%. (Because the note matures before the end of the year, the discount should be charged to Interest Expense.)

12 Gave Precision Windows $1,600 cash and a $6,800, 90-day, 14% note to secure an extension on Midtown's account that was due.

July 1 Paid the note discounted at American Security Bank on April 2.

11 Paid the note given Precision Windows on April 12.

Nov. 16 Borrowed money at American Security Bank by discounting Midtown's own $15,000 note payable for 60 days at 12%.

Dec. 16 Borrowed money at First Southwest Bank by giving an $18,500, 90-day, 12% note payable.

31 Made an adjusting entry to record interest on the November 16 note to American Security Bank.

31 Made an adjusting entry to record the accrued interest on the December 16 note to First Southwest Bank.

1994

Jan. 15 Paid the November 16 note to American Security Bank. Also recorded interest expense related to the note.

Mar. 16 Paid the principal and interest on the note given to First Southwest Bank on December 16.

Problem 12–3
Present values of alternative payment patterns
(LO 5)

Slawson Enterprises is negotiating with a contractor for the construction of a new office complex. The complex will be completed and ready for occupation two years from now. If Slawson pays for the complex immediately (Payment Plan A), it will cost $5,551,200. However, two alternative payment plans are available. Plan B would require a payment of $6,900,000 on completion. Plan C would require two annual payments of $3,600,000, the first of which would be made one year from now. In evaluating the three alternatives, the management of Slawson has decided to assume an interest rate of 14%.

Required

Calculate the present value of each payment plan and use the results to indicate which one Slawson Enterprises should choose.

Problem 12–4
Exchanging a noninterest-bearing note for a plant asset
(LO 6)

On January 1, 1993, Bertolet Company acquired an item of equipment by issuing a $500,000 noninterest-bearing, six-year note payable on December 31, 1998. A reliable cash price for the equipment was not readily available. The market rate of interest for notes like this one was 12% (annual) on the day of the exchange.

Required

(Round all amounts in your answers to the nearest whole dollar.)

1. Determine the initial net liability created by the issuance of this note.
2. Prepare a table showing the calculation of the amount of interest expense allocated to each year the note is outstanding and the carrying amount of the net liability at the end of each of those years.
3. Prepare general journal entries to record: (*a*) the acquisition of the equipment; (*b*) the amortization of the discount at the end of 1993, 1994, and 1995; and (*c*) the amortization of the discount and the payment of the note on December 31, 1998.
4. Show how the note should be presented on the December 31, 1995, balance sheet.

Problem 12–5
Capital leases and exchanges of plant assets
(LO 6)

Wesson Engineering Company leased a machine on January 1, 1993, under a contract calling for four annual payments of $15,000 on December 31 of 1993 through 1996, with the machine becoming the property of the lessee after the fourth payment. The machine was predicted to have a service life of six years and no salvage value, and the interest rate available to Wesson Engineering for equipment loans was 12% on the day the lease was signed. The machine was delivered on January 10, 1993, and was immediately placed in service. On January 4, 1998, it was overhauled at a total cost of $2,500. The overhaul did not increase the machine's efficiency but it did add two additional years to its expected service life. On June 30, 2000, the machine was traded in on a similar new machine having a $42,000 cash price. A $3,000 trade-in allowance was received, and the balance was paid in cash.

Required

(Round all amounts in your answers to the nearest whole dollar.)

1. Determine the initial net liability created by this lease and the cost of the leased asset.
2. Prepare a table showing the calculation of the amount of interest expense allocated to each year the lease is in effect and the carrying amount of the liability at the end of each of those years.
3. Prepare the entry to record the leasing of the machine.
4. Prepare entries that would be made on December 31, 1994, to record the annual depreciation on a straight-line basis, to record the lease payment,

and to amortize the discount. Also show how the machine and the lease liability should appear on the December 31, 1994, balance sheet.

5. Prepare the entries to record the machine's overhaul in 1998 and depreciation at the end of that year.
6. Prepare the entries that would be needed to record the exchange of the machines on June 30, 2000.

Problem 12–6
Accounting for capital and operating leases
(LO 6)

The Clearview Drilling Company needs two new trailers, each of which has an estimated service life of 12 years. The trailers could be purchased for $50,000 each, but Clearview does not have enough cash to pay for them. Instead, Clearview agrees to lease Trailer 1 for four years, after which the trailer remains the property of the lessor. In addition, Clearview agrees to lease Trailer 2 for six years, after which the trailer remains the property of the lessor. According to the lease contracts, Clearview must pay $13,000 annually for each trailer, with the payments to be made at the end of each lease year. Both leases were signed on December 31, 1993, at which time the prevailing interest rate available to Clearview for equipment loans was 14%.

Required

(Round all amounts in your answers to the nearest whole dollar.)

1. Determine whether each of these two leases is an operating or capital lease.
2. Prepare any required entries to record entering into the lease of (*a*) Trailer 1 and (*b*) Trailer 2.
3. Prepare the entries required on December 31, 1994, for (*a*) Trailer 1 and (*b*) Trailer 2. Use straight-line depreciation for any capital leases. (Remember, if the asset remains the property of the lessor, the lessee must take depreciation over the period of the capital lease.)
4. Trailer 1 was returned to the lessor on December 31, 1997, the end of the fourth and final year of the lease. Prepare the required entries as of December 31, 1997, for (*a*) Trailer 1 and (*b*) Trailer 2.
5. Show how Trailer 2 and the lease liability for the trailer should appear on the balance sheet as of December 31, 1997 (after the year-end lease payment).

[E]Problem 12–7
Reporting corporate tax expense with temporary differences between tax and financial accounting
(LO 9)

In each of the following cases, prepare a journal entry to record the income taxes on December 31, 1993. Each case involves a different company and is independent from the other cases.

Case 1

January 1, 1993, Deferred Income Tax Liability credit balance	$ 6,000
Taxable income on tax return	180,000
Tax rate in all years	15%

On December 31, 1993, an analysis of temporary differences shows that as a result of past transactions, future differences between taxable income and income before taxes will be:

In 1994, additional taxable income that will not appear on the income statement as income before taxes	$ 40,000

Case 2

January 1, 1993, Deferred Income Tax Liability credit balance	$ 6,000
Taxable income on tax return	120,000
Tax rate in all years	15%
On December 31, 1993, an analysis of temporary differences shows that as a result of past transactions, future differences between taxable income and income before taxes will be	None

Case 3

January 1, 1993, Deferred Income Tax Liability credit balance	$ 6,000
Taxable income on tax return	100,000
Tax rate in all years	15%
On December 31, 1993, an analysis of temporary differences shows that as a result of past transactions, future differences between taxable income and income before taxes will be:	
In 1994, additional taxable income that will not appear on the income statement as income before taxes	$ 30,000
In 1995, additional taxable income that will not appear on the income statement as income before taxes	60,000

Case 4

January 1, 1993, Deferred Income Tax Asset debit balance	$ 1,500
Taxable income on tax return	90,000
Tax rate in all years	15%
On December 31, 1993, an analysis of temporary differences shows that as a result of past transactions, future differences between taxable income and income before taxes will be	None

Case 5

January 1, 1993, Deferred Income Tax Liability credit balance	$ 9,000
Taxable income on tax return	130,000
Tax rate in 1993	15%
Tax rate in 1994 will be	20%
On December 31, 1993, an analysis of temporary differences shows that as a result of past transactions, future differences between taxable income and income before taxes will be:	
In 1994, additional taxable income that will not appear on the income statement as income before taxes	$ 60,000

[F]Problem 12–8
General journal entries for payroll transactions
(LO 7, 10)

A company has 10 employees, each of whom earns $1,300 per month and is paid on the last day of each month. All 10 have been employed continuously at this amount since January 1. On June 1, the following accounts and balances appeared in its ledger:

a. FICA Taxes Payable, $2,002. (The balance of this account represents the liability for both the employer and employees' FICA taxes for the May payroll only.)

b. Employees' Federal Income Taxes Payable, $1,850 (liability for May only).

c. Federal Unemployment Taxes Payable, $208 (liability for April and May together).

d. State Unemployment Taxes Payable, $1,040 (liability for April and May together).

e. Employees' Medical Insurance Payable, $2,400 (liability for April and May together).

During June and July, the company had the following payroll transactions:

June 5 Issued check payable to First State Bank, a federal depository bank authorized to accept employers' payments of FICA taxes and employee income tax withholdings. The $3,852 check was in payment of the May FICA and employee income taxes.

30 Prepared a general journal entry to record the June Payroll Record, which had the following column totals:

Office Salaries	Shop Wages	Gross Pay	FICA Taxes	Federal Income Taxes	Medical Insurance	Total Deductions	Net Pay
$5,200	$7,800	$13,000	$1,001	$1,850	$600	$3,451	$9,549

30 Recorded the employer's $600 liability for its matching contribution to the medical insurance plan of employees.

30 Issued checks payable to each employee in payment of the June payroll. (Record these with a single general journal entry.)

30 Prepared a general journal entry to record the employer's payroll taxes resulting from the June payroll. The company has a merit rating that reduces its state unemployment tax rate to 4.0% of the first $7,000 paid each employee. The federal rate is 0.8%.

July 9 Issued check payable to First State Bank in payment of the June FICA and employee income taxes.

11 Issued check payable to Independent Insurance Company in payment of the employee medical insurance premiums for the second quarter.

15 Issued check to the State Tax Commission for the April, May, and June state unemployment taxes. Mailed the check along with the second quarter tax return to the State Tax Commission.

31 Issued check payable to First State Bank. The check was in payment of the employer's federal unemployment taxes for the second quarter of the year.

31 Mailed Form 941 to the IRS, reporting the FICA taxes and the employees' federal income tax withholdings for the second quarter.

Required

Prepare the necessary general journal entries to record the transactions.

[F]Problem 12–9 •
The Payroll Register and the payroll bank account (LO 10)

On January 4, at the end of the first weekly pay period of the year, Stanwick Company's Payroll Register showed that its employees had earned $11,380 of office salaries and $32,920 of sales salaries. Withholdings from the employees' salaries were to include FICA taxes at an assumed rate of 7.7%, $6,430 of federal income taxes, $670 of medical insurance, and $420 of union dues. No employee earned more than $7,000.

Required

1. Calculate FICA taxes payable and prepare a general journal entry to record Stanwick Company's January 4 payroll.
2. Prepare a general journal entry to record Stanwick's payroll taxes resulting from the January 4 payroll. Assume Stanwick has a merit rating that reduces its state unemployment tax rate to 4.0% of the first $7,000 paid each employee. The federal unemployment tax rate is 0.8%.
3. Under the assumption Stanwick Company uses a payroll bank account and special payroll checks in paying its employees, give the general journal entry to transfer funds equal to the payroll from the regular bank account to the payroll bank account.
4. Answer this question: After the entry in requirement 3 is journalized and posted, are additional journal entries required to record the payroll checks and pay the employees?

Problem 12–10
Analytical essay
(LO 6)

On January 1, 1993, Compton Company made an entry like the following to record the receipt of cash in exchange for a six-year, noninterest-bearing note payable:

1993				
Jan.	1	Cash	xx,xxx.xx	
		Discount on Notes Payable	x,xxx.xx	
		Long-Term Notes Payable		xx,xxx.xx

Concerning the note, assume that the only dollar amounts you have knowledge of are the following:

a. The amount of the liability (net of discount) reported on the December 31, 1993, balance sheet.
b. The amount credited to the Discount on Notes Payable account on December 31, 1993.

Required

Explain how you would determine the following items, assuming you know only the preceding information. (Hint: You may find it helpful to review Illustration 12–4.)

1. The amount of the liability (net of discount) on the date the note was issued.
2. The market rate of interest on the date the note was issued.
3. The amount of the December 31, 1994, adjusting entry to amortize the discount for the note payable. (Adjustments are made annually on December 31.)
4. The face amount of the note. (Assume that you also have access to present value tables.)

Problem 12–11
Analytical essay
(LO 6)

On January 2, 1993, Hasting Company has decided to lease a delivery truck for four years. Lease payments are to be made on December 31, the end of Hasting's fiscal year. The truck has an estimated service life of eight years. The terms of the lease agreement are such that Hasting would account for the lease as an operating lease. At the last minute, Hasting and the lessor agree to change the period covered by the lease to be six years. Describe the entries Hasting Company should make in 1993 to account for the lease.

Alternate Problems

Problem 12–1A
Product warranty expense and property tax expense
(LO 2, 4)

Part 1. Harris & Sons buys and sells a single product subject to a one-year warranty that covers replacement parts but not labor. The company uses a periodic inventory system to account for merchandise. Prepare journal entries to record the following transactions completed by the company during the month of March. Cash was received or paid in each transaction.

Mar.	4	Purchased 7,200 units of product for $30 per unit.
	8	Purchased $18,500 of spare parts to be used in repairs to products that are expected to be returned for warranty work.
	11	Sold 3,900 units of product for $80 per unit, receiving cash.
	17	Repaired 150 units of product that customers returned under the warranty. Replacement parts cost $980 and the customers paid $1,250 for labor.
	20	Sold 4,100 units of product for $95 per unit.
	26	Repaired 176 units of product under the warranty. Replacement parts cost $1,125 and the customers paid $1,575 for labor.
	31	Recorded warranty expense for March. Past experience shows that 3% of the units sold require warranty work, and the average cost of replacement parts is $6.50 per unit returned. Average labor charges are $8.60 per unit.

Part 2. Odessa Paint Supply expects to accrue 1994 property taxes at the end of each month using the experience of 1993 to estimate the 1994 tax. In early 1993, Odessa's property was assessed at $300,000. The 1993 tax levy was $2.20 per $100. In April 1994, Odessa's property was reassessed at $330,000. (The reassessment was not expected to affect the tax levy of $2.20 per $100.) Early in June 1994, the annual tax levy was set at $2.40 per $100. On September 30, 1994, Odessa paid the 1994 tax. Complete financial statements are prepared by the company every month.

Required

Prepare entries to be recorded at the end of January, April, June, September, and October 1994, to accrue property tax expense for each of those months and to record the annual tax payment.

Problem 12–2A
Journalizing notes payable transactions
(LO 4)

Prepare general journal entries to record these transactions of Pine Company:

1993

Feb. 4 Purchased merchandise on credit from Ridgewood Supply Company, invoice dated February 3, terms 2/10, n/60, $35,200.

Mar. 2 Borrowed money at First Bank by discounting Pine's own $120,000 note payable for 30 days at 14%. (Because the note matures before the end of the year, the discount should be charged to Interest Expense.)

Apr. 1 Paid the note discounted at First Bank on March 2.

5 Gave Ridgewood Supply Company $11,200 cash and a $24,000, 30-day, 12% note to secure an extension on Pine's past-due account.

May 5 Paid the note given Ridgewood Supply Company on April 5.

Nov. 16 Borrowed money at First Bank by discounting Pine's own $108,000 note payable for 60 days at 10%.

Dec. 1 Borrowed money at Northwest National Bank by giving a $150,000, 90-day, 15% note payable.

31 Made an adjusting entry to record interest on the November 16 note to First Bank.

31 Made an adjusting entry to record the accrued interest on the December 1 note to Northwest National Bank.

1994

Jan. 15 Paid the November 16 note to First Bank and recorded interest expense on the note.

Mar. 1 Paid the principal and interest on the December 1 note given to Northwest National Bank.

Problem 12–3A
Present values of alternative payment patterns
(LO 5)

Seaside Amusement Park is negotiating with an engineering firm in planning the design and construction of a new roller coaster. The ride will be completed and ready for service five years from now. If Seaside pays for the roller coaster immediately (Payment Plan A), it will cost $950,000. However, two alternative payment plans are available. Plan B would require a payment of $1,325,000 on completion. Plan C would require five annual payments of $230,000, the first of which would be made one year from now. In evaluating the three alternatives, the management of Seaside has decided to assume an interest rate of 8%.

Required

Calculate the present value of each payment plan and use the results to indicate which one Seaside's management should choose.

Problem 12–4A
Exchanging a noninterest-bearing note for a plant asset
(LO 6)

On January 1, 1993, Fairview Manufacturing acquired an item of equipment by issuing a $390,000 noninterest-bearing, five-year note payable on December 31, 1997. A reliable cash price for the equipment was not readily available. The market rate of interest for notes like this one was 10% (annual) on the day of the exchange.

Required

(Round all amounts in your answers to the nearest whole dollar.)

1. Determine the initial net liability created by the issuance of this note.
2. Prepare a table showing the calculation of the amount of interest expense allocated to each year the note is outstanding and the carrying amount of the net liability at the end of each of those years.
3. Prepare general journal entries to record: (*a*) the acquisition of the equipment; (*b*) the amortization of the discount at the end of 1993, 1994, and 1995; and (*c*) the amortization of the discount and the payment of the note on December 31, 1997.
4. Show how the note should be presented on the December 31, 1996, balance sheet.

Problem 12–5A
Capital leases and exchanges of plant assets
(LO 6)

Stony Point Service Company leased a machine on January 1, 1993, under a contract calling for six annual payments of $130,000 on December 31 of 1993 through 1998, with the machine becoming the property of the lessee after the sixth payment. The machine was predicted to have a service life of seven years and no salvage value, and the interest rate available to Stony Point for equipment loans was 9% on the day the lease was signed. The machine was delivered on January 8, 1993, and was immediately placed in service. On January 2, 1996, it was overhauled at a total cost of $29,200. The overhaul did not increase the machine's efficiency but it did add an additional three years to its expected service life. On September 30, 1999, it was traded in on a similar new machine having a $330,000 cash price. A $65,000 trade-in allowance was received, and the balance was paid in cash.

Required

(Round all amounts in your answers to the nearest whole dollar.)

1. Determine the initial net liability created by this lease and the cost of the leased asset.
2. Prepare a table that shows the calculation of the amount of interest expense allocated to each year the lease is in effect and the carrying amount of the liability at the end of each of those years.
3. Prepare the entry to record the leasing of the machine.
4. Prepare entries that would be made on December 31, 1994, to record the annual depreciation on a straight-line basis, to record the lease payment, and to amortize the discount. Also show how the machine and the lease liability should appear on the December 31, 1994, balance sheet.
5. Prepare the entries to record the machine's overhaul in 1996 and depreciation at the end of that year.
6. Prepare the entries that would be needed to record the exchange of the machines on September 30, 1999.

Problem 12–6A
Accounting for capital and operating leases
(LO 6)

The Security Moving Company leased two new trucks. Each of the trucks has an estimated service life of six years. Truck 1 was leased for two years. Truck 2 was leased for three years. Each lease agreement calls for $75,000 annual lease payments at the end of that year. At the end of each lease, the truck will be returned to the lessor. Both leases were signed on December 31, 1993, at which time the prevailing interest rate available to Security Moving for equipment loans was 12%. Each of the trucks could have been purchased for $190,000 cash.

Required

(Round all amounts in your answers to the nearest whole dollar.)

1. Determine whether each of these two leases is an operating or capital lease.
2. Prepare any required entries to record entering into the lease of (*a*) Truck 1 and (*b*) Truck 2.
3. Prepare the entries required on December 31, 1994, for (*a*) Truck 1 and (*b*) Truck 2. Use straight-line depreciation for any capital leases. (Remember, if the asset remains the property of the lessor, the lessee must take depreciation over the period of the capital lease.)
4. Truck 1 was returned to the lessor on December 31, 1995, the end of the second and final year of the lease. Prepare the required entries as of December 31, 1995, for (*a*) Truck 1 and (*b*) Truck 2.
5. Show how Truck 2 and the lease liability for the truck should appear on the balance sheet as of December 31, 1995 (after the year-end lease payment).

[E]Problem 12–7A
Reporting corporate tax expense with temporary differences between tax and financial accounting (LO 9)

In each of the following cases, prepare a journal entry to record the income taxes on December 31, 1993. Each case involves a different company and is independent from the other cases.

Case 1

January 1, 1993, Deferred Income Tax Liability credit balance	$ 2,400
Taxable income on tax return	110,000
Tax rate in all years	15%
On December 31, 1993, an analysis of temporary differences shows that as a result of past transactions, future differences between taxable income and income before taxes will be:	
In 1994	None
In 1995, additional taxable income that will not appear on the income statement as income before taxes	$ 16,000

Case 2

January 1, 1993, Deferred Income Tax Liability credit balance	$ 7,200
Taxable income on tax return	190,000
Tax rate in all years	15%
On December 31, 1993, an analysis of temporary differences shows that as a result of past transactions, future differences between taxable income and income before taxes will be	None

Case 3

January 1, 1993, Deferred Income Tax Liability credit balance	$ 2,700
Taxable income on tax return	160,000
Tax rate in all years	15%
On December 31, 1993, an analysis of temporary differences shows that as a result of past transactions, future differences between taxable income and income before taxes will be:	
In 1994, additional taxable income that will not appear on the income statement as income before taxes	$ 30,000
In 1995, additional taxable income that will not appear on the income statement as income before taxes	24,000

Case 4

January 1, 1993, Deferred Income Tax Asset debit balance	$ 8,400
Taxable income on tax return	210,000
Tax rate in all years	15%
On December 31, 1993, an analysis of temporary differences shows that as a result of past transactions, future differences between taxable income and income before taxes will be	None

Case 5

January 1, 1993, Deferred Income Tax Liability credit balance	$ 9,600
Taxable income on tax return	150,000
Tax rate in 1993	15%
Tax rate in 1994 will be	22%
On December 31, 1993, an analysis of temporary differences shows that as a result of past transactions, future differences between taxable income and income before taxes will be:	
In 1994, additional taxable income that will not appear on the income statement as income before taxes	$ 64,000

[F]Problem 12–8A
General journal entries for payroll transactions
(LO 7, 10)

A company has six employees, each of whom earns $2,500 per month and is paid on the last day of each month. All six have been employed continuously at this amount since January 1. On March 1, the following accounts and balances appeared in its ledger:

a. FICA Taxes Payable, $2,310. (The balance of this account represents the liability for both the employer and employees' FICA taxes for the February payroll only.)

b. Employees' Federal Income Taxes Payable, $1,800 (liability for February only).

c. Federal Unemployment Taxes Payable, $240 (liability for January and February together).

d. State Unemployment Taxes Payable, $1,050 (liability for January and February together).

e. Employees' Medical Insurance Payable, $1,800 (liability for January and February together).

During March and April, the company had the following payroll transactions:

Mar. 10 Issued check payable to Union National Bank, a federal depository bank authorized to accept employers' payments of FICA taxes and employee income tax withholdings. The $4,110 check was in payment of the February FICA and employee income taxes.

31 Prepared a general journal entry to record the March Payroll Record, which had the following column totals:

Office Salaries	Shop Wages	Gross Pay	FICA Taxes	Federal Income Taxes	Medical Insurance	Total Deductions	Net Pay
$5,000	$10,000	$15,000	$1,155	$1,800	$450	$3,405	$11,595

31 Recorded the employer's $450 liability for its matching contribution to the medical insurance plan of employees.

31 Issued checks payable to each employee in payment of the March payroll. (Record these with a single general journal entry.)

31 Prepared a general journal entry to record the employer's payroll taxes resulting from the March payroll. The company has a merit rating that reduces its state unemployment tax to 3.5% of the first $7,000 paid each employee. The federal rate is 0.8%.

Apr. 4 Issued check payable to Union National Bank in payment of the March FICA and employee income taxes.

9 Issued check payable to Hawthorn Insurance Company in payment of the employee medical insurance premiums for the first quarter.

15 Issued check to the State Tax Commission for the January, February, and March state unemployment taxes. Mailed the check along with the first quarter tax return to the State Tax Commission.

30 Issued check payable to Union National Bank. The check was in payment of the employer's federal unemployment taxes for the first quarter of the year.

30 Mailed Form 941 to the IRS, reporting the FICA taxes and the employees' federal income tax withholdings for the first quarter.

Required

Prepare general journal entries to record the transactions.

[F]Problem 12–9A
The Payroll Register and the payroll bank account
(LO 10)

Talbot Company's first weekly pay period of the year ended on January 3. On that date, the column totals of Talbot's Payroll Register indicated its sales employees had earned $69,490, its office employees had earned $42,450, and its delivery employees had earned $2,060. The employees were to have FICA taxes withheld from their wages at an assumed 7.7% rate plus $17,250 federal income taxes, $2,320 medical insurance deductions, and $275 of union dues. No employee earned more than $7,000.

Required

1. Calculate FICA taxes payable and prepare a general journal entry to record Talbot Company's January 3 payroll.
2. Prepare a general journal entry to record Talbot's payroll taxes resulting from the January 3 payroll. Assume the company has a merit rating that reduces its state unemployment tax rate to 3.4% of the first $7,000 paid each employee. The federal unemployment tax rate is 0.8%.
3. Under the assumption Talbot Company uses special payroll checks and a payroll bank account in paying its employees, give the general journal entry to transfer funds equal to the payroll from the regular bank account to the payroll bank account.
4. After the entry in requirement 3 is journalized and posted, are additional journal entries required to record the payroll checks and pay the employees?

Problem 12–10A
Analytical essay
(LO 6)

On January 1, 1993, Steck Corporation made an entry like the following to record the receipt of cash in exchange for a five-year, noninterest-bearing note payable:

1993				
Jan.	1	Cash	xx,xxx.xx	
		Discount on Notes Payable	x,xxx.xx	
		Long-Term Notes Payable		xx,xxx.xx

Concerning the note, assume that the only dollar amounts you have knowledge of are the following:

a. The amount of the liability (net of discount) reported on the December 31, 1994, balance sheet.
b. The amount of the liability (net of discount) reported on the December 31, 1993, balance sheet.

Required

Explain how you would determine the following items, assuming you know only the preceding information. (Hint: You may find it helpful to review Illustration 12–4.)

1. The amount of the December 31, 1994, adjusting entry to amortize the discount on the note payable.
2. The market rate of interest on the date the note was issued.
3. The face amount of the note.

Problem 12–11A
Analytical essay
(LO 6)

On January 1, 1994, Jester Corporation is negotiating the lease of equipment for 10 years. The equipment has an estimated service life of 12 years. Tentatively, the lease agreement stipulates that lease payments are to be made on December 31, the end of Jester's fiscal year. Ownership does not transfer to Jester at the end of the 10 years. The lease agreement does not contain a bargain purchase option and the present value of the lease payments is 88% of the fair value of the equipment. Jester wants to account for the lease as an operating lease.

Required

Suggest a revision to the lease contract that would accommodate Jester. Describe the entries Jester Corporation would make in 1994 to account for the lease under the revised lease agreement. How should Jester report the lease on the 1994 financial statements?

Provocative Problems

Provocative Problem 12–1
Wiggins Supply Company
(LO 6)

Wiggins Supply Company is planning to acquire some new equipment from Clarksville Corporation and has asked you to assist in analyzing the situation. The equipment may be purchased for $750,000 and then leased by Wiggins under a six-year lease contract to a customer for $160,000 payable at the end of each year. After the lease expires, Wiggins expects to sell the equipment for $260,000.

1. Suppose Wiggins has $750,000 cash available to buy the equipment and requires a 12% rate of return on its investments. Should the company buy the equipment and lease it to the customer?
2. As an alternative to paying cash, Wiggins can invest the $750,000 in other operations for four years and earn 12% annually on its investment. If this is done, the equipment may be purchased by signing a $1,150,000, four-year, noninterest-bearing note payable to Clarksville Corporation. Should Wiggins pay $750,000 now or sign the $1,150,000 note?
3. Now suppose Wiggins does not have the option of signing a $1,150,000, four-year, noninterest-bearing note. Instead, the company may either pay $750,000 cash or lease the equipment from Clarksville Corporation for four years, after which the equipment would become the property of Wiggins. The lease contract would require $250,000 payments at the end of each year. If Wiggins leases the equipment, it will invest the $750,000 available cash in other operations and earn 12% on the investment. Should Wiggins pay cash or lease the equipment from Clarksville Corporation?

Provocative Problem 12–2
Quality Furniture Company
(LO 7)

Quality Furniture Company has 100 regular employees, each of whom earns more than $7,000 per year. The company's plant and office is located in a state with a maximum unemployment tax rate of 5.4% on the first $7,000 paid to each employee. The company's excellent past unemployment record has given it a merit rating that reduces its state unemployment tax rate to 4.0%.

The company has recently received an order for a line of leather sofas and chairs from a chain of department stores. The order should be very profitable and will probably be repeated each year. In filling the order, Quality Furniture can manufacture the furniture with its present equipment. However, it will have to add 40 persons to its work force for 40 hours per week for eight weeks to finish the furniture and pack it for shipment.

The company can hire these workers or it can secure the services of 40 people through TempServ, Inc. Quality Furniture would pay TempServ $10.00 for each hour worked by each person. The people will be employees of TempServ, which will pay their wages and all payroll taxes and benefits. On the other hand, if Quality Furniture employs the workers, it would pay them $8.25 per hour and also pay the following payroll taxes: FICA tax, 7.7%; federal unemployment tax, 0.8%; state unemployment tax, 5.0%. (The state unemployment tax rate will be 5.0% because, if the company hires the employees and terminates them each year after 8 weeks, it will receive a less favorable merit rating that will apply to all employees.) The company would also have to pay medical insurance benefits of $40 per employee per week.

On the basis of the costs under the two alternatives, should Quality Furniture hire additional workers or should it secure labor services through TempServ? Explain your answer.

Provocative Problem 12–3
Tridata Computer Company
(LO 7)

Tridata Computer Company employs a computer systems analyst at an annual salary of $58,800. The company pays federal unemployment taxes of 0.8% and state unemployment taxes of 4.2% on the first $7,000 of the analyst's wages. The social security portion of the FICA taxes is assumed to be 6.2% of the first $56,000, and the medicare portion 1.5% of the first $130,000. The company also pays $90 per month for the employee's medical insurance. Effective April 1, the company agreed to contribute 10% of the analyst's gross pay to a retirement program.

What was the total monthly cost of employing the analyst in January, March, May, and December? Assuming the employee works 170 hours each month, what is the average cost per hour in each of these four months? If the gross salary is increased by $6,000 for the next year, what will be the increase in the total annual cost of employing the analyst?

[E]**Provocative Problem 12–4**
Communication Services, Inc.
(LO 9)

Samuel and Lois Ungerson own all the outstanding stock of Communication Services, Inc., which they organized several years ago. The company is growing rapidly and needs additional capital. Lewis Trager, a potential investor, examined the following comparative income statement prepared by the company's bookkeeper:

COMMUNICATION SERVICES, INC.
Comparative Income Statement
For the Years 1993 and 1994

	1993	1994
Sales	$672,000	$768,000
Expenses other than income taxes	518,400	556,800
Income before income taxes	$153,600	$211,200
Federal income taxes	53,760	72,960
Net income	$ 99,840	$138,240

Trager expressed a tentative willingness to invest the required capital by purchasing a portion of the corporation's unissued stock. But, before making a final decision, Trager asked permission for his own accountant to examine the accounting records of the corporation. Because they needed the capital, the Ungersons granted permission. After the examination was made, the accountant prepared the following revised income statement covering the same periods:

COMMUNICATION SERVICES, INC.
Comparative Income Statement
For the Years 1993 and 1994

	1993	1994
Sales	$672,000	$768,000
Expenses other than income taxes	518,400	556,800
Income before income taxes	$153,600	$211,200
Income taxes expense	61,440	84,480
Net income	$ 92,160	$126,720

The accountant explained that the records were in good shape except for the measurement of the income tax expense. The adjustments arose from the fact that the bookkeeper did not consider the effects of temporary differences created by different financial and tax accounting procedures. No temporary differences existed prior to 1993 and those that occurred in 1993 and 1994 are expected to reverse in 1996.

The Ungersons were surprised at the change in the annual net incomes and did not understand the accountant's explanation. You have been asked to explain why there is a difference between the net income figures on the two sets of statements. Prepare calculations that will help you explain the difference. Assume a 40% income tax rate on all taxable income.

Provocative Problem 12–5
International Business Machines Corporation
(LO 1, 6, 7, 9)

Look in Appendix J at the financial statements for International Business Machines Corporation and the accompanying footnotes, and answer the following questions:

1. Examine the footnote on long-term debt, and find the discount on the liabilities. What does the amount of the discount in relation to total long-term debt indicate about the market interest rates compared to the face interest rates at the time the debt was issued?
2. Examine the footnote on rental expense and lease commitments. Is IBM a party to any lease contracts as a lessee? If so, are they capital leases or operating leases? How much expense was reported for 1990 from these leases? What kind of property is being leased?
3. Examine the footnote on retirement plans. Find the item labeled "Net periodic pension cost," and identify the cost for U.S. and non-U.S. pension plans for 1990, 1989, and 1988. Determine the combined net periodic pension cost for the two types of plans for each year. Also determine the percentage of earnings before income taxes that this cost represents for each year.

[E]4. Assume that IBM accounts for income taxes in accordance with the FASB's standard on accounting for income taxes (*SFAS 109*). Based on the (provision for) income taxes expense and the earnings before taxes reported on the income statement, what was the apparent income tax rate for 1990, 1989, and 1988? From the balance sheet, determine the change in the balance of the deferred income tax liability that occurred in 1990.

Comprehensive Problem

Corley Owney Exterminator Company (Review of Chapters 1–12)

The following December 31, 1993, unadjusted trial balance is for the Corley Owney Exterminator Company, which provides both interior and exterior pest control services. In addition, the company sells extermination products manufactured by other companies.

CORLEY OWNEY EXTERMINATOR COMPANY
Unadjusted Trial Balance
December 31, 1993

Cash	$ 62,700	
Accounts receivable	56,250	
Allowance for doubtful accounts		$ 750
Merchandise inventory	42,100	
Trucks	25,000	
Accumulated depreciation, trucks		–0–
Equipment	192,500	
Accumulated depreciation, equipment		129,000
Leasehold improvements	–0–	
Accounts payable		12,900
Estimated warranty liability		4,680
Unearned extermination services revenue		–0–
Long-term notes payable		75,000
Discount on notes payable	27,338	
Corley Owney, capital (December 31, 1992, balance)		63,778
Corley Owney, withdrawals	55,000	
Extermination services revenue		284,200
Interest earned		1,400
Sales		177,400
Purchases	119,900	
Depreciation expense, trucks	–0–	
Depreciation expense, equipment	–0–	
Wages expense	45,500	
Interest expense	–0–	
Rent expense	82,620	
Bad debts expense	–0–	
Miscellaneous expenses	9,800	
Repairs expense	16,800	
Utilities expense	13,600	
Warranty expense	–0–	
Totals	$749,108	$749,108

The following additional information is available:

a. The bank statement reconciliation on December 31, 1993, showed these items:

Balance per bank	$58,105
Balance per books	62,700
Outstanding checks	8,430
Deposit in transit	12,000
Interest earned	125
Service charges (miscellaneous expenses)	40
Included with the bank statement was a canceled check the company had failed to record (the amount of the check, which was a payment of an account payable, can be determined from the preceding information)	?

b. An examination of customers' accounts shows that accounts totaling $365 should be written off as uncollectible. In addition, the ending balance of the allowance account should be $840.

c. A truck was purchased and placed in service on July 1, 1993, and is being depreciated under the declining-balance method at twice the straight-line rate. These facts are also known:

Original cost	$25,000
Expected salvage value	3,000
Useful life	4 years

d. Two items of equipment (No. 7 and No. 9) were purchased in January 1990 and are being depreciated by the sum-of-the-years'-digits method. These facts are known about these assets:

	No. 7	No. 9
Original cost	$124,500	$68,000
Expected salvage value	19,500	5,000
Useful life	5 years	6 years

e. On October 1, 1993, Owney was paid $10,500 in advance to provide extermination services each month for an apartment complex for one year. Services began in October and the amount received was recorded in the Extermination Services Revenue account.

f. The expected cost of servicing items sold this year under warranty is estimated to be 3% of sales. No warranty expense has been recorded for 1993.

g. The $75,000 long-term note is a five-year, noninterest-bearing note obtained from First City Bank on December 31, 1991. The interest rate available to Corley Owney on the date of the loan was 12%.

h. In January 1993, Owney put a new storefront on the building she was leasing. These improvements totaled $16,800 and were recorded in the Repairs Expense account. The expected life of the improvements is six years but the remaining life of the lease is only four years. Owney is planning to move to a new location at the end of the four years.

i. In drafting the income statement and preparing the closing entries, a measure of the ending inventory is needed. It is measured with the retail method, and this information is known for 1993:

	Cost	Retail
Beginning inventory	$ 42,100	$ 64,600
Purchases	119,900	192,400
Additional markups		13,000
Markdowns		7,250
Sales		177,400

Required

1. Prepare a work sheet for the company using the preceding information.
2. Journalize entries resulting from the bank reconciliation and journalize the adjusting entries. Also present all calculations that support the entries.

3. Journalize closing entries for the company.
4. Prepare a single-step income statement with a supporting calculation of cost of goods sold, a statement of changes in owner's equity, and a classified balance sheet.

Answers to Objective Review Questions

LO 1 (*e*)	LO 5 (*e*)	LO 8 (*a*)
LO 2 (*b*)	LO 6 (*b*)	LO 9 (*d*)
LO 3 (*a*)	LO 7 (*d*)	LO 10 (*e*)
LO 4 (*e*)		

CHAPTER

13

Partnership Accounting

As a business enterprise becomes more complex, it needs more human and financial resources. A partnership allows the owners to pool their talents and funds to achieve more than they could individually. A partnership also creates needs for special accounting information.

Topical Coverage

The early chapters of this book introduced the three common types of business organizations: single proprietorships, partnerships, and corporations. In this chapter, we examine the partnership form of business in greater detail. The partnership form is widely used, especially in businesses where the owners know each other well. Many professional businesses, including CPA firms, are organized as partnerships.

Learning Objectives

After studying Chapter 13, you should be able to:

1. List the characteristics of a partnership and explain the concepts of mutual agency and unlimited liability in a partnership.
2. Allocate partnership earnings to partners (*a*) on a stated fractional basis, (*b*) in the partners' capital ratio, and (*c*) through the use of salary and interest allowances.
3. Prepare entries for (*a*) the sale of a partnership interest, (*b*) the admission of a new partner by investment, and (*c*) the retirement of a partner by the withdrawal of partnership assets.
4. Prepare entries required in the liquidation of a partnership.
5. Define or explain the words and phrases listed in the chapter glossary.

Characteristics of Partnerships

LO 1 List the characteristics of a partnership and explain the concepts of mutual agency and unlimited liability in a partnership.

Many businesses, such as small retail and service businesses, are organized as partnerships. Also, many professional practitioners—physicians, lawyers, and certified public accountants—have traditionally organized their practices as partnerships. In most states, the laws that govern the formation and operation of such partnerships are modeled after the Uniform Partnership Act. This act defines a **partnership** as "an association of two or more persons to carry on as co-owners a business for profit." Another definition of a partnership is "an association of two or more competent persons under a contract to combine some or all of their property, labor, and skills in the operation of a business." Both of these definitions say something about the legal nature of a partnership. However, the nature of the partnership form of business becomes clearer when you understand some of the specific features that characterize partnerships.

A Voluntary Association

A partnership is a voluntary association between the partners. This voluntary nature of a partnership is important because a person assumes some risk by entering a partnership. For example, each partner is responsible for the business acts of his or her partners when the acts are within the scope of the partnership. Also, a partner is personally liable for all of the debts of his or her partnership. As a result, you never have to join a partnership without agreeing who will be the partners. Normally, you should select only financially responsible people who have good judgment.

Based on a Contract

One advantage of a partnership as a form of business organization is that it is easy to organize. All that is necessary is for two or more legally competent people to agree to become partners. Their agreement becomes a **partnership contract.** This contract should be carefully written so that all anticipated points of future disagreement are covered. However, even if the partners make their agreement orally and fail to put it in writing, the partnership contract is binding.

Limited Life

The life of a partnership is always limited. Death, bankruptcy, or anything that takes away the ability of one of the partners to contract automatically ends a partnership. In addition, because a partnership is based on a contract, the contract may stipulate a period of time after which the partnership ends. If the contract does not specify a time period, the partnership ends when the business for which it was created is completed. Or, if no time is stated because the business is expected to go on indefinitely, the partnership may be terminated at will by any one of the partners.

Mutual Agency

In many partnerships, the relationship between the partners involves **mutual agency.** This means that every partner is an agent of the partnership. As its agent, a partner can commit or bind the partnership to any contract that is within the apparent scope of the partnership's business. For example, a partner in a merchandising business can sign contracts that bind the partnership to buy merchandise, lease a store building, borrow money, or hire employees. These activities are all within the scope of the business of a merchandising firm. On the other hand, a partner in a law firm, acting alone, cannot bind his or her partners to a contract to buy merchandise for resale or rent a retail store building. These actions are not within the normal scope of a law firm's business.

Partners may agree to limit the power of any one or more of the partners to negotiate certain contracts for the partnership. Such an agreement is binding on the partners and on outsiders who know that it exists. However, it is not binding on outsiders who do not know that it exists. Outsiders who are not aware of the agreement have the right to assume that each partner has the right to act as an agent for the partnership.

Because mutual agency exposes all partners to the risk of unwise actions by any one partner, carefully evaluate your potential partners before agreeing to join a partnership. The importance of this advice is underscored by the fact that most partnerships are also characterized by unlimited liability. Mutual agency and unlimited liability are the main reasons why most partnerships have only a few members.

Unlimited Liability

When a partnership cannot pay its debts, the creditors normally can satisfy their claims from the *personal* assets of the partners. Also, if the property of one partner is insufficient to meet his or her share of the partnership's debts, the creditors can turn to the assets of the remaining partners who are able to pay. Thus, a partner may be called on to pay all the debts of the partnership. This **unlimited liability of partners** is a very important characteristic of partnerships.

To illustrate the concept of unlimited liability, suppose that Tom Anderson and Carol Brown each invested $5,000 in a store to be operated as a partnership. They also agreed to share incomes and losses equally. Anderson has no property other than his $5,000 investment. However, Brown has sizable savings in addition to her investment. The partners rented a store and bought merchandise for $32,000. They paid $10,000 in cash and promised to pay the $22,000 balance later. However, before the business opened, the store burned and the merchandise was totally destroyed. There was no insurance and all the partnership assets were lost. Unlimited liability means that the partnership creditors can try to collect the full $22,000 of their claims from Brown because Anderson has no other assets. However, Brown can later try to collect $11,000 from Anderson, if he is ever able to save that much money. Partnerships in which all of the partners have unlimited liability are called **general partnerships.**

Limited Partnerships

So far, we have said that all partners normally have unlimited liability. Sometimes, however, individuals who want to invest in a partnership are not willing to accept the risk of unlimited liability. Their needs can be met by using a **limited partnership.** A limited partnership has two classes of partners, general and limited. At least one partner has to be a **general partner** who must assume unlimited liability for the debts of the partnership. The remaining **limited partners** have no personal liability beyond the amounts that they invest in the business. Usually, a limited partnership is managed by the general partner or partners. The limited partners have no active role except for major decisions specified in the partnership agreement.

Advantages and Disadvantages of a Partnership

Limited life, mutual agency, and unlimited liability are disadvantages of a partnership. Yet, there are other reasons why a partnership may be a preferred form of business organization. A partnership has the advantage of being able to bring together more money and skills than a single proprietorship. A partnership is easier to organize than a corporation. Also, a partnership may escape some of the federal and state regulations and taxes imposed on corporations. Finally, partners may act without having to hold stockholders' or directors' meetings, which are required of a corporation.

Partnership Accounting

Accounting for a partnership does not differ from accounting for a single proprietorship except for transactions directly affecting the partners' equities. Because ownership rights in a partnership are divided among two or more partners, partnership accounting requires the use of

- A capital account for each partner.
- A withdrawals account for each partner.
- An accurate measurement and division of earnings.

When a partner invests in a partnership, his or her capital account is credited for the amount invested. Withdrawals of assets by a partner are debited to his or her withdrawals account. And, in the end-of-period closing procedure, each partner's capital account is credited or debited for a share of the net income or loss. Finally, the withdrawals account of each partner is closed to that partner's capital account. These closing procedures are like those used for a single proprietorship. The only difference is that separate capital and withdrawals accounts are maintained for each partner. Thus, the closing procedures for a partnership require no further consideration. However, the matter of dividing the partnership's earnings among the partners requires additional discussion.

Nature of Partnership Earnings

Because they are its owners, partners cannot enter into an employer-employee contractual relationship with the partnership. They cannot legally hire themselves or pay themselves salaries. If partners devote their time and services to the affairs of their partnership, they are understood to do so for profit, not for salary. Therefore, when you calculate the net income of a partnership, salaries to partners are not deducted as expenses on the income statement. However, when the net income or loss of the partnership is allocated among the partners, the partners may agree to base part of the allocation on salary allowances that reflect the relative amounts of service provided by the partners. Likewise, if the services of one partner are much more valuable than those of another, salary allowances provide for the unequal service contributions.

Partners are also understood to have invested in a partnership for profit, not for interest. Nevertheless, partners may agree that the division of partnership earnings should include a return based on their invested capital. For example, if one partner contributes five times as much capital as another, it is only fair that this fact be taken into consideration when earnings are allocated among the partners. Thus, a partnership agreement may provide for interest allowances based on the partners' capital balances. Like salary allowances, interest allowances are not expenses to be reported on the income statement.

Division of Earnings

In the absence of a contrary agreement, the law states that the incomes and losses of a partnership are shared equally by the partners. However, partners may agree to any method of sharing. If they agree on how they will share incomes but say nothing about losses, then losses are shared in the same way as income.

LO 2 Allocate partnership earnings to partners (*a*) on a stated fractional basis, (*b*) in the partners' capital ratio, and (*c*) through the use of salary and interest allowances.

Several methods of sharing partnership earnings can be used. Three frequently used methods divide earnings: (1) on a stated fractional basis, (2) on the ratio of capital investments, or (3) partially on salary and interest allowances with any remainder in a fixed ratio.

Earnings Allocated on a Stated Fractional Basis

The easiest way to divide partnership earnings is to give each partner a fraction of the total. When this basis is used, the partners may receive equal fractions if their service and capital contributions are equal. Or, if their service and capital contributions are not equal, the agreement may provide for an unequal sharing. All that is necessary is for the partners to agree on the fractional share that each will receive.

For example, assume that the partnership agreement of Morse and North states that Morse will receive two thirds and North will receive one third of the partnership earnings. In accounting for the partnership, this agreement shapes the entry to close the Income Summary account. If the partnership's net income is $30,000, the following entry closes the Income Summary account and allocates the earnings to the partners.

Dec.	31	Income Summary	30,000.00	
		A. P. Morse, Capital		20,000.00
		R. G. North, Capital		10,000.00
		To close the Income Summary account and allocate the earnings.		

Division of Earnings Based on the Ratio of Capital Investments

If the nature of a partnership's business is such that earnings are closely related to money invested, a division of earnings based on the ratio of partners' investments offers a fair sharing method. To illustrate this method, assume that Chase, Davis, and Fall have agreed to share earnings in the ratio of their investments. These are: Chase, $50,000; Davis, $30,000; and Fall, $40,000. If net income for the year is $48,000, the following calculation indicates the respective shares of the partners:

Step 1:	Chase, capital	$ 50,000
	Davis, capital	30,000
	Fall, capital	40,000
	Total invested	$120,000

Step 2: Share of earnings to Chase: $\frac{\$50,000}{\$120,000} \times \$48,000 = \$20,000$

Share of earnings to Davis: $\frac{\$30,000}{\$120,000} \times \$48,000 = \$12,000$

Share of earnings to Fall: $\frac{\$40,000}{\$120,000} \times \$48,000 = \$16,000$

This entry allocates the earnings to the partners:

Dec.	31	Income Summary	48,000.00	
		T. S. Chase, Capital		20,000.00
		S. A. Davis, Capital		12,000.00
		R. R. Fall, Capital		16,000.00
		To close the Income Summary account and allocate the earnings.		

Salaries and Interest as Aids in Sharing

As we have mentioned, partners' service contributions are not always equal. Also, the capital contributions of the partners often are not equal. If the service contributions are not equal, the partners may use salary allowances to compensate for the differences. Or, when capital contributions are not equal, they may allocate part of the earnings with interest allowances that compensate for the unequal investments. When investment and service contributions are both unequal, the allocation of net incomes and losses may include both interest and salary allowances.

For example, in Hill and Dale's new partnership, Hill is to provide annual services that they agree are worth an annual salary of $36,000. Dale is less experienced in the business, so his service contribution to the business is worth only $24,000. Also, Hill will invest $30,000 in the business and Dale will invest $10,000. So that they are compensated fairly in light of the differences in their service and capital contributions, Hill and Dale agree to share incomes or losses as follows:

1. The partners grant annual salary allowances of $36,000 to Hill and $24,000 to Dale.
2. The partners grant an interest allowance equal to 10% of each partner's beginning-of-year capital balance.
3. The partners are to share equally the remaining balance of income or loss.

Note that the provisions for salaries and interest in this partnership agreement are called *allowances*. Also remember that, in the legal sense, partners do not work for salaries and do not invest in a partnership to earn interest. Rather, they work and invest for profits. Therefore, when a partnership agreement provides for salary and interest allowances to the partners, these allowances are not reported on the income statement as salaries and interest expense. They are only a means of splitting up the net income or net loss of the partnership.

Under the partnership agreement, Hill and Dale share the first year's net income of $70,000, as shown in Illustration 13–1. Notice that Hill gets $42,000, or 60% of the income, while Dale gets $28,000, or 40%.

In Illustration 13–1, notice that the $70,000 net income exceeds the salary and interest allowances of the partners. However, the method of sharing agreed to by Hill and Dale must be followed even if the net income is smaller than the salary and interest allowances. For example, if the first year's net

ILLUSTRATION 13–1

Sharing Income When Income Exceeds Interest and Salary Allowances

	Share to Hill	Share to Dale	Income to be Allocated
Total net income			$70,000
Allocated as salary allowances:			
Hill	$36,000		
Dale		$24,000	
Total allocated as salary allowances			60,000
Balance of income after salary allowances			$10,000
Allocated as interest:			
Hill (10% on $30,000)	3,000		
Dale (10% on $10,000)		1,000	
Total allocated as interest			4,000
Balance of income after salary and interest allowances			$ 6,000
Balance allocated equally:			
Hill	3,000		
Dale		3,000	
Total allocated equally			6,000
Balance of income			$ -0-
Shares of the partners	$42,000	$28,000	
Percentages of total net income	60%	40%	

income was $50,000, it would be allocated to the partners as shown in Illustration 13–2. Notice that this circumstance provides Hill with 64% of the total income, while Dale gets only 36%.

Hill and Dale would share a net loss in the same manner as the $50,000 net income. The only difference is that the income-and-loss-sharing procedure would begin with a negative amount of income because of the net loss. After the salary and interest allowances, the remaining balance to be allocated equally would then be a larger negative amount.

Partnership Financial Statements

In most respects, partnership financial statements are like those of a single proprietorship. On the balance sheet of a partnership, the owner's equity section often shows the separate capital account balance of each partner. The **statement of changes in partners' equity** shows the total capital balances at the beginning of the period, any additional investments made by the partners, the net income or loss of the partnership, withdrawals by the partners, and the ending capital balances. Usually, this statement shows these changes for each partner's capital account and includes the allocation of income among the partners.

For example, recall that Hill and Dale began their partnership by making investments of $30,000 and $10,000, respectively. During the first year of operations, in which the partnership earned $50,000, assume that Hill withdrew $20,000 and Dale withdrew $12,000. The statement of changes in partners' equity appears in Illustration 13–3.

ILLUSTRATION 13–2

Sharing Income When Interest and Salary Allowances Exceed Income

	Share to Hill	Share to Dale	Income to be Allocated
Total net income			$ 50,000
Allocated as salary allowances:			
Hill	$36,000		
Dale		$24,000	
Total allocated as salary allowances			60,000
Balance of income after salary allowances			$(10,000)
Allocated as interest:			
Hill (10% on $30,000)	3,000		
Dale (10% on $10,000)		1,000	
Total allocated as interest			4,000
Balance of income after salary and interest allowances			$(14,000)
Balance allocated equally:			
Hill	(7,000)		
Dale		(7,000)	
Total allocated equally			(14,000)
Balance of income			$ -0-
Shares of the partners	$32,000	$18,000	
Percentages of total net income	64%	36%	

ILLUSTRATION 13–3

A Statement of Changes in Partners' Equity

HILL AND DALE
Statement of Changes in Partners' Equity
For Year Ended December 31, 19—

	Hill		Dale		Total
Beginning capital balances		$ -0-		$ -0-	$ -0-
Plus:					
Investments by owners		30,000		10,000	40,000
Net income:					
Salary allowances	$36,000		$24,000		
Interest allowances	3,000		1,000		
Balance	(7,000)		(7,000)		
Total net income		32,000		18,000	50,000
Total		$62,000		$28,000	$90,000
Less partners' withdrawals		(20,000)		(12,000)	(32,000)
Ending capital balances		$42,000		$16,000	$58,000

Withdrawal or Addition of a Partner

A partnership is based on a contract between specific individuals. Therefore, when a partner withdraws from a partnership, the old partnership ceases to exist. Nevertheless, the business may continue to operate as a new partnership among the remaining partners.

LO 3 Prepare entries for (*a*) the sale of a partnership interest, (*b*) the admission of a new partner by investment, and (*c*) the retirement of a partner by the withdrawal of partnership assets.

The withdrawal of a partner from a partnership may take place in two ways. First, the withdrawing partner may sell his or her interest to another person who pays for the interest by transferring cash or other assets to the withdrawing partner. Second, cash or other assets of the partnership may be distributed to the withdrawing partner in settlement of his or her interest in the partnership.

When a new partner is admitted to a partnership, the old partnership technically ends and is replaced by a new partnership. Similar to the withdrawal of a partner, there are two ways a new partner may be admitted to an existing partnership: First, the new partner may purchase an interest directly from one or more of its partners. In other words, the new partner may pay cash to one or more of the existing partners in exchange for an interest in the partnership. Second, a new partner may join an existing partnership by investing cash or other assets in the business.

Sale of a Partnership Interest

Assume that the Abbott, Burns, and Camp partnership owes no liabilities and has the following assets and owners' equity:

Assets		Owners' Equity	
Cash	$ 3,000	Abbott, capital	$ 5,000
Other assets	12,000	Burns, capital	5,000
		Camp, capital	5,000
Total assets	$15,000	Total owners' equity	$15,000

Camp's equity in this partnership is $5,000. If Camp sells this equity to Davis for $7,000, Camp is selling a $5,000 recorded interest in the partnership assets. The entry on the partnership books to transfer the equity is:

Feb.	4	Camp, Capital	5,000.00	
		Davis, Capital		5,000.00
		To transfer Camp's equity in the partnership to Davis.		

After this entry is posted, the assets and owners' equity of the new partnership are:

Assets		Owners' Equity	
Cash	$ 3,000	Abbott, capital	$ 5,000
Other assets	12,000	Burns, capital	5,000
		Davis, capital	5,000
Total assets	$15,000	Total owners' equity	$15,000

Two aspects of this transaction are especially important. First, the $7,000 Davis paid to Camp is not recorded in the partnership books. Camp sold and transferred a $5,000 recorded equity in the partnership assets to Davis. The entry that records the transfer is a debit to Camp, Capital and a credit to Davis, Capital for $5,000. Furthermore, the entry is the same whether Davis pays Camp $7,000, or $70,000. The amount is paid directly to Camp. Because the partnership is not a party to the transaction, its assets and total equity are not affected by the transaction.

The second important aspect of this transaction is the question of whether Davis's purchase of Camp's interest qualifies Davis as a new partner. In fact, Abbott and Burns must agree if Davis is to become a partner. Abbott and Burns cannot prevent Camp from selling the interest to Davis. But Abbott and Burns do not have to accept Davis as a partner. If Abbott and Burns agree to accept Davis, a new partnership is formed and a new contract with a new income-and-loss-sharing ratio must be drawn.

What if either Abbott or Burns refuses to accept Davis as a partner? Under the Uniform Partnership Act, Davis gets Camp's share of partnership income and losses. And if the partnership is liquidated, Davis gets Camp's share of partnership assets. However, Davis gets no voice in the management of the firm until being admitted as a partner.

Investing Assets in an Existing Partnership

Instead of purchasing the equity of an existing partner, an individual may gain an equity by investing assets in the business. Then, the invested assets become the property of the partnership. For example, assume that the partnership of Evans and Gage has assets and owners' equity as follows:

Assets		Owners' Equity	
Cash	$ 3,000	Evans, capital	$20,000
Other assets	37,000	Gage, capital	20,000
Total assets	$40,000	Total owners' equity	$40,000

Also, assume that Evans and Gage have agreed to accept Hart as a partner with a one-half interest in the business on his investment of $40,000. This entry records Hart's investment:

Mar.	2	Cash	40,000.00	
		Hart, Capital		40,000.00
		To record the investment of Hart.		

After the entry is posted, the assets and owners' equity of the new partnership appear as follows:

Assets		Owners' Equity	
Cash	$43,000	Evans, capital	$20,000
Other assets	37,000	Gage, capital	20,000
		Hart, capital	40,000
Total assets	$80,000	Total owners' equity	$80,000

In this case, Hart has a 50% equity in the assets of the business. However, he does not necessarily have a right to one half of its net income. The sharing of incomes and losses is a separate matter on which the partners must agree. As you learned earlier in the chapter, the sharing of profits and losses may be in the ratio of the partners' relative capital contributions. However, the method of sharing also may depend on other factors.

A Bonus to the Old Partners

Sometimes, when the current value of a partnership is greater than the recorded amounts of equity, the partners may require an incoming partner to give a bonus for the privilege of joining the firm. For example, Judd and Kirk operate a partnership business, sharing its earnings equally. The partnership's accounting records show that Judd's recorded equity in the business is $38,000 and Kirk's recorded equity is $32,000. Judd and Kirk agree to accept Lee's $50,000 investment in the business in return for a one-third share of the partnership's earnings and a one-third equity in net assets. Lee's equity is determined with a calculation as follows:

Equities of the existing partners ($38,000 + $32,000) . .	$ 70,000
Investment of the new partner	50,000
Total partnership equity	$120,000
Equity of Lee (⅓ of total)	$ 40,000

Notice that although Lee invested $50,000 in the partnership, his equity in the recorded net assets of the partnership is only $40,000. The $10,000 difference usually is described as a bonus allocated to the existing partners (Judd and Kirk). Therefore, this entry records Lee's investment:

May	15	Cash	50,000.00	
		Lee, Capital		40,000.00
		Judd, Capital		5,000.00
		Kirk, Capital		5,000.00
		To record the investment of Lee.		

Notice that the $10,000 difference between the $50,000 invested by Lee and the $40,000 credited to his capital account is shared by Judd and Kirk according to their income-and-loss-sharing ratio. Such a bonus is always shared by the old partners in their income-and-loss-sharing ratio. This ratio is used because the bonus compensates the old partners for increases in the worth of the partnership that have not yet been recorded as income.

Recording Goodwill

As discussed previously, when a new partner's investment exceeds his or her equity in the partnership's net assets, the entry to record the new partner's admission normally allocates a bonus to the existing partners. Occasionally, however, firms use an alternative method to record the admission of a new partner. The alternative method involves recording goodwill on the books of the partnership. The debit to Goodwill is matched with credits that increase the equities of the existing partners.

The goodwill method of recording a new partner's admission would be used only if the evidence indicates that future earnings of the partnership are large enough to justify the increased partnership equity. Evidence of such future earnings might be provided by a historical record of earnings that are consistently in excess of the average for the industry.

In practice, goodwill is seldom recognized upon the admission of a new partner. Instead, the bonus method usually is used.

Bonus to the New Partner

Sometimes, the members of an existing partnership may be very eager to bring a new partner into their firm. The business may need additional cash or the new partner may have exceptional abilities or business contacts that will increase profits. Thus, the old partners may be willing to give the new partner a larger equity in the business than the amount of his or her investment. In this case, the old partners give a bonus to the new partner.

For example, Jay Moss and Mike Owen are partners with capital account balances of $30,000 and $18,000, respectively. They share incomes and losses in a 2:1 ratio. Anxious to have Kay Pitt join their partnership, the partners will grant her a one-fourth equity in the firm if she invests $12,000. If Pitt accepts, her equity in the new firm is calculated as follows:

Equity of the existing partners ($30,000 + $18,000) . .	$48,000
Investment of the new partner	12,000
Total equity in the new partnership	$60,000
Equity of Pitt (¼ of total)	$15,000

This entry records Pitt's investment:

June	1	Cash	12,000.00	
		Moss, Capital ($3,000 × ⅔)	2,000.00	
		Owen, Capital ($3,000 × ⅓)	1,000.00	
		Pitt, Capital		15,000.00
		To record the investment of Pitt.		

Note that Pitt's bonus is contributed by the old partners in their income-and-loss-sharing ratio. Also remember that Pitt's one-fourth equity does not necessarily entitle her to one fourth of the earnings of the business. The sharing of income and losses is a separate matter for agreement by the partners.

Withdrawal of a Partner

When a new partnership is formed, the contract should include the procedures to follow when a partner retires from the partnership. These procedures often state that a withdrawing partner shall withdraw assets equal to the current value of the partner's equity. To accomplish this, the procedures may require an audit of the accounting records and a revaluation of the partnership assets. The revaluation places the assets on the books at current values. It also causes the partners' capital accounts to reflect the current value of their equity.

For example, assume that Blue is retiring from the partnership of Smith, Blue, and Short. The partners have always shared incomes and losses in the ratio of one half to Smith, one fourth to Blue, and one fourth to Short. Their partnership agreement provides for an audit and asset revaluation on the retirement of a partner. Just prior to the audit and revaluation, their balance sheet shows the following assets and owners' equity:

Assets			**Owners' Equity**	
Cash		$11,000	Smith, capital	$22,000
Merchandise inventory		16,000	Blue, capital	10,000
Equipment	$20,000		Short, capital	10,000
Less accum. depr.	5,000	15,000		
Total assets		$42,000	Total owners' equity	$42,000

The audit and appraisal indicate that the merchandise inventory is overvalued by $4,000. Also, due to market changes, the partnership's equipment should be valued at $25,000, less accumulated depreciation of $8,000. The entries to record these revaluations are:

Oct.	31	Smith, Capital	2,000.00	
		Blue, Capital	1,000.00	
		Short, Capital	1,000.00	
		Merchandise Inventory		4,000.00
		To revalue the inventory.		
	31	Equipment	5,000.00	
		Accumulated Depreciation, Equipment		3,000.00
		Smith, Capital		1,000.00
		Blue, Capital		500.00
		Short, Capital		500.00
		To revalue the equipment.		

Note in these entries that the partners share the amount of the revaluations in their income-and-loss-sharing ratio. This is fair because revaluations of assets are actually gains and losses. If the partnership were not terminated, these gains and losses would sooner or later show up on the income statement as increases and decreases in net income. The revaluation simply records the effect of the gains and losses earlier than would have occurred.

After the entries revaluing the partnership assets are recorded, the balance sheet for the Smith, Blue, and Short partnership is as follows:

Assets			Owners' Equity	
Cash		$11,000	Smith, capital	$21,000
Merchandise inventory		12,000	Blue, capital	9,500
Equipment	$25,000		Short, capital	9,500
Less accum. depr.	8,000	17,000		
Total assets		$40,000	Total owners' equity	$40,000

After the revaluation, if Blue retires and takes cash equal to his revalued equity, this entry records the withdrawal:

Oct.	31	Blue, Capital	9,500.00	
		Cash		9,500.00
		To record the withdrawal of Blue.		

In withdrawing, Blue does not have to take cash in settlement of his equity. He may take any combination of assets to which the partners agree, or he may take the new partnership's promissory note. Also, the withdrawal of Blue generally creates a new partnership between the remaining partners. Therefore, a new partnership contract and a new income-and-loss-sharing agreement may be required.

Withdrawing Partner Takes Fewer Assets than Recorded Equity

Sometimes, when a partner retires, the remaining partners may not wish to revalue the assets on the books of the partnership. Nevertheless, they must determine the current values of the partnership assets to establish the amount of assets to be taken by the retiring partner. For example, the partners may agree that the assets are overvalued. As a result, the retiring partner should receive assets of less value than the book value of his or her equity. Also, even if the assets are not overvalued, a retiring partner may be willing to take less than the current value of his or her equity just to get out of the partnership.

When a partner retires and takes assets of less value than his or her recorded equity, the partner in effect leaves a portion of the equity in the business. The remaining partners share the unwithdrawn equity portion in their income-and-loss-sharing ratio. For example, assume that partners Black, Brown, and Green share incomes and losses in a 2:2:1 ratio. Their assets and equities are as follows:

Assets		Owners' Equity	
Cash	$ 5,000	Black, capital	$ 6,000
Merchandise inventory	9,000	Brown, capital	6,000
Store equipment	4,000	Green, capital	6,000
Total assets	$18,000	Total owners' equity	$18,000

Brown is anxious to withdraw from the partnership and offers to take $4,500 in cash in settlement for his equity. Black and Green agree to the $4,500 withdrawal, and Brown retires. This entry records the retirement:

Mar.	4	Brown, Capital	6,000.00	
		Cash		4,500.00
		Black, Capital		1,000.00
		Green, Capital		500.00
		To record the withdrawal of Brown.		

In retiring, Brown withdrew $1,500 less than his recorded equity. This is divided between Black and Green in their income-and-loss-sharing ratio. The income-and-loss-sharing ratio of the original partnership was Black, 2; Brown, 2; and Green, 1. Therefore, the ratio for sharing between Black and Green was 2:1, and the unwithdrawn book equity of Brown is shared by Black and Green in this ratio.

Withdrawing Partner Takes More Assets than Recorded Equity

There are two common reasons why a retiring partner might withdraw more assets than his or her recorded equity: First, the partnership assets may be undervalued on the books. Second, the continuing partners may want to encourage the retiring partner to withdraw by giving up assets of greater value than the retiring partner's recorded equity.

When assets are undervalued, the partners may not wish to change the recorded values. A retiring partner allowed to withdraw assets of greater value than that partner's recorded equity is, in effect, withdrawing his or her own equity plus a portion of the continuing partners' equities.

For example, assume that partners Jones, Thomas, and Finch share incomes and losses in a 3:2:1 ratio. The assets and owners' equity of the partnership are as follows:

Assets		**Owners' Equity**	
Cash	$ 5,000	Jones, capital	$ 9,000
Merchandise inventory	10,000	Thomas, capital	6,000
Equipment	3,000	Finch, capital	3,000
Total assets	$18,000	Total owners' equity	$18,000

Finch wishes to withdraw from the partnership. Jones and Thomas plan to continue the business. The partners agree that some of the partnership's assets are undervalued, but they do not wish to increase the recorded values. They further agree that if current values were recorded, the asset total would be increased by $6,000 and the equity of Finch would be increased by $1,000. Therefore, the partners agree that $4,000 is the proper value for Finch's equity

AS A MATTER OF
Ethics

Janis Carpenter is an accountant who has been engaged by Ed Hansen and Howard French, the remaining partners of the Hansen, Baker, French Partnership. Following the recent accidental death of the third partner, Renee Baker, Hansen and French have been negotiating with the executor of Baker's estate to settle the estate's claim against the partnership. The three partners had shared incomes and losses in the ratio of their capital balances, which were equal. Hansen and French have asked Carpenter to advise them in trying to reach a fair settlement.

Among the records is the partnership agreement, which has only a brief section dealing with settlements in the event of a partner's death. It says that a deceased partner's estate is entitled to the "deceased partner's percentage share of the partnership assets."

The executor of the estate has suggested that the estate is entitled to one third of the current value of the partnership's total assets. Hansen, on the other hand, has suggested that the distribution should be based on the book value of the assets, which is only 75% of the current value. French has pointed out that the others seem to ignore the liabilities of the partnership, which equal 40% of the assets' book value, and 30% of current value. French thinks the estate is entitled to only one third of the recorded equity. Given the close friendship of the three partners and the tragedy of Baker's death, both the executor and the remaining partners want a fair settlement for all parties. None of them are willing to file a lawsuit to resolve the difference. What would you suggest?

and that amount of cash may be withdrawn. This entry records the withdrawal:

May	7	Finch, Capital	3,000.00	
		Jones, Capital	600.00	
		Thomas, Capital	400.00	
		Cash		4,000.00
		To record the withdrawal of Finch.		

Death of a Partner

A partner's death automatically dissolves a partnership. As a result, the deceased partner's estate is entitled to receive the amount of his or her equity. The partnership contract should contain provisions for settlement in case a partner dies. Included should be provisions for (*a*) an immediate closing of the books to determine earnings since the end of the previous accounting period and (*b*) a method for determining and recording current values for the assets and liabilities. After these steps are taken, the remaining partners and the deceased partner's estate must agree to a disposition of the deceased partner's equity. This may involve selling the equity to the remaining partners or to an outsider, or it may involve the withdrawal of assets in settlement. We explained the appropriate entries for both cases in the previous paragraphs.

Liquidations

LO 4 Prepare entries required in the liquidation of a partnership.

When a partnership is liquidated, its business is ended. The assets are converted into cash, and the creditors are paid. The remaining cash is then distributed to the partners, and the partnership is dissolved. **Partnership liquidations** may follow a variety of different steps. However, we limit the following discussion to three typical situations.

All Assets Are Sold at a Net Gain

One typical partnership liquidation is the situation in which all of the partnership assets are converted into cash at a net gain. Then, the cash is distributed and the partnership is dissolved. The following example shows the necessary accounting entries to be made under these conditions.

Ottis, Skinner, and Parr have operated a partnership for a number of years, sharing incomes and losses in a 3:2:1 ratio. Due to several unsatisfactory conditions, the partners decide to liquidate as of December 31. On that date, the books are closed, and the income from operations is transferred to the partners' capital accounts. Thereafter, the partnership's balance sheet appears as follows:

Assets		Liabilities and Owners' Equity	
Cash	$10,000	Accounts payable	$ 5,000
Merchandise inventory	15,000	Ottis, capital	15,000
Other assets	25,000	Skinner, capital	15,000
		Parr, capital	15,000
Total assets	$50,000	Total liabilities and owners' equity	$50,000

In a liquidation, some gains or losses normally result from the sale of noncash assets. These losses and gains are called *losses and gains from liquidation*. Just like any other net incomes or losses, the partners share the losses and gains from liquidation in their income-and-loss-sharing ratio. Assume, for example, Ottis, Skinner, and Parr sell their inventory for $12,000 and their other assets for $34,000. This entry records the sales and the net gain allocation:

Jan.	12	Cash	12,000.00	
		Loss or Gain from Liquidation	3,000.00	
		Merchandise Inventory		15,000.00
		Sold the inventory at a loss.		
	15	Cash	34,000.00	
		Other Assets		25,000.00
		Loss or Gain from Liquidation		9,000.00
		Sold the other assets at a profit.		

Jan.	15	Loss or Gain from Liquidation	6,000.00	
		Ottis, Capital		3,000.00
		Skinner, Capital		2,000.00
		Parr, Capital		1,000.00
		To allocate the net gain from sale of assets to the partners in their 3:2:1 income-and-loss-sharing ratio.		

Notice in the last entry that the losses and gains from liquidation were shared in the partner's income-and-loss-sharing ratio. In solving liquidation problems, do not make the mistake of allocating the losses and gains in the ratio of the partners' capital balance.

After the merchandise inventory and other assets of Ottis, Skinner, and Parr are sold and the net gain is allocated, a new balance sheet shows the following:

Assets		**Liabilities and Owners' Equity**	
Cash	$56,000	Accounts payable	$ 5,000
		Ottis, capital	18,000
		Skinner, capital	17,000
		Parr, capital	16,000
Total assets	$56,000	Total liabilities and owners' equity	$56,000

Observe that the one asset, cash $56,000, exactly equals the sum of the liabilities and the equities of the partners.

After partnership assets are sold and the gain or loss shared, the realized cash is distributed to the proper parties. Because creditors have first claim, they are paid first. After the creditors are paid, the remaining cash is divided among the partners. Each partner has the right to cash equal to his or her equity or, in other words, cash equal to the balance of his or her capital account. These entries record the final cash payments and distribution to Ottis, Skinner, and Parr:

Jan.	15	Accounts Payable	5,000.00	
		Cash		5,000.00
		To pay the claims of the creditors.		
	15	Ottis, Capital	18,000.00	
		Skinner, Capital	17,000.00	
		Parr, Capital	16,000.00	
		Cash		51,000.00
		To distribute the remaining cash to the partners according to their capital account balances.		

Notice that after gains and losses are shared and the creditors are paid, each partner receives cash equal to the balance remaining in his or her capital account. The partners receive these amounts because cash is the only remaining partnership asset and a partner's capital account balance represents the partner's equity in that asset. In making the entry to distribute cash to the partners, be sure that you do not make the mistake of distributing it in the partners' income-and-loss-sharing ratio. Gains and losses from liquidation are allocated according to the income-and-loss-sharing ratio; but cash must be distributed to the partners in relation to their capital account balances.

All Assets Are Sold at a Net Loss; Each Partner's Capital Account Is Sufficient to Absorb His or Her Share of the Loss

In a liquidation, the partnership sometimes sells its assets at a net loss. For example, assume that the Ottis, Skinner, and Parr partnership does not sell its assets at a profit. Instead, assume that they sell the inventory for $10,000 and the other assets for $12,000. These entries record the sales and loss allocation:

Jan.	12	Cash	10,000.00	
		Loss or Gain on Liquidation	5,000.00	
		Merchandise Inventory		15,000.00
		Sold the inventory at a loss.		
	15	Cash	12,000.00	
		Loss or Gain on Liquidation	13,000.00	
		Other Assets		25,000.00
		Sold the other assets at a loss.		
	15	Ottis, Capital	9,000.00	
		Skinner, Capital	6,000.00	
		Parr, Capital	3,000.00	
		Loss or Gain on Liquidation		18,000.00
		To allocate the loss from sale of assets to the partners in their income-and-loss-sharing ratio.		

After the entries are posted, a balance sheet shows that the partnership cash exactly equals the liabilities and the equities of the partners, as follows:

Assets		**Liabilities and Owners' Equity**	
Cash	$32,000	Accounts payable	$ 5,000
		Ottis, capital	6,000
		Skinner, capital	9,000
		Parr, capital	12,000
Total assets	$32,000	Total liabilities and owners' equity	$32,000

The following entries record the distribution of the cash to the proper parties:

Jan.	15	Accounts Payable	5,000.00	
		Cash		5,000.00
		To pay the partnership creditors.		
	15	Ottis, Capital	6,000.00	
		Skinner, Capital	9,000.00	
		Parr, Capital	12,000.00	
		Cash		27,000.00
		To distribute the remaining cash to the partners according to the balances of their capital accounts.		

Notice again that after losses are shared and creditors are paid, the partners receive the remaining cash in the ratio of their capital account balances.

All Assets Are Sold at a Net Loss; a Partner's Capital Account Is Not Sufficient to Cover His or Her Share of the Loss

Sometimes, the liquidation losses allocated to a partner exceed that partner's capital account balance. In such cases, the partner must, if possible, cover the deficit by paying cash into the partnership. For example, contrary to the situations described in the previous illustrations, assume that the Ottis, Skinner, and Parr partnership sells its merchandise for $3,000 and sells its other assets for $4,000. These entries record the sales and the loss allocation:

Jan.	12	Cash	3,000.00	
		Loss or Gain on Liquidation	12,000.00	
		Merchandise Inventory		15,000.00
		Sold the inventory at a loss.		
	15	Cash	4,000.00	
		Loss or Gain on Liquidation	21,000.00	
		Other Assets		25,000.00
		Sold the other assets at a loss.		
	15	Ottis, Capital	16,500.00	
		Skinner, Capital	11,000.00	
		Parr, Capital	5,500.00	
		Loss or Gain on Liquidation		33,000.00
		To allocate the loss from sale of assets to the partners in their income-and-loss-sharing ratio.		

After posting the entry to allocate the loss, the capital account of Ottis has a $1,500 debit balance and appears as follows:

Ottis, Capital

Date		Explanation	Debit	Credit	Balance
Dec.	31	Balance			15,000.00
Jan.	15	Share of loss on sale	16,500.00		1,500.00

The partnership agreement states that one half of all losses or gains should be allocated to Ottis. Therefore, since Ottis's capital account balance is not large enough to absorb his share of the loss, he is obligated to pay $1,500 into the partnership to cover the deficit. If Ottis is able to pay, this entry records the receipt:

Dec.	31	Cash	1,500.00	
		Ottis, Capital		1,500.00
		To record the additional investment of Ottis to cover his share of loss.		

After the $1,500 is received, the partnership has $18,500 in cash. The following entries record the cash distributions to the proper parties:

Jan.	15	Accounts Payable	5,000.00	
		Cash		5,000.00
		To pay the partnership creditors.		
	15	Skinner, Capital	4,000.00	
		Parr, Capital	9,500.00	
		Cash		13,500.00
		To distribute the remaining cash to the partners according to the balances of their capital accounts.		

When a partnership's liquidation loss creates a debit balance in one partner's capital account balance, that partner may be unable to make up the deficit. In such cases, since each partner has unlimited liability, the deficit must be borne by the remaining partner or partners. For example, assume that Ottis is unable to pay the $1,500 necessary to cover the deficit in his capital account. If Ottis is unable to pay, his deficit must be shared by Skinner and Parr in their income-and-loss-sharing ratio. The partners share incomes and losses in the ratio of Ottis, 3; Skinner, 2; and Parr, 1. Therefore, Skinner and Parr share in a 2:1 ratio. This means that Skinner and Parr must share the $1,500 by which Ottis's share of the loss exceeded his capital account balance in a 2:1 ratio. Normally, the defaulting partner's deficit is transferred to the capital accounts of the remaining partners. This is accomplished for Ottis, Skinner, and Parr with the following entry:

ILLUSTRATION 13–4

Allocating Liquidation Loss and Partner's Deficit to Capital Accounts

Ottis, Capital

Date		Explanation	Debit	Credit	Balance
Dec.	31	Balance			15,000.00
Jan.	15	Share of loss on sale	16,500.00		(1,500.00)
	15	Deficit to Skinner and Parr		1,500.00	–0–

Skinner, Capital

Date		Explanation	Debit	Credit	Balance
Dec.	31	Balance			15,000.00
Jan.	15	Share of loss on sale	11,000.00		4,000.00
	15	Deficit to Skinner and Parr	1,000.00		3,000.00

Parr, Capital

Date		Explanation	Debit	Credit	Balance
Dec.	31	Balance			15,000.00
Jan.	15	Share of loss on sale	5,500.00		9,500.00
	15	Deficit to Skinner and Parr	500.00		9,000.00

Jan.	15	Skinner, Capital	1,000.00	
		Parr, Capital	500.00	
		Ottis, Capital		1,500.00
		To transfer the deficit of Ottis to the capital accounts of Skinner and Parr.		

After the deficit is transferred, the capital accounts of the partners appear as in Illustration 13–4. These entries record the final payments to creditors and distribution to the partners:

Jan.	15	Accounts Payable	5,000.00	
		Cash		5,000.00
		To pay the partnership creditors.		
	15	Skinner, Capital	3,000.00	
		Parr, Capital	9,000.00	
		Cash		12,000.00
		To distribute the remaining cash to the partners according to their capital account balances.		

Note that Ottis's inability to meet his loss share now does not relieve him of liability. If he becomes able to pay at some future time, Skinner and Parr may collect the full $1,500 from him. Skinner may collect $1,000, and Parr, $500.

Summary of the Chapter in Terms of Learning Objectives

LO 1. A partnership is a voluntary association between the partners that is based on a contract. The life of a partnership is limited by agreement or by the death or incapacity of a partner. Normally, each partner can act as an agent of the other partners and commit the partnership to any contract within the apparent scope of its business. All partners in a general partnership are personally liable for all the debts of the partnership. Limited partnerships include one or more general partners plus one or more (limited) partners whose liabilities are limited to the amount of their investments in the partnership. The risk of becoming a partner results in part from the fact that partnership characteristics include mutual agency and unlimited liability.

LO 2. A partnership's net incomes or losses are allocated to the partners according to the terms of the partnership agreement. The agreement may specify that each partner will receive a given fraction, or that the allocation of incomes and losses will reflect salary allowances and/or interest allowances. When salary and/or interest allowances are granted, the residual net income or loss usually is allocated equally or on a stated fractional basis.

LO 3. When a new partner buys a partnership interest directly from one or more of the existing partners, the amount of cash paid from one partner to another does not affect the total recorded equity of the partnership. The recorded equity of the selling partner(s) is simply transferred to the capital account of the new partner. Alternatively, a new partner may purchase an equity by investing additional assets in the partnership. When this occurs, part of the new partner's investment may be credited as a bonus to the capital accounts of the existing partners. Also, to gain the participation of the new partner, the existing partners may give the new partner a bonus whereby portions of the existing partners' capital balances are transferred to the new partner's capital account. Occasionally, goodwill is recorded when a new partner invests in a partnership.

LO 4. When a partnership is liquidated, losses and gains from selling the partnership assets are allocated to the partners according to their income-and-loss-sharing ratio. If a partner's capital account has a deficit balance that the partner cannot pay, the other partners must share the deficit in their relative income-and-loss-sharing ratio.

Demonstration Problem

The following events affect the partner's capital accounts in several successive partnerships. On a work sheet with six money columns, one for each of five partners and a totals column, show the effects of the following events on the partners' capital accounts:

4/13/89 Kelly and Emerson create K&E Co. Each invests $10,000, and they agree to share profits equally.

12/31/89 K&E Co. earns $15,000 in the year. Kelly withdraws $4,000 from the partnership, and Emerson withdraws $7,000.

1/1/90	Reed is made a partner in KE&R Co. after contributing $12,000 cash. The partners agree that each will get a 10% interest allowance on their beginning capital balances. In addition, Emerson and Reed are to receive $5,000 salary allowances. The remainder of the income is to be divided evenly.
12/31/90	The partnership's income for the year is $40,000, and these withdrawals occur: Kelly, $5,000; Emerson, $12,500; and Reed, $11,000.
1/1/91	For $20,000, Kelly sells her interest to Merritt, who is accepted by Emerson and Reed as a partner in the new ER&M Co. The profits are to be shared equally after Emerson and Reed each receive $25,000 salaries.
12/31/91	The partnership's income for the year is $35,000, and these withdrawals occur: Emerson, $2,500, and Reed, $2,000.
1/1/92	Davis is admitted as a partner after investing $60,000 cash in the new Davis & Associates partnership. Davis is given a 50% interest in capital after the other partners transfer $3,000 to his account from each of theirs. A 20% interest allowance (on the beginning-of-year capital balances will be used in sharing profits, but there will be no salaries. Davis will get 40% of the remainder, and the other three partners will each get 20%.
12/31/92	Davis & Associates earns $127,600 for the year, and these withdrawals occur: Emerson, $25,000; Reed, $27,000; Merritt, $15,000; and Davis, $40,000.
1/1/93	Davis buys out Emerson and Reed for the balances of their capital accounts, after a revaluation of the partnership assets. The revaluation gain is $50,000, which is divided in the previous 1:1:1:2 ratio. Davis pays the others from personal funds. Merritt and Davis will share profits on a 1:9 ratio.
2/29/93	The partnership had $10,000 of income since the beginning of the year. Merritt retires and receives partnership cash equal to her capital balance. Davis takes possession of the partnership assets in his own name, and the company is dissolved.

Solution to Demonstration Problem

Planning the Solution

- Evaluate each transaction's effects on the capital accounts of the partners.
- Each time a new partner is admitted or a partner withdraws, allocate any bonus based on the income-or-loss-sharing agreement.
- Each time a new partner is admitted or a partner withdraws, allocate subsequent net incomes or losses in accordance with the new partnership agreement.

Event	Kelly	Emerson	Reed	Merritt	Davis	Total
4/13/89						
Initial investment	$10,000	$10,000				$ 20,000
12/31/89						
Income (equal)	7,500	7,500				15,000
Withdrawals	(4,000)	(7,000)				(11,000)
Ending balance	$13,500	$10,500				$ 24,000
1/1/90						
New investment			$12,000			12,000
12/31/90						
10% interest	1,350	1,050	1,200			3,600
Salaries		5,000	5,000			10,000
Remainder (equal)	8,800	8,800	8,800			26,400
Withdrawals	(5,000)	(12,500)	(11,000)			(28,500)
Ending balance	$18,650	$12,850	$16,000			$ 47,500
1/1/91						
Transfer interest	(18,650)			$18,650		-0-
12/31/91						
Salaries		25,000	25,000			50,000
Remainder (equal)		(5,000)	(5,000)	(5,000)		(15,000)
Withdrawals		(2,500)	(2,000)			(4,500)
Ending balance	$ -0-	$30,350	$34,000	$13,650		$ 78,000
1/1/92						
New investment					$ 60,000	60,000
Bonuses to Davis		(3,000)	(3,000)	(3,000)	9,000	-0-
Adjusted balance		$27,350	$31,000	$10,650	$ 69,000	$138,000
12/31/92						
20% interest		5,470	6,200	2,130	13,800	27,600
Remain. (1:1:1:2)		20,000	20,000	20,000	40,000	100,000
Withdrawals		(25,000)	(27,000)	(15,000)	(40,000)	(107,000)
Ending balance		$27,820	$30,200	$17,780	$82,800	$158,600
1/1/93						
Gain (1:1:1:2)		10,000	10,000	10,000	20,000	50,000
Adjusted balance		$37,820	$40,200	$27,780	$102,800	$208,600
Transfer interests		(37,820)	(40,200)		78,020	-0-
Adjusted balance		$ -0-	$ -0-	$27,780	$180,820	$208,600
2/29/93						
Income (1:9)				1,000	9,000	10,000
Adjusted balance				$28,780	$189,820	$218,600
Settlements				(28,780)	(189,820)	(218,600)
Final balance				$ -0-	$ -0-	$ -0-

Glossary

LO 5 Define or explain the words and phrases listed in the chapter glossary.

General partner a partner who assumes unlimited liability for the debts of the partnership; the general partner in a limited partnership is usually responsible for its management. p. 690

General partnership a partnership in which all partners have unlimited liability for partnership debts. p. 690

Limited partners partners who have no personal liability for debts of the limited partnership beyond the amounts they have invested in the partnership. p. 690

Limited partnership a partnership that has two classes of partners, limited partners and one or more general partners. p. 690

Mutual agency the legal relationship among the partners whereby each partner is an agent of the partnership and is able to bind the partnership to contracts within the apparent scope of the partnership's business. p. 689

Partnership an unincorporated association of two or more persons to carry on a business for profit as co-owners. p. 688

Partnership contract the agreement between partners that sets forth the terms under which the affairs of the partnership will be conducted. p. 689

Partnership liquidations the winding up of a partnership business by converting its assets to cash and distributing the cash to the proper parties. p. 704–709

Statement of changes in partners' equity a financial statement that shows the total capital balances at the beginning of the period, any additional investments by the partners, the net income or loss of the period, the partners' withdrawals during the period, and the ending capital balances. p. 694

Unlimited liability of partners the legal relationship among general partners of a partnership that makes each general partner responsible for paying all the debts of the partnership if the other partners are unable to pay their shares. p. 690

Objective Review

Answers to the following questions are listed at the end of this chapter. Be sure that you decide which is the one best answer to each question *before* you check the answers.

LO 1 Which of the following is a characteristic of a partnership?

a. A partnership is a voluntary association between two or more persons that is based on a contract.

b. All partners in a general partnership are personally liable for all partnership debts.

c. The life of a partnership is always limited.

d. Unless the partnership contract specifies otherwise, each partner can act on behalf of the other partners and commit the partnership to any contract within the scope of its business.

e. All of the above are characteristics of a partnership.

LO 2 Slim and Jim form a partnership with initial investments of $50,000 and $25,000, respectively. The partners agree to annual salary allowances of $30,000 to Slim and $20,000 to Jim. Also, they agree to an interest allowance equal to 12% of each partner's beginning-of-year capital balance. The remaining balance of income or loss is to be shared equally. How would a first-year net income of $45,000 be shared between Slim and Jim?

a. Slim, $30,000; Jim, $15,000.
b. Slim, $29,000; Jim, $16,000.
c. Slim, $28,100; Jim, $16,900.
d. Slim, $27,000; Jim, $18,000.
e. Slim, $22,500; Jim, $22,500.

LO 3 Davis and Travis operate a partnership and share earnings equally. Davis's recorded equity is $80,000, and Travis's recorded equity is $70,000. Davis and Travis agree to accept Caldwell's $60,000 investment in the business in return for a one-quarter share of the partnership's earnings and a one-quarter equity in net assets. The entry to record Caldwell's investment in the partnership would include:

a. A credit to Davis, Capital for $7,500.
b. A credit to Travis, Capital for $3,750.
c. A credit to Caldwell, Capital for $52,500.
d. A credit to Caldwell, Capital for $60,000.
e. Both (*b*) and (*c*) are correct.

LO 4 The balance sheet for the partnership of Rome, Steele, and Robb before liquidation is as follows:

Assets		**Liabilities and Owners' Equity**	
Cash	$ 6,000	Accounts payable	$15,000
Merchandise inventory	42,000	Rome, capital	30,000
Other assets	27,000	Steele, capital	10,000
		Robb, capital	20,000
Total assets	$75,000	Total liabilities and owners' equity	$75,000

The merchandise inventory and other assets are sold for a total of $60,000. If incomes and losses are shared in a 3:2:1 ratio, what amount of cash should Rome receive on distribution of the remaining cash?

a. $20,000.
b. $30,000.
c. $33,000.
d. $25,500.
e. $17,000.

LO 5 In a relationship between partners, the characteristic whereby each partner is able to bind the partnership to contracts within the apparent scope of the partnership's business is:

a. Limited life.
b. Unlimited liability.
c. Mutual agency.
d. Voluntary association.
e. General partnership.

Questions for Class Discussion

1. Amey and Lacey are partners. Lacey dies, and her son claims the right to take his mother's place in the partnership. Does he have this right? Why?
2. If Roscoe cannot legally enter into a contract, can he become a partner?
3. If a partnership contract does not state the period of time the partnership is to exist, when does the partnership end?
4. As applied to a partnership, what does the term *mutual agency* mean?
5. Kurt and Ellen are partners in operating a store. Without consulting Kurt, Ellen enters into a contract for the purchase of merchandise for the store. Kurt contends that he did not authorize the order and refuses to take delivery. The vendor sues the partners for the contract price of the merchandise. Will the partnership have to pay? Why?
6. Would your answer to Question 5 differ if Kurt and Ellen were partners in a public accounting firm?
7. Can partners limit the right of a partner to commit their partnership to contracts? Would the agreement be binding (*a*) on the partners and (*b*) on outsiders?
8. What does the term *unlimited liability* mean when it is applied to members of a partnership?
9. Furst organized a limited partnership and is the only general partner. Nexx invested $20,000 in the partnership and was admitted as a limited partner with the understanding that he would receive 10% of the profits. After two unprofitable years, the partnership ceased doing business. At that point, partnership liabilities were $85,000 larger than partnership assets. How much money can the creditors of the partnership obtain from Nexx in satisfaction of the unpaid partnership debts?
10. How does a general partnership differ from a limited partnership?
11. George, Burton, and Dillman have been partners for three years. The partnership is being dissolved. George is leaving the firm, but Burton and Dillman plan to carry on the business. In the final settlement, George places a $75,000 salary claim against the partnership. He contends that he has a claim for a salary of $25,000 for each year because he devoted all of his time for three years to the affairs of the partnership. Is his claim valid? Why?
12. The partnership agreement of Barnes and Ardmore provides for a two-thirds, one-third sharing of income but says nothing about losses. The first year of partnership operations resulted in a loss and Barnes argues

that the loss should be shared equally because the partnership agreement said nothing about sharing losses. What do you think?

13. Ace and Bud are partners who agree that Ace will receive a $50,000 salary allowance after which remaining incomes or losses will be shared equally. If Bud's capital account is credited $1,000 as his share of the net income in a given period, how much net income did the partnership earn?
14. Van, Wink, and York are partners with capital account balances of $7,000 each. Zack pays Van $8,000 for his one-third interest and is admitted to the partnership. The bookkeeper debits Van, Capital and credits Zack, Capital for $7,000. Zack objects; he wants his capital account to show an $8,000 balance, the amount he paid for his interest. Explain why Zack's capital account is credited for $7,000.
15. If the partners in Blume Partnership want the financial statements to show the procedures used to allocate the partnership income among the partners, on what financial statement should the allocation appear?
16. After all partnership assets are converted to cash and all liabilities have been paid, the remaining cash should equal the sum of the balances of the partners' capital accounts. Why?
17. Kay, Kat, and Kim are partners. In a liquidation, Kay's share of partnership losses exceeds her capital account balance. She is unable to meet the deficit from her personal assets, and the excess losses are shared by her partners. Does this relieve Kay of liability?
18. A partner withdraws from a partnership and receives assets of greater value than the book value of his equity. Should the remaining partners share the resulting reduction in their equities in the ratio of their relative capital balances or in their income-and-loss-sharing ratio?

Exercises

Exercise 13–1
Journalizing partnership entries
(LO 2)

On March 1, 1993, Reed and Vaughn formed a partnership. Reed contributed $88,000 cash and Vaughn contributed land valued at $70,000 and a building valued at $120,000. Also, the partnership assumed responsibility for Vaughn's $80,000 long-term note payable associated with the land and building. The partners agreed to share profits as follows: Reed is to receive an annual salary allowance of $30,000, both are to receive an annual interest allowance of 10% of their original capital investment, and any remaining profit or loss is to be shared equally. On October 20, 1993, Reed withdrew cash of $32,000 and Vaughn withdrew $25,000. After the adjusting entries and the closing entries to the revenue and expense accounts, the Income Summary account had a credit balance of $79,000. Present general journal entries to record the initial capital investments of the partners, their cash withdrawals, and the December 31 closing of the withdrawals accounts. Finally, determine the balances of the partners' capital accounts as of the end of 1993.

Exercise 13–2
Income allocation in a partnership
(LO 2)

Newton and Berry began a partnership by investing $50,000 and $75,000, respectively. During its first year, the partnership earned $165,000.

Required

Prepare calculations showing how the income should be allocated to the partners under each of the following plans for sharing net incomes and losses:

a. The partners failed to agree on a method of sharing income.

b. The partners agreed to share incomes and losses in proportion to their initial investments.

c. The partners agreed to share income by allowing a $55,000 per year salary allowance to Newton, a $45,000 per year salary allowance to Berry, 10% interest on their initial investments, and the balance equally.

Exercise 13–3
Income allocation in a partnership
(LO 2)

Assume that the partners of Exercise 13–2 agreed to share net incomes and losses by allowing yearly salary allowances of $55,000 to Newton and $45,000 to Berry, 10% interest allowances on their investments, and the balance equally. (*a*) Determine the shares of Newton and Berry in a first-year net income of $94,400. (*b*) Determine the partners' shares in a first-year net loss of $15,700.

Exercise 13–4
Sale of a partnership interest
(LO 3)

The partners in the Royal Partnership have agreed that partner Prince may sell his $90,000 equity in the partnership to Duke, for which Duke will pay Prince $75,000. Present the partnership's journal entry to record the sale on September 30.

Exercise 13–5
Admission of a new partner
(LO 3)

The E-O Partnership has total partners' equity of $510,000, which is made up of Elm, Capital, $400,000, and Oak, Capital, $110,000. The partners share net incomes and losses in a ratio of 80% to Elm and 20% to Oak. On November 1, Ash is admitted to the partnership and given a 15% interest in equity and in incomes and losses. Prepare the journal entry to record the entry of Ash under each of the following unrelated assumptions: Ash invests cash of (*a*) $90,000; (*b*) $125,000; and (*c*) $60,000.

Exercise 13–6
Retirement of a partner
(LO 3)

Holland, Flowers, and Wood have been partners sharing net incomes and losses in a 5:3:2 ratio. On January 31, the date Wood retires from the partnership, the equities of the partners are Holland, $350,000; Flowers, $240,000; and Wood, $180,000. Present general journal entries to record Wood's retirement under each of the following unrelated assumptions:

a. Wood is paid $180,000 in partnership cash for his equity.

b. Wood is paid $200,000 in partnership cash for his equity.

c. Wood is paid $150,000 in partnership cash for his equity.

Exercise 13–7
Liquidation of a partnership
(LO 4)

The Red, White & Blue partnership was begun with investments by the partners as follows: Red, $175,000; White, $220,000; and Blue, $205,000. The first year of operations did not go well, and the partners finally decided to liquidate the partnership, sharing all losses equally. On August 31, after all assets were converted to cash and all creditors were paid, only $60,000 in partnership cash remained.

Required

1. Calculate the capital account balances of the partners after the liquidation of assets and payment of creditors.
2. Assume that any partner with a deficit pays cash to the partnership to cover the deficit. Then, present the general journal entries on August 31 to record the cash receipt from the deficient partner(s) and the final disbursement of cash to the partners.
3. Now make the contrary assumption that any partner with a deficit is not able to reimburse the partnership. Present journal entries (*a*) to transfer the deficit of any deficient partners to the other partners and (*b*) to record the final disbursement of cash to the partners.

Exercise 13–8
Liquidation of a partnership
(LO 4)

Sandburg, McArthur, and Cox are partners who share incomes and losses in a 1:4:5 ratio. After lengthy disagreements among the partners and several unprofitable periods, the partners decided to liquidate the partnership. Before the liquidation, the partnership balance sheet showed total assets, $116,000; total liabilities, $88,000; Sandburg, Capital, $1,200; McArthur, Capital, $11,700; and Cox, Capital, $15,100. The cash proceeds from selling the assets were sufficient to repay all but $24,000 to the creditors. Calculate the loss from selling the assets, allocate the loss to the partners, and determine how much of the remaining liability should be paid by each partner.

Exercise 13–9
Liquidation of a limited partnership
(LO 4)

Assume that the Sandburg, McArthur, and Cox partnership of Exercise 13–8 is a limited partnership. Sandburg and McArthur are general partners and Cox is a limited partner. How much of the remaining $24,000 liability should be paid by each partner?

Problems

Problem 13–1
Methods of allocating partnership income
(LO 2)

Tom Katz, Kaye Reeves, and Alice Troy invested $40,000, $56,000, and $64,000, respectively, in a partnership. During its first year, the firm earned $124,500.

Required

Prepare entries to close the firm's Income Summary account as of December 31 and to allocate the net income to the partners under each of the following assumptions:

a. The partners did not produce any special agreement on the method of sharing incomes.

b. The partners agreed to share net incomes and losses in the ratio of their beginning investments.

c. The partners agreed to share income by providing annual salary allowances of $33,000 to Katz, $28,000 to Reeves, and $40,000 to Troy; allowing 10% interest on the partners' beginning investments; and sharing the remainder equally.

Problem 13–2
Allocating partnership incomes and losses; sequential years
(LO 2)

Linda Nuñez and Ray Parker are in the process of forming a partnership to which Nuñez will devote one-half time and Parker will devote full time. They have discussed the following alternative plans for sharing net incomes and losses:

a. In the ratio of their initial investments, which they have agreed will be $21,000 for Nuñez and $31,500 for Parker.

b. In proportion to the time devoted to the business.

c. A salary allowance of $3,000 per month to Parker and the balance in accordance with their investment ratio.

d. A $3,000 per month salary allowance to Parker, 10% interest on their initial investments, and the balance equally.

The partners expect the business to generate income as follows: Year 1, $18,000 net loss; Year 2, $45,000 net income; and Year 3, $75,000 net income.

Required

1. Prepare three schedules with the following column headings:

Income/Loss Sharing Plan	Year ________		
	Calculations	Nuñez	Parker

2. Complete a schedule for each of the first three years by showing how the partnership net income or loss for each year would be allocated to the partners under each of the four plans being considered. Round your answers to the nearest whole dollar.

Problem 13–3
Partnership income allocation, statement of changes in partners' equity, and closing entries
(LO 2)

Brad Marshall, Jon Spiller, and Leigh Rand formed the MSR Partnership by making capital contributions of $183,750, $131,250, and $210,000, respectively. They anticipate annual net incomes of $225,000 and are considering the following alternative plans of sharing net incomes and losses: (*a*) equally; (*b*) in the ratio of their initial investments; or (*c*) salary allowances of $40,000 to Marshall, $30,000 to Spiller, and $45,000 to Rand; interest allowances of 10% on initial investments, with any remaining balance shared equally.

Required

1. Prepare a schedule with the following column headings:

Income/Loss Sharing Plan	Calculations	Share to Marshall	Share to Spiller	Share to Rand	Totals

Use the schedule to show how a net income of $225,000 would be distributed under each of the alternative plans being considered. Round your answers to the nearest whole dollar.

2. Prepare a statement of changes in partners' equity showing the allocation of income to the partners, assuming they agree to use alternative (*c*) and the net income earned is $105,000. During the year, Marshall, Spiller, and Rand withdrew $17,000, $24,000, and $32,000, respectively.
3. Prepare the December 31 journal entry to close Income Summary assuming they agree to use alternative (*c*) and the net income is $105,000. Also, close the withdrawals accounts.

Problem 13–4
Withdrawal of a partner
(LO 3)

Part 1. Godfrey, Gully, and Speck are partners with capital balances as follows: Godfrey, $84,000; Gully, $69,000; and Speck, $147,000. The partners share incomes and losses in a 3:2:5 ratio. Gully decides to withdraw from the partnership, and the partners agree to not have the assets revalued on his retirement. Prepare general journal entries to record the February 1 withdrawal of Gully from the partnership under each of the following unrelated assumptions:

a. Gully sells his interest to Goldman for $80,000 after Godfrey and Speck approve the entry of Goldman as a partner.

b. Gully gives his interest to a son-in-law, Spain. Godfrey and Speck accept Spain as a partner.

c. Gully is paid $69,000 in partnership cash for his equity.

d. Gully is paid $107,000 in partnership cash for his equity.

e. Gully is paid $15,000 in partnership cash plus computer equipment recorded on the partnership books at $35,000 less accumulated depreciation of $11,600.

Part 2. Assume that Gully does not retire from the partnership described in Part 1. Instead, Hatch is admitted to the partnership on February 1 with a 25% equity. Prepare general journal entries to record the entry of Hatch into the partnership under each of the following unrelated assumptions:

a. Hatch invests $100,000.

b. Hatch invests $72,500.

c. Hatch invests $131,000.

Problem 13–5
Liquidation of a partnership
(LO 4)

Swanson, Chapel, and Page plan to liquidate their partnership. They have always shared losses and gains in a 3:2:1 ratio, and on the day of the liquidation their balance sheet appeared as follows:

SWANSON, CHAPEL, AND PAGE
Balance Sheet
May 31, 19—

Assets		Liabilities and Owners' Equity	
Cash	$ 90,400	Accounts payable	$122,750
Inventory	268,600	David Swanson, capital	46,500
		Annie Chapel, capital	106,250
		Maria Page, capital	83,500
Total assets	$359,000	Total liabilities and owners' equity	$359,000

Required

Under the assumption the inventory is sold and the cash is distributed to the proper parties on May 31, prepare the general journal entries for the sale, the gain or loss allocation, and the distribution of the cash in each of the following unrelated cases:

a. The inventory is sold for $300,000.

b. The inventory is sold for $250,000.

c. The inventory is sold for $160,000, and any partners with resulting deficits can and do pay in the amount of their deficits.

d. The inventory is sold for $125,000, and the partners have no assets other than those invested in the business.

Problem 13–6
Withdrawal of a partner
(LO 3)

Until November 16, 1993, Rohan, Kovak, and Keene were partners that shared incomes and losses in the ratio of their beginning-of-year capital account balances. On November 16, Rohan suffered a heart attack and died. Kovak and Keene immediately ended the business operations and prepared the following adjusted trial balance:

ROHAN, KOVAK, AND KEENE
Adjusted Trial Balance
November 16, 1993

Cash	$ 10,625	
Accounts receivable	30,415	
Allowance for doubtful accounts		$ 1,115
Supplies inventory	46,875	
Equipment	148,860	
Accumulated depreciation, equipment		14,842
Building	227,325	
Accumulated depreciation, building		56,850
Land	14,800	
Accounts payable		22,688
Note payable (secured by mortgage)		37,005
Tracy Rohan, capital		141,040
Tracy Rohan, withdrawals	5,700	
Jackie Kovak, capital		141,040
Jackie Kovak, withdrawals	5,700	
Kerry Keene, capital		70,520
Kerry Keene, withdrawals	16,200	
Services revenue		75,150
Operating expense	53,750	
Totals	$560,250	$560,250

Required

1. Prepare the November 16 general journal entries to close the revenue, expense, income summary, and withdrawals accounts of the partnership.
2. Assume the estate of Rohan agreed to accept the land and building and to assume the mortgage note thereon in settlement of its claim against the partnership assets, and that Kovak and Keene planned to continue the business and rent the building from the estate. Prepare the partnership's December 1 general journal entry to transfer the land, building, and mortgage note in settlement with the estate.
3. Assume that, instead of the foregoing, the estate of Rohan demanded a cash settlement and the business had to be sold to a competitor, who gave $298,000 for the noncash assets and assumed the mortgage note but not the accounts payable. Prepare the December 1 general journal entry to transfer the noncash assets and mortgage note to the competitor, and the entries to allocate the gain or loss to the partners and to distribute the partnership cash.

Problem 13–7
Analytical essay
(LO 2)

Janet Koppen and Beverly Spikes want to form a partnership and are considering two methods of sharing incomes and losses. Method (*a*) splits all incomes and losses in a 2:3 ratio, or 40% to Koppen and 60% to Spikes. Method (*b*) depends on the income or loss of the partnership. If the partnership incurs a loss, the partners share it equally. If the income is in the range of $0 to $45,000, it is allocated based on an annual salary allowance of $15,000 to Koppen and $30,000 to Spikes. If the net income exceeds $45,000, the residual after the salary allowances is shared equally.

Koppen has retained you to write an evaluation of the two methods indicating which is more favorable to her. Your discussion should include a comparison of the two methods at each of the three possible net income levels. Also discuss the importance of asking Koppen to estimate the partnership's future earnings.

Problem 13–8
Analytical essay
(LO 3)

Guido, DeVito, and Vanelli have been operating a successful partnership for several years. Even though business is good, DeVito and Vanelli have disagreed with Guido on several occasions regarding the business, and Guido is now withdrawing from the partnership. The partners agree that the book values of the assets are less than their market values. However, they do not want to change the recorded values at this time. As a result, the partners have agreed that Guido should withdraw cash in an amount greater than his capital account balance.

DeVito and Vanelli are not sure how to calculate the adjustments to their capital accounts (brought about by the difference between Guido's equity and the cash he is withdrawing). DeVito thinks they should split the difference in the ratio of their capital account balances. Vanelli thinks the adjustments should be calculated using their original income-and-loss-sharing ratio. Which partner do you think is correct? Explain the reasons for your answers.

Alternate Problems

Problem 13–1A
Methods of allocating partnership income
(LO 1)

Paul Jones, Will Rogers, and Anne Thompson invested $82,000, $49,200, and $32,800, respectively, in a partnership. During its first year, the firm earned $135,000.

Required

Prepare entries to close the firm's Income Summary account as of December 31 and to allocate the net income to the partners under each of the following assumptions. (Round your answers to the nearest whole dollar.)

a. The partners did not specify any special method of sharing incomes.
b. The partners agreed to share net incomes and losses in the ratio of their beginning investments.
c. The partners agreed to share income by providing annual salary allowances of $48,000 to Jones, $36,000 to Rogers, and $25,000 to Thompson; allowing 10% interest on the partners' beginning investments; and sharing the remainder equally.

Problem 13–2A
Allocating partnership incomes and losses; sequential years
(LO 1)

Jacob Jackson and K. D. Fletcher are in the process of forming a partnership to which Jackson will devote one-third time and Fletcher will devote full time. They have discussed the following alternative plans for sharing net incomes and losses:

a. In the ratio of their initial investments, which they have agreed will be $52,000 for Jackson and $78,000 for Fletcher.
b. In proportion to the time devoted to the business.
c. A salary allowance of $2,000 per month to Fletcher and the balance in accordance with their initial investment ratio.
d. A $2,000 per month salary allowance to Fletcher, 10% interest on their initial investments, and the balance equally.

The partners expect the business to generate income as follows: Year 1, $18,000 net loss; Year 2, $38,000 net income; and Year 3, $94,000 net income.

Required

1. Prepare three schedules with the following column headings:

Income/ Loss Sharing Plan	Year ______		
	Calculations	Jackson	Fletcher

2. Complete a schedule for each of the first three years by showing how the partnership income or loss for each year would be allocated to the partners under each of the four plans being considered. (Round your answers to the nearest whole dollar.)

Problem 13–3A
Partnership income allocation, statement of changes in partners' equity, and closing entries
(LO 2)

Ella Phillips, Chet Fong, and Lou Campos formed the PFC Partnership by making capital contributions of $72,000, $108,000, and $60,000, respectively. They anticipate annual net incomes of $120,000 and are considering the following alternative plans of sharing net incomes and losses: (*a*) equally; (*b*) in the ratio of their initial investments; or (*c*) salary allowances of $20,000 to Phillips, $15,000 to Fong, and $40,000 to Campos; interest allowances of 12% on initial investments, with any remaining balance shared equally.

Required

1. Prepare a schedule with the following column headings:

Inc./Loss Sharing Plan	Calculations	Share to Phillips	Share to Fong	Share to Campos	Totals

   Use the schedule to show how a net income of $120,000 would be distributed under each of the alternative plans being considered. Round your answers to the nearest whole dollar.
2. Prepare a statement of changes in partners' equity showing the allocation of income to the partners, assuming they agree to use alternative (*c*) and the net income actually earned is $55,000. During the year, Phillips, Fong, and Campos withdrew $9,000, $19,000, and $12,000, respectively.
3. Prepare the December 31 journal entry to close Income Summary assuming they agree to use alternative (*c*) and the net income is $55,000. Also, close the withdrawals accounts.

Problem 13–4A
Withdrawal of a partner
(LO 3)

Part 1. Soltani, Sugimoto, and Suza are partners with capital balances as follows: Soltani, $303,000; Sugimoto, $74,000; and Suza, $223,000. The partners share incomes and losses in a 5:1:4 ratio. Soltani decides to withdraw from the partnership, and the partners agree to not have the assets revalued on her retirement. Prepare general journal entries to record the April 30 withdrawal of Soltani from the partnership under each of the following unrelated assumptions:

a. Soltani sells her interest to Samba for $250,000 after Sugimoto and Suza approve the entry of Samba as a partner.

b. Soltani gives her interest to a daughter-in-law, Shulak. Sugimoto and Suza accept Shulak as a partner.

c. Soltani is paid $303,000 in partnership cash for her equity.

d. Soltani is paid $175,000 in partnership cash for her equity.

e. Soltani is paid $100,000 in partnership cash plus manufacturing equipment recorded on the partnership books at $269,000 less accumulated depreciation of $168,000.

Part 2. Assume that Soltani does not retire from the partnership described in Part 1. Instead, Sung is admitted to the partnership on April 30 with a 20% equity. Prepare general journal entries to record the entry of Sung under each of the following unrelated assumptions:

a. Sung invests $150,000.
b. Sung invests $98,000.
c. Sung invests $213,000.

Problem 13–5A
Liquidation of a partnership
(LO 4)

Huggins, Hart, and Love, who have always shared incomes and losses in a 2:1:2 ratio, plan to liquidate their partnership. Just prior to the liquidation their balance sheet appeared as follows:

HUGGINS, HART, AND LOVE
Balance Sheet
January 18, 19—

Assets		Liabilities and Owners' Equity	
Cash	$174,300	Accounts payable	$171,300
Equipment	308,600	C. J. Huggins, capital	150,200
		D. C. Hart, capital	97,900
		J. D. Love, capital	63,500
Total assets	$482,900	Total liabilities and owners' equity	$482,900

Required

Under the assumption the equipment is sold and the cash is distributed to the proper parties on January 18, prepare general journal entries for the sale, the gain or loss allocation, and the distribution of cash in each of the following unrelated cases:

a. The equipment is sold for $325,000.
b. The equipment is sold for $265,000.
c. The equipment is sold for $100,000, and any partners with resulting deficits can and do pay in the amount of their deficits.
d. The equipment is sold for $75,000, and the partners have no assets other than those invested in the business.

Problem 13–6A
Withdrawal of a partner
(LO 3)

Until July 3, 1993, Daily, Murray, and Dryer were partners that shared incomes and losses in the ratio of their beginning-of-year capital account balances. On July 3, Murray suffered a heart attack and died. Daily and Dryer immediately terminated the partnership and prepared the following adjusted trial balance:

DAILY, MURRAY, AND DRYER
Adjusted Trial Balance
July 3, 1993

Cash	$ 31,418	
Accounts receivable	18,322	
Allowance for doubtful accounts		$ 725
Supplies inventory	54,910	
Equipment	110,660	
Accumulated depreciation, equipment		15,808
Building	303,300	
Accumulated depreciation, building		68,390
Land	27,400	
Accounts payable		25,975
Note payable (secured by mortgage)		64,012
Jess Daily, capital		146,800
Jess Daily, withdrawals	21,700	
Mel Murray, capital		206,000
Mel Murray, withdrawals	38,200	
Pat Dryer, capital		41,200
Pat Dryer, withdrawals	10,500	
Services revenue		195,600
Operating expense	166,100	
Totals	$782,510	$782,510

Required

1. Prepare the July 3 general journal entries to close the revenue, expense, income summary, and withdrawals accounts of the partnership.
2. Assume the estate of Murray agreed to accept the land and building and to assume the mortgage note thereon in settlement of its claim against the partnership assets, and that Daily and Dryer planned to continue the business and rent the building from the estate. Prepare the partnership's July 16 general journal entry to transfer the land, building, and mortgage note in settlement with the estate.
3. Assume that, instead of the foregoing, the estate of Murray demanded a cash settlement and the business had to be sold to a competitor, who gave $350,000 for the noncash assets and assumed the mortgage note but not the accounts payable. Prepare the July 16 general journal entry to transfer the noncash assets and mortgage note to the competitor, and the entries to allocate the gain or loss to the partners and to distribute the partnership cash.

Problem 13–7A
Analytical essay
(LO 2)

Janet Koppen and Beverly Spikes want to form a partnership and are considering two methods of sharing incomes and losses. Method (*a*) splits all profits and losses in a 2:3 ratio, or 40% to Koppen and 60% to Spikes. Method (*b*) depends on the income or loss of the partnership. If the partnership incurs a loss, the partners share it equally. If the income is in the range of $0 to $45,000, it is allocated based on an annual salary allowance of $15,000 to Koppen and $30,000 to Spikes. If the net income exceeds $45,000, the residual after the salary allowances is shared equally.

Spikes has retained you to write an evaluation of the two methods indicating which is most favorable to her. Your discussion should include a comparison of the two methods at each of the three possible net income levels. Also, discuss the importance of asking Spikes to estimate the partnership's future earnings.

Problem 13–8A
Analytical essay
(LO 3)

Kay Doobie, Ed Foley, and Brian McKenzie have been operating a partnership for several years. Business has not been good recently, and Doobie is withdrawing from the partnership. The partners agree that the market values of the assets are less than their recorded book values. However, they do not want to change the recorded values at this time. As a result, the partners have agreed that Doobie should withdraw cash in an amount that is less than her capital account balance.

Foley and McKenzie are not sure how to calculate the adjustments to their capital accounts (brought about by the difference between Doobie's equity and the cash she is withdrawing). Foley thinks they should split the difference in the ratio of their capital account balances. McKenzie thinks the adjustments should be calculated using their income-and-loss-sharing ratio. Which partner do you think is correct? Explain why.

Provocative Problems

Provocative Problem 13–1
Hartel and Huitt Partnership
(LO 1)

Keith Hartel and Todd Huitt agreed to share the annual net incomes or losses of their partnership as follows: if the partnership earns a net income, the first $60,000 is allocated 40% to Hartel and 60% to Huitt to reflect the time devoted to the business by each partner. Income in excess of $60,000 is shared equally. However, the partners have agreed to share any losses equally.

Required

1. Prepare a schedule showing how net income of $72,000 for 1993 should be allocated to the partners.
2. Sometime later in 1994, the partners discovered that $80,000 of accounts payable had existed on December 31, 1993, but had not been recorded. These accounts payable relate to expenses incurred by the business. They are now trying to determine the best way to correct their accounting records, particularly their capital accounts. Huitt suggests that they make a special entry crediting $80,000 to the liability account, and debiting their capital accounts for $40,000 each. Hartel, on the other hand, suggests that an entry should be made to record the accounts payable and retroactively correct the capital accounts to reflect the balance that they would have had if the expenses had been recognized in 1993. If they had been recognized, the partnership would have reported a loss of $8,000 instead of the $72,000 net income.
   (*a*) Present the journal entry suggested by Huitt for recording the accounts payable and allocating the loss to the partners.
   (*b*) Give the journal entry to record the accounts payable and correct the capital accounts according to Hartel's suggestion. Show how you calculated the amounts presented in the entry.

3. Which suggestion do you think complies with their partnership agreement? Why?

Provocative Problem 13–2
The Med Mart
(LO 3)

Martha Emerson and Florence Knight are partners who own and operate The Med Mart, a medical supply store. Emerson's recorded equity in the business is $129,000 and Knight's recorded equity is $69,000. They share incomes and losses by allowing annual salary allowances of $55,000 to Emerson and $30,000 to Knight, with any remaining balance being shared 70% to Emerson and 30% to Knight.

Gail Emerson, Martha Emerson's daughter, has been working in the store on a salary basis. In addition to working in the store, Gail is a registered nurse and works part time at a nearby hospital. Because Gail is well known and liked by many of the doctors, nurses, and other employees at the hospital, she attracts a great deal of business to the store. The partners believe that at least one third of the past three years' sales can be traced directly to Gail's association with the store, and it is reasonable to assume she was instrumental in attracting even more.

Gail is paid $2,000 per month, but feels this is not sufficient to induce her to remain with the store as an employee. However, she likes the work and plans to continue in the medical field. What she really wants is to become a partner in the business.

Her mother is anxious for her to remain in the business and proposes the following:

a. That Gail Emerson be admitted to the partnership with a 20% equity in the net assets.

b. That she, Martha Emerson, transfer from her capital account to Gail's capital account one half of the 20% interest; that Martha contribute cash to the firm for the other half of Gail's interest; and that Gail sign a note to Martha for the amount of cash paid by Martha.

c. That incomes and losses be shared by continuing the $55,000 and $30,000 salary allowances of the original partners and that Gail be given a $24,000 annual salary allowance, after which any remaining income or loss will be shared 50% to Martha Emerson, 30% to Florence Knight, and 20% to Gail Emerson.

Required

1. Prepare a schedule showing the partners' capital balances both before and immediately after Gail's admission to the partnership.
2. Assume the net incomes for the past three years were $87,600, $91,200, and $95,400, respectively. Prepare one schedule showing how net income was allocated during the past three years, and a second schedule showing how net income would have been allocated if Martha's proposal had been in effect all three years.
3. Describe how the admission of Gail would affect Florence's equity and share in future profits, and how the partnership might benefit from Gail's admission. Would you advise Florence to accept the proposal?

Provocative Problem 13–3
Baroque Partnership
(LO 3)

The balance sheet of the Baroque Partnership on December 31, 1993, is as follows:

Assets		Liabilities and Owners' Equity	
Cash	$ 20,000	Bonet, capital	$ 34,000
Other assets	80,500	Lebeaux, capital	50,500
Land	67,000	Dubois, capital	83,000
Total assets	$167,500	Total liabilities and owners' equity	$167,500

The income-and-loss-sharing percentages are Bonet, 20%; Lebeaux, 30%; and Dubois, 50%. Bonet wishes to withdraw from the partnership, and the partners finally agree that the land owned by the partnership should be transferred to Bonet in full payment for his equity. In reaching this decision, they recognize that the land has appreciated since it was purchased and is now worth $78,000. If Bonet retires on January 1, 1994, what journal entries should be made on that date?

Provocative Problem 13–4
As a Matter of Ethics: Essay

Ethics

Review the As a Matter of Ethics case on page 703. Then write a brief essay describing Janis Carpenter's engagement and the suggestions you would offer the partners. Your essay should include the reasons why your suggested settlement is fair.

Answers to Objective Review Questions

LO 1 (*e*)
LO 2 (*b*)
LO 3 (*e*)
LO 4 (*d*)
LO 5 (*c*)

PART

V

Accounting Principles, the FASB's Conceptual Framework, and Alternative Valuation Methods

Topical Coverage

Accounting principles or concepts are not laws of nature. They are broad ideas developed as a way of *describing* current accounting practices and *prescribing* new and improved practices. In studying Part V, you will learn about some new accounting concepts that the FASB developed in an effort to guide future changes and improvements in accounting. You also will learn about some major alternatives to the historical cost measurements reported in conventional financial statements. Studying these alternatives will help you understand the nature of the information that is contained in conventional statements. In addition, it will help you grasp the meaning of new reporting practices that may occur in future years.

Learning Objectives

After studying Part V, you should be able to:

1. Explain the difference between descriptive concepts and prescriptive concepts, and the difference between bottom-up and top-down approaches to the development of accounting concepts.
2. Describe the major components in the FASB's conceptual framework.
3. Explain why conventional financial statements fail to adequately account for price changes.
4. Use a price index to restate historical cost/nominal dollar costs into constant purchasing power amounts and to calculate purchasing power gains and losses.
5. Explain the current cost approach to valuation, including its effects on the income statement and balance sheet.
6. Explain the current selling price approach to valuation.
7. Define or explain the words and phrases listed in the Part V glossary.

ACCOUNTING PRINCIPLES AND THE FASB'S CONCEPTUAL FRAMEWORK

Descriptive and Prescriptive Accounting Concepts

LO 1 Explain the difference between descriptive concepts and prescriptive concepts, and the difference between bottom-up and top-down approaches to the development of accounting concepts.

To fully understand the importance of financial accounting concepts or principles, you must realize that they serve two purposes: First, they provide general descriptions of existing accounting practices. In doing this, concepts and principles serve as guidelines that help you learn about accounting. Thus, after learning how the concepts or principles are applied in a few situations, you develop the ability to apply them in different situations. This is easier and more effective than memorizing a very long list of specific practices.

Second, these concepts or principles help accountants analyze unfamiliar situations and develop procedures to account for those situations. This purpose is especially important for the Financial Accounting Standards Board (FASB), which is charged with developing uniform practices for financial reporting in the United States and with improving the quality of such reporting.

In prior chapters, we defined and illustrated several important accounting principles. These principles, which follow, describe in general terms the practices currently used by accountants.

Generally Accepted Principles		
Business entity principle	Full-disclosure principle	Objectivity principle
Conservatism principle	Going concern principle	Revenue recognition principle
Consistency principle	Matching principle	
Cost principle	Materiality principle	Time-period principle

To help you learn accounting, we first listed these principles in Chapter 1 (p. 23) and have referred to them frequently in later chapters. Although these ideas are labeled *principles,* in this discussion we use the term *concepts* to include both these principles as well as other general rules developed by the FASB. The FASB also uses the word *concepts* in this general manner.

The preceding concepts are useful for teaching and learning about accounting practice and are helpful for dealing with some unfamiliar transactions. As business practices have evolved in recent years, however, these concepts have become less useful as guides for accountants to follow in dealing with new and different types of transactions. This problem has occurred because the concepts are intended to provide general descriptions of current accounting practices. In other words, they describe what accountants currently do; they do not necessarily describe what accountants should do. Also, since these concepts do not identify weaknesses in accounting practices, they do not lead to major changes or improvements in accounting practices.

Because the FASB is charged with improving financial reporting, its first members decided that a new set of concepts should be developed. They also decided that the new set of concepts should not merely *describe* what was being done under current practice. Instead, the new concepts should *prescribe* what ought to be done to make things better. The project to develop a new set of prescriptive concepts was initiated in 1973, and quickly became known as the FASB's *conceptual framework project.*

However, before we examine the concepts developed by the FASB, we need to look more closely at the differences between descriptive and prescriptive uses of accounting concepts.

The Processes of Developing Descriptive and Prescriptive Accounting Concepts

Sets of concepts differ in how they are developed and used. In general, when concepts are intended to describe current practice, they are developed by looking at accepted specific practices, and then making some general rules to encompass them. This bottom-up approach is diagrammed in Illustration V–1, which shows the arrows going from the practices to the concepts. The outcome of the process is a set of general rules that summarize practice and that can be used for education and for solving some new problems. For example, this approach leads to the concept that assets are recorded at cost. However, these kinds of concepts often fail to show how new problems should be solved. For example, the concept that assets are recorded at cost does not provide much direct guidance for situations in which assets have no cost because they are donated to a company by a local government. Further, because these concepts are based on the presumption that current practices are adequate, they do not lead to the development of new and improved accounting methods. To continue the example, the concept that assets are initially recorded at cost

ILLUSTRATION V–1

A "Bottom-Up" Process of Developing Descriptive Accounting Concepts

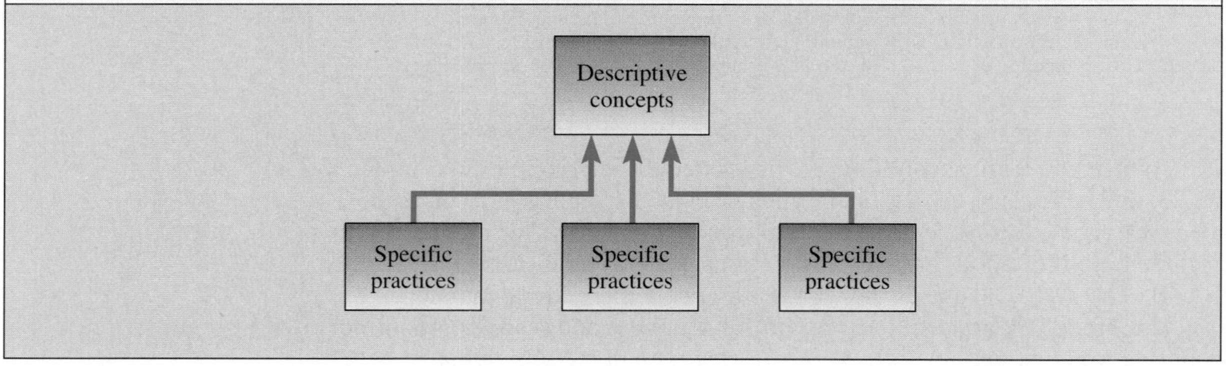

ILLUSTRATION V–2

A "Top–Down" Process of Developing Prescriptive Accounting Concepts

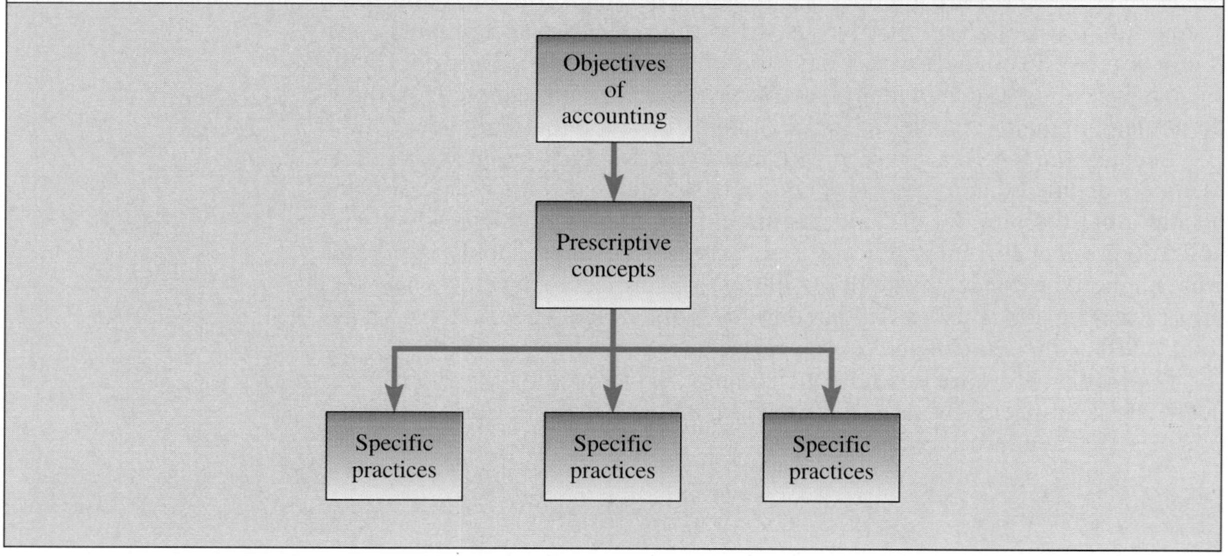

does not encourage asking the question of whether they should always be carried at that amount.

In contrast, if concepts are intended to *prescribe* improvements in accounting practices, they are likely to be designed by a top-down approach (Illustration V–2). Note that the top-down approach starts with broad accounting objectives. The process then generates broad concepts about the types of information that should be reported. Finally, these concepts should lead to specific practices that ought to be used. The advantage of this approach is that the concepts are good for solving new problems and evaluating old answers; its disadvantage is that the concepts may not be very descriptive of current practice. In fact, the suggested practices may not be in current use.

Since the FASB uses accounting concepts to prescribe accounting practices, the Board uses a top-down approach to develop its conceptual frame-

AS A MATTER OF

Opinion

Dennis R. Beresford, CPA

Mr. Beresford graduated from the University of Southern California in 1961 with a B.A. degree in accounting. After working 10 years in the Los Angeles office of Ernst & Ernst (now Ernst & Young), he was assigned to that firm's national office and made a partner. In 1987, he was appointed to the Financial Accounting Standards Board and named as its chairman. In 1991, he was reappointed for a second term, which will expire in 1997. Among his honors is the designation as the Beta Alpha Psi "Accountant of the Year" for 1986.

When the conceptual framework was being created, some thought that it would provide immediate answers for standard-setting issues. However, it could never do that all by itself. Rather, the framework is a tool that helps the FASB do its job.

Because getting to right answers depends on asking the right questions, I've come to realize that perhaps the most critical part of the standard-setting process is identifying and stating the issues properly. That's exactly what the conceptual framework helps us do by providing us with common objectives and terms. In effect, the conceptual framework brings discipline to those who participate in the standard-setting process. This discipline helps the Board to ask the right questions. It also helps other participants comment on our projects in a more consistent manner.

Although all Board members might not agree which answer to a question is best, the odds are much higher that the best answer will be among the alternatives that we consider if we ask the right questions. As a result, we are more likely to ultimately adopt the best answer.

work. The Board's concepts are not necessarily more correct than the previously developed concepts. However, the new concepts are intended to provide better guidelines for developing new and improved accounting practices. The Board has stated that it will use them as a basis for its future actions, and already has used them to justify important changes in financial reporting.

The FASB's Conceptual Framework

LO 2 Describe the major components in the FASB's conceptual framework.

The FASB's approach to developing its conceptual framework is diagrammed in Illustration V–3. Between 1978 and 1985, the Board issued six *Statements of Financial Accounting Concepts (SFAC)*. These concepts statements are not the same as the FASB's *Statements of Financial Accounting Standards (SFAS)*. The *SFAS*s are authoritative statements of generally accepted accounting principles that must be followed. The *SFAC*s are guidelines the Board uses in developing new standards. Accountants are not required to follow the *SFAC*s in practice.

The Objectives of Financial Reporting

The FASB's first *Statement of Financial Accounting Concepts (SFAC 1)* identified the broad objectives of financial reporting (Illustration V–3). The first and most general objective stated in *SFAC 1* is to "provide information that is useful to present and potential investors and creditors and other users in mak-

ILLUSTRATION V–3

The FASB's Conceptual Framework

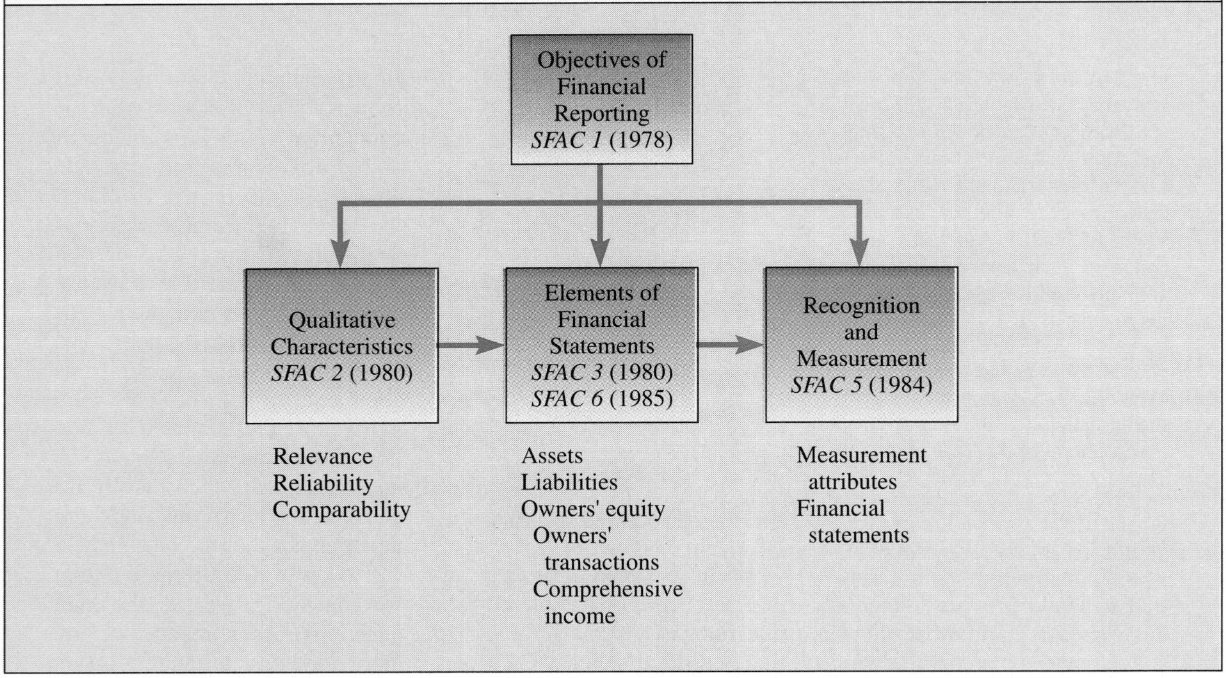

ing rational investment, credit, and similar decisions.''[1] From this beginning point in *SFAC 1,* the Board expressed other more specific objectives. These objectives recognize (1) that financial reporting should help users predict future cash flows, and (2) that information about a company's resources and obligations is useful in making such predictions. All the concepts in the conceptual framework are intended to be consistent with these general objectives. Of course, present accounting practice already provides information about a company's resources and obligations. Thus, although the conceptual framework is intended to be prescriptive of new and improved practices, the concepts in the framework are also descriptive of many current practices.

The Qualities of Useful Information

Illustration V–3 shows that the next step in the conceptual framework project was to identify the qualities (or qualitative characteristics) that financial information should have if it is to be useful in decision making. The Board discussed the fact that information can be useful only if it is understandable to users. However, the users are assumed to have the training, experience, and motivation to analyze financial reports. With this decision, the Board indicated that financial reporting should not try to meet the needs of unsophisticated or other casual report users.

[1] FASB, *Statement of Financial Accounting Concepts No. 1,* ''Objectives of Financial Reporting by Business Enterprises'' (Norwalk, Conn., 1978), par. 34.

In *SFAC 2,* the FASB said that information is useful if it is (1) relevant, (2) reliable, and (3) comparable. Information is *relevant* if it can make a difference in a decision. Information has this quality when it helps users predict the future or evaluate the past and is received in time to affect their decisions.

Information is *reliable* if users can depend on it to be free from bias and error. Reliable information is verifiable and faithfully represents what is supposed to be described. In addition, users can depend on information only if it is neutral. This means that the rules used to produce information should not be designed to lead users to accept or reject any specific decision alternative.

Information is *comparable* if users can use it to identify differences and similarities between companies. Comparability is possible only if companies follow uniform practices. However, even if all companies uniformly follow the same practices, comparable reports do not result if the practices are not appropriate. For example, comparable information would not be provided if all companies were to ignore the useful lives of their assets and depreciate all assets over two years.

Comparability also requires consistency (see Chapter 9, page 491), which means that a company should not change its accounting practices unless the change is justified as a reporting improvement. Another important concept discussed in *SFAC 2* is materiality (see Chapter 8, page 444).

Elements of Financial Statements

Illustration V–3 shows that another important step in developing the conceptual framework was to determine the elements of financial statements. This involved defining the categories of information that should be contained in financial reports. The Board's discussion of financial statement elements includes definitions of important elements such as assets, liabilities, equity, revenues, expenses, gains, and losses. In earlier chapters, we referred to many of these definitions when we explained various accounting procedures. The Board's pronouncement on financial statement elements was first published in 1980 as *SFAC 3*. In 1985, *SFAC 3* was replaced by *SFAC 6,* which modified the discussion of financial statement elements to include several elements for not-for-profit accounting entities.[2]

Recognition and Measurement

In *SFAC 5,* "Recognition and Measurement in Financial Statements of Business Enterprises," the FASB established concepts for deciding (1) when items should be presented (or recognized) in the financial statements, and (2) how to assign numbers to (or measure) those items. In general, the Board concluded that items should be recognized in the financial statements if they meet the following criteria: (1) *definitions*—the item meets the definition of an element of financial statements; (2) *measurability*—it has a relevant attribute measurable with sufficient reliability; (3) *relevance*—the information about it is capa-

[2] Among the six *Statements of Financial Accounting Concepts* issued by the FASB, one *(SFAC 4)* is directed toward accounting by not-for-profit organizations. Although *SFAC 4* is important, it is beyond the scope of this course.

ble of making a difference in user decisions, and (4) *reliability*—the information is representationally faithful, verifiable, and neutral.

The question of how items should be measured raises the fundamental question of whether financial statements should be based on cost or on value. Since this question is quite controversial, the Board's discussion of this issue is more descriptive of current practice than it is prescriptive of new measurement methods.

In *SFAC 5*, the Board stated that a full set of financial statements should show:

1. Financial position at the end of the period.
2. Earnings for the period. (This concept is very similar to the concept of net income used in current practice.)
3. Comprehensive income for the period. (This new concept is broader than earnings and includes all changes in owner's equity other than those that resulted from transactions with the owners. Some changes in asset values are included in this concept but are excluded from earnings.)
4. Cash flows during the period.
5. Investments by and distributions to owners during the period.

We should note that *SFAC 5* was the first official pronouncement to call for the presentation of a statement of cash flows. The statement of cash flows is now required under *SFAS 95*, which was issued two years after *SFAC 5*.

ALTERNATIVE ACCOUNTING VALUATION SYSTEMS

Conventional Financial Statements Fail to Account for Price Changes

LO 3 Explain why conventional financial statements fail to adequately account for price changes.

All accountants agree that conventional financial statements provide useful information for making economic decisions. However, many accountants also believe that conventional financial statements fail to adequately account for the impact of changing prices. Sometimes, this makes the statements misleading. That is, the statements may imply certain facts that are inconsistent with the real state of affairs. As a result, the information in the statements may lead decision makers to make decisions inconsistent with their objectives.

Failure to Account for Price Changes on the Balance Sheet

In what ways do conventional financial statements fail to account for changing prices? The general problem is that transactions are recorded in terms of the historical number of dollars paid. These amounts are not adjusted even though subsequent price changes may dramatically change the value of the purchased items. For example, Old Company purchased 10 acres of land for $25,000. Then, at the end of each accounting period, Old Company presented a balance sheet showing "Land . . . $25,000." Six years later, after price increases of 97%, New Company purchased 10 acres of land that was next to and nearly identical to Old Company's land. New Company paid $49,250 for the land.

Current Costs on the Balance Sheet

On the balance sheet, current cost accounting reports assets at the amounts that would have to be paid to purchase them as of the balance sheet date. Liabilities are reported at the amounts that would have to be paid to satisfy the liabilities as of the balance sheet date. Note that this valuation basis is similar to historical cost/constant purchasing power accounting in that a distinction exists between monetary and nonmonetary assets and liabilities. Monetary assets and liabilities are fixed in amount regardless of price changes. Therefore, monetary items are not adjusted for price changes. All of the nonmonetary items, however, must be evaluated at each balance sheet date to determine the best estimate of current cost.

For a moment, think about the large variety of assets reported on balance sheets. Given that there are so many different assets, you should not be surprised that accountants have difficulty obtaining reliable estimates of current costs. In some cases, they use price indexes that relate to specific categories of assets. Such specific price indexes may provide the most reliable source of current cost information. In other cases, when an asset is not new and has been partially depreciated, its current cost can be estimated by determining the cost to acquire a similar but new asset. Depreciation on the old asset is then based on the current cost of the new asset. Clearly, the accountant's professional judgment is an important factor in developing current cost data.

Current Selling Price Valuations

LO 6 Explain the current selling price approach to valuation.

In the previous discussion, you learned that conventional financial statements generally report historical costs in nominal dollars. That is, no adjustments are made for price changes. We also explained how accountants use a general price level index to adjust the nominal dollar amounts to measure the historical costs in terms of a constant purchasing power. Next, we discussed the alternative of reporting current (replacement) costs in the financial statements.

The final alternative to be considered is the reporting of assets (and liabilities) at current selling prices. On the balance sheet, this means assets would be reported at the amounts that would be received if the assets were sold. Similarly, liabilities would be reported at the amounts that would have to be paid to settle or eliminate the liabilities.

The argument for reporting the current selling prices of assets is based on the idea that the alternative to owning an asset is to sell it. Thus, the sacrifice a business makes to hold an asset is the amount it would receive if the asset were sold. Further, the benefit derived from owing a liability is the amount the business avoids paying by not eliminating the liability. If these current selling prices are reported on the balance sheet, the stockholders' equity represents the net amount of cash that would be realized by liquidating the business. This net liquidation value is the amount that could be invested in other projects if the business were liquidated. Therefore, one can argue that net liquidation value is the most relevant basis for evaluating whether the income the company earns is enough to justify remaining in business.

Some proponents of the current selling price approach believe that it should be applied to assets but not to liabilities. Others argue that it applies equally well to both. Still others believe that it should be applied only to assets held for sale. They would not apply it to assets held for use in the business.

A related issue is whether to report the adjustments to selling price as gains and losses in the income statement. Some businesses, especially banks, have expressed concern over the fact that reporting such gains or losses would cause large fluctuations in their reported net incomes. As an alternative to reporting the gains or losses on the income statement, they may be shown in stockholders' equity on the balance sheet as "unrealized gains and losses."

At the present time, the FASB has a project underway to evaluate the possibility of reporting the selling prices of marketable investments and marketable liabilities. A variety of individuals and groups have expressed both positive and negative opinions on the matter. The financial press describes the selling price approach to valuation as "mark to market" accounting.

Summary of Part V in Terms of Learning Objectives

LO 1. Some accounting concepts provide general descriptions of current accounting practices. Other concepts prescribe the practices accountants should follow. These prescriptive concepts are most useful in developing accounting procedures for new types of transactions and making improvements in accounting practice. A bottom-up approach to developing concepts examines current practices and then develops concepts to provide general descriptions of those practices. In contrast, a top-down approach begins by stating accounting objectives, and from there, develops concepts that prescribe the types of accounting practices accountants should follow.

LO 2. The FASB's conceptual framework begins with *SFAC 1* by stating the broad objectives of financial reporting. Next, *SFAC 2* identifies the qualitative characteristics accounting information should possess. The elements contained in financial reports are defined in *SFAC 6* and the recognition and measurement criteria to be used are identified in *SFAC 5*.

LO 3. Conventional financial statements report transactions in the historical number of dollars received or paid. Therefore, the statements are not adjusted to reflect general price level changes or changes in the specific prices of the items reported.

LO 4. To restate a historical cost/nominal dollar cost in terms of constant purchasing power, multiply the nominal dollar cost by a factor that represents the change in the general price level since the cost was incurred. On the balance sheet, monetary assets and liabilities should not be adjusted for changes in prices. However, purchasing power gains or losses result from holding monetary assets and owing monetary liabilities during a period of general price changes.

LO 5. Current costs on the balance sheet are the dollar amounts that would be spent to purchase the assets at the balance sheet date. On the income statement, current costs are the dollar amounts that would be necessary to acquire the consumed assets on the date they were consumed.

LO 6. Reporting current selling prices of assets and liabilities is supported by those who believe the balance sheet should show the net cost of not selling the assets and settling the liabilities. Some argue for applying selling price valuations to all assets and liabilities, or to marketable investments and marketable liabilities only, or to assets only. The related gains and losses may be reported on the income statement, but some would show them as unrealized stockholders' equity items on the balance sheet.

Glossary

LO 8 Define or explain the words and phrases listed in the Part V glossary.

Current cost In general, the cost that would be required to acquire (or replace) an asset or service at the present time. On the income statement, the number of dollars that would be required, at the time the expense is incurred, to acquire the resources consumed. On the balance sheet, the amounts that would have to be paid to replace the assets or satisfy the liabilities as of the balance sheet date. pp. 744–45

Historical cost/constant purchasing power accounting an accounting system that adjusts historical cost/nominal dollar financial statements for changes in the general purchasing power of the dollar. pp. 741–42

Historical cost/nominal dollar financial statements conventional financial statements that disclose revenues, expenses, assets, liabilities, and owners' equity in terms of the historical monetary units exchanged at the time the transactions occurred. p. 740

Monetary assets money or claims to receive a fixed amount of money; the number of dollars to be received does not change regardless of changes in the purchasing power of the dollar. pp. 741–42

Monetary liabilities fixed amounts that are owed; the number of dollars to be paid does not change regardless of changes in the general price level. pp. 741–42

Nonmonetary assets assets that are not claims to a fixed number of monetary units, the prices of which therefore tend to fluctuate with changes in the general price level. p. 743

Nonmonetary liabilities obligations that are not fixed in terms of the number of monetary units needed to satisfy them, and that therefore tend to fluctuate in amount with changes in the general price level. p. 743

Purchasing power gains or losses the gains or losses that result from holding monetary assets and/or owing monetary liabilities during a period in which the general price level changes. p. 741

Synonymous Terms

Selling price valuation in accounting mark to market accounting.

Objective Review

Answers to the following questions are listed at the end of Part V. Be sure that you decide which is the one right answer to each question *before* you check the answers.

LO 1 The FASB's conceptual framework is intended to:

a. Provide a historical analysis of accounting practice.
b. Describe current accounting practice.
c. Provide concepts that attempt to prescribe what should be done in accounting practice.
d. Describe every situation that may be encountered in accounting practice and prescribe an accounting principle for each one.
e. None of the above is correct.

LO 2 That a business should be consistent from year to year in its accounting practices most directly relates to the FASB's concept that information reported in financial statements should be:

a. Relevant. *b.* Material. *c.* Reliable. *d.* Measurable. *e.* Comparable.

LO 3 The following selected information is from the conventional balance sheets of Company A and Company B:

	Company A	Company B
Cash	$ 24,000	$ 40,000
Equipment, net	96,000	102,200
Land	130,000	157,800
Total assets	$250,000	$300,000

Based on this information, which of the following statements is true?

a. Company B's assets are worth $50,000 more than Company A's assets.
b. Company A's assets are worth at least $16,000 less than Company B's assets.
c. If Company A and Company B own identical equipment and depreciate the equipment on the same basis, Company A must have purchased its machinery at an earlier date than Company B.
d. If Company A and Company B own identical tracts of land, Company B must have purchased its land at a later date than Company A.
e. The relative values of Company A's and Company B's assets cannot be determined from this conventional balance sheet information.

LO 4 Foster Company purchased 150 acres of land for $100,000 in 1990 when the general price index was 145.0 and the specific price index for land was 142.0. In December 1993, the general price index was 150.0 and the specific price index for land was 140.0. The purchasing power gain or (loss) pertaining to land that would be reported on the 1993 historical cost/constant purchasing power income statement would be (rounded to the nearest dollar):

a. $ –0– . *b.* $ 3,448. *c.* $(3,448). *d.* $ 1,408. *e.* $(1,408).

LO 5 In the current cost approach to accounting:

a. All balance sheet items are restated to reflect general price level changes.
b. On the balance sheet, nonmonetary items are restated to reflect general price level changes.
c. On the balance sheet, monetary items are restated to reflect general price level changes.
d. Nonmonetary assets are reported at the amounts that would have to be paid to purchase them as of the balance sheet date.
e. None of the above is correct.

LO 6 If current selling price valuations were used to account for the assets and liabilities of a business:

a. Gains and losses from changing market values would not be recorded.

b. Losses from changing market values would be recorded but not gains.

c. All accountants agree that gains and losses from changes in market values would be reported on the income statement.

d. Some accountants believe that gains and losses from changes in market values should be accumulated and reported on the balance sheet as unrealized gains and losses.

e. None of the above is correct.

LO 7 Obligations that are not fixed in terms of the number of monetary units needed to satisfy them, and that therefore tend to fluctuate in amount with changes in the general price level, are called:

a. Monetary assets. *b*. Monetary liabilities. *c*. Nonmonetary assets. *d*. Nonmonetary liabilities. *e*. Current liabilities.

Questions for Class Discussion

1. Can a concept be used descriptively and prescriptively?
2. What is the starting point in a top-down approach to developing accounting concepts?
3. What is the starting point in a bottom-up approach to developing accounting concepts?
4. Explain the difference between the FASB's *Statements of Financial Accounting Concepts* and the *Statements of Financial Accounting Standards*.
5. Which three qualitative characteristics of accounting information did the FASB identify as being necessary if the information is to be useful?
6. What is implied by saying that financial information should have the qualitative characteristic of relevance?
7. What are the characteristics of accounting information that make it reliable?
8. What is the meaning of the phrase *elements of financial statements?*
9. What are the four criteria an item should satisfy to be recognized in the financial statements?
10. Some people argue that conventional financial statements fail to adequately account for inflation. What general problem with conventional financial statements generates this argument?
11. What is the fundamental difference in the adjustments made under current cost accounting and under historical cost/constant purchasing power accounting?
12. What are historical cost/nominal dollar financial statements?
13. What is the difference between monetary and nonmonetary assets?
14. Describe the meaning of *operating profit* under a current cost accounting system.
15. What is meant by the current selling price valuation of a liability?

Exercises

Exercise V–1
Adjusting costs for historical cost/constant purchasing power statements
(LO 4)

A company's plant and equipment consisted of land purchased in late 1987 for $225,000, machinery purchased in late 1989 for $85,000, and a building purchased in late 1991 for $330,000. Values of the general price index for December of 1987 through 1994 are as follows:

1987	100.0	1989	120.0	1991	150.0	1993	180.0
1988	112.0	1990	144.0	1992	165.5	1994	192.0

Required

1. Assuming the preceding price index adequately represents end-of-year price levels, calculate the amount of each asset's cost that would be shown on a historical cost/constant purchasing power balance sheet for (*a*) December 31, 1993, and (*b*) December 31, 1994. Ignore any accumulated depreciation.
2. Would the historical cost/constant purchasing power income statement for 1994 disclose any purchasing power gain or loss as a consequence of holding these assets? If so, how much?

Exercise V–2
Classifying monetary and nonmonetary items
(LO 4, 5)

Determine whether the following are monetary or nonmonetary items:

1. Wages payable. 2. Accounts payable. 3. Patents. 4. Preferred stock. 5. Product warranties liability. 6. Contributed capital in excess of par value, preferred stock. 7. Notes receivable. 8. Prepaid rent. 9. Merchandise inventory. 10. Equipment. 11. Goodwill. 12. Retained earnings. 13. Savings accounts. 14. Prepaid insurance.

Exercise V–3
Calculating amounts for current cost statements
(LO 5)

A company purchased land in 1991 at a cost of $245,000 and in 1992 at a cost of $120,000. What is the current cost of these land purchases in (*a*) 1993 and (*b*) 1994, given the following specific price index for land costs? (Round your answers to the nearest whole dollar.)

1991	102.0	1992	100.0	1993	107.1	1994	96.9

Exercise V–4
Calculating general purchasing power gain or loss
(LO 4)

Calculate the general purchasing power gain or loss in 1994 given the following price indexes: December 1993, 120.0; average during 1994, 125.0; and December 1994, 153.0

a. The cash balance on December 31, 1993, was $37,000. During 1994, cash sales occurred uniformly throughout the year and amounted to $235,500. Payments of expenses also occurred evenly throughout the year and amounted to $166,500. Accounts payable of $34,000 were paid in December.

b. Accounts payable amounted to $26,000 on December 31, 1993. Additional accounts payable amounting to $55,000 were recorded evenly throughout 1994. The only payment of accounts during the year was $34,000 in late December.

Problems

Problem V–1
Adjusting costs to historical cost/constant purchasing power amounts
(LO 4)

Levine Supply Company purchased machinery for $237,000 on December 30, 1990. They expected the equipment to last six years and to have no salvage value; straight-line depreciation was to be used. They sold the equipment on December 31, 1994, for $101,000. End-of-year general price index numbers were as follows:

1990	121.0	1992	138.2	1994	157.1
1991	135.3	1993	144.4		

Required

(Round all answers to the nearest whole dollar.)

1. What should be presented for the equipment and accumulated depreciation on a historical cost/constant purchasing power balance sheet dated December 31, 1993? Hint: Depreciation is the total amount of cost that has been allocated to expense. Therefore, the price index numbers used to adjust the nominal dollar cost of the asset should also be used to adjust the nominal dollar amount of depreciation.
2. How much depreciation expense should be shown on the historical cost/constant purchasing power income statement for 1993?
3. How much depreciation expense should be shown on the historical cost/constant purchasing power income statement for 1994?
4. How much gain on the sale of equipment should be reported on the historical cost/nominal dollar income statement for 1994?
5. After adjusting the equipment's cost and accumulated depreciation to the end-of-1994 price level, how much gain in (loss of) purchasing power was realized on the sale of the equipment?

Problem V–2
Calculating purchasing power gain or loss
(LO 4)

Setlaff Printing Company had three monetary items during 1994, cash, accounts receivable, and accounts payable. The changes in these accounts during the year were as follows:

Cash:	
Beginning balance	$ 45,250
Cash proceeds from sale of building (in March 1994)	25,600
Cash receipts from customers (spread evenly throughout the year)	179,700
Payments of accounts payable (spread evenly throughout the year)	(137,350)
Dividends declared and paid in June 1994.	(22,000)
Payments of other cash expenses during July 1994 . .	(38,900)
Ending balance	$ 52,300
Accounts receivable:	
Beginning balance	$ 46,400
Sales to customers (spread evenly throughout the year)	187,800
Cash receipts from customers (spread evenly throughout the year)	(179,700)
Ending balance	$ 54,500

Accounts payable:	
Beginning balance	$ 57,500
Merchandise purchases (spread evenly throughout the year)	115,800
Special purchase near end of December 1994	23,750
Payments of accounts payable (spread evenly throughout the year)	(137,350)
Ending balance	$ 59,700

General price index numbers at the end of 1993 and during 1994 are as follows:

Dec. 1993	234.1	June 1994	239.4	Avg. for 1994	240.2
Jan. 1994		July 1994	240.0		
Mar. 1994		Dec. 1994	245.8		

Required

Calculate the general purchasing power gain or loss experienced by Setlaff Printing Company in 1994. (Round all amounts to the nearest whole dollar.)

Problem V–3
Historical cost/nominal dollars, historical cost/constant purchasing power, and current costs
(LO 3, 4, 5)

Suffex Corporation purchased a tract of land for $425,000 in 1987, when the general price index was 174.9. At the same time, a price index for land values in the area of Suffex's tract was 181.2. In 1988, when the general price index was 188.5 and the specific price index for land was 203.7, Suffex Corporation bought another tract of land for $320,500. In late 1994, the general price index is 242.0 and the price index for land values is 259.9.

Required

1. In preparing a balance sheet at the end of 1994, show the amount that should be reported for land based on: (*a*) historical cost/nominal dollars; (*b*) historical cost/constant purchasing power; (*c*) current costs. (Round all amounts to the nearest whole dollar.)
2. In Suffex Corporation's December 1994 meeting of the board of directors, one director insists that Suffex has earned a gain in purchasing power as a result of owning the land. A second director argues that there could not have been a purchasing power gain or loss since land is a nonmonetary asset. Which director do you think is correct? Explain your answer.

Problem V–4
Analytical essay
(LO 1, 2)

Write a brief essay that explains the difference between descriptive and prescriptive concepts and that explains why the FASB's conceptual framework is designed to be prescriptive. Also discuss the question of whether specific concepts can be both descriptive and prescriptive.

Alternate Problems

Problem V–1A
Adjusting costs to historical cost/constant purchasing power amounts
(LO 4)

Bolton & Sykes Corporation purchased machinery for $720,000 on December 30, 1989. They expected the equipment to last eight years and to have no salvage value; straight-line depreciation was to be used. They sold the equipment on December 31, 1994, for $295,000. End-of-year general price index numbers were as follows:

1989	198.4	1991	209.6	1993	228.2
1990	202.0	1992	220.3	1994	234.7

Required

(Round all answers to the nearest whole dollar.)

1. What should be presented for the equipment and accumulated depreciation on a historical cost/constant purchasing power balance sheet dated December 31, 1992? Hint: Depreciation is the total amount of cost that has been allocated to expense. Therefore, the price index numbers used to adjust the nominal dollar cost of the asset should also be used to adjust the nominal dollar amount of depreciation.
2. How much depreciation expense should be shown on the historical cost/constant purchasing power income statement for 1993?
3. How much depreciation expense should be shown on the historical cost/constant purchasing power income statement for 1994?
4. How much gain on the sale of equipment should be reported on the historical cost/nominal dollar income statement for 1994?
5. After adjusting the equipment's cost and accumulated depreciation to the end-of-1994 price level, how much gain in (loss of) general purchasing power was realized on the sale of the equipment?

Problem V–2A
Calculating purchasing power gain or loss
(LO 4)

Pharmco, Inc., had three monetary items during 1994, cash, accounts receivable, and accounts payable. The changes in these accounts during the year were as follows:

Cash:	
Beginning balance	$122,000
Cash proceeds from sale of machinery (in February 1994).	45,200
Cash receipts from customers (spread evenly throughout the year)	397,800
Payments of accounts payable (spread evenly throughout the year)	(217,200)
Payments of other cash expenses in August 1994 . .	(152,050)
Dividends declared and paid during October 1994 . .	(104,600)
Ending balance	$ 91,150
Accounts receivable:	
Beginning balance	$187,450
Sales to customers (spread evenly throughout the year)	462,500
Cash receipts from customers (spread evenly throughout the year)	(397,800)
Ending balance	$252,150
Accounts payable:	
Beginning balance	$ 91,100
Merchandise purchases (spread evenly throughout the year)	175,350
Special purchase near end of October 1994	68,900
Payments of accounts payable (spread evenly throughout the year)	(217,200)
Ending balance	$118,150

General price index numbers at the end of 1993 and during 1994 are as follows:

Dec. 1993	76.8	Aug. 1994	72.4	Dec. 1994	76.0
Jan. 1994.	76.2	Oct. 1994	74.9	Avg. for 1994	73.3
Feb. 1994	74.7				

Required

Calculate the general purchasing power gain or loss experienced by Pharmco, Inc., in 1994. (Round all amounts to the nearest whole dollar.)

Problem V–3A
Historical cost/nominal dollars, historical cost/constant purchasing power, and current costs
(LO 1, 4)

Beta Company purchased a tract of land for $78,500 in 1986, when the general price index was 100.6. At the same time, a price index for land values in the area of Beta's tract was 97.0. In 1987, when the general price index was 107.2 and the specific price index for land was 106.8, Beta Company bought another tract of land for $115,000. In late 1994, the general price index is 134.5 and the price index for land values is 127.0.

Required

1. In preparing a balance sheet at the end of 1994, show the amount that should be reported based on: (*a*) historical cost/nominal dollars; (*b*) historical cost/constant purchasing power; (*c*) current costs.
   (Round all amounts to the nearest whole dollar.)
2. In Beta Company's December 1994 meeting of the board of directors, one director insists that Beta has incurred a loss of purchasing power as a result of owning the land. A second director argues that there could not have been a purchasing power gain or loss since land is a nonmonetary asset. Which director do you think is correct? Explain your answer.

Problem V–4A
Analytical essay
(LO 1, 2)

Write a brief essay that explains why a top-down approach to developing descriptive accounting concepts is not likely to be effective. Also explain why a bottom-up approach is more likely to be effective. Finally, explain why the FASB's conceptual framework reflects a top-down approach to developing concepts.

Answers to Objective Review Questions

LO 1 (*c*) LO 4 (*a*) LO 6 (*d*)
LO 2 (*e*) LO 5 (*d*) LO 7 (*d*)
LO 3 (*e*)

PART

VI

Accounting for Corporations, Long-Term Installment Notes, and Bonds

Most students of business will at some time work for a corporation. Perhaps all students will own (either directly or indirectly through a retirement fund) some debt or stock securities issued by corporations. For these reasons, you should have a basic understanding of corporations and the methods used to account for corporations and for stocks and bonds.

These topics are discussed in Part VI, which consists of the following chapters:

CHAPTER

14

Organization and Operation of Corporations

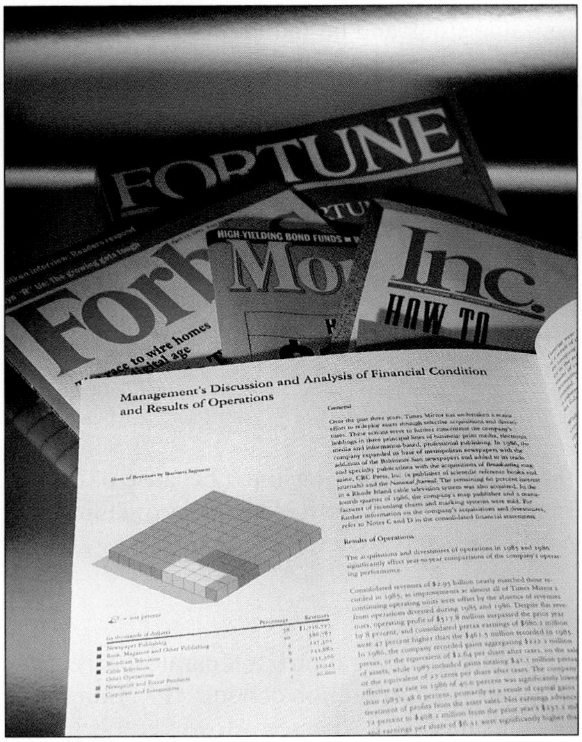

Business organizations that operate as corporations enjoy many advantages, including the ability to grow larger by selling stock to the public. The annual report presents accounting information that helps bridge the gap between a corporation's owners and its professional managers.

Topical Coverage

Of the three common types of business organizations (proprietorships, partnerships, and corporations), corporations are fewest in number. However, they transact more business than the other two combined. In the United States, the dollar sales volume of corporations is approximately nine times the combined sales of unincorporated businesses. Thus, from an overall economic point of view, corporations are clearly the most important form of business organization. As you study this chapter you will learn how corporations are organized and operated, and some of the procedures used to account for corporations.

Learning Objectives

After studying Chapter 14, you should be able to:

1. Explain the advantages, disadvantages, and organization of corporations, and the differences in accounting for partnerships and corporations.
2. Record the issuance of par value stock and no-par stock with or without a stated value, and explain the concept of minimum legal capital.
3. Record transactions that involve stock subscriptions and explain the effects of subscribed stock on a corporation's assets and stockholders' equity.
4. State the differences between common and preferred stock, and allocate dividends between the common and preferred stock of a corporation.
5. Explain convertible preferred stock and describe the meaning of the par value, call price, market value, and book value of corporate stock.
6. Define or explain the words and phrases listed in the chapter glossary.

Advantages of the Corporate Form

Corporations have become the dominant type of business because of the advantages created by the characteristics of this form of business organization. We describe these characteristics and their advantages next.

LO 1 Explain the advantages, disadvantages, and organization of corporations, and the differences in accounting for partnerships and corporations.

Corporations Are Separate Legal Entities

Unlike a proprietorship or partnership, a corporation is a separate legal entity. Separate and distinct from its owners, a corporation conducts its affairs with the same rights, duties, and responsibilities as a person. However, because it is not a real person, a corporation can act only through its agents, who are its officers and managers.

Stockholders Are Not Liable for the Corporation's Debts

As a separate legal entity, a corporation is responsible for its own acts and its own debts. Its shareholders are not liable for either. From the viewpoint of an investor, this lack of stockholders' liability is, perhaps, the most important advantage of the corporate form of business.

Ownership Rights of Corporations Are Easily Transferred

The ownership of a corporation is represented by shares of stock that generally can be transferred and disposed of any time the owners wish to do so. Also, the transfer of shares from one stockholder to another usually has no effect on the corporation or its operations.[1]

Corporations Have Continuity of Life

A corporation's life may continue indefinitely because it is not tied to the physical lives of its owners. In some cases, a corporation's life may be initially limited by the laws of the state of its incorporation. The corporation's charter can be renewed, however, and the life extended when the stated time expires. Thus, a corporation may have a perpetual life as long as it continues to be successful.

Stockholders Do Not Have a Mutual Agency Relationship

The stockholders of a corporation do not have the mutual agency relationship that exists for partners. Thus, a stockholder who is not a manager does not have the power to bind the corporation to contracts. Instead, a stockholder's participation in the affairs of the corporation is limited to the right to vote in the stockholders' meetings. Therefore, if you become a stockholder in a corporation, you may not have to worry about the character of the other stockholders to the same extent that you would if the business were a partnership. As a matter of ethical responsibility, however, you should always be interested in the character of those who are in business with you.

Ease of Capital Accumulation

Buying stock in a corporation is often more attractive to investors than investing in a partnership. Stock investments are attractive because: (1) stockholders are not liable for the corporation's actions and debts, (2) stock usually can be transferred easily, (3) the life of the corporation is not limited, and (4) stockholders do not have a relationship of mutual agency. These advantages make it possible for some corporations to accumulate large amounts of capital from the combined investments of many stockholders. In a sense, a corporation's capacity for raising capital is limited only by its ability to convince investors that it can use (and has used) their funds profitably. This situation is very different from the one faced by most partnerships, where mutual agency and unlimited liability reduce the number of investors who might be willing to become partners.

---

[1] However, a transfer of ownership can create significant effects if it brings about a change in who controls the company's activities.

Disadvantages of the Corporate Form

Governmental Regulation

Corporations are created by fulfilling the requirements of a state's incorporation laws. These laws subject a corporation to considerable state regulation and control. Single proprietorships and partnerships escape much of this regulation. In addition, they do not have to file many governmental reports required of corporations, particularly those that have issued stock to the public.

Taxation

Corporations are subject to the same property and payroll taxes as single proprietorships and partnerships. In addition, corporations are subject to taxes that are not levied on either of the other two. The most burdensome of these are federal and state income taxes that together may take 40% or more of a corporation's pretax income. However, the tax burden does not end there. The income of a corporation is taxed *twice,* first as income of the corporation and again as personal income to the stockholders when cash is distributed to them as dividends. This differs from single proprietorships and partnerships, which are not subject to income taxes as business units. Their income is taxed only as the personal income of their owners.[2]

The tax situation of a corporation is generally viewed as a disadvantage. However, in some cases, it can work to the advantage of stockholders because corporation and individual tax rates are progressive. That is, higher levels of income are taxed at higher rates and lower levels of income are taxed at lower rates. Therefore, taxes may be saved or at least delayed if a large amount of income is divided among two or more tax-paying entities. Thus, if an individual has a large personal income and pays taxes at a high rate, that person may benefit if some of the income is earned by a corporation that he or she owns, as long as the corporation avoids paying dividends. By not paying dividends, the corporation's income is taxed only once at the lower corporate rate, at least temporarily until dividends are paid.

Organizing a Corporation

A corporation is created by securing a charter from a state government. The requirements that must be met to be chartered vary among the states. Usually, a charter application must be signed by three or more subscribers to the prospective corporation's stock (such persons are called the *incorporators* or *promoters*). Then, the application must be filed with the appropriate state official. When it is properly completed and all fees are paid, the charter is issued and the corporation is formed. The subscribers then purchase the corporation's stock, meet as stockholders, and elect a board of directors. The directors are responsible for guiding the company's business affairs.

[2] Some corporations that have a limited number of shareholders can elect to be treated like a partnership for tax purposes. These companies are called *Subchapter S Corporations.*

Organization Costs

The costs of organizing a corporation, such as legal fees, promoters' fees, and amounts paid to secure a charter, are called **organization costs.** On the corporation's books, these costs are debited to an asset account entitled Organization Costs. In a sense, this intangible asset benefits the corporation throughout its life. Thus, you could argue that the cost should be amortized over the life of the corporation, which may be unlimited. However, generally accepted accounting principles preclude amortizing any intangible asset over a period longer than 40 years.[3]

In contrast, income tax rules permit a corporation to write off organization costs as a tax deduction over a minimum of five years. Thus, to make recordkeeping simple, many corporations use a five-year amortization period for financial statement purposes. Although the five-year period is clearly arbitrary, it is widely used in practice. Because organization costs are usually not material in amount, the *materiality principle* also supports the arbitrarily short amortization period.

Management of a Corporation

Although the organizational structures of all corporations are similar, they are not always the same. Illustration 14–1 diagrams two widely used alternatives. In all cases, the ultimate control of a corporation rests with its stockholders, but this control is exercised only indirectly through the election of the board of directors. Individual stockholders' rights to participate in management begin and end with a vote in the stockholders' meetings, where each of them has one vote for each share of stock owned.

Normally, a corporation holds a stockholders' meeting once each year to elect directors and transact other business as required by the corporation's bylaws. A group of stockholders that owns or controls the votes of 50% plus one share of a corporation's stock can easily elect the board and thereby control the corporation. However, in most companies, only a very few stockholders attend the annual meeting or even care about getting involved in the voting process. As a result, a much smaller percentage may be able to dominate the election of board members.

Stockholders who do not attend stockholders' meetings must be given an opportunity to delegate their voting rights to an agent. A stockholder does this by signing a document called a **proxy** that gives a designated agent the right to vote the stock. Prior to a stockholders' meeting, a corporation's board of directors typically mails to each stockholder an announcement of the meeting and a proxy that names the existing board chairperson as the voting agent of the stockholder. The announcement asks the stockholder to sign and return the proxy.

A corporation's board of directors is responsible for and has final authority for managing the corporation's activities. However, it can act only as a

[3] FASB, *Accounting Standards—Current Text* (Norwalk, Conn., 1990), sec. I60.110. First published in *APB Opinion No. 17,* par. 29.

ILLUSTRATION 14–1

Alternative Structures of Authority in a Corporation

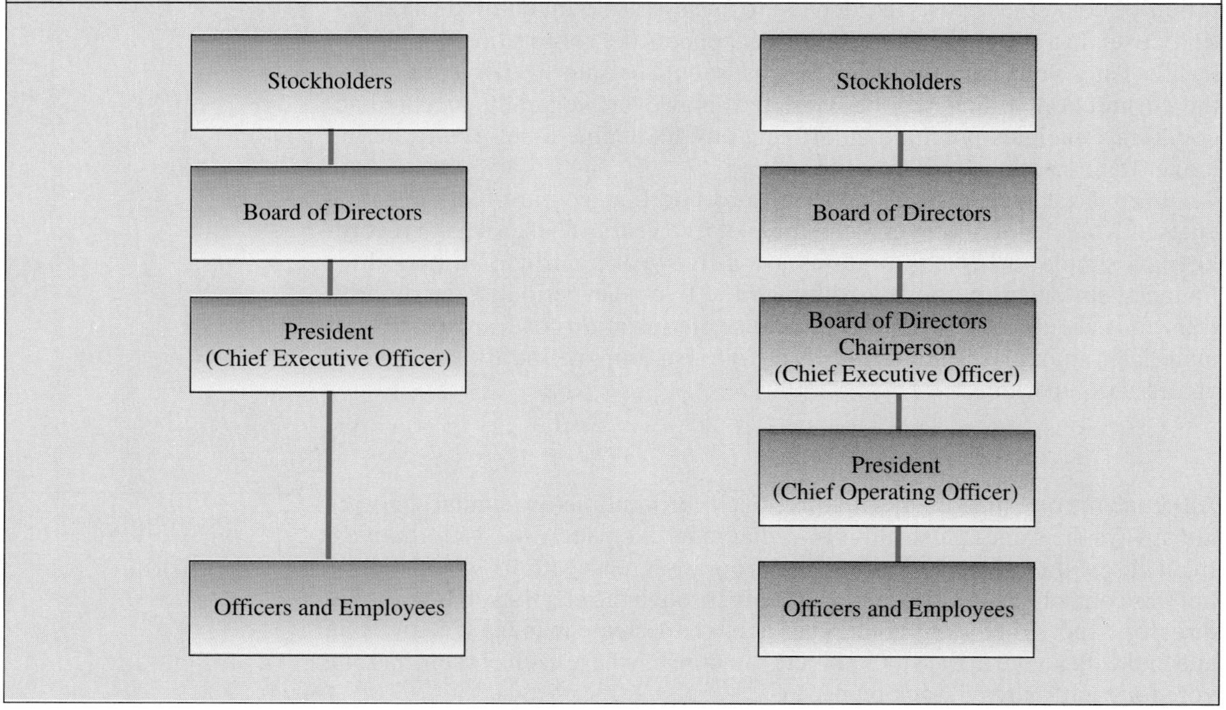

collective body. An individual director has no power to transact corporate business. Although the board has final authority, it usually limits its actions to establishing broad policy. Day-to-day direction of corporate business is delegated to executive officers appointed by the board to manage the business.

Traditionally, the chief executive officer (CEO) of the corporation is the president. Under the president, there may be several vice presidents who are assigned specific areas of management responsibility, such as finance, production, and marketing. In addition, the corporate secretary keeps the minutes of the meetings of the stockholders and directors and ensures that all legal responsibilities are fulfilled. In a small corporation, the secretary is also responsible for keeping a record of the stockholders and the changing amounts of their stock interest.

As shown on the right side of Illustration 14–1, many corporations have a different structure in which the chairperson of the board of directors also is the chief executive officer. With this arrangement, the president is usually designated the chief operating officer (COO), and the rest of the structure is essentially the same.

ILLUSTRATION 14–2

A Stock Certificate

NUMBER C9800

SHARES -50-

INCORPORATED UNDER THE LAWS OF THE STATE OF ILLINOIS

WESTFIELD PUBLISHING COMPANY, LTD.

THIS CERTIFIES that ROBERT WETZEL is the owner of

FIFTY

FULLY PAID AND NON-ASSESSABLE SHARES OF COMMON STOCK OF THE PAR VALUE OF $100.00 EACH OF THE WESTFIELD PUBLISHING COMPANY, LTD. transferable on the books of the Corporation in person or by duly authorized attorney upon surrender of this Certificate properly endorsed. This Certificate is not valid unless countersigned by the Transfer Agent and registered by the Registrar.

WITNESS the facsimile seal of the Corporation and the facsimile signatures of its duly authorized officers.

Dated: March 10, 1982

WESTFIELD PUBLISHING COMPANY SEAL ILLINOIS

SECRETARY PRESIDENT

Registered: By Registrar Authorized Signature

Countersigned: By Transfer Agent Authorized Signature

Stock Certificates and the Transfer of Stock

When investors buy a corporation's stock, they usually receive a stock certificate as proof that they purchased the shares.[4] In many corporations, only one certificate is issued for each block of stock purchased. This certificate may be for any number of shares. For example, the certificate of Illustration 14–2 is for 50 shares. Other corporations may use preprinted certificates, each of which represents 100 shares, plus blank certificates that may be made out for any number of shares.

When selling shares of a corporation, a stockholder completes and signs a transfer endorsement on the back of the certificate and sends it to the corporation's secretary or the transfer agent. The secretary or agent cancels and files the old certificate and issues a new certificate to the new stockholder. If the old certificate represents more shares than were sold, the corporation issues two new certificates. One certificate goes to the new stockholder for the sold shares and the other to the original stockholder for the remaining unsold shares.

[4] The issuance of certificates is less common than it used to be. Instead, many stockholders maintain accounts with the corporation or their stockbrokers and never receive certificates.

Transfer Agent and Registrar

If a corporation's stock is traded on a major stock exchange, the corporation must have a *registrar* and a *transfer agent*. The registrar keeps the stockholder records and prepares official lists of stockholders for stockholders' meetings and for dividend payments. Registrars and transfer agents usually are large banks or trust companies that have the computer facilities and staff to carry out this kind of work.

When a corporation has a transfer agent and a stockholder wants to transfer ownership of some shares to another party, the owner completes the transfer endorsement on the back of the stock certificate and sends the certificate to the transfer agent, usually with the assistance of a stockbroker. The transfer agent cancels the old certificate and issues one or more new certificates and sends them to the registrar. The registrar enters the transfer in the stockholder records and sends the new certificate or certificates to the proper owners.

Corporation Accounting

Corporation accounting was initially discussed in Chapter 4. In that discussion, we explained the entries to record several basic transactions of corporations. The entries included recording an issue of common stock for cash and closing a net income or a net loss from Income Summary to Retained Earnings. Also, the declaration and later payment of cash dividends were recorded. *At this point, you should review the Chapter 4 discussion of these entries on pages 207 through 208.* After completing that review, keep in mind that the stockholders' equity accounts of a corporation are divided into contributed capital accounts and retained earnings accounts. Also, remember that when a corporation's board of directors declares a cash dividend on the *date of declaration,* a legal liability of the corporation is incurred. The board of directors declares that on a specific future date, *the date of record,* the stockholders according to the corporation's records will be designated as those to receive the dividend. Finally, on the *date of payment,* the liability for the declared cash dividend is paid by the corporation.

The financial statements of a corporation were first illustrated in Chapter 5. The income statement was shown in Illustration 5–2 on page 259; the retained earnings statement was shown in Illustration 5–4 on page 265; and the balance sheet was shown in Illustration 5–5 on page 265. When you review these illustrations, note that income taxes were deducted on the income statement as an expense. Recall that a business organized as a corporation must pay income taxes, while a proprietorship or partnership does not pay income taxes. Also, cash dividends to stockholders are not an expense of the corporation; they are not deducted on the income statement. Instead, dividends are a *distribution of* net income and are subtracted on the retained earnings statement. Finally, notice that the stockholders' equity in Illustration 5–4 is divided into common stock and retained earnings.

Stockholders' Equity Accounts Compared to Partnership Accounts

To demonstrate the use of separate accounts for contributed capital and retained earnings as found in corporation accounting and to contrast their use with the accounts used in partnership accounting, assume the following: On January 5, 1993, a partnership involving two partners and a corporation having five stockholders were formed. Also assume that $25,000 was invested in each. In the partnership, J. Olm invested $10,000 and A. Baker invested $15,000. In the corporation, each of the five stockholders bought 500 shares of its $10 par value common stock at $10 per share. Without dates and explanations, general journal entries to record the investments are:

Partnership			Corporation		
Cash	10,000		Cash	25,000	
J. Olm, Capital . . .		10,000	Common Stock . . .		25,000
Cash	15,000				
A. Baker, Capital . .		15,000			

After the entries are posted, the owners' equity accounts of the two companies appear as follows:

Partnership

J. Olm, Capital

Date	Dr.	Cr.	Bal.
Jan. 5, 1993		10,000	10,000

A. Baker, Capital

Date	Dr.	Cr.	Bal.
Jan. 5, 1993		15,000	15,000

Corporation

Common Stock

Date	Dr.	Cr.	Bal.
Jan. 5, 1993		25,000	25,000

To continue the illustration, assume that during 1993, each company earned a net income of $8,000 and also distributed $5,000 to its owners. According to the partnership agreement, incomes are allocated 40% to Olm and 60% to Baker. The cash distribution to the partners was divided equally. The corporation declared the dividends on December 20, 1993, and both companies made the cash payments to owners on December 25, 1993. The entries to record the distribution of cash to partners and the declaration and payments of dividends to stockholders are as follows:

Partnership			Corporation		
J. Olm, Withdrawals	2,500		Dividends Declared	5,000	
A. Baker, Withdrawals . . .	2,500		Dividends Payable . . .		5,000
Cash		5,000	Dividends Payable	5,000	
			Cash		5,000

At the end of the year, the entries to close the Income Summary accounts are as follows:

Partnership

Income Summary	8,000	
J. Olm, Capital		3,200
A. Baker, Capital . . .		4,800

Corporation

Income Summary	8,000	
Retained Earnings . . .		8,000

Finally, the entries to close the withdrawals accounts and the Dividends Declared account are:

Partnership

J. Olm, Capital	2,500	
A. Baker, Capital	2,500	
J. Olm, Withdrawals . .		2,500
A. Baker, Withdrawals		2,500

Corporation

Retained Earnings	5,000	
Dividends Declared . .		5,000

After posting these entries, the owners' equity accounts of the two companies are as follows:

Partnership

J. Olm, Capital

Date	Dr.	Cr.	Bal.
Jan. 5, 1993		10,000	10,000
Dec. 31, 1993		3,200	13,200
Dec. 31, 1993	2,500		10,700

A. Baker, Capital

Date	Dr.	Cr.	Bal.
Jan. 5, 1993		15,000	15,000
Dec. 31, 1993		4,800	19,800
Dec. 31, 1993	2,500		17,300

J. Olm, Withdrawals

Date	Dr.	Cr.	Bal.
Dec. 25, 1993	2,500		2,500
Dec. 31, 1993		2,500	-0-

A. Baker, Withdrawals

Date	Dr.	Cr.	Bal.
Dec. 25, 1993	2,500		2,500
Dec. 31, 1993		2,500	-0-

Corporation

Common Stock

Date	Dr.	Cr.	Bal.
Jan. 5, 1993		25,000	25,000

Retained Earnings

Date	Dr.	Cr.	Bal.
Dec. 20, 1993	5,000		(5,000)
Dec. 31, 1993		8,000	3,000

Dividends Declared

Date	Dr.	Cr.	Bal.
Dec. 20, 1993	5,000		5,000
Dec. 31, 1993		5,000	-0-

Observe that in the partnership, after all entries have been posted, the $28,000 equity of the owners appears in the capital accounts of the partners:

J. Olm, capital	$10,700
A. Baker, capital	17,300
Total owners' equity	$28,000

By comparison, the stockholders' equity of the corporation is divided between contributed capital and the Retained Earnings account, as follows:

Common stock	$25,000
Retained earnings	3,000
Total stockholders' equity	$28,000

Authorization and Issuance of Stock

LO 2 Record the issuance of par value stock and no-par stock with or without a stated value, and explain the concept of minimum legal capital.

When a corporation is organized, its charter authorizes it to issue a specified number of shares of stock. If all of the authorized shares have the same rights and characteristics, the stock is called **common stock.** However, a corporation may be authorized to issue more than one class of stock, including preferred stock. (We discuss preferred stock later in this chapter.)

Because the corporation cannot issue more than the number of shares authorized in its charter, its founders will probably obtain authorization to issue more shares than they plan to sell when the company is first organized. By doing so, the corporation avoids having to get the state's approval to sell more shares when additional capital is needed to finance an expansion of the business. A corporation's balance sheet must disclose the numbers of shares authorized and issued. These facts are usually reported in the stockholders' equity section of the statement in a presentation similar to this:

Common stock, $10 par value, 25,000 shares authorized, 20,000 shares issued	$200,000

For example, IBM's balance sheet shows this information:

	1990	1989
	(in millions)	
Capital stock, $1.25 par value; Shares authorized, 750,000,000; Issued, 1990—571,618,795; 1989—574,775,560	$6,357	$6,341

Sale of Stock for Cash

When stock is sold for cash and immediately issued, an entry like the following is made to record the sale and issuance:

June	5	Cash	300,000.00	
		Common Stock, $10 Par Value		300,000.00
		Sold at par and issued 30,000 shares of $10 par value common stock.		

Exchanging Stock for Noncash Assets

A corporation may accept assets other than cash in exchange for its stock. In the process, the corporation also may assume some liabilities, such as a mortgage on some of the property. These transactions are recorded with an entry like this one:

June	10	Machinery	10,000.00	
		Buildings	65,000.00	
		Land	15,000.00	
		Long-Term Notes Payable		50,000.00
		Common Stock, $10 Par Value		40,000.00
		Exchanged 4,000 shares of $10 par value common stock for machinery, buildings, and land.		

Assets and liabilities are recorded at their fair market values as of the date of the transaction. If a reliable fair value for the assets cannot be determined, record the exchange by using the fair value of the stock as established by recent sales.

A corporation also may give shares of its stock to its promoters in exchange for their services in organizing the company. In this case, the corporation receives the intangible asset of being organized in exchange for its stock. Record this transaction as follows:

June	5	Organization Costs	5,000.00	
		Common Stock, $10 Par Value		5,000.00
		Gave the promotors 500 shares of $10 par value common stock in exchange for their services in organizing the corporation.		

Par Value and Minimum Legal Capital

Many stocks have a **par value**, which is an arbitrary value assigned to the stock when it is authorized. A corporation may choose to issue stock with a par value of any amount, but par values of $100, $25, $10, $5, $1, and even $0.01 are widely used. When a corporation issues par value stock, the par value is printed on each certificate and is used in accounting for the stock.

In many states, the par value of a corporation's stock also establishes the **minimum legal capital** for the corporation. Laws that establish minimum legal capital normally require stockholders to invest assets equal in value to at least the minimum legal capital. Otherwise, the stockholders are liable to the corporation's creditors for the deficiency. Usually, the minimum legal capital is defined as the par value of the issued stock. In other words, persons who buy stock from a corporation must give the corporation assets equal in value to at least the par value of the stock or be subject to making up the difference later. For example, if a corporation issues 1,000 shares of $100 par value stock, the minimum legal capital of the corporation is $100,000. Minimum legal capital requirements also make it illegal to pay any dividends if they reduce the stockholders' equity below the minimum amount.

The requirements for minimum legal capital are intended to protect the creditors of a corporation. Because a corporation's creditors cannot demand payment from the personal assets of the stockholders, the assets of the corporation are all that is available to satisfy the creditors' claims. To protect a corporation's creditors under these conditions, the minimum legal capital requirement limits a corporation's ability to distribute its assets to its stockholders. The idea is that assets equal to the amount of minimum legal capital must be retained in the corporation and cannot be paid to the stockholders unless all creditor claims are paid first.

Because par value determines the amount of minimum legal capital in many states, it is traditionally used in accounting for the part of stockholders' equity derived from the issuance of stock. However, par value does *not* establish a stock's market value or the price at which a corporation must issue the stock. If purchasers are willing to pay more, a corporation may sell and issue its stock at a price above par.

Stock Premiums and Discounts

Premiums on Stock

When a corporation sells its stock at a price above the par value, the stock is said to be issued at a premium. For example, if a corporation sells and issues its $10 par value common stock at $12 per share, the stock is sold at a $2 per share premium. A **premium on stock** is the amount in excess of par paid by the purchasers of newly issued stock. It is not a revenue and does not ever appear on the income statement. Rather, a premium is part of the investment of stockholders who pay more than par for their stock. It is simply a part of stockholders' equity.

In accounting for stock sold at a price greater than its par value, the premium is recorded separately from the par value and is called *contributed capital in excess of par value*. For example, assume that a corporation sells and issues 10,000 shares of its $10 par value common stock for cash at $12 per share. The sale is recorded as follows:

Dec.	1	Cash	120,000.00	
		Common Stock, $10 Par value		100,000.00
		Contributed Capital in Excess of Par Value, Common Stock		20,000.00
		Sold and issued 10,000 shares of $10 par value common stock at $12 per share.		

As we saw before, when stock is issued in exchange for assets other than cash, it is recorded at an amount equal to the fair value of the assets. If that fair value exceeds the par value of the stock, a premium is recorded as contributed capital in excess of par value.

When a balance sheet is prepared, any contributed capital in excess of par value is added to the par value of the stock in the equity section, as shown in the following example:

Stockholders' Equity

Common stock, $10 par value, 25,000 shares authorized, 20,000 shares issued	$200,000
Contributed capital in excess of par value, common stock	30,000
Total contributed capital	$230,000
Retained earnings	82,400
Total stockholders' equity	$312,400

Discounts on Stock

If stock is issued at a price below par value, the difference between par and the issue price is called a **discount on stock.** Most states prohibit the issuance of stock at a discount because the stockholders would be investing less than minimum legal capital. In states that allow stock to be issued at a discount, its purchasers usually become contingently liable to the corporation's creditors for the amount of the discount. Therefore, stock is seldom issued at a discount and a discussion of stock discounts has little practical importance. However, if stock is issued at less than par, the discount is not an expense and does not appear on the income statement. Rather, the discount is debited to a discount account, which is contra to the common stock account. In other words, the balance of the discount account is subtracted on the balance sheet from the par value of the stock.

No-Par Stock

At one time, all stocks were required to have a par value. Today, nearly all states permit the issuance of stocks that do not have a par value. The primary advantage of **no-par stock** is that it may be issued at any price without having a discount liability attached. Also, printing a par value of, say, $100 on a stock certificate may cause an inexperienced person to think that the share must be worth $100, when it actually may be worthless. Therefore, eliminating par value may encourage a closer analysis of the factors that give a stock value. These factors include such things as expectations about future earnings and dividends, and prospects for the economy as a whole.

In some states, the entire proceeds from the sale of no-par stock becomes minimum legal capital. In this case, the entire proceeds are credited to a no-par stock account. For example, if a corporation issues 1,000 shares of no-par stock at $42 per share, the transaction is recorded like this:

Oct.	20	Cash	,000.00	
		Common Stock, No-Par		,000.00
		Sold and issued 1,000 shares of no-par common stock at $42 per share.		

In other states, the board of directors of a corporation can place a **stated value** on its no-par stock. The stated value then becomes the minimum legal capital and is credited to the no-par stock account. If the stock is issued at an amount in excess of stated value, the excess is credited to an account called Contributed Capital in Excess of Stated Value, No-Par Common Stock. For example, suppose that a corporation issues 1,000 shares of no-par common stock with a stated value of $25 per share for cash equal to $42 per share. The transaction would be recorded as follows:

Oct.	20	Cash	42,000.00	
		Common Stock, No-Par		25,000.00
		Contributed Capital in Excess of Stated Value, No-Par Common Stock		17,000.00
		Sold 1,000 shares of no-par stock having a $25 per share stated value at $42 per share.		

Sale of Stock through Subscriptions

LO 3 Record transactions that involve stock subscriptions and explain the effects of subscribed stock on a corporation's assets and stockholders' equity.

Usually, stock is sold for cash and immediately issued. However, corporations sometimes sell stock through **stock subscriptions.** For example, when a new corporation is formed, the organizers may realize that the new business has limited immediate needs for cash but will need additional capital in the future. To get the corporation started on a sound footing, the organizers may sell the stock to investors who agree to contribute some cash now and to make additional contributions in the future. When stock is sold through subscriptions, the investor agrees to buy a certain number of the shares at a specified price. The agreement also states when payments are to be made. When the subscription is accepted by the corporation, it becomes a contract and the corporation acquires an asset. The asset is the right to receive payment from subscribers. At the same time, subscribers gain an equity in the corporation equal to the amount that they agree to pay.[5]

To illustrate the sale of stock through subscriptions, assume that on May 6, Northgate Corporation accepted subscriptions to 5,000 shares of its $10 par value common stock at $12 per share. The subscription contracts called for a 10% down payment to accompany the subscriptions with the balance to be paid in two equal installments due after three and six months. Northgate records the subscriptions with the following entry:

[5] Of course, there may be some doubt about the collectibility of the subscriptions for a new company because the subscribers may be inclined to withhold their payments if the company does not appear to be developing successfully.

May	6	Subscriptions Receivable, Common Stock	60,000.00	
		Common Stock Subscribed		50,000.00
		Contributed Capital in Excess of Par Value, Common Stock		10,000.00
		Accepted subscriptions to 5,000 shares of $10 par value common stock at $12 per share.		

At the time that subscriptions are accepted, the firm debits the Subscriptions Receivable account (an asset) for the sum of the stock's par value and premium. This is the total amount the subscribers agreed to pay. Notice that the **Common Stock Subscribed** account (an equity) is credited for par value and that the premium is credited to Contributed Capital in Excess of Par Value, Common Stock.

The receivables will be converted into cash when the subscribers pay for their stock. And, when all the payments are received, the subscribed stock will be issued and become outstanding. Northgate records the collections of the down payment and the two installment payments with these entries:

May	6	Cash	6,000.00	
		Subscriptions Receivable, Common Stock		6,000.00
		Collected 10% down payments on the common stock subscribed.		
Aug.	6	Cash	27,000.00	
		Subscriptions Receivable, Common Stock		27,000.00
		Collected the first installment payments on the common stock subscribed.		
Nov.	6	Cash	27,000.00	
		Subscriptions Receivable, Common Stock		27,000.00
		Collected the second installment payments on the common stock subscribed.		

In this case, the down payments accompanied the subscriptions. Therefore, the accountant could have combined the May 6 entries to record the receipt of the subscriptions and to record the down payments as follows:

May	6	Cash	6,000.00	
		Subscriptions Receivable, Common Stock	54,000.00	
		Common Stock Subscribed		50,000.00
		Contributed Capital in Excess of Par Value, Common Stock		10,000.00
		Accepted subscriptions to 5,000 shares of $10 par value common stock at $12 per share and received down payments of 10% of the subscription price.		

When stock is sold through subscriptions, the stock usually is not issued until the subscriptions are paid in full. Also, if dividends are declared before subscribed stock has been issued, the dividends go only to the holders of outstanding shares, not to the subscribers. However, as soon as the subscriptions are paid, the stock is issued. The entry to record the issuance of the Northgate common stock is as follows:

Aug.	5	Common Stock Subscribed	50,000.00	
		Common Stock, $10 Par Value		50,000.00
		Issued 5,000 shares of common stock sold through subscriptions.		

Subscriptions are usually collected in full, but not always. Sometimes, a subscriber fails to pay the agreed amount. When this default happens, the subscription contract is canceled. If the subscriber has made a partial payment on the contract, the amount may be refunded. Or, the company may issue a smaller amount of stock with a fair value equal to the partial payment. Or, the state law may allow the subscriber's partial payment to be kept by the corporation to compensate it for any damages.

Subscriptions Receivable and Subscribed Stock on the Balance Sheet

Subscriptions receivable are reported on the balance sheet as current or long-term assets, depending on when collection is expected. If a corporation prepares a balance sheet after accepting subscriptions to its stock but before the stock is issued, both the issued stock and the subscribed stock should be reported on the balance sheet as follows:

Common stock, $10 par value, 25,000 shares authorized, 20,000 shares issued	$200,000	
Common stock subscribed, 5,000 shares	50,000	
Total common stock issued and subscribed	$250,000	
Contributed capital in excess of par value, common stock	40,000	
Total contributed capital		$290,000

Rights of Common Stockholders

LO 4 State the differences between common and preferred stock, and allocate dividends between the common and preferred stock of a corporation.

When investors buy a corporation's common stock, they acquire all the *specific* rights granted by the corporation's charter to its common stockholders. They also acquire the *general* rights granted stockholders by the laws of the state in which the company is incorporated. State laws vary, but common stockholders usually have the following general rights:

1. The right to vote at stockholders' meetings.
2. The right to sell or otherwise dispose of their stock.
3. The right of first opportunity to purchase any additional shares of common stock issued by the corporation. This right is called the common stockholders' **preemptive right.** It gives stockholders the opportunity to protect their proportionate interest in the corporation. For example, a

stockholder who owns 25% of a corporation's common stock has the first opportunity to buy 25% of any new common stock issued. This arrangement enables the stockholder to maintain a 25% interest.
4. The right to share equally with other common stockholders in any dividends, with the result that each common share receives the same amount.
5. The right to share equally in any assets that remain after creditors are paid when the corporation is liquidated, with the result that each common share receives the same amount.

In addition, stockholders have the right to receive timely and accurate financial reports that describe the corporation's financial position and the results of its activities.

Preferred Stock

As mentioned earlier in this chapter, a corporation may be authorized to issue more than one kind or class of stock. If two classes are issued, one is generally called **preferred stock** and the other is called *common stock*. Preferred stock generally has a par value, but like common stock, may be sold at a price greater than par (or perhaps less). Separate contributed capital accounts are used to record the issuance of preferred stock. For example, if 50 shares of preferred stock with a $100 par value are issued for $6,000 cash, the entry is:

June	1	Cash	6,000.00	
		Preferred Stock		5,000.00
		Contributed Capital in Excess of Par Value, Preferred Stock		1,000.00
		Issued preferred stock for cash.		

The term *preferred* is used because the preferred shares have a higher priority (or senior status) relative to common shares in one or more ways. These typically include a preference for receiving dividends and a preference in the distribution of assets if the corporation is liquidated.

In addition to the preferences it receives, preferred stock carries all the rights of common stock, unless they are nullified in the corporation's charter. For example, most preferred stock does not have the right to vote. In effect, this disadvantage is accepted in return for the preferences.

Preferred Dividends

A preference for dividends gives preferred stockholders the right to receive their dividends before the common stockholders receive a dividend. In other words, a dividend cannot be paid to common stockholders unless preferred stockholders also receive one. The amount of dividends that the preferred stockholders must receive is usually expressed as a dollar amount per share or as a percentage applied to the par value. For example, holders of a 9%, $100 par value, preferred stock must be paid dividends at the rate of $9 per share per year before the common shareholders can receive any dividend. A preference for dividends does not, however, grant an absolute right to dividends. If the board of directors does not declare a dividend, neither the preferred nor the common stockholders receive one.

Cumulative and Noncumulative Preferred Stock

Preferred stock can be either **cumulative** or **noncumulative.** For cumulative, any undeclared dividends accumulate each year until they are received. For noncumulative, the right to receive dividends is forfeited in any year that the dividends are not declared.

When preferred stock is cumulative and the board of directors fails to declare a dividend to the preferred stockholders, the unpaid dividend is called a **dividend in arrears.** The accumulation of dividends in arrears on cumulative preferred stock does not guarantee that they will be paid. However, the cumulative preferred stockholders must be paid both the current dividend and all dividends in arrears before any dividend can be paid to the common stockholders.

To show the difference between cumulative and noncumulative preferred stock, assume that a corporation's outstanding stock includes 1,000 shares of $100 par, 9% preferred stock and 4,000 shares of $50 par common stock. During the first two years of the corporation's operations, the board of directors declared cash dividends of $5,000 in 1993 and $42,000 in 1994. The allocations of the total dividends are as follows:

	Preferred	Common
Assuming noncumulative preferred:		
1993	$ 5,000	$ -0-
1994:		
First: current preferred dividend	$ 9,000	
Remainder to common		$33,000
* * * * *		
Assuming cumulative preferred:		
1993	$ 5,000	$ -0-
1994:		
First: dividends in arrears	$ 4,000	
Next: current preferred dividend	9,000	
Remainder to common		$29,000
Totals	$13,000	$29,000

Notice that the allocation of the 1994 dividends depends on whether the preferred stock is noncumulative or cumulative. With noncumulative preferred stock, the preferred stockholders never receive the $4,000 that was skipped in 1993. However, when the preferred stock is cumulative, the $4,000 in arrears is paid in 1994 before the common stockholders receive a dividend.

Disclosure of Dividends in Arrears in the Financial Statements

Dividends are not like interest expense, which is incurred as time passes and therefore must be accrued. A liability for a dividend does not come into existence until the dividend is declared by the board of directors. Thus, if a preferred dividend date passes and the corporation's board fails to declare the dividend on its cumulative preferred stock, the dividend in arrears is not a liability. Accordingly, it does not appear as a liability on the balance sheet. However, when preparing financial statements, the *full-disclosure principle* requires you to report the amount of preferred dividends in arrears as of the balance sheet date. Normally, this information is given in a footnote to the financial statements. If there is no such disclosure, readers of the financial statements have the right to assume that preferred dividends are not in arrears.

Participating and Nonparticipating Preferred Stock

Dividends on preferred stock are generally limited each year to a maximum amount determined by applying the preferred percentage to the par value. When preferred stock is so limited, it is called *nonparticipating preferred stock*. Most preferred stock is nonparticipating. However, holders of some preferred stock may be paid additional dividends in excess of the stated percentage or amount. Such preferred stock is called **participating preferred stock.**

Large corporations with publicly traded stock rarely issue participating preferred stock. However, smaller corporations needing to raise more capital than the organizers can provide sometimes issue this stock. If the organizers are not willing to share control, but are willing to share profits with other investors, the corporation may issue participating preferred stock that has limited voting rights.

To illustrate participating preferred stock, assume that the 1,000 shares of $100 par, 9% preferred stock in the previous example are participating. Also, assume that cash dividends of $48,000 are declared in 1995. The allocation between preferred and common shares is as follows:

	Preferred	Common
Total par value	$100,000	$200,000
1995:		
First, to preferred (9% × $100,000)	$ 9,000	
Next, to common (9% × $200,000)		$ 18,000
The remainder ($21,000) as an equal percentage (7%):		
To preferred (7% × $100,000)	7,000	
To common (7% × $200,000)		14,000
Totals	$ 16,000	$ 32,000

Observe that the first step satisfies the preferred stockholders' right to 9% before any dividends are paid to the common stockholders. Next, the common shareholders receive 9% of the par value of their stock. Finally, the remaining

$21,000 of dividends are allocated in proportion to the par values of the two classes of stock. In this case, both the preferred and common shareholders are paid another 7% of the par value of their shares ($21,000/$300,000). Thus, the total amount paid is 16% of the par value.

In this example, no matter how large the total dividend might be, the preferred stock has the right to participate with common on an equal percentage basis. Therefore, the preferred stock in this example is called *fully participating preferred stock*. In other cases, the right to receive additional dividends beyond the basic preferred percentage is limited to a stated amount or percentage. For example, the holders of a 9%, $100 par value, preferred stock might have the right to participate in additional dividend declarations but only up to an additional 3%. This type of stock is called *partially participating preferred stock*.

Why Preferred Stock Is Issued

A corporation might issue preferred stock for several reasons. One reason is to raise capital without sacrificing control of the corporation. For example, suppose that the organizers of a business have $100,000 cash to invest but wish to organize a corporation that needs $200,000 of capital to get off to a good start. If they sold $200,000 of common stock, they would have only 50% control and would have to negotiate extensively with the other stockholders in making policy. However, if they issue $100,000 of common stock to themselves and can sell outsiders $100,000 of 8%, cumulative preferred stock that has no voting rights, they retain control of the corporation.

A second reason for issuing preferred stock is to boost the return earned by the common stockholders. Using the previous example to illustrate, suppose that the corporation's organizers expect the new company to earn an annual after-tax income of $24,000. If they sell and issue $200,000 of common stock, this income produces a 12% return on the $200,000 of common stockholders' equity. However, if they issue $100,000 of 8% preferred stock to the outsiders and $100,000 of common stock to themselves, their own return increases to 16% per year, as shown here:

Net after-tax income	$24,000
Less preferred dividends at 8%	(8,000)
Balance to common stockholders (equal to 16% on their $100,000 investment)	$16,000

In this case, the common stockholders earn 16% because the assets contributed by the preferred stockholders are invested to earn $12,000 while the preferred dividend payments amount to only $8,000.

The use of preferred stock to increase the return to common stockholders is an example of **financial leverage.** Whenever the dividend rate on preferred stock is less than the rate that the corporation earns on its assets, the effect of issuing preferred stock is to increase (or *lever*) the rate earned by common stockholders. Financial leverage also occurs when debt is issued and paid an interest rate less than the rate earned from using the assets the creditors loaned to the corporation.

There are other reasons for issuing preferred stock. For example, a corporation's preferred stock may appeal to some investors who believe that its common stock is too risky or that the dividend rate on the common stock will be too low. Also, if a corporation's management wants to issue common stock but believes the current market price for the common stock is too low, the corporation may issue preferred stock that is convertible into common stock. Later, if and when the price of the common stock increases, the preferred stockholders can convert their shares into common shares.

Convertible Preferred Stock

LO 5 Explain convertible preferred stock and describe the meaning of the par value, call price, market value, and book value of corporate stock.

As mentioned above, an issue of preferred stock can be made more attractive to some investors by giving them the right to exchange the preferred shares for a fixed number of common shares. **Convertible preferred stock** offers investors a higher potential return than does nonconvertible preferred stock. If the company prospers and its common stock increases in value, the convertible preferred stockholders can share in the prosperity by converting their preferred stock into the more valuable common stock. Conversion is at the option of the investors and therefore does not occur unless it is to their advantage. (You should realize that the investors can enjoy the results of the increased value of the common stock without converting the preferred stock because the preferred stock's market value reflects the change in the common stock's value.)

To see how the conversion of preferred stock is recorded, assume that a corporation's outstanding stock includes 1,000 shares of 10%, $100 par value convertible preferred stock. The stock was originally issued for $103 per share. Each preferred share is convertible into four shares of $10 par value common stock. If all of the preferred shares are converted on May 1, the entry to record the conversion is:

May	1	Preferred Stock	100,000.00	
		Contributed Capital in Excess of Par Value, Preferred Stock	3,000.00	
		Common Stock, $10 Par Value		40,000.00
		Contributed capital in Excess of Par Value, Common Stock		63,000.00
		To record the conversion of preferred stock.		

When the preferred stock is converted into common stock, the balances in the preferred stock accounts are removed and replaced with account balances related to common stock. No gain or loss is recorded, even though the market value of the common stock is probably greater than the $103,000 recorded in the common stock and paid-in capital accounts.

AS A MATTER OF

Fact

GM Plans to Sell Stock Issue that Features Higher Yield

Firm May Raise $600 Million in Its First Sale Since '87; But Buyers Face a Catch

General Motors Corp., in a move to bolster its dwindling cash reserves, plans to sell stock for the first time in nearly four years.

GM said it is seeking clearance from the Securities and Exchange Commission to offer as many as 16.1 million units of a special convertible preference stock. The securities, which could convert to as many as 16.1 million common shares on July 1, 1994, would pay a higher yield than GM common stock. But holders of the new stock would have little opportunity to profit if GM's common stock rose sharply because GM would likely call in the new issue, limiting the amount of appreciation.

GM hasn't priced the new securities yet, but company officials hope each unit will sell for about the same price as a share of GM common stock. GM common closed yesterday at $37.125, down 12.5 cents, in New York Stock Exchange composite trading, indicating that the offering could raise about $600 million.

* * *

Less-Costly Borrowing

Industry analysts said the new issue could allow GM to raise money at less cost than conventional borrowing. "The key is the pricing," said Lehman Brothers analyst Joseph Phillippi. GM has "plenty of borrowing room, but this may be cheaper than going to the debt markets," he said. Other analysts said the proposed stock issue is relatively small compared to GM's needs and predicted that the company will borrow more later in the year.

* * *

GM is joining a crowd of U.S. companies turning to the equity markets for capital, but in an unusual way. The new securities, called Preference Equity Redemption Cumulative Stock, or PERCS, are the creation of Morgan Stanley & Co., the lead underwriter and one of GM's longtime investment bankers.

In effect, GM is offering investors who were dismayed by February's 47% cut in the common-stock dividend a chance to earn higher dividends. And each new unit could be converted into a single share of GM common, or its cash equivalent, on July 1, 1994.

But there's a catch. If GM's common stock takes off, holders of the new securities won't get to go along for much of the ride. Instead, GM can call the new securities on 15 days' notice at any time before July 1, 1994. The call price will be set at the date of offering, and the premium over the regular common-share price at the time of the offering will decline over time. Thus, if GM common stock goes up, holders of the new securities likely would see their shares called in and replaced with less than one share of common.

Exactly how the pricing mechanism will work won't become clear until GM and Morgan Stanley get clearance to start selling the securities. That process could start as soon as this week, depending on SEC action, officials of the companies said. GM has agreed to sell 14 million of the new units through Morgan Stanley's underwriting group, but if demand is strong the underwriters have an option to buy up to 2.1 million more units for a total of 16.1 million.

Source: Joseph B. White, "GM Plans to Sell Stock Issue that Features Higher Yield," *The Wall Street Journal*, May 14, 1991, page A3. Reprinted by permission of *The Wall Street Journal*,

Stock Values

In addition to a par value, stocks may have a *call price*, a *market value*, and a *book value*.

Call Price of Callable Preferred Stock

Some issues of preferred stock are callable. This means that the issuing corporation has the right to retire the **callable preferred stock** by paying a specified amount to the preferred stockholders. The amount that must be paid to call and retire a preferred share is its **call price** or *redemption value*. This amount is set at the time the stock is issued. Normally, the call price includes the par value of the stock plus a premium that provides the stockholders with some additional return on their investment. When the issuing corporation calls and retires a preferred stock, it must pay not only the call price but also any dividends in arrears.

Market Value

The market value of a share of stock is the price at which it can be bought or sold. Market values are influenced by a wide variety of factors including expected future earnings, dividends, and events in the economy at large. Market values of frequently traded stocks are reported daily in newspapers such as *The Wall Street Journal*. The market values of stocks that are not actively traded can be more difficult to determine. Analysts use a variety of techniques to estimate the value of such stocks, and most of these techniques use accounting information as an important input to the valuation process.

Book Value

The **book value of a share of stock** is one share's portion of the corporation's net assets as recorded in its accounts. If a corporation has only common stock, divide total stockholders' equity by the number of outstanding shares to determine book value. For example, if total stockholders' equity is $285,000 and there are 10,000 shares outstanding, the book value per share is $28.50 ($285,000/10,000 shares).

Computing the book values of stock is more complex when both common and preferred shares are outstanding. To calculate the book values of each class of stock, first allocate the total stockholders' equity between the two classes. The preferred stockholders' portion equals the preferred stock's call price (or par value if the preferred is not callable) plus any cumulative dividends in arrears. The remaining stockholders' equity is then allocated to the common shares. To determine the book value per share of preferred, divide the portion of stockholders' equity assigned to preferred by the number of preferred shares outstanding. Similarly, the book value per share of common is the stockholders' equity assigned to common divided by the number of outstanding common shares. For instance, assume a corporation has the stockholders' equity as shown in Illustration 14–3.

If the preferred stock is callable at $108 per share and two years of cumulative preferred dividends are in arrears, the book values of the corporation's shares are calculated as follows:

ILLUSTRATION 14–3

Stockholders' Equity with Preferred and Common Stock

Stockholders' Equity

Preferred stock, \$100 par value, 7%, cumulative and nonparticipating, 2,000 shares authorized, 1,000 shares issued and outstanding	\$100,000	
Contributed capital in excess of par value, preferred stock	5,000	
Total capital contributed by preferred stockholders		\$105,000
Common stock, \$25 par value, 12,000 shares authorized, 10,000 shares issued and outstanding	\$250,000	
Contributed capital in excess of par value, common stock	10,000	
Total capital contributed by common stockholders		260,000
Total contributed capital		\$365,000
Retained earnings		82,000
Total stockholders' equity		\$447,000

Total stockholders' equity		\$447,000
Less equity applicable to preferred shares:		
Call price (1,000 × \$108)	\$108,000	
Cumulative dividends in arrears (\$100,000 × 7% × 2)	14,000	(122,000)
Equity applicable to common shares		\$325,000
Book value of preferred shares (\$122,000/1,000)		\$ 122.00
Book value of common shares (\$325,000/10,000)		\$ 32.50

In their annual reports to shareholders, corporations sometimes report the increase in the book value of the corporation's shares that has occurred during a year. Also, book value may have significance in contracts. For example, a stockholder may enter into a contract to sell shares at their book value at some future date. However, this agreement may not be wise because the stock is likely to have a market value that differs from its book value.

Similarly, book value should not be confused with the liquidation value of a stock. If a corporation is liquidated, its assets probably will sell at prices that are quite different from the amounts at which they are carried on the books.

Summary of the Chapter in Terms of Learning Objectives

LO 1. Advantages of the corporate form of business include the following: (*a*) status as separate legal entity, (*b*) lack of stockholder liability for the corporate debts, (*c*) easy transferability of ownership interests, (*d*) a corporation's continuity of life, and (*e*) the fact stockholders are not agents of the corporation. A disadvantage is that corporations are closely regulated by government. Also, the taxable status of corporations is often a disadvantage but sometimes may be an advantage.

A corporation is governed by the stockholders through the board of directors. Officers who manage the corporation include a president, perhaps one or more vice presidents, and a secretary. The chief executive officer may be the president or the board of directors chairperson.

LO 2. When stock is issued, the par or stated value is credited to the stock account and any excess is credited to a separate contributed capital account. If the stock has no par or stated value, the entire proceeds are credited to the stock account.

Stockholders must contribute assets equal to the minimum legal capital of a corporation or be potentially liable for the deficiency. And, as long as any liabilities remain unpaid, the minimum legal capital cannot be paid to stockholders.

LO 3. If a corporation sells stock through subscriptions, the right to receive payment is an asset of the corporation and the subscribers' equity is recorded in contributed capital accounts. The balance of the Common Stock Subscribed account is transferred to the Common Stock account when the shares are issued, which normally occurs after all payments are received.

LO 4. Preferred stock has a priority (or senior status) relative to common stock in one or more ways. Usually, this means that common stockholders cannot be paid dividends unless a specified amount of dividends is also paid to preferred shareholders. Preferred stock also may have a priority status if the corporation is liquidated. The dividend preference for many preferred stocks is cumulative, and a few preferred stocks also participate in dividends beyond the preferred amount.

LO 5. On the conversion of convertible preferred stock into common stock, the carrying value of the preferred stock is transferred to contributed capital accounts that relate to common stock. No gain or loss is recorded. Par value is an arbitrary amount assigned to a share of stock when the class of stock is authorized. If preferred stock is callable, the amount that must be paid to retire the stock is its call price plus any dividends in arrears. Market value is the price that a stock commands when it is bought or sold. The book value of preferred stock is any dividends in arrears plus its par value or, if it is callable, its call price. The remaining stockholders' equity is divided by the number of outstanding common shares to determine the book value per share of the common stock.

Demonstration Problem

Barton Corporation was created on January 1, 1993. The following transactions relating to stockholders' equity occurred during the first two years of the company's operations. Prepare the journal entries to record these transactions. Also prepare the balance sheet presentation of the organization costs, liabilities, and stockholders' equity as of December 31, 1993, and December 31, 1994. Include appropriate footnotes.

1993

Jan. 1 Authorized the issuance of 2 million shares of $5 par value common stock and 100,000 shares of $100 par value preferred stock.

The preferred stock pays a 10% annual dividend and is cumulative.

Jan.	1	Issued 200,000 shares of common stock at $12 per share.
	1	Issued 100,000 shares of common stock in exchange for a building valued at $820,000 and merchandise inventory valued at $380,000.
	1	Accepted subscriptions for 150,000 shares of common stock at $12 per share. The subscribers made no down payments, and the full purchase price was due on April 1, 1993.
	1	Paid a cash reimbursement to the company's founders for $100,000 of organization costs; these costs are to be amortized over 10 years.
	1	Issued 12,000 shares of preferred stock for $110 per share.
Apr.	1	Collected the full subscription price for the January 1 common stock and issued the stock.
Dec.	31	The Income Summary account for 1993 had a $125,000 credit balance before being closed to Retained Earnings; no dividends were declared on either the common or preferred stocks.
1994		
June	4	Issued 100,000 shares of common stock for $15 per share.
Dec.	10	Declared dividends payable on January 10, 1995, as follows: To preferred stockholders for 1993 . . . . $120,000 To preferred stockholders for 1994 . . . . 120,000 To common stockholders for 1994 300,000
	31	The Income Summary account for 1994 had a $1 million credit balance before being closed to Retained Earnings.

Solution to Demonstration Problem

Planning the Solution

- Record journal entries for the events in 1993.
- Close the accounts related to retained earnings.
- Determine the balances for the 1993 balance sheet.
- Determine the following amounts to use in the balance sheet and the accompanying note:
  a. The number of shares issued.
  b. The amount of dividends in arrears.
  c. The unamortized balance of organization costs.
- Prepare the specified portions of the 1993 balance sheet.
- Record journal entries for the events in 1994.
- Close the accounts related to retained earnings.
- Determine the balances for the 1994 balance sheet.
- Determine the following amounts to use in the balance sheet and the accompanying note:
  a. The number of shares issued.
  b. The unamortized balance of organization costs.
- Prepare the specified portions of the 1994 balance sheet.

1993 Jan.	1	Cash	2,400,000.00	
		Common Stock		1,000,000.00
		Contributed Capital in Excess of Par Value, Common Stock		1,400,000.00
		Issued 200,000 shares of common stock.		
	1	Building	820,000.00	
		Merchandise Inventory	380,000.00	
		Common Stock		500,000.00
		Contributed Capital in Excess of Par Value, Common Stock		700,000.00
		Issued 100,000 shares of common stock.		
	1	Subscriptions Receivable	1,800,000.00	
		Common Stock Subscribed		750,000.00
		Contributed Capital in Excess of Par Value, Common Stock		1,050,000.00
		Accepted subscriptions for 150,000 shares of common stock.		
	1	Organization Costs	100,000.00	
		Cash		100,000.00
		Reimbursed the founders for organization costs.		
	1	Cash	1,320,000.00	
		Preferred Stock		1,200,000.00
		Contributed Capital in Excess of Par Value, Preferred Stock		120,000.00
		Issued 12,000 shares of preferred stock.		
Apr.	1	Cash	1,800,000.00	
		Subscriptions Receivable		1,800,000.00
		Collected balance due on subscribed common stock.		
	1	Common Stock Subscribed	750,000.00	
		Common Stock		750,000.00
		Issued 150,000 shares of subscribed common stock.		
Dec.	31	Income Summary	125,000.00	
		Retained Earnings		125,000.00
		To close the Income Summary account and update Retained Earnings.		
1994 June	4	Cash	1,500,000.00	
		Common Stock		500,000.00
		Contributed Capital in Excess of Par Value, Common Stock		1,000,000.00
		Issued 100,000 shares of common stock.		
Dec.	10	Cash Dividends Declared	540,000.00	
		Common Dividend Payable		300,000.00
		Preferred Dividend Payable		240,000.00
		Declared current dividends and dividends in arrears to common and preferred stockholders, payable on January 10, 1995.		

1994				
Dec.	31	Income Summary	1,000,000.00	
		Retained Earnings		1,000,000.00
		To close the Income Summary account and update Retained Earnings.		
	31	Retained Earnings	540,000.00	
		Cash Dividends Declared		540,000.00
		To close the Cash Dividends Declared account.		

Balance sheet presentations:

	As of December 31,	
	1993	**1994**
Assets		
Organization costs	$ 90,000	$ 80,000
Liabilities		
Common dividend payable		$ 300,000
Preferred dividend payable		240,000
Total liabilities		$ 540,000
Stockholders' Equity		
Contributed capital:		
Preferred stock, $100 par value, 10% cumulative dividends, 100,000 shares authorized, 12,000 shares issued	$1,200,000	$1,200,000
Contributed capital in excess of par, preferred stock	120,000	120,000
Total capital contributed by preferred stockholders	$1,320,000	$1,320,000
Common stock, $5 par value, 2,000,000 shares authorized, 450,000 shares issued in 1993, and 550,000 shares in 1994	$2,250,000	$2,750,000
Contributed capital in excess of par, common stock	3,150,000	4,150,000
Total capital contributed by common stockholders	$5,400,000	$6,900,000
Total contributed capital	$6,720,000	$8,220,000
Retained earnings (see Note 1)	125,000	585,000
Total stockholders' equity	$6,845,000	$8,805,000

Note 1: As of December 31, 1993, there was $120,000 of dividends in arrears on the cumulative preferred stock.

Glossary

LO 6 Define or explain the words and phrases listed in the chapter glossary.

Book value of a share of stock one share's portion of the issuing corporation's net assets recorded in its accounts. pp. 782–83

Call price of preferred stock the amount that must be paid to call and retire a preferred share. p. 781

Callable preferred stock preferred stock that the issuing corporation, at its option, may retire by paying a specified amount (the call price) to the preferred stockholders plus any dividends in arrears. p. 781

Common stock stock of a corporation that has only one class of stock, or if there is more than one class, the class that has no preferences over the corporation's other classes of stock. p. 769

Common Stock Subscribed a stockholders' equity account in which a corporation records the par or stated value of unissued common stock that investors have contracted to purchase. p. 774

Convertible preferred stock a preferred stock that can be exchanged for shares of the issuing corporation's common stock at the option of the preferred stockholder. p. 780

Cumulative preferred stock preferred stock on which undeclared dividends accumulate until they are paid; common stockholders cannot receive a dividend until all cumulative dividends have been paid. p. 777

Discount on stock the difference between the par value of stock and its issue price when it is issued at a price below par value. p. 772

Dividend in arrears an unpaid dividend on cumulative preferred stock; it must be paid before any regular dividends on the preferred stock and before any dividends on the common stock. p. 777

Financial leverage the achievement of an increased return on common stock by paying dividends on preferred stock or interest at a rate that is less than the rate of return earned with the assets invested in the corporation by the preferred stockholders or creditors. pp. 779–80

Minimum legal capital an amount of assets defined by state law that stockholders must invest and leave invested in a corporation; this provision is intended to protect the creditors of the corporation. pp. 770–71

Noncumulative preferred stock a preferred stock on which the right to receive dividends is forfeited for any year that the dividends are not declared. p. 777

No-par stock a class of stock that does not have a par value; no-par stock can be issued at any price without creating a discount liability. pp. 772–73

Organization costs the costs of bringing a corporation into existence, including legal fees, promoters' fees, and amounts paid to the state to secure the charter. p. 763

Par value an arbitrary value assigned to a share of stock when the stock is authorized. p. 770

Participating preferred stock preferred stock that gives its owners the right to share in dividends in excess of the stated percentage or amount. p. 778

Preemptive right the right of common stockholders to protect their proportionate interest in a corporation by having the first opportunity to buy additional shares of common stock issued by the corporation. pp. 775–76

Preferred stock stock that gives its owners a priority status over common stockholders in one or more ways, such as the payment of dividends or the distribution of assets on liquidation. pp. 776–82

Premium on stock the difference between the par value of stock and its issue price when it is issued at a price above par value. pp. 771–72

Proxy a legal document that gives an agent of a stockholder the power to exercise the voting rights of that stockholder's shares. p. 763

Stated value of no-par stock an arbitrary amount assigned to no-par stock by the corporation's board of directors; this amount is credited to the no-par stock account when the stock is issued. p. 773

Stock subscription a contractual commitment by an investor to purchase unissued shares of stock and become a stockholder. pp. 773–75

Synonymous Terms

Call price redemption value.

Preferred senior status.

Subscribers incorporators; founders; promoters.

Objective Review

Answers to the following questions are listed at the end of this chapter. Be sure that you decide which is the one best answer to each question *before* you check the answers.

LO 1 An advantage of the corporate form of organization is:

a. That ownership rights are easily transferred.
b. That stockholders have a mutual agency relationship with the corporation.
c. The ease of capital assembly.
d. The lack of governmental regulation compared to single proprietorships and partnerships.
e. Both (*a*) and (*c*) are correct.

LO 2 Verde Corporation has no-par common stock with a stated value of $10 per share. The company issued 7,000 shares of its stock in exchange for some equipment valued at $105,000. The entry to record the transaction would include:

a. A credit to Retained Earnings for $35,000.
b. A credit to Contributed Capital in Excess of Stated Value, No-Par Common Stock for $35,000.
c. A debit to Equipment for $70,000.
d. A credit to Common Stock, No-Par for $105,000.
e. A credit to Contributed Capital in Excess of Stated Value, No-Par Common Stock for $70,000.

LO 3 Sweeps Publishing Corporation accepted subscriptions for 9,000 shares of $10 par value common stock at $48 per share. A 10% down payment was made on the date of the subscription contract, and the balance was to be paid in full six months later. The entries to record receipt of the final balance and the issuance of the stock would include:

a. A debit to Common Stock Subscribed for $432,000.
b. A credit to Contributed Capital in Excess of Par Value, Common Stock for $307,800.
c. A credit to Common Stock, $10 Par Value for $90,000.
d. A credit to Subscriptions Receivable, Common Stock for $432,000.
e. A debit to Subscriptions Receivable, Common Stock for $388,800.

LO 4 Bearcat Corporation has stockholders' equity as follows:

Preferred stock, $50 par value, 10%, cumulative and nonparticipating, 10,000 shares authorized, 9,000 shares issued and outstanding	$ 450,000
Contributed capital in excess of par value, preferred stock	50,000
Total capital contributed by preferred stockholders	$ 500,000
Common stock, $10 par value, 100,000 shares authorized, 27,000 shares issued and outstanding	$ 270,000
Contributed capital in excess of par value, common stock	540,000
Total capital contributed by common stockholders	$ 810,000
Total contributed capital	$1,310,000
Retained earnings	1,260,000
Total stockholders' equity	$2,570,000

Dividends have not been declared for the past two years, but in the third year, Bearcat Corporation declared $288,000 of dividends distributable to both preferred and common stockholders. Determine the amount of dividends to be paid to the common stockholders.

a. $ 90,000.
b. $135,000.
c. $153,000.
d. $243,000.
e. $288,000.

LO 5 World Cinema, Inc.'s callable preferred stock has a call price of $108 plus any dividends in arrears. The stockholders' equity of the company is as follows:

Preferred stock, $90 par value, 10%, cumulative and nonparticipating, 5,000 shares authorized, 1,000 shares issued and outstanding (dividends are in arrears for two years)	$ 90,000
Contributed capital in excess of par value, preferred stock	6,000
Total capital contributed by preferred stockholders	$ 96,000
Common stock, $20 par value, 50,000 shares authorized, 12,000 shares issued and outstanding	$240,000
Contributed capital in excess of par value, common stock	120,000
Total capital contributed by common stockholders	$360,000
Total contributed capital	$456,000
Retained earnings	174,000
Total stockholders' equity	$630,000

The book values per share of the preferred and common shares are:

a. Preferred, $126.00; common, $42.00.
b. Preferred, $96.00; common, $32.50.
c. Preferred, $90.00; common, $45.00.
d. Preferred, $108.00; common, $43.50.
e. Preferred, $114.00; common, $31.00.

LO 6 A preferred stock that can be exchanged for shares of its issuing corporation's common stock at the option of the stockholder is:

a. Participating preferred stock.
b. Noncumulative preferred stock.
c. Callable preferred stock.
d. Convertible preferred stock.
e. Cumulative preferred stock.

Questions for Class Discussion

1. What are the advantages and disadvantages of the corporate form of business organization?
2. Why is the income of a corporation said to be taxed twice?
3. Who is responsible for directing the affairs of a corporation?
4. What is a proxy?
5. What are organization costs? List several examples of these costs.
6. How are organization costs classified on the balance sheet?
7. What are the duties and responsibilities of a corporation's registrar and transfer agent?
8. Who serves as the chief executive officer of a corporation?
9. List the general rights of common stockholders.
10. What is the preemptive right of common stockholders?
11. Laws place no limit on the amounts that partners can withdraw from a partnership. On the other hand, laws regulating corporations place definite limits on the amount of dividends that stockholders can receive from a corporation. Why do you think there is a difference?
12. What is a stock premium? What is a stock discount?
13. Does a corporation earn a profit by selling its stock at a premium? Does it incur a loss by selling its stock at a discount?
14. Why do corporation laws make purchasers of stock at a discount contingently liable for the discount? To whom are they potentially liable?
15. What is the main advantage of no-par stock?
16. What distinguishes preferred stock from common stock?
17. What is the difference between cumulative and noncumulative preferred stock?
18. What is the difference between participating and nonparticipating preferred stock?

19. What are the balance sheet classifications of these accounts: (*a*) Subscriptions Receivable, Common Stock, and (*b*) Common Stock Subscribed?
20. What is the difference between the par value and the call price of a share of stock?
21. What is the difference between the market value and the book value of a share of stock?
22. Why would an investor find convertible preferred stock attractive?
23. Refer to the financial statements of McDonald's Corporation in Appendix K. During 1989, what was the total amount of: (*a*) dividends declared to common and preferred stockholders, and (*b*) dividends paid to common and preferred stockholders?
24. Using the consolidated financial statements of Federal Express Corporation, shown in Appendix K, calculate the book value per share of common stock (*a*) as of May 31, 1990, and (*b*) as of May 31, 1991.

Exercises

Exercise 14–1
Recording issuances of stock
(LO 2)

Prepare general journal entries to record the following issuances of stock by three different corporations:

1. One thousand shares of $5 par value common stock are issued for $45,000 cash.
2. Two hundred shares of no-par common stock are issued to promoters in exchange for their efforts in organizing the corporation. The promoters' efforts are estimated to be worth $7,000, and the stock has no stated value.
3. Assume the same facts as in (2), except that the stock has a $20 stated value.

Exercise 14–2
Comparative entries for partnership and corporation
(LO 1, 2)

Carl Tenbrink and Donna Mills began a new business on February 14 when each of them invested $125,000 in the company. On December 20, it was decided that $68,000 of the company's cash would be distributed equally between the owners. Two checks for $34,000 were prepared and given to the owners on December 23. On December 31, the company reported a $96,000 net income.

Prepare two sets of journal entries to record the investments by the owners, the distribution of cash to the owners, the closing of the Income Summary account, and the withdrawals or dividends under these alternative assumptions: (*a*) the business is a partnership, and (*b*) the business is a corporation that issued 1,000 shares of $10 par value, common stock to each owner.

Exercise 14–3
Accounting for par and no-par stock
(LO 2)

United Tire Corporation sold and issued 20,000 shares of its common stock for $840,000 on July 25. Give the entry to record the sale under each of the following independent assumptions: (*a*) the stock has no par value and the board of directors did not give it a stated value; (*b*) the stock has no par value and the board established a $1 per share stated value; and (*c*) the stock has a $10 par value.

Exercise 14–4
Stock subscriptions
(LO 3)

On May 15, Quality Dairy Corporation accepted subscriptions to 40,000 shares of its $5 par value common stock at $26.00 per share. The subscription contracts called for one fourth of the subscription price to accompany each contract as a down payment with the balance to be paid on November 15. Give the entries to record: (*a*) the subscriptions, (*b*) the down payments, (*c*) receipt of the remaining amount due on the subscriptions, and (*d*) issuance of the stock.

Exercise 14–5
Allocating dividends between common and cumulative preferred stock
(LO 4)

The outstanding stock of Cooper Realty Corporation includes 47,000 shares of $50 par value, 8%, cumulative and nonparticipating preferred stock and 82,000 shares of $10 par value common stock. During its first four years of operation, the corporation declared and paid the following amounts in dividends: first year, $0; second year, $200,000; third year, $420,000; and fourth year, $200,000. Determine the total dividends paid in each year to each class of stockholders. Also determine the total dividends paid to each class over the four years.

Exercise 14–6
Allocating dividends between common and noncumulative preferred stock
(LO 4)

Determine the total dividends paid in each year to each class of stockholders of the previous exercise under the assumption that the preferred stock is noncumulative. Also determine the total dividends paid to each class over the four years.

Exercise 14–7
Allocating dividends between common and participating preferred stock
(LO 4)

The outstanding stock of Chemco Corporation includes 8,000 shares of $100 par value, 6% cumulative and fully participating preferred stock and 16,000 shares of $10 par value common stock. It has regularly paid all dividends on the preferred stock. This year, the board of directors declared and paid a total of $96,000 in dividends to the two classes of stockholders. Determine the dividend per share to be paid to each class and the percent of par to be paid to each class of stockholders.

Exercise 14–8
Effect of preferred stock on rates of return
(LO 4)

Four individuals have agreed to begin a new business requiring a total investment of $600,000. Each of the four will contribute $100,000, and the remaining $200,000 will be raised from other investors. Two alternative plans for raising the money are being considered: (1) issue 6,000 shares of $100 par value common stock to all investors, or (2) issue 4,000 shares of $100 par value common stock to the four founders and 2,000 shares of $100 par value, 7%, cumulative and nonparticipating preferred stock to the remaining investors. In either case, all shares will be issued at par. If the business is expected to earn an after-tax net income of $84,000, what rate of return will the founders earn under each alternative? Which of the two plans will provide the higher return to the four founders?

Exercise 14–9
Effect of preferred stock on rates of return
(LO 4)

How would your answers to Exercise 14–8 be changed if the business is expected to earn an after-tax net income of only $36,000?

Exercise 14–10
Convertible preferred stock
(LO 5)

Camden Corporation has 8,000 outstanding shares of 8%, $100 par value preferred stock that is convertible into the corporation's no-par common stock at the rate of 5 shares of common for 1 share of preferred. The preferred stock was issued at a premium of $26 per share. Assume that all shares are presented for conversion.

Longview Manufacturing Corporation has issued 16,000 shares of 10%, $500 par value preferred stock at par. Each preferred share is convertible into 40 shares of the corporation's $1 par value common stock. Assume that one fourth of the convertible preferred stock is presented for conversion.

Present entries dated March 2 to record the conversions on the books of the two corporations.

Exercise 14–11
Book value per share of stock
(LO 5)

The stockholders' equity section from HeadStart Software Corporation's balance sheet is as follows:

Stockholders' Equity

Preferred stock, 8%, cumulative and nonparticipating, $100 par value, $110 call price, 6,000 shares issued and outstanding	$ 600,000
Common stock, $10 par value, 120,000 shares issued and outstanding	1,200,000
Retained earnings	780,000
Total stockholders' equity	$2,580,000

Required

1. Determine the book value per share of the preferred stock and of the common stock under the assumption that there are no dividends in arrears on the preferred stock.
2. Determine the book value per share for each kind of stock under the assumption that two years' dividends are in arrears on the preferred stock.

Problems

Problem 14–1
Stock subscriptions
(LO 2, 3, 4)

Micron Corporation is authorized to issue 60,000 shares of $50 par value, 8% cumulative and nonparticipating preferred stock and 250,000 shares of no-par value common stock. The board of directors established a $10 stated value for the no-par common stock. Micron Corporation then completed these transactions:

July 6 Accepted subscriptions to 80,000 shares of common stock at $18 per share. Down payments equal to 25% of the subscription price accompanied each subscription. The balance is due on August 10.

July 20 Gave the corporation's promoters 2,000 shares of common stock for their services in getting the corporation organized. The board valued the services at $35,000.

Aug. 4 Accepted subscriptions to 6,000 shares of preferred stock at $65 per share. The subscriptions were accompanied by 50% down payments. The balance is due on September 5.

10 Collected the balance due on the July 6 common stock subscriptions and issued the stock.

30 Accepted subscriptions to 1,000 shares of preferred stock at $62 per share. The subscriptions were accompanied by 50% down payments. The balance is due on October 30.

Sept. 5 Collected the balance due on the August 4 preferred stock subscriptions and issued the stock.

Required

1. Prepare general journal entries to record the transactions.
2. Prepare the stockholders' equity section of the corporation's balance sheet as of the close of business on September 30. Assume that retained earnings are $60,000.

Problem 14–2
Stockholders' equity transactions
(LO 2, 3, 4, 5)

Solar Energy Company is authorized by its charter to issue 500,000 shares of $10 par value common stock and 100,000 shares of 10%, noncumulative and nonparticipating, $100 par value convertible preferred stock. The company completed the following transactions:

1992

Feb. 5 Issued 70,000 shares of common stock at par for cash.

28 Gave the corporation's promoters 3,750 shares of common stock for their services in organizing the corporation. The directors valued the services at $40,000.

Mar. 3 Issued 44,000 shares of common stock in exchange for the following assets with the indicated reliable market values: land, $80,000; buildings, $210,000; and machinery, $155,000.

Dec. 31 Closed the Income Summary account. A $27,000 loss was incurred.

1993

Jan. 28 Issued 4,000 shares of preferred stock at par for cash.

Dec. 15 Solar Energy Company's preferred stockholders submitted 2,500 shares of their convertible stock for conversion into common shares on this date. The convertible preferred stockholders accepted 9 shares of common stock for each share of preferred stock.

31 Closed the Income Summary account. A $98,000 net income was earned.

1994

Jan. 1 The board of directors declared a 10% cash dividend to preferred shares and $0.20 per share cash dividend to outstanding common shares, payable on February 5 to the January 24 stockholders of record.

Feb. 5 Paid the previously declared dividends.

Oct. 20 Accepted subscriptions to 4,000 shares of common stock at $14.90 per share. Down payments of 40% accompanied the subscription contracts. The balance is due on January 20, 1995.

Dec. 31 Closed the Cash Dividends Declared and Income Summary accounts. A $159,000 net income was earned.

Required

1. Prepare general journal entries to record the transactions.
2. Prepare the stockholders' equity section of the balance sheet as of the close of business on December 31, 1994.

Problem 14–3
Calculating book values; allocating dividends between preferred and common stock
(LO 4, 5)

Part 1. The balance sheet of Desktop Services Corporation includes the following information:

Stockholders' Equity

Preferred stock, 8%, cumulative and nonparticipating, $100 par value, 2,500 shares authorized and issued	$250,000
Common stock, no-par value, 40,000 shares authorized and issued	400,000
Retained earnings	192,500
Total stockholders' equity	$842,500

Required

Assume that the preferred stock has a call price of $105 plus any dividends in arrears. Calculate the book value per share of the preferred and common stocks under each of the following assumptions:

a. There are no dividends in arrears on the preferred stock.
b. One year's dividends are in arrears on the preferred stock.
c. Three years' dividends are in arrears on the preferred stock.

Part 2. Since its organization, TVP Corporation has had 14,000 outstanding shares of $100 par value, 11% preferred stock and 235,000 shares of $10 par value common stock. No dividends have been paid this year, and none were paid during either of the past two years. However, the company has recently prospered and the board of directors wants to know how much cash would be required to provide a $1.50 per share dividend on the common stock.

Required

Prepare a schedule that shows the amounts of cash required for dividends to each class of stockholders to provide the desired $1.50 per share dividend to the common stockholders under each of the following assumptions:

a. The preferred stock is noncumulative and nonparticipating.
b. The preferred stock is cumulative and nonparticipating.

c. The preferred stock is cumulative and fully participating.

d. The preferred stock is cumulative and participating to 14%.

Problem 14–4
Allocating dividends in sequential years between preferred and common stock
(LO 4)

Alphalon Cookware Company has 4,000 outstanding shares of $100 par value, 8% preferred stock and 56,000 shares of $10 par value common stock. During a seven-year period, the company paid out the following amounts in dividends:

1990	$ –0–
1991	46,000
1992	–0–
1993	60,000
1994	74,000
1995	68,400
1996	144,000

No dividends were in arrears for the years prior to 1990.

Required

1. Prepare three schedules with column headings as follows:

Year	Calculations	Preferred Dividend per Share	Common Dividend per Share

2. Complete schedules under each of the following assumptions. (Round your answers to the nearest cent.)
   a. The preferred stock is noncumulative and nonparticipating.
   b. The preferred stock is cumulative and nonparticipating.
   c. The preferred stock is cumulative and fully participating.

Problem 14–5
Calculation of book values
(LO 5)

Simplex Clock Corporation's common stock is selling on a stock exchange today at $16.45 per share, and a just-published balance sheet shows the following information about the stockholders' equity of the corporation:

Stockholders' Equity

Preferred stock, 7.5%, cumulative and nonparticipating, $100 par value, 3,000 shares authorized and outstanding	$ 300,000
Common stock, $10 par value, 75,000 shares authorized and outstanding	750,000
Retained earnings	375,000
Total stockholders' equity	$1,425,000

Required

Answer these questions: (1) What is the market value of the corporation's common stock? (2) What are the par values of (*a*) the preferred stock and (*b*) the common stock? (3) If there are no dividends in arrears, what are the book values of (*a*) the preferred stock and (*b*) the common stock? (4) If two years' dividends are in arrears on the preferred stock, what are the book values of (*a*) the preferred stock and (*b*) the common stock? (Assume that the preferred stock is not callable.)

Problem 14–6
Analytical essay
(LO 1)

Daphne Thomas and Elizabeth White want to go into business as special event promoters. Both can contribute fairly large amounts of capital, but they will need to acquire additional equity capital from other investors in about a year. Thomas has the expertise to run the business, and White will handle the administrative details. They plan to hire about three employees initially and will distribute all profits annually. White wants to operate as a general partnership, but Thomas thinks they should form a corporation. Thomas asks you to write a brief essay supporting her view in favor of the corporate form. What would you include in your essay to convince White that a corporation would be preferable to a partnership in their situation?

Problem 14–7
Analytical essay
(LO 4, 5)

Refer to the stockholders' equity section of the balance sheet in Problem 14–3. Assume, however, that the common stock has 100,000 shares authorized instead of 40,000. Also, assume that the preferred stock is convertible into common stock at a rate of eight common shares for each share of preferred. If 1,000 shares of the preferred stock are converted into common stock, describe how this affects the stockholders' equity section of the balance sheet (immediately after the conversion). If you are a common stockholder in this company, and the company plans to pay total cash dividends of $300,000, does it make any difference to you whether or not the conversion takes place before the dividend declaration? Why?

Alternate Problems

Problem 14–1A
Stock subscriptions
(LO 2, 3, 4)

Conran Corporation is authorized to issue 50,000 shares of $100 par value, 9%, cumulative and nonparticipating preferred stock and 250,000 shares of no-par value common stock. The board of directors established a $5 stated value for the no-par common stock. Conran Corporation then completed these transactions:

Apr. 4 Accepted subscriptions to 65,000 shares of common stock at $17 per share. Down payments equal to 25% of the subscription price accompanied each subscription. The balance is due on June 3.

Apr. 11 Gave the corporation's promoters 1,300 shares of common stock for their services in organizing the corporation. The board valued the services at $26,000.

May 1 Accepted subscriptions to 5,000 shares of preferred stock at $120 per share. The subscriptions were accompanied by 40% down payments. The balance is due on July 31.

June 3 Collected the balance due on the April 4 common stock subscriptions and issued the stock.

July 1 Accepted subscriptions to 2,000 shares of preferred stock at $122 per share. The subscriptions were accompanied by 40% down payments. The balance is due on August 15.

31 Collected the balance due on the May 1 preferred stock subscriptions and issued the stock.

Required

1. Prepare general journal entries to record the transactions.
2. Prepare the stockholders' equity section of the corporation's balance sheet as of the close of business on July 31. Assume that retained earnings are $23,000.

Problem 14–2A
Stockholders' equity transactions
(LO 2, 3, 4, 5)

Coach Motor Company is authorized by its charter to issue 1 million shares of $1 par value common stock and 50,000 shares of 10%, noncumulative and nonparticipating, $100 par value convertible preferred stock. The company completed the following transactions:

1992

Feb. 2 Issued 110,000 shares of common stock at par for cash.

28 Gave the corporation's promoters 65,000 shares of common stock for their services in organizing the corporation. The directors valued the services at $80,000.

Mar. 10 Issued 150,000 shares of common stock in exchange for the following assets with the indicated reliable market values: land, $70,000; buildings, $130,000; and machinery, $89,000.

Dec. 31 Closed the Income Summary account. A $61,000 loss was incurred.

1993

Jan. 1 Issued 6,000 shares of preferred stock at par for cash.

Dec. 1 Coach Motor Company's preferred stockholders submitted 750 shares of their convertible stock for conversion into common shares on this date. The convertible preferred stockholders accepted 70 shares of common stock for each share of preferred stock.

31 Closed the Income Summary account. A $196,000 net income was earned.

1994

Jan. 1 The board of directors declared a 10% cash dividend to preferred shares and $0.20 per share cash dividend to outstanding common shares, payable on January 25 to the January 15 stockholders of record.

25 Paid the previously declared dividends.

Nov. 15 Accepted subscriptions to 30,000 shares of common stock at $3.20 per share. Down payments of 25% accompanied the subscription contracts. The balance is due on February 15, 1995.

Dec. 31 Closed the Cash Dividends Declared and Income Summary accounts. A $262,000 net income was earned.

Required

1. Prepare general journal entries to record the transactions.
2. Prepare the stockholders' equity section of the balance sheet as of the close of business on December 31, 1994.

Problem 14–3A
Calculating book values; allocating dividends between preferred and common stock
(LO 4, 5)

Part 1. The balance sheet of Global Filter Company includes the following information:

Stockholders' Equity

Preferred stock, 11%, cumulative and nonparticipating, $100 par value, 2,000 shares authorized and issued	$200,000
Common stock, no-par value, 60,000 shares authorized and issued	600,000
Retained earnings	120,000
Total stockholders' equity	$920,000

Required

Assume that the preferred stock has a call price of $106 plus any dividends in arrears. Calculate the book value per share of the preferred and common stocks under each of the following assumptions:

a. No dividends are in arrears on the preferred stock.
b. One year's dividends are in arrears on the preferred stock.
c. Three years' dividends are in arrears on the preferred stock.

Part 2. Since its organization, Newhouse Corporation has had 3,200 outstanding shares of $100 par value, 11% preferred stock and 64,000 shares of $10 par value common stock. No dividends have been paid this year, and none were paid during either of the past two years. However, the company has recently prospered and the board of directors wants to know how much cash would be required to provide a $1.50 per share dividend on the common stock.

Required

Prepare a schedule that shows the amounts of cash required for dividends to each class of stockholders to provide the desired $1.50 per share dividend under each of the following assumptions:

a. The preferred stock is noncumulative and nonparticipating.
b. The preferred stock is cumulative and nonparticipating.
c. The preferred stock is cumulative and fully participating.
d. The preferred stock is cumulative and participating to 13%.

Problem 14–4A
Allocating dividends in sequential years between preferred and common stock (LO 4)

Oxford Bros. Company has 2,000 outstanding shares of $100 par value, 12% preferred stock and 30,000 shares of $10 par value common stock. During a seven-year period, the company paid out the following amounts in dividends:

1990	$ -0-
1991	54,000
1992	-0-
1993	30,000
1994	39,000
1995	48,000
1996	90,000

No dividends were in arrears for the years prior to 1990.

Required

1. Prepare three schedules with column headings as follows:

Year	Calculations	Preferred Dividend per Share	Common Dividend per Share

2. Complete a schedule under each of the following assumptions. (Round your calculations of dividends per share to the nearest cent.)

   a. The preferred stock is noncumulative and nonparticipating.
   b. The preferred stock is cumulative and nonparticipating.
   c. The preferred stock is cumulative and fully participating.

Problem 14–5A
Calculation of book values
(LO 5)

Denver Plastics Corporation's common stock is selling on a stock exchange today at $12.80 per share, and a just-published balance sheet shows the following information about the stockholders' equity of the corporation:

Stockholders' Equity

Preferred stock, 10.5%, cumulative and nonparticipating, $100 par value, 7,800 shares authorized and outstanding	$ 780,000
Common stock, $10 par value, 165,000 shares authorized and outstanding	1,650,000
Retained earnings	330,000
Total stockholders' equity	$2,760,000

Required

Answer these questions: (1) What is the market value of the corporation's common stock? (2) What are the par values of (*a*) the preferred stock and (*b*) the common stock? (3) If there are no dividends in arrears, what are the book values of (*a*) the preferred stock and (*b*) the common stock? (4) If two years' dividends are in arrears on the preferred stock, what are the book values of (*a*) the preferred stock and (*b*) the common stock? (Assume that the preferred stock is not callable.)

Problem 14–6A
Analytical essay
(LO 1)

Daphne Thomas and Elizabeth White want to go into business as special event promoters. Both can contribute fairly large amounts of capital, but they will need to acquire additional cash in about a year. Thomas has the expertise to run the business, and White will handle the administrative details. They plan to hire about three employees initially and will distribute all profits annually. White wants to operate as a partnership, but Thomas thinks they should form a corporation. White asks you to write a brief essay supporting her view in favor of the partnership form. What would you include in your essay to convince Thomas that a partnership might be preferable to a corporation in their situation?

Problem 14–7A
Analytical essay
(LO 4, 5)

Refer to the stockholders' equity section of the balance sheet in Problem 14–3A. Assume, however, that the common stock has 100,000 shares authorized instead of 60,000. Also, assume that the preferred stock is convertible into common stock at a rate of eight common shares for each share of preferred. If 1,000 shares of the preferred stock are converted into common stock, describe how this affects the stockholders' equity section of the balance sheet (immediately after the conversion). If you are a common stockholder in this company, and cash dividends of $487,000 are to be paid out, does it make any difference to you whether or not the conversion takes place? Why?

Provocative Problems

Provocative Problem 14–1
M&M Fashions, Inc.
(LO 2)

Kara McLeod and Erin Morris have operated a clothing and tailoring company, M&M Fashions, for a number of years as partners sharing net incomes and losses in a 3 to 2 ratio. That is, McLeod gets 3/5 (60%) while Morris gets 2/5 (40%). Because the business is growing, the two partners entered into an agreement with Michael Lyon that includes converting their partnership into a corporation. The charter of the new corporation, M&M Fashions, Inc., authorizes the corporation to issue 65,000 shares of $10 par value common stock. On the date of the incorporation, July 31, 1993, a trial balance of the partnership ledger appears as follows:

M&M FASHIONS
Trial Balance
July 31, 1993

Cash	$ 26,600	
Accounts receivable	45,600	
Allowance for doubtful accounts		$ 1,450
Merchandise inventory	359,640	
Store equipment	91,100	
Accumulated depreciation, store equipment		27,330
Buildings	410,000	
Accumulated depreciation, buildings		123,000
Land	160,000	
Accounts payable		49,400
Notes payable		389,200
Kara McLeod, capital		288,800
Erin Morris, capital		213,760
Totals	$1,092,940	$1,092,940

The agreement between the partners and Lyon includes these provisions:

1. The partnership assets are to be revalued to reflect the following items. Changes in asset values should be allocated to the partners' capital accounts according to their income and loss ratio.
   a. The $1,100 account receivable of John O'Connell is known to be uncollectible and is to be written off as a bad debt.
   b. After writing off the O'Connell account, the allowance for doubtful accounts is to be increased to 4% of the remaining accounts receivable.
   c. The merchandise inventory is to be written down to $342,140 to allow for damaged and shopworn goods.
   d. Insufficient depreciation has been taken on the store equipment. Therefore, its book value is to be decreased to $45,550 by increasing the balance of the accumulated depreciation account.

e. The building is to be written up to its replacement cost, $492,000, and the balance of the accumulated depreciation account is to be increased to show the building to be three tenths depreciated.

2. After the partnership assets are revalued, the assets and liabilities are to be transferred to the corporation in exchange for its stock, with each partner accepting stock at par value for her equity in the partnership.
3. Michael Lyon is to buy any remaining authorized stock for cash at par value.

When this agreement was finalized, you were hired as the accountant for the new corporation. Your first job is to determine the amount of stock that each person should receive, and to prepare entries on the corporation's books to record the issuance of stock in exchange for the partnership assets and liabilities and the issuance of stock to Lyon for cash. In addition, prepare a balance sheet for the corporation as it should appear after all the adjustments have been recorded and the stock is issued.

Provocative Problem 14–2
Sonora Corporation
(LO 4)

The management of Sonora Corporation is considering expanding its operations into an additional innovative line of business. It is expected that assets invested in this expansion can earn a rate of return of 20% per year. At present, Sonora Corporation's outstanding stock includes only 40,000 shares of $20 par value common stock. There are no other contributed capital accounts and retained earnings equal $385,000. Existing operations consistently earn approximately $210,000 each year. To finance the expansion, management is considering three alternatives:

a. Issue 6,000 shares of $100 par, 12% cumulative, nonparticipating, nonvoting preferred stock. Investment advisors for the company have concluded that these shares could be issued at par.

b. Issue 3,000 shares of $100 par, 12% cumulative, fully participating, nonvoting preferred stock. The investment advisors have concluded that these shares could be sold for $200 per share.

c. Issue 15,000 shares of common stock at $40 per share.

In evaluating these three alternatives, Sonora Corporation management has asked you to calculate the dividends that would be distributed to each class of stockholder, assuming that the board of directors declares dividends each year equal to the total net income earned by the corporation. Your calculations should show the distribution of dividends to preferred and common stockholders under each of the three alternative financing plans. Also calculate dividends per share of preferred and dividends per share of common.

As a second part of your analysis, assume that you own 1,500 of the common shares outstanding prior to the expansion and that you will not acquire or purchase any of the newly issued shares. Based on your analysis, would you prefer that the proposed expansion in operations be rejected? If not, comment on the relative merits of each alternative from your point of view as a common stockholder.

Provocative Problem 14–3
Tricom Corporation and Beltline Company
(LO 4)

Having received a $150,000 lump sum of severance pay, Tom Campbell is thinking about investing the money in one of two securities: Tricom Corporation common stock or the preferred stock issued by Beltline Company. The companies manufacture competing products, and both have been in business about the same length of time—five years for Tricom and six years for Beltline. Also, the two companies have about the same amounts of stockholders' equity, as shown here:

Tricom Corporation

Common stock, $5 par value, 1 million shares authorized, 400,000 shares issued	$2,000,000
Retained earnings	900,000
Total stockholders' equity	$2,900,000

Beltline Company

Preferred stock, $100 par value, 10% cumulative and nonparticipating, 10,000 shares authorized and issued	$1,000,000*
Common stock, $10 par value, 150,000 shares authorized and issued	1,500,000
Retained earnings	130,000
Total stockholders' equity	$2,630,000

* The current and one prior year's dividends are in arrears on the preferred stock.

Tricom did not pay a dividend on its common stock during its first year's operations; however, in each of the past four years, it has paid a cash dividend of $0.25 per share. The stock is currently selling for $7.75 per share. In contrast, the preferred stock of Beltline Company is selling for $96 per share. Campbell has told you that he favors this stock as an investment. He feels that it is a bargain because it is selling not only $4 below par value but also $24 below book value, and as he says, "The dividends are guaranteed because it is a preferred stock." He also believes that the common stock of Tricom is overpriced at 7% above book value and 55% above par value, while paying only a $0.25 per share dividend.

a. Is the preferred stock of Beltline Company actually selling at a price $24 below its book value, and is the common stock of Tricom Corporation actually selling at a price 7% above book value and 55% above par?

b. From an analysis of the stockholders' equity sections, express your opinion of the two stocks as investments and describe some of the factors that Campbell should consider in choosing between the two stocks.

Provocative Problem 14–4
International Business Machines Corporation
(LO 3, 4, 5)

IBM®

Use the information provided in the financial statements of International Business Machines Corporation and the footnotes (see Appendix J) to answer the following questions:

1. Does it appear that IBM has been authorized to issue any preferred stock? If so, had any been issued as of December 31, 1990?
2. How many shares of common stock have been authorized? How many have been issued as of December 31, 1990?
3. What is the par value of the common stock? What is its book value at December 31, 1990?

4. Are any shares of common stock subscribed? Are there any shares that cannot be issued to the public because they have been promised to others?
5. What was the highest market value of the stock during 1990? What was the lowest?
6. Did IBM declare any dividends on its capital stock during 1990? If so, how large were the dividends (per share, and in total)?

Answers to Objective Review Questions

LO 1 (*e*) LO 2 (*b*) LO 3 (*c*) LO 4 (*c*) LO 5 (*a*) LO 6 (*d*)

CHAPTER

15

Additional Corporate Transactions; Reporting Income and Retained Earnings; Earnings per Share

One advantage of the corporate business form is that its owners can easily buy and sell their equity interests. Shares in large corporations are traded on the New York Stock Exchange or the NASDAQ over-the-counter market. Stock prices can be affected by information about stockholders' equity and earnings.

Topical Coverage

We begin this chapter with a discussion of dividends and other transactions between a corporation and its stockholders. In this section of the chapter, you will learn about stock dividends, stock splits, and repurchases of stock by the issuing corporation. The second section of the chapter explains how income and retained earnings information is classified and reported. The third section explains how accountants report the earnings per share of a corporation. Understanding these topics will help you interpret and evaluate corporate financial statements.

Learning Objectives

After studying Chapter 15, you should be able to:

1. Record cash dividends, stock dividends, and stock splits and explain their effects on the assets and stockholders' equity of a corporation.
2. Record purchases and sales of treasury stock and retirements of stock and describe their effects on stockholders' equity.
3. Describe restrictions and appropriations of retained earnings and the disclosure of such items in the financial statements.
4. Explain how the income effects of discontinued operations, extraordinary items, changes in accounting principles, and prior period adjustments are reported.
5. Calculate earnings per share for companies with simple capital structures and explain the difference between primary and fully diluted earnings per share.
6. Define or explain the words and phrases listed in the chapter glossary.

CORPORATE DIVIDENDS AND OTHER STOCK TRANSACTIONS

In Chapter 3, we first described a corporation's retained earnings as the total amount of its net incomes less its net losses and dividends declared since it began operations. Years ago, retained earnings were commonly called **earned surplus.** However, the term is rarely used anymore except in state laws that regulate corporations.

Retained Earnings and Dividends

LO 1 Record cash dividends, stock dividends, and stock splits and explain their effects on the assets and stockholders' equity of a corporation.

Most state laws say that a corporation cannot pay cash dividends unless retained earnings are available. However, the payment of a cash dividend reduces both cash and stockholders' equity. Therefore, a corporation cannot pay a cash dividend simply because it has a credit balance in Retained Earnings; it also must have enough cash on hand to pay the dividend. When cash or assets that will shortly become cash are not available, the board of directors may choose to avoid a dividend declaration even though the Retained Earnings balance is adequate. Even if a corporation has a large Retained Earnings balance, the board of directors may refuse to declare a dividend because the available cash is needed in the operations of the business.

In deciding whether to declare dividends, the board of directors must recognize that operating activities are a source of cash. Perhaps some cash from operating activities should be paid out in dividends and some should be retained for emergencies. In addition, some cash may be retained to pay dividends in years when current operating activities do not generate enough cash to pay normal dividends. Furthermore, management may want to retain some cash from operating activities to finance expanded operations. See page 207 for a discussion of entries for the declaration and distribution of a cash dividend.

Distributions from Contributed Capital

Generally, the Dividends Declared account may not be closed to any of the contributed capital accounts. However, in some states, dividends may be debited or charged to certain contributed capital accounts. Because contributed capital account balances result from stockholder contributions, dividends charged to contributed capital accounts are called **liquidating dividends.** Usually, the accounts that reflect the par or stated value of the outstanding stock cannot be used as a source of liquidating dividends. Whether or not other contributed capital accounts may be used depends on state law. For this reason, a board of directors should seek legal advice before voting to charge dividends to any contributed capital account.

Stock Dividends

Sometimes, a corporation distributes additional shares of its own stock to its stockholders without receiving any consideration from the stockholders. This type of distribution is called a **stock dividend.** A stock dividend and a cash dividend are very different. A cash dividend transfers assets from the corporation to the stockholders. As a result, a cash dividend reduces the corporation's assets and its stockholders' equity. On the other hand, a stock dividend does not transfer assets from the corporation to the stockholders; it has no effect on assets and no effect on total stockholders' equity.

Why Stock Dividends Are Distributed

If stock dividends have no effect on corporation assets and stockholders' equity, why are stock dividends declared and distributed? The primary reason for stock dividends is related to the market price of a corporation's common stock. For example, if a profitable corporation grows by retaining earnings, the price of its common stock also tends to grow. Eventually, the price of a share may become high enough to discourage some investors from buying the stock. Thus, the corporation may declare stock dividends to keep the price of its shares from increasing too much. For this reason, some corporations declare small stock dividends each year.

Another reason for declaring a stock dividend is to provide stockholders evidence of the company's expected future success without paying cash to the stockholders. If a corporation has the ability to earn a high rate of return on additional cash investments and thereby grow to be a larger business, management may prefer to avoid paying cash dividends. In this case, stock dividend declarations sometimes are said to be a substitute for cash dividends. Although assets are not transferred to the stockholders, a stock dividend communicates management's belief that the stockholders benefit by having the cash reinvested in the company.

Some stockholders may like stock dividends for another reason. Often, corporations that declare stock dividends continue to pay the same cash dividend per share after a stock dividend as before. The result is that stockholders receive more cash each time dividends are declared.

The Effect of Stock Dividends on Stockholders' Equity Accounts

Although a stock dividend does not affect the total assets or total stockholders' equity of a corporation, it does have an effect on the components of stockholders' equity. To record a stock dividend, you must transfer some of the Retained Earnings balance to contributed capital accounts. This action is described as *capitalizing* retained earnings.

If a corporation declares a **small stock dividend**, accounting principles require that the corporation capitalize an amount of retained earnings that equals the market value of the shares to be distributed. This rule is based on the concept that a small stock dividend is likely to have a small impact on the price of the stock. In applying this rule, a small stock dividend is defined as one that amounts to 25% or less of the previously outstanding shares. The rule makers concluded that some stockholders may incorrectly believe that earnings are distributed in a small stock dividend. Thus, the amount of retained earnings capitalized and made unavailable for future dividends should equal the market value of the shares to be distributed.[1]

On the other hand, a **large stock dividend** amounts to more than 25% of the shares outstanding before the dividend. A stock dividend of this magnitude has a pronounced impact on the stock's market price and is not apt to be perceived as a distribution of earnings. Therefore, in recording a stock dividend that is over 25%, you must capitalize retained earnings only to the extent required by law. Usually, this means ignoring the market value of the shares. Instead, debit Retained Earnings and credit the stock account for the par value or stated value of the shares issued.[2]

For example, assume that Northwest Corporation's stockholders' equity is as follows:

Northwest Corporation
Stockholders' Equity

Common stock, $10 par value, 15,000 shares authorized, 10,000 shares issued and outstanding . .	$100,000	
Contributed capital in excess of par value, common stock	8,000	
Total contributed capital	$108,000	
Retained earnings	35,000	
Total stockholders' equity		$143,000

[1] FASB, *Accounting Standards—Current Text* (Norwalk, Conn., 1990), sec. C20.103, 106. Previously published in *Accounting Research Bulletin No. 43*, ch. 7, sec. B, pars. 10, 13.

[2] Ibid., sec. C20.104.

Recording a Small Stock Dividend

To see how a small stock dividend is recorded, assume that on December 31, the directors of Northwest Corporation declared a 10% or 1,000-share stock dividend distributable on January 20 to the stockholders of record on January 15.

If the market value of Northwest Corporation's stock on December 31 is $15 per share, the dividend declaration is recorded as follows:

Dec.	31	Stock Dividends Declared	15,000.00	
		Common Stock Dividend Distributable		10,000.00
		Contributed Capital in Excess of Par Value, Common Stock		5,000.00
		To record the declaration of a 1,000-share common stock dividend.		

Note that the debit is to Stock Dividends Declared. Also recall that in previous chapters when we discussed cash dividends, they were debited to Cash Dividends Declared. A convenient system of accounts includes separate Cash Dividends Declared and Stock Dividends Declared accounts because the statement of retained earnings should disclose stock dividends declared and cash dividends declared as separate items.

In the year-end closing process, close the Stock Dividends Declared account to Retained Earnings as follows:

Dec.	31	Retained Earnings	15,000.00	
		Stock Dividends Declared		15,000.00

On January 20 record the distribution of the stock as follows:

Jan.	20	Common Stock Dividend Distributable	10,000.00	
		Common Stock		10,000.00
		To record the distribution of a 1,000-share common stock dividend.		

Note that these entries shift $15,000 of the stockholders' equity from retained earnings to contributed capital or, in other words, $15,000 of retained earnings is *capitalized*. Note also that the amount of retained earnings capitalized is equal to the market value of the 1,000 shares issued ($15 × 1,000 shares = $15,000).

Because stock dividends may not be declared very often, some companies do not use a Stock Dividends Declared account. Instead, they debit stock dividend declarations directly to Retained Earnings. However, if they do this, the accountant must remember to start the statement of retained earnings with the beginning balance and then subtract the amount debited to Retained Earnings when the stock dividends were recorded.

ILLUSTRATION 15–1

The Effect of Northwest Corporation's Stock Dividend on Stockholders

Before the 10% stock dividend:

Common stock (10,000 shares)	$100,000
Contributed capital in excess of par value, common stock	8,000
Retained earnings	35,000
Total contributed and retained capital	$143,000

$143,000/10,000 shares outstanding = $14.30 per share book value.
Book value of Johnson's 100 shares: $14.30 × 100 = $1,430.

After the 10% stock dividend is distributed:

Common stock (11,000 shares)	$110,000
Contributed capital in excess of par value, common stock	13,000
Retained earnings	20,000
Total contributed and retained capital	$143,000

$143,000/11,000 shares outstanding = $13 per share book value.
Book value of Johnson's 110 shares: $13 × 110 = $1,430.

As you already learned, a stock dividend does not distribute assets to the stockholders; it has no effect on the corporation's assets. Also, it has no effect on total stockholders' equity and no effect on the percentage of the company owned by each individual stockholder. To illustrate these last points, assume that Johnson owned 100 shares of Northwest Corporation's stock prior to the stock dividend. Then, the 10% stock dividend gave each stockholder 1 new share for each 10 shares previously held. Therefore, Johnson received 10 new shares.

Illustration 15–1 shows Northwest Corporation's total contributed and retained capital and the book value of Johnson's 100 shares before the dividend and after the dividend.

Illustration 15–1 shows that before the stock dividend, Johnson owned 100/10,000 or 1/100 of the Northwest Corporation stock, and his holdings had a $1,430 book value. After the dividend, he owns 110/11,000 or 1/100 of the corporation, and his holdings still have a $1,430 book value. In other words, there was no effect on Johnson's investment except that it was repackaged from 100 units into 110. Also, the only effect on the corporation's capital was a transfer of $15,000 from retained earnings to contributed capital. To summarize, there was no change in the corporation's total assets, no change in its total capital or equity, and no change in the percentage of that equity owned by Johnson.

Stock Dividends on the Balance Sheet

Because a stock dividend is payable in stock rather than in assets, it is not a liability of its issuing corporation. Therefore, if a balance sheet is prepared between the declaration and distribution dates of a stock dividend, the amount of the dividend distributable should appear on the balance sheet in the stockholders' equity section, as follows:

Common stock, $10 par value, 15,000 shares authorized, 10,000 shares issued and outstanding	$100,000
Common stock dividend distributable, 1,000 shares	10,000
Total common stock issued and to be issued	$110,000
Contributed capital in excess of par value, common stock	13,000
Total capital contributed and subscribed by common stockholders	$123,000
Retained earnings	20,000
Total stockholders' equity	$143,000

Recording a Large Stock Dividend

Recall that when the number of shares to be issued in a stock dividend exceeds 25% of the outstanding shares, you capitalize retained earnings equal to the minimum legal amount. Usually, this is the par value or stated value. For example, in the previous discussion, assume that Northwest Corporation's stock dividend declaration on December 31 was for 3,000 shares (30%) instead of 1,000 shares. Since this exceeds 25%, the company would ignore the $15 market value on the date of declaration and record the declaration as follows:

Dec.	31	Stock Dividends Declared	30,000.00	
		Common Stock Dividend Distributable		30,000.00
		To record the declaration of a 3,000 share stock dividend at par value.		

Stock Splits

Sometimes, when a corporation's stock is selling at a high price, the corporation calls it in and issues two, three, or more new shares in the place of each previously outstanding share. For example, a corporation that has $100 par value stock selling for $375 a share may call in the old shares and issue to the stockholders four shares of $25 par value in exchange for each $100 share formerly held. Or, the corporation may issue 10 shares of $10 par stock or any number of shares of no-par stock in exchange for each $100 share formerly held. This is known as a **stock split.** The usual purpose of a stock split is to reduce the market price of the stock and thereby facilitate trading in the stock.

A corporation also may have a **reverse stock split,** in which the outstanding shares are replaced by a smaller number of new shares. A reverse stock split is most likely to occur after a company has experienced large losses that have driven the company's stock price downward.

A stock split (or reverse split) has no effect on total stockholders' equity, and no effect on the equities of the individual stockholders. Also, the balances of the contributed capital and retained earnings accounts are not changed. Thus, a stock split (or reverse split) does not require a journal entry. All that is required is a memorandum entry in the stock account reciting the facts of the split. For example, such a memorandum might read, "Called in the outstanding $100 par value common stock and issued 10 shares of $10 par value com-

AS A MATTER OF

Ethics

Falcon Corporation's board of directors and officers have been meeting to discuss and plan the agenda for the corporation's 1994 annual stockholders' meeting. The first item considered by the directors and officers was whether to report a large government contract that Falcon has just obtained. Although this contract will significantly increase income and cash flows in 1994 and beyond, management decided that there is no need to reveal the news at the stockholders' meeting. "After all," one officer said, "the meeting is intended to be the forum for describing the past year's activities, not the plans for the next year."

After concluding that the contract will not be mentioned, the group has moved on to the next topic for the stockholders' meeting. This topic is a motion for the stockholders to approve a compensation plan that will award the managers the rights to acquire large quantities of shares over the next several years. According to the plan, the managers will have a three-year option to buy shares at a fixed price that equals the market value of the stock as measured 30 days after the upcoming stockholders' meeting. In other words, the managers will be able to buy stock in 1995, 1996, or 1997 by paying the 1994 market value. Obviously, if the stock increases in value over the next several years, the managers will realize large profits without having to invest any cash. The financial vice president asks the group whether they should reconsider the decision about the government contract in light of its possible relevance to the vote on the stock option plan.

mon stock for each old share previously outstanding." And when you prepare the balance sheet, the new par value and number of shares outstanding must be used in describing the stock.

Treasury Stock

LO 2 Record purchases and sales of treasury stock and retirements of stock and describe their effects on stockholders' equity.

Corporations often reacquire shares of their own stock. This is done for a variety of reasons. Some shares may be given to employees as bonuses. Others may be used to pay for the acquisition of another corporation. Sometimes, shares are repurchased to avoid a hostile takeover by an investor who seeks control of the company. Occasionally, shares are bought to maintain a favorable market for the stock. For example, in a recent annual report of W. R. Grace & Co., the chief executive officer described the reason for the company's repurchases of its stock as follows:

> The year began with the unexpected need to repurchase 13.6 million Grace common shares plus some preferred shares for nearly $600 million. This was an unplanned action made necessary when Grace's largest shareholder divested its entire holdings. And, it was done to avoid a potentially dangerous downturn in the market value of your Grace shares.

Whatever the reason, if a corporation reacquires shares of its own stock, the reacquired shares are called **treasury stock.** Treasury stock is a corporation's stock that was issued and then reacquired by the issuing corporation. Notice that the acquired stock must be the issuing corporation's own stock. The acquisition of another corporation's stock does not create treasury stock. Also, treasury stock is not the same as unissued stock. Treasury stock must

ILLUSTRATION 15–2

Curry Corporation's Balance Sheet Prior to the Purchase of Treasury Stock

CURRY CORPORATION
Balance Sheet
May 1, 1993

Assets		**Stockholders' Equity**	
Cash	$ 30,000	Common stock, $10 par value, authorized and issued 10,000 shares	$100,000
Other assets	95,000	Retained earnings	25,000
Total assets	$125,000	Total stockholders' equity	$125,000

have been issued and then reacquired. The distinction is important because stock once issued at par or above may be reacquired and then reissued at an amount below par without burdening the new stockholders with discount liability.

Although treasury stock differs from unissued stock in that it may be sold below par without discount liability, in other respects it has the same status as unissued stock. Neither is an asset. Neither receives cash dividends or stock dividends, and neither has a vote in the stockholders' meetings. Both are subtracted from authorized stock to determine outstanding stock when such things as book values are calculated.

Purchase of Treasury Stock

When a corporation purchases its own stock, it reduces both its assets and its stockholders' equity by equal amounts.[3] To illustrate, assume that on May 1, 1993, the condensed balance sheet of Curry Corporation appears as in Illustration 15–2.

On May 1, Curry Corporation purchases 1,000 shares of its outstanding stock at $11.50 per share, and records the transaction as follows:

May	1	Treasury Stock, Common	11,500.00	
		Cash		11,500.00
		Purchased 1,000 shares of treasury stock at $11.50 per share.		

The debit of the entry records a reduction in the equity of the stockholders. The credit records a reduction in assets. Both are equal to the cost of the

[3] This text discusses the *cost method* of accounting for treasury stock, which is the most widely used. Other methods are discussed in more advanced courses.

ILLUSTRATION 15–3

Curry Corporation's Balance Sheet Immediately after the Purchase of Treasury Stock

CURRY CORPORATION
Balance Sheet
May 1, 1993

Assets		Stockholders' Equity	
Cash	$ 18,500	Common stock, $10 par value, authorized and issued 10,000 shares of which 1,000 are in the treasury	$100,000
Other assets	95,000	Retained earnings of which $11,500 is restricted by the purchase of treasury stock	25,000
		Total	$125,000
		Less cost of treasury stock	11,500
Total assets	$113,500	Total stockholders' equity	$113,500

treasury stock. After the entry is posted, a new balance sheet shows the reductions as in Illustration 15–3.

In Illustration 15–3, notice that the cost of the treasury stock appears in the stockholders' equity section as a deduction from common stock and retained earnings. In comparing the two balance sheets (Illustrations 15–2 and 15–3), note that the treasury stock purchase reduced both assets and stockholders' equity by the $11,500 cost of the stock. Also, the amount of issued stock is not changed by the purchase of treasury stock. The dollar amount of issued stock remains at $100,000 and is unchanged from the first balance sheet. However, the purchase does reduce the amount of outstanding stock. Curry Corporation's outstanding stock was reduced from 10,000 to 9,000 shares.

Note the distinction between issued stock and outstanding stock. Issued stock may or may not be outstanding. Outstanding stock was issued and remains currently in the hands of stockholders. Also, remember that only outstanding stock receives dividends and has a vote in the meetings of stockholders.

Restricting Retained Earnings by the Purchase of Treasury Stock

LO 3 Describe restrictions and appropriations of retained earnings and the disclosure of such items in the financial statements.

The purchase of treasury stock by a corporation has the same effect on its assets and stockholders' equity as the payment of a cash dividend. Both transfer corporate assets to stockholders and thereby reduce assets and stockholders' equity. Therefore, in most states, a corporation may purchase treasury stock or it may pay cash dividends, but the sum of both cannot exceed the amount of its retained earnings available for dividends.

Unlike the payment of a cash dividend, the purchase of treasury stock does not reduce the balance of the Retained Earnings account. Instead, the purchase places a restriction on the amount of retained earnings available for dividends. Note the **restricted retained earnings** shown in Illustration 15–3. Usually, the restriction also is described in a footnote to the financial statements.

The restriction of retained earnings because of treasury stock purchases is a matter of state law. Other legal restrictions on retained earnings may be imposed by law or by contract.

Reissuing Treasury Stock

Treasury stock may be reissued at cost, above cost, or below cost. If reissued at cost, the entry to record the transaction is the reverse of the entry to record the purchase.

If treasury stock is sold at a price above cost, the amount received in excess of cost is credited to a contributed capital account called Contributed Capital, Treasury Stock Transactions. For example, if Curry Corporation sells for $12 per share 500 of the treasury shares purchased at $11.50 per share, the entry to record the transaction is as follows:

June	3	Cash	6,000.00	
		Treasury Stock, Common		5,750.00
		Contributed Capital, Treasury Stock Transactions		250.00
		Sold at $12 per share 500 treasury shares that cost $11.50 per share.		

When treasury stock is reissued at a price below cost, the entry to record the sale depends on whether there is a preexisting credit balance in the Contributed Capital, Treasury Stock Transactions account. If none exists, the excess of cost over the sales price is debited to Retained Earnings. However, if the contributed capital account has a credit balance, the excess of cost over sales price is charged to the contributed capital account to the extent possible. After the credit balance in the contributed capital account is eliminated, any remaining difference between cost and sales price is debited to Retained Earnings. For example, if Curry Corporation sells its remaining 500 shares of treasury stock at $10 per share, the entry to record the sale is:

July	10	Cash	5,000.00	
		Contributed Capital, Treasury Stock Transactions	250.00	
		Retained Earnings	500.00	
		Treasury Stock, Common		5,750.00
		Sold at $10 per share 500 treasury shares that cost $11.50 per share.		

Retirement of Stock

A corporation may purchase shares of its own stock to retire the stock rather than holding it as treasury stock. If so, such shares are permanently canceled on receipt. Like the purchase of treasury stock, the purchase and retirement of the stock is permissible only if the interests of creditors and other stockholders are not jeopardized.

When stock is purchased for retirement, all contributed capital amounts that relate to the retired shares are removed from the accounts. If the cash paid to purchase the shares exceeds the net amount removed from the contributed capital accounts, the difference is debited to Retained Earnings. And if the cash paid is less than the net amount removed from the contributed capital accounts, the difference is credited to a contributed capital account.

For example, assume a corporation originally issued its $10 par value common stock at $12 per share so that the $2 premium was credited to Contributed Capital in Excess of Par Value, Common Stock. If the corporation later purchased and retired 1,000 shares of this stock at the price for which it was issued, the entry to record the retirement is:

Apr.	12	Common Stock	10,000.00	
		Contributed Capital in Excess of Par Value, Common Stock	2,000.00	
		Cash		12,000.00
		Purchased and retired 1,000 shares of common stock at $12 per share.		

On the other hand, if the corporation paid $11 per share instead of $12, the entry for the retirement is:

Apr.	12	Common Stock	10,000.00	
		Contributed Capital in Excess of Par Value, Common Stock	2,000.00	
		Cash		11,000.00
		Contributed Capital from the Retirement of Common Stock		1,000.00
		Purchased and retired 1,000 shares of common stock at $11 per share.		

Or, if the corporation paid $15 per share, the entry for the purchase and retirement is:

Apr.	12	Common Stock	10,000.00	
		Contributed Capital in Excess of Par Value, Common Stock	2,000.00	
		Retained Earnings	3,000.00	
		Cash		15,000.00
		Purchased and retired 1,000 shares of common stock at $15 per share.		

Appropriations of Retained Earnings

A corporation may voluntarily designate an amount of retained earnings for some special purpose as a means of explaining to stockholders why dividends are not being declared. In contrast to retained earnings restrictions, which are binding by law or by contract, **appropriated retained earnings** result from a voluntary action by the board of directors. In earlier years, such appropriations were recorded by transferring portions of retained earnings from the Retained Earnings account to another stockholders' equity account such as Retained Earnings Appropriated for Contingencies or Retained Earnings Appropriated for Plant Expansion. When the contingency or other reason for an appropriation was passed, the appropriation account was eliminated by returning its balance to the Retained Earnings account.

Today, appropriations of retained earnings are seldom seen on balance sheets. Instead, management's reasons for not declaring dividends usually are conveyed in a letter to stockholders that is published with the financial statements.

REPORTING INCOME AND RETAINED EARNINGS INFORMATION

Income Statement Items Not Related to Continuing Operations

When the revenue and expense transactions of a company consist of routine, continuing operations, the company's single-step income statement shows revenues followed by a list of operating expenses and finally by net income. Often, however, the activities of a business include items not closely related to its continuing operations. In these cases, the income effects of such items should be separated from the revenues and expenses of continuing operations. Otherwise, the income statement fails to provide readers with clear information about the results of business activities.

LO 4 Explain how the income effects of discontinued operations, extraordinary items, changes in accounting principles, and prior period adjustments are reported.

To see how various income statement items should be classified, look at Illustration 15–4. Observe that the income statement is separated into five sections labeled 1 through 5. The first portion of the income statement (the portion labeled as 1) shows the revenues, expenses, and income generated by the company's continuing operations. This portion looks just like the single-step income statement we first discussed in Chapter 5. The next income statement section, labeled 2, relates to discontinued operations.

Discontinued Operations

Large companies often have several different lines of business operations or have several different classes of customers. A company's operations that involve a particular line of business or class of customers may qualify as a **segment of the business.** To qualify as a segment of a business, the assets, activities, and financial results of operations involving a particular line of business or class of customers must be distinguished from other parts of the business.

Separating Discontinued Operations on the Income Statement

Normally, the revenues and expenses of all business segments are added together and reported as the continuing operations of the business (as in section 1 of Illustration 15–4). However, when a business sells or disposes of a business segment, the results of that segment's operations must be separated and re-

ILLUSTRATION 15–4

Income Statement for a Corporation

CONNELLY CORPORATION
Income Statement
For Year Ended December 31, 1993

Section			
1	Net sales		$8,443,000
	Gain on sale of old equipment		30,000
	Total		$8,473,000
	Costs and expenses:		
	Cost of goods sold	$5,950,000	
	Depreciation expense	35,000	
	Other selling, general, and administrative expenses	515,000	
	Interest expense	20,000	
	Income taxes expense	792,000	(7,312,000)
	Unusual loss on sale of surplus land		(45,000)
	Infrequent gain on relocation of a plant		72,000
	Income from continuing operations		$1,188,000
2	**Discontinued operations:**		
	Income from operation of discontinued Division A (net of $166,000 income taxes)	$ 400,000	
	Loss on disposal of Division A (net of $60,000 tax benefit)	(150,000)	250,000
	Income before extraordinary items and cumulative effect of a change in accounting principle		$1,438,000
3	**Extraordinary items:**		
	Gain on sale of unused land expropriated by the state for a highway interchange (net of $35,000 income taxes)	$ 142,500	
	Loss from earthquake damage (net of $310,000 income tax benefit)	(670,000)	
4	**Cumulative effect of a change in accounting principle:**		
	Effect on prior years' income (to December 31, 1992) of changing to a different depreciation method (net of $18,000 income taxes)	27,000	(500,500)
	Net income		$ 937,500
5	**Earnings per common share** (250,000 shares outstanding):		
	Income from continuing operations		$4.75
	Discontinued operations		1.00
	Income before extraordinary items and cumulative effect of a change in accounting principle		$5.75
	Extraordinary items		(2.11)
	Cumulative effect of a change in accounting principle		.11
	Net income		$3.75

ported as you see in section 2 of Illustration 15–4.[4] In the illustration, the results of the discontinued operations are completely separated from the results of other activities. This separation makes it easier for financial statement readers to evaluate the continuing operations of the business.

[4] FASB, *Accounting Standards—Current Text* (Norwalk, Conn., 1990), sec. I13.105. First published as *APB Opinion No. 30,* par. 8.

Separating the Results of Operating a Segment that Is Being Discontinued from the Gain or Loss on Disposal

Within section 2 of Illustration 15–4, note that the income from *operating* Division A (the operation that is being discontinued) during the period is reported separately from the loss on the final *disposal* of Division A. Also, the income tax effects of the discontinued operations are separated from the income tax expense shown in section 1 of Illustration 15–4. Thus, the results of the discontinued operations are reported net of tax. Also, the amount of tax or tax benefit related to each item is disclosed.

The preceding discussion summarizes the method of reporting the results of discontinued operations on the income statement. The detailed requirements for measuring the income or losses of discontinued operations are discussed in more advanced accounting courses.

Extraordinary Items

Section 3 of the income statement in Illustration 15–4 reports gains and losses that are defined as extraordinary. To qualify as an **extraordinary gain or loss**, an item must be both unusual and infrequent. An **unusual gain or loss** is abnormal and unrelated or only incidentally related to the ordinary activities and environment of the business. An **infrequent gain or loss** is not expected to occur again, given the operating environment of the business.[5]

Given these definitions of *unusual* and *infrequent*, very few items meet both criteria; as a result, very few items qualify as extraordinary gains or losses. For example, none of the following generally qualify as extraordinary:

1. Write-down or write-off of assets unless caused by major casualty, an expropriation, or prohibition under a newly enacted law.
2. Gains or losses from exchange or translation of foreign currencies.
3. Gains and losses on disposal of a segment of a business.
4. Other gains and losses from sale or abandonment of property, plant, or equipment unless caused by a major casualty, an expropriation, or prohibition under a newly enacted law.
5. Effects of a strike, including those against competitors and major suppliers.
6. Adjustment of accruals on long-term contracts.[6]

Some gains or losses are neither unusual nor infrequent. They are reported among the revenues or costs and expenses of continuing operations. Other gains or losses may be unusual or infrequent but not both. Such gains or losses are not extraordinary items. On the income statement, items that are unusual or infrequent but not both are listed below the costs and expenses of continuing operations. Section 1 of Illustration 15–4 displays a "Gain on sale of old

[5] Ibid., sec. I17.107. First published as *APB Opinion No. 30*, par. 20.

[6] Ibid., sec. I17.110. First published as *APB Opinion No. 30*, par. 23.

ILLUSTRATION 15–5

Calculating the Cumulative Effect of a Change in an Accounting Principle

Year		Sum-of-the-Years'-Digits Depreciation	Straight-Line Depreciation	After-Tax Difference in Methods	
		a	*b*	(*a* − *b*) × 60%	
Prior years:					
1990	(6/21)	$ 60,000	$ 35,000	$25,000 × 60% =	$15,000
1991	(5/21)	50,000	35,000	15,000 × 60% =	9,000
1992	(4/21)	40,000	35,000	5,000 × 60% =	3,000
Totals				$45,000	$27,000*
Year of change:					
1993	(3/21)	30,000	35,000*	(5,000) × 60% =	(3,000)
Future years:					
1994	(2/21)	20,000	35,000	(15,000) × 60% =	(9,000)
1995	(1/21)	10,000	35,000	(25,000) × 60% =	(15,000)
Totals		$210,000	$210,000	$ -0-	$ -0-

* These two numbers are reported on the income statement in Illustration 15–4.

equipment'' that is neither unusual nor infrequent. The illustration also shows an unusual loss and an infrequent gain. Note that the correct classification of these items is not obvious from their descriptions. Instead, accountants carefully examine the circumstances surrounding each gain or loss to determine the correct classification.

Changes in Accounting Principles

The Consistency Principle Does Not Preclude Changes in Accounting Principles

After a company chooses to use a particular accounting method or principle, it must continue to use the same principle each period. This is required by the *consistency principle*. (In this discussion, methods such as FIFO and straight-line depreciation are called accounting principles.) Nevertheless, the *consistency principle* does not mean that a company may never make changes. A company may change from one accounting principle to another as long as it justifies the change as an improvement in financial reporting.

When a company changes from one accounting principle to another, the change often affects the amount of income reported. For example, assume a company has only one asset that cost $210,000, has no salvage value, and is being depreciated on a sum-of-the-years'-digits basis over six years. Also, assume a 40% income tax rate. Early in year 4, the company decides to switch to straight-line depreciation and justifies the change as an improvement in financial reporting. Illustration 15–5 compares the two depreciation methods during the six-year life of the asset.

Reporting Requirements for Changes in Accounting Principles

How should the change in depreciation methods be reported on the income statement? Illustration 15–4 shows the correct method of disclosure. In section 1 of Illustration 15–4, note that depreciation expense for the current year is $35,000. This is the straight-line amount in the year of change as calculated in Illustration 15–5. In section 4 of Illustration 15–4, the effect of the change on prior years' income is reported as $27,000 (net of $18,000 income taxes). Compare this with the calculations in Illustration 15–5, which show that the after-tax difference between the two depreciation methods in prior years is $27,000.

To summarize, a company that wants to make a change in accounting principles must report several items of information, including the following:

1. The nature of and justification for the change should be described in the footnotes to the financial statements.
2. The cumulative effect of the change on prior periods should be shown on the income statement below extraordinary items. Also, the effect on earnings per share must be shown separately. (See section 5 of Illustration 15–4.)
3. In the year of the change, the footnotes also should state the effect of the change on income before extraordinary items and on net income.[7]

Earnings per Share Section of the Income Statement

Observe in section 5 of Illustration 15–4 that separate earnings per share numbers are presented on the face of the income statement for each of the income statement categories. Although this section is slightly more complete than the minimum reporting requirements, many companies that have earnings or losses in all categories present their earnings per share information as shown in Illustration 15–4. Later in the chapter, we explain the procedures used to calculate earnings per share.

Prior Period Adjustments and the Statement of Retained Earnings

In the annual financial statements of a corporation, the income effect of one type of item is excluded entirely from the current income statement. This type of item is called a **prior period adjustment.** Very few items qualify as prior period adjustments. They are limited primarily to corrections of errors made in past years. The errors may have involved mathematical mistakes, or mistakes in applying accounting principles, or a failure to take known facts into consideration.[8] For example, the accountant may have forgotten to take depreciation on a plant asset, or calculated the depreciation incorrectly.

Prior period adjustments are reported in the statement of retained earnings as corrections to the beginning retained earnings balance. They are reported net of any related tax effect. For example, a statement of retained earnings with a prior period adjustment might appear as follows:

---

[7] Ibid., sec. A06.113–16. Originally published as *APB Opinion No. 20,* pars. 17–20.

[8] Ibid, sec. A35.104. First published as *APB Opinion No. 20,* par. 13.

CONNELLY CORPORATION
Statement of Retained Earnings
For Year Ended December 31, 1993

Retained earnings, December 31, 1992, as previously stated . .	$4,745,000
Prior period adjustment:	
Cost of land purchase that was incorrectly charged to expense (net of $60,000 income taxes)	130,000
Retained earnings, December 31, 1992, as adjusted	$4,875,000
Plus net income	937,500
Less cash dividends declared	(240,000)
Retained earnings, December 31, 1993	$5,572,500

Changes in Accounting Estimates

Errors of past periods that qualify as prior period adjustments must be distinguished from revisions or **changes in accounting estimates.** Errors include mathematical mistakes or failure to consider known facts. On the other hand, the preparation of financial statements requires many estimates about the future. For example, depreciation is based on estimates of useful life and estimates of salvage value. As new information becomes available, it may become necessary to change such estimates. Changes of this sort are not errors and do not qualify as prior period adjustments. Changes in accounting estimates are not allowed to affect the income of prior periods. Instead, the revised estimate is applied in calculating the appropriate revenue or expense of the current and future periods. We discussed one example of a change in an accounting estimate, the revision of depreciation rates, on pages 539 and 540 in Chapter 10.

Statement of Changes in Stockholders' Equity

In Chapter 5, we explained that some corporations do not present a separate statement of retained earnings. Instead, they present a combined statement of income and retained earnings, an example of which was shown in Illustration 5–8, on page 269. Other corporations show the statement of retained earnings information in an expanded statement called a **statement of changes in stockholders' equity.** In that statement, the beginning and ending balances of each stockholders' equity account are reconciled by listing all changes that occurred during the year. For example, the annual report of Winn-Dixie Stores, Inc., for the year ended June 27, 1990, included the financial statement shown in Illustration 15–6.

EARNINGS PER SHARE

Among the most commonly quoted statistics on the financial pages of daily newspapers is **earnings per share** of common stock. Investors use earnings per share data when they evaluate the past performance of a corporation, project its future earnings, and weigh investment opportunities.

ILLUSTRATION 15-6

Consolidated Statements of Stockholders' Equity

WINN-DIXIE STORES, INC.
Consolidated Statements of Stockholders' Equity
Years Ended June 27, 1990, June 28, 1989, and June 29, 1988

	1990	1989	1988
	Amounts in thousands		
Common stock:			
Beginning of year	**$ 40,130**	$ 42,299	$ 42,299
Deduct par value of common stock retired	**(484)**	(2,169)	—
End of year	**39,646**	40,130	42,299
Retained earnings:			
Beginning of year	**752,047**	754,764	713,832
Net earnings	**152,530**	134,545	116,694
Deduct cash dividends on common stock of $1.98, $1.92, and $1.86 per share in 1990, 1989, and 1988, respectively	**(77,944)**	(77,123)	(75,726)
Deduct excess of cost over par value of common stock retired	**(24,477)**	(60,095)	—
Deduct other	—	(44)	(36)
End of year	**802,156**	752,047	754,764
Cost of common stock held:			
Beginning of year 199,294, 2,391,931, and 1,066,514 shares	**9,004**	70,715	16,713
Add cost of 798,802, 163,410, and 1,325,417 shares reacquired	**45,756**	7,314	54,002
Deduct cost of 483,982 and 2,168,571 shares retired	**(24,960)**	(62,264)	—
Deduct cost of 25,126 and 187,476 shares issued under associates' stock purchase plan and management incentive plan	**(1,225)**	(6,761)	—
End of year 488,988, 199,294, and 2,391,931 shares	**28,575**	9,004	70,715
Total shareholders' equity	**$813,227**	$783,173	$726,348

Courtesy of Winn-Dixie Stores, Inc.

Companies with Simple Capital Structures

LO 5 Calculate earnings per share for companies with simple capital structures and explain the difference between primary and fully diluted earnings per share.

Earnings per share calculations may be simple or complex. The calculations are not as difficult for companies that have simple capital structures. A company has a **simple capital structure** if it has only common stock and perhaps nonconvertible preferred stock outstanding. In other words, to have a simple capital structure, the company cannot have any outstanding options or rights to purchase common stock at a specified price or any securities convertible into common stock.

Calculating Earnings per Share When the Number of Common Shares Outstanding Does Not Change

Consider a company that has only common stock and nonconvertible preferred stock outstanding. If the number of common shares outstanding does not change during the period, calculate earnings per share as follows:

$$\text{Earnings per share} = \frac{\text{Net income} - \text{Preferred dividends}^{9}}{\text{Common shares outstanding}}$$

For example, assume that in 1992, Blackwell Company earned a $40,000 net income and paid its preferred dividends of $7,500. On January 1, 1992, the company had 5,000 common shares outstanding and this number did not change during the year. Calculate earnings per share for 1992 as follows:

$$\text{Earnings per share} = \frac{\$40{,}000 - \$7{,}500}{5{,}000} = \$6.50$$

However, the calculation becomes more complex if the number of common shares outstanding changes during the period. The number of common shares outstanding may change (1) because the company sells additional shares or buys treasury shares or (2) because of stock dividends and stock splits.

Adjusting the Denominator for Sales or Purchases of Common Shares

If additional shares are sold or treasury shares are purchased during the year, earnings per share is based on the weighted-average number of shares outstanding during the year. For example, suppose that in 1993, Blackwell Company again earned $40,000 and preferred dividends were $7,500. However, on July 1, 1993, Blackwell sold 4,000 additional common shares. Also, on November 1, 1993, Blackwell purchased 3,000 treasury shares. In other words, 5,000 shares were outstanding for six months; then 9,000 shares were outstanding for four months; then 6,000 shares were outstanding for two months. When such changes occur, calculate the weighted-average number of shares outstanding during 1993 as follows:

Time Period	Shares Outstanding	Weighted by Portion of Year Outstanding
January–June.	5,000	(6/12) = 2,500
July–October.	(5,000 + 4,000)	(4/12) = 3,000
November–December	(9,000 − 3,000)	(2/12) = 1,000
Weighted-average common shares outstanding		6,500

The calculation of earnings per share for 1993 is:

$$\text{Earnings per share} = \frac{\$40{,}000 - \$7{,}500}{6{,}500} = \$5$$

---

[9] If preferred stock is cumulative, the current year's dividend must be subtracted even if it was not declared. If preferred stock is not cumulative, the current year's dividend is subtracted only if it was declared.

Adjusting the Denominator for Stock Splits and Stock Dividends

A stock split or stock dividend is different than a stock sale. When stock is sold, the company receives new assets that it uses to generate additional earnings. On the other hand, stock splits and stock dividends do not provide additional assets for the company. Instead, a stock split or stock dividend simply means that the company's earnings must be allocated to a larger number of outstanding shares.

Because of the nature of stock splits and stock dividends, treat them differently from stock sales when calculating the weighted-average number of shares outstanding. When a stock split or stock dividend occurs, the number of shares outstanding during previous portions of the year must be retroactively restated to reflect the stock split or dividend. For example, consider the previous example of Blackwell Company. Assume that the stock transactions in 1993 included a stock split, as follows:

Jan. 1: 5,000 common shares were outstanding.
July 1: Blackwell sold 4,000 additional shares of common stock.
Nov. 1: Blackwell purchased 3,000 common shares as treasury stock.
Dec. 1: Outstanding common shares were split **2 for 1.**

Given these changes in the number of shares outstanding during 1993, calculate the weighted-average number of shares outstanding as follows:

Time Period	Shares Outstanding	Restated for Stock Split	Weighted by Portion of Year Outstanding
January–June	5,000	2	(6/12) = 5,000
July–October	(5,000 + 4,000)	2	(4/12) = 6,000
November	(9,000 − 3,000)	2	(1/12) = 1,000
December	12,000	—	(1/12) = 1,000
Weighted-average common shares outstanding			13,000

Note that every time stock was sold or purchased, the resulting number of outstanding shares was restated for the subsequent stock split. The same type of restatement is required for stock dividends. If, for example, the 2 for 1 stock split on December 1 had been a 10% stock dividend, the previous amounts of outstanding shares would have been adjusted by a multiplier of 1.10 instead of 2. The calculation of Blackwell Company's earnings per share for 1993 is:

$$\text{Earnings per share} = \frac{\$40{,}000 - \$7{,}500}{13{,}000} = \$2.50$$

Companies with Complex Capital Structures

Companies with **complex capital structures** have outstanding securities such as bonds or preferred stock that are convertible into common stock. Earnings per share calculations for companies with complex capital structures are more complicated. Often, such companies must present two types of earnings per share calculations. One is called **primary earnings per share,** and the other is called **fully diluted earnings per share.**

Suppose that a corporation has convertible preferred stock outstanding throughout the current year. However, consider what the effects would have been if the preferred shares had been converted at the beginning of the year. The result of this assumed conversion would have been to increase the number of common shares outstanding and to reduce preferred dividends. The net result may have been to reduce earnings per share, or to increase earnings per share. When the assumed conversion of a security reduces earnings per share, the security is said to be **dilutive;** those that increase earnings per share are **antidilutive.**

Primary Earnings per Share

Based on detailed rules, convertible securities are evaluated at the time they are issued.[10] If eventual conversion appears highly probable, the convertible security is called a **common stock equivalent.** Primary earnings per share is calculated as if dilutive common stock equivalents had already been converted at the beginning of the period.

Fully Diluted Earnings per Share

Common stock equivalents have terms that make their eventual conversion very probable. Other convertible securities are less apt to be converted. Nevertheless, if we assume those securities were converted at the beginning of the period, the effect may be to reduce earnings per share; in other words, the assumed conversion may have a dilutive effect. Fully diluted earnings per share is calculated as if all dilutive securities had already been converted.

Presentations of Earnings per Share on the Income Statement

Because of the importance attached to earnings per share data, generally accepted accounting principles require earnings per share information to be shown on the face of a corporation's income statement. When a company's activities include all of the categories shown in Illustration 15–4 (page 820), separate earnings per share statistics usually are presented for each category. However, per share data on extraordinary items are not absolutely required. Also, gains or losses from discontinued operations per share may be reported in a footnote instead of on the face of the income statement.

Examples of earnings per share presentations are provided by the 1989 financial statements of Unocal Corporation and The May Department Stores Company. Illustrations 15–7 and 15–8 present the bottom portions of Unocal's and The May Department Stores' comparative income statements for 1989, 1988, and 1987.

In Illustration 15–7, notice that the earnings per share statistics of Unocal Corporation included each of the income statement categories discussed ear-

[10] FASB, *Accounting Standards—Current Text* (Norwalk, Conn., 1990), sec. E09.122–127. First published as *APB Opinion No. 15*, par. 31, 33, 35–37. Also see *FASB, Statement of Financial Accounting Standards No. 85* (March 1985), par. 2.

ILLUSTRATION 15–7

Reporting Earnings per Share on the Income Statement

CONSOLIDATED EARNINGS — UNOCAL CORPORATION
(dollars in millions except per share amounts)

Years ended December 31	1989	1988	1987
Net Earnings	$260	$480	$181
Earnings (Loss) per share			
Continuing operations	$1.53	$ .12	$ .79
Discontinued operations	(.42)	(.02)	(.01)
Cumulative effect of change in accounting principle	—	1.96	—
Net earnings per share	$1.11	$2.06	$ .78

Courtesy of Unocal Corporation

ILLUSTRATION 15–8

Reporting Primary and Fully Diluted Earnings per Share

CONSOLIDATED STATEMENT OF EARNINGS
The May Department Stores Company and Subsidiaries

(millions, except per share)	1989	1988	1987
Net earnings	$ 498	$ 534	$ 444
Primary Earnings per Share:			
Continuing operations	$3.75	$3.05	$2.56
Discontinued operations	.05	.38	.33
Gain (Loss) on disposal of discontinued operations	(.17)	.20	—
Primary Earnings per Share	$3.63	$3.63	$2.89
Fully Diluted Earnings per Share:			
Continuing operations	$3.64	$3.04	$2.56
Discontinued operations	.05	.38	.33
Gain (Loss) on disposal of discontinued operations	(.17)	.20	—
Fully Diluted Earnings per Share	$3.52	$3.62	$2.89

Courtesy of The May Department Stores Company

lier in the chapter, except for extraordinary items. Unocal has a simple capital structure and did not have to report both primary and fully diluted statistics. On the other hand, The May Department Stores Company report (Illustration 15–8) includes both primary earnings per share and fully diluted earnings per share.

Summary of Chapter in Terms of Learning Objectives

LO 1. Whereas cash dividends transfer corporate assets to the stockholders, stock dividends do not. Stock dividends and stock splits have no effect on assets, no effect on total stockholders' equity, and no effect on the equity of each stockholder. Small stock dividends are recorded by capitalizing retained earnings equal to the market value of the distributed shares. If the stock dividend is over 25% of the outstanding shares, only the par value or stated value of the distributed shares is capitalized.

LO 2. When outstanding shares are repurchased by the issuing corporation and held as treasury stock, the cost of the shares is debited to Treasury Stock, which is subtracted in the stockholders' equity section of the balance sheet. If treasury stock is reissued, proceeds in excess of cost are credited to Contributed Capital, Treasury Stock Transactions. If the proceeds are less than cost, the difference is debited to Contributed Capital, Treasury Stock Transactions to the extent a credit balance exists in that account. Any remaining amount is debited to Retained Earnings.

LO 3. In most states, retained earnings are legally restricted by an amount equal to the cost of treasury stock. Retained earnings also may be restricted by contract. Corporations may voluntarily appropriate retained earnings to inform stockholders why dividends are not larger in amount. More often, however, this information is expressed in a letter to the stockholders.

LO 4. If management has implemented a plan to discontinue a business segment, the net income or loss from operating the segment and the gain or loss on disposal are separately reported on the income statement below income from continuing operations. Next, extraordinary gains or losses, which are both unusual and infrequent, are listed and followed by the cumulative effect on past years' incomes of changes in accounting principles.

Prior period adjustments, which include the income effects of accounting errors made in prior periods, are reported on the statement of retained earnings. However, many companies omit the statement of retained earnings and report the changes in each stockholders' equity account on a statement of changes in stockholders' equity. Changes in accounting estimates are made because new information shows the old estimates to be invalid. When an accounting estimate is changed, the new estimate is used to calculate revenue or expense in the current and future periods.

LO 5. Companies with simple capital structures do not have outstanding securities convertible into common stock. For such companies, earnings per share is calculated by dividing net income less dividends to preferred stock by the weighted average number of outstanding common shares. In calculating the weighted average number of shares outstanding, the number of shares outstanding prior to a stock dividend or stock split must be restated to reflect the effect of the stock dividend or stock split.

Companies with complex capital structures have outstanding securities that are convertible into common stock. These companies may have to report both primary earnings per share and fully diluted earnings per share. In calculating primary earnings per share, the denominator is the weighted-average number of common shares outstanding plus dilutive common stock equivalents. Fully diluted earnings per share assumes the conversion of all dilutive securities.

Demonstration Problem

The Precision Company began 1993 with the following balances in its stockholders' equity accounts:

Common stock, $10 par, 500,000 shares authorized, 200,000 shares issued and outstanding	$2,000,000
Contributed capital in excess of par	1,000,000
Retained earnings	5,000,000
Total	$8,000,000

All of the outstanding stock was issued for $15 when the company was created.

Part 1. Prepare journal entries to account for the following transactions:

1993

Mar.	31	Declared a 20% stock dividend. The market value of the stock was $18 per share.
Apr.	15	Issued the common shares declared as a stock dividend on March 31.
June	30	Purchased 30,000 shares of treasury stock at $20 per share.
Aug.	31	Sold 20,000 of the treasury shares at $26 per share.
Nov.	30	Purchased and retired 50,000 shares at $24 per share.

Part 2. Use the following information to prepare an income statement for 1993, including earnings per share amounts for each category of income.

Cumulative effect on prior years' net incomes of a change in depreciation methods (net of income tax benefit)	$ (136,500)
Expenses of continuing operations	(2,072,500)
Extraordinary gain on legal settlement (net of income tax)	182,000
Gain on disposal of discontinued division (net of income tax)	29,000
Gain on sale of stock investment	400,000
Loss from operation of discontinued division (net of income tax benefit)	(120,000)
Income taxes on income from continuing operations	(225,000)
Prior period adjustment for error (net of income tax benefit)	(75,000)
Sales	4,140,000
Infrequent loss on purchase commitment	(650,000)

Part 3. Based on all of this information, prepare a statement of changes in stockholders' equity for 1993.

Solution to Demonstration Problem

Planning the Solution

- Decide whether the stock dividend should be treated as a small or large dividend. Then, analyze each transaction to determine the accounts affected and the appropriate amounts to be recorded.

- Based on the shares of stock outstanding at the beginning of the year and the transactions during the year that affected the number of outstanding shares, calculate the weighted-average number of shares outstanding during the year.
- Review the list of items related to income and decide the appropriate income statement category for each item.
- Prepare an income statement similar in format to Illustration 15–4, including appropriate earnings per share statistics.
- Follow the format in Illustration 15–6 to prepare a statement of changes in stockholders' equity.

Part 1

1993				
Mar.	31	Stock Dividends Declared	720,000.00	
		Common Stock Dividend Distributable		400,000.00
		Contributed Capital in Excess of Par Value, Common Stock		320,000.00
		Declared a stock dividend of 20% or 40,000 shares; market value is $18 per share.		
Apr.	15	Common Stock Dividend Distributable	400,000.00	
		Common Stock		400,000.00
		Distributed 40,000 shares of common stock.		
June	30	Treasury Stock, Common	600,000.00	
		Cash		600,000.00
		Purchased 30,000 shares of common stock at $20 per share.		
Aug.	31	Cash	520,000.00	
		Treasury Stock, Common		400,000.00
		Contributed Capital, Treasury Stock Transactions		120,000.00
		Sold 20,000 shares of treasury stock at $26 per share.		
Nov.	30	Common Stock	500,000.00	
		Contributed Capital in Excess of Par Value, Common Stock	250,000.00	
		Retained Earnings	450,000.00	
		Cash		1,200,000.00
		Purchased and retired 50,000 shares at $24 per share.		

Part 2. Calculation of the weighted average of outstanding shares:

Time Period	Shares Outstanding	Portion of Year Outstanding	Weighted by Portion of Year Outstanding
January–June	(200,000 × 1.2)	6/12	120,000
July–August	(240,000 − 30,000)	2/12	35,000
September–November	(210,000 + 20,000)	3/12	57,500
December	(230,000 − 50,000)	1/12	15,000
			227,500

PRECISION COMPANY
Income Statement
For Year Ended December 31, 1993

Sales		$4,140,000
Expenses of continuing operations		(2,072,500)
Income taxes		(225,000)
Gain on sale of stock investment		400,000
Infrequent loss on purchase commitment		(650,000)
Income from continuing operations		$1,592,500
Discontinued operations:		
Loss from operation of discontinued division (net of income tax benefit)	$(120,000)	
Gain on disposal of discontinued division's assets (net of income tax)	29,000	
Loss from discontinued division		(91,000)
Income before extraordinary items and cumulative effect of a change in accounting principle		$1,501,500
Extraordinary items:		
Extraordinary gain on legal settlement (net of income tax)		182,000
Cumulative effect of a change in accounting principle:		
Change in depreciation methods (net of income tax benefit)		(136,500)
Net income		$1,547,000
Earnings per share (227,500 average shares outstanding):		
Income from continuing operations		$ 7.00
Loss from discontinued operations		(0.40)
Income before extraordinary gain and cumulative effect of change in accounting principle		$ 6.60
Extraordinary gain		0.80
Cumulative effect of change in accounting principle		(0.60)
Net income		$ 6.80

(Note that the prior period adjustment for the error is not an income statement item.)

Part 3.

PRECISION COMPANY
Statement of Changes in Stockholders' Equity
For Year Ended December 31, 1993

Common stock	
Beginning of year	$2,000,000
Common stock dividend	400,000
Retirement of stock	(500,000)
End of year	$1,900,000
Other contributed capital	
Beginning of year	$1,000,000
Common stock dividend	320,000
Sale of treasury stock	120,000
Retirement of stock	(250,000)
End of year	$1,190,000
Retained earnings	
Beginning of year	$5,000,000
Prior period adjustment	(75,000)
Common stock dividend	(720,000)
Retirement of stock	(450,000)
Net income	1,547,000
End of year	$5,302,000
Treasury stock	
Purchase of treasury stock	$ (600,000)
Sale of treasury stock	400,000
End of year	$ (200,000)
Total stockholders' equity	$8,192,000

Glossary

LO 6 Define or explain the words and phrases listed in the chapter glossary.

Antidilutive securities convertible securities, the assumed conversion of which would have the effect of increasing earnings per share. p. 828

Appropriated retained earnings retained earnings voluntarily earmarked for a special use as a way of informing stockholders that assets from earnings equal to the appropriations are not available for dividends. pp. 818–19

Changes in accounting estimates adjustments to previously made assumptions about the future such as salvage values and the length of useful lives of buildings and equipment. p. 824

Common stock equivalent a security that is convertible into common stock and for which, according to detailed rules applied at the time of issuance, eventual conversion appears very probable. p. 828

Complex capital structure a capital structure that includes outstanding rights or options to purchase common stock or securities convertible into common stock. pp. 827–28

Dilutive securities convertible securities the assumed conversion of which would have the effect of decreasing earnings per share. p. 828

Earned surplus a synonym for retained earnings, no longer in general use. p. 808

Earnings per share the amount of net income (or components of income) that accrues to common shares divided by the weighted-average number of common shares outstanding. pp. 824–29

Extraordinary gain or loss a gain or loss that is both unusual and infrequent. pp. 821–22

Fully diluted earnings per share earnings per share statistics that are calculated as if all dilutive securities had already been converted. pp. 827–28

Infrequent gain or loss a gain or loss that is not expected to occur again, given the operating environment of the business. p. 821

Large stock dividend a stock dividend that amounts to more than 25% of the issuing corporation's shares outstanding before the dividend. pp. 810, 813

Liquidating dividends distributions of corporate assets to stockholders; these distributions are charged to contributed capital accounts and represent amounts originally contributed by the stockholders. p. 809

Primary earnings per share earnings per share statistics that are calculated as if outstanding dilutive common stock equivalents had already been converted. pp. 827–28

Prior period adjustment items reported in the current statement of retained earnings as corrections to the beginning retained earnings balance; limited primarily to corrections of errors that were made in past years. pp. 823–24

Restricted retained earnings retained earnings not available for dividends because of law or binding contract. p. 817

Reverse stock split the act of a corporation to call in its stock and issue one new share in the place of more than one share previously outstanding. p. 813

Segment of a business operations of a company that involve a particular line of business or class of customer, providing the assets, activities, and financial results of the operations can be distinguished from other parts of the business. p. 819

Simple capital structure a capital structure that does not include any rights or options to purchase common shares or any securities that are convertible into common stock. p. 825

Small stock dividend a stock dividend that amounts to 25% or less of the issuing corporation's previously outstanding shares. pp. 810–12

Statement of changes in stockholders' equity a financial statement that reconciles the beginning and ending balances of each stockholders' equity account by listing all changes that occurred during the year. pp. 824–25

Stock dividend a distribution by a corporation of shares of its own stock to its stockholders without the receipt of any consideration in return. pp. 809–813

Stock split the act of a corporation to call in its stock and issue more than one new share in the place of each share previously outstanding. p. 813

Treasury stock issued stock that has been reacquired and is currently held by the issuing corporation. pp. 814–17

Unusual gain or loss a gain or loss that is abnormal and unrelated or only incidentally related to the ordinary activities and environment of the business. p. 821

Synonymous Terms

Primary earnings per share earnings per common and common equivalent share.

Retained earnings earned surplus (a term no longer in use).

Statement of changes in stockholders' equity statement of stockholders' equity.

Objective Review

Answers to the following questions are listed at the end of this chapter. Be sure that you decide which is the one best answer to each question *before* you check the answers.

LO 1 Which of the following statements is true with regard to stock dividends and stock splits?

a. In a stock split, Retained Earnings is debited and the stock account is credited for the par value or stated value of the issued shares.

b. A corporation should capitalize an amount of retained earnings equal to the market value of the shares to be distributed if the stock dividend exceeds 25% of its outstanding shares.

c. The effect of stock dividends and stock splits on the total assets of the issuing corporation is equal to their effect on total retained earnings.

d. The distribution of stock dividends reduces both cash and stockholders' equity but a stock split reduces neither one.
e. A stock dividend does not transfer assets from a corporation to the stockholders but requires that an amount of retained earnings be capitalized.

LO 2 The purchase of treasury stock by a corporation:

a. Does not change the amount of outstanding stock.
b. Is recorded with an increase to assets and a decrease to assets.
c. Decreases the amount of issued stock.
d. Reduces in equal amounts both its total assets and its total stockholders' equity.
e. Requires a debit to Retained Earnings.

LO 3 When a corporation appropriates retained earnings:

a. The amount of the appropriation must be matched by available cash.
b. The board of directors becomes permanently committed not to pay dividends from those appropriated amounts.
c. The board of directors voluntarily allocates a portion of retained earnings for some special purpose, thereby indicating why dividends are not being declared.
d. The appropriation is recorded by transferring the appropriated amount from Retained Earnings to a contributed capital account.
e. None of the above.

LO 4 Which of the following qualifies as an extraordinary gain or loss?

a. A loss of plant and equipment damaged as a result of a meteorite shower.
b. A gain from the exchange of British pounds for dollars that resulted from credit sales of goods to British customers.
c. A loss incurred by a manufacturer of three-wheeled recreational vehicles as a result of a customer's lawsuit over injuries suffered from using the product.
d. A loss due to compensating a worker for injuries suffered while working at the company's plant.
e. None of the above are extraordinary items.

LO 5 Remington Corporation earned $250,000 in 1993, and preferred dividends were $70,000. On January 1, 1993, the company had 25,000 common shares outstanding. However, on July 1, 1993, Remington Corporation purchased 5,000 treasury shares. Earnings per share for 1993 is:

a. $7.20.
b. $8.00.
c. $9.00.
d. $10.00.
e. $11.11.

LO 6 A gain or loss that is not unusual but not expected to occur again given the operating environment of the business should be classified as:

a. Infrequent.
b. Unusual.
c. Extraordinary.
d. Abnormal.
e. Prior period adjustment.

Questions for Class Discussion

1. What effect does the declaration of a cash dividend have on the assets, liabilities, and stockholders' equity of the corporation that declares the dividend? What is the effect of the subsequent payment of the cash dividend?
2. Why are cash dividends charged against contributed capital accounts called liquidating dividends?
3. What effect does the declaration of a stock dividend have on the assets, liabilities, and total stockholders' equity of the corporation that declares the dividend? What is the effect of the subsequent distribution of the stock dividend?
4. In accounting for a stock dividend, what criterion distinguishes a small stock dividend?
5. What amount of retained earnings should be capitalized in accounting for a small stock dividend?
6. What is the difference between a stock dividend and a stock split?
7. Courts have held that a stock dividend is not taxable income to its recipients. Why?
8. If a balance sheet is prepared between the date of declaration and the date of payment or distribution of a dividend, how should the dividend be shown if it is (*a*) a cash dividend, or (*b*) a stock dividend?
9. What is treasury stock? How is it like unissued stock? How does it differ from unissued stock? What is the legal significance of this difference?
10. Southern Products Corporation bought 15,000 shares of Regional Steel Corporation stock and turned it over to the treasurer of Southern Products for safekeeping. Is this treasury stock? Why or why not?
11. What effect does the purchase of treasury stock have on assets and total stockholders' equity?
12. Distinguish between issued stock and outstanding stock.
13. Why do state laws place limitations on the purchase of treasury stock?
14. In the annual income statement of a corporation, what are four major sections of the statement that might appear below income from continuing operations?

15. If a company operates several different lines of business, which criteria must be met if the operations in a particular line of business are to qualify as a business segment?
16. If a company operates one of its business segments at a loss during much of 1993, and then finds a buyer and disposes of that segment during November of that year, which two items concerning that segment should appear on the company's 1993 income statement?
17. Where on the income statement should a company disclose a gain that is abnormal and unrelated to the ordinary activities of the business and that is not expected to recur more often than once every other year?
18. Which of the following items would qualify as an extraordinary gain or loss: (*a*) operating losses resulting from a strike against a major supplier; (*b*) a gain from the sale of surplus equipment; or (*c*) a loss from damage to a building caused by a tornado (a type of storm that rarely occurs in the geographical region of the company's operations)?
19. In past years, Daley Company paid its sales personnel annual salaries without additional incentive payments. This year, a new policy is being instituted whereby they receive sales commissions rather than annual salaries. Does this new policy require a prior period adjustment? Explain why or why not.
20. After taking five years' straight-line depreciation on an asset that was expected to have an eight-year life, a company concluded that the asset would last another six years. Does this decision involve a change in accounting principle? If not, how would you describe this change?
21. How is earnings per share calculated for a corporation with a simple capital structure?
22. In calculating the weighted-average number of common shares outstanding, how are stock splits and stock dividends treated?
23. Why are not all convertible securities considered to be common stock equivalents?
24. What is the difference between primary earnings per share and fully diluted earnings per share?
25. What is the difference between simple capital structures and complex capital structures?
26. Refer to the financial statements for Lands' End, Inc., presented in Appendix K. How many shares of treasury stock did Lands' End hold on January 31, 1991? When were these shares purchased?
27. Review the Consolidated Statements of Income for Federal Express Corporation presented in Appendix K and compare them with the income statement shown in Illustration 15–4. Which of the income statement sections shown in Illustration 15–4 are used in Federal Express Corporation's income statements? What dollar amounts are reported for sections other than "income from continuing operations?"

Exercises

Exercise 15–1
Stock dividends
(LO 1)

Ritchfield Corporation's stockholders' equity appeared as follows on August 10:

Common stock, $5 par value, 260,000 shares authorized, 80,000 shares issued	$400,000
Contributed capital in excess of par value, common stock	160,200
Total contributed capital	$560,200
Retained earnings	235,000
Total stockholders' equity	$795,200

On August 10, when the stock was selling at $9.00 per share, the corporation's directors voted a 10% stock dividend distributable on September 2 to the August 17 stockholders of record. The stock was selling at $9.50 per share at the close of business on September 5.

Required

1. Prepare general journal entries to record the declaration and distribution of the dividend.
2. Under the assumption that Cynthia McAllister owned 250 of the shares on August 10 and received her dividend shares on September 2, prepare a schedule showing the number of shares she held on August 10 and on September 5, with their total book values and total market values. Assume no change in total stockholders' equity from August 10 to September 5.

Exercise 15–2
Stock dividends and stock splits
(LO 1)

On March 31, 1993, Pacific Management Corporation's common stock was selling for $45 per share and the stockholders' equity section of the corporation's balance sheet appeared as follows:

Common stock, $30 par value, 150,000 shares authorized, 15,000 shares issued	$450,000
Contributed capital in excess of par value, common stock	220,450
Total contributed capital	$670,450
Retained earnings	298,900
Total stockholders' equity	$969,350

Required

1. Assume the corporation declares and immediately issues a 50% stock dividend and capitalizes the minimum required amount of retained earnings. Answer the following questions about the stockholders' equity of the corporation after the new shares are issued:
   a. What is the retained earnings balance?
   b. What is the total amount of stockholders' equity?
   c. How many shares are outstanding?
2. Assume that instead of declaring a 50% stock dividend, the corporation changes the par value of the stock to $20 and immediately effects a 3 for 2 stock split. Answer the following questions about the stockholders' equity of the corporation after the stock split takes place:

a. What is the retained earnings balance?
b. What is the total amount of stockholders' equity?
c. How many shares are outstanding?

Exercise 15–3
Treasury stock purchases
(LO 2, 3)

On October 31, Reynold Corporation's stockholders' equity section appeared as follows:

Stockholders' Equity

Common stock, $25 par value, 10,000 shares authorized and issued	$250,000
Retained earnings	220,100
Total stockholders' equity	$470,100

On October 31, the corporation purchased 900 shares of treasury stock at $50 per share. Give the entry to record the purchase and prepare a stockholders' equity section as it would appear immediately after the purchase.

Exercise 15–4
Sales of treasury stock
(LO 2)

On November 17, Reynold Corporation of Exercise 15–3 sold at $55 per share 300 of the treasury shares purchased on October 31; and on December 9, it sold the remaining treasury shares at $40 per share. Prepare general journal entries to record the sales.

Exercise 15–5
Retirement of stock
(LO 2)

The stockholders' equity section of Capital Vending, Inc.'s December 31, 1993, balance sheet is as follows:

Common stock, $10 par value, 600,000 shares authorized, 30,000 shares issued	$300,000
Contributed capital in excess of par value, common stock	240,000
Total contributed capital	$540,000
Retained earnings	105,800
Total stockholders' equity	$645,800

On January 1, 1994, the company purchased and retired 400 shares of its common stock. Prepare general journal entries to record the purchase and retirement under each of the following independent assumptions: (*a*) the stock was purchased for $15 per share, (*b*) the stock was purchased for $18 per share, and (*c*) the stock was purchased for $25 per share.

Exercise 15–6
Income statement categories
(LO 4)

The following list of items was extracted from the December 31, 1993, trial balance of Wesson Company. Using the information contained in this listing, prepare Wesson Company's income statement for 1993. You need not complete the earnings per share calculations.

	Debit	Credit
Salaries expense	$ 56,700	
Income tax expense (continuing operations)	48,380	
Loss from operating segment C (net of $10,200 tax benefit)	24,000	
Sales		$650,240
Cumulative effect on prior years' income of change from declining-balance to straight-line depreciation (net of $9,600 tax)		22,400

	Debit	Credit
Extraordinary gain on state's condemnation of land owned by Wesson Company (net of $24,800 tax)		58,000
Depreciation expense	42,100	
Gain on sale of segment C (net of $19,700 tax)		46,000
Cost of goods sold	390,200	

Exercise 15–7
Change in accounting principles
(LO 4)

Freemont Company has one depreciable asset that cost $270,000 and has decided to switch from sum-of-the-years'-digits depreciation to straight-line depreciation. In prior years, the company depreciated the asset for two years based on sum-of-the-years'-digits depreciation, no salvage value, and a five-year life. The company is subject to a 30% income tax rate. Calculate the amount of depreciation expense to be reported in the current year and the cumulative effect of the change on prior years' incomes. Indicate whether the cumulative effect of the change on prior years' incomes should be added or subtracted when calculating the current year's net income.

Exercise 15–8
Classifying income items not related to continuing operations
(LO 4)

In preparing the annual financial statements for Metro Electronics Company, the correct manner of reporting the following items was not clear to the company's employees. Explain where each of the following items should appear in the financial statements.

a. After depreciating office equipment for three years based on an expected useful life of eight years, the company decided this year that the office equipment should last seven more years. As a result, the depreciation for the current year is $10,000 instead of $12,500.

b. This year, the accounting department of the company discovered that last year, an installment payment on their five-year note payable had been charged entirely to interest expense. The after-tax effect of the charge to interest expense was $13,400.

c. The company keeps its repair trucks for several years before disposing of the old trucks and buying new trucks. This year, for the first time in 10 years, it sold old trucks for a gain of $18,900 and then purchased new trucks.

Exercise 15–9
Weighted-average shares outstanding and earnings per share
(LO 5)

Comfort Footware, Inc. reported $264,650 net income in 1993 and declared preferred dividends of $43,000. The following changes in common shares outstanding occurred during the year:

January 1:	60,000 common shares were outstanding.
June 1:	Sold 30,000 common shares for par.
September 1:	Declared and issued a 10% common stock dividend, or (90,000 × 10%) = 9,000 additional shares.

Calculate the weighted-average number of common shares outstanding during the year and earnings per share.

Exercise 15–10
Weighted-average shares outstanding and earnings per share
(LO 5)

Cromwell Production Company reported $736,500 net income in 1993 and declared preferred dividends of $66,500. The following changes in common shares outstanding occurred during the year.

January 1:	120,000 common shares were outstanding.
March 1:	Sold 20,000 common shares for par plus a $25 premium.
September 1:	Purchased 8,000 shares to be held as treasury stock.
December 1:	Declared and issued a 2 for 1 stock split.

Calculate the weighted-average number of common shares outstanding during the year and earnings per share.

Exercise 15–11
Reporting earnings per share
(LO 5)

Southside Corporation's 1993 income statement, excluding the earnings per share portion of the statement, was as follows:

Sales		$475,000
Costs and expenses:		
Depreciation	$ 51,900	
Income taxes	65,100	
Other expenses	205,000	322,000
Income from continuing operations		$153,000
Loss from operating discontinued business segment (net of $23,500 tax benefit)	$ 56,000	
Loss on sale of business segment (net of $9,400 tax benefit)	22,000	(78,000)
Income before extraordinary items and change in accounting principle		$ 75,000
Extraordinary gain (net of $18,400 taxes)	$ 43,200	
Cumulative effect of a change in accounting principle (net of $15,600 taxes)	36,000	79,200
Net income		$154,200

Throughout 1993, Southside had common stock equivalents and other potentially dilutive securities outstanding. If these particular securities had been converted, the number of common shares outstanding would have increased but the numerators in earnings per share calculations would not have been affected. Assuming the dilutive, common stock equivalents had been converted at the beginning of the year, the weighted-average number of common shares outstanding during the year would have been 60,000. Assuming all dilutive securities had been converted at the beginning of the year, the weighted-average number of common shares outstanding during the year would have been 84,000. Present the earnings per share portion of the 1993 income statement.

Problems

Problem 15–1
Treasury stock transactions and stock dividends
(LO 1, 2, 3)

Southwest Publications, Inc.'s stockholders' equity on December 31, 1992, consisted of the following:

Common stock, $5 par value, 225,000 shares authorized, 105,000 shares issued	$525,000
Contributed capital in excess of par value, common stock	78,750
Retained earnings	234,650
Total stockholders' equity	$838,400

During 1993, the company completed these transactions:

Mar.	6	Purchased 22,000 shares of treasury stock at $5.75 per share.
Apr.	17	The directors voted a $0.40 per share cash dividend payable on May 15 to the May 5 stockholders of record.
May	15	Paid the dividend declared on April 17.
Aug.	12	Sold 8,500 of the treasury shares at $6.00 per share.
Oct.	28	Sold 13,500 of the treasury shares at $5.00 per share.
Dec.	5	The directors voted a $0.30 per share cash dividend payable on January 3 to the December 26 stockholders of record, and they voted a 10% stock dividend distributable on January 26 to the December 26 stockholders of record. The market value of the stock was $5.90 per share.
	31	Closed the Income Summary account and credited the company's $100,250 net income to Retained Earnings.
	31	Closed the Cash Dividends Declared and Stock Dividends Declared accounts.

Required

1. Prepare general journal entries to record the transactions and closings for 1993.
2. Prepare a retained earnings statement for the year and the stockholders' equity section of the company's year-end balance sheet.

Problem 15–2
Cash dividend, stock dividend, and stock split
(LO 1)

Last April 30, Convenience Foods Corporation had an $862,500 credit balance in its Retained Earnings account. On that date, the corporation's contributed capital consisted of 750,000 authorized shares of $2 par common stock, of which 345,000 shares had been issued at $3 and were outstanding. It then completed the following transactions:

May	10	The board of directors declared a $1.50 per share cash dividend on the common stock, payable on June 16 to the May 31 stockholders of record.
June	16	Paid the dividend declared on May 10.
Aug.	5	The board declared a 1% stock dividend, distributable on September 2 to the August 20 stockholders of record. The stock was selling at $4.00 per share.
Sept.	2	Distributed the stock dividend declared on August 5.
	30	Because September 30 is the end of the company's fiscal year, closed the Income Summary account, which had a credit balance of $397,095. Also closed the Cash Dividends Declared and Stock Dividends Declared accounts.
Oct.	12	The board of directors voted to split the corporation's stock 2 for 1 by calling in the old stock and issuing two $1 par value shares for each $2 share held. The stockholders voted approval of the split and authorization of 1.6 million new $1 par value shares to replace the $2 shares. All legal requirements were met and the split was completed on November 17.

Required:

1. Prepare general journal entries to record these transactions and closings.
2. Under the assumption Phillip Bolton owned 5,000 of the $2 par value shares on April 30 and neither bought nor sold any shares during the period of the transactions, prepare a schedule with columns for the date, supporting calculations, book value per share, and book value of Bolton's shares. Then complete the schedule by calculating the book value per share of the corporation's stock and the book value of Bolton's shares at the close of business on April 30, May 10, June 16, September 2, September 30, and October 12. Assume that the only income earned by the company during these periods was the $397,095 earned and closed on September 30.
3. Prepare three stockholders' equity sections for the corporation, the first showing the stockholders' equity on April 30, the second on September 30, and the third on October 12.

Problem 15–3
Calculating net income from balance sheet comparison
(LO 1, 2, 3)

The equity sections from the 1992 and 1993 balance sheets of Fairfax Corporation appeared as follows:

Stockholders' Equity
(As of December 31, 1992)

Common stock, $5 par value, 450,000 shares authorized, 120,000 shares issued	$ 600,000
Contributed capital in excess of par value, common stock	260,000
Total contributed capital	$ 860,000
Retained earnings	698,260
Total stockholders' equity	$1,558,260

Stockholders' Equity
(As of December 31, 1993)

Common stock, $5 par value, 450,000 shares authorized, 145,000 shares issued of which 20,000 are in the treasury	$ 725,000
Contributed capital in excess of par value, common stock	372,500
Total contributed capital	$1,097,500
Retained earnings, of which $188,000 is restricted	574,500
Total	$1,672,000
Less cost of treasury stock	188,000
Total stockholders' equity	$1,484,000

On March 16, June 25, September 5, and again on November 22, 1993, the board of directors declared $0.80 per share cash dividends on the outstanding stock. The treasury stock was purchased on May 14. On October 5, while the stock was selling for $9.50 per share, the corporation declared a 25% stock dividend on the outstanding shares. The new shares were issued on November 8.

Required

Under the assumption that there were no transactions affecting retained earnings other than the ones given, determine the 1993 net income of Fairfax Corporation. Show your calculations.

Problem 15–4
Classifying income items in a published income statement
(LO 4)

Central Supply Company had several unusual transactions during 1993 and has prepared the following list of trial balance items. Select the appropriate items to use in constructing the 1993 income statement for the company.

	Debit	Credit
Accounts payable		$ 16,600
Loss from operation of Westside Division, a business segment to be discontinued (net of $14,000 income tax benefit)	$ 42,000	
Sales		398,500
Cost of goods sold	175,600	
Loss on sale of office equipment (an unusual transaction for the company that occurs only when administrative offices are redecorated, which happens about every eight years)	6,300	
Depreciation expense, buildings	35,620	
Depreciation expense, office equipment	12,450	
Income tax expense	20,950	
Payment received in November 1992 on customer account receivable incorrectly recorded in Sales account (net of $4,050 income tax benefit)	16,200	
Gain on sale of investment in land (The land was originally donated to Central Supply by a stockholder. Central Supply has never held land for investment purposes before and has no intention of doing so in the future.) (Net of $7,800 income taxes)		23,400
Loss on customer breach of contract suit. (This type of lawsuit is not unusual for companies in this industry. However, the lawsuit appears to have settled the matter in this case and the problem is not expected to arise in the foreseeable future.)	45,700	
Accumulated depreciation, buildings		108,000
Accumulated depreciation, office equipment		20,900
Gain on sale of Westside Division (net of $3,400 income taxes)		12,750
Interest earned		2,400
Other operating expenses	53,800	
Gain on payment from supplier to compensate for late delivery of materials purchased from supplier. (In this industry, such settlements with suppliers occur quite frequently.)		12,300
Effect on prior years' income of switching from straight-line depreciation to accelerated depreciation (net of $5,900 income tax benefit)	22,125	

Required

Prepare Central Supply Company's income statement for 1993, excluding the earnings per share statistics.

Problem 15–5
Changes in accounting principles
(LO 4)

On January 1, 1989, Fieldway Industries, Inc. purchased a large piece of equipment for use in its manufacturing operations. The equipment cost $350,000 and was expected to have a salvage value of $40,000. Depreciation was taken through 1992 on a declining-balance method at twice the straight-line rate assuming an eight-year life. Early in 1993, the company concluded that given the economic conditions in the industry, a straight-line method would result in more meaningful financial statements. They argue that straight-line depreciation would allow better comparisons with the financial results of other firms in the industry.

Required

1. Is Fieldway Industries allowed to change depreciation methods in 1993?
2. Prepare a table that shows the depreciation expense to be reported each year of the asset's life under both depreciation methods and the cumulative effect of the change on prior years' incomes. Assume an income tax rate of 25%, and round your answers to the nearest whole dollar.
3. State the amount of depreciation expense to be reported in 1993 and the cumulative effect of the change on prior years' incomes. How should the cumulative effect be reported? Does the cumulative effect increase or decrease net income?
4. Now assume that Fieldway Industries had used straight-line depreciation through 1992 and justified a change to declining-balance depreciation at twice the straight-line rate in 1993. What amount of depreciation expense should be reported in 1993? How does the reporting of the cumulative effect of the change differ from your answer to Requirement 3?

Problem 15–6
Earnings per share calculations and presentation
(LO 5)

Except for the earnings per share statistics, the 1993, 1992, and 1991 income statements of Custom Printing Company were originally presented as follows:

	1993	1992	1991
Sales	$998,900	$687,040	$466,855
Costs and expenses	383,570	234,500	157,420
Income from continuing operations	$615,330	$452,540	$309,435
Loss on discontinued operations	(107,325)	—	—
Income (loss) before extraordinary items and changes in accounting principles	$508,005	$452,540	$309,435
Extraordinary gains (losses)	—	80,410	(156,191)
Cumulative effect of change in accounting principle	(64,395)	—	—
Net income (loss)	$443,610	$532,950	$153,244

Information on common stock:

Shares outstanding on December 31, 1990	12,000
Purchase of treasury shares on March 1, 1991	− 1,200
Sale of shares on June 1, 1991	+ 5,200
Stock dividend of 5% on August 1, 1991	+ 800
Shares outstanding on December 31, 1991	16,800
Sale of shares on February 1, 1992	+ 2,400
Purchase of treasury shares July 1, 1992	− 600
Shares outstanding on December 31, 1992	18,600
Sale of shares on March 1, 1993	+ 6,900
Purchase of treasury shares on September 1, 1993	− 1,500
Stock split of 3 for 1 on October 1, 1993	+48,000
Shares outstanding on December 31, 1993	72,000

Required

1. Calculate the weighted-average number of common shares outstanding during (*a*) 1991, (*b*) 1992, and (*c*) 1993.
2. Present the earnings per share portions of (*a*) the 1991 income statement, (*b*) the 1992 income statement, and (*c*) the 1993 income statement.

Problem 15–7
Analytical essay
(LO 1)

The stockholders' equity section of Wernli Corporation's balance sheet at April 30 is as follows:

Common stock, $15 par value, 50,000 shares authorized, 20,000 shares issued and outstanding . .	$300,000
Contributed capital in excess of par value, common stock	60,000
Retained earnings	148,000
Total stockholders' equity	$508,000

Wernli is considering increasing the number of outstanding shares of common stock from 20,000 to 30,000 by one of the following alternative methods: (*a*) a 3 for 2 stock split or (*b*) declaring and issuing a 50% stock dividend.

Required

1. Describe the difference in how the declaration and issuance of the stock under the two alternative methods would be recorded in the accounting records of Wernli. Also explain why the Common Stock account must be increased if one alternative is used but is not increased if the other alternative is used.
2. Describe the effects on Wernli's balance sheet of using one alternative versus the other.

Problem 15–8
Analytical essay
(LO 5)

Compusub Corporation has tentatively prepared its financial statements for the year ended December 31, 1993, and has submitted them to you for review. The stockholders' equity section of Compusub's balance sheet at December 31 is as follows:

Preferred stock, $25 par value, 10% cumulative and nonparticipating, 30,000 shares authorized, 15,000 shares issued and outstanding	$ 375,000
Contributed capital in excess of par value, preferred stock	145,100
Common stock, $5 par value, 200,000 shares authorized, 110,000 shares issued and outstanding . .	550,000
Contributed capital in excess of par value, common stock	227,840
Retained earnings	996,200
Total stockholders' equity	$2,294,140

Compusub Corporation's 1993 net income was $600,000 and no cash dividends were declared. The only stock transaction that occurred during the year was the sale of 20,000 shares of common stock on March 31, 1993. Earnings per share for 1993 was calculated as follows:

$$\frac{\text{Net income}}{\text{Common plus preferred stock outstanding as of Dec. 31}} = \frac{\$600{,}000}{110{,}000 + 15{,}000} = \$4.80$$

Required

1. Explain what is wrong with the earnings per share calculation, indicating what corrections should be made to both the numerator and the denominator.
2. Explain how your answer to requirement 1 would be different if the preferred stock was not cumulative and if the issuance of 20,000 shares had been a stock dividend.

Alternate Problems

Problem 15–1A
Treasury stock transactions and stock dividends
(LO 1, 2, 3)

Fairlane Corporation's stockholders' equity on December 31, 1992, consisted of the following:

Common stock, $10 par value, 625,000 shares authorized, 370,000 shares issued	$3,700,000
Contributed capital in excess of par value, common stock	1,942,500
Retained earnings	627,200
Total stockholders' equity	$6,269,700

During 1993, the company completed these transactions:

Feb. 12 Purchased 15,000 shares of treasury stock at $27 per share.

18 The directors voted a $0.10 per share cash dividend payable on March 15 to the March 2 stockholders of record.

Mar. 15 Paid the dividend declared on February 18.

June 4 Sold 6,200 of the treasury shares at $34 per share.

Sept. 1 Sold 8,800 of the treasury shares at $22 per share.

Dec. 12 The directors voted a $0.20 per share cash dividend payable on January 19 to the January 2 stockholders of record, and they voted a 1% stock dividend distributable on February 4 to the January 22 stockholders of record. The market value of the stock was $25 per share.

31 Closed the Income Summary account and credited the company's $247,300 net income to Retained Earnings.

31 Closed the Cash Dividends Declared and Stock Dividends Declared accounts.

Required

1. Prepare general journal entries to record the transactions and closings for 1993.
2. Prepare a retained earnings statement for the year and the stockholders' equity section of the company's year-end balance sheet.

Problem 15–2A
Cash dividend, stock dividend, and stock split
(LO 1)

Last January 31, Richmond Corporation had a $3.5 million credit balance in its Retained Earnings account. On that date, the corporation's contributed capital consisted of 100,000 authorized shares of $60 par value common stock of which 50,000 shares had been issued at $75 and were outstanding. It then completed the following transactions:

Feb. 13 The board of directors declared a $10 per share cash dividend on the common stock, payable on March 14 to the March 1 stockholders of record.

Mar. 14 Paid the dividend declared on February 13.

May 22 The board declared a 25% stock dividend, distributable on June 18 to the June 4 stockholders of record. The stock was selling at $90 per share.

June 18 Distributed the stock dividend declared on May 22.

June 30 Because June 30 is the end of the accounting year, closed the Income Summary account, which had a credit balance of $1.5 million. Also closed the Cash Dividends Declared and Stock Dividends Declared accounts.

July 5 The board of directors voted to split the corporation's stock 3 for 1 by calling in the old stock and issuing three $20 par value shares for each $60 share held. The stockholders voted approval of the split and authorization of 200,000 new $20 par value shares to replace the $60 shares. All legal requirements were met and the split was completed on July 28.

Required

1. Prepare general journal entries to record these transactions and to close the Income Summary account at year-end.
2. Under the assumption Denise Shay owned 2,500 of the $60 par value shares on January 31 and neither bought nor sold any shares during the period of the transactions, prepare a schedule with columns for the date, supporting calculations, book value per share, and book value of Shay's shares. Then complete the schedule by calculating the book value per share of the corporation's stock and the book value of Shay's shares at the close of business on January 31, February 13, March 14, June 18, June 30, and July 28. Assume that the only income earned by the company during these periods was the $1.5 million which was earned and closed on June 30.
3. Prepare three stockholders' equity sections for the corporation, the first showing the stockholders' equity on January 31, the second on June 30, and the third on July 28.

Problem 15–3A
Calculating net income from balance sheet comparison
(LO 1, 2, 3)

The equity sections from the 1992 and 1993 balance sheets of Henneke Corporation appeared as follows:

Stockholders' Equity
(As of December 31, 1992)

Common stock, no-par, $20 stated value, 750,000 shares authorized, 350,000 shares issued	$ 7,000,000
Contributed capital in excess of stated value	1,760,000
Total contributed capital	$ 8,760,000
Retained earnings	1,950,720
Total stockholders' equity	$10,710,720

Stockholders' Equity
(As of December 31, 1993)

Common stock, no-par, $20 stated value, 750,000 shares authorized, 384,000 shares issued of which 10,000 are in the treasury	$ 7,680,000
Contributed capital in excess of stated value	1,964,000
Total contributed capital	$ 9,644,000
Retained earnings, of which $270,000 is restricted	1,260,640
Total	$10,904,640
Less cost of treasury stock	270,000
Total stockholders' equity	$10,634,640

On February 11, May 24, August 13, and again on December 12, 1993, the board of directors declared $0.25 per share cash dividends on the outstanding stock. The treasury stock was purchased on July 6. On November 1, while the stock was selling for $26.00 per share, the corporation declared a 10% stock dividend on the outstanding shares. The new shares were issued on December 5.

Required

Under the assumption that there were no transactions affecting retained earnings other than the ones given, determine the 1993 net income of Henneke Corporation. Show your calculations.

Problem 15–4A
Classifying income items in a published income statement
(LO 4)

Systems Communications Corporation had several unusual transactions during 1993 and has prepared the following list of trial balance items. Select the appropriate items to use in constructing the 1993 income statement for the company.

	Debit	Credit
Cost of goods sold	$245,800	
Effect on prior years' income of switching from accelerated depreciation to straight-line depreciation, (net of $24,500 income taxes)		$ 57,100
Gain on settlement with supplier to compensate for loss of major contract due to nondelivery of phone system from supplier. (In this industry, attempts to obtain such settlements with suppliers are not unusual but occur very infrequently.)		125,900
Accumulated depreciation, buildings		102,030
Income tax expense	151,290	
Income from operating Products Division, a business segment to be discontinued (net of $25,600 income taxes)		64,000
Three-year insurance policy paid in advance in January 1992 and recorded as prepaid insurance. No adjusting entry was made for expired portion in 1992. (net of $3,750 income tax benefit)	8,750	
Long-term note payable		86,500
Gain on sale of telegraph displayed in main entrance (an unusual transaction for the company that occurs about once every three years when a new display is obtained)		4,700
Depreciation expense	17,900	
Gain on sale of investment in stock (Systems Communications regularly maintains a large portfolio of stock investments as part of its business activities, expecting to enhance the earnings of the company through purchases and sales of such securities.)		46,500
Other operating expenses	235,680	
Gain on sale of Products Division (net of $45,800 income taxes)		106,900
Interest earned		36,200
Loss due to commercial plane crashing into warehouse (net of $16,200 income tax benefit)	37,800	
Sales		790,400

Required

Prepare Systems Communications Corporation's income statement for 1993, excluding the earnings per share statistics.

Problem 15–5A
Changes in accounting principles
(LO 4)

On January 1, 1989, the Blackwood Company purchased a major piece of equipment for use in its operations. The equipment cost $945,000 and was expected to have a salvage value of $105,000. Depreciation was taken through 1992 using the straight-line method assuming a seven-year life. Early in 1993, the company concluded that, given the economic conditions in the industry, a sum-of-the-years'-digits method would result in more meaningful financial statements. They argue that sum-of-the-years'-digits depreciation would allow better comparisons with the financial results of other firms in the industry.

Required

1. Is Blackwood Company allowed to change depreciation methods in 1993?
2. Prepare a table that shows the depreciation expense to be reported each year of the asset's life under both depreciation methods and the cumulative effect of the change on prior years' incomes. Assume an income tax rate of 30%, and round your answers to the nearest whole dollar.
3. State the amount of depreciation expense to be reported in 1993 and the cumulative effect of the change on prior years' incomes. How should the cumulative effect be reported? Does the cumulative effect increase or decrease net income?
4. Now assume that Blackwood Company had used sum-of-the-years'-digits depreciation through 1992 and justified a change to straight-line depreciation in 1993. What amount of depreciation expense should be reported in 1993? How does the reporting of the cumulative effect of the change differ from your answer to Requirement 3?

Problem 15–6A
Earnings per share calculations and presentation
(LO 5)

Except for the earnings per share statistics, the 1993, 1992, and 1991 income statements of Greggor Corporation were originally presented as follows:

	1993	1992	1991
Sales	$661,843	$696,250	$455,600
Costs and expenses	237,760	245,800	168,725
Income from continuing operations	$424,083	$450,450	$286,875
Loss on discontinued operations	(42,408)	(18,018)	—
Income (loss) before extraordinary items and changes in accounting principles	$381,675	$432,432	$286,875
Extraordinary gains (losses)	—	102,102	(33,750)
Cumulative effect of change in accounting principle	—	(72,072)	—
Net income (loss)	$381,675	$462,462	$253,125

Information on common stock:	
Shares outstanding on December 31, 1990	60,600
Sale of shares on March 1, 1991	+10,800
Purchase of treasury shares on July 1, 1991	− 4,200
Shares outstanding on December 31, 1991	67,200
Sale of shares on May 1, 1992	+18,000
Sale of shares on September 1, 1992	+ 2,640
Stock split of 3 for 2 on October 1, 1992	+43,920
Shares outstanding on December 31, 1992	131,760
Purchase of treasury shares on June 1, 1993	−15,000
Sale of shares on July 1, 1993	+11,000
Stock dividend of 10% on October 1, 1993	+12,776
Shares outstanding on December 31, 1993	140,536

Required

1. Calculate the weighted-average number of common shares outstanding during (*a*) 1991, (*b*) 1992, and (*c*) 1993.
2. Present the earnings per share portions of: (*a*) the 1991 income statement, (*b*) the 1992 income statement, and (*c*) the 1993 income statement.

Problem 15–7A
Analytical essay
(LO 1, 2)

The stockholders' equity section of Langhoffer Corporation's balance sheet at September 30 is as follows:

Common stock, $10 par value, 100,000 shares authorized, 50,000 shares issued and outstanding	$ 500,000
Contributed capital in excess of par value, common stock	150,000
Retained earnings	367,000
Total stockholders' equity	$1,017,000

Assume now that an event occurs on October 1 that impacts Langhoffer's stockholders' equity section, but does not involve net income nor additional investment of capital. The following are independent cases in which Langhoffer's stockholders' equity section has been revised to reflect that event.

	Case A	Case B	Case C
Common stock, 100,000 shares authorized:			
$10 par value, 50,000 shares issued and outstanding	$500,000		
$10 par value, 65,000 shares issued and outstanding		$ 650,000	
$20 par value, 25,000 shares issued and outstanding			$ 500,000
Contributed capital in excess of par value, common stock	150,000	150,000	150,000
Retained earnings	317,000	217,000	367,000
Total stockholders' equity	$967,000	$1,017,000	$1,017,000

Required

For each case, describe the differences in the September 30 and the October 1 stockholders' equity sections and state the event that must have occurred.

Problem 15–8A
Analytical essay
(LO 5)

Jaspin Company's financial statements for the year ended December 31, 1993, have been completed and submitted to you for review. The stockholders' equity section of Jaspin's balance sheet at December 31 is as follows:

Preferred stock, $40 par value, 7% noncumulative and nonparticipating, 10,000 shares authorized, 10,000 shares issued and outstanding	$ 400,000
Contributed capital in excess of par value, preferred stock	98,700
Common stock, $10 par value, 80,000 shares authorized, 60,000 shares issued of which 10,000 are in the treasury	600,000
Contributed capital in excess of par value, common stock	346,900
Retained earnings	450,530
Total	$1,896,130
Less cost of treasury stock	192,000
Total stockholders' equity	$1,704,130

The only stock transactions during 1993 were the purchase of 12,000 common shares as treasury stock on July 1 and the sale of 6,000 shares of treasury stock on October 31. Jaspin's 1993 net income was $240,000. A cash dividend on the preferred stock was declared on December 1, but was not paid as of December 31. Earnings per share for 1993 was calculated as follows:

$$\frac{\text{Net income}}{\text{Common stock outstanding on Dec. 31}} = \frac{\$240{,}000}{600{,}000} = \$4.00$$

Required

1. Explain what is wrong with the earnings per share calculation, indicating what corrections should be made to both the numerator and the denominator.
2. Explain how your answer to requirement 1 would be different if there had not been a cash dividend declaration to preferred stock and if the purchase of 12,000 treasury shares had taken place on January 1, 1993.

Provocative Problems

Provocative Problem 15–1
Valtech Corporation
(LO 1, 2, 3)

On January 1, 1991, Karen Martin purchased 500 shares of Valtech Corporation stock at $17.00 per share. On that date, the corporation had the following stockholders' equity:

Common stock, $10 par value, 400,000 shares authorized, 100,000 shares issued and outstanding	$1,000,000
Contributed capital in excess of par value, common stock	600,000
Retained earnings	1,200,000
Total stockholders' equity	$2,800,000

Since purchasing the 500 shares, Martin has neither purchased nor sold any additional shares of the company's stock. On December 31 of each year, she has received dividends on the shares held as follows: 1991, $1,320; 1992, $1,440; and 1993, $2,280.

On March 1, 1991, at a time when its stock was selling for $17.50 per share, Valtech Corporation declared a 20% stock dividend that was distributed one month later. On August 10, 1992, the corporation doubled the number of its authorized shares and split its stock 4 for 1. On April 5, 1993, it purchased 6,000 shares of treasury stock at $14.50 per share. The shares were still in its treasury at year-end.

Assume that Valtech Corporation's outstanding stock had a book value of $38.50 per share on December 31, 1991, a book value of $10.50 per share on December 31, 1992, and a book value of $11.75 on December 31, 1993.

Required

1. Prepare statements that show the components and amounts of the stockholders' equity in the corporation at the end of 1991, 1992, and 1993.
2. Prepare a schedule that shows the amount of the corporation's net income each year for 1991, 1992, and 1993. Assume that the changes in the company's retained earnings during the three-year period resulted from earnings and dividends.

Provocative Problem 15–2
Burtland Publishing Company
(LO 1)

Burtland Publishing Company's stockholders' equity on March 31 consisted of the following amounts:

Common stock, $30 par value, 350,000 shares authorized, 120,000 shares issued and outstanding	$3,600,000
Contributed capital in excess of par value, common stock	780,000
Retained earnings	4,700,400
Total stockholders' equity	$9,080,400

On March 31, when the stock was selling at $40 per share, the corporation's directors voted a 10% stock dividend, distributable on April 30 to the April 7 stockholders of record. The directors also voted an $8.90 per share annual cash dividend, payable on May 22 to the May 1 stockholders of record. The amount of the latter dividend was a disappointment to some stockholders, since the company had paid a $9.19 per share annual cash dividend for a number of years.

Ann Guerci owned 1,200 shares of Burtland Publishing Company stock on April 7, received her stock dividend shares, and continued to hold all of her shares until after the May 22 cash dividend. She also observed that her stock had a $40 per share market value on March 31, a market value it held until the close of business on April 7, when the market value declined to $38.50 per share. Give Burtland's entries to record the declaration and distribution or payment of the dividends involved here and answer these questions:

a. What was the book value of Guerci's total shares on March 31 (after taking into consideration the cash dividend declared on that day)? What was the book value on April 30, after she received the dividend shares?

b. What fraction of the corporation did Guerci own on March 31? What fraction did she own on April 30?

c. What was the market value of Guerci's total shares on March 31? What was the market value at the close of business on April 7?

d. What did Guerci gain from the stock dividend?

Provocative Problem 15–3
Quality Products, Inc.
(LO 4)

Quality Products, Inc. had the following rather special transactions and events in 1993:

a. Quality Products has distribution outlets in several foreign countries, one of which has been subject to political unrest. After a sudden change in governments, the new ruling body resolved that the amount of foreign investment in the country was excessive. As a result, Quality Products was forced to transfer ownership in its facility in that country to the new government. Quality Products was able to continue operations in a neighboring country and was allowed to transfer much of its inventory and equipment to the neighboring country. Nevertheless, the price paid to Quality Products for its facility resulted in a significant loss.

b. Quality Products, Inc.'s continuing operations involve a high technology production process. Technical developments in this area occur regularly and the production machinery becomes obsolete surprisingly often. Because such developments occurred recently, Quality Products decided that it was forced to sell certain items of machinery at a loss and replace those items with a different type of machinery. The problem is how to report the loss.

c. Three years earlier, Quality Products, Inc., purchased some highly specialized equipment that was to be used in the operations of a new division that Quality Products intended to acquire. The new division was in a separate line of business and would have been a separate segment of the business. After lengthy negotiations, the acquisition of the division was not accomplished and the company abandoned any hope of entering that line of business. Although the equipment had never been used, it was sold in 1993 at a loss. Quality Products, Inc., does not have a history of expanding into new lines of business and has no plans of doing so in the future.

d. Early in 1992, Quality Products purchased a new type of equipment for use in its production process. Although much of the production equipment is depreciated over four years, a careful analysis of the situation led the company to decide that the new equipment should be depreciated over eight years. Nevertheless, in the rush of year-end activities, the new equipment was included with the older equipment and depreciated on a four-year basis. In preparing adjustments at the end of 1993, the accountant discovered that $135,000 depreciation was taken on the new equipment in 1992, when only $67,500 should have been taken. The company is subject to a 25% income tax rate.

Required

Examine Quality Products, Inc.'s special transactions and events and describe how each one should be reported on the income statement or statement of retained earnings. Also state the item's specific characteristics that support your decision.

Provocative Problem 15–4
International Business Machines Corporation
(LO 1, 2, 3, 4, 5)

The financial statements and related disclosures from IBM's 1990 annual report are presented in Appendix J. Based on your examination of this information, answer the following:

1. Does IBM have a simple capital structure or a complex capital structure?
2. What was IBM's earnings per share in the second quarter of the 1990 year?
3. What was the total dollar amount of cash dividends declared by IBM during 1990?
4. What was the total dollar amount of cash dividends paid during 1990?
5. What was the total amount of cash dividends per share declared in 1990?
6. What was the total earnings per share for 1990?
7. How many shares of treasury stock did IBM sell during 1990?
8. What was the net cost of treasury stock purchased less the cost of treasury stock sold during 1990?
9. Did IBM have any extraordinary gains or losses during 1990?

10. Did IBM have any gains or losses on the disposal of a business segment during 1990?
11. According to IBM's Employees Stock Purchase Plan, what price does an employee have to pay for a share of IBM stock?

Provocative Problem 15-5
As a Matter of Ethics: Essay

Ethics

Review the As a Matter of Ethics case on page 814. Discuss the ethical implications of the tentative decision to avoid announcing Falcon Corporation's new government contract. What actions would you take if you were the financial vice president?

Answers to Objective Review Questions

LO 1 (*e*)	LO 3 (*c*)	LO 5 (*b*)
LO 2 (*d*)	LO 4 (*a*)	LO 6 (*a*)

CHAPTER

16

Installment Notes Payable and Bonds

Companies and other organizations, including governments, frequently need to borrow money for large, long-term projects, such as building a stadium. Special accounting techniques are used to measure interest expense and the amount of the liabilities.

Topical Coverage

In Chapter 12, you learned to account for notes payable that require a single payment on the date the note matures. In those cases, the single payment includes the entire amount borrowed plus interest. However, many notes require a series of payments that consist of interest plus a part of the amount borrowed. We begin this chapter with a discussion of these installment notes. Then, we turn to a discussion of bonds, which are liabilities issued by corporations as well as a variety of governmental bodies. The chapter concludes with a brief discussion of bond investments.

Learning Objectives

After studying Chapter 16, you should be able to:

1. Calculate and record the payments on an installment note payable.
2. Describe the various characteristics of different types of bond issues and prepare entries to record bonds that are issued between interest dates.
3. Calculate the price of a bond issue that sells at a discount and prepare entries to account for bonds issued at a discount.
4. Prepare entries to account for bonds issued at a premium.
5. Explain the purpose and operation of a bond sinking fund and prepare entries for sinking fund activities, for the retirement of bonds, and for the conversion of bonds into stock.
6. Describe the procedures used to account for investments in bonds.
7. Define or explain the words and phrases listed in the chapter glossary.

Although some promissory notes require a single lump-sum payment of the amount borrowed plus interest, most long-term notes require a series of payments. These notes are called **installment notes.** Each payment on an installment note includes interest and usually includes a partial repayment of the amount originally borrowed.

Installment Notes Payable

LO 1 Calculate and record the payments on an installment note payable.

When an installment note is used to borrow money, the borrower records the note just like a single-payment note. For example, suppose a company borrows $60,000 by signing an 8% installment note that requires six annual payments. The borrower records the note as follows:

1993 Dec.	31	Cash	60,000.00	
		Notes Payable		60,000.00
		Borrowed $60,000 by signing an 8% note.		

An installment note payable requires the borrower to pay back the debt in a series of periodic payments. Usually, each payment includes all of the interest accrued to the date of the payment plus some portion of the original amount borrowed (also called the *principal amount*). The terms of installment notes commonly call for one of two alternative payment patterns.

Installment Payments of Accrued Interest plus Equal Amounts of Principal

Some installment notes require payments that consist of interest accrued to date plus equal amounts of principal. Because each periodic payment reduces the amount owed, the next period's interest is reduced and the total amount of the next payment is smaller than the previous payment. For example, suppose that the $60,000, 8% note just recorded requires that the accrued interest plus $10,000 of principal be paid at the end of each year. To find the amount of interest accrued in each year, look at column *c* of the table at the top of Illustration 16–1. The table shows that the interest equals 8% of the principal of the note at the beginning of the year. It also shows that the unpaid principal balance is reduced by $10,000 each year.

The graph in Illustration 16–1 shows that: (1) the amount of principal in each payment remains constant at $10,000, (2) the amount of interest included in each payment gets steadily smaller, and (3) the total payment also gets smaller. Notice that the total interest expense of $16,800 equals the difference between the $76,800 paid back and the $60,000 borrowed.

The entries to record the first and the second annual payments are as follows:

1993				
Dec.	31	Notes Payable	10,000.00	
		Interest Expense	4,800.00	
		Cash		14,800.00
		To record first installment payment.		
1994				
Dec.	31	Notes Payable	10,000.00	
		Interest Expense	4,000.00	
		Cash		14,000.00
		To record second installment payment.		

Installment Payments that Are Equal in Total Amount

At this point, if you are not confident of your understanding of the concept of present value, turn back to Chapter 12 and review this concept. Also, see Appendix H at the end of the book for an expanded analysis of present and future values.

Many other installment notes require a series of equal-sized payments. Even though the payments are equal, they consist of changing amounts of interest and principal. For example, assume that the preceding $60,000, 8%

ILLUSTRATION 16–1

Installment Note with Payments of Accrued Interest and Equal Amount of Principal

Period Ending	(a) Beginning Principal Balance	(b) Periodic Payment	(c) Interest Expense for the Period *(a) x 8%*	(d) Portion of Payment that Is Principal *(b) – (c)*	(e) Ending Principal Balance *(a) – (d)*
12/31/93	$60,000	$14,800	$ 4,800	$10,000	$50,000
12/31/94	50,000	14,000	4,000	10,000	40,000
12/31/95	40,000	13,200	3,200	10,000	30,000
12/31/96	30,000	12,400	2,400	10,000	20,000
12/31/97	20,000	11,600	1,600	10,000	10,000
12/31/98	10,000	10,800	800	10,000	–0–
Total		$76,800	$16,800	$60,000	

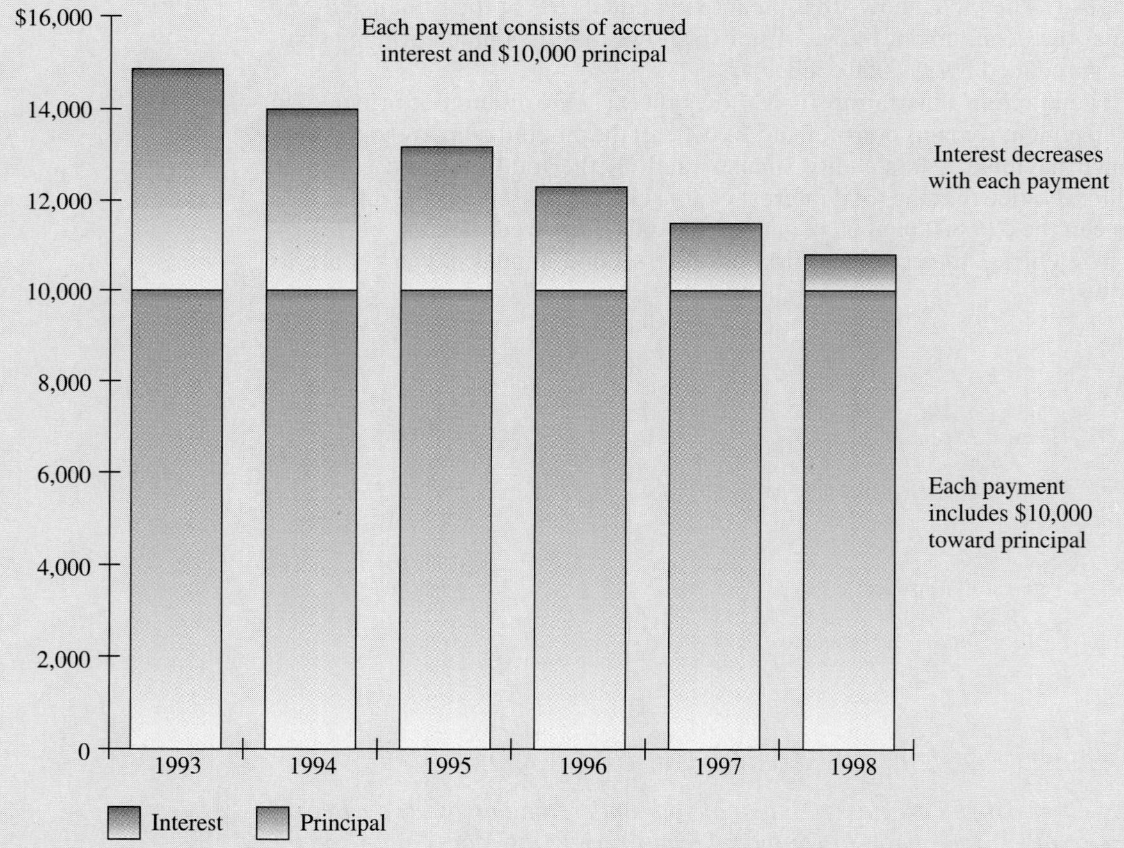

note requires a series of six equal payments to be made at the end of each year. Each payment is to be $12,979. The amount of each payment is $12,979 because $60,000 is the present value of six annual payments of $12,979, discounted at 8%. (In this chapter, all monetary amounts are rounded to the nearest whole dollar.)

Allocating Each Payment between Interest and Principal. Each payment of $12,979 includes both interest and principal. Illustration 16–2 shows the allocation of each payment between interest and principal. In the table at the top of the illustration, the amount of interest expense in each payment is calculated in column *c*. As you have seen before, the amount of interest expense is found by multiplying the rate of interest (8%) by the principal balance as of the beginning of the year. Notice that the amount of the payment in excess of the interest goes to repay the principal. For example, the interest on the first payment is $4,800. Because the payment is $12,979, the rest of the payment ($8,179) reduces the principal.

Observe that the amount of interest declines in 1994 to only $4,146 because the principal is smaller. Because the size of the payment remains constant at $12,979 and the interest decreases to $4,146, the repayment of principal increases to $8,833. This process continues until the full $60,000 of original principal has been paid back.

The graph in Illustration 16–2 shows that (1) the amount of interest declines each year, (2) the amount of principal repaid increases each year, and (3) the total payment remains constant. Because the tables in Illustrations 16–1 and 16–2 show how the principal balance is reduced through the periodic payments, they are often referred to as *installment note amortization schedules*.

The journal entries to record the first and second periodic payments are:

1993				
Dec.	31	Notes Payable	8,179.00	
		Interest Expense	4,800.00	
		Cash		12,979.00
		To record first installment payment.		
1994				
Dec.	31	Notes Payable	8,833.00	
		Interest Expense	4,146.00	
		Cash		12,979.00
		To record second installment payment.		

Similar entries record each of the remaining payments. Compare Illustration 16–1 with Illustration 16–2 to be sure that you understand the differences between the two payment patterns.

How to Calculate the Periodic Payments. In the example, the $60,000, 8% loan required six annual payments of $12,979. Illustration 16–2 shows that these payments are precisely the amounts needed to repay the loan. But, how do you know ahead of time that the $12,979 payment will work?

ILLUSTRATION 16–2

Installment Note with Equal Payments

Period Ending	*(a)* Beginning Principal Balance	*(b)* Periodic Payment	*(c)* Interest Expense for the Period *(a) x 8%*	*(d)* Portion of Payment that Is Principal *(b) – (c)*	*(e)* Ending Principal Balance *(a) – (d)*
12/31/93	$60,000	$12,979	$ 4,800	$ 8,179	$51,821
12/31/94	51,821	12,979	4,146	8,833	42,988
12/31/95	42,988	12,979	3,439	9,540	33,448
12/31/96	33,448	12,979	2,676	10,303	23,145
12/31/97	23,145	12,979	1,852	11,127	12,018
12/31/98	12,018	12,979	961	12,019	–0–
Total		$77,874	$17,874	$60,000	

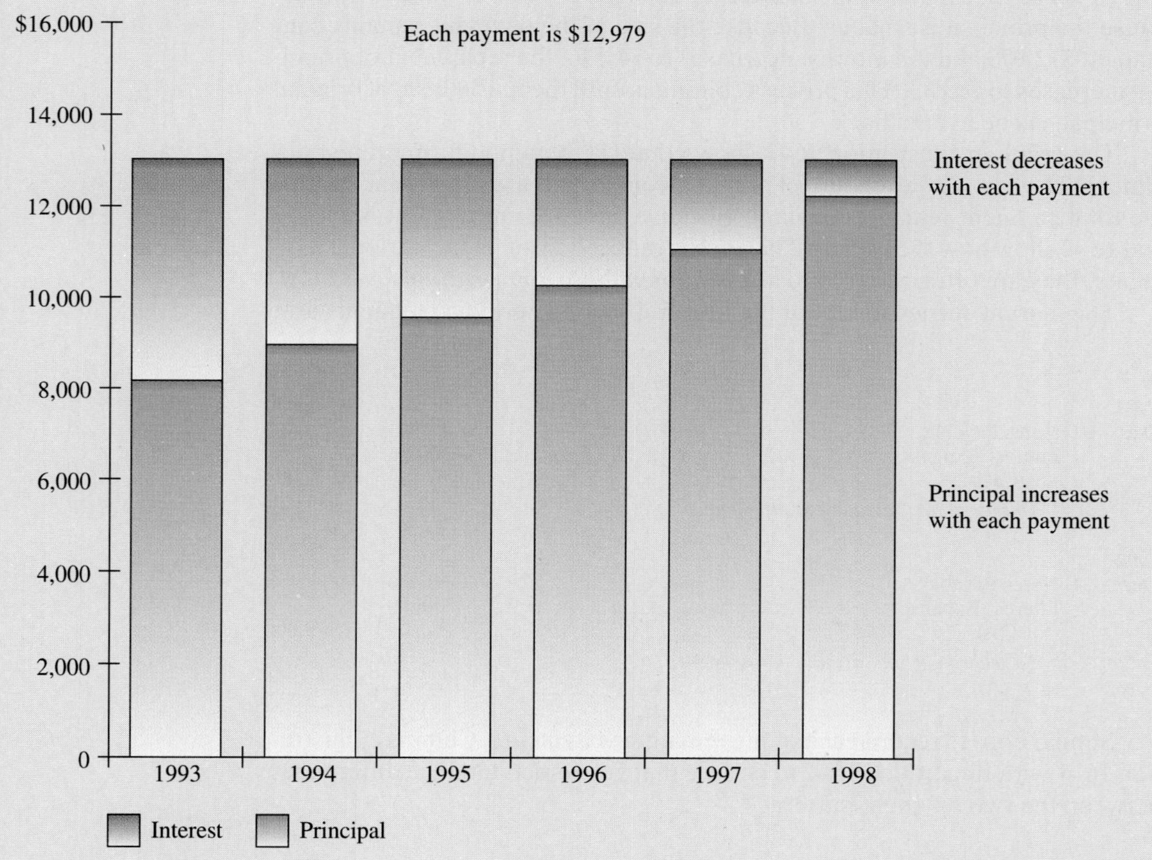

We can calculate the size of each payment using a table for the present value of an annuity such as Table 12–2 on page 625. To use the table for this purpose, we begin with the following equation:

$$\text{Payment} \times \text{Table value} = \text{Present value of the annuity}$$

Then, we can manipulate the equation to get this formula:

$$\text{Payment} = \frac{\text{Present value of the annuity}}{\text{Table value}}$$

Because the principal balance of an installment note equals the present value of the series of payments, the formula can now be presented as:

$$\text{Payment} = \frac{\text{Note balance}}{\text{Table value}}$$

The appropriate table value is based on the note's interest rate and the number of payments. For our example, the loan balance is \$60,000. The interest rate is 8% and there are six payments. Therefore, the value from Table 12–2 is 4.6229. These facts can now be combined in the formula to compute the size of the payment:

$$\text{Payment} = \frac{\$60{,}000}{4.6229} = \$12{,}979$$

Borrowing by Issuing Bonds

Corporations often borrow money by issuing **bonds.**[1] Similar to notes payable, bonds involve a written promise to pay interest at a stated annual rate and to pay the principal or **par value of the bonds.** Most bonds require that the borrower pay interest semiannually and pay the par value or **face amount** of the bonds at a fixed future date called the *maturity date of the bonds*. The annual amount of interest that must be paid is determined by multiplying the par value of the bonds by a stated rate of interest that was established before the bonds were issued.

Difference between Notes Payable and Bonds

When a business borrows money by signing a note payable, the money is generally borrowed from a single lender such as a bank. In contrast to a note payable, a bond issue typically includes a large number of bonds, usually in denominations of \$1,000, that are sold to many different lenders. After they are originally issued, bonds are frequently bought and sold by investors. Thus, any particular bond may actually be owned by a number of people before it matures.

[1] The federal government and other governmental units, such as cities, states, and school districts, also issue bonds. Although the examples in this chapter deal with bonds issued by business corporations, the methods used to account for bonds are the same for all organizations.

Difference between Stocks and Bonds

The phrase *stocks and bonds* may appear on the financial pages of newspapers or it may come up as a topic of conversation. Stocks and bonds are not the same things and you should understand the differences between them. A share of stock represents an equity or ownership right in a corporation. For example, a person who owns 1,000 of a corporation's 10,000 outstanding shares has an equity in the corporation measured at one tenth of the total stockholders' equity. Also, the person has a one-tenth interest in the corporation's future earnings. On the other hand, if a person owns a $1,000, 11%, 20-year bond issued by a corporation, the bond represents a debt or a liability of the corporation. The owner of the bond has two rights: (1) to receive 11% (or $110) interest each year the bond is outstanding and (2) to receive $1,000 when the bond matures 20 years after its date of issue.

Why Bonds Are Issued Instead of Stock

A corporation that needs funds for a long time may consider issuing either bonds or additional shares of stock. Each approach has its advantages and disadvantages. Present stockholders may see the issuance of additional shares as a disadvantage if the shares are issued to new stockholders. Because the new stockholders are owners, the additional stock potentially dilutes ownership, control of management, and earnings. On the other hand, bondholders are creditors and do not share in either management or earnings. However, a disadvantage of issuing bonds is that the interest on the bonds must be paid whether or not there are any earnings.

A potential advantage of issuing bonds is that doing so might increase earnings for the common stockholders. For example, assume that a corporation with 200,000 outstanding shares of common stock needs $1 million to expand its operations. Management estimates that, after the expansion, the company can earn $900,000 annually before bond interest, if any, and before corporate income taxes. Two plans for securing the needed funds are proposed: Plan A calls for issuing 100,000 additional shares of common stock at $10 per share. This plan increases the total outstanding shares to 300,000. Plan B calls for the sale of $1 million of 10% bonds at par. Illustration 16–3 shows how the plans would affect the corporation's earnings, under the assumption of a 40% income tax rate. Even though the projected total income under Plan B is smaller, the amount of income per share is larger.

Corporations must pay not only federal income taxes but also state income taxes in some states. These federal and state taxes may amount to as much as 40% or more of the corporation's before-tax income. However, interest expense is deductible in arriving at income subject to taxes. Therefore, when the combined state and federal tax rate is 40%, as in Illustration 16–3, the reduction in taxes from issuing bonds equals 40% of the annual interest on the bonds. In other words, the tax saving effectively pays 40% of the interest cost.

ILLUSTRATION 16–3

Financing with Stock or with Bonds

	Plan A	Plan B
Earnings before bond interest and income taxes . . .	$ 900,000	$ 900,000
Deduct interest expense		(100,000)
Income before income taxes	$ 900,000	$ 800,000
Deduct income taxes (40% rate)	(360,000)	(320,000)
Net income	$ 540,000	$ 480,000
Plan A income per share ($540,000/300,000 shares) . .	$1.80	
Plan B income per share ($480,000/200,000 shares) . .		$2.40

Characteristics of Bonds

Over the years, corporate lawyers and financial experts have created a wide variety of bonds with different combinations of characteristics. We describe some of the more common characteristics of various bond issues in the following paragraphs.

LO 2 Describe the various characteristics of different types of bond issues and prepare entries to record bonds that are issued between interest dates.

Serial Bonds

Some bond issues include bonds that mature at different dates. As a result, the entire bond issue is repaid gradually over a period of years. Bonds of this type are called **serial bonds.** For example, a $1 million issue of serial bonds might have $100,000 of the bonds mature each year from 6 to 15 years after the bonds were issued. In this case, the $1 million issue would consist of 10 groups or series of bonds, each of which would have a total par value of $100,000. Each group or series would have a unique maturity date. One series would mature after six years, another after seven years, and another each successive year until the entire $1 million issue had matured.

Sinking Fund Bonds

In contrast to serial bonds, **sinking fund bonds** all mature on the same date. However, sinking fund bonds require that the issuing corporation establish a separate pool of assets (called a *sinking fund*) for the purpose of providing the cash necessary to retire the bonds at maturity. We discuss sinking funds later in this chapter.

Registered Bonds and Bearer Bonds

The issuing corporation records the names and addresses of the owners of **registered bonds.** Interest payments on registered bonds are usually made by checks mailed to the registered owners. This arrangement also offers some protection from loss or theft.

Bonds that are not registered are called **bearer bonds;** they are payable to whoever holds them (the *bearer*). The holder of a bearer bond is presumed to be its rightful owner. Generally, bearer bonds are also **coupon bonds.** Coupon bonds get their name from the interest coupons attached to each bond. Each coupon calls for payment of the interest due on the bond on the interest payment date. The coupons are detached as they become due and are deposited with a bank for collection. At maturity, the holder or bearer usually follows the same process and deposits the bond certificates with a bank for collection.

Secured Bonds and Debentures

When bonds are secured, specific assets of the issuing corporation are pledged or mortgaged as security. This gives the bondholders additional protection. In the event the issuing corporation fails to make the required payments of interest or par value, the bondholders can demand that the mortgaged assets be sold and the proceeds used to repay the bondholders. In contrast to secured bonds, unsecured bonds depend on the general credit standing of the issuing corporation. Unsecured bonds are called **debentures.** A company generally must be financially strong if it is to successfully issue unsecured bonds at a favorable rate of interest.

The Process of Issuing Bonds

When a corporation issues bonds, it normally sells them to an investment firm called an *underwriter*. In turn, the underwriter resells the bonds to the public.

The legal document that states the rights and obligations of the bondholders and the issuer is called the **bond indenture.** In other words, the bond indenture is the written legal contract between the issuing company and the bondholders. Each bondholder may receive a bond certificate to serve as evidence of the corporation's debt to the bondholder. As a way to reduce costs, however, many corporations no longer issue bond certificates to registered bondholders.

If a bond issue is sold to a large number of investors, they are represented by a *trustee*. The trustee monitors the corporation's actions to ensure that the corporation fulfills its obligations as stated in the bond indenture. In most cases, the trustee is a large bank or trust company that is selected by the issuing company and identified in the indenture.

Accounting for the Issuance of Bonds

When a corporation issues bonds, the bond certificates (if any) are printed and the indenture is drawn and presented to the trustee of the bondholders. At that point, a memorandum describing the bond issue is commonly entered in the Bonds Payable account. The memorandum might read, "Authorized to issue $8 million of 9%, 20-year bonds dated January 1, 1993, due on December 31, 2012, with interest payable semiannually on each June 30 and December 31." The bonds in this example are typical of most bonds in that interest is paid two times each year.

After the bond indenture is deposited with the trustee of the bondholders, all or a portion of the bonds may be sold. If all are sold at their par value, this entry records the sale:

1993				
Jan.	31	Cash	8,000,000.00	
		Bonds Payable		8,000,000.00
		Sold 9%, 20-year bonds at par.		

When the semiannual interest is paid on these bonds, the transaction is recorded as follows:

1993				
June	30	Interest Expense	360,000.00	
		Cash		360,000.00
		Paid the semiannual interest on the bonds.		

And when the bonds are paid at maturity, the entry is:

2012				
Dec.	31	Bonds Payable	8,000,000.00	
		Cash		8,000,000.00
		Paid bonds at maturity.		

Bonds Sold between Interest Dates

As in the previous example, bonds are often sold on their date of issue. However, bonds also may be sold after their issue date and between interest dates. When this happens, the issuing corporation charges and collects from the purchasers the interest that has accrued on the bonds since the issue date or the preceding interest payment date. This accrued interest is then refunded to the purchasers on the next interest date. For example, on March 1, a corporation sold $100,000 of 9% bonds at par. The interest on the bonds is payable semiannually on each June 30 and December 31. The entry to record the sale two months after the issue date is:

Mar.	1	Cash	101,500.00	
		Interest Payable		1,500.00
		Bonds Payable		100,000.00
		Sold $100,000 of 9%, 20-year bonds on which two months' interest has accrued.		

The $1,500 equals two months' interest ($100,000 = 9% × 2/12.

At the end of four months, on the June 30 semiannual interest date, the purchasers of these bonds are paid a full six months' interest of $4,500 ($100,000 × 9% × 6/12). This payment includes four months' interest earned by the bondholders after March 1 and the two months' accrued interest collected from them at the time the bonds were sold. The entry to record the payment is:

June	30	Interest Payable	1,500.00	
		Interest Expense	3,000.00	
		Cash		4,500.00
		Paid the semiannual interest on the bonds.		

This practice of first collecting accrued interest from bond purchasers and then refunding it to them in the next interest payment may seem inefficient. However, bond transactions are executed on a plus-accrued-interest basis because it is easier for the bond issuer. For example, if a corporation were to sell bonds on a variety of dates during an interest period and not collect accrued interest, the amounts the bondholders would receive on the next payment date would vary depending on how long they owned the bonds. To make the correct payments, the issuing corporation would have to keep detailed records of the purchasers and the dates on which they bought their bonds. This extra record-keeping can be avoided if each buyer is charged for accrued interest at the time of purchase. Then, the corporation simply pays a full six months' interest to all purchasers, regardless of when they bought their bonds.

Bond Interest Rates

The interest rate to be paid by a corporation on its bonds is specified in the bond indenture and on each bond certificate. This rate is called the **contract rate.**[2] The contract rate of interest is applied to the par value of the bonds to determine the amount of interest to be paid each year. Even though bond interest is paid semiannually, the contract rate is usually stated on an annual basis.

For example, if a corporation issues a $1,000, 8% bond on which interest is paid semiannually, $80 will be paid each year in two payments of $40 each. Although the contract rate establishes the amount of interest that a corporation pays in cash, the contract rate is not necessarily the rate of interest expense that the corporation incurs. The interest expense the corporation incurs depends on how lenders assess their risks in lending to the corporation. This perceived risk is reflected in the **market rate for bond interest** available to the corporation. The market rate for bond interest is the rate borrowers are willing to pay and lenders are willing to accept for the use of money at the level of risk involved. The rate may change daily as the supply and demand for loanable funds changes. The market rate goes up when the demand for bond money increases and the supply decreases, and it goes down when the supply increases and the demand decreases.

Note that the market rate for bond interest is not the same for all corporations. The market rate for a specific corporation's bonds depends on the level of risk investors assign to those bonds. As the level of risk increases, the rate increases.

In many cases, a corporation that issues bonds offers a contract rate of interest equal to the rate it estimates the market will demand on the day the bonds are issued. If the estimate is correct, and the contract rate and market rate coincide on the day the bonds are issued, the bonds sell at par, which is

[2] This rate is also known as the *coupon rate*, the *stated rate*, or the *nominal rate*.

their face value. However, if the estimate is incorrect, the contract rate will not coincide with the market rate. As a result, bonds may sell below or above their par value (at a discount or a premium). Sometimes, the issuing corporation offers a low contract rate that results in a very large discount. Some companies even issue *zero-coupon bonds,* which do not provide for any periodic interest payments.

Bonds Sold at a Discount

LO 3 Calculate the price of a bond issue that sells at a discount and prepare entries to account for bonds issued at a discount.

A **discount on bonds payable** results when a corporation issues bonds that have a contract rate below the prevailing market rate. For the same level of risk, investors can get the market rate of interest elsewhere for the use of their money. Thus, they will buy the bonds only at a price that will yield the prevailing market rate on the investment. To estimate the expected market price of the bonds, find the *present value* of the expected cash flows by discounting the cash flows from the bond investment at the current market interest rate.

To illustrate how bond prices are determined, assume that a corporation offers to issue bonds with a $100,000 par value, an 8% annual rate, and a five-year life. Also assume that the market rate of interest for this corporation's bonds is 10%.[3] In exchange for the purchase price, the buyers of these bonds obtain the right to receive two different future cash inflows:

1. The right to receive $100,000 at the end of the bond issue's five-year life.
2. The right to receive $4,000 in interest at the end of each six-month interest period throughout the five-year life of the bonds.

To determine the price at which the bonds will be issued, you must calculate the present value of the future cash flows by discounting the amounts to be received at the market rate of interest. Although the market rate is expressed as an annual rate of 10%, this is understood to mean 5% semiannually. In five years, there are 10 semiannual periods. Therefore, use the number in the 10th row and the 5% column of Table 12–1 (page 623) to discount the $100,000 receipt at maturity. Then, use the number in the 10th row and the 5% column of Table 12–2 (page 625) to discount the series of $4,000 interest payments. Calculate the present value of these cash flows as follows:

Present value of $100,000 to be received after 10 periods, discounted at 5% per period ($100,000 × 0.6139)	$61,390
Present value of $4,000 to be received periodically for 10 periods, discounted at 5% ($4,000 × 7.7217)	30,887
Present value of the bonds	$92,277

Thus, the maximum price that informed buyers would offer for the bonds is $92,277.

If the corporation accepts $92,277 for its bonds and sells them on their date of issue (December 31, 1993), the sale is recorded with an entry like this:

[3] The spread between the contract rate and the market rate of interest on a new bond issue is seldom more than a fraction of a percent. However, we use a difference of 2% here to simplify the illustrations.

Dec.	31	Cash	92,277.00	
		Discount on Bonds Payable	7,723.00	
		Bonds Payable		100,000.00
		Sold 8%, 5-year bonds at a discount on their date of issue.		

In the corporation's financial statements, the bonds will appear in the long-term liability section of the December 31, 1993, balance sheet as follows:

Long-term liabilities:		
Bonds payable, 8%, due December 31, 1998	$100,000	
Less unamortized discount based on the 10% market rate for bond interest prevailing on the date of issue	7,723	$92,277

As shown above, any unamortized discount on bonds payable is deducted from the par value of the bonds on the balance sheet to show the **carrying amount of the bonds payable.** The carrying amount is the net amount at which the bonds are recorded in the accounts.

Amortizing the Discount

In the previous discussion, the corporation received $92,277 for its bonds, but, in five years, it must pay the bondholders $100,000. The difference, the $7,723 discount, is part of the cost of using the $92,277 for five years. The total interest cost is $47,723, which is the difference between the amount borrowed and the amount repaid:

Amount repaid:	
Ten payments of $4,000	$ 40,000
Maturity amount	100,000
Total repaid	$140,000
Less: Amount borrowed	(92,277)
Total interest expense	$ 47,723

This amount also equals the sum of the cash payments and the discount:

Ten payments of $4,000	$40,000
Discount	7,723
Total interest expense	$47,723

When accounting for these bonds, you must accomplish two things: First, the total interest expense must be allocated to the 10 six-month periods in the bonds' life. Second, the carrying value of the bonds must be determined on each balance sheet date. Two alternative accounting methods are used to accomplish these objectives. They are the straight-line method and the interest method.

ILLUSTRATION 16–4

Calculation of Interest Expense and Bond Discount Amortization: Staight-Line Method

Period Ending	(*a*) Beginning Carrying Amount	(*b*) Interest Expense for the Period (*c*) + (*d*)	(*c*) Interest to Be Paid the Bondholders	(*d*) Discount to Be Amortized *$7,723/10*	(*e*) Unamortized Discount at End of Period	(*f*) Ending Carrying Amount *$100,000* – (*e*)
6/30/93	$92,277	$ 4,772	$ 4,000	$ 772	$6,951	$ 93,049
12/31/93	93,049	4,772	4,000	772	6,179	93,821
6/30/94	93,821	4,772	4,000	772	5,407	94,593
12/31/94	94,593	4,772	4,000	772	4,635	95,365
6/30/95	95,365	4,772	4,000	772	3,863	96,137
12/31/95	96,137	4,772	4,000	772	3,091	96,909
6/30/96	96,909	4,772	4,000	772	2,319	97,681
12/31/96	97,681	4,772	4,000	772	1,547	98,453
6/30/97	98,453	4,772	4,000	772	775	99,225
12/31/97	99,225	4,775*	4,000	775	–0–	100,000
Total.		$47,723	$40,000	$7,723		

* Adjusted to compensate for accumulated rounding of amounts.

Straight-Line Method. The **straight-line method of amortizing bond discount or premium** is the simpler of the two methods. This method allocates an equal portion of the discount or premium (and the total interest expense) to each six-month interest period.

In applying the straight-line method in the present example, divide the $7,723 discount by 10, which is the number of interest periods in the life of the bond issue. The $772 answer ($7,723/10 = $772.30, or $772) is the amount of discount to be amortized at the end of each interest period.[4] Total interest expense for each interest period is the $4,772 sum of the $4,000 cash paid and the $772 amortized discount. This $4,772 amount is also equal to one tenth of the total expense of $47,723.

At the time of the semiannual cash payment, the following entry records the periodic interest expense:

June	30	Interest Expense	4,772.00	
		Discount on Bonds Payable		772.00
		Cash		4,000.00
		To record payment of six months' interest and amortization of the discount.		

Illustration 16–4 shows the interest expense to be recorded and the discount to be amortized each period when the straight-line method is applied to the present example. Notice the following points in Illustration 16–4:

[4] In this chapter and in the exercises and problems at the end of the chapter, all calculations involving bonds have been rounded to the nearest whole dollar.

1. In column *a*, the $92,277 beginning carrying amount equals the $100,000 face amount of the bonds less the $7,723 discount on the sale of the bonds.
2. The semiannual interest expense of $4,772 (column *b*) equals $4,000 paid to the bondholders (column *c*) plus the $772 discount amortization (column *d*).
3. Interest paid to bondholders each period (column *c*) is determined by multiplying the par value of the bonds by the semiannual contract rate of interest ($100,000 × 4% = $4,000).
4. The discount amortized each period is $772 (column *d*).
5. The unamortized discount at the end of each period (column *e*) is determined by subtracting the discount amortized that period from the unamortized discount at the beginning of the period.
6. The end-of-period carrying amount (column *f*) of the bonds is determined by subtracting the end-of-period amount of unamortized discount (column *e*) from the face amount of the bonds ($100,000). For example, at June 30, 1993: $100,000 − $6,951 = $93,049.

Interest Method. Straight-line amortization used to be widely applied in practice. However, generally accepted accounting principles now allow the straight-line method to be applied only when the results do not differ materially from those obtained by using the **interest method of amortizing bond discount or premium.**[5]

As you learned earlier in the case of installment notes with equal periodic payments, the amount of interest expense changes each period when the interest method is used. This is also true for bonds. To calculate the amount of interest expense allocated to each period, simply multiply the carrying amount of the bonds at the beginning of each period by the market rate for the bonds at the time they were issued.

After calculating interest expense for a period, you can determine the amount of discount to be amortized by subtracting the cash interest payment from the interest expense. Illustration 16–5 presents a table for applying the interest method to the bonds in the previous example. The table shows the interest expense to be recorded (column *b*), the cash interest payment (column *c*), the discount to be amortized (column *d*), and the remaining balance sheet amounts (columns *e* and *f*).

Compare Illustration 16–5 with Illustration 16–4 and note these points about the interest method:

1. The interest expense (column *b*) results from multiplying each beginning carrying amount by the 5% semiannual market rate that prevailed when the bonds were issued. For example, in the period ended June 30, 1993, the expense is $4,614 ($92,277 × 5%) and, in the period ended December 31, 1993, it is $4,645 ($92,891 × 5%).

[5] FASB, *Accounting Standards—Current Text* (Norwalk, Conn., 1990), sec. I69.108. First published in *APB Opinion No. 21*, par. 15.

ILLUSTRATION 16–5

Calculation of Interest Expense and Bond Discount Amortization: Interest Method

Period Ending	(a) Beginning Carrying Amount	(b) Interest Expense for the Period (a) × 5%	(c) Interest to Be Paid the Bondholders	(d) Discount to Be Amortized (b) − (c)	(e) Unamortized Discount at End of Period	(f) Ending Carrying Amount $100,000 − (e)
6/30/93	$92,277	$ 4,614	$ 4,000	$ 614	$7,109	$ 92,891
12/31/93	92,891	4,645	4,000	645	6,464	93,536
6/30/94	93,536	4,677	4,000	677	5,787	94,213
12/31/94	94,213	4,711	4,000	711	5,076	94,924
6/30/95	94,924	4,746	4,000	746	4,330	95,670
12/31/95	95,670	4,784	4,000	784	3,546	96,454
6/30/96	96,454	4,823	4,000	823	2,723	97,277
12/31/96	97,277	4,864	4,000	864	1,859	98,141
6/30/97	98,141	4,907	4,000	907	952	99,048
12/31/97	99,048	4,952	4,000	952	–0–	100,000
Total.		$47,723	$40,000	$7,723		

2. The amount of discount to be amortized each period is determined by subtracting the cash interest paid to the bondholders from the reported interest expense.

When the interest method is used to amortize a discount, the periodic entries involve the same accounts as straight-line method entries. However, the dollar amounts are different. For example, the entry to record the payment to the bondholders and to amortize the discount at the end of the first semiannual interest period of the bond issue in Illustration 16–5 is:

1993				
June	30	Interest Expense	4,614.00	
		Discount on Bonds Payable		614.00
		Cash		4,000.00
		To record payment to the bondholders and amortization of a portion of the discount.		

Similar entries, differing only in the amount of interest expense recorded and discount amortized, are made at the end of each semiannual interest period in the life of the bond issue.

Comparing the Straight-Line and Interest Methods. Now we can examine the differences between the interest method of amortizing a discount and the straight-line method. Illustration 16–6 presents useful information for observing the differences.

The first graph in Illustration 16–6 shows how the amounts of interest expense under straight-line are the same each period, while the amounts

ILLUSTRATION 16–6

Comparing Straight-Line Amortization with the Interest Method

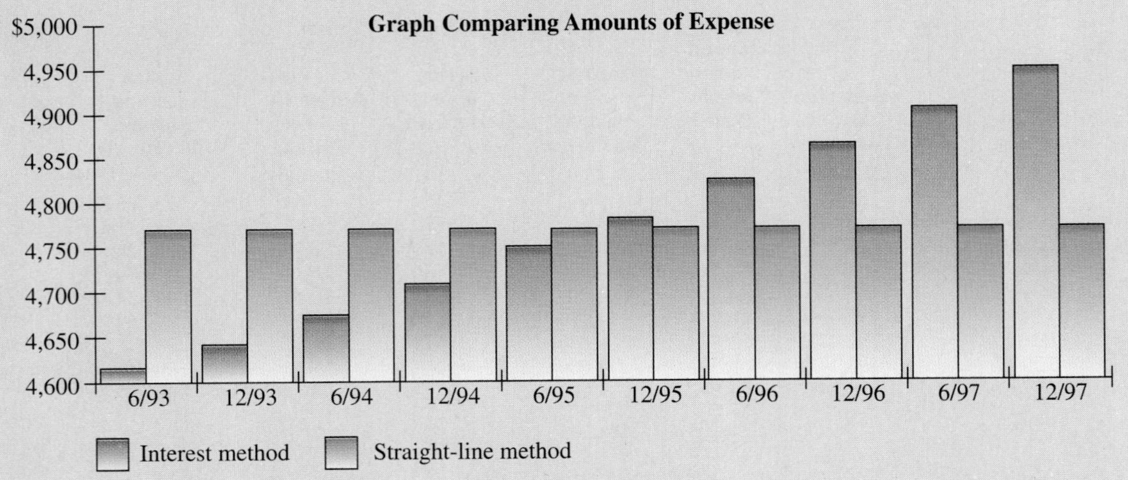

Table Comparing Rates of Expense

	Interest-Method Amortization			Straight-Line Amortization		
Period Ending	**Beginning-of-Period Carrying Amount**	**Interest Expense to Be Recorded**	**Interest Expense as a Percentage of Carrying Amount**	**Beginning-of-Period Carrying Amount**	**Interest Expense to Be Recorded**	**Interest Expense as a Percentage of Carrying Amount**
6/30/93	$92,277	$4,207	5.0	$92,277	$4,772	5.17
6/30/95	94,924	4,322	5.0	95,365	4,772	5.00
12/31/97	99,048	4,457	5.0	99,225	4,772	4.81

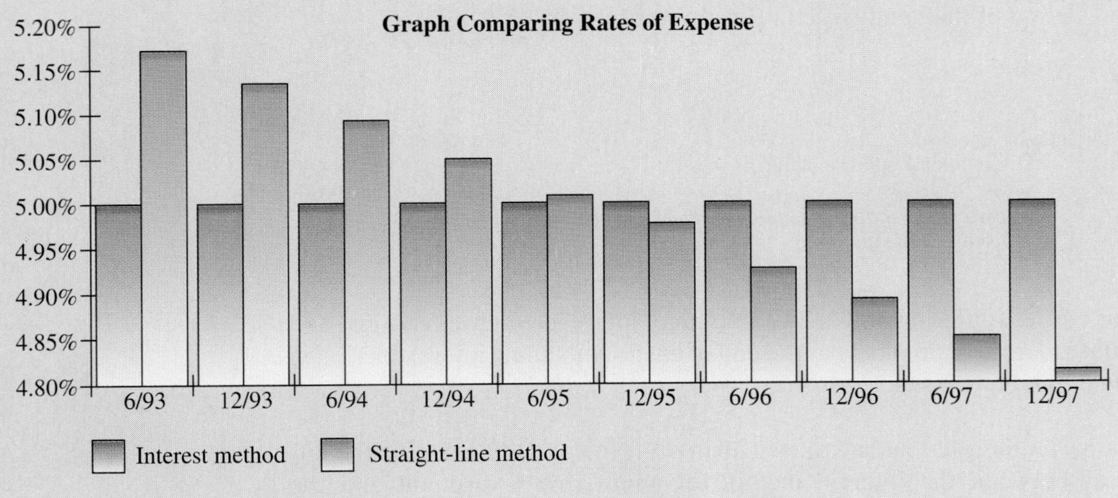

reported under the interest method increase each period. The table in the middle of Illustration 16–6 compares the two methods in three different interest periods. The table shows that when interest expense is expressed as a percentage of the beginning-of-period carrying value, the interest method results in the same percentages each period. On the other hand, when the straight-line method is used, the percentages change from period to period. This comparison extends to all 10 periods in the graph at the bottom of Illustration 16–6.

Recall that in this example, the corporation issued the bonds at a price that reflected a discounting of cash flows at 5% per six-month period. Thus, when the interest method is used, the amounts reported in the financial statements each period show an expense that is 5% of the beginning-of-period carrying value. For this reason, the interest method is preferred. In fact, the straight-line method can be used only where the results do not differ materially from those obtained through use of the interest method.

Bonds Sold at a Premium

LO 4 Prepare entries to account for bonds issued at a premium.

When a corporation offers to sell bonds carrying a contract rate of interest above the prevailing market rate for the risks involved, the bonds will sell at a **premium.** That is, buyers will bid up the price of the bonds, going as high, but no higher, than a price that will return the current market rate of interest on the investment. This price is the present value of the expected cash flows from the investment, determined by discounting these cash flows at the market rate of interest for the bonds.

For example, assume that a corporation offers to sell bonds that have a $100,000 par value and a five-year life. The interest is to be paid semiannually at a 12% annual rate. On the day of issue, the market rate of interest for the corporation's bonds is 10%. Buyers of these bonds discount the expected receipt of $100,000 after 10 six-month periods, and the expected receipt of $6,000 semiannually for 10 periods at the current market rate of 5% per six-month period. The calculation is:

Present value of $100,000 to be received after 10 periods, discounted at 5% per period ($100,000 × 0.6139)	$ 61,390
Present value of $6,000 to be received periodically for 10 periods, discounted at 5% ($6,000 × 7.7217)	46,330
Present value of the bonds	$107,720

If the bonds are sold for $107,720 on their issue date of May 1, 1993, the corporation records the sale as follows:

1993				
May	1	Cash	107,720.00	
		Premium on Bonds Payable		7,720.00
		Bonds Payable		100,000.00
		Sold bonds at a premium on their date of issue.		

When a balance sheet is prepared on May 1, 1993, the bonds appear as follows:

Long-term liabilities:		
12% bonds payable, due May 1, 1998.	$100,000	
Add unamortized premium based on the 10% market rate for bond interest prevailing on the date of issue.	7,720	$107,720

As you can see, any unamortized premium on bonds payable is added to the par value of the bonds to show the carrying amount of the bonds on the balance sheet.

Amortizing the Premium

Over the life of these bonds, the issuing corporation will pay back $160,000, which consists of the 10 periodic interest payments of $6,000 plus the $100,000 par value. Because it borrowed $107,720, the total interest expense will be $52,280:

Amount repaid:	
Ten payments of $6,000	$ 60,000
Maturity amount	100,000
Total repaid	$ 160,000
Less: Amount borrowed	(107,720)
Total interest expense	$ 52,280

This amount also equals the difference between the cash payments and the premium:

Ten payments of $6,000	$60,000
Premium.	(7,720)
Total interest expense	$52,280

The allocation of this total interest expense over 10 semiannual periods is accomplished by amortizing the premium. Illustration 16–7 shows an amortization schedule for the bonds using the interest method.

Observe in Illustration 16–7 that the premium to be amortized each period (column *d*) is determined by subtracting the interest expense (column *b*) from the cash interest paid to the bondholders (column *c*). The ending carrying amount equals the sum of the $100,000 par value and the unamortized premium (column *e*).

Based on Illustration 16–7, the entry to record the first semiannual interest payment and premium amortization is:

ILLUSTRATION 16–7

Calculation of Interest Expense and Bond Premium Amortization: Interest Method

Period Ending	(a) Beginning Carrying Amount	(b) Interest Expense for the Period (a) × 5%	(c) Interest to Be Paid the Bondholders	(d) Discount to Be Amortized (c) − (b)	(e) Unamortized Premium at End of Period	(f) Ending Carrying Amount $100,000 + (e)
11/1/93	$107,720	$ 5,386	$ 6,000	$ 614	$7,106	$107,106
5/1/94	107,106	5,355	6,000	645	6,461	106,461
11/1/94	106,461	5,323	6,000	677	5,784	105,784
5/1/95	105,784	5,289	6,000	711	5,073	105,073
11/1/95	105,073	5,254	6,000	746	4,327	104,327
5/1/96	104,327	5,216	6,000	784	3,543	103,543
11/1/96	103,543	5,177	6,000	823	2,720	102,720
5/1/97	102,720	5,136	6,000	864	1,856	101,856
11/1/97	101,856	5,093	6,000	907	949	100,949
5/1/98	100,949	5,051*	6,000	949	-0-	100,000
Total		$52,280	$60,000	$7,720		

* Adjusted to compensate for accumulated rounding of amounts.

1993				
Nov.	1	Interest Expense	5,386.00	
		Premium on Bonds Payable	614.00	
		Cash		6,000.00
		To record payment to the bondholders and amortization of a portion of the premium.		

Similar entries, with decreasing amounts of interest expense and increasing amounts of premium amortization, are made at the end of the remaining periods in the life of the bond issue. Note that the amortization of the premium has the effect of reducing interest expense below the amount paid in cash. In effect, each cash payment retires part of the principal balance of the bonds. This process continues until the final payment, when the carrying value equals the par value of $100,000.

Accrued Interest Expense

When bonds are sold, the bond interest periods often do not coincide with the issuing company's accounting periods. In these cases, you must make an adjustment for accrued interest at the end of each accounting period. For example, the bonds described in Illustration 16–7 were issued on May 1, 1993, and interest was first recorded and paid on November 1 of that year. By December 31, 1993, two months' interest has accrued on these bonds. If the accounting period ends on that date, the following adjusting entry is required:

1993				
Dec.	31	Interest Expense ($5,355 × 2/6)	1,785.00	
		Premium on Bonds Payable ($645 × 2/6)	215.00	
		Interest Payable ($6,000 × 2/6)		2,000.00
		To record two months' accrued interest and one third of the premium amortization applicable to the interest period.		

Two months are one third of a semiannual interest period. Therefore, the amounts in the entry are one third of the amounts applicable to the second interest period in the life of the bond issue. Similar entries will be made on each December 31 throughout the life of the issue. However, the amounts differ because the interest method of amortizing the premium produces a different measure of the expense in each interest period.

On May 1, 1994, this entry will record the semiannual payment of interest:

1994				
May	1	Interest Payable	2,000.00	
		Interest Expense ($5,355 × 4/6)	3,570.00	
		Premium on Bonds Payable ($645 × 4/6)	430.00	
		Cash		6,000.00
		Paid the interest on the bonds, a portion of which was previously accrued, and amortized four months' premium.		

Retirement of Bonds

Bond indentures commonly include a provision that gives the issuing corporation the option of retiring the bonds prior to their maturity date. The provision states that the corporation can exercise an option to *call* the bonds before they mature by paying the par value plus a *call premium*. These bonds are known as **callable bonds.** One reason corporations insert call provisions into the bond indenture is to allow them to take action if market interest rates decline sharply. Specifically, the provisions permit the company to retire the old bonds that have a high interest rate with new bonds that pay a lower interest rate. Even if a particular issue of bonds is not callable, the issuing corporation may be able to retire its bonds by purchasing them on the open market.

Whether bonds are called or purchased in the open market, the price paid is not likely to equal the carrying value of the bonds. Because the market interest rate changes as economic conditions change, the market value of a bond's remaining cash flows also changes. Therefore, the price paid to purchase and retire bonds may result in a gain or loss. For example, assume that a company has $1 million of outstanding bonds. After interest is recorded on the April 1 interest payment date, $12,000 of unamortized premium remains. Because the market interest rate has increased, the bonds are selling at the quoted price of 98½, which stands for 98.5% of par value.[6] If the company buys and retires one tenth of the outstanding bonds at this price, the entry to record the purchase and retirement is:

Apr.	1	Bonds Payable	100,000.00	
		Premium on Bonds Payable	1,200.00	
		Gain on Retirement of Bonds		2,700.00
		Cash		98,500.00
		To record the retirement of bonds.		

This retirement resulted in a $2,700 gain because the bonds were purchased for $2,700 below their carrying value.

Bond Sinking Fund

LO 5 Explain the purpose and operation of a bond sinking fund and prepare entries for sinking fund activities and for the retirement of bonds.

One reason investors buy bonds instead of stocks is that bonds usually provide greater security than stocks. To attract more investors, a corporation may give additional security to the bondholders by agreeing in the bond indenture to create a **bond sinking fund.** This fund consists of assets committed to be used for repaying the bondholders when the bonds mature.

A bond indenture that calls for a bond sinking fund to be created usually requires the issuing corporation to make regular periodic cash deposits with a sinking fund trustee. The trustee's duties are to safeguard the cash, invest it in securities of reasonably low risk, and add the earned interest and dividends to the accumulated balance in the sinking fund. When the bonds become due, the sinking fund trustee converts the sinking fund's investments to cash and pays the bondholders. Even though the sinking fund is in the custody of the trustee, it is the property of the bond issuer and should appear on its balance sheet in the long-term investments section.

The amounts that must be deposited to provide enough money to retire a bond issue at maturity depend on the net rate of return that can be earned on the invested funds. It is a net rate because the fee for the trustee's services is commonly deducted from the earnings.

To illustrate the accumulation of a sinking fund, assume that a corporation issues $1 million par value 10-year bonds on January 1, 1993. The bond indenture requires that the corporation make annual deposits with a sinking fund trustee on December 31 of each year in the bonds' life (1993 through 2002). Based on the assumption that the trustee will be able to earn an annual return of 8% on the invested assets, net of expenses, the corporation must deposit $69,029 each year.[7] Illustration 16–8 shows that these deposits and the earnings on the accumulated funds will generate enough cash to retire the bonds at maturity.

---

[6] Bond quotations are commonly expressed in this form. For example, a bond quoted at 101¼ can be bought or sold at 101.25% of its par value, plus accrued interest, if any. Broker's fees are added to this amount on purchases and deducted on sales.

[7] To understand how the periodic deposits to a sinking fund are calculated, study Appendix H at the end of the book. Using Table H–4, "Future Value of an Annuity of 1 per Period" in Appendix H, the payment of $69,029 is calculated as $1,000,000/14.4866 = $69.029.

ILLUSTRATION 16-8

Expected Asset Accumulation of a Bond Sinking Fund that Earns 8%

End of Year	Beginning-of-Period Sinking Fund Balance	8% Return Earned on Fund Balance	Amount Deposited	Total Increase in Sinking Fund	End-of-Period Sinking Fund Balance
1993	$ -0-	$ -0-	$ 69,029	$ 69,029	$ 69,029
1994	69,029	5,522	69,029	74,551	143,580
1995	143,580	11,486	69,029	80,515	224,095
1996	224,095	17,928	69,029	86,957	311,052
1997	311,052	24,884	69,029	93,913	404,965
1998	404,965	32,397	69,029	101,426	506,391
1999	506,391	40,511	69,029	109,540	615,931
2000	615,931	49,274	69,029	118,303	734,234
2001	734,234	58,739	69,029	127,768	862,002
2002	862,002	68,969*	69,029	137,998	1,000,000
Total		$309,710	$690,290	$1,000,000	

* Adjusted to compensate for accumulated rounding of amounts.

The entry to record the amount deposited each year appears as follows:

Dec.	31	Bond Sinking Fund	69,029.00	
		Cash		69,029.00
		To record the annual sinking fund deposit.		

The sinking fund trustee invests the deposits and sends the issuing corporation a report of the earnings on the investments at least once each year. The corporation then records the sinking fund earnings in its accounts and reports them on its income statement. For example, if 8% is earned during 1994, the corporation records the sinking fund earnings as follows:

1994				
Dec.	31	Bond Sinking Fund	5,522.00	
		Sinking Fund Earnings		5,522.00
		To record the sinking fund earnings.		

When sinking fund bonds mature, the trustee converts the fund's assets into cash and pays the par value of the bonds to the bondholders. When the sinking fund assets are sold, the amount of cash generated is often a little more or a little less than is needed to pay the bondholders. If excess cash is produced, it is returned to the corporation. If there is not enough, the corporation must make up the deficiency.

For example, if the securities in the sinking fund of a $1 million bond issue produce $1,010,325 when converted to cash, the trustee uses $1 million to pay the bondholders and returns the extra $10,325 to the corporation. The corporation then records the payment of its bonds and the return of the extra cash with this entry:

Jan.	3	Cash	10,325.00	
		Bonds Payable	1,000,000.00	
		Bond Sinking Fund		1,010,325.00
		To record payment of bonds and the return of extra cash from the sinking fund.		

Restrictions on Dividends Due to Outstanding Bonds

To protect a corporation's financial position and the interests of its bondholders, a bond indenture may restrict the dividends the corporation may pay while its bonds are outstanding. Commonly, the restriction provides that the corporation may pay dividends in any year only to the extent that the year's earnings exceed sinking fund requirements.

Converting Bonds to Stock

To make a bond issue more attractive, bondholders may be given the right to exchange their bonds for a fixed number of shares of the issuing company's common stock. Such **convertible bonds** offer investors initial investment security, and if the issuing company prospers and its stock increases in price, an opportunity to share in the prosperity by converting their bonds to the more valuable stock. Conversion is at the bondholders' option and therefore does not take place unless it is to their advantage. However, most convertible bonds also are callable bonds. Thus, if the common stock price rises enough to make conversion more attractive than being paid the call price, the issuing corporation can force bondholders to convert. To do this, the issuing corporation simply announces that the bonds are being called if the bondholders do not convert them without delay.

When bonds are converted into stock, the conversion changes a liability into owners' equity. The typical method of recording a conversion of bonds into stock transfers the carrying value of the converted bonds to contributed capital accounts. No gain or loss is recognized. For example, assume the following: (1) A company has outstanding $1 million of bonds on which there is $8,000 unamortized discount. (2) The bonds are convertible at the rate of a $1,000 bond for 90 shares of the company's $10 par value common stock. And (3), bonds with a par value of $100,000 have been presented for conversion on their interest date. The entry to record the conversion is:

May	1	Bonds Payable	100,000.00	
		Discount on Bonds Payable		800.00
		Common Stock		90,000.00
		Contributed Capital in Excess of Par Value, Common Stock		9,200.00
		To record the conversion of bonds.		

Note in this entry that the bonds' $99,200 carrying amount sets the accounting value for the capital contributed.

AS A MATTER OF

Fact

Wall Street Awaits Refinancing Boom as Interest Rates Show Sharp Decline

Your Money Matters

When does a 30-year bond turn into a 10-year bond or even a 5-year bond?

When the bond is "called," or redeemed before its maturity.

That's happening more and more, as states, municipalities, and corporations take advantage of today's low interest rates to refinance huge amounts of long-term debt. And it's bad news for bond investors.

At best, a call means that people who bought bonds for their retirement or their kids' college education will get their money back and be forced to reinvest the funds at a lower rate. "Nobody wants to see a bond yielding 10% called and receive principal back when bonds are yielding 6.5%," says Jeffrey Kratz, head of investor relations at John Nuveen & Co. in Chicago.

Paying a Premium

But people who bought high-yielding bonds or unit investment trusts at a premium—paying more than face value to get a higher yield investment—fare even worse. In addition to the lost investment opportunity, they actually lose money. That's because the bonds are typically called at par, costing investors the premium.

"The easiest way to get killed is if you paid a premium," says Herbert Davidson, vice president of fixed income at Financial Management Group Inc. in McLean, Va.

Holders of zero-coupon bonds are another group getting badly hurt by calls. These bonds sell at a deep discount, with the price curve rising as the bond gets closer to maturity. But when a zero is called, its value is still discounted and "the yields you hoped to earn turn out to be illusionary," says Mr. Davidson.

With interest rates continuing to head down, it's not just holders of the 10% or 12% bonds issued in the early 1980s that are being affected. "At 8.5% and upwards, look out," says Richard Lehmann, president of the Bond Investors Association, Miami Lakes, Fla. "And the lower rates get, the more this thing will accelerate."

A bond issuer usually retains the right to call the bond, albeit at a premium, after 10 years. The bond can usually be called at par a few years later. There are other sorts of calls, as well. Housing bonds, for example, are usually written with "extraordinary redemption features," meaning they can be redeemed at any time for a very wide range of reasons.

While call provisions are spelled out in the offering documents for bond issues, investors can still be caught unaware.

* * *

When bonds are called, most holders receive the unpleasant news by mail. But people who own bearer bonds—where the owner's name is nowhere on record—usually don't find out until they try to cash their next interest coupon at the bank, often months after the bond has been called. That means they can end up losing months of interest payments.

"At any one point in time, there are $100 million to $200 million in bearer bonds still outstanding held by people who did not hear about a call," says Robert Lamb [a New York University professor of municipal finance]. To protect themselves, he says holders of bearer bonds should either put their bonds with a broker or a depository so they can be informed of calls.

* * *

When shopping for new bonds, investors should be aware that call protection isn't what it used to be. With lower interest rates and heavy demand for bonds, "issuers can get away with shorter call features," says James F. Lynch, editor of the Lynch Municipal Bond Advisory in Santa Fe, N.M.

That means that the first call date on a bond may be only 7 or 8 years from issue, rather than the traditional 10 years. Some bonds can be called even sooner—with housing bonds, it can be as early as 12 to 36 months from issue.

And remember, while brokers may quote you an attractive yield to maturity, the only meaningful figure in today's market is yield to first call. Use that figure when making your investments, and you're less likely to be surprised.

Source: Lynn Asinof, "Bond Calls Leave Investors Hung Up," *The Wall Street Journal,* October 3, 1991, pp. C1, C18. Reprinted by permission of *The Wall Street Journal,*

Investments in Bonds

LO 6 Describe the procedures used to account for investments in bonds.

So far in this chapter, our discussion of bonds has focused on the issuing corporation. We now shift our attention to the purchasers of bonds. Bonds purchased as an investment are recorded at cost, including any broker's fees. If interest has accrued at the date of purchase, the purchaser also pays for the accrued interest and records it with a debit to Interest Receivable. The following entry records a purchase of $50,000 of 9%, 10-year bonds on May 1, 1993, four months after their initial issuance, at the price of 92, plus $400 of broker's fees:

1993				
May	1	Investment in AMCO Corporation Bonds	46,400.00	
		Interest Receivable	1,500.00	
		Cash		47,900.00
		Purchased fifty $1,000, 9%, 10-year bonds dated December 31, 1992, at a price of 92 plus a $400 broker's fee and accrued interest.		

The $46,400 cost of the bonds was their market value of $46,000 (92% × $50,000 par value) plus the $400 fee. This price created a discount of $3,600. Most bond investors do not record a discount (or a premium) in a separate account. The investment account is simply debited for the net cost. The accrued interest on May 1 was $1,500 ($50,000 × 9% × 4/12).

Short-Term Investments in Bonds

Assuming that AMCO Corporation pays interest semiannually on June 30 and December 31, the June 30, 1993, entry to record the receipt of interest from AMCO Corporation is as follows:

1993				
June	30	Cash	2,250.00	
		Interest Receivable.		1,500.00
		Interest Earned		750.00
		To record the first semiannual receipt of interest.		

This entry correctly reflects the fact that the purchaser owned the bonds for two months while the interest earned amounted to $750 ($50,000 × 9% × 2/12). However, recall that the bonds were purchased at a discount and then notice that this entry does not include any amortization of the discount. This practice is acceptable only if the bonds are held as a short-term investment. Under these conditions, the bond investment is reported at cost in the current asset section of the balance sheet. The market value of the bonds on the date of the balance sheet is also disclosed. For example, assume that the market value of the AMCO bonds is $49,000 on December 31, 1993. Thus, the investment would be reported as follows:

Current assets:	
Investment in AMCO Corporation bonds (market value is $49,000) . .	$46,400

When the bonds are sold, the gain or loss on the sale is calculated as the difference between the sale proceeds and cost.

Long-Term Investments in Bonds

What if the bonds are held to maturity as a long-term investment? Over the holding period, the market value of the bonds generally moves toward par value as the maturity date approaches. In a similar fashion, any discount or premium should be amortized so that the carrying value at maturity will equal the bonds' par value. This process also means that the interest earned in each period will include some discount or premium amortization. The procedures for amortizing a discount or premium on bond investments parallel those discussed and applied previously to bonds payable. The only difference is that the amortized discount or premium is debited or credited directly to the investment account.

Sales of Bonds by Investors

An investor who buys a bond might later decide to sell it after several months or years. The price at which the bond is sold is determined by the market interest rate for the bonds on the day of the sale. The market interest rate on the day of the sale determines the price because the new investor could get this current rate elsewhere. Therefore, the new investor discounts the right to receive the bond's face amount at maturity and the right to receive its interest for the remaining periods of life at the current market rate to determine the price to pay for the bond. As a result, since bond interest rates vary over time, a bond that originally sold at a premium may later sell at a discount, and vice versa. The seller should report a gain or loss for the difference between the proceeds of the sale and the bonds' carrying value as of the date of the sale.

Mortgages as Security for Notes Payable and Bonds

Earlier in this chapter, we said that some bonds are secured and some are unsecured. These arrangements are also possible for notes payable. When bonds (or notes) are unsecured, the obligation to pay interest and par (or principal) is equal in standing with other unsecured liabilities of the issuing company. If the company becomes financially troubled and is unable to pay its debts in full, none of the unsecured creditors has preference over any other.

The ability of a company to borrow money by issuing unsecured bonds (or signing an unsecured note) depends on the company's general credit standing. In many cases, a company cannot obtain debt financing without providing security to the creditors. In other cases, the rate of interest that creditors would charge to provide unsecured debt is very high. As a result, many notes payable and bond issues are secured by mortgages.

A **mortgage** is a legal agreement that helps protect a lender if a borrower fails to make the payments required by a note payable or bond indenture. A mortgage gives the lender the right to be paid out of the cash proceeds from the sale of the borrower's assets identified in the mortgage.

A separate legal document, called the **mortgage contract,** contains the terms of a mortgage. The mortgage contract is given to the trustee of the bond issue or to the lender along with the note payable. A mortgage contract normally requires the borrower to pay all property taxes on the mortgaged property, to keep the mortgaged property repaired, and to be sure that it is adequately insured. In addition, the mortgage normally grants its holder (the lender) the right to foreclose if the borrower fails to pay. In a foreclosure, a court either sells the property or grants possession of the mortgaged property to the lender who sells it. When the property is sold, the proceeds are first applied to court costs and then to the claims of the mortgage holder. The former owner of the property receives any cash that remains. Then, this amount may be used to pay the debts of the unsecured creditors.

Summary of the Chapter in Terms of Learning Objectives

LO 1. Installment notes typically require either of two alternative payment plans: (*a*) payments that include accrued interest plus an equal amount of principal or (*b*) payments that are equal in amount but consist of a declining amount of interest and an increasing amount of principal. If the second pattern is used, the payments are determined by dividing the amount borrowed (the present value of the payments) by the annuity table value for the interest rate and the number of payments.

LO 2. An installment note usually is given when a company borrows money from a single creditor. A bond issue, on the other hand, is divided into bonds that have a par value of $1,000 each so that many investors can participate in the issue. A share of stock represents an equity interest in a corporation while bonds and installment notes are liabilities of the corporation. A bond issue may consist of serial bonds, which mature at different points in time, or of bonds that all mature on the same date. Some of the latter are sinking fund bonds, for which a fund of assets is established to pay the bondholders the par value of the bonds at the maturity date. If bonds are registered, the name and address of each bondholder is recorded with the issuing corporation. In contrast, bearer bonds are payable to whoever holds, or bears, the bonds. Interest on bearer bonds is paid when coupons are detached and presented for payment. Mortgages secure some bonds, and other bonds, called *debentures,* are unsecured.

When bonds are sold between interest dates, the accrued interest is charged to the purchaser, who is then repaid that amount on the next interest payment date.

LO 3. The contract rate of interest is applied to the par value of bonds to determine the annual cash payment of interest, which is usually paid in two installments. The present value of a bond is determined by adding the present value of the interest payments and the present value of the par value.

When bonds are issued at a discount, the Bonds Payable account is credited for the par value of the bonds and the difference between the cash proceeds and the par value is debited to Discount on Bonds Payable. Each time interest is paid, part of the discount is amortized, with the effect of increasing interest expense above the amount of cash paid. The interest method of amortization is required by generally accepted accounting principles, but the straight-line method may be used if the results are not materially different from the interest method.

LO 4. When the market interest rate for a corporation's bonds is less than the contract rate, the bonds sell at a premium. The premium is recorded by the issuer in a separate account and is amortized over the life of the bonds in a manner similar to the amortization of bond discount.

LO 5. A corporation that issues sinking fund bonds makes periodic deposits of cash with a sinking fund trustee. The trustee invests the assets, reports the earnings to the issuing corporation, and uses the accumulated sinking fund assets to repay the bondholders on the maturity date of the bonds.

When convertible bonds are converted into common stock, the carrying value of the bonds is transferred to contributed capital accounts that relate to common stock. Generally, no gain or loss is recorded.

LO 6. The cost of a bond investment (including brokerage fees) is usually debited to an Investment in Bonds account without separately identifying any premium or discount on the investment. If held as a short-term investment, cash receipts of interest are recorded as interest earned, and no attempt is made to amortize the premium or discount on the bond investment. However, if bonds are held as a long-term investment, the difference between the cost and par value of the investment must be amortized. The methods used to amortize premiums or discounts on bond investments parallel the amortization of premiums or discounts on bonds payable.

Demonstration Problem

The Stanley Tile Company patented and successfully test-marketed a new product. However, to expand its ability to produce and market the product, the company needed $4 million of additional financing. On January 1, 1993, the company borrowed the money in the following ways:

1. Stanley signed an $800,000, 10% installment note that is to be repaid in five annual payments. Each payment is to include principal of $160,000 plus accrued interest. The payments will be made on December 31, 1993–97.
2. Stanley also signed a second $800,000, 10% installment note calling for five annual installment payments that are equal in amount. The payments will be made on December 31, 1993–97.
3. Stanley also issued three separate groups of five-year bonds, each of which has a face amount of $800,000. On January 1, 1993, the market interest rate for all three groups of bonds was 10% per year.
   a. Group A will pay 10% annual interest on June 30 and December 31, 1993–97.
   b. Group B will pay 12% annual interest on June 30 and December 31, 1993–97.
   c. Group C will pay 8% annual interest on June 30 and December 31, 1993–97.

Required

1. For the first installment note: (*a*) prepare an amortization schedule and (*b*) present the entry for the first installment payment on December 31, 1993.
2. For the second installment note: (*a*) calculate the amount of each installment payment; (*b*) prepare an amortization schedule; and (*c*) present the entry for the first installment payment on December 31, 1993.
3. For the 10% (Group A) bonds: present (*a*) the January 1, 1993, entry to record the issuance of the bonds and (*b*) the June 30, 1993, entry to record the first payment of interest.
4. For the 12% (Group B) bonds: (*a*) calculate the issuance price of the bonds; (*b*) present the January 1, 1993, entry to record the issuance of the bonds; (*c*) prepare a schedule that shows periodic interest expense and premium amortization using the interest method; (*d*) present the June 30, 1993, entry to record the first payment of interest; and (*e*) present a January 1, 1995, entry to record the retirement of the bonds at the contractual call price of $832,000.
5. For the 8% (Group C) bonds: (*a*) calculate the issuance price of the bonds; (*b*) present the January 1, 1993, entry to record the issuance of the bonds; (*c*) prepare a schedule that shows periodic interest expense and discount amortization using the interest method; and (*d*) present the June 30, 1993, entry to record the first payment of interest.

Solution to Demonstration Problem

Planning the Solution

- For the first installment note, prepare a table similar to the one in Illustration 16–1 and take the numbers for the entry from the first line.
- For the second installment note, divide the amount borrowed by the annuity table factor for 10% and five payments. Prepare a table similar to Illustration 16–2 and take the numbers for the entry from the first line.
- For the bonds in Group A, prepare the entries using the par value and the contractual interest.
- For the bonds in Group B, first calculate the present value of the bonds' cash flows using the market interest rate. Then, use the result to record the issuance. Next, develop an amortization table similar to Illustration 16–7 and take from it the numbers needed for the journal entry. Finally, use the table to get the carrying value as of the date of the retirement of the bonds, and use it in the journal entry.
- For the bonds in Group C, first calculate the present value of the bonds' cash flows using the market interest rate. Then, use the result to record the issuance. Next, develop an amortization table similar to Illustration 16–5 and take from it the numbers needed for the journal entry.

1. *a.* The amortization schedule for the first installment note:

Period Ending	Beginning Principal Balance	Periodic Payment	Interest Expense for the Period	Portion of Payment that Is Principal	Ending Principal Balance
12/31/93	$800,000	$ 240,000	$ 80,000	$160,000	$640,000
12/31/94	640,000	224,000	64,000	160,000	480,000
12/31/95	480,000	208,000	48,000	160,000	320,000
12/31/96	320,000	192,000	32,000	160,000	160,000
12/31/97	160,000	176,000	16,000	160,000	–0–
Total.		$1,040,000	$240,000	$800,000	

b. The entry for the first payment on this note on December 31, 1993:

1993				
Dec.		Interest Expense	80,000.00	
		Notes Payable	160,000.00	
		Cash		240,000.00
		Made first payment on installment note.		

2. *a.* Calculation of the dollar amount of the five equal payments for the second installment note:
From Table 12–2, the present value of $1 to be paid annually for five years, discounted at 10%, is $3.7908. Therefore:

Periodic payment = $800,000/3.7908 = $211,037

b. The amortization schedule for the second installment note:

Period Ending	Beginning Principal Balance	Periodic Payment	Interest Expense for the Period	Portion of Payment that Is Principal	Ending Principal Balance
12/31/93	$800,000	$ 211,037	$ 80,000	$131,037	$668,963
12/31/94	668,963	211,037	66,896	144,141	524,822
12/31/95	524,822	211,037	52,482	158,555	366,267
12/31/96	366,267	211,037	32,627	174,410	191,857
12/31/97	191,857	211,037	19,180*	191,857	–0–
Total.		$1,055,185	$255,185	$800,000	

* Adjusted to compensate for rounding.

c. The entry for the first payment on this note on December 31, 1993:

1993				
Dec.	31	Interest Expense	80,000.00	
		Notes Payable	131,037.00	
		Cash		211,037.00
		Made first payment on installment note.		

3. *a*. The entry for issuance of the 10% bonds on January 1, 1993:

1993				
Jan.	31	Cash	800,000.00	
		Bonds Payable, Group A		800,000.00
		Issued 10% bonds at face value.		

b. The entry for the first payment of interest on the bonds on June 30, 1993:

1993				
June	30	Interest Expense	40,000.00	
		Cash		40,000.00
		Paid interest on 10% bonds.		

4. *a*. Calculating the issue price of the 12% bonds:

Present value of \$800,000 to be paid after 10 periods, discounted at 5% (\$800,000 × 0.6139)	\$491,120
Present value of \$48,000 to be paid periodically for 10 periods, discounted at 5% (\$48,000 × 7.7217)	370,642
Present value of the bonds	\$861,762

b. The entry for issuance of the 12% bonds on January 1, 1993:

1993				
Jan.	1	Cash	861,762.00	
		Bonds Payable, Group B		800,000.00
		Premium on Bonds Payable, Group B		61,762.00
		Issued 12% bonds at a premium.		

c. The premium amortization table for the 12% bonds (interest method):

Period Ending	Beginning Carrying Amount	Interest Expense for the Period	Interest to Be Paid the Bondholders	Premium to Be Amortized	Unamortized Premium at End of Period	Ending Carrying Amount
6/30/93	\$861,762	\$ 43,088	\$ 48,000	\$ 4,912	\$56,850	\$856,850
12/31/93	856,850	42,843	48,000	5,157	51,693	851,693
6/30/94	851,693	42,585	48,000	5,415	46,278	846,278
12/31/94	846,278	42,314	48,000	5,686	40,592	840,592
6/30/95	840,592	42,030	48,000	5,970	34,622	834,622
12/31/95	834,622	41,731	48,000	6,269	28,353	828,353
6/30/96	828,353	41,418	48,000	6,582	21,771	821,771
12/31/96	821,771	41,089	48,000	6,911	14,860	814,860
6/30/97	814,860	40,743	48,000	7,257	7,603	807,603
12/31/97	807,603	40,397*	48,000	7,603	–0–	800,000
Total		\$418,238	\$480,000	\$61,762		

* Adjusted to compensate for accumulated rounding of amounts.

d. The entry for the first payment of interest of bonds on June 30, 1993:

Date		Account	Debit	Credit
1993				
June	30	Interest Expense	43,088.00	
		Premium on Bonds Payable, Group B	4,912.00	
		Cash		48,000.00
		Paid interest on 12% bonds.		

e. The entry that would be made on January 1, 1995, for the retirement of the 12% bonds at the contractual call price of $832,000:

Date		Account	Debit	Credit
1995				
Jan.	1	Bonds Payable, Group B	800,000.00	
		Premium on Bonds Payable, Group B	40,592.00	
		Gain on Retirement of Bonds		8,592.00
		Cash		832,000.00
		Retired 12% bonds at contractual call price of $832,000.		

5. *a.* Calculating the issue price of the 8% bonds:

Present value of $800,000 to be paid after 10 periods, discounted at 5% ($800,000 × 0.6139)	$491,120
Present value of $32,000 to be paid periodically for 10 periods, discounted at 5% ($32,000 × 7.7217)	247,094
Present value of the bonds	$738,214

b. The entry for issuance of the 8% bonds on January 1, 1993:

Date		Account	Debit	Credit
1993				
Jan.	1	Cash	738,214.00	
		Discount on Bonds Payable, Group C	61,786.00	
		Bonds Payable, Group C		800,000.00
		Issued 8% bonds at a discount.		

c. The discount amortization table for the 8% bonds (interest method):

Period Ending	Beginning Carrying Amount	Interest Expense for the Period	Interest to Be Paid the Bondholders	Discount to Be Amortized	Unamortized Discount at End of Period	Ending Carrying Amount
6/30/93	$738,214	$ 36,911	$ 32,000	$ 4,911	$56,875	$743,125
12/31/93	743,125	37,156	32,000	5,156	51,719	748,281
6/30/94	748,281	37,414	32,000	5,414	46,305	753,695
12/31/94	753,695	37,685	32,000	5,685	40,620	759,380
6/30/95	759,380	37,969	32,000	5,969	34,651	765,349
12/31/95	765,349	38,267	32,000	6,267	28,384	771,616
6/30/96	771,616	38,581	32,000	6,581	21,803	778,197
12/31/96	778,197	38,910	32,000	6,910	14,893	785,107
6/30/97	785,107	39,255	32,000	7,255	7,638	792,362
12/31/97	792,362	39,638*	32,000	7,638	–0–	800,000
Totals		$381,786	$320,000	$61,786		

* Adjusted to compensate for accumulated rounding of amounts.

d. The entry for the first payment of interest on the bonds on June 30, 1993:

1993				
June	30	Interest Expense	36,911.00	
		Discount on Bonds Payable, Group C		4,911.00
		Cash		32,000.00
		Paid interest on 8% bonds.		

Glossary

LO 7 Define or explain the words and phrases listed in the chapter glossary.

Bearer bond a bond that is made payable to whoever holds it (the bearer); this bond is not registered. p. 867

Bond a long-term liability of a corporation or governmental unit, usually issued in denominations of $1,000, that requires periodic payments of interest and payment of its par value when it matures. p. 865

Bond indenture the contract between the corporation that issued bonds and the bondholders; it states the obligations and rights of each party. p. 868

Bond sinking fund assets that are committed to be used for repaying the holders of bonds covered by a bond indenture that requires the fund to be created; the issuing company makes deposits to the fund, which is managed by an independent trustee; the fund is established to provide cash for repaying the bondholders when the bonds mature. pp. 881–83

Callable bond a bond that may be retired before maturity at the option of the issuing corporation. pp. 880–81

Carrying amount of bonds payable the net amount at which bonds are recorded in the issuer's accounts; equals the par value of the bonds less any unamortized discount or plus any unamortized premium. p. 872

Contract rate of bond interest the rate of interest specified in the bond indenture; it is applied to the par value of the bonds to determine the amount of interest to be paid each year. p. 870

Convertible bond a bond that may be exchanged for shares of its issuing corporation's stock at the option of the bondholder. p. 883

Coupon bond a bond that is issued with interest coupons attached to the bond certificate; the coupons are detached as they become due and are deposited with a bank for collection. p. 868

Debenture an unsecured bond that depends on the general credit standing of the issuing corporation. p. 868

Discount on bonds payable the difference between the par value of a bond and its issue price when the bond is sold for an amount less than its par value. p. 871

Face amount of a bond another term used to describe a bond's par value. p. 865

Installment notes promissory notes that require a series of payments, each of which consists of interest and a portion of the amount originally borrowed. pp. 861–65

Interest method of amortizing bond discount or premium a method of calculating interest expense for a period; it multiplies the bonds' beginning carrying value by the market rate of interest from the date of issuance; the periodic amortization of discount or premium equals the difference between the cash interest paid and the interest expense. pp. 874–75

Market rate for bond interest the rate borrowers are willing to pay and lenders are willing to accept for the use of money at the level of risk involved with that corporation's bonds. p. 870

Mortgage a legal agreement that helps protect a lender by giving the lender the right to be paid from the cash proceeds from the sale of the borrower's assets identified in the mortgage. pp. 886–87

Mortgage contract a legal document that states the rights of the lender and the obligations of the borrower with respect to assets pledged as security for a bond or note payable. p. 887

Par value of a bond the amount that the borrower agrees to repay at maturity and the amount on which interest payments are based; also called the face amount of the bond. p. 865

Premium on bonds payable the difference between the par value of a bond and its issue price when the bond is sold for an amount greater than its par value. p. 877

Registered bonds bonds that have the names and addresses of their owners recorded by the issuing corporation; interest payments are distributed by checks from the corporation to the owners. p. 867

Serial bonds an issue of bonds that mature at different dates, such that the total issue is repaid gradually over a period of years. p. 867

Sinking fund bonds bonds that require the issuing corporation to make deposits to a separate fund of assets during the life of the bonds; the bondholders are repaid at maturity from the assets in this fund. p. 867

Straight-line method of amortizing bond discount or premium a method that amortizes an equal amount of the original discount or premium in each accounting period in the life of the bonds. pp. 873–74

Synonymous Terms

Contract interest rate coupon rate; stated rate; nominal rate.

Principal of a bond par value; face value.

Objective Review

Answers to the following questions are listed at the end of this chapter. Be sure that you decide which is the one best answer to each question *before* you check the answers.

LO 1 When an installment note requires a series of payments that are equal in amount:

a. The interest expense for a given period is calculated by multiplying the face amount of the note by the interest rate.

b. The payments consist of an increasing amount of interest and a decreasing amount of principal.

c. The payments consist of changing amounts of the principal portion of the payment, but the interest portion of the payment remains constant.

d. The payments consist of changing amounts of interest, but the principal amount remains constant.

e. The portion of the payment that reduces principal is determined by multiplying the beginning-of-period principal balance by the interest rate and deducting that amount of interest expense from the payment.

LO 2 On May 1, a corporation sold $500,000 of 9% bonds on which interest is payable semiannually on each January 1 and July 1. If the bonds were sold at par value plus accrued interest, the entry to record the first semiannual interest payment on July 1 would include:

a. A debit to Interest Payable for $15,000.
b. A credit to Cash for $45,000.
c. A debit to Bonds Payable for $22,500.
d. A debit to Interest Payable for $7,500.
e. A credit to Interest Payable for $15,000 and a debit to Interest Expense for $22,500.

LO 3 What would be the selling price of 10% bonds that have a $100,000 par value and an eight-year life if interest is to be paid semiannually? Assume the market rate of interest is 12% and the bonds were sold six months before the first interest payment.

a. $100,000.
b. $ 89,900.
c. $ 86,050.
d. $115,644.
e. $110,836.

LO 4 On December 31, 1993, Cello Corporation received $109,444 from the sale of 16% bonds payable, $100,000 par value, interest payable June 30 and December 31. The bonds were sold to yield a 14% market rate of interest. Using the interest method, the entry to record the second payment of interest on December 31, 1994, would include a debit to Premium on Bonds Payable in the amount of:

a. $7,661.
b. $ 339.
c. $ 678.
d. $7,637.
e. $ 363.

LO 5 When the bond indenture requires the issuing corporation to establish a bond sinking fund:

a. The issuing corporation is usually required to make periodic cash deposits with a sinking fund trustee.
b. Interest and dividends earned from investing the assets in the sinking fund are credited to Sinking Fund Earnings and reported on the income statement of the issuing corporation.
c. The issuing corporation reports the accumulated amount of assets in the fund on its balance sheet as a long-term investment.
d. The final entry to retire the bonds with sinking fund assets may include a debit or credit to Cash if the total amount of sinking fund assets differs from the par value of the bonds.
e. All of the above.

LO 6 When an investor purchases corporate bonds:

a. Interest accrued on the date of purchase should be reported by the investor as interest earned.

b. And the purchase price includes a premium, the amount of interest earned and recorded in later periods will exceed the amount of cash received each period.

c. And the bonds are held as a long-term investment, any premium or discount on the investment must be amortized in the process of recording interest income.

d. The investment should be recorded at cost, excluding any brokerage fees.

e. And the bonds are held as a short-term investment, any premium or discount on the investment must be amortized in the process of recording interest income.

LO 7 A bearer bond is:

a. A bond for which the name and address of the owner are recorded by the issuing corporation.

b. An issue of bonds that mature at different points in time so that the entire bond issue is repaid gradually over a period of years.

c. A bond that may be exchanged for shares of its issuing corporation's stock at the option of the bondholder.

d. A bond that is not registered and is made payable to whoever holds the bond.

e. None of the above.

Questions for Class Discussion

1. What are two common payment patterns on installment notes?
2. How is the interest portion of an installment note payment calculated?
3. What is the difference between a note payable and a bond issue?
4. What is the primary distinction between a share of stock and a bond?
5. What advantages do bonds have over stock as a means of long-term financing?
6. What is a bond indenture? What are some of the provisions commonly included in an indenture?
7. What role is played by the underwriter when bonds are issued?
8. What is the function of the trustee on a bond issue?
9. Define or describe: (*a*) registered bonds, (*b*) coupon bonds, (*c*) serial bonds, (*d*) sinking fund bonds, (*e*) callable bonds, and (*f*) debenture bonds.
10. Why does a corporation that issues bonds between interest dates collect accrued interest from the purchasers of the bonds?
11. As it relates to a bond issue, what is the meaning of the phrase *contract rate of interest?* What is the meaning of the phrase *market interest rate for bonds?*

12. What determines market interest rates for bonds?
13. When the straight-line method is used to amortize bond discount, how is the interest expense for each period calculated?
14. When the interest method is used to amortize bond discount or premium, how is the interest expense for each period calculated?
15. If a $1,000 bond is sold at 98¼, at what price is it sold? If a $1,000 bond is sold at 101½, at what price is it sold?
16. If the quoted price for a bond is 97¾, does this price include accrued interest?
17. What purpose is served by creating a bond sinking fund?
18. How are bond sinking funds classified on the balance sheet?
19. Suppose that a bond issue matures when the sinking fund assets are insufficient for repaying the bondholders. Who makes up the deficiency before the bondholders are paid? If the sinking fund has more than enough cash to repay the bondholders at maturity, what happens to the excess?
20. Two legal documents are involved when a company borrows money in an arrangement secured by a mortgage. What are they and what is the purpose of each?
21. Why might a corporation issue convertible preferred stock or convertible bonds?
22. The financial statements for Federal Express Corporation are presented in Appendix K. On May 31, 1991, what amount of Federal Express's long-term debt was classified as a current liability?
23. Refer to the financial statements for Lands' End, Inc., presented in Appendix K. Assume that long-term debt consists solely of installment notes payable. What was the total amount of principal owed on these notes as of January 31, 1991?

Exercises

In solving the following exercises, round all dollar amounts to the nearest whole dollar. Also assume that none of the companies use reversing entries.

Exercise 16–1
Installment note with payments of accrued interest plus equal amounts of principal
(LO 1)

On December 31, 1993, Cleveland Cutlery Company borrowed $130,000 by signing a four-year, 11% installment note. The note requires annual payments of accrued interest plus equal amounts of principal on December 31 of each year from 1994 through 1997. Prepare journal entries to record the first payment on December 31, 1994, and the last payment on December 31, 1997.

Exercise 16–2
Installment note with equal payments
(LO 1)

On December 31, 1993, Custom Window & Door Company borrowed $80,000 by signing a five-year, 12% installment note. The note requires annual payments of $22,193 to be made on December 31. Prepare journal entries to record the first payment on December 31, 1994, and the second payment on December 31, 1995.

Exercise 16–3
Calculating installment note payments
(LO 1)

Rainbow Roofing Company borrowed $350,000 by signing a 10-year, 14% installment note. The terms of the note require 10 annual payments of an equal amount, the first of which is due one year after the date of the note. Calculate the amount of the installment payments, based on the present values contained in Table 12–2, page 625.

Exercise 16–4
Bonds sold between interest dates
(LO 2)

On April 30 of the current year, Salmonson Corporation sold $3 million of its 8.9% bonds at par plus accrued interest. The bonds were dated January 1 of the current year, with interest payable on each June 30 and December 31. (*a*) How many months of interest had accrued on these bonds when they were sold? (*b*) Give the entry to record the sale. (*c*) How many months of interest were paid on June 30 of the current year? (*d*) How many months of interest income did the bondholders earn during the first interest period? (*e*) Give the entry to record the first interest payment.

Exercise 16–5
Straight-line amortization of bond discount
(LO 3)

On June 1 of the current year, Tricon Corporation sold $2 million of its 10.4%, 20-year bonds. The bonds were dated June 1 of the current year, with interest payable on each December 1 and June 1. Give the entries to record the sale at 98½ and the first semiannual interest payment, using straight-line amortization for the discount.

Exercise 16–6
Calculating sales price of bonds sold at discount
(LO 3)

On September 1 of the current year, Computer Systems Corporation sold $1 million of its 10.5%, 10-year bonds at a price that reflected a 12% market rate for bond interest. Interest is payable each March 1 and September 1. Calculate the sales price of the bonds and prepare a general journal entry to record the sale of the bonds. (Use present value Tables 12–1 and 12–2, pages 623 and 625.)

Exercise 16–7
Interest method of amortizing bond discount
(LO 3)

Computer Systems Corporation of Exercise 16–6 uses the interest method of amortizing bond discount. Under the assumption that Computer Systems Corporation sold its bonds for $913,970 at the market rate of 12%, prepare a schedule with the column headings of Illustration 16–5 and present the amounts in the schedule for the first two interest periods. Also, prepare general journal entries to record the first payment of interest to the bondholders, the adjusting entry as of December 31, and the second payment of interest.

Exercise 16–8
Calculating sales price of bonds sold at premium
(LO 4)

Mirror Image Corporation sold $780,000 of its own 12%, seven-year bonds on October 1, 1993, at a price that reflected a 10% market rate of bond interest. The bonds pay interest each April 1 and October 1. Calculate the selling price of the bonds and prepare a general journal entry to record the sale. (Use present value Tables 12–1 and 12–2, pages 623 and 625.)

Exercise 16–9
Interest method of amortizing bond premium
(LO 4)

Assume that the bonds of Exercise 16–8 sold for $857,232 at the market interest rate of 10% and that Mirror Image Corporation uses the interest method to amortize the bond premium. Prepare general journal entries to accrue interest on December 31, 1993, and to record the first payment of interest on April 1, 1994.

Exercise 16–10
Retirement of bonds
(LO 5)

Amstead Construction Corporation sold $1.2 million of its 9.9%, 20-year bonds at 97¾ on their date of issue, January 1, 1993. Five years later, on January 1, 1998, after the bond interest for the period had been paid and 25% of the original discount on the issue had been amortized with the straight-line method, the corporation purchased and retired bonds with $200,000 par value on the open market at 101¾. Give the entry to record the purchase and retirement.

Exercise 16–11
Bond sinking fund
(LO 5)

On January 1, 1993, Dayton Paper Corporation sold $1.5 million of 15-year sinking fund bonds. The corporation is required to deposit $47,211 with the trustee at the end of each year in the life of the bonds. It expects to earn 10% on the assets in the sinking fund. (*a*) Prepare a general journal entry to record the first deposit of $47,211 with the trustee on December 31, 1993. (*b*) Prepare a general journal entry on December 31, 1994, to record the $4,721 earnings for 1994 reported to the corporation by the trustee. (*c*) After the final payment to the trustee, the sinking fund had an accumulated balance of $1,501,945. Prepare the general journal entry to record the payment to the bondholders on January 1, 2008.

Exercise 16–12
Convertible bonds
(LO 5)

Piper Corporation has outstanding $20 million of 9%, 20-year bonds on which there is $350,000 of unamortized bond premium. The bonds are convertible into the corporation's $1 par value common stock at the rate of one $1,000 bond for 200 shares of the stock, and $1 million of the bonds are presented for conversion.

Present an entry dated June 10 to record the conversion on the books of Piper Corporation.

Exercise 16–13
Bonds as temporary investments
(LO 6)

On May 1, 1993, Blanton Company purchased 75 USAM Corporation bonds dated December 31, 1992. Each bond has a par value of $1,000, a contract interest rate of 10%, and matures after 10 years. The bonds pay interest semiannually on June 30 and December 31. Blanton Company bought the bonds at 98½ plus accrued interest and a $1,000 brokerage fee. Blanton intends to hold the bonds as a temporary investment. Prepare journal entries for Blanton Company to record the purchase and the receipt of the interest payment on June 30, 1993.

Problems

In solving the following problems, round all dollar amounts to the nearest whole dollar. Also assume that none of the companies use reversing entries.

Problem 16–1
Installment notes
(LO 1)

On May 31, 1993, Myers Company borrowed $220,000 from a bank by signing a four-year, 14% installment note. The terms of the note require equal semiannual payments beginning on November 30, 1993.

Required

1. Calculate the size of the installment payments. (Use Table 12–2 on page 625.)
2. Complete an installment note amortization schedule for the Myers Company note similar to Illustration 16–2.
3. Prepare general journal entries to record the first and the last payments on the note.
4. Now, assume that the note requires payments of accrued interest plus equal amounts of principal. Prepare general journal entries to record the first and last payments on the note.

Problem 16–2
Straight-line method of amortizing bond discount
(LO 3)

Norcom Drug Corporation sold $1.2 million of its own 9.5%, five-year bonds on their date of issue, December 31, 1992. Interest is payable on each June 30 and December 31, and the bonds were sold at a price to yield the buyers a 10% annual return. The corporation uses the straight-line method of amortizing the discount.

Required

1. Calculate the price at which the bonds were sold. (Use present value Tables 12–1 and 12–2, pages 623 and 625.)
2. Prepare a bond discount amortization table similar to Illustration 16–4, but complete only the first two lines.
3. Prepare general journal entries to record the sale of the bonds and the first two interest payments.

Problem 16–3
Interest method of amortizing bond premium
(LO 4)

L&P Oil Corporation sold $5 million of its own 10%, 10-year bonds on December 31, 1992. The bonds were dated December 31, 1992, with interest payable on each June 30 and December 31, and were sold to yield the buyers a 9% annual return. The corporation uses the interest method of amortizing the premium.

Required

1. Calculate the price at which the bonds were sold. (Use present value Tables 12–1 and 12–2, pages 623 and 625.)
2. Prepare a bond premium amortization table similar to Illustration 16–7, but complete only the first two lines.
3. Prepare general journal entries to record the sale of the bonds and the first two interest payments.

Problem 16–4
Interest method of amortizing bond discount; bond sinking fund
(LO 3, 5)

Prepare general journal entries to record the following transactions of Turner Communications Corporation. Use present value Tables 12–1 and 12–2 (pages 000 and 000) as necessary, to calculate the amounts in your entries.

1992

Dec. 31 Sold $3.1 million of its own 11.6%, 10-year bonds dated December 31, 1992, with interest payable on each June 30 and December 31. The bonds sold for a price that reflected a 12% market rate of bond interest.

1993

June 30 Paid the semiannual interest on the bonds and amortized a portion of the discount calculated by the interest method.

Dec. 31 Paid the semiannual interest on the bonds and amortized a portion of the discount calculated by the interest method.

31 Deposited $160,312 with the sinking fund trustee to establish the sinking fund to repay the bonds.

1994

Dec. 31 Received a report from the sinking fund trustee that the sinking fund had earned $22,500.

2002

Dec. 31 Received a report from the sinking fund trustee that the bondholders had been paid $3.1 million on that day. Included was a $4,880 check for the excess cash accumulated in the sinking fund.

Problem 16–5
Straight-line method of amortizing bond premium; retirement of bonds
(LO 4, 5)

Prepare general journal entries to record the following bond transactions of Standard Corporation:

1993

Dec. 1 Sold $1.5 million par value of its own 12.6%, 10-year bonds at a price to yield the buyers a 12% annual return. The bonds were dated December 1, 1993, with interest payable on each June 1 and December 1.

31 Accrued interest on the bonds and amortized the premium for December 1993. Used the straight-line method to amortize the premium.

1994

June 1 Paid the semiannual interest on the bonds.

Dec. 1 Paid the semiannual interest on the bonds.

1995

Dec. 1 After paying the semiannual interest on the bonds on this date, Standard Corporation purchased one eighth of the bonds at 100½ and retired them. (Present only the entry to record the purchase and retirement of the bonds.)

Problem 16–6
Comparison of straight-line and interest methods
(LO 3, 4)

On December 31, 1992, Geneva Corporation sold $4 million of 10-year, 13.2% bonds payable at a price that reflected a 14% market rate of bond interest. The bonds pay interest on June 30 and December 31. Use present value Tables 12–1 and 12–2 (pages 623 and 625) as needed in calculating your answers.

Required

1. Present a general journal entry to record the sale of the bonds.
2. Present general journal entries to record the first and second payments of interest on June 30, 1993, and on December 31, 1993, using the straight-line method to amortize the premium or discount.
3. Present general journal entries to record the first and second payments of interest on June 30, 1993, and on December 31, 1993, using the interest method to amortize the premium or discount.
4. Prepare a schedule similar to the table in Illustration 16–6 on page 876. It should have columns for the beginning-of-period carrying amount, interest expense to be recorded, and interest expense as a percentage of carrying amount, as calculated under (*a*) the interest method, and (*b*) the straight-line method. In completing the schedule, present the amounts for the six-month periods ending on June 30, 1993, and December 31, 1993.

Problem 16–7
Bond Sinking Fund
(LO 6)

On January 1, 1993, the Palmgren Company entered into a bond covenant in which it agreed to accumulate $125,000 in a sinking fund by December 31, 1998. Management engaged the services of a trust company that agreed to pay 10% interest per year on the amount accumulated in the fund. The plan calls for six equal annual payments of $16,201 into the fund, starting on December 31, 1993, and ending on December 31, 1998.

Prepare a table similar to Illustration 16–8 showing the amount of annual earnings, the annual contribution, and the beginning and ending balances of the sinking fund for the years 1993 through 1998.

Problem 16–8
Analytical essay
(LO 3, 4, 5)

Review the transactions presented in Problem 16–4 for Turner Communications Corporation. Assume now that on December 31, 1992, the market rate of bond interest was 10% instead of 12%. Describe how the entries to record the sale of the bonds and the 1993 transactions are different as a result of this change in the facts.

Problem 16–9
Analytical essay
(LO 3, 5)

Review the transactions presented in Problem 16–4 for Turner Communications Corporation. Assume now that on December 31, 1992, Turner sold $3.1 million of its own 12%, 5-year bonds instead of 11.6%, 10-year bonds. Describe how the entries to record the sale of the bonds and the 1993 transactions are different as a result of this change in the facts.

Alternate Problems

In solving the following alternate problems, round all dollar amounts to the nearest whole dollar. Also assume that none of the companies use reversing entries.

Problem 16–1A
Installment notes
(LO 1)

Bisk Hardware Manufacturing Company financed a major expansion of its production capacity by borrowing $500,000 from a bank and signing an installment note. The five-year, 12%, $500,000 note is dated June 30, 1993, and requires equal semiannual payments beginning on December 31, 1993.

Required

1. Calculate the size of the installment payments. (Use Table 12–2 on page 625.)
2. Complete an installment note amortization schedule for the Bisk Hardware Manufacturing Company note similar to Illustration 16–2.
3. Prepare general journal entries to record the first and last payments on the note.
4. Now, assume that the note requires payments of accrued interest plus equal amounts of principal. Prepare general journal entries to record the first and last payments on the note.

Problem 16–2A
Straight-line method of amortizing bond premium
(LO 4)

On December 31, 1992, SONOS Corporation sold \$3.7 million of its own 12.9%, 10-year bonds. The bonds are dated December 31, 1992, with interest payable on each June 30 and December 31, and were sold to yield the buyers a 12% annual return. The corporation uses the straight-line method of amortizing the premium.

Required

1. Calculate the price at which the bonds were sold. (Use present value Tables 12–1 and 12–2, pages 623 and 625.)
2. Prepare a bond premium amortization table similar to Illustration 16–7, but complete only the first two lines.
3. Prepare general journal entries to record the sale of the bonds and the first two interest payments.

Problem 16–3A
Interest method of amortizing bond discount
(LO 3)

JBC Corporation sold \$800,000 of its own 9.7%, five-year bonds on their date of issue, December 31, 1992. Interest is payable on each June 30 and December 31, and the bonds were sold at a price to yield the buyers a 10% annual return. The corporation uses the interest method of amortizing the discount.

Required

1. Calculate the price at which the bonds were sold. (Use present value Tables 12–1 and 12–2, pages 623 and 625.)
2. Prepare a bond discount amortization table similar to Illustration 16–5, but complete only the first two lines.
3. Prepare general journal entries to record the sale of the bonds and the first two interest payments.

Problem 16–4A
Straight-line method of amortizing bond discount; bond sinking fund
(LO 3, 5)

Prepare general journal entries to record the following transactions of Dalcom Corporation. Use present value Tables 12–1 and 12–2 (pages 623 and 625), as necessary, to calculate the amounts in your entries.

1992

Dec. 31 Sold \$1.4 million of its own 8.7%, six-year bonds dated December 31, 1992, with interest payable on each June 30 and December 31. The bonds sold for a price that reflected a 9% market rate of bond interest.

1993

June 30 Paid the semiannual interest on the bonds and amortized a portion of the discount calculated by the straight-line method.

Dec. 31 Paid the semiannual interest on the bonds and amortized a portion of the discount calculated by the straight-line method.

31 Deposited $195,640 with the sinking fund trustee to establish the sinking fund to repay the bonds.

1994

Dec. 31 Received a report from the sinking fund trustee that the sinking fund had earned $19,600.

1998

Dec. 31 Received a report from the sinking fund trustee that the bondholders had been paid $1.4 million on that day. Included was a $4,770 check for the excess cash accumulated in the sinking fund.

Problem 16–5A
Interest method of amortizing bond premium; retirement of bonds
(LO 4, 5)

Prepare general journal entries to record the following bond transactions of Eco Paper Corporation:

1993

Oct. 1 Sold $2.8 million par value of its own 10.7%, five-year bonds at a price to yield the buyers a 10% annual return. The bonds were dated October 1, 1993, with interest payable on each April 1 and October 1.

Dec. 31 Accrued interest on the bonds and amortized the premium for October through December 1993. The interest method was used to amortize the premium.

1994

Apr. 1 Paid the semiannual interest on the bonds.

Oct. 1 Paid the semiannual interest on the bonds.

1995

Oct. 1 After paying the semiannual interest on the bonds on this date, Eco Paper Corporation purchased one fourth of the bonds at 101¾ and retired them. (Present only the entry to record the purchase and retirement of the bonds.)

Problem 16–6A
Comparison of straight-line and interest methods
(LO 3, 4)

On December 31, 1992, Trask Chemical Corporation sold $7 million of 10-year, 12.5% bonds payable at a price that reflected a 12% market rate of bond interest. The bonds pay interest on June 30 and December 31. Use present value Tables 12–1 and 12–2 (pages 623 and 625) as needed in calculating your answers.

Required

1. Present a general journal entry to record the sale of the bonds.
2. Present general journal entries to record the first and second payments of interest on June 30, 1993, and on December 31, 1993, using the straight-line method to amortize the premium or discount.

3. Present general journal entries to record the first and second payments of interest on June 30, 1993, and on December 31, 1993, using the interest method to amortize the premium or discount.
4. Prepare a schedule similar to the table in Illustration 16–6 on page 876. It should have columns for the beginning-of-period carrying amount, interest expense to be recorded, and interest expense as a percentage of carrying amount, as calculated under (*a*) the interest method, and (*b*) the straight-line method. In completing the schedule, present the amounts for the six-month periods ending on June 30, 1993, and December 31, 1993.

Problem 16–7A
Bond Sinking Fund
(LO 6)

On January 1, 1993, the Smith Company entered into a bond covenant in which it agreed to accumulate $400,000 in a sinking fund by December 31, 1999. Management engaged the services of a trust company that agreed to pay 15% interest per year on the amount accumulated in the fund. The plan calls for seven equal annual payments of $36,144 into the fund, starting on December 31, 1993, and ending on December 31, 1999.

Prepare a table similar to Illustration 16–8 showing the amount of annual earnings, the annual contribution, and the beginning and ending balances of the sinking fund for the years 1993 through 1999.

Problem 16–8A
Analytical essay
(LO 3, 4, 5)

Review the transactions presented in Problem 16–5A for Eco Paper Corporation. Assume now that on October 1, 1993, the market rate of bond interest was 13% instead of 10%. Describe how the entries to record the sale of the bonds and the December 31, 1993, accrual of interest are different as a result of this change in the facts.

Problem 16–9A
Analytical essay
(LO 4, 5)

Review the transactions presented in Problem 16–5A for Eco Paper Corporation. Assume now that on October 1, 1993, Eco sold $2.8 million of its own 10%, 10-year bonds instead of 10.7%, 5-year bonds. Describe how the entries to record the sale of the bonds and the December 31, 1993, accrual of interest are different as a result of this change in the facts.

Provocative Problems

In solving the following provocative problems, round all dollar amounts to the nearest whole dollar.

Provocative Problem 16–1
Sun Financial Company
(LO 2)

Sun Financial Company is planning major additions to its operating capacity and needs $4.5 million to finance the expansion. The company has been presented with three alternative proposals. Each involves issuing bonds that pay semiannual interest. The alternatives are

Plan A: Issue at par $4.5 million of 10-year, 12% bonds.
Plan B: Issue $5,094,000 of 10-year, 10% bonds.
Plan C: Issue $4,050,000 of 10-year, 14% bonds.

The market rate of interest for all of these bonds is expected to be 12%.

For each issue, calculate the expected cash outflow for interest for each six-month period, the expected cash proceeds from its sale, the interest expense for the first six-month period, and the amount that must be paid at maturity. Use the interest method to amortize bond premium or discount. Which plan has the smallest cash demands on the company prior to the final payment at maturity? Which requires the largest payment on maturity?

Provocative Problem 16–2
Capitol Tool Corporation
(LO 2)

The stockholders' equity of Capitol Tool Corporation includes 300,000 shares of outstanding common stock. Over the last three years, the corporation has earned an average of $0.60 per common share after taxes. To increase earnings, management is planning an expansion requiring the investment of an additional $1.8 million in the business. The cash is to be acquired either by selling an additional 180,000 shares of the company's common stock at $10 per share or by selling $1.8 million of 10%, 10-year bonds at par. Management predicts that the expansion will double the company's earnings (before taxes and any bond interest) in the first year after it is completed. Later years' earnings are expected to exceed the first year's earnings by another 25%. The company expects to continue to pay state and federal income taxes of 40% on its pre-tax earnings (after any bond interest).

Capitol Tool Corporation's management wants to finance the expansion in a manner that will serve the best interests of the present stockholders and has asked you to analyze the two alternatives from this perspective. Your report should describe the relative merits and disadvantages of the two proposed methods of financing the expansion. Prepare a schedule that shows expected after-tax earnings per share of common stock under each method.

Provocative Problem 16–3
Clark Corporation
(LO 3)

The Clark Corporation issued $1 million of zero-coupon bonds on January 1, 1993. These bonds are scheduled to mature after eight years on December 31, 2000. Clark Corporation will not make any periodic interest payments, but will simply pay out $1 million to the bondholders on the maturity date.

Part 1. Assume that the market priced these bonds to yield an annual compounded interest rate of 8%:

a. Determine the proceeds that Clark would realize from issuing these bonds.

b. Present the journal entry that would be made to record the issuance of these bonds.

c. Prepare a table showing the amount of interest allocated to each year in the bonds' life (use the interest method).

d. Present the journal entry that would be made to record the interest expense accrued for these bonds at December 31, 1993.

Part 2. Assume that the market priced these bonds to yield an annual compounded interest rate of 12%:

a. Determine the proceeds that Clark would realize from issuing these bonds.

b. Present the journal entry that would be made to record the issuance of these bonds.

c. Prepare a table showing the amount of interest allocated to each year in the bonds life (use the interest method).

d. Present the journal entry that would be made to record the interest expense accrued for these bonds at December 31, 1993.

Provocative Problem 16-4
International Business Machines Corporation
(LO 2, 5)

Turn to the debt footnote for International Business Machines Corporation in Appendix J. Use the information presented there to answer the following questions.

a. Has IBM issued any callable bonds? Any convertible bonds?

b. For the U.S. bonds and notes, what is the lowest interest rate? The highest?

c. For the U.S. bonds and notes, what is the earliest maturity date? The latest?

d. Are there any sinking fund bonds?

e. Were any new bonds issued during the year? Were any retired? How can you tell?

f. Identify bonds that were stated in currency from specific foreign countries. Which currencies are represented?

g. How much cash must be used to make sinking fund payments and to pay off bonds that mature in 1991? In 1993?

Answers to Objective Review Questions

LO 1	*(e)*	LO 4	*(e)*	LO 6	*(c)*
LO 2	*(a)*	LO 5	*(e)*	LO 7	*(d)*
LO 3	*(b)*				

PART

VII

Financial Statements: Interpretation and Modifications

Your study of Part VII will contribute a great deal to your ability to understand and use financial statements. You will learn about the statement of cash flows, which has only recently become required in public financial reports. Also, you will learn how businesses account for and report their investments in other companies and their operations in foreign countries. Finally, you will learn some important techniques used in analyzing financial statements.

Part VII consists of the following chapters:

CHAPTER

17

Statement of Cash Flows

Cash flows in and out of a company as the company makes sales, collects receivables, pays expenses, buys and sells assets, borrows cash, issues stock, repays debt, and pays dividends. Information about the cash generated and spent is useful for evaluating the past and predicting the future.

Topical Coverage

Cash is the lifeblood of a business enterprise. In a sense, cash is the fuel that keeps a business alive. With cash, employees and suppliers can be paid, loans can be repaid, and owners can receive dividends. But, without cash, none of these things can happen. In simple terms, a business must have an adequate amount of cash to operate. For these reasons, decision makers pay close attention to a company's cash position and the events and transactions causing that position to change. Information about the events and transactions that affect the cash position of a company is reported in a financial statement called the **statement of cash flows**. By studying this chapter, you will learn how to prepare and interpret a statement of cash flows.

Learning Objectives

After studying Chapter 17, you should be able to:

1. Describe the information provided in a statement of cash flows and classify the cash flows of a company as operating, investing, or financing activities.
2. Prepare a statement of cash flows in which cash flows from operating activities are reported according to the direct method and prepare a schedule of noncash investing and financing activities.
3. Calculate cash inflows and outflows by inspecting the noncash account balances of a company and related information about its transactions.
4. Prepare a working paper for a statement of cash flows so that cash flows from operating activities are reported according to the direct method.
5. Define or explain the words or phrases listed in the chapter glossary.

After studying Appendix G at the end of Chapter 17, you should be able to:

6. Calculate the net cash provided or used by operating activities according to the indirect method and prepare the statement of cash flows.
7. Prepare a working paper for a statement of cash flows so that the net cash flow from operating activities is calculated by the indirect method.

Why Cash Flow Information Is Important

Information about cash flows can influence decision makers in many ways. For example, if a company's regular operations bring in more cash than they use, investors will value the company higher than if property and equipment must be sold to finance operations. Information about cash flows can help creditors decide whether a company will have enough cash to pay its existing debts as they mature. And, investors, creditors, managers, and other users of financial statements use cash flow information to evaluate a company's ability to meet unexpected obligations. Cash flow information is also used to evaluate a company's ability to take advantage of new business opportunities that may arise. These are just a few of the many ways that different people use cash flow information.

The importance of cash flow information to decision makers has directly influenced the thinking of accounting authorities. For example, the FASB's objectives of financial reporting clearly reflect the importance of cash flow information. The FASB stated that financial statements should include information about:

- How a business obtains and spends cash.
- Its borrowing and repayment activities.
- The sale and repurchase of its ownership securities.
- Dividend payments and other distributions to its owners.
- Other factors affecting a company's liquidity or solvency.[1]

To accomplish these objectives, a financial statement is needed to summarize, classify, and report the periodic cash inflows and outflows of a business. This information is provided in a statement of cash flows.

Statement of Cash Flows

LO 1 Describe the information provided in a statement of cash flows and classify the cash flows of a company as operating, investing, or financing activities.

In November 1987, the FASB issued *Statement of Financial Accounting Standards No. 95,* "Statement of Cash Flows." This standard requires businesses to include a statement of cash flows in all financial reports that contain both a balance sheet and an income statement. The purpose of this statement is to present information about a company's cash receipts and disbursements during the reporting period.

Illustration 17–1 is a diagram of the information reported in a statement of cash flows. Note that the illustration shows three categories of cash flows: cash flows from operating activities, cash flows from investing activities, and cash flows from financing activities. Both inflows and outflows are included within each category. Because all cash inflows and outflows are reported, the statement reconciles the beginning-of-period and end-of-period balances of cash plus cash equivalents.

Direct Method of Presenting Cash Flows from Operating Activities

When preparing a statement of cash flows, you can calculate the net cash provided (or used) by operating activities two different ways. One is the **direct method of calculating net cash provided (or used) by operating activities.** The other is the indirect method. When using the direct method, you separately list each major class of operating cash receipts (for example, cash received from customers) and each major class of cash payments (such as payments for merchandise). Then, you subtract the payments from the receipts to determine the net cash provided (or used) by operating activities. The FASB encourages companies to use the direct method.

[1] FASB, *Statement of Financial Accounting Concepts No. 1,* "Objectives of Financial Reporting by Business Enterprises" (Norwalk, Conn., 1978), par. 49.

ILLUSTRATION 17–1

Categories of Information in the Statement of Cash Flows

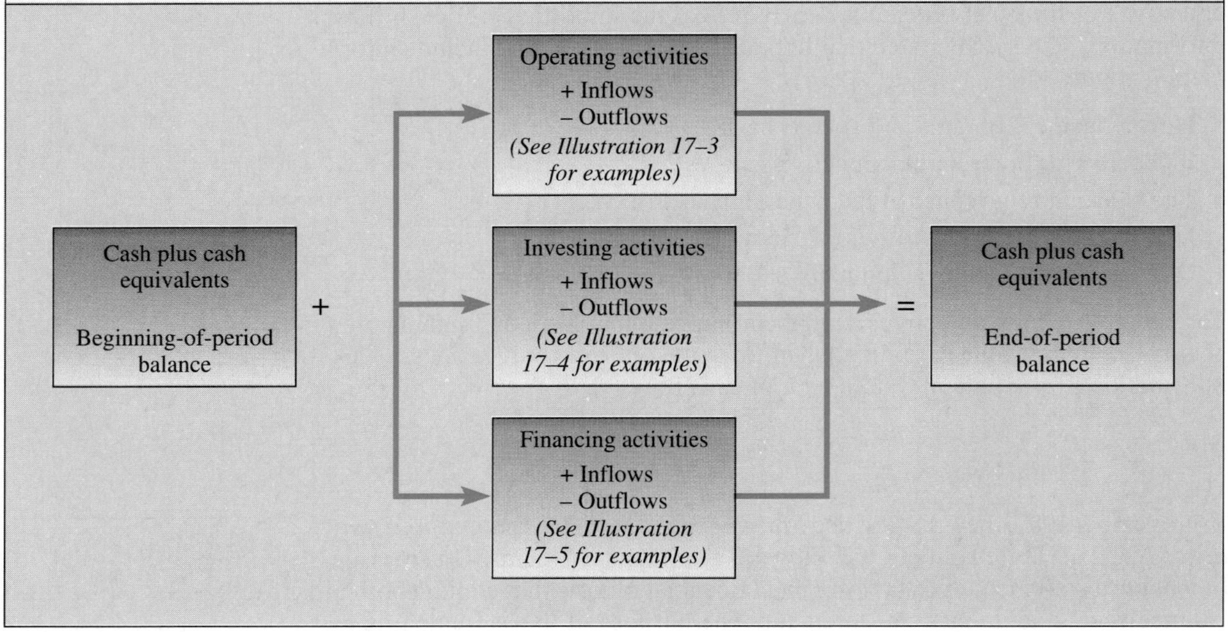

Indirect Method of Presenting Cash Flows from Operating Activities

The **indirect method of calculating net cash provided (or used) by operating activities** is not as informative as the direct method. The indirect method is not as informative because it does not disclose the individual categories of cash inflows and outflows from operating activities. Instead, the indirect method discloses only the net cash provided (or used) by operating activities.

When using the indirect method, list net income first. Next, adjust it for items that are necessary to reconcile net income to the net cash provided (or used) by operating activities. For example, in the calculation of net income, we subtract depreciation expense. However, depreciation expense does not involve a current cash payment. Therefore, add depreciation expense back to net income in the process of reconciling net income to the net cash provided (or used) by operating activities.

Because the direct method is most informative and is the method that the FASB recommends, the remainder of this chapter focuses on that approach. However, the indirect method is allowed, and most companies use that method in spite of the FASB's recommendation. Therefore, we explain and illustrate the indirect method in Appendix G at the end of this chapter.

The Format of the Statement of Cash Flows (Direct Method)

Illustration 17–2 shows the statement of cash flows for Grover Company. Notice that the major classes of cash inflows and cash outflows are listed separately in the operating activities section of the statement. This is the format of

ILLUSTRATION 17–2

GROVER COMPANY
Statement of Cash Flows
For Year Ended December 31, 1993

Cash flows from operating activities:		
Cash received from customers	$570,000	
Cash paid for merchandise	(319,000)	
Cash paid for wages and other operating expenses	(218,000)	
Cash paid for interest	(8,000)	
Cash paid for taxes	(5,000)	
Net cash provided by operating activities		$ 20,000
Cash flows from investing activities:		
Cash received from sale of plant assets	$ 12,000	
Cash paid for purchase of plant assets	(10,000)	
Net cash provided by investing activities		2,000
Cash flows from financing activities:		
Cash received from issuing stock	$ 15,000	
Cash paid to retire bonds	(18,000)	
Cash paid for dividends	(14,000)	
Net cash used in financing activities		(17,000)
Net increase in cash		$ 5,000
Cash balance at beginning of 1993		12,000
Cash balance at end of 1993		$ 17,000

the direct method. The operating cash outflows are subtracted from the operating cash inflows to determine the net cash provided (or used) by operating activities.

Also observe in Illustration 17–2 the other two categories of cash flows reported on the statement of cash flows. In both categories—investing activities and financing activities—we subtract the cash outflows from the cash inflows to determine the net cash provided (or used).

Compare the statement in Illustration 17–2 with the chart in Illustration 17–1. Notice that the beginning and ending balances are called *cash plus cash equivalents* in Illustration 17–1. However, in Illustration 17–2, the beginning and ending balances refer only to *cash*. The balances in Illustration 17–2 are called *cash* because Grover Company does not own any **cash equivalents.** However, this difference between the two illustrations raises the question: What are cash equivalents?

Cash and Cash Equivalents

In *Statement of Financial Accounting Standards No. 95,* the FASB concluded that a statement of cash flows should explain the difference between the beginning and ending balances of cash and cash equivalents. Prior to this new standard, cash equivalents were generally understood to be short-term, temporary

AS A MATTER OF

Opinion

Ms. Garza earned a BBA degree with a major in accounting at the University of Houston. Upon graduation she joined the audit staff of Ernst & Young where she specialized in bank auditing. She continued her education at The University of Texas at Austin, completing an MBA degree in 1982. Thereafter, Ms. Garza entered banking as a professional and executive lender. Presently, she is senior vice president and metropolitan manager of the Austin area, NationsBank of Texas, N.A.

Ms. Garza has served in a variety of public service positions with organizations such as United Way, the American Heart Association, and Easter Seals.

Mary E. Garza

After I left public accounting and entered the banking industry 10 years ago, there was not much emphasis placed on cash flow analysis. As a loan officer, the review of financial statements centered primarily on profitability. However, during the 10 years I have been in banking, there has been a shift in focus to the analysis of cash flows.

We now recognize that a lender must have a complete understanding of a borrower's cash flow in order to better assess both the borrowing needs and repayment sources. This requires historical and projected information about the major types of cash inflows and outflows.

The truth is that cash, and cash alone, is the source of repayment for all loans. Over the years, I have seen many companies, whose financial statements indicated good profitability, experience severe financial problems because the owners or managers lacked a good understanding of the companies' cash flow.

investments of cash. However, not all short-term investments meet the FASB's definition of cash equivalents. To qualify as a cash equivalent, an investment must satisfy these two criteria:

1. The investment must be readily convertible to a known amount of cash.
2. The investment must be sufficiently close to its maturity date so that its market value is relatively insensitive to interest rate changes.

In general, only investments purchased within three months of their maturity dates satisfy these criteria.[2] Examples of cash equivalents include short-term investments in U.S. Treasury bills, commercial paper (short-term corporate notes payable), and money market funds.

The idea of classifying short-term, highly liquid investments as cash equivalents is based on the assumption that companies make these investments to earn a return on idle cash balances. However, some companies have other reasons for investing in items that meet the criteria of cash equivalents. For example, an investment company that specializes in the purchase and sale of securities may buy cash equivalents as part of its investing strategy.

Sometimes, items that meet the criteria of cash equivalents are not held as temporary investments of idle cash balances. Companies that have such in-

[2] FASB, *Accounting Standards—Current Text* (Stamford, Conn., 1990), sec. C25.106. First published in *Statement of Financial Accounting Standards No. 95*, par. 8.

ILLUSTRATION 17–3

Cash Flows from Operating Activities

Cash Inflows	Cash Outflows
Cash sales to customers.	Payments to employees for salaries and wages.
Cash collections from credit customers.	Payments to suppliers of goods and services.
Receipts of cash dividends from stock investments in other entities.	Payments to government agencies for taxes, fines, and penalties.
Receipts of interest payments.	Interest payments, net of amounts capitalized.
Refunds from suppliers.	Cash refunds to customers.
Cash collected from a lawsuit.	Contributions to charities.

vestments are allowed to exclude them from the cash equivalents classification. However, the companies must develop a clear policy for determining which items to include and which to exclude. These policies must be disclosed in the footnotes to the financial statements and must be followed consistently from period to period.

Classifying Cash Transactions

On a statement of cash flows, cash and cash equivalents are treated as a single item. In other words, the statement reports the changes in cash plus cash equivalents. Therefore, cash payments to purchase cash equivalents and cash receipts from selling cash equivalents do not appear on the statement. All other cash receipts and payments are classified and reported on the statement as operating, investing, or financing activities. Within each category, individual cash receipts and payments are summarized in a manner that clearly describes the general nature of the company's cash transactions. Then, the summarized cash receipts and payments within each category are netted against each other. A category provides a net cash flow if the receipts in the category exceed the payments. And, if the payments in a category exceed the receipts, the category is a net use of cash during the period.

Operating Activities

Look at the cash flows classified as **operating activities** in Illustration 17–2. Notice that operating activities generally include transactions that relate to the calculation of net income. However, some income statement items are not related to operating activities. We discuss these items later.

As disclosed in a statement of cash flows, operating activities involve the production or purchase of merchandise and the sale of goods and services to customers. Operating activities also include expenditures that relate to administering the business. In fact, cash flows from operating activities include all cash flows from transactions that are not defined as investing or financing activities. Illustration 17–3 shows typical cash inflows and outflows from operating activities.

ILLUSTRATION 17–4

Cash Flows from Investing Activities

Cash Inflows	Cash Outflows
Proceeds from selling productive assets (for example, land, buildings, equipment, natural resources, and intangible assets).	Payments to purchase property, plant and equipment, or other productive assets (excluding merchandise inventory).
Proceeds from selling investments in the equity securities of other companies.	Payments to acquire equity securities of other companies.
Proceeds from selling investments in the debt securities of other entities, except cash equivalents.	Payments to acquire debt securities of other entities, except cash equivalents.
Proceeds from collecting the principal amount of loans.	Payments in the form of loans made to other parties.
Proceeds from the sale (discounting) of loans made by the enterprise.	

Investing Activities

Transactions that involve making and collecting loans or that involve purchasing and selling plant assets, other productive assets, or investments (other than cash equivalents) are called **investing activities.** Usually, investing activities involve the purchase or sale of assets classified on the balance sheet as plant and equipment, intangible assets, or long-term investments. However, the purchase and sale of short-term investments other than cash equivalents are also investing activities. Illustration 17–4 shows examples of cash flows from investing activities.

The fourth type of receipt listed in Illustration 17–4 involves proceeds from collecting the principal amount of loans. Regarding this item, carefully examine any cash receipts that relate to notes receivable. If the notes resulted from sales to customers, classify the cash receipts as operating activities. Use this classification even if the notes are long-term notes. But, if a company loans money to other parties, classify the cash receipts from collecting the principal of the loans as inflows from investing activities. Nevertheless, the FASB concluded that collections of interest are not investing activities. Instead, they are reported as operating activities.

Financing Activities

The **financing activities** of a business include transactions with its owners and transactions with creditors to borrow money or to repay the principal amounts of loans. Financing activities include borrowing and repaying both short-term loans and long-term debt. However, cash payments to settle credit purchases of merchandise, whether on account or by note, are operating activities. Payments of interest expense are also operating activities. Illustration 17–5 shows examples of cash flows from financing activities.

ILLUSTRATION 17–5

Cash Flows from Financing Activities

Cash Inflows	Cash Outflows
Proceeds from issuing equity securities (e.g., common and preferred stock).	Payments of dividends and other distributions to owners.
	Payments to purchase treasury stock.
Proceeds from issuing bonds and notes payable.	Repayments of cash loans.
Proceeds from other short- or long-term borrowing transactions.	Payments of the principal amounts involved in long-term credit arrangements.

ILLUSTRATION 17–6

Decco Company—Schedule of Noncash Investing and Financing Activities

The company issued 1,000 shares of common stock for the purchase of land and buildings with fair values of $5,000 and $15,000, respectively.

The company entered into a capital lease obligation of $12,000 for new computer equipment.

The company exchanged old machinery with a fair value of $7,000 and a book value of $8,000 for new machinery valued at $12,000. The balance of $5,000 was paid in cash.

Noncash Investing and Financing Activities

Some important investing and financing activities do not involve cash receipts or payments during the current period. For example, a company might purchase land and buildings and finance 100% of the purchase by giving a long-term note payable. Although this transaction clearly involves both investing and financing activities, we do not report it in the current period's statement of cash flows because it does not involve a cash inflow or outflow.

Other investing and financing activities may involve some cash receipt or payment but also involve giving or receiving other types of consideration. For example, suppose that you purchase machinery for $12,000 by paying cash of $5,000 and trading in old machinery that has a market value of $7,000. In this case, the statement of cash flows reports only the $5,000 cash outflow for the purchase of machinery. As a result, this $12,000 investing transaction is only partially described in the statement of cash flows.

In its 1987 pronouncement, the FASB concluded that the noncash portions of investing and financing activities should *not* be reported in the statement of cash flows. However, the Board recognized that noncash investing and financing activities are important events that should be disclosed. To accomplish this disclosure, a company may prepare a separate schedule of noncash investing and financing activities. Or, it can simply provide a narrative description of these activities. Illustration 17–6 shows an example of how a company might disclose its noncash investing and financing activities with a narrative.

In Illustration 17–6, notice that the last item describes an exchange of machinery. Following the requirements of the FASB, the schedule describes both the cash and noncash aspects of this transaction. The $5,000 cash payment is reported in Decco Company's statement of cash flows as an investing activity. Nevertheless, the schedule of noncash investing and financing activities includes both the cash and noncash aspects of the transaction.

Examples of transactions that must be disclosed as noncash investing and financing activities include the following:

- The retirement of debt securities by issuing equity securities.
- The conversion of preferred stock to common stock.
- The leasing of assets in a transaction that qualifies as a capital lease.
- The purchase of long-term assets by issuing a note payable to the seller.
- The exchange of a noncash asset for other noncash assets.
- The purchase of noncash assets by issuing equity or debt securities.

Preparing a Statement of Cash Flows

LO 2 Prepare a statement of cash flows in which cash flows from operating activities are reported according to the direct method and prepare a schedule of noncash investing and financing activities.

The information you need to prepare a statement of cash flows comes from a variety of sources. These include comparative balance sheets at the beginning and the end of the accounting period, an income statement for the period, and a careful analysis of each noncash balance sheet account in the general ledger. However, because cash inflows and cash outflows are to be reported, you might wonder why we do not focus our attention on the Cash account. For the moment, we should at least consider this approach.

Analyzing the Cash Account

All of a company's cash receipts and cash payments are recorded in the Cash account in the general ledger. Therefore, the Cash account would seem to be the logical place to look for information about cash flows from operating, investing, and financing activities. To demonstrate, review this summarized Cash account of Grover Company:

Summarized Cash Account

Balance, 12/31/92	12,000		
Receipts from customers	570,000	Payments for merchandise	319,000
Proceeds from sale of plant assets	12,000	Payments for wages and other operating expenses	218,000
Proceeds from stock issuance	15,000	Interest payments	8,000
		Tax payments	5,000
		Payments for purchase of plant assets	10,000
		Payments to retire bonds	18,000
		Dividend payments	14,000
Balance, 12/31/93	17,000		

In this account, the individual cash transactions are already summarized in major types of receipts and payments. For example, the account has only one debit entry for the total receipts from all customers. All that remains is to determine whether each type of cash inflow or outflow is an operating, investing, or financing activity and then place it in its proper category on the statement of cash flows. The completed statement of cash flows appears in Illustration 17–2 on page 917.

While an analysis of the Cash account may appear to be an easy way to prepare a statement of cash flows, it has two serious drawbacks: First, most companies have so many individual cash receipts and disbursements that it is not practical to review them all. Imagine what a problem this analysis would present for IBM, General Motors, Kodak, or Exxon, or even for a relatively small business. Second, the Cash account usually does not contain a description of each cash transaction. Therefore, even though the Cash account shows the amount of each debit and credit, you generally cannot determine the type of transaction by looking at the Cash account. Thus, the Cash account does not readily provide the information you need to prepare a statement of cash flows. To obtain the necessary information, you must analyze the changes in the noncash accounts.

Analyzing Noncash Accounts to Determine Cash Flows

LO 3 Calculate cash inflows and outflows by inspecting the noncash account balances of a company and related information about its transactions.

When a company records cash inflows and outflows with debits and credits to the Cash account, it also records credits and debits in other accounts. Some of these accounts are balance sheet accounts. Others are revenue and expense accounts that are closed to Retained Earnings, a balance sheet account. As a result, all cash transactions eventually affect noncash balance sheet accounts. Therefore, we can determine the nature of the cash inflows and outflows by examining the changes in the noncash balance sheet accounts. Illustration 17–7 shows this important relationship between the Cash account and the noncash balance sheet accounts.

In Illustration 17–7, notice that the balance sheet equation labeled (1) is expanded in (2) so that cash is separated from the other assets. Then, the equation is rearranged in (3) so that cash is set equal to the sum of the liability and equity accounts less the noncash asset accounts. The illustration then points out in (4) that changes in one side of the equation (cash) must be equal to the changes in the other side (noncash accounts). Part 4 shows that you can fully explain the changes in cash by analyzing the changes in liabilities, owners' equity, and noncash assets. This information is all that is needed to prepare a statement of cash flows.

This overall process has another advantage. The examination of each noncash account also identifies any noncash investing and financing activities that occurred during the period. As you learned earlier, these noncash items must be disclosed, but not on the statement of cash flows.

When beginning to analyze the changes in the noncash balance sheet accounts, recall that Retained Earnings is affected by revenues, expenses, and dividend declarations. Therefore, look at the income statement accounts to help explain the change in Retained Earnings. In fact, the income statement accounts provide important information that relates to the changes in several balance sheet accounts.

Illustration 17–8 summarizes some of these relationships between income statement accounts, balance sheet accounts, and possible cash flows. For example, to determine the cash receipts from customers during a period, adjust

ILLUSTRATION 17–7

Why an Analysis of the Noncash Accounts Explains the Change in Cash

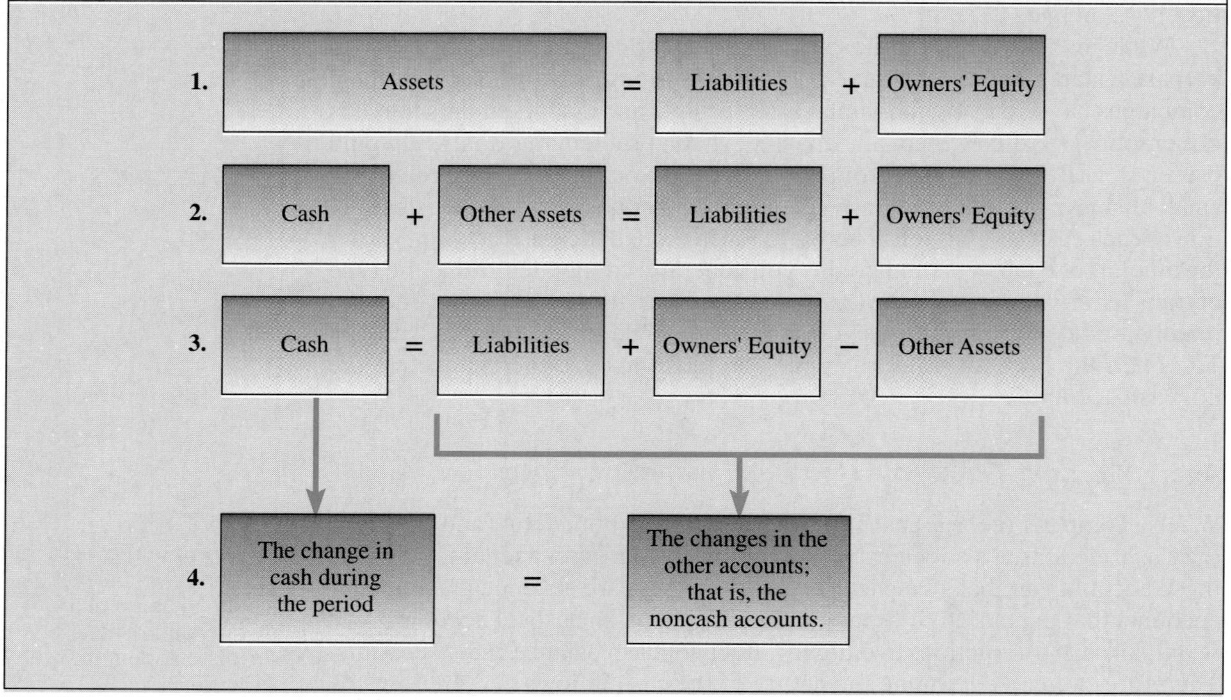

the amount of sales revenue for the increase or decrease in Accounts Receivable.[3] If the Accounts Receivable balance did not change, the cash collected from customers is equal to sales revenue. On the other hand, if the Accounts Receivable balance decreased, cash collections must have been equal to sales revenue plus the reduction in Accounts Receivable. And, if the Accounts Receivable balance increased, the cash collected from customers must have been equal to Sales less the increase in Accounts Receivable.

By analyzing all noncash balance sheet accounts and related income statement accounts in this fashion, you can obtain the necessary information for a statement of cash flows. So that you clearly understand this process, we illustrate it by examining the noncash accounts of Grover Company.

Grover Company: A Comprehensive Example

Grover Company's December 31, 1992 and 1993 balance sheets and its 1993 income statement are presented in Illustration 17–9. Our objective is to prepare a statement of cash flows that explains the $5,000 increase in cash, based on these financial statements and this additional information about the 1993 transactions:

[3] This introductory explanation assumes that there is no bad debts expense. However, if bad debts occur and are written off directly to Accounts Receivable, the change in the Accounts Receivable balance will be due in part to the write-off. The remaining change results from credit sales and from cash receipts. This chapter does not discuss the allowance method of accounting for bad debts since it would make the analysis unnecessarily complex at this time.

ILLUSTRATION 17–8

Key Relationships between Income Statement Items and Balance Sheet Accounts

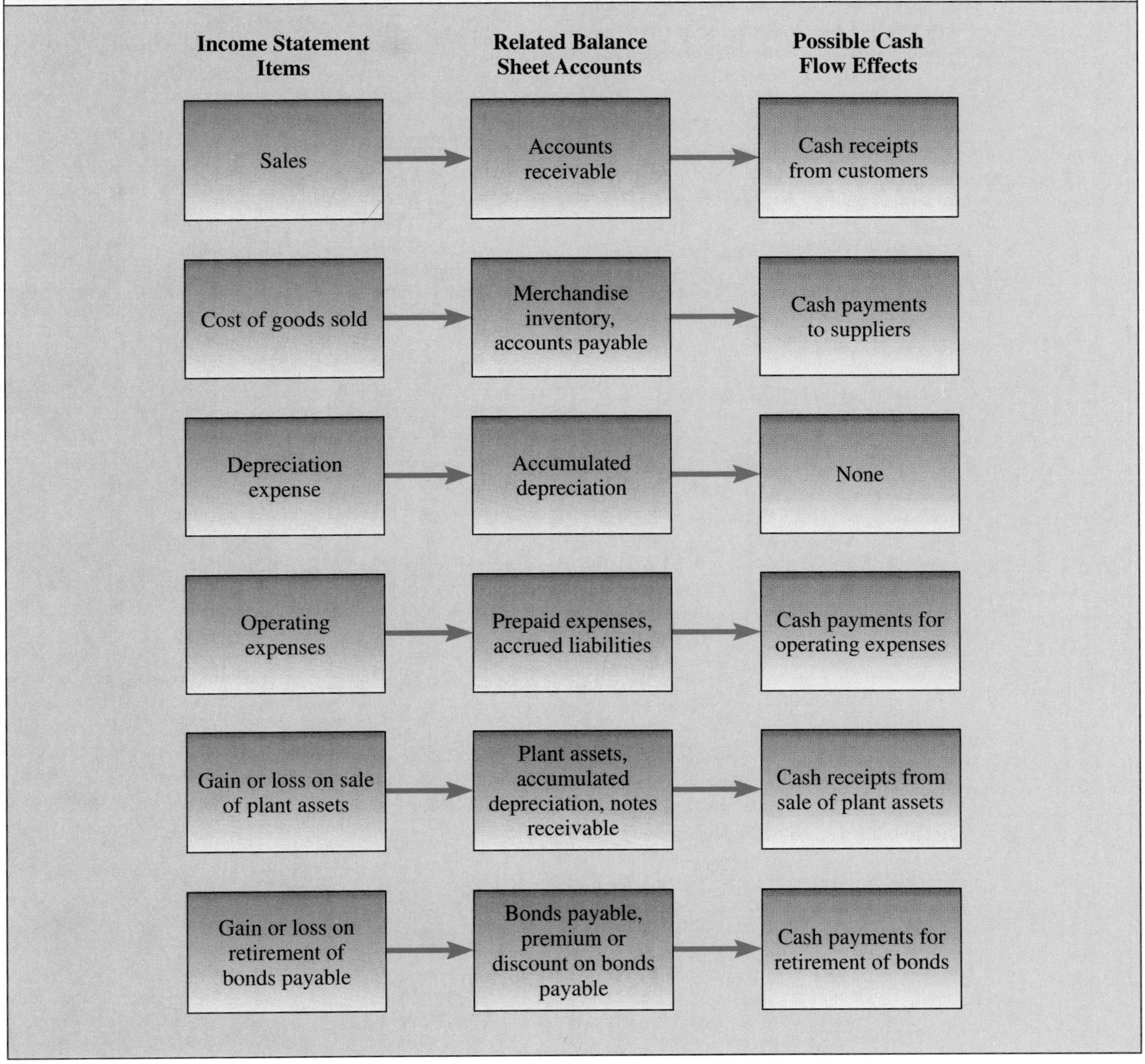

a. All accounts payable balances resulted from merchandise purchases.

b. Plant assets that cost $70,000 were purchased by paying $10,000 cash and issuing $60,000 of bonds payable to the seller.

c. Plant assets with an original cost of $30,000 and accumulated depreciation of $12,000 were sold for $12,000 cash. The result was a $6,000 loss.

d. The proceeds from issuing 3,000 shares of common stock were $15,000.

e. The $16,000 gain on the retirement of bonds resulted from paying $18,000 to retire bonds that had a book value of $34,000.

f. Cash dividends of $14,000 were declared and paid.

ILLUSTRATION 17–9

Financial Statements

GROVER COMPANY
Balance Sheet
December 31, 1993 and 1992

	1993		1992	
Assets				
Current assets:				
Cash		$ 17,000		$ 12,000
Accounts receivable		60,000		40,000
Merchandise inventory		84,000		70,000
Prepaid expenses		6,000		4,000
Total current assets		$167,000		$126,000
Long-term assets:				
Plant assets	$250,000		$210,000	
Less accumulated depreciation	60,000	190,000	48,000	162,000
Total assets		$357,000		$288,000
Liabilities				
Current liabilities:				
Accounts payable		$ 35,000		$ 40,000
Interest payable		3,000		4,000
Income taxes payable		22,000		12,000
Total current liabilities		$ 60,000		$ 56,000
Long-term liabilities:				
Bonds payable		90,000		64,000
		$150,000		$120,000
Stockholders' Equity				
Contributed capital:				
Common stock, $5 par value	$ 95,000		$ 80,000	
Retained earnings	112,000		88,000	
Total stockholders' equity		207,000		168,000
Total liabilities and stockholders' equity		$357,000		$288,000

GROVER COMPANY
Income Statement
For Year Ended December 31, 1993

Sales		$ 590,000
Cost of goods sold	$300,000	
Wages and other operating expenses	216,000	
Interest expense	7,000	
Income taxes expense	15,000	
Depreciation expense	24,000	(562,000)
Loss on sale of plant assets		(6,000)
Gain on retirement of debt		16,000
Net income		$ 38,000

Operating Activities

We begin the analysis by calculating the cash flows from operating activities. In general, this process involves adjusting the income statement items that relate to operating activities for changes in their related balance sheet accounts.

Cash Received from Customers. The calculation of cash receipts from customers begins with sales revenue. If all sales are for cash, the amount of cash received from customers is equal to sales. However, when sales are on account, you must adjust the amount of sales revenue for the change in Accounts Receivable to determine the cash received.

In Illustration 17–9, look at the Accounts Receivable balances on December 31, 1992, and 1993. The beginning balance was $40,000, and the ending balance was $60,000. The income statement shows that sales revenue was $590,000. With this information, you can reconstruct the Accounts Receivable account and determine the amount of cash received from customers, as follows:

Accounts Receivable

Balance, 12/31/92	40,000		
Sales, 1993	590,000	Collections =	570,000
Balance, 12/31/93	60,000		

This account shows that the balance of Accounts Receivable increased from $40,000 to $60,000. It also shows that cash receipts from customers are $570,000, which is equal to sales of $590,000 plus the $40,000 beginning balance less the $60,000 ending balance. This calculation can be restated in more general terms like this:

Cash received from customers = Sales − Increase in accounts receivable

And, if the balance of Accounts Receivable decreases, the calculation is:

Cash received from customers = Sales + Decrease in accounts receivable

Now turn back to Illustration 17–2 on page 917. Note that the $570,000 of cash Grover Company received from customers appears on the statement of cash flows as a cash inflow from operating activities.

Cash Payments for Merchandise. The calculation of cash payments for merchandise begins with cost of goods sold and merchandise inventory. For a moment, suppose that all merchandise purchases are for cash and that the ending balance of Merchandise Inventory is unchanged from the beginning balance. In this case, the total cash paid for merchandise equals the cost of goods sold. However, this case is not typical. Usually, you expect some change in a company's Merchandise Inventory balance during a period. Also, purchases of merchandise usually are made on account, causing some change in the Accounts Payable balance.

When the balances of Merchandise Inventory and Accounts Payable change, you must adjust cost of goods sold for the changes in these accounts to determine the cash payments for merchandise. This adjustment has two steps. First, combine the change in the balance of Merchandise Inventory with cost of goods sold to determine the cost of purchases during the period.[4] Second, combine the change in the balance of Accounts Payable with the cost of purchases to determine the total cash payments to suppliers of merchandise.

Consider again the Grover Company example. Begin by combining the reported amount of cost of goods sold ($300,000) with the Merchandise Inventory beginning balance ($70,000) and with the ending balance ($84,000) to determine the amount that was purchased during the period. To accomplish this, reconstruct the Merchandise Inventory account as follows:

Merchandise Inventory

Balance, 12/31/92	70,000		
Purchases =	**314,000**	Cost of goods sold	300,000
Balance, 12/31/93	84,000		

This account shows that we add the $14,000 increase in merchandise inventory to cost of goods sold of $300,000 to get purchases of $314,000.

To determine the cash paid for merchandise, adjust purchases for the change in accounts payable. This can be done by reconstructing the Accounts Payable account as follows:

Accounts Payable

		Balance, 12/31/92	40,000
Payments =	**319,000**	Purchases	314,000
		Balance, 12/31/93	35,000

In this account, purchases of $314,000 plus a beginning balance of $40,000 less the ending balance of $35,000 equals cash payments of $319,000. In other words, purchases of $314,000 plus the $5,000 decrease in accounts payable equals cash payments of $319,000.

To summarize the adjustments to cost of goods sold that are necessary to calculate cash payments for merchandise:

$$\text{Purchases} = \text{Cost of goods sold} \begin{bmatrix} + \text{ Increase in merchandise inventory} \\ \textit{or} \\ - \text{ Decrease in merchandise inventory} \end{bmatrix}$$

And,

$$\text{Cash payments for merchandise} = \text{Purchases} \begin{bmatrix} + \text{ Decrease in accounts payable} \\ \textit{or} \\ - \text{ Increase in accounts payable} \end{bmatrix}$$

Now, look at Illustration 17–2 on page 917. Notice that Grover Company's payments of $319,000 for merchandise are reported on the statement of cash flows as a cash outflow for operating activities.

[4] The amount of purchases is also in the Purchases account in the General Ledger.

Cash Payments for Wages and Other Operating Expenses. Grover Company's income statement shows wages and other operating expenses of $216,000 (see Illustration 17–9 on page 926). To determine the amount of cash paid during the period for wages and other operating expenses, we need to combine this amount with the changes in any related balance sheet accounts. In Grover Company's beginning and ending balance sheets in Illustration 17–9, look for prepaid expenses and any accrued liabilities that relate to wages and other operating expenses. In this example, the balance sheets show that Grover Company has prepaid expenses but does not have any accrued liabilities. Thus, the adjustment to the expense item is limited to the change in prepaid expenses. The amount of the adjustment can be determined by assuming that all cash payments of wages and other operating expenses were originally debited to Prepaid Expenses. With this assumption, we can reconstruct the Prepaid Expenses account as follows:

Prepaid Expenses

Balance, 12/31/92	4,000		
Payments =	**218,000**	Wages and other operating expenses	216,000
Balance, 12/31/93	6,000		

This account shows that prepaid expenses increased by $2,000 during the period. Therefore, the cash payments for wages and other operating expenses were $2,000 greater than the reported expense. Thus, the amount paid for wages and other operating expenses is $216,000 plus $2,000, or $218,000.

In reconstructing the Prepaid Expenses account, we assumed that all cash payments for wages and operating expenses were debited to Prepaid Expenses. However, this assumption does not have to be true for the analysis to work. If cash payments were debited directly to the expense account, the total amount of cash payments would be the same. In other words, the cash paid for operating expenses still equals the $216,000 expense plus the $2,000 increase in prepaid expenses.

On the other hand, if Grover Company's balance sheets had shown accrued liabilities, we would have to adjust the expense for the change in those accrued liabilities. In general terms, the calculation is as follows:

$$\text{Cash paid for wages and other operating expenses} = \text{Wages and other operating expenses} \begin{bmatrix} + \text{ Increase in prepaid expenses} \\ or \\ - \text{ Decrease in prepaid expenses} \end{bmatrix} \begin{bmatrix} + \text{ Decrease in accrued liabilities} \\ or \\ - \text{ Increase in accrued liabilities} \end{bmatrix}$$

Payments for Interest and Taxes. Grover Company's remaining operating cash flows involve cash payments for interest and for taxes. The analysis of these items is similar because both require adjustments for changes in related liability accounts. Grover Company's income statement shows interest expense of $7,000 and income taxes expense of $15,000. To calculate the related cash payments, adjust interest expense for the change in interest payable and adjust income taxes expense for the change in income taxes payable. These calculations are accomplished by reconstructing the liability accounts as follows:

Interest Payable

		Balance, 12/31/92	4,000
Interest paid =	8,000	Interest expense	7,000
		Balance 12/31/93	3,000

Income Taxes Payable

		Balance, 12/31/92	12,000
Income taxes paid =	5,000	Income taxes expense	15,000
		Balance, 12/31/93	22,000

These reconstructed accounts show that interest payments were $8,000 and income tax payments were $5,000. The general form of each calculation is:

$$\text{Cash Payment} = \text{Expense} \begin{bmatrix} + \text{ Decrease in related payable} \\ \textit{or} \\ - \text{ Increase in related payable} \end{bmatrix}$$

Both of these cash payments appear as operating items on Grover Company's statement of cash flows in Illustration 17–2 on page 917.

Investing Activities

Investing activities usually involve transactions that affect long-term assets. Recall from the information that was provided about Grover Company's transactions that the company purchased plant assets and also sold plant assets. Both of these transactions are investing activities.

Purchase of Plant Assets. Grover Company purchased plant assets that cost $70,000 by issuing $60,000 of bonds payable to the seller and paying the $10,000 balance in cash. The $10,000 payment is a cash outflow on the statement of cash flows (see Illustration 17–2). Also, because $60,000 of the purchase was financed by issuing bonds payable, this transaction involves noncash investing and financing activities. Therefore, it must be described in a schedule of noncash investing and financing activities or narratively in the financial statement footnotes. The schedule might appear as follows:

Schedule of noncash investing and financing activities:	
Purchased plant assets	$70,000
Issued bonds payable to finance purchase	60,000
Balance paid in cash	$10,000

Sale of Plant Assets. Grover Company sold plant assets that cost $30,000 when they had accumulated depreciation of $12,000. The result of the sale was a loss of $6,000 and a cash receipt of $12,000. This cash receipt is reported in the statement of cash flows as a cash inflow from investing activities (see Illustration 17–2).

Recall from Grover Company's income statement that depreciation expense was $24,000. Depreciation does not use or provide cash. Note, however, the effects of depreciation expense, the plant asset purchase, and the plant asset sale on the Plant Assets and Accumulated Depreciation accounts. These accounts are reconstructed as follows:

Plant Assets

Balance, 12/31/92	210,000		
Purchase	70,000	Sale	30,000
Balance 12/31/93	250,000		

Accumulated Depreciation, Plant Assets

		Balance, 12/31/92	48,000
Sale	12,000	Depreciation expense	24,000
		Balance, 12/31/93	60,000

The beginning and ending balances of these accounts were taken from Grover Company's balance sheets (Illustration 17–9). Reconstructing the accounts shows that the beginning and ending balances of both accounts are completely reconciled by the purchase, the sale, and the depreciation expense. Therefore, we did not omit any of the investing activities that relate to plant assets.

Financing Activities

Financing activities usually relate to a company's long-term debt and stockholders' equity accounts. In the information about Grover Company, four transactions involved financing activities. One of these, the $60,000 issuance of bonds payable to purchase plant assets, was discussed above as a noncash investing and financing activity. The remaining three transactions were the retirement of bonds, the issuance of common stock, and the payment of cash dividends.

Payment to Retire Bonds Payable. Grover Company's December 31, 1992, balance sheet showed total bonds payable of $64,000. Included within this balance for 1993 were bonds with a carrying value of $34,000 that were retired for an $18,000 cash payment during the year. The income statement reports the $16,000 difference as a gain. The statement of cash flows shows the $18,000 payments as a cash outflow for financing activities (see Illustration 17–2 on page 917).

Notice that the beginning and ending balances of Bonds Payable are reconciled by the $60,000 issuance of new bonds and the retirement of $34,000 of old bonds. The following reconstructed Bonds Payable account shows the results of these activities:

		Balance, 12/31/92	64,000
Retired bonds	34,000	Issued bonds	60,000
		Balance, 12/31/93	90,000

Receipt from Common Stock Issuance. During 1993, Grover Company issued 3,000 shares of common stock at par for $5 per share. This $15,000 cash receipt is reported on the statement of cash flows as a financing activity. Look at the December 31, 1992 and 1993 balance sheets in Illustration 17–9. Notice that the Common Stock account balance increased from $80,000 at the end of 1992 to $95,000 at the end of 1993. Thus, the $15,000 stock issue explains the change in the Common Stock account.

Payment of Cash Dividends. According to the facts provided about Grover Company's transactions, it paid cash dividends of $14,000 during 1993. This payment is a cash outflow for financing activities. Also, note that the effects of this $14,000 payment and the reported net income of $38,000 fully reconcile the beginning and ending balances of Retained Earnings. The following reconstructed Retained Earnings account shows this:

Retained Earnings

		Balance, 12/31/92	88,000
Cash dividend	14,000	Net income	38,000
		Balance, 12/31/93	112,000

We have described all of Grover Company's cash inflows and outflows and one noncash investing and financing transaction. In the process of making these analyses, we reconciled the changes in all of the noncash balance sheet accounts. The change in the Cash account is reconciled by the statement of cash flows, as seen in Illustration 17–2 on page 917.

Preparing a Working Paper for a Statement of Cash Flows (Direct Method)

LO 4 Prepare a working paper for a statement of cash flows so that cash flows from operating activities are reported according to the direct method.

When a company has a large number of accounts and many operating, investing, and financing transactions, the analysis of noncash accounts can be difficult and confusing. In these situations, a working paper can help organize the information needed to prepare a statement of cash flows. A working paper also makes it easier to check the accuracy of your work.

Designing the Working Paper

Examine the working paper for Grover Company in Illustration 17–10. Observe that the balance sheet account balances at the beginning and end of the period are entered in the first and fourth monetary columns, respectively. The middle two columns are used for reconciling the differences in these balances and for developing the statement of cash flows.

The process of reconciling the changes in the balance sheet accounts begins with the income statement. Enter the income statement below the balance sheet in the Analysis of Changes columns. Enter the revenues and gains in the Credit column and the expenses and losses in the Debit column. You will develop the statement of cash flows below the income statement. And, when noncash investing and financing activities are identified during the analysis, you will enter them in the very last lines of the working paper.

In Illustration 17–10, notice that the beginning and ending balances of each noncash balance sheet account are reconciled by the amounts in the Analysis of Changes columns. Look at the Cash account and note that the Analysis of Changes columns are empty. The reconciliation of the Cash account is not done on the Cash account row. Instead, the Cash account is reconciled by all of the items shown in the statement of cash flows section of the working paper.

Three characteristics of the working paper in Illustration 17–10 are particularly important: First, it provides the information needed to report cash flows from operating activities by the direct method. Second, it provides all the information necessary to prepare the statement of cash flows. To see this result, compare the statement of cash flows section of the working paper with the

ILLUSTRATION 17–10

GROVER COMPANY
Working Paper for Statement of Cash Flows (Direct Method)
For Year Ended December 31, 1993

	December 31, 1992	Analysis of Changes Debit		Analysis of Changes Credit		December 31, 1993
Balance sheet—debits:						
Cash	12,000					17,000
Accounts receivable	40,000	(*a1*)	590,000	(*a2*)	570,000	60,000
Merchandise inventory	70,000	(*b2*)	314,000	(*b1*)	300,000	84,000
Prepaid expenses	4,000	(*c2*)	218,000	(*c1*)	216,000	6,000
Plant assets	210,000	(*j1*)	70,000	(*g*)	30,000	250,000
	336,000					417,000
Balance sheet—credits:						
Accumulated depreciation, plant assets	48,000	(*g*)	12,000	(*f*)	24,000	60,000
Accounts payable	40,000	(*b3*)	319,000	(*b2*)	314,000	35,000
Interest payable	4,000	(*d2*)	8,000	(*d1*)	7,000	3,000
Income taxes payable	12,000	(*e2*)	5,000	(*e1*)	15,000	22,000
Bonds payable	64,000	(*h*)	34,000	(*j2*)	60,000	90,000
Common stock, $5 par value	80,000			(*k*)	15,000	95,000
Retained earnings	88,000	(*l*)	14,000	(*i*)	38,000	112,000
	336,000					417,000
Income statement:						
Sales				(*a1*)	590,000	
Cost of goods sold		(*b1*)	300,000			
Wages and other operating expenses		(*c1*)	216,000			
Interest expense		(*d1*)	7,000			
Income taxes expense		(*e1*)	15,000			
Depreciation expense		(*f*)	24,000			
Loss on sale of plant assets		(*g*)	6,000			
Gain on retirement of bonds				(*h*)	16,000	
Net income		(*i*)	38,000			
Statement of cash flows:						
Operating activities:						
Receipts from customers		(*a2*)	570,000			
Payments for merchandise				(*b3*)	319,000	
Payments for wages and other operating expenses				(*c2*)	218,000	
Payments for interest				(*d2*)	8,000	
Payments for taxes				(*e2*)	5,000	
Investing activities:						
Receipt from sale of plant assets		(*g*)	12,000			
Payment to purchase plant assets				(*j1*)	10,000	
Financing activities:						
Payment to retire bonds				(*h*)	18,000	
Receipts from issuing stock		(*k*)	15,000			
Payments of dividends				(*l*)	14,000	
Noncash investing and financing activities:						
Purchase of plant assets financed by bonds		(*j2*)	60,000	(*j1*)	60,000	
			2,847,000		2,847,000	

formal statement of cash flows in Illustration 17–2 on page 917. Third, the working paper also provides the information needed to disclose the noncash investing and operating activities.

Basic Steps to Prepare a Working Paper (Direct Method)

The information needed to prepare the working paper includes an income statement, the beginning and ending balance sheets, and other information about the activities of the period. Use the following six basic steps to prepare a working paper that includes enough information to report cash flows from operating activities by the direct method:

1. List the beginning balance sheet in the first column and the ending balance sheet in the fourth column. Debit balance accounts are listed first and credit balance accounts second. Total and prove the equality of the debits and credits in each balance sheet.
2. List each income statement item below the balance sheets and enter its amount in the Analysis of Changes column (debit for expense, credit for revenue). As you record each income statement credit, also record the corresponding debit next to the appropriate noncash balance sheet account. And as you record each income statement debit, record the corresponding credit next to the related noncash balance sheet account.

   After an income statement item is entered, analyze the changes in the noncash balance sheet accounts related to that income statement item. Illustration 17–8 on page 925 lists examples of these relationships. In the process of entering these changes, enter any cash flow effect in the statement of cash flows section of the working paper. [Entries *c1* and *c2* in Illustration 17–10 demonstrate this procedure for the operating expenses.]

   If an expense (or revenue) was paid (or received) in cash, it had no effect on any of the noncash balance sheet accounts. Therefore, if you record the expense (or revenue) in the income statement section of the working paper, enter the corresponding credit (or debit) as a cash outflow in the statement of cash flows section of the working paper.
3. As you enter income statement gains and losses, reconstruct the entries that created the gains or losses. These entries help reconcile the balance sheet accounts. Record the cash effects of gain and loss transactions as inflows or outflows in the investing or financing categories of the statement of cash flows.
4. Cross-reference the debits and credits of each entry by assigning them a letter (and number if more than one entry is needed to determine a specific cash flow). As you fill out the income statement and statement of cash flows sections of the working paper, leave some blank lines in each category to allow space for the rest of your analyses.
5. Review the entries for each balance sheet account to determine whether any differences between the beginning and ending balances remain unreconciled. If any remain, examine the additional information about the activities of the company and enter the necessary reconciling amounts in the Analysis of Changes columns.

6. To prove the arithmetic accuracy of your work, total the two middle columns and determine whether they are equal.

Entering the Analysis of Changes on the Working Paper

To help you understand the relationship between the items entered in the Analysis of Changes columns of the working paper and the facts of the Grover Company example, we will reexamine the information about the income statement and other transactions. For each item of information, a letter (and sometimes a number) corresponds to the entries on the working paper.

As you study the following information and the working paper in Illustration 17–10, clarify any items that appear confusing by reviewing the previous section of the chapter. Recall that we calculated and explained each cash flow by reconstructing the related noncash accounts.

Items *a1* and *a2* provide the facts and the analysis of changes that relate to receipts from customers.

a1. Sales revenue was $590,000. On the working paper, the analysis of the change labeled *a1* enters the sales revenue as a credit in the income statement section and as a debit to Accounts Receivable. This starts the reconciliation of the change in Accounts Receivable.

a2. Receipts from customers were the only source of decreases in Accounts Receivable. In the Statement of Cash Flows section of the working paper, the analysis of the change labeled *a2* enters the $570,000 of receipts from customers as an operating activity and as a decrease in Accounts Receivable. Note that this entry completes the reconciliation of the difference in Accounts Receivable between the two balance sheets.

Notice that the analysis of (*a1*) and (*a2*) assumes that all sales were on account. However, even if some sales were for cash, the analysis would correctly determine cash receipts from customers. Whether sales are for cash or on account, total cash receipts from customers equals sales revenue minus the increase (or plus the decrease) in Accounts Receivable.

Items *b1*, *b2*, and *b3* give the facts and the analysis of changes that relate to cash payments for merchandise.

b1. Cost of goods sold was $300,000. On the working paper, the analysis of change entry enters cost of goods sold in the income statement section with a debit and reduces Merchandise Inventory in the balance sheet section with a credit.

b2. Purchases of merchandise were on credit. On the working paper, this entry for $314,000 increases Merchandise Inventory and increases Accounts Payable. Note that Merchandise Inventory is now reconciled.

b3. The only decreases in Accounts Payable were payments to creditors. The entry labeled *b3* reconciles the Accounts Payable account and records the $319,000 cash payment for merchandise as an operating activity.

Items *c1* and *c2* provide the facts and the analysis of changes related to cash payments for wages and other operating expenses.

c1. Wages and other operating expenses were $216,000 and were paid in advance. On the working paper, entry *c1* records these expenses with a debit in the income statement section and a credit to the Prepaid Expenses account.

c2. Prepaid expenses increased by $2,000. Entry *c2* reconciles the Prepaid Expense account by showing a debit of $218,000. The credit is recorded as a cash outflow from operating activities in the lower section of the working paper.

Items *d1* and *d2* provide the facts and the analysis of changes related to payments for interest.

d1. Interest expense was $7,000. Under the assumption that all interest was accrued before being paid, entry *d1* debits Interest Expense and credits Interest Payable.

d2. Decreases in Interest Payable involved cash interest payments. Entry *d2* reconciles the Interest Payable account and classifies the $8,000 cash payment of interest as an operating activity.

Items *e1* and *e2* provide the facts and the analysis of changes related to payments for taxes.

e1. Income taxes expense was $15,000. Assuming that all taxes were accrued before being paid, entry *e1* records the expense with a debit and credits Income Taxes Payable.

e2. Payments of taxes were debited to Income Taxes Payable. Entry *e2* reconciles the Income Taxes Payable account and classifies the $5,000 cash payment of taxes as an operating activity.

Items *f*, *g*, *h*, and *i* provide the facts and the analysis of changes related to depreciation, the sale of plant assets, the retirement of bonds, and net income.

f. Depreciation expense was $24,000. Entry *f* records the expense and credits the Accumulated Depreciation account. This entry begins the reconciliation of Accumulated Depreciation. Notice that nothing appears in the operating cash flows section because depreciation expense does not involve a cash outflow.

g. Plant assets with an original cost of $30,000 and accumulated depreciation of $12,000 were sold for $12,000 cash. The result was a $6,000 loss. Entry *g* decreases Plant Assets by $30,000, completes the reconciliation of Accumulated Depreciation with a $12,000 debit, enters the $6,000 loss in the income statement section, and classifies the $12,000 cash receipt from sale of plant assets as an investing activity.

h. The $16,000 gain on retirement of bonds resulted from paying $18,000 to retire bonds with a book value of $34,000. Entry *h* decreases bonds payable by $34,000, enters the $16,000 gain in the income statement section, and classifies the $18,000 cash payment to retire bonds as a financing activity.

i. Net income was $38,000. Entry *i* completes the income statement section and helps start the reconciliation of Retained Earnings.

Items *j1* and *j2* provide the facts and the analysis of changes related to the purchase of plant assets, the issuance of bonds payable to finance part of the purchase, and the remaining cash payment to purchase plant assets.

j1. Plant assets that cost $70,000 were purchased by paying $10,000 cash and issuing $60,000 of bonds payable. Entry *j1* completes the reconciliation of Plant Assets, classifies the cash payment as an investing activity, and classifies $60,000 of the purchase as part of a noncash investing and financing transaction.

j2. The issuance of $60,000 of bonds to purchase plant assets was recorded by increasing Bonds Payable. Entry *j2* completes the reconciliation of Bonds Payable and classifies the bond issuance as part of a noncash investing and financing transaction.

Item *k* records the effects of issuing common stock, and item *l* records the effects of the cash dividend declared and paid to the stockholders.

k. The proceeds from issuing 3,000 shares of common stock were $15,000. Entry *k* reconciles the Common Stock account and classifies the receipt from issuing stock as a financing activity.

l. Cash dividends of $14,000 were declared and paid. Entry *l* completes the reconciliation of Retained Earnings and classifies the payment of dividends as a financing activity.

After all the analyses are performed, note that the balance of each *noncash* balance sheet account is completely reconciled. The Analysis of Changes columns can now be totaled to determine whether they are equal.

Reconciling Net Income to Net Cash Provided (or Used) by Operating Activities

As you learned earlier, the FASB recommends that the operating activities section of the statement of cash flows be prepared according to the direct method. Under this method, the statement reports each major class of cash inflows and outflows from operating activities. *However, when the direct method is used, the FASB also requires that companies disclose a reconciliation of net income to the net cash provided (or used) by operating activities.* This reconciliation is precisely what is accomplished by the *indirect* method of calculating the net cash provided (or used) by operating activities. Appendix G at the end of this chapter explains the indirect method.

Summary of Chapter in Terms of Learning Objectives

LO 1. The statement of cash flows reports cash receipts and disbursements as operating, investing, or financing activities. Operating activities include transactions related to producing or purchasing merchandise, selling goods and services to customers, and performing administrative functions. Investing activities include purchases and sales of noncurrent assets and short-term investments that are not cash equivalents. Financing activities include transactions with owners and transactions to borrow or repay the principal amounts of long-term and short-term debt.

LO 2. In using the direct method to report the net cash provided (or used) by operating activities, major classes of operating cash inflows and outflows are separately disclosed. On the statement, operating cash outflows are subtracted from operating cash inflows to derive the net inflow or outflow from operating activities. This method is encouraged by the FASB but is not required. A company must supplement its statement of cash flows with a schedule or narrative description of its noncash investing and financing activities. Two examples of these activities are the retirement of debt obligations by issuing equity securities and the exchange of a note payable for plant assets.

LO 3. Cash receipts and payments are recorded in the Cash account and in other noncash balance sheet accounts, or temporary accounts, such as revenues and expenses. The temporary accounts are closed to Retained Earnings. Therefore, to identify the cash receipts and cash payments, analyze the changes in the noncash balance sheet accounts created by income statement transactions and other events. For example, the amount of cash collected from customers is calculated by modifying sales revenues for the change in accounts receivable. Also, cash paid for interest is calculated by adjusting interest expense for the change in interest payable.

LO 4. On the working paper used to develop the statement of cash flows, enter the beginning and ending balances of each balance sheet account in the first and fourth columns. Then, enter the income statement items in the Analysis of Changes debit and credit columns. As each income statement item is credited or debited, the offsetting debit or credit is entered in the related noncash balance sheet accounts or in the statement of cash flows section. If a noncash current asset or current liability related to operations is involved, another entry must be made to completely reconcile its change and to record its related cash inflow or outflow. In this manner, the working paper identifies individual classes of cash receipts and payments, such as cash received from customers.

Demonstration Problem

The following summarized journal entries show the total debits and credits to the Pyramid Corporation's Cash account during 1993. Use the information to prepare a statement of cash flows for 1993. The cash provided (or used) by operating activities should be presented according to the direct method. In the statement, identify the entry that records each item of cash flow. Assume that the beginning balance of cash was $133,200.

a.	Cash	1,440,000.00	
	Common Stock, $10 par value		360,000.00
	Contributed Capital in Excess of Par Value, Common Stock		1,080,000.00
	Issued common stock for cash.		
b.	Cash	2,400,000.00	
	Notes Payable		2,400,000.00
	Borrowed cash with a note payable.		

c.	Purchases	480,000.00	
	Cash		480,000.00
	Purchased merchandise for cash.		
d.	Accounts Payable	1,200,000.00	
	Cash		1,200,000.00
	Paid for credit purchases of merchandise.		
e.	Wages Expense	600,000.00	
	Cash		600,000.00
	Paid wages to employees.		
f.	Rent Expense	420,000.00	
	Cash		420,000.00
	Paid rent for buildings.		
g.	Cash	3,000,000.00	
	Sales		3,000,000.00
	Made cash sales to customers.		
h.	Cash	1,800,000.00	
	Accounts Receivable		1,800,000.00
	Collected accounts from credit customers.		
i.	Machinery	2,136,000.00	
	Cash		2,136,000.00
	Purchased machinery for cash.		
j.	Investments	2,160,000.00	
	Cash		2,160,000.00
	Purchased investments for cash.		
k.	Interest Expense	216,000.00	
	Notes Payable	384,000.00	
	Cash		600,000.00
	Paid notes and accrued interest.		
l.	Cash	206,400.00	
	Dividends Earned		206,400.00
	Collected dividends from investments.		
m.	Cash	210,000.00	
	Loss on Sale of Investments	30,000.00	
	Investments		240,000.00
	Sold investments for cash.		
n.	Cash	720,000.00	
	Accumulated Depreciation, Machinery	420,000.00	
	Machinery		960,000.00
	Gain on Sale of Machinery		180,000.00
	Sold machinery for cash.		
o.	Common Dividend Payable	510,000.00	
	Cash		510,000.00
	Paid cash dividends to stockholders.		
p.	Income Taxes Payable	480,000.00	
	Cash		480,000.00
	Paid income taxes owed for the year.		

q.	Treasury Stock, Common	228,000.00	
	Cash		228,000.00
	Acquired treasury stock for cash.		

Solution to Demonstration Problem

Planning the Solution

- Prepare a blank statement of cash flows with sections for operating, investing, and financing activities.
- Examine each journal entry to determine whether it describes an operating, investing, or financing activity.
- Examine each journal entry to determine whether it describes an inflow or outflow of cash.
- Enter the cash effects of the entry in the appropriate section of the statement of cash flows, being sure to combine similar events, including *c* and *d*, as well as *g* and *h*.
- For entry *k*, identify the portions of the cash flow that should be assigned to operating and financing activities.
- Take subtotals of each section of the statement and determine the total change in cash.
- Add the net increase in cash to the beginning balance to get the ending balance.

PYRAMID CORPORATION
Statement of Cash Flows
For Year Ended December 31, 1993

Cash flows from operating activities:			
g, h.	Cash received from customers	$ 4,800,000	
l.	Cash received as dividends.	206,400	
c, d.	Cash paid for merchandise	(1,680,000)	
e.	Cash paid for wages	(600,000)	
f.	Cash paid for rent	(420,000)	
k.	Cash paid for interest	(216,000)	
p.	Cash paid for taxes.	(480,000)	
Net cash provided by operating activities			$ 1,610,400
Cash flows from investing activities:			
i.	Cash paid for purchases of machinery	$(2,136,000)	
j.	Cash paid for purchases of investments	(2,160,000)	
m.	Cash received from sale of investments	210,000	
n.	Cash received from sale of machinery	720,000	
Net cash used in investing activities			(3,366,000)
Cash flows from financing activities:			
a.	Cash received from issuing stock	$ 1,440,000	
b.	Cash received from borrowing	2,400,000	
k.	Cash paid for repayment of note payable. . . .	(384,000)	
o.	Cash paid for dividends	(510,000)	
q.	Cash paid for purchases of treasury stock . . .	(228,000)	
Net cash provided by financing activities			2,718,000
Net increase in cash			$ 962,400
Beginning balance of cash			133,200
Ending balance of cash			$ 1,095,600

APPENDIX

G

The Indirect Method of Calculating Net Cash Provided (or Used) by Operating Activities

LO 6 Calculate the net cash provided or used by operating activities according to the indirect method and prepare the statement of cash flows.

When using the indirect method, list net income first. Then, adjust net income to reconcile its amount to the net amount of cash provided (or used) by operating activities. To see the results of the indirect method, look at Illustration G–1. This illustration shows the reconciliation of Grover Company's net income to the net cash provided by operating activities.

In Illustration G–1, notice that the net cash provided by operating activities is $20,000. This same amount was reported on the statement of cash flows (direct method) in Illustration 17–2 on page 917. However, these illustrations show entirely different ways of calculating the $20,000 net cash inflow. Under the direct method in Illustration 17–2, we subtracted major classes of operating cash outflows from major classes of cash inflows. By comparison, we include none of the individual cash inflows or cash outflows under the indirect method in Illustration G–1. Instead, we modify net income to exclude those amounts included in the determination of net income but not involved in operating cash inflows or outflows during the period. Net income is also modified to include operating cash inflows and outflows not recorded as revenues and expenses.

Illustration G–1 shows three types of adjustments. The adjustments grouped under the section labeled (1) are for changes in noncash current assets and current liabilities that relate to operating activities. Adjustment (2) is for an item that relates to operating activities but that did not involve a cash inflow or outflow during the period. The adjustments grouped under (3) eliminate gains and losses that resulted from investing and financing activities. These gains and losses do not relate to operating activities.

ILLUSTRATION G-1

Grover Company—Reconciliation of Net Income to Net Cash Provided by Operating Activities

	Net income		
	Adjustments to reconcile net income to net cash provided by operating activities:		
(1)	Increase in accounts receivable	$(20,000)	
(1)	Increase in merchandise inventory	(14,000)	
(1)	Increase in prepaid expenses	(2,000)	
(1)	Decrease in accounts payable	(5,000)	
(1)	Decrease in interest payable	(1,000)	
(1)	Increase in income taxes payable	10,000	
(2)	Depreciation expense	24,000	
(3)	Loss on sale of plant assets	6,000	
(3)	Gain on retirement of bonds	(16,000)	
	Total adjustments		(18,000)
	Net cash provided by operating activities		$ 20,000

Adjustments for Changes in Current Assets and Current Liabilities

To help you understand why adjustments for changes in noncash current assets and current liabilities are part of the reconciliation process, we use the transactions of a very simple company as an example. Assume that Simple Company's income statement shows only two items, as follows:

Sales	$20,000
Operating expenses	(12,000)
Net income	$ 8,000

For a moment, assume that all of Simple Company's sales and operating expenses are for cash. The company has no current assets other than cash and has no current liabilities. Given these assumptions, the net cash provided by operating activities during the period is $8,000, which is the cash received from customers less the cash paid for operating expenses. The net cash provided by operating activities also equals net income.

Adjustments for Changes in Noncash Current Assets

Now assume that Simple Company's sales are on account. Also assume that its Accounts Receivable balance was $2,000 at the beginning of the year and $2,500 at the end of the year. Under these assumptions, cash receipts from customers equal sales of $20,000 minus the $500 increase in Accounts Receivable, or $19,500. Therefore, using the *direct* method, the net cash provided by operating activities is $7,500 ($19,500 − $12,000).

When the *indirect* method is used to calculate the net cash flow, net income of $8,000 is adjusted for the $500 increase in accounts receivable to get $7,500 as the net amount of cash provided by operating activities. Both calculations are as follows:

Direct Method

Receipts from customers ($20,000 − $500)	$19,500
Payments for operating expenses	(12,000)
Cash provided (or used) by operating activities . .	$ 7,500

Indirect Method

Net income	$8,000
Less the increase in accounts receivable	(500)
Cash provided (or used) by operating activities . .	$7,500

Notice that the direct method calculation subtracts the increase in Accounts Receivable from Sales, while the indirect method calculation subtracts the increase in Accounts Receivable from net income.

As another example, assume instead that the Accounts Receivable balance decreased from $2,000 to $1,200. Under this assumption, cash receipts from customers equal sales of $20,000 plus the $800 decrease in Accounts Receivable, or $20,800. By the direct method, the net cash provided by operating activities is $8,800 ($20,800 − $12,000). And when the indirect method is used, the $800 decrease in Accounts Receivable is added to the $8,000 net income to get $8,800 net cash provided by operating activities.

When the indirect method is used, adjustments like those for Accounts Receivable are required for all noncash current assets related to operating activities. When a noncash current asset increases, part of the assets derived from operating activities goes into the increase. This leaves a smaller amount as the net cash inflow. Therefore, when you calculate the net cash inflow using the indirect method, subtract the noncash current asset increase from net income. But when a noncash current asset decreases, additional cash is produced, and you should add this amount to net income. These modifications of income for changes in current assets related to operating activities are as follows:

Net income
Add: Decreases in current assets
Subtract: Increases in current assets
Net cash provided (or used) by operating activities

Adjustments for Changes in Current Liabilities

To illustrate the adjustments for changes in current liabilities, return to the original assumptions about Simple Company. Sales of $20,000 are for cash, and operating expenses are $12,000. However, assume now that Simple Company has Interest Payable as its only current liability. Also assume that the beginning-of-year balance in Interest Payable was $500 and the end-of-year balance was $900. This increase means that the operating expenses of $12,000 include $400 of interest that was not paid in cash during the period. Therefore, the cash payments for operating expenses were only $11,600, or ($12,000 −

$400). Under these assumptions, the direct method calculation of net cash provided by operating activities is $8,400, or $20,000 receipts from customers less $11,600 payments for expenses. The indirect method calculation of $8,400 is net income of $8,000 plus the $400 increase in Interest Payable.

Alternatively, if the Interest Payable balance decreased, for example by $300, the cash outflow for operating expenses would have been the $12,000 expense plus the $300 liability decrease, or $12,300. Then, the direct calculation of net cash flow is $20,000 − $12,300 = $7,700. The indirect calculation is $8,000 − $300 = $7,700. In other words, when using the indirect method, subtract a decrease in Interest Payable from net income.

Using the indirect method requires adjustments like those for Interest Payable for all current liabilities related to operating activities. When a current liability decreases, part of the cash derived from operating activities pays for the decrease. Therefore, subtract the decrease from net income to determine the remaining net cash inflow. And when a current liability increases, it finances some operating expenses. In other words, cash was not used to pay for the expense and the liability increase must be added to net income when you calculate cash provided by operating activities. These adjustments for changes in current liabilities related to operating activities are:

Net income
Add: Increases in current liabilities
Subtract: Decreases in current liabilities
Net cash provided (or used) by operating activities

One way to remember how to make these modifications to net income is to observe that a *debit* change in a noncash current asset or a current liability is *subtracted* from net income. And, a *credit* change in a noncash current asset or a current liability is *added* to net income.

Adjustments for Other Operating Items that Do Not Provide or Use Cash

Some operating items that appear on an income statement do not provide or use cash during the current period. One example is depreciation. Other examples are amortization of intangible assets, depletion of natural resources, and bad debts expense.

Record these expenses with debits to expense accounts and credits to noncash accounts. They reduce net income but do not require cash outflows during the period. Therefore, when adjustments to net income are made under the indirect method, add these noncash expenses back to net income.

In addition to noncash expenses such as depreciation, net income may include some revenues that do not provide cash inflows during the current period. An example is equity method earnings from a stock investment in another entity (see Chapter 18). If net income includes revenues that do not provide cash inflows, subtract the revenues from net income in the process of reconciling net income to the net cash provided by operating activities.

The indirect method adjustments for expenses and revenues that do not provide or use cash during the current period are as follows:

Net income
Add: Expenses that do not use cash
Subtract: Revenues that do not provide cash
Net cash provided (or used) by operating activities

Adjustments for Nonoperating Items

Some income statement items are not related to the operating activities of the company. These gains and losses result from investing and financing activities. Examples are gains or losses on the sale of plant assets and gains or losses on the retirement of bonds payable.

Remember that the indirect method reconciles net income to the net cash provided (or used) by operating activities. Therefore, net income must be modified to exclude gains and losses created by investing and financing activities. In making the modifications under the indirect method, subtract gains from financing and investing activities from net income and add losses back to net income:

Net income
Add: Losses from investing or financing activities
Subtract: Gains from investing or financing activities
Net cash provided (or used) by operating activities

Applying the Indirect Method to Grover Company

LO 7 Prepare a working paper for a statement of cash flows so that the net cash flow from operating activities is calculated by the indirect method.

Determining the net cash flows provided (or used) by operating activities according to the indirect method requires balance sheets at the beginning and end of the period, the current period's income statement, and other information about selected transactions. Illustration 17–9 on page 926 shows the income statement and balance sheet information for Grover Company. Based on this information, Illustration G–1 presents the indirect method of reconciling net income to net cash provided by operating activities.

Preparing the Indirect Method Working Paper

In addition to Grover Company's comparative balance sheets and income statement presented in Illustration 17–9, the information needed to prepare the working paper follows. The letters identifying each item of information also cross-reference related debits and credits on the working paper.

a. Net income was $38,000.
b. Accounts receivable increased by $20,000.
c. Merchandise inventory increased by $14,000.

d. Prepaid expenses increased by $2,000.
e. Accounts payable decreased by $5,000.
f. Interest payable decreased by $1,000.
g. Income taxes payable increased by $10,000.
h. Depreciation expense was $24,000.
i. Loss on sale of plant assets was $6,000; assets that cost $30,000 with accumulated depreciation of $12,000 were sold for $12,000 cash.
j. Gain on retirement of bonds was $16,000; bonds with a book value of $34,000 were retired with a cash payment of $18,000.
k. Plant assets that cost $70,000 were purchased; the payment consisted of $10,000 cash and the issuance of a $60,000 note payable.
l. Sold 3,000 shares of common stock for $15,000.
m. Paid cash dividends of $14,000.

Illustration G–2 shows the indirect method working paper for Grover Company. Notice that the beginning and ending balance sheets are recorded on the working paper the same as when using the direct method. Following the balance sheets, we enter information in the Analysis of Changes columns about cash flows from operating, investing, and financing activities and about noncash investing and financing activities. Note that the working paper does not reconstruct the income statement. Instead, net income is entered as the first item used in computing the amount of cash flows from operating activities.

Entering the Analysis of Changes on the Working Paper

After the balance sheets are entered, we recommend using the following sequence of procedures to complete the working paper:

1. Enter net income as an operating cash inflow (a debit) and as a credit to Retained Earnings.
2. In the statement of cash flows section, adjustments to net income are entered as debits if they increase cash inflows and as credits if they decrease cash inflows. Following this rule, adjust net income for the change in each noncash current asset and current liability related to operating activities. For each adjustment to net income, the offsetting debit or credit should reconcile the beginning and ending balances of a current asset or current liability.
3. Enter the adjustments to net income for income statement items, such as depreciation, that did not provide or use cash during the period. For each adjustment, the offsetting debit or credit should help reconcile a noncash balance sheet account.
4. Adjust net income to eliminate any gains or losses from investing and financing activities. Because the cash associated with a gain must be excluded from operating activities, the gain is entered as a credit in the operating activities section. On the other hand, losses are entered with debits. For each of these adjustments, the related debits and/or credits

ILLUSTRATION G–2

GROVER COMPANY
Working Paper for Statement of Cash Flows (Indirect Method)
For Year Ended December 31, 1993

	December 31, 1992	Analysis of Changes Debit	Analysis of Changes Credit	December 31, 1993
Balance sheet—debits:				
Cash	12,000			17,000
Accounts receivable	40,000	(*b*) 20,000		60,000
Merchandise inventory	70,000	(*c*) 14,000		84,000
Prepaid expenses	4,000	(*d*) 2,000		6,000
Plant assets	210,000	(*k1*) 70,000	(*i*) 30,000	250,000
	336,000			417,000
Balance sheet—credits:				
Accumulated depreciation, plant assets	48,000	(*i*) 12,000	(*h*) 24,000	60,000
Accounts payable	40,000	(*e*) 5,000		35,000
Interest payable	4,000	(*f*) 1,000		3,000
Income taxes payable	12,000		(*g*) 10,000	22,000
Bonds payable	64,000	(*j*) 34,000	(*k2*) 60,000	90,000
Common stock, $5 par value	80,000		(*l*) 15,000	95,000
Retained earnings	88,000	(*m*) 14,000	(*a*) 38,000	112,000
	336,000			417,000
Statement of cash flows:				
Operating activities:				
Net income		(*a*) 38,000		
Increase in accounts receivable			(*b*) 20,000	
Increase in merchandise inventory			(*c*) 14,000	
Increase in prepaid expenses			(*d*) 2,000	
Decrease in accounts payable			(*e*) 5,000	
Decrease in interest payable			(*f*) 1,000	
Increase in income taxes payable		(*g*) 10,000		
Depreciation expense		(*h*) 24,000		
Loss on sale of plant assets		(*i*) 6,000		
Gain on retirement of bonds			(*j*) 16,000	
Investing activities:				
Receipt from sale of plant assets		(*i*) 12,000		
Payment for purchase of plant assets			(*k1*) 10,000	
Financing activities:				
Payment to retire bonds			(*j*) 18,000	
Receipts from issuing stock		(*l*) 15,000		
Payments of dividends			(*m*) 14,000	
Noncash investing and financing activities:				
Purchase of plant assets financed by bonds		(*k2*) 60,000	(*k1*) 60,000	
		337,000	337,000	

help reconcile balance sheet accounts and also involve entries to show the cash flow from investing or financing activities.

5. After reviewing any unreconciled balance sheet accounts and related information, enter the reconciling entries for all remaining investing and financing activities. These include items such as purchases of plant assets, issuances of long-term debt, sales of capital stock, and dividend payments. Some of these may require entries in the noncash investing and financing activities section of the working paper.
6. Confirm the accuracy of your work by totaling the Analysis of Changes columns and by determining that the change in each balance sheet account has been explained.

For Grover Company, these steps were performed in Illustration G–2:

Step	Entries
1	(*a*)
2	(*b*) through (*g*)
3	(*h*)
4	(*i*) through (*j*)
5	(*k*) through (*m*)

Because adjustments *i, j,* and *k* are more complex, we show them in the following debit and credit format. This format is similar to the one used for general journal entries, except that the changes in the Cash account are identified as sources or uses of cash.

i.	Loss from Sale of Plant Assets	6,000.00	
	Accumulated Depreciation	12,000.00	
	Receipt from Sale of Plant Assets	12,000.00	
	Plant Assets		30,000.00
	To describe the sale of plant assets.		
j.	Bonds Payable	34,000.00	
	Payments to Retire Bonds		18,000.00
	Gain on Retirement of Bonds		16,000.00
	To describe the retirement of bonds.		
k1.	Plant Assets	70,000.00	
	Payment to Purchase Plant Assets		10,000.00
	Purchase of Plant Assets Financed by Bonds		60,000.00
	To describe the purchase of plant assets, the cash payment, and the use of noncash financing.		
k2.	Purchase of Plant Assets Financed by Bonds	60,000.00	
	Bonds Payable		60,000.00
	To show the issuance of bonds payable to finance the purchase of plant assets.		

Summary of Appendix G in Terms of Learning Objectives

LO 6. In using the indirect method to calculate the net cash provided (or used) by operating activities, first list the net income and then modify it for these three types of events: (*a*) changes in noncash current assets and current liabilities related to operating activities; (*b*) revenues and expenses that did not provide or use cash; and (*c*) gains and losses from investing and financing activities. If using the direct method, report the reconciliation between net income and net cash provided (or used) by operating activities on a separate schedule.

LO 7. To prepare an indirect method working paper, first enter the beginning and ending balances of the balance sheet accounts in columns 1 and 4. Then, establish the three sections of the statement of cash flows. Enter net income as the first item in the operating activities section. Then, adjust the net income for events (*a*) through (*c*) identified in the preceding paragraph. This process reconciles the changes in the noncash current assets and current liabilities related to operations. Reconcile any remaining balance sheet account changes and report their cash effects in the appropriate sections. Enter noncash investing and financing activities at the bottom of the working paper.

Glossary

LO 5 Define or explain the words or phrases listed in the chapter Glossary.

Cash equivalent an investment that is readily convertible to a known amount of cash and that is sufficiently close to its maturity date so that its market value is relatively insensitive to interest rate changes. p. 917–19

Direct method of calculating net cash provided or used by operating activities a calculation of the net cash provided or used by operating activities that lists the major classes of operating cash receipts, such as receipts from customers, and subtracts the major classes of operating cash disbursements, such as cash paid for merchandise. p. 915

Financing activities transactions with the owners of a business or transactions with its creditors to borrow money or to repay the principal amounts of loans. p. 920

Indirect method of calculating net cash provided or used by operating activities a calculation that begins with net income and then adjusts the net income amount by adding and subtracting items that are necessary to reconcile net income to the net cash provided or used by operating activities. p. 916

Investing activities transactions that involve making and collecting loans or that involve purchasing and selling plant assets, other productive assets, or investments other than cash equivalents. p. 920

Operating activities activities that involve the production or purchase of merchandise and the sale of goods and services to customers, including expenditures related to administering the business. p. 919

Statement of cash flows a financial statement that reports the cash inflows and outflows for an accounting period, and that classifies those cash flows as operating activities, investing activities, and financing activities. p. 914

Synonymous Terms

Cash inflow source of cash.

Cash outflow use of cash.

Objective Review

Answers to the following questions are listed at the end of this chapter. Be sure that you decide which is the one best answer to each question *before* you check the answers.

LO 1 A payment in the form of a loan made by a manufacturing company to another company is an example of:

a. A cash flow from operating activities.
b. A cash flow from investing activities.
c. A cash flow from financing activities.
d. A noncash investing and financing activity.
e. A cash payment to purchase a cash equivalent.

LO 2 The following T-account is a summary of the Cash account of Outland Shirt Company.

Summarized Cash Account

Balance, 12/31/92	5,000		
Receipts from customers	273,000	Payments for merchandise	150,000
Proceeds from dividends from stock investments	4,500	Payments for other operating expenses	105,000
Proceeds from issuance of bonds payable	75,000	Interest payments	7,500
		Tax payments	6,000
Proceeds from sale of stock investment	27,000	Payments to purchase treasury stock	75,000
		Dividend payments	22,500
Balance, 12/31/93	18,500		

A statement of cash flows prepared according to the direct method would state:

a. Net cash provided (or used) by financing activities, $(22,500).
b. Net cash provided (or used) by investing activities, $31,500.
c. Net cash provided (or used) by operating activities, $4,500.
d. Net cash provided (or used) by investing activities, $(48,000).
e. Net cash provided (or used) by operating activities, $18,500.

LO 3 Snyder Company's Merchandise Inventory account balance decreased during a period from a beginning balance of $32,000 to an ending balance of $28,000. Cost of goods sold for that same period was $168,000. If the Accounts Payable balance increased $2,400 during the period, what was the amount of cash paid for merchandise?

a. $161,600.
b. $166,400.
c. $168,000.
d. $169,600.
e. $174,400.

LO 4 In preparing a working paper for a statement of cash flows with the cash flows from operating activities reported according to the direct method:

a. Sales revenue is entered as a credit in the income statement section and as a debit to Accounts Receivable.
b. The amount of net income is credited to Retained Earnings.
c. The net effect on cash of entries under the noncash investing and financing activities section for the purchase of plant assets financed by bonds is $–0– (the debits equal the credits).
d. Expenses paid in cash may be analyzed as having no effect on the noncash balance sheet accounts, in which case the expense payments are recorded as debits in the income statement section and credits in the statement of cash flows section.
e. All of the above are correct.

LO 5 Transactions with the owners or long-term creditors of the business or that involve borrowing cash on a short-term basis are classified as:

a. Noncash investing and financing activities.
b. Operating activities.
c. Financing activities.
d. Investing activities.
e. None of the above.

LO 6 Determine the net cash provided (or used) by operating activities based on the following data:

Net income	$74,900
Decrease in accounts receivable	4,600
Increase in inventory	11,700
Decrease in accounts payable	1,000
Loss on sale of equipment	3,400
Payment of dividends	21,500

a. $48,700.
b. $61,000.
c. $63,400.
d. $70,200.
e. $79,600.

LO 7 In preparing a working paper for a statement of cash flows with the cash flows from operating activities reported according to the indirect method:

a. A decrease in accounts receivable is analyzed with a debit in the statement of cash flows section and a credit in the balance sheet section.
b. A cash dividend paid is analyzed with a debit to retained earnings and a credit in the investing activities section.
c. The analysis of a cash payment to retire bonds payable at a loss would require one debit and two credits.
d. Depreciation expense would not require analysis on the working paper because there is no cash inflow or outflow.
e. None of the above is correct.

A letter ^{G} identifies the questions, exercises, and problems based on Appendix G at the end of the chapter.

Questions for Class Discussion

1. What information is shown on a statement of cash flows?
2. What are the three categories of cash flows shown on a statement of cash flows?
3. What are some examples of items reported on a statement of cash flows as investing activities?
4. What are some examples of items reported on a statement of cash flows as financing activities?
5. When a statement of cash flows is prepared by the direct method, what are some examples of items reported as cash flows from operating activities?

6. A machine that was held as a long-term asset for use in business operations is sold for cash. Where should this cash flow appear on the statement of cash flows?
7. A business purchases merchandise inventory for cash. Where should this cash flow appear on the statement of cash flows?
8. If a corporation pays cash dividends, where on the corporation's statement of cash flows should the payment be reported?
9. A company purchases land for $200,000 and finances 100% of the purchase with a long-term note payable. Should this transaction be reported on a statement of cash flows? If so, where on the statement should it be reported?
10. A company purchases land for $100,000, paying $20,000 cash and borrowing the remainder on a long-term note payable. How should this transaction be reported on a statement of cash flows?
11. What is the direct method of reporting cash flows from operating activities?
12. What is the indirect method of reporting cash flows from operating activities?
13. Do the direct and indirect methods of calculating cash flows from operating activities lead to the same net amount?
14. Is depreciation a source of cash?
15. On June 3, a company borrowed $50,000 by giving its bank a 60-day, interest-bearing note. On the statement of cash flows, where should this item be reported?
16. A company borrowed $50,000 by giving its bank a 60-day, 12% interest-bearing note. When the note was repaid, the company also paid interest of $1,000. On the statement of cash flows, where should the $1,000 interest payment be reported?
17. When a working paper for the preparation of a statement of cash flows is prepared, all changes in noncash balance sheet accounts are accounted for on the working paper. Why?
18. A company retired a long-term note payable by issuing, at par, shares of common stock equal in value to the carrying amount of the note. How is this event analyzed on the statement of cash flows working paper?

[G]19. If a company reports a net income for the year, is it possible for the company to show a net cash outflow from operating activities? Explain your answer.

[G]20. Why are expenses such as depreciation and amortization of goodwill added to net income when cash flow from operations is calculated by the indirect method?

[G]21. A company had $70,000 of merchandise inventory at the beginning of a period and $40,000 of merchandise inventory at the end of the same period. If the net cash flow from operating activities is calculated by the indirect method, how should this decrease in inventory be treated in the calculation?

G22. A company reports a net income of $15,000 that includes a $3,000 gain on sale of plant assets. Why is this gain subtracted from net income in the process of reconciling net income to the net cash provided or used by operating activities?

23. Refer to the consolidated statements of cash flows for Federal Express Corporation in Appendix K. (*a*) What type and amount of noncash activities took place during the year ended May 31, 1991? (*b*) How much cash was used for income taxes during the year ended May 31, 1990?

G24. Refer to McDonald's Corporation's consolidated statement of cash flows shown in Appendix K. (*a*) Which method was used to calculate cash provided by operating activities? (*b*) Why was the decrease in accrued interest subtracted rather than added in the calculation of cash provided by operations during 1990?

Exercises

Exercise 17–1
Classifying transactions on statement of cash flows
(LO 1)

The following seven events occurred during the year. Assume that the company presents a statement of cash flows using the direct method of reporting cash provided by operating activities. Place an *x* in one of the columns next to each event. If the item should appear in the statement of cash flows, place the *x* in the column for the section in which it would be presented. If the event is not to appear in the statement, indicate with the *x* whether it should be presented in the supplemental schedule of noncash investing and financing activities or not reported at all.

	Statement of Cash Flows			Schedule of Noncash Investing and Financing Activities	Not Reported on Statement or Schedule
	Operating Activities	Investing Activities	Financing Activities		
a. Paid cash to purchase a trademark.					
b. Long-term bonds payable were retired by issuing common stock.					
c. A cash dividend that was declared in a previous period was paid in the current period.					
d. Surplus merchandise inventory was sold for cash.					
e. Borrowed cash from the bank by signing a six-month note payable.					
f. A six-month note receivable was accepted in exchange for a building that had been used in operations.					
g. Recorded depreciation expense on all plant assets.					

Exercise 17–2
Organizing the statement of cash flows and supporting schedule
(LO 1, 2)

Use the following information about the 1993 cash flows of Union Sales Company to prepare a statement of cash flows under the direct method and a schedule of noncash investing and financing activities.

Cash and cash equivalents balance, December 31, 1992 . .	$ 20,000
Cash and cash equivalents balance, December 31, 1993 . .	56,000
Cash paid to retire long-term notes payable	100,000
Cash received from sale of equipment	49,000
Cash paid for merchandise	202,000
Cash paid for store equipment	19,000
Cash borrowed on six-month note payable	20,000
Cash dividends paid	12,000
Bonds payable retired by issuing common stock (there was no gain or loss on the retirement)	150,000
Cash paid for salaries	58,000
Cash paid for other expenses	32,000
Land purchased and financed by long-term note payable .	85,000
Cash received from customers	388,000
Cash received as interest	2,000

Exercise 17–3
Calculating cash flows
(LO 3)

In each of the following cases, use the information provided about the 1993 operations of Dayton Window Company to calculate the indicated cash flow:

Case A:	Calculate cash paid for rent:	
	Rent expense	$11,400
	Prepaid rent, January 1	1,900
	Prepaid rent, December 31	2,850
Case B:	Calculate cash paid to employees:	
	Salaries expense	$34,000
	Salaries payable, January 1	2,100
	Salaries payable, December 31	2,500
Case C:	Calculate cash received from customers:	
	Sales revenue	$85,000
	Accounts receivable, January 1	4,200
	Accounts receivable, December 31	5,800

Exercise 17–4
Calculating cash flows
(LO 3)

In each of the following cases, use the information provided about the 1993 operations of Greenleaf Company to calculate the indicated cash flow:

Case A:	Calculate cash received from interest:	
	Interest revenue	$17,000
	Interest receivable, January 1	1,500
	Interest receivable, December 31	1,800
Case B:	Calculate cash paid for utilities:	
	Utilities expense	$5,100
	Utilities payable, January 1	1,100
	Utilities payable, December 31	900
Case C:	Calculate cash paid for merchandise:	
	Cost of goods sold	$88,000
	Merchandise inventory, January 1	26,600
	Accounts payable, January 1	11,300
	Merchandise inventory, December 31 . .	21,900
	Accounts payable, December 31	14,000

Exercise 17–5
Cash flows from operating activities (direct method)
(LO 2, 3)

Use the following income statement and information about changes in noncash current assets and current liabilities to present the cash flows from operating activities using the direct method:

ACE SECURITY SYSTEMS COMPANY
Income Statement
For Year Ended December 31, 1993

Sales		$404,000
Cost of goods sold		198,000
Gross profit from sales		$206,000
Operating expenses:		
Salaries and wages	$55,230	
Depreciation expense	9,600	
Rent expense	10,800	
Amortization of goodwill	1,200	
Interest expense	4,250	81,080
Total		$124,920
Loss on sale of equipment		1,600
Net income		$123,320

Changes in current asset and current liability accounts during the year, all of which related to operating activities, were as follows:

Accounts receivable	$9,000 increase
Merchandise inventory	6,000 increase
Accounts payable	3,000 decrease
Salaries and wages payable	1,000 decrease

[G]Exercise 17–6
Cash flows from operating activities (indirect method) (LO 3, 6)

Refer to the information about Ace Security Systems Company presented in Exercise 17–5. Use the indirect method and calculate the cash provided (or used) by operating activities.

[G]Exercise 17–7
Cash flows from operating activities (indirect method) (LO 6)

REC Corporation's 1993 income statement showed the following: net income, $364,000; depreciation expense, $45,000; amortization expense, $8,200; and gain on sale of plant assets, $7,000. An examination of the company's current assets and current liabilities showed that the following changes occurred because of operating activities: accounts receivable decreased $18,100; merchandise inventory decreased $52,000; prepaid expenses increased $3,700; accounts payable decreased $9,200; other payables increased $1,400. Use the indirect method to calculate the cash flow from operating activities.

Exercise 17–8
Noncash investing and financing activities (LO 2)

Use the following information to prepare a schedule of noncash investing and financing activities for Analog Corporation:

a. The income statement shows a $4,200 loss on exchange of machinery. The loss relates to an old machine that had a book value of $47,200 when it was exchanged for a new machine that had a cash price of $43,000.

b. Outstanding bonds payable carried on the books at $200,000 were retired by issuing 8,000 shares of $10 par, common stock that had a market value of $200,000.

c. A building valued at $430,000 was purchased by paying cash of $75,000 and signing a long-term note payable for the balance.

d. The income statement shows a $82,000 gain on the sale of land. The land had a book value of $90,000 and was sold for $172,000. Analog Corporation received $72,000 cash and accepted a long-term promissory note for the balance of the sales price.

Exercise 17–9
Statement of cash flows (direct method)
(LO 2, 3)

Dominion Company's 1993 and 1992 balance sheets showed the following items:

	December 31	
	1993	**1992**
Debits		
Cash	$ 26,000	$ 31,000
Accounts receivable	16,000	14,000
Merchandise inventory	107,000	115,000
Equipment	98,000	78,000
Totals	$247,000	$238,000
Credits		
Accumulated depreciation, equipment	$ 45,800	$ 31,200
Common stock, $10 par value	120,000	120,000
Retained earnings	81,200	86,800
Totals	$247,000	$238,000

An examination of the company's activities during 1993, including the income statement, reveals the following:

a.	Sales (all on credit)		$356,000
b.	All credits to Accounts Receivable during the period were receipts from customers.		
c.	Cost of goods sold	$182,000	
d.	All merchandise purchases were for cash.		
e.	Depreciation expense	14,600	
f.	Other operating expenses	105,000	301,600
g.	Net income		$ 54,400
h.	Equipment was purchased for $20,000 cash.		
i.	The company declared and paid $60,000 of cash dividends during the year.		

Required

Prepare a statement of cash flows that follows the direct method to calculate the net cash provided (or used) by operating activities. Do not prepare a working paper but show any supporting calculations.

[G]Exercise 17–10
Statement of cash flows (indirect method)
(LO 3, 6)

Refer to the facts about Dominion Company presented in Exercise 17–9. Prepare a statement of cash flows that follows the indirect method of calculating the net cash provided (or used) by operating activities. Do not prepare a working paper but show any supporting calculations.

Problems

Problem 17–1
Statement of cash flows (direct method)
(LO 1, 2, 3)

Montego Tool Corporation's 1993 and 1992 balance sheets carried the following items:

	December 31	
	1993	**1992**
Debits		
Cash	$ 58,000	$ 39,000
Accounts receivable	31,000	27,000
Merchandise inventory	203,000	178,000
Equipment	111,000	99,000
Totals	$403,000	$343,000
Credits		
Accumulated depreciation, equipment	$ 52,000	$ 34,000
Accounts payable	23,000	32,000
Income taxes payable	9,000	8,000
Common stock, $10 par value		
Contributed capital in excess of par value, common stock	66,000	54,000
Retained earnings	59,000	29,000
Totals	$403,000	$343,000

An examination of the company's activities during 1993, including the income statement, shows the following:

a1.	Sales (all on credit)		$664,000
a2.	Credits to Accounts Receivable during the period were receipts from customers.		
b1.	Cost of goods sold	$398,000	
b2.	Purchases of merchandise were on credit.		
b3.	Debits to Accounts Payable during the period resulted from payments for merchandise.		
c.	Depreciation expense	18,000	
d.	Other operating expenses (paid with cash)	167,000	
e1.	Income taxes expense	14,000	597,000
e2.	The only decreases in Income Taxes Payable were payments of taxes.		
f.	Net income		$ 67,000

g. Equipment was purchased for $12,000 cash.
h. Eight hundred shares of stock were issued for cash at $25 per share.
i. The company declared and paid $37,000 of cash dividends during the year.

Required

Prepare a statement of cash flows that reports the cash inflows and outflows from operating activities according to the direct method. Do not prepare a working paper. Instead, prepare the statement directly from your examination of the balance sheets and the additional information provided about the income statement and other transactions of the company. Show your supporting calculations.

Problem 17–2
Cash flows working paper (direct method)
(LO 1, 4)

Refer to the information about Montego Tool Corporation presented in Problem 17–1. Prepare a working paper for a statement of cash flows according to the direct method.

[G]Problem 17–3
Reconciling net income to cash flows from operating activities
(LO 6)

Refer to Montego Tool Corporation's balance sheets presented in Problem 17–1. The additional information about the company's activities during 1993 is restated as follows:

a. Net income was $67,000.
b. Accounts receivable increased.
c. Merchandise inventory increased.
d. Accounts payable decreased.
e. Income taxes payable increased.
f. Depreciation expense was $18,000.
g. Equipment was purchased for $12,000 cash.
h. Eight hundred shares of stock were issued for cash at $25 per share.
i. The company declared and paid $37,000 of cash dividends during the year.

Required

Prepare a schedule that reconciles net income to the net cash provided or used by operating activities.

[G]Problem 17–4
Cash flows working paper (indirect method)
(LO 1, 7)

Refer to the facts about Montego Tool Corporation presented in Problem 17–1 and Problem 17–3. Prepare a statement of cash flows working paper that follows the indirect method of calculating cash flows from operating activities. Identify the debits and credits in the Analysis of Changes columns with letters that correspond to the list of information about the company presented in Problem 17–3.

Problem 17–5
Statement of cash flows (direct method)
(LO 1, 2, 3)

Clarion Corporation's 1993 and 1992 balance sheets included the following items:

	December 31	
	1993	**1992**
Debits		
Cash	$ 43,100	$ 61,300
Accounts receivable	52,000	39,700
Merchandise inventory	219,000	202,000
Prepaid expenses	4,300	5,000
Equipment	127,600	88,000
Totals	$446,000	$396,000
Credits		
Accumulated depreciation, equipment	$ 27,700	$ 35,200
Accounts payable	70,500	93,300
Short-term notes payable	8,000	5,000
Long-term notes payable	75,000	43,000
Common stock, $10 par value	135,000	125,000
Contributed capital in excess of par value, common stock	26,000	
Retained earnings	103,800	94,500
Totals	$446,000	$396,000

a1.	Sales revenue, all on credit		$397,000
a2.	Credits to Accounts Receivable during the period were receipts from customers.		
b1.	Cost of goods sold	$200,000	
b2.	All merchandise purchases were on credit.		
b3.	Debits to Accounts Payable during the period resulted from payments to creditors.		
c.	Depreciation expense	15,000	
d1.	Other expenses	109,200	
d2.	The other expenses were paid in advance and were initially debited to Prepaid Expenses.		
e.	Income taxes expense (paid with cash)	9,700	
f.	Loss on sale of equipment	4,100	338,000
	The equipment cost $37,500, was depreciated by $22,500, and was sold for $10,900.		
g.	Net income		$ 59,000

h1. Equipment that cost $77,100 was purchased by paying cash of $20,000 and (*h2*) by signing a long-term note payable for the balance.
i. Borrowed $3,000 by signing a short-term note payable.
j. Paid $25,100 to reduce a long-term note payable.
k. Issued 1,000 shares of common stock for cash at $36 per share.
l. Declared and paid cash dividends of $49,700.

Required

Prepare a statement of cash flows that reports the cash inflows and outflows from operating activities according to the direct method. Do not prepare a working paper. Instead, prepare the statement directly from your examination of the balance sheets and the additional information provided about the income statement and other transactions of the company. Show your supporting calculations. Also prepare a schedule of noncash investing and financing activities.

Problem 17–6
Cash flows working paper (direct method)
(LO 1, 4)

Refer to the information about Clarion Corporation presented in Problem 17–5. Prepare a working paper for a statement of cash flows according to the direct method.

[G]Problem 17–7
Reconciling net income to cash flows from operating activities
(LO 6)

Refer to Clarion Corporation's balance sheets presented in Problem 17–5. The additional information about the company's activities during 1993 is restated as follows:

a. Net income was $59,000.
b. Accounts receivable increased.
c. Merchandise inventory increased.
d. Prepaid expenses decreased.
e. Accounts payable decreased.
f. Depreciation expense was $15,000.
g. Equipment that cost $37,500 with accumulated depreciation of $22,500 was sold for $10,900 cash, which caused a loss of $4,100.
h. Equipment that cost $77,100 was purchased by paying cash of $20,000 and (*i*) by signing a long-term note payable for the balance.

j. Borrowed $3,000 by signing a short-term note payable.
k. Paid $25,100 to reduce a long-term note payable.
l. Issued 1,000 shares of common stock for cash at $36 per share.
m. Declared and paid cash dividends of $49,700.

Required

Prepare a schedule that reconciles net income to the net cash provided or used by operating activities.

[G]Problem 17–8
Cash flows working paper (indirect method)
(LO 1, 7)

Refer to the facts about Clarion Corporation presented in Problem 17–5 and Problem 17–7. Prepare a statement of cash flows working paper that follows the indirect method of calculating cash flows from operating activities. Identify the debits and credits in the Analysis of Changes columns with letters that correspond to the list of information about the company presented in Problem 17–7.

Problem 17–9
Analytical essay
(LO 3)

Write a brief essay explaining why, in preparing a statement of cash flows according to the direct method, it is generally better to determine the changes in cash by analyzing the changes in the noncash accounts rather than by examining the Cash account directly. Include in your essay an explanation of why the changes in cash for the period equal the changes in the noncash balance sheet accounts.

Problem 17–10
Analytical essay
(LO 4, 7)

The following items might be found on a working paper for a statement of cash flows. Write a brief essay describing where each item appears on a working paper for a statement of cash flows according to the direct method. Also describe the nature of any debits and/or credits that should be entered in the Analysis of Changes columns next to each item.

1. Accounts receivable.
2. Sales.
3. Depreciation expense.
4. Payment to purchase equipment.

Alternate Problems

Problem 17–1A
Statement of cash flows (direct method)
(LO 1, 2, 3)

Trilon Corporation's 1993 and 1992 balance sheets carried the following items:

	December 31 1993	December 31 1992
Debits		
Cash	$ 71,900	$ 42,400
Accounts receivable	25,900	31,000
Merchandise inventory	233,800	186,500
Equipment	140,600	102,000
Totals	$472,200	$361,900
Credits		
Accumulated depreciation, equipment	$ 64,400	$ 40,800
Accounts payable	51,300	47,500
Income taxes payable	6,000	9,000
Common stock, $10 par value	220,000	200,000
Contributed capital in excess of par value, common stock	56,000	20,000
Retained earnings	74,500	44,600
Totals	$472,200	$361,900

An examination of the company's activities during 1993, including the income statement, shows the following:

a1.	Sales (all on credit)		$813,000
a2.	The only decreases in Accounts Receivable were receipts from customers.		
b1.	Cost of goods sold	$372,000	
b2.	Purchases of merchandise were on credit.		
b3.	Debits to Accounts Payable during the period resulted from payments for merchandise.		
c.	Depreciation expense	23,600	
d.	Other operating expenses (paid with cash)	239,700	
e1.	Income taxes expense	59,800	695,100
e2.	The only decreases in Income Taxes Payable were payments of taxes.		
f.	Net income		$117,900

g. Equipment was purchased for $38,600 cash.
h. Two thousand shares of stock were issued for cash at $28 per share.
i. The company declared and paid $88,000 of cash dividends during the year.

Required

Prepare a statement of cash flows that reports the cash inflows and outflows from operating activities according to the direct method. Do not prepare a working paper. Instead, prepare the statement directly from your examination of the balance sheets and the additional information provided about the income statement and other transactions of the company. Show your supporting calculations.

Problem 17–2A
Cash flows working paper (direct method)
(LO 1, 4)

Refer to the information about Trilon Corporation presented in Problem 17–1A. Prepare a working paper for a statement of cash flows according to the direct method.

[G]Problem 17–3A
Reconciling net income to cash flows from operating activities
(LO 6)

Refer to Trilon Corporation's balance sheets presented in Problem 17–1A. Additional information about the company's activities during 1993 is as follows:

a. Net income was $117,900.
b. Accounts receivable decreased.
c. Merchandise inventory increased.
d. Accounts payable increased.
e. Income taxes payable decreased.
f. Depreciation expense was $23,600.
g. Equipment was purchased for $38,600 cash.
h. Two thousand shares of stock were issued for cash at $28 per share.
i. The company declared and paid $88,000 of cash dividends during the year.

Required

Prepare a schedule that reconciles net income to the net cash provided or used by operating activities.

[G]Problem 17–4A
Cash flows working paper (indirect method)
(LO 1, 7)

Refer to the facts about Trilon Corporation presented in Problem 17–1A and Problem 17–3A. Prepare a statement of cash flows working paper that follows the indirect method of calculating cash flows from operating activities. Identify the debits and credits in the Analysis of Changes columns with letters that correspond to the list of information about the company presented in Problem 17–3A.

Problem 17–5A
Statement of cash flows (direct method)
(LO 1, 2, 3)

Systems Corporation's 1993 and 1992 balance sheets included the following items:

	December 31	
	1993	**1992**
Debits		
Cash	$ 91,000	$ 47,700
Accounts receivable	49,400	60,500
Merchandise inventory	303,000	326,800
Prepaid expenses	11,400	12,800
Equipment	185,500	144,000
Totals	$640,300	$591,800
Credits		
Accumulated depreciation, equipment	$ 72,500	$ 62,000
Accounts payable	78,300	82,300
Short-term notes payable	11,500	7,500
Long-term notes payable	75,000	55,000
Common stock, $5 par value	310,000	300,000
Contributed capital in excess of par value, common stock	12,000	
Retained earnings	81,000	85,000
Totals	$640,300	$591,800

Additional information about the 1993 activities of the company is as follows:

a1.	Sales revenue, all on credit		$722,000
a2.	Decreases in Accounts Receivable were only from receipts from customers.		
b1.	Cost of goods sold	$390,000	
b2.	All merchandise purchases were on credit.		
b3.	Credits to Accounts Payable during the period were from payments for merchandise.		
c.	Depreciation expense	24,400	
d1.	Other expenses	261,900	
d2.	The other expenses were paid in advance and were initially debited to Prepaid Expenses.		
e.	Income taxes expense	6,300	
f.	Loss on sale of equipment	1,400	684,000
	The equipment cost $34,000, was depreciated by $13,900, and was sold for $18,700.		
g.	Net income		$ 38,000

h1. Equipment that cost $75,500 was purchased by paying cash of $25,500 and (*h2*) by signing a long-term note payable for the balance.
i. Borrowed $4,000 by signing a short-term note payable.
j. Paid $30,000 to reduce a long-term note payable.
k. Issued 2,000 shares of common stock for cash at $11 per share.
l. Declared and paid cash dividends of $42,000.

Required

Prepare a statement of cash flows that reports the cash inflows and outflows from operating activities according to the direct method. Do not prepare a working paper. Instead, prepare the statement directly from your examination of the balance sheets and the additional information provided about the income statement and other transactions of the company. Show your supporting calculations. Also prepare a schedule of noncash investing and financing activities.

Problem 17–6A
Cash flows working paper (direct method)
(LO 1, 4)

Refer to the information about Systems Corporation presented in Problem 17–5A. Prepare a working paper for a statement of cash flows according to the direct method.

ᴳProblem 17–7A
Reconciling net income to cash flows from operating activities
(LO 6)

Refer to Systems Corporation's balance sheets presented in Problem 17–5A. The additional information about the company's activities during 1993 is restated as follows:

a. Net income was $38,000.
b. Accounts receivable decreased.
c. Merchandise inventory decreased.
d. Prepaid expenses decreased.
e. Accounts payable decreased.
f. Depreciation expense was $24,400.
g. Equipment that cost $34,000 with accumulated depreciation of $13,900 was sold for $18,700 cash, which caused a loss of $1,400.

h. Equipment that cost $75,500 was purchased by paying cash of $25,500 and by signing a long-term note payable for the balance.
i. Borrowed $4,000 by signing a short-term note payable.
j. Paid $30,000 to reduce a long-term note payable.
k. Issued 2,000 shares of common stock for cash at $11 per share.
l. Declared and paid cash dividends of $42,000.

Required

Prepare a schedule that reconciles net income to the net cash provided or used by operating activities.

[G]Problem 17–8A
Cash flows working paper (indirect method)
(LO 1, 7)

Refer to the facts about Systems Corporation presented in Problem 17–5A and Problem 17–7A. Prepare a statement of cash flows working paper that follows the indirect method of calculating cash flows from operating activities. Identify the debits and credits in the Analysis of Changes columns with letters that correspond to the list of information about the company presented in Problem 17–7A.

Problem 17–9A
Analytical essay
(LO 3)

When preparing a statement of cash flows according to the direct method, changes in noncash balance sheet accounts are analyzed to explain the changes in cash. Following are some income statement items that provide important information related to changes in noncash balance sheet accounts. Briefly explain how each of these income statement items and their related balance sheet accounts are used to identify specific cash inflows and outflows:

1. Sales.
2. Cost of goods sold.
3. Operating expenses.
4. Gain on sale of plant assets.

Problem 17–10A
Analytical essay
(LO 4, 7)

The following items might be found on a working paper for a statement of cash flows. Write a brief essay describing where each item appears on a working paper for a statement of cash flows according to the direct method. Also describe the nature of any debits and/or credits that should be entered in the Analysis of Changes columns next to each item.

1. Accounts payable.
2. Cost of goods sold.
3. Loss on sale of equipment.
4. Payments of cash dividends.

Provocative Problems

Provocative Problem 17–1
Opticon, Inc.
(LO 3)

Opticon, Inc.'s 1993 statement of cash flows appeared as follows:

Cash flows from operating activities:		
Cash receipts from customers	$602,400	
Cash payments for merchandise	(315,700)	
Payments for other operating expenses	(163,000)	
Payments of income taxes	(17,400)	
Net cash provided by operating activities		$106,300
Cash flows from investing activities:		
Receipt from sale of office equipment	$ 9,300	
Purchase of store equipment	(14,000)	
Net cash used by investing activities		(4,700)
Cash flows from financing activities:		
Payment to retire bonds payable	$ (51,100)	
Payment of dividends	(25,000)	
Net cash used by financing activities		(76,100)
Net increase in cash		$ 25,500
Cash balance at beginning of year		31,900
Cash balance at end of year		$ 57,400

Opticon, Inc.'s beginning and ending balance sheets were as follows:

	December 31	
	1993	1992
Debits		
Cash	$ 57,400	$ 31,900
Accounts receivable	45,500	53,100
Merchandise inventory	208,000	195,300
Prepaid expenses	4,800	2,200
Equipment	181,100	195,600
Totals	$496,800	$478,100
Credits		
Accumulated depreciation, equipment	$ 82,600	$ 63,400
Accounts payable	38,400	45,000
Income taxes payable	6,800	5,900
Dividends payable	–0–	6,000
Bonds payable	–0–	50,000
Common stock, $5 par value	225,000	225,000
Retained earnings	144,000	82,800
Totals	$496,800	$478,100

An examination of the company's statements and accounts showed:

a. All sales were made on credit.

b. All merchandise purchases were on credit.

c. Accounts Payable balances resulted from merchandise purchases.

d. Prepaid expenses relate to other operating expenses.

e. Equipment that cost $28,500 with accumulated depreciation of $14,800 was sold for cash.

f. Equipment was purchased for cash.

g. The change in the balance of Accumulated Depreciation resulted from depreciation expense and from the sale of equipment.

h. The change in the balance of Retained Earnings resulted from dividend declarations and net income.

Required

Present Opticon, Inc.'s income statement for 1993. Show your supporting calculations.

Provocative Problem 17–2
St. Thomas Company
(LO 1, 2, 3, 6)

The following items include the 1993 and 1992 balance sheets and the 1993 income statement of the St. Thomas Company. Additional information about the company's 1993 transactions is presented after the financial statements.

ST. THOMAS COMPANY
Balance Sheet
December 31, 1993, and 1992

	1993		1992	
Assets				
Current assets:				
Cash and cash equivalents	$ 3,100		$ 3,400	
Accounts receivable	5,500		5,900	
Merchandise inventory	23,000		22,000	
Total current assets		$31,600		$31,300
Long-term investments:				
Straun Corporation common stock		8,000		10,000
Plant assets:				
Land		12,000		9,000
Buildings	$50,000		$50,000	
Less accumulated depreciation	25,000	25,000	22,500	27,500
Equipment	$32,000		$26,000	
Less accumulated depreciation	13,000	19,000	10,000	16,000
Total assets		$95,600		$93,800
Liabilities				
Current liabilities:				
Notes payable	$14,000		$12,500	
Accounts payable	5,400		5,900	
Other accrued liabilities	3,900		4,300	
Interest payable	1,200		1,100	
Taxes payable	200		400	
Total current liabilities		$24,700		$24,200
Long-term liabilities:				
Bonds payable, due in 1999		25,000		20,000
Total liabilities		$49,700		$44,200
Stockholders' Equity				
Contributed capital:				
Common stock, $1 par value	$25,000		$23,000	
Contributed capital in excess of par value	9,000		7,000	
Retained earnings	13,500		19,600	
Total	$47,500		$49,600	
Less cost of treasury stock	1,600		-0-	
Total stockholders' equity		45,900		49,600
Total liabilities and stockholders' equity		$95,600		$93,800

ST. THOMAS COMPANY
Income Statement
For Year Ended December 31, 1993

Revenues:		
Sales	$87,000	
Gain on sale of stock investment	400	
Dividend income	500	
Interest income	100	$88,000
Expenses and losses:		
Cost of goods sold	$38,200	
Other expenses	19,800	
Interest expense	1,300	
Income taxes expense	3,100	
Depreciation expense, buildings	2,500	
Depreciation expense, equipment	5,000	
Loss on sale of equipment	400	
Total expenses and losses		70,300
Net income		$17,700

Additional information:

1. All the other expenses were initially credited to the Other Accrued Liabilities account.
2. Received $2,400 from the sale of Straun Corporation common stock, which originally cost $2,000.
3. Received a cash dividend of $500 from the Straun Corporation.
4. Received $100 cash from the First National Bank on December 31, 1993, as interest income.
5. Sold old equipment for $3,600. The old equipment originally cost $6,000 and had accumulated depreciation of $2,000.
6. Purchased land costing $3,000 on December 31, 1993, in exchange for a note payable. Both principal and interest are due on June 30, 1994.
7. Purchased new equipment for $12,000 cash.
8. Purchased treasury stock for $1,600 cash.
9. Paid $1,500 of notes payable.
10. Sold additional bonds payable at par of $5,000 on January 1, 1993.
11. Issued 2,000 shares of common stock for cash at $2 per share.
12. Declared and paid a $23,800 cash dividend on October 1, 1993.

(The working papers that accompany the text include forms for this problem.)

Required

a. Prepare a direct method working paper for St. Thomas Company's 1993 statement of cash flows.

b. Prepare the statement of cash flows for 1993.

c. Prepare a schedule that reconciles net income to the company's net cash provided (or used) by operating activities for 1993.

Provocative Problem 17–3
International Business Machines Corporation
(LO 1)

Look in Appendix J at the end of the book to find International Business Machines Corporation's Statement of Cash Flows. Based on your examination of that statement, answer the following questions:

1. Was IBM's statement of cash flows prepared according to the direct method or the indirect method?
2. During each of the years 1988, 1989, and 1990, was the cash provided from operating activities more or less than the cash paid for dividends?
3. In calculating the net cash provided from operating activities, which single item represented the largest addition to net income during 1990? During 1989?
4. In calculating the net cash provided from operating activities, which single item represented the largest subtraction from net income during 1990? During 1989?
5. What was the largest cash inflow from investing activities during 1990?
6. What was the largest cash outflow from investing activities during 1990?
7. Did the company issue any new stock for cash during the three-year period 1988 through 1990?
8. Compare the payments to purchase and retire capital stock during 1990 and 1989.

Answers to Objective Review Questions

LO 1 (*b*)
LO 2 (*a*)
LO 3 (*a*)
LO 4 (*e*)
LO 5 (*c*)
LO 6 (*d*)
LO 7 (*a*)

CHAPTER

18

Stock Investments, Consolidations, and International Operations

Astonishing growth of global markets is leading even small companies to customers and investors in other countries. In addition, today's complex world requires complex financial structures. In many cases, parent corporations control subsidiaries operating in different industries, states, or countries.

Topical Coverage

Most large corporations invest in the stock of other corporations, and many have operations in foreign countries. The financial statement effects of such investments and foreign operations often are very important. As a result, your study of these topics in this chapter will enrich your ability to understand and interpret the financial reports of most large businesses.

Learning Objectives

After studying Chapter 18, you should be able to:

1. State the criteria for classifying stock investments as current assets or as long-term investments.
2. Describe the circumstances under which the cost method, the equity method, and consolidated financial statements are used in accounting for long-term stock investments.
3. Prepare entries to account for long-term stock investments according to the cost method and the equity method and to reflect lower of cost or market.
4. Prepare consolidated balance sheets and explain how to report any excess of investment cost over book value and minority interests.
5. Describe the primary problems of accounting for international operations and prepare entries to account for sales to foreign customers.
6. Define or explain the words and phrases listed in the chapter glossary.

Stocks as Investments

In Chapters 14 and 15, we discussed stock transactions in which the issuing corporation sold or repurchased its own stock. The focus of our discussion was the stockholders' equity accounts of the issuing corporation. However, such transactions represent only a small portion of the stock transactions that take place every day. In fact, most stock transactions are between stockholders and do not involve the issuing corporation. These purchase and sale transactions between investors are usually arranged through agents, called *brokers,* who charge a commission for their services.

In acting as agents for their customers, brokers buy and sell many stocks and bonds on exchanges, such as the New York Stock Exchange. Other stocks and bonds are not listed or traded on an organized stock exchange. Instead, they are bought and sold in the *over-the-counter market*. Each security in this market is handled by brokers who receive offers to buy or sell the security at specific *bid* or *asked* prices through a network of other brokers.

Recall that per share stock prices are quoted on the basis of dollars and one-eighth fractions of dollars. A stock quoted at 29¼ will sell for $29.25 per share, and a stock quoted at 28⅞ will sell for $28.875 per share. For example, the purchases and sales of American Telephone & Telegraph's common stock and Apple Computer Company's common stock were reported in many newspapers on Wednesday, April 24, 1991, as follows:

Stock	High	Low	Close	Net Change
AT&T	36⅝	35⅞	36	−⅛
Apple C	63	60¼	60½	—

These reported prices are the highest and lowest prices at which the stock traded during Tuesday, April 23, and the price of the last transaction that occurred at the end of the day. The net change is the difference between the closing price on Tuesday and the closing price for Monday, April 22.

Classifying Investments

LO 1 State the criteria for classifying stock investments as current assets or as long-term investments.

Equity securities include common and preferred stocks. **Marketable equity securities** are identified by the FASB as those that have "sales prices or bid and ask prices . . . currently available on a national securities exchange or in the over-the-counter market."[1] To have this price information available, these securities must be actively traded.

If an investment in marketable equity securities is held as "an investment of cash available for current operations," it is classified as a current asset.[2] (You learned how to account for short-term investments in marketable equity securities in Chapter 8.)

Investments that are not held as a ready source of cash are called **long-term investments.** They include funds earmarked for a special purpose, such as bond sinking funds, as well as land or other assets that are owned but not used in the regular operations of the business. Long-term investments also include investments in bonds and stocks that are not marketable or that, although marketable, are not intended to serve as a ready source of cash. These assets are reported on the balance sheet in a separate category called *Long-term investments*.

Accounting for Long-Term Investments in Stock

LO 2 Describe the circumstances under which the cost method, the equity method, and consolidated financial statements are used in accounting for long-term stock investments.

The method used to account for a long-term stock investment depends on the relationship between the investor and the investee. This relationship takes one of three forms:

1. The investor is not able to significantly influence the operations of the investee.
2. The investor has a significant influence but does not control the investee.
3. The investor controls the investee.

When a company invests in another company's stock, the shares owned by the investor may represent only a small percentage of the total amount of stock outstanding. In this case, the investor usually does not have the ability to

1 FASB, *Accounting Standards—Current Text* (Norwalk, Conn., 1990), sec. I89.404. First published in *Statement of Financial Accounting Standards No. 12,* par. 7.

2 Ibid., sec. B05.105. Previously published in *Accounting Research Bulletin No. 43,* ch. 3, sec. A, par. 4.

influence the operations of the investee corporation. Normally, an investor does not have a significant influence if it owns less than 20% of the investee's voting stock.[3]

Sometimes, an investor buys a large block of a corporation's voting stock and is able to exercise a significant influence over the investee corporation. An investor who owns 20% or more of a corporation's voting stock is normally presumed to have a significant influence over the investee. There may be cases, however, where the accountant concludes that the 20% test of significant influence should be overruled by other, more persuasive, evidence.[4]

If an investor owns more than 50% of a corporation's voting stock, the investor can dominate all of the other stockholders in electing the corporation's board of directors. Thus, the investor has control over the investee corporation's management.[5]

As we stated earlier, the method of accounting for a stock investment depends on the relationship between the investor and the investee. Illustration 18–1 shows each type of investor/investee relationship and the corresponding accounting methods used. In studying this illustration, note that if the investor does not have a significant influence, the accounting method used is either the **cost method** or the *lower of cost or market* method. Also note that the marketability of the stock determines which of these two methods will be applied. If the investor has a significant influence, the accounting method used is the **equity method.** Finally, if the investor controls the investee, the investor reports **consolidated financial statements** to the public. As shown in Illustration 18–1, an investor that controls an investee presents consolidated financial statements but uses the equity method in its records. Also note that the marketability of the shares does not affect the choice between the equity method and consolidation. We explain each of these accounting methods in the following sections.

The Cost Method of Accounting for Stock Investments

LO 3 Prepare entries to account for long-term stock investments according to the cost method and the equity method and to reflect lower of cost or market.

When stock is purchased as an investment, the asset is recorded at its total cost, which includes any commission paid to the broker. For example, Gordon Company purchased 1,000 (1%) of Dot Corporation's 100,000 outstanding common shares as a long-term investment at 23¼ plus a $300 broker's commission. Gordon's entry to record the transaction is:

Sept.	10	Investment in Dot Corporation Stock	23,550.00	
		Cash		23,550.00
		Purchased 1,000 shares of stock for $23,250 plus a $300 broker's commission.		

[3] Ibid., sec. I82.104. First published in *APB Opinion No. 18,* par. 17.

[4] Ibid., sec. I82.107–108. First published in *FASB Interpretation No. 35,* pars. 3–4.

[5] Ibid., sec. C51.102. First published in *Statement of Financial Accounting Standards No. 94,* par. 13.

ILLUSTRATION 18–1

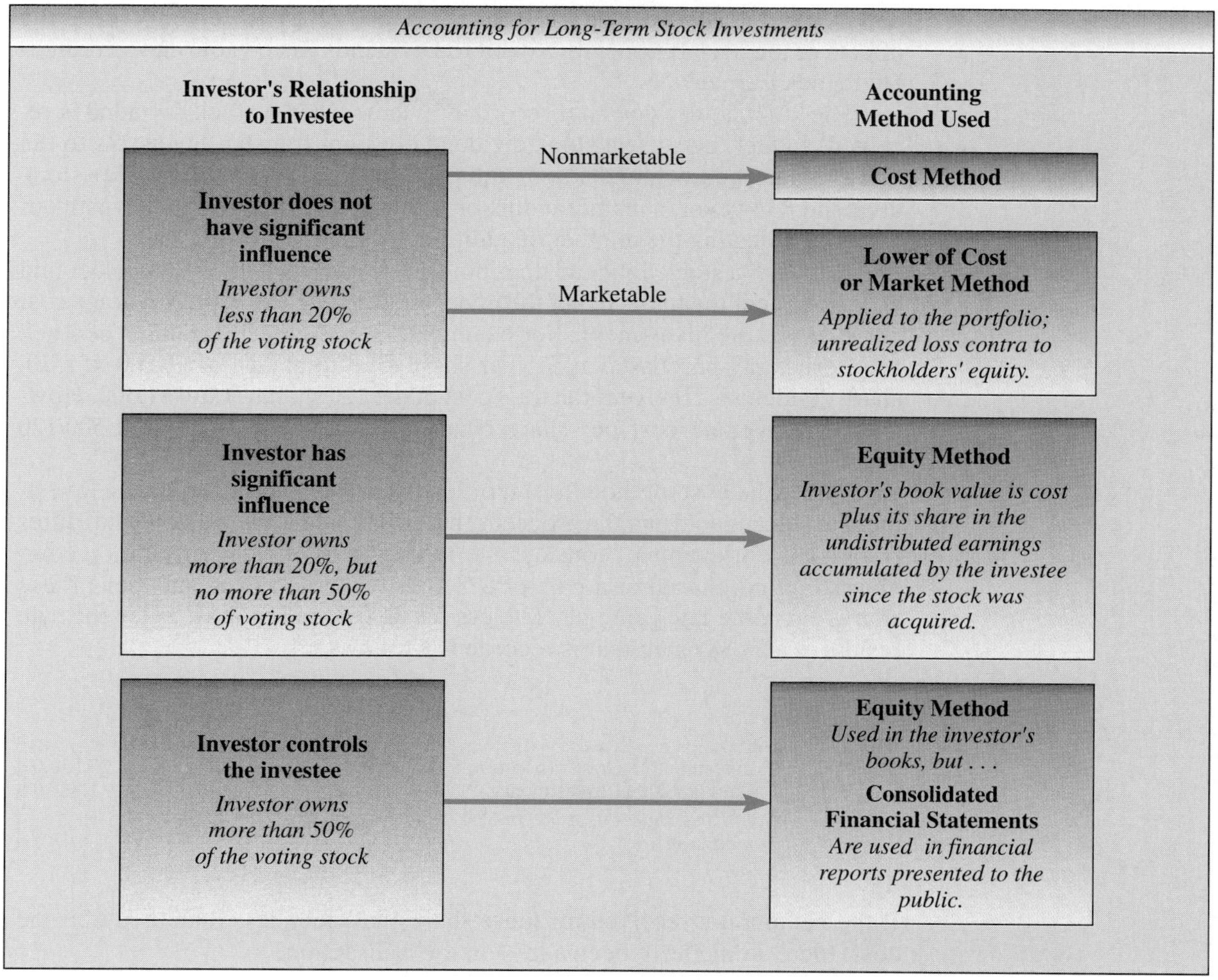

Observe that nothing about the par value is recorded nor is any premium or discount. Only the corporation that issues the stock records premiums and discounts. An investor records the entire cost as a debit to the investment account, even though the cost may be above or below par value.

When the cost method is used and a cash dividend is received on the stock, record the dividend as follows:

Oct.	5	Cash	1,000.00	
		Dividends Earned		1,000.00
		Received a $1 per share dividend on the Dot Corporation stock.		

Unlike interest on bonds and notes, dividends are not earned merely as time passes. Therefore, you never make an end-of-period entry to accrue dividends that have not been declared. However, if the investor's balance sheet is prepared after a cash dividend is declared but before it is received, record the effects of the declaration with a debit to Dividends Receivable and a credit to Dividends Earned.

The stockholder does not record a revenue when a stock dividend is received. In fact, because a stock dividend does not transfer any assets to the stockholder, the stockholder does not make any journal entry to record a stock dividend. However, a memorandum or note may be written in the investment account indicating the number of additional shares received.

Although a stock dividend does not transfer assets to the stockholder and does not affect the total cost of the investment, it does affect the average cost per share of the investment. For example, suppose that 100 shares of stock were originally purchased at $15 per share for a total cost of $1,500. If a 20-share dividend is received, the total cost of the 120 shares is still $1,500. However, the average cost per share changes from $15 to $12.50 ($1,500/120 shares).

Under the cost method, a gain or loss must be recorded when an investment in stock is sold and the proceeds (net of any sales commission paid) differ from cost. For example, consider the 1,000 shares of Dot Corporation common stock purchased at a cost of $23,550. If Gordon Company sells these shares on some later date at 25¾ less a sales commission of $315, the sale results in a $1,885 gain that is recorded as follows:

Jan.	7	Cash	25,435.00	
		Investment in Dot Corporation Stock		23,550.00
		Gain on Sale of Investments		1,885.00
		Sold 1,000 shares of stock for $25,750 less a $315 commission.		

If the net amount received for these shares had been less than their $23,550 cost, there would have been a loss on the transaction.

Lower of Cost or Market

When using the cost method to account for a stock investment that is not marketable, report the asset on the balance sheet at cost. However, as you learned in Chapter 8, investments in marketable equity securities are divided into (1) a short-term portfolio and (2) a long-term portfolio. Then, the total market value of each portfolio is calculated and compared to the total cost of each portfolio. Each portfolio is reported at the lower of cost or market.[6]

Recall from Chapter 8 that a decline in total market value of the current portfolio below its cost is reported on the income statement as a loss. Any later recoveries of market value (up to but not exceeding cost) are reported in the income statement as gains.[7]

---

[6] Ibid., sec. I89.102–103. First published in *Statement of Financial Accounting Standards No. 12*, pars. 8–9.

[7] Ibid., sec. I89.105.

In the case of a long-term portfolio of marketable equity securities, market value declines are always reported on the balance sheet but are reported on the income statements only if they appear to be permanent. Usually, they are not assumed to be permanent, in which case the market value decline is called an *unrealized loss* and is reported as a separate contra stockholders' equity item on the balance sheet.[8]

For example, assume that a company purchased a portfolio of long-term investments in marketable equity securities at a cost of $67,000. On December 31, the end of the accounting period, the market value of the portfolio had declined to $58,000. However, the decline was believed to be temporary. The entry to record the market decline is:

Dec.	31	Unrealized Loss on Market Decline of Long-Term Investments	9,000.00	
		Allowance to Reduce Long-Term Investments to Market		9,000.00
		To record market decline of long-term investments in marketable stocks.		

In the long-term investments section of the balance sheet, the company reports its investments portfolio at its original cost of $67,000 less the $9,000 allowance, or $58,000. The stockholders' equity section appears as follows (the common stock and retained earnings amounts are assumed):

Common stock	$100,000	
Retained earnings	80,000	
Less unrealized loss on market decline of long-term investments	(9,000)	
Total stockholders' equity		$171,000

In future years, the balances of the unrealized loss account and the allowance account will receive equal adjustments to reflect additional changes in market value in the range below the original cost. Note that their balances will always be equal to each other; that is, the debit balance in the unrealized loss account will always equal the credit balance in the allowance account.

The Equity Method of Accounting for Common Stock Investments

If a common stock investor has significant influence over the investee, the *equity method* of accounting for the investment must be used. When the stock is acquired, the investor records the purchase at cost, just as under the cost method. For example, on January 1, 1993, Gordon Company purchased 3,000 shares (30%) of JWM, Inc., common stock for a total cost of $70,650. This entry would be made to record the purchase on Gordon's books:

---

[8] Ibid., sec. I89.105, 115.

Jan.	1	Investment in JWM, Inc. . . . . Cash . . . . *Purchased 3,000 shares of common stock.*	70,650.00	 70,650.00

Under the equity method, the earnings of the investee corporation not only increase the investee's net assets but also increase the investor's equity claims against the investee's assets. Therefore, when the investee closes its books and reports the amount of its earnings, the investor takes up its share of those earnings in its investment account. For example, assume that JWM, Inc., reported net income of $20,000 for 1993. Gordon's entry to record its 30% share of these earnings is:

Dec.	31	Investment in JWM, Inc. . . . . Earnings from Investment in JWM, Inc. . . . . *To record 30% equity in investee's earnings of $20,000.*	6,000.00	 6,000.00

The debit records the increase in Gordon Company's equity in JWM, Inc. The credit causes 30% of JWM, Inc.'s net income to appear on Gordon's income statement as earnings from the investment. As with any other revenue, Gordon closes the equity method earnings to Income Summary and then to Retained Earnings.

If the investee corporation incurs a net loss instead of a net income, the investor debits its share of the loss to an account called Loss from Investment and reduces (credits) its Investment in Stock account. Then, the investor closes the loss to Income Summary and finally to Retained Earnings.

Dividends paid by the investee corporation decrease its assets and retained earnings. Dividends also decrease the investor's equity in the investee. Under the equity method, the receipt of cash dividends is not recorded as revenue because the investor has already recorded its share of the earnings reported by the investee. Instead, dividends received from the investee are nothing more than a conversion of the form of the investor's asset from a stock investment to cash. In effect, part of the investor's equity claim against the investee is settled by the dividend. Thus, the equity method records dividends as a reduction in the balance of the investment account.

For example, assume that JWM, Inc., declared and paid $10,000 in cash dividends on its common stock. Gordon's entry to record its 30% share of these dividends, which it received on January 9, 1994, is:

Jan.	9	Cash . . . . Investment in JWM, Inc. . . . . *To record receipt of 30% of the $10,000 dividend paid by JWM, Inc.*	3,000.00	 3,000.00

Thus, when the equity method is used, the carrying value of a common stock investment equals the cost of the investment plus the investor's equity in the *undistributed* earnings of the investee. For example, after the preceding transactions are recorded on the books of Gordon Company, the investment account appears as follows:

Investment in JWM, Inc.

Date		Explanation	Debit	Credit	Balance
1993					
Jan.	1	Investment	70,650		70,650
Dec.	31	Share of earnings	6,000		76,650
1994					
Jan.	9	Share of dividend		3,000	73,650

When an equity method stock investment is sold, the gain or loss on the sale is determined by comparing the proceeds from the sale with the carrying value (book value) of the investment on the date of sale. For example, suppose that Gordon Company sold its JWM, Inc., stock for $80,000 on January 10, 1994. The entry to record the sale is:

Jan.	10	Cash	80,000.00	
		Investment in JWM, Inc.		73,650.00
		Gain on Sale of Investments		6,350.00
		Sold 3,000 shares of stock for $80,000.		

Parent and Subsidiary Corporations

Corporations frequently own stock in and may even control other corporations. For example, if Par Company owns more than 50% of the voting stock of Sub Company, Par Company can elect Sub Company's board of directors and thus control its activities and resources. In this case, the controlling corporation, Par Company, is known as the **parent company** and Sub Company is called a **subsidiary.**

When a corporation owns all the outstanding stock of a subsidiary, it can take over the subsidiary's assets, cancel the subsidiary's stock, and merge the subsidiary into the parent company. However, there often are financial, legal, and tax advantages if a large business is operated as a parent corporation that controls one or more subsidiary corporations. In fact, most large companies are parent corporations that own one or more subsidiaries.

Some parent corporations are organized solely for the purpose of holding the stock of their subsidiaries. In such cases, the parent corporations have no operating activities of their own and are called *holding companies.*

When a business operates as a parent company with subsidiaries, separate accounting records are maintained by each corporation. From a legal viewpoint, the parent and each subsidiary are still separate entities with all the rights, duties, and responsibilities of individual corporations. However, investors in the parent company indirectly are investors in the subsidiaries. To evaluate their investments, parent company investors must consider the financial status and operations of the subsidiaries as well as the parent. This information is provided in *consolidated financial statements.*

ILLUSTRATION 18–2

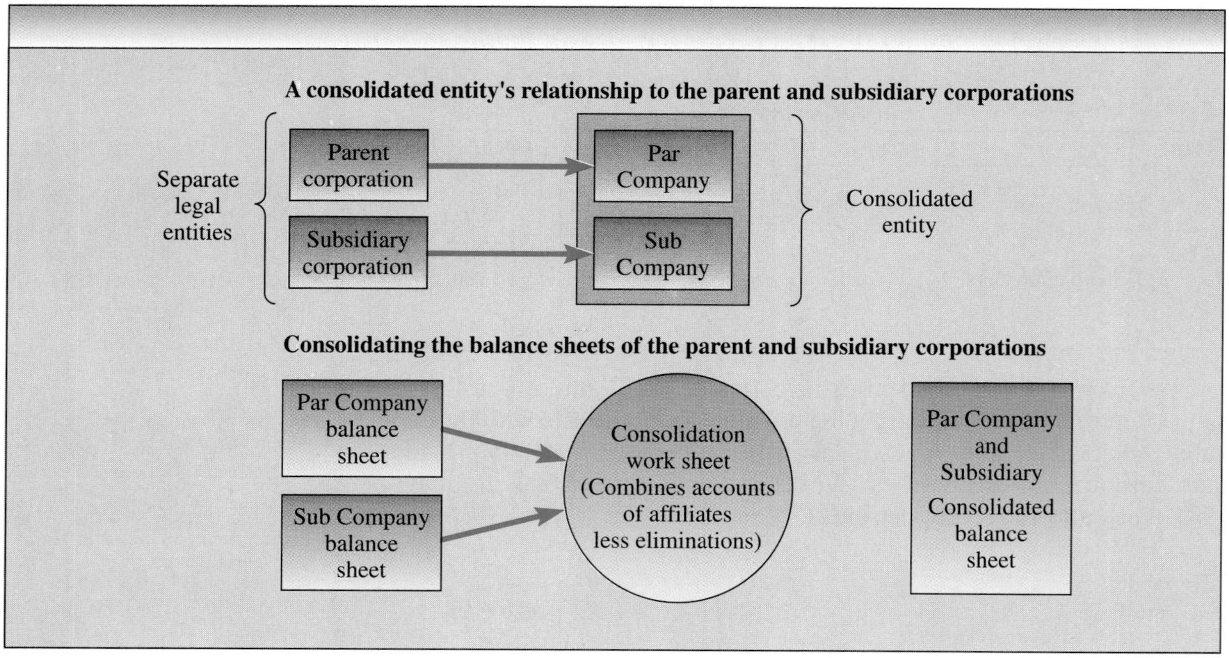

Consolidated statements show the financial position, the results of operations, and the cash flows of all corporations under the parent stockholders' control, including the subsidiaries. These statements are prepared as if the business is organized as a single company. In other words, the assets and liabilities of all affiliated companies are combined on a single balance sheet. Also, their revenues and expenses are combined on a single income statement and their cash flows are combined on a single statement of cash flows. The relationship between the consolidated entity and the separate parent and subsidiary corporations is represented in the top section of Illustration 18–2.

Consolidated Balance Sheets

LO 4 Prepare consolidated balance sheets and explain how to report any excess of investment cost over book value and minority interests.

The bottom section of Illustration 18–2 depicts the process of preparing a consolidated balance sheet from the separate balance sheets of the parent and the subsidiary. When parent and subsidiary balance sheets are consolidated, the two companies' assets and liabilities are combined. However, duplications in items are eliminated so that the combined figures do not show more assets and equities than actually exist. For example, a parent's investment in the shares of a subsidiary's stock is carried as an asset in the parent company's records. But, these shares actually represent an equity in the subsidiary's assets. Therefore, if the parent's investment in a subsidiary and the subsidiary's assets were both shown on the consolidated balance sheet, the same resources would be counted twice. To prevent this double counting, the parent's investment account and the subsidiary's capital accounts are offset and eliminated in preparing a consolidated balance sheet.

Likewise, a single enterprise cannot owe a debt to itself. For example, suppose that the parent company has loaned $10,000 to the subsidiary. The

ILLUSTRATION 18–3

Consolidation Work Sheet for 100% Owned Subsidiary; Stock Purchased at Book Value

PAR COMPANY AND SUB COMPANY
Work Sheet for a Consolidated Balance Sheet
December 31, 1993

	Par Company	Sub Company	Eliminations Debit	Eliminations Credit	Consolidated Amounts
Assets					
Cash	5,000	15,000			20,000
Notes receivable	10,000			(*a*) 10,000	
Investment in Sub Company	115,000			(*b*) 115,000	
Other assets	190,000	117,000			307,000
	320,000	132,000			327,000
Liabilities and Equities					
Accounts payable	15,000	7,000			22,000
Notes payable		10,000	(*a*) 10,000		
Common stock	250,000	100,000	(*b*) 100,000		250,000
Retained earnings	55,000	15,000	(*b*) 15,000		55,000
	320,000	132,000	125,000	125,000	327,000

parent's accounts would reflect a $10,000 receivable, while the subsidiary would reflect a $10,000 payable. From the consolidated point of view, however, there is no receivable and no payable. Therefore, receivables and payables between the parent and the subsidiary are eliminated in preparing a consolidated balance sheet.

Balance Sheets Consolidated at Time of Acquisition

When a parent's balance sheet and a subsidiary's balance sheet are combined in the process of preparing a consolidated balance sheet, a work sheet normally is used to organize the data. Illustration 18–3 shows a work sheet to consolidate the accounts of Par Company and its subsidiary, Sub Company. In the work sheet, the account balances are presented as of December 31, 1993, the date on which Par Company acquired its interest in Sub Company. Par Company paid cash to purchase all of Sub Company's outstanding $10 par value common stock from the Sub Company stockholders. The stock had a book value of $115,000, or $11.50 per share, on Sub Company's books. In this first illustration, we assume that Par Company simply paid $115,000, or book value, for the outstanding shares.

In Illustration 18–3, notice that the *Eliminations* columns include two sets of debits and credits. One set is identified by the letter *a*, and the other set is identified by the letter *b*. These two sets of debits and credits are sometimes called elimination entries. However, the eliminations on a consolidation work sheet are not like the adjustments entered on work sheets in earlier chapters. Elimination entries appear only on the consolidation work sheet. Elimination entries are not journalized on the books of the parent or on the books of the subsidiary.

Elimination *a*. On December 31, 1993, Par Company loaned Sub Company $10,000 cash to use in its operations. In exchange for the cash, Sub Company signed a promissory note to Par Company. This intercompany debt was in reality a transfer of funds within the consolidated entity. Because this transaction did not increase the total assets and total liabilities of the affiliated companies, elimination *a* is made to keep both balances from appearing on the consolidated balance sheet. To understand this elimination, recall that the subsidiary's promissory note appears as a $10,000 debit in Par Company's Notes Receivable account. Then, observe that the first credit in the Eliminations column exactly offsets, or *eliminates,* this item. Next, recall that the subsidiary's note appears as a credit in Sub Company's Notes Payable account. In the Eliminations columns, the $10,000 debit completes the elimination of this intercompany debt. As a result of this elimination, neither the receivable nor the payable appears in the last column of the work sheet.

Elimination *b*. When buying a subsidiary's stock, a parent company records the investment as an asset. This investment represents an equity in the subsidiary's net assets. However, you must not show both the subsidiary's net assets (equity) and the parent company's investment in the subsidiary on the consolidated balance sheet. Doing so would double count those items. On the work sheet, the credit portion of elimination *b* eliminates Par Company's investment and avoids double counting of the subsidiary's net assets.

Note that the debits of elimination *b* eliminate the stockholders' equity account balances of Sub Company. This prevents Sub Company's stockholders' equity account balances from appearing on the consolidated balance sheet. These eliminations are necessary because, in the present example, Par Company owns all of Sub Company's stock. None of the Sub Company shares are held by outside investors.

After the intercompany items are eliminated on a work sheet like the one in Illustration 18–3, the assets of the parent and the subsidiary and the remaining equities in these assets are combined and carried into the work sheet's last column. The combined amounts are then used to prepare a consolidated balance sheet that shows all the assets and equities of the parent and its subsidiary.

Parent Company Does Not Buy All of Subsidiary's Stock and Pays More than Book Value

In the preceding example, Par Company purchased 100% of its subsidiary's stock at a cost that equaled the book value of the stock. However, a parent company may purchase less than 100% of a subsidiary's stock and very likely will pay a price that is different from book value. To illustrate, assume that Par Company purchased only 80% of Sub Company's outstanding stock. Also assume that Par Company paid $13 per share, or $1.50 more than the stock's book value. Illustration 18–4 presents the consolidation work sheet for this example.

ILLUSTRATION 18–4

Consolidation Work Sheet; 80% of Subsidiary Stock Purchased at More than Book Value

PAR COMPANY AND SUB COMPANY
Work Sheet for a Consolidated Balance Sheet
December 31, 1993

	Par Company	Sub Company	Eliminations Debit	Eliminations Credit	Consolidated Amounts
Assets					
Cash	16,000	15,000			31,000
Notes receivable	10,000			(*a*) 10,000	
Investment in Sub Company	104,000			(*b*) 104,000	
Other assets	190,000	117,000			307,000
Excess of cost over book value			(*b*) 12,000		12,000
	320,000	132,000			350,000
Liabilities and Equities					
Accounts payable	15,000	7,000			22,000
Notes payable		10,000	(*a*) 10,000		
Common stock	250,000	100,000	(*b*) 100,000		250,000
Retained earnings	55,000	15,000	(*b*) 15,000		55,000
Minority interest				(*b*) 23,000	23,000
	320,000	132,000	137,000	137,000	350,000

These new assumptions do not change the work sheet treatment of the intercompany debt. Therefore, elimination *a* is exactly the same as the one presented in Illustration 18–3.

However, the new assumptions require a more complicated work sheet entry to eliminate the parent's investment and the subsidiary's stockholders' equity accounts. The elimination is complicated because it must deal with (1) the *minority interest* in the subsidiary and (2) the *excess over book value* paid by the parent company for the subsidiary's stock.

Minority Interest. When a parent company buys a controlling interest in a subsidiary, it becomes the subsidiary's majority stockholder. If the parent owns less than 100% of the subsidiary's stock, the subsidiary has other stockholders who hold a **minority interest** in its assets and earnings.

When you prepare a consolidated balance sheet for a parent and a subsidiary that has a minority interest, the equity of the minority stockholders must be recognized. You can use the consolidation work sheet to calculate the minority interest in the process of eliminating the stockholders' equity balances of the subsidiary. The procedures are shown in Illustration 18–4. In this case, the minority stockholders have a 20% interest in the subsidiary. Therefore, 20% of the subsidiary's stockholders' equity, or $23,000 [($100,000 + $15,000) × 20%], is reclassified on the work sheet as the minority interest in the consolidated entity.

Excess of Investment Cost over Book Value. Illustration 18–4 is also based on the assumption that Par Company paid $13 per share for its 8,000 shares of Sub Company's stock. Therefore, the cost of these shares exceeded their book value by $12,000, calculated as follows:

Cost of stock (8,000 shares at $13.00 per share) . .	$104,000
Book value (8,000 shares at $11.50 per share) . . .	92,000
Excess of cost over book value (8,000 shares at $1.50 per share)	$ 12,000

Now observe how the process of eliminating the parent's investment in the subsidiary identifies and measures this excess of cost over book value on the work sheet. Then, the excess is carried into the asset portion of the Consolidated Amounts column.

To summarize elimination *b,* notice that it has three debits and two credits. First, notice that the $104,000 credit to Investment in Sub Company eliminates the balance of that account. Second, note the elimination of the stockholders' equity accounts of Sub Company with a $100,000 debit to Common Stock and a $15,000 debit to Retained Earnings. The $23,000 credit recognizes the equity of the Sub Company's minority interest stockholders. Finally, a $12,000 debit recognizes the cost in excess of book value paid by the parent. This debit also balances the debits and credits of elimination *b*.

After the work sheet of Illustration 18–4 is completed, the consolidated amounts in the last column are used to prepare the consolidated balance sheet shown in Illustration 18–5. Notice the treatment of the minority interest in the balance sheet. The minority stockholders have a $23,000 equity in the consolidated entity. Some accountants believe that this item should be reported in the stockholders' equity section. Others believe that it should be reported in the long-term liabilities section. As a compromise, most companies show the minority interest as a separate item between the liabilities and stockholders' equity sections. This approach is used in Illustration 18–5.

Next, observe that the $12,000 excess over book value that Par Company paid for Sub Company's stock appears on the consolidated balance sheet as an asset called *Goodwill from consolidation*.

There are several reasons why a parent might pay more than book value for its equity in a subsidiary. One reason may be that some of the subsidiary's assets are carried on the subsidiary's books at less than their fair values. Another reason may be that some of the subsidiary's liabilities are carried at book values greater than their fair values. A third reason might be that the subsidiary's earnings prospects are good enough to justify paying more for the stock than the net fair (market) value of the subsidiary's assets and liabilities.

In this illustration, we assume that the book values of Sub Company's assets and liabilities equal their fair values. However, Sub Company's high expected earnings justified paying $104,000 for an 80% interest.

If a company pays more than book value because the subsidiary's assets are undervalued or its liabilities are overvalued, the cost in excess of book

ILLUSTRATION 18-5

PAR COMPANY AND SUBSIDIARY
Consolidated Balance Sheet
December 31, 1993

Assets		
Cash		$ 31,000
Other assets		307,000
Goodwill from consolidation		12,000
Total assets		$350,000
Liabilities and Stockholders' Equity		
Liabilities:		
Accounts payable		$ 22,000
Minority interest		23,000
Stockholders' equity:		
Common stock	$250,000	
Retained earnings	55,000	
Total stockholders' equity		305,000
Total liabilities and stockholders' equity		$350,000

value must be allocated to those assets and liabilities so that they are restated at their fair values. After the subsidiary's assets and liabilities have been restated to reflect fair values, any remaining cost in excess of book value is reported on the consolidated balance sheet as Goodwill from consolidation.[9]

Occasionally, a parent company pays less than book value for its interest in a subsidiary. One likely reason for a price below book value is that some of the subsidiary's assets are carried on its books at amounts in excess of fair value. Therefore, the APB ruled that the excess of book value over cost should be allocated to reduce the balance sheet valuations of the overvalued assets.[10]

Earnings and Dividends of a Subsidiary

As you have already learned, a parent uses the equity method in its books to account for its investment in a subsidiary. Thus, the parent's recorded net income and Retained Earnings account include the parent's share of the net income earned by the subsidiary since the date of acquisition. Also, the balance of the parent's Investment in Subsidiary account increases (or decreases) each year by an amount equal to the parent's share of the subsidiary's earnings (or loss) less the parent's share of any dividends paid by the subsidiary.

[9] Ibid., sec. B50.403. First published in *APB Opinion No. 16*, par. 87.

[10] Ibid., sec. B50.160.

AS A MATTER OF
Fact

Since December 15, 1988, generally accepted accounting principles have required companies to consolidate their subsidiaries even though the operations of the parent and the subsidiaries are not similar or homogeneous. In a survey of 600 industrial and merchandising companies, 86 disclosed information about nonhomogeneous subsidiaries that were consolidated. The nature of the nonhomogeneous operations consolidated by the survey companies is shown in the following chart:

Nonhomogeneous Operations Consolidated by 86 Industrial and Merchandising Companies

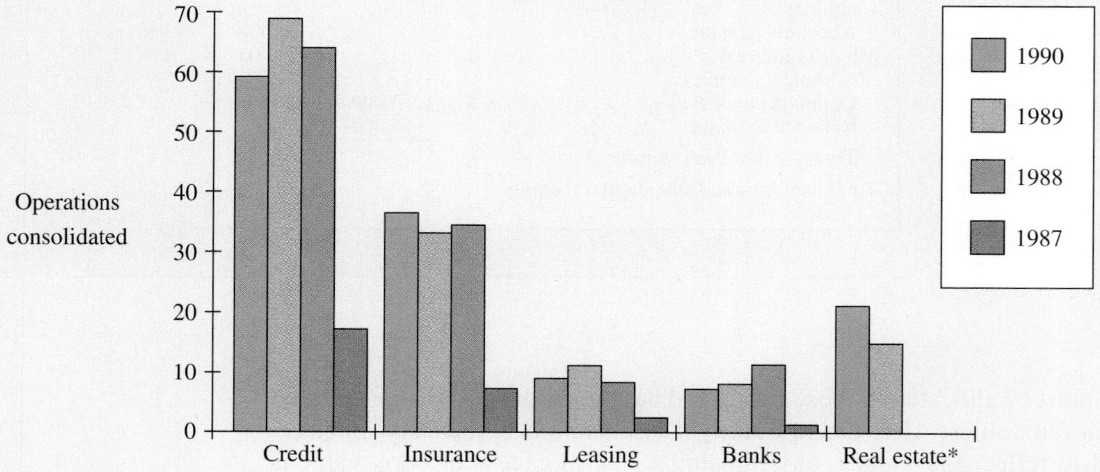

*Not compiled in 1987 or 1988

Data for chart excerpted with permission from *Accounting Trends & Techniques*, Annual Survey of Accounting Practices followed in 600 Stockholders' Reports, 45th ed., Copyright © 1991 by American Institute of Certified Public Accountants, Inc., Table 1–9, p. 52.

For example, assume that Sub Company earned $12,500 during 1994, its first year as a subsidiary, and at year-end paid out $7,500 in dividends. Par Company records its 80% share of these earnings and dividends as follows:

Dec.	31	Investment in Sub Company	10,000.00	
		Earnings from Investment in Subsidiary		10,000.00
		To record 80% of the 1994 net income reported by Sub Company.		
Dec.	31	Cash	6,000.00	
		Investment in Sub Company		6,000.00
		To record the receipt of 80% of the $7,500 dividends paid by Sub Company.		

ILLUSTRATION 18–6

Work Sheet for a Consolidated Balance Sheet; One Year after Acquisition

PAR COMPANY AND SUB COMPANY
Work Sheet for a Consolidated Balance Sheet
December 31, 1993

	Par Company	Sub Company	Eliminations Debit	Eliminations Credit	Consolidated Amounts
Assets					
Cash	22,000	20,000			42,000
Notes receivable	10,000			(*a*) 10,000	
Investment in Sub Company	108,000			(*b*) 108,000	
Other assets	190,000	117,000			307,000
Excess of cost over book value			(*b*) 12,000		12,000
	330,000	137,000			361,000
Liabilities and Equities					
Accounts payable	15,000	7,000			22,000
Notes payable		10,000	(*a*) 10,000		
Common stock	250,000	100,000	(*b*) 100,000		250,000
Retained earnings	65,000	20,000	(*b*) 20,000		65,000
Minority interest				(*b*) 24,000	24,000
	330,000	137,000	142,000	142,000	361,000

Consolidated Balance Sheets at a Date after Acquisition

Illustration 18–6 shows the December 31, 1994, work sheet for consolidating the balance sheets of Par Company and Sub Company. To simplify the illustration, we assume that Par Company had no transactions during the year, and thus had no journal entries other than those made to record its share of Sub Company's earnings and dividends. Also, the other assets and liabilities of Sub Company did not change, the subsidiary has not paid the note payable to Par Company, and there is no interest on that note.

Compare Illustration 18–6 with Illustration 18–4 to see the changes that have occurred since the beginning of the year in Par Company's balance sheet (the first column). Par Company's cash increased from $16,000 to $22,000 because of the $6,000 cash dividend received from Sub Company. The Investment in Sub Company account increased from $104,000 to $108,000 as a result of the equity method entries during the year. Finally, Par Company's retained earnings increased by $10,000, which was the parent's share of the subsidiary's earnings.

The second column of Illustration 18–6 contains only two changes: (1) Sub Company's cash balance increased by $5,000, which is the difference between its $12,500 net income and the $7,500 cash dividends paid out, and (2) retained earnings increased from $15,000 to $20,000, which is also explained by the $12,500 net income less $7,500 dividends.

Entry *a* is still needed to eliminate the intercompany debt, and is exactly the same as before. However, elimination *b* is different in several respects.

The credit to the investment account is now increased to $108,000 to eliminate the larger balance. The debit to common stock is still for $100,000, but the debit to retained earnings is increased to $20,000 to reflect the increased balance in that account. Because the subsidiary had a $5,000 addition to its retained earnings, the size of the credit to the 20% minority interest is greater in 1994 by the minority's $1,000 share of the $5,000.

Finally, the $12,000 excess cost over book value shown in Illustration 18–6 is unchanged from a year earlier. We have left it unchanged merely to simplify the example. As you know from Chapter 11, generally accepted accounting principles require this cost to be amortized.[11] The procedures for computing and recognizing this cost for the consolidated financial statements are not explained here. You will learn about them in a more advanced course.

Other Consolidated Statements

In addition to the balance sheet, the consolidated financial statements include a consolidated income statement, a consolidated retained earnings statement, and a consolidated statement of cash flows. You can gain a general understanding of these statements without further discussion of the procedures used to prepare them. At this point, you only need to understand that all duplications in items are eliminated. Thus, when one affiliated company records profit on sales to another affiliate, the profit is eliminated in the consolidated statements. Also, the amounts of net income and retained earnings reported in consolidated statements equal the amounts recorded by the parent under the equity method.

The Corporation Balance Sheet

This and preceding chapters have described several different components of balance sheets. Illustration 18–7 presents an example that includes a number of these components.

Three items of information in this balance sheet reveal that it is a consolidated balance sheet. They are the title and the two items *Goodwill from consolidation* and *Minority interest*. In Illustration 18–7, notice the asset called Investment in Toledo Corporation common stock. Note that Toledo Corporation is not a consolidated subsidiary. When the balance sheet was prepared, Betco Corporation's investments in its subsidiaries' stock were eliminated. Therefore, the Toledo Corporation stock is an investment in an unconsolidated company.

Accounting for International Operations

In today's complex world, many companies conduct business activities in more than one country. In fact, the operations of some large corporations involve so many different countries that they are called **multinational businesses.** The problems of managing and accounting for companies that have international operations can be very complex. Because of this complexity, the

[11] Ibid., sec. I60.108–112. First published in *APB Opinion No. 17,* pars. 27–31.

ILLUSTRATION 18-7

Consolidated Balance Sheet

BETCO CORPORATION
Consolidated Balance Sheet
December 31, 1994

Assets

Current assets:			
Cash		$ 15,000	
Marketable securities		5,000	
Accounts receivable	$ 50,000		
Less allowance for doubtful accounts	1,000	49,000	
Subscriptions receivable, common stock		15,000	
Merchandise inventory		115,000	
Prepaid expenses		1,000	
Total current assets			$200,000
Long-term investments:			
Toledo Corporation common stock (cost approximates market)		$ 5,000	
Bond sinking fund		15,000	
Total long-term investments			20,000
Plant assets:			
Store equipment	$ 85,000		
Less accumulated depreciation	20,000	$ 65,000	
Buildings	$285,000		
Less accumulated depreciation	30,000	255,000	
Land		50,000	
Total plant assets			370,000
Intangible assets:			
Goodwill from consolidation			10,000
Total assets			$600,000

Liabilities

Current liabilities:			
Accounts payable	$ 14,000		
State and federal income taxes payable	16,000		
Notes payable	10,000		
Total current liabilities		$ 40,000	
Long-term liabilities:			
Bonds payable, 8%, secured by mortgage, due in 2000	$100,000		
Less unamortized discount based on the 8¼% market rate for bond interest prevailing on the date of issue	2,000	98,000	
Total liabilities			$138,000
Minority interest			15,000

Stockholders' Equity

Contributed capital:			
Common stock, $10 par value, authorized 50,000 shares, issued 30,000 shares of which 1,000 are in the treasury	$300,000		
Unissued common stock subscribed, 2,500 shares	25,000		
Contributed capital in excess of par value, common stock	33,000		
Total contributed capital		$358,000	
Retained earnings (Note 1)		105,000	
Total contributed and retained capital		$463,000	
Less cost of treasury stock		16,000	
Total stockholders' equity			447,000
Total liabilities and stockholders' equity			$600,000

Note 1: Retained earnings in the amount of $31,000 is restricted under an agreement with the corporation's bondholders and because of the purchase of treasury stock, leaving $74,000 of retained earnings not restricted.

LO 5 Describe the primary problems of accounting for international operations and prepare entries to account for sales to foreign customers.

following pages present only a brief discussion. A more detailed study of these issues is reserved for advanced business courses.

Two primary problems in accounting for international operations occur because businesses with transactions in more than one country have to deal with more than one currency. These two problems are (1) accounting for sales or purchases denominated in a foreign currency and (2) preparing consolidated financial statements with foreign subsidiaries. To clarify the analysis, we discuss these problems from the perspective of companies that have a base of operations in the United States. Therefore, we assume that the companies in our examples prepare financial statements in terms of the U.S. dollar. Hence, the **reporting currency** of such firms is the U.S. dollar.

Exchange Rates between Currencies

Active markets for the purchase and sale of foreign currencies exist all over the world. In these markets, U.S. dollars can be exchanged for Canadian dollars, British pounds, French francs, Japanese yen, or other currencies. The price of one currency can be stated in another currency and is called a **foreign exchange rate.** For example, assume that the current exchange rate for British pounds and U.S. dollars was $1.7515 on January 31, 1993. This rate means that one pound could have been acquired for $1.7515. On the same day, assume that the exchange rate between German marks and U.S. dollars was $0.5321. This number means that one mark could be purchased for $0.5321. Foreign exchange rates fluctuate daily (or even hourly) in accordance with the changing supply and demand for each currency and expectations about future events.

Sales or Purchases Denominated in a Foreign Currency

When a U.S. company makes a sale to a foreign customer, a special problem can arise in accounting for the sale and the account receivable. If the sales terms require the foreign customer's payment to be in U.S. dollars, no special accounting problem arises. But, if the terms of the sale state that payment is to be made in a foreign currency, the U.S. company must go through special steps to account for the sale and the account receivable.

For example, suppose that a U.S. company, the Boston Company, makes a credit sale to London Outfitters, a British company. The sale occurs on December 12, 1993, and the price is £10,000, which is due on February 10, 1994. Naturally, Boston Company keeps its accounting records in terms of U.S. dollars. Therefore, to record the sale, Boston Company must translate the sales price from pounds to dollars. This is done using the current exchange rate on the date of the sale. Assuming that the current exchange rate on December 12 is $1.80, Boston records the sale as follows:

Dec.	12	Accounts Receivable—London Outfitters	18,000.00	
		Sales (10,000 × $1.80)		18,000.00
		To record a sale at £10,000, when the exchange rate equals $1.80.		

Now, assume that Boston Company prepares annual financial statements on December 31, 1993. On that date, the current exchange rate has increased to \$1.84. Therefore, the current dollar value of Boston Company's receivable is \$18,400 (10,000 × \$1.84). This amount is now \$400 greater than the amount originally recorded on December 12. According to generally accepted accounting principles, the receivable must be reported in the balance sheet at its current dollar value. Hence, Boston Company must make the following entry to record the increase in the dollar value of the receivable:

Dec.	31	Accounts Receivable—London Outfitters	400.00	
		Foreign Exchange Gain or Loss		400.00
		To record the effects of the increased value of the British pound on our receivable.		

The Foreign Exchange Gain or Loss is closed to the Income Summary account and reported on the income statement.[12]

Assume that Boston Company receives London Outfitters' payment of £10,000 on February 10, and immediately exchanges the pounds for U.S. dollars. On this date, the exchange rate for pounds has declined to \$1.78. Therefore, Boston Company receives only \$17,800 (10,000 × \$1.78). The firm records the receipt and the loss associated with the decline in the exchange rate as follows:

Feb.	10	Cash.	17,800.00	
		Foreign Exchange Gain or Loss.	600.00	
		Accounts Receivable—London Outfitters		18,400.00
		Received foreign currency payment of account and converted it into dollars.		

Accounting for credit purchases from a foreign supplier is similar to the previous example of a credit sale to a foreign customer. If the U.S. company is required to make a payment in a foreign currency, the account payable must be translated into dollars before it can be recorded by the U.S. company. Then, if the exchange rate changes, an exchange gain or loss must be recognized by the U.S. company at any intervening balance sheet date and at the payment date.

Consolidated Statements with Foreign Subsidiaries

A second problem of accounting for international operations involves the preparation of consolidated financial statements when the parent company has one or more foreign subsidiaries. For example, suppose that a U.S. company owns a controlling interest in a French subsidiary. The reporting currency of the U.S. parent is the dollar. However, the French subsidiary main-

[12] Ibid, sec. F60.122. First published as FASB, *Statement of Financial Accounting Standards No. 52,* par. 15.

tains its financial records in francs. Before preparing a consolidated working paper, the parent must translate the financial statements of the French company into U.S. dollars. After the translation is completed, the preparation of consolidated statements is not any different than for any other subsidiary.[13]

The procedures for translating a foreign subsidiary's account balances depend on the nature of the subsidiary's operations. In simple terms, the general process requires the parent company to select appropriate foreign exchange rates and then to apply those rates to the account balances of the foreign subsidiary.

Summary of the Chapter in Terms of Learning Objectives

LO 1. Stock investments are classified as current assets if they are marketable and are held as a source of cash to be used in current operations. All other stock investments are classified as long-term investments.

LO 2. The cost method is used if the investor does not have a significant influence over the investee corporation and the stock is not readily marketable. The lower of cost or market method is applied to the long-term portfolio of marketable stock investments. Usually, significant control does not exist if the investor owns less than 20% of the investee's voting stock.

The equity method is used if the investor has a significant influence over the investee. This situation usually exists when the investor owns 20% or more of the investee's voting stock. If an investor owns more than 50% of another corporation's voting stock and controls the investee, the investor's financial reports are prepared on a consolidated basis.

LO 3. Under the cost method, the investment account is maintained at cost and dividends received are credited to a revenue account. The lower of cost or market method is applied to the long-term portfolio of investments in marketable equity securities. However, declines and recoveries in the market value of the long-term portfolio are not reported on the income statement. Instead, the amount by which market value is less than cost is deducted from stockholders' equity on the balance sheet.

Under the equity method, the investor records its share of the investee's earnings with a debit to the investment account and a credit to a revenue account. Dividends received satisfy the investor's equity claims and reduce the investment account balance.

LO 4. To prepare a consolidated balance sheet, all items duplicated on the books of the subsidiary and the parent are eliminated. These eliminations always include offsetting the parent's investment account against the subsidiary's stockholders' equity accounts. If some of the subsidiary's stock is held by outside parties, that portion of the subsidiary's stockholders' equity is reclassified as minority interest. Also, if the cost of the parent's investment differs from the book value of the investment, the difference is recognized. The remaining account balances of the affiliates are added to get the consolidated amounts.

[13] The problem grows much more complicated when the accounts of the French subsidiary are maintained in accordance with the French version of GAAP. The French statements must be converted to U.S. GAAP before the consolidation can be completed.

LO 5. If a U.S. company makes a credit sale to a foreign customer and the sales terms call for payment with a foreign currency, the company must translate the foreign currency into dollars to record the receivable. Then, if the exchange rate changes before payment is received, foreign exchange gains or losses must be recognized in the year in which they occur. The same treatment is used if a U.S. company makes a credit purchase from a foreign supplier and is required to make payment in a foreign currency. Also, if a U.S. company has a foreign subsidiary that maintains its accounts in a foreign currency, the account balances must be translated into dollars before they can be consolidated with the parent's accounts.

Demonstration Problem

The following series of events and facts are related to Brown Company's investment activities during 1993 and 1994. Show the appropriate journal entries and the portions of each year's balance sheet and income statement that describe these events and facts.

1993

Sept. 9 Purchased as a long-term investment 1,000 shares of Packard, Inc. common stock for $80,000 cash. These shares represent less than 3% of the outstanding shares and are not marketable.

Oct. 2 Purchased as a long-term investment 2,000 shares of AT&T common stock for $60,000 cash. The stock is actively traded on the New York Stock Exchange.

17 Purchased as a long-term investment 1,000 shares of Apple Computers common stock for $40,000 cash. The stock is actively traded in the over-the-counter market.

Nov. 1 Received $5,000 cash dividends from Packard.

30 Received $3,000 cash dividends from AT&T.

Dec. 15 Received $1,400 cash dividends from Apple.

31 Market values for the investments in marketable equity securities are AT&T, $48,000 and Apple Computers, $45,000.

31 After closing the accounts, selected account balances on Brown Company's books are:

Common stock	$1,000,000
Contributed capital in excess of par value	2,000,000
Retained earnings	750,000

1994

Jan. 5 Purchased 120,000 shares (a 30% interest) of Hanson Company common stock, a corporation that was just created by two former employees. Brown paid $600,000 cash, will have influence over the management of the company, and plans to hold the stock as a long-term investment.

Feb. 15 Packard, Inc., was taken over by other investors, and Brown sold its shares for $125,000 cash.

May 30 Received $3,100 cash dividends from AT&T.

June	15	Received $1,600 cash dividends from Apple.
Aug.	17	Sold the AT&T stock for $52,000 cash.
	19	Purchased 2,000 shares of Coca-Cola common stock for $50,000 as a long-term investment. The stock is actively traded on the New York Stock Exchange.
Dec.	15	Received $1,800 cash dividends from Apple.
	19	Received $13,000 cash dividends from Hanson Company.
	31	Total profits for Hanson Company for 1994 are determined to be $140,000.
	31	Market values of the investments in marketable equity securities are Apple, $39,000 and Coca-Cola, $48,000.
	31	After closing the accounts, selected account balances on Brown Company's books are:

Common stock	$1,100,000
Contributed capital in excess of par value . .	2,300,000
Retained earnings	970,000

Solution to Demonstration Problem

Planning the Solution

- Account for the investment in Packard under the cost method.
- Account for the investments in AT&T, Apple, and Coca-Cola as long-term investments in marketable equity securities.
- Account for the investment in Hanson under the equity method.
- Prepare the information for the two balance sheets by including the appropriate assets, contra assets, stockholders' equity accounts, and contra stockholders' equity accounts.

Journal entries during 1993:

Sept.	9	Investment in Packard, Inc., Common Stock	80,000.00	
		Cash		80,000.00
		Acquired 1,000 shares as a long-term nonmarketable investment.		
Oct.	2	Investment in AT&T Common Stock	60,000.00	
		Cash		60,000.00
		Acquired 2,000 shares as a long-term marketable investment.		
	17	Investment in Apple Common Stock	40,000.00	
		Cash		40,000.00
		Acquired 1,000 shares as a long-term marketable investment.		

Journal entries continued

Nov.	1	Cash	5,000.00	
		Dividends Earned		5,000.00
		Received dividend from Packard, Inc.		
	30	Cash	3,000.00	
		Dividends Earned		3,000.00
		Received dividend from AT&T.		
Dec.	15	Cash	1,400.00	
		Dividends Earned		1,400.00
		Received dividend from Apple.		
	31	Unrealized Loss on Market Decline of Long-Term Investments	7,000.00	
		Allowance to Reduce Long-Term Investments to Market		7,000.00
		To record market decline of long-term marketable equity securities portfolio.		

	Cost	Market
AT&T	$ 60,000	$48,000
Apple	40,000	45,000
Total	$100,000	$93,000
Required allowance balance		$ 7,000
Existing balance		–0–
Necessary increase		$ 7,000

December 31, 1993, balance sheet items:

Assets		
Long-term investments in equity securities:		
Nonmarketable, at cost		$ 80,000
Marketable:		
Cost	$100,000	
Less: Allowance to reduce to market	(7,000)	93,000
Total		$ 173,000
Stockholders' Equity		
Common stock		$1,000,000
Contributed capital in excess of par value		2,000,000
Total contributed capital		$3,000,000
Retained earnings		750,000
Less: Unrealized loss on market decline of long-term investments		(7,000)
Total		$3,743,000

Income statement items for the year ended December 31, 1993:

Dividends earned	$ 9,400

Journal entries during 1994:

Jan.	5	Investment in Hanson Company Common Stock	600,000.00	
		Cash		600,000.00
		Acquired 120,000 shares as long-term nonmarketable investment. The equity method is to be used.		
Feb.	15	Cash	125,000.00	
		Investment in Packard, Inc., Common Stock		80,000.00
		Gain on Sale of Investments		45,000.00
		Sold 1,000 shares for cash.		
May	30	Cash	3,100.00	
		Dividends Earned		3,100.00
		Received dividend from AT&T.		
June	15	Cash	1,600.00	
		Dividends Earned		1,600.00
		Received dividend from Apple.		
Aug.	17	Cash	52,000.00	
		Loss on Sale of Investments	8,000.00	
		Investment in AT&T Common Stock		60,000.00
		Sold 2,000 shares for cash.		
	19	Investment in Coca-Cola Common Stock	50,000.00	
		Cash		50,000.00
		Acquired 2,000 shares as a long-term marketable investment.		
Dec.	15	Cash	1,800.00	
		Dividends Earned		1,800.00
		Received dividend from Apple.		
	19	Cash	13,000.00	
		Investment in Hanson Company Common Stock		13,000.00
		Received dividend from Hanson Company, deducted from investment account under the equity method.		
	31	Investment in Hanson Company Common Stock	42,000.00	
		Earnings from Investment in Hanson Company ($140,000 × 30%)		42,000.00
		Recorded our 30% share of the annual earnings reported by Hanson Company.		
	31	Allowance to Reduce Long-Term Investments to Market	4,000.00	
		Unrealized Loss on Market Decline of Long-Term Investments		4,000.00
		To record the market value recovery of the long-term marketable equity securities portfolio.		

	Cost	Market
Apple	$40,000	$39,000
Coca-Cola	50,000	48,000
Total	$90,000	$87,000
Required allowance balance		$ 3,000
Existing balance		7,000
Necessary decrease		$ 4,000

December 31, 1994, balance sheet items:

Assets		
Long-term investments in equity securities:		
Nonmarketable, under equity method		$ 629,000
Marketable:		
Cost	$90,000	
Less: Allowance to reduce to market	(3,000)	87,000
Total		$ 716,000
Stockholders' Equity		
Common stock		$1,100,000
Contributed capital in excess of par value		2,300,000
Total contributed capital		$3,400,000
Retained earnings		970,000
Less: Unrealized loss on market decline of long-term investments		(3,000)
Total		$4,367,000

Income statement items for the year ended December 31, 1994:

Dividends earned	$ 6,500
Earnings from equity method investment	42,000
Gain on sale of investments	45,000
Loss on sale of investments	(8,000)
Total	$ 85,500

Glossary

LO 6 Define or explain the words and phrases listed in the chapter glossary.

Consolidated financial statements financial statements that show the results of all operations under the parent's control, including those of any subsidiaries; assets and liabilities of all affiliated companies are combined on a single balance sheet, revenues and expenses are combined on a single income statement, and cash flows are combined on a single statement of cash flows as though the business were in fact a single company. pp. 974, 979–88

Cost method of accounting for stock investments an accounting method whereby the investment is recorded at total cost and maintained at that amount; any earnings subsequently reported and dividends paid by the investee do not affect the investment account balance. pp. 974–77

Equity method of accounting for stock investments an accounting method used when the investor has influence over the investee, but does not control it; under this method, the investment is initially recorded at its total cost, and the investment account balance is subsequently increased to reflect the investor's share of the investee's earnings and decreased to reflect the investor's receipt of dividends paid by the investee. pp. 974, 977–79

Foreign exchange rate the price of one currency stated in terms of another currency. p. 990

Long-term investments investments that are not intended to be a ready source of cash in case of need, such as bond sinking funds, land, bonds, and stocks that are not marketable, or, if they are marketable, it is not management's intent to dispose of them within the next year or operating cycle, whichever is longer. p. 973

Marketable equity securities common and preferred stocks that are actively traded, such that sales prices or bid and ask prices are currently available on a national securities exchange or in the over-the-counter market. p. 973

Minority interest the portion of a subsidiary company's stockholders' equity that is not owned by the parent corporation. p. 983

Multinational business a company that operates in a large number of different countries. p. 988

Parent company a corporation that owns a controlling interest in another corporation (more than 50% of the voting stock is required). p. 979

Reporting currency the currency in which a company presents its financial statements. p. 990

Subsidiary a corporation that is controlled by another corporation (the parent) because the parent owns more than 50% of the subsidiary's voting stock. p. 979

Objective Review

Answers to the following questions are listed at the end of this chapter. Be sure that you decide which is the one best answer to each question *before* you check the answers.

LO 1 Which of the following criteria must be satisfied for a stock investment to be classified as long term?

a. The stock must not be held longer than one year.
b. The stock must not be a marketable security.
c. The stock must be common shares.
d. The stock must not be a marketable security that is held as a ready source of cash.
e. The stock must be a marketable security.

LO 2 Under which of the following circumstances would a company account for its investment in another company's stock according to the equity method?

a. The investment represents 35% of the investee's outstanding bonds payable.
b. The investor owns 23% of the investee company's voting stock but other facts disclose that the investor does not have a significant influence over the investee.
c. The investment represents 4% of the investee's outstanding common shares.
d. The investment represents 45% of the investee's outstanding preferred (nonvoting) stock.
e. The investor company owns 16% of the investee company's common stock and exercises a significant influence over the operations of the investee company.

LO 3 On January 1, 1993, Brenner Wholesale Corporation purchased 7,000 shares (35%) of Outback Cargo Company's common stock at a total cost of $140,000. Outback Cargo's net income over the next three years totaled $450,000, and the company declared and paid $200,000 in dividends on its outstanding common shares. Brenner Wholesale sold its Outback Cargo Company shares on January 3, 1996, for $34.50 per share. The entry to record the sale is as follows:

a.	Cash	241,500.00	
	Investment in Outback Cargo Company		70,000.00
	Gain on Sale of Investments		171,500.00
b.	Cash	241,500.00	
	Investment in Outback Cargo Company		140,000.00
	Gain on Sale of Investments		101,500.00
c.	Cash	241,500.00	
	Loss on Sale of Investments	56,000.00	
	Investment in Outback Cargo Company		297,500.00
d.	Cash	241,500.00	
	Investment in Outback Cargo Company		227,500.00
	Gain on Sale of Investments		14,000.00
e.	Cash	241,500.00	
	Investment in Outback Cargo Company		241,500.00

LO 4 Hart Corporation purchased 75% of Western Supply Company's stock at a total cost of $300,000, which amounted to $25 per share. The book value of the stock was $22 per share. Calculate the following amounts to report in Hart's consolidated balance sheet on the date of acquisition: (1) investment in Western Supply Company, (2) excess of cost over book value, and (3) minority interest.

a. (1) $300,000; (2) $36,000; (3) $ 88,000.
b. (1) $300,000; (2) $27,000; (3) $100,000.
c. (1) $300,000; (2) $ –0– ; (3) $100,000.
d. (1) $ –0– ; (2) $36,000; (3) $ 88,000.
e. Cannot be determined from information given.

LO 5 If a U.S. company makes a credit sale of merchandise to a French customer and the sales terms require the customer's payment to be in francs:

a. The United States company will incur an exchange loss if the foreign exchange rate between francs and dollars increases from $0.189 at the date of sale to $0.199 at the date the account is settled.
b. The French company will incur an exchange loss if the foreign exchange rate between francs and dollars decreases from $0.189 at the date of sale to $0.179 at the date the account is settled.
c. The French company may eventually have to record an exchange gain or loss.
d. The U.S. company may be required to record an exchange gain or loss on the date of the sale.
e. None of the above is correct.

LO 6 The name of the method of accounting for stock investments whereby the investment is recorded at total cost, the account balance is maintained at that amount, and subsequent investee earnings and dividends do not affect the investment account is the:

a. Equity method.
b. Consolidated method.
c. Fair value method.
d. Cost method.
e. Cash equivalent method.

Questions for Class Discussion

1. What evidence allows an accountant to identify a security as being marketable?
2. Under what conditions should a stock investment be classified on the balance sheet as a long-term investment?
3. What types of assets are classified as long-term investments?
4. In accounting for common stock investments, when should the cost method be used? When should the equity method be used?

5. Under what circumstances would a company prepare consolidated financial statements?
6. When the cost method is used to account for a long-term stock investment, what events cause the investor to record revenue from the investment?
7. If a company prepares consolidated financial statements, what method would the company normally use on its books to account for its investment in the subsidiary?
8. When a parent corporation uses the equity method to account for its investment in a subsidiary, what recognition is given by the parent corporation to the income or loss reported by the subsidiary? What recognition is given to dividends declared by the subsidiary?
9. Under what circumstances is lower of cost or market applied to long-term investments in stock?
10. When a long-term portfolio of investments in marketable equity securities is written down to a market value that is less than cost, how is the loss reported on the financial statements?
11. What are consolidated financial statements?
12. What account balances must be eliminated in preparing a consolidated balance sheet?
13. Why are the stockholders' equity accounts of a subsidiary eliminated in the process of preparing a consolidated balance sheet?
14. What is meant by minority interest? Where is this item disclosed on a consolidated balance sheet?
15. Why would a parent corporation pay more than book value for the stock of a subsidiary?
16. When a parent pays more than book value for the stock of a subsidiary, how should this additional cost be reported on the consolidated balance sheet?
17. What are two basic problems of accounting for international operations?
18. If a U.S. company makes a credit sale to a foreign customer and the customer is required to make payment in U.S. dollars, can the U.S. company have an exchange gain or loss as a result of the sale?
19. A U.S. company makes a credit sale to a foreign customer, and the customer is required to make payment in a foreign currency. The foreign exchange rate was $1.40 on the date of the sale and is $1.30 on the date the customer pays the receivable. Will the U.S. company record an exchange gain or an exchange loss?
20. On December 31, 1993, a U.S. company has an account receivable from a British customer that requires the customer to pay £6,000 to the U.S. company. How do you determine the amount to be reported on the U.S. company's December 31 balance sheet?
21. In preparing its December 31, 1993, financial statements, a U.S. company had to report an account receivable that was denominated in a foreign currency. The receivable stemmed from a sale made on No-

vember 14, 1993. In translating the receivable into dollars, should the accountant use the foreign exchange rate on November 14 or on December 31?

McDonald's® What you want is what you get.

FEDERAL EXPRESS

22. Refer to McDonald's Corporation's consolidated balance sheet presented in Appendix K. Which line item indicates that McDonald's activities include international operations?
23. Refer to the financial statements of Federal Express Corporation presented in Appendix K. Does Federal Express own any stock issued by other corporations? How did you determine your answer?

Exercises

Exercise 18–1
Classifying stock investments; lower of cost or market
(LO 1, 3)

During 1993. Lormont Corporation made five investments in equity securities. These securities, with their December 31, 1993, market values, are as follows:

a. Feyland Materials Corporation preferred stock: 1,440 shares, $45,000 cost, $46,800 market value. Purpose of the investment is to earn a return on surplus cash balances.

b. Terrific Toys Company common stock: 2,160 shares, $79,200 cost, $73,800 market value. Purpose of investment is expected gains from increases in market value during next three years.

c. Wedford Company preferred stock: 1,800 shares, $39,600 cost, $42,300 market value. Purpose of investment is to earn dividends while holding as a source of cash for operations.

d. Stellen Industries, Inc. common stock: 2,700 shares, $66,600 cost, $70,200 market value. Purpose of investment is to hold for expected increase in value over the next few years.

e. Clarion Corporation common stock: 5,400 shares, $64,800 cost, $57,600 market value. Purpose of investment is to develop a stronger supplier relationship with Clarion Corporation.

Calculate the lower-of-cost-or-market amount of the long-term portfolio of stock investments as of December 31, 1993. If necessary, prepare a journal entry dated December 31, 1993, to record any decline in market value. If a loss is recorded, explain how it should be reported by Lormont Corporation.

Exercise 18–2
Stock investment transactions
(LO 2, 3)

Prepare general journal entries to record the following events on the books of The Shoe Depot, Inc.:

1993

Jan. 4 Purchased 23,000 shares of Crestway Company common stock for $72,500 plus broker's fee of $3,400. Crestway Company has 287,500 shares of common stock outstanding, and The Shoe Depot does not have a significant influence on Crestway Company policies.

June 3 Crestway Company declared and paid a cash dividend of $0.20 per share.

Dec. 31 Crestway Company announced that net income for the year amounted to $338,900.

1994

Feb. 14 Crestway Company declared and paid a cash dividend of $0.75 per share.

May 1 Crestway Company declared and issued a stock dividend of one additional share for each four shares already outstanding.

Dec. 30 The Shoe Depot sold 8,000 shares of Crestway Company for $29,600.

31 Crestway Company announced that net income for the year amounted to $526,250.

Exercise 18–3
Stock investment transactions
(LO 2, 3)

Prepare general journal entries to record the following events on the books of Quorum Company:

1993

Jan. 5 Purchased 13,500 shares of Maxey Corporation for $172,800 plus broker's fee of $5,000. Maxey Corporation has 67,500 shares of common stock outstanding and has acknowledged the fact that its policies will be significantly influenced by Quorum Company.

Aug. 24 Maxey Corporation declared and paid a cash dividend of $1.20 per share.

Dec. 31 Maxey Corporation announced that net income for the year amounted to $232,800.

1994

Feb. 22 Maxey Corporation declared and paid a cash dividend of $1.50 per share.

Oct. 5 Maxey Corporation declared and issued a stock dividend of one additional share for each five shares already outstanding.

Dec. 31 Maxey Corporation announced that net income for the year amounted to $332,950.

31 Quorum Company sold 5,400 shares of Maxey Corporation for $91,000.

Exercise 18–4
Comparison of cost and equity methods
(LO 2, 3)

On December 31, 1992, Clark Management Company and Cumberland Company each purchased 11,400 shares of AA Service Company stock from an existing stockholder at a cost of $7.00 per share. On that date, the stockholders' equity of AA Service Company appeared as follows:

Common stock ($5 par)	$285,000
Retained earnings	85,500
Total.	$370,500

Because of some contractual limitations, Cumberland Company does not have a significant influence over AA Service Company. However, Clark

Management Company does have a significant influence over AA Service Company.

During 1993 and 1994, AA Service Company earned an annual net income of $80,000 and paid cash dividends of $16,000 each year. Calculate the carrying value as of December 31, 1994, for (*a*) Clark Management Company's investment in AA Service Company and (*b*) Cumberland Company's investment in AA Service Company.

Exercise 18–5
Consolidated statement elimination entry at acquisition
(LO 4)

On December 31, Roadway Company had the following stockholders' equity:

Common stock, $25 par value, 27,000 shares issued and outstanding	$ 675,000
Retained earnings	559,000
Total stockholders' equity	$1,234,000

On the same day (December 31), Reisner Products, Inc., purchased 21,600 of Roadway Company's outstanding shares, paying $50 per share, and prepared a work sheet to consolidate the balance sheets of the two companies. In general journal form, give the entry that should be made on this work sheet to eliminate Reisner Products, Inc.'s investment and the related stockholders' equity accounts of Roadway Company.

Exercise 18–6
Consolidated statement elimination entry after acquisition
(LO 4)

During the year following its acquisition by Reisner Products, Inc. (see Exercise 18–5), Roadway Company earned $220,000 and paid out $55,000 in dividends. In general journal form, give the entry under these assumptions to eliminate Reisner Products, Inc.'s investment and Roadway Company's stockholders' equity account balances as of the end of the year.

Exercise 18–7
Consolidated balance sheet
(LO 4)

On December 31, 1993, Value Mart, Inc. purchased 80% of REM Optical Company's outstanding stock. The balance sheets of the two companies on that date were as follows:

	Value Mart	REM Optical
Assets		
Investment in REM Optical Company	$201,600	
Other assets	723,600	$288,000
Total assets	$925,200	$288,000
Liabilities and Stockholders' Equity		
Liabilities	$205,200	$ 36,000
Common stock, $5 par value	450,000	180,000
Retained earnings	270,000	72,000
Total liabilities and stockholders' equity	$925,200	$288,000

Present the consolidated balance sheet for Value Mart, Inc., and its subsidiary on December 31, 1993. (Do not prepare a consolidated work sheet.)

Exercise 18–8
Calculating consolidated net income
(LO 3, 4)

On January 1, 1993, Farrow Company purchased 70% of Allen Corporation's outstanding stock. During the year ended December 31, 1993, Farrow earned a net income (excluding its share of the earnings of Allen Corporation) of $145,000. Allen Corporation earned a net income of $64,000 and paid cash dividends of $24,000 during 1993. Calculate the net income to be reported on Farrow Corporation's consolidated income statement for 1993.

Exercise 18–9
Receivables denominated in a foreign currency
(LO 5)

On May 5, 1993, Digital, Inc. made a credit sale to a German company. The terms of the sale required the German company to pay DM 120,000 (deutsche marks) on January 18, 1994. Digital, Inc. prepares quarterly financial statements on March 31, June 30, September 30, and December 31. The foreign exchange rates for marks during the time the receivable was outstanding were:

May 5, 1993	$0.6700
June 30, 1993	0.6880
September 30, 1993	0.6920
December 31, 1993	0.6820
January 18, 1994.	0.6750

Calculate the foreign exchange gain or loss that Digital, Inc., should report on each of its quarterly income statements during the last three quarters of 1993 and the first quarter of 1994. Also calculate the amount that should be reported on Digital Inc.'s balance sheets at the end of each of those quarters.

Exercise 18–10
Foreign currency transactions
(LO 5)

Fiore Company of Poughkeepsie, New York, sells its products to customers in the United States and in Italy. On November 25, 1993, Fiore Company sold merchandise on credit to Pacioli Imports Company of Naples, Italy, at a price of 20.5 million lira. The exchange rate on that day was 1 lira equals $0.0009600. On December 31, 1993, when Fiore Company prepared its financial statements, the exchange rate was 1 lira for $0.0009000. Pacioli Imports paid its bill in full on January 6, 1994, at which time the exchange rate was 1 lira for $0.0009090. Fiore Company immediately exchanged the 20.5 million lira for U.S. dollars. Prepare journal entries on November 25, December 31, and January 6 to account for the sale and account receivable on the books of Fiore Company.

Problems

Problem 18–1
Stock investments—cost and equity methods
(LO 2, 3)

Holden Enterprises, Inc., was organized on January 3, 1993, for the purpose of investing in the shares of other companies. Holden Enterprises immediately issued 150,000 shares of $1 par, common stock for which it received $150,000 cash. On January 6, 1993, Holden Enterprises purchased 30,000 shares (20%) of Compusystem Corporation's outstanding stock at a cost of $150,000. The following transactions and events subsequently occurred:

1993

June 5 Compusystem Corporation declared and paid a cash dividend of $.60 per share.

Dec. 31 Compusystem Corporation announced that its net income for 1993 was $160,000.

1994

Mar. 10 Compusystem Corporation declared and issued a stock dividend of 1 share for each 10 shares already outstanding.

July 25 Compusystem Corporation declared and paid a cash dividend of $0.50 per share.

Dec. 31 Compusystem Corporation announced that its net income for 1994 was $120,000.

1995

Jan. 3 Holden Enterprises, Inc. sold all of its investment in Compusystem Corporation for $168,000 cash.

Part 1. Holden Enterprises is presumed to have a significant influence over Compusystem Corporation because it owns 20% of the stock.

Required

1. Give the entries on the books of Holden Enterprises, Inc. to record the preceding events regarding its investment in Compusystem Corporation.
2. Calculate the carrying value per share of Holden Enterprises, Inc.'s investment as reflected in the investment account on January 2, 1995.
3. Calculate Holden Enterprises, Inc.'s retained earnings balance on January 4, 1995, including any gain or loss from the sale of the Compusystem stock.

Part 2. Although Holden Enterprises, Inc., owns 20% of Compusystem Corporation's outstanding stock, a thorough investigation of the surrounding circumstances indicates that it does not have a significant influence over the investee. Therefore, the cost method is the appropriate procedure to use in accounting for the investment.

Required

1. Give the entries on the books of Holden Enterprises, Inc. to record the preceding events regarding its investment in Compusystem Corporation.
2. Calculate the cost per share of Holden Enterprises, Inc.'s investment as reflected in the investment account on January 2, 1995.
3. Calculate Holden Enterprises, Inc.'s retained earnings balance on January 4, 1995, including any gain or loss from the sale of the Compusystem stock.

Problem 18–2
Consolidated statements, at acquisition and one year later
(LO 4)

On January 1, 1993, Glasner Company purchased 75% of Chemco Corporation's outstanding stock at $32 per share. On that date, Glasner Company had retained earnings of $745,000. Chemco Corporation had retained earnings of $243,000, and had 27,000 outstanding shares of $10 par common stock, all of which were originally issued at par.

Part 1.

Required

1. Give the elimination entry to be used on a work sheet for a consolidated balance sheet dated January 1, 1993.
2. Determine the amount of consolidated retained earnings that should be shown on a consolidated balance sheet dated January 1, 1993.

Part 2. During the year ended December 31, 1993, Glasner Company paid cash dividends of $134,500 and earned net income of $278,000 excluding earnings from its investment in Chemco Corporation. Chemco Corporation earned net income of $95,000 and paid dividends of $43,200. Except for Glasner Company's Retained Earnings account and the Investment in Chemco Corporation account, the balance sheet accounts for the two companies on December 31, 1993, are as follows:

	Glasner Company	Chemco Corporation
Assets		
Cash	$386,500	$228,900
Notes receivable	23,900	
Merchandise inventory	455,600	195,200
Building (net)	557,200	246,000
Land	450,300	167,400
Investment in Chemco Corporation	?	
Total assets	$?	$837,500
Liabilities and Stockholders' Equity		
Accounts payable	$363,250	$248,800
Notes payable	436,850	23,900
Common stock	800,500	270,000
Retained earnings	?	294,800
Total liabilities and stockholders' equity	$?	$837,500

Glasner Company loaned $23,900 to Chemco Corporation during 1993, for which Chemco Corporation signed a note. On December 31, 1993, the note had not been repaid.

Required

1. Calculate the December 31, 1993, balances in Glasner Company's Investment in Chemco Corporation account and Retained Earnings account.
2. Complete a work sheet to consolidate the balance sheets of the two companies as of December 31, 1993.

Problem 18–3
Consolidated work sheet and balance sheet
(LO 4)

The following items appeared in the first two columns of a work sheet prepared to consolidate the balance sheets of Leisure World, Inc., and Seabreeze Corporation on the day that Leisure gained control of Seabreeze by purchasing 5,400 shares of its $20 par value common stock at $34 per share.

	Leisure World, Inc.	Seabreeze Corporation
Assets		
Cash	$ 65,750	$ 22,300
Accounts receivable, net	98,700	25,150
Notes receivable, Seabreeze Corporation	20,200	
Merchandise inventory	121,630	37,800
Investment in Seabreeze Corporation	183,600	
Equipment, (net)	140,200	120,250
Buildings, (net)	218,350	
Land	102,100	
Total assets	$950,530	$205,500
Liabilities and Stockholders' Equity		
Accounts payable	$ 67,680	$ 19,300
Notes payable, Leisure World, Inc.		20,200
Common stock	546,000	120,000
Retained earnings	336,850	46,000
Total liabilities and stockholders' equity	$950,530	$205,500

At the time that Leisure acquired control of Seabreeze, it took Seabreeze's note in exchange for $20,200 in cash. Leisure also sold and delivered $10,450 of equipment at cost to Seabreeze Corporation on open account (account receivable). Both transactions are reflected in the preceding accounts.

Required

1. Prepare a work sheet to consolidate the balance sheets of the two companies and prepare a consolidated balance sheet. Assume that any difference between cost and book value of Leisure World, Inc.'s, investment in Seabreeze Corporation should be described as excess of cost over book value.
2. Under the assumption that Seabreeze Corporation earned $65,600 during the first year after it was acquired by Leisure World, Inc., and paid out $32,400 in dividends, give the work sheet entry to eliminate Leisure's investment in the subsidiary and Seabreeze's stockholders' equity accounts at the end of the year.

Problem 18–4
Foreign currency transactions
(LO 5)

Industrial Products Corporation is a U.S. company that has customers in several foreign countries. The company had the following transactions in 1993 and 1994:

1993

July 13 Sold merchandise for 6.5 million pesos to Garza Import Company of Mexico, payment in full to be received in 90 days. On this day, the foreign exchange rate for pesos was $0.0003350.

Aug. 27 Sold merchandise to Takahashi Corporation of Japan for $12,360 cash. The exchange rate for yen was $0.007700.

Oct. 14 Received Garza Import Company's payment for its purchase of July 13 and exchanged the pesos for dollars. The current foreign exchange rate for pesos was $0.0004050.

Nov. 3 Sold merchandise on credit to Rive Noir Company, located in Paris, France. The price of 135,700 francs was to be paid 60 days from the date of sale. The exchange rate for francs was $0.19900 on November 3.

Dec. 15 Sold merchandise for 16,500 pounds to Stanton, Ltd. of England, payment in full to be received in 30 days. The exchange rate for pounds was $1.9800.

Dec. 31 Prepared adjusting entries to recognize exchange gains or losses on the annual financial statements. Rates for exchanging foreign currencies on this day included the following:

Pesos (Mexico)	$0.0003200
Yen (Japan)	0.007610
Francs (France)	0.20150
Pounds (England)	1.9620

1994

Jan. 2 Received Rive Noir Company's full payment for the sale of November 3 and immediately exchanged the francs for dollars. The exchange rate for francs was $0.20360.

Jan. 16 Received full payment from Stanton, Ltd. for the sale of December 15 and immediately exchanged the pounds for dollars. The exchange rate for pounds was $1.9560.

Required

1. Prepare general journal entries to account for these transactions of Industrial Products Corporation.
2. Calculate the foreign exchange gain or loss to be reported on Industrial Products Corporation's 1993 income statement.

Problem 18–5
Analytical essay
(LO 4)

Refer to the facts presented in Problem 18–3. Note that Leisure World acquired 5,400 shares of Seabreeze common stock at $34 per share, a total cost of 5,400 × $34 = $183,600. This purchase gives Leisure World 90% ownership of Seabreeze and excess cost over book value of $183,600 − ($120,000 + $46,000) × .9 = $34,200.

Required

For the following independent assumptions, describe the impact on the consolidated balance sheet prepared at acquisition date:

1. Instead of 5,400 shares, Leisure World purchased 6,000 shares of Seabreeze common stock at $34 per share.
2. Leisure World purchased 5,400 shares of Seabreeze common stock for a total of $149,400 instead of $183,600.

Problem 18–6
Analytical essay
(LO 2, 3)

Apex Corporation began operations in January 1993. During the year, Apex invested in several companies by purchasing common stock. The following information pertains to the investment portfolio of Apex at December 31, 1993:

Investment	Cost	Market
A	$20,000	$21,000
B	3,100	3,000
C	56,900	49,000
	$80,000	$73,000

Assume that all the investments are marketable and that Apex's ownership in each investee is less than 20%.

Required

Consider the two alternatives of classifying the portfolio as short-term investments or long-term investments. For these two alternatives, briefly discuss the similarities and the differences in accounting for the investment portfolio during 1993, including the effects of the investments on the 1993 financial statements. (Short-term investments are discussed in Chapter 8.)

Alternate Problems

Problem 18–1A
Stock investments—cost and equity methods
(LO 2)

Global Securities Company was organized on January 3, 1993, for the purpose of investing in the shares of other companies. Global Securities immediately issued 200,000 shares of $3 par, common stock for which it received $600,000 cash. On January 8, 1993, Global Securities Company purchased 50,000 shares (25%) of Syntex Company's outstanding stock at a cost of $600,000. The following transactions and events subsequently occurred:

1993

July 7 Syntex Company declared and paid a cash dividend of $1.10 per share.

Dec. 31 Syntex Company announced that its net income for 1993 was $490,000.

1994

June 13 Syntex Company declared and issued a stock dividend of one share for each five shares already outstanding.

Aug. 2 Syntex Company declared and paid a cash dividend of $0.80 per share.

Dec. 31 Syntex Company announced that its net income for 1994 was $380,000.

1995

Jan. 5 Global Securities Company sold all of its investment in Syntex Company for $716,000 cash.

Part 1. Global Securities Company is presumed to have a significant influence over Syntex Company because it owns 25% of the stock.

Required

1. Give the entries on the books of Global Securities Company to record the events regarding its investment in Syntex Company.

2. Calculate the carrying value per share of Global Securities Company's investment as reflected in the investment account on January 1, 1995.
3. Calculate Global Securities Company's retained earnings balance on January 6, 1995, including any gain or loss from the sale of the Syntex stock.

Part 2. Although Global Securities Company owns 25% of Syntex Company's outstanding stock, a thorough investigation of the surrounding circumstances indicates that Global Securities Company does not have a significant influence over Syntex Company, and the cost method is the appropriate method of accounting for the investment.

Required

1. Give the entries on the books of Global Securities Company to record the preceding events regarding its investment in Syntex Company.
2. Calculate the cost per share of Global Securities Company's investment as reflected in the investment account on January 1, 1995.
3. Calculate Global Securities Company's retained earnings balance on January 6, 1995, including any gain or loss from the sale of the Syntex stock.

Problem 18–2A
Consolidated statements, at acquisition and one year later
(LO 4)

On January 1, 1993, Matrix Company purchased 80% of Digitcomp, Inc.'s outstanding stock at $90 per share. On that date, Matrix Company had retained earnings of $437,000. Digitcomp, Inc. had retained earnings of $156,000 and had 5,000 outstanding shares of $50 par common stock, all of which were originally issued at par.

Part 1.

Required

1. Give the elimination entry to be used on a work sheet for a consolidated balance sheet dated January 1, 1993.
2. Determine the amount of consolidated retained earnings that should be shown on a consolidated balance sheet dated January 1, 1993.

Part 2. During the year ended December 31, 1993, Matrix Company paid cash dividends of $78,000 and earned net income of $389,500 excluding earnings from its investment in Digitcomp, Inc. Digitcomp earned net income of $92,000 and paid dividends of $30,000. Except for Matrix Company's Retained Earnings account and the Investment in Digitcomp, Inc., account, the balance sheet accounts for the two companies on December 31, 1993, are as follows:

	Matrix Company	Digitcomp, Inc.
Assets		
Cash	$360,400	$ 98,200
Notes receivable	25,500	
Merchandise inventory	289,000	104,150
Building (net)	314,100	196,900
Land	225,450	158,550
Investment in Digitcomp, Inc.	?	
Total assets	$?	$557,800

	Matrix Company	Digitcomp, Inc.
Liabilities and Stockholders' Equity		
Accounts payable	$241,450	$ 64,300
Notes payable		25,500
Common stock	560,500	250,000
Retained earnings	?	218,000
Total liabilities and stockholders' equity	$?	$557,800

Matrix Company loaned $25,500 to Digitcomp, Inc. during 1993, for which Digitcomp, Inc. signed a note. On December 31, 1993, the note had not been repaid.

Required

1. Calculate the December 31, 1993, balances in Matrix Company's Investment in Digitcomp, Inc., account and Retained Earnings account.
2. Complete a work sheet to consolidate the balance sheets of the two companies as of December 31, 1993.

Problem 18–3A
Consolidated work sheet and balance sheet
(LO 4)

The following items appeared in the first two columns of a work sheet prepared to consolidate the balance sheets of Wilcox Company and Monroe Company on the day that Wilcox gained control of Monroe by purchasing 19,125 shares of its $30 par value common stock at $47 per share.

	Wilcox Company	Monroe Company
Assets		
Cash	$ 157,950	$ 57,600
Accounts receivable, (net)	316,105	105,300
Notes receivable, Monroe Company	132,100	
Merchandise inventory	250,060	312,400
Investment in Monroe Company	898,875	
Equipment, (net)	289,000	205,620
Buildings, (net)	401,500	323,200
Land	157,890	192,880
Total assets	$2,603,480	$1,197,000
Liabilities and Stockholders' Equity		
Accounts payable	$ 324,780	$ 69,500
Note payable, Wilcox Company		132,100
Common stock	1,450,800	675,000
Retained earnings	827,900	320,400
Total liabilities and stockholders' equity	$2,603,480	$1,197,000

At the time that Wilcox acquired control of Monroe, it took Monroe Company's note in exchange for $132,100 in cash. Wilcox also sold and delivered $40,600 of equipment at cost to Monroe on open account (account receivable). Both transactions are reflected in the preceding accounts.

Required

1. Prepare a work sheet to consolidate the balance sheets of the two companies and prepare a consolidated balance sheet. Assume that any difference between cost and book value of Wilcox Company's investment

in Monroe Company should be described as excess of cost over book value.

2. Under the assumption that Monroe Company earned $213,660 during the first year after it was acquired by Wilcox Company and paid out $90,000 in dividends, give the work sheet entry to eliminate Wilcox's investment in the subsidiary and Monroe's stockholders' equity accounts at the end of the year.

Problem 18–4A
Foreign currency transactions
(LO 5)

International Supply Company is a United States corporation that has customers in several foreign countries. The company had the following transactions in 1993 and 1994:

1993

Aug. 6 Sold merchandise for 8,900 pounds to Nottingham Service Company of England, payment in full to be received in 30 days. On this day, the current foreign exchange rate for pounds was $1.9500.

Sept. 1 Sold merchandise to Saiku Company of Japan for $28,620 cash. The foreign exchange rate for yen was $0.007703.

Sept. 7 Received Nottingham Service Company's payment for its purchase of August 6, and exchanged the pounds for dollars. The exchange rate for pounds was $2.1100.

Nov. 17 Sold merchandise on credit to D'Ambrosio Import Company, a company located in Venice, Italy. The price of 7.5 million lira was to be paid 60 days from the date of sale. On November 17, the foreign exchange rate for lira was $0.0009050.

Dec. 20 Sold merchandise for 6,200 punts to Shamrock Distributors, Inc. of Dublin, payment in full to be received in 30 days. The exchange rate for Irish punts was $1.8120.

31 Prepared adjusting entries to recognize exchange gains or losses on the annual financial statements. Rates of exchanging foreign currencies on this day included the following:

Pounds (England)	2.1500
Yen (Japan)	0.007742
Lira (Italy).	0.0008900
Punts (Ireland).	1.7960

1994

Jan. 18 Received D'Ambrosio Import Company's full payment for the sale of November 17, and immediately exchanged the lira for dollars. The exchange rate for lira was $0.0009000.

20 Received full payment from Shamrock Distributors, Inc., for the sale of December 20, and immediately exchanged the punts for dollars. The exchange rate for punts was $1.8060.

Required

1. Prepare general journal entries to account for these transactions of International Supply Company.

2. Calculate the foreign exchange gain or loss to be reported on International Supply Company's 1993 income statement.

Problem 18–5A
Analytical essay
(LO 4)

Refer to the facts presented in Problem 18–3A. Note that Wilcox acquired 19,125 shares of Monroe common stock at $47 per share, a total cost of 19,125 × $47 = $898,875. This purchase gives Wilcox 85% ownership of Monroe and excess cost over book value of $898,875 – .85($675,000 + $320,400) = $52,785.

Required

For the following independent assumptions, describe the impact on the consolidated balance sheet prepared at acquisition date:

1. Instead of 19,125 shares, Wilcox purchased 20,250 shares of Monroe common stock at $47 per share.
2. Wilcox purchased 19,125 shares of Monroe common stock for a total of $846,090 instead of $898,875.

Problem 18–6A
Analytical essay
(LO 2, 3)

Juarez Corporation began operations in January 1992. Since Juarez's inception, it has invested in several companies by purchasing common stock. The following information pertains to the investment portfolio of Juarez at December 31, 1993:

Investment	Cost	Market
A	$45,200	$46,500
B	15,000	18,200
C	10,600	9,100
	$70,800	$73,800

Prior to December 31 adjusting entries, the balance in the allowance account reducing the investments to market is $2,000. Assume that all the investments are marketable and that Juarez's ownership in each investee is less than 20%.

Required

Consider the two alternatives of classifying the portfolio as short-term investments or as long-term investments. For these two alternatives, briefly discuss the similarities and the differences in accounting for the investment portfolio during 1993, including the effects of the investments on the 1993 financial statements. (Short-term investments are discussed in Chapter 8.)

Provocative Problems

Provocative Problem 18–1
Omega Corporation
(LO 2, 3)

When corporations have their annual meetings with stockholders, the managements often have to deal with difficult questions from stockholders. For example, at a recent stockholders' meeting of Omega Corporation, one of the stockholders said:

I have owned shares of Omega for several years, but I am now questioning whether management is telling the truth in the annual financial statements. At the end of 1992, you announced that Omega had just acquired a 35% interest in the outstanding stock of Intex Corporation. You also stated that the 250,000 shares had cost Omega about $4.25 million. In the financial statements for 1993, you told us that the investments of Omega were proving to be very profitable and reported that earnings from all investments had amounted to more than $3.75 million. In the financial statements for 1994, you explained that Omega had sold the Intex shares during the first week of the year, receiving $5,025,000 cash proceeds from the sale. Nevertheless, the income statement for 1994 reports a $12,500 loss on the sale before taxes. I realize that Intex Corporation did not pay any dividends during 1993, but it was very profitable. As I recall, it reported net income of $2.25 million for 1993. Personally, I do not think you should have sold the shares. But, much more importantly, you reported to us that our company had a loss of $12,500 from the sale. How can that be true if the shares were purchased for $4,250,000 and were sold for $5,025,000?

Explain to this stockholder why the $12,500 loss is correctly reported.

Provocative Problem 18–2
Segments, Inc.
(LO 4)

Segments, Inc. is a retail clothing company. A recent annual report of Segments, Inc. included the following footnote to its financial statements:

(4) Minority Interest in Subsidiary

In December, the Company's previously wholly owned subsidiary, ComfortFit, Inc., sold 230,000 shares of its common stock to the public, resulting in net proceeds of $2,990,000. This sale reduced the Company's holding in that subsidiary to approximately 77% of the outstanding common stock.

Given this information, would you expect the future consolidated financial statements of Segments, Inc., to report its investment in ComfortFit, Inc., according to the equity method? Why or why not? Also, assume that Segments, Inc. prepared a consolidated balance sheet immediately after the subsidiary's sale of stock to the public. Did the sale of stock have any effects on that balance sheet? If so, explain the effects.

Provocative Problem 18–3
International Business Machines Corporation
(LO 4, 5)

IBM

Examine IBM's financial statements and supplemental information presented in Appendix J and answer the following questions:

1. Are IBM's financial statements consolidated? How can you tell?
2. Does IBM have more than one subsidiary? How can you tell?
3. An examination of the balance sheet reveals that no minority interest is reported. Give two possible explanations for this omission.
4. Find the footnote that explains Investments and Sundry Assets. Has IBM paid more for the stock of one or more of its subsidiaries than the fair value of the underlying assets and liabilities? How can you tell?
5. Look again at the footnote that explains Investments and Sundry Assets. Does IBM own any nonmarketable stocks? Describe any details that you can find.

6. Does IBM have any foreign operations? How can you tell?
7. Is there a foreign exchange gain or loss on the income statement? Provide a reasonable explanation for what you find or do not find.

Answers to Objective Review Questions

LO 1 (*d*)	LO 3 (*d*)	LO 5 (*e*)
LO 2 (*e*)	LO 4 (*d*)	LO 6 (*d*)

CHAPTER

19

Analyzing Financial Statements

Financial reports are highly summarized descriptions of complex organizations. Analyzing and understanding the information they present requires a lot of effort. The people who prepare reports need to know what their readers are looking for and how to help them find it.

Topical Coverage

As a result of studying the previous 18 chapters, you have learned the fundamental methods and principles used to generate financial statements. The focus of this chapter is on the analysis of financial statements. In studying this chapter, you will increase your understanding of how the information in financial statements can be used to evaluate the activities and financial status of a business.

Learning Objectives

After studying Chapter 19 you should be able to:

1. Explain the relationship between financial reporting and general purpose financial statements.
2. Describe, prepare, and interpret comparative financial statements and common-size comparative statements.
3. Calculate and explain the interpretation of the ratios, turnover, and rates of return used to evaluate (*a*) short-term liquidity, (*b*) long-term risk and capital structure, and (*c*) operating efficiency and profitability.
4. State the limitations associated with using financial statement ratios and the sources from which standards for comparison may be obtained.
5. Describe the segment information disclosed in financial reports of large companies with operations in several lines of business and list the four basic issues faced by accountants in dealing with segment information.
6. Define or explain the words and phrases listed in the chapter glossary.

Financial Reporting

LO 1 Explain the relationship between financial reporting and general purpose financial statements.

Many people receive and analyze financial information about business firms. These people include managers, employees, directors, customers, suppliers, owners, lenders, potential investors, potential creditors, brokers, regulatory authorities, lawyers, economists, labor unions, financial advisors, and the financial press. Some of these groups, such as managers and some regulatory agencies, are able to gain access to specialized financial reports that meet their specific interests. However, the other groups usually must rely on the **general purpose financial statements** that companies publish periodically. General purpose financial statements include (1) an income statement, (2) a balance sheet, (3) a statement of retained earnings (or statement of changes in stockholders' equity), and (4) a statement of cash flows. In addition to the information contained in the body of general purpose financial statements, the information contained in the footnotes is an integral part of the statements.

Financial reporting is intended to provide useful information to investors, creditors, and others for making investment, credit, and similar decisions. The information should help the users assess the amounts, timing, and uncertainty of prospective cash inflows and outflows.

Financial reporting includes financial statements but is much broader. Financial reporting includes communicating information in a variety of ways. Some examples are annual reports filed with the Securities and Exchange

Commission, news releases, and management letters or analyses included in annual reports. One such example is in Appendix J; look at the pages from IBM's annual report identified at the top as MANAGEMENT DISCUSSION.

Comparative Statements

LO 2 Describe, prepare, and interpret comparative financial statements and common-size comparative statements.

When the financial information of a business is analyzed, individual items usually are not particularly significant in and of themselves. However, relationships between items and groups of items plus changes that occurred are significant. As a result, financial statement analysis involves identifying and describing relationships between items and groups of items and changes in items.

You can see changes in financial statement items more clearly when amounts for two or more successive accounting periods are placed side by side in columns on a single statement. Statements prepared in this manner are called **comparative statements.** Each financial statement can be presented in the comparative format.

In its simplest form, a comparative balance sheet consists of the amounts from two or more successive balance sheets arranged side by side so that you can see the changes in the amounts. However, the usefulness of the statement can be improved by also showing the changes in terms of absolute dollar amounts and as percentages. When this presentation is provided, as shown in Illustration 19–1, large dollar and large percentage changes are more readily apparent.

A comparative income statement is prepared in the same way. Income statement amounts for two or more successive periods are placed side by side, with dollar and percentage changes in additional columns. Illustration 19–2 shows such a statement.

Analyzing and Interpreting Comparative Statements

In analyzing and interpreting comparative data, study any items that show significant dollar or percentage changes. Then, try to identify the reasons for each change and, if possible, determine whether they are favorable or unfavorable. For example, in Illustration 19–1, the first item, "Cash," shows a decrease of $5,500. The next item, "Short-term investments," shows an extremely large decrease. Also, the "Long-term investments" were completely eliminated during the year. At first glance these changes appear to be unfavorable. However, these decreases must be evaluated in light of other changes that occurred. The increases in "Store equipment," "Buildings," and "Land," show that the company materially increased its plant assets between the two balance sheet dates. Further study suggests that the company has apparently constructed a new building on land that was held as an investment until needed for this expansion. Also, the company apparently paid for the new plant assets by reducing cash, selling the investment in Apex Company common stock, and issuing a $50,000 note payable.

In gaining control over operations, a comparative income statement can be especially useful to management. For example, in Illustration 19–2, "Gross sales" increased 14.1% and "Net sales" increased 13.9%. At the same time,

ILLUSTRATION 19–1

Comparative Balance Sheet with Dollar and Percentage Changes

RANGER WHOLESALE COMPANY
Comparative Balance Sheet
December 31, 1994, and December 31, 1993

	December 31		Amount of Increase or (Decrease) during 1994	Percent of Increase or (Decrease) during 1994
	1994	1993		
Assets				
Current assets:				
Cash	$ 15,000	$ 20,500	$ (5,500)	(26.8)%
Short-term investments	3,000	70,000	(67,000)	(95.7)
Accounts receivable, net	68,000	64,000	4,000	6.3
Merchandise inventory	90,000	84,000	6,000	7.1
Prepaid expenses	5,800	6,000	(200)	(3.3)
Total current assets	$181,800	$244,500	$ (62,700)	(25.6)
Long-term investments:				
Real estate	$ –0–	$ 30,000	$ (30,000)	(100.0)
Apex Company common stock	–0–	50,000	(50,000)	(100.0)
Total long-term investments	$ –0–	$ 80,000	$ (80,000)	(100.0)
Plant and equipment:				
Office equipment, net	$ 3,500	$ 3,700	$ (200)	(5.4)
Store equipment, net	17,900	6,800	11,100	163.2
Buildings, net	176,800	28,000	148,800	531.4
Land	50,000	20,000	30,000	150.0
Total plant and equipment	$248,200	$ 58,500	$189,700	324.3
Total assets	$430,000	$383,000	$ 47,000	12.3
Liabilities				
Current liabilities:				
Accounts payable	$ 43,600	$ 55,000	$ (11,400)	(20.7)
Wages payable	800	1,200	(400)	(33.3)
Taxes payable	4,800	5,000	(200)	(4.0)
Notes payable	5,000	–0–	5,000	
Total current liabilities	$ 54,200	$ 61,200	$ (7,000)	(11.4)
Long-term liabilities:				
Notes payable (secured by mortgage on land and buildings)	60,000	10,000	50,000	500.0
Total liabilities	$114,200	$ 71,200	$ 43,000	60.4
Stockholders' Equity				
Common stock, $10 par value	$250,000	$250,000	$ –0–	–0–
Retained earnings	65,800	61,800	4,000	6.5
Total stockholders' equity	$315,800	$311,800	$ 4,000	1.3
Total liabilities and equity	$430,000	$383,000	$ 47,000	12.3

ILLUSTRATION 19–2

Comparative Income Statement with Dollar and Percentage Changes

RANGER WHOLESALE COMPANY
Comparative Income Statement
For Years Ended December 31, 1994 and 1993

	Years Ended December 31		Amount of Increase or (Decrease) during 1994	Percent of Increase or (Decrease) during 1994
	1994	1993		
Gross sales	$973,500	$853,000	$120,500	14.1%
Sales returns and allowances	13,500	10,200	3,300	32.4
Net sales	$960,000	$842,800	$117,200	13.9
Cost of goods sold	715,000	622,500	92,500	14.9
Gross profit from sales	$245,000	$220,300	$ 24,700	11.2
Operating expenses:				
Selling expenses:				
Advertising expense	$ 7,500	$ 5,000	$ 2,500	50.0
Sales salaries expense	109,500	97,500	12,000	12.3
Store supplies expense	3,200	2,800	400	14.3
Depreciation expense, store equipment	2,400	1,700	700	41.2
Delivery expense	14,800	14,000	800	5.7
Total selling expenses	$137,400	$121,000	$ 16,400	13.6
General and administrative expenses:				
Office salaries expense	$ 41,000	$ 40,050	950	2.4
Office supplies expense	1,300	1,250	50	4.0
Insurance expense	1,600	1,200	400	33.3
Depreciation expense, office equipment	300	300	-0-	-0-
Depreciation expense, buildings	2,850	1,500	1,350	90.0
Bad debts expense	2,250	2,200	50	2.3
Total general and administration expenses	$ 49,300	$ 46,500	$ 2,800	6.0
Total operating expenses	$186,700	$167,500	$ 19,200	11.5
Operating income	$ 58,300	$ 52,800	$ 5,500	10.4
Less interest expense	6,300	1,500	4,800	320.0
Income before taxes	$ 52,000	$ 51,300	$ 700	1.4
Income taxes	19,000	18,700	300	1.6
Net income	$ 33,000	$ 32,600	$ 400	1.2
Earnings per share	$ 1.32	$ 1.30	$ 0.02	1.5

"Sales returns and allowances" increased 32.4%, or at a rate more than twice that of gross sales. Returned sales usually represent wasted sales effort and dissatisfied customers. Therefore, the increased rate of "Sales returns and allowances" should be investigated, and the reason for the increase should be determined.

In addition to the large increase in the "Sales returns and allowances," note that the rate of increase of "Cost of goods sold" is greater than the rate of increase of "Net sales." This unfavorable trend should be corrected if possible.

In attempting to find reasons for Ranger Wholesale Company's increase in sales, the increases in advertising and in plant assets must be considered. For example, an increase in advertising may increase sales. Also, the increase in plant assets may have been necessary to support larger sales and production volumes.

Calculating Percentage Increases and Decreases

To calculate the percentage increases and decreases shown on comparative statements, divide the dollar increase or decrease of an item by the amount shown for the item in the base year. If no amount is shown in the base year, or if the base year amount is negative (such as a net loss), a percentage increase or decrease cannot be calculated. For example, in Illustration 19–1, there were no notes payable at the end of 1993, and a percentage change for this item cannot be calculated.

In this text, percentages and ratios typically are rounded to one or two decimal places. However, there is no uniform practice on this matter. In general, percentages should be carried out far enough to ensure that meaningful information is obtained. They should not be carried so far that the significance of relationships becomes lost in the length of the numbers.

Trend Percentages

Trend percentages (also known as *index numbers*) can be used to describe changes that have occurred from one period to the next. They are also used to compare data that cover a number of years. Calculate trend percentages as follows:

1. Select a base year and assign each item on the base year statement a weight of 100%.
2. Then, express each item from the statements for the years after the base year as a percentage of its base year amount. To determine these percentages, divide the amounts in the years after the base year by the amount of the item in the base year.

For example, if 1988 is selected as the base year for the following data, divide the amount of *Sales* in each year by $210,000 to get the trend percentages for sales. To get the trend percentages for cost of goods sold, divide the *Cost of goods sold* amount in each year by $145,000. And, the gross profit trend percentages equal the *Gross profit* amount in each year divided by $65,000.

	1993	1992	1991	1990	1989	1988
Sales	$400,000	$367,000	$320,000	$278,000	$241,500	$210,000
Cost of goods sold . .	260,000	212,000	190,000	165,000	159,500	145,000
Gross profit. . .	$140,000	$155,000	$130,000	$113,000	$ 82,000	$ 65,000

When the percentages are calculated, the trends for these three items appear as follows:

ILLUSTRATION 19–3

Trend Lines Showing Percentage Changes in Sales, Cost of Goods Sold, and Gross Profit

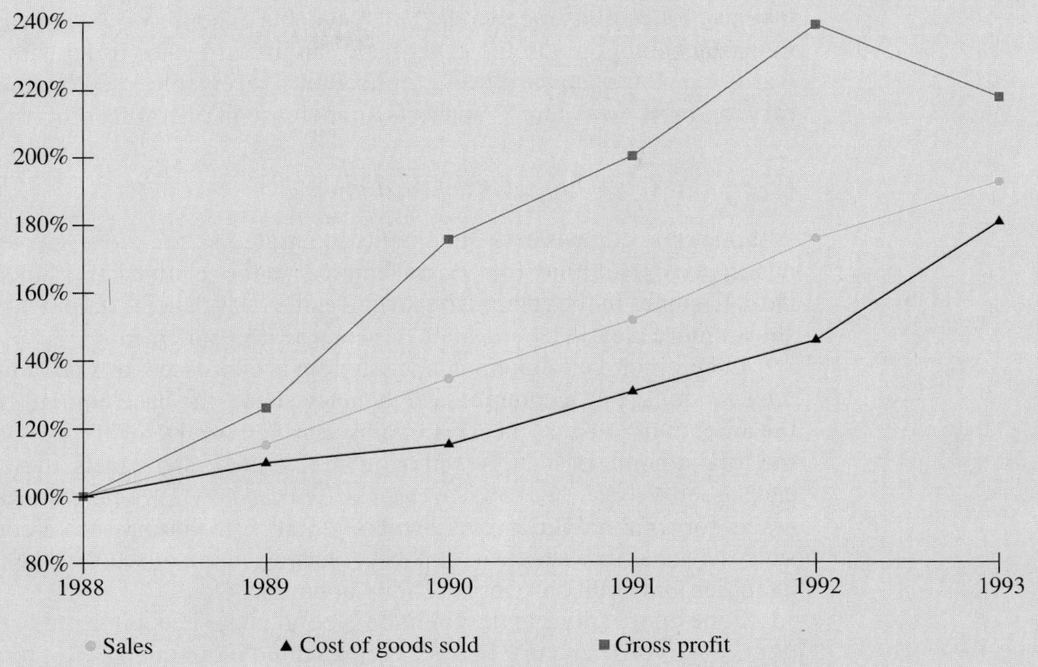

	1993	1992	1991	1990	1989	1988
Sales	190%	175%	152%	132%	115%	100%
Cost of goods sold . .	179	146	131	114	110	100
Gross profit. . .	215	238	200	174	126	100

Illustration 19–3 presents the same data in a graphical format. A graph can help identify trends and detect changes in their direction or growth rates. For example, note that although the trend for sales was consistently upward, the rate of increase declined slightly in 1993.

A graph also may help you identify and understand the relationships between items. For example, Illustration 19–3 shows that through 1992, cost of goods sold increased at a rate that was somewhat less than the increase in sales. Further, the differing trends in these two items had a pronounced effect on the percentage changes in gross profit. In 1993, while sales increased (at a slower rate), cost of goods sold increased at a much greater rate. The net effect of these 1993 changes was to sharply decrease gross profit, which reversed the trend of the past four years.

This presentation and analysis of the data suggest a problem that management needs to address. The graph also provides a warning to outside analysts that they should perhaps reconsider their past predictions of future cash flows.

The analysis of financial statement items may also include the relationships between items on different financial statements. For example, the combination of a downward sales trend with an upward trend for merchandise inventory, accounts receivable, and bad debts expense would indicate an unfavorable situation. On the other hand, an upward sales trend with a downward or a slower upward trend for accounts receivable, merchandise inventory, and selling expenses suggests an increase in operating efficiency.

Common-Size Comparative Statements

Although the comparative statements illustrated so far show how each item has changed over time, they do not emphasize the relative importance of each item. Changes in the relative importance of each financial statement item are shown more clearly by **common-size comparative statements.**

In common-size statements, each item is expressed as a percentage of a *base amount*. For a common-size balance sheet, the base amount is usually the amount of total assets. This total is assigned a value of 100%. (Of course, the total amount of liabilities plus owners' equity also equals 100%.) Then, each asset, liability, and owners' equity item is shown as a percentage of total assets (or total liabilities plus owners' equity). If you present a company's successive balance sheets in this way, changes in the mixture of the assets or liabilities and equity are more readily apparent.

For example, look at the common-size balance sheet presented in Illustration 19–4. Note that current assets represented more than 63% of total assets in 1993, whereas current assets amounted to less than 43% of total assets in 1994. Most of this change can be attributed to short-term investments, which fell from over 18% to less than 1% of total assets.

In producing a common-size income statement, the amount of net sales is usually the base amount and is also assigned a value of 100%. Then, each statement item appears as a percentage of net sales. This format can be informative and useful. If you think of the 100% sales amount as representing one sales dollar, then the remaining items show how each sales dollar was distributed among costs, expenses, and profit. For example, the comparative income statement in Illustration 19–5 shows that the 1993 cost of goods sold consumed 73.86 cents of each sales dollar. In 1994, cost of goods sold consumed 74.48 cents of each sales dollar. While this increase is small, almost $6,000 of additional gross profit would have been earned if the cost of goods sold percentage in 1994 had remained at the 1993 level.

Common-size percentages help the analyst identify potential efficiencies and inefficiencies that may otherwise be difficult to see. To illustrate, even though the dollar amounts of office and sales salaries expense were greater in 1994 than they were in 1993, both of these expenses represented smaller percentages of sales in 1994 than they did in 1993. These comparisons do not tell you why such changes took place, but they raise the possibility that the office and sales staffs were more productive in 1994 than in 1993.

Many corporate annual reports include graphic presentations of common-size information. Typical examples of these graphs appear in Illustration 19–6. The pie chart on the left side of the illustration shows the composition of Ranger Wholesale Company's assets on December 31, 1994. The chart on the

ILLUSTRATION 19–4

Common-Size Comparative Balance Sheet

RANGER WHOLESALE COMPANY
Common-Size Comparative Balance Sheet
December 31, 1994, and December 31, 1993

	December 31		Common-Size Percentages	
	1994	1993	1994	1993
Assets				
Current assets:				
Cash	$ 15,000	$ 20,500	3.49%	5.35%
Short-term investments	3,000	70,000	0.70	18.28
Accounts receivable, net	68,000	64,000	15.81	16.71
Merchandise inventory	90,000	84,000	20.93	21.93
Prepaid expenses	5,800	6,000	1.35	1.57
Total current assets	$181,800	$244,500	42.28	63.84
Long-term investments:				
Real estate	$ –0–	$ 30,000		7.83
Apex Company common stock	–0–	50,000		13.05
Total long-term investments	$ –0–	$ 80,000		20.88
Plant and equipment:				
Office equipment, net	$ 3,500	$ 3,700	0.81	0.97
Store equipment, net	17,900	6,800	4.16	1.78
Buildings, net	176,800	28,000	41.12	7.31
Land	50,000	20,000	11.63	5.22
Total plant and equipment	$248,200	$ 58,500	57.72	15.28
Total assets	$430,000	$383,000	100.00%	100.00%
Liabilities				
Current liabilities:				
Accounts payable	$ 43,600	$ 55,000	10.14%	14.36%
Wages payable	800	1,200	0.19	0.31
Taxes payable	4,800	5,000	1.12	1.31
Notes payable	5,000	–0–	1.16	
Total current liabilities	$ 54,200	$ 61,200	12.61	15.98
Long-term liabilities:				
Notes payable (secured by a mortgage on land and buildings)	60,000	10,000	13.95	2.61
Total liabilities	$114,200	$ 71,200	26.56	18.59
Stockholders' Equity				
Common stock, $10 par value	$250,000	$250,000	58.14	65.27
Retained earnings	65,800	61,800	15.30	16.14
Total stockholders' equity	$315,800	$311,800	73.44	81.41
Total liabilities and equity	$430,000	$383,000	100.00%	100.00%

ILLUSTRATION 19-5

Common-Size Comparative Income Statement

RANGER WHOLESALE COMPANY
Common-Size Comparative Income Statement
For Years Ended December 31, 1994 and 1993

	Years Ended December 31		Common-Size Percentages	
	1994	**1993**	**1994**	**1993**
Gross sales	$973,500	$853,000	101.41%	101.21%
Sales returns and allowances	13,500	10,200	1.41	1.21
Net sales	$960,000	$842,800	100.00	100.00
Cost of goods sold	715,000	622.500	74.48	73.86
Gross profit from sales	$245,000	$220,300	25.52	26.14
Operating expenses:				
Selling expenses:				
Advertising expense	$ 7,500	$ 5,000	0.78	0.59
Sales salaries expense	109,500	97,500	11.41	11.57
Store supplies expense	3,200	2,800	0.33	0.33
Depreciation expense, store equipment	2,400	1,700	0.25	0.20
Delivery expense	14,800	14,000	1.54	1.66
Total selling expenses	$137,400	$121,000	14.31	14.35
General and administrative expenses:				
Office salaries expense	$ 41,000	$ 40,050	4.27	4.75
Office supplies expense	1,300	1,250	0.14	0.15
Insurance expense	1,600	1,200	0.17	0.14
Depreciation expense, office equipment	300	300	0.03	0.04
Depreciation expense, buildings	2,850	1,500	0.30	0.18
Bad debts expense	2,250	2,200	0.23	0.26
Total general and administrative expenses	$ 49,300	$ 46,500	5.14	5.52
Total operating expenses	$186,700	$167,500	19.45	19.87
Operating income	$ 58,300	$ 52,800	6.07	6.27
Less interest expense	6,300	1,500	0.66	0.18
Income before taxes	$ 52,000	$ 51,300	5.41	6.09
Income taxes	19,000	18,700	1.98	2.22
Net income	$ 33,000	$ 32,600	3.43%	3.87%
Earnings per share	$ 1.32	$ 1.30	—	—

right side shows the portions of each 1994 sales dollar that were consumed by cost of goods sold, operating expenses, and interest and tax expense. It also shows the portion that ended up as net income.

Analysis of Short-Term Liquidity

The amount of current assets less current liabilities is called the **working capital** or *net working capital* of a business. A business must maintain an adequate amount of working capital to meet current debts, carry sufficient inventories, and take advantage of cash discounts. Indeed, a business that runs out of working capital cannot continue its operations. Because current assets and

ILLUSTRATION 19–6

Common Size Financial Statement Information

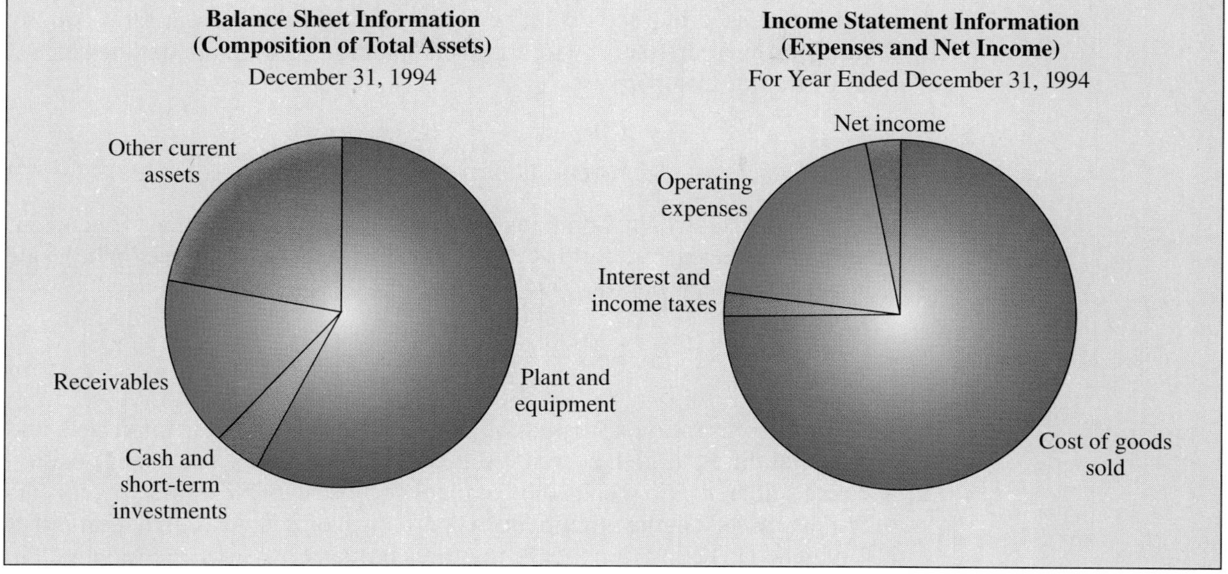

current liabilities are so necessary for efficient operations, an important part of evaluating the financial position of a business involves the analysis of working capital.

LO 3 Calculate and explain the interpretation of the ratios, turnovers, and rates of return used to evaluate (*a*) short-term liquidity, (*b*) long-term risk and capital structure, and (*c*) operating efficiency and profitability.

When evaluating the working capital of a business, you must look beyond the simple dollar amount of the excess of the current assets over the current liabilities. Instead, you need to consider the amount of the excess in relation to the amount of current liabilities. To see why this is true, consider the following example of Ace Company and Brown Company:

	Ace Company	Brown Company
Current assets	$100,000	$20,000
Current liabilities . .	90,000	10,000
Working capital . . .	$ 10,000	$10,000

Ace and Brown both have the same $10,000 amount of working capital. However, Ace must be able to convert its current assets to at least 90% of their book value in order to pay the liabilities. On the other hand, Brown Company has a much greater cushion when it converts its current assets to cash. In theory, it could lose as much as 50% of the assets' book value and still be able to pay its liabilities. Thus, Brown faces a much less risky situation than Ace does.

As a general rule, the dollar amount of a company's working capital does not adequately describe the strength of its working capital position. The ratio of its current assets to its current liabilities is often a more useful description.

Current Ratio

The relationship between a company's current assets and its current liabilities can be expressed by the **current ratio.** To calculate the current ratio, simply divide total current assets by total current liabilities. For example, the current ratio of Brown Company is:

$$\frac{\text{Current assets, \$20,000}}{\text{Current liabilities, \$10,000}} = 2.0$$

In other words, Brown Company's current assets are two times its current liabilities, or the current ratio is 2 to 1. The current ratio of Ranger Wholesale Company at December 31, 1994, is:

$$\frac{\text{Current assets, \$181,800}}{\text{Current liabilities, \$54,200}} = 3.4$$

The current ratio expresses the relationship between current assets and current liabilities. A high current ratio generally indicates a stronger position because a higher ratio means the company is more capable of meeting its current obligations. On the other hand, a company might have a current ratio that is too high. This condition means that the company has invested too much in current assets compared to its needs. Normally, current assets do not generate very much additional revenue. Therefore, if a company invests too much in current assets, the investment is not being used efficiently.

Years ago, bankers and other creditors often used a current ratio of 2 to 1 as a rule of thumb in evaluating the debt-paying ability of a credit-seeking company. A company with a 2 to 1 current ratio was generally thought to be a good credit risk in the short run. However, most lenders realize that the 2 to 1 rule of thumb is not an adequate test of debt-paying ability. They realize that whether a company's current ratio is good or bad depends on at least three factors:

1. The nature of the company's business.
2. The composition of its current assets.
3. The turnover rate for some of its current assets.

In addition, the ratio can be affected by a company's choice of an inventory flow assumption. For example, a company that uses LIFO tends to have a smaller reported amount of current assets than if it uses FIFO. Therefore, consider the underlying factors before deciding that a given current ratio (or any other ratio, for that matter) is acceptable.

Whether a company's current ratio is adequate depends on the nature of its business. A service company that has no inventories other than supplies and that grants little or no credit may be able to operate on a current ratio of less than 1 to 1 if its sales generate enough cash to pay its current liabilities on time. On the other hand, a company that sells high-fashion clothing or furniture may occasionally misjudge future styles. If this happens, the company's inventory may not generate much cash until after a relatively long period of time. A company that faces risks like these may need a current ratio of much more than 2 to 1 to protect its liquidity.

Therefore, when you study the adequacy of working capital, consider the type of business under review. Before you decide that a company's current ratio is too low (or too high), compare the company's current ratio with ratios of other successful companies in the same industry. Another important source of insight is to observe how the ratio compares to its values in past periods.

Also consider the composition of a company's current assets when you evaluate its working capital position. Cash and short-term investments are more liquid than accounts and notes receivable. And, short-term receivables normally are more liquid than merchandise inventory. Cash can be used to pay current debts at once. But, accounts receivable and merchandise must be converted into cash before payments can be made. Therefore, an excessive amount of receivables and inventory could weaken the company's ability to pay its current liabilities.

Acid-Test Ratio

An easily calculated check on current asset composition is the **acid-test ratio**, also called the *quick ratio* because it is the ratio of quick assets to current liabilities. Quick assets are cash, short-term investments, accounts receivable, and notes receivable. These are the most liquid types of current assets. We calculate the acid-test ratio of Ranger Wholesale Company at the end of 1994 as follows:

Quick assets:		Current liabilities:	
Cash	$15,000	Accounts payable	$43,600
Short-term investments	3,000	Wages payable	800
Accounts receivable	68,000	Taxes payable	4,800
		Notes payable	5,000
Total	$86,000	Total	$54,200

$$\frac{\text{Quick assets, \$86,000}}{\text{Current liabilities, \$54,200}} = 1.59\text{, or } 1.6 \text{ to } 1$$

A traditional rule of thumb for an acceptable acid-test ratio is 1 to 1. However, as is true for all financial ratios, you should be skeptical about rules of thumb.

The working capital requirements of a company are also affected by how frequently the company converts and replaces its current assets. For example, assume that Dash Company and Fox Company sell the same amounts of merchandise on credit each month. However, Dash Company grants 30-day terms to its customers, while Fox Company grants 60 days. Both collect their accounts at the end of these credit periods. As a result of the difference in terms, Dash Company turns over, or collects, its accounts twice as fast as Fox Company. Also, as a result of the more rapid turnover, Dash Company makes only one half the investment in accounts receivable that is required of Fox Company. Thus, Dash can operate successfully with smaller current and acid-test ratios.

Accounts Receivable Turnover

One way to measure how frequently a company converts its accounts receivable into cash is to calculate the **accounts receivable turnover.** To calculate the accounts receivable turnover, divide credit sales (or net sales, if the amount of credit sales is not readily available) for a year by the average accounts receivable balance during the year. If the company has short-term notes receivable, those balances should be included with the accounts receivable. The average balance can be approximated by averaging the beginning and ending balances. For example, calculate Ranger Wholesale Company's accounts receivable turnover for 1994 as follows:

a. December 31, 1993, accounts receivable . .	$ 64,000
b. December 31, 1994, accounts receivable . .	68,000
c. Average balance $(a + b)/2$	66,000
d. Net sales for year	960,000

$$\frac{\text{Net Sales, \$960,000}}{\text{Average Accounts Receivable, \$66,000}} = 14.5$$

Thus, it can be said that Ranger creates and collects its receivables approximately 14.5 times per year.

If accounts receivable are collected quickly, the accounts receivable turnover is high. In general, this situation is favorable because it means that the company does not have to commit large amounts of capital to accounts receivable. However, an accounts receivable turnover may be too high, especially if it results from the fact that credit terms are so restrictive that they have a negative effect on sales volume.

Sometimes, the ending accounts receivable balance can substitute for the average balance in calculating accounts receivable turnover. This approximation is suitable if the effect on the ratio is not significant. If possible, credit sales should be used rather than the sum of cash and credit sales. Also, using gross accounts receivable (before subtracting the allowance for doubtful accounts) is more likely to provide helpful information. However, information about credit sales is seldom available in published financial statements. Likewise, published balance sheets may report accounts receivable at their net amount. Therefore, an external analyst may be forced to use total sales and net accounts receivable.

Days' Sales Uncollected

Accounts receivable turnover is only one way to measure how frequently a company collects its accounts. Another method is to calculate the **days' sales uncollected.** To illustrate the calculation of days' sales uncollected, assume that a company had credit sales of $250,000 during a year and $25,000 of accounts and short-term notes receivable at the year's end. Thus, one tenth of its credit sales are uncollected. In other words, the charge sales made during one tenth of a year, or 36.5 days ($\frac{1}{10} \times 365$ days in a year), are uncollected. In equation form, this calculation of days' sales uncollected is as follows:

$$\frac{\text{Accounts receivable, \$25,000}}{\text{Credit sales, \$250,000}} \times 365 = 36.5 \text{ day's sales uncollected}$$

Days' sales uncollected has more meaning if you know the credit terms. According to a rule of thumb, a company's days' sales uncollected should not exceed one and one third times the days in its *credit* period if it does not offer discounts and one and one third times the days in its *discount* period if it does offer discounts. If the company offers 30-day terms without a discount, then 36.5 days is within the rule-of-thumb amount. However, if its terms are 2/10, n/30, the size of its days' sales uncollected seems excessive.

Turnover of Merchandise Inventory

Working capital requirements are also affected by how long a company holds merchandise inventory before selling it. This effect can be measured by calculating the **merchandise turnover**, which is the number of times the average inventory is sold during a reporting period. A high turnover generally indicates good merchandising. Also, from a working capital point of view, a company with a high turnover requires a smaller investment in inventory than one that produces the same sales with a low turnover. On the other hand, the merchandise turnover may be too high if a company keeps such a small inventory that sales volume is restricted.

To calculate merchandise turnover, divide the cost of goods sold during a period by the average inventory for the same period. Cost of goods sold measures the amount of merchandise (at cost) that was sold during an accounting period. Average inventory is the average amount of merchandise (at cost) on hand during the period. The 1994 merchandise turnover of Ranger Wholesale Company is calculated as follows:

$$\frac{\text{Cost of goods sold, \$715,000}}{\text{Average merchandise inventory, \$87,000}} = \text{Merchandise turnover of 8.2 times}$$

In this calculation, the cost of goods sold was taken from the company's 1994 income statement. The average inventory was estimated by averaging the beginning inventory for 1994 ($84,000) and the ending inventory for 1994 ($90,000), which is $87,000 [($84,000 + $90,000)/2]. In case the beginning and ending inventories do not represent the amount of inventory normally on hand, a more accurate turnover may be computed by using the average of its monthly or quarterly inventories, if that information is readily available.

Standards of Comparison

LO 4 State the limitations associated with using financial statement ratios and the sources from which standards for comparison may be obtained.

After you compute ratios and turnovers in the process of analyzing financial statements, you then have to decide whether the calculated amounts suggest good, bad, or merely average performance by the company. To make these judgments, you must have some basis for comparison. The following are possibilities:

1. An experienced analyst may compare the ratios and turnovers of the company under review with *subjective* standards acquired from past experiences.

2. For purposes of comparison, an analyst may calculate the ratios and turnovers of a selected group of competing companies in the same *industry* as the one whose statements are under review.
3. *Published* ratios and turnovers (such as those provided by Dun & Bradstreet) may be used for comparison.
4. Some local and national trade associations gather data from their members and publish *standard* or *average* ratios for their trade or industry. When available, these data can give the analyst a useful basis for comparison.
5. *Rule-of-thumb* standards can be used as a basis for comparison.

Of these five standards, the ratios and turnovers of a selected group of competing companies normally are the best bases for comparison. Rule-of-thumb standards should be applied with great care and then only if they seem reasonable in light of past experience and the industry's norms.

Analysis of Long-Term Risk and Capital Structure

LO 3 Calculate and explain the interpretation of the ratios, turnovers, and rates of return used to evaluate (*a*) short-term liquidity, (*b*) long-term risk and capital structure, and (*c*) operating efficiency and profitability.

An analysis of working capital evaluates the short-term liquidity of the company. However, analysts are also interested in a company's ability to meet its obligations and provide security to its creditors over the long-run. Indicators of this ability include *debt* and *equity* ratios, the relationship between *pledged plant assets and secured liabilities*, and the company's capacity to earn *sufficient income to pay its fixed interest charges*.

Debt and Equity Ratios

Financial analysts are always interested in the portion of a company's assets contributed by its owners and the portion contributed by creditors. This relationship is described by ratios that express (1) total liabilities as a percentage of total assets and (2) total stockholders' equity as a percentage of total assets. Calculate the debt and equity ratios of Ranger Wholesale Company as follows:

	1994	1993
a. Total liabilities	$114,200	$ 71,200
b. Total owners' equity	315,800	311,800
c. Total liabilities and stockholders' equity	$430,000	$383,000
Percentages provided by creditors: (*a*/*c*)	26.6%	18.6%
Percentages provided by stockholders: (*b*/*c*)	73.4%	81.4%

In general, a company is less risky if it has only a small amount of debt in its capital structure. With a small amount of debt, the obligation to pay interest is less burdensome. Also, the greater the equity of the owners in relation to liabilities, the greater the losses that can be absorbed by the owners before the remaining assets become inadequate to satisfy the claims of creditors.

From the stockholders' point of view, however, including debt in the capital structure of a company may be desirable, so long as the risk is not too great. If a business can earn a return on borrowed capital that is higher than the cost of borrowing, the difference represents increased income to stockholders.

Because debt can have the effect of increasing the return to stockholders, the inclusion of debt is sometimes described as *financial leverage*. Companies are said to be highly leveraged if a large portion of their assets are financed by debt.

Pledged Plant Assets to Secured Liabilities

Companies often borrow by issuing notes or bonds secured by mortgages on some of their plant assets. The ratio of pledged plant assets to secured liabilities is calculated to measure the protection provided to the secured creditors by the pledge of assets. To calculate this ratio, divide the book value of the pledged assets by the liabilities secured by the mortgages on those assets. The ratio for Ranger Wholesale Company is calculated as of the end of 1994 and 1993 as follows:

	1994	1993
Buildings, net	$176,800	$ 28,000
Land	50,000	20,000
a. Book value of pledged plant assets	$226,800	$ 48,000
b. Notes payable (secured by mortgage)	$ 60,000	$ 10,000
Ratio of pledged assets to secured liabilities (*a*/*b*)	3.8 to 1	4.8 to 1

The usual rule-of-thumb minimum value for this ratio is 2 to 1. However, the ratio needs careful interpretation because it is based on the book value of the pledged assets. As you know, book values are often unrelated to the amount that would be received for the assets in a foreclosure sale or other liquidation. Thus, estimated foreclosure or liquidation values are a better measure of the protection provided by pledged assets. Also, the long-term earning ability of the company with pledged assets is equally as important to secured creditors as the pledged assets' value because debts can be paid with cash generated by operating activities as well as cash obtained by selling assets.

Times Fixed Interest Charges Earned

The number of **times fixed interest charges were earned** is often calculated to describe the security of the return offered to creditors. The amount of income before the deduction of fixed interest charges and income taxes is the amount available to pay the fixed interest charges. To calculate the number of times fixed interest charges were earned, divide income *before* fixed interest charges and income taxes by the amount of fixed interest charges. The result is the number of times fixed interest charges were earned. The larger this number, the greater is the security for the lenders. A rule of thumb for this statistic is that creditors are reasonably safe if the company earns its fixed interest charges two or more times each year.

Calculate the number of times fixed interest charges were earned by Ranger Wholesale Company as follows:

	1994	1993
a. Income before interest and taxes	$58,300	$52,800
b. Interest expense	6,300	1,500
Times fixed interest charges earned (*a*/*b*)	9.3	35.2

Thus, there would appear to be little risk for the creditors of this company. Although the ratio dropped substantially from 1993 to 1994, the cause of the increase was the change in the amount of interest, not the amount of income.

Analysis of Operating Efficiency and Profitability

Financial analysts are especially interested in the ability of a company to use its assets efficiently to produce profits for its owners and thus to provide cash flows to them. Several ratios are available to help you evaluate operating efficiency and profitability.

Profit Margin

The operating efficiency of a company can be expressed in terms of two components. The first is the company's **profit margin,** which describes the company's ability to earn a net income from sales. This quality is measured by expressing net income as a percentage of sales. For example, calculate the profit margin of Ranger Wholesale Company in 1994 as follows:

$$\frac{\text{Net income, \$33,000}}{\text{Net sales, \$960,000}} = 3.4\%$$

To evaluate the profit margin of a company, consider the nature of the industry in which the company operates. For example, a publishing company might be expected to have a profit margin between 10 and 15%, while a retail supermarket might have a normal profit margin of 1 or 2%. The profit margin is also affected by the marketing strategy that the company uses. That is, a low margin strategy requires a high sales volume, while a high margin strategy allows a lower volume of sales to be adequate.

Total Asset Turnover

The second component of operating efficiency is **total asset turnover,** which describes the ability of the company to use its assets to generate sales. To calculate this statistic, divide net sales by the average total assets employed in the business. For Ranger Wholesale Company, the total asset turnover is

$$\frac{\text{Net sales, \$960,000}}{\text{Average total assets, \$406,500}} = 2.4$$

The average total assets is usually estimated by averaging the total assets at the beginning ($383,000) and end ($430,000) of the period.

In general, the higher the total asset turnover, the more efficiently the company is using its assets. However, as in the case of profit margin, the evaluation of total asset turnover depends on the nature of the industry in which the company operates. The relationship between the assets' book value and their current market value should also be considered.

Both profit margin and total asset turnover describe the two basic components of operating efficiency. However, they also evaluate management performance because the management of a company is fundamentally responsible for its operating efficiency.

Return on Total Assets Employed

Because operating efficiency has two basic components (profit margin and total asset turnover), analysts frequently calculate a summary measure of these components. The summary measure is called the **return on total assets employed.** To calculate this measure, divide net income by the average total assets employed during the year. For example, calculate the return on the total assets employed by Ranger Wholesale Company during 1994 as follows:

a. Net income	$ 33,000
b. Average total assets employed ($430,000 + $383,000)/2 . .	406,500
Return on total assets employed (*a*/*b*)	8.1%

The preceding calculation shows that Ranger Wholesale Company earned an 8.1% return on its average total assets employed in the business during 1994. However, you cannot tell whether this rate of return is good or bad without some basis for comparison. An especially useful basis for comparison is the rates of return earned by companies of similar size engaged in the same kind of business. You would also want to compare this rate with the rates produced on other kinds of investments. And, you should evaluate the trend in the rates of return earned by the company in recent years.

Earlier, we said that the return on total assets employed summarizes the two components of operating efficiency—profit margin and total asset turnover. The following calculation shows the relationship between these three measures. Notice that both profit margin and total asset turnover contribute to overall operating efficiency, as measured by return on total assets employed.

Profit margin × Total asset turnover = Return on total assets employed

$$\frac{\text{Net Income}}{\text{Net Sales}} \times \frac{\text{Net Sales}}{\text{Average Total Assets}} = \frac{\text{Net Income}}{\text{Average Total Assets}}$$

For Ranger Wholesale Company:

$$3.4\% \times 2.4 = 8.1\%$$

Return on Common Stockholders' Equity

Perhaps the most important reason for operating a business is to earn a net income for its owners. The **return on common stockholders' equity** measures the success of a business in reaching this goal. Usually, you should use an average of the beginning-of-year and end-of-year amounts of stockholders' equity in calculating the return. For Ranger Wholesale Company, the 1994 calculation is as follows:

	1994
a. Net income after taxes	$ 33,000
b. Average stockholders' equity [($311,800 + $315,800)/2]	313,800
Rate of return on stockholders' equity (*a*/*b*)	10.5%

When preferred stock is outstanding, subtract the preferred dividend requirements from net income to arrive at the common stockholders' share of income to be used in this calculation. And, the denominator of the ratio should be the average book value of the common stock.

Price Earnings Ratio

A commonly used statistic in comparing stock investment opportunities is the **price earnings ratio.** To calculate the price earnings ratio, divide market price per share by earnings per share. For example, if Ranger Wholesale Company's common stock sold at $15 per share at the end of 1994, calculate the stock's end-of-year price earnings ratio as:

$$\frac{\text{Market price per share, \$15}}{\text{Earnings per share, \$1.32}} = 11.4$$

In comparing price earnings ratios of different stocks, remember that these ratios are likely to vary from industry to industry. For example, a price earnings ratio of 8 to 10 is normal in the steel industry, while a price earnings ratio of 20 might be expected in a growth industry, such as high-tech electronics.

Dividend Yield

When investors evaluate whether to buy a stock at a given price per share, they often consider how much return they can expect to receive from cash dividends. **Dividend yield** is a statistic used to compare the dividend-paying performance of different investment alternatives. To calculate the dividend yield of stock, divide the amount of dividends paid annually by the market price per share. For example, Ranger Wholesale Company paid cash dividends in 1994 of $29,000, which amounted to $1.16 per share. If the market price per share is $15, the dividend yield is:

$$\frac{\text{Annual dividends per share, \$1.16}}{\text{Recent market price per share, \$15}} = 7.7\%$$

Review of Financial Statement Ratios and Statistics for Analysis

To evaluate short-term liquidity, use these ratios:

$$\text{Current ratio} = \frac{\text{Current assets}}{\text{Current liabilities}}$$

$$\text{Acid-test ratio} = \frac{\text{Cash + Short-term investments + Current receivables}}{\text{Current liabilities}}$$

$$\text{Accounts receivable turnover} = \frac{\text{Credit sales}}{\text{Average accounts receivable}}$$

$$\text{Days' sales uncollected} = \frac{\text{Accounts Receivable}}{\text{Charge sales}} \times 365$$

$$\text{Merchandise turnover} = \frac{\text{Cost of goods sold}}{\text{Average merchandise inventory}}$$

To evaluate long-term risk and capital structure, use these ratios:

$$\text{Debt ratio} = \frac{\text{Total liabilities}}{\text{Total assets}}$$

$$\text{Equity ratio} = \frac{\text{Total stockholders' equity}}{\text{Total assets}}$$

$$\frac{\text{Pledged plant assets}}{\text{to secured liabilities}} = \frac{\text{Book value of pledged plant assets}}{\text{Total secured liabilities}}$$

$$\text{Times fixed interest charges earned} = \frac{\text{Income before interest and taxes}}{\text{Interest expense}}$$

To evaluate operating efficiency and profitability, use these ratios:

$$\text{Profit margin} = \frac{\text{Net income}}{\text{Net sales}}$$

$$\text{Total asset turnover} = \frac{\text{Net sales}}{\text{Average total assets}}$$

$$\text{Return on total assets employed} = \frac{\text{Net income}}{\text{Average total assets}}$$

$$\text{Return on common stockholders' equity} = \frac{\text{Net income} - \text{Preferred dividends}}{\text{Average common stockholders' equity}}$$

$$\text{Price earnings ratio} = \frac{\text{Market price per common share}}{\text{Earnings per share}}$$

$$\text{Dividend yield} = \frac{\text{Annual dividends declared}}{\text{Market price per share}}$$

Reporting Information on Business Segments

Financial analysis is more complicated when a company is large and operates in more than one line of business. When information is provided about each **business segment** of the company, outside users of the financial statements can gain a better understanding of the overall business. A business segment is a portion of the company that can be separately identified by the products or services that it provides or a geographic market that it serves. The usefulness of segment information comes from the insight it provides about the relative performance of the segments and the dependence of the entire company on the profits derived from one or more of the segments.

Segment information must be published by public companies, which are those that have issued securities (either stock or bonds) traded in public mar-

LO 5 Describe the segment information disclosed in financial reports of large companies with operations in several lines of business and list the four basic issues faced by accountants in dealing with segment information.

kets.[1] As an example, Illustration 19–7 shows segment information provided in the annual report of The Walt Disney Company. The company's income statement reports some of the segment information, and a footnote presents the rest.

Segment Information to Be Disclosed

In Illustration 19–7, observe that The Walt Disney Company has three segments: theme parks and resorts, filmed entertainment, and consumer products. Also notice that these items of information are presented for each segment:

1. Revenues or net sales.
2. Operating profits (before interest and taxes).
3. Capital expenditures.
4. Depreciation and amortization expense.
5. Identifiable assets.

Public companies with material operations in more than one industry must disclose these items of information for each segment. In addition, they may be required to report (1) a geographical distribution of sales and (2) sales to major customers. Notice that The Walt Disney Company identifies the export revenues generated by its domestic operations.

Four Basic Segment Reporting Issues

Companies face four basic issues in compiling information about their segments. The FASB provides detailed guidelines for dealing with these issues. Although these guidelines are too complex to be fully explained at this introductory level, you should be aware of each basic issue.

Identifying Significant Segments. The operations of a business may not be neatly organized in segments that are important to financial statement readers. For purposes of segment reporting, the business must be divided into enough segments to show the basic industries in which it operates. On the other hand, it should not be divided into so many segments that the information becomes overwhelming.

Transfer Pricing between Segments. In many companies, one or more of their segments sell products or services to the other segments. Sales between segments provide revenues to the selling segment and create costs for the purchasing segment. To avoid double counting them, these sales and costs are eliminated when preparing the financial statements for the entire business. However, sales between segments are not eliminated when describing the

---

[1] FASB, *Accounting Standards—Current Text* (Norwalk, Conn., 1992), sec. S20.101. First published as *FASB Statement No. 15*.

ILLUSTRATION 19–7

Segment Information

THE WALT DISNEY COMPANY
Segment Information in the 1990 Annual Report
(in millions)

Income statement	1990	1989	1988
Revenues [or net sales]			
Theme parks and resorts	$3,019.6	$2,595.4	$2,042.0
Filmed entertainment	2,250.3	1,587.6	1,149.2
Consumer products	573.8	411.3	247.0
	5,843.7	4,594.3	3,438.2
Operating income [before interest and taxes]			
Theme parks and resorts	889.3	785.4	564.8
Filmed entertainment	313.0	256.5	186.3
Consumer products	223.2	187.1	133.7
	1,425.5	1,229.0	884.8
Footnote 11			
Capital expenditures			
Theme parks and resorts	$ 519.8	$ 665.4	$ 559.0
Filmed entertainment	39.5	27.2	16.9
Consumer products	34.3	21.6	6.6
Corporate	122.7	35.4	13.2
	$ 716.3	$ 749.6	$ 595.7
Depreciation [and amortization] expense			
Theme parks and resorts	$ 177.4	$ 172.4	$ 137.2
Filmed entertainment	12.9	12.2	6.8
Consumer products	5.8	3.1	0.6
Corporate	7.0	3.8	4.0
	$ 203.1	$ 191.5	$ 148.6
Identifiable assets			
Theme parks and resorts	$4,420.3	$4,066.9	$3,195.6
Filmed entertainment	1,672.8	1,252.1	631.2
Consumer products	236.4	193.1	148.8
Corporate	1,692.8	1,145.1	1,133.3
	$8,022.3	$6,657.2	$5,108.9
Supplemental revenue data			
Theme parks and resorts			
Admissions	$1,179.9	$1,021.7	$ 816.3
Merchandise, food, and beverage	1,113.5	1,019.5	829.1
Filmed entertainment			
Theatrical product	1,545.7	1,090.1	824.9

Export revenues by domestic operations for the three years ended September 30, 1990, 1989, and 1988 were $938.8 million, $653.3 million, and $400.1 million, respectively.

AS A MATTER OF

Ethics

Diane Coleman is the manager of Lacto Corporation's Tech Division. Jay Smiley is the manager of the company's Salnic Division. Tech Division's product is not sold to the public but is transferred to Salnic Division, where it is added to other components to produce the finished product. Tech Division's profit equals the difference between its costs and the revenue that it earns on sales to Salnic Division. Salnic Division is also affected by this price, but in the opposite direction. That is, the transfer price paid to Tech Division is one of the costs incurred by Salnic Division. Several managers in each division are compensated in proportion to the profit that their divisions earn. As a result, Coleman and other Tech Division managers benefit if the transfer price is high. Smiley and the Salnic Division managers, on the other hand, benefit if the transfer price is low.

The components manufactured by Tech Division are also produced by outside companies. If Salnic Division were allowed to buy the components from other suppliers, it would have to pay approximately $5 million for next year's supply. However, the costs Tech Division will incur to produce the next year's components will be about $3.2 million. Because of this difference, top management will not let Salnic Division buy from outsiders.

In making plans for the upcoming year, Coleman is dealing with the issue of what price Salnic Division should be charged for Tech Division's components. Coleman is tempted to try for a price in excess of $5 million, because top management will not really let Smiley buy from outsiders. Coleman wonders how Smiley and top management will react to the price she will try to establish.

performance of each segment. The issue is how to determine a fair price (called a **transfer price**) for these sales that allows the profit of both the selling and the buying segments to be usefully measured.

Measuring Segment Profitability Even if each segment of a business operates as a highly independent unit, some general expenses of the business benefit more than one segment. Some of these **common expenses** can be allocated to the segments on a reasonable basis. Others may not be usefully allocated. For example, notice that The Walt Disney Company reported $7 million of depreciation expense for the corporate segment in 1990. When preparing segment profit information, you first must determine which expenses to allocate and which to leave unallocated. Then, for these expenses to be allocated, you must determine the most reasonable basis for allocation.

Identifying Segment Assets. Many assets are easily identified with specific segments because they are used by only one segment. Other assets are shared by more than one segment. To report the amount invested in the assets in each segment, you must determine reasonable bases for allocating the book value of shared assets among the segments that benefit from them. You will probably find that the cost of some assets cannot be allocated among the segments. For example, The Walt Disney Company identified nearly $1.7 billion of assets as belonging to the corporate segment as of the end of 1990.

Summary of the Chapter in Terms of Learning Objectives

LO 1. Financial reporting is intended to provide information useful to investors, creditors, and others in making investment, credit, and similar decisions. The information is communicated in a variety of ways, including general purpose financial statements. These statements normally include an income statement, balance sheet, statement of retained earnings or statement of changes in stockholders' equity, and statement of cash flows.

LO 2. Comparative financial statements show amounts for two or more successive periods, sometimes with the changes in the items disclosed in absolute and percentage terms. In common-size statements, each item is expressed as a percentage of a base amount. The base amount for the balance sheet is usually total assets, and the base amount for the income statement is usually net sales.

LO 3. To evaluate the short-term liquidity of a company, calculate a current ratio, an acid-test ratio, the accounts receivable turnover, the days' sales uncollected, and the merchandise turnover.

In evaluating the long-term risk and capital structure of a company, calculate debt and equity ratios, pledged plant assets to secured liabilities, and the number of times fixed interest charges were earned.

In evaluating operating efficiency and profitability, calculate profit margin, total asset turnover, return on total assets employed, and return on common stockholders' equity. Other statistics used to evaluate the profitability of alternative investments include the price earnings ratio and the dividend yield.

LO 4. In deciding whether financial statement ratio values are satisfactory, too high, or too low, you must have some bases for comparison. These bases may come from past experience and personal judgment, from ratios of similar companies, or from ratios published by trade associations and other public sources. Traditional rules of thumb should be applied with great care and only if they seem reasonable in light of past experience.

LO 5. Large companies that operate in more than one industry disclose the following information on each industrial segment: revenues, operating profits (before interest and taxes), depreciation and amortization expense, capital expenditures, and identifiable assets. They may also report a geographical distribution of sales and sales to major customers. The four problems accountants face in preparing segment information include: identifying significant segments, transfer pricing between segments, measuring segment profitability, and identifying segment assets.

Demonstration Problem

Use the financial statements of Precision Company to satisfy the following requirements:

1. Prepare a comparative income statement showing the percentage increase or decrease for 1994 over 1993.
2. Prepare common-size comparative balance sheets for 1994 and 1993.

3. Compute the following ratios as of December 31, 1994, or for the year ended December 31, 1994:
   a. Current ratio.
   b. Acid-test ratio.
   c. Accounts receivable turnover.
   d. Days' sales uncollected.
   e. Merchandise turnover.
   f. Debt ratio.
   g. Pledged plant assets to secured liabilities.
   h. Times fixed interest charges earned.
   i. Profit margin.
   j. Total asset turnover.
   k. Return on total assets employed.
   l. Return on common stockholders' equity.

PRECISION COMPANY
Comparative Income Statement
For Years Ended December 31, 1994 and 1993

	1994	1993
Sales	$2,486,000	$2,075,000
Cost of goods sold	1,523,000	1,222,000
Gross profit from sales	$ 963,000	$ 853,000
Operating expenses:		
Advertising expense	$ 145,000	$ 100,000
Sales salaries expense	240,000	280,000
Office salaries expense	165,000	200,000
Insurance expense	100,000	45,000
Supplies expense	26,000	35,000
Depreciation expense	85,000	75,000
Miscellaneous expense	17,000	15,000
Total operating expenses	$ 778,000	$ 750,000
Operating income	$ 185,000	$ 103,000
Less interest expense	44,000	46,000
Income before taxes	$ 141,000	$ 57,000
Income taxes	47,000	19,000
Net income	$ 94,000	$ 38,000
Earnings per share	$ 0.99	$ 0.40

PRECISION COMPANY
Comparative Balance Sheet
December 31, 1994, and December 31, 1993

	1994	1993
Assets		
Current assets:		
Cash	$ 79,000	$ 42,000
Short-term investments	65,000	96,000
Accounts receivable (net)	120,000	100,000
Merchandise inventory	250,000	265,000
Total current assets	$ 514,000	$ 503,000
Plant and equipment:		
Store equipment (net)	$ 400,000	$ 350,000
Office equipment (net)	45,000	50,000
Buildings (net)	625,000	675,000
Land	100,000	100,000
Total plant and equipment	$1,170,000	$1,175,000
Total assets	$1,684,000	$1,678,000

	1994	1993
Liabilities		
Current liabilities:		
Accounts payable	$ 164,000	$ 190,000
Short-term notes payable	75,000	90,000
Taxes payable	26,000	12,000
Total current liabilities	$ 265,000	$ 292,000
Long-term liabilities:		
Notes payable (secured by mortgage on building and land)	400,000	420,000
Total liabilities	$ 665,000	$ 712,000
Stockholders' Equity		
Common stock, $5 par value	$ 475,000	$ 475,000
Retained earnings	544,000	491,000
Total stockholders' equity	$1,019,000	$966,000
Total liabilities and equity	$1,684,000	$1,678,000

Solution to Demonstration Problem

Planning the Solution

- Set up a four column income statement; enter the 1994 and 1993 amounts in the first two columns, and then enter the dollar change in the third column and the percentage change from 1993 in the fourth column.
- Set up a four column balance sheet; enter the 1994 and 1993 amounts in the first two columns, and then compute and enter the amount of each item as a percent of total assets.
- Compute the given ratios using the provided numbers; be sure to use the average of the beginning and ending amounts where appropriate.

1.

PRECISION COMPANY
Comparative Income Statement
For Years Ended December 31, 1994 and 1993

			Increase (Decrease) in 1994	
	1994	**1993**	**Amount**	**Percent**
Sales	$2,486,000	$2,075,000	$411,000	19.8
Cost of goods sold	1,523,000	1,222,000	301,000	24.6
Gross profit from sales	$ 963,000	$ 853,000	$110,000	12.9
Operating expenses:				
Advertising expense	$ 145,000	$ 100,000	$ 45,000	45.0
Sales salaries expense	240,000	280,000	(40,000)	(14.3)
Office salaries expense	165,000	200,000	(35,000)	(17.5)
Insurance expense	100,000	45,000	55,000	122.2
Supplies expense	26,000	35,000	(9,000)	(25.7)
Depreciation expense	85,000	75,000	10,000	13.3
Miscellaneous expense	17,000	15,000	2,000	13.3
Total operating expenses	$ 778,000	$ 750,000	$ 28,000	3.7
Operating income	$ 185,000	$ 103,000	$ 82,000	79.6
Less interest expense	44,000	46,000	(2,000)	(4.3)
Income before taxes	$ 141,000	$ 57,000	$ 84,000	147.4
Income taxes	47,000	19,000	28,000	147.4
Net income	$ 94,000	$ 38,000	$ 56,000	147.4
Earnings per share	$ 0.99	$ 0.40	$ 0.59	147.5

2.

PRECISION COMPANY
Common-Size Comparative Balance Sheet
December 31, 1994, and December 31, 1993

	December 31		Common-Size Percentages	
	1994	**1993**	**1994**	**1993**
Assets				
Current assets:				
Cash	$ 79,000	$ 42,000	4.69%	2.50%
Short-term investments	65,000	96,000	3.86	5.72
Accounts receivable (net)	120,000	100,000	7.13	5.96
Merchandise inventory	250,000	265,000	14.85	15.79
Total current assets	$514,000	$ 503,000	30.53	29.97
Plant and equipment:				
Store equipment (net)	$ 400,000	$ 350,000	23.75	20.86
Office equipment (net)	45,000	50,000	2.67	2.98
Buildings (net)	625,000	675,000	37.11	40.23
Land	100,000	100,000	5.94	5.96
Total plant and equipment	$1,170,000	$1,175,000	69.47	70.03
Total assets	$1,684,000	$1,678,000	100.00%	100.00%
Liabilities				
Current liabilities:				
Accounts payable	$ 164,000	$ 190,000	9.74%	11.32%
Short-term notes payable	75,000	90,000	4.45	5.36
Taxes payable	26,000	12,000	1.54	0.72
Total current liabilities	$ 265,000	$ 292,000	15.73	17.40
Long-term liabilities:				
Notes payable (secured by mortgage on building and land)	400,000	420,000	23.75	25.03
Total liabilities	$ 665,000	$ 712,000	39.48	42.43
Stockholders' Equity				
Common stock, $5 par value	$ 475,000	$ 475,000	28.21	28.31
Retained earnings	544,000	491,000	32.31	29.26
Total stockholders' equity	$1,019,000	$ 966,000	60.52	57.57
Total liabilities and equity	$1,684,000	$1,678,000	100.00%	100.00%

3. Ratios for 1994:
   a. Current ratio: $514,000/$265,000 = 1.9
   b. Acid-test ratio: ($79,000 + $65,000 + $120,000)/$265,000 = 1.0
   c. Average receivables: ($120,000 + $100,000)/2 = $110,000
   Accounts receivable turnover: $2,486,000/$110,000 = 22.6
   d. Days' sales uncollected: ($120,000/$2,486,000) × 365 = 17.6 days
   e. Average inventory: ($250,000 + $265,000)/2 = $257,500
   Merchandise turnover: $1,523,000/$257,500 = 5.9 times
   f. Debt ratio: $665,000/$1,684,000 = 39.5%
   g. Pledged assets to secured liabilities:
   ($625,000 + $100,000)/$400,000 = 1.8
   h. Times fixed interest charges earned: $185,000/$44,000 = 4.2 times
   i. Profit margin: $94,000/$2,486,000 = 3.8%
   j. Average total assets: ($1,684,000 + $1,678,000)/2 = $1,681,000
   Total asset turnover: $2,486,000/$1,681,000 = 1.48
   k. Return on total assets employed: $94,000/$1,681,000 = 5.6% or
   3.8% × 1.48 = 5.6%
   l. Average total equity: ($1,019,000 + $966,000)/2 = $992,500
   Return on common stockholders' equity: $94,000/$992,500 = 9.5%

Glossary

LO 6 Define or explain the words and phrases listed in the chapter glossary.

Accounts receivable turnover a measure of how long it takes a company to collect its accounts, calculated by dividing credit sales (or net sales) by the average accounts receivable balance. p. 1030

Acid-test ratio the relationship between quick assets (cash, short-term investments, accounts receivable, and notes receivable) and current liabilities, calculated as quick assets divided by current liabilities. p. 1029

Business segment a portion of the business that can be separately identified by the products or services that it provides or a geographic market that it serves. p. 1037

Common expenses expenses incurred for the benefit of more than one segment of a business; some common expenses can be allocated among the segments, while others cannot be allocated. p. 1040

Common-size comparative statements comparative financial statements in which each amount is expressed as a percentage of a base amount. In the balance sheet, the amount of total assets is usually selected as the base amount and is expressed as 100%. In the income statement, net sales is usually selected as the base amount. pp. 1024–26

Comparative statements financial statements with data for two or more successive accounting periods placed in columns side by side, sometimes with changes shown in dollar amounts and percentages. pp. 1019–22

Current ratio the relationship of a company's current assets to its current liabilities, that is, current assets divided by current liabilities. pp. 1028–29

Days' sales uncollected the number of days of average credit sales volume accumulated in the accounts receivable balance, calculated as the product of 365 times the accounts receivable balance divided by credit sales. p. 1030

Dividend yield the annual cash dividends paid per share of stock expressed as a percentage of the market price per share; used to compare the dividend paying performance of different investment alternatives. p. 1036

Financial reporting the process of providing information that is useful to investors, creditors, and others in making investment, credit, and similar decisions. pp. 1018–19

General purpose financial statements statements published periodically for use by a wide variety of interested parties; include the income statement, balance sheet, statement of retained earnings (or statement of changes in stockholders' equity), and statement of cash flows. p. 1018

Merchandise turnover the average number of times a company's inventory is sold during an accounting period, calculated by dividing cost of goods sold by the average merchandise inventory balance. p. 1031

Price earnings ratio a measure used to evaluate the profitability of alternative common stock investments, calculated as market price per share of common stock divided by earnings per share. p. 1036

Profit margin a component of operating efficiency and profitability, calculated by expressing net income as a percentage of net sales. p. 1034

Return on common stockholders' equity a measure of profitability in the use of assets provided by common stockholders, measured by expressing net income less preferred dividends as a percentage of average common stockholders' equity. pp. 1035–36

Return on total assets employed a summary measure of operating efficiency and management performance, calculated by expressing net income as a percentage of average total assets. p. 1035

Times fixed interest charges earned a measure of a company's ability to satisfy fixed interest charges, calculated as income before interest and income taxes divided by fixed interest charges. pp. 1033–34

Total asset turnover a component of operating efficiency and profitability, calculated by dividing net sales by average total assets. pp. 1034–35

Transfer price a price assigned to products or services sold by one segment of a business to another. p. 1040

Working capital current assets minus current liabilities. p. 1026

Synonymous Terms

Acid-test ratio quick ratio.

Business segment line of business.

Trend percentages index numbers.

Working capital net working capital.

Objective Review

Answers to the following questions are listed at the end of this chapter. Be sure that you decide which is the one best answer to each question *before* you check the answers.

LO 1 Which of the following is not an objective of financial reporting?

a. Financial reporting includes reporting information in general purpose financial statements and in other ways such as news announcements and management discussions in annual reports.
b. Financial reporting should provide information that is useful primarily for meeting the needs of corporation managers.
c. Financial reporting should provide information that is useful to investors and creditors and other users in making investment, credit, and similar decisions.
d. Financial reporting should provide information to help users assess the amounts, timing, and uncertainty of prospective cash inflows and outflows.
e. All of the above are objectives of financial reporting.

LO 2 Given the following information for Moyers Corporation, determine the common-size percentages for gross profit from sales.

	1994	1993
Net sales	$134,400	$114,800
Cost of goods sold	72,800	60,200

a. 45.8% in 1994; 47.6% in 1993.
b. 113% in 1994; 100% in 1993.
c. 12.8% increase during 1994.
d. 100% in 1994; 88.8% in 1993.
e. 54.2% in 1994; 52.4% in 1993.

LO 3 Times fixed interest charges earned describes:

a. How fast a company collects its accounts.
b. The security of the return offered to creditors.
c. Short-term liquidity.
d. Operating efficiency and profitability.
e. The protection provided to the secured creditors by the mortgages on the assets.

LO 4 Which of the following may be used as a standard for comparing ratios and turnovers computed in the process of analyzing financial statements?

a. Rule-of-thumb standards.
b. Past experience of the analyst with the company under review as well as other companies.
c. Ratios and turnovers of a selected group of companies competing in the same industry as the one whose statements are under review.
d. Data gathered and published by local and national trade associations as standard or average ratios for their industry.
e. All of the above.

LO 5 Which of the following is not one of the items of segment information that must be disclosed in the financial reports of large companies having operations in several lines of business?

a. Depreciation and amortization expense.
b. Extraordinary gains and losses.
c. Operating profits (net of interest and taxes).
d. Revenues.
e. All of the above must be disclosed.

LO 6 A summary measure of operating efficiency and management performance, calculated by expressing net income as a percentage of average total assets, is called:

a. Times fixed interest charges earned.
b. Total asset turnover.
c. Return on total assets employed.
d. Price earnings ratio.
e. Profit margin.

Questions for Class Discussion

1. Who are the intended users of general purpose financial statements?
2. What statements are usually included in the general purpose financial statements published by corporations?
3. Explain the difference between financial reporting and financial statements.
4. Financial reporting should help users make what kind of predictions?

5. Why are some comparative balance sheets prepared with columns that show increases and decreases in both dollar amounts and percentages?
6. Under what circumstances is it impossible to calculate a useful percentage increase or decrease in a comparative financial statement item?
7. When trends are calculated and compared, it is often informative to compare the trend of sales with the trends of several other financial statement items. What are some of the items that should be compared to sales in this fashion?
8. What are common-size financial statements?
9. What items are usually assigned a value of 100% on (*a*) a common-size balance sheet and (*b*) a common-size income statement?
10. Why is working capital given special attention in the process of analyzing balance sheets?
11. Which ratio provides the better indication of a company's ability to meet its debt obligations in the very near future, the current ratio or the acid-test ratio?
12. Indicate whether each of the following transactions increases working capital, decreases working capital, or has no effect on working capital:
    a. Collected accounts receivable.
    b. Borrowed money by giving a 90-day, interest-bearing note.
    c. Declared a cash dividend.
    d. Paid a cash dividend previously declared.
    e. Sold plant assets for cash.
    f. Sold merchandise at a profit.
13. List several factors that affect the need for working capital.
14. Suggest several reasons why a 2-to-1 current ratio may not be adequate for a particular company.
15. Why does accounts receivable turnover provide information about a company's short-term liquidity?
16. What is the significance of the number of days' sales uncollected?
17. Why does merchandise inventory turnover provide information about a company's short-term liquidity?
18. Why do creditors like to see a high proportion of total assets being financed by owners' equity?
19. Why is the capital structure of a company, as measured by debt and equity ratios, of importance to financial statement analysts?
20. Why must the ratio of pledged plant assets to secured liabilities be interpreted with caution?
21. What is the relationship between profit margin, total asset turnover, and return on total assets employed?
22. Why would a company's return on total assets employed be different from its return on common stockholders' equity?
23. What ratios would you calculate for the purpose of evaluating management performance?
24. How can you use the information provided by the price earnings ratio and dividend yield?

25. What insights are provided to financial statement users by segment information?
26. Which five items of segment information must be disclosed in the annual report of a public company?
27. Which four basic issues must be dealt with in preparing information about the segments of a business?
28. What difficulty is created by common expenses when segment information is being prepared?
29. The financial statements for Federal Express Corporation are presented in Appendix K. Calculate Federal Express's return on total assets employed for the fiscal year ended May 31, 1991.
30. Refer to the financial statements for McDonald's Corporation presented in Appendix K. Calculate McDonald's equity ratio as of December 31, 1990.

What you want is what you get.

Exercises

Exercise 19–1
Calculating trend percentages
(LO 2)

Calculate trend percentages for the following items, using 1990 as the base year. Then, state whether the situation shown by the trends appears to be favorable or unfavorable:

	1994	1993	1992	1991	1990
Sales	$785,200	$742,920	$694,600	$646,280	$604,000
Cost of goods sold	359,040	337,280	315,520	293,760	272,000
Accounts receivable	52,800	50,000	47,200	44,000	40,000

Exercise 19–2
Reporting percentage changes
(LO 2)

Where possible, calculate percentages of increase and decrease for the following items. The parentheses indicate negative balances.

	1994	1993
Equipment, net	$70,400	$55,000
Notes receivable.	8,000	16,000
Notes payable	20,000	-0-
Retained earnings	(3,000)	15,000
Cash	8,400	(2,100)

Exercise 19–3
Calculating common-size percentages
(LO 2)

Express the following income statement information in common-size percentages and assess whether the situation is favorable or unfavorable.

GRUNDFEST CORPORATION
Comparative Income Statement
For Years Ended December 31, 1993 and 1992

	1993	1992
Sales	$640,000	$490,000
Cost of goods sold.	352,000	257,250
Gross profit from sales	$288,000	$232,750
Operating expenses	181,760	125,440
Net income	$106,240	$107,310

Exercise 19–4
Evaluating short-term liquidity
(LO 3)

Fitzwater Company's December 31 balance sheets included the following data:

	1993	1992	1991
Cash	$ 17,200	$ 28,500	$ 33,400
Accounts receivable, net	69,000	54,000	48,000
Merchandise inventory	81,000	46,000	29,000
Prepaid expenses	9,800	5,500	4,600
Plant assets, net	175,000	182,000	170,000
Total assets	$352,000	$316,000	$285,000
Accounts payable	$ 69,200	$ 44,600	$ 32,700
Long-term notes payable secured by mortgage on plant assets	85,000	85,000	75,000
Common stock, $10 par value	125,000	125,000	125,000
Retained earnings	72,800	61,400	52,300
Total liabilities and stockholders' equity	$352,000	$316,000	$285,000

Required

Compare the short-term liquidity positions of the company at the end of 1993, 1992, and 1991, by calculating: (*a*) the current ratio and (*b*) the acid-test ratio. Comment on any changes that occurred.

Exercise 19–5
Evaluating short-term liquidity
(LO 3)

Refer to the information in Exercise 19–4 about Fitzwater Company. The company's income statements for the years ended December 31, 1993, and 1992, included the following data:

	1993	1992
Sales	$610,000	$575,000
Cost of goods sold	$366,000	$352,000
Other operating expenses	201,000	185,000
Interest expense	10,200	10,200
Income taxes	4,900	4,200
Total costs and expenses	$582,100	$551,400
Net income	$ 27,900	$ 23,600
Earnings per share	$ 2.23	$ 1.89

Required

For the years ended December 31, 1993, and 1992, calculate the following (assume all sales were on credit): (*a*) days' sales uncollected, (*b*) accounts receivable turnover, and (*c*) merchandise turnover. Comment on any changes that occurred from 1992 to 1993.

Exercise 19–6
Evaluating long-term risk and capital structure
(LO 3)

Refer to the information in Exercises 19–4 and 19–5 about Fitzwater Company. Compare the long-term risk and capital structure positions of the company at the end of 1993 and 1992 by calculating the following ratios: (*a*) debt and equity ratios, (*b*) pledged plant assets to secured liabilities, and (*c*) times fixed interest charges earned. Comment on any changes that occurred.

Exercise 19–7
Evaluating operating efficiency and profitability
(LO 3)

Refer to the financial statements of Fitzwater Company presented in Exercises 19–4 and 19–5. Evaluate the operating efficiency and profitability of the company by calculating the following: (*a*) profit margin, (*b*) total asset turnover, and (*c*) return on total assets employed. Comment on any changes that occurred.

Exercise 19–8
Evaluating profitability (LO 3)

Refer to the financial statements of Fitzwater Company presented in Exercises 19–4 and 19–5. This additional information about the company is known:

Common stock market price, December 31, 1993	$24.00
Common stock market price, December 31, 1992	16.00
Annual cash dividends per share in 1993.	1.32
Annual cash dividends per share in 1992.	1.16

Required

To evaluate the profitability of the company, calculate the following for 1993 and 1992: (*a*) return on common stockholders' equity, (*b*) price earnings ratio on December 31, and (*c*) dividend yield.

Exercise 19–9
Determining income effects from common-size and trend percentages (LO 3)

Common-size and trend percentages for a company's sales, cost of goods sold, and expenses follow:

	Common-Size Percentages			Trend Percentages		
	1994	**1993**	**1992**	**1994**	**1993**	**1992**
Sales	100.0%	100.0%	100.0%	95.9%	98.0%	100.0%
Cost of goods sold	56.3	60.0	61.4	87.9	95.8	100.0
Expenses.	28.8	28.7	28.8	95.8	97.6	100.0

Required

Determine whether the company's net income increased, decreased, or remained unchanged during this three-year period.

Exercise 19–10
Segment reporting with sales between segments (LO 5)

The following operating information is available about the two business segments of the Chicago Corporation:

	Segment P	Segment Q
Sales to outside parties	$200,000	$520,000
Sales to Segment Q	?	
Purchases from Segment P		?
Other expenses of each segment	240,000	316,000

The items that Segment P sold to Segment Q were processed further and then sold by Q to outside parties. In measuring the intersegment sales, the manager of Segment P believes that they should be priced at $100,000, which is approximately the same price that would have been paid by outside buyers. The Segment Q manager argues that the price should be lower because Segment Q is part of the Chicago Corporation family and is not an outside buyer. According to the Segment Q manager, a price of $50,000 would more than cover Segment P's cost.

Required

Prepare reports that show the sales, expenses, and income from operating each segment under the alternate assumptions that the intersegment sales are priced at (*a*) $100,000 and (*b*) $50,000. Then, express each segment's income from operations as a percent of its sales. Comment on the importance of the transfer pricing decision in evaluating the performance of each segment.

Problems

Problem 19–1
Calculating ratios and percentages
(LO 2, 3)

The condensed statements of Compton Car Company follow:

COMPTON CAR COMPANY
Comparative Income Statement
For Years Ended December 31, 1994, 1993, and 1992
($000)

	1994	1993	1992
Sales	$74,000	$68,000	$59,000
Cost of goods sold	45,658	40,052	33,866
Gross profit from sales	$28,342	$27,948	$25,134
Selling expenses	$12,306	$11,506	$10,095
Administrative expenses	8,658	8,262	7,304
Total expenses	$20,964	$19,768	$17,399
Income before taxes	$ 7,378	$ 8,180	$ 7,735
State and federal income taxes	2,140	2,372	2,243
Net income	$ 5,238	$ 5,808	$ 5,492

COMPTON CAR COMPANY
Comparative Balance Sheet
December 31, 1994, 1993, and 1992
($000)

	1994	1993	1992
Assets			
Current assets	$12,780	$11,940	$14,140
Long-term investments	–0–	100	930
Plant and equipment	19,150	20,000	16,250
Total assets	$31,930	$32,040	$31,320
Liabilities and Stockholders' Equity			
Current liabilities	$ 5,050	$ 4,990	$ 4,870
Common stock	13,500	13,500	13,390
Other contributed capital	1,850	1,850	1,460
Retained earnings	11,530	11,700	11,600
Total liabilities and stockholders' equity	$31,930	$32,040	$31,320

Required

1. Calculate each year's current ratio.
2. Express the income statement data in common-size percentages.
3. Express the balance sheet data in trend percentages with 1992 as the base year.
4. Comment on any significant relationship revealed by the ratios and percentages.

Problem 19–2
Calculation and analysis of trend percentages
(LO 2)

The condensed comparative statements of Federal Stamp Corporation follow:

FEDERAL STAMP CORPORATION
Comparative Income Statement
For Years Ended December 31, 1995–1989
($000,000)

	1995	1994	1993	1992	1991	1990	1989
Sales	$500	$455	$416	$364	$334	$299	$260
Cost of goods sold	247	228	204	179	157	142	120
Gross profit from sales	$253	$227	$212	$185	$177	$157	$140
Operating expenses	203	170	147	102	100	87	75
Net income	$ 50	$ 57	$ 65	$ 83	$ 77	$ 70	$ 65

FEDERAL STAMP CORPORATION
Comparative Balance Sheet
December 31, 1995–1989
($000,000)

	1995	1994	1993	1992	1991	1990	1989
Assets							
Cash	$ 13	$ 17	$ 19	$ 22	$ 23	$ 20	$ 25
Accounts receivable, net	99	97	95	73	64	61	51
Merchandise inventory	250	243	230	194	174	148	130
Other current assets	6	8	5	9	8	8	5
Long-term investments	–0–	–0–	–0–	34	34	34	34
Plant and equipment, net	400	418	386	215	222	200	206
Total assets	$768	$783	$735	$547	$525	$471	$451
Liabilities and Equity							
Current liabilities	$143	$147	$133	$107	$ 93	$ 77	$ 68
Long-term liabilities	179	202	215	98	100	104	99
Common stock	200	200	200	175	175	160	160
Other contributed capital	48	48	48	40	40	40	40
Retained earnings	198	186	139	127	117	90	84
Total liabilities and equity	$768	$783	$735	$547	$525	$471	$451

Required

1. Calculate trend percentages for the items of the statements using 1989 as the base year.
2. Analyze and comment on the situation shown in the statements.

Problem 19–3
Calculation of financial statement relationships
(LO 3)

The 1993 financial statements of Karlin Corporation follow:

KARLIN CORPORATION
Income Statement
For Year Ended December 31, 1993

Sales		$888,700
Cost of goods sold:		
Merchandise inventory, December 31, 1992	$ 77,500	
Purchases	410,900	
Goods available for sale	$488,400	
Merchandise inventory, December 31, 1993	52,000	
Cost of goods sold		436,400
Gross profit from sales		$452,300
Operating expenses		267,400
Operating income		$184,900
Interest expense		13,200
Income before taxes		$171,700
Income taxes		36,000
Net income		$135,700

KARLIN CORPORATION
Balance Sheet
December 31, 1993

Assets		Liabilities and Stockholders' Equity	
Cash	$ 29,100	Accounts payable	$ 48,900
Short-term investments	47,600	Accrued wages payable	5,400
Accounts receivable, net	55,500	Income taxes payable	7,100
Notes receivable (trade)	8,000	Long-term note payable, secured by mortgage on plant assets	120,000
Merchandise inventory	52,000	Common stock, $5 par value	250,000
Prepaid expenses	3,900	Retained earnings	147,900
Plant assets, net	383,200		
Total assets	$579,300	Total liabilities and stockholders' equity	$579,300

Assume that all sales were on credit. On the December 31, 1992, balance sheet, the assets totaled $480,300, common stock was $250,000, and retained earnings were $103,800.

Required

Calculate the following: (*a*) current ratio, (*b*) acid-test ratio, (*c*) days' sales uncollected, (*d*) merchandise turnover, (*e*) ratio of pledged plant assets to secured liabilities, (*f*) times fixed interest charges earned, (*g*) profit margin, (*h*) total asset turnover, (*i*) return on total assets employed, and (*j*) return on common stockholders' equity.

Problem 19–4
Comparative analysis of financial statement ratios
(LO 3)

Two companies that operate in the same industry as competitors are being evaluated by a bank that can lend money to only one of them. Summary information from the financial statements of the two companies follows:

Data from the current year-end balance sheets

	Monarch Company	Command Company
Assets		
Cash	$ 18,700	$ 33,000
Accounts receivable	34,500	53,800
Notes receivable (trade)	8,500	6,000
Merchandise inventory	88,600	119,700
Prepaid expenses	4,200	6,200
Plant and equipment, net	284,100	288,600
Total assets	$438,600	$507,300
Liabilities and Equity		
Current liabilities	$ 60,300	$ 94,700
Long-term notes payable	80,000	100,000
Common stock, $10 par value	175,000	180,000
Retained earnings	123,300	132,600
Total liabilities and equity	$438,600	$507,300

	Monarch Company	Command Company
Data from the current year's income statements		
Sales	$625,000	$780,500
Cost of goods sold	372,500	465,200
Interest expense	8,000	11,000
Income tax expense	13,800	21,900
Net income	75,300	95,800
Beginning-of-year data		
Accounts receivable, net	$ 28,800	$ 52,900
Notes receivable	-0-	-0-
Merchandise inventory	54,900	101,000
Total assets	388,100	422,500
Common stock, $10 par value	175,000	180,000
Retained earnings	100,500	90,800

Required

1. Calculate current ratios, acid-test ratios, accounts (including notes) receivable turnovers, merchandise turnovers, and days' sales uncollected for the two companies. Then, identify the company that you consider to be the better short-term credit risk and explain why.
2. Calculate profit margins, total asset turnovers, returns on total assets employed, and returns on common stockholders' equity. Assuming that each company paid cash dividends of $3.00 per share and each company's stock can be purchased at $40 per share, calculate their price earnings ratios and the dividend yield. Also, identify which company's stock you would recommend as the better investment and explain why.

Problem 19–5
Analysis of working capital
(LO 3)

Davis Corporation began the month of October with $360,000 of current assets, a current ratio of 2.4 to 1, and an acid-test ratio of 1.4 to 1. During the month, it completed the following transactions:

Oct.	2	Bought $40,000 of merchandise on account. (The company uses a perpetual inventory system.)
	4	Sold merchandise that cost $35,000 for $64,000.
	10	Collected a $12,000 account receivable.
	14	Paid a $14,000 account payable.
	20	Wrote off a $6,000 bad debt against the Allowance for Doubtful Accounts account.
	21	Declared a $0.50 per share cash dividend on the 50,000 shares of outstanding common stock.
	25	Paid the dividend declared on October 21.
	27	Borrowed $50,000 by giving the bank a 60-day, 12% note.
	30	Borrowed $75,000 by signing a long-term secured note.
	31	Used the $125,000 proceeds of the notes to buy additional machinery.

Required

Prepare a schedule showing the company's current ratio, acid-test ratio, and working capital after each of the transactions. Round to two decimal places.

Problem 19–6
Analytical essay
(LO 3)

Visican Company and Stockton Company are similar companies that operate within the same industry. The following information is available:

	Visican			Stockton		
	1994	**1993**	**1992**	**1994**	**1993**	**1992**
Working capital	$105,000	$81,000	$60,000	$50,000	$45,000	$52,000
Current ratio	3.5	2.7	2.0	1.9	2.0	2.1
Acid test ratio	2.7	2.2	1.6	1.0	1.1	1.2
Accounts receivable turnover	15.2	14.6	15.0	32.8	26.7	28.4
Merchandise inventory turnover	13.2	12.1	12.0	22.1	19.4	16.8

Required

Write a brief essay comparing Visican Company and Stockton Company based on the information provided. Your discussion should include their relative ability to meet current obligations and to use current assets efficiently.

Problem 19–7
Analytical essay
(LO 3)

Roster Company and Farleigh Company are similar companies that operate within the same industry. Roster Company began operations in 1992 and Farleigh Company in 1980. In 1994, both companies paid 7% interest to creditors. The following information is also available:

	Roster			Farleigh		
	1994	**1993**	**1992**	**1994**	**1993**	**1992**
Sales	$300,000	$220,000	$100,000	$600,000	$560,000	$578,000
Profit margin	3.2	3.4	3.3	2.7	2.9	2.6
Total asset turnover	2.0	1.8	1.6	3.6	3.4	3.3
Return on total assets employed	6.4	6.1	5.3	9.7	9.9	8.6

Required

Write a brief essay comparing Roster Company and Farleigh Company based on the information provided. Your discussion should include their relative ability to use assets efficiently to produce profits. Also comment on their relative success in employing financial leverage in 1994.

Alternate Problems

Problem 19–1A
Calculating ratios and percentages
(LO 2, 3)

The condensed statements of Stanton Corporation follow:

STANTON CORPORATION
Comparative Income Statement
For Years Ended December 31, 1994, 1993, and 1992
($000)

	1994	**1993**	**1992**
Sales	$111,000	$95,500	$82,800
Cost of goods sold	61,100	49,700	39,500
Gross profit from sales	$ 49,900	$45,800	$43,300
Selling expenses	$ 14,800	$11,700	$12,600
Administrative expenses	11,100	11,800	10,700
Total expenses	$ 25,900	$23,500	$23,300
Income before taxes	$ 24,000	$22,300	$20,000
State and federal income taxes	3,600	3,300	3,000
Net income	$ 20,400	$19,000	$17,000

STANTON CORPORATION
Comparative Balance Sheet
December 31, 1994, 1993, and 1992
($000)

	1994	1993	1992
Assets			
Current assets	$29,400	$18,700	$20,100
Long-term investments	-0-	1,500	6,600
Plant and equipment	59,900	61,200	47,400
Total assets	$89,300	$81,400	$74,100
Liabilities and Stockholders' Equity			
Current liabilities	$12,300	$10,100	$ 8,600
Common stock	20,000	20,000	18,000
Other contributed capital	6,500	6,500	4,500
Retained earnings	50,500	44,800	43,000
Total liabilities and stockholders' equity	$89,300	$81,400	$74,100

Required

1. Calculate each year's current ratio.
2. Express the income statement data in common-size percentages.
3. Express the balance sheet data in trend percentages with 1992 as the base year.
4. Comment on any significant relationships revealed by the ratios and percentages.

Problem 19–2A
Calculation and analysis of trend percentages
(LO 2)

The condensed comparative statements of Great Outdoors Company follow:

GREAT OUTDOORS COMPANY
Comparative Income Statement
For Years Ended December 31, 1995–1989
($000,000)

	1995	1994	1993	1992	1991	1990	1989
Sales	$500	$520	$510	$540	$580	$570	$610
Cost of goods sold	210	217	214	228	239	232	234
Gross profit from sales	$290	$303	$296	$312	$341	$338	$376
Operating expenses	221	228	226	245	252	256	276
Net income	$ 69	$ 75	$ 70	$ 67	$ 89	$ 82	$100

GREAT OUTDOORS COMPANY
Comparative Balance Sheet
December 31, 1995–1989
($000,000)

	1995	1994	1993	1992	1991	1990	1989
Assets							
Cash	$ 35	$ 38	$ 37	$ 41	$ 50	$ 47	$ 51
Accounts receivable, net	103	114	110	112	123	121	129
Merchandise inventory	157	163	161	160	173	183	176
Other current assets	23	24	25	27	26	29	31
Long-term investments	87	67	47	94	94	94	97
Plant and equipment, net	398	404	408	323	328	333	338
Total assets	$803	$810	$788	$757	$794	$807	$822

	1995	1994	1993	1992	1991	1990	1989
Liabilities and Equity							
Current liabilities	$178	$185	$168	$135	$161	$187	$232
Long-term liabilities	147	162	177	192	210	222	237
Common stock	160	160	160	160	160	160	160
Other contributed capital	65	65	65	65	65	65	65
Retained earnings	253	238	218	205	198	173	128
Total liabilities and equity	$803	$810	$788	$757	$794	$807	$822

Required

1. Calculate trend percentages for the items of the statements using 1989 as the base year.
2. Analyze and comment on the situation shown in the statements.

Problem 19–3A
Financial statement ratios
(LO 3)

The 1994 financial statements of Heartland Corporation follow:

HEARTLAND CORPORATION
Income Statement
For Year Ended December 31, 1994

Sales		$647,000
Cost of goods sold:		
Merchandise inventory, December 31, 1993	$ 50,100	
Purchases	400,000	
Goods available for sale	$450,100	
Merchandise inventory, December 31, 1994	38,600	
Cost of goods sold		411,500
Gross profit from sales		$235,500
Operating expenses		182,100
Operating income		$ 53,400
Interest expense		7,500
Income before taxes		$ 45,900
Income taxes		8,100
Net income		$ 37,800

HEARTLAND CORPORATION
Balance Sheet
December 31, 1994

Assets		Liablities and Stockholders' Equity	
Cash	$ 13,800	Accounts payable	$ 32,500
Short-term investments	16,300	Accrued wages payable	4,100
Accounts receivable, net	34,700	Income taxes payable	4,600
Notes receivable (trade)	7,000	Long-term note payable, secured by mortgage on plant assets	75,000
Merchandise inventory	38,600		
Prepaid expenses	3,800		
Plant assets, net	217,600	Common stock, $10 par value	125,000
		Retained earnings	90,600
Total assets	$331,800	Total liabilities and stockholders' equity	$331,800

Assume that all sales were on credit. On the December 31, 1993, balance sheet, the assets totaled $288,400, common stock was $125,000, and retained earnings were $58,800.

Required

Calculate the following: (*a*) current ratio, (*b*) acid-test ratio, (*c*) days' sales uncollected, (*d*) merchandise turnover, (*e*) ratio of pledged plant assets to secured liabilities, (*f*) times fixed interest charges earned, (*g*) profit margin, (*h*) total asset turnover, (*i*) return on total assets employed, and (*j*) return on common stockholders' equity.

Problem 19–4A
Comparative analysis of financial statement ratios (LO 3)

Two companies that operate in the same industry as competitors are being evaluated by a bank that can lend money to only one of them. Summary information from the financial statements of the two companies follows:

Data from the current year-end balance sheets	Sun Company	Lakeway Company
Assets		
Cash	$ 22,600	$ 42,800
Accounts receivable	79,000	88,800
Notes receivable (trade)	13,500	12,300
Merchandise inventory	88,800	120,000
Prepaid expenses	11,800	13,400
Plant and equipment, net	178,500	255,000
Total assets	$394,200	$532,300
Liabilities and Stockholders' Equity		
Current liabilities	$ 85,000	$106,300
Long-term notes payable	90,000	101,000
Common stock, $10 par value	136,500	159,000
Retained earnings	82,700	166,000
Total liabilities and equity	$394,200	$532,300
Data from the current year's income statements		
Sales	$527,500	$744,000
Cost of goods sold	388,500	529,000
Interest expense	10,600	13,200
Income tax expense	8,600	15,100
Net income	48,800	67,200
Beginning-of-year data		
Accounts receivable, net	$ 73,500	$ 75,300
Notes receivable	–0–	–0–
Merchandise inventory	106,300	84,500
Total assets	385,700	450,000
Common stock, $10 par value	136,500	159,000
Retained earnings	47,550	114,700

Required

1. Calculate current ratios, acid-test ratios, accounts (including notes) receivable turnovers, merchandise turnovers, and days' sales uncollected for the two companies. Then, identify the company that you consider to be the better short-term credit risk and explain why.
2. Calculate profit margins, total asset turnovers, returns on total assets employed, and returns on common stockholders' equity. Assuming that each company paid cash dividends of $1 per share and each company's stock can be purchased at $33 per share, calculate their price earnings ratios and dividend yield. Also, identify which company's stock you would recommend as the better investment and explain why.

Problem 19–5A
Analysis of working capital
(LO 3)

Country Comfort Corporation began the month of August with $845,000 of current assets, a current ratio of 2.6 to 1, and an acid-test ratio of 1.1 to 1. During the month, it completed the following transactions:

Aug. 2 Sold merchandise that cost $41,000 for $69,000.
4 Collected a $53,000 account receivable.
8 Bought $75,000 of merchandise on account. (The company uses a perpetual inventory system.)
10 Borrowed $50,000 by giving the bank a 60-day, 12% note.
14 Borrowed $100,000 by signing a long-term secured note.
20 Used the $150,000 proceeds of the notes to buy additional machinery.
22 Declared a $1.50 per share cash dividend on the 50,000 shares of outstanding common stock.
25 Wrote off a $14,000 bad debt against Allowance for Doubtful Accounts.
27 Paid a $66,000 account payable.
31 Paid the dividend declared on August 22.

Required

Prepare a schedule showing the company's current ratio, acid-test ratio, and working capital after each of the transactions. Round to two decimal places.

Problem 19–6A
Analytical essay
(LO 3)

Lamar Company and Guadalupe Company are similar companies that operate within the same industry. The following information is available:

	Lamar			Guadalupe		
	1994	1993	1992	1994	1993	1992
Working capital	$240,000	$190,000	$195,000	$240,000	$190,000	$195,000
Current ratio	2.3	2.4	2.2	0.8	1.0	0.9
Acid test ratio	1.2	1.1	1.3	0.4	0.5	0.6
Accounts receivable turnover	16.7	16.4	15.9	6.9	7.8	14.7
Merchandise inventory turnover	10.5	11.2	16.7	10.2	11.8	16.1

Required

Write a brief essay comparing Lamar Company and Guadalupe Company based on the information provided. Your discussion should include their relative ability to meet current obligations and to use current assets efficiently.

Problem 19–7A
Analytical essay
(LO 3)

Information pertaining to Gaynor Corporation's operation for the three-year period ending December 31, 1994, follows:

	1994	1993	1992
Sales	$560,000	$400,000	$250,000
Income before taxes	100,000	90,000	50,000
Interest expense	50,000	30,000	15,000
Debt ratio	20.8%	28.4%	32.2%
Equity ratio	79.2%	71.6%	67.8%
Times fixed interest charges earned	3.0	4.0	4.3

Required

Based on the information provided, evaluate Gaynor Corporation's ability to meet obligations and provide security to its creditors. Would your answer be different if Gaynor's $100,000 income before taxes in 1994 included an extraordinary loss of $60,000? How?

Provocative Problems

Provocative Problem 19–1
The Clorox Company
(LO 2, 3)

The Clorox Company is a diversified firm that develops, manufactures, and markets premium-quality household products, architectural coatings, and food service products. In addition to the liquid bleach product from which it takes its name, the company markets the leading line of dry salad dressing mixes. Founded in 1913, the Clorox Company has become an international company with sales in excess of $1 billion. A recent annual report included a 10-year summary, from which the following information has been extracted:

(In thousands, except per-share data)

	Year 4	Year 3	Year 2	Year 1
Operations				
Net sales	**$1,089,070**	$1,054,847	$974,566	$913,807
Percent change	**+ 3.2**	+8.2	+ 6.6	+ 5.4
Net earnings	**$95,610**	$86,124	$79,709	$65,507
Percent change	**+11.0**	+8.0	+21.7	+45.2
Common Stock				
Per share:				
Earnings from continuing operations	**$3.60**	$3.27	$3.09	$2.72
Earnings from discontinued operations	—	—	—	—
Net earnings				
Assuming no dilution	**$3.60**	$3.27	$3.09	$2.72
Assuming full dilution	**$3.50**	$3.17	$3.01	$2.64
Dividends	**$1.40**	$1.24	$1.08	$0.95
Shareholders' equity at end of year	**20.61**	18.37	16.40	13.48
Other Data				
Working capital	**$240,180**	$203,011	$144,424	$117,333
Total assets	**849,225**	778,062	701,396	603,875
Long-term debt	**38,151**	38,945	43,174	72,597
Shareholders' equity	**549,793**	485,856	431,313	325,998
Current ratio	**2.4**	2.0	1.8	1.7
Percent return on net sales—continuing operations	**8.8**	8.2	8.2	7.2
Percent return on average shareholders' equity	**18.5**	18.8	20.2	21.6

Courtesy of The Clorox Company.

Discuss the format of the Clorox Company's presentation relative to the illustrations in the chapter. Then evaluate the company's performance over the four-year period.

Provocative Problem 19–2
T. J. Topp Company
(LO 2, 3)

In your position as controller of T. J. Topp Company, you are responsible for keeping the board of directors informed about the financial activities and status of the company. In preparing for the next board meeting, you have calculated the following ratios, turnovers, and percentages to enable you to answer questions:

	1994	1993	1992
Current ratio	2.6 to 1	2.4 to 1	2.1 to 1
Acid-test ratio	0.8 to 1	1.1 to 1	1.2 to 1
Merchandise turnover	7.5 times	8.7 times	9.9 times
Accounts receivable turnover	6.7 times	7.4 times	8.2 times
Return on stockholders' equity	9.75%	11.50%	12.25%
Profit margin	3.3%	3.5%	3.7%
Total asset turnover	2.6 times	2.6 times	3.0 times
Return on total assets	8.8%	9.4%	10.1%
Sales to plant assets	3.8 to 1	3.6 to 1	3.3 to 1
Sales trend	128.00	117.00	100.00
Selling expenses to net sales	9.8%	13.7%	15.3%

Required

Use the given data to answer each of the following questions. Explain your answers.

1. Is it becoming easier for the company to meet its current debts on time and to take advantage of cash discounts?
2. Is the company collecting its accounts receivable more rapidly?
3. Is the company's investment in accounts receivable decreasing?
4. Are dollars invested in inventory increasing?
5. Is the company's investment in plant assets increasing?
6. Is the stockholders' investment becoming more profitable?
7. Is the company using its assets efficiently?
8. Did the dollar amount of selling expenses decrease during the three-year period?

Provocative Problem 19–3
Davis, Inc., and Crawford, Inc.
(LO 3)

Davis, Inc., and Crawford, Inc., are competing companies with similar backgrounds. The stock of each company is traded locally, and each stock can be purchased at its book value. Joan Rogers has an opportunity to invest in only one of the companies; she is undecided as to which company is better managed and which stock is the better investment. Prepare a report for Rogers stating which company you think is better managed and which company's stock you think may be the better investment. Back your report with any ratios, turnovers, and other analyses that provide relevant information.

Balance Sheets
December 31, 1993

	Davis, Inc.	Crawford, Inc.
Assets		
Cash	$ 34,200	$ 34,900
Accounts receivable, net	86,300	92,100
Merchandise inventory	119,600	126,200
Prepaid expenses	3,600	4,500
Plant and equipment, net	392,900	376,700
Total assets	$ 636,600	$ 634,400

	Davis, Inc.	Crawford, Inc.
Liabilities and Stockholders' Equity		
Current liabilities	$ 110,700	$ 124,400
Long-term notes payable	128,200	117,000
Common stock, $10 par value	231,600	203,600
Retained earnings	166,100	189,400
Total liabilities and equity	$ 636,600	$ 634,400

Income Statements
For Year Ended December 31, 1993

	Davis, Inc.	Crawford, Inc.
Sales	$1,657,500	$1,747,600
Cost of goods sold	1,147,800	1,235,400
Gross profit on sales	$ 509,700	$ 512,200
Operating expenses	439,100	469,500
Operating income	$ 70,600	$ 42,700
Interest expense	10,500	10,100
Income before taxes	$ 60,100	$ 32,600
Income taxes	10,000	4,900
Net income	$ 50,100	$ 27,700
December 31, 1992, Data		
Accounts receivable	$ 106,600	$ 144,800
Merchandise inventory	101,100	116,600
Total assets	595,500	563,000
Common stock	231,200	203,100
Retained earnings	150,700	162,000

Provocative Problem 19–4
International Business Machines Corporation
(LO 5)

IBM

Use the financial statements and related footnotes of the IBM Corporation shown in Appendix J to answer the following questions:

1. What segments (or classes of product) are identified on IBM's Consolidated Statement of Earnings?
2. What were the revenues and costs attributed to Software in 1990?
3. Calculate the 1990 gross profit (revenue minus cost) of IBM's four identified segments (or classes of product). Which one earned the largest profit? Which earned the smallest?
4. Which geographic segments are identified by IBM?
5. Which geographic segment has the greatest revenue from customers for 1990? Which one has the smallest?
6. Which geographic segment has the greatest investment in assets at the end of 1990? Which one has the smallest?
7. What kinds of products are transferred between areas?

Provocative Problem 19–5
As a Matter of Ethics: Essay

Ethics

Review the As a Matter of Ethics case on page 1040 and write a brief essay discussing Coleman's ethical responsibility as the manager of Tech Division. Your discussion should consider the possibility that Coleman has the ability to dominate the pricing decision and the alternative possibility that the division managers are expected to negotiate a price for top management's approval.

Answers to Objective Review Questions

LO 1 (*b*)
LO 2 (*a*)
LO 3 (*b*)
LO 4 (*e*)
LO 5 (*b*)
LO 6 (*c*)

PART

VIII

Managerial Accounting and Accounting for Manufacturing Costs

In this part of *Fundamental Accounting Principles,* we focus our attention on managerial accounting. Managerial accounting provides information that helps managers make decisions about their organizations. Although managerial accounting and financial accounting are different in many ways, they are also similar. In fact, many of the same techniques for measuring manufacturing costs are used in both managerial and financial accounting. Therefore, this topic of accounting for manufacturing costs is especially suitable for your introduction to managerial accounting. To get you started, Chapter 20 explains the basic flows of goods through manufacturing and shows how these flows are described by manufacturing accounting systems. The general accounting systems described in Chapter 20 use periodic inventory measurements. In Chapter 21, you will learn about job order cost accounting systems that use perpetual inventory measurements. They provide more detailed information about the costs of unique products manufactured individually or in small batches. Chapter 22 describes process cost accounting systems, which also use perpetual inventory measurements to provide information about the cost of products manufactured in large quantities. And, in Chapter 23, you will see how accountants develop information to evaluate the performance of managers and the success achieved by the part of the business that they manage.

Part VIII consists of the following chapters:

CHAPTER

20

An Introduction to Managerial Accounting and Cost Accounting Concepts

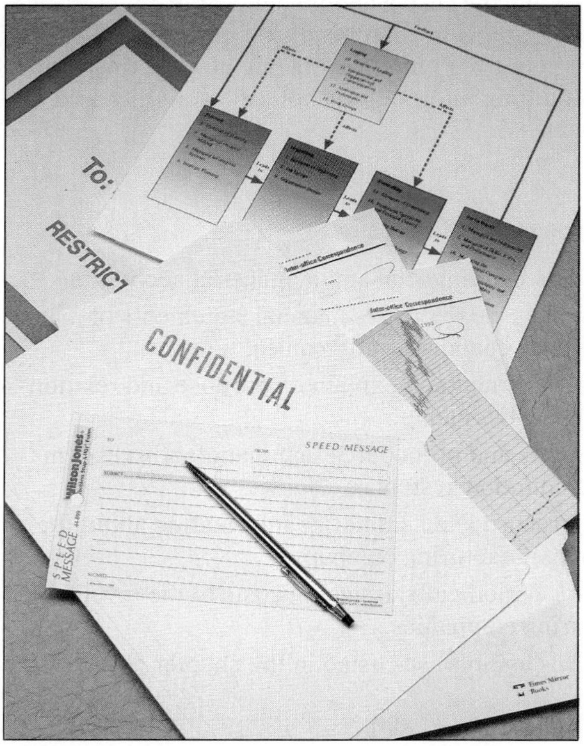

Financial accounting information is useful for investors and creditors outside a company, but managers need information that is not presented in the financial statements. Unlike financial accounting information, managerial accounting information is kept inside the company and is not available to the public.

Topical Coverage

Managerial and financial accounting are similar because they both provide information that helps people make decisions about organizations. However, managerial and financial accounting are also quite different. To help you understand the distinction, this chapter first describes 10 differences between managerial and financial accounting.

The chapter also compares the accounting and reporting practices used by manufacturing and merchandising companies. Both types of companies earn revenues by selling goods. On one hand, a merchandising company sells goods without changing their condition. On the other hand, a manufacturing company buys raw materials and turns them into finished products that it sells to customers. The differences between merchandising and manufacturing create needs for different kinds of information, which, in turn, lead to different accounting practices.

Most of what you have already learned about accounting in previous chapters applies to both merchandising and manufacturing companies. However, when we discussed inventories and the cost of goods sold in prior chapters, we limited the examples and illustrations to merchandising companies. In this chapter, you will learn more about the unique problems of gathering useful managerial and financial accounting information about the activities and assets of manufacturing companies.

Learning Objectives

After studying Chapter 20, you should be able to:

1. Describe 10 differences between financial and managerial accounting.
2. Describe the basic differences between the financial statements of manufacturing companies and merchandising companies.
3. Prepare a manufacturing statement and explain its purpose and relationship to the primary financial statements.
4. Describe the unique accounts and procedures that manufacturing companies use in a general accounting system.
5. Prepare journal entries to record and summarize information about the activities and assets of a manufacturing company.
6. Explain the procedures for periodically assigning costs to the inventories owned by manufacturing companies.
7. Define or explain the words and phrases listed in the chapter glossary.

Introduction to Managerial Accounting

Most of the discussions in the first 19 chapters of this book focus on financial accounting, which provides information primarily to people who are not managers of an organization. As described in the first chapter, *managerial accounting,* or *management accounting,* provides information to the managers of an organization. Thus, both financial and managerial accounting share the

LO 1 Describe 10 differences between financial and managerial accounting.

common purpose of providing information. Financial and managerial accounting also share the common practice of reporting monetary information. In fact, they even report some of the same information. We have already seen some areas in which the two types of accounting overlap. For example, the financial statements for a company contain information that is useful for both the managers of a company (insiders) and other persons who are interested in the company (outsiders).

This chapter takes a more careful look at managerial accounting information, how it is gathered, and how it is used. The main topic of this chapter and Chapters 21 and 22 is accounting for manufacturing activities. We look at the concepts and procedures used to determine the costs of the products that a company manufactures and sells. A firm reports these costs on its balance sheet as inventory and on its income statement as cost of goods sold.

Information about the cost of products is also very important for managers. For example, managers use information about the past cost of producing goods to predict the cost of producing the same or similar items in the future. Then, they use the predicted cost to set an appropriate selling price. Sometimes, the manufacturer cannot set the price because it is determined in the marketplace. Then, managers may use the predicted cost in deciding whether the product can be produced profitably.

Managers also use information about costs as they control the production process. For example, information about manufacturing costs helps managers identify costs that should be reduced. In later chapters, you will learn more about how managers use cost information in controlling business operations.

Differences between Financial and Managerial Accounting

Despite the overlap of financial and managerial accounting, there are a number of differences between them. The following paragraphs discuss the 10 differences summarized in Illustration 20–1.

Users of the Information. As mentioned before, financial and managerial accounting provide information for different groups of people. Companies provide financial accounting information to external users, including investors, creditors, and others. These external users do not have a part in managing the activities of the organization. Firms prepare managerial accounting information for internal users, who are managers responsible for making and implementing decisions about the organization's activities.

Purpose of the Information. Investors, creditors, and other users of financial accounting information must decide whether to invest in or lend to the organization, and on what terms. If they have already invested in the organization or loaned to it, they must decide whether to continue holding the stock or the loan.

Managers are concerned with planning the future of the organization to take advantage of opportunities or to overcome obstacles. Managers also try to control present activities to ensure that they are being carried out efficiently. Managerial accounting information helps managers make both planning and control decisions.

ILLUSTRATION 20–1

Differences between Financial and Managerial Accounting

	Financial Accounting	Managerial Accounting
1. Users of the information	Investors, creditors, and other users external to the organization	Managers internal to the organization
2. Purpose of the information	Assist external users in making investment, credit, and other financial decisions	Assist managers in planning and controlling the organization's activities
3. Source of the need for the informaion	Required by law and by contract and to maintain good public relations	Needed by managers to help them make better decisions
4. Structure of practice	Tends to be rigid	Relatively flexible
5. Standards for acceptability	Generally accepted accounting principles	Guided only by usefulness to managers
6. Reporting the information	General purpose financial statements	Specific management reports
7. Verification of the information	Usually audited by independent CPAs	Not independently audited
8. Timeliness of the information	Available only after the audit is completed	Available quickly without the need to wait for an audit
9. Subject of the information	Primary focus is on whole organization	Includes focus on specific projects and subdivisions of the organization
10. Time dimensions covered by the information	Primarily past events and present condition	Includes future predictions as well as past events and present condition

Source of the Need for the Information. Companies provide financial accounting information to outsiders because it is required by law or by the company's contracts with investors and creditors. Providing financial accounting information also helps companies maintain good relations with investors and the community.

In contrast, companies are not required to produce managerial accounting information by law or by contract. Instead, the information is created because management makes better decisions when it has useful information about the company's past activities and future prospects. No one outside the organization forces managerial accounting information to be produced. It is produced simply because managers find it to be useful.

Structure of Practice. Because of the long history behind financial accounting, and because many external users need to be protected against false or misleading information, financial accounting practices tend to have a rigid structure. In other words, an extensive set of rules and guidelines, known as generally accepted accounting principles, govern financial accounting practices.

The internal users of managerial accounting information are not in the same position as the external users. In general, managers do not need to be protected against false or misleading information. Thus, managerial accounting practices are flexible. This flexibility allows various companies to custom design their managerial accounting systems. Even within a single company, different managers often can design their own systems to meet their special needs. This flexibility also allows managers to modify their systems quickly in response to changes in the environment.

Standards for Acceptability. Earlier chapters describe many requirements of generally accepted accounting principles, or GAAP. These principles or standards guide an organization in meeting its reporting obligations to outsiders. As you learned in Chapter 1, GAAP are developed through complex political processes that are designed to protect the public's interest.

Managerial accounting is not constrained by the authoritative standards that make up GAAP. The managers of a company can decide for themselves what information they want and how they want it to be reported. Managerial accountants do not have to comply with any specific external standards. Of course, this does not mean that managerial accountants can safely ignore common sense and report irrelevant or unreliable information. It does mean that they can use whatever practices they believe will work best, even if very few other companies use them. Of course, managerial accountants use many common practices, and we focus on some of them in the remaining chapters. However, you should realize that managerial accountants use these practices because they produce useful information, not because they are required.

Reporting the Information. Because financial accounting information has many different users, special reports cannot possibly be designed for each user. Instead, companies usually present financial accounting information in the form of general purpose financial statements. By providing a complete set of statements and footnotes, financial accountants try to report most of the information that most external users need. However, general purpose financial statements contain more information than some users need and less than others would like to receive.

In contrast, managerial accountants design management reports to meet the special needs of specific managers. Users of managerial accounting information and managerial accountants often know each other and can interact to learn exactly what information is desired and what information can be made available. Ideally, the reports should include all the information about the company's operations that the manager needs and nothing beyond that.

Verification of the Information. Typically, the external users of financial accounting information do not have a personal relationship with the managers of a company. Thus, external users need some additional assurance before they can accept the company's financial statements as trustworthy. To provide this assurance, general purpose financial statements often are audited by independent certified public accountants. The independent audit adds credibility to the financial statements.

In contrast, managerial accounting information is not independently audited. Those who send and receive the reports are usually in frequent communication concerning the reports. They also work for the same organization and have the common goal of making the company successful. Thus, managerial accountants have nothing to gain by providing false or misleading information to managers. In very large companies, managerial accounting reports may be examined by internal auditors. This process is designed more to identify inefficiencies than to provide assurances to managers about the dependability of the information.

Timeliness of the Information. In most cases, the financial statements that a company sends to external users must be audited. Because audits can take two to three months to complete, annual financial reports to outsiders usually are not available to users until well after the end of the year.

On the other hand, managerial accountants can deliver information to managers more quickly because it does not have to be audited. To get the information quickly, however, managers may have to accept some lack of precision in the reports. For example, an early internal report to management produced right after the end of the year might indicate that net income for the year was between $4.2 million and $4.75 million. Later, the audited income statement might show that net income for the year was $4.55 million. Even though the internal report is not precise, the information may be more useful because it is available so much earlier.

Subject of the Information. Although a corporation might be organized in divisions and departments, investors do not buy stock in one division or department of a corporation. Similarly, creditors do not lend money to a single division or department of a company. Instead, they own shares in or make loans to the whole company. Thus, since they are interested in the entire company, the financial accounting information that goes to external users focuses primarily on the organization as a whole. You may recall from Chapter 19 that large companies must report segmental information according to GAAP. However, the purpose of this requirement is to help external users understand more about the whole company.

The focus of managerial accounting is quite different. Only the top-level managers are concerned with managing the entire organization. Most managers in the organization are responsible for much smaller sets of activities. These middle and lower level managers are best served when their managerial accounting reports deal with the specific activities, projects, and subdivisions for which they are responsible. For example, divisional sales managers are directly responsible only for the results achieved in their divisions. Even though they may be interested in seeing the results for all divisions, they probably do not need a companywide sales report. What divisional sales managers need to improve their sales representatives' performance is detailed information about the results achieved in their specific divisions, including information about the level of success achieved by each of their sales representatives.

Time Dimensions Covered by the Information. As mentioned earlier, a company's managers must be cautious in constructing financial accounting reports. Otherwise, they may find themselves in trouble for using overly optimistic predictions. To protect external users from excessive optimism, financial reports according to GAAP deal primarily with the results of past activities and conditions that exist in the present. Although some predictions are necessary, such as the service lives and salvage values of plant assets, predictions about the future are avoided whenever possible.

In contrast, managerial accounting often includes predictions of future conditions and events. For example, an important managerial accounting report is a budget, which consists of predictions of future sales, expenses, and other costs. If managerial accounting reports were restricted to the past and present, managers would not be able to use budgets and would not be able to manage very effectively.

A Reminder. Although the preceding paragraphs have emphasized the differences between financial and managerial accounting, you should not conclude that they are completely separate. Much information is useful to both external and internal users. In particular, information about the costs of manufacturing products is useful to both external investors and creditors and internal managers. So that you can understand more about manufacturing activities, we now take a closer look at the differences between merchandising and manufacturing.

Comparing Merchandising and Manufacturing Activities

As we mentioned at the beginning of the chapter, the basic difference between merchandising and manufacturing companies is that merchandisers buy goods that are ready for sale while manufacturers produce goods from raw materials. For example, a shoe store buys and sells shoes without doing anything to physically change them. In contrast, the shoe manufacturer must buy leather, cloth, plastic, rubber, glue, and laces and then use employees' labor in a factory to convert these raw materials into shoes. These unique operations of a manufacturer require special accounting practices.

Financial Statements for a Manufacturing Company

In prior chapters, we focused on the financial statements of merchandising and service companies. However, manufacturing is different from selling merchandise and providing services. As a result, the financial statements for manufacturing companies have some unique features.

The Balance Sheet

LO 2 Describe the basic differences between the financial statements of manufacturing companies and merchandising companies.

Manufacturers have several kinds of assets that other companies do not have. In particular, manufacturers usually have three inventories instead of the single inventory that is held by merchandising companies. For example, in Illustration 20–2, notice the three different inventories in the current asset section of the balance sheet for Excel Manufacturing Company.

ILLUSTRATION 20–2

Balance Sheet for a Manufacturing Company

EXCEL MANUFACTURING COMPANY
Balance Sheet
December 31, 1994

Assets

Current assets:		
Cash		$ 11,000
Accounts receivable	$ 32,000	
Allowance for doubtful accounts	(1,850)	30,150
Raw materials inventory		9,000
Goods in process inventory		7,500
Finished goods inventory		10,300
Supplies		350
Prepaid insurance		300
Total current assets		$ 68,600
Plant assets:		
Small tools		$ 1,100
Delivery equipment	$ 9,000	
Accumulated depreciation	(4,000)	5,000
Office equipment	$ 1,700	
Accumulated depreciation	(400)	1,300
Factory machinery	$ 72,000	
Accumulated depreciation	(6,500)	65,500
Factory building	$ 90,000	
Accumulated depreciation	(3,300)	86,700
Land		9,500
Total plant assets		$169,100
Intangible assets:		
Patents		$ 11,200
Total assets		$248,900

Liabilities and Stockholders' Equity

Current liabilities:		
Accounts payable	$ 14,000	
Wages payable	540	
Interest payable	2,000	
Income taxes payable	32,600	
Total current liabilities	$ 49,140	
Long-term liabilities:		
Long-term notes payable	50,000	
Total liabilities		$ 99,140
Stockholders' equity:		
Common stock, $5 par value	$100,000	
Retained earnings	49,760	
Total stockholders' equity		149,760
Total liabilities and stockholders' equity		$248,900

The first inventory consists of the **raw materials** the company acquires to use in making products. It uses these materials in two ways—directly and indirectly. Most raw materials physically become part of the product and therefore are clearly identified with specific units or batches of product. Raw materials used in this manner are called **direct materials.** Other materials used in support of the production process are not as clearly identified with specific units or batches of product. For example, companies need lubricants for machinery and supplies for cleaning up the factory. These materials are called **indirect materials** because they do not become a part of the product and are not clearly identified with units or batches of product. Items used as indirect materials often appear on the balance sheet as factory supplies. In other cases, they are included in raw materials.

Another inventory held by manufacturers is the **goods in process inventory,** also called the *work in process inventory*. It consists of products that are in the process of being manufactured but are not yet complete. The goods in process inventory may or may not be large, depending on the nature of the production process. If the time required to produce a unit of product is very short, the goods in process inventory is likely to be small. But, if weeks or months are needed to produce a unit, the goods in process inventory is larger.

The third inventory owned by a manufacturer is the **finished goods inventory,** which consists of the completed products waiting to be sold. This inventory is similar to the merchandise inventory owned by a retailing company because both inventories contain items ready for sale.

Manufacturers also have unique plant assets such as *small tools, factory buildings,* and *factory equipment*. An intangible asset often owned by manufacturers is *patents*. Companies use these assets to manufacture products. The balance sheet in Illustration 20–2 shows that Excel Manufacturing Company owns all of these assets. Some manufacturers invest millions or even billions of dollars in their production facilities and patents.

The Income Statement

One difference between the income statements of manufacturers and merchandisers is the way in which they describe the elements that make up the cost of goods sold. Observe these cost of goods sold schedules for a merchandiser and a manufacturer:

Merchandising Company		Manufacturing Company	
Cost of goods sold:		Cost of goods sold:	
Beginning *merchandise* inventory	$ 14,200	Beginning *finished goods* inventory	$ 11,200
Cost of goods *purchased*. . . .	234,150	Cost of goods *manufactured* (see the manufacturing statement)	170,500
Goods available for sale	$248,350	Goods available for sale	$181,700
Ending *merchandise* inventory.	12,100	Ending *finished goods* inventory .	10,300
Cost of goods sold	$236,250	Cost of goods sold	$171,400

Notice that the merchandiser uses the term *merchandise* inventory while the manufacturer uses the term *finished goods* inventory. (The manufacturer's inventories of raw materials and goods in process are not included because they are not available for sale.) Next, observe that the manufacturing company shows the cost of goods *manufactured* instead of the cost of goods *purchased*. This difference exists because the manufacturer produces its

ILLUSTRATION 20–3

Income Statement for a Manufacturing Company

EXCEL MANUFACTURING COMPANY
Income Statement
For Year Ended December 31, 1994

Sales			$310,000
Cost of goods sold:			
Finished goods inventory, December 31, 1993		$ 11,200	
Cost of goods manufactured (see manufacturing statement)		170,500	
Goods available for sale		$181,700	
Finished goods inventory, December 31, 1994		(10,300)	
Cost of goods sold			171,400
Gross profit			$138,600
Operating expenses:			
Selling expenses:			
Sales salaries expense	$18,000		
Advertising expense	5,500		
Delivery wages expense	12,000		
Shipping supplies expense	250		
Insurance expense, delivery equipment	300		
Depreciation expense, delivery equipment	2,100		
Total selling expenses		$ 38,150	
General and administrative expenses:			
Office salaries expense	$15,700		
Miscellaneous expense	200		
Bad debts expense	1,550		
Office supplies expense	100		
Depreciation expense, office equipment	200		
Interest expense	4,000		
Total general and administrative expenses		21,750	
Total operating expenses			59,900
Income before income taxes			$ 78,700
Less income taxes expense			(32,600)
Net income			$ 46,100
Net income per common share (20,000 shares)			$2.31

goods instead of purchasing them ready for sale. The line showing the cost of goods manufactured also includes a reference to the *manufacturing statement,* which we discuss later in this chapter.

Other than these differences, the cost of goods sold calculations appear the same for both companies. However, we want to emphasize that the numbers used in the calculations represent different activities. The merchandiser's cost of goods purchased is the cost of buying the products to be sold. The manufacturer's cost of goods manufactured includes the sum of the *materials, labor,* and *overhead* costs incurred by the manufacturer in producing the products.

In Illustration 20–3, notice that the operating expenses of Excel Manufacturing Company include sales salaries, office salaries, and depreciation of the delivery and office equipment. However, the operating expenses do not in-

ILLUSTRATION 20–4

Product and Period Costs in the Financial Statements

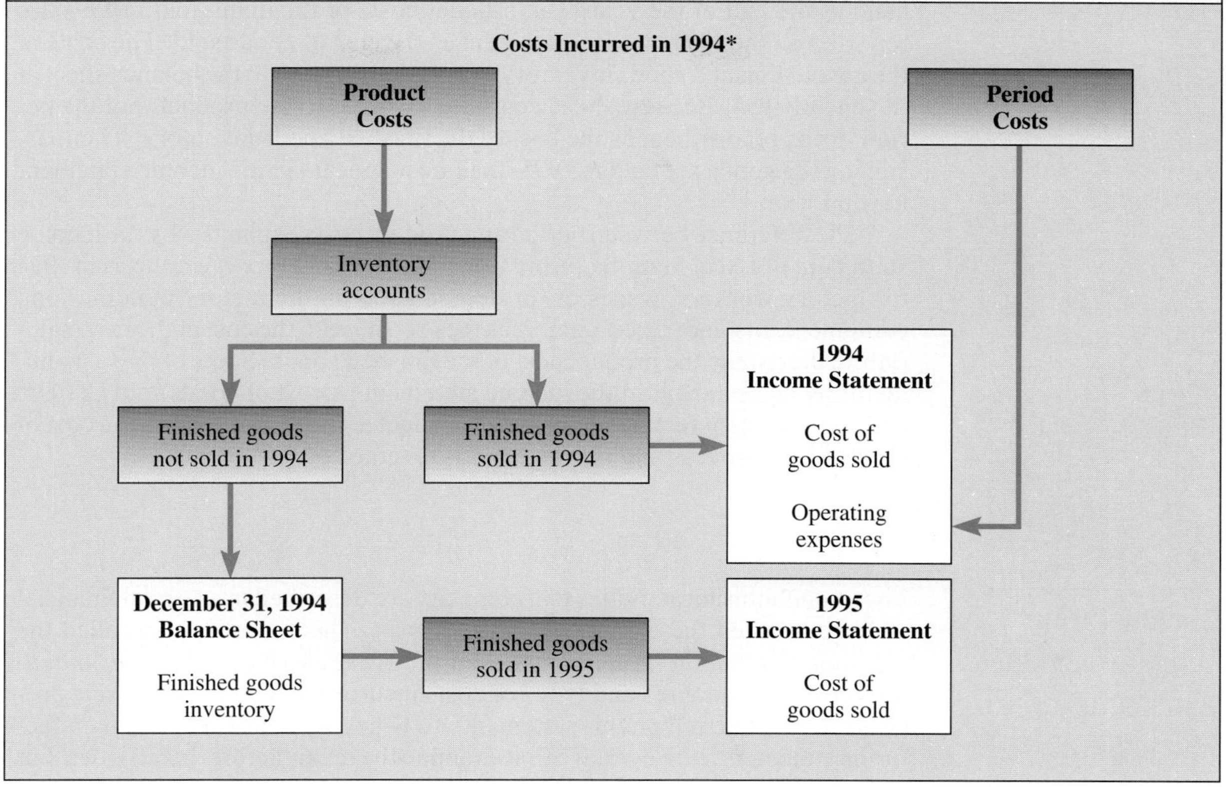

*Excluded from this diagram are costs to acquire assets other than inventory, costs to retire debt, and costs of payments to owners.

clude manufacturing costs such as factory workers' wages and depreciation of the production equipment and the factory. These are not reported as operating expenses. Instead, as we explain in the next section, they are capitalized as product costs and then go into the income statement as cost of goods sold.

The Difference between Period and Product Costs

You have already learned in prior chapters that some costs are capitalized or debited to asset accounts and other costs are charged to expense as they are incurred. Costs are capitalized if they produce benefits that are expected to have value in the future. Costs are expensed if their benefits appear to expire as the costs are incurred. In the case of manufacturing companies, costs that are capitalized as inventory are called **product costs.** Costs that are charged to expense as they are incurred are called **period costs.**

Illustration 20–4 shows the difference between the product costs and period costs incurred by a manufacturer during 1994. The period costs flow directly to the 1994 income statement as expenses because they do not produce assets. In contrast, product costs are initially assigned to inventory accounts.

The final treatment of product costs depends on what happens to the finished goods. That is, the finished goods are either sold in 1994 or are still on hand at the end of the year. The product costs of the items sold in 1994 are reported on the 1994 income statement as the cost of goods sold. The costs of the unsold finished goods inventory are carried forward to the balance sheet at the end of 1994. Because these costs are assigned to the product, not the period, firms report them as the cost of the finished goods inventory. Then, assuming the goods are sold in 1995, their cost appears in the income statement for that year.

The difference between period and product costs explains why the income statement of Excel Manufacturing Company does not report expenses in 1994 for factory workers' wages or for depreciation on the factory buildings and equipment. Instead, Excel combines these costs with the cost of the raw materials to determine the product cost of the finished goods. Some of these manufacturing costs appear in the income statement as cost of goods sold in 1994, and some of them remain on the balance sheet at the end of 1994 as the cost of the goods in process and finished goods inventories.

Manufacturing Activities and the Manufacturing Statement

The manufacturing activities of a company are described in a special financial statement called the **manufacturing statement.** This report is also called the *schedule of manufacturing activities* or the *schedule of cost of goods manufactured.* The amounts and types of costs incurred in the manufacturing process are summarized on this statement. To help you understand the manufacturing statement, however, we first examine the manufacturer's activities that relate to inventories.

Manufacturing Activities that Relate to Inventories

Illustration 20–5 represents the flow of a manufacturer's activities that relate to its inventories. Note that the diagram has three sections. The top section represents the flow of raw materials. A company starts an accounting period with a beginning raw materials inventory. During the period, it acquires additional raw materials. When the purchases are added to the beginning inventory, the result is the raw materials available for use in production. Two things can happen to these materials. Either they are used in production or they remain on hand at the end of the period for use in the next period.

The middle section of Illustration 20–5 shows four factors that come together in the production activity of the period. They are *direct materials, direct labor, factory overhead,* and the *beginning goods in process inventory.*

Direct Materials. The first factor used in production is the direct materials that come into the manufacturing process from the raw materials inventory. Recall that the cost of direct materials is clearly associated with units or batches of production because the materials go into and become part of the finished products.

ILLUSTRATION 20–5

Flows of Resources through the Inventories and the Production Process to Customers

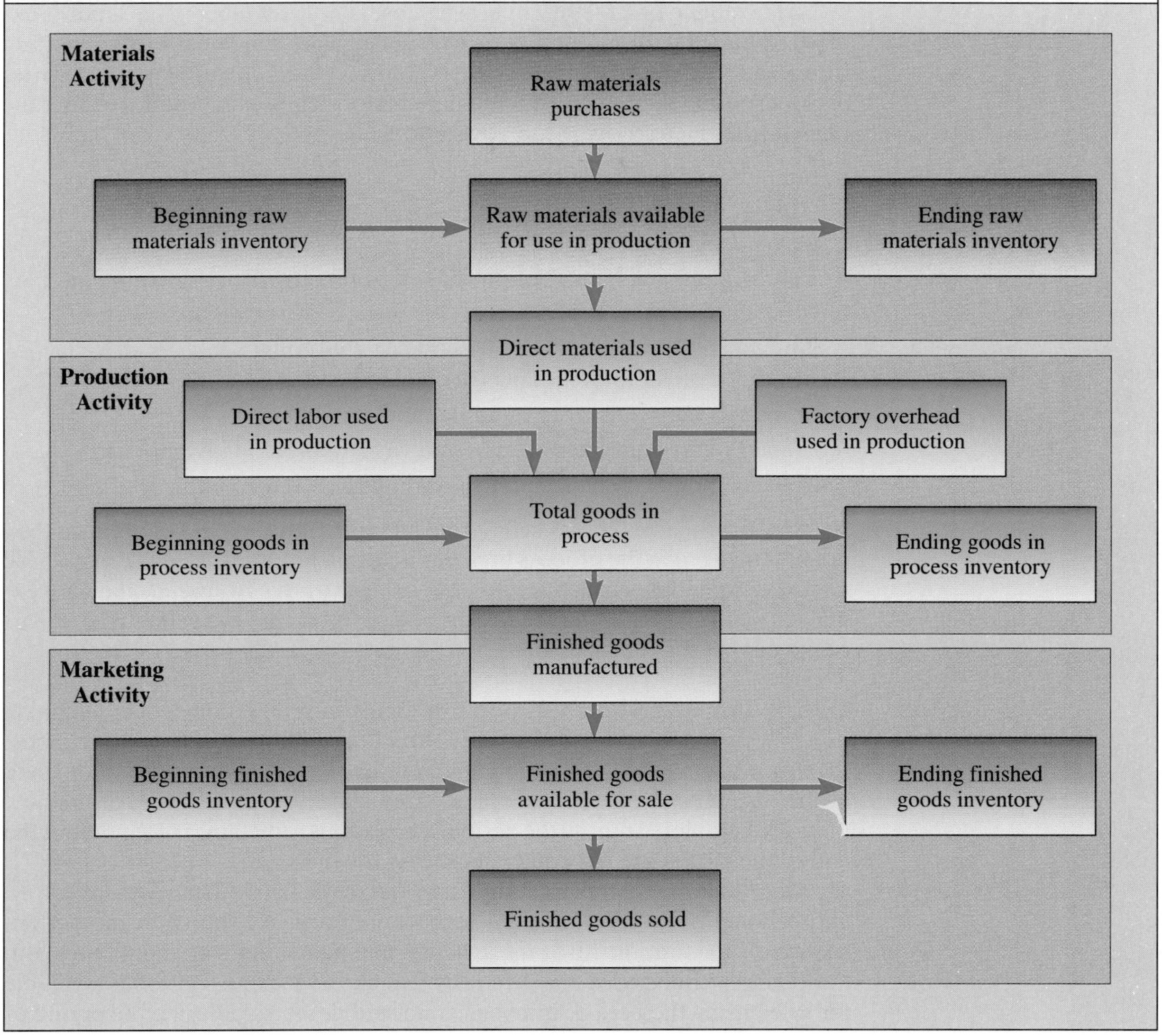

Direct Labor. The second factor, shown in the middle section of Illustration 20–5, is **direct labor.** The cost of direct labor is clearly associated with specific units or batches of production because direct labor converts raw materials into finished products.

Factory Overhead. The third factor applied in production is **factory overhead,** also called *manufacturing overhead* or *factory burden*. Although they are incurred as part of the manufacturing process, factory overhead costs are not clearly associated with specific units of product or batches of production.

Factory overhead includes all manufacturing costs other than direct materials and direct labor costs.

An example of a factory overhead cost is **indirect labor.** This labor is exerted by manufacturing employees who do not work specifically on converting direct materials into finished products. Indirect labor includes such activities as supervising employees, maintaining factory equipment, and cleaning the plant. Other factory overhead costs are:

- Indirect materials: Cleaning supplies and lubricants.
- Indirect labor (including related payroll taxes and fringe benefits): Maintenance and supervision.
- Depreciation and amortization: Factory building, factory equipment, patents, and tools.
- Factory utilities: Electricity, natural gas, and water.
- Insurance on factory buildings and equipment.
- Property taxes on factory buildings and equipment.
- Property taxes on raw materials and work in process inventories.
- Repairs and maintenance on factory buildings and equipment.

Factory overhead excludes selling and administrative expenses because they are not incurred in the process of manufacturing products. Even though these costs are sometimes called *selling and administrative overhead,* they are expensed on the income statement as period costs and are not capitalized as part of the cost of the finished goods.

Goods in Process Inventory. The fourth factor in production is the beginning *goods in process inventory*. In many situations, companies direct their labor, material, and overhead to completing all units of product that were incomplete at the beginning of the period. Then, they start new units. Most of the new units are completed during the period. Those units remaining incomplete at the end of the period are the goods in process inventory.

Once units are completed, they pass out of the goods in process inventory and become part of the finished goods inventory. As shown in the bottom section of Illustration 20–5, these newly completed units are combined with the beginning finished goods inventory to make up the finished goods available for sale during the period. Finished goods either are sold during the period or remain on hand at the end of the period. When they are sold, their cost is reported on the income statement as the cost of goods sold. If they are not sold, their cost appears on the balance sheet as the ending finished goods inventory.

The Manufacturing Statement

LO 3 Prepare a manufacturing statement, and explain its purpose and relationship to the primary financial statements.

Illustration 20–6 presents the manufacturing statement of Excel Manufacturing Company for 1994. This statement summarizes the costs of the manufacturing activity that took place during the period.

The top section of the statement calculates the cost of the raw materials that were used. The calculation starts with the beginning raw materials inventory of $8,000. Then, purchases of $86,500 are added to get the $94,500 cost of raw materials available for use in 1994. Based on a physical count, the ending

ILLUSTRATION 20–6

Manufacturing Statement

EXCEL MANUFACTURING COMPANY
Manufacturing Statement
For Year Ended December 31, 1994

Direct materials:		
Raw materials inventory, December 31, 1993	$ 8,000	
Raw materials purchases	86,500	
Raw materials available for use	$94,500	
Raw materials inventory, December 31, 1994	(9,000)	
Direct materials used		$ 85,500
Direct labor		60,000
Factory overhead costs:		
Indirect labor	$ 9,000	
Factory supervision	6,000	
Factory utilities	2,600	
Repairs, factory equipment	2,500	
Property taxes, factory building	1,900	
Factory supplies used	600	
Factory insurance expired	1,100	
Small tools written off	200	
Depreciation, factory equipment	3,500	
Depreciation, factory building	1,800	
Amortization, patents	800	
Total factory overhead costs		30,000
Total manufacturing costs		$175,500
Add goods in process inventory, December 31, 1993		2,500
Total goods in process during the year		$178,000
Deduct goods in process inventory, December 31, 1994		(7,500)
Cost of goods manufactured		$170,500

raw materials inventory is estimated to be $9,000, and the total cost of raw materials used during the period is calculated as $85,500 ($94,500 − $9,000).

The total direct labor cost of $60,000 includes related payroll taxes and fringe benefits. Note that the statement lists the cost of each factory overhead item and shows that the total factory overhead cost for the year was $30,000. Some companies show only the total factory overhead on the manufacturing statement. Then, a separate schedule of overhead items is prepared in support of the manufacturing statement.

In Illustration 20–6, notice that the total manufacturing costs incurred during the year are calculated as $175,500 ($85,500 + $60,000 + $30,000). Then, in the bottom section of the statement, this amount is added to the beginning goods in process inventory of $2,500 to compute the $178,000 total cost of goods that were in process during the year. Because the ending goods in process inventory had an estimated cost of $7,500, the net cost of goods manufactured (or *cost of goods completed*) during the year was $170,500. Now turn to Illustration 20–3 on page 1076 and find this same item and amount listed in the cost of goods sold section of Excel Manufacturing Company's income statement.

AS A MATTER OF
Ethics

Three former college classmates got together to have dinner at an expensive restaurant to talk over the past and to share recent news about what they and their companies were doing. The evening was long but entertaining and fruitful with respect to business ideas. When the check arrived, it was grabbed by one of the three. Because he was a self-employed entrepreneur, he said, "Here, let me pay it—I'll deduct it as a business expense on my tax return, and it won't cost me as much." One of the others was the vice president of a medium-sized corporation. She snatched the check out of his hand and said, "I'll put this on a company credit card, and it won't cost us anything at all." The third, who was a factory manager for a company that sold products to the government, smiled and folded his hands. When his silence got the attention of the other two, he said, "Neither of you understands the system yet. I'll put this on my company's credit card and call it overhead on a cost-plus contract my company has with the government.* That way, my company will pay for our dinner *and* make a profit on it."

* Under a cost-plus contract, the seller receives its costs plus a percentage of those costs.

The manufacturing statement contains information that management uses in planning and controlling the company's production activities. To provide timely information, the statement is likely to be produced monthly for internal use or even weekly or more often. Although the manufacturing statement may contain information useful to outside parties, it is not a general purpose financial statement. Because GAAP does not require companies to publish the statement, most of them do not.

Accounting for Manufacturing Activities with a General Accounting System

So far, our focus has been on how the reports generated by the accounting system reflect what happens when production activities take place. We now turn to the accounting procedures used to compile the information presented in the reports. In this introductory chapter, we describe simple manufacturing accounting systems based on *periodic* inventories. These systems estimate the costs of the raw materials, goods in process, and finished goods inventories based on physical counts of the quantities on hand at the end of each period. This information is then used to compute the amounts consumed, finished, and sold during the period. A manufacturing company that applies these periodic inventory procedures is said to have a **general accounting system.**

Many manufacturing companies use more complex accounting systems based on *perpetual* inventories. These systems are called **cost accounting systems.** By keeping running records of the costs of materials, goods in process, and finished goods inventories, these systems provide more timely information about those inventories and changes in their levels. They also provide timely information about manufacturing costs per unit of product, which managers use in their efforts to control costs. Chapter 21 describes *job order* cost accounting systems that provide more detailed information about the costs of unique products manufactured individually or in small batches. Chapter 22 describes *process* cost accounting systems that provide information about the costs of products manufactured in large quantities.

Despite their differences, general accounting systems and cost accounting systems have similar features. They both focus on the three elements of manufacturing cost: *direct materials, direct labor,* and *factory overhead*. They also provide information about the three inventories—raw materials, goods in process, and finished goods. However, they do not keep these records in the same way. The next sections describe how general accounting systems work.

Accounts Unique to a General Accounting System

LO 4 Describe the unique accounts and procedures that manufacturing companies use in a general accounting system.

Many of the accounts used by manufacturing companies and merchandising companies are the same. Both have accounts for such things as cash, accounts receivable, accounts payable, common stock, retained earnings, sales, and selling and administrative expenses. However, because of the complexity of a manufacturing company's operations, its General Ledger usually contains more accounts than a merchandising company's ledger. The accounts that are used only by manufacturing companies include Factory Equipment, Accumulated Depreciation on Factory Equipment, Factory Supplies, Factory Supplies Used, Raw Materials Inventory, Raw Materials Purchases, Direct Labor, Factory Overhead, Goods in Process Inventory, Finished Goods Inventory, and Manufacturing Summary. The last seven accounts in this list are explained next.

Raw Materials Inventory. Under a periodic inventory system, a firm records the cost of the raw materials on hand at the end of the period in the Raw Materials Inventory account. Throughout the following accounting period, this amount remains in the account as its beginning balance. Then, when the period ends, the balance is updated in the closing process.

Companies determine the end-of-period cost of raw materials by counting the materials on hand and assigning costs to them based on actual purchase prices. Management may choose to assign costs to the account based on FIFO, LIFO, weighted average, or specific invoice prices. To avoid unnecessary complexity, we assume a FIFO flow throughout our discussion of manufacturing accounting.

Raw Materials Purchases. In a general accounting system, the cost of raw materials purchased during a period is debited to the Raw Materials Purchases account. This account is similar to the Purchases account that you have used for merchandise purchases. Raw Materials Purchases is a temporary holding account for costs that are later allocated between the ending raw materials inventory and the production of the period. The account starts each period with a zero balance. The balance increases as materials purchases are recorded and returns to zero when the account is closed at the end of the period.

Many companies use supplemental and contra accounts to record other events that affect the cost of the purchased materials. For example, the ledger might include accounts for transportation-in, materials purchases returns and allowances, and materials purchases discounts. To simplify the illustrations in this chapter, we do not include these accounts in the examples.

Direct Labor. General accounting systems use a special temporary account to record direct labor costs. The Direct Labor account is similar to the Raw Materials Purchases account because it accumulates direct labor costs until they are allocated to other accounts at the end of the year. The account begins the year with a zero balance, receives debits throughout the year as direct labor costs are incurred, and then is closed at the end of the period. When the Direct Labor account is closed, the accumulated costs are assigned to the fully and partially completed units of product manufactured during the year.

To help managers control direct labor costs, the accounting system may include several accounts for different categories of direct labor costs. Other accounts distinguish base pay from fringe benefits and payroll taxes. However, all these costs end up being assigned to products. To simplify the discussion, the illustrations in the chapter use only one Direct Labor account.

Factory Overhead. Firms use another temporary holding account to record manufacturing overhead costs. The Factory Overhead account is like the Direct Labor account because it starts the year with a zero balance. During the year, it is debited as overhead costs are incurred. Then, when the accumulated costs are allocated to products in the year-end closing process, the account balance is returned to zero.

As in the case of direct labor, a company may use a group of individual overhead accounts to accumulate information about different overhead costs. This information often helps management control specific overhead costs such as indirect labor, indirect materials, and utilities. Although the upcoming example uses only a single overhead account, it also shows how multiple overhead accounts could be used.

Goods in Process Inventory. As we described earlier, a manufacturing company often has an inventory of partially completed goods in process. These units have received at least some of their direct materials, and probably some direct labor and overhead costs. However, the units remain unfinished. At the end of the period, the estimated cost of the unfinished units is debited to the Goods in Process Inventory account.

Because a general accounting system is based on periodic inventory methods, the balance of this account remains unchanged throughout the following period. In other words, the account is not updated during a period to reflect the completion of units or the introduction of new units into production. Finally, the next year-end closing process updates the account balance to reflect the cost of the ending goods in process inventory.

The costs to be recorded in the Goods in Process Inventory account can seldom be determined with precision under a periodic system. Even though the number of units might be countable, the process of assigning costs to those units is not precise. Imagine, for example, a workshop with 120 partially completed lawn mowers. Some of them are just barely started, others are part way along in production, and still others are nearly complete. Determining the cost of these mowers involves many estimates and compromises. We describe these measurement problems in more detail later in the chapter.

Finished Goods Inventory. Finished goods are completed units ready for sale. Like the other two inventory accounts, the initial balance of the Finished Goods Inventory account equals the cost of the prior year's ending inventory. As additional units are completed and sales occur, the account is not updated. No entries are made to the account until it is updated by the year-end closing process to reflect the estimated cost of the finished goods on hand.

A physical count of the ending finished goods inventory provides some of the information needed to determine the ending balance in the account. However, with a general accounting system, accountants often encounter measurement difficulties when they assign costs to completed goods. The difficulties arise because the system does not keep precise records of costs incurred in producing each unit. The next two chapters show how perpetual inventory systems provide more precise measures of unit costs. As a result, the valuation of the goods in process and finished goods inventories is more precise.

Manufacturing Summary. A general accounting system also uses the Manufacturing Summary account. This temporary account is similar to the Income Summary account. The Manufacturing Summary account has a zero balance throughout the year until the closing process starts. During closing, all manufacturing costs are transferred to this account. Then, the account balance is returned to zero as this total cost is allocated among the three ending inventory accounts and the cost of goods sold.

Journal Entries under a General Accounting System

LO 5 Prepare journal entries to record and summarize information about the activities and assets of a manufacturing company.

Now that you have a background for manufacturing and general accounting systems, we can describe the journal entries that account for manufacturing activities. The entries are based on the following information about the inventories and events for Excel Manufacturing Company for 1994.

Beginning inventories:	
Raw materials	$ 8,000
Goods in process	2,500
Finished goods	11,200
Production costs for the year:	
Raw materials purchases	$86,500
Direct labor	60,000
Factory overhead	30,000
Ending inventories:	
Raw materials	$ 9,000
Goods in process	7,500
Finished goods	10,300

For now, the costs of the ending inventories are assumed. Later, we describe how you can determine the amounts.

Illustrations 20–7 through 20–11 (following page 1091) include a series of four transparency overlays. As you turn each transparency, note that the top section traces how the costs flow through the manufacturing process and the three inventories. The middle section shows how costs are accumulated in the accounts. The bottom section explains the events in the diagrams.

Beginning Balances

The top portion of Illustration 20–7 presents five boxes that represent the sources of manufacturing costs described earlier. They include the beginning materials inventory, the beginning goods in process inventory, the purchases of raw materials, the direct labor costs, and the factory overhead. The middle section shows the beginning balances of the accounts affected by the 1994 activities of Excel Manufacturing. Initially, only the Raw Materials Inventory and Goods in Process Inventory accounts have balances. The amounts of $8,000 and $2,500 are carried forward from the end of 1993. The other three accounts (Raw Materials Purchases, Direct Labor, and Factory Overhead) receive entries in recording the events of 1994.

Phase 1—Recording the Period's Manufacturing Activities

Move the first overlay into place to produce Illustration 20–8. In this illustration, the arrows labeled "1" represent the manufacturing events of the year. They symbolize purchasing raw materials for $86,500, using direct labor at a cost of $60,000, and incurring $30,000 of factory overhead costs.

The middle section of Illustration 20–8 adds three accounts to the previous illustration. They are Cash, Accounts Payable, and Other Accounts. These accounts, together with Raw Materials Purchases, Direct Labor, and Factory Overhead, are used to record the production costs for 1994. The journal entries used to record the 1994 activities are represented in Illustration 20–8 by the arrows labeled "1". For example, the arrows pointing to Accounts Payable and Raw Material Purchases summarize all of the credit purchases of raw materials during the period. In general journal form, one of those transactions would be recorded as follows:

1994				
May	15	Raw Materials Purchases	800.00	
		Accounts Payable		800.00
		Purchased raw materials on credit.		

This entry increases the balance of Raw Materials Purchases by the cost of the acquired materials. It also increases the balance of Accounts Payable to reflect the new liability created by the transaction.

As another example, the arrows pointing to Direct Labor and Other Accounts represent all of the 1994 accruals of direct labor costs. Again in general journal form, one of those transactions (ignoring withholdings) would be recorded as follows:

Aug.	21	Direct Labor	2,550.00	
		Wages Payable		2,550.00
		To accrue direct labor payroll.		

This entry increases the balance of the temporary Direct Labor account and increases Wages Payable (Other Accounts in the illustration) by the amount accrued.

The arrow pointing to Factory Overhead represents all overhead costs incurred during the year. One of those, for example, might have been $1,800 of depreciation on the factory building, as recorded with this adjusting entry at the end of the year:

Dec.	31	Factory Overhead.	1,800.00	
		Accumulated Depreciation, Building		1,800.00
		To record depreciation on the factory building.		

This entry increases the balance of the temporary Factory Overhead account for the depreciation of the factory building. It also increases the credit balance of the Accumulated Depreciation account for the building.

To simplify the diagram, Illustration 20–8 uses a summary account called Other Accounts to represent all accounts—other than Cash and Accounts Payable—that are credited during the year in recording manufacturing costs. The illustration also uses only one Factory Overhead account instead of the many detailed accounts that a company might use.

Notice that the Raw Materials Inventory and Goods in Process Inventory accounts do not receive any entries during the year under the periodic system. Thus, their balances still equal the costs of these inventories as of December 31, 1993, when the current year began.

The balances in all five production accounts are presented as they exist at the end of 1994, after the adjusting entries are posted but before the accounts are closed.

Phase 2—Closing the Temporary Manufacturing Accounts

Now move the next overlay into place to create Illustration 20–9. The flowchart at the top shows that the five sources of manufacturing costs generated a total cost of $187,000 to be accounted for during 1994. We calculate this total as follows:

Beginning inventories:	
Raw materials	$ 8,000
Goods in process	2,500
Production costs for the year:	
Raw materials purchases	86,500
Direct labor	60,000
Factory overhead	30,000
Total costs to be accounted for during 1994 . .	$187,000

The middle section of Illustration 20–9 shows the effects of the first closing entry, labeled "2", which transfers the balances of the five accounts into the temporary Manufacturing Summary account at the end of 1994. In general journal form, that closing entry appears as follows:

1994				
Dec.	31	Manufacturing Summary	187,000.00	
		Raw Materials Inventory		8,000.00
		Goods in Process Inventory		2,500.00
		Raw Materials Purchases		86,500.00
		Direct Labor		60,000.00
		Factory Overhead		30,000.00
		To close the production accounts to Manufacturing Summary.		

Posting this entry closes the Raw Materials Purchases, Direct Labor, and Factory Overhead accounts. As a result, they have zero balances and are ready to be used in 1995 to record the production costs for that year. The entry also creates zero balances in the Raw Materials Inventory and Goods in Process Inventory accounts. However, the next closing entry updates them to reflect the correct end-of-period inventory amounts.

You can gain a better understanding of systems that use more than one overhead account by considering the following alternative version of the closing entry. It uses the specific overhead cost accounts listed in the manufacturing statement in Illustration 20–6 on page 1081.

1994				
Dec.	31	Manufacturing Summary	187,000.00	
		Raw Materials Inventory		8,000.00
		Goods in Process Inventory		2,500.00
		Raw Materials Purchases		86,500.00
		Direct Labor		60,000.00
		Indirect Labor		9,000.00
		Factory Supervision		6,000.00
		Factory Utilities		2,600.00
		Repairs, Factory Equipment		2,500.00
		Property Taxes on Factory Building		1,900.00
		Factory Supplies Used		600.00
		Factory Insurance Expired		1,100.00
		Small Tools Written Off		200.00
		Depreciation of Factory Equipment		3,500.00
		Depreciation of Factory Building		1,800.00
		Amortization of Patents		800.00
		To close the production accounts to Manufacturing Summary.		

Phase 3—Recording the Ending Balances of the Manufacturing Inventory Accounts

Turn the third transparency to see Illustration 20–10. The flowchart shows that part of the $187,000 total costs for 1994 is assigned to the inventories of unused raw materials ($9,000). Part is assigned to goods in process ($7,500), and the remaining $170,500 is the cost of the finished units. The flowchart also adds the beginning balance of the finished goods inventory.

The middle section of Illustration 20–10 shows the next step in closing the manufacturing accounts. The entry represented by arrow "3" records the cost of the raw materials and goods in process inventories at the end of the year. The balances of these accounts are presented on Excel Manufacturing Company's balance sheet as of December 31, 1994.

In general journal form, closing entry "3" is

1994				
Dec.	31	Raw Materials Inventory	9,000.00	
		Goods in Process Inventory	7,500.00	
		Manufacturing Summary		16,500.00
		To update the raw materials and goods in process inventories.		

Notice that this entry increases the balance of the two inventory accounts from zero to the amounts that they need to have for the balance sheet. This entry also reduces the balance of the Manufacturing Summary account to $170,500, which equals the cost of goods manufactured for 1994. Look at Illustration 20–6 on page 1081 to see this amount on the bottom line of the Manufacturing Statement. You can also see it in the Cost of Goods Sold section of the income statement in Illustration 20–3 on page 1076.

Illustration 20–10 also adds the Finished Goods Inventory account to the diagram. Note that at this point in the closing process, the account still has its beginning balance.

Phase 4—Closing the Manufacturing Summary Account and Updating the Finished Goods Inventory Account

Moving the fourth transparency overlay into place creates Illustration 20–11. Arrow "4" in the flowchart shows how to determine the $181,700 cost of goods available for sale in 1994. It is the sum of the $11,200 beginning finished goods inventory and the $170,500 cost of goods completed during the year. Arrow "5" shows how the cost of goods available for sale is divided between the cost of the ending finished goods inventory and the cost of goods sold. The ending inventory consists of goods with a cost of $10,300, and the cost of goods sold is $171,400.

The middle section of the illustration shows how the accounts are affected by the two closing entries labeled with arrows "4" and "5". The $181,700 debit to Income Summary in entry "4" is the sum of the $170,500 balance of the Manufacturing Summary account and the $11,200 beginning balance of Finished Goods Inventory. As shown in Illustration 20–11, entry "4" closes the Manufacturing Summary account. It also clears the beginning balance from Finished Goods Inventory and prepares that account for the next closing entry. The $181,700 debit to Income Summary is the cost of goods available for sale. In Illustration 20–3 on page 1076, notice that this $181,700 amount is reported on the income statement.

The complete closing entry is not represented in Illustration 20–11 because the focus of the illustration is on the accounts that relate to manufacturing costs. The following complete closing entry closes all the 1994 expense accounts for Excel Manufacturing Company. The balances of the expense accounts are taken from the 1994 income statement in Illustration 20–3.

1994				
Dec.	31	Income Summary	274,200.00	
		Manufacturing Summary		**170,500.00**
		Finished Goods Inventory		**11,200.00**
		Sales Salaries Expense		18,000.00
		Advertising Expense		5,500.00
		Delivery Wages Expense		12,000.00
		Shipping Supplies Expense		250.00
		Insurance Expense, Delivery Equipment		300.00
		Depreciation Expense, Delivery Equipment		2,100.00
		Office Salaries Expense		15,700.00
		Miscellaneous Expense		200.00
		Bad Debts Expense		1,550.00
		Office Supplies Expense		100.00
		Depreciation Expense, Office Equipment		200.00
		Interest Expense		4,000.00
		Income Taxes Expense		32,600.00
		To close the Manufacturing Summary and expense accounts, and to clear the Finished Goods Inventory account.		

Note the first two credits in the complete closing entry. In Illustration 20–11, the $181,700 debit to Income Summary is the sum of these two credits.

Arrow "5" in Illustration 20–11 divides the $181,700 cost of the available goods into the ending finished goods inventory ($10,300) and the cost of goods sold ($171,400). In the middle section of Illustration 20–11, entry "5" completes the process of accounting for Excel Manufacturing Company's manufacturing costs during 1994. Excel allocated the total cost as follows:

Total manufacturing costs to be accounted for during 1994 (See page 1088)	$187,000	
Beginning finished goods inventory	11,200	
Total costs to be accounted for		$198,200
Allocation of costs:		
Ending raw materials inventory	$ 9,000	
Ending goods in process inventory	7,500	
Ending finished goods inventory	10,300	
Cost of goods sold	171,400	
Total costs accounted for		$198,200

Although Illustration 20–11 does not show the Sales account, the complete closing entry also includes a debit to Sales:

1994				
Dec.	31	Finished Goods Inventory	10,300.00	
		Sales	310,000.00	
		Income Summary		320,300.00
		To close the Sales account and update the Finished Goods Inventory account.		

After this entry is posted, the Income Summary account has a credit balance of $46,100, which equals the net income for 1994. The following entry closes the Income Summary account and updates the Retained Earnings account:

1994				
Dec.	31	Income Summary	46,100.00	
		Retained Earnings		46,100.00
		To close Income Summary and update Retained Earnings.		

Observe that the last closing entry is exactly the same whether the company is engaged in merchandising, manufacturing, or providing services. After the closing process is completed, the Income Summary account appears as follows:

Income Summary — **Acc. No. 901**

Date		Explanation	Debit	Credit	Balance
1994					
Dec.	31		274,200		274,200
	31			320,300	46,100
	31		46,100		-0-

Reporting Overhead Costs to Managers and to External Parties

Illustration 20–12 shows how manufacturing cost information flows from managerial accounting reports to the financial statements. In the illustration, overhead cost information flows from a schedule of overhead costs to the manufacturing statement and on to the income statement. Note that the individual factory overhead costs are listed in a separate schedule. The schedule supports and explains the total factory overhead cost item shown on the manufacturing statement. Recall that some companies include a detailed list of overhead costs in the manufacturing statement and others use a supporting schedule. The manufacturing statement includes the total factory overhead in its calculation of the cost of goods manufactured. Then, the cost of goods manufactured is carried over to the income statement and shown as part of the cost of goods sold calculation.

As we mentioned earlier, the manufacturing statement and the supporting schedule of overhead items are prepared for managers. They are rarely published. Nevertheless, the manufacturing statement explains and is consistent with the income statement. As you already know, the financial statements published for use by outsiders always include an income statement. Thus, you can see that even though managerial accounting and financial accounting are designed to serve different users, some managerial reports are closely related to the financial statements.

ILLUSTRATION 20–7

Beginning Balances

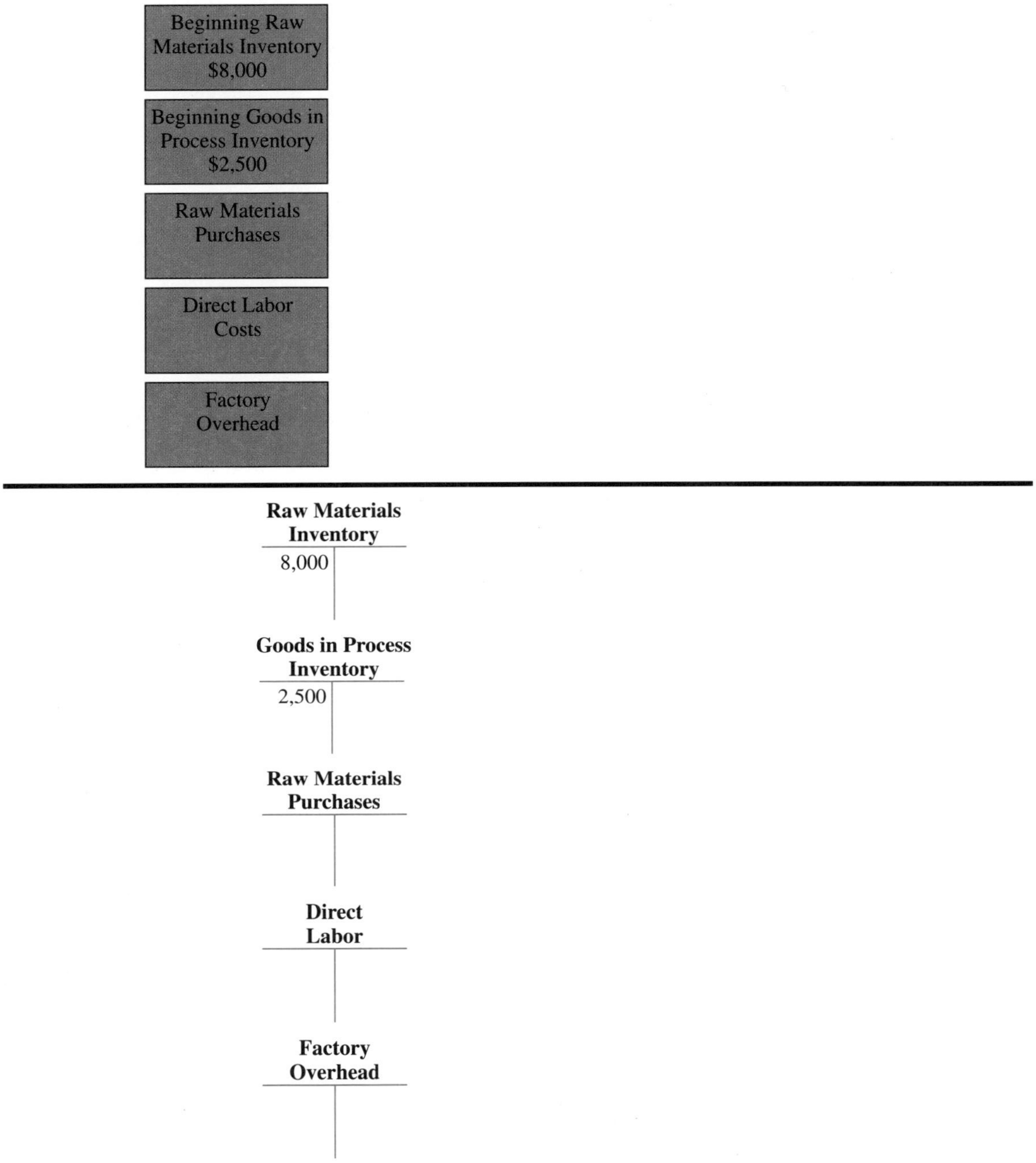

Explanation

At the beginning of the year, the only manufacturing accounts with balances are the Raw Materials Inventory and the Goods in Process Inventory accounts. The Finished Goods Inventory account will be shown later.

ILLUSTRATION 20–9

Phase 2—Closing the Temporary Manufacturing Accounts

ILLUSTRATION 20-9

Phase 2—Closing the Temporary Manufacturing Accounts

ILLUSTRATION 20–12

Relationships between Overhead Items, the Manufacturing Statement, and the Income Statement

Schedule of Overhead Items
For Year Ended 12/31/94

Indirect labor	$ 9,000
Supervision	6,000
Other overhead items .	15,000
Total overhead	$30,000

→

Manufacturing Statement
For Year Ended 12/31/94

Direct materials. . . .	$ 85,500
Direct labor.	60,000
Factory overhead . . .	30,000
Total manuf. costs . .	$175,500
Goods in process:	
Beginning.	2,500
Ending	(7,500)
Cost of goods manuf. .	$170,500

→

Income Statement
For Year Ended 12/31/94

Sales	$310,000
Cost of goods sold:	
Beg. finished goods. .	$ 11,200
Cost of goods manuf. .	170,500
End. finished goods. .	(10,300)
Cost of goods sold . .	$171,400
Gross profit.	$138,600
Expenses	(59,900)
Income before taxes .	$ 78,700
Income taxes	(32,600)
Net income	$ 46,100

Inventory Valuation Problems under a General Accounting System

LO 6 Explain the procedures for periodically assigning costs to the inventories owned by manufacturing companies.

When a company uses a general accounting system, it bases the ending inventories of raw materials, goods in process, and finished goods on physical counts of the units on hand. Assigning cost to the raw materials inventory does not involve a new problem. It is no different than assigning cost to the merchandise inventory of a retailer. The items in both inventories are generally in the same condition as when they were purchased.

However, determining the costs of goods in process and finished goods inventories is more complex. Because these inventories have been partially or wholly converted from raw materials into finished products, firms cannot simply measure the costs of goods in process and finished goods as the amounts paid to suppliers. Instead, the manufacturing cost of these inventories must be estimated.

Estimating Direct Material and Direct Labor Costs in the Ending Inventories

In some manufacturing processes, the direct materials and direct labor costs in the goods in process and finished goods inventories can be determined precisely. More often, however, a production manager who understands the manufacturing process must estimate these costs.

After the manager estimates the quantity of direct materials in each unit, costs are assigned based on a cost flow assumption such as FIFO. Finally, the estimated direct material costs for the units in the inventory are totaled to approximate the direct material cost of the entire inventory. Companies use the same process to calculate the cost of direct materials in the finished goods inventory.

The procedures for estimating the direct labor cost of goods in process are similar to those used for direct materials. Normally, a production manager estimates the hours of direct labor that have been applied to the units in the inventory. Then, based on the cost per hour of labor, the manager calculates the total direct labor cost of the units. The manager makes similar estimates of the direct labor cost added to the finished goods on hand.

Estimating Factory Overhead Cost in the Ending Inventories

Because factory overhead is not clearly associated with specific units or batches of product, estimating the overhead cost that should be assigned to the ending inventories is a challenging problem. The traditional approach to assigning overhead relates factory overhead to some other factor that is used throughout most of the manufacturing process. For example, many companies express total factory overhead cost as a percentage of total direct labor cost. Then, they assign overhead cost to units of product by multiplying that percentage by the direct labor cost assigned to each unit.

To see how this procedure is followed, consider the example of Excel Manufacturing Company. The company's total overhead costs for 1994 were \$30,000 and its total direct labor costs were \$60,000. Thus, \$1 of factory overhead cost was incurred for each \$2 of direct labor cost. In other words, overhead costs as a percentage of direct labor cost were:

$$\frac{\text{Factory overhead, \$30,000}}{\text{Direct labor, \$60,000}} = 50\%$$

Next, Excel applies this percentage to management's estimates of direct labor cost per unit to determine the factory overhead cost per unit.

The following table shows the assignments of all three types of cost to the units in the ending inventories:

	Goods in Process			Finished Goods		
	Cost per Unit	**Units of Product**	**Total Cost**	**Cost per Unit**	**Units of Product**	**Total Cost**
Direct materials (estimated) . .	\$3.75	1,000	\$3,750	\$11.00	515	\$ 5,665
Direct labor (estimated)	2.50	1,000	2,500	6.00	515	3,090
Factory overhead (50% of direct labor)	1.25	1,000	1,250	3.00	515	1,545
Total cost.			\$7,500			\$10,300

The table shows that management estimated direct materials costs at \$3.75 per unit in process and \$11 per finished unit. The estimates of direct labor cost were \$2.50 per unit in process and \$6.00 per finished unit. Then, factory overhead cost was assigned at the rate of 50% of the direct labor cost. Physical counts of the ending inventories showed that there were 1,000 partially finished units in process and 515 units in the finished goods inventory. Finally, each per unit cost was multiplied by the number of units in each inventory to calculate the total cost assigned to the two inventories. Notice that the $7,500 cost of the ending goods in process and the $10,300 cost of the ending finished goods inventory are the amounts used in Illustration 20–12.

Companies commonly relate factory overhead to direct labor when assigning overhead to inventories. However, this method is not the only one that can be used. Another possibility relates factory overhead to machine-hours used in manufacturing. Thus, if the products are manufactured on a machine, total overhead cost may be divided by total machine-hours used to get overhead cost per machine-hour. Then, firms can assign overhead to units based on the number of machine-hours used to produce a unit.

Other factors, such as the quantity of direct materials used in production, also may be used as the basis for assigning overhead to inventories. However, all assignment methods are somewhat arbitrary. They are all based on the assumption that the amount of overhead incurred in producing a unit of product is proportional to the amount of the related factor (such as direct labor) that it takes to produce a unit. Chapter 23 describes a more sophisticated approach to the problem called *activity-based costing*.

Summary of the Chapter in Terms of Learning Objectives

LO 1. Despite their similarities, financial and managerial accounting differ in many ways. These include who uses the information, what they use the information for, why they need it, the flexibility of the practices, the existence of standards for acceptability, and the nature of the reports. The information provided by financial and managerial accounting also differs in the need for its verification, its timeliness, its subject matter, and the extent to which it includes predictions about future events.

LO 2. The financial statements of manufacturers and merchandisers are different in their descriptions of inventories and cost of goods sold. In the cost of goods sold calculations, manufacturers report the cost of goods manufactured while merchandisers report the cost of purchases. The balance sheets of manufacturers include three inventories (raw materials, goods in process, and finished goods) while merchandisers report only merchandise inventory. Manufacturers also may identify some of their plant assets as factory equipment and buildings.

LO 3. The manufacturing statement presents a calculation of the cost of goods manufactured during the period. It begins by showing the period's costs for direct materials, direct labor, and overhead, and then combines these numbers with the beginning and ending inventories of goods in process to calculate the cost of the completed goods.

LO 4. Unique accounts used by manufacturers with general accounting systems include Raw Materials Inventory, Raw Materials Purchases, Direct Labor, Factory Overhead, Goods in Process Inventory, Finished Goods Inventory, and Manufacturing Summary. Additional accounts may provide more detailed information for management use in planning and controlling operations.

LO 5. During each period, manufacturers use separate accounts to record their raw materials purchases, direct labor costs, and factory overhead costs. After end-of-period adjustments are recorded in the closing process, all manufacturing costs are transferred to the Manufacturing Summary account. Next, the Manufacturing Summary balance is allocated to cost of goods manufactured (Income Summary) and to the ending inventories of materials and goods in process. At the same time, the beginning finished goods inventory balance is transferred to Income Summary. Another closing entry records the ending finished goods inventory.

LO 6. When determining the costs of ending inventories, a manufacturer allocates the raw materials and direct labor costs to goods in process and finished goods based on estimates by production managers. Factory overhead cost is related to another factor used in production, such as direct labor or machine hours. Then, the manufacturer allocates overhead cost to the ending work in process and finished goods inventories based on the estimated direct labor or machine-hours used to produce the units in the inventories.

Demonstration Problem

The following account balances and other information were taken from the accounting records of Sunny Corporation for the year ended December 31, 1994. Use the information to prepare a schedule of factory overhead costs, a manufacturing statement (show only the total overhead cost), and an income statement.

Advertising expense	$ 85,000
Amortization of patents	16,000
Bad debts expense	28,000
Depreciation expense, office equipment	37,000
Depreciation of factory building	133,000
Depreciation of factory equipment	78,000
Direct labor	250,000
Factory insurance expired	62,000
Factory supervision	74,000
Factory supplies used	21,000
Factory utilities	115,000
Finished goods inventory, December 31, 1993	15,000
Finished goods inventory, December 31, 1994	12,500
Goods in process inventory, December 31, 1993	8,000
Goods in process inventory, December 31, 1994	9,000
Income taxes expense	53,400
Indirect labor	26,000
Interest expense	25,000
Miscellaneous expense	55,000
Property taxes on factory equipment	14,000
Raw materials inventory, December 31, 1993	60,000
Raw materials inventory, December 31, 1994	78,000
Raw materials purchases	313,000
Repairs, factory equipment	31,000
Salaries expense	150,000
Sales	1,630,000

Solution to Demonstration Problem

Planning the Solution

- Analyze the list of the costs and select those items that are factory overhead.
- Arrange these costs in a schedule of factory overhead costs for 1994.
- Analyze the items remaining on the list and select the ones related to production activity for the year; the selected items should include the materials and goods in process inventories and direct labor.
- Prepare a manufacturing statement for 1994 showing the calculation of the cost of materials used in production, the cost of direct labor, and the total factory overhead cost. When presenting the overhead cost on this statement, show only the total overhead cost from the schedule of overhead costs for 1994. Then, show the costs of the beginning and ending goods in process inventory to determine the total cost of goods manufactured.
- Combine the remaining revenue and expense items from the list into the income statement for 1994. Combine the cost of goods manufactured from the manufacturing statement with the finished goods inventory amounts to calculate the cost of goods sold for 1994.

SUNNY CORPORATION
Schedule of Factory Overhead Costs
For Year Ended December 31, 1994

Amortization of patents	$ 16,000
Depreciation of factory building	133,000
Depreciation of factory equipment	78,000
Factory insurance expired	62,000
Factory supervision	74,000
Factory supplies used	21,000
Factory utilities	115,000
Indirect labor	26,000
Property taxes on factory equipment	14,000
Repairs, factory equipment	31,000
Total factory overhead	$570,000

SUNNY CORPORATION
Manufacturing Statement
For Year Ended December 31, 1994

Direct materials:		
Raw materials inventory, December 31, 1993	$ 60,000	
Raw materials purchases	313,000	
Raw materials available for use	$373,000	
Raw materials inventory, December 31, 1994	(78,000)	
Direct materials used		$ 295,000
Direct labor		250,000
Factory overhead costs		570,000
Total manufacturing costs		$1,115,000
Goods in process inventory, December 31, 1993		8,000
Total goods in process		$1,123,000
Goods in process inventory, December 31, 1994		(9,000)
Cost of goods manufactured		$1,114,000

SUNNY CORPORATION
Income Statement
For Year Ended December 31, 1994

Sales		$1,630,000
Cost of goods sold:		
Finished goods inventory, December 31, 1993	$ 15,000	
Cost of goods manufactured	1,114,000	
Goods available for sale	$1,129,000	
Finished goods inventory, December 31, 1994	(12,500)	
Cost of goods sold		(1,116,500)
Gross profit		$ 513,500
Operating expenses:		
Advertising expense	$ 85,000	
Bad debts expense	28,000	
Depreciation expense, office equipment	37,000	
Interest expense	25,000	
Miscellaneous expense	55,000	
Salaries expense	150,000	
Total operating expenses		(380,000)
Income before income taxes		$ 133,500
Income taxes expense		(53,400)
Net income		$ 80,100

Glossary

LO 7 Define or explain the words and phrases listed in the chapter glossary.

Cost accounting system a system of accounting for manufacturing operations that uses perpetual inventory records. p. 1082

Direct labor labor with a cost that is clearly associated with specific units or batches of product because the labor is used to convert raw materials into finished products. p. 1079

Direct materials raw materials that physically become part of the product and therefore are clearly identified with specific units or batches of product. p. 1074

Factory overhead costs that are incurred as part of the manufacturing process but are not clearly associated with specific units or batches of product; includes all manufacturing costs other than direct material and direct labor costs. p. 1079

Finished goods inventory products that have completed the manufacturing process and are ready to be sold by the manufacturer. p. 1075

General accounting system a system of accounting for manufacturing operations that uses periodic inventories. p. 1082

Goods in process inventory products that are in the process of being manufactured but that are not yet complete. p. 1075

Indirect labor labor that is included in factory overhead because it is exerted by manufacturing employees who do not work specifically on converting direct materials into finished products. p. 1080

Indirect materials materials that are used in support of the production process but that do not become a part of the product and are not clearly identified with units or batches of product. p. 1075

Manufacturing statement a financial report that summarizes the amounts and types of costs that were incurred in the manufacturing process during the period. p. 1078

Period costs costs that are charged to expense because their benefits appear to expire as the costs are incurred. p. 1077

Product costs costs that are capitalized as inventory because they produce benefits that are expected to have value in the future. p. 1077

Raw materials materials that are purchased for use in making products; most are used as direct materials but some are used as indirect materials. p. 1074

Synonymous Terms

Cost of goods manufactured cost of goods completed.

Factory overhead manufacturing overhead; factory burden.

Goods in process inventory work in process inventory.

Managerial accounting management accounting.

Manufacturing statement schedule of manufacturing activities; schedule of cost of goods manufactured.

Objective Review

Answers to the following questions are listed at the end of this chapter. Be sure that you decide which is the one best answer to each question *before* you check the answers.

LO 1 Managerial accounting produces information that is

a. Designed to meet the needs of managers internal to the organization.
b. Prepared according to the specific needs of the user.
c. Often focused heavily on the future.
d. Generally concerned with subunits of the organization rather than the overall entity.
e. All of the above.

LO 2 The financial statements of a manufacturer

a. Include only a merchandise inventory on the balance sheet.
b. Present the calculation of the cost of goods sold using the cost of goods manufactured during the year.
c. Include expenses for direct labor, material, and overhead on the income statement.
d. Show the calculation of the cost of goods sold using the cost of goods purchased during the year.
e. None of the above.

LO 3 A manufacturing statement

a. Shows the elements of manufacturing costs incurred during the period and calculates the cost of goods sold during the period.
b. Shows the changes that occurred during the period in raw materials inventory, goods in process inventory, and finished goods inventory.
c. Shows the elements of manufacturing costs incurred during the period and calculates the cost of goods manufactured during the period.
d. Shows all cost items that make up the operating expenses incurred during the period.
e. None of the above.

LO 4 Which of the following statements is true with regard to the procedures used in a general accounting system for a manufacturing company?

a. Perpetual inventory records are maintained for raw materials and goods in process but not for finished goods.
b. Labor that contributes to production but that is not directly applied to units of product is accounted for as factory overhead.
c. Examples of direct labor include the labor of supervisors and maintenance engineers.
d. All manufacturing costs other than direct materials are called factory overhead.
e. Product costs are recorded in expense accounts.

LO 5 In preparing closing entries for a manufacturing company that uses a general accounting system

a. The beginning balance of Finished Goods Inventory is credited to Finished Goods Inventory and debited to Income Summary.
b. The beginning balance of Finished Goods Inventory plus the cost of goods completed during the period is debited to Finished Goods Inventory and credited to Income Summary.
c. The beginning balances of Raw Materials Inventory, Goods in Process Inventory, and Finished Goods Inventory are credited to those accounts and debited to Manufacturing Summary.
d. The balances of all manufacturing overhead accounts are credited to those accounts and debited to Manufacturing Summary.
e. Both (*a*) and (*d*) are correct.

LO 6 In measuring the ending inventories of goods in process and finished goods, which one of the following is not done in typical circumstances?

a. The physical quantities of units on hand are counted at the end of the year.
b. The amount of factory overhead included in each product is estimated by relating overhead to another factor used in production.
c. A production manager estimates the amount of direct material cost that is included in each product.
d. A production manager estimates the amount of direct labor cost that is included in each product.
e. All of the above are typically done.

LO 7 Factory overhead consists of

a. Direct materials.
b. Direct materials and direct labor.
c. Indirect materials and direct labor.
d. All manufacturing costs other than direct materials and direct labor.
e. Direct materials, direct labor, and all other manufacturing costs.

Questions for Class Discussion

1. What is the difference between the intended users of financial and managerial accounting information?
2. Are companies required to produce both financial and managerial accounting reports?
3. Why does the structure of financial accounting tend to be rigid while managerial accounting is relatively flexible?
4. Do generally accepted accounting principles control the practice of managerial accounting?
5. Why are the financial statements of a company subjected to an independent audit? Are managerial accounting reports audited? Why or why not?
6. Why is financial accounting focused on the entire organization while managerial accounting tends to focus on parts of the organization?

7. Why does managerial accounting tend to include more predictions of the future than financial accounting?
8. What is the basic difference between a manufacturing company and a merchandising company?
9. What are the three inventories that manufacturers present on their balance sheets?
10. What is the difference between direct materials and indirect materials?
11. In addition to inventories, what other assets may appear on the balance sheet of a manufacturer but not on the balance sheet of a merchandiser?
12. What differences exist between manufacturing companies and merchandising companies in their cost of goods sold calculations?
13. What is the difference between product and period costs?
14. What are the three categories of manufacturing cost?
15. What is the difference between direct labor and indirect labor?
16. How is the cost of indirect labor treated in accounting for production?
17. List several examples of factory overhead costs.
18. What is the difference between factory overhead and selling and administrative overhead?
19. Which inventories of a manufacturing company appear on its manufacturing statement? Which appear on the income statement? Which appear on the balance sheet?
20. How are the beginning and ending goods in process inventories used on the manufacturing statement?
21. What is the difference between a general accounting system for manufacturers and a cost accounting system?
22. Identify the seven accounts used in general accounting systems for manufacturers that are not used by merchandising or service companies.
23. If a general accounting system is used, at what point in the accounting cycle are the costs of raw materials purchases, direct labor, and factory overhead allocated to the cost of goods sold and to the ending raw materials, goods in process, and finished goods inventories?
24. What accounts are summarized in the Manufacturing Summary account? What accounts are summarized in the Income Summary account?
25. Describe the relationships among the income statement, the manufacturing statement, and a detailed schedule of factory overhead costs.
26. Why are the assignments of direct materials and direct labor costs to goods in process and finished goods inventories usually based on estimates by managers familiar with the production process?
27. Republic Company used an overhead rate of 60% of direct labor cost to add overhead cost to the cost of the items of its goods in process inventory. Given that the manufacturing statement of the company reported total overhead cost of $156,000, how much direct labor did it report?

28. A footnote to the Land's End financial statements states in part: "Inventory, primarily merchandise held for sale . . ." What other types of inventories might the company hold?
29. Notice that the current assets on the balance sheet of Federal Express in Appendix K do not include any inventories. Explain why this situation is not unusual.

Exercises

Exercise 20–1
Calculating cost of goods sold
(LO 2)

Calculate the cost of goods sold for these two companies:

	Adams Retail	Brown Manufacturing
Beginning inventory:		
Merchandise	$125,000	
Finished goods		$ 250,000
Purchases	524,000	
Cost of goods manufactured		1,235,000
Ending inventory:		
Merchandise	75,000	
Finished goods		322,000

Exercise 20–2
Classifying product costs and period costs
(LO 1)

The following costs were incurred by a manufacturing company. Classify each one as either a product or a period cost.

Accident insurance on factory workers
Advertising
Amortization of patents
Bad debts expense
Depreciation of factory building
Direct materials used
Interest on long-term debt
Office salaries
Repairs to factory machinery
Sales salaries
Small tools used
State and federal income taxes

Exercise 20–3
Calculating the cost of goods manufactured and the cost of goods sold
(LO 2)

The following information was taken from the accounting records of Candele Company and Dortmund Company:

	Candele Company	Dortmund Company
Beginning finished goods inventory . . .	$ 7,500	$ 8,900
Beginning goods in process inventory . .	6,200	11,000
Beginning raw materials inventory	3,200	4,120
Depreciation of factory equipment	12,000	17,500
Direct labor	5,000	7,000
Ending finished goods inventory	6,150	10,900
Ending goods in process inventory	7,700	9,500
Ending raw materials inventory	2,300	1,700
Factory utilities	3,000	2,200
Factory supplies used	1,800	2,400
General and administrative expenses . .	17,000	25,000
Indirect labor	650	960
Repairs, factory equipment	1,660	2,550
Raw materials purchases	13,500	16,300
Sales salaries	15,000	14,000

Calculate the cost of goods manufactured and the cost of goods sold for each company.

Exercise 20–4
Identifying components of financial statements
(LO 3)

For each of the following account balances in a manufacturing company's ledger, indicate by a ✓ in the appropriate column whether it will appear on the balance sheet, the income statement, the manufacturing statement, or a detailed schedule of factory overhead costs. Assume that the income statement shows the calculation of cost of goods sold and the manufacturing statement shows only the total amount of factory overhead.

Note that an account balance may appear on more than one report. For example, the ending inventory of finished goods appears on both the balance sheet and the income statement.

Account	Balance Sheet	Income Statement	Manufacturing Statement	Overhead Schedule
Accounts receivable				
Bad debts expense				
Beginning finished goods inventory				
Beginning goods in process inventory				
Beginning raw materials inventory				
Cash				
Depreciation of factory building				
Depreciation of factory equipment				
Depreciation expense, office building				
Depreciation expense, office equipment				
Direct labor				
Ending finished goods inventory				
Ending goods in process inventory				
Ending raw materials inventory				
Factory supervision				
Factory supplies used				
Income taxes				
Insurance on factory building				
Insurance expense, office building				
Office supplies used				
Property taxes on factory building and equipment				
Raw materials purchases				
Sales				

Exercise 20–5
Preparing a manufacturing statement
(LO 3)

After Ennunzi Corporation posted its adjusting entries on December 31, 1994, the General Ledger included the following account balances. (Some accounts in the General Ledger have not been listed.)

Sales	$1,425,000
Raw materials inventory, December 31, 1993	78,000
Goods in process inventory, December 31, 1993	91,050
Finished goods inventory, December 31, 1993	114,750
Raw materials purchases	229,650
Direct labor	273,300
Factory supplies used	27,600
Indirect labor	67,200
Repairs, factory equipment	12,000
Rent on factory building	99,000
Selling expenses	172,800
General and administrative expenses	201,900

The ending inventories are

Raw materials inventory, December 31, 1994. . . .	$ 71,250
Goods in process inventory, December 31, 1994 . .	63,300
Finished goods inventory, December 31, 1994 . . .	106,950

Given this information, prepare a manufacturing statement for Ennunzi Corporation. Include the individual overhead account balances.

Exercise 20–6
Preparing a manufacturing company's income statement
(LO 2, 3)

Use the information provided in Exercise 20–5 to prepare an income statement for Ennunzi Corporation.

Exercise 20–7
Understanding the manufacturing process
(LO 4)

The following partially completed flowchart is similar to Illustration 20–5 on page 1079. Some of the boxes in the flowchart show cost amounts while other boxes contain question marks. Calculate the cost that should appear in each box with a question mark.

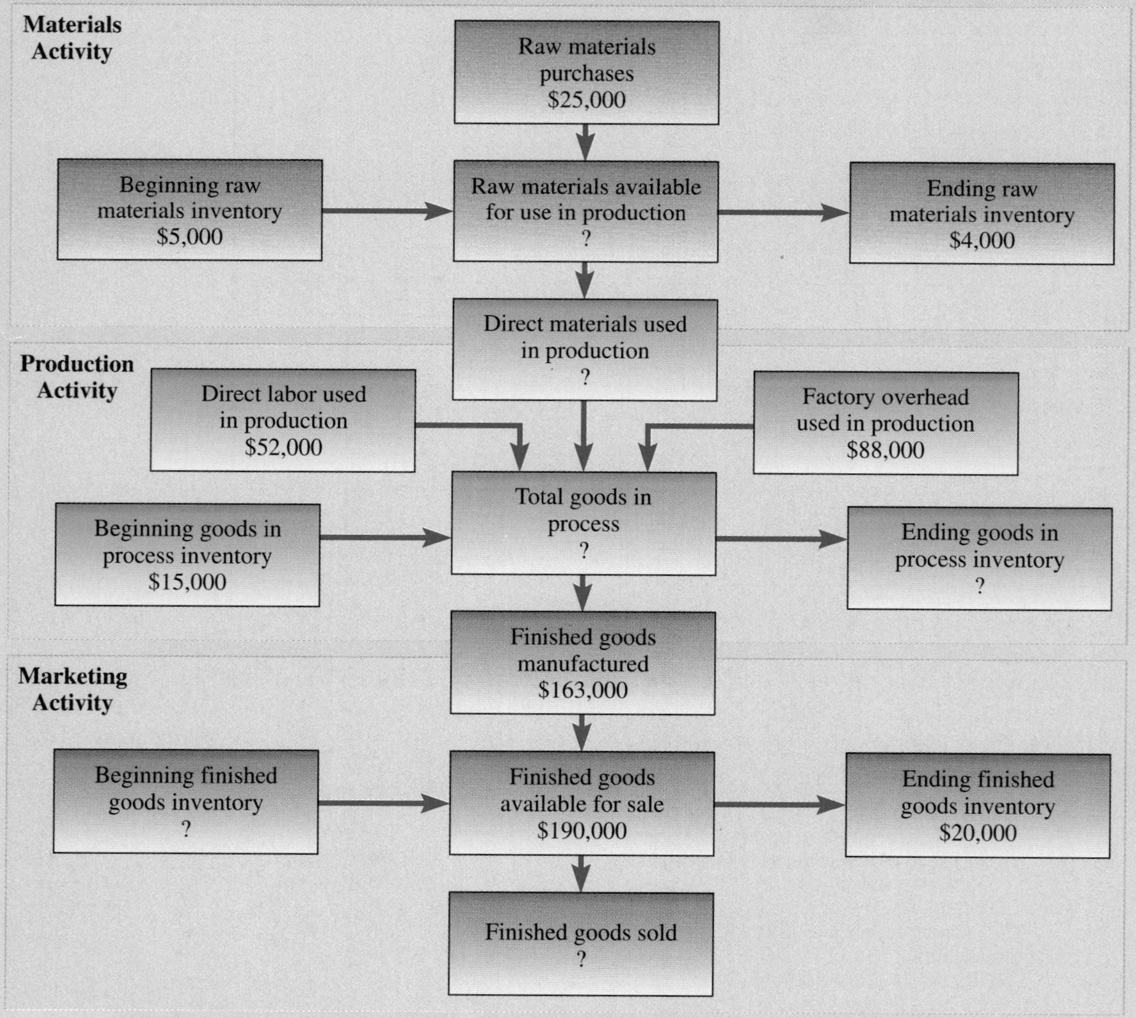

Exercise 20–8
Identifying facts about manufacturing accounts (LO 4)

The following chart lists seven accounts used in general accounting systems for manufacturers. Fill in the requested facts for each account. The first row is completed for you.

Account	Balance at Beginning of Year	Entries to Account Prior to Closing	Closing Entries Made to Account	Closed at End of Year?	Financial Statements on which Balance Is Reported
Raw Materials Inventory	Cost of raw materials on hand at end of prior year	None	Credited for beginning balance, Debited for ending balance	No	Manufacturing Statement Balance Sheet
Raw Materials Purchases					
Direct Labor					
Factory Overhead					
Goods in Process Inventory					
Finished Goods Inventory					
Manufacturing Summary					

Exercise 20–9
Making closing entries to the Manufacturing Summary account (LO 5)

The International Company manufactures products and accounts for its activities using a general accounting system. The following account balances are taken from the company's ledger at the end of the year before closing:

Raw Materials Inventory	$ 10,000
Goods in Process Inventory	8,000
Raw Materials Purchases	42,000
Direct Labor	55,000
Factory Overhead	110,000

Physical counts at the end of the year show:

Raw Materials Inventory	$ 9,000
Goods in Process Inventory	8,800

Prepare the closing entries that should be made to the Manufacturing Summary account, except for the entry to the Income Summary account.

Exercise 20–10
Making closing entries to the Income Summary account
(LO 5)

These additional account balances are taken from the ledger of The International Company described in Exercise 20–9.

Finished Goods Inventory	$ 15,000
Sales	400,000
Selling Expenses	61,000
General and Administrative Expenses	43,500
Income Taxes Expense	36,720

A physical count at the end of the year shows:

Finished Goods Inventory	$ 18,500

Prepare the closing entries that should be made to the Income Summary account. Assume that the balance of the Manufacturing Summary account is $207,200 (debit) after the entries in Exercise 20–9 are posted.

Exercise 20–11
Closing entries for a manufacturing company
(LO 5)

Use the information provided in Exercise 20–5 and prepare closing entries for Ennunzi Corporation.

Exercise 20–12
Closing entries for a manufacturing company
(LO 5)

The following account balances are taken from the Gibraltar Corporation's accounting records after adjustments as of December 31, 1994. Also presented are the results of physical counts and valuations of the ending inventories.

Sales	$140,800
Raw materials purchases	22,400
Direct labor	33,040
Factory overhead	27,200
Selling expenses	15,280
General and administrative expenses	13,920
Income taxes expense	15,840
Raw materials inventory	4,160
Goods in process inventory	5,680
Finished goods inventory	3,440
Ending inventories:	
Raw materials	$ 6,480
Goods in process	8,400
Finished goods	5,280

Prepare closing entries for the company.

Exercise 20–13
Overhead rate calculation and analysis
(LO 6)

Fantastic Company uses the proportional relationship between factory overhead and direct labor costs to assign factory overhead to its inventories of goods in process and finished goods. The company incurred the following costs during 1994:

Direct materials used	$425,000
Direct labor costs	960,000
Factory overhead costs	864,000

a. Determine the company's overhead rate.

b. Under the assumption that the company's $38,000 ending goods in process inventory had $12,000 of direct labor costs, determine the inventory's direct material costs.

c. Under the assumption that the company's $225,000 ending finished goods inventory had $130,000 of direct material costs, determine the inventory's direct labor cost and its factory overhead costs.

Exercise 20–14
Allocating costs to ending inventories
(LO 6)

According to physical counts, Harding Company's ending goods in process inventory consisted of 1,000 units of partially completed product and its finished goods inventory consisted of 3,000 units of product. The factory manager determined that the goods in process inventory included direct materials cost of $2.20 per unit and direct labor cost of $1.50 per unit. Finished goods were estimated to have $3.50 of direct materials cost per unit and $2.00 of direct labor cost per unit. During the period, the company incurred these costs:

Direct materials	$125,000
Direct labor	40,000
Factory overhead	72,000

The company allocates factory overhead to goods in process and finished goods inventories by relating overhead to direct labor cost.

a. Calculate the overhead rate (overhead as a percentage of direct labor).

b. Calculate the total cost of the two ending inventories.

c. Because this was Harding Company's first year, there were no beginning inventories. Calculate the cost of goods sold for the year, and show how much direct material, direct labor, and factory overhead are included in the cost of goods sold.

Problems

Problem 20–1
Allocating costs to goods in process; preparing the manufacturing statement
(LO 3, 4, 6)

Dominion Company's General Ledger included the following items related to its manufacturing activities for 1994. The accounts have been adjusted, but have not yet been closed.

Raw materials inventory	$ 56,400
Goods in process inventory	66,240
Raw materials purchases	207,600
Direct labor	300,000
Indirect labor	129,480
Factory utilities	72,960
Repairs, factory equipment	20,040
Rent on factory building	56,400
Property taxes on factory equipment	12,840
Factory insurance expired	10,680
Factory supplies used	23,280
Depreciation of factory equipment	55,200
Amortization of patents	9,120

In addition, the ending inventory of raw materials is $60,720. The ending inventory of goods in process is not known, but it is known that the company makes a single product and that 3,000 units of goods were in process on December 31, 1994. Each unit contained an estimated $12.00 of direct materials and had $5.00 of direct labor cost assigned to it.

Required

1. Calculate the overhead rate based on the relationship between total factory overhead cost and total direct labor cost. Then, determine the cost of the ending goods in process inventory.
2. Prepare a manufacturing statement for 1994.
3. Prepare entries to close the manufacturing accounts to Manufacturing Summary and to close the Manufacturing Summary account.

Problem 20–2
Preparing manufacturing and income statements
(LO 2, 3, 4)

The following alphabetical list of items was taken from the adjusted trial balance and other records of Jackson Manufacturing Company before the year-end closing entries were recorded:

Advertising expense	$ 6,480
Depreciation expense, office equipment	2,700
Depreciation expense, selling equipment	3,240
Depreciation of factory equipment	11,340
Direct labor	209,520
Factory supervision	38,880
Factory supplies used	5,940
Factory utilities	10,800
Income taxes expense	43,740
Indirect labor	18,900
Inventories:	
Raw materials, January 1	52,920
Raw materials, December 31	54,540
Goods in process, January 1	4,280
Goods in process, December 31	4,500
Finished goods, January 1	56,700
Finished goods, December 31	45,360
Miscellaneous production costs	2,700
Office salaries expense	22,680
Raw materials purchases	278,100
Rent expense, office space	7,560
Rent expense, selling space	8,640
Rent on factory building	25,920
Repairs, factory equipment	9,720
Sales	972,540
Sales discounts	18,360
Sales salaries expense	94,500
Transportation-in on raw materials	8,100

Required

Prepare a manufacturing statement and an income statement for the company. The income statement should present separate categories for (*a*) selling expenses and (*b*) general and administrative expenses.

Problem 20–3
Calculating cost components and preparing the manufacturing statement
(LO 3, 4, 6)

Kennedy Company began this year with the following inventories: raw materials, $40,000; goods in process, $60,000; and finished goods, $70,000. The company uses the ratio between its total factory overhead and total direct labor costs to assign overhead cost to its inventories of goods in process and finished goods. At the end of this year, this information was known about the costs of the inventories (one amount is missing):

	Raw Materials	Goods in Process	Finished Goods
Direct materials costs	$22,000	$13,000	$20,000
Direct labor costs	–0–	10,000	25,000
Factory overhead costs	–0–	?	30,000
Totals	$22,000	$?	$75,000

This additional information was available from the company's records:

Total factory overhead costs incurred during the year	$360,000
Cost of all goods manufactured during the year	900,000

Required

Prepare a manufacturing statement for Kennedy Company for the year. You can develop all the missing data from what you have been given.

Problem 20–4
Adjusting and closing entries, allocating overhead costs
(LO 4, 5, 6)

Following is the unadjusted trial balance of the Browning Company as of December 31, 1994:

Cash	$ 25,000	
Accounts receivable	100,000	
Raw materials inventory	80,000	
Goods in process inventory	40,000	
Finished goods inventory	90,000	
Factory equipment	200,000	
Accumulated depreciation, factory equipment		$ 45,000
Accounts payable		65,000
Wages payable		
Income taxes payable		
Common stock		175,000
Retained earnings		151,000
Sales		625,000
Raw materials purchases	250,000	
Direct labor	93,000	
Indirect labor	35,000	
Factory utilities	27,000	
Repairs, factory equipment	6,000	
Depreciation of factory equipment		
Selling expenses	65,000	
General and administrative expenses	50,000	
Income taxes expense		
Total	$1,061,000	$1,061,000

The following adjusting entries need to be made:

a. Depreciation on the factory equipment for the year is $30,000.

b. Accrued direct labor wages are $7,000.

c. Accrued indirect labor wages are $2,000.

d. Accrued income taxes are estimated to be $32,000.

The raw materials ending inventory was $84,000. These facts were known about the other ending inventories:

	Materials Cost per Unit	Labor Cost per Unit	Units
Goods in process	$10.00	$4.00	2,000
Finished goods	16.00	9.00	5,000

Required

1. Present the prescribed adjusting entries.
2. Determine the total adjusted overhead cost, the total adjusted direct labor cost, and the overhead cost to direct labor cost ratio.
3. Determine the cost of the ending inventories of goods in process and finished goods.
4. Present the closing entries.

Problem 20–5
Preparing manufacturing schedules and financial statements
(LO 3)

Using the answers to Problem 20–4, prepare the following financial statements for the Browning Company:

1. Schedule of overhead costs for 1994.
2. Manufacturing statement for 1994 (show only one line for factory overhead).
3. Income statement for 1994.
4. Balance sheet for December 31, 1994.

Problem 20–6
Analytical essay
(LO 3, 4)

Analyze Illustration 20–5 on page 1079 and describe how the activities represented by the flowchart are presented in a company's managerial and financial accounting reports.

Problem 20–7
Analytical essay
(Review problem)

Review the facts given in Problem 20–2 for Jackson Manufacturing Company. If the cost of goods sold for the year equals $629,420, what is the cost of goods manufactured? Given that the cost of materials used during the year is $284,580, recall what you learned in Chapter 19 about merchandise turnover and calculate the turnover rates for Jackson's raw materials and finished goods inventories. Then, discuss some possible reasons for the differences between the turnover rates for the two inventories.

Alternate Problems

Problem 20–1A
Allocating costs to goods in process; preparing the manufacturing statement
(LO 3, 4, 6)

Delevan Company's General Ledger included the following items related to its manufacturing activities for 1994. The accounts have been adjusted, but have not yet been closed.

Raw materials inventory	$ 45,800
Goods in process inventory	38,000
Raw materials purchases	175,000
Direct labor	250,000
Indirect labor	35,000
Factory utilities	26,000
Repairs, factory equipment	19,000
Rent on factory building	13,500
Property taxes on factory equipment	18,000
Factory insurance expired	4,000
Factory supplies used	7,000
Depreciation of factory equipment	16,000
Amortization of patents	36,500

In addition, the ending inventory of raw materials is known to be $50,000. The ending inventory of goods in process is not known, but it is known that the company makes a single product and that 500 units of goods were in process on December 31, 1994. Each unit contained an estimated $10.00 of direct materials and had $32.00 of direct labor cost assigned to it.

Required

1. Calculate the overhead rate based on the relationship between total factory overhead cost and total direct labor cost. Then, determine the cost of the ending goods in process inventory.
2. Prepare a manufacturing statement for 1994.
3. Prepare entries to close the manufacturing accounts to Manufacturing Summary and to close the Manufacturing Summary account.

Problem 20–2A
Preparing manufacturing and income statements
(LO 2, 3, 4)

The following alphabetical list of items was taken from the adjusted trial balance and other records of Jefferson Manufacturing Company before the year-end closing entries were recorded:

Advertising expense	$ 8,100
Depreciation expense, office equipment	3,375
Depreciation expense, selling equipment	4,050
Depreciation of factory equipment	14,175
Direct labor	261,900
Factory supervision	48,600
Factory supplies used	7,425
Factory utilities	13,500
Income taxes expense	54,675
Indirect labor	23,625
Inventories:	
Raw materials, January 1	66,150
Raw materials, December 31	68,175
Goods in process, January 1	5,350
Goods in process, December 31	7,625
Finished goods, January 1	70,875
Finished goods, December 31	56,700
Miscellaneous production costs	3,375
Office salaries expense	28,350
Raw materials purchases	347,625
Rent expense, office space	9,450
Rent expense, selling space	10,800
Rent on factory building	32,400
Repairs, factory equipment	12,150
Sales	1,215,675
Sales discounts	22,950
Sales salaries expense	118,125
Transportation-in on raw materials	10,125

Required

Prepare a manufacturing statement and an income statement for the company. The income statement should present separate categories for (*a*) selling expenses and (*b*) general and administrative expenses.

Problem 20–3A
Calculating cost components and preparing the manufacturing statement
(LO 3, 4, 6)

Carter Company began this year with the following inventories: raw materials, $50,000; goods in process, $30,000; and finished goods, $80,000. The company uses the ratio between its total factory overhead and total direct labor costs to assign overhead costs to its inventories of goods in process and finished goods. At the end of this year, this information was known about the costs of the inventories (one amount is missing):

	Raw Materials	Goods in Process	Finished Goods
Direct material costs.	$15,000	$20,000	$ 40,000
Direct labor costs	–0–	25,000	42,000
Factory overhead costs	–0–	?	63,000
Totals	$15,000	$?	$145,000

This additional information was available from the company's records:

Total factory overhead costs incurred during the year . .	$240,000
Cost of all goods manufactured during the year.	800,000

Required

Prepare a manufacturing statement for Carter Company for the year. You can develop all the missing data from what you have been given.

Problem 20–4A
Adjusting and closing entries, allocating overhead costs
(LO 4, 5, 6)

Following is the partially adjusted trial balance of the Colt Company as of December 31, 1994:

Cash	$ 43,000	
Accounts receivable	120,000	
Raw materials inventory	60,000	
Goods in process inventory	50,000	
Finished goods inventory	150,000	
Factory equipment	400,000	
Accumulated depreciation, factory equipment		$ 65,000
Accounts payable		100,000
Wages payable		
Income taxes payable		
Common stock		200,000
Retained earnings		259,000
Sales		950,000
Raw materials purchases	350,000	
Direct labor	137,500	
Indirect labor	55,000	
Factory utilities	44,500	
Repairs, factory equipment	14,000	
Depreciation of factory equipment		
Selling expenses	85,000	
General and administrative expenses	65,000	
Income taxes expense		
Total	$1,574,000	$1,574,000

The following adjusting entries need to be made:

a. Depreciation on the factory equipment for the year is $62,500.

b. Accrued direct labor wages are $12,500.

c. Accrued indirect labor wages are $4,000.

d. Accrued income taxes are estimated to be $30,000.

The raw materials ending inventory was $54,000. These facts were known about the other ending inventories:

	Materials Cost per Unit	Labor Cost per Unit	Units
Goods in process	$ 8.00	$5.00	3,500
Finished goods	15.00	7.50	4,000

Required

1. Present the prescribed adjusting entries.
2. Determine the total adjusted overhead cost, the total adjusted direct labor cost, and the overhead cost to direct labor cost ratio.
3. Determine the cost of the ending inventories of goods in process and finished goods.
4. Present the closing entries.

Problem 20–5A
Preparing manufacturing schedules and financial statements
(LO 3)

Using the answers to Problem 20–4, prepare the following financial statements for the Colt Company:

1. Schedule of overhead costs for 1994.
2. Manufacturing statement for 1994 (show only one line for factory overhead).
3. Income statement for 1994.
4. Balance sheet for December 31, 1994.

Problem 20–6A
Analytical essay
(LO 3, 4, 5)

Analyze Illustration 20–5 on page 1079 and describe the journal entries used to record the activities represented by the flowchart.

Problem 20–7A
Analytical essay
(Review problem)

Review the facts given in Problem 20–2A for Jefferson Manufacturing Company. If the cost of goods sold for the year equals $784,775, what is the cost of goods manufactured? Given that the cost of materials used during the year is $355,725, recall what you learned in Chapter 19 about merchandise turnover and calculate the turnover rates for Jefferson's raw materials and finished goods inventories. Then, discuss some possible reasons for the differences between the turnover rates for the two inventories.

Provocative Problems

Provocative Problem 20–1
Ranger Manufacturing Company
(LO 4, 6)

Ranger Manufacturing Company has operated for three years. Its business is manufacturing and selling a single product. Although annual sales increased by 20% and 25% in the last two years, it appears that net income increased by only about 7% and 14%. The company president, Ryan Knowland, has asked you to analyze the situation and tell him why profits have lagged behind sales. Knowland is primarily a production expert and knows little about accounting. Also, the person who keeps the company's books has a limited understanding of accounting for manufacturing.

The company's condensed income statements for the past three years show:

	1994	1995	1996
Sales	$500,000	$600,000	$750,000
Cost of goods sold:			
Finished goods inventory, beginning	$ -0-	$ 33,000	$ 49,500
Cost of goods manufactured	165,000	218,750	314,000
Goods available for sale	$165,000	$251,750	$363,500
Finished goods inventory, ending	33,000	49,500	72,600
Cost of goods sold	$132,000	$202,250	$290,900
Gross profit from sales	$368,000	$397,750	$459,100
Selling and administrative expenses	80,000	90,000	108,750
Net income	$288,000	$307,750	$350,350

As you have checked into things, you have uncovered the following additional information:

a. The company sold 5,000 units of its product during the first year it was in business, 6,000 units during the second year, and 7,500 units during the third. All sales were priced at $100 per unit, and no discounts were granted.

b. The finished goods inventory consisted of 500 units at the end of the first year, 750 at the end of the second, and 1,100 at the end of the third.

c. The bookkeeper valued the units in each year's ending finished goods inventory at $66 per unit. The amount reported by the bookkeeper on the income statement as the cost of goods manufactured in each year was the sum of the costs for materials, labor, and overhead incurred in each year.

d. Because the time needed to produce the product is very short, no in-process inventories existed at any of the reporting dates.

Required

Prepare a report for Knowland that shows: (1) the number of units of product manufactured each year, (2) each year's cost to manufacture a unit of product, (3) the cost of each year's ending inventory of finished goods, and (4) each year's selling and administration expenses per unit of product sold. As part of your report, (5) prepare income statements for all three years that show the net income each year (use FIFO for finding the cost of the finished goods inventory). Finally, (6) provide a possible explanation of why the net income has not kept pace with the rising sales volume.

Provocative Problem 20–2
Northwestern Motor Homes
(LO 6)

Several years ago, Samantha Sedalia took over the operation of her family's motor home manufacturing company. The company previously manufactured basic motor homes. However, it recently has turned more and more to building custom vehicles to individual customers' specifications. The seasonal nature of this business means that shop activity is rather slow during October, November, and December when customers are not interested in buying motor homes.

Sedalia has tried to increase business during these slow months. However, most prospective customers who come to the business during these months just don't end up buying. When Sedalia quotes a price for a motor home, most customers during the slow months say that the product is nice but the price is too high, and then leave without placing an order. Sedalia thinks the trouble may lie in using the rule that her father used when he ran the business (before many custom orders were taken). His rule was to "always set the price high enough to make a 10% profit over and above all costs, and be sure that all costs are included."

Sedalia has found that the direct material and direct labor costs are pretty easy to figure but that overhead is another thing. The overhead consists of depreciation of the factory building and machinery, utility costs, property taxes, and so on. In total, these amount to about $20,000 each month, whether she builds any motor homes or not. In applying her father's rule, she finds that she has to charge more for a motor home built during the slow fourth quarter because the overhead is spread over fewer jobs. She readily admits that this practice seems to drive away business during the months when she could most easily handle extra volume. However, she really finds it hard to break her father's rule because, as she says, "Dad did all right in this business for a long time."

Required

Explain why the old price rule leads to higher bids for motor homes that would be built in December than for those built in May, which is a very busy month. You may want to assume some figures to make your point. Suggest how to solve this pricing problem and still follow the rule.

Provocative Problem 20–3
International Business Machines Corporation (LO 2)

Use the financial statements and related footnotes of the IBM annual report shown in Appendix J to complete the following requirements:

a. What types of inventories does IBM own?

b. What method does IBM use to value the inventories?

c. Given the information IBM provides about its inventories, is it certain that IBM is a manufacturing company?

Provocative Problem 20–4
As a Matter of Ethics: Essay

Ethics

Examine the ethics case on page 1082 and provide answers to these questions, together with explanations for your answers:

1. Do you think it is ethical for businessmen and businesswomen to use a social occasion to discuss business?
2. Do you think it is ethical for them to receive tax deductions for the cost of social occasions in which business is discussed?
3. Do you think it is ethical for a person in business to be reimbursed by an employer for a social occasion in which business is discussed?
4. Do you think that it is ethical for a person employed by a corporation to be reimbursed with a profit for a social occasion in which business is discussed?

Answers to Objective Review Questions

LO 1 (*e*)
LO 2 (*b*)
LO 3 (*c*)
LO 4 (*b*)
LO 5 (*e*)
LO 6 (*e*)
LO 7 (*d*)

CHAPTER

21

New Production Management Concepts and Job Order Cost Accounting

Many companies perform unique jobs to satisfy specific customers. For example, a house painter has to understand each customer's desires, buy paint and supplies, hire assistants, do the painting, and collect the bills. Careful accounting helps the painter manage jobs and know how much to charge.

Topical Coverage

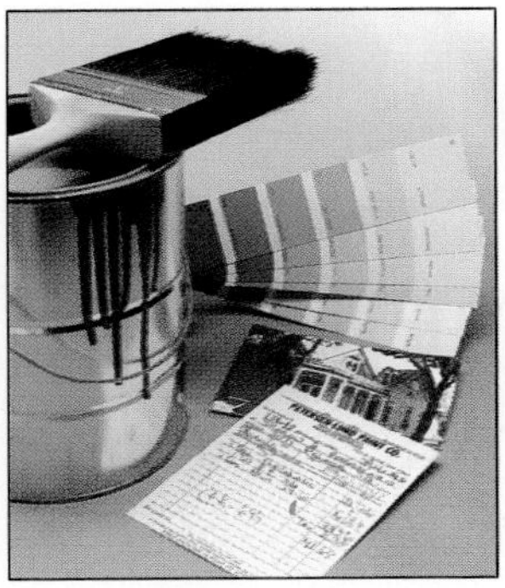

In Chapter 20, you learned some basic concepts about manufacturing and about the general accounting systems that some firms use to account for costs incurred in producing goods. This chapter expands your understanding of manufacturing by looking at five new production management concepts that are changing the way many companies manufacture their products. These concepts are customer orientation, total quality management, just-in-time manufacturing, the theory of constraints, and continuous improvement.

To put these concepts into practice, managers must have more up-to-date and precise information than general accounting systems can provide. General accounting systems are not adequate because they are based on periodic inventory methods. Cost accounting systems based on perpetual inventory methods are much more effective. They constantly track the quantities of materials, goods in process, and finished goods inventories, and thus provide more up-to-date information. In this chapter, we explain one type of cost accounting system called job order cost accounting. These systems are used by companies that manufacture single units or small groups of unique products.

Learning Objectives

After studying Chapter 21, you should be able to:

1. Identify five new production management concepts and explain how they affect the management of manufacturing processes.
2. Describe the type of manufacturing operations in which job order cost accounting systems are used.
3. Explain how job cost sheets are used in job order cost accounting systems.
4. Describe and record the flow of materials, labor, and overhead costs in a job order cost accounting system.
5. Explain how the accounts are adjusted for any overapplied or underapplied factory overhead.
6. Define or explain the words and phrases listed in the chapter glossary.

New Production Management Concepts

LO 1 Identify five new production management concepts and explain how they affect the management of manufacturing processes.

Several factors have encouraged the development of new ideas about how companies should manage their production operations. These factors include increased demands by customers for higher quality products, for custom-designed products, and for faster delivery. In addition, the movement toward a worldwide economy and increased competition between United States, Japanese, German, and other foreign manufacturers have forced domestic companies to look for new and more effective management processes.

During the 1970s and 1980s, many companies began to apply several new concepts for managing their manufacturing processes. These new concepts have changed the way they manufacture their products. Many of these changes were not possible earlier because of a lack of computing power. Since that time, dramatic advances in computers have brought about a variety of improvements in manufacturing processes. New kinds of manufacturing equipment, such as computer-controlled robots and machine tools, are now widely used. In addition, the information available to production managers has been greatly expanded. Accounting and other types of information are often available on demand. Coupled with improved communication devices, computers allow companies to transmit data and reports over long distances at low cost, without any delays.

As a result of these forces, new philosophies of management have developed quickly and spread around the world. Among these are five new concepts of how managers should approach their tasks. The following sections of the chapter explain these ideas more completely.

Customer Orientation

The management concept of **customer orientation** means that a company's managers and employees need to be in tune with the wants and needs of customers. This concept extends all the way back into the factory. In effect, customer orientation bends the company's productive ability toward meeting customers' wants and needs. This approach is far different from using advertising and selling efforts to bend customers' wants toward accepting the company's products.

The concept of customer orientation calls for flexible product designs that include options to support individual customer choices. Instead of presenting buyers with products that the seller has already manufactured, the goal is to meet buyers' needs by modifying the products as they are manufactured. The idea is to offer customers more attention and service.

In addition to flexible product designs, the concept of customer orientation calls for flexible production processes that allow a manufacturer to respond quickly to changes in buyers' needs and preferences.

Total Quality Management

A major focus of many companies across the United States as well as in other countries has been to improve the quality of their products and services. Because of the worldwide attention given to the high quality of several Japanese and German manufacturers and the increased demands of customers for high quality, managers have identified quality as one of the most important keys to success in manufacturing. In an effort to implement this new emphasis, many firms have adopted a concept called **total quality management (TQM).**

Under TQM, all managers and employees strive toward higher standards in their work and in the products and services they offer to customers. (Note that these new concepts of production management apply to the production of both products and services. Customers look for flexibility and quality in services as much as they look for them in products.)

Traditional production processes tend to leave the responsibility for quality in the hands of a somewhat independent group of quality control inspec-

AS A MATTER OF
Fact

In the '50s, Japanese products were a joke. They lacked quality and many times totally missed the market. But Japanese people spent years learning to understand the United States, and in the '70s the situation changed. The Japanese have applied quality techniques to manufacturing consumer products and the world has benefited.

Following World War II, the United States could make almost any product, and if it was close to usable and affordable, customers would buy it. The United States produced about half of the world's total production, and we consumed an equal amount. We dominated and customers had no choice. Now, we have formidable foreign competition . . . [that] has excellent education, ample capital, and is strongly motivated. There is a beneficial payoff from these advantages in price, performance, and ease of use. If we wish to increase, or even maintain our current living standard, we must be a net contributor in the world market.

American industries need to start employing Total Quality Management, a philosophy that has been credited with the Japanese success. Before embarking on TQM in any organization, there are two basic facts that must be understood.

First, customer focus—satisfying customer needs is the No. 1 reason for the existence of any business. The cars that Chrysler is trying to sell in Japan still have the steering wheel on the left side, [even though the Japanese] drive on the left side of the road. How successful would the Japanese have been in this country if they had insisted on sending us cars with the steering wheel on the right? We must learn to make things the way the customer wants, not the way we dictate.

Second, we must understand that virtually everything we do is a process. A process is defined as having inputs, outputs, and a series of steps between them. It is important to understand that businesses are processes because that allows us to define them, measure them, and make improvements in them.

Let's get on with the task. We need to be totally committed to quality in business, education, and government. We need to be competitive in the world marketplace so that we can contribute to the welfare of others. As author and TQM expert W. Edwards Deming has said, improved quality yields higher productivity through decreased scrap, rework, mistakes, delays, snags, and better use of resources. Higher productivity allows us to capture market share with lower prices and provide more jobs.

Dave Kent, "Bashing Japan won't improve quality in America," *Colorado Springs Gazette-Telegraph*, January 19, 1992, p. G2.

tors. The focus usually is on an inspection of completed products. In contrast, TQM requires a focus on quality throughout the production process. The strategy is to identify defective work when and where it occurs. This constant focus on quality reminds each employee of the need to eliminate defective work at all stages of production activity. The expected results are fewer defects in completed products and potential reductions of costs associated with reworking rejected products.

A company that uses TQM rewards employees when they find defects. Without this emphasis, employees are more likely to ignore defects in partially completed units that arrive at their workstations. After all, pointing out problems may require extra effort, paperwork, and hostile reactions from other employees. Thus, an essential ingredient of TQM is changing the attitudes of employees to encourage a new commitment to quality. TQM also encourages employees to try new ways to improve quality. By keeping an open mind and rewarding innovation, managers committed to TQM can tap the knowledge and abilities of the people closest to the work.

A company that operates under TQM has a strong emphasis on the value of reaching higher quality levels. For example, a TQM company will establish quality standards and measure quality results at each stage of production. Many companies set maximum rejection rates as targets for each workstation. Then, they encourage employees by rewarding those who reach their targets and by displaying actual rejection rates.

Just-in-Time Manufacturing

Managers recognize that commitments to customers and quality lead to profits only if the company's activities are carried out efficiently. Customer orientation promotes efficiency because fewer unmarketable products are manufactured. Total quality management promotes efficiency because it reduces the cost of reworking or repairing defective products. Another strategy for improving efficiency is to use a **just-in-time (JIT)** manufacturing system.

Under a JIT approach, companies acquire or produce inventory only as it is needed. Thus, manufacturing activity is scheduled so that finished products are assembled only as they are needed for delivery to customers. Furthermore, firms produce components of the finished product only as needed in the assembly process. In addition, raw materials are obtained from suppliers only when the company is ready to use them. In effect, the company tries to keep no more than bare minimum amounts of finished goods, goods in process, and raw materials inventories.

Installing a JIT system can be a way of implementing the concept of customer orientation. In other words, companies manufacture products in response to predicted or actual customer orders. The orientation of JIT is that products are *pulled* through the manufacturing process by the orders received from customers. This is in contrast to a more traditional approach in which products are *pushed* through production by the insertion of raw materials and the application of labor and overhead. The traditional approach then relies on marketing and sales forces to push the finished units on to customers.

In 1991, Toyota announced a striking example of using JIT with a customer orientation. Toyota declared that all automobiles sold in Japan are to be produced only in response to specific orders from individual customers. Under this system, customers place orders through dealers and wait only two weeks to take delivery. The advantages are that customers get exactly what they want with a relatively short wait and that neither the manufacturer nor dealers have to invest in large inventories of automobiles.

Note that JIT may be applied to raw materials and goods in process as well as to finished products. Consider the following production line for a product that has four components added in sequence as the units move toward completion:

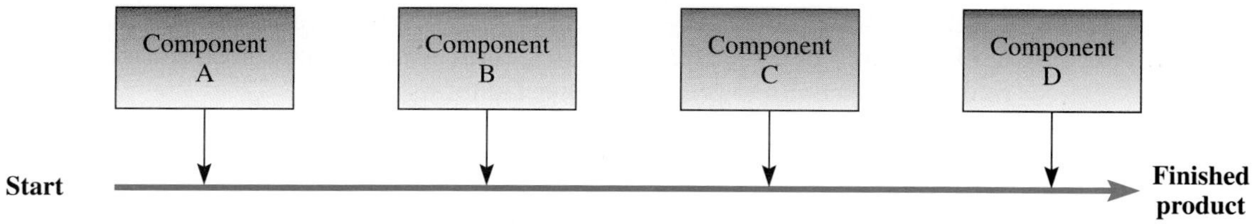

The traditional approach to manufacturing accumulates inventories of the components between the workstations to avoid the risk of shutting down the production line because of a shortage of any of the four components. In contrast, the JIT management goal calls for the four components to arrive at the production line *just in time* to be used. If this goal can be accomplished, the company will have less invested in inventories and will be able to use the funds to reduce debt or invest in other profitable activities.

A JIT approach can be even more efficient when a product consists of several components that are manufactured in separate production lines. For example, the components of an air conditioner include a case, a compressor, a fan, a heat exchanger, and a control system. Each component is the output of a separate production line. If the JIT approach can be implemented throughout the entire air conditioner factory, large gains in efficiency are possible.

Not all manufacturing situations allow the use of JIT methods. A JIT company must be able to predict the timing and nature of customer orders. An effective total quality management system must be in place to carefully control the manufacturing processes. Otherwise, unexpected numbers of defective units may cause all production activity to stop. JIT also requires dependable suppliers who are willing to make frequent shipments of small quantities. Computers and good communication equipment are essential. For example, some companies use systems that send orders directly from the manufacturer's production line to the supplier's production line.

Theory of Constraints

The fourth new concept for improving a company's productive operations is the **theory of constraints (TOC).** The basic idea is that management should focus on the factors that limit or constrain the operations of the business. After the constraints have been identified, management should develop ways of relaxing or overcoming these constraining processes.

From a TOC perspective, the company's overall goal is to minimize the goods in process inventory waiting to be processed while maximizing the throughput. **Throughput** is the added value of finished products processed through the system. The added value per unit is the selling price minus the direct costs of production.

Management can apply the theory of constraints to the whole production process, including plant layout, the numbers of employees and the mix of their skills, the quantity and nature of the machinery, the availability of raw materials, and the methods used to distribute finished goods to customers. The ideal outcome has all machines and workers fully occupied without limiting, or constraining, any other machines or workers. Furthermore, the output level should be high enough to meet market demand for the product. The key to increasing throughput is to find the most constraining process or bottleneck that creates excess in-process inventories. These inventories are said to be upstream of the bottleneck when they are waiting to be processed. A bottleneck also creates downstream inefficiencies because employees and machines must wait for units to reach their workstations.

Consider the previous example of the production line that combines four components to produce finished goods. If the workstation for adding Component B to the product is a bottleneck, partially completed units back up behind it until they are processed. In addition, the workers and machines used to add Components C and D are starved, or waiting unproductively to do their jobs. If Components C and D are themselves outputs from other production lines, they will stack up at the main line, and excess inventories will also accumulate behind them. The final result is that the resources of the company are not used efficiently and finished products are not produced or sold to customers as quickly as they could be.

Once a bottleneck is identified, management figures out how to relieve it and increase throughput. The solution may be as simple as adding more machinery or extra shifts of workers, or it may require redesigning the production line or the product.

Applying the theory of constraints is a continuous process. After the first constraint is identified and relieved, you search for the next one. That is, as soon as one bottleneck is cleared up, some other constraint begins to act as the factor that is limiting throughput. Management should then focus attention on locating this constraint and improving performance.

Continuous Improvement

The fifth new production management concept calls for an attitude of **continuous improvement** throughout the entire organization. With this attitude, every manager and employee constantly looks for ways to improve company operations. This includes customer service, product quality, product features, the production process, and employee interactions. An attitude of continuous improvement rejects the tendency to think that anything is ever "good enough." New ideas are constantly being tried and old ideas are constantly being questioned.

The relationship between continuous improvement and the other production management concepts should be clear. With this attitude, the company's employees are committed to meeting customers' needs, to improving quality, and to increasing efficiency. With continuous improvement, there is no place for resistance to change. Instead, managers and employees seek every opportunity for growth and increased profitability. Because of the intense competition in today's world economy, a company is less likely to fall behind if its employees are committed to continuous improvement.

Production Management and Cost Accounting

With this background in place, we now begin to examine cost accounting systems that help management gain control over the production process. In Chapter 20, you learned several basic concepts of manufacturing. You saw that companies employ three components of production (materials, labor, and overhead) and move products through three inventories (raw materials, goods in process, and finished goods). Chapter 20 explained how a general accounting system can account for manufacturing activity. Although general accounting systems are still used by smaller companies, cost accounting systems generate more timely and more precise information.

Under a general accounting system, managers have to wait for physical counts of the inventories to learn what has happened. Even then, the information may not be very precise because the costs of the goods in process and finished goods inventories are based on subjective estimates.

Under a cost accounting system, production information is available quickly. Because perpetual records are used for the inventories, the information in the accounts is as up to date as the most recent transactions. Computer systems can record events in the factory almost as soon as they occur. Cost accounting information is also based on more precise measures of product costs.

With so many different kinds of companies operating today, many different cost accounting systems are used in practice. The cost accounting system used by a company depends on the nature of its products and its manufacturing activities. The variety of cost accounting systems is so extensive that it would not be possible to explain all of them even in an advanced textbook. However, most cost accounting systems are either job order or process cost accounting systems. The rest of this chapter explains job order cost accounting systems, where they are used, and how they work. We explain process cost accounting systems in the next chapter.

Job order and process cost accounting systems were developed long before the new production management concepts described earlier. Nevertheless, these cost accounting systems have proven to be flexible and adaptable to different environments. In fact, they are still used to meet the new needs created by these recent developments.

Characteristics of Job Order Manufacturing Operations

LO 2 Describe the type of manufacturing operations in which job order cost accounting systems are used.

Many companies manufacture products that are individually designed to meet the needs of each customer. Each unique product is manufactured separately. Because the products are often produced in response to special orders, their production is called **job order manufacturing.** In this type of manufacturing, the production of a unique product is called a **job.** Some items that might be produced as jobs include a special machine tool, a building, a yacht, or a piece of custom-made jewelry. All of these items are built to meet the unique demands of specific customers. When a job involves producing more than one unit of a unique product, it is often called a **job lot.** Products produced as job lots might include benches for a new church, imprinted tee shirts for a 10K race or a company picnic, and advertising signs for a chain of stores.

Although job order operations are usually described using examples of manufacturing operations, they also apply to service companies. Many, if not most, service companies meet their customers' needs by performing a unique service for each customer. Examples of such services include a CPA's audit of a client's financial statements, an interior designer's remodelling of an office, a wedding consultant's planning and supervision of a reception, and a lawyer's defense of a client in a lawsuit. Whether the setting is manufacturing or service, job order operations involve meeting the needs of customers by producing or performing unique jobs.

AS A MATTER OF
Opinion

Management Accounting for Service Firms

Mr. Ward received his BBA in accounting from Baylor University in 1990. He has had audit experience with manufacturing firms, but currently is dealing with firms in service industries, such as real estate and insurance.

Timothy P. Ward
Staff Accountant
KPMG Peat Marwick
Dallas, Texas

Service firms face some of the same problems as manufacturing firms. Customers of all firms now demand better service, delivered in less time, and at a lower cost. Firms maintain their competitive edge by meeting and exceeding their customers' expectations.

I see many parallels between manufacturing firms and service firms. Manufacturing firms have large investments in inventories and capital equipment. They seek to ensure that their production processes are efficient, quality of output is high, and costs are under control. Service firms, however, have most of their investment in personnel, but want the services that they deliver to their customers to be provided with utmost efficiency and at reasonable costs. Success in the service industry requires excellence in every measure of efficiency.

Because their processes appear much simpler than those of manufacturing firms, service firms might appear to have uncomplicated cost or managerial accounting systems; yet, they must schedule and coordinate their resources as carefully as their manufacturing counterparts. Such firms must continually maintain and upgrade the skills of their people in order to take advantage of new opportunities.

With new opportunities constantly developing in this world of perpetual change, I am excited about the prospect of learning even more about how techniques developed for manufacturing firms can be used in service firms.

Like all manufacturing processes, job order manufacturing requires the use of materials, labor, and other manufacturing costs. When materials used in manufacturing can be clearly identified with a particular job, they are defined as direct materials. Similarly, labor used on a particular job is defined as direct labor. Other costs that contribute to the production of more than one job are manufacturing overhead. As you learned in Chapter 20, typical manufacturing overhead items are depreciation on factory buildings and equipment, factory supplies, supervision, maintenance, cleaning, and utilities.

Sequence of Events in a Job Order Manufacturing Operation

In a typical job order manufacturing operation, the arrival of a customer's order for a unique product causes the manufacturer to begin working on a job. In other cases, management may decide to begin work on a job before a contract has been signed with a customer. Such jobs are said to be manufactured on speculation. Regardless of the job's source, the first step is often to predict the cost of completing the job based on the design of the product. The design

ILLUSTRATION 21–1

Manufacturing Activities during March 1994, Medford Machine Tools Company

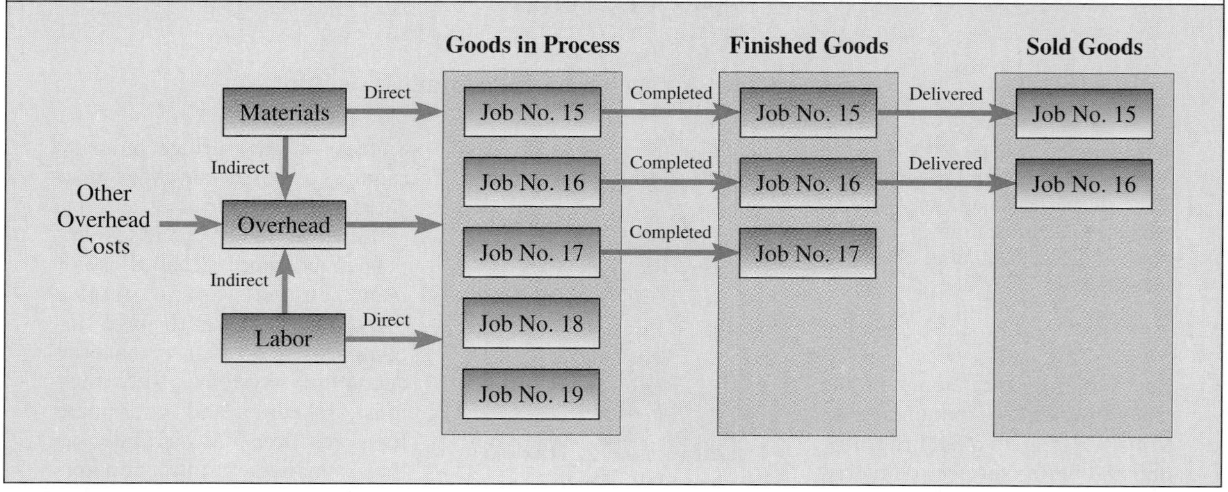

may be prepared by the customer or the manufacturer. This leads to negotiating the sales price and deciding whether to take on the job. Some jobs are priced on a cost-plus basis. Under this arrangement, the customer pays the manufacturer or contractor for the costs incurred on the job plus an agreed amount or rate of profit.

Next, the manufacturer schedules production of the job to fit the needs of the customer and to fit within its available production capacity. The work schedule should provide adequate facilities in the workplace, including tools, machinery, and supplies. Once the schedule is completed, the manufacturer can place orders for raw materials. Under JIT, the orders for materials call for delivery just in time to be used in production. Thereafter, production occurs as materials and labor are applied to the job.

To get an overall view of job order production activity, look at Illustration 21–1. The illustration diagrams the March 1994 production activity of Medford Machine Tools Company. Observe that materials, labor, and overhead were added to Job Nos. 15, 16, 17, 18, and 19 during the month. The company completed Job Nos. 15, 16, and 17 during the month, and delivered Job Nos. 15 and 16 to customers. At the end of the month, Job Nos. 18 and 19 remain in the goods in process inventory and Job No. 17 is in the finished goods inventory. Also notice that labor and materials are divided into their direct and indirect components. The indirect costs are added to other types of overhead, and the total overhead cost is then allocated to the jobs.

Job Order Operations of Service Companies

If a job consists of a service instead of a product, there generally is no lag between working on the job and delivering it to the customer. Typically, the company recognizes the revenue in its financial statements as the service is performed, even though the whole job is not complete. For example, if a service job is estimated to be 60% complete at the end of a period, 60% of the revenues from the job are accrued and reported in the income statement. At

ILLUSTRATION 21–2

Job Cost Sheet

Medford Machine Tools — Medford, Oregon

Customer's name *Cone Lumber Company* Job no. *15*
Address *1542 Clark Center Dr.* City & State *Bend, Oregon*
Job description *High-speed (variable) drill press*
Date promised *March 15* Date started *March 3* Date completed *March 11*

Direct Materials			Direct Labor			Manufacturing Overhead		
Date	Requisition	Cost	Date	Time Ticket	Cost	Date	Rate	Cost
3/3/94	*R-4698*	*100.00*	*3/3/94*	*L-3393*	*120.00*	*3/11/94*	*160% of direct labor cost*	*1,600.00*
3/7/94	*R-4705*	*225.00*	*3/4/94*	*L-3422*	*150.00*			
3/9/94	*R-4725*	*180.00*	*3/5/94*	*L-3456*	*180.00*			
3/10/94	*R-4777*	*95.00*	*3/8/94*	*L-3479*	*60.00*			
			3/9/94	*L-3501*	*90.00*			
			3/10/94	*L-3535*	*240.00*			
			3/11/94	*L-3559*	*160.00*			
Total		*600.00*	Total		*1,000.00*	Total		*1,600.00*

Remarks: *Completed job on March 11 and shipped to customer on March 15. Met all specifications and requirements.*

Summary:	
Materials	*600.00*
Labor	*1,000.00*
Overhead	*1,600.00*
Total cost	*3,200.00*

Signed: *C. Luther, Supervisor*

the same time, the costs of the job incurred to date are reported as expenses. Thus, a service company does not report an inventory of in-process or finished services.

Job Order Cost Accounting

LO 3 Explain how job cost sheets are used in job order cost accounting systems.

Much of the accounting information that managers of job cost operations use to plan and control production activities is not stored in general ledger accounts. Because the information includes a lot of detailed data, it is usually stored in a variety of subsidiary records that are controlled by general ledger accounts. Subsidiary records can be used to store information about raw materials, overhead costs, job in process, and finished goods. You will learn about each of these records as you study the rest of the chapter.

The primary purpose of a **job order cost accounting system** is to determine the cost of producing each job or job lot. To serve this purpose, the accounting system must include a separate record for each job. As production activity occurs, the system must capture information about the costs incurred and charge those costs to the jobs in process.

The separate record that is maintained for each job is called a **job cost sheet.** Illustration 21–2 shows the job cost sheet for a drill press that Medford

Machine Tools Company manufactured for Cone Lumber Company. The job cost sheet identifies the customer, the number assigned to the job, the product, and various dates. The costs of producing the job were recorded on the sheet as the costs were incurred. When the job was completed, the supervisor entered the date of completion, recorded any remarks, and signed the sheet.

In Illustration 21–2, note that the costs are classified as direct materials, direct labor, and overhead. The job cost sheet shows that the direct materials added to Job No. 15 on four different dates totaled $600. The seven entries for direct labor costs totaled $1,000. In addition, Medford charged overhead costs of $1,600 to the job.

During the time a job is being manufactured, its accumulated costs are included in the cost of the goods in process inventory. The collection of job cost sheets for all of the jobs in process make up a subsidiary ledger controlled by the Goods in Process Inventory account in the General Ledger. Managers use the job cost sheets to monitor the costs incurred to date and to predict and control the costs to complete each job.

When a job is finished, the job cost sheet is completed and moved from the file of jobs in process to the file of finished jobs that have not yet been delivered to customers. This latter file acts as a subsidiary ledger controlled by the Finished Goods Inventory account. When a finished job is delivered to the customer, the job cost sheet is moved again to a permanent file that supports the total cost of goods sold reported in the current and prior periods.

The next sections of the chapter describe the documents used in job order cost accounting and the flow of costs through the system. We discuss materials costs, labor costs, and overhead costs in separate sections.

Materials Cost Flows and Related Documents

LO 4 Describe and record the flow of materials, labor, and overhead costs in a job order cost accounting system.

Illustration 21–3 shows the flow of materials cost data through the subsidiary records of the job cost accounting system. As items of material are received from suppliers, workers count and inspect them. They also note the quantity and cost of the items on a receiving report. This report serves as a source document for recording the receipt on a **materials ledger card** and in the general ledger accounts. In nearly all job order cost accounting systems, materials ledger cards are perpetual records that are updated each time units are purchased and each time units are issued for use in production.

As Illustration 21–3 shows, materials may be requisitioned to be used on a specific job (direct materials) or to be used as overhead (indirect materials). The cost of direct materials flows from the materials ledger card to the job cost sheet. The cost of indirect materials flows from the materials ledger card to the Indirect Materials account in the Factory Overhead Ledger. (This is a subsidiary ledger controlled by the Factory Overhead account in the General Ledger.)

Illustration 21–4 shows a materials ledger card for a material used by Medford Machine Tools. Notice that the card identifies the item as a high-speed drill motor. The card also shows the item's stock number, its location in the storeroom, information about the maximum and minimum quantities that should be on hand, and the quantity to be ordered. In Illustration 21–4, note the issue of a motor that was recorded on March 7, 1994. The job cost sheet in Illustration 21–2 shows that this motor was used in manufacturing Job No. 15.

ILLUSTRATION 21–3

Flow of Materials Costs through the Subsidiary Records

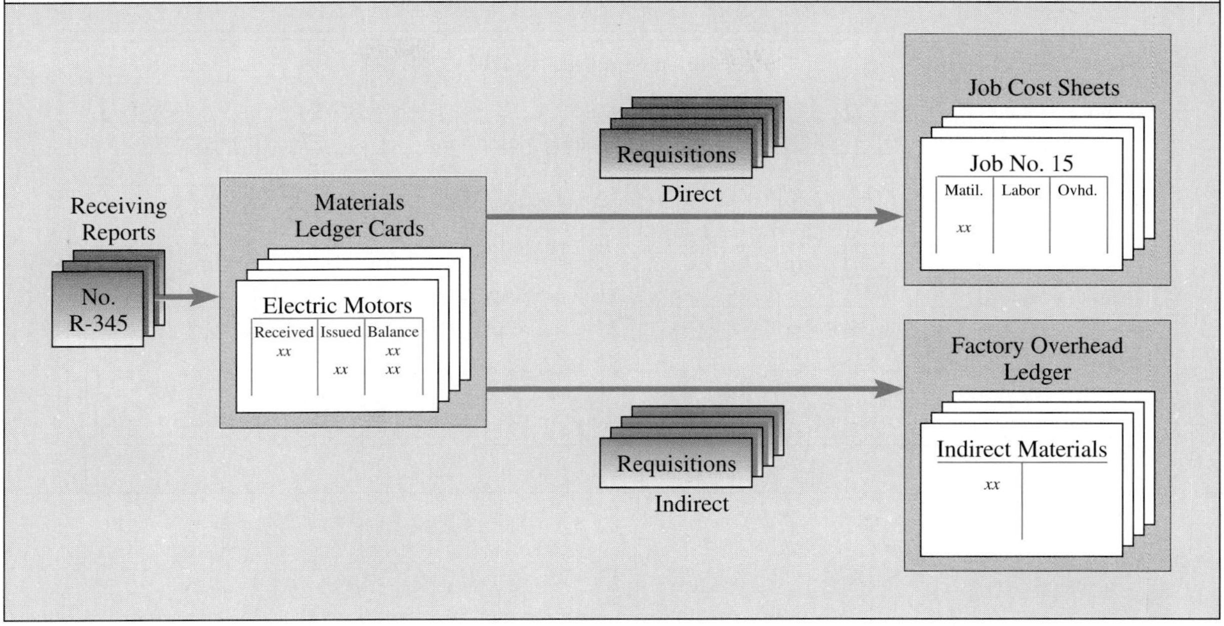

ILLUSTRATION 21–4

Raw Materials Ledger Card

Medford Machine Tools

Item *High-speed drill motor* Stock no. *M-347* Location in storeroom *Bin 137*
Maximum quantity *5 units* Minimum quantity *1 unit* Quantity to reorder *2 units*

	Received				Issued				Balance		
Date	Receiving Report Number	Units	Unit Price	Total Price	Requisition Number	Units	Unit Price	Total Price	Units	Units Price	Total Price
									1	225.00	225.00
3/4/94	C-7117	2	225.00	450.00					3	225.00	675.00
3/7/94					R-4705	1	225.00	225.00	2	225.00	450.00

ILLUSTRATION 21–5

Materials Requisition

Requisition Number R-4705

Job no.	15	Date	3/7/94
Material stock no.	M-347	Material description	Electric motor
Quantity requested	1	Requested by	C. Luther
Quantity provided	1	Date provided	3/7/94
Filled by	M. Bateman	Material received by	C. Luther
Remarks			

Medford Machine Tools

When materials are needed in production, a production manager prepares a **materials requisition** and sends it to the materials manager. Illustration 21–5 shows the materials requisition for the high-speed drill motor for Job No. 15. Notice that the requisition shows the number of the job, the type of material, the quantity needed, and the signature of the manager authorized to make the requisition. To see how the requisition relates to the flow of costs, compare the information on Illustration 21–5 with the March 7, 1994, entries in Illustrations 21–2 and 21–4.

This entry records the use of the motor on Job No 15:

Mar.	7	Goods in Process Inventory—Job No. 15	225.00	
		Raw Materials Inventory—M-347		225.00
		To record use of material on Job No. 15.		

This entry is posted to the general ledger accounts and to the subsidiary records. Posting to the subsidiary records includes a debit to a job cost sheet and a credit to a materials ledger card. An entry to record the use of indirect materials is the same except the debit is to Factory Overhead. In the subsidiary Factory Overhead Ledger, this entry is posted to Indirect Materials.

Labor Cost Flows and Related Documents

Illustration 21–6 shows the flow of labor costs from the Factory Payroll account to the subsidiary records of the job cost accounting system. We mentioned previously that the cost flows in the subsidiary records provide the detailed information needed to manage operations.

ILLUSTRATION 21–6

Flow of Labor Costs to the Subsidiary Records

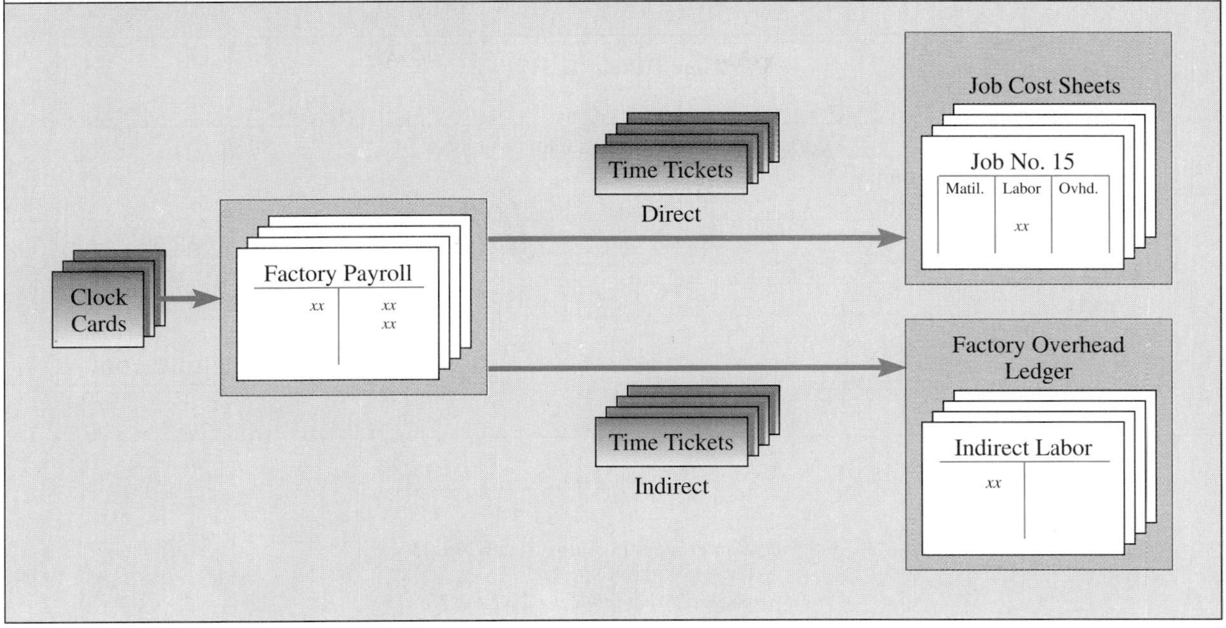

LO 4 Describe and record the flow of materials, labor, and overhead costs in a job order cost accounting system.

The flow of costs in Illustration 21–6 begins with the **clock cards** used by employees to record the number of hours they are at work. Clock cards serve as source documents for the entries to record labor costs. Each pay period, payroll clerks use the clock card data on the number of hours worked to determine total labor cost, which is then debited to the Factory Payroll account. Factory Payroll is a temporary account that holds the total payroll cost (both direct and indirect) until it is allocated to specific jobs and to overhead.

To assign labor costs to specific jobs and to overhead, the clerks must know how each employee's time at work was used and how much it cost. Source documents called **time tickets** usually capture this data. Employees fill out time tickets each day to report how much time they spent on each job. An employee who works on several jobs during a day completes a separate time ticket for each job. Tickets are also prepared for time that should be charged to overhead as indirect labor.

Illustration 21–7 shows a time ticket reporting the time a Medford Machine Tools employee spent working on Job No. 15. Note that the employee's supervisor signed the ticket to confirm its accuracy. The hourly rate and total labor cost were calculated after the time ticket reached the accounting department. To see the effect of this time ticket on the job cost sheet, look in Illustration 21–2 on page 1127 for the entry dated March 8, 1994.

When time tickets report labor used on a specific job, the cost should be recorded as direct labor. For example, this entry records the time ticket in Illustration 21–7:

ILLUSTRATION 21–7

Labor Time Ticket

Time Ticket L-3479

Job no. 15 Date 3/8/94
Employee name T. Thompson Employee number 3969
Time and rate information:
Start time 9:00 Finish time 12:00
Elapsed time 3.0 Hourly rate $20.00 Total Cost $60.00
Approved by C. Luther
Remarks

Medford Machine Tools

Mar.	8	Goods in Process Inventory—Job No. 15.	60.00	
		Factory Payroll.		60.00
		To record direct labor used on Job No. 15.		

The debit in this entry is posted to both the general ledger account and to the appropriate job cost sheet. An entry to record indirect labor debits Factory Overhead and credits Factory Payroll. In the subsidiary Factory Overhead Ledger, the debit in this entry is posted to the Indirect Labor account.

Overhead Cost Flows and Related Documents

LO 4 Describe and record the flow of materials, labor, and overhead costs in a job order cost accounting system.

The cost flows diagrammed in Illustration 21–8 are associated with manufacturing overhead. Note that the four sources of overhead costs include indirect materials and indirect labor. As we already discussed, these costs are recorded in response to requisitions for indirect materials and time tickets for indirect labor. The remaining sources of overhead are vouchers that authorize payments for items such as supplies or utilities and adjusting entries for costs such as depreciation.

Recall that factory overhead includes all manufacturing costs other than direct materials and direct labor. Because factory overhead usually includes many different costs, a separate account for each overhead cost often is maintained in a subsidary Factory Overhead Ledger. This ledger is controlled by the Factory Overhead account in the General Ledger. Like the Factory Payroll account, Factory Overhead is a temporary account that accumulates costs until they are applied to jobs.

As you learned in Chapter 20, manufacturing overhead costs are recorded with debits to the Factory Overhead account and credits to other accounts such as Cash, Accounts Payable, and Accumulated Depreciation, Equipment. In the subsidiary Factory Overhead Ledger, the debits are posted to the appropriate accounts such as Depreciation of Factory Equipment, Insurance on Factory Equipment, or Amortization of Patents.

ILLUSTRATION 21–8

Flow of Manufacturing Overhead Costs

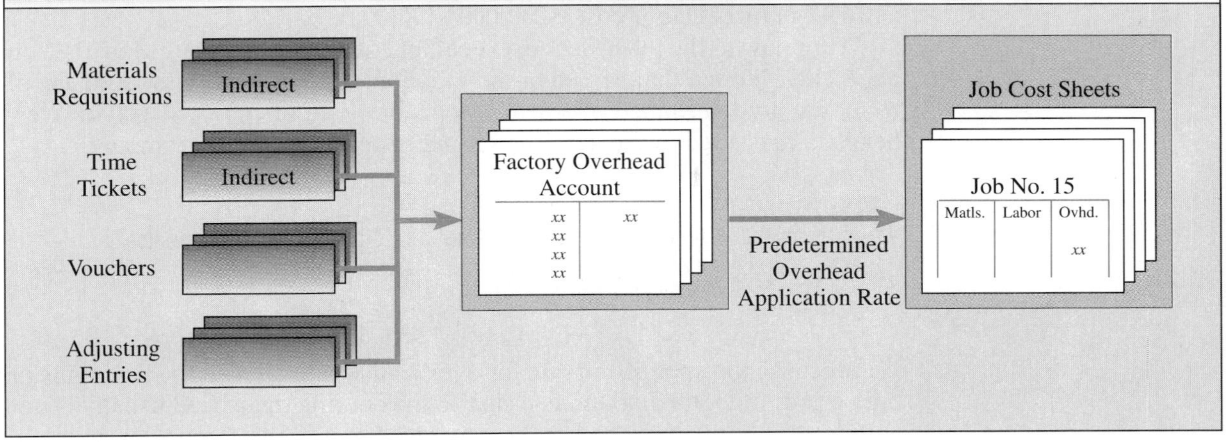

In Illustration 21–8, observe that overhead costs flow from the Factory Overhead account to the job cost sheets. This assignment of overhead to jobs is difficult because manufacturing overhead, by definition, is made up of costs that are not clearly associated with specific units or batches of product. In other words, the accountant cannot clearly determine that a specific dollar amount of overhead was incurred to produce one job while another dollar amount was incurred to produce another job. Nevertheless, manufacturing overhead costs are necessary if any manufacturing activity is to take place. Therefore, if the calculated total cost of a job is to include all of the costs needed to manufacture the job, some amount of manufacturing overhead must be included in the total.

In Chapter 20, you learned how to assign overhead to inventories and cost of goods sold by relating overhead to some other variable used in production, such as direct labor or machine-hours. In that chapter, for example, total overhead cost incurred during a period was expressed as a percentage of total direct labor cost incurred. Then, overhead was applied by multiplying that percentage by the estimated amount of direct labor in each ending inventory and in cost of goods sold.

Job order cost accounting systems often use a similar procedure to assign overhead costs to jobs. However, the fact that perpetual inventory records are used means that the assignment of overhead to jobs cannot wait until the end of the period. Instead, overhead must be predicted in advance and assigned to jobs by using a **predetermined overhead application rate.** To set this rate, the total overhead cost and total direct labor cost (or other variable) are estimated prior to the beginning of the period. Even though financial reports may be prepared monthly or quarterly, the estimates are usually for annual amounts. Then, the relationship between these predicted amounts is used during the period to assign overhead to jobs.

For example, assume that Medford Machine Tools assigns overhead to jobs by relating overhead to direct labor. At the beginning of 1994, management predicted that total direct labor cost for 1994 would be $125,000. They also predicted that total factory overhead costs would be $200,000. Based on these estimates, they calculated the predetermined overhead application rate as 160% of direct labor cost ($200,000/$125,000).

Turn now to the job order cost sheet for Job No. 15 in Illustration 21–2 on page 1127. Notice that $1,000 of direct labor was assigned to the job. Then, using the predetermined overhead application rate of 160%, $1,600 of overhead was assigned to the job. The journal entry to record this amount is

Mar.	11	Goods in Process Inventory—Job No. 15.	1,600.00	
		Factory Overhead		1,600.00
		To assign overhead to Job No. 15.		

Because the application rate for overhead is estimated at the beginning of the period, the total amount assigned to jobs during the period usually is not equal to the total amount actually incurred. Later in the chapter, we explain how this difference is treated at the end of the period.

Summary of All Manufacturing Cost Flows during the Period

In the previous sections, we showed journal entries that charged Goods in Process and Job No. 15 for the cost of a direct material requisition, for the cost of a direct labor time ticket, and for manufacturing overhead. Although separate entries for each material requisition and labor time ticket are appropriate, each item typically is not recorded with a separate entry. Instead, materials requisitions may be collected for a day or a week and recorded with a single entry that summarizes the requisitions. The same may be done with labor time tickets. When such summary entries are made, supporting schedules of the jobs to be charged and the types of materials used provide the basis for postings to the subsidiary records.

As described in the previous paragraph, summary entries are usually recorded more often than monthly. Nevertheless, to show all of the manufacturing cost flows during a period and the related entries, we continue with the example of Medford Machine Tools. Illustration 21–9 presents the costs related to all of Medford's manufacturing activities during March 1994. Recall that Medford did not have any jobs in process at the beginning of the month. The firm applied materials, labor, and overhead to five jobs during the month; workers completed Job Nos. 15 and 16 and delivered them to the customers. At the end of the month, Job No. 17 was completed but not delivered and Job Nos. 18 and 19 were still in process. In Illustration 21–9, note that raw materials were purchased for $2,750, labor costs incurred were $5,300, and overhead costs incurred were $6,720.

Illustration 21–10 shows the flow of these costs through the general ledger accounts and the resulting end-of-month status of the subsidiary records. The numbered arrows at the top of the illustration show the flows of total costs for the month. Keep in mind that each numbered cost flow represents several entries made during March. However, to review the form of those entries, we represent each cost flow with a single entry that summarizes the actual entries made during the month. The numbers of the following entries correspond to the arrows in Illustration 21–10:

ILLUSTRATION 21–9

Medford Machine Tools—Costs of All Manufacturing Activities during March 1994

Explanation	Materials	Labor	Overhead Incurred	Overhead Assigned	Goods in Process	Finished Goods	Cost of Goods Sold
Job 15	$ 600	$1,000		$1,600			$3,200
Job 16	300	800		1,280			2,380
Job 17	500	1,100		1,760		$3,360	
Job 18	150	700		1,120	$1,970		
Job 19	250	600		960	1,810		
Total job costs	$1,800	$4,200		$6,720	$3,780	$3,360	$5,580
Indirect materials	550		$ 550				
Indirect labor		1,100	1,100				
Other overhead			5,070				
Total costs used in production	$2,350	$5,300	$6,720				
Ending inventory	1,400						
Materials available	$3,750						
Less beginning inventory	(1,000)						
Purchases	$2,750						

		Debit	Credit
1.	Raw Materials Inventory	2,750.00	
	Accounts Payable		2,750.00
	Acquired materials on credit for use in the factory		
2.	Goods in Process Inventory	1,800.00	
	Raw Materials Inventory		1,800.00
	To assign the cost of direct materials used in producing jobs.		
3.	Factory Overhead	550.00	
	Raw Materials Inventory		550.00
	To record the use of indirect materials in production.		
4.	Factory Payroll	5,300.00	
	Cash (and other accounts)		5,300.00
	To record salaries and wages of factory personnel (other accounts include various payroll liabilities).		
5.	Goods in Process Inventory	4,200.00	
	Factory Payroll		4,200.00
	To assign the cost of direct labor used in producing jobs.		
6.	Factory Overhead	1,100.00	
	Factory Payroll		1,100.00
	To record indirect labor costs as overhead.		
7.	Factory Overhead	5,070.00	
	Cash (and other accounts)		5,070.00
	To record overhead costs incurred such as insurance on factory equipment, utilities, rent of factory building, and depreciation of equipment.		

ILLUSTRATION 21–10

Flows of All Manufacturing Costs and End-of-Month Job Cost Sheets

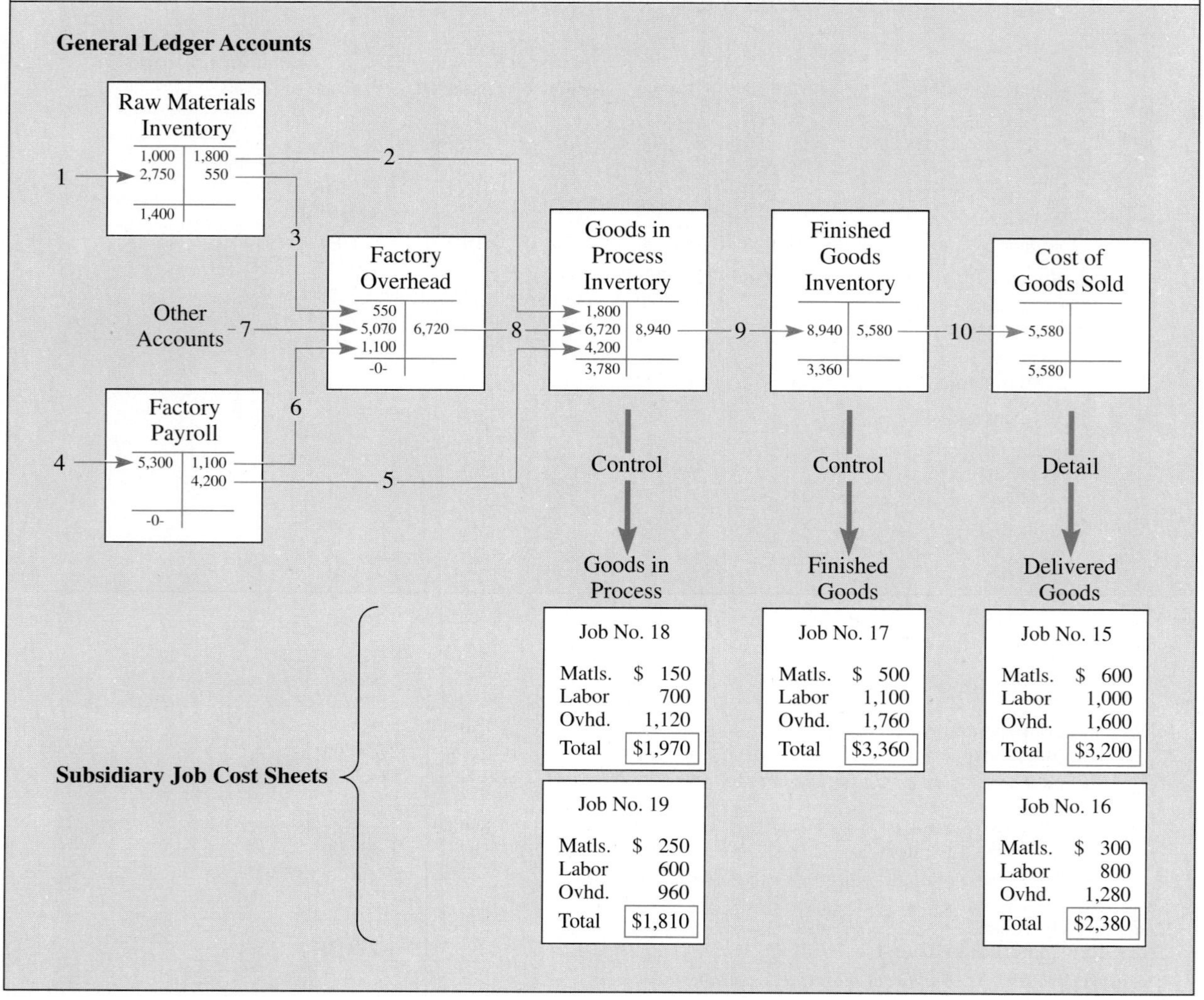

8.	Goods in Process Inventory	6,720.00	
	Factory Overhead		6,720.00
	To apply overhead costs to jobs at the rate of 160% of direct labor cost.		
9.	Finished Goods Inventory	8,940.00	
	Goods in Process Inventory		8,940.00
	To record the completed production of Job Nos. 15, 16, and 17.		
10.	Cost of Goods Sold	5,580.00	
	Finished Goods Inventory		5,580.00
	To record the sale of Job Nos. 15 and 16 to customers.		

ILLUSTRATION 21–11

MEDFORD MACHINE TOOLS, INC.
Manufacturing Statement
For Month Ended March 31, 1994

Direct materials used	$ 1,800
Direct labor	4,200
Factory overhead	6,720
Total manufacturing costs	$12,720
Add goods in process inventory, February 28, 1994	–0–
Total goods in process during the month	$12,720
Deduct goods in process inventory, March 31, 1994	(3,780)
Cost of goods manufactured	$ 8,940

The bottom of Illustration 21–10 shows the status of the job cost sheets at the end of the month. Note that the sum of the costs assigned to the jobs in process ($1,970 + $1,810) equals the $3,780 balance in Goods in Process Inventory. Also, the costs assigned to Job No. 17 equal the $3,360 balance in Finished Goods Inventory. Finally, the sum of the costs assigned to Job Nos. 15 and 16 ($3,200 + $2,380) equals the $5,580 balance in Cost of Goods Sold.

The Manufacturing Statement

A manufacturing statement prepared under a job order cost accounting system appears just like one prepared under a general accounting system. Under both systems, the statement summarizes the total costs of manufacturing activities during the period. The manufacturing statement for Medford Machine Tools appears in Illustration 21–11.

Adjusting for Underapplied and Overapplied Factory Overhead

LO 5 Explain how the accounts are adjusted for any overapplied or underapplied factory overhead.

In Illustration 21–10, look at the debits in the Factory Overhead account and notice that the total cost of factory overhead actually incurred during the period was $550 + $5,070 + $1,100 = $6,720. Then, notice that this $6,720 is exactly equal to the amount applied to production in entry 8. We made the overhead incurred and overhead applied equal to each other to simplify the previous discussion. However, in a real company, the amount of overhead incurred would rarely, if ever, equal the amount of overhead applied.

Recall that a job order cost accounting system uses a predetermined overhead application rate to apply factory overhead costs to jobs. Also remember that the firm calculates a predetermined overhead application rate before the accounting period begins. The rate is, in fact, an estimated relationship between future overhead costs and another variable such as future direct labor costs. After the period is over, the amounts of overhead and direct labor costs actually incurred rarely are exactly equal to the estimated amounts. Thus, the amount of overhead incurred rarely equals the amount of overhead applied.

ILLUSTRATION 21–12

Allocation of Underapplied Overhead to Jobs

	Direct Labor Assigned to Jobs		Allocation of Underapplied Overhead Percentage × $480		
Job	**Dollars**	**Percentages**	**Goods in Process**	**Finished Goods**	**Cost of Goods Sold**
15.	$1,000	23.8%			$114
16.	800	19.0			91
17.	1,100	26.2		$126	
18.	700	16.7	$ 80		
19.	600	14.3	69		
Total	$4,200	100.0%	$149	$126	$205

Underapplied Overhead

If less overhead was applied than was actually incurred, the remaining debit balance in the Factory Overhead account at the end of a period is **underapplied overhead.** For example, suppose that Medford Machine Tools incurred a total overhead cost of $7,200 during March 1994. Since the amount of overhead applied was only $6,720, the Factory Overhead account is left with a $480 debit balance, as shown here:

Factory Overhead — **Acct. No.** 540

Date		Explanation	Debit	Credit	Balance	
1994						
Mar.	31	Indirect materials cost	550		550	
Mar.	31	Indirect labor cost	1,100		1,650	
Mar.	31	Other overhead costs	5,550		7,200	
Mar.	31	Overhead costs applied to jobs		6,720	480	*(debit)*

The $480 debit balance represents manufacturing costs that were not charged to jobs. As a result, the balances in Goods in Process Inventory, Finished Goods Inventory, and Cost of Goods Sold fail to include all the manufacturing costs incurred. Thus, the Factory Overhead balance should be allocated among those accounts. Ideally, the method of allocating the underapplied overhead should be consistent with the allocation method used during the period. In the case of Medford Machine Tools, the underapplied overhead should be allocated to jobs based on direct labor.

Illustration 21–12 shows the necessary calculations. In that illustration, note that the direct labor is assigned to each job as a percentage of total direct labor. Then, these percentages are multiplied by $480 to determine how much of the underapplied overhead should be allocated to each job. This adjusting entry records the allocation of the underapplied overhead:

Mar.	31	Goods in Process Inventory	149.00	
		Finished Goods Inventory	126.00	
		Cost of Goods Sold	205.00	
		Factory Overhead		480.00
		To adjust the cost of the jobs worked on in March for underapplied overhead cost.		

Overapplied Overhead

If the amount of overhead applied during a period exceeds the overhead incurred, the resulting credit balance in the Factory Overhead account is **overapplied overhead.** The treatment of overapplied overhead at the end of the period is the same as the treatment of underapplied overhead. In other words, whether the remaining Factory Overhead balance is a debit or credit makes no difference. It should be allocated to goods in process, finished goods, and cost of goods sold.

Underapplied and Overapplied Amounts That Are Not Material

Sometimes, the amount of underapplied or overapplied overhead is not material compared to the total manufacturing costs incurred during the period. When this is the case, many companies prefer to avoid the calculations that must be made to allocate the underapplied or overapplied amount to goods in process, finished goods, and cost of goods sold. Instead, they simply transfer the remaining Factory Overhead account balance to Cost of Goods Sold. For most companies, a large portion of the overhead cost ends up in this account anyway. If the Medford Machine Tools management had decided that the $480 of underapplied overhead was immaterial, the entry would have been

Mar.	31	Cost of Goods Sold	480.00	
		Factory Overhead		480.00
		To adjust cost of goods sold for underapplied overhead.		

Summary of the Chapter in Terms of Learning Objectives

LO 1. Production management experienced important changes in the 1970s and 1980s as five new concepts began to be widely implemented. These concepts include customer orientation, total quality management (TQM), just-in-time (JIT) manufacturing, the theory of constraints (TOC), and continuous improvement. These concepts have helped production managers change the kinds of products, the attitudes of employees toward quality and improvement, and the way that they operate production facilities.

LO 2. Job order cost accounting systems account for operations involving the manufacture of products that are individually designed to meet the needs of each customer. Job order cost accounting systems also may be used by companies that provide a unique service for each customer.

LO 3. In a job order cost accounting system, the costs of producing each job are accumulated on a separate job cost sheet. On a job cost sheet, the costs of direct materials, direct labor, and manufacturing overhead are accumulated separately and then added to determine the total cost of the job. Job cost sheets for the jobs in process, finished jobs, and jobs that have been sold are subsidiary records that are controlled by related general ledger accounts.

LO 4. In the subsidiary records, the costs of materials flow from receiving reports to materials ledger cards and then to job cost sheets or to the Indirect Materials account in the Factory Overhead Ledger. The costs of labor flow from clock cards to the Factory Payroll account and then to job cost sheets or to the Indirect Labor account in the Factory Overhead Ledger. Manufacturing overhead costs are first accumulated in the Factory Overhead account, which controls the subsidiary Factory Overhead Ledger. Then, based on a predetermined overhead application rate, overhead costs are charged to jobs.

LO 5. At the end of each period, the Factory Overhead account normally has a residual debit or credit balance. A debit balance represents underapplied overhead and a credit balance represents overapplied overhead. If this balance is material, it is allocated to Goods in Process Inventory, Finished Goods Inventory, and Cost of Goods Sold. The allocation should be based on the same variable, such as direct labor, that was used to apply overhead during the period. If the balance is not material, it is usually transferred to Cost of Goods Sold.

Demonstration Problem

The following information describes the job order manufacturing activities of Peak Manufacturing Company for May:

Raw materials purchases	$16,000
Factory payroll cost	15,400
Overhead costs incurred:	
Indirect materials	5,000
Indirect labor	3,500
Factory rent	1,450
Factory utilities	2,650
Factory equipment depreciation	5,400

The predetermined overhead rate was 150% of the direct labor cost. These costs were allocated to the five jobs worked on during May:

Job	401	402	403	404	405
Balances at April 30:					
Direct materials	$1,700	$1,900			
Direct labor	1,000	700			
Applied overhead	1,500	1,050			
Costs during May:					
Direct materials	50	3,500	$2,200	$1,300	$1,400
Direct labor	1,100	4,000	3,200	2,800	800
Applied overhead	?	?	?	?	?
Status at May 31	Finished (sold)	Finished (sold)	Finished (unsold)	Finished (unsold)	In process

Required

1. Determine the total cost of
   a. The April 30 inventory of jobs in process.
   b. The materials used during May.
   c. The labor used during May.
   d. The factory overhead incurred and applied during May and the amount of any over- or underapplied overhead on May 31.
   e. Each of the five jobs as of May 31.
   f. The four jobs completed during the month.
   g. The May 31 inventory of goods in process.
   h. The May 31 inventory of finished goods.
   i. The goods sold during May.
2. Present summarized journal entries for the month to record
   a. The materials purchases (all of which were on credit), the factory payroll (paid with cash), and the actual overhead costs, including indirect materials and indirect labor (the factory rent and utilities were paid with cash).
   b. The assignment of direct materials, direct labor, and overhead costs to the Goods in Process Inventory account. (Use separate debit entries for each job.)
   c. The transfer of each completed job to the Finished Goods Inventory account.
   d. The cost of goods sold.
   e. The removal of any underapplied or overapplied overhead from the Factory Overhead account. (Assume the amount is not material.)
3. Prepare a manufacturing statement for May.

Solution to Demonstration Problem

Planning the Solution

- Determine the cost of the April 30 in-process inventory by adding up the materials, labor, and applied overhead costs for Jobs 401 and 402.
- Calculate the cost of materials used and labor by adding up the amounts assigned to jobs and to overhead.
- Calculate the total overhead incurred by adding the amounts of the five components; calculate the amount of applied overhead by multiplying the total direct labor cost by the predetermined overhead rate; compute the underapplied or overapplied amount as the difference between the actual cost and the applied cost.
- Determine the total cost charged to each job by adding any costs incurred in April to the materials, labor, and overhead applied during May.
- Group the costs of the jobs according to their status as completed (Jobs 401, 402, 403, and 404); in process (Job 405); on hand (Jobs 403 and 404); and sold (Jobs 401 and 402).
- Record the direct materials costs assigned to the five jobs, using a separate Goods in Process Inventory account for each job; do the same thing for the direct labor and the applied overhead.

- Transfer the costs of Jobs 401, 402, 403, and 404 from Goods in Process Inventory to Finished Goods Inventory.
- Record the costs of Jobs 401 and 402 as the cost of goods sold.
- Record the transfer of the underapplied overhead from the Factory Overhead account to the Cost of Goods Sold account.
- On the manufacturing statement, remember to include the beginning and ending in-process inventories, and to deduct the underapplied overhead.

1. Total cost of:

a. April 30 inventory of jobs in process:

Job 401:	
Direct materials	$1,700
Direct labor	1,000
Applied overhead	1,500
Total	$4,200
Job 402:	
Direct materials	$1,900
Direct labor	700
Applied overhead	1,050
Total	$3,650
Total in process inventory	$7,850

b. Materials used during May:

Direct materials:	
Job 401	$ 50
Job 402	3,500
Job 403	2,200
Job 404	1,300
Job 405	1,400
Total direct materials	$ 8,450
Indirect materials	5,000
Total materials	$13,450

c. Labor used during May:

Direct labor:	
Job 401	$ 1,100
Job 402	4,000
Job 403	3,200
Job 404	2,800
Job 405	800
Total direct labor	$11,900
Indirect labor	3,500
Total labor	$15,400

d. Factory overhead incurred during May:

Indirect materials	$ 5,000
Indirect labor	3,500
Factory rent	1,450
Factory utilities	2,650
Factory equipment depreciation	5,400
Total actual overhead	$18,000
Overhead applied (150% × $11,900)	17,850
Underapplied overhead	$ 150

e. Total cost of each job:

	401	402	403	404	405
From April:					
Direct materials	$1,700	$1,900			
Direct labor	1,000	700			
*Applied overhead	1,500	1,050			
From May:					
Direct materials	50	3,500	$ 2,200	$1,300	$1,400
Direct labor	1,100	4,000	3,200	2,800	800
*Applied overhead	1,650	6,000	4,800	4,200	1,200
Total costs	$7,000	$17,150	$10,200	$8,300	$3,400

*Equals 150% of the direct labor cost.

f. Total cost of the jobs completed during May:

Job 401	$ 7,000
Job 402	17,150
Job 403	10,200
Job 404	8,300
Total	$42,650

g. Total cost of the May 31 inventory of goods in process:

Job 405	$ 3,400

h. Total cost of the May 31 inventory of finished goods:

Job 403	$10,200
Job 404	8,300
Total	$18,500

i. Total cost of goods sold during May:

Job 401	$ 7,000
Job 402	17,150
Total	$24,150

2. Journal entries:

a.	Raw Materials Inventory	16,000.00	
	Accounts Payable		16,000.00
	To record materials purchases.		
	Factory Payroll	15,400.00	
	Cash		15,400.00
	To record factory payroll.		
	Factory Overhead	5,000.00	
	Raw Materials Inventory		5,000.00
	To record indirect materials.		
	Factory Overhead	3,500.00	
	Factory Payroll		3,500.00
	To record indirect labor.		
	Factory Overhead	1,450.00	
	Cash		1,450.00
	To record factory rent.		
	Factory Overhead	2,650.00	
	Cash		2,650.00
	To record factory utilities.		
	Factory Overhead	5,400.00	
	Accumulated Depreciation, Factory Equipment		5,400.00
	To record depreciation of manufacturing equipment.		
b.	Assignment of costs to goods in process:		
	Goods in Process Inventory (Job 401)	50.00	
	Goods in Process Inventory (Job 402)	3,500.00	
	Goods in Process Inventory (Job 403)	2,200.00	
	Goods in Process Inventory (Job 404)	1,300.00	
	Goods in Process Inventory (Job 405)	1,400.00	
	Raw Materials Inventory		8,450.00
	To assign direct materials to jobs.		
	Goods in Process Inventory (Job 401)	1,100.00	
	Goods in Process Inventory (Job 402)	4,000.00	
	Goods in Process Inventory (Job 403)	3,200.00	
	Goods in Process Inventory (Job 404)	2,800.00	
	Goods in Process Inventory (Job 405)	800.00	
	Factory Payroll		11,900.00
	To assign direct labor to jobs.		
	Goods in Process Inventory (Job 401)	1,650.00	
	Goods in Process Inventory (Job 402)	6,000.00	
	Goods in Process Inventory (Job 403)	4,800.00	
	Goods in Process Inventory (Job 404)	4,200.00	
	Goods in Process Inventory (Job 405)	1,200.00	
	Factory Overhead		17,850.00
	To apply overhead to jobs.		
c.	Finished Goods Inventory	42,650.00	
	Goods in Process Inventory (Job 401)		7,000.00
	Goods in Process Inventory (Job 402)		17,150.00
	Goods in Process Inventory (Job 403)		10,200.00
	Goods in Process Inventory (Job 404)		8,300.00
	To record completion of jobs.		

d.	Cost of Goods Sold	24,150.00	
	Finished Goods Inventory		24,150.00
	To record sale of Jobs 401 and 402.		
e.	Cost of Goods Sold	150.00	
	Factory Overhead		150.00
	To assign underapplied overhead.		

3.

PEAK MANUFACTURING COMPANY
Manufacturing Statement
For Month Ended May 31

Direct materials used		$ 8,450
Direct labor used		11,900
Factory overhead:		
Indirect materials	$5,000	
Indirect labor	3,500	
Factory rent	1,450	
Factory utilities	2,650	
Factory equipment depreciation	5,400	18,000
Total manufacturing costs		$38,350
Add goods in process, April 30 (Jobs 401 and 402)		7,850
Total goods in process during the month		$46,200
Deduct goods in process, May 31 (Job 405)		(3,400)
Deduct underapplied overhead		(150)
Cost of goods manufactured (Jobs 401, 402, 403, 404)		$42,650

Glossary

LO 6 Define or explain the words and phrases listed in the chapter glossary.

Clock card a source document that an employee uses to record the number of hours at work and that is used to determine the total labor cost for each pay period. p. 1131

Continuous improvement an attitude of constantly seeking ways to improve company operations, including customer service, product quality, product features, the production process, and employee interactions. p. 1123

Customer orientation a management concept that encourages all managers and employees (including those in the factory) to be in tune with the wants and needs of customers; leads to flexible product designs and production processes. p. 1119

Job a unique product or service that is produced to meet the demands of a particular customer. p. 1124

Job cost sheet a subsidiary record in a job order cost accounting system used to record the costs of producing a job. p. 1127

Job lot a group of unique products that is produced for a particular customer. p. 1124

Job order cost accounting system a cost accounting system that is designed to determine the cost of producing each job or job lot and that accumulates manufacturing costs by job. p. 1127

Job order manufacturing a type of manufacturing that produces unique products (or services) for each customer. p. 1124

Just-in-time (JIT) an approach to managing inventories and production operations such that units of materials and products are obtained and provided only as they are needed. p. 1121

Materials ledger card a subsidiary record of a raw materials item that records data on the quantity and cost of units purchased, units issued for use in production, and units that remain in the raw materials inventory. p. 1128

Materials requisition a source document that production managers use to request materials for manufacturing and that is used to assign materials cost to specific jobs or to overhead. p. 1130

Overapplied overhead the amount by which the overhead applied to jobs during a period with the predetermined overhead application rate exceeds the overhead incurred during the period. p. 1138

Predetermined overhead application rate the rate established prior to the beginning of a period that relates estimated overhead to another variable such as estimated direct labor, and that is used to assign overhead cost to jobs. p. 1133

Theory of constraints (TOC) a management concept that asserts the primary focus of managers should be to discover and then relax or overcome the factors that limit the throughput of the company's operations. p. 1122

Throughput the added value (selling price minus direct costs of production) of finished products processed through the system. p. 1122

Time ticket a source document that an employee uses to report how much time was spent working on a job or on overhead and that is used to determine the amount of direct labor to charge to the job or to determine the amount of indirect labor to charge to factory overhead. p. 1131

Total quality management (TQM) a management concept under which all managers and employees at all stages of operations strive toward higher standards and a reduced number of defective units. p. 1119

Underapplied overhead the amount by which overhead incurred during a period exceeds the overhead applied to jobs with the predetermined overhead application rate. p. 1138

Synonymous Terms

Assign (overhead) apply (overhead).

Goods in process work in process; jobs in process.

Overhead allocation overhead application.

Objective Review

Answers to the following questions are listed at the end of the chapter. Be sure that you decide which is the one best answer to each question *before* you check the answers.

LO 1 Which of the following management concepts involves an attitude of constantly looking for better ways of operating a business?

a. Continuous improvement.
b. Customer orientation.
c. Just-in-time manufacturing.
d. Total quality management.
e. Theory of constraints.

LO 2 Which of the following products is likely to involve a job order manufacturing operation?

a. Inexpensive watches.
b. Bicycles.
c. Microcomputers.
d. Luggage.
e. Apartment buildings.

LO 3 Which of the following statements about job cost sheets is true?

a. Job cost sheets are financial statements reported to outside investors in manufacturing companies.
b. A separate job cost sheet is maintained in the General Ledger for each job in process.
c. The collection of job cost sheets of unfinished jobs makes up a subsidiary ledger that is controlled by the Goods in Process account.
d. The collection of job cost sheets for jobs that have been finished and delivered to customers make up a subsidiary ledger that is controlled by the Finished Goods Inventory account.

e. One collection of job cost sheets serves as a subsidiary Factory Overhead Ledger.

LO 4 In a job order cost accounting system

a. The information recorded on a materials requisition indicates whether the cost of issued materials should be charged to a job or to the Indirect Materials subsidiary account.
b. The assignment of labor cost to jobs or to the Indirect Labor subsidiary account is based on the information recorded on employees' time tickets.
c. Indirect labor costs are assigned to jobs as part of manufacturing overhead.
d. Overhead costs are recorded in the Factory Overhead account in response to materials requisitions, time tickets, vouchers, and adjusting entries.
e. All of the above are correct.

LO 5 At the beginning of a period, Zip Company established a predetermined overhead application rate of 150% of direct labor. During that period, actual direct labor costs incurred were $14,700 and actual overhead costs incurred were $24,550. Overhead applied during the period appeared in the following categories at the end of the period:

Jobs still in process.	20%
Jobs finished but unsold	15
Jobs finished and sold	65

Assuming the underapplied overhead is material, the adjusting entry to allocate the underapplied overhead to jobs will include a

a. Debit to Goods in Process Inventory for $500.
b. Credit to Finished Goods Inventory for $375.
c. Credit to Factory Overhead for $500.
d. Debit to Cost of Goods Sold for $2,500.
e. Credit to Factory Overhead for $24,550.

LO 6 Just-in-time manufacturing

a. Requires an attitude of constantly looking for ways to improve the company's operations.
b. Attempts to find bottlenecks in the production process so that they can be relieved and throughput increased.
c. Must be used in a job order manufacturing system.
d. Attempts to maintain minimum or even zero levels of inventories.
e. Requires flexible product designs and flexible production processes.

Questions for Class Discussion

1. What factors have encouraged the development of new ideas about production management?
2. What is the essence of customer orientation?

3. What attitude pervades a company under total quality management?
4. What does just-in-time manufacturing try to accomplish for finished goods and raw materials inventories?
5. When managers use the theory of constraints to streamline a company's production process, what do they look for?
6. Which management concept emphasizes most clearly the importance of not resisting change?
7. Which of the following products call for a job order cost accounting system to be used: (*a*) custom-designed homes, (*b*) flat-bed truck trailers, and (*c*) videocassette recorders?
8. What is the difference between a job and a job lot?
9. Which three costs are accumulated on job cost sheets?
10. When services are provided to customers on a job order basis, when is revenue usually recognized?
11. What types of information are recorded on a job cost sheet? How are job cost sheets used by management?
12. In a job order cost accounting system, what records serve as a subsidiary ledger for Goods in Process Inventory? For Finished Goods Inventory?
13. What is a materials ledger card? Why are materials ledger cards used in job order cost accounting systems and not used in a general accounting system for manufacturing companies?
14. What entries are recorded when a materials manager receives a materials requisition and then issues materials for use in the factory?
15. What are the purposes of clock cards and time tickets?
16. What are the three source documents that lead to debits to the Factory Overhead account?
17. Why does a job order cost accounting system use a predetermined overhead application rate?
18. Refer to the job cost sheet of Illustration 21–2. How did the accountant determine the amount of overhead costs to charge to the job?
19. From the time of their purchase to the sale of the job, what general ledger accounts do direct materials costs flow through in a job order cost accounting system?
20. What events cause debits to be recorded in the Factory Payroll account? What events cause credits to be recorded in the account?
21. What events cause debits to be recorded in the Factory Overhead account? What events cause credits to be recorded in the account?
22. How does the process of determining the ending goods in process in a job order cost accounting system differ from the process used in a general accounting system?
23. In a job order cost accounting system, why does the Factory Overhead account usually have an overapplied or underapplied balance at the end of every accounting period?

24. At the end of a period, the Factory Overhead account has a debit balance. Does this represent overapplied or underapplied overhead?
25. What method should be used to eliminate a material amount of overapplied or underapplied overhead from the Factory Overhead account?
26. Suppose that Land's End produces 1,000 sweaters of a particular style. Do you suppose that this production project would be accounted for as a job lot? Explain briefly.
27. Essentially each package delivered by Federal Express represents a unique job because it is taken from one specific location to another. Do you think that each package is accounted for separately using a job cost accounting system? Why?

Exercises

Exercise 21–1
Analysis of cost flows
(LO 3)

As of the end of August, the job cost sheets of the Chopin Company showed that the following total costs had been accumulated on these three jobs:

	Job 77	Job 78	Job 79
Direct materials	$5,000	$11,000	$9,000
Direct labor	3,000	4,400	7,000
Overhead	3,750	5,500	8,750

Job 77 had been started in production during July and the following costs had already been assigned to it in that month: direct materials of $2,000, direct labor of $600, and overhead of $750. Jobs 78 and 79 were started during August. Overhead cost was applied with a predetermined application rate based on direct labor cost. Only Jobs 77 and 78 were finished during August, and it is expected that Job 79 will be finished in September. No raw materials were used indirectly during August. Using this information, answer the following questions:

a. What was the cost of the raw materials requisitioned during August?
b. How much direct labor cost was incurred during August?
c. What predetermined overhead application rate was used during August?
d. How much cost was transferred to finished goods during August?

Exercise 21–2
Documents used in job order cost accounting systems
(LO 4)

The left column below and on the next page includes the names of several documents used in job order cost accounting systems. The right column presents short descriptions of the purposes of the documents. In the blank space beside each of the numbers in the right column, write the letter of the document that serves the described purpose.

a. Factory Payroll account	__1. Communicates to the storeroom that materials are needed to complete a job.

b. Materials ledger card	__2. Shows only the total amount of time that an employee works each day.
c. Time ticket	__3. Shows the amount approved for payment of an overhead cost.
d. Voucher	__4. Shows the amount of time an employee worked on a specific job.
e. Materials requisition	__5. Temporarily accumulates the cost of incurred overhead until the cost is assigned to specific jobs.
f. Factory Overhead account	__6. Temporarily accumulates labor costs incurred until they are assigned to specific jobs or to overhead.
g. Clock card	__7. Perpetual inventory record of raw materials received, used, and on hand.

Exercise 21–3
Completing the job cost sheet
(LO 3)

The following information was found on materials requisitions and time tickets for Job 9-1005 that was completed by Beaufort Boat Trailers, Inc. for Redfish Rentals. The requisitions are identified by code numbers starting with the letter Q and the time tickets start with W:

Date	Document	Amount
7/1/94	Q-4698	625.00
7/1/94	W-3393	300.00
7/2/94	Q-4705	900.00
7/2/94	W-3422	300.00
7/3/94	W-3456	300.00
7/5/94	Q-4725	500.00
7/5/94	W-3479	225.00
7/8/94	Q-4777	100.00
7/8/94	W-3501	225.00
7/10/94	W-3559	150.00

Before the year started, management estimated that the overhead cost would equal 200% of the direct labor cost for each job or job lot. With this information, determine the cost of the job lot that Beaufort produced for Redfish Rentals.

Exercise 21–4
Calculating overhead application rate; assigning costs to jobs
(LO 3, 4)

In December 1993, Willie Company's management established the 1994 overhead application rate based on direct labor cost. The information used in setting the rate included the cost accountant's estimates that the company would incur $960,000 of overhead costs and $600,000 of direct labor cost during 1994. During January of 1994, Willie Company began and completed Job 4-22. Calculate the overhead application rate for 1994 and use the information on the following job cost sheet to determine the total cost of the job.

JOB COST SHEET

Customer's name *Chilly Corp.* Job no. *4-22*

Job description *5 Two-Page Color Monitors—21 inch*

	Direct Materials		Direct Labor		Overhead Costs Applied	
Date	Requisition No.	Amount	Time-Ticket Number	Amount	Rate	Amount
Jan. 14	*1-032*	*2,500.00*	*1T-150*	*320.00*		
15	*1-045*	*3,525.00*	*1T-159*	*640.00*		
20	*1-180*	*1,775.00*	*1T-221*	*640.00*		
Total						

Exercise 21–5
Analysis of costs assigned to goods in process
(LO 4)

Grange Company uses a job order cost accounting system that charges overhead to jobs on the basis of direct labor cost. At the end of last year, the company's Goods in Process Inventory account showed the following:

Goods in Process Inventory — Acct. No. 121

Date		Explanation	Debit	Credit	Balance
1994					
Dec.	31	Direct materials cost	250,000		250,000
	31	Direct labor cost	40,000		290,000
	31	Overhead costs	48,000		338,000
	31	To finished goods		228,000	110,000

Required

1. Determine the overhead application rate (based on direct labor cost) used by the company.
2. Only one job was in the goods in process inventory at the end of December. Its direct materials cost was $88,000. How much direct labor cost must have been assigned to it? How much overhead cost must have been assigned to it?

Exercise 21–6
Journal entries in a job order cost accounting system
(LO 4)

During one month, a company that uses a job order cost accounting system purchased raw materials for $25,000 cash. It then used $6,000 of the raw materials inventory indirectly as factory supplies and used $21,000 as direct materials. The monthly factory payroll was paid in cash, and amounted to $60,000. Of this amount, $14,000 was classified as indirect labor and the remainder as direct. Prepare general journal entries to record these events.

Exercise 21–7
Understanding cost flows in a job order cost accounting system
(LO 4)

The Cool Manufacturing Company produces special order products and uses a job order cost accounting system. The system provided the following information:

	June 30	July 31
Inventories:		
Raw materials	$13,000	$ 16,000
Goods in process	3,200	6,500
Finished goods	22,000	14,400
Information about July:		
Raw materials purchases (paid with cash)		$ 63,000
Factory payroll (paid with cash)		125,000
Factory overhead:		
Indirect materials		4,000
Indirect labor		25,000
Other overhead costs		33,500
Sales (received in cash)		380,000
Predetermined overhead application rate based on direct labor cost		62.5%

Calculate the following amounts for July:

a. Cost of direct materials used.

b. Cost of direct labor used.

c. Cost of goods manufactured.

d. Cost of goods sold.

e. Gross profit.

Exercise 21–8
Recording journal entries for a job order cost accounting system
(LO 4)

Using the information provided in Exercise 21–7 and your answers to the questions for that exercise, prepare general journal entries to record the following events for July:

a. Raw materials purchases.

b. Direct materials usage.

c. Indirect materials usage.

d. Factory payroll costs.

e. Direct labor usage.

f. Indirect labor usage.

g. Factory overhead other than indirect materials and indirect labor (record the credit in Other Accounts).

h. Application of overhead to goods in process.

i. Transfer of finished jobs to the finished goods inventory.

j. Sale and delivery of finished goods to customers.

Exercise 21–9
Posting entries to T-accounts
(LO 4)

Set up six T-accounts like those shown in Illustration 21–10. Using the information in Exercise 21–7, enter the beginning inventory balances and show the flows of manufacturing costs during July. (Use arrows like those in Illustration 21–10.)

Exercise 21–10
Eliminating the end-of-period balance in Factory Overhead
(LO 5)

In December 1993, Pointer Company established its predetermined overhead application rate for jobs produced during 1994 by using the following predictions:

Overhead costs	$600,000
Direct labor costs	500,000

At the end of 1994, the company's records showed that actual overhead costs for the year had been $525,000. The actual direct labor cost had been assigned to jobs as follows:

Jobs completed and sold	$360,000
Jobs still in the finished goods inventory	63,000
Jobs in the goods in process inventory	27,000
Total actual direct labor cost	$450,000

Required

1. Calculate the predetermined overhead application rate for 1994.
2. Set up a T-account for Factory Overhead and enter the overhead costs incurred and the amounts applied to jobs during the year with the predetermined rate. Determine whether overhead was overapplied or underapplied during the year.
3. Prepare the general journal entry to allocate any over- or underapplied overhead among the cost of goods sold, the ending finished goods inventory, and the goods in process inventory.

Exercise 21–11
Eliminating the end-of-period balance in Factory Overhead
(LO 5)

In December 1993, Setter Company established its predetermined overhead application rate for jobs produced during 1994 by using the following predictions:

Overhead costs	$450,000
Direct labor costs	300,000

At the end of 1994, the company's records showed that actual overhead costs for the year had been $505,000. The actual direct labor cost had been assigned to jobs as follows:

Jobs completed and sold	$210,000
Jobs still in the finished goods inventory	42,000
Jobs in the goods in process inventory	28,000
Total actual direct labor cost	$280,000

Required

1. Calculate the predetermined overhead application rate for 1994.
2. Set up a T-account for Factory Overhead and enter the overhead costs incurred and the amounts applied to jobs during the year with the predetermined rate. Determine whether overhead was overapplied or underapplied during the year.
3. Prepare the general journal entry to allocate any over- or underapplied overhead among the cost of goods sold, the ending finished goods inventory, and the goods in process inventory.

Problems

Problem 21–1
Recording manufacturing costs and preparing financial reports
(LO 4, 5)

The following information refers to the job order manufacturing activities of Superior Company for June:

The May 31 inventory of raw materials was $5,000. Raw materials purchases during June were $20,000. Factory payroll cost during June was $11,000. Overhead costs incurred during June were

Indirect materials	$1,500
Indirect labor	700
Factory rent	1,000
Factory utilities	600
Factory equipment depreciation	1,400

The predetermined overhead rate was 50% of the direct labor cost.

Costs allocated to the three jobs worked on during June were

	Job 888	Job 889	Job 890
Balances at May 31:			
Direct materials	$ 700	$ 900	
Direct labor	900	800	
Applied overhead	450	400	
Costs during June:			
Direct materials	5,000	8,500	$4,000
Direct labor	1,500	2,800	6,000
Applied overhead	?	?	?
Status at June 30	Finished (sold)	Finished (unsold)	In process

Job 888 was sold for $19,000 cash during June.

Required

1. Determine the total of each manufacturing cost incurred for June (direct labor, direct materials, allocated overhead), and the total cost assigned to each of the three jobs (including the balances from May 31).
2. Present journal entries for the month to record
   a. The materials purchases (on credit), the factory payroll (paid with cash), and the actual overhead costs, including indirect materials and indirect labor. (The factory rent and utilities were paid with cash.)
   b. The assignment of direct materials, direct labor, and applied overhead costs to the Goods in Process Inventory.
   c. The transfer of Jobs 888 and 889 to the Finished Goods Inventory.
   d. The cost of goods sold for Job 888.
   e. The revenue from the sale of Job 888.
   f. The assignment of any underapplied or overapplied overhead to the Cost of Goods Sold account. (The amount is not material.)
3. Prepare a manufacturing statement for June (use a single line presentation for direct materials and show the details of overhead cost). Also, present a calculation of gross profit for June and show how the inventories would be presented on the June 30 balance sheet.

Problem 21–2
Source documents, journal entries, and financial statements
(LO 3, 4, 5)

The following trial balance of the Edinburgh Company was generated by the computer system on the morning of December 31, 1994. Terry Scott, the company's accountant, knows that something is wrong with the trial balance because it does not show any balance for the goods in process inventory and it still shows balances in the Factory Payroll and Factory Overhead accounts:

Cash	$ 16,000	
Accounts receivable	14,000	
Raw materials inventory	8,000	
Goods in process inventory	–0–	
Finished goods	3,000	
Prepaid rent	1,000	
Accounts payable		$ 3,500
Notes payable		4,500
Common stock		10,000
Retained earnings		29,000
Sales		60,000
Cost of goods sold	35,000	
Factory payroll	6,000	
Factory overhead	9,000	
Miscellaneous expenses	15,000	
Total	$107,000	$107,000

After a few moments of searching a cluttered in-box, Scott finds these six source documents that need to be processed to bring the accounting records up to date:

Materials requisition 94-1005:	$1,200 direct materials to Job 815
Materials requisition 94-1006:	$2,200 direct materials to Job 817
Materials requisition 94-1007:	$700 indirect materials
Labor time ticket 94-9765:	$2,000 direct labor to Job 815
Labor time ticket 94-9766:	$3,000 direct labor to Job 817
Labor time ticket 94-9767:	$1,000 indirect labor

Jobs 815 and 817 are the only units in process at the end of the year. The predetermined overhead application rate is 210% of direct labor cost.

Required

1. Use the information on the six source documents to prepare journal entries to assign the following costs:
   a. Direct materials costs to goods in process inventory.
   b. Direct labor costs to goods in process inventory.
   c. Overhead costs to goods in process inventory.
   d. Indirect materials costs to the overhead account.
   e. Indirect labor costs to the overhead account.
2. Determine the new balance of the Factory Overhead account after making the entries in requirement 1. Determine whether there is any under- or overapplied overhead for the year. If so, prepare the appropriate adjusting entry to close the overhead account, assuming that the amount is not material.
3. Prepare a revised trial balance.
4. Prepare an income statement for 1994 and a balance sheet as of December 31, 1994.

Problem 21–3
Source documents and journal entries under job order cost accounting (LO 3, 4)

Estonia Company's predetermined overhead application rate during a recent month was 200% of direct labor. The company's activities related to manufacturing during the month were

a. Purchased raw materials on account, $50,000.

b. Paid factory wages with cash, $42,000.

c. Paid miscellaneous factory overhead costs with cash, $5,500.

d. Materials requisitions for the month show that the following materials were used on jobs and indirectly:

Job 92	$10,000
Job 93	5,000
Job 94	11,000
Job 95	12,000
Job 96	2,000
Total direct materials	$40,000
Indirect materials	6,000
Total materials used	$46,000

e. Labor time tickets for the month show the following labor was used on jobs and indirectly:

Job 92	$ 4,000
Job 93	7,000
Job 94	9,000
Job 95	13,000
Job 96	1,000
Total direct labor	$34,000
Indirect labor	8,000
Total	$42,000

f. Overhead was applied to Jobs 92, 94, and 95.

g. Jobs 92, 94, and 95 were transferred to finished goods.

h. Jobs 92 and 94 were sold on account for a total price of $120,000.

i. Overhead costs incurred during the month were as follows. (Credit Prepaid Insurance for the expired factory insurance.)

Depreciation of factory building	$18,500
Depreciation of factory equipment	15,500
Expired factory insurance	3,500
Accrued property taxes payable	10,500

j. At the end of the month, overhead is applied to the goods in process (Jobs 93 and 96) using the predetermined rate of 200% of direct labor cost.

Required

1. Prepare general journal entries to record the events and transactions *a* through *j*.
2. Set up T-accounts for each of the following general ledger accounts, each of which started the month with a zero balance. Then, post the

journal entries to these T-accounts and determine the balance of each account.

Raw Materials Inventory	Factory Payroll
Goods in Process Inventory	Factory Overhead
Finished Goods Inventory	Cost of Goods Sold

3. Prepare a job cost sheet for each job worked on during the month. Use the following simplified form:

Job No.	
Materials	$
Labor	
Overhead	
Total	$

4. Prepare a schedule showing the total cost of each job in process and proving that the sum of the costs equals the Goods in Process Inventory account balance. Prepare similar schedules for the finished goods inventory and the cost of goods sold.

Problem 21–4
Allocating overhead based on predetermined overhead application rate (LO 5)

In December 1993, Winston Company's accountant estimated the next year's direct labor as the cost of 20 persons, working an average of 1,900 hours each at an average wage rate of $12 per hour. The accountant also estimated the following manufacturing overhead costs for 1994:

Indirect labor	$ 79,800
Factory supervision.	60,000
Rent on factory building	35,000
Factory utilities	22,000
Factory insurance expired	17,000
Depreciation of factory equipment	120,000
Repairs, factory equipment	15,000
Factory supplies used	7,000
Miscellaneous production costs	9,000
Total	$364,800

At the end of 1994, the cost records showed the company had incurred $350,000 of overhead costs. It had completed and sold five jobs with the following direct labor costs:

711	$ 77,000
712	65,000
713	87,500
714	110,000
715	92,000

In addition, Job 716 was in process at the end of the year and had been charged $5,000 for direct labor. The company's predetermined overhead application rate is based on direct labor cost.

Required

1. Determine:
   a. The predetermined overhead application rate for 1994.

b. The total overhead cost applied to each of the six jobs during 1994.
c. The over- or underapplied overhead at year-end.

2. Assuming that the amount of over- or underapplied overhead is not material, prepare the appropriate journal entry to close the Factory Overhead account at the end of 1994.

Problem 21–5
Recording manufacturing transactions; subsidiary records
(LO 4, 5)

If the working papers that accompany this text are not available, do not attempt to solve this problem.

The Tennessee Company manufactures special variations of its product (called a photomach) in response to special orders from its customers. On March 1, the company had no inventories of goods in process or finished goods but held the following raw materials:

Material G	60 units @ $100 =	$6,000
Material P	40 units @ 80 =	3,200
Paint	22 units @ 36 =	792
Total		$9,992

On March 2, the company began working on two photomachs: Job 47 for Hill Company and Job 48 for Dale, Inc.

Required

Follow the instructions given in the below list of activities and then complete the statements provided in the working papers:

a. Purchased raw materials on credit and recorded the following information from the receiving reports and invoices:

Receiving Report No. 28, Material G, 75 units at $100 each.
Receiving Report No. 29, Material P, 35 units at $80 each.

(Instructions: Record the purchases with a single general journal entry and post it to the appropriate general ledger T-accounts, using the transaction letter to identify the entries. Also, enter the receiving report information on the materials ledger cards.)

b. Requisitioned the following raw materials for production:

Requisition No. 73, for Job 47, 40 units of Material G.
Requisition No. 74, for Job 47, 30 units of Material P.
Requisition No. 75, for Job 48, 20 units of Material G.
Requisition No. 76, for Job 48, 15 units of Material P.
Requisition No. 77, for 6 units of paint.

(Instructions: Enter the amounts for the direct materials requisitions only on the materials ledger cards and the job cost sheets. Enter the indirect material amount on the raw materials ledger card and record a debit to the Indirect Materials account in the subsidiary Factory Overhead Ledger. Do not record a general journal entry at this time.)

c. Employees turned in the following time tickets for work in March:

Time tickets Nos. 1 to 10 for direct labor on Job 47, $10,000.
Time tickets Nos. 11 to 30 for direct labor on Job 48, $8,000.
Time tickets Nos. 31 to 36 for equipment repairs, $3,000.

(Instructions: Record the direct labor reported on the time tickets only on the job cost sheets and debit the indirect labor to the Indirect Labor account in the subsidiary Factory Overhead Ledger. Do not record a general journal entry at this time.)

d. The company paid cash for the following items during the month:

Factory payroll, $21,000.
Miscellaneous overhead items, $9,000.

(Instructions: record the payments with general journal entries and then post them to the general ledger accounts. Also record a debit in the Miscellaneous Overhead account in the subsidiary Factory Overhead Ledger.)

e. Finished Job 47 and transferred it to the warehouse. The company assigns overhead to each job with a predetermined overhead application rate equal to 70% of direct labor cost.

(Instructions: enter the allocated overhead on the cost sheet for Job 47, fill in the cost summary section of the cost sheet, and then mark the cost sheet as "Finished." Next, prepare a journal entry to record the job's completion and transfer to finished goods, and then post it to the general ledger accounts.)

f. Delivered Job 47 and accepted the customer's promise to pay $72,500 within 30 days.

(Instructions: Prepare general journal entries to record the sale of Job 47 and the cost of goods sold. Post them to the general ledger accounts.)

g. Applied overhead to Job 48, based on the job's direct labor to date.

(Instructions: Enter the overhead on the job cost sheet but do not make a general journal entry at this time.)

h. Recorded the total direct and indirect materials costs as reported on all the requisitions for the month.

(Instructions: Prepare a general journal entry to record these costs, and post it to the general ledger accounts.)

i. Recorded the total direct and indirect labor costs as reported on all the time tickets for the month.

(Instructions: Prepare a general journal entry to record these costs, and post it to the general ledger accounts.)

j. Recorded the total overhead costs applied to jobs.

(Instructions: Prepare a general journal entry to record the application of these costs, and post it to the general ledger accounts.)

Problem 21–6
Analytical essay
(LO 5)

Problem 21–1 describes the practices used by Superior Company in its job order cost accounting system. Superior uses a predetermined overhead application rate of 50% of direct labor cost. Problem 21–1 assumes that any over- or underapplied overhead is not material and should be assigned to cost of goods sold.

Assume now that the overhead is underapplied and is material. Superior is still considering assigning all of it to cost of goods sold. Describe how this treatment of the underapplied overhead will affect the financial statements for the current year and the following year.

Problem 21–7
Analytical essay
(LO 4, 5)

The president of Dunner Corporation has hired you as the new accountant. He has asked you to prepare the financial statements for the year ended December 31, 1994, based on the adjusted trial balance that follows:

DUNNER CORPORATION
Adjusted Trial Balance
December 31, 1994

Cash	$ 25,720	
Accounts receivable	28,500	
Raw materials inventory	2,100	
Goods in process inventory	14,250	
Finished goods inventory	23,800	
Store equipment	36,890	
Accumulated depreciation, store equipment		$ 13,540
Accounts payable		12,600
Long-term notes payable		34,800
Common stock		35,800
Retained earnings		31,970
Sales		96,500
Sales returns and allowances	1,250	
Cost of goods sold	69,200	
Factory payroll	2,400	
Factory overhead	1,200	
Miscellaneous expenses	19,900	
	$225,210	$225,210

The president has informed you that this trial balance was prepared by the previous accountant and is supposedly ready to be used in preparing the statements. He has also told you that Dunner uses a job order cost accounting system and assigns factory overhead using a predetermined overhead rate that relates overhead to direct labor.

After taking a brief look at the adjusted trial balance, you tell the president that you suspect some items of information for the period were not processed, or were processed incorrectly, and that you need some time to research the problem. Explain the basis of your suspicions to the president and describe the nature of the entries that will probably be required to correct the adjusted trial balance.

Alternate Problems

Problem 21–1A
Recording manufacturing costs and preparing financial reports
(LO 4, 5)

The following information refers to the job order manufacturing activities of Michigan Company for July:

The June 30 inventory of raw materials was $8,000. Raw materials purchases during July were $30,000. Factory payroll cost during July was $34,000. Overhead costs incurred during the month of July were

Indirect materials	$ 3,000
Indirect labor	2,000
Factory rent	13,000
Factory utilities	11,000
Factory equipment depreciation	12,500

The predetermined overhead rate was 130% of the direct labor cost. Costs allocated to the three jobs worked on during July were

	Job 313	Job 314	Job 315
Balances at June 30:			
Direct materials	$ 2,000	$ 3,000	
Direct labor	1,000	1,100	
Applied overhead	1,300	1,430	
Costs during July:			
Direct materials	5,000	15,000	$ 8,000
Direct labor	8,000	14,000	10,000
Applied overhead	?	?	?
Status at July 31	Finished (sold)	Finished (unsold)	In process

Job 313 was sold for $50,000 cash during July.

Required

1. Determine the total of each manufacturing cost incurred for July (direct labor, direct materials, allocated overhead), and the total cost assigned to each of the three jobs (including the balances from June 30).
2. Present journal entries for the month to record
   a. The materials purchases (on credit), the factory payroll (paid with cash), and the actual overhead costs, including indirect materials and indirect labor. (The factory rent and utilities were paid with cash.)
   b. The assignment of direct materials, direct labor, and applied overhead costs to the Goods in Process Inventory.
   c. The transfer of Jobs 313 and 314 to the Finished Goods Inventory.
   d. The cost of Job 313 in the Cost of Goods Sold account.
   e. The revenue from the sale of Job 313.
   f. The assignment of any underapplied or overapplied overhead to the Cost of Goods Sold account. (The amount is not material.)
3. Prepare a manufacturing statement for July (use a single line presentation for direct materials and show the details of overhead cost). Also, present a calculation of gross profit for July and show how the inventories would be presented on the July 31 balance sheet.

Problem 21–2A
Source documents, journal entries, and preparing financial statements
(LO 3, 4, 5)

The following trial balance of the Glasgow Company was generated by the computer system on the morning of December 31, 1994. Hillary Tartan, the company's accountant, knows that something is wrong with the trial balance because it does not show any balance for the goods in process inventory and it still shows balances in the Factory Payroll and Factory Overhead accounts:

Cash	$ 20,000	
Accounts receivable	40,000	
Raw materials inventory	12,000	
Goods in process inventory	-0-	
Finished goods	25,000	
Prepaid rent	2,000	
Accounts payable		$ 8,000
Notes payable		15,000
Common stock		30,000
Retained earnings		16,900
Sales		125,000
Cost of goods sold	70,000	
Factory payroll	10,000	
Factory overhead	4,900	
Miscellaneous expenses	11,000	
Total	$194,900	$194,900

After a few moments of searching a cluttered in-box, Tartan finds these six source documents that need to be processed to bring the accounting records up to date:

Materials requisition 94-7878:	$2,200 direct materials to Job 929
Materials requisition 94-7879:	$3,500 direct materials to Job 930
Materials requisition 94-7880:	$1,250 indirect materials
Labor time ticket 94-3454:	$4,000 direct labor to Job 929
Labor time ticket 94-3455:	$5,000 direct labor to Job 930
Labor time ticket 94-3456:	$1,000 indirect labor

Jobs 929 and 930 are the only units in process at the end of the year. The predetermined overhead application rate is 80% of direct labor cost.

Required

1. Use the information in the six source documents to prepare journal entries to assign the following costs:
   a. Direct materials costs to goods in process inventory.
   b. Direct labor costs to goods in process inventory.
   c. Overhead costs to goods in process inventory.
   d. Indirect materials costs to the overhead account.
   e. Indirect labor costs to the overhead account.
2. Determine the new balance of the Factory Overhead account after making the entries in requirement 1. Determine whether there is under- or overapplied overhead for the year. If so, prepare the appropriate adjusting entry to close the overhead account, assuming that the amount is not material.
3. Prepare a revised trial balance.
4. Prepare an income statement for 1994 and a balance sheet as of December 31, 1994.

Problem 21–3A
Source documents and journal entries under job order cost accounting (LO 3, 4)

Lithuania Company's predetermined overhead application rate during a recent month was 90% of direct labor. The company's activities related to manufacturing during the month were:

a. Purchased raw materials on account, $38,000.
b. Paid factory wages with cash, $66,500.

c. Paid miscellaneous factory overhead costs with cash, $7,500.

d. Materials requisitions for the month show that the following materials were used on jobs and indirectly:

Job 60	$ 9,000
Job 61	6,000
Job 62	8,000
Job 63	7,000
Job 64	1,000
Total direct materials	$31,000
Indirect materials	2,500
Total materials used	$33,500

e. Labor time tickets for the month show the following labor was used on jobs and indirectly:

Job 60	$11,000
Job 61	13,000
Job 62	17,000
Job 63	12,000
Job 64	5,000
Total direct labor	$58,000
Indirect labor	8,500
Total	$66,500

f. Jobs 60, 62, and 63 were completed and overhead was allocated to them with the predetermined overhead application rate of 90% of direct labor cost.

g. Jobs 60, 62, and 63 were transferred to finished goods.

h. Jobs 60 and 62 were sold on account for a total price of $150,000.

i. Overhead costs incurred during the month were as follows. (Credit Prepaid Insurance for the expired factory insurance.)

Depreciation of factory building	$16,500
Depreciation of factory equipment	12,500
Expired factory insurance	1,500
Accrued property taxes payable	3,500

j. At the end of the month, overhead is applied to the goods in process (Jobs 61 and 64) using the predetermined rate of 90% of direct labor cost.

Required

1. Prepare general journal entries to record the events and transactions *a* through *j*.
2. Set up T-accounts for each of the following general ledger accounts, each of which started the month with a zero balance. Then, post the journal entries to these T-accounts and determine the balance of each account.

Raw Materials Inventory	Factory Payroll
Goods in Process Inventory	Factory Overhead
Finished Goods Inventory	Cost of Goods Sold

3. Prepare a job cost sheet for each job worked on during the month. Use the following simplified form:

Job. No.	
Materials	$
Labor	
Overhead	
Total cost	$

4. Prepare a schedule showing the total cost of each job in process and proving that the sum of the costs equals the Goods in Process Inventory account balance. Prepare similar schedules for the finished goods inventory and the cost of goods sold.

Problem 21–4A
Allocating overhead based on predetermined overhead application rate (LO 5)

In December 1993, Salem Company's accountant estimated the next year's direct labor as the cost of 40 persons, working an average of 1,800 hours each at an average wage rate of $20 per hour. The accountant also estimated the following manufacturing overhead costs for 1994:

Indirect labor	$ 360,000
Factory supervision	300,000
Rent on factory building	240,000
Factory utilities	98,000
Factory insurance expired	40,000
Depreciation of factory equipment	200,000
Repairs, factory equipment	150,000
Factory supplies used	140,000
Miscellaneous production costs	200,000
Total	$1,728,000

At the end of 1994, the cost records showed the company had incurred $1,750,000 of actual overhead costs. It had completed and sold five jobs with the following direct labor costs:

929	$200,000
930	150,000
931	650,000
932	160,000
933	250,000

In addition, Job 934 was in process at the end of the year and had been charged $50,000 for direct labor. The company's predetermined overhead application rate is based on direct labor cost.

Required

1. Determine:
   a. The predetermined overhead application rate for 1994.
   b. The total overhead cost applied to each of the six jobs during 1994.
   c. The over- or underapplied overhead at year-end.
2. Assuming that the amount of over- or underapplied overhead is not material, prepare the appropriate journal entry to close the Factory Overhead account at the end of 1994.

Problem 21–5A
Recording manufacturing transactions; subsidiary records
(LO 4, 5)

If the working papers that accompany this text are not available, do not attempt to solve this problem.

The Kentucky Company manufactures special variations of its product (called an electroscope) in response to orders from its customers. On October 1, the company had no inventories of goods in process or finished goods but held the following raw materials:

Material G	50 units @ $ 60 =	$3,000
Material P	20 units @ 200 =	4,000
Paint	10 units @ 20 =	200
Total		$7,200

On October 2, the company began working on two electroscopes: Job 20 for Hither Company and Job 21 for Yon, Inc.

Required

Follow the instructions given in the list of activities below and then complete the statements provided in the working papers.

a. Purchased raw materials on credit and recorded the following information from the receiving reports and invoices:

Receiving Report No. 80, Material G, 50 units at $60 each.
Receiving Report No. 81, Material P, 80 units at $200 each.

(Instructions: Record the purchases with a single general journal entry and post it to the appropriate general ledger T-accounts, using the transaction letter to identify the entries. Also, enter the receiving report information on the materials ledger cards.)

b. Requisitioned the following raw materials for production:

Requisition No. 60, for Job 20, 20 units of Material G.
Requisition No. 61, for Job 20, 40 units of Material P.
Requisition No. 62, for Job 21, 10 units of Material G.
Requisition No. 63, for Job 21, 30 units of Material P.
Requisition No. 64, for 5 units of paint.

(Instructions: Enter the amounts for the direct materials requisitions only on the materials ledger cards and the job cost sheets. Enter the indirect material amount on the raw materials ledger card and record a debit to the Indirect Materials account in the subsidiary Factory Overhead Ledger. Do not record a general journal entry at this time.)

c. Employees turned in the following time tickets for work in October:

Time tickets Nos. 1 to 10 for direct labor on Job 20, $12,000.
Time tickets Nos. 11 to 20 for direct labor on Job 21, $10,000.
Time tickets Nos. 21 to 24 for equipment repairs, $2,000.

(Instructions: Record the direct labor reported on the time tickets only on the job cost sheets and debit the indirect labor to the Indirect Labor account in the subsidiary Factory Overhead Ledger. Do not record a general journal entry at this time.)

d. The company paid cash for the following items during the month:

Factory payroll, $24,000.
Miscellaneous overhead items, $23,500.

(Instructions: Record the payments with general journal entries and then post them to the general ledger accounts. Also record a debit in the Miscellaneous Overhead account in the subsidiary Factory Overhead Ledger.)

e. Finished Job 20 and transferred it to the warehouse. The company assigns overhead to each job with a predetermined overhead application rate equal to 120% of direct labor cost.

(Instructions: Enter the allocated overhead on the cost sheet for Job 20, fill in the cost summary section of the cost sheet, and then mark the cost sheet as "Finished." Next, prepare a journal entry to record the job's completion and transfer to finished goods, and then post it to the general ledger accounts.)

f. Delivered Job 20 and accepted the customer's promise to pay $65,000 within 30 days.

(Instructions: Prepare general journal entries to record the sale of Job 20 and the cost of goods sold. Post them to the general ledger accounts.)

g. At the end of the month, used the predetermined rate to assign overhead cost to Job 21, based on the direct labor cost used on the job up to that date.

(Instructions: Enter the overhead on the job cost sheet but do not make a general journal entry at this time.)

h. Recorded the total direct and indirect materials costs as reported on all the requisitions for the month.

(Instructions: Prepare a general journal entry to record these costs, and post it to the general ledger accounts.)

i. Recorded the total direct and indirect labor costs as reported on all the time tickets for the month.

(Instructions: Prepare a general journal entry to record these costs, and post it to the general ledger accounts.)

j. Recorded the total overhead costs applied to jobs.

(Instructions: Prepare a general journal entry to record the application of these costs, and post it to the general ledger accounts.)

Problem 21–6A
Analytical essay
(LO 5)

Problem 21–1A describes the practices used by Michigan Company in its job order cost accounting system. Michigan uses a predetermined overhead rate of 130% of direct labor cost to assign factory overhead. Problem 21–1A assumes that any over- or underapplied overhead is not material and should be assigned to cost of goods sold.

Assume now that the overhead is overapplied and is material. Michigan is still considering assigning all of it to cost of goods sold. Describe how this treatment of the overapplied overhead will affect the financial statements for the current year and the following year.

Problem 21–7A
Analytical essay
(LO 4, 5)

The president of Bostec Manufacturing Company is anxious to see some figures on the results of operations for 1994. She does not want to wait until the financial statements are prepared and has asked you, the accountant for Bostec, for an adjusted trial balance. Bostec uses a job order cost accounting system and assigns overhead based on a predetermined overhead rate. You prepare the following adjusted trial balance and submit it to her as requested:

BOSTEC MANUFACTURING COMPANY
Adjusted Trial Balance
December 31, 1994

Cash	$ 13,450	
Accounts receivable	26,200	
Raw materials inventory	9,300	
Goods in process inventory	17,090	
Finished goods inventory	15,860	
Store equipment	24,220	
Accumulated depreciation, store equipment		$ 7,400
Accounts payable		12,600
Long-term notes payable		15,000
Common stock		20,000
Retained earnings		39,820
Sales		75,800
Cost of goods sold	52,100	
Factory payroll	–0–	
Factory overhead	–0–	
Miscellaneous expenses	12,400	
	$170,620	$170,620

The president calls you to her office and wants to know why factory payroll and factory overhead are reported as zero when she knows costs were incurred for both. Explain this result to the president. Include in your explanation a brief description of the entries that are made to these accounts.

Provocative Problems

Provocative Problem 21–1
Gagne Manufacturing Co.
(LO 1)

The Gagne Manufacturing Co. produces and sells a single product that consists of three components. One component is an electronics package that detects an intrusion in a building and sends a radio signal to the police. The other two components are a control mechanism and a metal box. Gagne builds each component and then combines them into the finished product. The following flowchart shows the whole manufacturing operation:

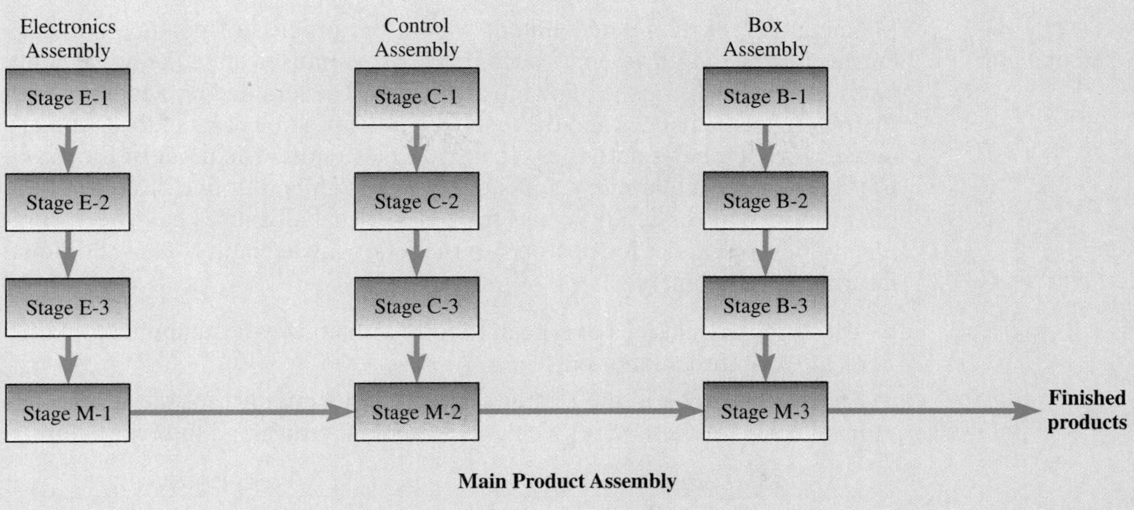

The electronics package is fabricated in three stages (E-1, E-2, and E-3), as are the control mechanism (C-1, C-2, and C-3) and the metal box (B-1, B-2, and B-3). The final product assembly also requires three production stages (M-1, M-2, and M-3). To avoid production delays, inventories of materials (or components) are held at each of the 12 stages.

Recently, management has begun to consider just-in-time manufacturing. All of the company's suppliers have agreed to fill smaller, more frequent orders. Some have even agreed to send several orders during a single day so that they can operate without building up inventories of finished goods. In comparing the current operations with a JIT system, Gagne's managers prepared the following table:

Stage	Cost of Materials Processed in One Day	Days' Stock Currently Held	Days' Stock That Must Be Held Under JIT
E-1	$ 4,000	4.00	1.00
E-2	5,000	3.00	0.50
E-3	2,000	2.00	0.25
C-1	7,000	2.00	0.00
C-2	8,000	10.00	3.00
C-3	3,000	5.00	1.00
B-1	9,000	5.00	1.00
B-2	6,000	5.00	1.00
B-3	9,500	3.00	0.50
M-1	7,000	2.00	0.25
M-2	10,000	4.00	0.50
M-3	14,000	10.00	3.00

Required

Calculate the amount by which Gagne's investment in inventories can be reduced by changing to a JIT system. Also calculate the effect of the change on net income, assuming that Gagne can earn 15% per year on additional investments in other operations.

Provocative Problem 21–2
Majestic Corporation
(LO 4, 5)

Majestic Corporation's accountant was in the process of posting summary entries for the month when he became ill. In a confused state, he posted only parts of several entries. Following are selected general ledger accounts with their October 1 balances and the results of posting some parts of the summary entries for October's activities. In some cases, either the debit or the credit portion of a particular entry appears in the accounts, but one or more of the offsetting credits or debits is missing. Assume that all entries have been completely posted except for postings to the following accounts. This additional information is available:

- The company charges overhead to jobs with an overhead application rate of 125% of direct labor cost.
- The $72,000 debit in the Factory Overhead account is the sum of all overhead costs for October other than indirect materials and indirect labor.

Raw Materials Inventory

Oct. 1 Bal.	60,000	70,000
	96,000	

Factory Payroll

130,000	

Goods in Process Inventory

Oct. 1 Bal.	20,000	200,000
Dir. mat'l.	50,000	
Dir. labor	100,000	

Cost of Goods Sold

Finished Goods Inventory

Oct. 1 Bal.	25,000	188,000

Factory Overhead

72,000	

Required

1. Copy the accounts on a sheet of paper and add the missing debits and credits. Identify the debits and credits of each entry with a code letter. (Hint: You may find it helpful to first draft the entries in general journal form.)
2. Answer the following questions before considering overapplied or underapplied overhead:
   a. What is the October 31 balance of the Finished Goods account?
   b. How much factory labor cost (direct and indirect) was incurred during October?
   c. What was the cost of the goods sold for October?
   d. How much overhead was incurred during the month?
   e. How much overhead was charged to jobs during the month?
3. Was overhead overapplied or underapplied during the month? By how much?

Provocative Problem 21–3
Fleet Company
(LO 3)

Fleet Company's factory was completely destroyed by an explosion and fire on August 17, 1994. All inventories were lost and many accounting records were destroyed, although some were salvaged from the ashes, and others were available from off-site back ups. In preparing to settle with the fire insurance company, Fleet's management has asked you to help estimate the costs of the destroyed raw materials, goods in process, and finished goods. The company uses job order cost accounting and the following information is available:

a. The company's December 31, 1993, balance sheet reported these costs for the inventories: raw materials, $90,000; goods in process, $100,000; and finished goods, $120,000.

b. The cost of raw materials purchased between January 1 and August 17 was $165,000. Direct and indirect materials costing $112,000 (combined) were issued to the factory during the same period.

c. Between January 1 and August 17, factory wages totaling $400,000 were paid and charged to jobs or overhead.

d. The total debits to Factory Overhead during the period before the fire amounted to $300,000. Indirect materials represented $40,000 of this balance, and indirect labor represented $80,000.

e. The overhead application rate used by the company was 90% of direct labor cost.

f. The cost of jobs transferred to the finished goods inventory during the January 1 to August 17 period was $700,000.

g. Jobs costing $625,000 were sold and delivered to customers between January 1 and August 17, 1994.

h. The August 17 Factory Overhead account balance should be allocated among the goods in process inventory, the finished goods inventory, and the cost of goods sold. The allocation should be made in proportion to the direct labor charged to the three groups of jobs between January 1 and August 17. The direct labor charges were

Sold jobs	$220,800
Finished but unsold jobs	51,200
Jobs in process	48,000
Total direct labor	$320,000

Required

To determine the August 17 inventories, set up T-accounts for the following accounts and enter the appropriate balances and postings based on the available information: Raw Materials Inventory, Goods in Process Inventory, Finished Goods Inventory, Factory Payroll, Cost of Goods Sold, and Factory Overhead.

Answers to Objective Review Questions

LO 1 (*a*) LO 2 (*e*) LO 3 (*c*) LO 4 (*e*) LO 5 (*a*) LO 6 (*d*)

CHAPTER

22

Process Cost Accounting

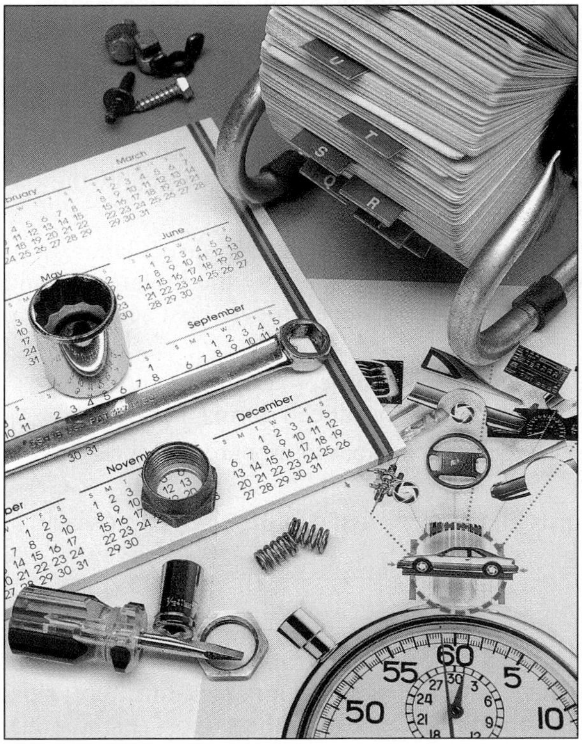

Many products are produced in large quantities with complex processes, for example, cars emerge from an assembly line as a result of the efforts by many different people in a variety of departments. Managerial accounting techniques gather information about the costs of these processes.

Topical Coverage

In Chapter 21, you learned about job order cost accounting systems. Companies use these systems to account for manufacturing when each product or job consists of one unit (or a group of units) that is uniquely designed to meet the requirements of a particular customer. In other words, each unit (or group of units) is a distinct product or job that requires unique applications of material, labor, and overhead. As we explained in Chapter 21, manufacturing operations of this nature are best served by a job order cost accounting system that maintains a separate accounting record for each job and accumulates costs by job.

Of course, not all products are manufactured in this way. Many products have standard designs, and one unit is no different from any other unit. Typically, a large number of units are produced on a more or less continuous basis, period after period. In producing this kind of product, all units pass through the same series of manufacturing steps or processes. In this chapter, you will learn how to use a process cost accounting system to account for products like this. We will explain how manufacturing costs are accumulated for each process and then assigned to the units that pass through the processes.

Learning Objectives

After studying Chapter 22, you should be able to:

1. Explain the nature of process manufacturing operations and how they differ from job order operations.
2. Describe the process of accumulating direct materials, direct labor, and manufacturing overhead costs according to each production process and prepare entries to record the flow of costs in a process cost accounting system.
3. Explain how equivalent units are used in process cost accounting systems and calculate the equivalent units produced during a period.
4. Describe the purposes served by and be able to prepare a process cost summary.
5. Define or explain the words and phrases listed in the chapter glossary.

Process Manufacturing Operations

LO 1 Explain the nature of process manufacturing operations and how they differ from job order operations.

Many companies produce large quantities of identical products. Examples of such products are carpeting, hand tools, personal computers, furniture, skis, television sets, compact disks, building supplies (lumber, doors, paint, etc.), greeting cards, calculators, and small pleasure boats. Products like these are produced in a manufacturing operation that passes the products through a series of *processes,* or steps in production. Each process involves a different set of activities. For example, a manufacturing operation that produces prefabricated doors might include these four processes:

1. Cutting the wood for the door and frame.
2. Planing and sanding the wood, and fabricating the door and frame from the wood components.

ILLUSTRATION 22–1

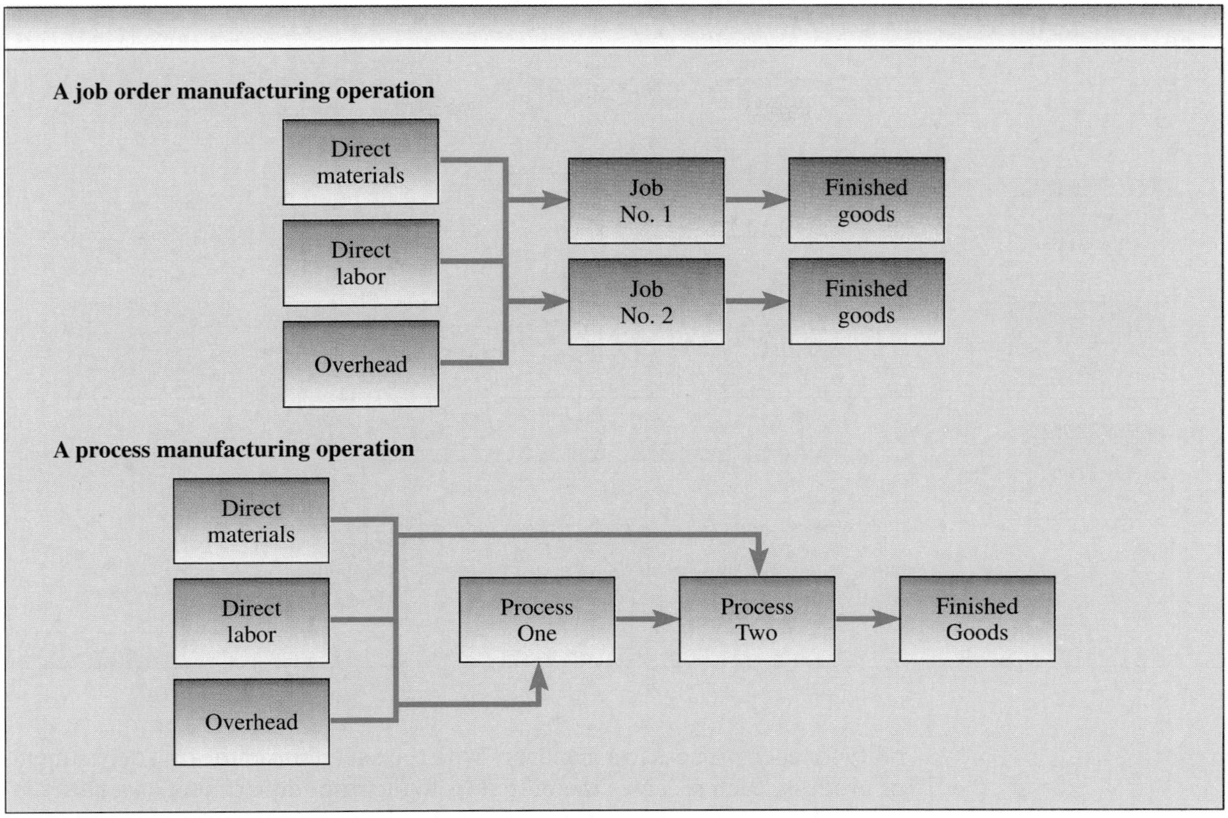

3. Mounting the hardware, including the hinges, latch, and knob, and assembling the finished door and the finished frame.
4. Packaging the completed unit for shipment.

Comparing Process and Job Order Manufacturing Operations

Process and job order manufacturing operations are similar because they both combine materials, labor, and other manufacturing overhead items in the process of producing products. However, they differ in the way they are organized and managed. Illustration 22–1 shows that direct materials, direct labor, and overhead are applied to specific jobs in a job order operation. By comparison, a process manufacturing operation applies direct materials, direct labor, and overhead to specific manufacturing processes. Thus, the focus of job order operations is on specific jobs while the focus of process operations is on the series of processes used to complete the product.

Organization of Process Manufacturing Operations

In a process manufacturing operation, each process is identified as a separate *production department* or *workstation* or *work center*. Unlike a job order operation that assigns each job to a manager, a process operation assigns responsi-

ILLUSTRATION 22–2

A Manufacturing Operation with Parallel and Sequential Processes

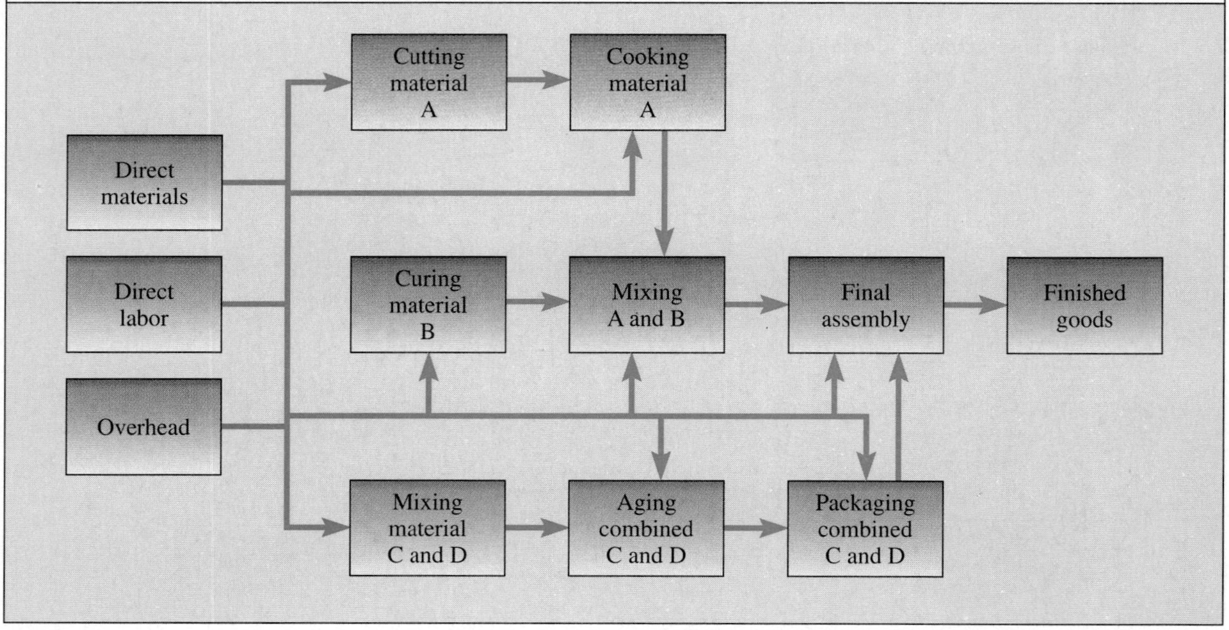

bility for each process to a manager. With the exception of the first department or process, each receives the output from the prior department as a partially processed product. Depending on the nature of the process, direct labor, manufacturing overhead, and, perhaps, additional direct materials are combined to move the product further toward completion. Only the last department in the series produces finished goods ready for sale to customers.

Most process manufacturing operations are more complex than the one show in Illustration 22–1. For example, Illustration 22–2 shows an operation in which components of a final product are manufactured in three parallel processes and then combined at different stages of production. Although this illustration may appear complex, many manufacturing operations involve hundreds of different components and related production processes.

Delta Processing Company—A Comprehensive Case

To provide a basis for illustrating process cost accounting, consider Delta Processing Company. Delta produces a simple product called Noxall, which is an over-the-counter remedy for upset stomachs. Delta sells Noxall to wholesale distributors who in turn sell it to retailers. Noxall is produced in two steps. The first step uses a grinding process to pulverize large blocks of the active ingredient, called Noxalene. The second step mixes this powder with flavorings and preservatives, and molds it into Noxall tablets. This process also puts the Noxall tablets into packages.

Illustration 22–3 shows a simplified floor plan of the Delta factory, which has five rooms:

ILLUSTRATION 22–3

Floor Plan of Delta Processing Company's Factory

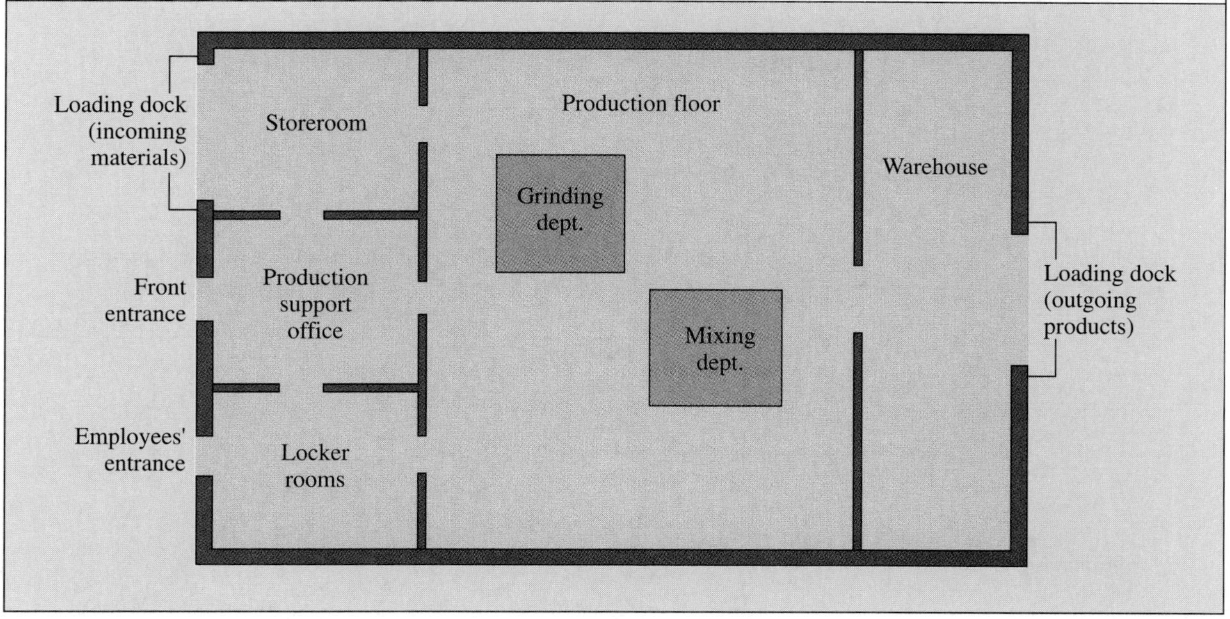

- The *storeroom,* where materials are received and then distributed in response to requisitions.
- The *production support office,* which is used by administrative and maintenance employees who support manufacturing operations.
- The employees' *locker rooms,* where workers change from street clothes into uniforms before working in the factory.
- The *production floor,* which is divided into two areas for use by the grinding and mixing departments.
- The *warehouse,* in which finished products are stored before being shipped to wholesalers.

Even though Delta Processing Company's product is relatively simple, the factory could have five or more managers, as shown in this diagram:

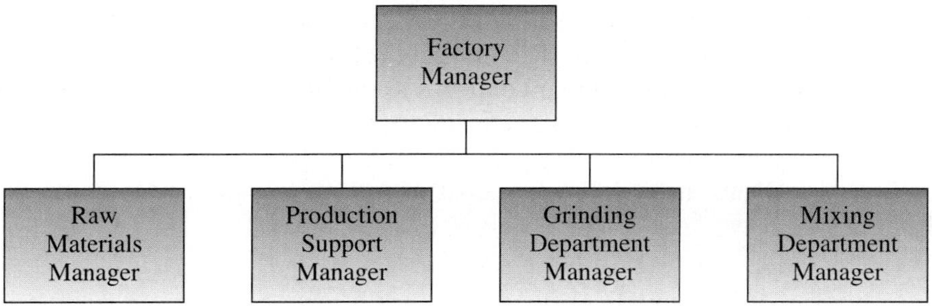

ILLUSTRATION 22–4

Process Manufacturing Operations Delta Processing Company

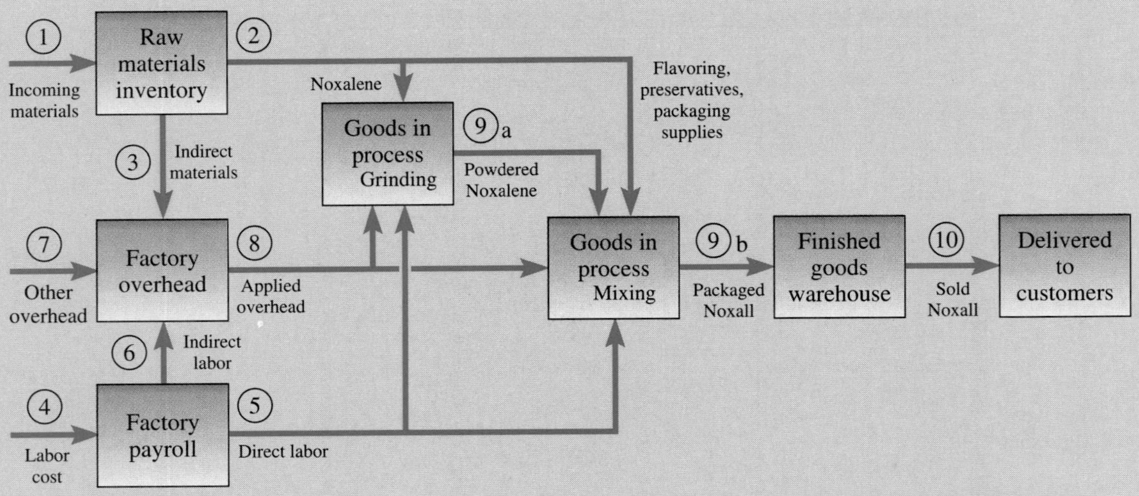

Manufacturing Costs during April 1994

	Raw Materials	Factory Payroll	Factory Overhead	Grinding Department	Mixing Department
Beginning balance	$ 4,000			$ 4,250	$ 3,520
Purchases and costs incurred	14,135	$14,020	$ 880		
Application of costs:					
Direct materials	(11,940)			9,900	2,040
Indirect materials	(1,195)		1,195		
Direct labor		(10,800)		5,700	5,100
Indirect labor		(3,220)	3,220		
Overhead applied			(5,295)	4,275	1,020

The first step in process manufacturing is the decision to produce a specific product. Management must determine the types and quantities of materials and labor needed and then schedule the work for the departments. Based on these plans, production begins.

The flowchart at the top of Illustration 22–4 shows the production steps for Delta Processing Company. The table at the bottom of the illustration summarizes Delta's manufacturing inventories at the beginning of April 1994, the manufacturing costs Delta incurred during April, and the application of those costs to the grinding and mixing departments. In the following sections, we explain how Delta uses a process cost accounting system to account for these costs.

Accumulating the Costs of Each Manufacturing Process

LO 2 Describe the process of accumulating direct materials, direct labor, and manufacturing overhead costs according to each production process and prepare entries to record the flow of costs in a process cost accounting system.

In a job order operation, managers are responsible for planning and controlling the costs of manufacturing each job. To provide managers with relevant cost information, a job order cost accounting system accumulates the costs of each job on a separate job cost sheet. By comparison, managers in a process operation are responsible for planning and controlling the costs of each process. Thus, a **process cost accounting system** accumulates the manufacturing costs of each process. Then, the cost per unit is determined by dividing the total cost assigned to a process by the number of units that passed through the process. You will learn more about calculating unit costs later in the chapter.

Direct and Indirect Costs in Process Cost Accounting

In Chapter 20, you learned that direct material and direct labor costs can be clearly associated with specific units or batches of product. Other manufacturing costs that cannot be clearly associated with specific units or batches of product are defined as manufacturing overhead. Chapter 21 explained how the concepts of direct and indirect materials and labor are used in job order cost accounting. In summary, materials and labor used on jobs are charged to the jobs as direct costs. Materials and labor that contribute to manufacturing but are not clearly associated with specific jobs are indirect costs and are allocated to jobs as manufacturing overhead.

Process cost accounting systems also use the concepts of direct and indirect manufacturing costs. Materials and labor that are clearly associated with specific manufacturing processes are assigned to those processes as direct costs. Materials and labor that are not clearly associated with a specific process are indirect costs and are assigned to overhead.[1]

Accounting for Materials Costs

In Illustration 22–4, arrow 1 represents the arrival of materials at Delta Processing Company's factory. These materials include Noxalene, flavorings, preservatives, packaging supplies, and supplies for the production support office. Assuming that Delta uses a perpetual inventory system and makes all purchases on credit, this entry summarizes the receipts of raw materials during April:

1	Raw Materials Inventory	14,135.00	
	Accounts Payable		14,135.00
	Acquired materials on credit for use in the factory.		

[1] Some costs classified as manufacturing overhead in a job order system may be classified as direct costs in process cost accounting. For example, depreciation on a machine used entirely by one process is a direct cost of that process. In this introductory discussion, however, all manufacturing costs other than direct materials and direct labor are treated as overhead.

The accounting department makes entries to record the receipt of materials when it receives copies of receiving reports from the storeroom.

Arrow 2 in Illustration 22–4 represents the flow of direct materials to the grinding and mixing departments, where they are used in producing Noxall. Most direct materials are physically incorporated into the finished product. However, in process cost accounting, direct materials include supplies used in a specific process because they can be clearly associated with that process.

As in a job order system, the manager of a process usually obtains material for use in the process by submitting a materials requisition to the raw materials storeroom manager. However, in some situations, materials move continuously from the raw materials inventory to a manufacturing process. In these cases, a **materials consumption report** summarizes the materials used by a department during a reporting period and replaces materials requisitions.

The following entry records the use of direct materials by Delta Processing Company's two production departments during April:

2	Goods in Process Inventory—Grinding	9,900.00	
	Goods in Process Inventory—Mixing	2,040.00	
	Raw Materials Inventory		11,940.00
	To assign costs of direct materials used in the grinding and mixing departments.		

Two goods in process inventory accounts allow the costs incurred by each process to be separately accumulated. Note that the entry does not increase or decrease the company's assets because it merely transfers costs from one asset account to two other asset accounts.

In Illustration 22–4, arrow 3 shows the flow of indirect materials from the storeroom to factory overhead. These materials are not clearly associated with either the grinding or the mixing departments. They are used in support of production. The production support office is called a **service department** because its activities are not directly involved in manufacturing products. By comparison, the grinding and mixing departments are called **production departments** because they produce the products.

The following entry records the cost of indirect materials used by Delta during April:

3	Factory Overhead	1,195.00	
	Raw Materials Inventory		1,195.00
	To record indirect materials used in April.		

After the entries for materials are posted, the Raw Materials Inventory account looks like this:

Raw Materials Inventory **Acct. No.** 132

Date		Explanation	Debit	Credit	Balance
1994					
Mar.	31	Beginning balance			4,000
Apr.	30	Materials purchases	14,135		18,135
	30	Direct materials usage		11,940	6,195
	30	Indirect materials usage		1,195	5,000

The April 30 balance sheet presents the balance of this account as a current asset.

Accounting for Labor Costs

Illustration 22–4 represents the factory payroll cost for Delta Processing Company with arrow 4. The total labor cost of $14,020 is paid with cash and is recorded in the Factory Payroll account with this entry:

4	Factory Payroll	14,020.00	
	Cash		14,020.00
	To record factory wages for April.		

This entry is triggered by time reports sent to the company's account from the two production departments and the production support office. (For simplicity, we have not identified withholdings and additional payroll taxes for the employees.)

In a process operation, the direct labor of a production department includes all labor used exclusively by that department, even if it is not applied to the product itself. For example, if a production department has a full-time manager and a full-time maintenance worker, their salaries are direct labor costs, not factory overhead.

Arrow 5 in Illustration 22–4 shows Delta's use of direct labor in the grinding and mixing departments. The following entry transfers April's direct labor costs from the Factory Payroll account to the two goods in process accounts:

5	Goods in Process Inventory—Grinding	5,700.00	
	Goods in Process Inventory—Mixing	5,100.00	
	Factory Payroll		10,800.00
	To assign costs of direct labor used in the grinding and mixing departments.		

Arrow 6 in Illustration 22–4 represents the indirect labor used by Delta Processing Company. These employees provide the clerical, maintenance, and other services that help the grinding and mixing departments produce Noxall more efficiently. For example, they order materials, deliver them to the factory floor, repair equipment, operate and program computers used in production, keep payroll and other production accounting records, clean up, and move the finished goods to the warehouse. The following entry charges these indirect labor costs to factory overhead:

6	Factory Overhead	3,220.00	
	Factory Payroll		3,220.00
	To record indirect labor as overhead.		

After these entries for labor are posted, the Factory Payroll account looks like this:

Factory Payroll					Acct. No. 530
Date		Explanation	Debit	Credit	Balance
1994					
Mar.	31	Beginning balance			-0-
Apr.	30	Total payroll for April	14,020		14,020
	30	Direct labor costs		10,800	3,220
	30	Indirect labor costs		3,220	-0-

This account is now closed and ready to receive entries for May.

Accounting for Factory Overhead

Overhead costs other than indirect materials and indirect labor are represented by arrow 7 in Illustration 22–4. These overhead items include the costs of insuring manufacturing assets, renting the factory building, using factory utilities, and depreciating the equipment. The following entry records these costs for the month of April:

7	Factory Overhead	880.00	
	Prepaid Insurance		80.00
	Accrued Utilities Payable		200.00
	Cash		250.00
	Accumulated Depreciation, Factory Equipment		350.00
	To record manufacturing overhead items incurred during April.		

After this entry is posted, the Factory Overhead account balance is $5,295. This total overhead cost for April includes indirect materials of $1,195, indirect labor of $3,220, and $880 of other overhead items.

Arrow 8 in Illustration 22–4 represents the application of factory overhead to the production departments. Recall from Chapters 20 and 21 that factory overhead is applied to products or jobs by relating the overhead cost to another variable such as direct labor hours or machine hours used in production. Job order and process cost systems both use predetermined application rates.

In many situations, a single allocation basis (like direct labor hours) fails to provide useful allocations. As a result, management may use different rates for different production departments. For example, based on an analysis of each department's operations, Delta Processing Company applies overhead as follows:

	Predetermined Overhead Application Rate
Grinding department	75% of its direct labor cost
Mixing department	20% of its direct labor cost

The results of multiplying April's direct labor costs by these rates are:

Production Department	Direct Labor Cost	Predetermined Rate	Overhead Applied
Grinding	$5,700	75%	$4,275
Mixing	5,100	20%	1,020
Total			$5,295

Delta records these overhead applications with the following entry:

8	Goods in Process Inventory—Grinding	4,275.00	
	Goods in Process Inventory—Mixing	1,020.00	
	Factory Overhead.		5,295.00
	Allocated factory overhead costs to the grinding department at 75% of direct labor cost and to the mixing department at 20% of direct labor cost.		

After posting this entry, the Factory Overhead account looks like this:

Factory Overhead — **Acct. No. 540**

Date		Explanation	Debit	Credit	Balance
1994					
Mar.	31	Beginning balance			-0-
Apr.	30	Indirect materials	1,195		1,195
	30	Indirect labor costs	3,220		4,415
	30	Other overhead costs	880		5,295
	30	Applied to production departments		5,295	-0-

To simplify the Delta Processing Company example, the amount of overhead applied exactly equals the actual overhead incurred during April. In actual practice, however, using a predetermined overhead application rate almost certainly leaves an overapplied or underapplied balance in the Factory Overhead account. At the end of the period, this overapplied or underapplied balance should be allocated among the cost of goods sold and the goods in process and finished goods inventories. The procedures for making this allocation are the same as the ones used in Chapter 21 for job order cost accounting systems.

Calculating and Using Equivalent Units of Production

LO 3 Explain how equivalent units are used in process cost accounting systems and calculate the equivalent units produced during a period.

In the previous sections, we explained how the manufacturing costs for a period are accumulated in separate Goods in Process accounts for each manufacturing process. However, note that we have not explained the flows labeled 9_a, 9_b, and 10 in Illustration 22–4. These arrows represent the transfer of products from the grinding department to the mixing department, from the mixing department to finished goods inventory, and from finished goods inventory to cost of goods sold. To determine the costs that should be recorded for these flows, you must first determine the cost per unit of product and then apply this result to the number of units transferred.

Accounting for Beginning and Ending Goods in Process Inventories

If a manufacturing process does not have any beginning or ending goods in process inventory, the unit cost calculation is simple. The unit cost of goods transferred out of a process is:

$$\frac{\text{Total cost assigned to the process}}{\text{Total number of units started and finished during the period}}$$

However, if a process has a beginning or ending inventory of partially processed units, the cost assigned to the process should be allocated to all units that were worked on during the reporting period. In other words, the denominator must be a measure of the entire production activity of the process during the period. This measure is called the **equivalent units of production.** Equivalent units of production measure the activity of a process as the number of units that would have been completed if all effort during a period had been applied to units that were started and finished.

Equivalent Units May Not Be the Same for Materials and for Direct Labor and Overhead

In many manufacturing processes, the equivalent units of production for materials is not the same as equivalent units for labor and overhead. To see why this condition exists, consider the following manufacturing process:

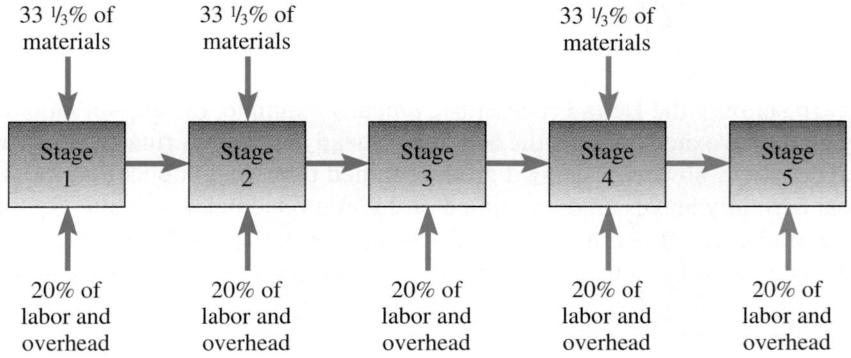

This diagram shows a single production process that consists of five stages. One third of the direct materials cost is added at each Stage 1, Stage 2, and Stage 4. One fifth of the direct labor cost is added to each of the five stages. Because overhead is applied as a percentage of direct labor, one fifth of the overhead is also added at each of the five stages.

If units have gone through Stage 1, they are one-third complete with respect to materials but only one-fifth complete with respect to labor and overhead. If they have gone through Stage 2, they are two-thirds complete with respect to materials, but only two-fifths complete with respect to labor and overhead. If they have gone through Stage 3, they are still two-thirds complete with respect to materials, but three-fifths complete with respect to labor and overhead. And, if they are through Stage 4, they are 100% complete with respect to materials but only four-fifths complete with respect to labor and overhead.

Assume that 300 units of product were started and processed through Stage 1 during a month. At the end of the month, they are one-third complete *with respect to materials*. Expressed in terms of equivalent finished units, the processing of these 300 units is equivalent to finishing 100 units; that is, 300 × 33⅓% = 100.

Although the processing of the 300 units equals 100 equivalent units of production with respect to materials, only one fifth of the direct labor and overhead were added to the 300 units at the end of Stage 1. Therefore, the equivalent units of production with respect to direct labor and overhead equals 300 × 20% = 60 units.

Accounting for Delta Processing Company's Grinding Department

The following table shows the information needed to calculate equivalent units of production for Delta's grinding department:

Beginning inventory:	
Units of product	30,000
Percentage of completion—direct materials	100%
Percentage of completion—direct labor	33⅓%
Units started during April	90,000
Units transferred from grinding to mixing	100,000
Ending inventory:	
Units of product	20,000
Percentage of completion—direct materials	100%
Percentage of completion—direct labor	25%

In calculating equivalent units, we assume that each of Delta's production departments processes units on a first-in, first-out basis.[2] Thus, the 100,000 units transferred from grinding to mixing during April include the 30,000 units from the beginning inventory. The remaining 70,000 units transferred out were started during April. In the preceding table, note that a total of 90,000 units were started during April. Because 70,000 of these units were completed, 20,000 units remain unfinished at the end of the month.

[2] We assume a FIFO flow throughout the calculations of this chapter. Weighted-average and LIFO measures can be used but they are less useful for measuring how effectively costs were controlled during a period.

Equivalent Units of Production and Cost per Unit—Direct Materials

LO 3 Explain how equivalent units are used in process cost accounting systems and calculate the equivalent units produced during a period.

In the grinding department, all materials (the Noxalene blocks) are added at the beginning of the process. That is, a unit of product is 100% complete with respect to materials as soon as it is started. Therefore, the beginning goods in process inventory for April received all its materials in March and should not be assigned any additional materials cost. The units started and completed during April and the April 30 goods in process inventory received all their materials during April. Thus, with respect to materials, the grinding department's equivalent units of production are calculated as follows:

Grinding—Equivalent Units of Production (Direct Materials)

	Units of Product	Percent Added	Equivalent Units
Beginning goods in process	30,000	0%	-0-
Goods started and completed	70,000	100%	70,000
Ending goods in process	20,000	100%	20,000
Total units	120,000		90,000

The table in Illustration 22–4 on page 1178 shows that the total direct materials cost for the grinding department was $9,900. Thus, the direct materials cost per equivalent unit is $0.11 ($9,900/90,000 units).

Equivalent Units of Production and Cost per Unit—Direct Labor

Recall from Illustration 22–4 that Delta's grinding department incurred $5,700 of direct labor cost during April. In Illustration 22–5, the square represents this direct labor activity. The illustration shows how the direct labor was applied to three different groups of products.

Part of the direct labor was used to finish the beginning goods in process. In the diagram, the white portion of the upper left circle represents the unfinished portion of the 30,000 units in the beginning goods in process inventory. The lower circle on the left shows that this portion was completed during April. Direct labor was also applied to 70,000 units that were both started and completed during April. In addition, the rest of the direct labor was used to start work on the 20,000 units that remain unfinished in the April 30 goods in process inventory. In Illustration 22–5, the shaded portion of the lower right circle represents the fact that they are only 25% complete.

The grinding department's total direct labor cost of $5,700 must be allocated among all units worked on during April. Therefore, we must calculate direct labor cost per unit based on the department's equivalent units of production. The following table summarizes the calculation:

Grinding—Equivalent Units of Production (Direct Labor)

	Units of Product	Percent Added	Equivalent Units
Beginning goods in process	30,000	66⅔%	20,000
Goods started and completed	70,000	100%	70,000
Ending goods in process	20,000	25%	5,000
Total units	120,000		95,000

ILLUSTRATION 22-5

Use of Direct Labor during April — Grinding Department

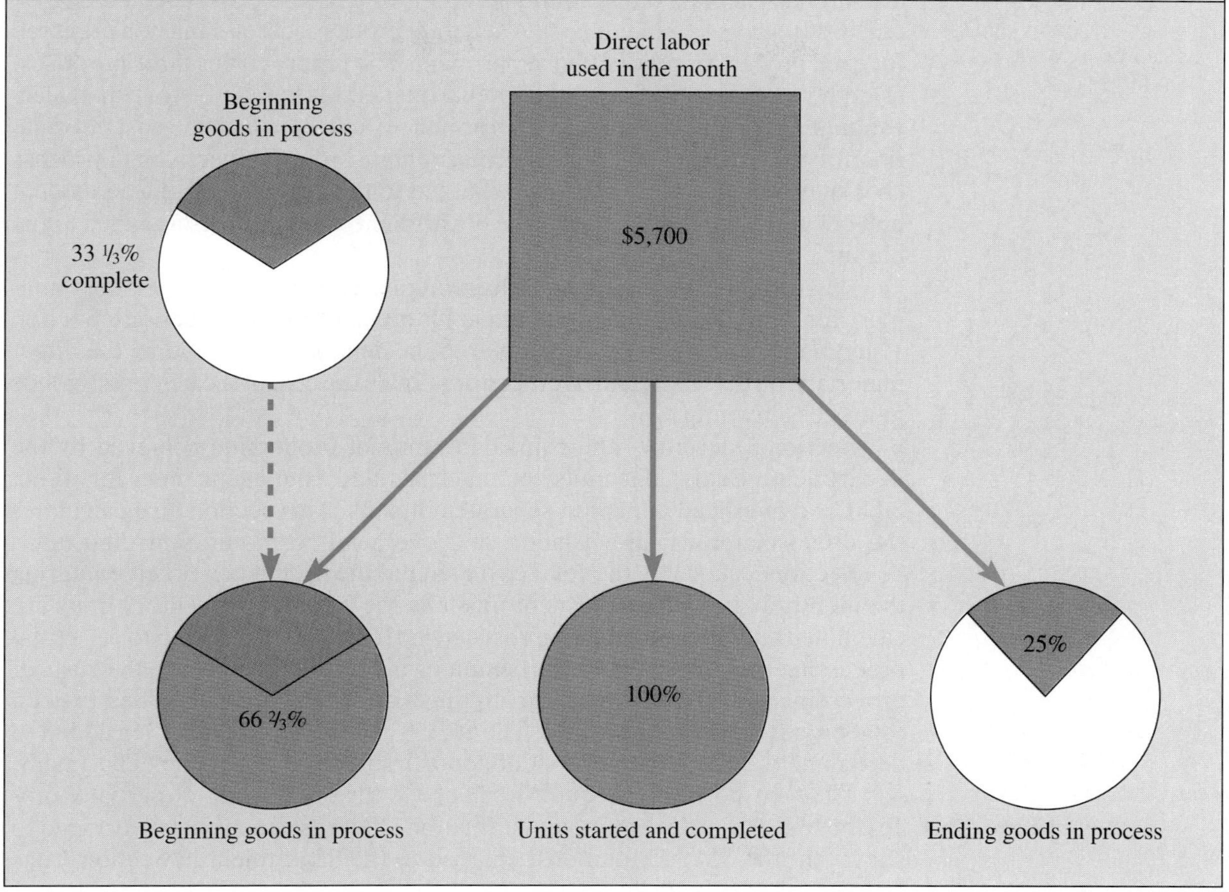

Note that the direct labor used to finish the beginning inventory was equivalent to the labor that would be used to start and finish 20,000 units. An additional 70,000 units were started and completed during the month. Finally, the work performed on the 20,000 units in the ending inventory was equivalent to starting and finishing 5,000 units. Total equivalent units of production with respect to direct labor is 95,000 units. Because the total direct labor cost was $5,700, the cost per equivalent unit was $0.06 ($5,700/95,000).

Equivalent Units of Production and Cost per Unit—Overhead

Earlier we explained that Delta assigns overhead to the grinding department at the rate of 75% of the direct labor cost. As a result, the total overhead applied to the department was $4,275 ($5,700 × 75%). Because overhead is assigned on the basis of direct labor cost, the equivalent units of production is the same for overhead as for direct labor. Therefore, the overhead cost per unit is $0.045 ($4,275/95,000).

Process Cost Summary—Grinding Department

LO 4 Describe the purposes served by and be able to prepare a process cost summary.

The primary managerial accounting report for a process cost accounting system is the **process cost summary.** A separate process cost summary is prepared for each process or production department. The report serves three purposes: (1) to help managers control their departments; (2) to help factory managers evaluate department managers' performance; and (3) to provide cost information for the financial statements. To accomplish these objectives, a process cost summary describes the costs charged to the department, the equivalent units of production achieved by the department, and the costs assigned to the output.

Illustration 22–6 shows the Delta grinding department's process cost summary for April. Notice that the summary is divided into three sections. Section 1 summarizes the total costs charged to the department, including the direct materials, direct labor, and overhead costs plus the cost of the beginning goods in process inventory.

Section 2 describes the equivalent units of production achieved by the department. Equivalent units for materials and equivalent units for direct labor and overhead appear in separate columns. This section also calculates the direct materials, direct labor, and overhead costs per equivalent unit.

Section 3 allocates the total costs among the products worked on during the month. Note that the costs of finishing the beginning inventory units are calculated and then added to the cost carried forward from March to get a total processing cost of $6,350 for the beginning inventory units. Next, the costs of processing 70,000 units from start to finish are calculated and added to get a total processing cost of $15,050. The $6,350 and the $15,050 are then added to determine the $21,400 total cost of goods transferred out of the department.

The next portion of section 3 calculates the $2,725 cost of partially processing the ending inventory units. Finally, all the assigned costs are added to show that the $24,125 total cost charged to the department in Section 1 has been assigned to units in Section 3.

Transferring Goods between Departments

LO 2 Describe the process of accumulating direct materials, direct labor, and manufacturing overhead costs according to each production process and prepare entries to record the flow of costs in a process cost accounting system.

Arrow 9_a in Illustration 22–4 on page 1178 represents the transfer of units (powdered Noxalene) from the grinding department to the mixing department. The $21,400 cost of this transfer, as calculated in Section 3 of the process cost summary, is recorded with the following entry:

9_a	Goods in Process Inventory—Mixing	21,400.00	
	Goods in Process Inventory—Grinding		21,400.00
	To record the transfer of partially completed goods from the grinding department to the mixing department.		

After this entry is posted, the Goods in Process Inventory account for the grinding department appears as follows:

ILLUSTRATION 22–6

DELTA PROCESSING COMPANY
Process Cost Summary for the Grinding Department
For Month Ended April 30, 1994

	Costs Charged to the Department	
	Direct materials requisitioned	$ 9,900
	Direct labor charged	5,700
1	Overhead allocated (at predetermined rate)	4,275
	Total processing costs for the month	$19,875
	Goods in process at the beginning of the month	4,250
	Total costs to be accounted for	$24,125

	Equivalent Unit Processing Costs		Equivalent Units	
		Units of Product	Direct Materials	Labor and Overhead
	Units processed:			
	Beginning goods in process	30,000	–0–	20,000
	Units started and completed	70,000	70,000	70,000
	Ending goods in process	20,000	20,000	5,000
2	Total	120,000	90,000	95,000

Total direct materials cost for April	$9,900
Direct materials cost per equivalent unit ($9,900/90,000 units)	$0.110
Total direct labor cost for April	$5,700
Direct labor cost per equivalent unit ($5,700/95,000 units)	$0.060
Total overhead cost for April	$4,275
Overhead cost per equivalent unit ($4,275/95,000 units)	$0.045

	Assignment of Costs to the Output of the Department	Equivalent Units	Cost per Unit	Total Cost
	Goods in process, March 31, 1994, and completed during April:			
	Costs from prior month			$ 4,250
	Direct materials added (none)			–0–
	Direct labor added	20,000	$0.060	1,200
	Overhead applied	20,000	$0.045	900
	Total costs to process			$ 6,350
3	Goods started and completed during April:			
	Direct materials added	70,000	$0.110	$ 7,700
	Direct labor added	70,000	$0.060	4,200
	Overhead applied	70,000	$0.045	3,150
	Total costs to process			$15,050
	Total costs transferred to mixing department (unit cost = $21,400/100,000 units = $0.214)			$21,400
	Goods in process, April 30, 1994:			
	Direct materials added	20,000	$0.110	$ 2,200
	Direct labor added	5,000	$0.060	300
	Overhead applied	5,000	$0.045	225
	Total costs to process			$ 2,725
	Total costs accounted for			$24,125

Goods in Process Inventory—Grinding **Acct. No. 133**

Date		Explanation	Debit	Credit	Balance
1994					
Mar.	31	Beginning balance			4,250
Apr.	30	Direct materials	9,900		14,150
	30	Direct labor costs	5,700		19,850
	30	Applied overhead	4,275		24,125
	30	Transfer to mixing department		21,400	2,725

Notice that the $2,725 ending balance equals the cost assigned to these partially completed units in Section 3 of the process cost summary in Illustration 22–6.

Accounting for Delta Processing Company's Mixing Department

LO 3 Explain how equivalent units are used in process cost accounting systems and calculate the equivalent units produced during a period.

The mixing department starts working on the Noxalene as soon as it is received from the grinding department. Then, it gradually adds direct materials in the form of flavoring, preservatives, and packaging supplies. Direct labor and overhead are added at the same rate as direct materials.

Equivalent Units of Production—Mixing Department

In the grinding department, the equivalent units of production for direct labor and overhead were not the same as for direct materials. However, the mixing department requires only one calculation of equivalent units of production because direct materials, direct labor, and overhead are all used at the same rate. The following table provides the data needed to calculate equivalent units of production:

Beginning inventory:	
Units of product	16,000
Percentage of completion—Direct materials, direct labor, and overhead	25%
Units received from grinding department	100,000
Units transferred to finished goods	101,000
Ending inventory:	
Units of product	15,000
Percentage of completion—Direct materials, direct labor, and overhead	33⅓%

Note that 101,000 units were transferred to finished goods during April. Based on a first-in, first-out assumption, 16,000 of these units came from the beginning goods in process inventory and 85,000 were started and completed during the period. Because 100,000 units were received from the grinding department during April and 85,000 of those units were completed, the ending goods in process inventory contains 15,000 units. The following table calculates the department's equivalent units of production during April:

Mixing—Equivalent Units of Production (Direct Materials, Direct Labor, and Overhead)

	Units of Product	Percent Added	Equivalent Units
Beginning goods in process	16,000	75%	12,000
Goods started and completed	85,000	100%	85,000
Ending goods in process.	15,000	33⅓%	5,000
Total units	116,000		102,000

Process Cost Summary—Mixing Department

LO 4 Describe the purposes served by and be able to prepare a process cost summary.

Illustration 22–7 shows the process cost summary for the mixing department. Notice that the costs charged to the department in Section 1 include $21,400 transferred in from the grinding department. Section 2 shows the equivalent units of production for the direct materials, direct labor, and overhead added by the mixing department. Section 2 also calculates the costs per equivalent unit added during the mixing process. Section 3 shows how the costs charged to the department are assigned to the output of the department. The $29,470 cost of the units transferred to finished goods is calculated as the combined cost of the beginning units in process and the started and completed units.

Because all Noxalene received from the grinding department enters production at the beginning of the mixing process, the beginning goods in process inventory is 100% complete with respect to Noxalene. None of the Noxalene transferred in during April was used to finish the beginning inventory units. Therefore, the $21,400 cost transferred in during April relates to the 100,000 units that the mixing department started to process during April. In section 3 of Illustration 22–7, notice that $18,190 of the $21,400 was assigned to the 85,000 units started and finished during April (85,000 × $0.214). The remaining $3,210 was assigned to the 15,000 units in the ending inventory (15,000 × $0.214).

Tranferring Costs to Finished Goods Inventory and to Cost of Goods Sold

LO 2 Describe the process of accumulating direct materials, direct labor, and manufacturing overhead costs according to each production process and prepare entries to record the flow of costs in a process cost accounting system.

Arrow 9_b in Illustration 22–4 on page 1178 represents the transfer of finished products from the mixing department to the finished goods inventory. The process cost summary for the mixing department shows that 101,000 units of packaged Noxall were assigned a cost of $29,470. The following entry records the transfer:

9_b	Finished Goods Inventory	29,470.00	
	Goods in Process Inventory—Mixing.		29,470.00
	To record the transfer of completed units of Noxall out of production.		

After this entry is posted, the mixing department's Goods in Process Inventory account appears as follows:

ILLUSTRATION 22–7

DELTA PROCESSING COMPANY
Process Cost Summary for the Mixing Department
For Month Ended April 30, 1994

	Costs Charged to the Department	
	Direct materials requisitioned	$ 2,040
	Direct labor charged	5,100
	Overhead allocated (at predetermined rate)	1,020
1	Total processing costs for the month	$ 8,160
	Goods in process at the beginning of the month	3,520
	Costs transferred in from the grinding department (100,000 units at $0.214 each)	21,400
	Total costs to be accounted for	$33,080

	Equivalent Unit Processing Costs	Units of Product	Equivalent Units of Production
	Units processed:		
	Beginning goods in process	16,000	12,000
	Units started and completed	85,000	85,000
	Ending goods in process	15,000	5,000
2	Total	116,000	102,000
	Total direct materials cost for April		$ 2,040
	Direct materials cost per equivalent unit ($2,040/102,000 units)		$ 0.020
	Total labor cost for April		$ 5,100
	Labor cost per equivalent unit ($5,100/102,000 units)		$ 0.050
	Total overhead cost for April		$ 1,020
	Overhead cost per equivalent unit ($1,020/102,000 units)		$ 0.010

	Assignment of Costs to the Output of the Department	Equivalent Units	Cost per Unit	Total Cost
	Goods in process, March 31, 1994, and completed during April:			
	Costs from prior month			$ 3,520
	Direct materials added	12,000	$0.020	240
	Direct labor added	12,000	$0.050	600
	Overhead applied	12,000	$0.010	120
	Total costs to process			$ 4,480
	Goods started and completed during April:			
3	Costs transferred in (85,000 × $0.214)			$18,190
	Direct materials added	85,000	$0.020	1,700
	Direct labor added	85,000	$0.050	4,250
	Overhead applied	85,000	$0.010	850
	Total costs to process			$24,990
	Total costs transferred to finished goods (unit cost = $29,470/101,000 units = $0.2918)			$29,470
	Goods in process, April 30, 1994:			
	Costs transferred in (15,000 × $0.214)			$ 3,210
	Direct materials added	5,000	$0.020	100
	Direct labor added	5,000	$0.050	250
	Overhead applied	5,000	$0.010	50
	Total costs to process			$ 3,610
	Total costs accounted for			$33,080

Goods in Process Inventory—Mixing **Acct. No. 134**

Date		Explanation	Debit	Credit	Balance
1994					
Mar.	31	Beginning balance			3,520
Apr.	30	Direct materials	2,040		5,560
	30	Direct labor costs	5,100		10,660
	30	Applied overhead	1,020		11,680
	30	Transfer from grinding department	21,400		33,080
	30	Transfer to warehouse		29,470	3,610

Assume that Delta Processing Company sold 106,000 units of Noxall during April. The beginning inventory of finished goods consisted of 23,000 units with a cost of $6,440. The remaining 83,000 units sold came from the 101,000 that were completed during April. Thus, the ending finished goods inventory amounted to 18,000 units. Notice in section 3 of Illustration 22–7 that the total manufacturing cost per unit finished during April was $0.2918 ($29,470/101,000). Thus, the cost of goods sold for April was:

23,000 units from the beginning inventory	$ 6,440
83,000 units manufactured during April (83,000 × $0.2918) . .	24,219
Total cost of goods sold	$30,659

The following entry records the cost of goods sold for the month:

10	Cost of Goods Sold	30,659.00	
	Finished Goods Inventory		30,659.00
	To record cost of goods sold during April.		

After the entry is posted, the Finished Goods Inventory account appears as follows:

Finished Goods Inventory **Acct. No. 135**

Date		Explanation	Debit	Credit	Balance
1994					
Mar.	31	Beginning balance			6,440
Apr.	30	Transfer from mixing department	29,470		35,910
	30	Cost of goods sold		30,659	5,251

Summary of Delta Processing Company's Manufacturing Cost Flows

Illustration 22–8 summarizes the flows of Delta Processing Company's manufacturing costs during April. Previous sections of the chapter explained each of these flows and showed the entries to record them. The flow of costs through the accounts reflects the flow of manufacturing activities and products in the factory.

New Production Management Concepts and Process Manufacturing Systems

You learned about several new production management concepts in Chapter 21. Adopting these concepts brings about changes in some process manufacturing operations. For example, management concerns with throughput and just-in-time manufacturing have caused boundary lines between departments to become less distinct. In some cases, higher quality and better efficiency are obtained by reorganizing the production processes. For example, instead of producing both doors and cabinets in a series of departments, a separate work center for each product may be established within one department. When this rearrangement occurs, the process cost accounting system must be modified to accumulate the costs of each work center.

When a company adopts just-in-time (JIT) manufacturing techniques, the inventories described in this chapter may virtually disappear. For example, if raw materials are not ordered or received until they are needed, a Raw Materials Inventory account is not necessary. Instead, the materials cost is immediately debited to the Goods in Process Inventory account. Similarly, a Finished Goods Inventory account may not be needed. Instead, the cost of the finished goods can be debited directly to the Cost of Goods Sold account instead of the Finished Goods Inventory account.

When a company uses the theory of constraints to increase throughput, the cost accounting system should help the managers locate bottlenecks. For example, the presence of a bottleneck may be signaled by the existence of large upstream or downstream inventories. Based on their analysis of inventories, managers may be able to pinpoint and eliminate the bottleneck.

In Chapter 23, you will learn about *activity-based costing,* which uses several factors to allocate overhead. Activity-based costing is widely used because many manufacturing operations have reduced the amount of direct labor used in production. In many automated factories, for example, direct labor cost is often reduced to less than 10% of a product's total cost. If direct labor cost is this small, it is not likely to be closely correlated with overhead. Therefore, allocations of overhead based on direct labor cost are not useful in these circumstances. Instead, other factors lead to more useful information.

Process Cost Accounting Systems for Service Companies

Many service companies also use process departments to perform specific tasks for consumers. For example, hospitals have radiology and physical therapy facilities with special equipment and trained employees. When patients need services, they are processed through the appropriate departments and receive the prescribed care.

ILLUSTRATION 22-8

Flows of Costs through Delta Processing Company for April 1994

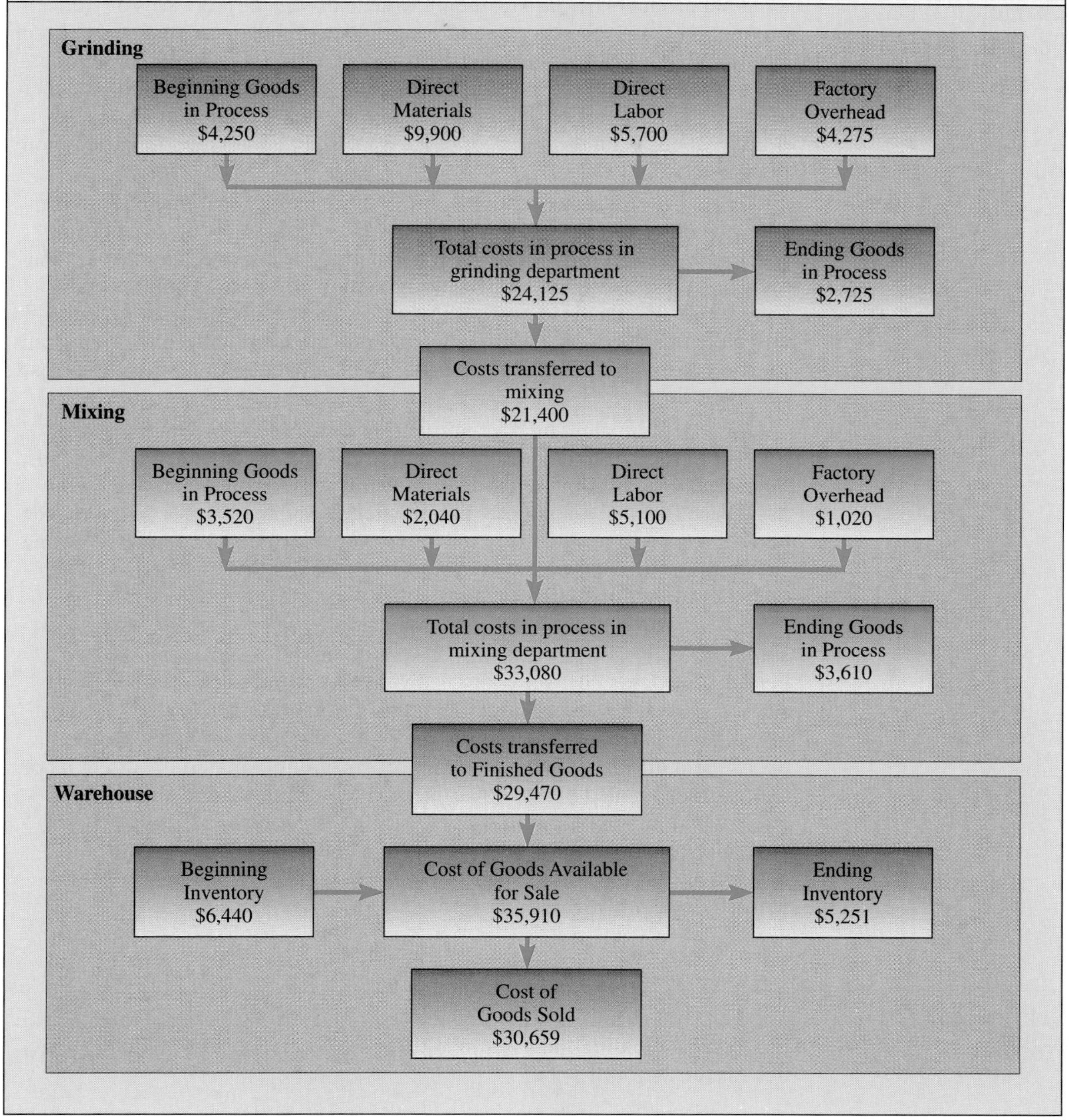

Cost accounting information is needed by service providers as much as by manufacturers. Managers of service processes use information about the cost of providing services to plan future operations, to control costs, and to determine prices to charge customers. Although manufacturing operations are used in this chapter to illustrate process accounting systems, the basic techniques of process cost accounting may be applied equally well to service operations.

Summary of the Chapter in Terms of Learning Objectives

LO 1. Process manufacturing operations produce large quantities of identical products by passing them through a series of processes or steps in production. Like job order operations, they combine direct materials, direct labor, and overhead in the manufacturing operation. Unlike job order operations that assign the responsibility for each job to a manager, process operations assign the responsibility for each process to a manager. Thus, the primary focus is on the series of processes used to complete the production of products.

LO 2. A process cost accounting system uses a separate goods in process inventory account for each process and accumulates manufacturing costs in these accounts. As units of product are transferred from one manufacturing process to the next, the accumulated cost of those units is transferred from one goods in process inventory account to the next. As units complete the last manufacturing process and are eventually sold, their accumulated cost is transferred to Finished Goods Inventory and finally to Cost of Goods Sold.

LO 3. Equivalent units of production measure the productivity of a process in respect to its use of direct materials or direct labor or overhead. To calculate equivalent units, determine the number of units that would have been finished if all of the direct materials (or direct labor or overhead) had been used to manufacture units that were started and completed during the period. The costs incurred by a process are divided by its equivalent units of production to determine cost per unit.

LO 4. A process cost summary is a managerial accounting report that summarizes the activity of a production process or department during a period. A process cost summary is divided into three sections. The first section shows the costs charged to the department. These include the cost of the beginning goods in process, the cost transferred in from a preceding department during the period, and the costs of direct materials, direct labor, and overhead added by the department. The second section shows the equivalent units of output produced during the period and the costs per equivalent unit. The third section uses the equivalent units and the unit costs to allocate the total cost from the first section among the products worked on during the period.

Demonstration Problem

The Pennsylvania Company produces a product in an operation that has two processes—molding and assembling. These facts are known about the activities for the factory for July:

Raw materials:	
Beginning inventory	$100,000
Raw materials purchased on credit	300,000
Direct materials used in molding	(190,000)
Direct materials used in assembling	(88,600)
Indirect materials used	(51,400)
Ending inventory	$ 70,000

Factory payroll:	
Direct labor used in molding	$ 42,000
Direct labor used in assembling	55,375
Indirect labor used	50,625
Total payroll cost (paid with cash)	$148,000
Factory overhead incurred:	
Indirect materials used	$ 51,400
Indirect labor used	50,625
Other overhead costs	71,725
Total factory overhead incurred	$173,750
Factory overhead applied:	
Molding (150% of direct labor)	$ 63,000
Assembling (200% of direct labor)	110,750
Total factory overhead applied	$173,750
Molding Department:	
Beginning goods in process inventory (units)	5,000
Percentage completed—materials	100%
Percentage completed—labor and overhead	60%
Units started and completed	17,000
Ending goods in process inventory (units)	8,000
Percentage completed—materials	100%
Percentage completed—labor and overhead	25%
Costs:	
Beginning in process inventory	$ 53,000
Direct materials added	190,000
Direct labor added	42,000
Overhead applied (150% of direct labor)	63,000
Total costs	$348,000
Assembling Department:	
Beginning goods in process inventory	$154,800
Ending goods in process inventory	108,325
Finished goods inventory:	
Beginning inventory	$ 96,400
Cost transferred in from Assembling	578,400
Cost of goods sold	(506,100)
Ending inventory	$168,700

Required

1. Compute the equivalent units of production for the molding department for July and determine the costs per equivalent unit for direct materials, direct labor, and overhead.
2. Compute the cost of the units transferred from molding to assembling during the month and the cost of the ending goods in process inventory for the molding department.
3. Prepare summary journal entries to record the events of July.

Solution to Demonstration Problem

Planning the Solution

- Calculate the molding department's equivalent units of production with respect to direct materials. Determine the cost per unit by dividing the total direct materials cost charged to the department by the number of equivalent units.

- Calculate the molding department's equivalent units of production with respect to direct labor and overhead. Determine the cost per unit by dividing total direct labor cost charged to the department by the number of equivalent units. Then, do the same thing for the overhead charged to the department.
- Compute the total cost of the goods transferred to the assembly department by using the equivalent units and unit costs to determine: (*a*) the cost of the beginning in process inventory; (*b*) the materials, labor, and overhead costs added to the beginning in process inventory; and (*c*) the materials labor, and overhead costs added to the units started and completed in the month.
- Use the information to record entries for (*a*) raw materials purchases, (*b*) direct materials usage, (*c*) indirect materials usage, (*d*) factory payroll costs, (*e*) direct labor usage (*f*) indirect labor usage, (*g*) other overhead costs (credit Other Accounts), (*h*) application of overhead to the two departments, (*i*) transferring partially completed goods from molding to assembling, (*j*) transferring finished goods out of assembling, and (*k*) the cost of goods sold.

1. Equivalent units of production—direct materials:

	Units of Product	Percent Added	Equivalent Units
Beginning goods in process	5,000	0%	–0–
Goods started and completed	17,000	100%	17,000
Ending goods in process.	8,000	100%	8,000
Total units	30,000		25,000

Materials cost per equivalent unit = $190,000/25,000 = $7.60 per unit

Equivalent units of production—direct labor and overhead:

	Units of Product	Percent Added	Equivalent Units
Beginning goods in process	5,000	40%	2,000
Goods started and completed	17,000	100%	17,000
Ending goods in process.	8,000	25%	2,000
Total units	30,000		21,000

Labor cost per equivalent unit = $42,000/21,000 = $2.00 per unit

Overhead cost per equivalent unit = $63,000/21,000 = $3.00 per unit

2. Cost of units transferred from Molding to Assembling during the month:

	Equivalent Units	Cost per Unit	Total Cost
Beginning goods in process:			
Costs from prior month			$ 53,000
Direct materials added.	–0–	$7.60	–0–
Direct labor added.	2,000	2.00	4,000
Overhead applied	2,000	3.00	6,000
Total cost to process.			$ 63,000

	Equivalent Units	Cost per Unit	Total Cost
Units started and completed:			
Direct materials added	17,000	$7.60	$129,200
Direct labor added	17,000	2.00	34,000
Overhead applied	17,000	3.00	51,000
Total cost to process			$214,200
Cost of transferred units			$277,200

3. Summary general journal entries for July:

Raw materials purchases:

Raw Materials Inventory	300,000.00	
Accounts Payable		300,000.00

Direct materials usage:

Goods in Process Inventory—Molding	190,000.00	
Goods in Process Inventory—Assembling	88,600.00	
Raw Materials Inventory		278,600.00

Indirect materials usage:

Factory Overhead	51,400.00	
Raw Materials Inventory		51,400.00

Factory payroll costs:

Factory Payroll	148,000.00	
Cash		148,000.00

Direct labor usage:

Goods in Process Inventory—Molding	42,000.00	
Goods in Process Inventory—Assembling	55,375.00	
Factory Payroll		97,375.00

Indirect labor usage:

Factory Overhead	50,625.00	
Factory Payroll		50,625.00

Other overhead costs:

Factory Overhead	71,725.00	
Other Accounts		71,725.00

Application of overhead:

Goods in Process Inventory—Molding	63,000.00	
Goods in Process Inventory—Assembling	110,750.00	
Factory Overhead		173,750.00

Transferring partially completed goods from Molding to Assembling:

Goods in Process Inventory—Assembling	277,200.00	
Goods in Process Inventory—Molding		277,200.00

Transferring finished goods:

Finished Goods Inventory	578,400.00	
Goods in Process Inventory—Assembling		578,400.00

Cost of goods sold:

Cost of Goods Sold	506,100.00	
Finished Goods Inventory		506,100.00

Glossary

LO 5 Define or explain the words and phrases listed in the chapter glossary.

Equivalent units of production a measure of the productivity of a process with respect to its use of direct materials or direct labor or overhead; expresses the activity of a process as the number of units that would have been processed during a period if all effort had been applied to units that were started and finished during the period. p. 1184

Materials consumption report a document that shows the raw materials issued to a department during a period and that substitutes for materials requisitions. p. 1180

Process cost accounting system a system of accounting in which the costs of each process are accumulated separately and then assigned to the units of product that passed through the process. p. 1179

Process cost summary a managerial accounting report that describes the costs charged to a department, the equivalent units of production by the department, and how the costs were assigned to the output. p. 1188

Production department an organizational unit of a factory that has the responsibility for partially manufacturing or producing a product. p. 1180

Service department an organizational unit of a factory that has the responsibility for providing support for the work of the production departments. p. 1180

Synonymous Terms

Equivalent units of production equivalent finished units.

Process cost summary cost of production report.

Production department manufacturing process; work center; workstation.

Objective Review

Answers to the following questions are listed at the end of the chapter. Be sure that you decide which is the one best answer to each question *before* you check the answers.

LO 1 A process manufacturing operation:

a. Is another name for a job order operation.
b. Is used when each product or job has a unique design so that the manufacturing operation focuses on the production of each specific job.
c. Is a manufacturing operation in which the concepts of direct materials and direct labor have no meaning.
d. Is used when a company produces large quantities of standard products.
e. Assigns a manager responsibility for the production of each job.

LO 2 When Department X sends partially completed units to Department Y, the entry that records the transfer includes:

a. A debit to Goods in Process Inventory—Department X
b. A debit to Goods in Process Inventory—Department Y
c. A credit to Goods in Process Inventory—Department X
d. A credit to Goods in Process Inventory—Department Y
e. Both *b* and *c*.

LO 3 Equivalent units are:

a. Units of a proposed new product that are intended to be reproduced as the final product.

b. Units of a product produced by a foreign competitor that are of the same quality as units produced by a domestic company.

c. Units of a product that a manufacturer produces for sale under another company's brand name which are otherwise exactly like the units the manufacturer produces and sells under its own brand name.

d. A measure of a production department's productivity in using direct materials, direct labor, or overhead.

e. None of the above

LO 4 The following information for a company's assembly department relates to the manufacturing operations for one month:

Costs charged to the department:	
Direct materials requisitioned	$ 60,000
Direct labor cost incurred	30,000
Overhead costs (predetermined overhead rate is 50% of direct labor)	15,000
Total processing costs	$105,000
Goods in process at the beginning of the month	10,000
Cost transferred from prior department (32,000 units at $3.25 each)	104,000
Total costs to be accounted for	$219,000

Equivalent unit information for direct materials, direct labor, and overhead:

	Units of Product	Percent Added
Beginning in process inventory	6,000	66⅔%
Units started and completed	24,000	100
Ending in process inventory	8,000	25

The units transferred to the assembly department were immediately placed in production, with the result that none of their $104,000 cost was added to the beginning in process inventory. Their cost was divided between the units started and completed and the units in the ending goods in process inventory.

What is the total cost of the units transferred from the assembly department to finished goods during the month?

a. $ 98,500.

b. $162,000.

c. $176,000.

d. $186,000.

e. $192,500.

LO 5 Which of the following tasks would be the responsibility of a service department in a factory?

a. To manufacture a product from start to finish.

b. To partially manufacture units of product that are then transferred to another department for further processing.

c. To service and maintain the equipment used by the production departments.

d. To market and sell the products made in the factory.

e. None of the above.

Questions for Class Discussion

1. Under what conditions is a process cost accounting system more suitable for measuring manufacturing costs than a job order cost accounting system?
2. What types of cost are typically charged to a production department in a process manufacturing operation?
3. Can services be delivered by process operations? Give an example.
4. What types of costs are incurred by both job order and process manufacturing operations?
5. What procedure is used to assign service department costs to production departments?
6. Why is it possible for direct labor in a process manufacturing operation to include the labor of employees who do not work specifically on products?
7. What effect does the transfer of a partially completed product from one production department to another have on the total assets of the company?
8. What purposes are served by a process cost summary?
9. A manufacturing company produces a single product by processing it first through a mixing department and next through a cutting department. What accounts do direct labor costs flow through in this company's process cost system?
10. How many goods in process inventory accounts are needed in a process cost accounting system?
11. After all labor costs for a period are allocated, what balance should remain in the Factory Payroll account?
12. Is it possible to have underapplied or overapplied overhead costs in a process cost accounting system?
13. How should managers interpret a department's equivalent units of production with respect to direct labor?
14. Suppose that a production department began an accounting period with 8,000 units of product that were one fourth complete, started and completed 50,000 units, and ended with 6,000 units that were one third processed. How many equivalent units did it produce during the period?
15. A process cost summary for a department has three sections. What information is presented in each of them?
16. Assume that a company successfully uses just-in-time manufacturing drastically shorten the time needed to manufacture its products. By doing so, it essentially eliminates its goods in process inventories. How does this result affect its calculations of equivalent units of production?

17. The Walt Disney Company has two major segments: motion pictures and amusement parks. What types of cost accounting systems are likely to be used in accounting for the activities in these segments? Why?

LANDS' END DIRECT MERCHANTS

18. Suppose that Lands' End produces work shirts through a multiple process production line. Starting with cutting the fabric, what are some of the processes that might be included in manufacturing the shirts?

Exercises

Exercise 22–1
Documents used in process cost accounting systems
(LO 2)

Match each document listed on the left with the appropriate description of its purpose.

a. Materials consumption report
b. Process cost summary
c. Goods in Process Inventory—Department A
d. Raw Materials Inventory account
e. Materials requisition
f. Finished Goods Inventory account
g. Factory Overhead account

__1. Holds costs of finished products until sold to customers.
__2. Holds costs for indirect materials, indirect labor, and other similar costs until assigned to production departments.
__3. Describes the direct materials used in a production department.
__4. Notifies the materials manager that materials should be sent to a production department.
__5. Holds costs of materials until they are used in production departments or as factory overhead.
__6. Holds costs of direct materials, direct labor, and applied overhead until products are transferred from Department A.
__7. A periodic report that describes the activity and output of a production department.

Exercise 22–2
Journal entries in a process cost accounting system
(LO 2)

The Arizona Company manufactures products with two processes: bending and gluing. Prepare entries to record the following activities for October:

a. Purchased raw materials on credit at a cost of $10,000.
b. Used direct materials with costs of $3,000 in the bending department and $5,000 in the gluing department.
c. Used indirect materials with cost of $3,500.
d. Incurred total labor cost of $25,000, all of which was paid in cash.

e. Used direct labor with costs of $10,000 in the bending department and $8,000 in the gluing department.

f. Used indirect labor with a cost of $7,000.

g. Incurred other overhead costs of $8,000 (credit Cash).

h. Applied overhead at the rates of 125% of direct labor in the bending department and 75% of direct labor in the gluing department.

i. Transferred partially completed products with a cost of $23,300 from the bending department to the gluing department.

j. Transferred completed products with a cost of $45,000 from the gluing department to the finished goods inventory.

k. Sold products on credit for $97,000. Their accumulated cost was $47,000.

Exercise 22–3
Journal entries in a process cost accounting system
(LO 2)

The Sew What Company manufactures textile products with three process departments: spinning, weaving, and sewing. Prepare entries to record the following activities for January:

a. Purchased raw materials on credit at a cost of $50,000.

b. Used direct materials with costs of $17,000 in spinning, $5,000 in weaving, and $8,000 in sewing.

c. Used indirect materials with costs of $19,000.

d. Incurred total labor cost of $70,000, all of which was paid in cash.

e. Used direct labor with costs of $20,000 in spinning, $6,000 in weaving, and $10,000 in sewing.

f. Used indirect labor with cost of $34,000.

g. Incurred other overhead costs of $12,000 (credit Cash).

h. Applied overhead at the rates of 140% of direct labor in the spinning department, 200% of direct labor in the weaving department, and 250% of direct labor in the sewing department.

i. Transferred partially completed products with a cost of $60,000 from the spinning department to the weaving department.

j. Transferred partially completed products with a cost of $85,000 from the weaving department to the sewing department.

k. Transferred completed products with a cost of $120,000 from the sewing department to the finished goods inventory.

l. Sold products on credit for $280,000. Their accumulated cost was $125,000.

Exercise 22–4
Interpreting journal entries in a process cost accounting system
(LO 2)

The following journal entries were recorded by the Brown Bag Company's process cost accounting system. The company produces its products by passing them through a cutting department and an assembling department. Overhead is applied to production departments based on the direct labor cost during the period. Provide a brief explanation of the event recorded by each entry.

a.	Factory Overhead	2,500.00	
	Other Accounts		2,500.00
b.	Finished Goods Inventory	22,000.00	
	Goods-in-Process Inventory—Assembling		22,000.00
c.	Factory Paryoll	8,000.00	
	Cash		8,000.00
d.	Raw Materials Inventory	13,000.00	
	Accounts Payable		13,000.00
e.	Goods in Process Inventory—Cutting	6,000.00	
	Goods in Process Inventory—Assembling	4,500.00	
	Raw Materials Inventory		10,500.00
f.	Goods in Process Inventory—Cutting	4,000.00	
	Goods in Process Inventory—Assembling	2,500.00	
	Factory Payroll		6,500.00
g.	Accounts Receivable.	62,500.00	
	Sales		62,500.00
	Cost of Goods Sold	25,000.00	
	Finished Goods Inventory		25,000.00
h.	Goods in Process Inventory—Assembling	15,000.00	
	Goods in Process Inventory—Cutting		15,000.00
i.	Factory Overhead	1,500.00	
	Factory Payroll		1,500.00
j.	Goods in Process Inventory—Cutting	3,000.00	
	Goods in Process Inventory—Assembling	3,500.00	
	Factory Overhead		6,500.00
k.	Factory Overhead	2,500.00	
	Raw Materials Inventory		2,500.00

Exercise 22–5
Recording cost flows in a process cost system (LO 2)

Greenspan Company manufactures a product by processing it through the rolling department and then through the wrapping department. The following information describes the manufacturing operations for August:

	Rolling Dept.	Wrapping Dept.
Direct materials used	$ 80,000	$120,000
Direct labor used	15,000	25,000
Predetermined overhead application rate	120%	200%
Goods transferred from Rolling to Wrapping	$(115,000)	$115,000
Goods transferred from Wrapping to finished goods		(201,000)

In addition, sales for the month totaled $300,000 on credit and the cost of goods sold was $214,000.

Required

Prepare summary general journal entries to record the August activities.

Exercise 22–6
Calculating equivalent units
(LO 3)

During a recent month, a production department in a process manufacturing system completed a number of units of product and transferred them to finished goods. Of these units, 25,000 were in process in the department at the beginning of the month and 110,000 were started and completed during the month. The beginning inventory units were 70% completed when the month began. At the end of the month, 33,000 additional units were in process in the department and were 40% completed.

Required

Calculate (*a*) the number of physical units transferred to finished goods and (*b*) the number of equivalent units produced in the department during the month.

Exercise 22–7
Assigning costs to inventories in a process cost system
(LO 3, 4)

The production department described in Exercise 22–6 had $156,840 of direct labor cost charged to it during the month. The direct labor is applied evenly throughout the process.

Required

Calculate the direct labor cost per equivalent unit in the department and allocate the direct labor cost among the units in the goods in process inventories and the units started and completed during the month.

Exercise 22–8
Calculating equivalent units
(LO 3)

A production department in a process manufacturing system completed 100,000 units of product and transferred them to finished goods during a recent week. Of these units, 30,000 were in process at the beginning of the week. The other 70,000 units were started and completed during the week. At the end of the period, 20,000 units were in process.

Required

Calculate the department's equivalent units of production with respect to direct materials under each of the following unrelated assumptions:

1. All direct materials are added to the products when processing begins.
2. The direct materials are added to the products evenly throughout the process. The beginning goods-in-process inventory was 25% complete and the ending goods in process inventory was 35% complete.
3. One half the direct materials are added to the products when the process begins and the other half is added when the process is 75% complete as to direct labor. The beginning goods in process inventory was 20% complete as to direct labor and the ending goods in process inventory was 50% complete as to direct labor.

Exercise 22–9
Complete a flowchart for a process system
(LO 2)

The following flowchart shows the production activity of the cutting and baking departments of the Cramer Cookie Company for May. Use the amounts shown on the flowchart to calculate the missing numbers identified by question marks.

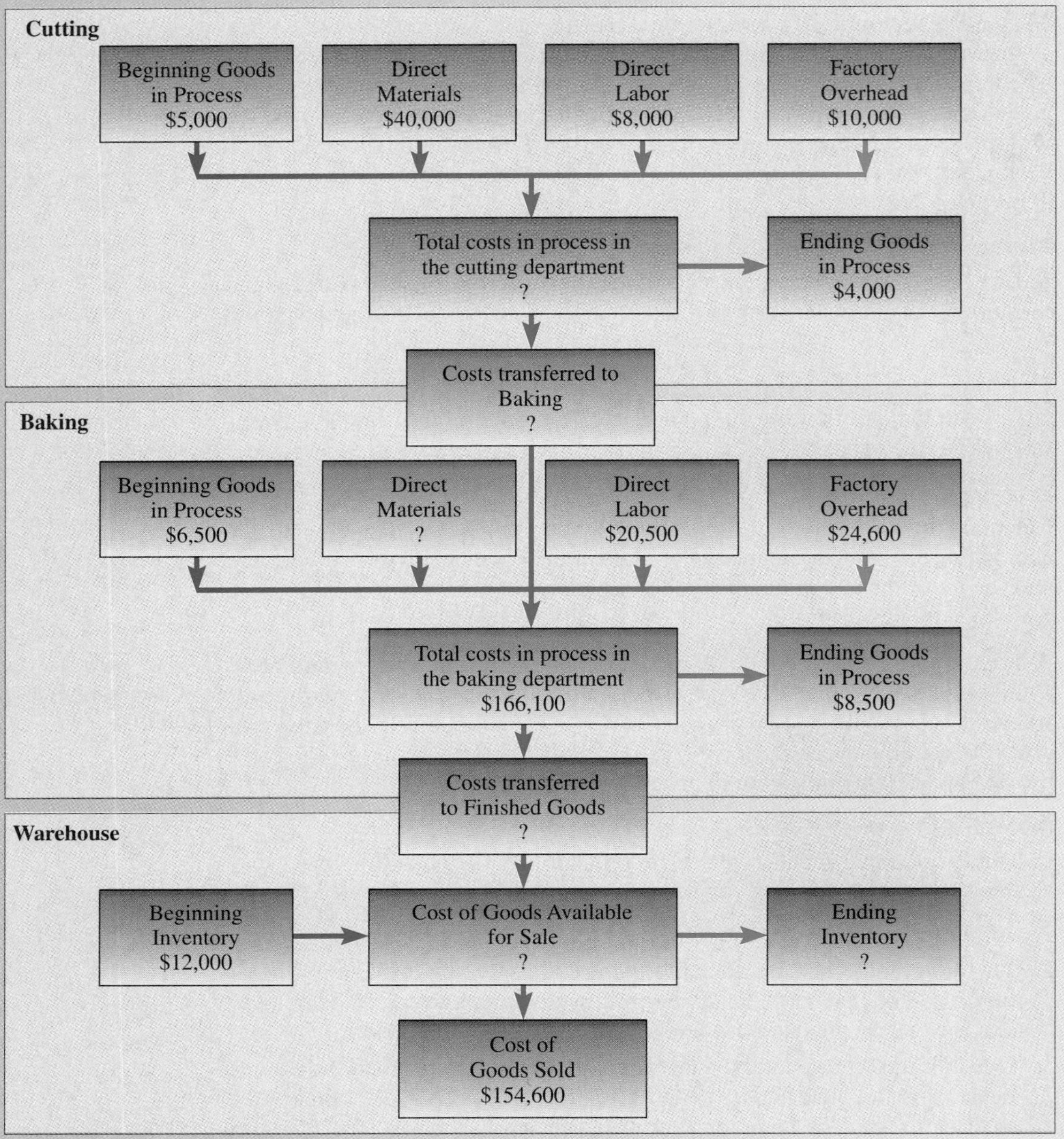

Exercise 22–10
Completing a process cost summary
(LO 4)

The following partially completed process cost summary describes the activities of the blending department of the Mission Valley Company. The output of the blending department is sent to the packaging department, which sends the finished goods to the warehouse for shipping. Complete the unfinished sections of the process cost summary.

Costs Charged to the Department

Direct materials requisitioned	$ 62,000
Direct labor charged	19,500
Overhead allocated (at 150% predetermined rate)	29,250
Total processing costs for the month	$110,750
Goods in process at the beginning of the month	9,000
Total costs to be accounted for	$119,750

Equivalent Unit Processing Costs

		Equivalent Units	
	Units of Product	Direct Materials	Labor and Overhead
Beginning goods in process	800	400	600
Units started and completed	5,000	5,000	5,000
Ending goods in process	1,200	800	900
Total	7,000	6,200	6,500

Total direct materials cost for May	$
Direct materials cost per equivalent unit ($ / units)	$
Total direct labor cost for May	$
Direct labor cost per equivalent unit ($ / units)	$
Total overhead cost for May	$
Overhead cost per equivalent unit ($ / units)	$

Assignment of Costs to the Output of the Department

	Equivalent Units	Cost per Unit	Total Cost
Goods in process, April 30 and completed during May:			
Costs from prior month			$
Direct materials added			
Direct labor added			
Overhead applied			
Total costs to process			$
Goods started and completed during May:			
Direct materials added			$
Direct labor added			
Overhead applied			
Total costs to process			$
Total costs transferred to packaging dept. (unit cost = $ /5,800 units = $)			$
Goods in process, May 31:			
Direct materials added			$
Direct labor added			
Overhead applied			
Total costs to process			$
Total costs accounted for			$

Problems

Problem 22–1
Measuring production costs and preparing journal entries
(LO 2, 3)

The Plentiful Puppets Company manufactures small wooden puppets by passing the products through a carving department and an assembly department. This information is known about its inventories for October:

	Beginning Inventory	Ending Inventory
Raw materials	$ 40,000	$ 35,000
Goods in process—carving	100,000	110,000
Goods in process—assembly	190,000	235,000
Finished goods	422,000	402,000

The following information relates to the company's activities during October:

Raw materials purchases (on credit)	$140,000
Factory payroll cost (paid with cash)	400,000
Other overhead cost (credit Other Accounts)	52,000
Materials used:	
Direct—carving	80,000
Direct—assembly	25,000
Indirect	40,000
Labor used:	
Direct—carving	200,000
Direct—assembly	60,000
Indirect	140,000
Overhead rates as % of direct labor:	
Carving	80%
Assembly	120%
Sales (on credit)	$875,000

Required

1. Compute (*a*) the cost of products transferred from carving to assembly, (*b*) the cost of products transferred from assembly to finished goods, and (*c*) the cost of goods sold.
2. Prepare summary general journal entries to record the activities during October.

Problem 22–2
Calculating costs per equivalent unit and allocating costs to products
(LO 3)

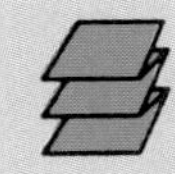

The Tarkson Manufacturing Company passes its product through several departments, including the mixing department. Direct labor is added evenly throughout the process in this department. During June, 190,000 units of product were transferred to finished goods from the mixing department. Of these units, 40,000 units were 30% complete at the beginning of the period and 150,000 were started and completed during the period. At the end of June, the goods in process inventory consisted of 90,000 units that were 20% complete.

The mixing department's direct labor cost for June was $282,240.

Required

Determine (*a*) the mixing department's equivalent units of production with respect to direct labor, (*b*) the direct labor cost per equivalent unit, and (*c*) the amount of direct labor cost assigned to the beginning goods in process inventory, to the units started and completed, and to the ending goods in process inventory.

Problem 22–3
Journal entries in a process cost accounting system and using equivalent units
(LO 2, 3)

The Rhode Island Company produces large quantities of a product that goes through two processes—smelting and tooling. These facts are known about the factory's activities for August:

Raw materials:	
Beginning inventory	$ 8,000
Raw materials purchased (on credit)	55,280
Direct materials used in smelting	(40,000)
Direct materials used in tooling	(9,280)
Indirect materials used	(10,140)
Ending inventory	$ 3,860
Factory payroll:	
Direct labor used in smelting	$ 17,000
Direct labor used in tooling	13,920
Indirect labor used	9,080
Total payroll cost (paid with cash)	$ 40,000
Factory overhead incurred:	
Indirect materials used	$ 10,140
Indirect labor used	9,080
Other overhead costs	22,910
Total factory overhead incurred	$ 42,130
Factory overhead applied:	
Smelting (125% of direct labor)	$ 21,250
Tooling (150% of direct labor)	20,880
Total factory overhead applied	$ 42,130

The following facts are known about the inventory in the Smelting Department:

Units:	
Beginning in process inventory	1,000
Started and completed	3,000
Ending in process inventory	2,000
Percentage completed:	
Beginning in process inventory	
Materials	100%
Labor and overhead	25%
Ending in process inventory	
Materials	100%
Labor and overhead	25%
Costs:	
Beginning in process inventory	$ 10,250
Direct materials added	40,000
Direct labor added	17,000
Overhead applied (125% of direct labor)	21,250
Total costs	$ 88,500
Transferred out to tooling department	(68,000)
Ending in process inventory	$ 20,500

These facts are known about the goods in process inventories for the tooling department:

Beginning in process inventory	$43,500
Ending in process inventory	44,280

These facts are known about the finished goods:

Beginning inventory	$ 37,100
Cost transferred in from tooling	111,300
Cost of goods sold	(132,500)
Ending inventory.	$ 15,900

During the month, 5,000 units of finished goods were sold for cash at the price of $60 each.

Required

1. Prepare entries to record the activities of August.
2. Calculate the equivalent units of production for the Smelting Department for August, and calculate the costs per equivalent unit for direct materials, direct labor, and overhead.
3. Calculate the cost of the ending goods in process inventory for the Smelting Department.

Problem 22–4
Preparing a process cost summary
(LO 3, 4)

Badge Manufacturing Company produces its product by passing it through a single processing department. Direct materials, direct labor, and overhead are added to the product evenly throughout the process. The company uses month-long reporting periods for its process cost accounting system.

The Goods in Process Inventory account appears as follows after posting entries for direct materials, direct labor, and overhead costs during April:

Goods in Process Inventory **Acct. No.** 133

Date		Explanation	Debit	Credit	Balance
Apr.	1	Beginning balance			27,200
	30	Direct materials	61,500		88,700
	30	Direct labor costs	205,000		293,700
	30	Applied overhead	82,000		375,700

During April, the company finished and transferred 100,000 units of the product to finished goods. Of these units, 20,000 were in process at the beginning of the month and 80,000 were started and completed during the month. The beginning goods in process inventory was 40% complete. At the end of the month, the goods in process inventory consisted of 15,000 units that were 70% complete.

Required

1. Calculate the number of equivalent units of production for April.
2. Prepare the department's process cost summary for April.
3. Prepare an entry to transfer the cost of the completed units to Finished Goods Inventory.

Problem 22–5
Preparing a process cost summary
(LO 3, 4)

Buttons Production Company manufactures a single product in one department. All direct materials are added at the beginning of the manufacturing process. Direct labor and overhead are added evenly throughout the process. The company uses month-long reporting periods for its process cost accounting system.

During September, the company completed and transferred 7,400 units of product to the finished goods inventory. The beginning goods in process inventory consisted of 1,000 units that were 100% complete with respect to direct materials and 40% complete with respect to direct labor and overhead. The other 6,400 completed units were started during the month. In addition, 800 units were in process at the end of the month. They were 100% complete with respect to direct materials and 75% complete with respect to direct labor and overhead.

After posting the entries to record direct materials, direct labor, and overhead during September, the company's Goods in Process Inventory account appears as follows:

Goods in Process Inventory — **Acct. No.** 133

Date		Explanation	Debit	Credit	Balance
Sep.	1	Beginning balance			60,440
	30	Direct materials	165,600		226,040
	30	Direct labor costs	395,200		621,240
	30	Applied overhead	316,160		937,400

Required

1. Calculate the department's equivalent units of production for September.
2. Prepare the department's process cost summary for September.
3. Prepare the entry to transfer the cost of the completed units to Finished Goods Inventory.

Problem 22–6
Analytical essay
(LO 3, 4)

Refer to the information presented in Problem 22–2 for Tarkson Manufacturing Company. Assume that the mixing department is the final process in Tarkson's manufacturing operation and that all units are sold and shipped to customers as soon as they are completed. Also assume that an error was made in determining the percentage of completion for the units in ending inventory. Instead of being 20% complete, they were really 40% complete.

Required

Write a brief essay describing the effects that this error would have on Tarkson's June financial statements.

Problem 22–7
Analytical essay
(LO 2, 3, 4)

The Grundfest Company uses a process cost accounting system for its manufacturing operation in which products are passed through the shredding and the bagging departments. The predetermined overhead application rates are

100% of direct labor cost for the shredding department and 180% of the direct labor cost for the bagging department. In a recent month, the following costs were reported:

	Shredding	Bagging
Direct materials	$40,000	$ 65,000
Direct labor	15,000	22,000
Factory overhead applied	15,000	39,600
Totals	$70,000	$126,600

Because both departments have very short processing times, there are no beginning or ending goods in process inventories. There is no finished goods inventory because units of product are sold and delivered to customers as soon as they are completed.

Assume that two employees who worked in the bagging department incorrectly coded their time sheets. As a result, the shredding department's reported direct labor cost incorrectly includes $2,500 that should have been charged to the bagging department.

Required

Write a brief essay explaining the effects of the error on the company's financial statements and process cost summaries.

Alternate Problems

Problem 22–1A
Measuring production costs and preparing journal entries
(LO 2, 3)

The Biggo Bassets Company manufactures stuffed basset hounds by passing the products through a cutting department and a stuffing department. This information is known about its inventories for October:

	Beginning Inventory	Ending Inventory
Raw materials	$12,000	$15,000
Goods in process—cutting	4,000	7,000
Goods in process—stuffing	22,000	18,000
Finished goods	26,000	33,000

The following information relates to the company's activities during October:

Raw materials purchases (on credit)	$ 30,000
Factory payroll cost (paid with cash)	50,000
Other overhead cost (credit Other Accounts)	4,000
Materials used:	
Direct—cutting	$ 2,000
Direct—stuffing	18,000
Indirect	7,000
Labor used:	
Direct—cutting	$ 22,000
Direct—stuffing	16,000
Indirect	12,000
Overhead rates as % of direct labor:	
Cutting	50%
Stuffing	75%
Sales (on credit)	$140,000

Required

1. Compute (*a*) the cost of products transferred from cutting to stuffing, (*b*) the cost of products transferred from stuffing to finished goods, and (*c*) the cost of goods sold.
2. Prepare entries to record the activities during October.

Problem 22–2A
Calculating costs per equivalent unit and allocating costs to products
(LO 3)

The Radial Manufacturing Company passes its product through several departments, including the turning department. Direct materials are added evenly throughout the process in this department. During November, 38,000 units of product were transferred to finished goods from the turning department. Of these units, 7,000 units were 60% complete at the beginning of the period and 31,000 were started and completed during the period. At the end of November, the goods in process inventory consisted of 9,000 units that were 75% complete. The turning department's direct materials cost for November was $171,121.

Required

Determine (*a*) the turning department's equivalent units of production with respect to direct materials, (*b*) the direct materials cost per equivalent unit, and (*c*) the amount of direct materials cost assigned to the beginning goods in process inventory, to the units started and completed, and to the ending goods in process inventory.

Problem 22–3A
Journal entries in a process cost accounting system and using equivalent units
(LO 2, 3)

The East Carolina Company produces large quantities of a food product that goes through two processes—slicing and canning. These facts are known about the factory's activities for September:

Raw materials:	
Beginning inventory	$ 42,000
Raw materials purchased (on credit)	250,000
Direct materials used in slicing	(124,100)
Direct materials used in canning	(89,100)
Indirect materials used	(50,800)
Ending inventory	$ 28,000
Factory payroll:	
Direct labor used in slicing	$159,000
Direct labor used in canning	17,820
Indirect labor used	23,180
Total payroll cost (paid with cash)	$200,000
Factory overhead incurred:	
Indirect materials used	$ 50,800
Indirect labor used	23,180
Other overhead costs	25,260
Total factory overhead incurred	$ 99,240
Factory overhead applied:	
Slicing (40% of direct labor)	$ 63,600
Canning (200% of direct labor)	35,640
Total factory overhead applied	$ 99,240

The following facts are known about the inventory in the slicing department:

Units:	
Beginning in process inventory	20,000
Started and completed	60,000
Ending in process inventory	10,000
Percentage completed:	
Beginning in process inventory	
Materials	80%
Labor and overhead	40%
Ending in process inventory	
Materials	90%
Labor and overhead	75%
Costs:	
Beginning in process inventory	$ 49,600
Direct materials added	124,100
Direct labor added	159,000
Overhead applied (40% of direct labor)	63,600
Total costs	$396,300
Transferred out to canning department	(360,000)
Ending in process inventory	$ 36,300

These facts are known about the goods in process inventories for the canning department:

Beginning in process inventory	$124,500
Ending in process inventory	114,660

These facts are known about the finished goods:

Beginning inventory	$ 18,300
Cost transferred in from canning	512,400
Cost of goods sold	(500,200)
Ending inventory	$ 30,500

During the month, 82,000 units of finished goods were sold for cash at the price of $12 each.

Required

1. Prepare entries to record the activities of September.
2. Calculate the slicing department's equivalent units of production for September, and calculate the costs per equivalent unit for direct materials, direct labor, and overhead.
3. Calculate the cost of the ending goods in process inventory for the slicing department.

Problem 22–4A
Preparing a process cost summary
(LO 3, 4)

Buckle Manufacturing Company produces its product by passing it through a single processing department. Direct materials, direct labor, and overhead are added to the product evenly throughout the process. The company uses month-long reporting periods for its process cost accounting system.

The Goods in Process Inventory account appears as follows after posting entries for direct materials, direct labor, and overhead costs:

Goods in Process Inventory **Acct. No.** 133

Date		Explanation	Debit	Credit	Balance
June	1	Beginning balance			46,800
	30	Direct materials	75,600		122,400
	30	Direct labor costs	283,500		405,900
	30	Applied overhead	378,000		783,900

During June, the company finished and transferred 65,000 units of the product to finished goods. Of these units, 5,000 were in process at the beginning of the month, and 60,000 were started and completed during the month. The beginning goods in process inventory was 80% complete. At the end of the month, the goods in process inventory consisted of 8,000 units that were 25% completed.

Required

1. Calculate the number of equivalent units of production for June.
2. Prepare the department's process cost summary for June.
3. Prepare an entry to transfer the cost of the completed units to Finished Goods Inventory.

Problem 22–5A
Preparing a process cost summary
(LO 3, 4)

Bows Production Company manufactures a single product in one department. Direct labor and overhead are added evenly throughout the process. Direct materials are added as needed. The company uses month-long reporting periods for its process cost accounting system.

During April, the company completed and transferred 110,000 units of product to the finished goods inventory. The beginning in process inventory consisted of 10,000 units that were 75% complete with respect to direct materials and 60% complete with respect to direct labor and overhead. The other 100,000 completed units were started during the month. In addition, 20,000 units were in process at the end of the month. They were 50% complete with respect to direct materials and 30% complete with respect to direct labor and overhead.

The company has only one Goods in Process Inventory account. At the end of the month, the account appeared as follows after entries for direct materials, direct labor, and overhead had been posted:

Goods in Process Inventory **Acct. No.** 133

Date		Explanation	Debit	Credit	Balance
Apr.	1	Beginning balance			20,550
	30	Direct materials	56,250		76,800
	30	Direct labor costs	88,000		164,800
	30	Applied overhead	220,000		384,800

Required

1. Calculate the equivalent units of production for direct materials and for direct labor and overhead.

2. Prepare the department's process cost summary for April.
3. Prepare an entry to transfer the cost of the completed units to Finished Goods Inventory.

Problem 22–6A
Analytical essay
(LO 3, 4)

Refer to the information presented in Problem 22–2A for Radial Manufacturing Company. Assume that the turning department is the final process in Radial's manufacturing operation and that all units are sold and shipped to customers as soon as they are completed. Also assume that an error was made in determining the percentage of completion for the units in ending inventory. Instead of being 75% complete, they were really 25% complete.

Required

Write a brief essay describing the effects that this error would have on Radial's November financial statements.

Problem 22–7A
Analytical essay
(LO 2, 3, 4)

The Sampson Company uses a process cost accounting system for its manufacturing operation in which the products are passed through the machining and the finishing departments. The predetermined overhead application rates are 50% of direct labor cost for the machining department and 220% of direct labor cost for the finishing department. In a recent month, the following costs were reported:

	Machining	Finishing
Direct materials	$ 80,000	$110,000
Direct labor	100,000	90,000
Factory overhead applied	50,000	198,000

Because both departments have very short processing times, there are no beginning or ending goods in process inventories. There is no finished goods inventory because units of products are sold and delivered to customers as soon as they are completed.

Assume that two employees who worked in the finishing department incorrectly coded their time sheets. As a result, the machining department's reported direct labor cost incorrectly includes $6,000 that should have been charged to the finishing department.

Required

Write a brief essay explaining the effects of the error on the company's financial statements and the process cost summaries.

Provocative Problems

Provocative Problem 22–1
London Company
(LO 3)

A processing department of the London Company started August with 50,000 units in its goods in process inventory, each of which was 80% complete. During August, an additional 440,000 units were started in the department. A total of 450,000 units were completed and transferred to finished goods. If August's production was measured as 424,000 equivalent units, how many units of product were in process at the end of the month and what was their stage of completion?

Provocative Problem 22–2
Dublin Manufacturing Company
(LO 2, 4)

Following is an excerpt from the process cost summary for the Dublin Manufacturing Company's bending department for June. The department receives partially processed units from the cutting department and transfers its output to the assembly department. Use the information in the process cost summary to prepare journal entries to record:

a. The transfer of units into Bending from Cutting.
b. The use of direct materials in Bending.
c. The use of direct labor in Bending.
d. The application of overhead to Bending.
e. The transfer of units from Bending to Assembly.

DUBLIN MANUFACTURING COMPANY
Process Cost Summary for the Bending Department
For Month Ended June 30

Costs Charged to the Department

Direct materials requisitioned	$ 77,500
Direct labor charged	128,000
Overhead allocated (at 150% of direct labor)	192,000
Total processing costs for the month	$397,500
Goods in process at the beginning of the month	90,000
Costs transferred in from the Cutting Department	212,500
Total costs to be accounted for	$700,000

Equivalent Unit Processing Costs

(not needed)

Assignment of Costs to the Output of the Department

	Equivalent Units	Cost per Unit	Total Cost
Goods in process, May 31, and completed during June:			
Costs from prior month			$ 90,000
Direct materials added	800	$25.00	20,000
Direct labor added	1,000	$40.00	40,000
Overhead applied	1,000	$60.00	60,000
Total costs to process			$210,000
Goods started and completed during June:			
Costs transferred in (2,000 × $85.00)			$170,000
Direct materials added	2,000	$25.00	50,000
Direct labor added	2,000	$40.00	80,000
Overhead applied	2,000	$60.00	120,000
Total costs to process			$420,000
Total costs transferred to Assembly (unit cost = $630,000/3,000 units = $210.00)			$630,000
Goods in process, June 30:			
Costs transferred in (500 × $85.00)			$ 42,500
Direct materials added	300	$25.00	7,500
Direct labor added	200	$40.00	8,000
Overhead applied	200	$60.00	12,000
Total costs to process			$ 70,000
Total costs accounted for			$700,000

Provocative Problem 22–3
International Business Machines Corporation
(LO 1)

IBM

The financial statements in Appendix J reflect the fact that IBM is a large and complicated company. Its most significant activity is manufacturing many different kinds of computers, including small personal computers (which are highly standardized) and large custom-designed mainframe computers. The company also produces various kinds of software, including custom programs written to meet specific customers' needs. In addition, IBM provides repair services for both small and large computers.

For each of the following activities, indicate the type of cost accounting system most likely used by IBM. Provide a brief statement justifying your answers.

a. Manufacturing personal computers.

b. Manufacturing custom-designed mainframe computer systems.

c. Producing custom-designed software for specific customers.

d. Providing repair services.

Comprehensive Problem

Albert Company
(Review of Chapters 2, 5, 9, 20, 22)

The Albert Company produces a product by sending it through two processes, one of which takes place in Department One and the other in Department Two. All of Department One's output is transferred to Department Two. In addition to the goods in process inventories in Departments One and Two, Albert maintains inventories of raw materials and finished goods. Albert uses raw materials as direct materials in Departments One and Two and as indirect materials. Its factory payroll costs include direct labor for each department and indirect labor.

In this problem, you are to maintain certain records and produce various measures of the inventories to reflect the events of May. Round all calculations of unit costs to the nearest penny and all other dollar amounts to the nearest whole dollar. To begin, set up the following general ledger accounts and enter their April 30 balances:

Raw Materials Inventory	$ 32,000
Goods in Process Inventory—Department One	64,220
Goods in Process Inventory—Department Two	25,000
Finished Goods Inventory	110,000
Sales	–0–
Cost of Goods Sold	–0–
Factory Payroll	–0–
Factory Overhead	–0–

1. Prepare entries to record the following events that occurred during May:
   a. Purchased raw materials for $100,000 cash (use a perpetual inventory system).
   b. Used raw materials as follows:

Department One	$36,530
Department Two	42,000
Indirect materials	21,000

   c. Incurred factory payroll cost of $180,000, paid with cash (ignore income and other taxes).
   d. Assigned factory payroll costs as follows:

Department One	$100,000
Department Two	50,000
Indirect labor	30,000

   e. Incurred additional factory overhead costs of $24,000, paid in cash.
   f. Allocated factory overhead to Departments One and Two as a percentage of the direct labor costs. (To make this entry, you must first compute the overhead allocation rate using direct labor and overhead costs incurred during May.)

2. Information about the units of product on hand or worked on during May follows:

	Department One	Department Two
Units in beginning inventory	300	500
Percent completed with respect to:		
Materials	65%	80%
Labor and overhead	40%	46%
Units started and finished in May	1,000	900
Percent completed with respect to:		
Materials	100%	100%
Labor and overhead	100%	100%
Units in ending inventory.	500	800
Percent completed with respect to:		
Materials	60%	25%
Labor and overhead	84%	10%

Use this information and the facts from part 1 to make the following calculations:

a. Equivalent units of production in Department One and the per unit costs for labor, materials, and overhead.

b. Equivalent units of production in Department Two and the per unit costs for labor, materials, and overhead.

3. Using the results from part 2 and previously given information, make the following calculations, and prepare general journal entries to record:
   g. Total cost of units transferred from Department One to Department Two during May.
   h. Total cost of units transferred from Department Two to finished goods during May.
   i. Sale of finished goods that cost $265,700 for $625,000 cash.
4. Post the journal entries from parts 1 and 3 to the ledger accounts that you set up at the beginning of the problem.
5. Compute the amount of gross profit from the sales in May.

Answers to Objective Review Questions

LO 1 (*d*)
LO 2 (*e*)
LO 3 (*d*)
LO 4 (*d*)
LO 5 (*c*)

CHAPTER

23

Accounting for the Departments of a Business and Responsibility Accounting

As a company grows, it divides into departments so that tasks may be carried out more efficiently. But delegating duties to departments creates challenges for managers. Managerial accounting information can help them make and keep departments productive and profitable.

Topical Coverage

The three preceding chapters have focused your attention on measuring the costs of products manufactured in factories, with some emphasis on using the results in published financial statements. This chapter shifts our focus to managerial accounting reports that can be used in directing a company's activities. In particular, it explains how and why management divides companies into departments. It also describes the kinds of information generated by departmental and responsibility accounting systems. This information is useful for evaluating the contributions made by individual departments and the performances achieved by departmental managers. Finally, the chapter describes activity-based cost accounting.

Learning Objectives

After studying Chapter 23, you should be able to:

1. Explain why businesses are divided into subunits or departments and explain the difference between cost centers and profit centers.
2. Describe the difference between direct and indirect expenses of departments, the bases used to allocate indirect expenses, and the procedures used in the allocation process.
3. Prepare reports that measure the performance of a profit center and describe the factors that should be considered in eliminating an unprofitable department.
4. Explain the concept of controllable costs and prepare reports to be used in evaluating the performance of a department manager.
5. Describe the problems associated with allocating joint costs between products.
6. Describe activity-based costing and its advantages for generating useful information for management.
7. Define or explain the words and phrases listed in the chapter glossary.

Departmental Accounting

LO 1 Explain why businesses are divided into subunits or departments and explain the difference between cost centers and profit centers.

Chapter 19 described the usefulness of and practices for reporting segment information in a large company's external financial statements. Managerial accounting information about smaller subunits of a business is also very useful for managers of both large and small companies. In fact, almost all businesses are divided into subunits or departments when they get to be too large to be managed effectively as a single unit. For example, the discussion of process cost accounting in Chapter 22 showed you how many manufacturing systems are subdivided into departments so that they can be more easily managed.

Managerial accounting for the departments of a business has two primary goals. The first goal is to provide information that management can use to evaluate the profitability or cost effectiveness of each department's activities. This goal is met by **departmental accounting systems.** The second goal is to assign costs and expenses to the particular managers who are responsible for controlling those costs and expenses. This information is then used to evaluate the performance of those managers in meeting those responsibilities. This information is provided by **responsibility accounting systems.** Departmental and responsibility accounting systems are closely related and share much of the same information.

Creating Departments within a Business

Most businesses are sufficiently large and complex to be divided into subunits or departments. When a business is departmentalized, each department is usually placed under the direction of a manager. As the business grows larger, management may divide a department into new departments. This division is needed so that the responsibilities for the activities of a unit do not overwhelm the manager's ability to oversee and control the unit effectively. Where possible, the company also establishes departments to take full advantage of the specialized skills of particular managers.

Basis for Departmentalization

Chapter 22 described the two most basic categories of departments. These categories include *production departments* and *service departments.*

In a factory, production departments engage directly in manufacturing. Factory departments are usually organized to put each manufacturing process under the direction of a single manager. The process is identified by the activities that it carries out or the products or components that it manufactures.

In a store, production departments make sales directly to customers. In this setting, management usually organizes departments around the goods that each of them sells. That is, each *selling department* has the task of selling one or more lines of merchandise.

In either a factory or a store, service departments help manufacturing or selling departments by providing support services. For example, these services include advertising, purchasing, payroll processing, human resource management, and corporate-level management. The service departments assist or otherwise perform services for the production departments. Service departments do not directly manufacture products or produce revenues through sales. However, their activities are important for the profitability of each production department and the entire company.

Using Information to Evaluate Departments

When a business is divided into departments, company managers need to know how well each department is performing. Therefore, the departmental accounting system must supply information about the resources used and outputs achieved by each department. This evaluation requires the system to measure and accumulate revenue and expense information for each department wherever possible. Because of its potential usefulness to competitors, this managerial accounting information is not distributed to the public. Instead, information about departments is prepared exclusively for internal managers to help control operations, appraise performance, allocate resources, and take corrective actions. For example, if one of several departments is particularly profitable, management may decide to expand its operations. Or, if a department is showing poor results, information about its revenues, costs, and expenses may suggest useful changes.

The kind of accounting information used to evaluate a department depends on whether it is a **cost center** or a **profit center.** A cost center is a department that incurs costs (or expenses) without directly generating revenues. For example, the manufacturing departments of a factory and service departments (such as the accounting, advertising, and purchasing departments) are generally cost centers. A profit center not only incurs costs but also generates revenues. The selling departments of a business are often profit centers.

The information used to evaluate a department's contribution to the overall profitability of a business depends on whether it is a cost center or a profit center. In addition, the kind of responsibility accounting information used to evaluate managers depends on whether they are responsible for cost centers or profit centers. Managers of cost centers are judged on their ability to control costs by keeping them within a satisfactory range. Managers of profit centers are judged on their ability to generate revenues in excess of the department's expenses.

Obtaining Information about Departments

Different companies use various methods to generate information about their departments. The methods actually used depend on the extent to which they use computers and sophisticated cash registers.

Computerized Systems

Sophisticated cash registers allow the managers of a merchandising company to accumulate information about each department's sales and sales returns. In a networked system, the registers transfer this information directly to the store's computer. Sophisticated cash registers are actually capable of doing much more than accumulating sales information for each department. They also print relevant information on the sales ticket given to the customer, total the ticket, and initiate entries to record credit sales in the customer's account. If information about the sold goods is recorded at the register (by a scanner or a keyboard), the system can produce detailed daily departmental summaries of the items that were sold and those that remain in the inventory.

Using Separate Accounts for Each Department

The preceding sophisticated systems allow a business to easily determine daily total sales and sales returns for each department. More clerical effort is needed for less sophisticated systems that do not connect the registers to a computer. In these systems, the totals are usually accumulated by one of two methods. First, a business may provide separate Sales and Sales Returns accounts in its general ledger for each department. Alternatively, the business may produce a *supplementary spreadsheet analysis* of departmental sales and sales returns. These methods can also be used to accumulate information about purchases and purchases returns for the departments.

ILLUSTRATION 23–1

A Departmentalized Sales Journal

Sales Journal

Date		Account Debited	Invoice Number	PR	Accounts Receivable Debit	Departmental Sales		
						Dept. 1 Credit	Dept. 2 Credit	Dept. 3 Credit
Oct.	1	Walter Marshfield	737		145.23	90.15	55.08	
	1	Thomas Higgins	738		85.90		40.30	45.60
	.	.	.		.	.	.	.
	.	.	.		.	.	.	.
	.	.	.		.	.	.	.
Total					10,400.85	4,056.75	4,292.10	2,052.00

If a business chooses to provide separate Sales, Sales Returns, Purchases, and Purchases Returns accounts in its ledger for each selling department, it will find advantages in providing columns in its special journals to record transactions by departments. Illustration 23–1 shows a sales journal used to record information for each selling department. The amounts to be debited to the customers' accounts are entered in the Accounts Receivable Debit column and posted to these accounts daily. Less frequently, perhaps monthly, this column's total is debited to the Accounts Receivable controlling account. The amounts sold to the customers from each department are entered in the last three columns. The totals of these columns are posted to the ledger accounts at least monthly.

Departmental Sales Spreadsheet Analyses

If separate accounts are not maintained in the general ledger for each department, a business can develop departmental information by using a supplemental spreadsheet analysis. In applying this approach, the firm uses nondepartmentalized general ledger accounts for sales, sales returns, purchases, and purchases returns. Transactions are recorded in these accounts as if the business is not departmentalized. However, the company's accountant identifies each department's transactions and enters the amounts on a spreadsheet.

For example, after recording sales in its usual manner, the system may find daily total sales for each department and then enter the daily totals on a sales spreadsheet like the one in Illustration 23–2. At the end of a month or other period, the column totals of the spreadsheet show sales by departments, and the combined total of all the columns should equal the balance of the Sales account.

When a store uses a spreadsheet analysis of department sales, it may use separate spreadsheets to accumulate sales, sales returns, purchases, and purchases returns. At the end of the period, the several spreadsheets show the store's sales, sales returns, purchases, and purchases returns by departments.

ILLUSTRATION 23-2

Departmental Sales Spreadsheet

Date		Men's Wear Dept.	Boys' Wear Dept.	Shoe Dept.	Leather Goods Dept.	Women's Wear Dept.	Total Sales
May	1	957.15	775.06	615.00	575.25	927.18	3,849.64
	2	898.55	736.27	545.80	410.20	887.27	3,478.09
	.	.	.	.	.	.	.
	.	.	.	.	.	.	.
	.	.	.	.	.	.	.
Total		24,124.10	19,647.29	15,090.40	12,810.85	23,587.85	95,260.49

If each department counts its inventory, it can also calculate its gross profit.

Accumulating information and computing the gross profit for each selling department in a departmentalized business is not difficult. However, some companies do not even attempt to measure the net income generated by each department because of the complexities of allocating expenses among departments. Nonetheless, this information can be very useful and many companies do gather it.

Allocating Expenses among Departments

If a business attempts to measure departmental net income, its management must solve some special managerial accounting problems. The problems involve allocating the company's expenses among its selling departments.

LO 2 Describe the difference between direct and indirect expenses of departments, the bases used to allocate indirect expenses, and the procedures used in the allocation process.

Direct Expenses Do Not Require Allocation

A company's **direct expenses** are easily traced to a specific department because they are incurred for the sole benefit of that department. For example, the salary of an employee who works in only one department is a direct expense of that department.

Notice that the concept of direct expense is very similar to the concept of direct cost that was first introduced in Chapter 20. There, we used the term *direct cost* in the context of a manufacturing operation where all manufacturing costs are product costs rather than period costs (expenses). In nonmanufacturing departments, costs are charged to expense as they are incurred. In these situations, the term *direct expense* is used instead of *direct cost*.

Allocating Indirect Expenses

A company's expenses also include **indirect expenses.** Indirect expenses (like indirect costs) are incurred for the joint benefit of more than one department. For example, if two or more departments share a single building, they jointly enjoy the benefits of the expenses of renting, heating, and lighting the building. These expenses are indirect because they cannot be easily traced to any specific department. However, if there is a need for managerial accounting information about the income produced by each department, the indirect expenses should be allocated among the departments that benefited from them. If so, each indirect expense should be allocated on a basis that fairly approximates the relative benefit received by each department. However, measuring the benefit each department receives from an indirect expense is usually difficult or impossible. Even after a reasonable allocation basis is chosen, considerable doubt often exists regarding the share to be charged to each department.

To illustrate how an indirect expense can be allocated, assume that a jewelry store purchases janitorial services from an outside firm. The management then decides to allocate the cost among the store's three departments according to the floor space that each occupies. The cost of janitorial services for a recent month is $300. This table shows the square feet of floor space occupied by each department, computes the percentage of the total square feet, and then allocates this $300 cost among them by using those percentages:

Department	Square Feet	Percent of Total	Allocated Cost
Jewelry	1,000	25.0%	$ 75
Watch repair	600	15.0	45
China and silver	2,400	60.0	180
Total	4,000	100.0%	$300

For example, the table shows that the jewelry department occupies 25% of the floor space in the store. Thus, it is likely that 25% of the janitorial services are applied to cleaning its space. Therefore, 25% of the total $300 cost is assigned to the jewelry department. When the allocation process is completed, these and other allocated costs are deducted from the gross profits generated by each department to determine the net income that each produced.

You can apply the concepts of *direct* and *indirect costs* or *expenses* in a variety of situations. In general, you can easily trace or associate direct costs or expenses with a *cost object*. In this chapter, the relevant cost object is a department. However, other cost objects may be relevant for other decisions. In general accounting systems for manufacturing operations (Chapter 20) and job order cost systems (Chapter 21), the cost object is a job or a group of products. In process cost systems (Chapter 22), the cost object is a process.

Bases for Allocating Indirect Expenses

The following paragraphs describe some bases that are often used to allocate common indirect expenses among departments. There are no hard-and-fast rules about which basis is most useful for a given expense. Such rules are not appropriate because an expense allocation often involves several factors, and the relative importance of the factors varies from situation to situation. Judgment is required, and people may not agree on the most useful basis for allocating an indirect expense.

Wages and Salaries. Employees' wages may be either a direct or an indirect expense. If their time is spent entirely in one department, their wages are a direct expense of that department. But, if the employees work in more than one department, their wages are an indirect expense to be allocated among the benefited departments. In general, an employee's contribution to a department depends on the hours worked in the department. Thus, a reasonable basis for allocating employees' wages is the relative amount of time they spend in each department.

A supervisory employee may supervise more than one department. In such cases, the time spent in each department can be a useful basis for allocating the supervisor's salary. However, a supervisor is frequently on the move, and it may not be practical to record the time spent in each department. Therefore, some companies allocate supervisory salaries to the departments on the basis of the number of employees in each department. This basis is reasonable if the supervisor's primary task is managing people. Others make the allocation on the basis of the sales achieved in the supervised departments. This basis is reasonable if the supervisor's relative contributions to the departments are reflected by their levels of selling activity.

Rent, Depreciation, and Related Building Expenses. Rent expense for a building is reasonably allocated to departments on the basis of the amount of the floor space occupied by each department. However, some floor space may be more valuable than other space because of its location. If so, the allocation method should charge some departments with more expense per square foot than other departments. For example, ground-floor retail space is usually more valuable than basement or upper-floor space because all customers must pass the departments near the entrance while fewer of them go beyond the first floor. Because there are no precise measures of floor space values, however, it may be helpful to base the allocation on other data, including statistics about customer traffic and opinions of real estate leasing experts. In any case, all allocations of rent ultimately depend on management's judgment.

If the company owns the building, depreciation, taxes, insurance, and similar expenses are usually allocated like rent expense.

Advertising. When a store effectively advertises a department's products, people come into the store to buy them. Of course, a customer may buy unadvertised products during the same visit. Thus, advertising products for some departments may help the sales of all departments. Accordingly, many stores treat advertising as an indirect expense in their departmental income statements. A common technique allocates this cost on the basis of each department's proportion of total sales. For example, a department that has 10% of the store's total sales will be assigned 10% of the advertising expense.

Other stores try to be more precise in their allocations and analyze each advertisement to determine the column inches of newspaper space or minutes of TV or radio time devoted to the products of a department. Then, each department is charged with the actual costs of producing and publishing the advertisements. However, management must consider whether this precision creates sufficient added usefulness to justify the effort.

Equipment Depreciation. To account for each department's equipment depreciation expense, a company should keep sufficiently detailed records to show which departments use specific assets. Depreciation on equipment used only in one department is a direct expense of that department. Depreciation for an asset used by more than one department is an indirect expense to be allocated among all of them. In these cases, the relative numbers of hours that the equipment is used by the departments is a reasonable basis for allocating depreciation to them.

Utilities Expenses. Firms usually allocate utilities expenses (such as for heating and lighting) on the basis of floor space occupied by departments. This practice should be based on an observation that the amount of heat and the number of lights, their wattage, and the extent of their use are uniform throughout the business. Should there be significant differences in these factors among the departments, further analysis and a separate allocation may produce more useful information. Again, there is a trade-off between the usefulness of the more precise information and the effort of getting it.

Service Departments. In order to manufacture products and make sales, production departments must have services provided by such departments as the general office, personnel, payroll, advertising, and purchasing departments. Because service departments do not produce revenues, companies evaluate them as cost centers. To assist these evaluations, the departmental accounting system can accumulate and report costs incurred directly by each service department. If the service departments' evaluations are based on all costs, the departmental accounting system should allocate indirect costs to each department that benefits from them.

By definition, a service department supports the activities of other departments. Therefore, when any production department's effectiveness is assessed, managers should consider the cost of any benefits it receives from service departments. *Thus, after the costs of operating service departments have been compiled, they should be allocated to the production (or selling) departments.* In effect, the costs of service departments are shared indirect expenses of production departments. If management wants to evaluate selling departments as profit centers using net income instead of gross profit, service department costs should be allocated to them. The following list shows some commonly used bases for allocating service department costs to production and selling departments:

Service Departments	Commonly Used Expense Allocation Bases
General office	Number of employees or sales in each department
Personnel	Number of employees in each department
Payroll	Number of employees in each department
Advertising	Sales or amounts of advertising charged directly to each department
Purchasing	Dollar amounts of purchases or number of purchase orders processed
Cleaning and maintenance	Square feet of floor space occupied

Procedures for Allocating Expenses

Each profit center must be assigned its full expenses to produce a complete income statement. These costs include direct expenses and indirect expenses shared with other departments. As we just described, it may be useful to compile the full amount of expenses incurred in the service departments and then assign them to the production departments. To illustrate, suppose that the Alphamax Hardware Store has five departments. Two of them (general office and purchasing) are service departments and the other three (hardware, housewares, and appliances) are selling departments. There are three stages in allocating costs to the selling departments.

The first stage assigns *direct* expenses to each production and selling department, as follows:

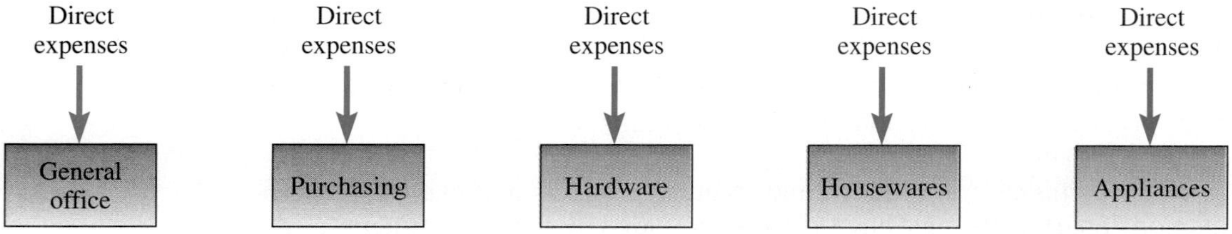

The direct expenses include salaries and other expenses that each department incurs but does not share with any other department. This information is accumulated in departmental expense accounts maintained in the accounting system.

The second step allocates the *indirect* expenses among all five departments according to the allocation base used for each expense. This process is represented as follows:

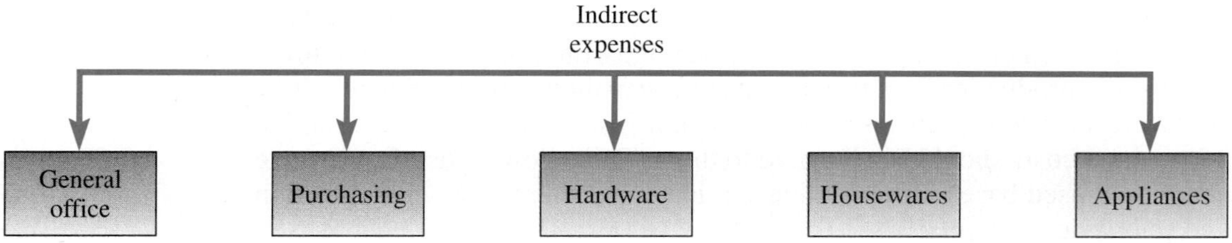

The indirect expenses include the items discussed earlier, such as depreciation, rent, and supervisory costs. These indirect costs are recorded in general expense accounts, and the allocation is accomplished with a *departmental expense allocation spreadsheet* like the one in Illustration 23–3.

The third step allocates the *service department expenses* of the general office and purchasing departments to the three sales departments. The following chart represents this process:

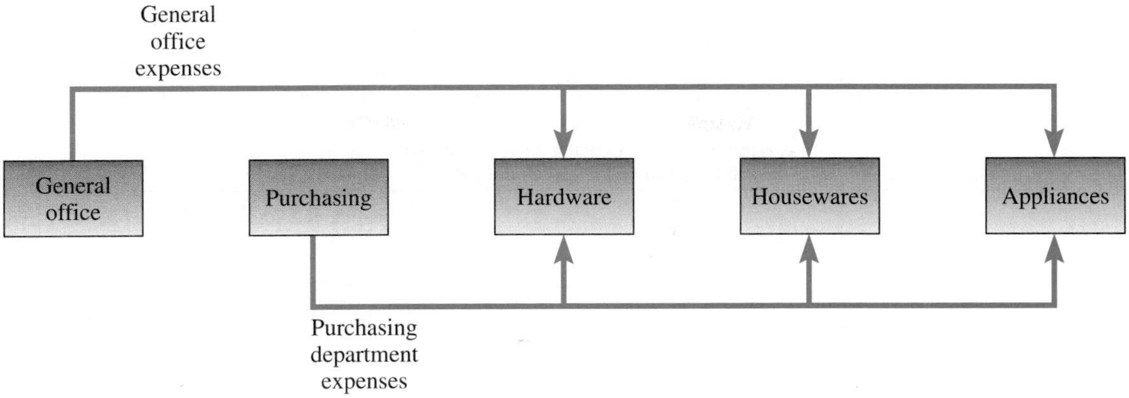

The expenses are allocated by using one of the bases listed previously. The calculations are made on a spreadsheet like the one in Illustration 23–3.[1]

Notice that the first column in Illustration 23–3 lists the direct and indirect expense categories. The lower section of the first column lists the names of the service departments. The allocation bases are in the second column, and the total expense amounts are in the third.

The first stage of the allocation assigns the three direct expenses (salaries, equipment depreciation, and supplies) to the five departments. The second stage allocates the four indirect expenses (rent, utilities, advertising, and insurance) using the listed allocation bases.

For example, consider the allocation of the rent expense. The five departments occupy the following square feet of space:

General office	1,500
Purchasing	1,500
Hardware	4,050
Housewares	2,700
Appliances	2,250
Total	12,000

Even though the two service departments occupy 25% of the total space (3,000 square feet/12,000 square feet), they are located in the rear of the building, which has a lower value than the space in the front occupied by the selling departments. Management estimates that the space in the rear produces only $1,200 of the total rent expense of $12,000. This table allocates the $1,200 rent expense between the two departments in proportion to their square footage:

[1] In some circumstances, a company may allocate costs of a service department to other service departments because they use its services. For example, the costs of the payroll office benefit all service and production departments, with the possible result that some of its costs could be assigned to all of them. In this book, virtually all the examples and assignment materials allocate service cost only to production departments.

ILLUSTRATION 23–3

A Departmental Expense Allocation Spreadsheet

ALPHAMAX HARDWARE STORE
Departmental Expense Allocations
For Year Ended December 31, 1994

	Allocation Bases	Expense Account Balance	Allocation of Expenses to Departments: General Office Dept.	Purchasing Dept.	Hardware Dept.	Housewares Dept.	Appliances Dept.
Direct expenses							
Salaries expense	Payroll records	51,900	13,300	8,200	15,600	7,000	7,800
Depreciation on equipment	Depreciation records	1,500	500	300	400	100	200
Supplies expense	Requisitions	900	200	100	300	200	100
Indirect expenses							
Rent expense	Amount and value of space	12,000	600	600	4,860	3,240	2,700
Utilities expense	Floor space	2,400	300	300	810	540	450
Advertising expense	Sales	1,000			500	300	200
Insurance expense	Value of insured assets	2,500	400	200	900	600	400
Total department expenses		72,200	15,300	9,700	23,370	11,980	11,850
Service department expenses							
General office department	Sales		15,300		7,650	3,825	3,825
Purchasing department	Purchase orders			9,700	3,880	3,395	2,425
Total expenses allocated to selling departments		72,200			34,900	19,200	18,100

Department	Square Feet	Percent of Total	Allocated Cost
General office	1,500	50.0%	$ 600
Purchasing	1,500	50.0	600
Total	3,000	100.0%	$1,200

Then, the next table allocates the remaining $10,800 of rental cost among the three selling departments:

Department	Square Feet	Percent of Total	Allocated Cost
Hardware	4,050	45.0%	$ 4,860
Housewares	2,700	30.0	3,240
Appliances	2,250	25.0	2,700
Total	9,000	100.0%	$10,800

The square footage occupied by the five departments is used more simply for allocating the utilities expense of $2,400:

ILLUSTRATION 23–4

ALPHAMAX HARDWARE STORE
Departmental Income Statement
For Year Ended December 31, 1994

	Hardware Department	Housewares Department	Applicances Department	Combined
Sales	$119,500	$71,700	$47,800	$239,000
Cost of goods sold	73,800	43,800	30,200	147,800
Gross profit on sales	$ 45,700	$27,900	$17,600	$ 91,200
Operating expenses:				
Salaries expense	$ 15,600	$ 7,000	$ 7,800	$ 30,400
Depreciation expense, equipment	400	100	200	700
Supplies expense	300	200	100	600
Rent expense	4,860	3,240	2,700	10,800
Utilities expense	810	540	450	1,800
Advertising expense	500	300	200	1,000
Insurance expense	900	600	400	1,900
Share of general office expenses	7,650	3,825	3,825	15,300
Share of purchasing expenses	3,880	3,395	2,425	9,700
Total operating expenses	$ 34,900	$19,200	$18,100	$ 72,200
Net income (loss)	$ 10,800	$ 8,700	$ (500)	$ 19,000
Analysis:				
Gross profit as percentage of sales	38.2%	38.9%	36.8%	38.2%

Department	Square Feet	Percent of Total	Allocated Cost
General office	1,500	12.50%	$ 300
Purchasing	1,500	12.50	300
Hardware	4,050	33.75	810
Housewares	2,700	22.50	540
Appliances	2,250	18.75	450
Total	12,000	100.00%	$2,400

Examine the lines in Illustration 23–3 for the rent and utilities expenses to see that they show the amounts from these tables. For simplicity, the details of the other allocations are not shown.

Notice that each of the four indirect expenses is allocated to all five departments, except for the advertising expense. Because the advertising expense is allocated on the basis of sales, and because the service departments do not have any sales, it is allocated to only the three selling departments.

The third stage allocates the total expenses of the two service departments to the three selling departments. The allocations are accomplished with the listed allocation bases.

When the spreadsheet is completed, the amounts in the departmental columns can be used to prepare the departmental income statements that appear in Illustration 23–4.

ILLUSTRATION 23–5

ALPHAMAX HARDWARE STORE
Income Statement Showing Departmental Contributions to Overhead
For Year Ended December 31, 1994

	Hardware Department	Housewares Department	Appliances Department	Combined
Sales	$119,500	$71,700	$47,800	$239,000
Cost of goods sold	73,800	43,800	30,200	147,800
Gross profit on sales	$ 45,700	$27,900	$17,600	$ 91,200
Direct expenses:				
Salaries expense	$ 15,600	$ 7,000	$ 7,800	$ 30,400
Depreciation expense, equipment	400	100	200	700
Supplies expense	300	200	100	600
Total direct expenses	$ 16,300	$ 7,300	$ 8,100	$ 31,700
Departmental contributions to overhead	$ 29,400	$20,600	$ 9,500	$ 59,500
Indirect expenses:				
Rent expense				$ 10,800
Utilities expense				1,800
Advertising expense				1,000
Insurance expense				1,900
General office department expense				15,300
Purchasing department expense				9,700
Total indirect expenses				$ 40,500
Net income				$ 19,000
Contribution percentages	24.6%	28.9%	19.9%	24.9%

Departmental Contributions to Overhead

LO 3 Prepare reports that measure the performance of a profit center and describe the factors that should be considered in eliminating an unprofitable department.

Measures of departmental net incomes like those in Illustration 23–4 do not necessarily provide a valid basis for evaluating each department's performance, especially if the indirect expenses are a large portion of total expenses. The weakness exists in these situations because the net income numbers are greatly affected by the somewhat arbitrary assumptions and decisions involved in allocating indirect expenses. This limitation of departmental net income numbers can be overcome by evaluating departmental performance on the basis of their **departmental contributions to overhead.** A department's contribution to overhead is the amount by which its revenues exceed its *direct* costs and expenses.[2]

Illustration 23–5 shows the departmental contributions to overhead for Alphamax Company. Using the information in Illustrations 23–4 and 23–5, we can now perform a more complete evaluation of the profitability of the three sales departments. Compare the performance of the appliance department as

[2] The department's contribution is said to be "to overhead" because of the old practice of considering all indirect expenses to be "overhead." Thus, the excess of a department's revenues over its expenses represents a contribution toward paying the company's total overhead.

AS A MATTER OF
Fact

On a sunny spring afternoon, Sears CEO Edward Brennan strolls into the yawning boardroom on the 68th floor of the Sears Tower in Chicago. "I just heard the news," he says sadly. "The Cubs fired Don Zimmer. Why didn't they give him a chance?" Such empathy for the ousted Cubs manager comes not just from Brennan's love of baseball but also from the fact that he is feeling major-league pressure himself. By taking control of Sears Roebuck's beleaguered $32-billion-a-year retail business, Brennan told his board of directors, shareholders, employees, and customers that he can fix what's ailing Sears better and faster.

What that means financially: The merchandise group—the stores, the catalogue, and the Sears credit card—watched net income plunge 60% last year, to $257 million, the lowest level since 1980, while sales grew an anemic 1.2%, to $32 billion. U.S. operations, which account for 78.5% of Sears' total merchandise revenues, lost $100 million.

Brennan looks and sounds remarkably calm for a man facing the unenviable task of trying to make Sears competitive again. Consider the retailers that are setting the pace for the next decade, and you'll see companies that are miles ahead of Sears in cost control, distribution capabilities, and merchandising skill.

If Sears is to achieve the kind of success Brennan is banking on, its best shot comes from what it insists on calling "power formats." Ordinary people would call them departments, as in "Where is the children's department?" The merchandise group is divided into seven of them: home appliances and electronics; automotive supplies; home improvement products; home furnishings; and men's, women's, and children's apparel.

Carving up the merchandise group this way gave Sears something it never had before: a way of accurately measuring how profitable each category was. Believe it or not, Sears' practice before 1989 had been simply to allocate costs based on company averages for each business. For instance, managers didn't know the apparel group's actual warehouse or distribution charges or its employee health costs. Without throwing real costs up against actual sales, management had no way of knowing how much money each business was making. Explains an executive who was close to the planning: "The exercise was brutal in its truthfulness. A lot of things we were selling turned out not to be as profitable as everyone thought."

Source: Susan Caminiti, *Fortune,* July 15, 1991, pp. 88–90,

described in the two reports. Illustration 23–4 shows a net loss of $500 resulting from the department's operations. On the other hand, Illustration 23–5 shows a positive contribution to overhead of $9,500, which is 19.9% of sales. Although the contribution of the appliance department is not as large as those of the other departments, a $9,500 contribution to overhead appears much better than a $500 loss.

Eliminating an Unprofitable Department

When a department shows poor performance by reporting a net loss or a low contribution to overhead, management may consider eliminating it. However, in considering this action, neither the net income figure nor the contribution to overhead provides sufficient information for the decision. In fact, the department's **escapable expenses** and **inescapable expenses** must be considered. Escapable expenses (sometimes called *avoidable expenses*) are the expenses that would not be incurred if the department were eliminated. Inescapable expenses (sometimes called *unavoidable expenses*) are the expenses that would continue even if the department were eliminated. For example, the management of Alphamax Company is considering whether to eliminate its appliances department. An analysis of the various operating expenses for the whole company and the department shows that the expenses assigned to the appliances department fall into these categories:

	Total Expenses	Escapable Expenses	Inescapable Expenses
Cost of goods sold	$30,200	$30,200	
Direct expenses:			
Salaries expense	7,800	7,800	
Depreciation expense, equipment	200		$ 200
Supplies expense	100	100	
Indirect expenses:			
Rent expense	3,600		3,600
Utilities expense	600		600
Advertising expense	200	200	
Insurance expense	400	300	100
Service department costs:			
Share of office department expenses	3,000	2,200	800
Share of purchasing expenses	2,100	1,000	1,100
Total	$48,200	$41,800	$6,400

This analysis shows that Alphamax would avoid total expenses of $41,800 if it eliminated the appliances department. But, the department's sales are $47,800, which means that the company will lose $6,000 of income if it eliminates the department. *As a general rule, a department can be considered a candidate for elimination if its revenues are less than its escapable expenses.* In effect, the escapable expenses are the cost of obtaining the department's revenues. When the escapable expenses are greater than the revenues, the company is better off if it eliminates the department.

In considering the elimination of an unprofitable department, you also need to determine whether its presence increases the revenues of other departments. Even though one department is unprofitable on its own, it may still contribute to the sales and profits of other departments by bringing in more customers. In this case, a department might be continued even when its revenues are less than its escapable expenses. On the other hand, even a profitable department might be discontinued if its space, assets, and staff can be more profitably used by expanding an existing department or by creating a completely new one.

From this discussion, you should understand that the decision to keep or eliminate a department requires a more complex analysis than simply looking at the bottom line of a departmental income statement or another managerial accounting report. Even though these reports provide useful information, they are only the starting point for the decision.

Controllable Costs and Expenses

LO 4 Explain the concept of controllable costs and prepare reports to be used in evaluating the performance of a department manager.

Management can use *departmental accounting* reports of net income and contributions to overhead in assessing whether a department should remain in the company. However, are these numbers useful for assessing how well a department *manager* has performed? In these situations, neither a department's net income nor its contribution to overhead may be very useful because many expenses that enter into them are beyond the control of the manager. Instead, the performance of a manager should be evaluated with information provided in *responsibility accounting* reports that describe the department's activities in terms of **controllable costs.** A cost is controllable if the manager has the power to determine or at least strongly influence the amounts incurred. An **uncontrollable cost** is not within the manager's control or influence.

Controllable Costs and Direct Costs

You should understand that controllable costs are not necessarily the same as direct costs. Direct costs are easily traced to a specific department, but their amounts may or may not be under the control of the department's manager. For example, department managers often have little or no control over the amount of depreciation expense because they cannot do anything to affect the amount of equipment assigned to their departments. Also, managers usually have no control over their own salaries. On the other hand, department managers can control or influence the cost of goods sold and the supplies used in the department.

When controllable costs are used to judge managers' performances, managers should rely on data that describes the departments' outputs and their controllable costs and expenses. A manager's performance should be judged by comparing the current period's results with planned levels and the results of prior periods.

Circumstances that Make Costs Controllable or Uncontrollable

Controllable and uncontrollable costs must be identified with a particular manager and a definite time period. Without defining these two reference points, it is not possible to know whether a cost is controllable or uncontrollable. For example, the cost of property insurance may not be controllable at the department manager's level, but it is subject to control by the executive responsible for obtaining the company's insurance coverage. Likewise, this executive may not have any control over expenses resulting from insurance policies already in force. But, when a policy eventually expires, the executive is free to renegotiate the replacement policy and thus gain some control or influence over the cost in the long run. Thus, all costs are controllable at some level of management if the time period is sufficiently long.

Responsibility Accounting

The concept of controllable costs and expenses provides the basis for a responsibility accounting system. In a responsibility accounting system, managers are responsible for the costs and expenses that fall under their control. Prior to each reporting period, the company develops plans that specify the expected costs or expenses under the control of each manager. Those plans

ILLUSTRATION 23–6

Levels of Organizational Responsibility

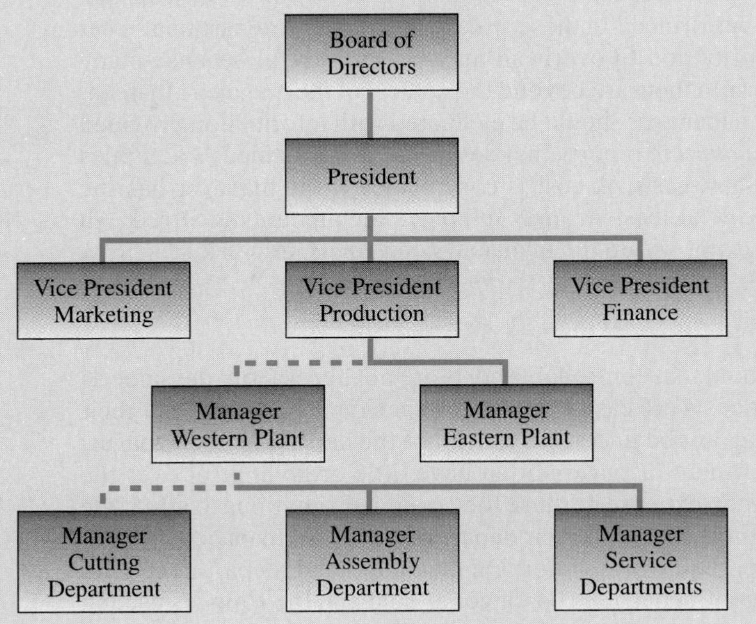

are called **responsibility accounting budgets.** To enlist the cooperation of each manager and to be sure that the budgets establish reasonable goals, the managers should be closely involved in preparing their budgets.

The responsibility accounting system accumulates costs and expenses to include in timely reports to the managers about the costs for which they are responsible. These reports are **performance reports.** They compare actual costs and expenses to the budgeted amounts. Managers use performance reports to focus their attention on specific actual costs that differ from the budgeted amounts. With this information in hand, they can decide what corrective action to take.

Higher management levels also use performance reports to evaluate the effectiveness of lower-level managers in controlling costs and keeping within budgeted amounts. To achieve proper motivation, managers should not be evaluated using costs that they do not control. Chapter 26 gives further consideration to the nature and use of performance reports.

A responsibility accounting system should reflect the fact that control over costs and expenses belongs to several levels of management. For example, consider the organization chart in Illustration 23–6. In the chart, the lines connecting the various managerial positions represent channels of authority. Thus, while the three department managers are responsible for the controllable costs and expenses incurred in their departments, those same costs are subject to the general control of the Western plant manager. And, the Western plant's costs are also subject to the control of the vice president of production, the president, and ultimately the board of directors.

At the lowest levels, managers have only limited responsibilities and relatively little control over costs. As a result, performance reports for this management level should cover only a few controllable costs. Responsibilities and control broaden at higher levels in the company. Reports to higher-level managers are therefore broader and cover a wider range of costs. However, reports to managers at these levels normally do not contain all the details reported to their subordinates. Instead, the details reported to lower-level managers are normally summarized on the reports to their superiors. The details are summarized for two reasons: (1) lower-level managers are primarily responsible for the costs described by the details and (2) reports with too many details can obscure more important points. If reports to higher-level managers are too detailed, they may draw attention from the broader, more important issues confronting the company.

Illustration 23–7 presents summarized performance reports for the three management levels highlighted in Illustration 23–6. Observe in Illustration 23–7 that costs under the control of the cutting department manager are totaled and included among the controllable costs of the Western plant manager. Also, the costs under the control of the plant manager are totaled and included among the controllable costs of the vice president for production. In this manner, a responsibility accounting system provides relevant information for each management level.

Before going on, we need to acknowledge that computers have caused our ability to produce vast amounts of information to far outstrip our ability to use the information. Good managers need to select relevant data for planning and controlling the areas under their responsibility. A good responsibility accounting system reflects this need and makes every effort to get the right information to the right person at the right time. The right person is the person who can control the cost and the right time is before the cost gets out of control.

Joint Costs

LO 5 Describe the problems associated with allocating joint costs between products.

Most manufacturing processes involve **joint costs.** A joint cost is a single cost incurred in producing or purchasing two or more essentially different products. A joint cost is somewhat similar to an indirect expense in the sense that it is shared among more than one cost object. For example, a petroleum refining company incurs a joint cost when it buys crude oil that it breaks apart to produce different grades of gasoline, lubricating oil, kerosene, paraffin, ethylene, and a variety of other products. Likewise, a sawmill incurs joint costs when it buys a log and cuts it into boards classified as Clear, Select Structural, No. 1 Common, No. 2 Common, No. 3 Common, as well as other types of lumber and by-products.

When a joint cost is incurred, a question arises as to whether its amount should be allocated to the different products produced from it. Because the allocation of a joint cost is always arbitrary, the best answer is to avoid allocating the cost to the products whenever possible. Many managerial decisions, such as whether to continue buying logs and cutting lumber, should be based on unallocated cost information.

ILLUSTRATION 23–7

Responsibility Accounting Performance Reports

Vice president, production

Controllable Costs	For July Budgeted Amount	Actual Amount	Over (Under) Budget
Salaries, plant managers	$ 80,000	$ 80,000	$ –0–
Quality control costs	21,000	22,400	1,400
Office costs	29,500	28,800	(700)
Western plant	276,700	279,500	2,800
Eastern plant	390,000	380,600	(9,400)
Total	$797,200	$791,300	$(5,900)

Manager, western plant

Controllable Costs	For July Budgeted Amount	Actual Amount	Over (Under) Budget
Salaries, department managers	$ 75,000	$ 78,000	$ 3,000
Depreciation	10,600	10,600	–0–
Insurance	6,800	6,300	(500)
Cutting department	79,600	79,900	300
Assembly department	61,500	60,200	(1,300)
Service department 1	24,300	24,700	400
Service department 2	18,900	19,800	900
Total	$276,700	$279,500	$ 2,800

Manager, cutting department

Controllable Costs	For July Budgeted Amount	Actual Amount	Over (Under) Budget
Raw materials	$ 26,500	$ 25,900	$ (600)
Direct labor	32,000	33,500	1,500
Indirect labor	7,200	7,000	(200)
Supplies	4,000	3,900	(100)
Other controllable costs	9,900	9,600	(300)
Total	$ 79,600	$ 79,900	$ 300

ILLUSTRATION 23–8

Allocating a Joint Cost on a Physical Basis

Grade of Lumber	Board Feet Produced	Percent of Total	Allocated Cost	Selling Price	Gross Profit
Structural	10,000	10.0%	$ 3,000	$12,000	$ 9,000
No. 1 Common	30,000	30.0	9,000	18,000	9,000
No. 2 Common	40,000	40.0	12,000	16,000	4,000
No. 3 Common	20,000	20.0	6,000	4,000	(2,000)
Total	100,000	100.0%	$30,000	$50,000	$20,000

However, when GAAP financial statements are prepared, the full joint cost must be assigned to specific products. Thus, the financial accountant faces the problem of deciding how to allocate the joint cost among the products that result from incurring the cost. For example, if some products are sold and others remain in inventory, allocating the joint cost allows the accountant to assign costs to the cost of goods sold and the ending inventory.

A joint cost could be allocated on some physical basis, such as the ratio of pounds, cubic feet, or gallons of each joint product to the total pounds, cubic feet, or gallons of all joint products flowing from the cost. However, this method is not usually applied because the resulting cost allocations do not reflect the relative market values acquired with the joint cost or produced from the joint cost. For example, certain parts of a log are more valuable than others because of the products that can be produced from them. A simple physical basis for allocating the joint cost would not reflect the extra value flowing into some products or the inferior value flowing into others. In turn, a physical basis could cause the sale of some joint products to appear more profitable than others. Some joint products may even be reported as selling at a loss while others show a profit.

As an example of using a physical measure to allocate a joint cost, suppose that a sawmill bought logs for $30,000. When cut, the logs produced 100,000 board feet of lumber in the grades and amounts shown in Illustration 23–8. Observe that the logs produced 20,000 board feet of No. 3 Common lumber, which is 20% of the total lumber produced from the logs. Under the physical allocation, the No. 3 lumber would be assigned 20% of the $30,000 cost of the logs, or $6,000 ($30,000 × 20%). Because this low-grade lumber can be sold for only $4,000, this allocation would cause a $2,000 loss to be reported from its production and sale.

The disadvantage of the physical allocation approach is that it does not reflect the fact that some portions of the raw materials (such as logs) are more valuable than others. For example, the portion of a log used to produce Structural grade lumber is worth more than the portion used to produce No. 3 Common lumber. A potentially more useful analysis would attempt to find the cost of the specific subcomponents of the materials used to produce specific products. However, we cannot easily know what certain parts of a log are worth.

ILLUSTRATION 23–9

Allocating a Joint Cost on a Value Basis

Grade of lumber	Selling Price	Percent of Total	Allocated Cost	Gross Profit
Structural	$12,000	24.0%	$ 7,200	$ 4,800
No. 1 Common	18,000	36.0	10,800	7,200
No. 2 Common	16,000	32.0	9,600	6,400
No. 3 Common	4,000	8.0	2,400	1,600
Total	$50,000	100.0%	$30,000	$20,000

Accountants have developed an approach that allocates the joint cost in proportion to the value of the output produced by the process at the point of separation. Illustration 23–9 demonstrates this approach to allocation. Here, the percentages of the total cost allocated to each grade are determined by the ratio of each grade's selling price to the total selling price of $50,000. Thus, for example, the Structural grade lumber receives 24% of the total cost ($12,000/$50,000) instead of the 10% portion based on the physical measure. And, the No. 3 Common lumber receives only 8% of the total cost, or $2,400, which is materially less than the $6,000 assigned to it with the physical basis. Notice that one outcome of the value-based allocation is that *every* grade produces exactly the same 40% gross profit on its selling price. This 40% rate also equals the gross profit rate from selling all the lumber made from the $30,000 logs for a combined price of $50,000.

Activity-Based Costing

LO 6 Describe activity-based costing and its advantages for generating useful information for management.

In reading the preceding section, you may have recognized that the factory overhead costs in job order and process cost accounting systems are special cases of joint indirect costs. Factory overhead is an indirect cost because it cannot be clearly associated with specific jobs, processes, or products. Factory overhead is also a joint cost because it is incurred in producing more than one product. In earlier chapters, this special joint cost was allocated in proportion to the direct labor cost incurred for a job or a process.

From the discussion in this chapter, you should have gained the insight that indirect costs are produced by many different factors. In reality, overhead cost is really too complex to be explained as the result of the variation of only one factor, such as direct labor.[3] To gain more precision and therefore more complete and useful information, the practices of **activity-based costing** have been developed.

As suggested by the name, activity-based costing (ABC) assigns costs to departments and products on the basis of a variety of activities instead of only

[3] Because technological advances keep increasing the extent of automated manufacturing, direct labor cost has generally declined as a percentage of total production cost. In some companies, direct labor cost has declined so significantly that it is actually treated as overhead.

ILLUSTRATION 23–10

Costs and Cost Drivers in Activity-Based Costing

Cost	Cost Driver
Materials purchasing	Number of purchase orders received from a department
Materials handling	Number of materials requisitions received from a department or for a job
Personnel processing	Number of employees hired or laid off
Equipment depreciation	Number of products produced or hours of use
Quality inspection costs	Number of defective units
Indirect labor for setting up equipment for production	Number of setups required by a department
Engineering costs for product modifications	Number of modifications initiated by a department or for a product

one. To a certain extent, ABC is similar to the practices used in this chapter for allocating indirect costs among departments and for allocating service department costs to production departments. However, ABC offers several advantages.

Implementing ABC requires managers to carefully analyze each component of overhead cost to identify the factors that affect its amount. These factors are the **cost drivers** for the various components of cost. Once the cost drivers are identified, they are used to assign costs to products and processes, just like the overhead allocation bases described in earlier sections. The difference between traditional allocation methods and ABC is that there are many more cost drivers than allocation bases. Using the traditional allocation methods described in this chapter, the entire costs assigned to service departments are assigned to production departments with a single allocation basis. Under ABC, individual cost items in service departments are allocated to products manufactured or sold in the production or selling departments. Illustration 23–10 lists some examples of indirect costs and their cost drivers. The accounting system uses these cost drivers to assign overhead costs to departments (for departmental and responsibility accounting) or to products.

ABC is best applied in situations where many different kinds of products are manufactured by single departments. For example, some products produced in a department might be simple, while others are more complex. The more complex products are likely to require additional assistance from certain service departments, such as engineering, maintenance, and materials handling. However, if the same amount of direct labor is applied to the complex and simple products, a traditional overhead allocation system assigns the same overhead cost to them, despite their differences. With the more detailed approach of ABC, the more complex products are assigned a greater portion of the overhead cost. As a result, pricing and other decisions may be affected. In addition, production department managers can more usefully focus on managing the activities that drive overhead cost instead of merely trying to reduce allocated overhead cost by reducing direct labor cost.

Another benefit of ABC is that it causes management to pay closer attention to all the activities that take place in the business. If overhead costs are grouped together in a single account, managers may not direct their attention to controlling any of them individually. But, when ABC is implemented, managers must look very closely at each item. In turn, the system encourages them to manage each cost more carefully to increase the benefit obtained for each dollar spent. In addition, this analysis encourages managers to cooperate because it allows them to see how their efforts are interrelated. When these things occur, the company is said to have implemented *activity-based management*. In effect, implementing activity-based costing can bring about many improvements in a company that reach far beyond cost accounting information.

Summary of the Chapter in Terms of Learning Objectives

LO 1. Businesses are divided into departments whenever they become too large to be effectively managed as a single unit. Production departments either manufacture products in a factory or sell products in a store. Service departments support the activities of these production departments. Departmental accounting systems provide information for evaluating departments' performances and responsibility accounting systems provide information for evaluating the performance of department managers. Departments are evaluated as cost centers if they incur costs but do not generate revenues. Departments are evaluated as profit centers if they generate revenues.

LO 2. Direct expenses are easily traced to a specific department because they are incurred for the sole benefit of one department. Indirect expenses, on the other hand, benefit more than one department. If departmental net incomes are measured, indirect expenses are allocated to the departments on some reasonable basis. The allocation basis selected for an indirect expense is a matter of judgment but should reflect the relative benefit the departments receive from the expense.

LO 3. Departmental income statements can be used to evaluate the profitability of the departments that generate revenues. But, if indirect expenses are large and difficult to allocate, the departments should be evaluated on the basis of their contributions to overhead. In general, an unprofitable department should not be eliminated if its revenues exceed its escapable expenses. However, a decision to eliminate a department should also consider how it affects the performance of the other departments as well as alternative uses of the space, assets, and staff.

LO 4. A controllable cost must be identified with a specific level of management and a specific time period. The total expenses of operating a department often include items that are not controllable by the department manager. To be useful, performance reports produced by a responsibility accounting system for evaluating departmental managers should include only the expenses (and revenues) controllable by the managers.

LO 5. A joint cost is a single cost incurred in producing or purchasing two or more different products. When income statements are prepared, joint costs should be allocated to the resulting joint products based on the relative market value of the joint products at the point of separation.

LO 6. Activity-based costing is a system for assigning overhead costs to products and departments in accordance with cost drivers. ABC differs from traditional cost accounting systems that allocate overhead in proportion to a single allocation base, such as direct labor-hours. The main purpose of ABC is to gain more understanding about the costs of producing different products. Beyond providing this information, a major advantage of ABC is that it forces managers to analyze and then control individual overhead cost items instead of merely lumping them together in a single unmanageable group.

Demonstration Problem

Use the following information to prepare departmental income statements for Hacker's Haven, a computer store. The store has five departments. Three of them are selling departments (hardware, software, and repairs), and two are service departments (general office and purchasing).

Some accounting information about the five departments' activities for 1994 follows:

	General Office	Purchasing	Hardware	Software	Repairs
Sales	—	—	$960,000	$600,000	$840,000
Cost of goods sold	—	—	500,000	300,000	200,000
Direct expenses:					
Payroll	$60,000	$45,000	80,000	25,000	325,000
Depreciation	6,000	7,200	33,000	4,200	9,600
Supplies	15,000	10,000	10,000	2,000	25,000

In addition, several indirect expenses are incurred in the departments. In preparing an income statement, these indirect expenses are allocated among the five departments. Then, the expenses of the two service departments are allocated to the three production departments. The total amounts and the allocation bases for each expense are as follows:

Type of Indirect Expense	Total Cost	Allocation Basis
Rent	$150,000	Square footage occupied
Utilities	50,000	Square footage occupied
Advertising	125,000	Dollars of sales
Insurance	30,000	Value of assets insured
Service departments:		
General office	?	Number of employees
Purchasing	?	Dollars of cost of goods sold

The following information is needed for the allocations:

Department	Square Feet	Sales	Insured Assets	Employees	Cost of Goods Sold
General office	500		$ 60,000		
Purchasing	500		72,000		
Hardware	4,000	$ 960,000	330,000	5	$ 500,000
Software	3,000	600,000	42,000	5	300,000
Repairs	2,000	840,000	96,000	10	200,000
Total	10,000	$2,400,000	$600,000	20	$1,000,000

Required:

1. Complete a departmental expense allocation worksheet for Hacker's Haven.
2. Prepare a departmental income statement reporting net income for each selling department and for all selling departments combined.

Solution to Demonstration Problem

Planning the Solution

- Set up and complete four schedules to allocate the indirect expenses for rent, utilities, advertising, and insurance.
- Allocate the departments' indirect expenses with a six-column worksheet like the one in Illustration 23–3. Enter the given amounts of the direct expenses for each department. Then enter the allocated amounts of the indirect expenses that were just calculated.
- Complete two schedules for allocating the general office and purchasing department costs to the three selling departments. Enter these amounts on the worksheet, and determine the total expenses allocated to the three selling departments.
- Prepare a four-column departmental income statement like the one in Illustration 23–4. Show sales, cost of goods sold, the gross profit from sales, the individual direct and indirect expenses, and the net income for each of the three selling departments and for the entire company.

Allocations of indirect expenses among the five departments:

Rent	Square Feet	Percent of Total	Allocated Cost
General office	500	5.0%	$ 7,500
Purchasing	500	5.0	7,500
Hardware	4,000	40.0	60,000
Software	3,000	30.0	45,000
Repairs	2,000	20.0	30,000
Total	10,000	100.0%	$150,000

Utilities	Square Feet	Percent of Total	Allocated Cost
General office	500	5.0%	$ 2,500
Purchasing	500	5.0	2,500
Hardware	4,000	40.0	20,000
Software	3,000	30.0	15,000
Repairs	2,000	20.0	10,000
Total	10,000	100.0%	$50,000

Advertising	Sales Dollars	Percent of Total	Allocated Cost
Hardware	$ 960,000	40.0%	$ 50,000
Software	600,000	25.0	31,250
Repairs	840,000	35.0	43,750
Total	$2,400,000	100.0%	$125,000

Insurance	Assets Insured	Percent of Total	Allocated Cost
General office	$ 60,000	10.0%	$ 3,000
Purchasing	72,000	12.0	3,600
Hardware	330,000	55.0	16,500
Software	42,000	7.0	2,100
Repairs	96,000	16.0	4,800
Total	$600,000	100.0%	$30,000

Departmental Expense Allocation Spreadsheet
For Year Ended December 31, 1994

Expense	Allocation Bases	Expense Account Balance	General Office	Purchasing	Hardware Dept.	Software Dept.	Repairs Dept.
Direct expenses:							
Payroll		$ 535,000	$60,000	$45,000	$ 80,000	$ 25,000	$325,000
Depreciation . . .		60,000	6,000	7,200	33,000	4,200	9,600
Supplies		62,000	15,000	10,000	10,000	2,000	25,000
Indirect expenses:							
Rent	Square ft.	150,000	7,500	7,500	60,000	45,000	30,000
Utilities	Square ft.	50,000	2,500	2,500	20,000	15,000	10,000
Advertising . . .	Sales	125,000	—	—	50,000	31,250	43,750
Insurance	Assets	30,000	3,000	3,600	16,500	2,100	4,800
Total		$1,012,000	$94,000	$75,800	269,500	124,550	448,150
Service dept. expenses:							
General office . .	Employees		$94,000		23,500	23,500	47,000
Purchasing	Goods sold			$75,800	37,900	22,740	15,160
Total expenses allocated to selling departments . . .		$1,012,000			$330,900	$170,790	$510,310

Allocations of service department expenses among the three selling departments:

General office	Employees	Percent of Total	Allocated Cost
Hardware	5	25.0%	$23,500
Software	5	25.0	23,500
Repairs	10	50.0	47,000
Total	20	100.0%	$94,000

Purchasing	Cost of Goods Sold	Percent of Total	Allocated Cost
Hardware	$ 500,000	50.0%	$37,900
Software	300,000	30.0	22,740
Repairs	200,000	20.0	15,160
Total	$1,000,000	100.0%	$75,800

HACKER'S HAVEN COMPUTER STORE
Departmental Income Statement
For Year Ended December 31, 1994

	Hardware	Software	Repairs	Combined
Sales	$960,000	$600,000	$840,000	$2,400,000
Cost of goods sold	500,000	300,000	200,000	1,000,000
Gross profit	$460,000	$300,000	$640,000	$1,400,000
Expenses:				
Payroll	$ 80,000	$ 25,000	$325,000	$ 430,000
Depreciation	33,000	4,200	9,600	46,800
Supplies	10,000	2,000	25,000	37,000
Rent	60,000	45,000	30,000	135,000
Utilities	20,000	15,000	10,000	45,000
Advertising	50,000	31,250	43,750	125,000
Insurance	16,500	2,100	4,800	23,400
General office	23,500	23,500	47,000	94,000
Purchasing	37,900	22,740	15,160	75,800
Total expenses	$330,900	$170,790	$510,310	$1,012,000
Net income	$129,100	$129,210	$129,690	$ 388,000

Glossary

LO 7 Define or explain the words and phrases listed in the chapter glossary.

Activity-based costing a system of assigning costs to departments and products on the basis of a variety of activities instead of only one. p. 1244

Controllable costs costs with amounts that the manager has the power to determine or at least strongly influence. p. 1239

Cost center a department that incurs costs (or expenses) without directly generating revenues. p. 1226

Cost driver a factor that affects the amount of a component of overhead; cost drivers are used in activity-based costing. p. 1226

Departmental accounting system an accounting system that provides information management can use to evaluate the profitability or cost effectiveness of a department's activities. p. 1224

Departmental contribution to overhead the amount by which a department's revenues exceed its direct costs and expenses. p. 1236

Direct expenses expenses that are easily traced and assigned to a specific department because they are incurred for the sole benefit of that department. p. 1228

Escapable expenses expenses that would not be incurred if a department were eliminated. pp. 1237–38

Indirect expenses expenses that are not easily associated with a specific department; they are incurred for the benefit of more than one department. pp. 1228–29

Inescapable expenses expenses that will continue even if a department is eliminated. pp. 1237–38

Joint cost a single cost incurred in producing or purchasing two or more essentially different products. p. 1241

Performance report a responsibility accounting report that compares actual costs and expenses for a department with the budgeted amounts. p. 1240

Profit center a unit of a business that not only incurs costs but also generates revenues. p. 1226

Responsibility accounting budget a plan that specifies the expected costs and expenses under the control of a manager. p. 1240

Responsibility accounting system an accounting system that provides information management can use to evaluate the performance of a department's manager. p. 1225

Uncontrollable costs costs that the manager does not have the power to determine or at least strongly influence. p. 1239

Synonymous Terms

Activity-based costing ABC.

Escapable expenses avoidable expenses.

Inescapable expenses unavoidable expenses.

Joint costs common costs; shared costs.

Objective Review

Answers to the following questions are listed at the end of the chapter. Be sure that you decide which is the one best answer to each question *before* you check the answers.

LO 1 If a business is divided into departments

a. All departments will probably be evaluated as cost centers.
b. Only departments that produce revenues can be evaluated as cost centers.
c. All departments will probably be evaluated as profit centers.
d. Each department must represent a separable industrial segment of the company's operations.
e. None of the above is correct.

LO 2 If a company has two sales departments (shoes and hats) and two service departments (payroll and advertising), which of the following statements is correct?

a. All wages incurred in the payroll department should be allocated to the advertising department.
b. Wages incurred in the payroll department are indirect expenses of the sales departments.
c. Wages incurred in the payroll department are direct expenses of the payroll department.
d. Advertising department expenses should be allocated to the other three departments.
e. Both (*b*) and (*c*) are true.

LO 3 This information describes the results produced by the fixtures department of The Decorator Store in the last reporting period:

Sales	$21,000
Net loss	$ (6,000)
Departmental contribution to overhead	10% of sales
Escapable expenses	$17,400
Inescapable expenses	$ 9,600

Which of the following is the best reason for eliminating or not eliminating the fixtures department?

a. The fixtures department should be eliminated because it has a net loss.
b. The fixtures department should be eliminated because of the combination of its net loss and its poor contribution to overhead.
c. The fixtures department should be eliminated because $17,400 of escapable expenses could be avoided by eliminating it.
d. The Decorator Store is better off continuing the fixtures department because its revenues exceed its escapable expenses.
e. None of the above is correct.

LO 4 Which of the following best describes how well a sales department manager has performed?

a. Net income figures.
b. Contribution to overhead.
c. Escapable expenses.
d. Controllable revenues and expenses.
e. All of the above.

LO 5 Kilian Co. produces three products: T1, T2, and T3. The joint costs incurred for the current month on these products is $90,000. The following data relate to this month's production:

Product	Units	Unit Sales Price
T1	48,000	$3.00
T2	32,000	6.00
T3	16,000	9.00

The joint cost that should be allocated to T3 is

a. $15,000.
b. $24,000.
c. $27,000.
d. $42,000.
e. $45,000.

LO 6 Activity-based costing offers these advantages over traditional approaches to allocating overhead:

a. Providing more precision and more complete information about overhead.
b. Basing the allocations on many cost-drivers instead of just one.
c. Forcing managers to examine and thus manage every component of overhead.
d. Increasing cooperation among managers because they can see how their efforts are interrelated.
e. All of the above.

LO 7 A department's contribution to overhead is

a. The amount by which its revenues exceed its direct expenses.
b. The amount of overhead cost that it contributes to the total overhead for the company.
c. The amount by which its revenues exceed its total direct and indirect expenses.
d. The amount by which its revenues exceed its controllable expenses.
e. The amount by which its revenues exceed its inescapable expenses.

Questions for Class Discussion

1. What is the difference between departmental accounting systems and responsibility accounting systems?
2. Why are businesses divided into departments?
3. What is the difference between production departments and service departments?
4. Give several examples of service departments.
5. Is it possible to evaluate the profitability of a cost center? Why?
6. Are service departments evaluated as cost centers or as profit centers? Why?
7. If a company with a computerized accounting system uses sophisticated cash registers networked with its computer, is the company likely to use departmental sales analysis spreadsheets? Why?
8. How is a departmental sales analysis spreadsheet used in determining sales by departments?
9. What is the difference between direct and indirect expenses?
10. In a merchandising company, what are the typical cost objects for classifying expenses as direct or indirect?
11. Suggest a reasonable basis for allocating each of the following indirect expenses to departments: (*a*) salary of a supervisor who manages several departments, (*b*) rent, (*c*) heat, (*d*) electricity used for lighting, (*e*) janitorial services, (*f*) advertising, (*g*) expired insurance on equipment, and (*h*) property taxes on equipment.
12. Describe the three steps of preparing a spreadsheet for allocating expenses to departments.
13. How useful is information about the net income of a department when it includes allocated indirect expenses?
14. How is a department's contribution to overhead measured?
15. What are escapable and inescapable expenses?
16. What are controllable costs?
17. Why should managers be closely involved in preparing their responsibility accounting budgets?
18. In responsibility accounting, who is the right person to be given timely reports and statistics for a specific cost?
19. What is a joint cost? How are joint costs usually allocated among the products produced from them?
20. What is the activity-based costing? What is a cost driver?
21. Lands' End receives telephone orders for merchandise presented in different catalogs sent to different groups of customers. Why would it be useful to (*a*) collect information from customers that identifies the particular catalog they are ordering from, and (*b*) treat each catalog as a profit center?
22. Federal Express flies packages from drop off points to Memphis, sorts them in a central facility, and then delivers them the next morning to their destinations. In evaluating the profitability of a manager of a field office (such as Fresno, California), would it be useful to allocate any of the central sorting facility costs to that manager's performance report?

Exercises

Exercise 23–1
Departmental expense allocations
(LO 2)

The Eagle Company has four departments: materials, personnel, manufacturing, and packaging. In a recent month, the four departments incurred three shared indirect costs. The amounts of these expenses and the bases used to allocate them are listed below:

Expense	Cost	Allocation Base
Supervision	$100,000	Number of employees
Utilities	80,000	Square feet occupied
Insurance	22,000	Value of assets in use
Total expense	$202,000	

Use these quantities in allocating the costs for the month:

Department	Employees	Square Feet	Assets Value
Materials	12	12,000	$ 16,000
Personnel	4	2,000	4,000
Manufacturing	44	20,000	100,000
Packaging	20	6,000	40,000
Total	80	40,000	$160,000

Using this information, prepare allocations of each of the three indirect expenses among the four departments. Then, prepare a table that shows the total expenses assigned to the four departments.

Exercise 23–2
Allocating rent expense to departments
(LO 2)

Hammer's Department Store pays $160,000 rent every year for its two-story building. The space in the building is occupied by five departments as follows:

Men's department	2,400 square feet of first-floor space
Women's department	3,600 square feet of first-floor space
Kids' department	2,100 square feet of second-floor space
Tall department	1,050 square feet of second-floor space
Bargains department	2,850 square feet of second-floor space

The company allocates 62.5% of the total rent expense to the first floor and 37.5% to the second floor. It then allocates the rent expense for each floor to the departments on that floor on the basis of the space occupied. Determine the rent to be allocated to each department. (Round all amounts to the nearest whole dollar.)

Exercise 23–3
Allocating service department expenses to production departments
(LO 2)

The following partially completed lower section of a departmental allocation spreadsheet is being prepared for Lew Staynard's One-Stop Department Store. At this stage, it shows only the amounts of direct and indirect expenses allocated to the five departments:

Expense	Allocation Bases	Expense Account Balance	Advertising Dept.	Purchasing Dept.	Groceries Dept.	Drugs Dept.	Garden Dept.
Total		$1,635,000	$55,000	$75,000	$400,000	$625,000	$480,000
Service Dept. expenses:							
Advertising	Sales		?		?	?	?
Purchasing.	Purchase orders			?	?	?	?
Total expenses allocated to selling departments		?			?	?	?

Complete the spreadsheet by allocating the two service departments' expenses to the three selling departments. These amounts were known about the allocation bases for the three selling departments:

	Sales	Purchase Orders
Groceries	$1,000,000	380
Drugs	1,600,000	260
Garden	1,400,000	610
Total.	$4,000,000	1,250

Exercise 23–4
Allocating indirect payroll expense to departments
(LO 2)

Dana Wilson works in both the sweaters department and the pants department of Sudstrom's Fashions Store. Wilson assists customers in both departments and also straightens and stocks the merchandise in both departments as needed. The store allocates Wilson's annual wages of $23,600 between the two departments based on a sample of the time worked in the two departments. The sample was obtained from a diary that Wilson kept of hours worked in a randomly chosen week. The diary showed that the following hours were spent in these activities:

Selling in the sweaters department	27
Straightening and stocking in the sweaters department	9
Selling in the pants department	12
Straightening and rearranging merchandise in the pants department	2
Idle time spent waiting for a customer to enter one of the selling departments . .	1

Required

Prepare calculations to allocate Wilson's wages between the departments.

Exercise 23–5
Departmental expense allocation spreadsheet
(LO 2)

ProShop Sales Company has two service departments (advertising and purchasing), and two sales departments (golf clubs and clothes). During 1994, the departments had the following direct expenses:

Advertising department	$10,000
Purchasing department	16,000
Clubs department	65,000
Clothes department	80,000

The departments occupy the following square feet of floor space:

Advertising department	1,000
Purchasing department	800
Clubs department	3,600
Clothes department	2,600

The advertising department developed and distributed 60 ad pieces during the year. Of these, 39 promoted club sales and 21 promoted clothes. The purchasing department placed orders for $640,000 of merchandise during the year. Of this amount, $240,000 was for the clubs department while the remainder was for the clothes department.

Required

Prepare an expense allocation sheet for ProShop Sales Company that assigns the direct expenses to all four departments and the year's $80,000 of utilities expense to the four departments on the basis of floor space occupied. In addition, allocate the advertising department expenses on the basis of the number of ads placed and the purchasing department expenses on the basis of the cost of the merchandise purchased. Provide supplemental schedules showing how you computed the expense allocations.

Exercise 23–6
Income effects of eliminating departments
(LO 3)

The Green Company's management expects the next year to produce the following net incomes for its five departments:

	Dept. J	Dept. K	Dept. L	Dept. M	Dept. N
Sales	$ 25,000	$40,000	$30,000	$ 20,000	$45,000
Expenses:					
Escapable	$ 26,000	$16,000	$10,000	$ 27,000	$ 7,000
Inescapable	9,000	3,000	21,000	7,000	37,000
Total expenses	$ 35,000	$19,000	$31,000	$ 34,000	$44,000
Net income (loss)	$(10,000)	$21,000	$ (1,000)	$(14,000)	$ 1,000

Required

Prepare a combined income statement for the company under each of the following conditions:

a. Management does not eliminate any departments.
b. Management eliminates those departments expected to show net losses.
c. Management eliminates only those departments not expected to increase the company's net income (or reduce its net loss).

Exercise 23–7
Evaluating managerial performance
(LO 4)

Terry Johnson manages the appliance service department of a large department store. This is the 1994 income statement for the department:

Revenues:		
Sales of services	$350,000	
Sales of parts	240,000	$590,000
Costs and expenses:		
Cost of parts sold	$100,000	
Wages (hourly)	20,000	
Manager's salary	40,000	
Payroll taxes	27,000	
Supplies	53,000	
Building depreciation	31,000	
Utilities	48,000	
Interest on long-term debt	25,000	
Income taxes allocated to department	29,000	
Total costs and expenses		373,000
Department net income		$217,000

Analyze the items on the income statement to identify those that clearly should be included on a performance report used to evaluate Johnson's performance. List them and explain why you have chosen them. Then, list and explain the items that should clearly be excluded. Finally, list the items that are not clearly included or excluded and explain why they fall in that category.

Exercise 23–8
Assigning joint real estate costs
(LO 5)

Mountain Real Estate Company just completed developing a subdivision that includes 180 home sites. The 160 lots in the Meadow section are below a ridge and do not have a view of the nearby mountain range, while the 20 lots in the High Ridge section offer unobstructed views. The Meadow lots are expected to sell for $30,000 each, while the High Ridge lots are expected to sell for $80,000 each. The developer acquired the land for $1,750,000 and spent another $850,000 on street and utilities improvements. Assign the joint land and improvement costs to the lots and determine the average cost per lot. (Round all amounts to the nearest whole dollar.)

Exercise 23–9
Assigning joint product costs
(LO 5)

Down East Lobster Company purchases lobsters and processes them into tails and flakes. It then sells the lobster tails for $20.00 per pound and sells the flakes for $12.50 per pound. On average, 100 pounds of lobster can be processed into 50 pounds of tails and 20 pounds of flakes, with 30 pounds of waste.

Assume that 1,000 pounds of lobster are purchased for $5 per pound. The lobsters are then processed with an additional labor cost of $600. No materials or labor costs are assigned to the waste. If 400 pounds of tails are sold and 125 pounds of flakes are sold, what is the allocated cost of the sold items and the cost of the remaining inventory?

Exercise 23–10
Activity-based costing
(LO 6)

The Mildenhall Company manufactures two products, sprockets and gears, on the same production line. Last month, the company experienced the following costs and results:

	Sprockets	Gears	Total
Direct materials	$12,000	$18,000	$ 30,000
Direct labor	6,000	14,000	20,000
Overhead (250% of labor)	15,000	35,000	50,000
Total cost	$33,000	$67,000	$100,000
Quantity produced	1,000	5,000	
Average cost per unit	$33.00	$13.40	

Several of the managers have approached the cost accounting department for help in understanding activity-based costing. Their specific request is that ABC be applied to the production results to see whether the average cost per unit is significantly changed. This additional information is extracted from the production records for the month:

- The overhead cost for supervision was $2,000. The cost driver for supervision is direct labor cost.
- The overhead cost for machinery depreciation was $28,000. The cost driver for this cost is hours of use. The machinery was used 600 hours for the sprockets and 200 hours for the gears.

- The overhead cost for preparing the line to produce products was $20,000. The line was set up 36 times to produce different sprockets and only 14 times to produce different gears.

Required

Use this information to:

a. Assign the overhead cost to the products using activity-based costing cost drivers.

b. Determine the average cost per unit of the two products using direct materials, direct labor, and overhead allocated under ABC.

Problems

Problem 23–1
Allocation of building occupancy costs
(LO 2)

High Fashion, Inc., has several departments that occupy both floors of a two-story building. The departmental accounting system has a single account in the ledger called Building Occupancy Cost. These types and amounts of costs were recorded in this account for last year:

Depreciation, building	$ 40,000
Interest, building mortgage	60,000
Taxes, building and land	18,000
Heating expenses	6,000
Lighting expense	7,000
Cleaning expense	13,000
Total	$144,000

The building has 4,000 square feet on each floor. For simplicity, the bookkeeper merely divided the $144,000 occupancy cost by 8,000 square feet to find an average cost of $18.00 per square foot. Then, each department was charged with a building occupancy cost equal to this rate times the number of square feet that it occupies.

Jackie Baldwin manages a first-floor department that occupies 1,200 square feet and Carey Gardner manages a second-floor department that occupies 1,500 square feet of floor space. In discussing the departmental reports, they have questioned whether using the same rate per square foot for all departments makes sense because the first-floor space has a greater value. Looking further into the issue, the two managers checked a recent real estate study of average rental costs for similar space. The amounts do not include costs for heating, lighting, and cleaning. They found that ground-floor space is worth $21.00 per square foot while second-floor space is worth only $14.00.

Required

Use the preceding information to

1. Allocate the occupancy cost to the two departments by the bookkeeper's method.
2. Allocate the occupancy cost to the two departments in proportion to the relative market values of the space, except for the heating, lighting, and cleaning costs, which should be allocated on an equal basis per square foot occupied.

Problem 23–2
Departmental income statement
(LO 3)

Gander Corporation began operating in January 1994 with two selling departments and one office department. The 1994 departmental net incomes are shown below:

GANDER CORPORATION
Departmental Income Statement
For Year Ended December 31, 1994

	Chairs	Sofas	Combined
Sales	$300,000	$200,000	$500,000
Cost of goods sold	180,000	140,000	320,000
Gross profit from sales	$120,000	$ 60,000	$180,000
Direct expenses			
Sales salaries	$ 25,000	$ 15,000	$ 40,000
Advertising	2,400	4,000	6,400
Store supplies used	2,000	1,000	3,000
Depreciation of equipment	5,000	6,000	11,000
Total direct expenses	$ 34,400	$ 26,000	$ 60,400
Allocated expenses			
Rent expense	$ 12,000	$ 18,000	$ 30,000
Utilities expense	4,000	6,000	10,000
Share of office department expenses	12,000	8,000	20,000
Total allocated expenses	$ 28,000	$ 32,000	$ 60,000
Total expenses	$ 62,400	$ 58,000	$120,400
Net income	$ 57,600	$ 2,000	$ 59,600

Starting in January 1995, Gander plans to open a third department that will sell rugs. Management predicts that the new department will produce $175,000 in sales with a 35% gross profit margin and that it will require the following direct expenses: sales salaries, $18,000; advertising, $6,000; store supplies, $1,000; and equipment depreciation, $4,000.

Since opening, the store has rented space in a building. It will be possible to fit the new department into the same overall space by taking some square footage from the other two departments. When the new rugs department is opened, it will fill one fourth of the space presently used by the chairs department and one sixth of the space used by the sofas department. Management does not predict any increase in utilities costs, which are allocated among the departments in proportion to occupied space.

The company allocates its office department expenses among the selling departments in proportion to their sales. It expects the rugs department to increase office department expenses by $5,000.

Because the rugs department will bring new customers into the store, management expects sales in the chairs and sofas departments to increase by 5%. Those departments' gross profit percentages are not expected to change. No changes are expected in their direct expenses, except for store supplies used, which will increase in proportion to sales.

Required

Prepare a departmental income statement that shows the company's predicted results of operations for 1995 with three selling departments. (Round all amounts to the nearest whole dollar.)

Problem 23–3
Analysis of escapable and inescapable expenses
(LO 3)

The management of the New Hampshire Company is trying to decide whether to eliminate department K, which has produced losses or low profits for several years. The company's 1994 departmental income statement shows a similar result:

NEW HAMPSHIRE COMPANY
Income Statement
For Year Ended December 31, 1994

	Dept. J	Dept. K	Combined
Sales	$525,000	$350,000	$875,000
Cost of goods sold	315,000	255,000	570,000
Gross profit from sales	$210,000	$ 95,000	$305,000
Operating expenses:			
Direct expenses:			
Advertising	$ 20,000	$ 15,000	$ 35,000
Store supplies used	5,000	4,400	9,400
Depreciation of store equipment	6,000	4,000	10,000
Total direct expenses	$ 31,000	$ 23,400	$ 54,400
Allocated expenses:			
Sales salaries	$ 87,360	$ 37,440	$124,800
Rent expense	11,400	5,700	17,100
Bad debts expense	12,000	10,000	22,000
Office salary	18,096	12,064	30,160
Insurance expense	2,500	1,250	3,750
Miscellaneous office expenses	3,000	2,000	5,000
Total allocated expenses	$134,356	$ 68,454	$202,810
Total expenses	$165,356	$ 91,854	$257,210
Net income (loss)	$ 44,644	$ 3,146	$ 47,790

In analyzing the decision to eliminate department K, the management has looked at the following items of information:

a. The company has one office worker who earns $580 per week or $30,160 per year and five sales clerks who each earn $480 per week or $24,960 per year.

b. Currently, the full salaries of three sales clerks are charged to department J. The full salary of one sales clerk is charged to department K. Because the fifth clerk works half-time in both departments, her salary is divided evenly between the two departments.

c. The sales salaries and the office salary currently assigned to department K would be avoided if the department were eliminated. However, management prefers another plan. Three sales clerks have indicated that they will be quitting soon. Management thinks that their work can be done by the other two clerks if the one office worker works in sales half-time. The office worker's schedule will allow this shift of duties if department K is eliminated. If this change is implemented, half the office worker's salary would be reported as sales salaries and half would be reported as office salary.

d. The store building is rented under a long-term lease that cannot be changed. Therefore, the space presently occupied by department K will have to be used by the current department J. The equipment used by department K will be used by the current department J.

e. Closing department K will eliminate its expenses for advertising, bad debts, and store supplies. It will also eliminate 60% of the insurance expense allocated to the department for coverage on its merchandise inventory. In addition, 20% of the miscellaneous office expenses presently allocated to department K will be eliminated.

Required

1. Prepare a three-column schedule that lists (*a*) the company's total expenses (including cost of goods sold), (*b*) the expenses that would be eliminated by closing department K, and (*c*) the expenses that will continue.
2. Prepare a forecasted income statement for the company reflecting the elimination under the assumption that sales and the gross profit will not be affected. The statement should also reflect the reassignment of the office worker to one-half time as a sales clerk.

Problem 23–4
Allocating joint costs (LO 5)

Pat and Tom Bloome own a tomato farm. After preparing the following income statement, Pat remarked to Tom that they should have fed the no. 3 tomatoes to the pigs and saved a lot of trouble.

PAT AND TOM BLOOME
Income from Tomatoes
For Year Ended December 31, 1994

	No. 1	No. 2	No. 3	Combined
Sales:				
Grade				
No. 1: 500,000 lbs. @ $0.60	$300,000			
No. 2: 400,000 lbs. @ $0.25		$100,000		
No. 3: 500,000 lbs. @ $0.20			$100,000	
Combined				$500,000
Costs:				
Land preparation, seed, planting, and cultivating @ $0.102/lb	$ 51,000	$ 40,800	$ 51,000	$142,800
Harvesting, sorting, and grading @ $0.075/lb	37,500	30,000	37,500	105,000
Marketing @ $0.010/lb	5,000	4,000	5,000	14,000
Total costs	$ 93,500	$ 74,800	$ 93,500	$261,800
Net income or loss	$206,500	$ 25,200	$ 6,500	$238,200

In preparing the statement, Pat and Tom allocated the joint costs among the grades as an equal amount per pound. Records about the marketing costs show that $10,000 of the $14,000 was the cost of crating the no. 1 and no. 2 tomatoes and hauling them to the buyer. The remaining $4,000 of marketing costs was the cost of crating the no. 3 tomatoes and hauling them to the cannery where they were stewed and canned.

Required

1. Prepare allocation schedules showing how the Bloomes computed the costs per pound of tomatoes.
2. Prepare allocation schedules showing how the costs would be allocated on the basis of the relative sales values of the three grades. Separate the

marketing costs into the amounts directly identifiable to the grades. Then, allocate any shared marketing costs on the basis of the relative sales values of the grades. (Round all percents to the nearest one tenth and all dollar amounts to the nearest whole dollar.)

3. Using your answers to requirement 2, prepare an income statement that shows the results of producing and marketing the tomatoes.

Problem 23–5
Departmental expense allocation spreadsheet
(LO 2, 3)

The Giant Gourmet Store has three selling departments (cookware, gadgets, and linens) and two service departments (general office and purchasing). After the end of the year, the following information was available for preparing financial statements and internal reports:

	Cookware	Gadgets	Linens
Sales	$500,000	$300,000	$200,000
Purchases	250,000	120,000	130,000
January 1 (beginning) inventory	25,000	28,000	12,000
December 31 (ending) inventory	32,000	23,000	13,000

The Giant Gourmet Store classifies salaries, supplies used, and depreciation as direct expenses of the departments. Payroll, requisition, and plant asset records showed these amounts of direct expenses for the year:

	Salaries Expense	Supplies Used	Depreciation
General office	$15,000	$1,000	$2,000
Purchasing department	16,000	1,200	2,200
Cookware department	40,000	300	1,100
Gadgets department	25,000	200	1,000
Linens department	30,000	500	1,300

The company incurred the following amounts of indirect expenses:

Rent expense	$22,000
Advertising expense	16,000
Expired insurance	10,000
Utilities expense	30,000
Custodial expense	20,000

In preparing financial statements and internal reports, The Giant Gourmet Store allocates the indirect expenses among the departments as follows:

a. Rent expense is first allocated between the selling and service departments on the basis of the value of floor space. The general office and purchasing departments occupy space in the rear of the store that is not as valuable as space in the front. Thus, only $2,000 of the total rent is allocated to these two departments. This amount is allocated between them in proportion to the space that they occupy. The remaining rent is divided among the three selling departments in proportion to the space that they occupy. The five departments occupy these amounts of space:

General office	1,800 square feet
Purchasing department	2,200 square feet
Cookware department	4,800 square feet
Gadgets department	4,000 square feet
Linens department	7,200 square feet

b. Advertising expense is allocated among the selling departments on the basis of sales.

c. Insurance expense is allocated in proportion to the insured value of the equipment in the five departments. The insured values of the equipment in the departments are:

General office	$ 8,000
Purchasing department	10,000
Cookware department	12,000
Gadgets department.	4,000
Linens department	6,000

d. Utilities and custodial care expenses are assigned to the departments on the basis of floor space occupied.

The Giant Gourmet Store then allocates its general office department expenses among its three selling departments on the basis of their dollars of sales, and allocates the purchasing department expenses on the basis of the dollars of purchases.

Required

1. Prepare allocation schedules for the shared indirect expenses.
2. Prepare a departmental expense allocation spreadsheet for the company. Show the allocation tables for the costs of the service departments. (Round all amounts to the nearest whole dollar.)
3. Prepare a departmental income statement showing sales, cost of goods sold, expenses, and net incomes by departments and for the entire store.
4. Prepare a departmental income statement that displays each selling department's contribution to overhead.

Problem 23–6
Responsibility accounting performance reports
(LO 4)

Winnie Sanborn, the manager of Martinez Manufacturing Company's Northern plant, is responsible for all costs of the plant's operation other than her own salary. The plant has two production departments and one service department. The doors and windows departments manufacture different products and have their own managers. The office department provides services equally to the two production departments. Sanborn manages the office department. Martinez Manufacturing prepares a monthly budget for each production department and the office department. After the end of each month, the responsibility accounting system assembles information and presents budgeted and actual costs in performance reports for each of the production department managers and the plant manager.

Each performance report includes only those costs that the particular manager can control. The production department managers control the costs of raw materials, wages, supplies used, and equipment depreciation. The plant manager is responsible for the department managers' salaries, utilities, building rent, office salaries other than her own, other office costs, and the total costs of the two production departments.

The production departments' budgets and cost accumulations for July were as follows:

	Budget		Actual		
	Doors	Windows	Doors	Windows	Combined
Raw materials	$250,000	$120,000	$242,000	$111,000	$353,000
Wages	100,000	40,000	107,500	37,000	144,500
Salary—dept. manager	50,000	46,000	50,000	43,200	93,200
Supplies used	10,000	6,000	9,500	6,300	15,800
Equip. depreciation	35,000	25,000	35,000	25,000	60,000
Utilities	20,000	12,000	23,000	13,500	36,500
Building rent.	40,000	10,000	40,000	10,000	50,000
Office dept. costs	49,000	49,000	50,000	50,000	100,000
Total	$554,000	$308,000	$557,000	$296,000	$853,000

Office department costs consisted of the following:

	Budget	Actual
Plant manager salary	$59,000	$ 59,000
Other office salaries	25,000	26,500
Other office costs	14,000	14,500
Total	$98,000	$100,000

Required

Prepare responsibility accounting performance reports that list the costs controlled by the following managers:

1. Manager of the doors department.
2. Manager of the windows department.
3. Manager of the Northern plant.

In each report, include the budgeted and actual costs for the month, and show the amount that each actual cost is over or under the budgeted amount.

Problem 23–7
Analytical essay
(LO 3)

The Griffin Department Store is considering the possibility of closing its hat department, which has been experiencing declining performance over several years. Information from the department's most recent income report shows these results:

Sales	$900,000
Expenses:	
Direct escapable	350,000
Indirect escapable	250,000
Indirect inescapable	435,000

1. What is the hat department's net income?
2. What is the hat department's contribution to overhead?
3. What is the excess of the hat department's revenues over its escapable expenses?
4. Assuming that eliminating the hat department will not reduce sales in other departments, should it be closed down?
5. A marketing manager has proposed replacing the hat department with a games department. The proposal includes these forecasted amounts:

Sales	$1,200,000
Expenses:	
Direct escapable	400,000
Indirect escapable	425,000
Indirect inescapable	300,000

Taking this alternative into consideration, should the hat department be eliminated? Explain your answer.

Problem 23–8
Analytical essay
(LO 3, 4)

Marla Mitchell is the manager of the Harleyville store of Amalgamated Stores, Inc. Amalgamated is a chain with more than 500 stores located all over the country. The manager of each store receives a salary as well as a bonus equal to a percent of the store's net profit for the reporting period. The following net income calculation appeared on a performance report for a recent three-month period:

Sales	$1,000,000
Cost of goods sold	(600,000)
Wages expense	(190,000)
Utilities expense	(20,000)
Home office expense	(90,000)
Net income	$ 100,000
Manager's bonus (5%)	$ 5,000

In previous periods, the bonus percentage had been 5% but the performance report had not included any changes for the home office expense. The home office expense is assigned to every store as a percent of its sales. This reporting period's rate is 9%.

1. Describe a valid reason for including a charge for the expenses of operating the home office in a performance report for store managers.
2. Describe the main disadvantages of imposing a new charge for the home office based on a percent of the sales achieved by a store manager.
3. Suggest an alternative approach that offers more advantages than the one being used by Amalgamated Stores, Inc.

Alternate Problems

Problem 23–1A
Allocation of building occupancy costs
(LO 2)

The Corner Hardware Store, Inc., has several departments that occupy all floors of a two-story building with a partial basement. The store has rented this building under a long-term lease negotiated years ago when rental rates were much lower. The departmental accounting system has a single account in the ledger called Building Occupancy Cost. These types and amounts of costs were recorded in this account for last year:

Building rent	$200,000
Lighting expense	15,000
Cleaning expense	9,000
Total	$224,000

The building has 8,000 square feet on each floor but only 4,000 square feet in the basement. For simplicity, the bookkeeper merely divided the $224,000 occupancy cost by 20,000 square feet to find an average cost of $11.20 per square foot. Then, each department was charged with a building occupancy cost equal to this rate times the number of square feet that it occupies.

Tony Amado manages a basement level department that occupies 2,200 square feet of floor space. In discussing the departmental reports, Amado questioned whether using the same rate per square foot for all departments makes sense because the different floor levels have different values. Looking further into the issue, the manager checked a recent real estate study of average rental costs for similar space. The amounts do not include costs for lighting and cleaning. The report shows that ground-floor space is worth $30.00 per square foot while second-floor space is worth $16.00 and basement space is worth only $8.00.

Required

Use the preceding information to:

1. Allocate the occupancy cost to Amado's department by the bookkeeper's method.
2. Allocate the occupancy cost to Amado's department in proportion to the relative market value of the space, except for the lighting and cleaning costs, which should be allocated on an equal basis per square foot occupied.

Problem 23–2A
Departmental income statement
(LO 3)

Serenity Sales, Inc., began operating in January 1994 with two selling departments and one office department. The 1994 departmental net incomes are shown below:

SERENITY SALES, INC.
Departmental Income Statement
For Year Ended December 31, 1994

	Paint	Wallcovers	Combined
Sales	$600,000	$360,000	$960,000
Cost of goods sold	360,000	270,000	630,000
Gross profit from sales	$240,000	$ 90,000	$330,000
Direct expenses			
Sales salaries	$ 30,000	$ 25,000	$ 55,000
Advertising	15,000	5,000	20,000
Store supplies used	4,000	1,000	5,000
Depreciation of equipment	7,000	3,000	10,000
Total direct expenses	$ 56,000	$ 34,000	$ 90,000
Allocated expenses			
Rent expense	$ 30,000	$ 20,000	$ 50,000
Utilities expense	9,000	6,000	15,000
Share of office department expenses	53,125	31,875	85,000
Total allocated expenses	$ 92,125	$ 57,875	$150,000
Total expenses	$148,125	$ 91,875	$240,000
Net income	$ 91,875	$ (1,875)	$ 90,000

Starting in January 1995, Serenity plans to open a third department that will sell drapes. Management predicts that the new department will produce

$264,000 in sales with a 30% gross profit margin and that it will require the following direct expenses: sales salaries, $15,000; advertising, $11,000; store supplies, $2,500; and equipment depreciation, $5,000.

Since opening, the store has rented space in a building. It will be possible to fit the new department into the same overall space by taking some square footage from the other two departments. When the new drapes department is opened, it will fill one fourth of the space presently used by the paint department and one fourth of the space used by the wallcovers department. Management does not predict any increase in utilities costs, which are allocated among the departments in proportion to occupied space.

The company allocates its office department expenses among the selling departments in proportion to their sales. It expects the drapes department to increase office department expenses by $7,000.

Because the drapes department will bring new customers into the store, management expects sales in the paint and wallcovers departments to increase by 10%. Those departments' gross profit percentages are not expected to change. No changes are expected in their direct expenses, except for store supplies used, which will increase in proportion to sales.

Required

Prepare a departmental income statement that shows the company's predicted results of operations for 1995 with three selling departments. (Round all amounts to the nearest whole dollar.)

Problem 23–3A
Analysis of escapable and inescapable expenses
(LO 3)

The management of the Vermont Company is trying to decide whether to eliminate department 2, which has produced losses or low profits for several years. The company's 1994 departmental income statement shows a similar result:

VERMONT COMPANY
Income Statement
For Year Ended December 31, 1994

	Dept. 1	Dept. 2	Combined
Sales	$500,000	$125,000	$625,000
Cost of goods sold	300,000	80,000	380,000
Gross profit from sales	$200,000	$ 45,000	$245,000
Operating expenses:			
Direct expenses:			
Advertising	$ 20,000	$ 2,000	$ 22,000
Store supplies used	4,000	1,000	5,000
Depreciation of store equipment	10,000	5,000	15,000
Total direct expenses	$ 34,000	$ 8,000	$ 42,000
Allocated expenses:			
Sales salaries	$ 62,400	$ 31,200	$ 93,600
Rent expense	16,000	4,000	20,000
Bad debts expense	20,000	2,000	22,000
Office salary	20,800	5,200	26,000
Insurance expense	3,000	1,000	4,000
Miscellaneous office expenses	1,000	2,000	3,000
Total allocated expenses	$123,200	$ 45,400	$168,600
Total expenses	$157,200	$ 53,400	$210,600
Net income (loss)	$ 42,800	$ (8,400)	$ 34,400

In analyzing the decision to eliminate department 2, the management has looked at the following items of information:

a. The company has one office worker who earns $500 per week or $26,000 per year and three sales clerks who each earn $600 per week or $31,200 per year.

b. Currently, the full salaries of two sales clerks are charged to department 1. The full salary of one sales clerk is charged to department 2.

c. The sales salaries and the office salary currently assigned to department 2 would be avoided if the department were eliminated. However, management prefers another plan. Two sales clerks have indicated that they will be quitting soon. Management thinks that their work can be done by the one remaining clerk if the one office worker works in sales half-time. The office worker's schedule will allow this shift of duties if department 2 is eliminated. If this change is implemented, half the office worker's salary would be reported as sales salaries and half would be reported as office salary.

d. The store building is rented under a long-term lease that cannot be changed. Therefore, the space presently occupied by department 2 will have to be used by the current department 1. The equipment used by department 2 will be used by the current department 1.

e. Closing department 2 will eliminate its expenses for advertising, bad debts, and store supplies. It will also eliminate 75% of the insurance expense allocated to the department for coverage on its merchandise inventory. In addition, 40% of the miscellaneous office expenses presently allocated to department 2 will be eliminated.

Required

1. Prepare a three-column schedule that lists (*a*) the company's total expenses (including cost of goods sold), (*b*) the expenses that would be eliminated by closing department 2, and (*c*) the expenses that will continue.
2. Prepare a forecasted income statement for the company reflecting the elimination under the assumption that sales and the gross profit will not be affected. The statement should also reflect the reassignment of the office worker to one-half time as a sales clerk.

Problem 23–4A
Allocating joint costs
(LO 5)

Eduardo Villanueva's orchards produced a good crop of kiwi fruit in 1994. After preparing the following income statement, Villanueva concluded that he should have given the no. 3 kiwis to charity and saved a lot of money.

EDUARDO VILLANUEVA
Income from Kiwis
For the Year Ended December 31, 1994

	No. 1	**No. 2**	**No. 3**	**Combined**
Sales:				
Grade				
No. 1: 200,000 lbs. @ $1.50	$300,000			
No. 2: 200,000 lbs. @ $1.00		$200,000		
No. 3: 250,000 lbs. @ $0.50			$125,000	
Combined				$625,000
Costs:				
Tree pruning and care, @ $0.50/lb.	$100,000	$100,000	$125,000	$325,000
Picking, sorting, and grading @ $0.15/lb	30,000	30,000	37,500	97,500
Marketing @ $0.02/lb	4,000	4,000	5,000	13,000
Totla costs.	$134,000	$134,000	$167,500	$435,500
Net income or loss.	$166,000	$ 66,000	$ (42,500)	$189,500

In preparing the statement, Villanueva allocated the joint costs among the grades as an equal amount per pound. Records about the marketing costs show that $9,000 of the $13,000 was the cost of crating the no. 1 and no. 2 kiwis and hauling them to the buyer. The remaining $4,000 of marketing costs was the cost of crating the no. 3 kiwis and hauling them to the cannery where they were used to make jelly.

Required

1. Prepare allocation schedules showing how Villanueva computed the costs per pound of kiwis.
2. Prepare allocation schedules showing how the costs would be allocated on the basis of the relative sales values of the three grades. Separate the marketing costs into the amounts directly identifiable to the grades. Then, allocate any shared marketing costs on the basis of the relative sales values of the grades. (Round all percents to the nearest one tenth and all dollar amounts to the nearest whole dollar.)
3. Using your answers to requirement 2, prepare an income statement that shows the results of producing and marketing the kiwis.

Problem 23–5A
Departmental expense allocation spreadsheet
(LO 2, 3)

The Favorite Games Store has three selling departments (soccer, hockey, and baseball) and two service departments (general office and purchasing). After the end of the year, the following information was available for preparing financial statements and internal reports:

	Soccer	**Hockey**	**Baseball**
Sales	$400,000	$337,500	$512,500
Purchases	256,000	200,000	344,000
January 1 (beginning) inventory	30,000	50,000	10,000
December 31 (ending) inventory	35,000	42,000	10,000

The Favorite Games Store classifies salaries, supplies used, and depreciation as direct expenses of the departments. Payroll, requisition, and plant asset records showed these amounts of direct expenses for the year:

	Salaries Expense	Supplies Used	Depreciation
General office	$25,500	$1,500	$3,000
Purchasing department	24,000	2,000	1,500
Soccer department	50,000	500	1,000
Hockey department	55,000	600	1,200
Baseball department	75,000	800	1,500

The company incurred the following amounts of indirect expenses:

Rent expense	$30,000
Advertising expense	22,000
Expired insurance	6,000
Utilities expense	16,000
Custodial expense	12,000

In preparing financial statements and internal reports, The Favorite Games Store allocates the indirect expenses among the departments as follows:

a. Rent expense is first allocated between the selling and service departments on the basis of the value of floor space. The general office and purchasing departments occupy space in the rear of the store that is not as valuable as space in the front. Thus, only $4,000 of the total rent is allocated to these two departments. This amount is allocated between them in proportion to the space that they occupy. The remaining rent is divided among the three selling departments in proportion to the space that they occupy. The five departments occupy these amounts of space:

General office	800 square feet
Purchasing department	1,200 square feet
Soccer department	4,500 square feet
Hockey department	6,300 square feet
Baseball department	7,200 square feet

b. Advertising expense is allocated among the selling departments on the basis of sales.

c. Insurance expense is allocated in proportion to the insured value of the equipment in the five departments. The insured values of the equipment in the departments are

General office	$21,000
Purchasing department	12,000
Soccer department	54,000
Hockey department	30,000
Baseball department	33,000

d. Utilities and custodial care expenses are assigned to the departments on the basis of floor space occupied.

The Favorite Games Store then allocates its general office department expenses among its three selling departments on the basis of their dollars of sales, and allocates the purchasing department expenses on the basis of the dollars of purchases.

Required

1. Prepare allocation schedules for the shared indirect expenses.

2. Prepare a departmental expense allocation spreadsheet for the company. Show the allocation tables for the costs of the service departments. (Round all amounts to the nearest whole dollar.)
3. Prepare a departmental income statement showing sales, cost of goods sold, expenses, and net incomes by departments and for the entire store.
4. Prepare a departmental income statement that displays each selling department's contribution to overhead.

Problem 23–6A
Responsibility accounting performance reports
(LO 4)

Sharon Krocesky, the manager of Nakasone Strings and Skins Company's Connecticut plant, is responsible for all costs of the plant's operation other than her own salary. The plant has two production departments and one service department. The guitars and drums departments manufacture different products and have their own managers. The office department provides services equally to the two production departments. Krocesky manages the office department. Nakasone Strings and Skins prepares a monthly budget for each production department and the office department. After the end of each month, the responsibility accounting system assembles information and presents budgeted and actual costs in performance reports for each of the production department managers and the plant manager.

Each performance report includes only those costs that the particular manager can control. The production department managers control the costs of raw materials, wages, supplies used, and equipment depreciation. The plant manager is responsible for the department managers' salaries, utilities, building rent, office salaries other than her own, other office costs, and the total costs of the two production departments.

The production departments' budgets and cost accumulations for March were as follows:

	Budget		Actual		
	Guitars	Drums	Guitars	Drums	Combined
Raw materials	$310,000	$125,000	$300,000	$132,000	$432,000
Wages	155,000	65,000	151,000	68,000	219,000
Salary—dept. manager	35,000	38,000	35,000	37,500	72,500
Supplies used	29,000	28,000	28,000	30,000	58,000
Equip. depreciation	50,000	63,000	50,000	63,000	113,000
Utilities	3,000	4,000	2,400	3,600	6,000
Building rent	2,800	3,500	2,800	3,500	6,300
Office dept. costs	46,000	46,000	43,250	43,250	86,500
Total	$630,800	$372,500	$612,450	$380,850	$993,300

Office department costs consisted of the following:

	Budget	Actual
Plant manager salary	$47,000	$47,500
Other office salaries	22,000	18,000
Other office costs	23,000	21,000
Total	$92,000	$86,500

Required

Prepare responsibility accounting performance reports that list the costs controlled by the following managers:

1. Manager of the guitars department.
2. Manager of the drums department.
3. Manager of the Connecticut plant.

In each report, include the budgeted and actual costs for the month, and show the amount that each actual cost is over or under the budgeted amount.

Problem 23–7A
Analytical essay
(LO 3)

The Jacobson Department Store is considering the possibility of closing its shoe department, which has been experiencing declining performance over several years. Information from the department's most recent income report shows these results:

Sales	$800,000
Expenses:	
Direct escapable	400,000
Indirect escapable	300,000
Indirect inescapable	205,000

1. What is the shoe department's net income?
2. What is the shoe department's contribution to overhead?
3. What is the excess of the shoe department's revenues over its escapable expenses?
4. Assuming that eliminating the shoe department will not reduce sales in other departments, should it be closed down?
5. A marketing manager has proposed replacing the shoe department with a chocolate department. The proposal includes these forecasted amounts:

Sales	$500,000
Expenses:	
Direct escapable	125,000
Indirect escapable	300,000
Indirect inescapable	120,000

Taking this alternative into consideration, should the shoe department be eliminated? Explain your answer.

Problem 23–8A
Analytical essay
(LO 3, 4)

Bill Tyler is the manager of the Coopertown store of Allied Merchants, Inc. Allied is a chain with more than 1,000 stores located all over the country. The manager of each store receives a salary as well as a bonus equal to a percent of the store's net profit for the reporting period. The following net income calculation appeared on a performance report for a recent three-month period:

Sales	$777,000
Cost of goods sold	(422,000)
Wages expense	(166,000)
Utilities expense	(12,000)
Depreciation	(92,700)
Net income	$ 84,300
Manager's bonus (6%)	$ 5,058

In previous periods, the bonus percentage had been 6% but the performance report had included much smaller charges for depreciation. The depreciation expense was changed starting this period to include costs of assets used in the corporate office, including a new building. The extra amount of depreciation is assigned to every store as a percent of its sales. This reporting period's rate is 10%.

1. Describe a valid reason for including a charge for the expenses of depreciating the headquarters building in a performance report for store managers.
2. Describe the main disadvantages of imposing a new charge for depreciation based on a percent of the sales achieved by a store manager.
3. Suggest an alternative approach that offers more advantages than the one being used by Allied Merchants, Inc.

Provocative Problems

Provocative Problem 23–1
Southgate, A Real Estate Partnership
(LO 5)

Chris Eastwood, Pat Weston, and Jan Northrup formed a partnership to develop and sell a plot of land that was owned by Eastwood. Eastwood invested the land at its $500,000 fair market value, Weston invested $300,000 cash in the partnership, and Northrup invested $50,000 cash. The partners agreed to share losses and gains equally. Weston and Northrup were able to invest less than Eastwood in acknowledgement of their expertise and an agreement that they would do all the work needed to make the project a success.

Subsequently, the partnership developed the subdivision, called Southgate, by installing utility hookups and streets at a cost of $340,000. The subdivision contained 20 lots, with 4 in the Southeast section, 10 in the Southwest section, and 6 in the South section. The lots were priced as follows:

Southeast	$ 50,000
Southwest	80,000
South	100,000

In return for special work on the project, Northrup was allowed to take (at cost) one of the lots from the South section for a personal home site. After the remaining 19 lots were sold at the listed prices for cash, the partnership was dissolved and all the cash was distributed to the partners.

Required

1. Using their relative market values, allocate the total joint costs of the developed land among the three categories of lots and compute the average cost per lot in each section.
2. Determine the amount of cash that each of the partners should have received when the partnership was dissolved. Set up a six-column spreadsheet with columns for the cash, the cost of the land, the gain on the sale of the lots, and each of the three partners' equity balances. Enter the events in the order of their occurrence, allocate the gain equally among the partners, and then compute the cash distributions.

Provocative Problem 23–2
Sunray Company
(LO 2, 3)

The new bookkeeper for the Great Openings Company prepared the following internal report:

GREAT OPENINGS COMPANY
Income Statement
For August 1994

	Windows Department	Doors Department	Combined
Sales	$360,000	$240,000	$600,000
Cost of goods sold	160,000	160,000	320,000
Gross profit on sales	$200,000	$ 80,000	$280,000
Selling expenses	$ 50,000	$ 32,500	$ 82,500
Warehousing expenses	40,000	40,000	80,000
General and administrative expenses	11,750	11,750	23,500
Total expenses	$101,750	$ 84,250	$186,000
Net income	$ 98,250	$ (4,250)	$ 94,000

The company buys windows and doors and then resells them at wholesale prices to contractors. The sales efforts are carried out by two departments, one for each product. In addition, the company has two service departments for warehousing and general office services. After receiving the report, the company's manager is not convinced that it properly reflects the relative profitability of the two departments. The manager has asked you to analyze the underlying data and to work with the bookkeeper to redraft the report and to prepare any supporting schedules or comments that will make the report more useful. Your research uncovers the following facts:

1. The manager likes the form of the internal report. Specifically, all the direct and allocated indirect expenses of the two selling departments should be reported as "selling expenses"; the expenses of the warehouse department should be allocated to the selling departments and reported as "warehousing expenses"; and, the expenses of the general office department should be allocated to the selling departments and reported as "general and administrative expenses."
2. The company sold 2,000 windows and 1,500 doors during August. Although the total cost of goods sold is correct, the bookkeeper could not find the detailed records and merely allocated the total between the two departments equally. A more careful search shows that the cost of each window was $100 and the cost of each door was $80.
3. Although a window and a door require approximately the same amount of storage space in the warehouse, there are three styles of windows and nine styles of doors. As a result, the company must carry an inventory of doors that takes up three times more space in the warehouse than the inventory of windows.
4. The space in the company's building has been divided as follows:

	Square Footage	Value of Space
Warehouse	75%	40%
General office	5	10
Window sales office	12	30
Door sales office	8	20

5. Warehousing expenses for August consisted of the following:

Wages expense	$24,000
Warehouse equipment depreciation	4,000
Building depreciation	40,000
Utilities expenses	12,000
Total	$80,000

The bookkeeper had classified all of the building's depreciation and utilities expense as warehousing expenses.

6. Selling expenses for August consisted of the following:

	Window Department	Door Department
Sales salaries	$36,000	$19,000
Office equipment depreciation	3,000	2,500
Advertising	11,000	11,000
Totals	$50,000	$32,500

Sales salaries and equipment depreciation were assigned to the two departments on the basis of actual amounts incurred. The bookkeeper allocated the correct total amount of advertising expense evenly between the two departments. In fact, the company ties its advertising expenditures closely to the amounts of sales generated by the two departments.

7. General and administrative expenses attributable to the general office department for August were:

Salaries and wages	$20,000
Office equipment depreciation	2,500
Miscellaneous expenses	1,000
Total	$23,500

These costs are proportionally related to the amount of sales of each of the two products.

Provocative Problem 23–3
Vista Grande Corporation
(LO 3)

Vista Grande Corporation retails two models of large computer monitors used by professional desktop publishers. The company's operations produced these results in the quarter that just ended:

	VG-19	VG-21
Units sold	1,500	1,000
Selling price per unit	$500	$850
Cost per unit	275	425
Sales commission per unit	20	30
Indirect selling and administrative expenses per unit	$62.50	$106.25

The total indirect selling and administrative expenses were $200,000. They were allocated to the models on the basis of their relative sales volumes. The VG-19 model produced $750,000 of revenue and the VG-21 model produced $850,000. Thus, the VG-19 model was assigned 46.875% of the $200,000 of indirect expenses, or $93,750. Then, this amount was divided by the number of units to get $62.50 per unit. The same calculations produced the $106.25 per unit indirect cost for the VG-21 model.

The management of Vista Grande Corporation is in the process of selecting among three management strategies for the next quarter. The three alternatives are (1) do no special advertising, in which case sales of each model will continue at present levels; (2) increase the sales of the VG-19 model by a special advertising effort; or (3) increase the sales of the VG-21 model by a special advertising effort. Because the demand for large monitors is stable, an increase in the unit sales of one model will cause an equal decrease in unit sales of the other model. By spending $22,500 on advertising for the VG-19, the company can sell 300 additional units of the VG-19 model and lose 300 units of sales of the VG-21 model. Or, the opposite effect will occur if the company advertises the VG-21 model.

Recommend the best action to Vista Grande management and support your recommendation with income statements that show the contribution to overhead achieved under each alternative.

Provocative Problem 23–4
Fastnet Company
(LO 2)

Fastnet Company has five departments, including service departments A, B, and C and production departments 1 and 2. Because the services of department A are used by the other four departments, its costs are allocated to all four of them. The services of department B are used by departments C, 1, and 2, and its costs (including the allocation of department A's costs) are allocated to all three of them. The costs accumulated in department C (including its share of the costs of departments A and B) are allocated to departments 1 and 2.

The direct and indirect costs of all five departments are shown below, as well as the percentages used to allocate the three service department costs to the other departments:

	Dept. A	Dept. B	Dept. C	Dept. 1	Dept. 2
Direct costs incurred by each department	$20,000	$30,000	$40,000	$80,000	$90,000
Allocation rates:					
Department A		10%	20%	40%	30%
Department B			30%	50%	20%
Department C				60%	40%

In determining the total costs allocated to the production departments:

1. What dollar amount of department C's direct costs will be charged to department 2?
2. What dollar amount of department B's direct costs will be charged to department 2?
3. What dollar amount of department A's direct costs will be charged to department 2?

Provocative Problem 23–5
International Business Machines Corporation
(LO 3)

A footnote to the financial statements of the IBM Corporation in Appendix J describes a restructuring that occurred in 1989. Read the footnote and explain what happened in the company and the effects produced on the income statement.

Answers to Objective Review Questions

LO 1 (*e*)
LO 2 (*e*)
LO 3 (*d*)
LO 4 (*d*)
LO 5 (*c*)
LO 6 (*e*)
LO 7 (*a*)

PART

IX

Planning and Controlling Business Operations

The essence of managing a business or other organization can be summarized in two words: planning and controlling. Managerial accounting information plays a critical role in helping managers perform both of these functions. Planning relates to the future and predicted future events are described in the budget. The budget is the most central managerial accounting document. Budgeting involves forecasting future activities and compiling their expected results. Controlling relates to the present. By monitoring reports about recent events and their effects, managers can design actions to expand their successes and limit their setbacks. As you study the remaining chapters of this book, you will learn how managerial accounting information is developed and used in planning and controlling.

Part IX consists of the following chapters:

CHAPTER

24

Cost-Volume-Profit Analysis

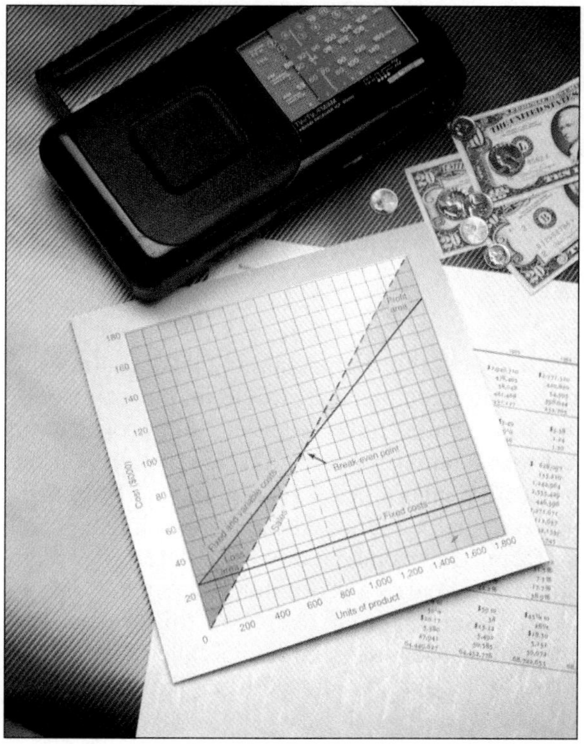

Managers must anticipate events and their results when planning future activities such as bringing a new product to market. Because profits are essential, managers must try to predict future costs and revenues. Cost-volume-profit analysis is useful for starting to form profit plans.

Topical Coverage

This chapter explains different kinds of costs and shows how they are affected by changes in the operating volume of a business. By studying the chapter, you will learn to analyze the costs and revenues of a business so that you can describe how different operating strategies affect its profit or loss. Managers use this kind of analysis to forecast what will happen if changes are made in costs, sales volume, selling prices, or product mix. They then use the forecasts to select the best strategy for the future.

Learning Objectives

After studying Chapter 24, you should be able to:

1. Describe different types of cost behavior in relation to sales volume.
2. State the assumptions used in cost-volume-profit analysis and explain how they limit the usefulness of the analysis.
3. Prepare and interpret a scatter diagram of past costs and sales volume.
4. Calculate a break-even point for a single product company and present its costs and revenues in a graph.
5. Describe several applications of cost-volume-profit analysis.
6. Calculate the break-even point for a multiproduct company by constructing a composite sales unit.
7. Define or explain the words and phrases listed in the chapter glossary.

Questions Addressed by Cost-Volume-Profit Analysis

The first phase in managing a company's future is planning its activities and other events. The first step in the planning phase is predicting the volume of activity, the costs to be incurred, revenues to be received, and profits to be earned. An important tool that helps managers carry out this first step in the planning phase is **cost-volume-profit analysis**, or *CVP analysis*. CVP analysis helps managers predict how income will be affected by changes in costs and sales levels. In its most basic form, CVP analysis involves determining the sales level at which a company neither earns a profit nor incurs a loss, or, in other words, the point at which it is said to break even. For this reason, this most basic form of cost-volume-profit analysis is sometimes called *break-even analysis*. However, managers use other applications of the analysis to answer questions like these:

- What sales volume is needed to earn a desired net income?
- How much net income will be earned if unit selling prices are reduced and sales volume is increased?
- How much net income will be earned if we install a new machine that reduces labor costs?
- How much net income will be earned if we change the sales mix of our products?

When the technique is expanded to answer these additional questions, the phrase *cost-volume-profit analysis* is more descriptive than break-even analysis.

Cost Behavior

LO 1 Describe different types of cost behavior in relation to sales volume.

Conventional cost-volume-profit analysis requires management to classify all costs as either *fixed* or *variable*. Some costs are definitely fixed in nature while others are definitely variable. However, when you examine various costs, you will find that some are neither completely fixed nor completely variable.

Fixed Costs

The amount of a **fixed cost**incurred each period remains unchanged even when production volume varies from period to period. For example, $5,000 rent paid for a factory building remains the same each month, whether the factory operates with a single eight-hour shift or around the clock with three shifts. Furthermore, the rent cost is the same each month at any level of output from zero on up to the full production capacity of the plant. Although the total fixed cost remains constant as the level of production changes, the fixed cost per unit of product decreases as volume increases. For example, if 20 units are produced in a month, the average factory building rent cost per unit is $250. When production increases to 100 units per month, the average cost per unit decreases to $50. And, the average cost decreases to $10 per unit if production increases to 500 units per month. Other examples of fixed costs include depreciation, property taxes, office salaries, and many other service department costs. In effect, fixed costs are incurred to create productive and marketing capacity for a particular period of time.

When production volume and costs are presented on a graph, units of product are usually plotted on the horizontal axis, and dollars of cost are plotted on the vertical axis. Fixed costs are then represented as a horizontal line because the total amount remains constant at all levels of production. The graph in Illustration 24–1 represents this behavior. Note that the fixed costs remain at $32,000 at all production levels up to the factory's monthly capacity of 2,000 units of output.

Variable Costs

The total amount of a **variable cost**changes in proportion to changes in volume. For example, the direct material cost of a product is a variable cost. If one unit of product requires materials that cost $20, total materials costs are $200 when 10 units of product are manufactured, $400 for 20 units, $600 for 30 units, and so on. Notice that the variable cost per unit produced remains constant while the total amount of variable cost changes in direct proportion to changes in the level of production. Other variable costs include direct labor (if workers are paid for completed units), some overhead costs, selling commissions, and shipping costs. Variable costs are plotted on a graph of cost and volume as a straight line that starts at the zero cost level. It also has an upward (positive)

ILLUSTRATION 24–1

Relationships of Fixed Costs, Variable Costs, and Total Costs to Volume

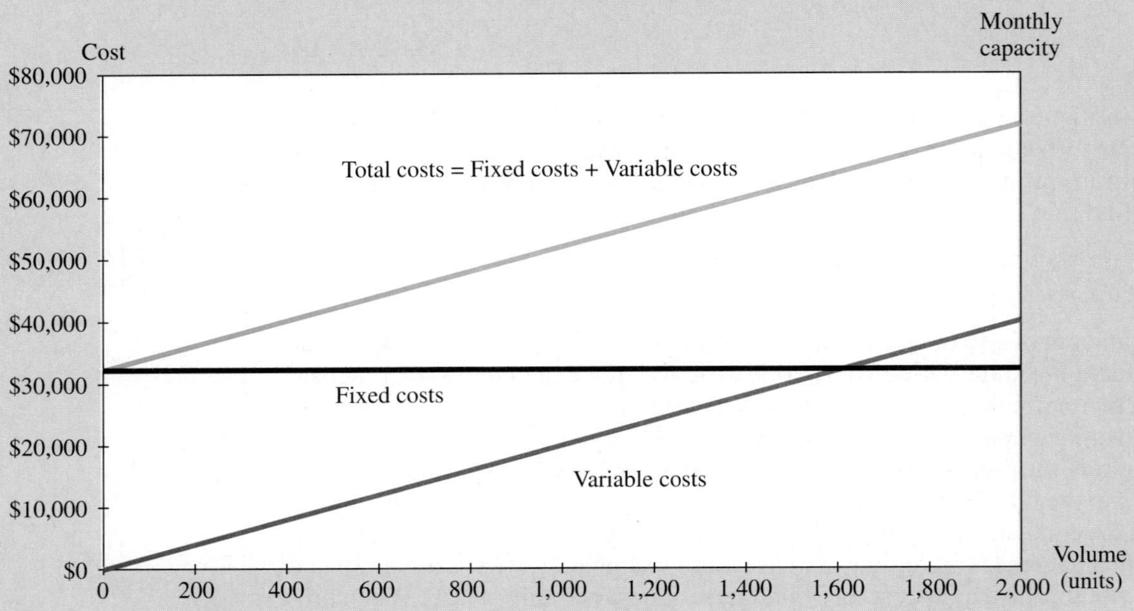

slope. That is, the line rises as the production volume increases. Notice that the variable cost line for this example of $20 per unit appears in Illustration 24–1. In effect, variable costs are incurred in using the productive and marketing capacity created by the fixed costs.

Total Cost

In simple cases, the total cost to be incurred equals the sum of the fixed costs and the variable costs. The upper line in Illustration 24–1 represents the total cost. It originates on the vertical axis at the $32,000 fixed cost point. Thus, at the zero level of output, the total cost equals only the fixed costs. Then, the total cost increases as the activity level increases. The amount of the increase equals the variable cost per unit for each additional unit produced. (The slope of the total cost line equals the slope of the variable cost line, which also equals the variable cost per unit.) The total cost reaches its maximum level at the limit of the productive capacity for the planned period.

Step-Variable Costs and Semivariable Costs

In real situations, many costs are neither completely fixed nor completely variable. For example, some costs go up in steps, such as the salaries of production supervisors. Their salaries are fixed for a particular production volume from zero up to the maximum that can be completed on one shift. When an additional shift is added to increase production, additional supervisors must

ILLUSTRATION 24–2

Step-Variable Costs, Semivariable Costs, and the Relevant Range

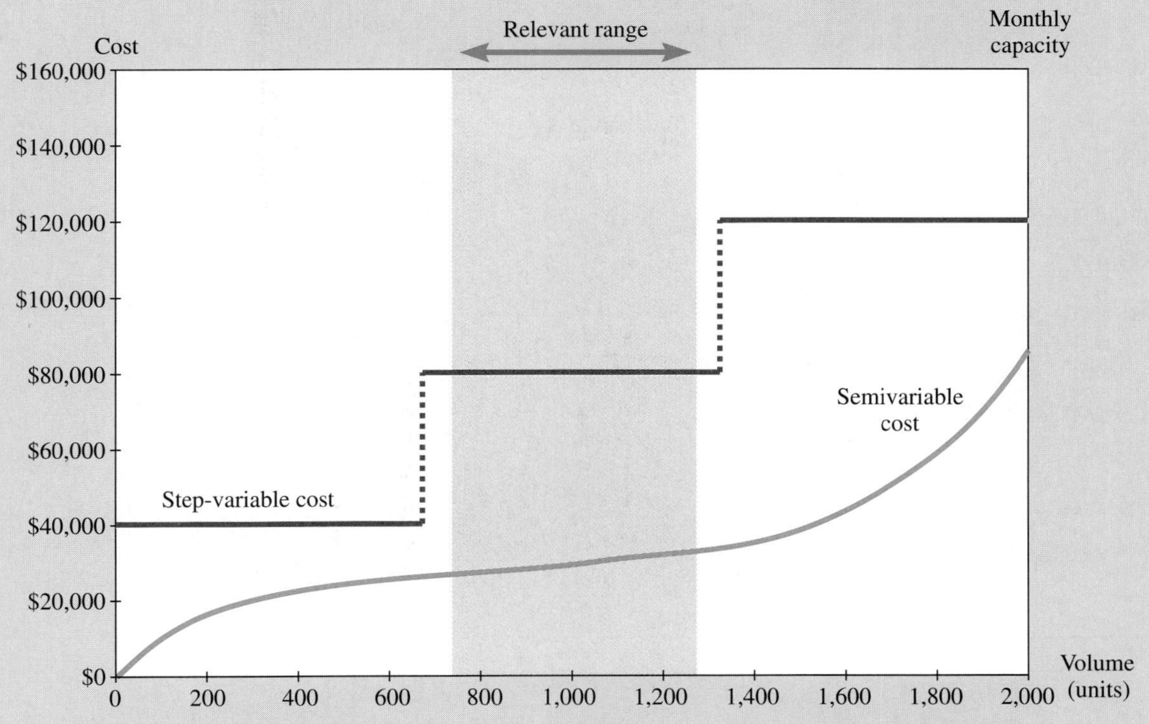

be hired, and the total cost for supervisory salaries goes up by a lump-sum amount. Total supervisory salaries then remain fixed at this new level until a third shift is added, in which case the cost increases by another lump sum. Costs that show this behavior are **step-variable costs.** They are also called *step-wise costs* or *stair-step costs*. A step-variable cost is represented graphically in Illustration 24–2. Notice how it is flat within a narrow range until a maximum volume is reached. Then it jumps up to the next higher level and stays there until a new maximum volume is reached. In a conventional CVP analysis, a step-variable cost must be treated as either a fixed cost or a variable cost. The specific treatment depends on the cost's behavior in the expected range of operations.

Other costs may be semivariable or *nonlinear* in nature. **Semivariable costs** increase as volume increases but not at a constant rate like pure variable costs. These costs change with production-level changes, but not proportionately. Thus, they must be plotted on a graph as a curved line. Illustration 24–2 represents a semivariable cost as the curved line beginning at zero when production is zero and increasing at different rates, with its highest rate as the sales volume approaches the maximum capacity for the month.

An example of a semivariable cost is total direct labor cost when workers are paid by the hour or other time period. At low levels of production, adding

ILLUSTRATION 24–3

A Mixed Cost and Its Components

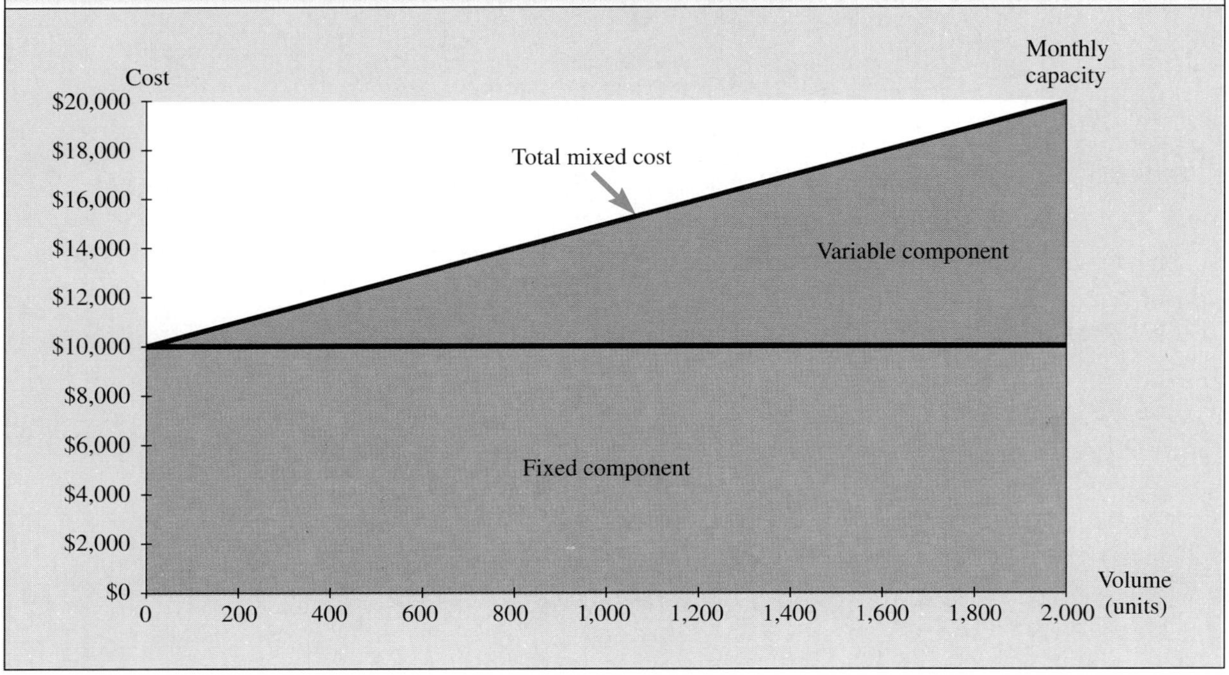

more workers allows each of them to specialize by doing the same task over and over again instead of doing several different tasks. Thus, the whole crew becomes more efficient and able to produce additional units for lower costs. Eventually, however, a point of diminishing returns is reached and adding more workers begins to create inefficiencies. For example, workers may have to spend more time and effort in merely communicating with each other or coordinating their efforts. As a result, adding more workers does increase output, but the labor cost per unit increases, and the total labor cost goes up with a steeper slope. Note these effects in Illustration 24–2 where the semi-variable cost curve starts at zero, rises, flattens out, and then increases at a faster rate as the volume approaches the productive capacity for the month.

Mixed Costs. Other costs act like a combination of a fixed and a variable cost. These costs are **mixed costs.** For example, the compensation cost for sales representatives can include a fixed monthly salary and a variable commission based on sales. Illustration 24–3 presents a graph of a mixed cost. Like a fixed cost, it is greater than even when volume is at zero. Then, unlike a fixed cost, it increases steadily in proportion to the increase in volume.

In a CVP analysis, the simplest way to include mixed costs is to divide them into their fixed and variable components. Notice that Illustration 24–3 identifies these two components of the mixed cost. Then, the fixed component is added to other fixed costs for the planning period and the variable component is added to the other variable costs.

Assumptions Used in Cost-Volume-Profit Analysis

LO 2 State the assumptions used in cost-volume-profit analysis and explain how they limit the usefulness of the analysis.

Conventional cost-volume-profit analysis techniques are based on relationships that can be expressed as straight lines similar to those in Illustration 24–1. Thus, users of conventional CVP analysis classify all costs as either fixed or variable. In addition, they assume that revenues are constant for every unit sold during the month. Once they identify the costs and revenues, they can use the data to answer a variety of questions. To summarize, the usefulness of the answers to those questions depends on the validity of at least these three basic assumptions:

1. The per unit selling price must be constant at all levels.
2. The variable costs must remain constant per unit of output.
3. The fixed costs must remain constant within the planning period's physical capacity.

Even though these assumptions are not always realistic, they do not necessarily limit the usefulness of CVP analysis as a first step in forecasting the effects of a plan.

Relationship between Production Output and Sales Volume

So far in this discussion, we have defined variable costs and fixed costs in terms of levels of *output produced*. However, conventional CVP analysis typically describes the planning period's level of activity in terms of *sales volume* rather than output. This sales volume can be described as either the number of units sold or the dollars of sales.

To simplify the analysis, we can assume that the level of production will be the same as the level of sales. Thus, we do not have to be concerned with costs that would flow into the inventory instead of being sold, or with costs that would flow into the cost of goods sold from the prior period's inventory. This simplifying assumption is justified because CVP analysis provides only a tentative plan that does not include the details of inventory management.

Working with the Assumptions

If the expected events are consistent with the previous assumptions, costs and revenues for the planning period can be represented by straight lines in a graph. Often, however, the behavior of actual individual costs and revenues is not perfectly consistent with these assumptions. If the expected cost and revenue behavior is significantly inconsistent with the assumptions, the results of a CVP analysis are not very useful. However, there are several reasons why we can perform useful analyses while using these assumptions.

Aggregating Costs May Offset Deviations. Although individual components of total variable costs may not be perfectly variable, aggregating the many components may allow their individual deviations to offset each other. In other words, the assumption of variable behavior may be satisfied with respect to total variable costs even though it is not satisfied by individual variable cost items. Similarly, the assumption that fixed costs are constant may be satisfied for total fixed costs even though individual fixed cost items may not be perfectly consistent with the assumption.

Relevant Range of Operations. Revenues, variable costs, and fixed costs also can be reasonably represented as straight lines in a graph if the assumptions are intended to apply only over a **relevant range of operations.** The relevant range of operations is the normal operating range for the business. Except for unusually difficult or prosperous times, management makes plans for operating within a relatively narrow range of volume that is neither close to zero nor approaching full capacity. Thus, the relevant range for planning excludes extremely high and low operating levels that are not likely to be encountered. Within the relevant range, then, specific fixed cost items can be expected to be truly fixed. As shown in Illustration 24–2, a semivariable cost can be treated as perfectly variable if the relevant range encompasses the volumes in which it has a constant slope. Beyond the limits of the relevant range, none of the costs may behave as we expect within the range. However, these deviations would not concern us because we would not plan to operate at those levels.

Cost-Volume-Profit Analysis Is Not Precise. As a very practical matter, you should understand that CVP analysis yields, at best, approximate first answers to questions about costs, volumes, and profits. These first answers do not have to be precise because the analysis makes only initial predictions about the future. As long as managers understand that the answers are nothing more than approximations, cost-volume-profit analysis can be a useful tool for starting the planning process.

Identifying Cost Behavior

LO 3 Prepare and interpret a scatter diagram of past costs and sales volume.

Identifying the behavior of a company's costs requires a careful examination of experience and, to a certain extent, management's judgment in interpreting that data. Initially, individual costs should be analyzed and classified as fixed or variable based on the manager's understanding of how each cost is likely to behave in the relevant range. Some costs can be classified easily at this stage. For example, raw material costs for a manufacturer or cost of goods sold for a merchandiser are clearly variable. And, monthly expenses for rent or administrative salaries are clearly fixed.

Scatter Diagrams. If a cost is not obviously fixed or variable, an analysis of past behavior can be useful. One helpful technique for analyzing past behavior is to display data about past costs on a **scatter diagram** like the one presented in Illustration 24–4. In preparing a scatter diagram, one period's volume in dollars or units is plotted on the horizontal axis and the cost for that period is plotted on the vertical axis. Thus, the cost and volume for each operating period appear as a single point on the diagram.

Illustration 24–4 shows a scatter diagram of a company's total costs and sales for each of 12 months. Each point represents the total costs incurred and the sales volume for a specific month. As an example, note the point labeled "May." That month's sales were $25,000 and its total costs were $25,000.

Estimated Line of Cost Behavior. Illustration 24–4 includes a line drawn among the scattered points. This line is the **estimated line of cost behavior.** It is drawn to identify the past relationship between total cost and sales volume. If the

ILLUSTRATION 24-4

A Scatter Diagram with an Estimated Line of Cost Behavior

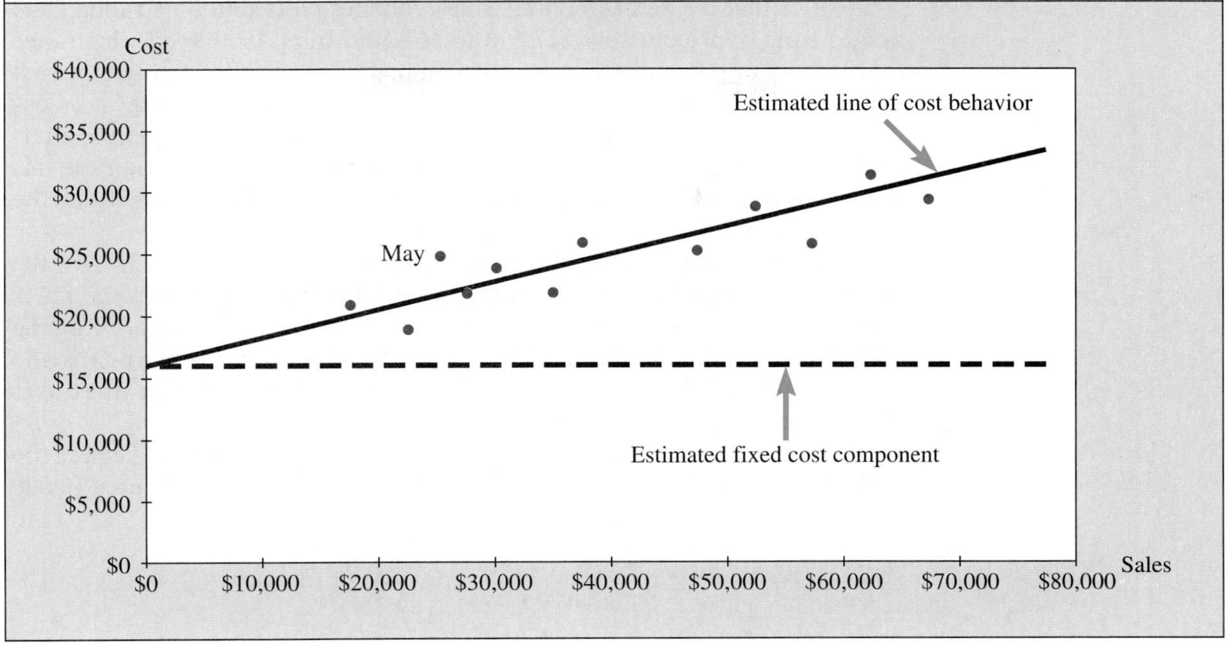

factors that shaped this line in the past are still in effect, management can use it to predict future cost levels at different sales volumes. Three alternative methods can be used to derive this line.

First, the **high-low method** is a simple way to draw the estimated line of behavior. However, its results are likely to be imprecise. To apply this method, you merely connect the two points in the diagram representing the highest and lowest total cost. The obvious deficiency of the high-low method is that it totally ignores all the available cost and sales volume points except the highest and lowest. The outcome is likely to be imprecise because it is based on the most extreme points rather than more typical conditions that are likely to occur in future periods.

A second simple but potentially more useful approach is to visually assess the scattered points and draw a line through them that represents the relationship between cost and volume. Like the high-low method, this approach can be satisfactory for quick and rough estimates.

Third, a more sophisticated method of identifying cost behavior is also commonly used. The statistical method of **least-squares regression** requires potentially complex calculations that can be readily accomplished with spreadsheet or statistical applications computer programs. The result of applying this technique is a line that best fits the actual cost and sales volume experience of the company.[1] The techniques for producing least-squares re-

[1] The method is called *least-squares* because the line minimizes the squares of the distance between each point and the line.

gressions are usually covered in statistics courses and their uses in accounting situations are described in more advanced cost accounting courses.

Notice that the actual monthly sales volumes plotted in Illustration 24–4 ranges from approximately \$17,500 to \$67,500. In all likelihood, this range represents the relevant range for the company. If the estimated line of cost behavior is extended too far beyond this range in either direction, it is less likely to be useful for predicting future costs. Also, notice that the line intercepts the vertical axis at \$16,000. As shown in the diagram, you can use this amount as the fixed costs for a month, as long as the sales volume is within the relevant range.

Variable costs per dollar of sales are represented in Illustration 24–4 by the slope of the estimated line of cost behavior. The slope of any straight line is found by comparing any two points that lie on the line. To estimate variable cost per sales dollar, divide the change in total cost between the two points (the vertical distance) by the change in dollar sales volume between those two points (the horizontal distance).

For example, in Illustration 24–4, we can select the two points where the sales volume equals zero and \$40,000. At these points, the costs were \$16,000 and \$25,000. Therefore, calculate the slope as follows:

$$\frac{\text{Change in cost}}{\text{Change in sales}} = \frac{\$25,000 - \$16,000}{\$40,000 - \$\ \text{-0-}} = \frac{\$9,000}{\$40,000} = \$0.225 \text{ per sales dollar}$$

If you analyze a company's past costs, you might be able to use these statistical techniques to predict fixed and variable costs without analyzing each individual cost component. However, you may have greater confidence in the predictions if you classify individual cost components and then test your results against past observations. To test the classifications, you can prepare scatter diagrams and estimated lines of cost behavior for individual cost items, total variable costs, total fixed costs, and total costs.

Finding the Break-Even Point

LO 4 Calculate a break-even point for a single product company and present its costs and revenues in a graph.

The **break-even point** is the unique sales level at which a company neither earns a profit nor incurs a loss. The break-even point can be expressed either in units of product or in dollars of sales. For example, assume that Carson Company sells a single product for \$100 per unit and incurs \$70 of variable costs per unit sold. The fixed costs are \$24,000 per month and the monthly capacity is 1,800 units of product. Therefore, the company breaks even for a month as soon as it sells 800 units or as soon as sales volume reaches \$80,000. You can determine this break-even point as follows:

1. Each unit sold at \$100 recovers \$70 of variable costs and contributes \$30 toward the fixed costs.
2. Sales of 800 units contribute exactly \$24,000 toward the fixed costs, which are fully recovered at this volume.
3. And, if 800 units are sold at \$100 each, the total sales volume is \$80,000.

The amount by which the sales price per unit exceeds variable costs per unit is a product's **contribution margin per unit.** In effect, the contribution margin per

ILLUSTRATION 24–5

Derivation of Break-Even Formulas

Let:	S = sales in units	R = revenue per unit
	F = fixed costs per month	V = variable cost per unit
	$S \times R$ = dollar sales	$S \times V$ = total variable cost
Then:	Contribution margin per unit = $R - V$	
At break-even:	Sales = Fixed Costs + Variable Costs	
	$(S \times R) = F + (S \times V)$	
	$(S \times R) - (S \times V) = F$	
	$S \times (R - V) = F$	
	$S = F/(R - V)$	
	$S = F/\textit{Contribution margin per unit}$	
And:	Contribution rate = $(R - V)/R$	
At break-even:	$S = F/(R - V)$	
	$S \times R = (F \times R)/(R - V)$	
	$S \times R = F \times [R/(R - V)]$	
	$S \times R = F/[(R - V)/R]$	
	$S \times R = F/\textit{Contribution rate}$	

unit is the amount that the sale of one unit contributes toward recovering the fixed costs and profit.

The contribution margin for a product also can be expressed as a percentage of its sales price. This percentage is the product's **contribution rate.** For the Carson Company, the contribution rate of its product is 30% ($30/$100).

The contribution margin per unit can be used to calculate the break-even point in units of product. And, the contribution rate can be used to calculate a break-even point in dollars. These formulas are

$$\text{Break-even point in units} = \frac{\text{Fixed costs}}{\text{Contribution margin per unit}}$$

$$\text{Break-even point in dollars} = \frac{\text{Fixed costs}}{\text{Contribution rate}}$$

For those readers interested in the mathematics, Illustration 24–5 presents the derivations of these formulas.

Inserting Carson Company's fixed costs and contribution rate in the second formula gives this result:

$$\text{Break-even point in dollars} = \frac{\$24{,}000}{30\%} = \$80{,}000$$

In this example, the solution comes out evenly. In other circumstances, carry the contribution rate out to several decimal places to avoid rounding errors when calculating the break-even point in dollars. The calculated break-even point in units may include a fraction of a unit, such as 520.25 units. In solving the exercises and problems, round the result normally, even though the company would not actually break even at a rounded-down volume (520 units, in this case). The practice of always rounding up (to 521 units) is sometimes

ILLUSTRATION 24–6

Income Statement at a Break-Even Sales Level

CARSON COMPANY
Forecasted Income Statement

Sales (800 units @ $100 each)		$80,000
Costs:		
Fixed costs	$24,000	
Variable costs (800 units @ $70 each)	56,000	80,000
Net income.		$ -0-

encouraged, but doing so assumes a precision that cannot be justified because of the predictions used in the calculation.

To verify that Carson Company's break-even point equals $80,000 and 800 units, prepare a simple income statement similar to the one in Illustration 24–6. It shows that the $80,000 revenue from the sales of 800 units exactly equals the sum of the fixed and variable costs.

Drawing a CVP Chart

Illustration 24–7 is a graphic representation of the cost-volume-profit relationships for Carson Company for a month. This type of presentation is a **CVP chart.** It is also sometimes called a *break-even graph* or *break-even chart.* Notice that the horizontal axis represents the units sold and the vertical axis represents dollars of sales and costs. In accordance with the simplifying assumptions used in basic analyses, straight lines depict costs and revenues on the graph. To prepare a CVP chart like the one in Illustration 24–7, complete the following steps:

1. Plot the amount of fixed costs on the vertical axis. If you wish, draw a horizontal line at this level to show that fixed costs remain unchanged regardless of sales volume. So that you can see this effect, Illustration 24–7 includes this line. However, the fixed cost line is not essential to the analysis and is usually omitted.
2. Draw a line to represent total costs (variable costs plus fixed costs). For any sales level on the graph, the line shows the sum of the fixed costs and the variable costs for that level. This line starts at the fixed-costs level on the vertical axis because total costs equal the fixed costs at the zero sales level. The slope of the total cost line equals the variable cost per unit. To draw the line, compute the total costs for any sales level, and connect this point with the vertical axis intercept. Do not extend this line beyond the productive capacity for the planning period.
3. Draw a sales line starting at the origin (zero units and zero dollars of sales). The slope of this line equals the selling price per unit. To draw the line, compute the total revenues for any sales level, and connect this point with the origin. Do not extend this line beyond the productive capacity for the planning period. The total revenue should be at its maxi-

ILLUSTRATION 24–7

Cost-Volume-Profit Chart

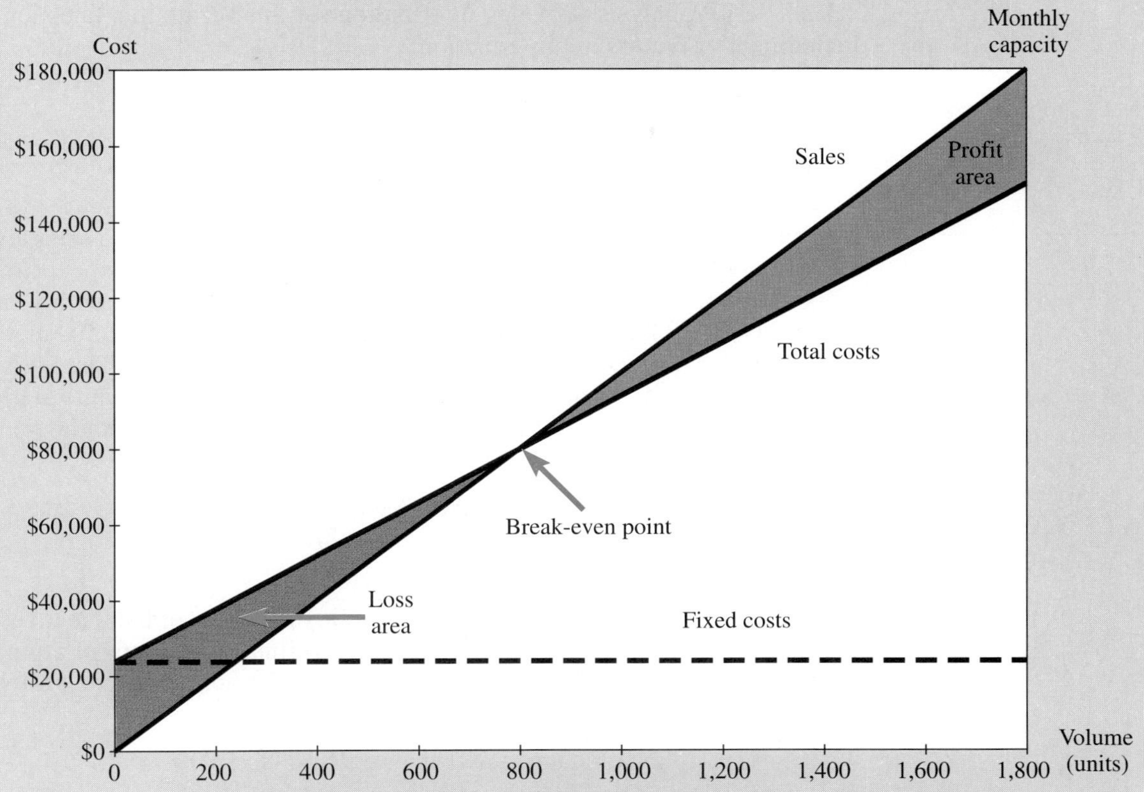

mum level at maximum capacity. It is likely that the relevant range will be near the middle of the graph.[2]

As you examine Illustration 24–7, observe that the total cost line and the sales line intersect at 800 units of product. This intersection is the break-even point because the total sales revenue of $80,000 equals the $80,000 sum of the fixed and variable costs.

On either side of the break-even point, the vertical distance between the sales line and the total cost line at any specific sales volume measures the profit or loss expected at that volume. At volume levels to the left of the break-even point, this vertical distance is the amount of the loss because the total cost line is above the total sales line. And, at volume levels to the right of the break-even point, the vertical distance represents the amount of profit because the total sales line is above the total cost line.

[2] These instructions are provided to guide you through a manual drafting process. The graph can also be drawn with computer assistance including spreadsheet programs that can convert numeric data to graphs.

Finding the Income from an Expected Sales Level

LO 5 Describe several applications of cost-volume-profit analysis.

Cost-volume-profit analysis can be used to develop preliminary answers to a variety of planning questions. Generally, the first question that managers need an answer to is, "How much income will we have from our expected level of sales?" CVP analysis provides information for answering this question by including four factors in this equation:

$$\text{Profit} = \text{Sales} - (\text{Fixed costs} + \text{Variable costs})$$

or

$$\text{Profit} = \text{Sales} - \text{Fixed costs} - \text{Variable costs}$$

You can use this equation to calculate the profit from an expected sales level. For example, assume that the management of Carson Company expects to sell 1,500 units of its product. How much profit will result if the monthly sales reach this level? At this volume, revenues would be $150,000 (1,500 units × $100). Carson Company's fixed costs are $24,000 per month. The variable costs per unit are $70 per unit, and total variable costs for 1,500 units of product are $105,000 ($70 × 1,500 units). By substituting these amounts in the equation, we can calculate the profit this way:

$$\begin{aligned}\text{Profit} &= \$150{,}000 - \$24{,}000 - \$105{,}000\\ &= \$150{,}000 - \$129{,}000\\ &= \$21{,}000\end{aligned}$$

Notice that the $21,000 profit does not include the effects of income taxes. If the management of Carson Company wants to find the amount of after-tax income from selling 1,500 units, they must apply the appropriate tax rates to the $21,000. If the tax rate is 25%, the equation becomes:

$$\begin{aligned}\text{Net income} &= \$21{,}000 - (25\% \times \$21{,}000)\\ &= \$21{,}000 - \$5{,}250\\ &= \$15{,}750\end{aligned}$$

Then, the management must determine whether this profit is an adequate return on the assets invested in providing the operating capacity. Management should also consider whether total dollars of sales can be increased by raising or lowering prices. CVP is a good tool for answering these kinds of "what if" questions.

Finding the Amount of Sales Needed for a Target Net Income

CVP analysis also can be used to find the sales level needed to produce a target net income. The formula is

$$\text{Dollar sales} = \frac{\text{Fixed costs} + \text{Target net income} + \text{Income taxes}}{\text{Contribution rate}}$$

For those interested in the underlying mathematics, Illustration 24–8 presents the derivation of the formula.

ILLUSTRATION 24–8

Derivation of Target Income Formula

Let: S = sales in units R = revenue per unit
F = fixed costs per month V = variable cost per unit
N = target net income T = income taxes
$S \times R$ = dollar sales $S \times V$ = total variable cost

And: Contribution rate = $(R - V)/R$

Then:
$$N = (S \times R) - F - (S \times V) - T$$
$$(S \times R) - (S \times V) = F + N + T$$
$$S \times (R - V) = F + N + T$$
$$S = (F + N + T)/(R - V)$$
$$S \times R = [(F + N + T) \times R]/(R - V)$$
$$S \times R = (F + N + T) \times [R/(R - V)]$$
$$S \times R = (F + N + T)/[(R - V)/R]$$
$$S \times R = (F + N + T)/\textit{Contribution rate}$$

To illustrate the formula's use, recall that Carson Company has monthly fixed costs of \$24,000 and a 30% contribution rate. Now, assume that the management has set a target monthly income of \$18,000 after considering income taxes at the rate of 25%. At this rate, the before-tax income needs to be \$24,000 [\$18,000/(1 − .25)] and the tax is \$6,000. Under these assumptions, \$160,000 of sales are necessary to produce a \$18,000 net income. Calculate this amount as follows:

$$\text{Dollar sales at target income level} = \frac{\text{Fixed costs} + \text{Net income} + \text{Income taxes}}{\text{Contribution rate}}$$
$$= \frac{\$24,000 + \$18,000 + \$6,000}{30\%}$$
$$= \frac{\$48,000}{30\%} = \$160,000$$

You can also use this formula with the contribution margin as the denominator. If so, the result is the number of units that must be sold to reach the target income level. This calculation applies to the Carson Company's situation:

$$\text{Unit sales at target income level} = \frac{\text{Fixed costs} + \text{Net income} + \text{Income taxes}}{\text{Contribution margin}}$$
$$= \frac{\$24,000 + \$18,000 + \$6,000}{\$30}$$
$$= \frac{\$48,000}{\$30} = 1,600 \text{ units}$$

AS A MATTER OF

Ethics

A small management group in a major corporation is discussing a proposal they are about to submit to the division manager for approval. If approved, several million dollars will be committed to new equipment and to new employees working for this group. The critical factor in the decision is the range of possible profits that will result from different sales volume projections. The data under consideration are the likely sales figures and operating costs of the project.

The sales figures are subjective because the proposed product has not been produced before. One team member suggests that they might as well pick some numbers that will produce a profit because any estimate is "as good as any other."

The cost predictions are based on experience with a manufacturing system similar to the proposed process. As a result, the management team has assumed that the fixed and variable costs of the proposed project would occur in the same relationship as they do in the comparable manufacturing system. The fixed and variable cost components for the proposal are being estimated from a scatter diagram of 20 months' production by the comparable manufacturing system. However, the results are not as supportive of an investment in the project as the group thinks may be necessary to get the proposal approved.

At this point, a team member asks whether some of the less favorable data points might be dropped from the analysis to see if the cost picture could be improved. This person has picked up on the familiar argument that the innovative nature of this venture makes one cost estimate "as good as any other." The accountant member of the team has been asked to produce a cost-volume-profit analysis to reflect the proposed modifications but wonders whether it is the right thing to do.

These two calculations have equivalent answers because sales of 1,600 units at $100 per unit will yield $160,000 of revenue.

The next step in the planning process is to determine whether the company can sell 1,600 units at the assumed price. If not, other alternatives need to be examined.

Finding the Margin of Safety

The excess of expected sales over the sales at the break-even point is a company's **margin of safety.** This difference is called the margin of safety because it is the amount that sales could drop before the company will incur a loss. The margin of safety can be expressed in units of product, in dollars, or even as a percentage of the predicted level of sales. For example, if Carson Company's expected sales are $100,000, the margin of safety is $20,000 over the break-even sales of $80,000. As a percentage, the margin of safety is 20% of the expected sales:

$$\text{Margin of safety} = \frac{\text{Expected sales} - \text{Break-even sales}}{\text{Expected sales}}$$

or

$$\text{Margin of safety} = \frac{\$100{,}000 - \$80{,}000}{\$100{,}000} = 20\%$$

Then, management should assess whether this margin of safety is adequate in light of the variability of sales volumes that might be expected in the future.

Finding the Answers to Other Questions

In planning business operations, managers often consider a variety of strategies. These possible strategies often affect the costs and revenues of the business. Cost-volume-profit analysis is useful for helping managers complete preliminary evaluations of likely effects of new strategies. For example, managers may want to know what would happen if they reduced the selling price of the product to increase sales. Or, managers might want to know what would happen to profits if they installed a new automated machine that would increase fixed costs while reducing variable costs. If the managers can describe how the change would affect the company's fixed costs, variable costs, selling price, and volume, they can use CVP analysis to predict the resulting profit.

To illustrate the possible effect of a change, assume that the manager of Carson Company is thinking about buying a new machine that would increase the monthly fixed costs from \$24,000 to \$30,000. If the purchase is made, the machine will reduce variable costs from \$70 per unit to \$60 per unit. Because the product's selling price will remain unchanged at \$100, the contribution margin and the contribution rate will both increase. The new contribution margin will be \$40 per unit (\$100 − \$60) and the new contribution rate will be 40% of the selling price (\$40/\$100). The manager wants to know what the break-even point will be if the machine is bought.

If the machine is purchased, the company's new break-even point in dollars will be:

$$\text{New break-even point in dollars} = \frac{\text{New fixed costs}}{\text{New contribution rate}}$$

$$= \frac{\$30{,}000}{40\%} = \$75{,}000$$

The new fixed costs and the new contribution rate also can be used to determine the expected income at a given sales level, to find the sales level needed to earn a target net income, or to answer other questions management may raise before purchasing the new machine.

Multiproduct Break-Even Point

LO 6 Calculate the break-even point for a multiproduct company by constructing a composite sales unit.

Up to this point, we have considered only those situations in which the company produces a single product because the basic model requires this simplicity. However, it is possible to modify the basic model slightly for use when a company produces and sells several products in a fairly consistent ratio. Specifically, a company that sells more than one product can estimate the break-even point by using a *composite unit* composed of specific numbers of units of each product in proportion to their expected **sales mix.** The sales mix is the ratio of the volumes of the various products. Then, CVP analysis treats the composite unit as though it is a single product.

To illustrate the use of a composite unit, assume that Denson Company sells three products, A, B, and C. Management wants to estimate the company's break-even point for the next month. Unit selling prices for the three products are

Product A	$5
Product B	8
Product C	4

Because the sales mix is the ratio of 4 units of A to 2 units of B to 1 unit of C (more conveniently expressed as 4:2:1), the selling price of a composite unit consisting of the three products is calculated as follows:

4 units of Product A @ $5 per unit . .	$20
2 units of Product B @ $8 per unit . .	16
1 unit of Product C @ $4 per unit . . .	4
Selling price of a composite unit . . .	$40

The company's fixed costs are $48,000 per month and the variable costs of the three products are

Product A	$3.25
Product B	4.50
Product C	2.00

Thus, the variable costs of a composite unit of the products are

4 units of Product A @ $3.25 per unit	$13
2 units of Product B @ $4.50 per unit	9
1 unit of Product C @ $2.00 per unit	2
Variable costs of a composite unit	$24

After the variable costs and selling price of a composite unit of the company's products are found, the Denson Company can calculate the contribution margin for a composite unit by subtracting the variable costs of a composite unit from its selling price:

$$\text{Contribution margin per composite unit} = \text{Selling price} - \text{Variable costs} = \$40 - \$24 = \$16$$

The management then uses the $16 contribution margin to determine the company's break-even point in composite units. The break-even point is found as follows:

$$\text{Break-even point in composite units} = \frac{\text{Fixed costs}}{\text{Contribution margin per composite unit}} = \frac{\$48{,}000}{\$16} = 3{,}000 \text{ composite units}$$

According to this calculation, Denson Company breaks even when it sells 3,000 composite units of its products. To determine how many units of each product must be sold to break even, the number of units of each product in the composite unit is multiplied by 3,000:

Product A: 4 × 3,000	12,000 units
Product B: 2 × 3,000	6,000 units
Product C: 1 × 3,000	3,000 units

ILLUSTRATION 24–8

DENSON COMPANY
Forecasted Product Income Statement
at the Break-Even Point

	Product A	Product B	Product C	Combined
Sales:				
Product A (12,000 @ $5)	$60,000			
Product B (6,000 @ $8)		$48,000		
Product C (3,000 @ $4)			$12,000	$120,000
Total revenues				
Variable costs:				
Product A (12,000 @ $3.25)	39,000			
Product B (6,000 @ $4.50)		27,000		
Product C (3,000 @ $2.00)			6,000	
Total variable costs				72,000
Contribution margin	$21,000	$21,000	$ 6,000	$ 48,000
Fixed costs				48,000
Net income				$ -0-

The schedule in Illustration 24–8 verifies these results by showing the company's revenues and costs at the break-even point.

A cost-volume-profit analysis based on composite units can answer a variety of planning questions. Once a product mix is established, all answers are based on the assumption that it remains constant at all sales levels, just like the other factors in the analysis. And, like the other factors, the sales mix can be varied to see what would happen under alternative strategies.

Evaluating the Usefulness of Cost-Volume-Profit Analyses

Cost-volume-profit analysis is useful when management begins the planning process and needs to predict the results of alternative strategies for selling prices, fixed costs, variable costs, sales volume, and product mix. But, you should keep two points in mind before using the results of a CVP analysis. First, the data used in the analysis are predictions of future conditions. Therefore, the output of the analysis can be no better than the quality of those predictions. Second, the simplified CVP analysis presented in this chapter is based on assumptions that the selling price will remain constant, that fixed costs are truly fixed, and that variable costs are truly variable. These assumptions do not always correspond to reality. Therefore, the results of the analyses are rough approximations at best. If you keep these limits in mind, CVP analysis can be useful for starting to plan the activities of a business.

More complex CVP analyses can be designed to reflect such things as nonlinear revenue and cost behaviors. These analyses are described in more advanced managerial accounting courses.

Summary of the Chapter in Terms of Learning Objectives

LO 1. A cost's behavior is described in terms of how its amount changes in relation to production and sales volume changes. As volume increases, total fixed costs remain unchanged. Total variable costs change in direct proportion to volume changes. Step-variable costs remain constant over a small volume range, increase by a lump sum, then remain constant over another volume range, and so on. Semivariable costs change in a nonlinear relationship to volume changes. Mixed costs display the effects of fixed and variable components.

LO 2. Conventional cost-volume-profit analysis is based on assumptions that the selling price of the single product remains constant and that variable and fixed costs behave consistently with those classifications. These assumptions are not likely to hold at volume levels outside the relevant range of operations of the business. If the assumptions do not lead to valid predictions of future costs, the CVP analysis will not be helpful.

LO 3. A scatter diagram is a graph that plots points representing the actual cost and sales volume for a number of past periods. To predict future costs, an estimated line of cost behavior needs to be drawn through the points. This line can be fitted to the points by the high-low method, a visual approximation, or a least-squares regression. The vertical intercept approximates the fixed costs and the slope approximates the variable cost per unit.

LO 4. A company's break-even point for a period is the sales volume at which total revenues equal the total costs. To calculate a break-even point in terms of units, divide total fixed costs by the contribution margin per unit. To calculate a break-even point in terms of sales dollars, divide total fixed costs by the contribution rate.

LO 5. Cost-volume-profit analysis can be used to develop initial predictions of what would happen under alternative strategies concerning sales volume, selling prices, variable costs, or fixed costs.

LO 6. CVP analysis can be applied to a multiproduct company by expressing the predicted sales volume in terms of composite units of product.

Demonstration Problem

The Tate Manufacturing Co. produces and sells a single product on a simple production line. The fixed costs of operating the business have averaged about $150,000 per month, and the variable costs have been about $5 per unit. All the manufactured product can be sold at $8 per unit and the fixed costs provide a production capacity of up to 100,000 units per month. Use this information to answer requirements 1, 2, and 3. Requirements 4 and 5 are based on additional facts provided later.

Required

1. Use formulas to calculate the following:
   a. Contribution margin per unit.
   b. Break-even point in terms of the number of units produced and sold.
   c. Amount of profit at 30,000 units per month (ignore income taxes).

   d. Amount of profit at 85,000 units per month (ignore income taxes).
   e. Quantity of units to be produced and sold to provide $45,000 of after-tax profits, assuming an income tax rate of 25%.
2. Draw a CVP chart for the company, showing units of output on the horizontal axis. Identify the break-even point and the amount of pre-tax profit when the level of production is 75,000 units. (Omit the fixed cost line.)
3. Use formulas to calculate the following:
   a. Contribution rate.
   b. Break-even point in terms of sales dollars.
   c. Amount of profit at $250,000 of sales per month (ignoring income taxes).
   d. Amount of profit at $600,000 of sales per month (ignoring income taxes).
   e. Dollars of sales needed to provide $45,000 of after-tax profits, assuming an income tax rate of 25%.

Terry Tate, the company's president, is considering new plans for operating the production line and marketing the product. If implemented, the plans would produce the following changes:

- The monthly fixed costs would increase to $300,000.
- The variable costs would decrease to $3.25 per unit.
- All units would be sold for $7 each.
- The increased fixed costs would allow Tate to produce up to 200,000 units per month.

4. Calculate the following:
   a. The change in the contribution margin per unit.
   b. The change in the break-even point in units.
   c. The change in the amount of profit at 30,000 units per month (ignore income taxes).
   d. The change in the amount of profit at 85,000 units per month (ignore income taxes).
   e. The change in the quantity of units to be produced and sold to provide $45,000 of after-tax profits, assuming an income tax rate of 25%.
5. Draw a CVP chart for the company under the proposed new operating plan, showing units of output on the horizontal axis. Identify the break-even point and the amount of pre-tax profit when the level of production is 150,000 units. (Omit the fixed cost line.)

Solution to Demonstration Problem

Planning the Solution

- Find the formulas in the chapter for the required items concerning volumes expressed in units and solve them using the original data given in the problem.

- Draw a CVP chart that reflects the facts given in the problem. The horizontal axis should plot the volume in units up to 100,000, and the vertical axis should plot the total dollars up to $800,000. Plot the total cost line as upward-sloping, starting at the fixed cost level ($150,000) on the vertical axis and increasing until it reaches $650,000 at the maximum volume of 100,000 units. Verify that the break-even point (where the two lines cross) equals the amount you computed in Part 1.
- Find the formulas in the chapter for the required items concerning volumes expressed in units and solve them using the original data given in the problem.
- Use the predictions for the new plans to calculate the described changes.
- Draw a CVP chart that reflects the revised facts given for the problem. The horizontal axis should plot the volume in units up to 200,000, and the vertical axis should plot the total dollars up to $1.4 million. Plot the total cost line as upward-sloping, starting at the proposed new fixed cost level ($300,000) on the vertical axis and increasing until it reaches $950,000 at the maximum volume of 200,000 units. Verify that the break-even point (where the two lines cross) equals the amount you computed in Part 4.

Part 1.

a. Contribution margin per unit = Selling price per unit − Variable cost per unit

= $8 − $5 = $3

b. Break-even point in units $= \dfrac{\text{Fixed costs}}{\text{Contribution margin per unit}}$

$= \dfrac{\$150{,}000}{\$3} = 50{,}000$ units

c. Profit at 30,000 unit sales = (Units × Contribution margin per unit) − Fixed costs

= (30,000 × $3) − $150,000 = −$60,000 (a loss)

d. Profit at 85,000 unit sales = (Units × Contribution margin per unit) − Fixed costs

= (85,000 × $3) − $150,000 = $105,000 profit

e. Pretax profit = $45,000/75% = $60,000

Income taxes = $60,000 × 25% = $15,000

Units needed for $45,000 profit $= \dfrac{\text{Fixed costs + Net income + Income taxes}}{\text{Contribution margin per unit}}$

$= \dfrac{\$150{,}000 + \$45{,}000 + \$15{,}000}{\$3} = 70{,}000$ units

Part 2. CVP chart:

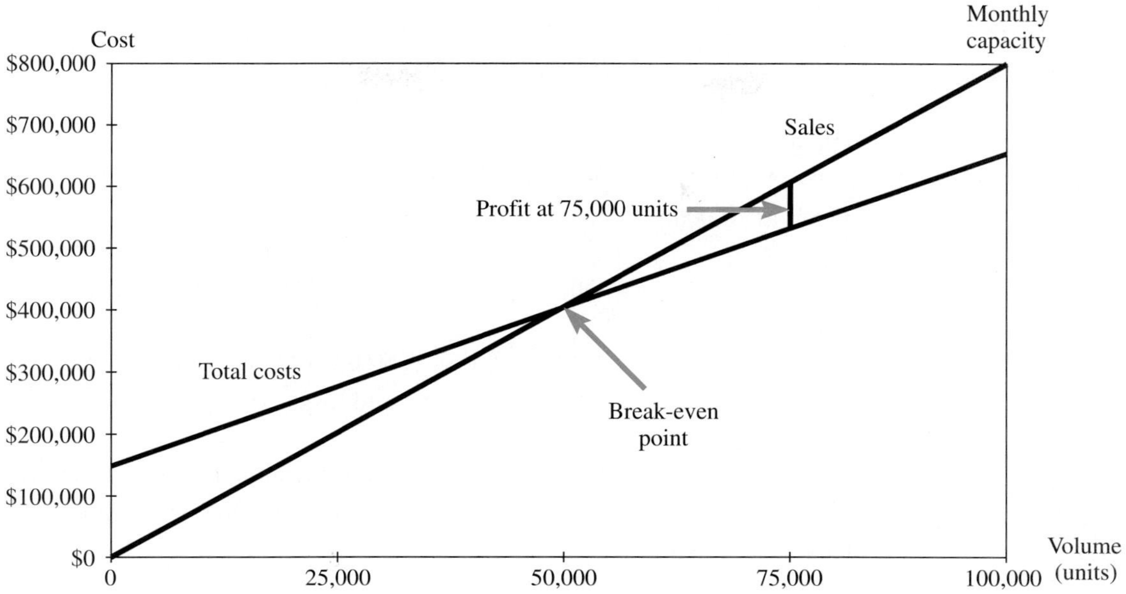

Part 3.

a. Contribution rate $= \dfrac{\text{Contribution margin per unit}}{\text{Selling price per unit}} = \dfrac{\$3}{\$8} = .375$, or 37.5%

b. Break-even point in dollars $= \dfrac{\text{Fixed costs}}{\text{Contribution rate}} = \dfrac{\$150{,}000}{37.5\%} = \$400{,}000$

c. Profit at sales of $250,000
= (Sales × Contribution rate) − Fixed costs
= ($250,000 × 37.5%) − $150,000
= −$56,250 (a loss)

d. Profit at sales of $600,000
= (Sales × Contribution rate) − Fixed costs
= ($600,000 × 37.5%) − $150,000
= $75,000 profit

e. Dollars of sales to have $45,000 profits $= \dfrac{\text{Fixed costs + Net income + Income taxes}}{\text{Contribution rate}}$

$$= \frac{\$150{,}000 + \$45{,}000 + \$15{,}000}{37.5\%} = \$560{,}000$$

Part 4.

a. Contribution margin per unit = Selling price per unit − Variable cost per unit
= $7.00 − $3.25 = $3.75

Change created by proposal = $3.75 − $3.00 = $0.75 per unit increase

b. Break-even point in units $= \dfrac{\text{Fixed costs}}{\text{Contribution margin per unit}}$

$= \dfrac{\$300{,}000}{\$3.75} = 80{,}000$ units

Change created by proposal = 80,000 − 50,000 = 30,000 units increase

c. Profit at 30,000 unit sales = (Units × Contribution margin per unit) − Fixed costs

= (30,000 × \$3.75) − \$300,000 = −\$187,500 (a loss)

Change created by proposal = \$(187,500) loss − \$(60,000) loss

= −\$127,500 (increased loss)

d. Profit at 85,000 unit sales = (Units × Contribution margin per unit) − Fixed costs

= (85,000 × \$3.75) − \$300,000 = \$18,750 profit

Change created by proposal = \$18,750 − \$105,000

= −\$86,250 (decreased profit)

e. Units needed for \$45,000 profit $= \dfrac{\text{Fixed costs + Net income + Income taxes}}{\text{Contribution margin per unit}}$

$= \dfrac{\$300{,}000 + \$45{,}000 + \$15{,}000}{\$3.75} = 96{,}000$ units

Change created by proposal = 96,000 − 70,000 = 26,000 units increase

Part 5. CVP chart:

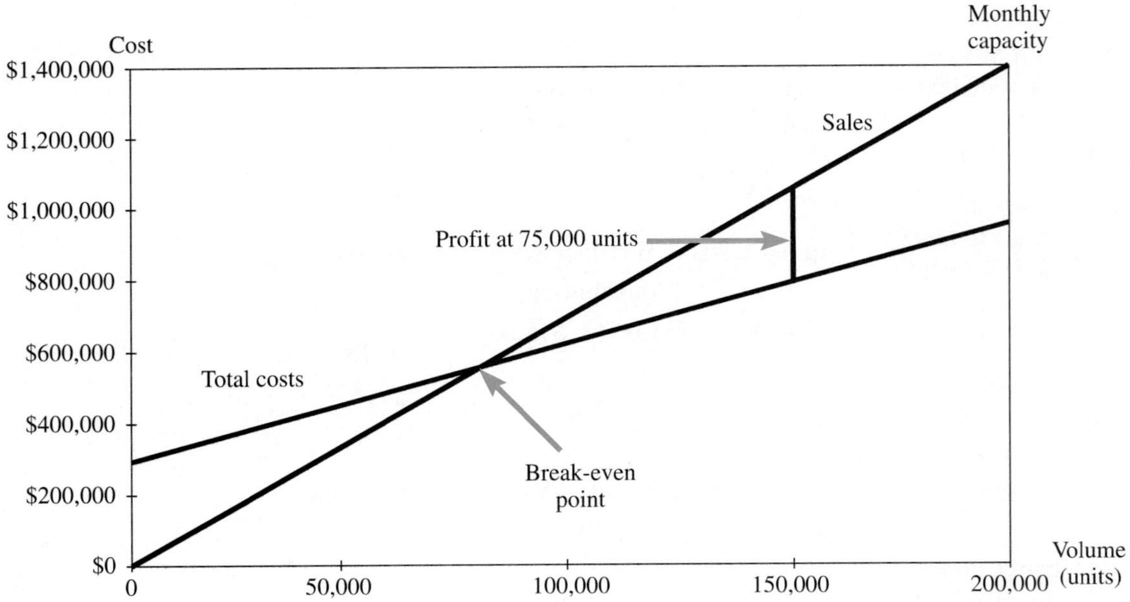

Glossary

LO 7 Define or explain the words and phrases listed in the chapter glossary.

Break-even point the unique sales level at which a company neither earns a profit nor incurs a loss. p. 1290

Contribution margin per unit the amount that the sale of one unit contributes toward recovering fixed costs and profit. pp. 1290–91

Contribution rate the contribution margin per unit expressed as a percentage of the product's selling price. p. 1291

Cost-volume-profit analysis the first initial step in the planning phase of operating a business; the analysis predicts the effects of changes in costs and sales level on the income of a business. p. 1282

CVP chart a graph that plots volumes on the horizontal axis and costs and revenues on the vertical axis. p. 1292

Estimated line of cost behavior a line on a scatter diagram that is intended to reflect the past relationship between cost and volume. p. 1288

Fixed cost a cost that remains unchanged in total amount even when production volume varies from period to period. p. 1283

High-low method a simple way to draw an estimated line of cost behavior by connecting the highest and lowest costs on a scatter diagram with a straight line. p. 1289

Least-squares regression a statistical method for deriving an estimated line of cost behavior that is more precise than the high-low method. p. 1289

Margin of safety the excess of expected sales over the sales at the break-even point. p. 1296

Mixed cost a cost that can be separated into fixed and variable components. p. 1286

Relevant range of operations a business's normal operating range; excludes extremely high and low volumes that are not likely to be encountered. p. 1288

Sales mix the ratio of the volumes of the various products sold by a company. p. 1297

Scatter diagram a graph used to analyze past cost behaviors by displaying costs and volumes for each period as points on the diagram. p. 1288

Semivariable cost a cost that changes with volume but not at a constant rate. p. 1285

Step-variable cost a cost that remains constant over limited ranges of volumes but increases by a lump sum when volume increases beyond maximum amounts. p. 1285

Variable cost a cost that changes in proportion to changes in production volume. p. 1283

Synonymous Terms

Cost-volume-profit analysis CVP analysis; break-even analysis.

CVP chart CVP graph; break-even chart; break-even graph.

Step-variable cost step-wise cost; stair-step cost.

Objective Review

Answers to the following questions are listed at the end of the chapter. Be sure that you decide which is the one best answer to each question before you check the answers.

LO 1 Which of the following statements about the behavior of typical costs is true?

a. The amount of a fixed cost per unit of product decreases as volume increases.
b. The amount of variable cost per unit of product increases as volume increases.
c. A semivariable cost includes both fixed and variable elements and should be divided into its separate components for a useful analysis classification.
d. As volume decreases, total costs decrease at the rate of variable costs per unit.
e. Both (*a*) and (*d*) are correct.

LO 2 In conventional cost-volume-profit analysis:

a. Costs are assumed to be either fixed or variable.
b. The relationships of costs to volume can be plotted as straight lines on a graph.
c. The selling price per unit is assumed to remain constant at all volumes.
d. The basic assumptions of linear relationships are intended to apply only over the relevant range of operations.
e. All of the above.

LO 3 In a scatter diagram of a company's past cost experience:

a. Cost per unit is usually plotted on the vertical axis with volume in dollars or units plotted on the horizontal axis.
b. Each point shows the total cost for a given period and the sales price per unit during that period.
c. The high-low method results in an estimated line of cost behavior that is described as being the best fit of the cost and volume data on the graph.
d. The estimated line of cost behavior is intended to represent the average relationship between costs and sales volume.
e. The cost and volume of each period are entered as two points on the diagram.

LO 4 Global Company sells a single product for $80 per unit and incurs $55 of variable costs per unit. If fixed costs are $17,475 per month:

a. The contribution margin is $55 per unit.
b. The break-even point is 318 units.
c. The break-even point in dollars is $55,920.
d. The contribution rate is 68.75%.
e. The break-even point is 219 units.

LO 5 Use the following data to find the margin of safety:

Units sold	9,000
Revenue	$270,000
Fixed costs.	$108,000
Variable costs	$108,000

a. $18 per unit.
b. 6,000 units.
c. $90,000.
d. 60%.
e. $54,000.

LO 6 The sales mix of Bell Corporation's three products (P1, P2, and P3) is 2:1:4. Fixed costs total $160,000 and unit price and variable cost data are:

	P1	P2	P3
Unit sales price	$5	$4	$4
Unit variable cost	2	2	3

Bell Corporation's break-even point is

a. $266,667.
b. $320,000.
c. $355,555.
d. $400,000.
e. $480,000.

LO 7 A mixed cost displays which one of the following behaviors?

a. Starts at zero cost at zero volume and increases proportionately to increases in volume.
b. Starts at a non-zero positive cost at zero volume and increases proportionately to increases in volume.
c. Starts at zero cost at zero volume and increases disproportionately to increases in volume.
d. Starts at a non-zero positive cost at zero volume and increases disproportionately to increases in volume.
e. Starts at a non-zero positive cost at zero volume and remains at that level over all ranges in volume.

Questions for Class Discussion

1. Why is cost-volume-profit analysis used?
2. What is a fixed cost? Identify two examples of fixed costs.
3. When volume increases, do fixed costs per unit increase or decrease? Why?
4. What is a variable cost? Identify two variable costs.
5. If volume increases, what happens to the amount of variable costs per unit?

6. What is a semivariable cost?
7. How do step-variable costs and semivariable costs differ?
8. How should a mixed cost be treated in a cost-volume-profit analysis?
9. The usefulness of cost-volume-profit analysis rests on the validity of three basic assumptions. What are they?
10. In performing a conventional CVP analysis for a manufacturing company, what simplifying assumption is usually made about the volume of production and the volume of sales?
11. What two factors tend to justify classifying all costs as either fixed or variable even though individual costs might not behave perfectly consistently with these classifications?
12. How does assuming a relevant range affect cost-volume-profit analysis?
13. Does cost-volume-profit analysis provide precise answers to questions about the effect of cost changes on profits?
14. How can a scatter diagram be used in identifying the behavior of a company's costs?
15. What is the primary weakness of the high-low method of deriving an estimated line of cost behavior?
16. What is a company's break-even point?
17. A company sells a product for $90 per unit that has variable costs of $54 per unit. What is the product's contribution margin per unit? What is its contribution rate?
18. Assume that a straight line on a CVP chart intersects the vertical axis at the level of fixed costs and has a positive slope. It rises with each additional unit of volume by the amount of the variable costs per unit. What would this line represent?
19. Why are fixed costs depicted as a horizontal line on a CVP chart?
20. Two similar companies each have sales of $100,000 and total costs of $80,000 for a month. Company A's total costs include $20,000 of variable costs and $60,000 of fixed costs. If Company B's total costs include $60,000 of variable costs and $20,000 of fixed costs, which company will enjoy a greater profit if sales double?
21. What is a company's margin of safety?
22. What is a company's sales mix?
23. If a company produces and sells more than one product, the usefulness of a conventional cost-volume-profit analysis depends on an additional assumption about sales mix. What is that assumption?
24. Consider the process of preparing sandwiches for sale during the lunch rush hour at a McDonald's store. Identify some of the variable and fixed costs associated with that process.
25. Federal Express flies packages from drop off points to Memphis, sorts them there in a central facility, and then delivers them the next morning to their destinations. Is is likely that some flights produce more costs than revenues?

McDonald's®
What you want is what you get.™

FEDERAL EXPRESS

Exercises

Exercise 24–1
Identifying categories of cost behavior
(LO 1)

The left column presents the names of several categories of costs. The right column presents short definitions of those costs. In the blank space beside each of the numbers in the right column, write the letter of the cost described by the definition.

a. Fixed cost	__1. This cost is the combined amount of all the other costs.
b. Mixed cost	__2. This cost increases in direct proportion to increases in volume because its amount is constant for each unit produced.
c. Variable cost	__3. This cost increases when volume increases, but the increase is not constant for each unit produced.
d. Semivariable cost	__4. This cost remains the same over all volume levels within the productive capacity for the planning period.
e. Step-variable cost	__5. This cost has a component that remains the same over all volume levels and another component that increases in direct proportion to increases in volume.
f. Total cost	__6. This cost remains constant over a limited range of volume that is less than the total productive capacity; when it reaches the end of its limited range, it increases by a lump sum and remains at that level until another limited range is exceeded.

Exercise 24–2
Recognizing cost behavior graphs
(LO 1)

The five graphs on the following page represent various cost behaviors. Identify the type of cost behavior that each graph represents:

1.

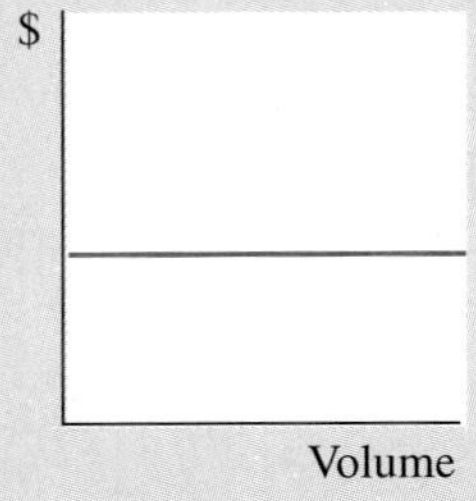

2.

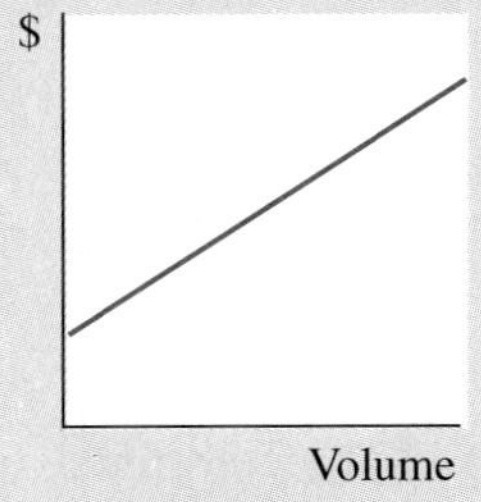

3.

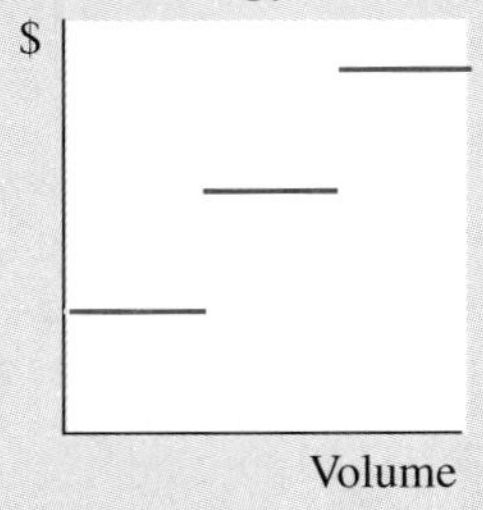

4.

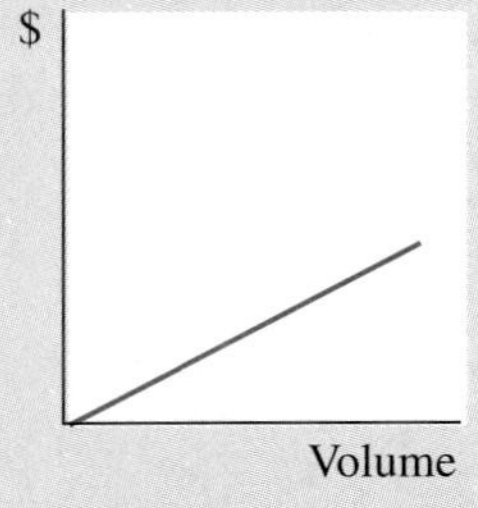

5.

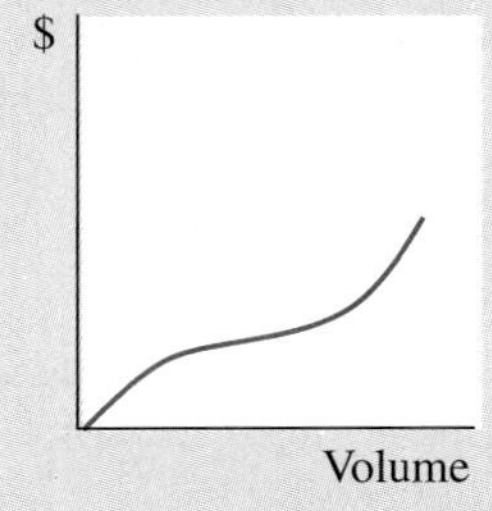

Exercise 24–3
Recognizing cost behavior patterns
(LO 1)

Five series of costs measured at various volume levels follow. Examine each series and identify which is fixed, variable, mixed, semivariable, and step-variable:

Volume (units)	Series A	Series B	Series C	Series D	Series E
0	$ -0-	$ -0-	$900	$ 400	$ 650
50	400	1,000	900	400	720
100	800	1,100	900	400	790
150	1,200	1,200	900	800	860
200	1,600	1,300	900	800	930
250	2,000	1,600	900	1,200	1,000
300	2,400	2,250	900	1,200	1,070

Exercise 24–4
Recognizing cost behavior patterns
(LO 1)

Five series of costs measured at various volume levels follow. Examine each series and identify which is fixed, variable, mixed, semivariable, and step-variable:

Volume (units)	Series A	Series B	Series C	Series D	Series E
0	$ -0-	$1,600	$ -0-	$1,000	$1,600
200	3,000	1,850	1,600	1,000	1,600
400	3,300	2,100	3,200	1,000	1,600
600	3,600	2,350	4,800	2,000	1,600
800	3,900	2,600	6,400	2,000	1,600
1,000	4,800	2,850	8,000	3,000	1,600
1,200	6,750	3,100	9,600	3,000	1,600

Exercise 24–5
Scatter diagram and cost behavior—six data points
(LO 3)

A company's accounting system provides the following information about its monthly sales volume and the amount of a specific cost in those months:

Month	Sales	Cost
1	$30,000	$16,200
2	21,000	11,000
3	21,000	14,000
4	15,000	11,000
5	18,000	12,000
6	25,000	13,000

Use this data to prepare a scatter diagram. Then, draw an estimated line of cost bbehavior and determine whether the cost appears to be variable, fixed, or mixed.

Exercise 24–6
Scatter diagram and cost behavior—15 data points
(LO 3)

Use the following information about monthly sales volume and the amount of a specific cost to prepare a scatter diagram. Then, draw a cost line that reflects the behavior displayed by this cost. Finally, determine whether the cost is variable, semivariable, step-variable, fixed, or mixed.

Period	Sales	Cost	Period	Sales	Cost
1	$76,000	$59,000	9	$58,000	$39,000
2	80,000	56,000	10	33,000	24,000
3	21,000	23,000	11	25,000	24,500
4	41,000	40,000	12	72,000	55,000
5	49,000	39,000	13	28,000	26,000
6	63,000	55,000	14	44,000	41,000
7	68,000	59,000	15	38,000	26,500
8	55,000	43,000			

Exercise 24–7
Calculating contribution margin and rate
(LO 4)

Ballfour Corporation manufactures a single product that sells for $28 per unit. The total variable costs of the product are $21 per unit and the company's annual fixed costs are $105,000. Use this data to calculate the company's:

a. Contribution margin per unit.

b. Contribution rate.

c. Break-even point in units.

d. Break-even point in dollars of sales.

Exercise 24–8
Calculating additional sales necessary to break even
(LO 5)

Prepare an income statement for Ballfour Corporation's operations (from Exercise 24–7) showing sales, variable costs, and fixed costs at the break-even point. If Ballfour Corporation's fixed costs were to increase by $15,000, how many sales (in dollars) would be needed to break even?

Exercise 24–9
Calculating sales required to obtain desired income
(LO 5)

The management of Ballfour Corporation (in Exercise 24–7) wants to earn an annual after-tax income of $120,000. The company is subject to a combined federal and state income tax rate of 40%. Calculate:

a. The units of product that must be sold to earn the target after-tax net income.

b. The dollars of sales that must be reached to earn the target after-tax net income.

Exercise 24–10
Estimating the income result from increased volume
(LO 5)

In looking ahead, the sales manager of Ballfour Corporation (in Exercise 24–7) predicts that the annual sales of the company's product will soon reach 51,000 units even though the price will increase to $40 per unit. According to the production manager, the variable costs are expected to increase to $28 per unit but fixed costs will remain at $105,000. The company's tax adviser expects that the combined federal and state income tax rate will still be 40%. What amounts of before-tax and after-tax income can the company expect to earn from selling units at this expected level with these expected costs?

Exercise 24–11
Calculating total variable and fixed costs
(LO 5)

Grosch Company expects to sell 80,000 units of its product next year, which should produce total revenues of $4.8 million. Management predicts that the pre-tax net income for the year will be $960,000 and that the contribution margin per unit will be $16. Using this information, compute (*a*) the total expected variable costs and (*b*) the total expected fixed costs for next year.

Exercise 24–12
Calculating unit and dollar sales using contribution margin
(LO 5)

In predicting the events of the upcoming quarter, the management of the Partridge Company thinks that it will incur a total of $250,000 of variable costs and $400,000 of fixed costs while earning a pre-tax income of $100,000. The management predicts that the contribution margin per unit will be $50. Using this information, determine (*a*) the total expected dollar sales for the quarter and (*b*) the number of units expected to be sold in the quarter.

Exercise 24–13
Calculating sales and variable costs using contribution rate
(LO 5)

The management of the Young Company predicts that it will incur fixed costs of $240,000 next year and that the pre-tax income will be $96,000. The expected contribution rate is 75%. Use this information to compute the amounts of (*a*) total dollar sales and (*b*) total variable costs.

Exercise 24–14
CVP analysis using composite units
(LO 6)

The Big Diamond Company sells bats and gloves in the ratio of 5:3 (5 bats for every 3 gloves). The selling price of each bat is $40 and the selling price of each glove is $50. The variable cost of a bat is $21 and the variable cost of a glove is $27. Next year's fixed costs are expected to be $803,600. Use this information to determine:

a. The selling price of a composite unit of these products.

b. The variable costs per composite unit.

c. The break-even point in composite units.

d. The number of units of each product that will be sold at the break-even point.

Problems

Problem 24–1
Scatter diagram with estimated line of cost behavior
(LO 3)

The accounting system of the Heinmets Company collected the following monthly total sales and cost data about its operating activities for the past year:

Period	Sales	Total Cost
1	$125,000	$ 85,000
2	95,000	65,000
3	117,000	100,000
4	105,000	80,000
5	150,000	115,000
6	105,000	85,000
7	135,000	100,000
8	125,000	95,000
9	85,000	65,000
10	100,000	90,000
11	90,000	70,000
12	85,000	75,000

The management of the company wants to use this historical data to predict future fixed and variable costs.

Required

1. Prepare a scatter diagram with sales volume plotted on the horizontal axis (scale this axis in $20,000 intervals) and with total cost plotted on the vertical axis (scale this axis in $20,000 intervals). Then, plot the sales and cost data for the Heinmets Company.
2. Develop an estimated line of cost behavior by a visual inspection and draw it on the scatter diagram. (Assume a linear relationship, which means that you should draw a straight line on the graph.)
3. Based on the estimated line of cost behavior and the assumption that the future will be like the past, predict the amount of monthly fixed costs for the Heinmets Company. Also, predict future variable cost per sales dollar.
4. Use the estimated line of cost behavior to predict future total costs when the sales volume is $100,000 and $140,000.

Problem 24–2
Completing CVP analyses, including a chart
(LO 4)

Pine Creek Company manufactures and markets a number of products. Management is considering the future of Product 18, which has not been as profitable as planned. Because this product is manufactured and marketed independently from the other products, its total costs can be precisely measured. The plan for the next year calls for a selling price of $320 per unit. The fixed costs for the year are expected to be $200,000, up to the maximum capacity of 2,500 units. The forecasted variable costs are $120 per unit.

Required

1. Predict the break-even point for Product 18 in terms of (*a*) units and (*b*) dollars of sales.

2. Prepare a CVP chart for Product 18. Use 2,500 as the maximum number of units on the graph and $800,000 as the maximum number of dollars.
3. Prepare an income statement showing sales, fixed costs, and variable costs for Product 18 at the break-even point.
4. Determine the sales volume in dollars that the company must achieve to earn a $154,000 income from Product 18, after income taxes are assessed at 30%.
5. Determine the after-tax income that the company would earn from sales of $800,000.

Problem 24–3
CVP chart and income statements to confirm projections
(LO 4, 5)

In 1994, the Yosemite Company sold 5,000 units of its only product, and incurred a $28,000 loss (ignoring income taxes), as follows:

YOSEMITE COMPANY
Income Statement
For Year Ended December 31, 1994

Sales		$250,000
Costs:		
Fixed	$128,000	
Variable	150,000	278,000
Net loss		$ (28,000)

During a planning session for 1995's activities, the production manager has pointed out that variable costs can be reduced 50% by installing a machine that automates several operations presently being done by hand. To obtain these savings, the company must increase its annual fixed costs by $40,000. The maximum capacity of the system would be 10,000 units per year.

Required

1. Calculate 1994's break-even point in terms of dollars.
2. Calculate the dollar break-even point for 1995 under the assumption that the new machine is installed.
3. Prepare a CVP chart for 1995 under the assumption that the new machine is installed.
4. Prepare a forecasted income statement for 1995 that shows the expected results with the new machine installed. Assume that there will be no change in the selling price and no change in the number of units sold. The combined federal and state income tax rate is 30%.
5. Calculate the sales level required to earn $49,000 of after-tax income in 1995 with the new machine installed and with no change in the selling price. Prepare a forecasted income statement that shows the results at this sales level.

Problem 24–4
Analyzing the effects of price and volume changes on profits
(LO 5)

Last year, Gillespie Company earned a disappointing 4.2% after-tax return on sales from marketing 100,000 packages of its only product, Garden Green. The company buys Garden Green in bulk and repackages it in bags for resale at the price of $10 per bag. Gillespie incurred these costs last year:

Cost of bulk product for 100,000 packages	$400,000
Packaging materials and other variable packaging costs	40,000
Fixed costs	500,000
Income tax rate	30%

The marketing manager has reported that this year's results will be the same as last year's unless some changes are made. The manager has suggested that the company can increase the number of bags sold by 80% by reducing the selling price by 20% and upgrading the packaging. The change would increase variable packaging costs by 25%, but increased sales would allow the company to take advantage of a 20% quantity discount on the product's bulk purchase price. Neither the packaging nor the volume change would affect fixed costs, which provide an annual capacity of 200,000 units.

Required

1. Calculate the dollar break-even points for selling Garden Green (*a*) under the existing price strategy and (*b*) under the new strategy that alters the selling price and the variable costs.
2. Prepare a CVP chart for each strategy.
3. Prepare side-by-side condensed forecasted income statements showing the anticipated results of (*a*) continuing the existing strategy and (*b*) changing to the new strategy. Determine whether the after-tax return on sales will be changed by the new strategy.

Problem 24–5
Break-even analysis comparing different cost structures
(LO 5)

Hornbaker Company produces and sells two products, B and C. These products are manufactured in separate factories and marketed through completely different channels. Thus, they do not have any shared costs. Last year, Hornbaker sold 60,000 units of each product. The following income statements describe the financial results:

	Product B	Product C
Sales	$1,500,000	$1,500,000
Costs:		
Fixed costs	$ 300,000	$ 900,000
Variable costs	900,000	300,000
Total costs	$1,200,000	$1,200,000
Income before taxes	$ 300,000	$ 300,000
Income taxes (35% rate)	105,000	105,000
Net income	$ 195,000	$ 195,000

Required

1. Calculate the break-even point in dollars for each product.
2. Prepare a CVP chart for each product. Use 100,000 as the annual capacity.
3. Assume that the company expects the sales of each product to decline to 52,000 units in the upcoming year, even though the price will remain unchanged. Prepare a forecasted income statement that shows the expected profits from the two products. Follow the format of the preceding statement.
4. Assume that the company expects the sales of each product to increase

to 95,000 units in the upcoming year, even though the price will remain unchanged. Prepare a forecasted income statement that shows the expected profits from the two products. Follow the format of the preceding statement.

Problem 24–6
Break-even analysis with composite units
(LO 6)

Geneva Company manufactures and sells three products, A1, B2, and C3. Their individual selling prices are

Product A1	$20.00 per unit
Product B2	$30.00 per unit
Product C3	$50.00 per unit

The variable costs of manufacturing and selling the products have been:

Product A1	$12.00 per unit
Product B2	$20.00 per unit
Product C3	$30.00 per unit

Their sales mix is a ratio of 5:4:2, and the annual fixed costs shared by all three products are $48,000. One particular item of raw materials is used in manufacturing all three products. Management has learned that a new material is just as good and cheaper. The new material would reduce the variable costs as follows: Product A1 by $2.00, Product B2 by $2.50, and Product C3 by $4.00. But, the new material requires new equipment, which will increase annual fixed costs by $3,800.

Required

1. Assuming that the company continues to use the old material, determine the company's break-even point in dollars and the units of each product that would be sold at the break-even point.
2. Assuming that the company decides to use the new material, determine the company's new break-even point in dollars and the units of each product that would be sold at the break-even point.

Problem 24–7
Analytical essay
(LO 1)

Exercise 24–3 presents measures of five types of costs. Assume that the relevant range of operation for the planning period is 101 to 200 units. Determine the total variable costs per unit (including any semivariable costs and the variable component of any mixed costs) within this range. Also, determine the total fixed costs (including any step-variable costs and the fixed component of any mixed costs) within this range. Predict the total cost that would be incurred if the volume equals 160 units.

Problem 24–8
Analytical essay
(LO 1, 5)

Examine the product income statements presented in Problem 24–5 and answer the following:

a. Describe the cost structures for these two products.
b. Despite the differences in their cost structures, why do they experience identical incomes at the volume given in the problem?
c. If sales were to greatly decrease, which of these products would experience the greater loss? Why?

d. If sales were to greatly increase, which of these products would experience the greater profit? Why?

e. Describe some factors that might have created the different cost structures for these two products.

Alternate Problems

Problem 24–1A
Scatter diagram with estimated line of cost behavior
(LO 3)

The accounting system of the Stanley Company collected the following monthly total sales and cost data about its operating activities for the past year:

Period	Sales	Total Cost
1	$100,000	$46,000
2	65,000	41,000
3	55,000	34,000
4	80,000	42,000
5	50,000	38,000
6	110,000	52,500
7	75,000	44,000
8	95,000	50,000
9	70,000	40,000
10	45,000	30,000
11	90,000	45,000
12	60,000	37,000

The management of the company wants to use this historical data to predict future fixed and variable costs.

Required

1. Prepare a scatter diagram with sales volume plotted on the horizontal axis (scale this axis in $20,000 intervals) and with total cost plotted on the vertical axis (scale this axis in $10,000 intervals). Then, plot the sales and cost data for the Stanley Company.
2. Develop an estimated line of cost behavior by a visual inspection and draw it on the scatter diagram. (Assume a linear relationship, which means that you should draw a straight line on the graph.)
3. Based on the estimated line of cost behavior and the assumption that the future will be like the past, predict the amount of monthly fixed costs for the Stanley Company. Also, predict future variable cost per sales dollar.
4. Use the estimated line of cost behavior to predict future total costs when the sales volume is $50,000 and $80,000.

Problem 24–2A
Completing CVP analyses, including a chart
(LO 4)

Woodmoor Company manufactures and markets a number of products. Management is considering the future of Product 27, which has not been as profitable as planned. Because this product is manufactured and marketed independently from the other products, its total costs can be precisely measured. The plan for the next year calls for a selling price of $50 per unit. The fixed costs for the year are expected to be $75,000, up to the maximum capacity of 10,000 units. The forecasted variable costs are $35 per unit.

Required

1. Predict the break-even point for Product 27 in terms of (*a*) units and (*b*) dollars of sales.
2. Prepare a CVP chart for Product 27. Use 10,000 as the maximum number of units on the graph and $500,000 as the maximum number of dollars.
3. Prepare an income statement showing sales, fixed costs, and variable costs for Product 27 at the break-even point.
4. Determine the sales volume in dollars that the company must achieve to earn a $39,000 income from Product 27, after income taxes are assessed at 35%.
5. Determine the after-tax income that the company would earn from sales of $400,000.

Problem 24–3A
CVP chart and income statements to confirm projections
(LO 4, 5)

In 1994, the Sequoia Company sold 20,000 units of its only product, and incurred a $100,000 loss (ignoring income taxes), as follows

SEQUOIA COMPANY
Income Statement
For Year Ended December 31, 1994

Sales		$ 600,000
Costs:		
Fixed	$250,000	
Variable	450,000	700,000
Net loss		$(100,000)

During a planning session for 1995's activities, the production manager has pointed out that variable costs can be reduced 50% by installing a machine that automates several operations presently being done by hand. To obtain these savings, the company must increase its annual fixed costs by $100,000. The maximum capacity of the system would be 40,000 units per year.

Required

1. Calculate 1994's break-even point in terms of dollars.
2. Calculate the dollar break-even point for 1995 under the assumption that the new machine is installed.
3. Prepare a CVP chart for 1955 under the assumption that the new machine is installed.
4. Prepare a forecasted income statement for 1995 that shows the expected results with the new machine installed. Assume that there will be no change in the selling price and no change in the number of units sold. The combined federal and state income tax rate is 40%.
5. Calculate the sales level required to earn $96,000 of after-tax income in 1995 with the new machine installed and with no change in the selling price. Prepare a forecasted income statement that shows the results at this sales level.

Problem 24–4A
Analyzing the effects of price and volume changes on profits
(LO 5)

Last year, Monte Carlo Company sold 35,000 units of product at $8 per unit. Manufacturing and selling the product required $60,000 of fixed manufacturing costs and $90,000 of fixed selling and administrative expenses. Last year's variable costs and expenses per unit were

Material	$2.00
Direct labor (paid on the basis of completed units)	1.50
Variable manufacturing overhead costs	0.20
Variable selling and administrative expenses	0.10

A new raw material has recently become available that is both easier to work with and cheaper than the old material. Management has already established that the company will switch to the new material because material costs can be decreased by 60% and direct labor costs can be decreased by 40%. The new material will not affect the product's quality or marketability. The next set of decisions concerns the marketing strategy to be used. Because the factory's output is creeping up to its annual capacity of 40,000 units, some consideration is being given to increasing the selling price to reduce the number of units sold. At this point, two strategies have been identified. Under Plan 1, the company will keep the price at the current level and sell the same volume as last year. This plan increases profits because of the materials change. Under Plan 2, the product's price will be increased by 25%, but unit sales volume will fall only 10%. Under both Plan 1 and Plan 2, all of the fixed costs and variable costs (per unit) will be exactly the same.

Required

1. Calculate the break-even point in dollars for Plan 1 and Plan 2.
2. Prepare CVP charts for Plan 1 and Plan 2.
3. Prepare side-by-side condensed forecasted income statements showing the anticipated results of Plan 1 and Plan 2. The statements should show sales, total fixed costs, total variable costs and expenses, income before taxes, income taxes (30% rate), and net income.

Problem 24–5A
Break-even analysis comparing different cost structures
(LO 5)

Tomberlin Company produces and sells two products, T and L. These products are manufactured in separate factories and marketed through completely different channels. Thus, they do not have any shared costs. Last year, Tomberlin sold 50,000 units of each product. The following income statements describe the financial results:

	Product T	Product L
Sales	$400,000	$400,000
Costs:		
Fixed costs	$ 50,000	$280,000
Variable costs	280,000	50,000
Total costs	$330,000	$330,000
Income before taxes	$ 70,000	$ 70,000
Income taxes (32% rate)	22,400	22,400
Net income	$ 47,600	$ 47,600

Required

1. Calculate the break-even point in dollars for each product.
2. Prepare a CVP chart for each product. Use 80,000 as the annual capacity.
3. Assume that the company expects the sales of each product to decline to 33,000 units in the upcoming year, even though the price will remain unchanged. Prepare a forecasted income statement that shows the expected profits from the two products. Follow the format of the preceding statement.
4. Assume that the company expects the sales of each product to increase to 64,000 units in the upcoming year, even though the price will remain unchanged. Prepare a forecasted income statement that shows the expected profits from the two products. Follow the format of the preceding statement.

Problem 24–6A
Break-even analysis with composite units
(LO 6)

Lucerne Company manufactures and sells three products, Red, Blue, and Gray. Their individual selling prices are

Product Red.	$ 80.00 per unit
Product Blue	$120.00 per unit
Product Gray	$ 60.00 per unit

The variable costs of manufacturing and selling the products have been:

Product Red.	$ 50.00 per unit
Product Blue	$ 80.00 per unit
Product Gray	$ 30.00 per unit

Their sales mix is a ratio of 1:2:3, and the annual fixed costs shared by all three products are $180,000. One particular item of raw materials is used in manufacturing all three products. Management has learned that a new material is just as good and cheaper. The new material would reduce the variable costs as follows: Product Red by $2.00, Product Blue by $8.00, and Product Gray by $2.00. But, the new material requires new equipment, which will increase annual fixed costs by $32,800.

Required

1. Assuming that the company continues to use the old material, determine the company's break-even point in dollars and the units of each product that would be sold at the break-even point.
2. Assuming that the company decides to use the new material, determine the company's new break-even point in dollars and the units of each product that would be sold at the break-even point.

Problem 24–7A
Analytical essay
(LO 1)

Exercise 24–4 presents measures of five types of costs. Assume that the relevant range of operation for the planning period is 401 to 800 units. Determine the total variable costs per unit (including any semivariable costs and the variable component of any mixed costs) within this range. Also, determine the total fixed costs (including any step-variable costs and the fixed component of any mixed costs) within this range. Predict the total cost that would be incurred if the volume equals 550 units.

Problem 24–8A
Analytical essay
(LO 1, 5)

Examine the product income statements presented in Problem 24–5A and answer the following;

a. Describe the cost structures for these two products.

b. Despite the differences in their cost structures, why do they experience identical incomes at the volume given in the problem?

c. If sales were to greatly decrease, which of these products would experience the greater loss? Why?

d. If sales were to greatly increase, which of these products would experience the greater profit? Why?

e. Describe some factors that might have created the different cost structures for these two products.

Provocative Problems

Provocative Problem 24–1
Thunder Corporation
(LO 4, 5)

Thunder Corporation produces replacement steering wheels for cars. Last year, the company's plant operated at a level near its capacity with the results shown in the following condensed income statement:

Sales (10,000 wheels)	$500,000
Cost of goods manufactured and sold (fixed, $100,000; variable, $180,000)	280,000
Gross profit	$220,000
Selling and administrative expenses (fixed, $50,000; variable, $40,000)	90,000
Income before taxes	$130,000

Aishi Motors has offered Thunder a two-year contract whereby it would buy 6,000 steering wheels each year for $40 each. Aishi would export these wheels overseas and these sales would not reduce domestic sales. To produce that many additional wheels, the company's plant would have to be expanded, with the result that all fixed manufacturing costs would be doubled. Variable manufacturing costs per unit would be the same in the new plant as in the old plant. The expansion would not affect either fixed or variable selling and administrative expenses.

Required

The manager is not sure whether Thunder should enter into the contract and has asked for your help in identifying information to help decide whether to accept the offer. Present your advice, based on the following information:

1. The predicted income before taxes for each year under the contract, assuming that there is no change in domestic sales.
2. A comparison of break-even sales levels before and after the plant addition. Because management is concerned about what happens after the contract expires, compute the break-even point, assuming no export sales.
3. The predicted income before taxes after the plant expansion but assuming no contract sales, and assuming that domestic sales continue at the current level.

Provocative Problem 24–2
TropiCall Beverages
(LO 4, 5, 6)

TropiCall Beverages sells three products called Citrus, Punchy, and Cooler. Last year's sales mix for the three products was in the ratio of 5:3:2, with combined sales of all products totaling 2 million cases. Citrus sells for $25 per case and has a 40% contribution rate. Punchy sells for $32 per case and has a 25% contribution rate, and Cooler sells for $40 per case and has a 35% contribution rate. The fixed costs of manufacturing and selling the products amount to $500,000. The company estimates that next year's combined sales of the three products will again be 2 million cases.

The sales manager has suggested that slanting the company's advertising and sales efforts toward Punchy and Cooler during the coming year, with no increases in cost, the sales mix of the three products will change to the ratio of 4:3:3.

Required

Explain why the company should change its sales mix as suggested. Support your answer with figures.

Provocative Problem 24–3
Great Blades Company
(LO 5)

Great Blades Company operated at near capacity during the last year and its management expects a 30% increase in this year's unit sales. As a result, the management is trying to decide how to provide adequate capacity for this year. The search for a solution has ended up with two alternatives. In both cases, the selling price would remain at last year's level to discourage competitors from entering the market. The first alternative would keep fixed costs constant but would increase variable costs to 50% of the product's selling price. The second alternative would increase fixed costs over current levels by 18% but would not affect variable costs as a percent of sales.

Last year's income statement for Great Blades provided the following summarized information:

Sales	$1,200,000
Costs:	
Variable costs	(480,000)
Fixed costs	(500,000)
Pretax income	$ 220,000

Required

Which alternative do you recommend? Support your recommendation with any relevant data.

Provocative Problem 24–4
International Business Machines Corporation

Turn to the annual report for IBM in Appendix J and find the "five-year comparison of selected financial data" for 1986 through 1990. Use this information to determine the total revenues and the total costs deducted from revenues for each year (without considering the cumulative effect of changes in accounting for income taxes in 1988). Then, plot the revenues and the costs on a scatter diagram. Draw in an estimated line of total cost behavior, and discuss your findings. (If you have access to a computer program that executes a least-squares regression, use it.)

Provocative Problem 24–5
As a Matter of Ethics: Essay

Ethics

Read the ethics case on page 1295. What do you think the accountant should do? Who would gain from manipulating the predicted figures? Who would lose? What would happen if the project was accepted and then turned out to be a disaster?

Answers to Objective Review Questions

LO 1 (*e*)
LO 2 (*e*)
LO 3 (*d*)
LO 4 (*c*)
LO 5 (*c*)
LO 6 (*d*)
LO 7 (*b*)

CHAPTER

25

The Master Budget: A Formal Plan for the Business

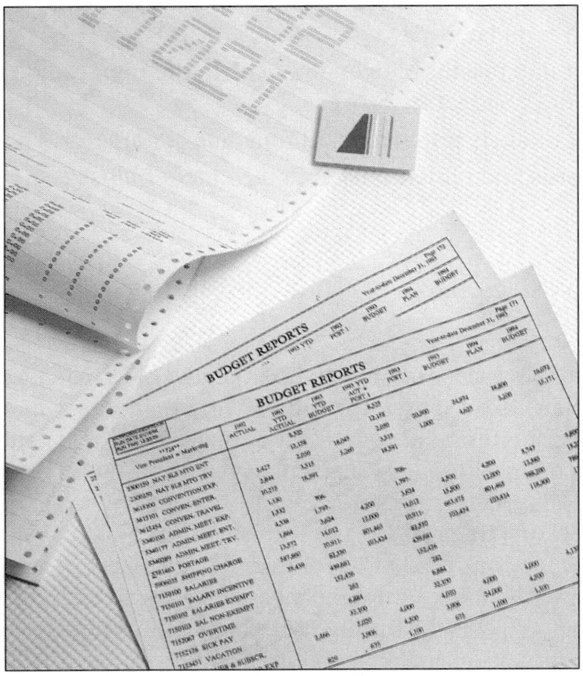

Once an overall business plan has been created, top management must communicate it to the managers and other employees who will put it into effect. They need to know what specific goals to work toward and what capital and human resources will be available. Budgets are used to communicate these plans.

Topical Coverage

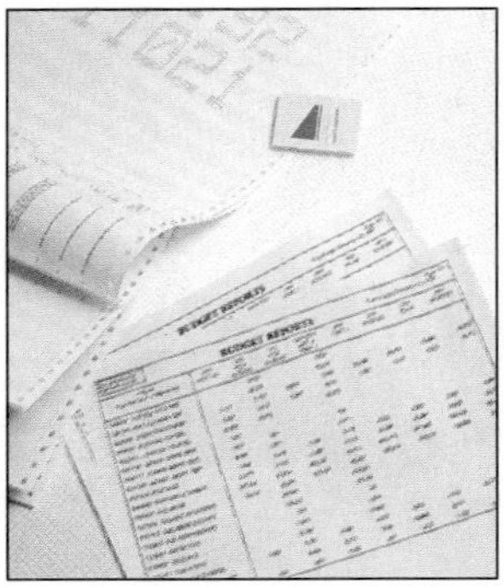

Once management has used cost-volume-profit analysis to select an operating strategy for the upcoming period, it must turn that strategy into specific plans. These plans are usually compiled in a master budget. The budgeting process serves several purposes, including motivation and communication. The budget also coordinates the activities of all parts of the company toward its objectives. And, the budget later serves as a standard for evaluating actual results and performance. In this chapter, you learn how to prepare a master budget as the formal plan for the future activities of a company. If you ever go into business for yourself, your ability to prepare this kind of formal plan could very well help you achieve success.

Learning Objectives

After studying Chapter 25, you should be able to:

1. Explain the importance of budgeting and describe its benefits.
2. Describe the components of a master budget and list the sequence of steps in preparing a master budget.
3. Prepare each component of a master budget and explain the importance of each budget to the overall budgeting process.
4. Integrate the component budgets into budgeted financial statements.
5. Define or explain the words and phrases listed in the chapter glossary.

The Importance of Budgeting

LO 1 Explain the importance of budgeting and describe its benefits.

If a business is to accomplish the variety of objectives expected of it, management must first carefully plan its activities for future weeks, months, and years. Then, managers should monitor and control the actual activities so that they conform to the plan. In many situations, particularly in a continuous improvement environment, management finds it useful to replace the original version of the plan with a new one that reflects new information. This revised plan then serves as the basis for controlling the company's activities.

Budgeting is the process of planning future business actions and expressing them as formal plans. The **budget** is the formal statement of the company's future plans. Because the economic or financial aspects of the business are the primary relevant factors involved in management decisions, budgets are usually expressed in monetary terms.

Benefits from Budgeting

All business managers should engage in planning because it is absolutely necessary if business activities are to succeed in the long run. Managers who plan carefully and formalize plans with a complete budgeting process can expect to obtain the benefits described in the following paragraphs.

Budgeting Promotes Study, Research, and a Focus on the Future

When management plans the future with the care and attention to detail needed for preparing the budget, the process involves thorough study and research. This process should not only lead to the best conceivable plans but also instill in the managers the good habit of making careful analyses before reaching decisions. In effect, a careful budgeting process tends to promote good decision making.

In addition, the relevant items for a budgetary analysis are concerned with the future. Thus, the budgeting process focuses management's attention on future events and the opportunities available to the business. The pressures of daily operating problems often divert management's attention and take precedence over planning. If so, the company can be left without carefully considered objectives. A good budgeting system counteracts this tendency by formalizing the planning process. Budgeting makes planning an explicit management responsibility.

Budgeting Provides a Basis for Evaluating Performance

The control function requires management to evaluate business operations in comparison to norms or objectives. Then, using these evaluations, management can implement appropriate corrective actions. In evaluating operations, they can compare actual results against these two alternative norms or objectives: (1) past performance or (2) expected performance as described in the budget.

Although past performance is occasionally used as the basis of evaluation, budgeted performance is potentially superior for determining whether actual results are acceptable or show a need for corrective action. Past performance is often inferior as a standard for evaluation because it fails to take into account changes that may affect current activities. For example, a firm achieved past sales under economic conditions that may be dramatically different from those shaping current sales results. Changes in overall economic conditions, shifts in competitive advantages within the industry, new product developments, increased or decreased advertising commitments, and other factors all tend to reduce the usefulness of comparisons between past results and recent performance.

On the other hand, managers develop budgeted performance levels after careful research that attempts to anticipate such broad factors and take their effects into account. Thus, budgets provide the benefit of a superior basis for evaluating performance. In turn, management has a more effective control system.

Budgeting Is a Source of Motivation

Because budgeting provides standards for evaluating actual performance, the budget and how it is used can significantly affect the attitudes of the employees who are evaluated. If management is not careful, the budgeting process can have a negative effect on employees' attitudes. For example, budgeted levels of performance must be realistic to avoid discouraging employees. Also, the personnel who will be evaluated should be consulted and involved in preparing the budget in order to increase their commitment to meeting it. In addition, evaluations of performance must allow the affected employees to explain the reasons for apparent performance deficiencies. After all, the managerial accounting reports may not tell the complete story.

In summary, these three guidelines are important:

1. The employees who will be affected by a budget should be consulted when the budget is prepared.
2. The objectives reflected in a budget should be obtainable.
3. The subsequent evaluations of performance should be made carefully with opportunities to explain apparent deficiencies.

When these guidelines are followed, budgeting can be a strongly positive motivating force in the organization. Budgeted performance levels can provide goals that individuals strive to attain or even exceed as they fulfill their responsibilities to the organization.

Budgeting Is a Means of Coordinating Business Activities

When a business is large enough to be organized into departments, an important management task is to be sure that the departments' activities all contribute to meeting the overall goals of the company. This task requires careful coordination. Budgeting provides a way to achieve this coordination.

When a budget is prepared, each department's objectives are determined in advance. Carefully designed objectives can lead each department to contribute to achieving overall goals for the company. For example, managers can budget a production department to produce approximately the number of units the selling department is expected to sell. Then, they can budget the purchasing department to buy raw materials on the basis of budgeted production. Also, they can budget the hiring activities of the personnel department to consider the budgeted production levels. In this way, the budgeting process coordinates the activities of various departments to meet the company's overall goals.

Budgeting Is a Means of Communicating Plans and Instructions

In a very small business, the manager can adequately explain business plans directly to the employees. For example, the manager can communicate specific operating plans to the employees with frequent conversations. However, conversations can create uncertainty and confusion if they are not supported by documents that clearly state the plans. Further, such conversations are inadequate for all but the smallest companies. It is better to use a written budget that informs employees throughout the organization about management's broad plans for the business. The budget also communicates management's specific plans for actions to be taken by responsible employees during the budget period.

AS A MATTER OF
Ethics

In the course of working in the budget office of a large public corporation, an accounting clerk discovers that the actual earnings for the current quarter are going to be far below what was budgeted and announced in the business press as the expected amount. In light of this information, the clerk calls a stockbroker and gives an order to sell short 1,000 shares of the corporation's stock. (Under this arrangement, the broker borrows shares from another customer who owns them, sells the borrowed shares in the market, and then later buys the same number of shares to go back into that customer's account. If the value of the shares declines, the short-seller makes a profit.)

At about the same time, one of the company's top officers decides to take a higher position with a competitor in the same industry but in a different part of the country. Before his departure is announced to the public, he sells all the shares of the company that were granted to him or bought by him as part of his compensation plan. He intends to use the proceeds to acquire a new house and to buy shares issued by his new employer. At the time he sells, he knows about the coming news of the earnings shortfall. He also knows that his leaving will significantly hamper the company's ability to improve earnings, and that his arrival at the new company will greatly enhance its ability to capture market share.

Do any of these actions seem unethical?

The Budget Committee

To achieve the best results, the task of preparing a budget should not be the sole responsibility of any one department. Similarly, the budget generally should not be simply handed down as top management's final word. Rather, budget figures and budget estimates are often more useful if they are developed through a *bottom up* process. For example, the sales department should have a hand in preparing sales estimates. Likewise, the production department should have initial responsibility for preparing its own expense budget. Otherwise, sales representatives and production employees may believe that the budget figures are meaningless because they may think that they were prepared by people who know little, if anything, about sales and production problems and needs.

Although budgets usually should be developed by this bottom up process, the budgeting system also requires central guidance to keep matters in balance. This guidance can be supplied by a budget committee of department heads and other high-level executives who are responsible for seeing that budgeted amounts are realistic and coordinated. If a department submits initial budget figures that do not reflect efficient performance, the budget committee should return them to the department with explanatory comments on how to improve them. Then, the originating department must either adjust its proposals or explain why they should be accepted. Communication between the originating department and the budget committee should continue as needed to ensure that both parties accept the budget as reasonable, attainable, and desirable.

The Budget Period

For convenience, budget periods usually coincide with accounting periods. Thus, most companies prepare at least an annual budget. In addition to their annual budgets, many companies prepare long-range budgets that set forth major objectives for periods of 3, 5, or even 10 years in advance. Long-range budgets should plan the accomplishment of long-range objectives. These budgets are particularly important in planning major expenditures for plant and equipment. Additionally, long-range budgets are useful for deciding whether to finance major projects by issuing bonds, issuing stock, or retaining cash generated by operating activities.

The annual budget for a business reflects the objectives adopted for the next year. To provide more specific guidance, the annual budget is usually broken down into quarterly or monthly budgets. Short-term budgets like these are useful because they allow management to promptly evaluate actual performance and take corrective action. Once they know quarterly or monthly results, managers can compare them to budgeted amounts in a report similar to Illustration 25–1. Notice that the report shows the actual results, the budgeted results, and any difference (called a *variance*). Management can use the third column of variances to quickly identify potential areas for improvement.

Many businesses follow the practice of **continuous budgeting** by preparing **rolling budgets.** As each monthly or quarterly budget period goes by, these firms revise their entire set of budgets, adding new monthly or quarterly budgets to replace the ones that have lapsed. Thus, at any point in time, monthly or quarterly budgets are available for the next 12 months or four quarters. Illustration 25–2 represents the five rolling budgets that would be prepared starting in December 1994. The first one covers the next four quarters through December 1995. Then, in March 1995, the company would prepare another rolling budget for the next four quarters through March 1996. The same process would be repeated every three months. As a result, management is continuously planning ahead. Also notice that any particular quarter's budget is drawn up four times using the most recent information available. For example, Illustration 25–2 shows that the budget for the fourth quarter of 1995 would be prepared in December 1994, and in March, June, and September of 1995. In contrast, if continuous budgeting is not used, the budget for this fourth quarter will be nine months old when it is finally implemented. In a rapidly changing environment, this plan could easily be out of date.

The Master Budget

When a company formalizes a comprehensive or overall plan for the future, the resulting budget is a **master budget.** As an overall plan, the master budget includes specific plans for expected sales, the units of product to be produced, the merchandise (or materials) to be purchased, the expenses to be incurred, the long-term assets to be purchased, and the amounts of cash to be borrowed or loans to be repaid. The planned activities of each subunit of the business should be separately presented within the master budget.

To include definite plans for all activities, a master budget contains several subbudgets. The subbudgets connect with each other, or *articulate,* to form the overall coordinated plan for the business. Thus, the master budget typically includes budgets for sales, purchases, production, various expenses,

ILLUSTRATION 25–1

Comparing Actual Performance with Budgeted Performance

CONSOLIDATED STORES, INC.
Income Statement with Variations from Budget
For Month Ended April 30, 1994

	Actual	Budget	Variance
Sales	$63,500	$60,000	$+3,500
Less: Sales returns and allowances	1,800	1,700	+100
Sales discounts	1,200	1,150	+50
Net sales	$60,500	$57,150	$+3,350
Cost of goods sold:			
Merchandise inventory, April 1, 1994	$42,000	$44,000	$−2,000
Purchases, net	39,100	38,000	+1,100
Transportation-in	1,250	1,200	+50
Goods available for sale	$82,350	$83,200	$ −850
Merchandise inventory, April 30, 1994	41,000	44,100	−3,100
Cost of goods sold	$41,350	$39,100	$+2,250
Gross profit	$19,150	$18,050	$+1,100
Operating expenses:			
Selling expenses:			
Sales salaries	$ 6,250	$ 6,000	$ +250
Advertising	900	800	+100
Store supplies	550	500	+50
Depreciation, store equipment	1,600	1,600	
Total selling expenses	$ 9,300	$ 8,900	$ +400
General and administrative expenses:			
Office salaries	$ 2,000	$ 2,000	
Office supplies used	165	150	$ +15
Rent	1,100	1,100	
Insurance	200	200	
Depreciation, office equipment	100	100	
Total general and administrative expenses	$ 3,565	$ 3,550	$ +15
Total operating expenses	$12,865	$12,450	$ +415
Income from operations	$ 6,285	$ 5,600	$ +685

capital expenditures, and cash. Also, managers may express the expected financial results of the planned activities in a budgeted income statement for the budget period and a budgeted balance sheet as of the end of the budget period.

Preparing the Master Budget

In general, the number and types of budgets included in the master budget depend on the size and complexity of the business. As a minimum, a master budget should include the following items:

1. Operating budgets.
   a. *Sales budget.*
   b. For merchandising companies: *merchandise purchases budget* (describing the number of units to be purchased).

ILLUSTRATION 25–2

Rolling Budgets

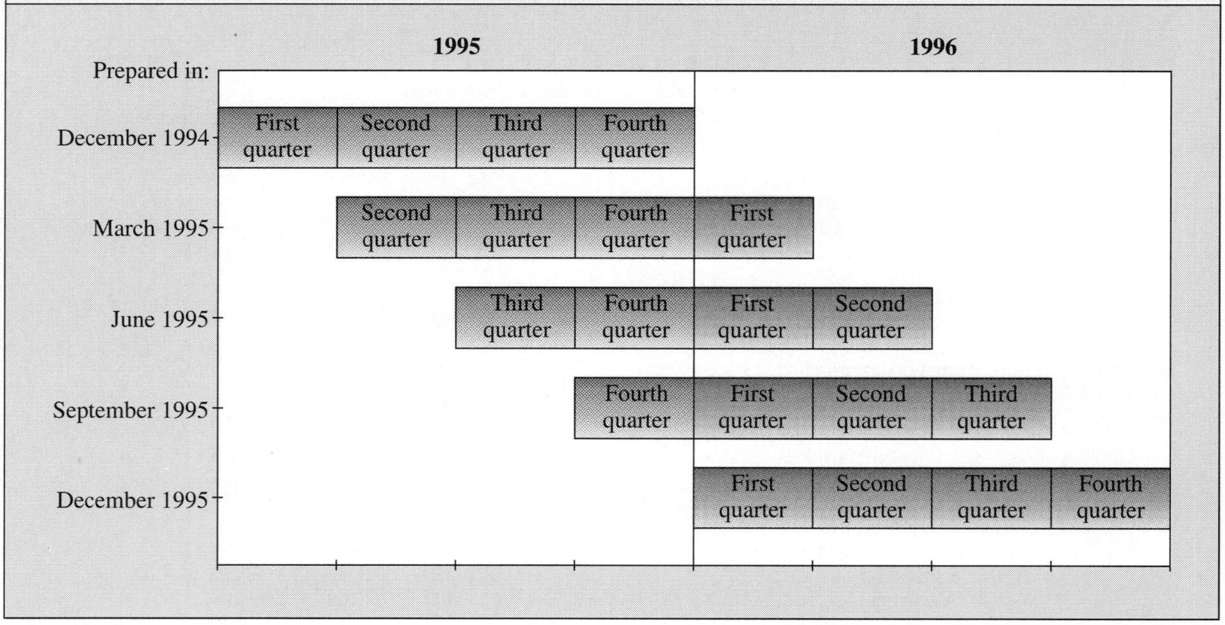

LO 2 Describe the components of a master budget and list the sequence of steps in preparing a master budget.

   c. For manufacturing companies:
      (1) *Production budget* (describing the number of units to be produced).
      (2) *Manufacturing budget* (describing the planned manufacturing costs).
   d. *Selling expense budget.*
   e. *General and administrative expense budget.*
2. *Capital expenditures budget* (describing the budgeted expenditures for new plant and equipment).
3. Financial budgets.
   a. *Cash budget* (describing the budgeted cash receipts and disbursements).
   b. *Budgeted income statement.*
   c. *Budgeted balance sheet.*

In addition to these budgets, managers may include supporting calculations and schedules in the master budget.

Management cannot prepare some budgets until other budgets are complete. For example, the merchandise purchases budget cannot be prepared until the sales budget is available because the number of units to be purchased depends on how many units are expected to be sold. As a result, you must prepare the budgets within the master budget in the following sequence, which is also represented as flowcharts in Illustration 25–3:

First: The *sales budget* must be prepared first because the amount of sales determines the level of activity in all parts of the company.

ILLUSTRATION 25-3

Sequence of Budgeting Steps

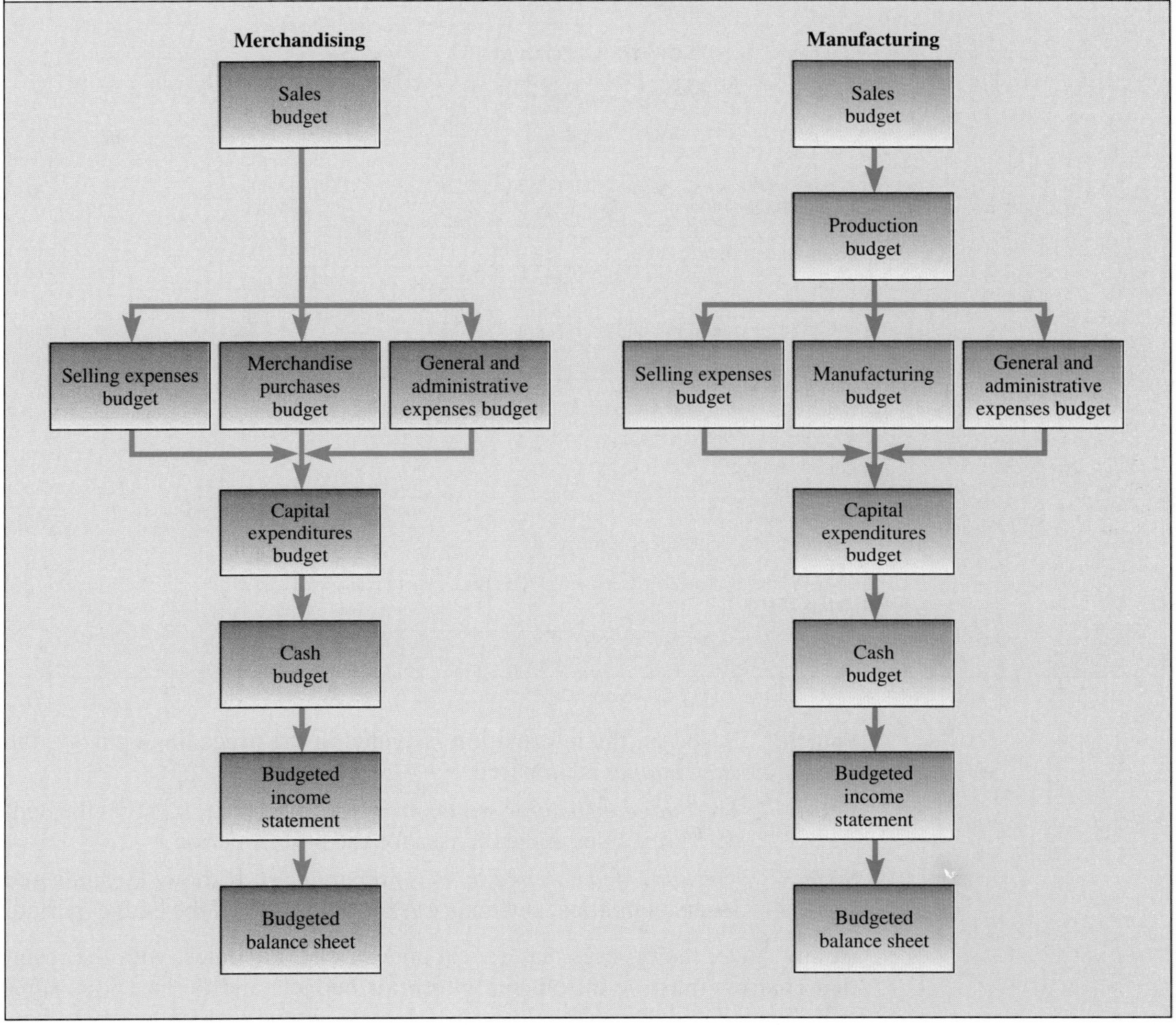

Second: The other *operating budgets* are prepared next. For merchandising companies, the budgets for merchandise purchases, selling expenses, and general and administrative expenses can be prepared in any sequence. For manufacturing companies, the production budget must be prepared before the manufacturing budget because the number of units to be produced clearly shapes the quantities of materials, direct labor, and overhead to be budgeted. The budgets for selling expenses and general and administrative expenses can also be prepared at this stage.

Third: The *capital expenditures budget* is prepared next, but only if capital expenditures are anticipated during the budget period.

ILLUSTRATION 25–4

The Balance Sheet Immediately Prior to Future Budgeted Periods

NORTHERN COMPANY
Balance Sheet
September 30, 1994

Assets

Cash		$ 20,000
Accounts receivable		42,000
Inventory (9,000 units @ $6)		54,000
Equipment*	$200,000	
Less accumulated depreciation	(36,000)	164,000
Total assets		$280,000

Liabilities and Stockholders' Equity

Liabilities:		
Accounts payable	$ 58,200	
Income taxes payable (due October 31, 1994)	20,000	
Note payable to bank	10,000	$ 88,200
Stockholders' equity:		
Common stock	$150,000	
Retained earnings	41,800	191,800
Total liabilities and stockholders' equity		$280,000

* The equipment is being depreciated on a straight-line basis over 10 years. Predicted salvage value is $20,000.

Fourth: Based on the information provided in the preceding budgets, the *cash budget* is prepared.

Fifth: The *budgeted income statement* is prepared next. It shows the budgeted revenues and expenses for the budget period.

Sixth: The *budgeted balance sheet* is prepared last. It shows the budgeted assets, liabilities, and equity as of the last day of the budget period.

At any stage, the process may reveal undesirable outcomes, with the result that changes must be introduced into prior budgets and the previous steps must be repeated. For example, an early version of the cash budget may show that an inadequate amount of cash would be generated under the existing plan unless cash outlays are reduced. Or, a preliminary budgeted balance sheet may indicate that too much debt would result from an ambitious capital expenditures budget. In either case, revised plans may be needed.

Illustrating the Preparation of the Master Budget

This section of the chapter explains the procedures used to prepare the master budget for Northern Company, a retailer of a single product. The company's master budget includes operating, capital expenditure, and cash budgets for each month in a quarter. It also includes a budgeted income statement for each quarter and a budgeted balance sheet as of the last day of each quarter. On the following pages, Northern Company budgets are prepared for October, November, and December 1994. Illustration 25–4 presents the beginning balance sheet for this budgeting period.

ILLUSTRATION 25–5

Sales Budget Showing Planned Unit Sales and Dollar Sales

NORTHERN COMPANY
Monthly Sales Budget
October 1994–January 1995

	Budgeted Unit Sales	Budgeted Unit Price	Budgeted Total Sales
September 1994 (actual)	7,000	$10	$ 70,000
October 1994.	10,000	10	100,000
November 1994	8,000	10	80,000
December 1994	14,000	10	140,000
January 1995.	9,000	10	90,000

Preparing a Sales Budget

LO 3 Prepare each component of a master budget and explain the importance of each budget to the overall budgeting process.

The first step in preparing the master budget is the development of the **sales budget.** This plan shows the units of goods to be sold and the revenue to be derived from the sales. The sales budget is the starting point in the budgeting process because the plans for most departments are related to sales. The sales budget should emerge from a careful analysis of forecasted economic and market conditions, plant capacity, proposed selling expenses (such as advertising), and predictions of unit sales. Because people normally feel a greater commitment to goals they have had a hand in setting, the sales personnel of a company are usually asked to develop predictions of sales for each territory and department. Another advantage of using this participatory approach to budgeting is that it applies the knowledge and experience of those people actually engaged in the activity. The final sales budget is then based on these predictions after the budget committee has considered the forecasted business conditions, selling expenses, and other factors.

During September 1994, Northern Company sold 7,000 units of product at $10 per unit. After obtaining predictions from sales personnel and considering the market conditions affecting Northern Company's product, the sales budget in Illustration 25–5 is established. Because the purchasing department must base December 1994 purchases on estimated sales for January 1995, the sales budget is expanded to include January 1995, as well as the three months in the fourth quarter.

The sales budget in Illustration 25–5 is more detailed than simple projections of total sales. Specifically, it contains forecasts of both unit sales and unit prices. Some companies prepare a sales budget expressed only in terms of total sales dollars. In practice, most sales budgets are more detailed because they must show units and unit prices for many different products, classified by sales representative, by department, and by territory.

Preparing a Merchandise Purchases Budget

A variety of sophisticated techniques help management make inventory purchasing decisions. These techniques all recognize that the number of units to be added to inventory depends on the budgeted sales volume. Whether a company manufactures or purchases the product it sells, budgeted future sales volume is the primary factor to consider in most inventory management decisions.

Just-in-Time Inventory Systems. The managers of *just-in-time* inventory systems use sales budgets for very short periods (covering perhaps as few as one or two days) to order just enough merchandise or materials to satisfy the immediate sales demand. As a result, the level of inventory on hand is held to a minimum (including zero in ideal situations). A just-in-time system minimizes the costs of maintaining an inventory. However, just-in-time systems are practical only if customers are content to order in advance or if managers can determine short-term sales demand with very little error. Also, suppliers must be able and willing to ship small quantities regularly and promptly.

Safety Stock Inventory System. The market conditions and manufacturing processes for many products do not allow a just-in-time system to be used. Instead, many companies keep enough inventory on hand to reduce the risk of running out. This practice requires sufficient purchases to satisfy the budgeted sales amounts and to maintain an additional quantity of inventory as a **safety stock.** The safety stock provides protection against lost sales caused by unfulfilled demands from customers or delays in shipments from suppliers.

Merchandise Purchases Budget. Companies usually express a **merchandise purchases budget** in both units and dollars. This table shows the general formula for compiling a purchases budget:

	Units
Budgeted ending inventory	7,200
Add budgeted sales	10,000
Required units of available merchandise	17,200
Deduct the beginning inventory	(9,000)
Inventory to be purchased	8,200

In equation form, the formula is

$$\begin{array}{ccccccc} \text{Inventory} & & \text{Budgeted} & & \text{Budgeted} & & \text{Budgeted} \\ \text{to be} & = & \text{ending} & + & \text{sales for} & - & \text{beginning} \\ \text{purchased} & & \text{inventory} & & \text{the period} & & \text{inventory} \end{array}$$

If the calculation is expressed in units and only one product is involved, the number of dollars of inventory to be purchased can be budgeted simply by multiplying the units to be purchased by the cost per unit.

After considering the cost of maintaining an inventory and the risk associated with a temporary inventory shortage, Northern Company has decided that the number of units in its inventory at the end of each month should equal 90% of the next month's predicted sales. In other words, the inventory at the end of October should equal 90% of the budgeted November sales, the November ending inventory should equal 90% of the expected December sales, and so on. Also, the company's suppliers have indicated that the September

ILLUSTRATION 25–6

NORTHERN COMPANY
Merchandise Purchases Budget
October, November, and December 1994

	October	November	December
Next month's budgeted sales (units)	8,000	14,000	9,000
Ratio of inventory to future sales	× 90%	× 90%	× 90%
Budgeted ending inventory (units)	7,200	12,600	8,100
Add: Budgeted sales for the month (units) . .	10,000	8,000	14,000
Required units of available merchandise . . .	17,200	20,600	22,100
Deduct beginning inventory (units)	(9,000)	(7,200)	(12,600)
Number of units to be purchased	8,200	13,400	9,500
Budgeted cost per unit	$6	$6	$6
Budgeted cost of merchandise purchases . . .	$49,200	$80,400	$57,000

1994 per unit cost of $6 should remain unchanged through January 1995. Based on these factors and on the fact that 9,000 units were on hand at September 30 (see Illustration 25–4), the company prepared the merchandise purchases budget in Illustration 25–6.

The first three lines of Northern Company's merchandise purchases budget determine the required ending inventories. Then, budgeted unit sales are added to the desired ending inventory and the beginning inventory is subtracted to determine the budgeted number of units to be purchased. Finally, the last lines calculate the budgeted cost of the purchases by multiplying the units to be purchased by the predicted cost per unit.

Recall from the previous discussion that some budgeting systems describe only the total dollars of budgeted sales. Likewise, a system may state a merchandise purchases budget only in terms of the total cost of merchandise to be purchased without stating the number of units to be purchased. When this practice is used, however, you must assume a constant relationship between sales and cost of goods sold. For example, Northern Company expects the cost of goods sold to equal 60% of sales. (Note that the budgeted sales price is $10 and the budgeted unit cost is $6.) Thus, its cost of goods sold could be budgeted in dollars on the basis of budgeted sales without requiring information on the number of units involved. However, it would still be necessary to consider the effects of the beginning and ending inventories in determining the amounts to be purchased.

Preparing Production Budgets and Manufacturing Budgets

Because Northern Company does not manufacture its product, its budget for acquiring goods to be sold is a *merchandise purchases budget,* as shown in Illustration 25–6. A manufacturing company must prepare a **production budget** instead of a merchandise purchases budget. A production budget shows

ILLUSTRATION 25–7

NORTHERN COMPANY
Selling Expense Budget
October, November, and December 1994

	October	November	December	Total
Budgeted sales	$100,000	$80,000	$140,000	$320,000
Sales commission percentage	× 10%	× 10%	× 10%	× 10%
Sales commissions	$ 10,000	$ 8,000	$ 14,000	$ 32,000
Salary for sales manager	2,000	2,000	2,000	6,000
Total selling expenses	$ 12,000	$10,000	$ 16,000	$ 38,000

the number of units to be produced each month. Production budgets are similar to merchandise purchases budgets except that the number of units to be purchased each month (as shown in Illustration 25–6) would be replaced by the number of units to be manufactured each month. Also, a production budget does not show costs because it is always expressed entirely in units of product. The budgeted production costs (for materials, direct labor, and overhead) are shown in the **manufacturing budget**, which is based on the production volume in the production budget.

A manufacturing budget shows the budgeted costs for raw materials, direct labor, and manufacturing overhead. In many companies, the manufacturing budget actually consists of three subbudgets: a raw materials purchases budget, a direct labor budget, and an overhead budget. These budgets show the total cost of goods to be manufactured during the budget period.

Preparing a Selling Expense Budget

The initial responsibility for preparing a **selling expense budget** typically belongs to the vice president of marketing or an equivalent sales manager. This budget is a plan listing the types and amounts of selling expenses expected during the budget period. Typically, the sales budget is prepared and then the selling expense budget is created to provide sufficient selling expenses to meet those sales goals. Thus, predictions of selling expenses are based on both the tentative sales budget and on the experience of previous periods adjusted for expected changes.

After some or all of the master budget is tentatively prepared, management may decide that the projected sales volume is inadequate. If so, subsequent adjustments in the sales budget may require corresponding adjustments in the selling expense budget.

Northern Company's selling expenses consist of commissions paid to sales personnel and a $2,000 monthly salary paid to the sales manager. Sales commissions equal 10% of total sales and are paid during the month the sales are made. No advertising expenses are budgeted for this particular quarter. Illustration 25–7 shows the selling expense budget for Northern Company.

ILLUSTRATION 25–8

NORTHERN COMPANY
General and Administrative Expense Budget
October, November, and December 1994

	October	November	December	Total
Administrative salaries	$4,500	$4,500	$4,500	$13,500
Depreciation of equipment	1,500	1,500	1,500	4,500
Total general and administrative expenses	$6,000	$6,000	$6,000	$18,000

Preparing a General and Administrative Expense Budget

The office manager usually has the responsibility for preparing the initial proposal for the **general and administrative expense budget.** This budget is a plan that shows the predicted operating expenses that are not included in the selling expenses budget. The amounts of variable general and administrative expenses depend on budgeted sales volume. However, many of these expenses are fixed and do not vary in proportion to changes in sales volume.

Although interest expense and income tax expense are often classified as general and administrative expenses in published income statements, they generally cannot be planned at this stage of the budgeting process. The prediction of interest expense must follow the preparation of the cash budget, which determines the extent to which any loans are needed. The predicted income tax expense depends on the amount of pretax income on the budgeted income statement. In addition, interest and income taxes are usually beyond the control of the office manager. As a result, they should not be used in evaluating that person's performance in comparison to the budget.

General and administrative expenses for Northern Company include administrative salaries of $54,000 per year, or $4,500 per month. The salaries are paid each month when they are earned. Using the facts described in Illustration 25–4, the depreciation on the company's equipment is $18,000 per year [($200,000 – $20,000)/10 years], or $1,500 per month ($18,000/12 months). Illustration 25–8 shows the budget for these expenses.

Preparing a Capital Expenditures Budget

The next step is preparing the **capital expenditures budget.** This budget lists dollar amounts to be received from disposing of equipment and to be spent on purchasing additional equipment if the proposed production program is carried out. Because production capacity is limited by the company's plant and equipment, this budget is usually affected by long-range plans for the business instead of short-term sales budgets for the next year or quarter. Nevertheless, the process of preparing a sales or manufacturing budget may reveal that the

AS A MATTER OF *Opinion*

Mr. Van Gelder received his B.S. degree from Rensselaer Polytechnic Institute and his MBA degree from the University of Michigan.

After working at a number of different positions during a 19-year career at Monsanto Company, he was named president of Koch Engineering Company in 1984. He is currently chairman of Koch Engineering Company and vice president, chemical technology for Koch Industries, Inc.

John M. Van Gelder

Budgeting forms a major part of the acquisition economics package that Koch Industries prepares for potential acquisition candidates.

When evaluating a company for potential purchase, we project the firm's net income, capital requirements, and personnel requirements for 15 years into the future—the normal estimated time period an acquired firm is expected to contribute to Koch's overall performance. We begin by projecting sales volumes, prices, and total revenues for each year. Constantly looking for synergistic opportunities to combine resources and services of the new firm with our existing operations, we derive the planned cost of sales for each revenue amount and estimate periodic selling, general, and administrative expenses. We combine these elements to form projected net income for the purchase candidate for each of the 15 years of the estimated life of the project. At the same time income statements are being built, and for the same time period, we model capital requirements and personnel requirements to support the income projections.

Comparing the budgeted investment cost of a potential acquisition with resource (capital and personnel) availability and the expected future income, we decide the appropriate price to offer for the candidate firm. If our acquisition occurs, we then compare the actual earnings generated, by year, to those budgeted in the acquisition model to measure our performance.

company needs more capacity and that additional equipment must be purchased.

The process of evaluating and planning capital expenditures is called *capital budgeting*. Because capital expenditures often involve long-run commitments of large amounts, planning those expenditures is an important responsibility of higher levels of management. Typically, capital expenditures involve large dollar amounts that have a major effect on the predicted cash flows and perhaps on the company's need for debt or equity financing. Accordingly, the capital expenditures budget may be closely tied to management's evaluation of the company's ability to service more debt. You will learn more about capital budgeting in Chapter 27.

Northern Company does not anticipate any disposals of equipment through December 1994. However, management plans to acquire additional equipment for $25,000 cash near the end of December 1994. Because of the limited capital expenditures, no separate budget for them is presented here. However, the cash budget in Illustration 25–9 includes this amount.

ILLUSTRATION 25–9

NORTHERN COMPANY
Cash Budget
October, November, and December 1994

	October	November	December
Beginning cash balance	$ 20,000	$ 20,000	$ 22,272
Cash receipts from customers	82,000	92,000	104,000
Total cash available	$102,000	$112,000	$126,272
Cash disbursements:			
Payments for merchandise	$ 58,200	$ 49,200	$ 80,400
Sales commissions (Illustration 25–7)	10,000	8,000	14,000
Salaries:			
Sales (Illustration 25–7)	2,000	2,000	2,000
Administrative (Illustration 25–8)	4,500	4,500	4,500
Accrued income taxes payable (Illustration 25–4)	20,000		
Dividends ($150,000 × 2%)		3,000	
Interest on bank loan:			
October ($10,000 × 1%)	100		
November ($22,800 × 1%)		228	
Purchase of equipment			25,000
Total cash disbursements	$ 94,800	$ 66,928	$125,900
Preliminary balance	$ 7,200	$ 45,072	$ 372
Additional loan from bank	12,800		19,628
Repayment of loan from bank		(22,800)	
Ending cash balance	$ 20,000	$ 22,272	$ 20,000
Loan balance, end of month	$ 22,800	$ -0-	$ 19,628

Preparing a Cash Budget

After developing tentative budgets for sales, merchandise purchases, expenses, and capital expenditures, the next step is preparing the **cash budget.** This budget shows the expected cash inflows and outflows during the budget period. The cash budget is especially helpful in maintaining a cash balance adequate for meeting the company's obligations. Thus, by preparing a cash budget, management can prearrange loans to cover any anticipated cash shortages well before they are needed. On the other hand, the cash budget also helps management avoid having a cash balance that is too large. Too much cash is undesirable because it earns a relatively low rate of return, if any. For these reasons, a company that prepares a cash budget usually has better control over its cash balances.

In preparing the cash budget, you add expected receipts to the beginning cash balance and deduct expected expenditures. If the expected cash balance is inadequate, the required additional cash appears in the budget as a planned increase from short-term loans. If the tentative ending balance exceeds the minimum, the excess should be applied to repaying the loans or to acquiring temporary investments.

Much of the information needed for preparing the cash budget can be obtained directly from the previously prepared operating and capital expenditures budgets. However, further investigation and additional calculations may be necessary to determine the amounts to be included.

Illustration 25–9 shows the cash budget for Northern Company. In the illustration, October's beginning cash balance was obtained from the September 30, 1994, balance sheet in Illustration 25–4.

Budgeted sales of Northern Company were shown in Illustration 25–5. An analysis of past sales records indicates that 40% of Northern Company's sales are for cash. The remaining 60% are credit sales and these customers can be expected to pay in full during the month after the sales. The budgeted cash receipts from customers are calculated as follows:

	September	October	November	December
Sales	$70,000	$100,000	$80,000	$140,000
Ending accounts receivable (60%)	$42,000	$ 60,000	$48,000	$ 84,000
Cash receipts from:				
Cash sales (40%)		$ 40,000	$32,000	$ 56,000
Collections of prior month's receivables		42,000	60,000	48,000
Total cash receipts		$ 82,000	$92,000	$104,000

The calculation shows that October's budgeted cash receipts consist of $40,000 from expected cash sales ($100,000 × 40%) plus the anticipated collection of $42,000 of accounts receivable from the end of September. Also note that each month's total cash receipts are listed on the second line of Illustration 25–9.

Northern Company's purchases of merchandise are entirely on account, and full payments are made during the month following the purchases. Thus, in Illustration 25–9, the cash disbursements for purchases are obtained from the September 30, 1994, balance sheet (Illustration 25–4) and from the merchandise purchases budget (Illustration 25–6) as follows:

October payments (September 30 balance)	$58,200
November payments (October purchases)	49,200
December payments (November purchases)	80,400

Because sales commissions and all salaries are paid monthly, the budgeted cash disbursements for these expenses came from the selling expense budget (Illustration 25–7) and the general and administrative expense budget (Illustration 25–8). Notice that the cash budget is not affected by the depreciation expense in the general and administrative expenses budget.

As indicated in the September 30, 1994, balance sheet (Illustration 25–4), accrued income taxes are due and payable in October. The cash budget in

Illustration 25–9 shows this $20,000 expected expenditure in that month. Predicted income tax expense for the quarter ending December 31 is 40% of net income and is due in January 1995. This amount appears in the budgeted income statement as income tax expense. The same amount appears on the budgeted balance sheet as the income tax liability.

During the second month of each quarter, the Northern Company pays a cash dividend equal to 2% of the par value of the common stock. The cash budget in Illustration 25–9 shows a November payment of $3,000 for this planned disbursement.

Northern Company has an agreement with the bank that grants additional loans to the company at the end of each month if needed to maintain a minimum cash balance of $20,000. Interest is paid at the end of each month at the rate of 1% of the beginning balance of the loans. And, if the cash balance exceeds $20,000 at the end of a month, the firm uses the excess to repay any outstanding loans. The interest payments in Illustration 25–9 equal 1% of the prior month's ending loan balance. For October, this expenditure is 1% of the $10,000 balance in the balance sheet in Illustration 25–4. For November, the company expects to pay interest of $228, which is 1% of the $22,800 expected loan balance as of October 31. No interest is scheduled for December because the company anticipates repaying the loans in full at the end of November.

Illustration 25–9 shows that the October 31 preliminary balance (before any loan-related activity) falls to $7,200, which is below the $20,000 minimum. Thus, Northern Company expects to bring the balance up to the minimum by borrowing $12,800 through another short-term note. At the end of November, the budget shows a preliminary cash balance of $45,072 before any loan activity. As a result, the company expects to repay the $22,800 loan. Note, however, that the equipment purchase budgeted for December will again draw the preliminary cash balance to only $372, which is well below the $20,000 minimum. Thus, the company expects to borrow $19,628 in that month to get back up to the minimum ending balance.

Preparing a Budgeted Income Statement

LO 4 Integrate the component budgets into budgeted financial statements.

The next-to-last step in preparing a master budget is summarizing the effects of the various plans in the **budgeted income statement.** The budgeted income statement is a managerial accounting report that presents predicted amounts of the company's revenues and expenses for the budget period. The information needed for preparing a budgeted income statement comes primarily from the previously prepared budgets and the research conducted in the process of preparing them.

For many companies, the volume of information summarized in the budgeted income statement and the budgeted balance sheet is so large that the managerial accountants use work sheets. These work sheets accumulate the budgeted transactions and classify them by their effects on the income statement and the balance sheet. In this example, the Northern Company has only a few expected transactions and account balances. Thus, the budgeted financial statements can be prepared by analyzing the other budgets and by using information from the related discussions. Northern Company's budgeted income

ILLUSTRATION 25–10

NORTHERN COMPANY
Budgeted Income Statement
For Three Months Ended December 31, 1994

Sales (Illustration 25–5, 32,000 units @ $10)		$320,000
Cost of goods sold (32,000 units @ $6)		192,000
Gross profit		$128,000
Operating expenses:		
Sales commissions (Illustration 25–7)	$32,000	
Sales salaries (Illustration 25–7)	6,000	
Administrative salaries (Illustration 25–8)	13,500	
Depreciation on equipment (Illustration 25–8)	4,500	
Interest expense (Illustration 25–9)	328	(56,328)
Net income before income taxes		$ 71,672
Income tax expense ($71,672 × 40%)		(28,669)
Net income		$ 43,003

statement is shown in Illustration 25–10. Notice that it is now possible to predict the amount of income tax expense for the quarter as 40% of the budgeted pretax net income.

Preparing a Budgeted Balance Sheet

The final step in preparing the master budget is the compilation of the **budgeted balance sheet.** This managerial accounting report presents predicted amounts of the company's assets, liabilities, and stockholders' equity as of the end of the budget period.

As previously mentioned, the Northern Company has only a few transactions and account balances. Thus, its budgeted balance sheet, which appears in Illustration 25–11, can be prepared by analyzing the other budgets and using information in the related discussions of those budgets. The sources of the amounts shown in the budgeted balance sheet are as follows:

Item	Amount	Explanation
Cash	$ 20,000	Ending balance for December from the cash budget in Illustration 25–9.
Accounts receivable	$ 84,000	60% of $140,000 sales budgeted for December from the sales budget in Illustration 25–5.
Inventory	$ 48,600	8,100 units in budgeted December ending inventory at the budgeted cost of $6 per unit (from the purchases budget in Illustration 25–6).
Equipment	$225,000	September 30 balance of $200,000 from the beginning balance sheet in Illustration 25–4 plus $25,000 cost of new equipment from the cash budget in Illustration 25–9.
Accumulated depreciation	$ 40,500	September 30 balance of $36,000 from the beginning balance sheet in Illustration 25–4 plus $4,500 expense from the general and administrative expense budget in Illustration 25–8.

ILLUSTRATION 25–11

NORTHERN COMPANY
Budgeted Balance Sheet
December 31, 1994

Assets		
Cash		$ 20,000
Accounts receivable		84,000
Inventory (8,100 units @ $6)		48,600
Equipment	$225,000	
Less accumulated depreciation	(40,500)	184,500
Total assets		$337,100
Liabilities and Stockholders' Equity		
Liabilities:		
Accounts payable	$ 57,000	
Income taxes payable	28,669	
Bank loan payable	19,628	$105,297
Stockholders' equity:		
Common stock	$150,000	
Retained earnings	81,803	231,803
Total liabilities and stockholders' equity		$337,100

Item	Amount	Explanation
Accounts payable	$ 57,000	Budgeted cost of merchandise purchases for December from the purchases budget in Illustration 25–6.
Income taxes payable	$ 28,669	Budgeted income tax expense from the budgeted income statement for the fourth quarter in Illustration 25–10.
Bank loan payable	$ 19,628	Budgeted December 31 balance from the cash budget in Illustration 25–9.
Common stock	$150,000	Unchanged from the beginning balance sheet in Illustration 25–4.
Retained earnings	$ 81,803	September 30 balance of $41,800 from the beginning balance sheet in Illustration 25–4 plus budgeted net income of $43,003 from the budgeted income statement in Illustration 25–10 minus budgeted cash dividends of $3,000 from the cash budget in Illustration 25–9.

An 8-column work sheet can be used to prepare the budgeted income statement and budgeted balance sheet. The first two columns of the work sheet show the post-closing trial balance as of the last day of the period prior to the budget period. Next, the budgeted transactions and adjustments are entered in the second pair of work sheet columns in the same manner as end-of-period adjustments are entered on an ordinary work sheet. For example, if the budget calls for credit sales of $250,000, the title of the Sales account is entered on the work sheet in the Account Titles column. Then, the Sales account is credited and Accounts Receivable is debited for $250,000 in the second pair of money columns. After all budgeted transactions and adjustments are entered on the work sheet, the post-closing trial balance amounts in the first pair of money columns are combined with the budget amounts in the second pair of columns and sorted to the proper Income Statement and Balance Sheet columns of the work sheet. Finally, the balances in these columns are used to prepare the budgeted income statement and balance sheet.

Summary of the Chapter in Terms of Learning Objectives

LO 1. Planning is a management responsibility of critical importance to business success, and budgeting is the process used by management to formalize its plans. Budgeting promotes study and research by management and focuses its attention on the future. Budgeting also provides a basis for evaluating performance, serves as a source of motivation, is a means of coordinating business activities, and communicates management's plans and instructions to the company's employees.

LO 2. A master budget is a formal overall plan for a business that consists of specific plans for business operations, capital expenditures, and the financial results of those activities. The budgeting process begins with preparing a sales budget. Based on the expected sales volume, merchandising companies can budget merchandise purchases, selling expenses, and administrative expenses. Manufacturing companies also must budget production quantities, raw materials purchases, direct labor costs, and overhead. Next, the capital expenditures budget is prepared, followed by the cash budget, and the budgeted financial statements.

LO 3. In the process of preparing a master budget, each component budget is designed to provide guidance for the persons responsible for the activities covered by that budget. The budgets show how much revenue is to be received from sales and how much expense is to be incurred. The budgets are designed to reflect the fact that the activities of one area (such as manufacturing) support the activities of the others (such as marketing). As a result, the various components of the business are directed to pursue activities that are consistent with and supportive of the overall objectives of the business.

LO 4. The operating budgets, the capital expenditures budget, and the cash budget, along with their supporting calculations and the balance sheet prior to the first budget period, contain the information needed to prepare a budgeted income statement for the budget period and a budgeted balance sheet as of the end of the budget period. A small company can prepare these budgeted financial statements by extracting the necessary information from the budgets, related calculations, and beginning balance sheet. The budgeted financial statements show the expected financial consequences of the planned activities described in the budgets.

Demonstration Problem

The management of Daredevil Company has asked you to prepare a master budget for the company from the following information. The budget is to cover the months of April, May, and June of 1994.

DAREDEVIL COMPANY
Balance Sheet
March 31, 1994

Assets

Cash	$ 50,000	
Accounts receivable	175,000	
Inventory	126,000	
Total current assets		$351,000
Equipment	$480,000	
Accumulated depreciation	(90,000)	390,000
Total assets		$741,000

Liabilities and Stockholders' Equity

Accounts payable	$156,000	
Short-term notes payable	12,000	
Total current liabilities		$168,000
Long-term note payable		200,000
Total liabilities		$368,000
Common stock	$235,000	
Retained earnings	138,000	
Total stockholders' equity		373,000
Total liabilities and stockholders' equity		$741,000

a. Actual unit sales for March were 10,000 units. Each month's sales are expected to exceed the prior month's results by 5%. The selling price of the product is $25 per unit.

b. The company's policy calls for the ending inventory of a given month to equal 80% of the next month's expected unit sales. The March 31 inventory was 8,400 units, which was in compliance with the policy.

c. Sales representatives' commissions are 12.5%, and are paid in the month of the sales. The sales manager's salary will be $3,500 in April and $4,000 thereafter.

d. The general and administrative expenses include administrative salaries of $8,000 per month, depreciation of $5,000 per month, and 0.9% monthly interest on the long-term note payable.

e. Thirty percent of the company's sales are expected to be for cash and the remaining 70% will be on credit. Receivables are collected in full in the month following the sale (none is collected in the month of the sale).

f. All purchases of merchandise are on credit, and no payables arise from any other transactions. The purchases of one month are fully paid in the next month. The purchase price is $15 per unit.

g. The minimum ending cash balance for all months is $50,000. If necessary, the company will borrow enough cash to reach the minimum. The resulting short-term note will require an interest payment of 1% at the end of each month. If the ending cash balance exceeds the minimum, the excess will be applied to repaying the short-term notes payable.

h. Dividends of $100,000 are to be declared and paid in May.

i. No cash payments for income taxes are to be made during the second quarter. Income taxes will be assessed at 35% in the quarter.

j. Equipment purchases of $55,000 are scheduled for June.

Required

Prepare the following budgets and other financial information:

1. The sales budget, including sales for July.
2. The purchases budget, the budgeted cost of goods sold for each month and the quarter, and the cost of the June 30 budgeted inventory.
3. The selling expense budget.
4. The general and administrative expense budget.
5. The expected cash receipts from customers and the expected June 30 balance of accounts receivable.
6. The expected cash payments for purchases and the expected June 30 balance of accounts payable.
7. The cash budget.
8. The budgeted income statement.
9. The budgeted statement of retained earnings.
10. The budgeted balance sheet.

Solution to Demonstration Problem

Planning the Solution

- The sales budget shows the expected sales for each month in the quarter. Start by multiplying March sales by 105%, and do the same thing for the remaining months. July's sales are needed for the purchases budget. To complete the budget, multiply the expected unit sales by the selling price of $25 per unit.
- Use these results and the 80% inventory policy to budget the size of the ending inventory for April, May, and June. Then, add the budgeted sales to these numbers, and subtract the actual or expected beginning inventory for each month. The result will be the number of units to be purchased in each month. Multiply these numbers by the per unit cost of $15. Find the budgeted cost of goods sold by multiplying the unit sales in each month by the $15 cost per unit. And, find the cost of the June 30 ending inventory by multiplying the units expected to be on hand at that date by the $15 cost per unit.
- The selling expense budget has only two items. Find the amount of sales representatives' commissions by multiplying the expected dollar sales in each month by the 12.5% commission rate. Then, add the sales manager's salary of $3,500 in April and $4,000 in May and June.
- The general and administrative expense budget should show three items. Administrative salaries are fixed at $8,000 per month and depreciation is to be $5,000 per month. Budget the monthly interest expense on the long-term note by multiplying its $200,000 balance by the 0.9% monthly interest rate.

- Determine the amounts of cash sales in each month by multiplying the budgeted sales by 30%. Add to this amount the credit sales of the prior month, which you can compute as 70% of the prior month's sales. April's cash receipts from collecting receivables will equal the March 31 balance of $175,000. The expected June 30 accounts receivable balance equals 70% of June's total budgeted sales.
- Determine expected cash payments on accounts payable for each month by making them equal to the merchandise purchases in the prior month. The payments for April equal the March 31 balance of accounts payable shown on the beginning balance sheet. The June 30 balance of accounts payable equals merchandise purchases for June.
- Prepare the cash budget by combining the given information and the amounts of cash receipts and payments on account that you just calculated. The cash disbursements will also include: sales commissions, sales salaries, administrative salaries, interest on the long-term note, dividends, the June asset purchase, and interest on the short-term notes.
- Complete the cash budget for each month by either borrowing enough to raise the preliminary balance up to the minimum or paying off the short-term note as much as the balance will allow without falling below the minimum. Also show the ending balance of the short-term notes in the budget. One month's ending cash balance becomes the next month's beginning balance.
- Prepare the budgeted income statement by combining these budgeted items for all three months: sales, cost of goods sold, sales commissions, sales salaries, administrative salaries, depreciation, interest on the long-term note, and interest on the short-term note. Then, determine the income before income taxes and multiply it by the 35% rate to find the quarter's income tax expense. Finish the statement by showing the amount of budgeted net income.
- The budgeted statement of retained earnings should show the March 31 balance plus the quarter's net income minus the quarter's dividends.
- The budgeted balance sheet includes updated balances for all the items that appear in the beginning balance sheet and an additional liability for unpaid income taxes. The amounts for all asset, liability, and equity accounts can be found either in the budgets and schedules or by adding amounts found there to the beginning balances.

1. The sales budget:

	April	May	June	July
Prior month's sales	10,000	10,500	11,025	11,576
Plus 5% growth	500	525	551	579
Projected unit sales	10,500	11,025	11,576	12,155

	April	May	June	Quarter
Projected unit sales	10,500	11,025	11,576	
Selling price per unit	× $25	× $25	× $25	
Projected sales revenue	$262,500	$275,625	$289,400	$827,525

2. The purchases budget:

	April	May	June	Quarter
Next month's unit sales	11,025	11,576	12,155	
Ending inventory percentage	× 80%	× 80%	× 80%	
Desired ending inventory	8,820	9,261	9,724	
This month's unit sales	10,500	11,025	11,576	
Units to be available	19,320	20,286	21,300	
Beginning inventory	(8,400)	(8,820)	(9,261)	
Units to be purchased	10,920	11,466	12,039	
Budgeted cost per unit	$15	$15	$15	
Projected purchases	$163,800	$171,990	$180,585	$516,375

Budgeted cost of goods sold:

	April	May	June	Quarter
This month's unit sales	10,500	11,025	11,576	
Budgeted cost per unit	× $15	× $15	× $15	
Projected cost of goods sold	$157,500	$165,375	$173,640	$496,515

Budgeted inventory for June 30:

Units	9,724
Cost per unit	× $15
Total	$145,860

3. Selling expense budget:

	April	May	June	Quarter
Budgeted sales	$262,500	$275,625	$289,400	$827,525
Commission percentage	× 12.5%	× 12.5%	× 12.5%	× 12.5%
Sales commissions	$ 32,813	$ 34,453	$ 36,175	$103,441
Manager's salary	3,500	4,000	4,000	11,500
Projected selling expenses	$ 36,313	$ 38,453	$ 40,175	$114,941

4. General and administrative expense budget:

	April	May	June	Quarter
Administrative salaries	$ 8,000	$ 8,000	$ 8,000	$ 24,000
Depreciation	5,000	5,000	5,000	15,000
Interest on long-term note payable (0.9% × $200,000)	1,800	1,800	1,800	5,400
Projected expenses	$ 14,800	$ 14,800	$ 14,800	$ 44,400

5. Expected cash receipts from customers:

	April	May	June	Quarter
Budgeted sales	$262,500	$275,625	$289,400	
Ending accounts receivable (70%)	$183,750	$192,938	$202,580	
Cash receipts				
Cash sales (30%)	$ 78,750	$ 82,687	$ 86,820	$248,257
Collections of prior month's receivables	175,000	183,750	192,938	551,688
Total cash to be collected	$253,750	$266,437	$279,758	$799,945

6. Expected cash payments to suppliers:

	April	May	June	Quarter
Cash payments (equal to prior month's purchases)	$156,000	$163,800	$171,990	$491,790
Expected June 30 balance of accounts payable (June purchases)			$180,585	

7. Cash budget:

	April	May	June
Beginning cash balance	$ 50,000	$ 89,517	$ 50,000
Cash received from customers	253,750	266,437	279,758
Total cash available	$303,750	$355,954	$329,758
Cash payments:			
Payments for merchandise	$156,000	$163,800	$171,990
Sales commissions	32,813	34,453	36,175
Salaries:			
Sales	3,500	4,000	4,000
Administrative	8,000	8,000	8,000
Interest on long-term note	1,800	1,800	1,800
Dividends		100,000	
Equipment purchase			55,000
Interest on short-term notes:			
April ($12,000 × 1.0%)	120		
June ($6,099 × 1.0%)			61
Total	$202,233	$312,053	$277,026
Preliminary balance	$101,517	$ 43,901	$ 52,732
Additional loan		6,099	
Loan repayment	(12,000)		(2,732)
Ending cash balance	$ 89,517	$ 50,000	$ 50,000
Ending short-term notes	$ –0–	$ 6,099	$ 3,367

8.

DAREDEVIL COMPANY
Budgeted Income Statement
Quarter Ended June 30, 1994

Sales		$827,525	*(part 1)*
Cost of goods sold		(496,515)	*(part 2)*
Gross profit		$331,010	
Operating expenses:			
Sales commissions	$103,441		*(part 3)*
Sales salaries	11,500		*(part 3)*
Administrative salaries	24,000		*(part 4)*
Depreciation	15,000		*(part 4)*
Interest on long-term note	5,400		*(part 4)*
Interest on short-term notes	181		*(part 7)*
Total operating expenses		(159,522)	
Income before income taxes		$171,488	
Income taxes (35%)		(60,021)	
Net income		$111,467	

9.

DAREDEVIL COMPANY
Budgeted Statement of Retained Earnings
For the Quarter Ended June 30, 1994

Beginning retained earnings . . .	$138,000	*(given)*
Net income	111,467	*(income statement)*
Total	$249,467	
Dividends	(100,000)	*(given)*
Ending retained earnings	$149,467	

10.

DAREDEVIL COMPANY
Budgeted Balance Sheet
June 30, 1994

Cash	$ 50,000		*(part 7)*
Accounts receivable	202,580		*(part 5)*
Inventory	145,860		*(part 2)*
Total current assets		$398,440	
Equipment	$535,000		*(given plus purchase)*
Accumulated depreciation . . .	(105,000)	430,000	*(given plus expense)*
Total assets		$828,440	
Accounts payable	$180,585		*(part 6)*
Short-term notes payable	3,367		*(part 7)*
Estimated income taxes payable	60,021		*(income statement)*
Total current liabilities		$243,973	
Long-term note payable		200,000	*(given)*
Total liabilities		$443,973	
Common stock	$235,000		*(given)*
Retained earnings	149,467		*(retained earnings statement)*
Total stockholders' equity . . .		384,467	
Total liabilities and equity		$828,440	

Glossary

LO 5 Define or explain the words and phrases listed in the chapter glossary.

Budget a formal statement of future plans, usually expressed in monetary terms. p. 1326

Budgeted balance sheet a managerial accounting report that presents predicted amounts of the company's assets, liabilities, and stockholders' equity as of the end of the budget period. pp. 1332, 1344

Budgeted income statement a managerial accounting report that presents predicted amounts of the company's revenues and expenses for the budget period. pp. 1332, 1343

Budgeting the process of planning future business actions and expressing them as formal plans. p. 1326

Capital expenditures budget a plan that lists dollar amounts to be received from disposing of equipment and dollar amounts to be spent on purchasing additional equipment if the proposed production program is carried out. pp. 1332, 1339

Cash budget a plan that shows the expected cash inflows and outflows during the budget period, including receipts from loans needed to maintain a minimum cash balance and repayments of such loans. pp. 1332, 1341

Continuous budgeting the practice of preparing budgets for each of several future periods and revising those budgets as each period is completed; as one period is completed, a new budget is added, with the result that the budget always covers the same number of future periods. p. 1330

General and administrative expense budget a plan that lists the types and amounts of general and administrative expenses expected during the budget period. pp. 1332, 1339

Manufacturing budget a plan that shows the predicted costs for materials, direct labor, and overhead to be incurred in manufacturing the units in the production budget. pp. 1332, 1338

Master budget a comprehensive or overall formal plan for a business that includes specific plans for expected sales, the units of product to be produced, the merchandise (or materials) to be purchased, the expense to be incurred, the long-term assets to be purchased, and the amounts of cash to be borrowed or loans to be repaid, as well as a budgeted income statement and balance sheet. p. 1330

Merchandise purchases budget a plan that states the units or costs of merchandise to be purchased by a merchandising company during the budget period. pp. 1331, 1336

Production budget a plan that states the number of units to be manufactured during each future period covered by the budget, based on the budgeted sales for the period and the levels of inventory needed to support future sales. pp. 1332, 1337–1338

Rolling budgets the set of periodic budgets that are prepared and periodically revised in the practice of continuous budgeting. p. 1330

Safety stock a quantity of merchandise or materials over the minimum needed to satisfy budgeted demand; provides protection against lost sales caused by unfulfilled demands from customers or delays in shipments from suppliers. p. 1336

Sales budget a plan showing the units of goods to be sold and the revenue to be derived from the sales; the starting point in the budgeting process because the plans for most departments are related to sales. pp. 1331, 1335

Selling expense budget a plan that lists the types and amounts of selling expenses expected during the budget period. pp. 1332, 1338

Synonymous Terms

Articulated interconnected.

Budget formal plan.

Capital budget asset purchase plan.

Variance difference.

Objective Review

Answers to the following questions are listed at the end of the chapter. Be sure that you decide which is the one best answer to each question *before* you check the answers.

LO 1 Budgeting is useful because it:

a. Is a means of communicating management's plans and directives to employees.
b. Promotes good decision-making processes by focusing management's attention on studying, researching, and planning the future.
c. Can help motivate employees to meet established goals.
d. Provides a basis for evaluating performance.
e. All of the above.

LO 2 A master budget:

a. Always includes a manufacturing budget that specifies the number of units to be produced.
b. Is prepared with a process that starts with the operating budgets and continues with the capital expenditures budget, the cash budget, and the budgeted financial statements.
c. Is prepared with a process that starts with the budgeted income statement.
d. Is prepared with a process that ends with the budgeted income statement.
e. Always includes a sales budget that specifies the units of product to be purchased or manufactured.

LO 3 In preparing monthly budgets for the third quarter, Doran, Inc., budgeted the following unit sales for each month: July, 120; August, 140; September, 150; and October, 200. The June 30 finished goods inventory consists of 50 units and management wants each month's ending inventory to be 60% of the next month's sales. The production budget for the third quarter should call for producing these units of product:

	July	August	September
a.	84	90	120
b.	132	146	180
c.	154	140	150
d.	154	146	180
e.	120	140	150

LO 4 In the process of preparing a budgeted balance sheet:

a. The cost of plant and equipment can be determined by analyzing the capital expenditures budget and the balance sheet from the beginning of the budget period.
b. The cash balance is determined by comparing the sales budget with the merchandise purchases budget.
c. Retained earnings are calculated from information contained in the cash budget and the balance sheet from the beginning of the budget period.
d. Liabilities can be determined by analyzing the general and administrative expense budget.
e. All of the above.

LO 5 A rolling budget is

a. Prepared at the beginning of a year and left unrevised throughout the entire year.
b. Prepared once each year and updated during the year only if some significant event happens.
c. Covers a specific calendar year, with each remaining quarter's budget being revised as the year passes.
d. Covers a fixed number of time periods (months or quarters) and is updated by revising each period's amounts and by adding a new budget for an additional period.
e. None of the above.

Questions for Class Discussion

1. What are the two most basic activities in managing a business?
2. What is a budget? What is a master budget?
3. How does budgeting help managers control a business?
4. What are the major benefits of budgeting?
5. How does budgeting promote good decision making?
6. What two alternative norms or objectives can be used to evaluate actual performance? Which of the two is generally more useful?
7. What three guidelines should be followed to effectively motivate employees with budgeting?
8. Why should each department participate in preparing its own budget?
9. How does budgeting help management coordinate business activities?
10. If the managers of a business are able to communicate plans to their employees through direct conversations, are budgets still useful in communicating expectations?

11. What is the responsibility of the budget committee?
12. What is the usual time period covered by a master budget? How far in advance can long-range budgets be prepared?
13. What is continuous budgeting? What are rolling budgets?
14. What are the three primary categories of budgets in the master budget?
15. What is the difference between operating budgets for merchandising and manufacturing companies?
16. What sequence is followed in preparing the budgets that comprise the master budget?
17. What is a sales budget? A selling expense budget? A capital expenditures budget?
18. What is the difference between a production budget and a manufacturing budget?
19. How does a just-in-time inventory system differ from a safety stock system?
20. What is a cash budget? Why do operating budgets and the capital expenditures budget need to be prepared before the cash budget?
21. Federal Express has managers in its local branches and in its headquarters in Memphis. What kinds of capital expenditures would these different kinds of managers plan?
22. Because of the nature of the business, do you think that the management of a local McDonald's store would do much long-term budgeting?

What you want is what you get.

Exercises

Exercise 25–1
Merchandise purchases budget
(LO 3)

The April sales budget of the Quickstop Drivein calls for sales of $650,000. The store expects to begin April with a $100,000 inventory and end the month with a $110,000 inventory. The cost of goods sold is typically around 70% of sales.

Required

Prepare a merchandise purchases budget for the store showing the cost of the goods that should be purchased during April under this plan.

Exercise 25–2
Production budget for two quarters
(LO 3)

Simpson Company manufactures a single product. The management predicts that the first quarter's ending inventory will consist of 40,000 units. The following unit sales of the product are expected during the rest of the year:

Second quarter	70,000
Third quarter	100,000
Fourth quarter	150,000

Management's policy calls for a quarter's ending inventory to equal 60% of the next quarter's budgeted sales.

Required

Prepare a production budget showing the units of product that should be manufactured during the year's second and third quarters.

Exercise 25–3
Cash budget for three months
(LO 3)

Georgia Company budgeted the following cash receipts and cash disbursements from operations for the first quarter of the next year:

	Receipts	Disbursements
January	$145,000	$138,800
February	175,000	155,860
March	200,000	210,500

According to a credit agreement with the company's bank, Georgia promises to have a minimum cash balance of $10,000 at the end of each month. In return, the bank has agreed that the company can borrow up to $50,000 with interest of 12% per year, paid on the last day of each month. The interest is calculated on the beginning balance of the loan for the month. The company is expected to have a cash balance of $10,000 and a loan balance of $20,000 on January 1.

Required

Prepare monthly cash budgets for the first quarter.

Exercise 25–4
Cash budget from transaction data
(LO 3)

Use the following information to prepare a cash budget for the Wagner Company. The budget should show expected cash receipts and disbursements for May and the balance expected on May 31.

a. Beginning cash balance on May 1: $25,000.

b. Cash receipts from sales: 30% are collected in the month of sale, 50% in the next month, 18% in the second month, and 2% are uncollectible. The following amounts are actual and budgeted sales:

March (actual)	$860,000
April (actual)	600,000
May (budgeted) . . .	700,000

c. Payments on purchases: 60% in the month of purchase and 40% in the month following purchase. The following amounts are actual and budgeted merchandise purchases:

April (actual)	$215,000
May (budgeted) . . .	300,000

d. Budgeted cash disbursements for salaries in May: $105,500.

e. Budgeted depreciation expense for May: $6,000.

f. Other cash expenses budgeted for May: $75,000.

g. Accrued income taxes due in May: $40,000.

h. Bank loan interest due in May: $3,300.

Exercise 25–5
Budgeted income statement and balance sheet
(LO 4)

Based on the information provided in Exercise 25–4 and the additional information that follows, prepare a budgeted income statement for May and a budgeted balance sheet for May 31.

a. Cost of goods sold is 44% of sales.

b. The inventory at the end of April was $40,000.

c. Salaries payable on April 30 were $25,000 and are expected to be $20,000 on May 31.

d. The Equipment account has a balance of $800,000. On April 30, accumulated depreciation was $140,000.

e. The $3,300 cash payment of interest represents the 1% monthly expense on a bank loan of $330,000.

f. Income taxes payable on April 15 were $40,000, and the income tax rate applicable to the company is 30%.

g. The 2% of sales that prove to be uncollectible are debited to Bad Debts Expense and credited to the Allowance for Doubtful Accounts during the month of sale. Specific accounts that prove to be uncollectible are written off at the end of the second month after the sale.

h. The only other balance sheet accounts are Common Stock, which has a balance of $300,000, and Retained Earnings, which has a balance of $506,800 on April 30.

Exercise 25–6
Merchandise purchases budget for three months
(LO 3)

Garson Company prepared monthly budgets for the current year. The budgets planned for an October 31 inventory of 5,000 units. The company follows a policy of ending each month with merchandise inventory on hand equal to a specified percentage of the budgeted sales for the following month. Budgeted sales and merchandise purchases for three months were as follows:

	Units	
	Sales	**Purchases**
August	40,000	46,000
September	70,000	68,000
October	60,000	53,000

Based on the preceding information, calculate the following amounts:

a. The percentage relationship between a month's ending inventory and sales budgeted for the following month.

b. The units budgeted to be sold in November.

c. The units budgeted for August's beginning inventory.

Then, show how the company compiled the merchandise purchases budgets for August, September, and October.

Exercise 25–7
Calculations of budgeted cash payments
(LO 3)

Payson Company's cost of goods sold is consistently 40% of sales. The company plans to have a merchandise inventory at the beginning of each month with a cost equal to 30% of that month's budgeted cost of goods sold. All merchandise is purchased on credit, and 50% of the purchases made during a month are paid in that month. Another 35% is paid for during the first month after purchase, and the remaining 15% is paid for during the second month after purchase.

Use the following sales budgets to calculate the expected cash payments to be made during April:

February	$125,000
March.	100,000
April	150,000
May	175,000

Exercise 25–8
Budgeting monthly cost of goods sold
(LO 3)

Super Sales Company purchases its merchandise on credit. It has recently budgeted the following accounts payable balances and merchandise inventory balances:

	Accounts Payable	Merchandise Inventory
March 31	$40,000	$100,000
April 30	50,000	120,000
May 31	44,000	112,000
June 30	57,000	99,000

Cash payments on accounts payable during each month are expected to be:

March	$335,000
April	385,000
May	325,000
June	395,000

a. Calculate the budgeted amounts of purchases for April, May, and June.

b. Calculate the budgeted amounts of cost of goods sold for April, May, and June.

Exercise 25–9
Budgeting accounts payable balances
(LO 3)

Daily Braid, a merchandising company, budgets its monthly cost of goods sold to equal 70% of sales. The inventory policy calls for a beginning inventory in each month equal to 25% of the budgeted cost of goods sold for that month.

All purchases are on credit, and 20% of the purchases in any month are paid for during the same month. Another 50% is paid during the first month after purchase, and the remaining 30% is paid in the second month after purchase. The following sales budgets have been established:

May	$400,000
June	320,000
July.	360,000
August	320,000
September	280,000

a. Calculate the budgeted purchases for May, June, July, and August.

b. Calculate the budgeted payments on accounts payable for July and August.

c. Calculate the budgeted ending balances of accounts payable for July and August.

Problems

Problem 25–1
Production budget and materials purchases budget
(LO 3)

Zippee Manufacturing Company produces a winter sports product called a Slipper. Each Slipper requires one-half pound of plastic and is produced in a single operation by an extrusion process. The company's management predicts that there will be 35,000 units of the product and 16,000 pounds of plastic on hand on September 30 of the current year, and that 100,000 units of the product will be sold during the year's fourth quarter. Because the peak selling season will have passed, management wants to start the first quarter of the next year with only 10,000 finished Slippers and only 3,000 pounds of plastic in the materials inventory. Plastic can be purchased for approximately $25.00 per pound.

Required

Prepare a fourth-quarter production budget and a fourth-quarter plastic purchases budget for the company (include the dollar cost of the purchases).

Problem 25–2
Production budget and merchandise purchases budget
(LO 3)

Boardwalk Corporation retails three products that it buys ready for sale. The company's March 31 inventories are

Product 1	30,000 units
Product 2	50,000 units
Product 3	145,000 units

The company's management realizes that excessive inventories have accumulated for all three products. As a result, the managers have created a new policy that the ending inventory in any month should equal 20% of the expected unit sales for the following month.

Expected sales in units for April, May, June, and July are as follows:

	Budgeted Sales in Units			
	April	**May**	**June**	**July**
Product 1	40,000	50,000	60,000	70,000
Product 2	65,000	55,000	45,000	35,000
Product 3	160,000	132,000	162,000	130,000

Required

Prepare separate purchases budgets (in units) for each of the three products covering April, May, and June.

Problem 25–3
Monthly cash budgets
(LO 3)

During the last week of April, the owner of the Homewood Store approached the bank for a $100,000 loan to be made on May 1 and repaid on July 31 with annual interest of 9%. The owner planned to increase the store's inventory by $80,000 during May and needed the loan to pay for the merchandise in June and July. The bank's loan officer needed more information about Homewood Store's ability to repay the loan and asked the owner to forecast the store's July 31 cash position.

On May 1, Homewood Store was expected to have a $4,000 cash balance, $90,000 of accounts receivable, and $60,000 of accounts payable. Its budgeted sales, purchases, and cash expenditures for the coming three months are as follows:

	May	**June**	**July**
Sales	$250,000	$300,000	$350,000
Merchandise purchases	240,000	150,000	180,000
Payroll	15,000	20,000	25,000
Rent	8,000	8,000	8,000
Other cash expenses	6,000	9,000	11,000
Repayment of bank loan			100,000
Interest on the loan			2,250

The budgeted May purchases include the inventory increase. All sales are on account. The company's regular past experience shows that 10% is collected in the month of the sale, 60% is collected in the month following the sale, 25% in the second month, 3% in the third, and the remainder is not collected. Applying these percentages to the May 1 accounts receivable balance shows that $54,000 of the $90,000 will be collected during May, $22,500 during June, and $2,700 during July. All merchandise is purchased on credit. Eighty percent of the balance is paid in the month following a purchase and the remaining 20% is paid in the second month. The $60,000 of accounts payable at the end of April will be paid as follows: $48,000 in May and $12,000 in June.

Required

Prepare cash budgets for May, June, and July for the Homewood Store. Provide additional supplemental schedules as needed.

Problem 25–4
Cash budgets with supporting schedules
(LO 3)

Tomlinson Company has a cash balance of $15,000 on May 1. The company's product sells for $20 per unit. Actual and projected sales are

	Units	Dollars
March (actual)	6,000	$120,000
April (actual)	9,000	180,000
May (budgeted). . . .	5,000	100,000
June (budgeted). . . .	9,000	180,000
July (budgeted)	11,000	220,000

All sales are on credit. Recent experience shows that 40% of the revenues are collected in the month of the sale, 30% in the month after the sale, 25% in the second month after the sale, and 5% prove to be uncollectible.

The purchase price of the product is $12 per unit. All purchases are payable within 21 days. Thus, 30% of the purchases made in a month are paid in that month and the other 70% are paid in the next month. Tomlinson Company's management has a policy of maintaining an ending monthly inventory of 30% of the next month's unit sales plus a safety stock of 100 units. The March 31 and April 30 actual inventory levels were consistent with this policy.

Selling and administrative expenses for the year of $480,000 are paid in cash evenly throughout the year. The company's minimum cash balance for the end of a month is $15,000. This minimum is maintained, if necessary, by borrowing cash from the bank. If the balance goes over $15,000, the company repays as much of the loan as it can without going below the minimum. This loan carries an annual 12% interest rate, which is paid monthly as 1% of the beginning balance. At April 30, the balance of the loan was $4,000.

Required

1. Prepare a schedule that shows how much cash will be collected in May and June from the credit customers.
2. Prepare a schedule that shows the budgeted ending inventories for March, April, May, and June.
3. Prepare a schedule showing the purchases budgets for the product for April, May, and June. Present the calculation in terms of units and then show the dollar amount of purchases for each month.

4. Prepare a schedule showing the cash to be paid out during May and June for product purchases.
5. Prepare monthly cash budgets for May and June, including any loan activity and interest expense. Also, show the loan balance at the end of each month.

Problem 25–5
Preparation and analysis of budgeted income statements
(LO 4)

Barrington Company buys one kind of merchandise at $12 per unit and sells it at $25 per unit. The company's sales representatives receive a 20% commission on each sale. The March income statement shows the following information:

BARRINGTON COMPANY
Income Statement
For Month Ended March 31

Sales	$500,000
Cost of goods sold	240,000
Gross profit	$260,000
Expenses:	
Sales commissions	$100,000
Advertising	50,000
Store rent	5,000
Administrative salaries	10,000
Depreciation	6,000
Other	12,000
Total	$183,000
Net income	$ 77,000

The company's management believes that the March results would be repeated during April, May, and June without any changes in strategy. However, some changes are being considered. Management believes that unit sales will increase at a rate of 8% each month during the next quarter (including April) if the item's selling price is reduced to $22.50 per unit and if advertising expenses are increased by 40% and remain at that level for all three months. Even if these changes are made, the purchase price will remain at $12 per unit. Under this plan, the sales representatives would continue to earn a 20% commission and all other expenses would remain unchanged.

Required

Using a three-column format, prepare budgeted income statements for April, May, and June that show the expected results of implementing the proposed changes. Based on the information in the budgeted income statements, recommend whether management should implement the plan.

Problem 25–6
Preparing a complete master budget
(LO 2, 3, 4)

Shortly before the end of 1994, the management of Glaser Corporation prepared the following budgeted balance sheet for December 31, 1994:

GLASER CORPORATION
Budgeted Balance Sheet
As of December 31, 1994

Cash		$ 40,000
Accounts receivable		100,000
Inventory		45,000
Total current assets		$185,000
Equipment	$300,000	
Accumulated depreciation	(30,000)	270,000
Total		$455,000
Accounts payable	$ 75,000	
Loan from bank	5,000	
Taxes payable (due March 15, 1995)	50,000	
Total liabilities		$130,000
Common stock	$375,000	
Retained earnings (deficit)	(50,000)	
Total stockholders' equity		325,000
Total		$455,000

In anticipation of preparing a master budget for January, February, and March 1995, management has gathered the following information:

a. Glaser Corporation's single product is purchased for $5 per unit and resold for $12. The expected inventory level on December 31 (9,000 units) is greater than management's desired level for 1995 of 40% of the next month's expected unit sales. Budgeted sales are

January	15,000 units
February	12,000
March	20,000
April	25,000

b. Cash sales are 40% of total sales and credit sales are 60% of total sales. Of the credit sales, 70% are collected in the first month after the sale and 30% in the second month after the sale. Seventy percent of the December 31, 1994, balance of accounts receivable will be collected during January and 30% will be collected during February.

c. Merchandise purchased by the company is paid for as follows: 80% in the month after purchase, and 20% in the second month after purchase. Eighty percent of the Accounts Payable balance on December 31, 1994, will be paid during January, and 20% will be paid during February.

d. Sales commissions of 10% of sales are paid each month. Additional sales salaries are $72,000 per year.

e. General and administrative salaries are $84,000 per year. Repair expenses equal $1,500 per month and are paid in cash.

f. The equipment shown in the December 31, 1994, balance sheet was purchased in January 1994. It is being depreciated over 10 years under the straight-line method with no salvage value. The following new purchases of equipment are planned in the coming quarter:

January	$60,000
February	30,000
March	24,000

This equipment will also be depreciated with the straight-line method over 10 years, with no salvage value. A full month's depreciation is taken for the month in which the equipment is purchased.

g. The company plans to acquire some land at the end of March at a cost of $58,000. The purchase price will be paid with cash on the last day of the month.

h. Glaser Corporation has a working arrangement with the bank to obtain additional loans as needed. The interest rate is 12% per year, and the interest is paid at the end of each month based on the beginning balance. Partial or full payments on these loans can be made on the last day of the month. Glaser Corporation has agreed to maintain a minimum ending cash balance of $40,000 in every month.

i. The income tax rate applicable to the company is 30%. However, income taxes on the first quarter's income will not be paid until April 15.

Required

Prepare a master budget for the first quarter of 1995. It should include the following component budgets:

1. Monthly sales budgets (showing both budgeted unit sales and dollar sales).
2. Monthly merchandise purchases budgets.
3. Monthly selling expense budgets.
4. Monthly general and administrative expense budgets.
5. Monthly capital expenditures budgets.
6. Monthly cash budgets.
7. Budgeted income statement for the first quarter.
8. Budgeted balance sheet as of March 31, 1995.

Provide as many supplemental schedules as you need. Round all amounts to the nearest dollar.

Problem 25–7
Analytical essay
(LO 3)

Examine your answer to Problem 25–2 about the merchandise purchase budget for the Boardwalk Corporation. It should reflect much smaller purchases of all three products in April compared to May and June.

What factor caused these smaller purchases to be planned? Suggest some conditions in the business that would cause this factor to affect Boardwalk as it apparently has.

Problem 25–8
Analytical essay
(LO 3)

In Problem 25–4, the Tomlinson Company's cash budget indicates that the company will need to borrow nearly $4,000 in May, and that it will be able to repay that new loan plus a prior loan of $4,000 in June.

Suggest some reasons why knowing this information in April would be helpful to Tomlinson's management.

Alternate Problems

Problem 25–1A
Production budget and materials purchases budget
(LO 3)

Earthware Manufacturing Company produces a planter called an Earthpot. Each Earthpot requires four pounds of clay and is produced in a molding and firing process. The company's management predicts that there will be 2,000 units of the product and 4,000 pounds of clay on hand on December 31 of the current year, and that 50,000 units of the product will be sold during the next year's first quarter. Because the peak selling season will be just beginning, management wants to end the first quarter with 24,000 finished Earthpots and 12,000 pounds of clay in the materials inventory. Clay can be purchased for approximately $1.60 per pound.

Required

Prepare a first-quarter production budget and a first-quarter clay purchases budget for the company (include the dollar cost of the purchases).

Problem 25–2A
Production budget and merchandise purchases budget
(LO 3)

Airlift Corporation retails three products that it buys ready for sale. The company's July 31 inventories are

Product 50	4,900 units
Product 60	22,900 units
Product 70	11,900 units

The company's management realizes that excessive inventories have accumulated for all three products. As a result, the managers have created a new policy that the ending inventory in any month should equal 25% of the expected unit sales for the following month.

Expected sales in units for August, September, October, and November are as follows:

	Budgeted Sales in Units			
	August	**September**	**October**	**November**
Product 50	5,000	7,000	9,000	11,000
Product 60	22,000	30,000	38,000	26,000
Product 70	12,000	10,000	8,000	6,000

Required

Prepare separate purchases budgets (in units) for each of the three products covering August, September, and October.

Problem 25–3A
Monthly cash budgets
(LO 3)

During the last week of May, the owner of the Greenwood Store approached the bank for a $35,000 loan to be made on June 1 and repaid on August 31 with annual interest of 12%. The owner planned to increase the store's inventory by $30,000 during June and needed the loan to pay for the merchandise in July and August. The bank's loan officer needed more information about Greenwood Store's ability to repay the loan and asked the owner to forecast the store's August 31 cash position.

On June 1, Greenwood Store was expected to have a $1,500 cash balance, $60,000 of accounts receivable, and $50,000 of accounts payable. Its budgeted sales, purchases, and cash expenditures for the coming three months are as follows:

	June	July	August
Sales	$100,000	$150,000	$180,000
Merchandise purchases	115,000	80,000	100,000
Payroll	8,000	8,500	9,000
Rent	3,000	3,000	3,000
Other cash expenses	32,000	4,000	3,500
Repayment of bank loan			35,000
Interest on the loan			1,050

The budgeted June purchases include the inventory increase. All sales are on account. The company's regular past experience shows that 25% is collected in the month of the sale, 45% is collected in the month following the sale, 20% in the second month, 9% in the third, and the remainder is not collected. Applying these percentages to the June 1 accounts receivable balance shows that $40,500 of the $70,000 will be collected during June, $18,000 during July, and $8,100 during August. All merchandise is purchased on credit. Eighty percent of the balance is paid in the month following a purchase and the remaining 20% is paid in the second month. The $50,000 of accounts payable at the end of May will be paid as follows: $40,000 in June and $10,000 in July.

Required

Prepare cash budgets for June, July, and August for the Greenwood Store. Provide additional supplemental schedules as needed.

Problem 25–4A
Cash budgets with supporting schedules (LO 3)

Boland Company has a cash balance of $30,000 on April 1. The company's product sells for $125 per unit. Actual and projected sales are

	Units	Dollars
February (actual)	4,000	$500,000
March (actual)	2,000	250,000
April (budgeted)	6,000	750,000
May (budgeted)	3,000	375,000
June (budgeted)	3,800	475,000

All sales are on credit. Recent experience shows that 20% of the revenues are collected in the month of the sale, 30% in the month after the sale, 48% in the second month after the sale, and 2% prove to be uncollectible.

The purchase price of the product is $100 per unit. All purchases are payable within 12 days. Thus, 60% of the purchases made in a month are paid in that month and the other 40% are paid in the next month. Boland Company's management has a policy of maintaining an ending monthly inventory of 25% of the next month's unit sales plus a safety stock of 50 units. The February 28 and March 31 actual inventory levels were consistent with this policy.

Selling and administrative expenses for the year of $600,000 are paid in cash evenly throughout the year. The company's minimum cash balance for the end of a month is $30,000. This minimum is maintained, if necessary, by borrowing cash from the bank. If the balance goes over $30,000, the company repays as much of the loan as it can without going below the minimum. This loan carries an annual 9% interest rate, which is paid monthly as 0.75% of the beginning balance. At March 31, the balance of the loan was $16,000.

Required

1. Prepare a schedule that shows how much cash will be collected in April and May from the credit customers.
2. Prepare a schedule that shows the budgeted ending inventories for February, March, April, and May.
3. Prepare a schedule showing the purchases budgets for the product for March, April, and May. Present the calculation in terms of units and then show the dollar amount of purchases for each month.
4. Prepare a schedule showing the cash to be paid out during April and May for product purchases.
5. Prepare monthly cash budgets for April and May, including any loan activity and interest expense. Also, show the loan balance at the end of each month.

Problem 25–5A
Preparation and analysis of budgeted income statements
(LO 4)

Jordan Company buys one kind of merchandise at $32 per unit and sells it at $60 per unit. The company's sales representatives receive an 8% commission on each sale. The December income statement shows the following information:

JORDAN COMPANY
Income Statement
For Month Ended December 31

Sales	$600,000
Cost of goods sold	320,000
Gross profit	$280,000
Expenses:	
Sales commissions	$ 48,000
Advertising	80,000
Store rent	12,000
Administrative salaries	20,000
Depreciation	25,000
Other	6,000
Total	$191,000
Net income	$ 89,000

The company's management believes that the December results would be repeated during January, February, and March without any changes in strategy. However, some changes are being considered. Management believes that unit sales will increase at a rate of 10% each month during the next quarter (including January) if the item's selling price is reduced to $56 per unit and if advertising expenses are increased by 25% and remain at that level for all three months. Even if these changes are made, the purchase price will remain at $32 per unit. Under this plan, the sales representatives would continue to earn an 8% commission and all other expenses would remain unchanged.

Required

Using a three-column format, prepare budgeted income statements for January, February, and March that show the expected results of implementing the proposed changes. Based on the information in the budgeted income statements, recommend whether management should implement the plan.

Problem 25–6A
Preparing a complete master budget
(LO 2, 3, 4)

Shortly before the end of 1994, the management of Arnold Corporation prepared the following budgeted balance sheet for December 31, 1994:

ARNOLD CORPORATION
Budgeted Balance Sheet
As of December 31, 1994

Cash		$ 24,000
Accounts receivable		350,000
Inventory		100,000
Total current assets		$474,000
Equipment	$540,000	
Accumulated depreciation	(67,500)	472,500
Total		$946,500
Accounts payable	$240,000	
Loan from bank	10,000	
Taxes payable (due March 15, 1995)	60,000	
Total liabilities		$310,000
Common stock	$450,000	
Retained earnings	186,500	
Total stockholders' equity		636,500
Total		$946,500

In anticipation of preparing a master budget for January, February, and March 1995, management has gathered the following information:

a. Arnold Corporation's single product is purchased for $20 per unit and resold for $30. The expected inventory level on December 31 (5,000 units) is greater than management's desired level for 1995 of 25% of the next month's expected unit sales. Budgeted sales are

January	6,000 units
February	8,000
March	10,000
April	9,000

b. Cash sales are 25% of total sales and credit sales are 75% of total sales. Of the credit sales, 60% are collected in the first month after the sale and 40% in the second month after the sale. Sixty percent of the December 31, 1994, balance of accounts receivable will be collected during January and 40% will be collected during February.

c. Merchandise purchased by the company is paid for as follows: 20% in the month after purchase, and 80% in the second month after purchase. Twenty percent of the Accounts Payable balance on December 31, 1994, will be paid during January, and 80% will be paid during February.

d. Sales commissions of 20% of sales are paid each month. Additional sales salaries are $60,000 per year.

e. General and administrative salaries are $96,000 per year. Repair expenses equal $2,000 per month and are paid in cash.

f. The equipment shown in the December 31, 1994, balance sheet was purchased in January 1994. It is being depreciated over eight years under the straight-line method with no salvage value. The following new purchases of equipment are planned in the coming quarter:

January	$48,000
February	60,000
March	19,200

This equipment will also be depreciated with the straight-line method over eight years, with no salvage value. A full month's depreciation is taken for the month in which the equipment is purchased.

g. The company plans to acquire some land at the end of March at a cost of $100,000. The purchase price will be paid with cash on the last day of the month.

h. Arnold Corporation has a working arrangement with the bank to obtain additional loans as needed. The interest rate is 12% per year, and the interest is paid at the end of each month based on the beginning balance. Partial or full payments on these loans can be made on the last day of the month. Arnold Corporation has agreed to maintain a minimum ending cash balance of $24,000 in every month.

i. The income tax rate applicable to the company is 40%. However, income taxes on the first quarter's income will not be paid until April 15.

Required

Prepare a master budget for the first quarter of 1995. It should include the following component budgets:

1. Monthly sales budgets (showing both budgeted unit sales and dollar sales).
2. Monthly merchandise purchases budgets.
3. Monthly selling expense budgets.
4. Monthly general and administrative expense budgets.
5. Monthly capital expenditures budgets.
6. Monthly cash budgets.
7. Budgeted income statement for the first quarter.
8. Budgeted balance sheet as of March 31, 1995.

Provide as many supplemental schedules as you need. Round all amounts to the nearest dollar.

Problem 25–7A
Analytical essay
(LO 3)

Examine your answer to Problem 25–2A about the merchandise purchase budgets for the Airlift Corporation. It should reflect much smaller purchases of all three products in August compared to September and October.

What factor caused these smaller purchases to be planned? Suggest some conditions in the business that would cause this factor to affect Airlift as it apparently has.

Problem 25–8A
Analytical essay
(LO 3)

In Problem 25–4A, the Boland Company's cash budget indicates that the company will need to borrow more than $20,000 in April and more than $30,000 in May. Suggest some reasons why knowing this information in March would be helpful to Boland's management.

Provocative Problems

Provocative Problem 25–1
Norton Company
(LO 3)

Norton Company produces a candy bar that requires 2 pounds of chocolate per unit. The owner of the company is negotiating with the bank for approval to obtain loans as they are needed. An important item in the discussion has been the question of how much cash Norton will require to pay for purchases of chocolate.

Norton Company purchases its chocolate on account, and the resulting payables are paid in cash as follows: 40% during the month after purchase and 60% during the second month after purchase.

The company plans to manufacture enough candy bars to maintain an ending monthly inventory equal to 30% of the next month's sales. Sufficient chocolate is to be purchased each month to maintain an ending inventory equal to 20% of the next month's production requirements.

During the coming months, budgeted unit sales are as follows:

March	40,000
April	60,000
May	75,000
June	25,000

The following data are available on February 28:

Candy bars on hand	15,000
Pounds of chocolate on hand	33,000
Accounts payable	
Due in March	$300,000
Due in April	450,000

Recent prices of chocolate have varied substantially and the owner speculates that the price could range from $4 to $10 per pound during the next few months. You are asked to assist the owner by predicting the cash payments to be made in the months of March, April, and May. Prepare separate predictions based on a low price of $4 and a high price of $10.

Provocative Problem 25–2
Stingray Corporation
(LO 3)

The Stringray Corporation has budgeted the following unit sales volumes:

May	140,000
June	120,000
July	100,000
August	125,000

The company's inventory policy is to maintain an ending finished goods inventory of 20% of the next month's budgeted sales plus a safety stock of 5,000 units. The May 1 inventory was 26,000 units.

An analysis of Stingray Corporation's manufacturing costs shows:

Material cost	$10.00 per unit
Direct labor cost	$ 4.00 per unit
Variable overhead cost	$22.00 per unit
Fixed overhead costs	$550,000 per month

Required

Prepare production budgets and manufacturing budgets for the months of May, June, and July. The manufacturing budgets should show the total manufacturing costs expected in each of the three months.

Provocative Problem 25–3
As a Matter of Ethics
Essay

Ethics

Examine the ethics case on page 1329. What specific factor in the first situation makes the accounting clerk's action unethical? In the second situation, the executive's activity concerning his stock seems to be prompted by his resignation and his need for cash. Do you think that these considerations change the ethics of the situation?

Answers to Objective Review Questions

LO 1 (*e*)	LO 3 (*d*)	LO 5 (*d*)
LO 2 (*b*)	LO 4 (*a*)	

CHAPTER

26

Flexible Budgets and Standard Costs

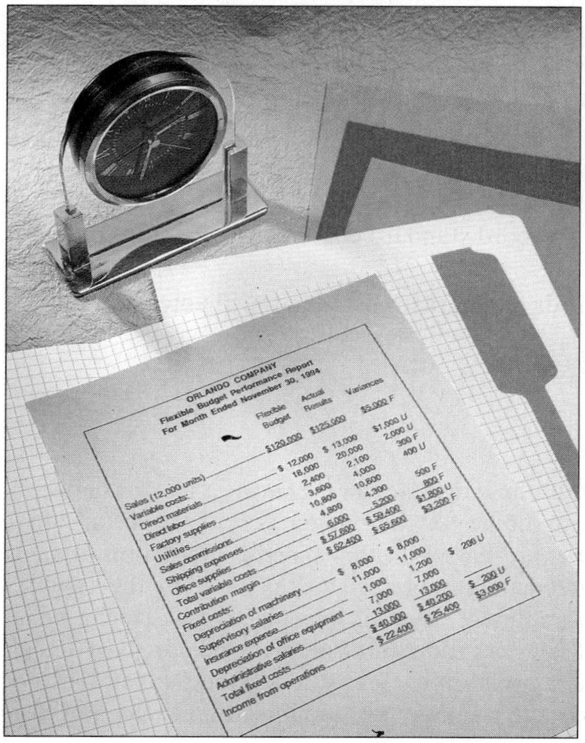

A plan is based on predictions. Because the future is seldom predicted accurately, managers must be flexible in evaluating performance. It would be too simple to conclude that success or failure occurred just because profits were higher or lower than expected. Flexible budgeting leads to more useful evaluations.

Topical Coverage

In Chapter 25, you learned that budgeting organizes and formalizes management's planning activities. You also learned that budgets can provide a basis for evaluating actual performance. In this chapter, we look more closely at how budgets can be used to evaluate performance. These evaluations are important for controlling business operations. By studying this chapter, you will learn another way that managerial accounting contributes to fulfilling management's control responsibility.

Learning Objectives

After studying Chapter 26, you should be able to:

1. Describe the differences between and relative advantages of fixed budgets and flexible budgets and be able to prepare a flexible budget.
2. State what standard costs represent, how they are determined, and how they are used by management to evaluate performance.
3. Calculate material, labor, and overhead variances, and describe what each variance indicates about the performance of a company.
4. Explain how standard cost accounting information is useful for the technique of management by exception.
5. Prepare journal entries to record standard costs and to account for price and quantity variances.
6. Define or explain the words and phrases listed in the chapter glossary.

Fixed Budgets and Performance Reports

You learned in Chapter 25 that the initial step in preparing a master budget is selecting the expected sales volume for the budget period. Then, all other budgets in the master budget are based on this specific prediction of sales volume. In effect, the predicted amount of each cost is based on the assumption that a specific (or *fixed*) amount of sales will take place. A budget based on a single predicted amount of sales or production volume is called a **fixed budget** or a *static budget*. The total amount of each cost in a fixed budget does not reflect the possibility that the actual sales or production volume may be different from the fixed budgeted amount.

Remember from Chapter 25 that one benefit of a budget is that it provides a useful basis for analyzing the success of actual results. Information useful for this analysis is often presented as a comparison in a **performance report** like the one in Illustration 26–1. This particular report compares actual results for the Orlando Company for November 1994 with the results expected under a fixed budget for 10,000 units of product. (In this example, the production volume equals sales volume so that the amount of inventory does not change.) Notice that the performance report designates the differences between budgeted and actual performance as *variances*. You should also note the letters *F* and *U*

ILLUSTRATION 26–1

A Performance Report Based on a Fixed Budget

ORLANDO COMPANY
Performance Report
For Month Ended November 30, 1994

	Fixed Budget	Actual Performance	Variances
Sales: In units	10,000	12,000	
In dollars	$100,000	$125,000	$25,000 *F*
Cost of goods sold:			
Direct materials	$ 10,000	$ 13,000	$ 3,000 *U*
Direct labor	15,000	20,000	5,000 *U*
Overhead:			
Factory supplies	2,000	2,100	100 *U*
Utilities	3,000	4,000	1,000 *U*
Depreciation of machinery	8,000	8,000	
Supervisory salaries	11,000	11,000	
Selling expenses:			
Sales commissions	9,000	10,800	1,800 *U*
Shipping expenses	4,000	4,300	300 *U*
General and administrative expenses:			
Office supplies	5,000	5,200	200 *U*
Insurance expense	1,000	1,200	200 *U*
Depreciation of office equipment	7,000	7,000	
Administrative salaries	13,000	13,000	
Total expenses	$ 88,000	$ 99,600	$11,600 *U*
Income from operations	$ 12,000	$ 25,400	$13,400 *F*

F = Favorable variance
U = Unfavorable variance

beside the numbers in the third column of the performance report. Their meanings are

> *F = Favorable variance*—compared to the budget, the actual cost or revenue contributes to a *higher* income.
>
> *U = Unfavorable variance*—compared to the budget, the actual cost or revenue contributes to a *lower* income.

This convention is followed throughout the chapter.

In evaluating Orlando Company's operations, management is likely to ask a variety of questions, including these:

- Why is actual income from operations $13,400 higher than the budgeted amount?
- Are the amounts paid for each expense item too high?
- Is the manufacturing department using too much direct material?
- Is the manufacturing department using too much direct labor?

In fact, the performance report in Illustration 26–1 provides little help in answering these questions because the actual sales volume was 2,000 units higher than budgeted. The manager might assume that this higher level caused total dollar sales and many of the expenses to be higher, but other factors also could have influenced their amounts. This fixed budget performance report has limited usefulness because it fails to show whether actual costs were out of line for the actual sales volume. The report really does not provide management much useful information beyond the simple fact that the sales volume was 2,000 units higher than expected.

FLEXIBLE BUDGETS

LO 1 Describe the differences between and relative advantages of fixed budgets and flexible budgets and be able to prepare a flexible budget.

To help management answer questions like the ones presented on page 1375, many companies prepare **flexible budgets**, which are also called *variable budgets*. Unlike the planning budgets described in Chapter 25, flexible budgets are prepared after a specific period's activities are completed. Their purpose is to help managers evaluate past performance instead of helping them plan future events. In contrast to fixed budgets based on one *expected* amount of budgeted sales or production, flexible budgets describe the amounts of revenue and expense that should have occurred at the *actual* level of output. Flexible budgets are more useful for evaluations because they reflect the fact that different levels of activity produce disproportionately different amounts of cost. As a result, comparisons of actual results with budgeted performance are more likely to direct management to the reasons why the actual results differed from what should have happened.

Preparing a Flexible Budget

Flexible budgeting is designed to reveal the effects of volume on the level of costs. To prepare a flexible budget, management depends on the distinctions between fixed and variable costs used in the cost-volume-profit analyses described in Chapter 24. Remember from Chapter 24 that the variable cost per unit of activity remains constant. Thus, the total amount of a variable cost changes in direct proportion to a change in the level of activity. On the other hand, the total amount of a fixed cost remains unchanged regardless of changes in the level of activity within the relevant (or normal) operating range of activity.[1]

In generating the numbers used in a flexible budget, the accountant expresses each variable cost as a constant amount per unit of sales (or as percentage of a sales dollar). In contrast, the budgeted amount of each fixed cost is expressed as the total amount expected to occur at any sales volume.

Illustration 26–2 shows a set of possible flexible budgets for Orlando Company for November 1994. Notice that seven of the expenses listed in Illustra-

[1] In Chapter 24, we acknowledged that some costs are neither strictly variable nor strictly fixed. In the present discussion, we continue using the assumption that all costs can be reasonably classified as either variable or fixed within the relevant range.

ILLUSTRATION 26–2

A Set of Flexible Budgets

ORLANDO COMPANY
Possible Flexible Budgets
For Month Ended November 30, 1994

	Variable Amount per Unit	Total Fixed Cost	Unit Sales of 10,000	Unit Sales of 12,000	Unit Sales of 14,000
Sales	$10.00		$100,000	$120,000	$140,000
Variable costs:					
Direct materials	$ 1.00		$ 10,000	$ 12,000	$ 14,000
Direct labor	1.50		15,000	18,000	21,000
Factory supplies	0.20		2,000	2,400	2,800
Utilities	0.30		3,000	3,600	4,200
Sales commissions	0.90		9,000	10,800	12,600
Shipping expenses	0.40		4,000	4,800	5,600
Office supplies	0.50		5,000	6,000	7,000
Total variable costs	$ 4.80		$ 48,000	$ 57,600	$ 67,200
Contribution margin	$ 5.20		$ 52,000	$ 62,400	$ 72,800
Fixed costs:					
Depreciation, machinery		$ 8,000	$ 8,000	$ 8,000	$ 8,000
Supervisory salaries		11,000	11,000	11,000	11,000
Insurance expense		1,000	1,000	1,000	1,000
Depreciation, office equipment		7,000	7,000	7,000	7,000
Administrative salaries		13,000	13,000	13,000	13,000
Total fixed costs		$40,000	$ 40,000	$ 40,000	$ 40,000
Income from operations			$ 12,000	$ 22,400	$ 32,800

tion 26–1 are variable costs. The remaining five expenses are fixed costs. These classifications result from management's investigation of each of the company's expenses. (You should avoid drawing general rules from these examples. These particular expense categories are not always the same for every company. For example, depending on the nature of the company's operations, office supplies expense may be fixed or variable with respect to sales. In the present example, the company's management concluded that the office supplies cost is variable.)

The flexible budgets in Illustration 26–2 list sales and then the variable costs. They show the total variable costs and then subtract the total from sales. As you learned in Chapter 24, this difference between sales and variable costs equals the *contribution margin*. The budgets then list the expected amounts of fixed costs and present the expected income from operations before income taxes.

In Illustration 26–2, the first and second columns show the flexible budget amounts that can be applied to any volume of sales within the relevant range. The other columns illustrate the flexible budgets that would be generated by applying these amounts to three selected sales volumes. For example, the first flexible budget (for 10,000 units) shows the same amounts that appeared in

Illustration 26–1 on page 1375. The numbers are the same because that volume was assumed when the company prepared the fixed budget for November.

Remember that Orlando Company's actual sales volume for November was 12,000 units. This level was 2,000 units more than the 10,000 units originally forecasted in the master budget. To find the difference in expected costs for these two levels, compare the flexible budget for 10,000 units in the third column of Illustration 26–2 with the flexible budget for 12,000 units in the fourth column.

To identify opportunities for improving performance, the company's managers should compare the actual income of $25,400 (from Illustration 26–1) with the $22,400 income expected at the actual sales volume of 12,000 units. Thus, the total variance in income to be explained and understood is only $3,000 instead of the $13,400 variance identified in Illustration 26–1. After receiving the flexible budget based on November's actual volume, management's next step is to determine what caused this $3,000 difference. A flexible budget performance report provides useful guidance for answering this question.

Flexible Budget Performance Report

A **flexible budget performance report** helps management analyze the difference between actual performance and budgeted performance based on the actual sales volume (or other level of activity). The report should direct management's attention toward those particular costs or revenues with actual amounts that differ substantially from the budgeted amounts.

Illustration 26–3 shows the flexible budget performance report for Orlando Company for November. The managerial accountant prepared this report after the actual volume was known to be 12,000 units. Observe that Illustration 26–3 shows a $5,000 favorable variance in total dollar sales. Because the actual and budgeted volumes are both 12,000 units, the $5,000 sales variance must have resulted solely from a selling price that was higher than expected. Further analysis of the facts surrounding this $5,000 sales variance produces these results:

Actual average price per unit	$125,000/12,000 = $10.4167
Budgeted price per unit	$120,000/12,000 = 10.0000
Favorable sales variance per unit	$ 5,000/12,000 = $ 0.4167

Management would use this information to assess whether the decision to increase the selling price met its goals. Then, they would consider which pricing strategy to use in the future.

The other variances in Illustration 26–3 should direct management's attention to areas where corrective actions could help them control Orlando Company's operations. Each variance can be analyzed like the previous sales variance. That is, think of each expense as the joint result of using a given number of units of the expense item and paying a specific price per unit. According to this approach, a variance in Illustration 26–3 can be created in part by a difference between the actual price per unit and the budgeted price per

ILLUSTRATION 26-3

ORLANDO COMPANY
Flexible Budget Performance Report
For Month Ended November 30, 1994

	Flexible Budget	Actual Results	Variances
Sales (12,000 units)	$120,000	$125,000	$5,000 *F*
Variable costs:			
Direct materials	$ 12,000	$ 13,000	$1,000 *U*
Direct labor	18,000	20,000	2,000 *U*
Factory supplies	2,400	2,100	300 *F*
Utilities	3,600	4,000	400 *U*
Sales commissions	10,800	10,800	
Shipping expenses	4,800	4,300	500 *F*
Office supplies	6,000	5,200	800 *F*
Total variable costs	$ 57,600	$ 59,400	$1,800 *U*
Contribution margin	$ 62,400	$ 65,600	$3,200 *F*
Fixed costs:			
Depreciation of machinery	$ 8,000	$ 8,000	
Supervisory salaries	11,000	11,000	
Insurance expense	1,000	1,200	$ 200 *U*
Depreciation of office equipment	7,000	7,000	
Administrative salaries	13,000	13,000	
Total fixed costs	$ 40,000	$ 40,200	$ 200 *U*
Income from operations	$ 22,400	$ 25,400	$3,000 *F*

F = Favorable variance
U = Unfavorable variance

unit. If so, there is a **price variance.** And, a variance also can be created in part by a difference between the actual number of units used and the budgeted number of units expected to be used. If so, there is a **quantity variance.** You will learn more about this technique of **variance analysis** in the following section on standard costs.

STANDARD COSTS

LO 2 State what standard costs represent, how they are determined, and how they are used by management to evaluate performance.

In Chapters 21 and 22, you learned about job order and process cost accounting systems. Accountants use many different variations of these two basic types of systems in practice. One important variation is a standard cost accounting system based on standard costs.

The costs described in Chapters 21 and 22 are **historical costs** because they are the dollar amounts paid by the business in past transactions. These historical (or actual) costs provide useful information for some purposes. However, management needs a basis of comparison to decide whether the amounts of the historical costs are reasonable or excessive.

Because they are budgeted amounts, **standard costs** offer a useful basis for these evaluations. Standard costs are the costs that should be incurred under normal conditions to produce a specific product or component, or to perform a specific service. Standard costs are established through personnel, engineering, and accounting studies of past experience and other data. Then, management uses standard costs to assess the reasonableness of the actual costs incurred when producing the product or service during the past period. When actual costs vary from standard, management can use that information to help them identify possible problems and corrective actions.

Standard costs are used in preparing budgets because they should be incurred under normal conditions. Thus, standard costs are budgeted costs, and terms such as *standard material cost, standard labor cost,* and *standard overhead cost* refer to the amounts budgeted for direct materials, direct labor, and overhead in normal circumstances.

Setting the Amounts of Standard Costs

Managerial accountants, engineers, personnel administrators, and other managers combine their efforts to set the amounts of standard costs. To identify standard direct labor costs, management can conduct time and motion studies for each labor operation in the process for manufacturing a product or providing a service. From these studies, management can both learn the best way to perform the operation and set the standard labor time required for the operation under normal conditions. Management also investigates the quantity, grade, and cost of each material used in the process. Detailed management studies of machines and other productive equipment also help the company achieve greater efficiency and learn what standard overhead costs should be.

Regardless of the care exercised in setting standard costs and in revising them as conditions change, actual costs frequently differ from standard costs. If so, the difference may result from more than one factor. For example, the actual quantity of material used may differ from standard and the price paid per unit of material also may differ from standard. Similar quantity and price differences from standard amounts can occur for labor. That is, the actual labor time and the actual labor price may have varied from what was expected. Later in the chapter, you will learn about factors that may cause actual overhead cost to differ from standard.

Variances

LO 3 Calculate material, labor, and overhead variances, and describe what each variance indicates about the performance of a company.

The differences between actual and standard costs are called **cost variances.** As you have learned, variances can be favorable or unfavorable. A variance from standard cost is considered favorable if the actual cost is below the standard cost, and it is considered unfavorable if the actual cost is above the standard cost.[2]

[2] Rules are seldom as simple as they seem. For example, if management spends less than the budgeted amount on maintenance or insurance, the performance report would identify the difference as a favorable variance. However, cutting these expenses could lead to major losses in the long run if the machinery wears out prematurely or the insurance coverage proves to be inadequate.

ILLUSTRATION 26–4

The Variance Analysis Cycle

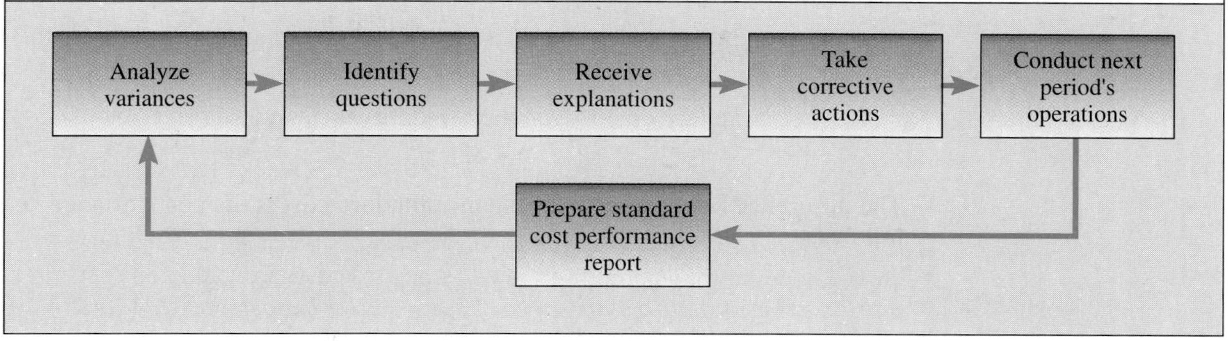

When a cost variance occurs, management should examine the circumstances to determine the factors that created it. By doing so, management should be able to identify who is responsible for the variance and then help them correct the problem. For example, assume that the standard material cost for producing 2,000 units of a product is $8,000, but that material costing $9,000 was actually used. The $1,000 unfavorable variance may have resulted from paying a price for the material that was higher than the standard price. Alternatively, the process may have used a greater quantity of material than standard. Or, there may have been some combination of these factors.

The purchasing department is usually responsible for the price paid for a material. Therefore, responsibility for explaining the problem rests with the purchasing manager if the variance was caused by a price greater than standard. On the other hand, the production department is usually responsible for the amount of material used. Thus, the production department manager is responsible for explaining the problem if the process used more than the standard amount of materials. However, the production department may have used more than the standard amount of material because its quality was below specifications, with the result that more waste was created. In this case, the purchasing manager is responsible for explaining why the inferior materials were acquired. On the other hand, the production manager is responsible for explaining what happened if the analysis shows that the waste was caused by inefficiencies. In summary, the performance report may identify the existence of the problem, but it can do no more than point the direction for further investigation to find out what can be done to improve future results.

In effect, the cost variances trigger questions. These questions call for answers that, in turn, should lead to changes designed to correct the problem and eliminate the variances for the next reporting period. The diagram in Illustration 26–4 shows the flow of events in this management cycle.

Isolating Material and Labor Variances

You can break down a cost variance into components that provide more information about the factors that caused it to occur. The total materials cost or labor cost can be expressed as the following equation:

$$\text{Actual cost} = \text{Actual quantity} \times \text{Actual price}$$
$$AC = AQ \times AP$$

Also, the standard cost that should have been incurred can be expressed in this formula:

$$\text{Standard cost} = \text{Standard quantity} \times \text{Standard price}$$
$$SC = SQ \times SP$$

The difference between actual cost and standard cost is the cost variance, as follows:

$$\text{Cost variance} = \text{Actual cost} - \text{Standard cost}$$
$$CV = AC - SC$$

We explained earlier that a cost variance can be created by two factors: (1) a difference between the actual quantity and the standard quantity and (2) a difference between the actual price and the standard price. To assess the effects of these two factors, we can express the cost variance as the sum of the quantity variance and the price variance. The quantity variance can be calculated with this formula:

$$\text{Quantity variance} = \left(\text{Actual quantity} - \text{Standard quantity}\right) \times \text{Standard price}$$
$$QV = (AQ - SQ) \times SP$$

This amount represents the additional cost incurred because the actual quantity (*AQ*) was greater than the expected standard quantity (*SQ*). Or, if the variance is favorable, it shows how much was saved by reducing the quantity below the standard amount.

The price variance is calculated as follows:

$$\text{Price variance} = (\text{Actual price} - \text{Standard price}) \times \text{Actual quantity}$$
$$PV = (AP - SP) \times AQ$$

This variance shows how much additional cost was incurred because the actual price was higher than standard. Or, if the variance is favorable, it shows how much the company saved by negotiating a lower price.

To illustrate cost variances, the following discussion is based on the example of the Green Company. For this example, assume that the company has established the following standard quantities for materials and labor, and these standard costs per unit for Product Z:

Direct materials (1 lb. per unit at $1 per lb.) . . .	$1.00
Direct labor (1 hr. per unit at $6 per hr.).	6.00
Overhead ($2 per standard direct labor hour) . .	2.00
Total standard cost per unit	$9.00

Material Variances

During May, Green Company started and completed 3,500 units of Product Z and used 3,600 pounds of direct materials that cost $1.05 per pound. Thus, the total material cost was $3,780. Under these facts, the actual and standard direct material costs for the 3,500 units and the direct material cost variance are

Actual cost	3,600 lbs. @ $1.05 per lb. =	$3,780
Standard cost	3,500 lbs. @ $1.00 per lb. =	3,500
Direct material cost variance (unfavorable)	=	$ 280

Initially, it is apparent that the total variance is the combined result of using more materials than planned and buying those materials at a higher price than was anticipated.

Using the equations presented earlier, the actual cost also can be calculated as follows:

$$\begin{aligned} AC &= AQ \times AP \\ &= 3{,}600 \times \$1.05 \\ &= \$3{,}780 \end{aligned}$$

The standard cost for the 3,500 units can be calculated as follows:

$$\begin{aligned} SC &= SQ \times SP \\ &= 3{,}500 \times \$1.00 \\ &= \$3{,}500 \end{aligned}$$

Therefore, the direct material cost variance is

$$\begin{aligned} CV &= AC - SC \\ &= \$3{,}780 - \$3{,}500 \\ &= \$280 \text{ (unfavorable)} \end{aligned}$$

Regardless of how the information is presented, the actual direct material cost for these units is $280 greater than the standard cost. We can get dollar measures of the contributions of the factors that created this unfavorable variance by calculating a direct material quantity variance and a direct material price variance. These calculations are presented in the following table:

Quantity variance:			
Actual units at the standard price	3,600 lbs. @ $1.00 =	$3,600	
Standard units at the standard price	3,500 lbs. @ $1.00 =	3,500	
Variance (unfavorable)	100 lbs. @ $1.00 =		$100
Price variance:			
Actual units at the actual price	3,600 lbs. @ $1.05 =	$3,780	
Actual units at the standard price	3,600 lbs. @ $1.00 =	3,600	
Variance (unfavorable)	3,600 lbs. @ $0.05 =		180
Direct material cost variance (unfavorable)			$280

The formulas also can be used to calculate the variances in this table. Thus, the quantity variance can be calculated like this:

$$\begin{aligned} QV &= (AQ - SQ) \times SP \\ &= (3{,}600 - 3{,}500) \times \$1.00 \\ &= \$100 \text{ (unfavorable)} \end{aligned}$$

And, the price variance can be computed with this formula:

$$\begin{aligned} PV &= (AP - SP) \times AQ \\ &= (\$1.05 - \$1.00) \times 3{,}600 \\ &= \$180 \text{ (unfavorable)} \end{aligned}$$

Regardless of how it is presented, the analysis shows that $100 of the excess direct material cost resulted from using 100 more pounds than standard, and $180 resulted from a unit purchase price that was $0.05 above standard. With this information, management can go to the responsible individuals for explanations. The excess usage of 100 pounds should be explained by the manager of the production department and the higher price of $1.05 needs to be explained by the manager of the purchasing department.

Labor Variances

The labor cost for a specific product or service depends on the number of hours worked (the quantity) and the wage rate paid to the employees (the price). Therefore, when actual amounts for a task differ from standard, the labor cost variance can be divided into a quantity variance and a price variance, just like the material cost variance.

For example, the direct labor standard for 3,500 units of Product Z is one hour per unit, or 3,500 hours at $6 per hour. If 3,400 hours at $6.30 per hour were actually used to complete the units, the actual and standard labor costs for these units are

Actual cost	3,400 hrs. @ $6.30 per hr. =	$21,420
Standard cost	3,500 hrs. @ $6.00 per hr. =	21,000
Direct labor cost variance (unfavorable)		$ 420

The actual cost is only $420 over the standard but computing the quantity and price variances reveals the following additional data:

Quantity variance:			
Actual hours at standard price	3,400 hrs. @ $6.00 =	$20,400	
Standard hours at standard price	3,500 hrs. @ $6.00 =	21,000	
Variance (favorable)	(100) hrs. @ $6.00 =		$ (600)
Price variance:			
Actual hours at actual price	3,400 hrs. @ $6.30 =	$21,420	
Actual hours at standard price	3,400 hrs. @ $6.00 =	20,400	
Variance (unfavorable)	3,400 hrs. @ $0.30 =		1,020
Direct labor cost variance (unfavorable)			$ 420

The information in this table also can be computed with the formulas. Thus, the quantity variance can be calculated as follows:

$$\begin{aligned} QV &= (AQ - SQ) \times SP \\ &= (3{,}400 - 3{,}500) \times \$6.00 \\ &= -\$600 \text{ (favorable)} \end{aligned}$$

And, the price variance can be determined with this formula:

$$\begin{aligned} PV &= (AP - SP) \times AQ \\ &= (\$6.30 - \$6.00) \times 3{,}400 \\ &= \$1{,}020 \text{ (unfavorable)} \end{aligned}$$

The analysis shows that a favorable quantity variance of $600 resulted from using 100 fewer direct labor hours than standard for the units produced. However, this favorable variance was more than offset by a wage rate that was $0.30 above standard. Thus, the production manager should explain how the labor hours were reduced. (If the experience can be repeated and transferred to other departments, the savings can be multiplied.) And, the personnel administrator should explain why the wage rate was higher than expected.

One possible explanation of the factors that led to these labor variances might lie in the fact that the factory or department has workers of various skill levels. If so, it is the responsibility of the foreman or other production manager to assign each task to workers with the skill level appropriate for getting it done. In this case, an investigation might show that higher skilled workers were used to produce the 3,500 units of Product Z. As a result, fewer labor hours were required for the work. However, the wage rate paid to the workers was higher than standard because of their greater skills. In Green Company's situation, the effect of this strategy was a higher than standard total cost. Thus, steps should be taken to change the strategy in the future.

Assigning Standard Overhead Costs to Products and Services

When standard costs are used, the predetermined overhead rate assigns standard overhead costs to the goods or services produced during the period. The rate may be based on the relationship between standard overhead and standard labor cost, or standard labor hours, or standard machine-hours, or some other measure of production. For example, Green Company charges its Product Z with $2 of standard overhead cost per standard direct labor hour. Because the direct labor standard for Product Z is one hour per unit, the 3,500 units manufactured in May were charged with $7,000 of standard overhead costs.

Before going on, recall that only 3,400 actual direct labor-hours were used in producing these units. But, overhead costs are assigned to the units on the basis of standard labor hours, not on the basis of actual labor hours. Standard labor hours are used because the total amount of overhead charged to all units produced should equal the total expected overhead cost for the period. Thus, the total overhead costs should be assigned to the products even though less than the standard amount of labor was used in producing them. In other words, the allocated costs should not vary from the expected amount simply because the amount of direct labor used was different from expected.

Establishing Overhead Standards

Standard overhead costs, like other standard costs, are the amounts expected to occur at the projected level of operation for the planned period. Unlike direct materials and direct labor, however, overhead includes both variable and fixed cost components. As a result, the average overhead cost per unit changes as the projected volume changes. Because standard costs are budgeted costs, they must be established before the reporting period begins. Therefore, standard overhead costs are average per unit costs, based on the projected volume of output.

To establish the standard overhead cost rate for a future period, management uses the same cost structure that will be used to construct a flexible budget after the period is completed. This cost structure identifies the different overhead cost components and classifies them as variable or fixed. To produce the standard overhead rate, management must select a specific volume and predict the total overhead cost. Then, they divide this total by the allocation base to produce the standard rate. In many cases, the allocation base is the standard direct labor hours expected to be used to produce the projected volume.

Illustration 26–5 presents the overhead cost structure used in developing flexible budgets for the Green Company. It also establishes the predetermined standard overhead rate for May before the month begins. The first column lists the per unit amounts of the variable costs and the monthly amounts of fixed costs. The next four columns show the total costs expected to occur at four possible levels of output. Notice that the overhead cost per unit gets smaller as the volume increases. This result occurs because the fixed costs remain constant for the month.

In setting the standard overhead cost for May, management selects a volume that they expect to occur. As indicated in Illustration 26–5, the managers of the Green Company chose the 80% level for a volume of 4,000 units. At this volume, they budgeted $8,000 for the total overhead for May. This total cost produces a $2 per unit average overhead cost. And, because the company has a standard of one direct labor hour for each unit, the predetermined standard overhead application rate for May is $2 per standard direct labor hour.

When selecting the expected operating level for the plant, management must consider a number of factors. Theoretically, the level could be set as high as 100% of capacity, but it is almost always set at a lower level. Some factors that can put the expected operating level below full capacity include difficulties in scheduling work, equipment that is unavailable because of maintenance, and insufficient demand for the product. In addition, a good long-run management practice calls for having some plant capacity in excess of current operating needs to allow future growth. Because of a combination of these factors, the management of the Green Company determined that the expected production level for May would be at 80% of capacity, or 4,000 units.

ILLUSTRATION 26–5

GREEN COMPANY
Possible Total Overhead Costs
For Month Ended May 31, 1994

	Flexible Budget Amounts	Possible Production Levels (Percent of Monthly Capacity) 70%	80%	90%	100%
Production in units	1 unit	3,500	*4,000*	4,500	5,000
Factory overhead:					
Variable costs (per unit):					
Indirect labor	$0.40	$1,400	*$1,600*	$1,800	$2,000
Indirect materials	0.30	1,050	*1,200*	1,350	1,500
Power and lights	0.20	700	*800*	900	1,000
Maintenance	0.10	350	*400*	450	500
Totals	$1.00	$3,500	*$4,000*	$4,500	$5,000
Fixed costs (per month):					
Building rent	$1,000	$1,000	*$1,000*	$1,000	$1,000
Depreciation, machinery	1,200	1,200	*1,200*	1,200	1,200
Supervisory salaries	1,800	1,800	*1,800*	1,800	1,800
Totals	$4,000	$4,000	*$4,000*	$4,000	$4,000
Total factory overhead		$7,500	*$8,000*	$8,500	$9,000
Standard direct labor hours	1 hr./unit	3,500	*4,000*	4,500	5,000
Predetermined overhead rate per standard direct labor hour		$2.143	*$2.000*	$1.889	$1.800

Expected production level during May (↑ 80% column)

Overhead Variances

When standard costs are used, the cost accounting system applies overhead to production on the basis of the predetermined standard overhead cost rate. Then, at the end of a cost period, the difference between the total overhead cost applied to products and the total overhead cost actually incurred is called the **overhead cost variance.** Calculate this variance as follows:

$$\text{Overhead cost variance} = \text{Actual overhead incurred} - \text{Standard overhead applied}$$

$$\text{OCV} = \text{AOI} - \text{SOA}$$

To help management identify the factors that created the overhead cost variance, the managerial accountant can divide it into two components.[3] First, the

[3] It is also possible to divide the total overhead variance into three components. This three-way analysis of overhead variance is left for more advanced cost accounting courses.

actual production volume during the period may have been different from the *expected* production volume used to establish the standard overhead application rate. Thus, the amount of overhead assigned to the product during the month was based on an assumed level of production that did not occur. Second, the *actual* overhead costs may have differed from the *expected* amounts for the actual volume. In other words, the total difference between the allocated cost and the actual cost arose from two factors: (1) an inaccurate prediction of the volume of operation and (2) actual costs that did not match the expected amounts. To describe the effects of these two factors, the total overhead cost variance is the sum of the volume variance and the controllable variance.

Volume Variance

The **volume variance** is the difference between two dollar amounts of overhead cost. The first amount equals the total overhead cost that would have been expected if the actual operating volume had been accurately predicted. The second number is the overhead cost allocated to the month's products using the predetermined standard overhead rate. Thus, the volume variance can be described with this formula:

Volume variance = Overhead budgeted at the actual production volume Achieved − Standard overhead applied

VV = OB − SOA

For example, the Green Company actually operated at 70% of capacity during May even though the expected production volume was 80% of capacity when the predetermined overhead application rate was set. From the facts shown in Illustration 26–5, we can see that the company would have budgeted only $7,500 of overhead at this volume instead of $8,000. If this volume had been predicted, the standard overhead rate would have been $2.143 per hour instead of $2.00 per hour. But, the company did produce only 3,500 units of Product Z and did assign overhead to those units at the predetermined standard rate of $2 per direct labor hour. In light of these facts, the company's volume variance for May is

Volume variance:	
Budgeted overhead at 3,500 units	$7,500
Standard overhead applied to products (3,500 standard labor hours at the $2 per hour standard rate)	7,000
Variance (unfavorable)	$ 500

The table shows the same result as this equation:

VV = OB − SOA
= $7,500 − $7,000
= $500 (unfavorable)

ILLUSTRATION 26–6

The Overhead Volume Variance

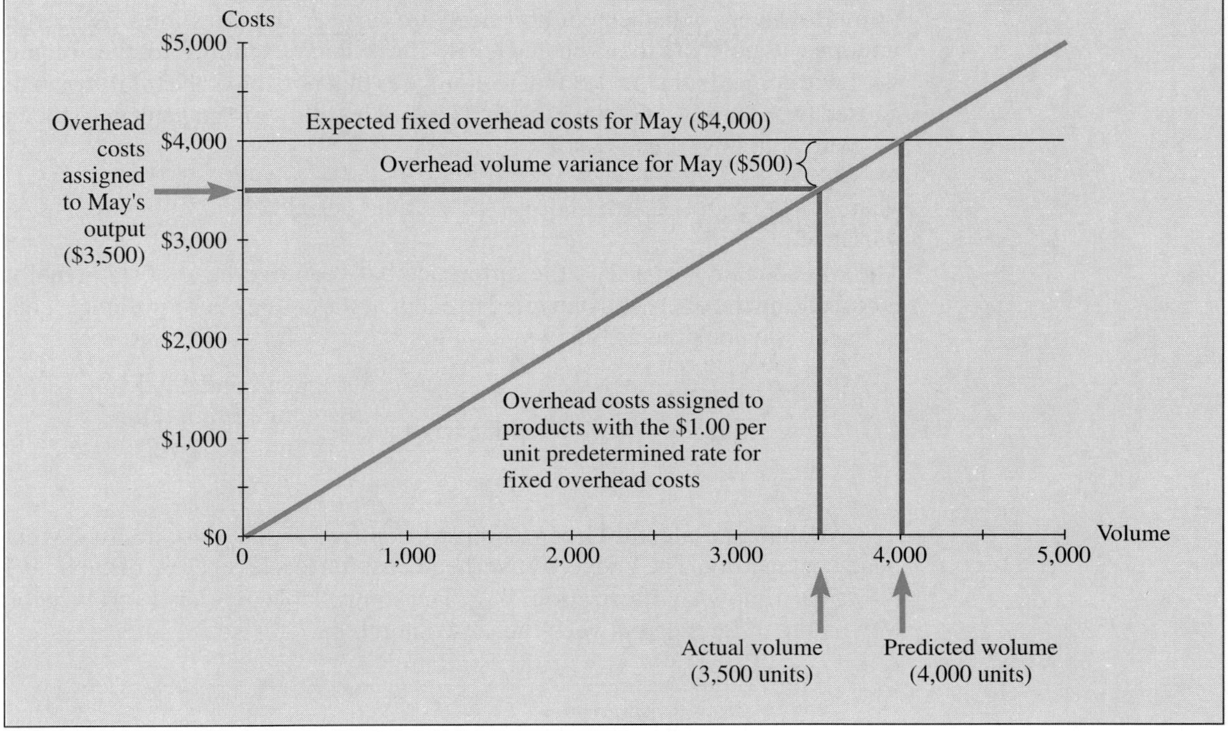

In summary, the company expected to assign $8,000 of overhead to 4,000 units during May but actually assigned only $7,000 of overhead to 3,500 units.

To understand this volume variance more completely, examine the detailed amounts in Illustration 26–5 for the possible volumes of 70% and 80% of capacity. Observe that the company can subdivide the $2 per hour overhead rate at the 80% level into $1 per hour for variable overhead and $1 per hour for fixed overhead only at that level. Thus, when the $2 overhead rate was applied to the 3,500 units produced at the actual 70% level, the $1 fixed cost portion of the rate fell short by $500 in allocating the total budgeted fixed overhead cost of $4,000.

This result is shown graphically in Illustration 26–6. In the graph, the upward sloping line represents the amount of fixed overhead costs that was expected to be applied to the units produced in May. The horizontal line represents the $4,000 of total fixed costs expected for May. These two lines intersect at the planned operating volume of 4,000 units. At the 3,500 unit volume, the application line falls $500 below the budgeted overhead line. This shortfall below the budgeted amount is the volume variance.

An unfavorable volume variance simply reflects the fact that the plant did not reach its expected operating level. In every case, management would already know this result, and the variance would not convey any new information. However, management still needs to answer the question of why the volume was not up to the expected level. The primary usefulness of the volume variance comes from the fact that it eliminates that portion of the total variance caused by failing to meet the expected level. This allows management to focus on controlling overhead costs.

Controllable Variance

The **controllable variance** is the difference between overhead costs actually incurred and the overhead budgeted to occur at the actual operating level. This variance is calculated as follows:

$$\text{Controllable variance} = \text{Actual overhead incurred} - \text{Overhead budgeted at the actual production volume achieved}$$

$$CV = AOI - OB$$

For this example, the Green Company incurred $7,650 of total actual overhead cost in May. The budgeted overhead cost for this level (70% of capacity) is $7,500, a shown in Illustration 26–5. The controllable overhead variance for May is the difference between these two numbers:

Controllable variance:	
Actual overhead incurred	$7,650
Overhead budgeted at operating level achieved . .	7,500
Variance (unfavorable).	$ 150

The calculation can also be made with this formula:

$$\begin{aligned} CV &= AOI - OB \\ &= \$7{,}650 - \$7{,}500 \\ &= \$150 \text{ (unfavorable)} \end{aligned}$$

The controllable overhead variance shows how well management controlled the total overhead cost (particularly the variable components) at the actual operating level. In this case, management exceeded the budget by $150 at the actual 70% level.

A complete overhead variance report provides managers with more detailed information about the specific overhead costs and how they differed from the budgeted amounts. Illustration 26–7 shows the May overhead variance report for Green Company. It shows that the fixed costs and maintenance cost occurred as expected. However, the costs for indirect labor and power and lights were higher than expected at the actual volume. And, the indirect materials cost was slightly below the expected amount.

ILLUSTRATION 26–7

GREEN COMPANY
Factory Overhead Variance Report
For Month Ended May 31, 1994

Volume variance:

Expected production level	80% of capacity
Production level achieved	70% of capacity
Volume variance	$500 (unfavorable)

Controllable variance:

	Flexible Budget	Actual Results	Variances
Variable overhead costs:			
Indirect labor	$1,400	$1,525	$125 *U*
Indirect materials	1,050	1,025	$ 25 *F*
Power and lights	700	750	50 *U*
Maintenance	350	350	
Total variable costs	$3,500	$3,650	$150 *U*
Fixed overhead costs:			
Building rent	$1,000	$1,000	
Depreciation, machinery	1,200	1,200	
Supervisory salaries	1,800	1,800	
Total fixed costs	$4,000	$4,000	
Total overhead costs	$7,500	$7,650	$150 *U*

F = Favorable variance
U = Unfavorable variance

Combining the Volume and Controllable Variances

The total overhead variance was measured earlier at $650. This amount equals the sum of the volume and controllable variances:

Overhead Cost Variance = Volume Variance + Controllable Variance
OCV = VV + CV

You can also combine the volume and controllable variances as shown in this table:

Volume variance:		
Overhead budgeted at operating level achieved	$7,500	
Standard overhead applied to production (3,500 standard hours at $2 per hour)	7,000	
Variance (unfavorable)		$500
Controllable variance:		
Actual overhead incurred	$7,650	
Overhead budgeted at actual operating level	7,500	
Variance (unfavorable)		150
Overhead cost variance [Actual overhead incurred in excess of overhead charged to production] (unfavorable)		$650

AS A MATTER OF *Ethics*

You are an internal auditor looking into your company's procedures for comparing actual results with budgeted amounts. You notice that for several years running, one manager (who has managed several different departments over the years) always spends exactly what is budgeted for discretionary supplies and small items of equipment.

Looking into the records further, you find that 25 to 35% of the annual budget for these items has been spent by this manager in November and December, right before the end of the budget year. An interview with the manager reveals that he always spends what is budgeted, whether or not the supplies and equipment are really needed. He offers three reasons to justify his actions. First, he doesn't want his budget to be cut back and thinks it will be if he doesn't spend all that he is allocated. Second, the company's practice of following management by exception calls attention to big deviations from the budget, and he would just as soon avoid that kind of attention. Third, he feels that the practice doesn't hurt anyone because the money was budgeted to be spent.

Although there is some logic in the manager's actions and explanation, you wonder whether you should comment on this matter in your report. You also wonder what recommendations, if any, you should offer.

Using Standard Costs to Control a Business

LO 4 Explain how standard cost accounting information is useful for the technique of management by exception.

To control business activities, top management must be able to influence the actions of the lower-level managers responsible for the company's revenues, costs, and expenses. After a budget is prepared and standard costs are established, management should take appropriate action to gain control when actual costs differ from the standard or budgeted amounts.

Reports like the ones in this chapter call management's attention to variances from business plans and other standards. When managers use these reports to focus on problem areas, the budgeting process contributes to the control function. As a matter of efficiency in using the budget performance reports, management should practice the analytical technique known as **management by exception.** Under this approach, managers focus on the most significant variances and give less attention to the areas where performance is close enough to the standard to be satisfactory. In effect, management concentrates on the exceptional or irregular situations and defers dealing with areas showing actual results that are reasonably close to the plan.

Using Standard Costs for Service and Other Nonmanufacturing Activities

Managers of many companies use standard costs and variance analysis only for manufacturing costs. If so, the master budget includes selling and general and administrative expenses, but subsequent control over these expenses is not based on standard costs and variances. However, managers of other companies recognize that standard costs and variances can help them control their nonmanufacturing expenses. In addition, companies that provide services to customers (instead of products) can use standard costs. The previous uses of variances can be easily adapted to these nonmanufacturing situations.

Standard Costs in the Accounts

LO 5 Prepare journal entries to record standard costs and to account for price and quantity variances.

As shown in this chapter's example, companies use standard costs in management reports. In addition, most standard cost systems also record the costs and the variances in the accounts. This practice simplifies record-keeping and helps the managerial accountant prepare the reports more easily. You do not need a detailed knowledge of standard cost accounting practices to understand standard costs and how they are used. However, you should know how to record standard costs and variances in the accounts. The following entries briefly illustrate the process for Green Company's standard costs and variances for May.

The first entry records the standard materials cost incurred in May in the Goods in Process Inventory account. This part of the entry should be familiar from your prior study of cost accounting. Notice especially that the amount of the debit equals the standard cost ($3,500) instead of the actual cost ($3,780). The entry credits the Raw Materials Inventory for the actual cost. The difference between the standard and actual costs is recorded with debits to two separate materials variance accounts. In this case, the material quantity variance and material price variance are both recorded as debits because they represent additional costs above the standard cost. This treatment also reflects the fact that they are unfavorable because they represent higher costs and lower net income.

May	31	Goods in Process Inventory	3,500.00	
		Direct Material Quantity Variance	100.00	
		Direct Material Price Variance	180.00	
		Raw Materials Inventory		3,780.00
		To charge production for the standard quantity of materials used (3,500 pounds) at the standard price ($1 per pound) and to record the direct material quantity and price variances.		

The next entry debits the Goods in Process Inventory account for the standard labor cost of the goods manufactured during May ($21,000) instead of the actual cost ($21,420). The actual cost is recorded with a credit to the Factory Payroll account. The difference between the standard and actual costs is explained by two variances. The direct labor price variance is unfavorable and debited to an account with that name. Then, a credit is recorded for the direct labor quantity variance, which was favorable.

May	31	Goods in Process Inventory	21,000.00	
		Direct Labor Price Variance	1,020.00	
		Direct Labor Quantity Variance		600.00
		Factory Payroll		21,420.00
		To charge production with 3,500 standard hours of direct labor at the standard $6 per hour rate and to record the direct labor quantity and price variances.		

The direct labor quantity variance is favorable because it represents a lower cost and a higher net income.

The next entry assigns the standard predetermined overhead to the cost of the goods manufactured during the period. It debits the predetermined amount ($7,000) to the Goods in Process Inventory account instead of the actual cost ($7,650). To account for the difference, the entry includes a debit of $500 to the Volume Variance account and a $150 debit to the Controllable Variance account.

May	31	Goods in Process Inventory	7,000.00	
		Volume Variance	500.00	
		Controllable Variance	150.00	
		Factory Overhead		7,650.00
		To apply overhead at the standard rate of $2 per standard direct labor hour (3,500 hours) and to record overhead variances.		

The balances of these six separate variance accounts accumulate until the end of the accounting period. Thus, unfavorable variances of some months offset against favorable variances of others. Because these amounts represent the results of events during the year, their balances must be closed at the end of the year. And, because their balances represent differences between actual and standard costs, they must be added to or subtracted from the manufacturing costs recorded during the year. By doing so, the recorded manufacturing costs equal the actual costs incurred during the year. The company must use these actual amounts in external financial statements prepared in accordance with generally accepted accounting principles. If the variances are material, they need to be added to or subtracted from the balances of the Goods in Process Inventory, the Finished Goods Inventory, and the Cost of Goods Sold accounts. If the amounts are immaterial, they are merely added to or subtracted from the balance of the Cost of Goods Sold account.[4]

Summary of the Chapter in Terms of Learning Objectives

LO 1. A fixed budget shows the revenues, costs, and expenses expected to occur at the specified production and sales volume. Therefore, if the actual production and sales volume is at some other level, the amounts in the fixed budget do not provide a reasonable basis for evaluating actual performance. A flexible budget expresses variable costs in per unit terms so that it can be used to develop budgeted amounts for any production and sales volume within the relevant range. As a result, managers calculate budgeted amounts after a period for the volume that actually occurred. Then, this budget can be more usefully applied in evaluating the actual performance.

LO 2. Standard costs are the normal costs that should be incurred to produce a product or perform a service. As such, they are the amounts that should be budgeted ahead of time and used in evaluations. Standard costs

[4] This process is similar to the one demonstrated in Chapter 21 for eliminating an underapplied or overapplied balance in the Factory Overhead account.

should be based on a careful examination of the processes used to produce a product or perform a service and the quantities and prices that should be incurred in carrying out those processes. On a performance report, these standard costs (which are really flexible budget amounts) are compared to actual costs and the differences are presented as variances. The variances suggest areas for management attention and possible corrective action.

LO 3. Material and labor cost variances are the differences between the actual costs incurred and the budgeted costs. These total cost variances can be broken into quantity variances and price variances to direct management's attention to the actions of the lower-level managers responsible for quantities used or prices paid. The overhead cost variance is the difference between actual overhead incurred and overhead applied to the output produced in the period. This total variance can be broken into a volume variance and a controllable variance. The volume variance occurs because the standard overhead application rate is applied to an actual volume that differs from the expected or budgeted volume. The controllable variance is the difference between actual overhead incurred and the overhead that should have been incurred at the actual volume achieved during the period.

LO 4. Standard cost accounting provides management with information about costs that differ from budgeted amounts. Performance reports disclose the costs or areas of operations that have significant variances from normal or budgeted amounts. This disclosure of differences from expected levels allows managers to devote their attention to the exceptions and pay less attention to areas in which operations are proceeding normally.

LO 5. When a company records standard costs in its accounts, the standard costs of materials, labor, and overhead are debited to the Goods in Process Inventory account. Based on an analysis of the material, labor, and overhead costs, each quantity variance, price variance, volume variance, and controllable variance is recorded in a separate account. At the end of the period, if the variances are material, they are allocated among the balances of the Goods in Process Inventory, Finished Goods Inventory, and Cost of Goods Sold accounts. If they are not material, they may be simply debited or credited to the Cost of Goods Sold account.

Demonstration Problem

The Gregory Company provides the following information about its budgeted and actual results for April 1994. Although the expected volume for April was 25,000 units produced and sold, the company actually produced and sold 27,000 units.

Budget data—25,000 units (asterisks identify factory overhead items):

Selling price	\$5.00 per unit
Variable costs (per unit of output):	
Direct materials	1.24 per unit
Direct labor	1.50 per unit
*Factory supplies	0.25 per unit
*Utilities	0.50 per unit
Selling costs	0.40 per unit

Fixed costs (per month):	
*Depreciation of machinery	$3,750
*Depreciation of building	2,500
General liability insurance	1,200
Property taxes on office equipment	500
Other administrative expense	750

Actual results during April—27,000 units produced:

Selling price (per unit of output)	$5.23 per unit
Variable costs (per unit of output):	
Direct materials	1.12 per unit
Direct labor	1.40 per unit
*Factory supplies	0.37 per unit
*Utilities	0.60 per unit
Selling costs	0.34 per unit
Fixed costs (per month):	
*Depreciation of machinery	$3,710
*Depreciation of building	2,500
General liability insurance	1,250
Property taxes on office equipment	485
Other administrative expense	900

Standard manufacturing costs based on expected output of 25,000 units:

	Per Unit of Output	Quantity to Be Used	Total Cost
Direct materials, 4 oz. @ $0.31/oz.	$1.24/unit	100,000 oz.	$31,000
Direct labor, 0.25 hrs. @ $6.00/hr.	1.50/unit	6,250 hrs.	37,500
Overhead	1.00/unit		25,000

Actual costs incurred to produce 27,000 units:

	Per Unit of Output	Quantity Used	Total Cost
Direct materials, 4 oz. @ $0.28/oz.	$1.12/unit	108,000 oz.	$30,240
Direct labor, 0.20 hrs. @ $7.00/hr.	1.40/unit	5,400 hrs.	37,800
Overhead	1.20/unit		32,400

If standards had been based on an expected output of 27,000 units, standard manufacturing costs would have been:

	Per Unit of Output	Quantity to Be Used	Total Cost
Direct materials, 4 oz. @ $0.31/oz.	$1.24/unit	108,000 oz.	$33,480
Direct labor, 0.25 hrs. @ $6.00/hr.	$1.50/unit	6,750 hrs.	40,500
Overhead			26,500

Required

1. Develop possible flexible budgets for April showing expected revenues, costs, and income under assumptions of 20,000, 25,000, and 30,000 units of output made and sold.
2. Prepare a performance report that contrasts the actual results with the amounts that would have been budgeted if the actual volume had been expected.
3. Present variance analyses for direct materials, direct labor, and manufacturing overhead.

Planning the Solution

Solution to Demonstration Problem

- Prepare a three-column table showing the expected results at the three specified possible levels of output. Compute the variable costs by multiplying the per unit variable costs by the expected volumes. Include fixed costs at the given amounts. Combine the amounts on the table to show the total variable costs, the total contribution margin, total fixed costs, and income from operations.
- Prepare another three-column table that shows the actual results and the amounts that should have been incurred at 27,000 units. Show any differences in the third column and label them with either an *F* for favorable if they increase income or a *U* for unfavorable if they decrease income.
- Using the table format from the chapter, compute these total variances and the individual variances:

  Total materials variance (including the direct materials quantity variance and the direct materials price variance

  Total direct labor variance (including the direct labor quantity variance and the direct labor price variance)

  Total overhead variance (including the overhead volume variance and the overhead controllable variance)

1. Flexible budgets:

	20,000 Units	25,000 Units	30,000 Units
Sales	$100,000	$125,000	$150,000
Variable costs:			
Direct materials	$ 24,800	$ 31,000	$ 37,200
Direct labor	30,000	37,500	45,000
Factory supplies	5,000	6,250	7,500
Utilities	10,000	12,500	15,000
Selling costs	8,000	10,000	12,000
Total variable costs	$ 77,800	$ 97,250	$116,700
Contribution margin	$ 22,200	$ 27,750	$ 33,300
Fixed costs:			
Depreciation of machinery	$ 3,750	$ 3,750	$ 3,750
Depreciation of building	2,500	2,500	2,500
General liability insurance	1,200	1,200	1,200
Property taxes on office equipment	500	500	500
Other administrative expense	750	750	750
Total fixed costs	$ 8,700	$ 8,700	$ 8,700
Income from operations	$ 13,500	$ 19,050	$ 24,600

2.

THE GREGORY COMPANY
Flexible Budget Performance Report
For Month of April 1994

	Flexible Budget	Actual Results	Variance
Sales (27,000 units)	$135,000	$141,210	$6,210 *F*
Variable costs:			
Direct materials	$ 33,480	$ 30,240	$3,240 *F*
Direct labor	40,500	37,800	2,700 *F*
Factory supplies	6,750	9,990	3,240 *U*
Utilities	13,500	16,200	2,700 *U*
Selling costs	10,800	9,180	1,620 *F*
Total variable costs	$105,030	$103,410	$1,620 *F*
Contribution margin	$ 29,970	$ 37,800	$7,830 *F*
Fixed costs:			
Depreciation of machinery	$ 3,750	$ 3,710	$ 40 *F*
Depreciation of building	2,500	2,500	
General liability insurance	1,200	1,250	50 *U*
Property taxes on office equipment	500	485	15 *F*
Other administrative expense	750	900	150 *U*
Total fixed costs	$ 8,700	$ 8,845	$ 145 *U*
Income from operations	$ 21,270	$ 28,955	$7,685 *F*

F = Favorable variance
U = Unfavorable variance

3. Variance analyses of manufacturing costs:

Material variances:			
Actual cost	108,000 oz. @ $0.28	$30,240	
Standard cost	108,000 oz. @ $0.31	33,480	
Direct material cost variance (favorable)			$(3,240)
Quantity variance:			
Actual units at standard price	108,000 oz. @ $0.31	$33,480	
Standard units at standard price	108,000 oz. @ $0.31	33,480	
Variance (none)			$ –0–
Price variance:			
Actual units at actual price	108,000 oz. @ $0.28	$30,240	
Actual units at standard price	108,000 oz. @ $0.31	33,480	
Variance (favorable)	108,000 oz. @ ($0.03)		(3,240)
Direct material cost variance (favorable)			$(3,240)
Labor variances:			
Actual cost	5,400 hrs. @ $7.00	$37,800	
Standard cost	6,750 hrs. @ $6.00	40,500	
Direct labor cost variance (favorable)			$(2,700)
Quantity variance:			
Actual hours at standard price	5,400 hrs. @ $6.00	$32,400	
Standard hours at standard price	6,750 hrs. @ $6.00	40,500	
Variance (favorable)	(1,350) hrs. @ $6.00		$(8,100)
Price variance:			
Actual hours at actual price	5,400 hrs. @ $7.00	$37,800	
Actual hours at standard price	5,400 hrs. @ $6.00	32,400	
Variance (unfavorable)	5,400 hrs. @ $1.00		5,400
Direct labor cost variance (favorable)			$(2,700)
Overhead variances:			
Total overhead cost incurred	27,000 units @ $1.20	$32,400	
Total overhead applied	27,000 units @ $1.00	27,000	
Overhead cost variance (unfavorable)			$ 5,400
Volume variance:			
Budgeted overhead at 27,000 units		$26,500	
Standard overhead applied to production (27,000 units @ $1.00 per unit rate)		27,000	
Variance (favorable)			$ (500)
Controllable variance:			
Actual overhead incurred		$32,400	
Overhead budgeted at operating level achieved		26,500	
Variance (unfavorable)			5,900
Total overhead variance (unfavorable)			$ 5,400

Glossary

LO 6 Define or explain the words and phrases listed in the chapter glossary.

Controllable variance the difference between the overhead costs actually incurred and the overhead budgeted at the actual operating level. p. 1390

Cost variance the difference between the actual incurred cost and the standard amount. p. 1380

Fixed budget a planning budget based on a single predicted amount of sales or production volume; unsuitable for evaluations if the actual volume differs from the predicted volume. p. 1374

Flexible budget a budget prepared after an operating period is complete to help managers evaluate past performance; uses fixed and variable costs in determining total costs. p. 1376

Flexible budget performance report an internal report that helps management analyze the difference between actual performance and budgeted performance based on the actual sales volume (or other level of activity); presents the differences between actual and budgeted amounts as variances. p. 1378

Historical costs dollar amounts paid by the business in past transactions. p. 1379

Management by exception an analytical technique used by management to focus on the most significant variances and give less attention to the areas where performance is satisfactory. p. 1392

Overhead cost variance the difference between the actual overhead incurred during a period and the standard overhead applied to products. p. 1387

Performance report an internal report that compares actual cost and revenue amounts with budgeted amounts and identifies the differences between them as favorable or unfavorable variances. p. 1374

Price variance a difference between actual and budgeted revenue or cost caused by the difference between the actual price per unit and the budgeted price per unit. p. 1379

Quantity variance the difference between actual and budgeted revenue or cost caused by the difference between the actual number of units sold or used and the budgeted number of units. p. 1379

Standard costs the costs that should be incurred under normal conditions to produce a specific product (or component) or to perform a specific service. p. 1380

Variance analysis a process of examining the differences between actual and budgeted revenues or costs and describing them in terms of the amounts that resulted from price and quantity differences. p. 1379

Volume variance the difference between the total overhead cost that would have been expected if the actual operating volume had been accurately predicted and the amount of overhead cost that was allocated to products using the predetermined standard overhead rate. p. 1388

Synonymous Terms

Fixed budget static budget.
Flexible budget variable budget.
Historical costs actual costs.

Objective Review

Answers to the following questions are listed at the end of the chapter. Be sure that you decide which is the one best answer to each question *before* you check the answers.

LO 1 A flexible budget:

a. Cannot be prepared without first classifying each cost as variable or fixed.
b. Shows each fixed cost as the amount expected regardless of the sales volume.
c. Shows variable costs as constant amounts of cost per unit of activity.
d. Is prepared after a period is completed to provide a sound basis for evaluating performance.
e. All of the above.

LO 2 Standard costs:

a. Change in direct proportion to changes in the level of activity.
b. Equal the amounts that should be incurred under normal conditions to produce a given product or component or to perform a particular service.
c. Are the amounts incurred at the actual level of production for the period.
d. Are compared to fixed budget costs for the purpose of presenting a flexible budget performance report.
e. Are calculated as the average of the historical costs incurred during recent periods of production.

LO 3 Use the following data to compute the total direct labor cost variance:

Actual hours worked per unit.	2.5
Standard direct labor hours per unit . .	2.0
Actual production (units).	2,500
Budgeted production (units)	3,000
Actual price per hour.	$3.10
Standard cost per hour	$3.00

a. $3,750 *U*
b. $1,375 *U*
c. $4,375 *F*
d. $4,375 *U*
e. $5,000 *U*

LO 4 To use management by exception with standard costs:

a. A company must record standard costs in its accounts.

b. Fixed budget performance reports must be presented to management on a timely basis.

c. Variances from flexible budget amounts must be calculated to allow management to focus its attention on significant differences between actual and budgeted performance.

d. Only quantity and price variances for direct materials and direct labor can be analyzed.

e. None of the above.

LO 5 Carlo Company uses a standard cost system. Select the journal entry that records these material variances:

Direct material cost actually incurred	$73,200
Direct material quantity variance (favorable) . .	3,800
Direct material price variance (unfavorable). . .	1,300

a.	Goods in Process Inventory	73,200.00	
	Direct Material Price Variance.	1,300.00	
	Direct Material Quantity Variance		3,800.00
	Raw Materials Inventory		70,700.00
b.	Goods in Process Inventory	70,700.00	
	Direct Material Quantity Variance.	3,800.00	
	Direct Material Price Variance		1,300.00
	Raw Materials Inventory		73,200.00
c.	Goods in Process Inventory	73,200.00	
	Direct Material Quantity Variance.	3,800.00	
	Direct Material Price Variance		1,300.00
	Raw Materials Inventory		75,700.00
d.	Direct Material Quantity Variance.	3,800.00	
	Direct Material Price Variance		1,300.00
	Goods in Process Inventory.		2,500.00
e.	Goods in Process Inventory	75,700.00	
	Direct Material Price Variance.	1,300.00	
	Direct Material Quantity Variance		3,800.00
	Raw Materials Inventory		73,200.00

LO 6 A flexible budget:

a. Is not particularly useful for planning but is very useful for evaluating performance after the budget period is over.

b. Is very useful for planning but is not particularly useful for evaluating performance after the budget period is over.

c. Is prepared as a plan when management has some idea of the amount of costs that could be incurred but is not certain about the exact volume.

d. Includes only variable costs because the fixed costs are covered in the fixed budget.

e. None of the above.

Questions for Class Discussion

1. What is a fixed budget?
2. What limits the usefulness of fixed budget performance reports?
3. What are the differences between fixed and flexible budgets?
4. What is the initial step in preparing a flexible budget?
5. In what sense can a variable cost be considered to be constant?
6. Is it possible for a category of costs to be classified as variable by some companies and fixed by others?
7. What is the contribution margin?
8. What type of analysis does a flexible budget performance report help management make?
9. In standard cost accounting, what is a cost variance?
10. What is a price variance? What is a quantity variance?
11. If the material quantity variance is favorable and the material price variance is favorable, can the total material cost variance be unfavorable?
12. What is the purpose of using standard costs?
13. What department is usually responsible for a direct material price variance? What department is usually responsible for a direct material quantity variance?
14. Can the total labor cost variance be favorable if the labor quantity variance is favorable and the labor price variance is unfavorable?
15. What is the predetermined standard overhead rate? How is it created?
16. In a two-way analysis of the overhead variance, what is the volume variance?
17. Under what conditions is the overhead volume variance considered to be favorable?
18. In a two-way analysis of the overhead variance, what is the controllable variance and what creates it?
19. If a company is budgeted to operate at 80% of capacity and actually operates at 84% of capacity, what effect will the 4% excess have on the controllable variance?
20. If a company's overhead costs consisted of only variable costs and the actual sales volume was 5% lower than the budgeted sales volume, what kind of volume variance would the company experience?
21. If the standard overhead cost applied to products exceeds the budgeted overhead at the actual volume, is the volume variance favorable or unfavorable?
22. What is the relationship among standard costs, variance analysis, and management by exception?
23. If standard manufacturing costs are recorded in the accounts, how are the recorded variances treated at the end of an accounting period?
24. Suppose that Federal Express has a standard fuel cost for a particular flight from an outlying location into its sorting facility in Memphis. List several factors that might cause the actual cost incurred to vary from the standard.

25. Would a flexible budget be useful for a moviemaking project conducted by Disney? Would a flexible budget be useful for one of its amusement parks?

Exercises

Exercise 26–1
Classifying costs as fixed or variable
(LO 1)

Speed Roller Company manufactures and sells roller blades. It normally operates eight hours a day, five days per week. On the basis of this general information, classify each of the following costs as fixed or variable. If certain facts would affect your choice, describe at least one reason that would cause you to change your conclusion.

a. Management salaries.
b. Direct labor.
c. Bolts and screws.
d. Electricity for power tools.
e. Repair expense for power tools.
f. Rollers.
g. Incoming shipping expenses.
h. Natural gas used for heating.
i. Depreciation on power tools.
j. Fire insurance on property.
k. Plastic.
l. Pension cost.
m. Office supplies.
n. Sales commissions.

Exercise 26–2
Preparing a flexible budget
(LO 1)

Campbell Company prepared the following fixed budget for the second quarter of 1994:

Sales (20,000 units)		$1,000,000
Cost of goods sold:		
Direct materials	$320,000	
Direct labor	170,000	
Production supplies	132,000	
Plant manager's salary	15,000	(637,000)
Gross profit		$ 363,000
Selling expenses:		
Sales commissions	$ 80,000	
Packaging	105,000	
Advertising	50,000	(235,000)
Administrative expenses:		
Administrative salaries	$ 30,000	
Depreciation, office equipment	15,000	
Insurance	9,000	
Office rent	6,000	(60,000)
Income from operations		$ 68,000

Following the format of Illustration 26–2, prepare a schedule that shows the amounts of the variable costs per unit and the fixed costs per quarter and three possible flexible budgets for sales volumes of 15,000, 20,000, and 25,000 units.

Exercise 26–3
Analysis of fixed budget performance report
(LO 1)

Camellia Company's fixed budget performance report for a recent month shows this information:

	Fixed Budget	Actual Results	Variance
Unit sales.	1,400	1,800	
Sales	$231,000	$297,000	$66,000 *F*
Expenses.	160,000	195,400	35,400 *U*
Income from operations	$ 71,000	$101,600	$30,600 *F*

The budgeted expenses of $160,000 included $140,000 of variable expenses and $20,000 of fixed expenses. The actual expenses included $19,000 of fixed expenses.

Prepare a flexible budget performance report that shows any variances between the budgeted results and the actual results. (List the fixed and variable expenses separately.)

Exercise 26–4
Analysis of fixed budget performance report
(LO 1)

Carnation Company's fixed budget performance report for a recent month shows this information:

	Fixed Budget	Actual Results	Variance
Unit sales.	3,000	2,400	
Sales	$120,000	$105,600	$14,400 *U*
Expenses.	110,000	98,500	11,500 *F*
Income from operations	$ 10,000	$ 7,100	$ 2,900 *U*

The budgeted expenses of $110,000 included $75,000 of variable expenses and $35,000 of fixed expenses. The actual expenses included $32,500 of fixed expenses.

Prepare a flexible budget performance report that shows any variances between the budgeted results and the actual results. (List the fixed and variable expenses separately.)

Exercise 26–5
Direct material variances
(LO 2, 3)

CheapButNice Company has just finished making 2,000 small tables using 31,000 pounds of plastic that cost $94,550. The company's direct material standards for one table are 15 pounds of plastic at $3.25 per pound.

Required

Measure the direct material variances incurred in manufacturing these tables.

Exercise 26–6
Direct labor variances
(LO 2, 3)

After evaluating the Anchor Company's manufacturing process, management decided to establish standards of 0.4 hour of direct labor per unit of product, and $12.00 per hour for the labor rate.

During May, the company used 1,550 hours of direct labor at a total cost of $18,755 to produce 4,000 units of product. In June, the company used 2,020 hours of direct labor at a total cost of $24,745 to produce 5,000 units of product.

Calculate the quantity variance, the price variance, and the total direct labor cost variance for each of these two months.

Exercise 26–7
Calculation of quantity used based on variance information
(LO 2, 3)

During a recent period, Gibraltar Company's manufacturing operations experienced a favorable price variance of $3,000 on its direct materials usage. The actual price per liter of the material was $38.50 while the standard price was $38.90. How many liters of material were used during the period?

Exercise 26–8
Calculations of costs based on variance information
(LO 2, 3)

Calculate the answers for each of the following independent cases:

a. Anderson Company's output for the period required a standard direct material cost of $50,000. During the period, the direct material variances included a favorable price variance of $3,000 and a favorable quantity variance of $1,235. What was the actual total direct materials cost for the period?

b. Bronson Company's output for the period had an unfavorable direct labor price variance of $6,555 and an unfavorable direct labor quantity variance of $1,777. The goods produced during the period required a standard direct labor cost of $85,550. What was the actual total direct labor cost incurred during the period?

c. Carson Company's output for the period had a favorable overhead volume variance of $20,000 and an unfavorable overhead controllable variance of $33,600. Standard overhead charged to production during the period amounted to $150,000. What was the actual total overhead cost incurred during the period?

Exercise 26–9
Calculating volume and controllable variances
(LO 3)

The Luling Company expected to operate last month at 80% of its productive capacity of 25,000 units per month. At this planned level, the company expected to use 20,000 standard hours of direct labor. The overhead is allocated to products using a predetermined standard rate based on direct labor hours. At the 80% level of operation, the total budgeted cost includes $50,000 of fixed overhead cost and $62,000 of variable overhead cost.

During the month, the company actually incurred $99,650 of overhead while producing 19,200 units of product. Find the overhead volume variance, the overhead controllable variance, and the total overhead variance.

Exercise 26–10
Overhead variances
(LO 3)

The Blackstone Company established the following standard costs for one unit of its product for a recent month:

Direct material (4 kg. @ $5.00 per kg.)	$20.00
Direct labor (3 hrs. @ $16.00 per hr.)	48.00
Factory overhead (3 hrs. @ $6.00 per hr.) . .	18.00
Standard cost	$86.00

The $6.00 per direct labor hour overhead rate is based on an expected operating level equal to 75% of the factory's capacity of 50,000 units per month. The following monthly flexible budget information applies to the situation:

	Operating Levels		
	70%	75%	80%
Budgeted output (units)	35,000	37,500	40,000
Budgeted labor (standard hours)	105,000	112,500	120,000
Budgeted overhead:			
Variable overhead	$525,000	$562,500	$600,000
Fixed overhead	112,500	112,500	112,500
Total overhead	$637,500	$675,000	$712,500

During the past month, the company operated at 70% of capacity and incurred the following actual overhead costs:

Variable overhead costs	$507,000
Fixed overhead costs.	114,000
Total overhead costs	$621,000

Required

1. Show how the company calculated the predetermined overhead application rate of $6.00 per hour.
2. Calculate the overhead volume variance, the overhead controllable variance, and the total overhead variance.

Exercise 26–11
Recording material variances in the accounts
(LO 5)

Refer to the facts in Exercise 26–5 in working this exercise. CheapButNice Company records standard costs in its accounts. Thus, it records its material variances in separate accounts when it assigns raw materials costs to the Goods in Process Inventory account.

Required

1. Show the general journal entry that would be made to change the direct materials costs to the Goods in Process Inventory account and to record the material variances in their accounts.
2. Assume that the material variances created by the facts in Exercise 26–5 were the only variances accumulated in the accounting period and that they are not considered material. Show the adjusting journal entry that would be made to close the variance accounts at the end of the period.

Problems

Problem 26–1
Preparing and using a flexible budget
(LO 1)

Castañeda Company's master budget for 1994 included the following budgeted income statement. It was based on an expected production and sales volume of 10,000 units.

CASTAÑEDA COMPANY
Fixed Budget
For Year Ended December 31, 1994

Sales		$770,000
Cost of goods sold:		
Direct materials	$295,000	
Direct labor.	65,000	
Machinery repairs (variable cost). . . .	14,300	
Depreciation of plant (annual)	60,000	
Utilities (variable cost is 25%)	50,000	
Supervisory salaries	35,000	(519,300)
Gross profit		$250,700
Selling expenses:		
Packaging	$ 15,000	
Shipping	29,000	
Sales salary (a fixed annual amount) . .	45,000	(89,000)
General and administrative expenses:		
Insurance expense	$ 20,200	
Salaries	60,400	
Rent expense	27,100	(107,700)
Income from operations		$ 54,000

Required

1. Classify the items in the fixed budget as variable or fixed and determine their amounts per unit or for the year, as appropriate.
2. Prepare one schedule showing two possible flexible budgets for the company for sales and production volumes of 9,000 and 12,000 units.
3. A consultant has suggested that business conditions are improving. One possible effect could be a sales volume of approximately 14,000 units. The president of the company is confident that this volume is within the relevant range of existing capacity. How much would operating income increase over the 1994 budgeted amount if this level could be reached without having to increase capacity?
4. The consultant's report also describes the possibility of an unfavorable change, in which case production and sales volume for 1994 could fall to 7,000 units. How much income from operations would occur if the volume falls to this level?

Problem 26–2
Flexible budget performance report
(LO 1)

Refer to the facts in Problem 26–1 in working this problem. Castañeda Company's actual statement of income for 1994 follows:

CASTAÑEDA COMPANY
Statement of Income from Operations
For Year Ended December 31, 1994

Sales (12,000 units)		$960,000
Cost of goods sold:		
Direct materials	$350,000	
Direct labor	90,000	
Machinery repairs (variable cost)	11,600	
Depreciation of plant (annual)	60,000	
Utilities (fixed cost is $38,500)	54,500	
Supervisory salaries	37,500	(603,600)
Gross profit		$356,400
Selling expenses:		
Packaging	$ 21,000	
Shipping	31,000	
Sales salary (annual)	45,500	(97,500)
General and administrative expenses:		
Insurance expense	$ 26,000	
Salaries	58,000	
Rent expense	27,000	(111,000)
Income from operations		$147,900

Required

1. Using the flexible budget prepared for Problem 26–1, present a flexible budget performance report for 1994.
2. Explain the sales variance.

Problem 26–3
Calculating material, labor, and overhead variances
(LO 2, 3)

George Manufacturing Company established the following standard unit costs for its single product:

Direct material (8 lbs. @ $7.00 per lb.)	$ 56.00
Direct labor (2 hrs. @ $14.00 per hr.)	28.00
Factory overhead (2 hrs. @ $18.00 per hr.)	36.00
Total standard cost	$120.00

The overhead rate was based on an expectation that the operating volume would equal 80% of the productive capacity of 30,000 units per quarter. The following additional flexible budget information is also available:

	Operating Levels		
	70%	**80%**	**90%**
Production in units	21,000	24,000	27,000
Standard direct labor hours	42,000	48,000	54,000
Budgeted overhead:			
Fixed factory overhead	$500,000	$500,000	$500,000
Variable factory overhead	318,500	364,000	409,500

During a recent quarter, the company actually operated at 70% of capacity and produced 21,000 units of product. These units were assigned the following standard costs:

Direct material (168,000 lbs. @ $7.00 per lb.)	$1,176,000
Direct labor (42,000 hrs. @ $14.00 per hr.)	588,000
Factory overhead (42,000 hrs. @ $18.00 per hr.)	756,000
Total standard cost	$2,520,000

Actual costs incurred during the quarter were

Direct material (170,000 lbs. @ $6.50)	$1,105,000
Direct labor (44,000 hrs. @ $13.75)	605,000
Fixed factory overhead costs	490,000
Variable factory overhead costs	325,000
Total actual costs	$2,525,000

Required

1. Compute the total direct material cost variance and the price and quantity variances.
2. Compute the total direct labor cost variance and the price and quantity variances.
3. Compute the total overhead cost variance and the volume and controllable variances.

Problem 26–4
Calculating and reporting material, labor, and overhead variances
(LO 2, 3)

Augusta Company has established the following standard costs per unit for the product it manufactures:

Direct material (5 kgs. @ $6.00 per kg.)	$30.00
Direct labor (2 hrs. @ $12.00 per hr.)	24.00
Overhead (2 hrs. @ $5.00 per hr.)	10.00
Total standard cost	$64.00

The overhead rate was based on an expectation that the operating volume would equal 80% of the productive capacity of 5,000 units per month. The following additional flexible budget information is also available:

	Operating Levels		
	70%	80%	90%
Production in units	3,500	4,000	4,500
Standard direct labor hours	7,000	8,000	9,000
Budgeted overhead:			
Variable costs:			
Indirect materials	$ 4,375	$ 5,000	$ 5,625
Indirect labor	7,000	8,000	9,000
Power	1,750	2,000	2,250
Maintenance	875	1,000	1,125
Total variable costs	$14,000	$16,000	$18,000
Fixed costs:			
Rent of factory building	$ 6,000	$ 6,000	$ 6,000
Depreciation, machinery	10,000	10,000	10,000
Taxes and insurance	1,200	1,200	1,200
Supervisory salaries	6,800	6,800	6,800
Total fixed costs	$24,000	$24,000	$24,000
Total overhead costs	$38,000	$40,000	$42,000

During October, the company operated at 90% of capacity and produced 4,500 units. The following actual costs were incurred:

Direct material (23,000 kgs. @ $5.90 per kg.)		$135,700
Direct labor (9,400 hrs. @ $12.05 per hr.)		113,270
Overhead costs:		
Indirect materials	$5,000	
Indirect labor	8,000	
Power	2,250	
Maintenance	1,500	
Rent of factory building	6,000	
Depreciation, machinery	9,600	
Taxes and insurance	1,500	
Supervisory salaries	7,000	40,850
Total costs		$289,820

Required

1. Compute the direct material variances, including the quantity and price variances.
2. Compute the direct labor variances, including the quantity and price variances.
3. Prepare a factory overhead variance report that shows the total volume and controllable variances.
4. Prepare a detailed factory overhead variance report (like Illustration 26–7) that shows the variances for the individual items of overhead.

Problem 26–5
Flexible budget, variance analysis, and report for overhead costs
(LO 1, 2, 3, 4)

The Ernst Company has established the following standard costs for one unit of its product:

Direct material (12 liters $ $4.00 per liter)	$48.00
Direct labor (3 hrs. @ $9.00 per hr.)	27.00
Overhead (3 hrs. @ $4.50 per hr.)	13.50
Total standard cost	$88.50

The predetermined overhead application rate ($4.50 per direct labor hour) is based on an expected volume of 50% of the factory's capacity of 20,000 units per month. Thus, the expected monthly output is 10,000 units. Following are the company's budgeted overhead costs for one month at the 50% level:

ERNST COMPANY
Monthly Factory Overhead Budget (at 50% of capacity)

Variable costs:		
Indirect materials	$20,000	
Indirect labor	40,000	
Power	10,000	
Repairs and maintenance	15,000	
Total variable costs		$ 85,000
Fixed costs:		
Depreciation, building	$10,000	
Depreciation, machinery	15,000	
Taxes and insurance	5,000	
Supervision	20,000	
Total fixed costs		50,000
Total overhead costs		$135,000

The company incurred the following actual costs when it unexpectedly operated at 40% of capacity during July:

Direct material (98,000 liters @ $4.00)		$392,000
Direct labor (23,000 hrs. @ $9.15)		210,450
Overhead costs:		
Indirect materials	$15,000	
Indirect labor	33,000	
Power	7,800	
Repairs and maintenance	10,500	
Depreciation, building	10,000	
Depreciation, machinery	15,000	
Taxes and insurance	4,800	
Supervision	19,800	115,900
Total costs		$718,350

Required

1. Classify the items in the overhead budget as variable or fixed and determine their amounts per unit or for the month, as appropriate.
2. Prepare a set of possible flexible overhead budgets for July showing the amounts of each variable and fixed cost at the 40%, 50%, and 60% levels.
3. Compute the direct material variances, including the quantity and price variances.
4. Compute the direct labor variances, including the quantity and price variances.
5. Prepare a factory overhead variance report that shows the total volume and controllable variances.
6. Prepare a detailed factory overhead variance report (like Illustration 26–7) that shows the variances for the individual items of overhead.

Problem 26–6
Recording material, labor, and overhead variances
(LO 4, 5)

Springfield Company's standard cost accounting system recorded the following information concerning its operations during September:

Standard direct material cost	$250,000
Direct material quantity variance (favorable)	10,500
Direct material price variance (unfavorable)	2,200
Actual direct labor cost	125,000
Direct labor quantity variance (unfavorable)	15,000
Direct labor price variance (favorable)	1,600
Actual overhead cost	498,000
Volume variance (favorable)	22,000
Controllable variance (unfavorable)	17,600

Required

1. Prepare general journal entries dated September 30 to record the company's costs and variances for the month.
2. Identify areas that would attract the attention of a manager who uses management by exception.

Problem 26–7
Analytical essay
(LO 1)

The Scandinavia Company recently prepared a fixed budget for the coming year based on an expected volume of 100,000 units. At this volume, the fixed costs were expected to be $600,000 and the variable costs were also expected to be $600,000.

Required

1. What amount would be expected for the fixed, variable, and total costs at 50,000 units? At 200,000 units?
2. Explain why the amount of total expected costs at 50,000 units is not 25% of the amount of total expected costs at 200,000 units.
3. Suppose that the company could reduce fixed costs by 25% while increasing variable costs by 50%. What would be the expected amounts of fixed, variable, and total costs at 50,000 units? At 100,000 units? At 200,000 units?
4. Explain why knowledge of the fixed and variable nature of a company's costs is essential for preparing useful plans for the future and useful evaluations of the past.

Problem 26–8
Analytical essay
(LO 1)

In Exercise 26–3, the Camellia Company's fixed budget analysis shows a favorable variance for sales, an unfavorable variance for expenses, and a favorable variance for income from operations.

However, the flexible budget analysis prepared in solving the exercise shows no variance for sales, a favorable variance for expenses, and a much smaller favorable variance for income from operations.

Explain why the analyses produce such different outcomes.

Alternate Problems

Problem 26–1A
Preparing and using a flexible budget
(LO 1)

Canyon Company's master budget for 1994 included the following budgeted income statement. It was based on an expected production and sales volume of 50,000 units.

CANYON COMPANY
Fixed Budget
For Year Ended December 31, 1994

Sales		$550,000
Cost of goods sold:		
Direct materials	$194,000	
Direct labor	32,000	
Patent royalties paid (based on units)	5,500	
Depreciation of machinery (annual)	29,800	
Utilities (variable cost is 80%)	20,000	
Supervisory salaries	15,000	(296,300)
Gross profit		$253,700
Selling expenses:		
Commissions	$ 22,000	
Shipping	75,000	
Sales salary (annual)	45,000	(142,000)
General and administrative expenses:		
Property taxes	$ 9,600	
Salaries	23,400	
Rent expense	18,000	(51,000)
Income from operations		$ 60,700

Required

1. Classify the items in the fixed budget as variable or fixed and determine their amounts per unit or for the year, as appropriate.
2. Prepare one schedule showing two possible flexible budgets for the company for sales and production volumes of 40,000 and 60,000 units.
3. A consultant has suggested that business conditions are improving. One possible effect could be a sales volume of approximately 72,000 units. The president of the company is confident that this volume is within the relevant range of existing capacity. How much would operating income increase over the 1994 budgeted amount if this level could be reached without having to increase capacity?
4. The consultant's report also describes the possibility of an unfavorable change, in which case production and sales volume for 1994 could fall to 25,000 units. How much income from operations would occur if the volume falls to this level?

Problem 26–2A
Flexible budget performance report
(LO 1)

Refer to the facts in Problem 26–1A in working this problem. Canyon Company's actual statement of income for 1994 follows:

CANYON COMPANY
Statement of Income from Operations
For Year Ended December 31, 1994

Sales (60,000 units)		$642,000
Cost of goods sold:		
Direct materials	$234,000	
Direct labor	39,000	
Patent royalties paid (based on units)	6,600	
Depreciation of machinery (annual)	29,800	
Utilities (variable cost is $17,900)	21,300	
Supervisory salaries	16,800	(347,500)
Gross profit		$294,500
Selling expenses:		
Commissions	$ 25,680	
Shipping	93,000	
Sales salary (annual)	48,000	(166,680)
General and administrative expenses:		
Property taxes	$ 10,500	
Salaries	23,400	
Rent expense	18,000	(51,900)
Income from operations		$ 75,920

Required

1. Using the flexible budget prepared for Problem 26–1A, present a flexible budget performance report for 1994.
2. Explain the sales variance.

Problem 26–3A
Calculating material, labor, and overhead variances
(LO 2, 3)

Charlie Company established the following standard unit costs for its single product:

Direct material (3 kgs. @ $4.00 per kg.)	$12.00
Direct labor (2 hrs. @ $9.00 per hr.)	18.00
Factory overhead (2 hrs. @ $3.00 per hr.)	6.00
Total standard cost	$36.00

The overhead rate was based on an expectation that the operating volume would equal 90% of the productive capacity of 20,000 units per quarter. The following additional flexible budget information is also available:

	Operating Levels		
	80%	**90%**	**100%**
Production in units	16,000	18,000	20,000
Standard direct labor hours	32,000	36,000	40,000
Budgeted overhead:			
Fixed factory overhead	$45,000	$45,000	$45,000
Variable factory overhead	56,000	63,000	70,000

During a recent quarter, the company actually operated at 80% of capacity and produced 16,000 units of product. These units were assigned the following standard costs:

Direct material (48,000 kgs. @ $4.00 per kg.)	$192,000
Direct labor (32,000 hrs. @ $9.00 per hr.)	288,000
Factory overhead (32,000 hrs. @ $3.00 per hr.)	96,000
Total standard cost	$576,000

Actual costs incurred during the quarter were

Direct material (49,000 kgs. @ $4.10)	$200,900
Direct labor (31,000 hrs. @ $8.75)	271,250
Fixed factory overhead costs	44,000
Variable factory overhead costs	56,000
Total actual costs	$572,150

Required

1. Compute the total direct material cost variance and the price and quantity variances.
2. Compute the total direct labor cost variance and the price and quantity variances.
3. Compute the total overhead cost variance and the volume and controllable variances.

Problem 26–4A
Calculating and reporting material, labor, and overhead variances (LO 2, 3)

Carolina Company has established the following standard costs per unit for the product it manufactures:

Direct material (20 ozs. @ $0.75 per oz.)	$15.00
Direct labor (1 hr. @ $20.00 per hr.)	20.00
Overhead (1 hr. @ $53.50 per hr.)	53.50
Total standard cost	$88.50

The overhead rate was based on an expectation that the operating volume would equal 60% of the productive capacity of 1,500 units per month. The following additional flexible budget information is also available:

	Operating Levels		
	50%	60%	70%
Production in units	750	900	1,050
Standard direct labor hours	750	900	1,050
Budgeted overhead:			
Variable costs:			
Indirect materials	$ 4,500	$ 5,400	$ 6,300
Indirect labor	2,625	3,150	3,675
Power	1,875	2,250	2,625
Maintenance	1,125	1,350	1,575
Total variable costs	$10,125	$12,150	$14,175
Fixed costs:			
Rent of factory building	$12,000	$12,000	$12,000
Depreciation, machinery	11,000	11,000	11,000
Taxes and insurance	5,000	5,000	5,000
Supervisory salaries	8,000	8,000	8,000
Total fixed costs	$36,000	$36,000	$36,000
Total overhead costs	$46,125	$48,150	$50,175

During April, the company operated at 70% of capacity and produced 1,050 units. The following actual costs were incurred:

Direct material (22,000 ozs. @ $0.70 per oz.)		$15,400
Direct labor (1,000 hrs. @ $19.50 per hr.)		19,500
Overhead costs:		
Indirect materials	$ 5,900	
Indirect labor	3,700	
Power	2,500	
Maintenance	800	
Rent of factory building	12,000	
Depreciation, machinery	11,000	
Taxes and insurance	6,000	
Supervisory salaries	7,900	49,800
Total costs		$84,700

Required

1. Compute the direct material variances, including the quantity and price variances.
2. Compute the direct labor variances, including the quantity and price variances.
3. Prepare a factory overhead variance report that shows the total volume and controllable variances.
4. Prepare a detailed factory overhead variance report (like Illustration 26–7) that shows the variances for the individual items of overhead.

Problem 26–5A
Flexible budget, variance analysis, and report for overhead costs
(LO 1, 2, 3, 4)

The Young Company has established the following standard costs for one unit of its product:

Direct material (3 kgs. @ $3.00 per kg.)	$ 9.00
Direct labor (1 hr. @ $6.00 per hr.)	6.00
Overhead (1 hr. @ $8.00 per hr.)	8.00
Total standard cost	$23.00

The predetermined overhead application rate ($8.00 per direct labor hour) is based on an expected volume of 75% of the factory's capacity of 10,000 units per month. Thus, the expected monthly output is 7,500 units. Following are the company's budgeted overhead costs for one month at the 75% level:

YOUNG COMPANY
Monthly Factory Overhead Budget (at 75% of capacity)

Variable costs:		
Indirect materials	$ 3,750	
Indirect labor	15,000	
Power	3,750	
Repairs and maintenance	7,500	
Total variable costs		$30,000
Fixed costs:		
Depreciation, building	$ 4,000	
Depreciation, machinery	12,000	
Taxes and insurance	3,000	
Supervision	11,000	
Total fixed costs		30,000
Total overhead costs		$60,000

The company incurred the following actual costs when it operated as expected at 75% of capacity during May:

Direct material (23,000 kgs. @ $3.05)		$ 70,150
Direct labor (7,600 hrs. @ $6.15)		46,740
Overhead costs:		
Indirect materials	$ 3,600	
Indirect labor	13,710	
Power	3,850	
Repairs and maintenance	7,800	
Depreciation, building	4,000	
Depreciation, machinery	12,500	
Taxes and insurance	2,750	
Supervision	11,000	59,210
Total costs		$176,100

Required

1. Classify the items in the overhead budget as variable or fixed and determine their amounts per unit or for the month, as appropriate.
2. Prepare a set of possible flexible overhead budgets for May showing the amounts of each variable and fixed cost at the 65%, 75%, and 85% levels.
3. Compute the direct material variances, including the quantity and price variances.
4. Compute the direct labor variances, including the quantity and price variances.
5. Prepare a factory overhead variance report that shows the total volume and controllable variances.
6. Prepare a detailed factory overhead variance report (like Illustration 26–7) that shows the variances for the individual items of overhead.

Problem 26–6A
Recording material, labor, and overhead variances
(LO 4, 5)

Plymouth Company's standard cost accounting system recorded the following information concerning its operations during March:

Standard direct material cost	$145,000
Direct material quantity variance (favorable)	12,500
Direct material price variance (favorable)	900
Actual direct labor cost	210,000
Direct labor quantity variance (favorable)	17,800
Direct labor price variance (unfavorable)	1,650
Actual overhead cost	242,000
Volume variance (unfavorable)	1,100
Controllable variance (unfavorable)	21,200

Required

1. Prepare general journal entries dated March 31 to record the company's costs and variances for the month.
2. Identify areas that would attract the attention of a manager who uses management by exception.

Problem 26–7A
Analytical essay
(LO 1)

The Scarlatti Company recently prepared a fixed budget for the coming year based on an expected volume of 50,000 units. At this volume, the fixed costs were expected to be $500,000 and the variable costs were expected to be $250,000.

Required

1. What amount would be expected for the fixed, variable, and total costs at 25,000 units? At 100,000 units?
2. Explain why the amount of total expected costs at 25,000 units is not 25% of the amount of total expected costs at 100,000 units.
3. Suppose that the company could reduce fixed costs by 40% while increasing variable costs by 40%. What would be the expected amounts of fixed, variable, and total costs at 25,000 units? At 50,000 units? At 100,000 units?
4. Explain why knowledge of the fixed and variable nature of a company's costs is essential for preparing useful plans for the future and useful evaluations of the past.

Problem 26–8A
Analytical essay
(LO 1)

In Exercise 26–4, the Carnation Company's fixed budget analysis shows an unfavorable variance for sales, a favorable variance for expenses, and an unfavorable variance for income from operations.

However, the flexible budget analysis prepared in solving the exercise shows a favorable variance for sales, an unfavorable variance for expenses, and a favorable variance for income from operations.

Explain why the analyses produce such different outcomes.

Provocative Problems

Provocative Problem 26–1
Ambassador Sweets Company
(LO 2, 3)

In preparing its budget for April, Ambassador Sweets Company's management planned to sell chocolate candy for $15 a box. Each box was expected to require 2 pounds of a special chocolate that the company planned to purchase for $4.50 per pound. The boxes were expected to be produced at the rate of five per direct labor hour, and the company expected to hire workers for $9.00 per hour. Each box was to be packaged in a cardboard container, which the company planned to buy at $1 each.

For volumes ranging between 3,000 and 6,000 boxes, the management expected to incur these fixed expenses in April:

Administrative and sales salaries	$5,000
Depreciation	3,000
Utilities	1,050
Insurance	880

During April, Ambassador Sweets actually produced and sold 4,000 boxes of chocolates at $16.25 each. It used 8,100 pounds of chocolate, which had been purchased at $4.80 per pound. Workers were paid $8.80 per hour and worked 750 hours to produce the chocolates. The company used 4,025 containers, which it actually purchased for $1.20 each. All the fixed expenses occurred as planned.

Although these facts are available to the company's managers, they have not yet been able to clearly evaluate the operating performance of the company's separate activities. They can see that the actual operating income differed from the expected amount but have not established how much of that amount was contributed by the different activities. They have asked you to describe how the differences between the actual and expected amounts affected the company's performance. Do what you can to help them.

Provocative Problem 26–2
Missouri Manufacturing Company
(LO 2, 3)

Terry Green has been employed by Missouri Manufacturing Company for 10 years, with the last 3 in one of the assembly departments. About a year ago, Green was made the department manager and has achieved a strong performance in that position. Since the promotion, internal complaints and employee turnover and absenteeism have declined, while output has increased and employee morale has soared. During the past two months, the department has been operating below its standard costs, which hasn't happened for four or five years.

Recently, Pat Hayward, one of Green's crew, suggested that the company modify the department's machinery to make it more versatile and automatic. The modifications would cost $45,000 and would have an eight-year life and no salvage value. They should increase the rate of production by 10%, reduce maintenance costs $1,000 per year, and reduce the size of the crew by one person. The wages of the least senior person in the department are about $20,000 per year.

Upon receiving the suggestion, Green's response was, "I appreciate the suggestion, but let's forget it for now. We have been doing real well in meeting our standards, and the company doesn't need the extra capacity right now. Besides, the job market is tough, and whoever we let go could be on unemployment for a long time. I think our team's relationships are real strong, and I don't want to have to pick somebody to lay off. We just can't do anything as drastic as this and keep up the head of steam that we have going for us."

Is it possible that the company's use of standard costs to evaluate Green has affected Green's assessment of Hayward's suggestion? Explain your answer. Does your analysis of the recommendation lead you to agree with Green's initial response? Is it advantageous for decisions like these to be made at the department level, or should they be handled at a higher level in the company? Is there an appropriate way for Hayward to pass this suggestion to a manager at a level higher than Green?

Provocative Problem 26–3
Wisconsin Company
(LO 2)

The Wisconsin Company manufactures a product with a seasonal demand and a short shelf life. As a result, the product cannot be accumulated in advance of its sale, and the numbers of units manufactured in different quarters vary a great deal.

The company's cost accounting system operates on a quarterly cycle, and adds actual costs to the Goods in Process Inventory. In turn, these costs flow into the Cost of Goods Sold account for each quarter and into the Finished Goods Inventory account. At the end of last year, which reflected a typical set of seasonal variations, this summarized cost report was prepared for the company manager:

WISCONSIN COMPANY
Quarterly Reports of Average Product Costs
Year Ended December 31

	First Quarter	Second Quarter	Third Quarter	Fourth Quarter
Direct materials	$132,000	$ 523,200	$1,093,750	$395,550
Direct labor	47,250	192,000	406,250	148,500
Variable overhead costs	73,350	300,000	631,250	222,750
Fixed overhead costs	200,000	200,000	200,000	200,000
Total costs	$452,600	$1,215,200	$2,331,250	$966,800
Units of output	15,000	60,000	125,000	45,000
Average cost per unit	$30.17	$20.25	$18.65	$21.48

Because of some difficulty in interpreting the report, the manager has asked you to explain why the average cost per unit varies so much among quarters. The manager has also asked you to suggest any improvements in the cost accounting system that could lead to more useful information. The manager believes that quarterly reports are needed for a timely response to apparent control problems, so your suggestion should include a schedule showing how last year's material, labor, and overhead costs per unit would have been reported under your suggestion.

Provocative Problem 26–4
As a Matter of Ethics: Essay

Ethics

Examine the ethics case on page 1392. Evaluate the reasons given by the department manager for his behavior in ordering supplies in the pattern described in the case. Do these actions seem ethical to you? As the internal auditor, what would you do next?

Answers to Objective Review Questions

LO 1 (*e*)	LO 3 (*d*)	LO 5 (*e*)
LO 2 (*b*)	LO 4 (*c*)	LO 6 (*a*)

CHAPTER

27

Capital Budgeting and Other Managerial Decisions

Managing an organization requires many decisions, some of which involve acquiring assets and investing large amounts of capital. In making good capital budgeting and other decisions, managers need to focus on the relevant information and disregard the irrelevant.

Topical Coverage

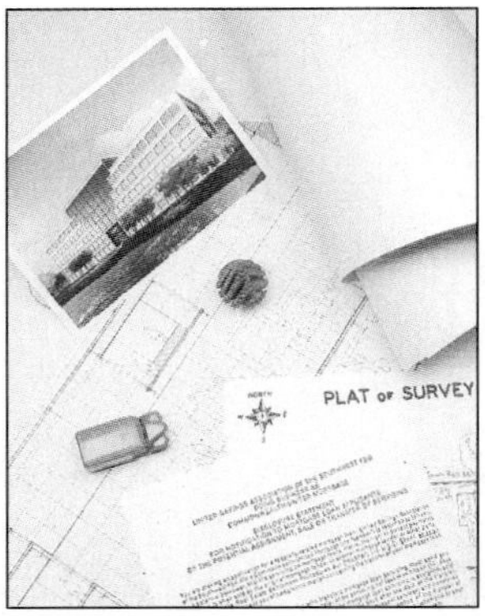

Business decisions involve choosing between alternative courses of action. Although many factors can affect these decisions, the analysis typically begins by looking for the alternative that offers the highest return on the investment or the greatest reduction in costs. Some decisions are based on little more than an intuitive understanding of the situation because the available information is too inadequate to allow a more systematic approach. In other circumstances, intangible factors such as convenience, prestige, and environmental considerations are more important than strictly quantitative factors. Even in these situations, you can reach a more sound decision if you can describe the consequences of alternative choices in quantitative terms. This chapter examines several systematic methods of analysis that can help managers make decisions.

Learning Objectives

After studying Chapter 27, you should be able to:

1. Explain the importance of capital budgeting.
2. Calculate the expected payback period of an investment and describe its limitations.
3. Calculate the expected average rate of return on an investment and describe its limitations.
4. Calculate the net present value of the cash flow from a proposed investment, and describe the procedures used in this method and its advantages and disadvantages.
5. Explain how information about incremental costs affects decisions about accepting or rejecting additional volume and about making or buying a component of a product.
6. Describe the importance of sunk costs, out-of-pocket costs, and opportunity costs for decisions, including the choice between scrapping or reworking defective units and between selling a product or processing it further.
7. Define or explain the words and phrases listed in the chapter glossary.

CAPITAL BUDGETING

LO 1 Explain the importance of capital budgeting.

Chapter 25 described the *capital expenditures budget,* which is management's plan for acquiring and selling plant assets. The process of analyzing alternative investments and deciding which assets to acquire or sell is called **capital budgeting.** The plans may involve buying such things as a new machine, a new building, or a whole new project. In all cases, a fundamental goal for implementing the decision is to earn a satisfactory return on the investment. Capital budgeting decisions require a careful analysis because they are generally the most difficult and risky decisions that management faces. The decisions are difficult because they are usually based on predictions of numerous events that might occur well into the future. At best, these predictions are highly

ILLUSTRATION 27–1

Expected Net Income and Net Cash Flow from an Investment

	Expected Net Income	Expected Cash Flows
Annual sales of new product	$30,000	$30,000
Deduct annual expenses:		
Cost of materials, labor and overhead (other than depreciation)	(15,500)	(15,500)
Depreciation	(2,000)	
Additional selling and administrative expenses	(9,500)	(9,500)
Annual pre-tax income	$ 3,000	
Income taxes (30%)	(900)	(900)
Annual net income	$ 2,100	
Annual net cash flow		$ 4,100

tentative and potentially undependable. A capital budgeting decision is risky because (1) the outcome is highly uncertain, (2) large amounts of money are usually involved, (3) the investment involves a long-term commitment, and (4) the decision may be difficult or impossible to reverse, no matter how poor it turns out to be.

The practice of capital budgeting involves a wide range of decisions. As a result, managers have developed a variety of techniques for helping them make these decisions. Despite this variety, essentially all of these techniques involve predicting the cash inflows and outflows of each proposed investment, assessing the advantages of those flows, and then choosing the investments to be made. In this chapter, we consider three widely recognized methods for comparing alternative investments. These methods call for calculating the *payback period,* the *rate of return on average investment,* and the *net present value.*

Payback Period

LO 2 Calculate the expected payback period of an investment and describe its limitations.

Any investment project, whether it involves a machine or some other long-term asset, produces cash inflows and requires cash outflows. The difference between these inflows and outflows in a period is the *net cash flow*. The **payback period** for an investment is the time expected to pass before the net cash flows return the investment's initial cost. In general, managers prefer assets with shorter payback periods to reduce the risk that the investment might not be profitable over the long run. As a result of acquiring assets with short payback periods, the company is less vulnerable to inaccurate long-term predictions of future cash flows.

For example, assume that the Murray Company is considering several capital investments. One involves purchasing a machine to be used in manufacturing a new product. The machine would cost $16,000 and is expected to have an eight-year life with no salvage value. Management also predicts that the machine will produce 10,000 units of product each year and that the product will be sold for $3 per unit. Illustration 27–1 shows the expected annual revenues and expenses (including depreciation and income taxes) from the asset. The illustration also shows the cash flows the asset is expected to generate each year in its life.

Illustration 27–1 calculates the cash flows from the investment by subtracting the expected cash outflows from the expected cash inflows. The second column simply excludes noncash items (in this case depreciation is the only noncash item). An alternative approach adjusts the projected net income for revenue and expense items that do not involve cash flows. For this example, the $4,100 annual net cash flow equals the net income of $2,100 plus the $2,000 depreciation.

The payback period for an investment is calculated as follows:

$$\text{Payback period} = \frac{\text{Cost of asset}}{\text{Annual net cash flow}}$$

This ratio shows how long it will take the investment project to generate enough net cash flow to return (or pay back) the cash initially invested to buy it. The calculation for this example is as follows:

$$\text{Payback period} = \frac{\$16,000}{\$\ 4,100} = 3.9 \text{ years}$$

Because of the uncertainty associated with the predicted annual net cash flows, the result of 3.9 years is rounded to only one decimal place. Carrying it any further would not add any meaning or usefulness to the result. The cash flows are expected to occur over as many as eight future years. Predictions like these are not dependable enough to justify more precise calculations and carrying the decimals further would suggest an inappropriate degree of accuracy. In light of this uncertainty, we might even question carrying the calculation to one decimal place. Perhaps the most appropriate interpretation of the statistic is to say that the payback period appears to be approximately four years long.[1]

Calculating Payback Periods When Cash Flows Are Not Uniform

The previous example assumed net cash flows were $4,100 each and every year. The payback period can also be calculated when the predicted cash flows vary from year to year. Instead of taking a ratio, it is necessary to find the cumulative total of the net cash inflows.

For example, assume that an investment costing $15,000 is expected to produce the following net cash flows over the next four years:

	Annual Net Cash Flows
Year 1	$3,000
Year 2	4,000
Year 3	5,000
Year 4	6,000

[1] This caution in interpreting the results is suitable for all calculations involving predictions. Managers and managerial accountants need to avoid a spurious accuracy that looks reasonable but that is not justified by the potential imprecision of the predictions.

The net cash flows accumulate as shown in the second column of this schedule:

	Annual Net Cash Flows	Cumulative Net Cash Flows
Year 1	$3,000	$ 3,000
Year 2	4,000	7,000
Year 3	5,000	12,000
Year 4	6,000	18,000

The cumulative net cash flows are $12,000 at the end of year 3 and $18,000 at the end of year 4. Thus, the expected payback period for the $15,000 investment is somewhere between three and four years. The project is expected to pay back $12,000 of the $15,000 investment during the first three years. If the cash flows occur evenly throughout each year, the remaining $3,000 will be paid back around the middle of year 4. Thus, the payback period is about 3.5 years.

Evaluating the Payback Period as a Method of Comparing Investments

A short payback period is desirable because the more quickly cash is received, the more quickly it is available for other uses. Furthermore, a short payback period also means the invested funds are at risk for a shorter time. This short period improves the company's ability to respond to unanticipated changes. In effect, a short payback period reduces the company's risk of having to hold an unprofitable investment.

The payback period should never be the only consideration in evaluating investments because it ignores at least two important factors. First, it fails to reflect differences in the timing of net cash flows within the payback period. In the previous example, the net cash flows in the first four years were $3,000, $4,000, $5,000, and $6,000. If another asset had predicted cash flows of $9,000, $3,000, $2,000, and $2,000 in the four years, its payback period would also be 3.5 years. However, the second pattern would be more desirable because it would provide more cash more quickly.

Second, the payback period is deficient because it ignores *all* cash flows after the period. For example, one investment may pay back its cost in 3 years but stop producing cash after another year, while a second investment would require 5 years to pay back its cost but continue to produce net cash flows for another 15 years. Anyone considering only the payback period would mistakenly choose the first investment.

Rate of Return on Average Investment

To overcome these disadvantages of the payback period as a capital budgeting tool, it is possible to use the **rate of return on average investment** for an asset or a project. This approach takes into consideration all cash flows from the investment. In addition, it provides a more appropriate way to compare and rank alternatives that have differing life spans. This rate is calculated by dividing the after-tax net income from the project by the average investment in the

ILLUSTRATION 27–2

Calculating Average Investment When Net Cash Flows Are Received Evenly throughout Each Year

	Beginning Book Value	Annual Depreciation	Ending Book Value	Average Book Value
Year 1	$16,000	$ 2,000	$14,000	$15,000
Year 2	14,000	2,000	12,000	13,000
Year 3	12,000	2,000	10,000	11,000
Year 4	10,000	2,000	8,000	9,000
Year 5	8,000	2,000	6,000	7,000
Year 6	6,000	2,000	4,000	5,000
Year 7	4,000	2,000	2,000	3,000
Year 8	2,000	2,000	0	1,000
Total		$16,000		

LO 3 Calculate the expected average rate of return on an investment and describe its limitations.

project. Despite its superiority over the payback period, the rate of return on the average investment has its own limitations, which we discuss later.

Rate of Return When Net Cash Flows Are Received Evenly throughout the Year

In calculating the average investment to use in finding the rate, management must make an assumption about the timing of the cash flows that represent the recovery of the asset's annual depreciation. In most cases, net cash flows are received evenly throughout the year. If this pattern can be assumed, the average investment for each year should be calculated as the average of its beginning and ending book values. If the Murray Company's $16,000 machine is depreciated $2,000 each year, the average amount invested in the machine for each year can be calculated as shown in Illustration 27–2. The average for any year is the average of the beginning and ending book values.

To perform this analysis, we need the average book value during the asset's entire life. The amount can be found by taking the average of the eight yearly averages. This approach is necessary if an accelerated depreciation method is used. If we use straight-line depreciation, we can find the average book value for the eight years as the sum of the beginning and ending book values divided by 2:

$$\text{Average investment} = \frac{\text{Beginning book value} + \text{Ending book value}}{2}$$

$$= \frac{\$16{,}000 + \$\ -0-}{2}$$

$$= \$8{,}000$$

This example is simplified by the assumption that the machine has no salvage value. If the machine had a salvage value, the average investment would be calculated as (Original cost + Salvage value)/2.

After the average investment is determined, the rate of return on average investment can be calculated. This step divides the estimated annual after-tax net income by the average investment. In equation form, the calculation appears as follows:

$$\text{Return on average investment} = \frac{\text{Annual after-tax net income}}{\text{Average investment}}$$

Because the Murray Company expects an after-tax annual net income of \$2,100, the expected rate of return (rounded to the nearest percentage) is

$$\text{Return on average investment} = \frac{\$2{,}100}{\$8{,}000} = 26\%$$

Average Investment When the Net Cash Flows Are Received at Year-End

In some cases, the revenue from an investment is not spread evenly over each year but is received in a lump-sum near the end of each year. For example, a financial investment might pay interest in a lump sum at the end of the year. Or, a building's owner might receive a year's annual rent near the end of a year. In analyzing these cases, depreciation can be considered to be recovered near the end of the year. Thus, the asset's book value equals the beginning balance during the entire year, up until the very end. As a result, the average investment during the year is the asset's beginning book value. As applied to the example in Illustration 27–2, an assumption of year-end flows produces the following calculation of the average investment:

$$\begin{aligned}\text{Average investment} &= \frac{\text{First year's book value} + \text{Final year's book value}}{2}\\ &= \frac{\$16{,}000 + \$2{,}000}{2}\\ &= \$9{,}000\end{aligned}$$

If the machine had a salvage value, the book value at the beginning of (and throughout) the final year would equal the salvage value plus the final year's depreciation expense.

With this \$9,000 average investment, the return on average investment for the Murray Company's asset is calculated as follows:

$$\text{Return on average investment} = \frac{\$2{,}100}{\$9{,}000} = 23\%$$

The result is a lower rate of return because the average investment is higher by \$1,000.

Evaluating the Return on Average Investment

At this point, the question should arise whether 26% (or 23%) is a satisfactory rate of return. On the surface, 26% appears better than a lower rate, such as 10 or 15%. However, this conclusion is valid only if the alternatives have similar lives and involve similar levels of risk. And, other available investment alternatives might yield even higher returns. In other words, an investment's return can be considered to be satisfactory or unsatisfactory only when it is related to returns from other investments with similar lives and risk. When average investment returns are used to select between capital investments, the one with the least risk, the shortest payback period, and the highest return for the longest time is often identified as the best.

Perhaps because the rate of return on average investment is relatively easy to calculate, it has long been used in evaluating investment opportunities. However, its usefulness is limited because the measure of the amount invested is based on a systematic prediction of the asset's values in the future. Depreciation methods were created to allocate costs among years, not to predict market values of the assets. The usefulness is also limited when the asset's net incomes are expected to vary from year to year because the rate's calculation must be based on the *average* annual net income. Two investments with the same average annual net income are not equivalent if one is expected to have higher amounts in the early years and lower amounts in the later years. The rate of return on average investment simply fails to distinguish between these two investments. Because of these deficiencies, a comparison of *net present values* generally offers a better method of selecting the preferred investment.

Net Present Values

LO 4 Calculate the net present value of the cash flows from a proposed investment, and describe the procedures used in this method and its advantages and disadvantages.

To use net present values, you need a good understanding of the concepts of discounting. We explain these concepts in Chapter 12, beginning on page 621. Review that discussion before going on if you do not fully understand these concepts. An expanded explanation of discounting is presented in Appendix H. In addition, you can use the present value tables in Appendix H, on pages H-10 and H-12, to solve several of the problems at the end of this chapter.

When a business invests in a new plant asset, it expects that asset to produce a stream of future net cash flows. Normally, a business should not acquire the asset unless its expected cash flows are sufficient to provide a satisfactory return on that investment and recover the amount initially invested. For example, assume that the cash flows from the Murray Company's investment are received at the end of each year. Will the asset provide a satisfactory return while recovering the amount of the investment? If the company considers a 12% compounded annual return to be satisfactory, we can answer this question with the calculations shown in Illustration 27–3. The table shows the calculation of the **net present value** of the investment, which is an estimate of the asset's value to the company. The net present value is calculated by discounting the future cash flows from the investment at a satisfactory rate and then subtracting the initial cost of the investment.

The Murray Company must invest $16,000 to purchase the machine described in Illustration 27–3. The company expects to sell the machine's output and receive net cash flows of $4,100 each year for the next eight years. The first column of Illustration 27–3 shows the amounts of the annual cash flows. The table values in the second column are based on the assumption that the net cash flows are received at the end of each year. (To simplify the discussion of net present values and the related problems at the end of the chapter, we assume that the net cash flows are received at the end of the year. More complex calculations are presented in advanced accounting and finance courses.)

ILLUSTRATION 27–3

Net Present Value Analysis of Future Cash Inflows from a Proposed Investment

	Net Cash Flows	Present Value of $1 at 12%	Present Value of Net Cash Flows
Year 1	$ 4,100	0.8929	$ 3,661
Year 2	4,100	0.7972	3,269
Year 3	4,100	0.7118	2,918
Year 4	4,100	0.6355	2,606
Year 5	4,100	0.5674	2,326
Year 6	4,100	0.5066	2,077
Year 7	4,100	0.4523	1,854
Year 8	4,100	0.4039	1,656
Total	$32,800		$20,367
Amount to be invested			(16,000)
Net present value of investment			$ 4,367

The annual net cash flows in the first column of Illustration 27–3 are multiplied by the table values in the second column to determine the present values in the third column. In the lower section of the illustration, the asset's $16,000 initial cost is deducted from the $20,367 total present value of the future cash inflows. Notice that the total present value exceeds the amount to be invested by $4,367. Therefore, this machine is expected to recover its cost, provide a 12% compounded return, and generate another $4,367. The analysis can also be summarized by saying that the value of the future cash flows to the Murray Company exceeds their $16,000 cost by $4,367.[2]

Generally, when the expected cash flows from an asset are discounted at a satisfactory rate and have a *positive* net present value, the asset should be acquired. Also, when comparing several investment opportunities of about the same cost and the same risk, the one with the highest positive net present value is preferred.

Simplifying the Calculation

The calculation in Illustration 27–3 uses the separate present values of $1 at 12% for each of the eight years. Each year's cash flow is multiplied by the present value of $1 at 12% for that number of years to determine its present value. Then, the present values of the eight cash flows are added to determine their total. The calculation can be simplified in two different ways because the annual cash flows are the same size. One simplification adds the eight yearly

[2] Another calculation shows that the *internal rate of return* for this investment is 19.4% per year, well in excess of the 12% minimum rate specified by the company's management. This calculation finds the discount rate that makes the present value of the net cash inflows equal the $16,000 cost of the investment. Notice that this rate differs from the rate of return on average investment for this asset. The difference arises from the fact that the two calculations use different bases for the amount invested and received each year.

present values of $1 at 12% to get a total of 4.9676. Then, this amount is multiplied by the annual cash flow of $4,100 to get the $20,367 total present value of the cash flows.

An even simpler calculation is based on Table H–3, which shows the present value of $1 to be received periodically for a number of periods. (A series of equal payments is called an *annuity*.) In this case, $4,100 is expected to be received annually for eight years. To determine the present value of these annual receipts discounted at 12%, go down the 12% column of Table H–3 to the amount on the eighth line. The table value is 4.9676. Then, the present value of the eight annual $4,100 receipts is $20,367 (4.9676 × $4,100).

The easiest way to simplify the calculation is to use a hand-held calculator with compound interest functions. You can also find the answers by using a spreadsheet program on a personal computer. Of course, the actual technique that you use does not matter, as long as the calculation is properly made.

Unequal Future Cash Flows

Net present value analysis can also be used when cash flows are not uniform. For example, assume that a company can choose only one capital investment from among projects A, B, and C. Each would have a cost of $12,000. The future cash flows are shown in the first column of the tables for each asset in Illustration 27–4.

All three projects in Illustration 27–4 are expected to produce the same total cash flows of $15,000. However, project A is expected to produce equal amounts each year, project B is expected to produce a greater amount in the first year, and project C is expected to produce a greater amount in the third year. Therefore, if the present values of the cash flows are found at the 10% rate used in the illustration, the projects will not produce the same net present values.[3]

Project A has a $435 positive net present value. Project B has a higher positive net present value of $908 because it brings in more cash more quickly. However, project C has a $197 *negative* net present value because it has a small cash flow in the first year and a large one in the third year. If a minimum 10% return is required, project C should be rejected because the investment's net present value indicates that it will not earn at that rate. Furthermore, if only one project can be accepted, project B appears to be the better investment because its cash flows have a higher net present value.

Considering the Effects of Salvage Value and Accelerated Depreciation

We assumed that the $16,000 machine in the Murray Company example will have no salvage value at the end of its useful life. In many cases, a machine or other asset is expected to have a salvage value. If so, this amount is an additional cash flow that will be received at the end of the final year in the asset's life.

[3] The amounts in Illustration 27-4 are rounded to the nearest whole dollar. However, it is likely that this much precision is spurious accuracy because future cash flows and their present values are always based on predictions.

ILLUSTRATION 27-4

Comparing Net Present Values of Projects When the Timing and Amounts of the Future Cash Flows Are Different

	Net Cash Flows	Present Value of $1 at 10%	Present Value of Net Cash Flows
Project A			
Year 1	$ 5,000	0.9091	$ 4,546
Year 2	5,000	0.8264	4,132
Year 3	5,000	0.7513	3,757
Total	$15,000		$12,435
Amount to be invested			(12,000)
Net present value of investment			$ 435
Project B			
Year 1	$ 8,000	0.9091	$ 7,273
Year 2	5,000	0.8264	4,132
Year 3	2,000	0.7513	1,503
Total	$15,000		$12,908
Amount to be invested			(12,000)
Net present value of investment			$ 908
Project C			
Year 1	$ 1,000	0.9091	$ 909
Year 2	5,000	0.8264	4,132
Year 3	9,000	0.7513	6,762
Total	$15,000		$11,803
Amount to be invested			(12,000)
Net present value of investment			$ (197)

The Murray Company example computed depreciation using the straight-line method. In practice, however, accelerated depreciation is often used for income tax reporting. Accelerated depreciation produces larger depreciation deductions in the early years of an asset's life and smaller deductions in the later years. This pattern results in smaller income tax payments in the early years and larger payments in later years. This variation does not change the basic nature of a present value analysis, but it can change the result. Using accelerated depreciation for tax reporting affects the net present value of the asset's cash flows because it produces larger net cash inflows in the early years of the asset's life and smaller ones in later years. Because early cash flows are more valuable than later ones, being able to use accelerated depreciation for tax reporting always makes an investment more desirable.

Selecting the Earnings Rate

Top management should select the earnings rate to be used for evaluating capital investments. Although financial formulas can aid this selection, the choice of a satisfactory minimum rate is largely subjective. Management may do something as simple as deciding that many investment opportunities can be

AS A MATTER OF *Ethics*

Several months ago, Colfax Corporation's top management adopted new policies to control equipment purchases. According to the new policy, any proposal for a purchase in excess of $5,000 must be submitted for a careful review and capital budgeting analysis. When preparing a proposal, the manager must include predictions of future cash flows that are expected to result from the equipment purchase. These predictions are appraised by a central financial analysis group and modified as necessary. This group has the authority to approve or disapprove the proposal based on an analysis of its merits and the availability of funds.

Gary Waters, one of Colfax's middle-level managers, has recently decided that his group can perform more efficiently and effectively with a major upgrade of its personal computer network. The upgrade requires several new computers, large capacity hard disks, additional internal memory, a new network controller, software, and various other items. All items can be delivered quickly, and the benefits are expected to be realized within a short time.

Although the total cost of the items Waters wants to purchase is approximately $25,000, he is thinking about planning the purchase in a way that will avoid the hassle of preparing a lengthy proposal. No single component costs more than $5,000, and if he prepares six or seven purchase orders, all of the proposed items could be purchased without exceeding $5,000 for any one order.

You are a close friend of Waters, and he asks your opinion. He says that the new equipment would definitely improve profits. It would take a lot of effort to develop suitable predictions of cash flows, and the financial analysis group's decision will probably take two months. By that time, Waters is confident that he could receive the equipment, add it to the network, and start getting the job done.

What is your advice to your friend?

found that will earn, say, a 10% compounded return. This rate then becomes the minimum. The company should refuse to make an investment at less than this rate if it has average risk.

The required earnings rate should always be higher than the rate at which money can be borrowed because the return on an investment must cover the interest and provide an additional profit to reward the company for its risk. For example, if money can be borrowed at around 10%, a required after-tax return of 15% may be acceptable in industrial companies with average risk. A lower rate may be suitable for public utilities with lower risks, while a higher rate is needed for other companies facing unusually high risks.

OTHER MANAGERIAL DECISIONS

This section describes six general categories of decisions that managers must make in many different situations. The objective of the discussions is to show you which cost and other financial factors are relevant to those decisions. The descriptions also show you how to structure an analysis to reach a decision more easily.

Replacing Plant Assets

New and better machines are continuously coming on the market. As a result, managers must frequently decide whether to replace an existing machine with a new and better one. In many cases, an existing machine is in good physical condition and is still producing the company's product. However, a new machine should be considered if it can do the job with a large savings in operating costs. In this situation, management must decide whether the after-tax savings in operating costs justify the investment.

The decision analysis should compare the cash savings with the cash outflows needed to obtain the new machine, net of any cash inflow from selling the old one. The net present value method is the best way to analyze these predicted cash flows.

Finding the amount of after-tax cash effects of replacing an existing machine may be complicated by the fact that the annual tax depreciation on the new machine could be based on the book value of the old machine plus the cash paid. This complexity arises only if the old asset is given in exchange for the new one (see Chapter 11). Because other complications can also arise, a complete discussion of these decisions is left to more advanced managerial accounting courses.

Accepting Additional Business

LO 5 Explain how information about incremental costs affects decisions about accepting or rejecting additional volume and about making or buying a component of a product.

We have seen in prior chapters that the measures of costs provided by cost accounting systems are average historical costs. Although useful in product pricing and in controlling operations, historical costs are not necessarily relevant to decisions about accepting additional business. Instead, the relevant costs are the additional costs, which are generally called the **incremental costs** or *differential costs*. The incremental costs are incurred only if the company accepts the additional volume.

For example, assume that a company operates at its normal level, which is 80% of full capacity. The company produces and sells approximately 100,000 units of product annually, with the following average and total costs:

	Per Unit	Total
Sales (100,000 units)	$10.00	$1,000,000
Direct materials	$ 3.50	$ 350,000
Direct labor	2.20	220,000
Factory overhead	1.10	110,000
Selling expenses	1.40	140,000
Administrative expenses	0.80	80,000
Total expenses	$ 9.00	$ 900,000
Operating income	$ 1.00	$ 100,000

The marketing department reports it has found a customer who wants to buy and export the company's product to another country. This potential customer has offered to buy 10,000 units of product at the lower than average price of $8.50 per unit. The price reduction is being considered because this sale would be several times larger than any previous sale made by the company. Because the units are being exported, the new business would not affect domestic sales. To determine whether this order should be accepted or rejected, management needs to know whether net income will increase if the offer is accepted. If the managerial accountant simply relied on the per unit average costs, these numbers would be reported:

	Per Unit	Total
Sales (10,000 units)	$ 8.50	$85,000
Direct materials	$ 3.50	$35,000
Direct labor	2.20	22,000
Factory overhead	1.10	11,000
Selling expenses	1.40	14,000
Administrative expenses	0.80	8,000
Total expenses	$ 9.00	$90,000
Operating loss	$(0.50)	$(5,000)

If the decision were to be based on these average costs, the new business would be rejected because it would generate a loss. However, average costs are not relevant to this decision.

Instead, the *incremental* costs are relevant for deciding whether to accept the new business. Therefore, before making the decision, the costs of the new business must be analyzed more closely. Assume that the analysis reveals the following information:

- Manufacturing 10,000 additional units of product would require additional direct materials of $3.50 per unit and additional direct labor of $2.20 per unit (just like the units already being produced).
- The 10,000 units can be manufactured with only $5,000 of incremental factory overhead costs for power, packaging, and indirect labor for handling materials.
- Incremental commissions and other selling expenses resulting from the sale would be only $2,000.
- Incremental administrative expenses of $1,000 for clerical efforts would be needed.

Based on this added information, Illustration 27–5 shows how the additional business would affect the company's net income.

The analysis in the illustration suggests that the additional business should be accepted. The additional business would provide $85,000 of revenue while creating only $65,000 of additional costs. When this analysis is made, it shows that accepting the additional business at $8.50 per unit should generate $20,000 of additional pretax income. In fact, the company would have more income at any price above $6.50 per unit.

Incremental costs of additional volume are always relevant, but they may greatly exceed the relatively small amounts in this example. The incremental costs were small because the additional volume was within the existing available capacity of the factory. If the additional volume requires the company to expand its capacity by obtaining more equipment, more space, or more supervisory personnel, the incremental costs could easily exceed the incremental revenue.

ILLUSTRATION 27–5

The Effects of Accepting Additional Business

	Present Business	Additional Business	Combined
Sales	$1,000,000	$85,000	$1,085,000
Direct materials	$ 350,000	$35,000	$ 385,000
Direct labor	220,000	22,000	242,000
Factory overhead	110,000	5,000	115,000
Selling expenses	140,000	2,000	142,000
Administrative expense	80,000	1,000	81,000
Total expenses	$ 900,000	$65,000	$ 965,000
Operating income	$ 100,000	$20,000	$ 120,000

Another factor relevant to a decision to accept additional volume is the effect on existing sales. In the example, all the new units were to be sold elsewhere without affecting domestic sales. However, if the order would cause existing sales to decline, that fact would need to be included in the analysis.

And, if the future cash flows are to be received over several time periods, their net present value should be calculated and used in making the analysis for management.

In summary, the key point is that management should not use the average costs generated by a cost accounting system, especially allocated overhead. In their place, the managerial accounting system needs to provide information about the incremental costs that would be incurred only if the additional business is accepted.

Make or Buy Decisions

Incremental costs are also relevant to a decision between making or buying a particular component of a product. For example, assume that a manufacturer has excess productive capacity. The idle machines can be used to manufacture part 417, a component of the company's product. This component is presently purchased and delivered to the plant at a cost of $1.20 per unit. The manufacturer estimates that making part 417 would cost $0.45 for direct materials, $0.50 for direct labor, and an undetermined amount of factory overhead. At this point, we need to figure out how much overhead should be added to these costs to provide useful information for the decision. If the normal predetermined overhead application rate is 100% of direct labor cost, we might say that the overhead cost is $0.50 per unit. If so, the total cost would be $1.45, and we would decide that the company would be better off to buy the part at $1.20 each.

The prior section shows that only the incremental overhead costs are relevant and that we should ignore the normal predetermined overhead rate. The incremental overhead costs might include, for example, power for operating the machines, supplies, cleanup, materials handling, and quality control. If these incremental overhead costs are less than $0.25 per unit, the total cost of making the component would be less than $1.20. If so, the manufacturer may be justified in manufacturing the part in the short run. If the decision to make the part would require the company to incur major incremental fixed costs to expand its capacity, the cost of making the part could increase to the point that buying it would be more economical.

As we saw, any amount of overhead less than $0.25 per unit results in a total cost for Part 417 that is less than the $1.20 purchase price. Nevertheless, in deciding whether to make or buy the part, the manufacturer should consider other factors, including such things as quality, timeliness of delivery (especially in a just-in-time setting), the reactions of customers and suppliers, and other intangible items. When these additional factors are considered, small cost differences may not matter.

Again, a key point is that the full average cost provided by a cost accounting system is not likely to be relevant to this decision. Instead, only the incremental costs must be considered.

Other Cost Concepts

LO 6 Describe the importance of sunk costs, out-of-pocket costs, and opportunity costs for decisions, including the choice between scrapping or reworking defective units and between selling a product or processing it further.

Additional categories of costs related to managerial decisions include *sunk costs, out-of-pocket costs,* and *opportunity costs.*

A **sunk cost** arises from a past decision. It is considered sunk in the sense that it cannot be avoided or changed in any way. As a result, sunk costs are irrelevant to decisions. For example, the historical cost of a machine is a sunk cost. Nothing can be done in the future to change that cost. Instead, we need to consider the current market value of the machine in any decision about what to do with it in the future.

An **out-of-pocket cost** requires a current outlay of cash. Costs for materials, labor, supplies, and utilities are examples of out-of-pocket costs. Generally, out-of-pocket costs are incurred or avoided as a result of management's decisions. Thus, they are relevant to those decisions. Most *allocated* costs, especially fixed overhead costs such as depreciation and amortization, are not out-of-pocket costs.

The costs discussed previously result from expenditures to obtain goods or services. In addition, the concept of cost should be broadened to include **opportunity costs.** These costs are the potential benefits lost by choosing an alternative course of action. For example, if a student must turn down a job in order to attend summer school, the $3,000 salary that is not received must be considered part of the cost of going to school. As another example, suppose that a company decides to make a component instead of buying it. By choosing to do so, the company gives up the benefit that could be obtained by using the productive capacity for another activity. If the capacity cannot be used, there is no opportunity cost. On the other hand, if the capacity can be used to produce net cash flows of $100,000, that amount is the opportunity cost that must be considered in the make-or-buy decision. In retailing, the commitment of shelf space to one class of merchandise (such as snacks) means that the space is not available for another type of merchandise (such as cereal). In deciding whether to try selling more snacks, management's analysis should include an opportunity cost equal to the lost profits from not being able to sell the cereal.

Opportunity costs are not entered in the accounting records. However, they are always relevant to decisions involving rejected opportunities. As an example of a situation in which both sunk costs and opportunity costs must be identified, we next turn to decisions between scrapping or reworking defective units of product.

Scrapping or Reworking Defective Units

Any costs incurred in manufacturing units of product that do not meet quality standards are sunk costs. They have been incurred and cannot be changed. Thus, they are irrelevant and should not enter into a decision between selling the units as scrap or reworking them so that they meet the quality standards. For example, assume that a company has 10,000 defective units of product that cost $1 per unit to manufacture. The units can be sold as they are for $0.40 each, or they can be reworked for $0.80 per unit, after which they can be sold for their full price of $1.50 per unit. Should the company rework the units or should it sell them as scrap?

Note that the original manufacturing costs of $1 per unit are sunk and *completely* irrelevant to the decision. Based on the given information, the comparative returns from scrapping or reworking the units are as follows:

	Scrap	Rework
Sales of defective units	$4,000	$15,000
Less cost to rework.		(8,000)
Net return.	$4,000	$ 7,000

Reworking is a better tactic as long as it does not interfere with normal operations. However, suppose that reworking the defective units would cause the company to be unable to manufacture 10,000 new units with an incremental cost of $1 per unit. If they can be sold for $1.50 per unit, the comparative returns should be analyzed as follows:

	Scrap	Rework
Sales of defective units.	$ 4,000	$15,000
Sales of new units	15,000	
Less cost to rework the old units		(8,000)
Less cost to manufacture the new units . .	(10,000)	
Net return from using capacity.	$ 9,000	$ 7,000

If the defective units are scrapped, the plant's limited capacity can be used to manufacture new units that will be sold for a net profit of $5,000. This tactic produces a $9,000 total return from selling the new and scrapping the defective units. Obviously, this outcome is better than the $7,000 net return generated by using the productive capacity to rework the defective units.

This situation can also be analyzed using an opportunity cost. If reworking the defective units requires the company to give up manufacturing the new units, the company incurs the opportunity cost of the lost $5,000 net return from making and selling new units. This opportunity cost is the difference between the $15,000 revenue from selling the new units and their $10,000 manufacturing costs. The following analysis shows how the opportunity cost should be included:

	Scrap	Rework
Sales of defective units	$4,000	$15,000
Less cost to rework the old units		(8,000)
Less opportunity cost (return lost by not manufacturing the new units) . . .		(5,000)
Net return from using capacity	$4,000	$ 2,000

Observe that the two analyses lead to the same conclusion. Either way, there is a $2,000 difference in favor of scrapping the defective units. But, this result is different from the first analysis that showed a $3,000 advantage for reworking the units. That analysis was incomplete because it omitted the $5,000 opportunity cost.

Process or Sell

Sunk costs, out-of-pocket costs, and opportunity costs also enter into deciding whether to sell partially completed products as they are or to process them further. If the completed products are processed further, the company will be able to sell them to customers.

For example, suppose that the Monarch Company has 40,000 units of partially finished product Q. These units cost $0.75 per unit to manufacture, for a total cost of $30,000. The 40,000 units can be sold to another manufacturer as a raw material for $50,000. Alternatively, Monarch Company can process them further and turn them into finished products X, Y, and Z at an incremental cost of $2 per unit. The additional processing would produce the following numbers of each product, which could be sold at the indicated unit prices:

Product	Price	Units	Revenue
X.	$4.00	10,000	$ 40,000
Y.	6.00	22,000	132,000
Z.	8.00	6,000	48,000
Spoilage	0.00	2,000	–0–
Total		40,000	$220,000

The company's management must determine whether the additional revenue from selling these finished products exceeds the cost of finishing them. Illustration 27–6 shows the analysis that should be completed.

Observe that the revenue that would be received by selling product Q is an opportunity cost of doing additional processing on the units. Also notice that the $30,000 manufacturing cost for the 40,000 units of product Q does not appear in Illustration 27–6. This cost is the same regardless of which alternative is chosen. Therefore, it is sunk and irrelevant to the decision.

ILLUSTRATION 27-6

Analyzing the Effect of Selling an Unfinished Product or Processing It Further

Revenue if processed further		$220,000
Less:		
Additional costs of processing (40,000 @ $2)	$80,000	
Opportunity cost (lost sales of Product Q)	50,000	
Total cost of processing		130,000
Net advantage of additional processing		$ 90,000

Another way to analyze this decision is to compare the incremental revenue from further processing with the incremental cost of the additional work. This table shows the relevant calculations:

Revenue if processed further	$220,000
Revenue if sold as is	50,000
Incremental revenue	$170,000
Incremental cost of processing	80,000
Incremental advantage	$ 90,000

This analysis leads to the same conclusion that the company is better off incurring the cost to produce products X, Y, and Z because the additional revenue generated by selling them is greater than the additional cost.

Selecting a Sales Mix

When a company sells a variety of products, some are likely to be more profitable than others. If so, management may be wise to concentrate its sales efforts on the more profitable products. However, if production facilities or other factors are limited, an increase in the production and sale of one product may require the company to reduce the production and sale of others. In this situation, management must identify the most profitable combination (or *sales mix*) of the products and concentrate on selling the products in this combination.

To identify the best sales mix for its products, management must know the contribution margin of each product. In addition, management must know about the facilities required to produce the products and any limits, or constraints, on these facilities and the markets for the products. For example, assume that the Keystone Company produces and sells two products, A and B. The same machines are used to produce both products, which have the following selling prices and variable costs per unit:

	Product A	Product B
Selling price	$5.00	$7.50
Variable costs	3.50	5.50
Contribution margin	$1.50	$2.00

The variable costs are included in the analysis because they are the incremental costs of producing the products within the existing capacity of 100,000 machine-hours per month.

If both products use one machine-hour per unit and there is an unlimited market for product B, the Keystone Company should produce as much of product B as it possibly can because of its larger contribution margin per unit. At full capacity, the company would generate $200,000 of contribution margin.

Alternatively, suppose that product A uses one machine-hour per unit while product B requires two machine-hours for each unit. If the market for product A is unlimited, the company should commit all of its efforts to this product because it produces $1.50 of contribution margin per machine-hour while product B produces only $1 per machine-hour. This calculation is as follows:

	Product A	**Product B**
Selling price	$5.00	$7.50
Variable costs	3.50	5.50
Contribution margin	$1.50	$2.00
Machine-hours per unit	1.0	2.0
Contribution margin per machine-hour	$1.50	$1.00

Thus, by using the entire capacity of 100,000 machine-hours to produce 100,000 units of product A, the Keystone Company can generate $150,000 of contribution margin. If the entire 100,000 hours were used to produce 50,000 units of product B, the company would generate a contribution margin of only $100,000. Thus, when a company has no excess capacity, only the most profitable product should be manufactured.

The need for a mix of different products arises if market demand is not sufficient to allow the company to sell all that it can produce. To see how this need arises, assume that the Keystone Company can sell no more than 80,000 units of product A, even though it can produce as many as 100,000 units. With this market constraint in place, the company should produce no more than 80,000 units of product A. This level will leave another 20,000 machine-hours of capacity available for manufacturing product B. Therefore, the company should use the spare capacity to produce 10,000 units of product B. This sales mix maximizes the company's contribution margin at $140,000 for the time period.[4]

[4] The sophisticated mathematical technique called *linear programming* is especially useful for finding the optimal sales mix of a large number of products subject to many different market and production constraints.

Summary of the Chapter in Terms of Learning Objectives

LO 1. Capital budgeting is the process of analyzing alternative investments and deciding which assets to acquire or sell. Generally, capital budgeting involves predicting the cash flows to be received from alternative possibilities, evaluating their merits, and then choosing which ones should be pursued.

LO 2. One method of comparing possible investments calculates and compares their payback periods. This period is an estimate of the time that can be expected to pass before the cumulative net cash inflow from the investment equals its initial cost. The payback period analysis is limited because it fails to reflect the riskiness of the cash flows, differences in the timing of cash flows within the payback period, and all cash flows that occur after the payback period.

LO 3. A project's expected rate of return on the average investment is calculated by dividing the periodic after-tax net income by the average investment in the project. When the net cash flows are received evenly throughout each period, the average investment is calculated as the average of the investment's initial book value and its salvage value. If the net cash flows are expected to be received at the end of each year, the average investment is calculated as the average of the investment's initial book value and its book value at the beginning of the last year in its life. One major limitation of rate of return on average investment is its dependence on predictions of future value derived from depreciation methods. It also fails to reflect year-to-year variations in expected net incomes.

LO 4. The net present value of an investment is determined by predicting the future cash flows that it is expected to generate, discounting them at a rate that represents an acceptable return, and then subtracting the initial cost of the investment from the sum of the present values. This technique can deal with any pattern of expected cash flows and applies a superior concept of return on investment. However, it is limited by the subjectivity inherent in predicting future cash flows and in selecting the discount rate.

LO 5. In deciding whether to produce and sell additional units of product, the relevant factors are the incremental costs and revenues from the additional volume. Costs that will not change as a result of the decision are irrelevant and must not be considered. Incremental costs and revenues are also relevant to a decision between making or buying a component of a product.

LO 6. Sunk costs cannot be avoided because they result from past decisions. Out-of-pocket costs require current outlays of cash. Opportunity costs are potential benefits that are lost as a result of choosing a particular course of action. Because sunk costs have already been incurred, they are not relevant to any decision, including the choice between scrapping or reworking defective units. Out-of-pocket costs that change as a result of choosing an alternative are incremental and relevant to the choice between alternatives. Also, when one course of action precludes taking an alternative, the lost benefits of the rejected alternative should be included among the costs of taking the chosen course of action. All of these costs apply in decisions between selling a partially completed product or processing it further and in decisions about the company's sales mix.

Demonstration Problem

Part 1.
Davenport Company is considering three investment opportunities that would involve purchasing Asset X, Asset Y, or Asset Z. Straight-line depreciation would be used in each case, and the salvage value would be received at the end of the life of the investment. In estimating the periodic net incomes from each asset, the only noncash expense is depreciation. The following predictions are available about these investments:

	Asset		
	X	Y	Z
Purchase price	$40,000	$40,000	$40,000
Salvage value	$ 1,000	$ -0-	$10,000
Useful life	6 years	8 years	8 years
Expected net incomes (losses):			
Year 1	$ 3,500	$11,000	$ (3,750)
Year 2	3,500	9,000	4,250
Year 3	3,500	7,000	8,250
Year 4	3,500	5,000	16,250
Year 5	3,500	3,000	(1,750)
Year 6	3,500	1,000	(1,750)
Year 7	-0-	(1,000)	(1,750)
Year 8	-0-	(3,000)	21,250
Total income	$21,000	$32,000	$41,000

Required
Rank the three investments from first to third, based on each of the following analytical techniques:

a. Payback period, assuming that the cash flows from each investment are received evenly throughout each year.

b. Return on average investment, assuming that the net income from each investment is received evenly throughout each year.

c. Net present value, using 8% per year as the discount rate. For this analysis, assume that the cash flows are received at the end of each year.

Part 2.
Determine the appropriate action in each of the following decision situations:

a. The Eagleview Company has been operating at 80% of its 100,000 unit per year capacity for manufacturing its product. A chain store has offered to buy an additional 10,000 units at $22 each and sell them in an area where Eagleview currently has no outlet. Consider the following facts:

	Per Unit	Total
Costs at 80% of capacity:		
Direct materials	$ 8.00	$ 640,000
Direct labor	7.00	560,000
Total (fixed and variable) overhead	12.50	1,000,000
Totals	$27.50	$2,200,000

In producing the 10,000 additional units, fixed overhead costs would remain at their present level but incremental variable overhead costs of $3.00 per unit would be incurred. Should the company accept or reject this order?

b. The Foothills Company uses Part JR345 in manufacturing its products. In the past, it has always purchased this part from a supplier for $40 each. It recently upgraded its own manufacturing capabilities and has enough excess capacity (including trained workers) to begin manufacturing Part JR345 instead of buying it. The bookkeeper has prepared the following projection of the cost of making the part, assuming that overhead should be allocated to the part with the normal predetermined application rate of 200% of the direct labor cost.

Direct materials	$11.00
Direct labor	15.00
Total fixed and variable overhead (200% of direct labor cost)	30.00
Total	$56.00

The company's accountant reviewed these calculations and determined that the volume of output of the part will not require any incremental fixed overhead cost. Incremental variable overhead cost will be $17 per unit. Should the company make or buy this part?

c. Georgetown Company's manufacturing process causes a relatively large number of defective parts to be produced. The defective parts can be (*1*) sold for scrap, (*2*) melted down to recover the metal for reuse, or (*3*) reworked and otherwise repaired. If defective parts are reworked, the output of other good units is reduced because there is no excess capacity. In fact, each unit reworked means that one new unit cannot be produced. The following information is available about 500 defective parts that are currently on hand:

Proceeds of selling as scrap	$2,500
Additional cost of melting down all defective parts	$ 400
Cost of metal purchases that can be avoided by using recycled metal	$4,800
Cost to rework 500 defective parts:	
Direct materials	$ -0-
Direct labor	1,500
Incremental overhead	1,750
Cost to produce 500 new parts:	
Direct materials	$6,000
Direct labor	5,000
Incremental overhead	3,200

Should the company melt down the parts, sell them as scrap, or rework them?

Solution to Demonstration Problem

Planning the Solution

- Begin solving Part 1 by calculating the annual depreciation cost for each of the three assets. Then, predict the annual net cash flows for the three alternatives for each of the eight years by adding the predicted net income, the depreciation expense, and the salvage value (only in the asset's final year).
- Find the payback period for each of the three assets. The calculation for Asset X can be found as a ratio. The payback periods for Assets Y and Z must be found by calculating their cumulative cash flows. Then, rank the three opportunities, with the shortest payback period receiving the highest rank.
- Find the return on average investment for each of the three assets. To begin, find each asset's average annual net income by dividing the total income by the number of years in its life. Then, find the average investment over that life by finding the average of their initial cost and their salvage values. Third, divide the average annual income by the annual investment to get a percentage. Finally, rank the three alternatives, with the highest rate of return getting the highest ranking.
- Find the net present value of the future net cash flows from the three investments. Set up a three-column table for each asset. The first column should show the net cash inflow for each year in the asset's life. The second column should show table values from Table H–1 for the present value of $1 discounted at 8%. The third column should be the product of the future cash flow and the table value. Then, take the sum of the yearly present values and subtract the initial cost. The result is the net present value of each project. Finally, rank the three proposals, with the largest net present value getting the highest ranking.
- In Part 2, determine whether the Eagleview Company should accept the additional business by finding the incremental costs of materials, labor, and overhead that will be incurred if the order is accepted. Leave out those fixed costs that will not be increased by the order. If the incremental revenue will exceed the incremental cost, accept the order.
- Determine whether the Foothills Company should make or buy the component by finding the incremental cost of making each unit. If the incremental cost exceeds the purchase price, the component should be purchased.
- Determine whether the Georgetown Company should sell the defective parts, melt them down and recycle the metal, or rework them. To compare the three choices, examine all costs incurred and disposal proceeds received in going from the current condition of having 500 defective units to the condition of having 500 new units. For the scrapping tactic, include the costs of producing 500 brand new units and subtract the $2,500 proceeds from selling the old ones. For the melting tactic, include the costs of melting the defective units, add the net cost of new materials in excess over those obtained from recycling, and add the direct labor and overhead costs. For the reworking tactic, merely add the costs of direct

labor and incremental overhead. Then, select the alternative that has the lowest cost. Notice that the cost assigned to the 500 defective units is sunk and not considered in choosing among the three alternatives.

Part 1.

Annual depreciation and cash flows from each of the three investments:

Annual depreciation expense:

	X	Y	Z
Cost	$40,000	$40,000	$40,000
Salvage value	(1,000)	–0–	(10,000)
Depreciable base	$39,000	$40,000	$30,000
Life	6 years	8 years	8 years
Annual depreciation	$ 6,500	$ 5,000	$ 3,750

Annual cash flows (Net income plus depreciation plus salvage in final year):

	X	Y	Z
Year 1	$10,000	$16,000	$ –0–
Year 2	10,000	14,000	8,000
Year 3	10,000	12,000	12,000
Year 4	10,000	10,000	20,000
Year 5	10,000	8,000	2,000
Year 6	11,000	6,000	2,000
Year 7	–0–	4,000	2,000
Year 8	–0–	2,000	35,000
Total	$61,000	$72,000	$81,000

a. Payback period:

Investment X:

$$\text{Payback period} = \frac{\text{Cost of asset}}{\text{Annual net cash flow}} = \frac{\$40{,}000}{\$10{,}000} = 4 \text{ years}$$

Investment Y:

	Annual Net Cash Flows	Cumulative Net Cash Flows
Year 1	$16,000	$16,000
Year 2	14,000	30,000
Year 3	12,000	42,000

Thus, the $40,000 cost is paid back in slightly less than three years.

Investment Z:

	Annual Net Cash Flows	Cumulative Net Cash Flows
Year 1	$ –0–	$ –0–
Year 2	8,000	8,000
Year 3	12,000	20,000
Year 4	20,000	40,000

Thus, the $40,000 cost is paid back in four years.

Ranking:

Investment Y is ranked first because it will pay back the cost in less than three years. Investments X and Z are tied for second with payback periods of four years.

b. Return on average investment:

Because the cash flows are spread evenly throughout each period, the average investment is calculated as the average of the original cost and the salvage value.

	X	Y	Z
Average net income per year:			
Total income over life	$21,000	$32,000	$41,000
Estimated useful life	6 years	8 years	8 years
Average annual net income	$ 3,500	$ 4,000	$ 5,125
Average investment:			
Purchase price (initial book value)	$40,000	$40,000	$40,000
Salvage value (final book value)	1,000	–0–	10,000
Sum	$41,000	$40,000	$50,000
Average (sum/2)	$20,500	$20,000	$25,000
Average return on average investment	17.1%	20.0%	20.5%
Rank	Third	Second	First

c. Net present value (using 8% per year as the discount rate):

Investment X:

	Net Cash Flows	Present Value at 8%	Present Value of Cash Flows
Year 1	$10,000	0.9259	$ 9,259
Year 2	10,000	0.8573	8,573
Year 3	10,000	0.7938	7,938
Year 4	10,000	0.7350	7,350
Year 5	10,000	0.6806	6,806
Year 6	11,000	0.6302	6,932
Total	$61,000		$46,858
Original cost of asset			(40,000)
Net present value			$ 6,858

Investment Y:

	Net Cash Flows	Present Value at 8%	Present Value of Cash Flows
Year 1	$16,000	0.9259	$14,814
Year 2	14,000	0.8573	12,002
Year 3	12,000	0.7938	9,526
Year 4	10,000	0.7350	7,350
Year 5	8,000	0.6806	5,445
Year 6	6,000	0.6302	3,781
Year 7	4,000	0.5835	2,334
Year 8	2,000	0.5403	1,081
Total	$72,000		$56,333
Original cost of asset			(40,000)
Net present value			$16,333

Investment Z:

	Net Cash Flows	Present Value at 8%	Present Value of Cash Flows
Year 1	$ -0-	0.9259	$ -0-
Year 2	8,000	0.8573	6,858
Year 3	12,000	0.7938	9,526
Year 4	20,000	0.7350	14,700
Year 5	2,000	0.6806	1,361
Year 6	2,000	0.6302	1,260
Year 7	2,000	0.5835	1,167
Year 8	35,000	0.5403	18,911
Total	$81,000		$53,783
Original cost of asset			(40,000)
Net present value			$13,783

On the basis of the net present values, the investments are ranked as follows:

Y	$16,333	First
Z	13,783	Second
X	6,858	Third

Part 2.

a. This decision concerns accepting additional business. Because the unit costs seem to be $27.50, it appears as if the offer to sell for $22.00 should be rejected. However, the $27.50 cost includes some fixed costs. When the analysis includes only the incremental cost, the per unit cost is reduced as follows:

Direct materials	$ 8.00
Direct labor	7.00
Variable overhead	3.00
Total incremental cost	$18.00

Therefore, the offer should be accepted because it will produce $4.00 of additional profit per unit, which is a total profit of $40,000 for the 10,000 units.

b. This is a make or buy decision. The bookkeeper's analysis is faulty because it includes the nonincremental overhead of $13 per unit. When only the incremental overhead of $17 is included, the unit cost of manufacturing the part is

Direct materials	$11.00
Direct labor	15.00
Variable overhead	17.00
Total incremental cost	$43.00

Therefore, it would be better to continue buying the part for $40 instead of making it for $43. (This analysis shows that it is possible to reach the right decision even though the information is incorrect.)

c. This is a scrap or rework decision. The goal is to identify the alternative that produces the greatest benefit to the company. To compare the alternatives on an equal basis, determine the net cost of obtaining 500 marketable units. The comparison is as follows:

	Sell as Is	Melt and Recycle	Rework Old Units
Incremental cost to produce 500 marketable units:			
Direct material:			
Cost of new materials	$ 6,000	$ 6,000	
Value of recycled metal		(4,800)	
Net materials cost		$ 1,200	
Melting costs		400	
Total direct material cost	$ 6,000	$ 1,600	
Direct labor	5,000	5,000	$1,500
Incremental overhead	3,200	3,200	1,750
Total cost to produce 500 marketable units	$14,200	$ 9,800	$3,250
Less proceeds of selling defective units as scrap	(2,500)		
Net cost	$11,700	$ 9,800	$3,250

The incremental cost of obtaining 500 marketable parts is smallest if the defective parts are reworked.

Glossary

LO 7 Define or explain the words and phrases listed in the chapter glossary.

Capital budgeting the process of analyzing alternative investments and deciding which assets to acquire or sell. p. 1422

Incremental cost an additional cost incurred only if a particular action is taken. p. 1433

Net present value an estimate of an asset's value to the company; calculated by discounting the future cash flows from the investment at a satisfactory rate and then subtracting the initial cost of the investment. p. 1428

Opportunity cost the potential benefits of one alternative that are lost by choosing another. p. 1436

Out-of-pocket cost a cost that requires a current outlay of cash; usually an incremental cost. p. 1436

Payback period the time expected to pass before the net cash flows from an investment return its initial cost. p. 1423

Rate of return on average investment a rate used to evaluate the acceptability of an investment; equals the after-tax periodic income divided by the average investment in the asset. p. 1425

Sunk cost a cost that cannot be avoided or changed in any way because it arises from a past decision; irrelevant to future decisions. p. 1436

Synonymous Terms

Incremental costs differential costs; additional costs; marginal costs.

Limitations constraints.

Sales mix combination of products.

Objective Review

Answers to the following questions are listed at the end of the chapter. Be sure that you decide which is the one best answer to each question *before* you check the answers.

LO 1 Capital budgeting is

a. An optional activity that only a few companies should engage in.
b. Concerned with analyzing alternative sources of capital, including debt and preferred stock.
c. An essential activity for all companies as they consider what assets to acquire.
d. Best accomplished by intuitive assessments of the value of assets and their potential usefulness to the company.
e. None of the above.

LO 2 Collins Corporation is considering the purchase of a new piece of equipment that costs $75,000. Annual net cash flows to be produced by this investment are $30,000, $25,000, $15,000, $10,000, and $5,000. The payback period is

a. 2.5 years.
b. 3 years.

c. 3.5 years.
d. 4 years.
e. 5 years.

LO 3 The following data relate to a machinery purchase that the Alright Company is considering:

Cost	$180,000
Salvage value	$ 5,000
Estimated useful life	8 years
Annual income before depreciation	$ 39,450

Calculate the expected rate of return on average investment, assuming that the net cash flows from the investment are received evenly throughout the year (ignore income taxes):

a. 18%.
b. 19%.
c. 20%.
d. 38%.
e. 43%.

LO 4 Casco Bay Company can invest in only one of four projects. Each project requires a $20,000 investment and is expected to generate end-of-period cash flows as follows:

	Annual Cash Flows			
	Project 1	**Project 2**	**Project 3**	**Project 4**
Year 1	$ 8,500	$12,000	$ 4,500	$ –0–
Year 2	8,500	8,500	8,500	9,200
Year 3	8,500	4,000	13,000	9,200
Year 4	–0–	–0–	–0–	9,200
Total	$25,500	$24,500	$26,000	$27,600

Assuming a discount rate of 10%, which project has the greatest net present value?

a. Project 1.
b. Project 2.
c. Project 3.
d. Project 4.
e. Cannot be determined.

LO 5 Brown Company has just received a special order for 200 units of its product. To be able to stamp the buyer's name on each unit, Brown must incur an additional fixed cost of $400 above its normal manufacturing costs. Without the order, the company would be operating at 75% of capacity. At this level, it would produce 7,500 units of product and incur the following costs:

Direct materials	$37,500
Direct labor	60,000
Factory overhead (30% variable)	20,000
Selling expenses (60% variable)	25,000

This order will not affect Brown's normal unit sales and will not increase fixed overhead and selling costs. Also, variable selling expenses on the special order will be reduced to one-half the normal amount. What price per unit will Brown Company need to earn $1,000 on the order?

a. $14.80.
b. $15.80.
c. $19.80.
d. $20.80.
e. $21.80.

LO 6 Jimbo, Inc., incurs a joint cost of $1,000 in producing its four products. The selling prices in the following list are for partially and fully processed products. Also shown are the additional costs incurred in finishing the partially processed units:

Product	Unfinished Selling Price	Finished Selling Price	Additional Processing Costs
Alpha	$300	$600	$150
Beta	450	900	300
Gamma	275	425	125
Delta	150	210	75

Which of these products should not be processed further?

a. Alpha.
b. Beta.
c. Gamma.
d. Delta.
e. All should be processed further.

LO 7 A sunk cost should not be considered in making a decision because it

a. Was incurred in the past.
b. Is not an out-of-pocket cost to be incurred in the future.
c. Is not incremental with any future course of action.
d. Cannot be changed by any future decision.
e. All of the above.

Questions for Class Discussion

1. What is capital budgeting? Why are capital budgeting decisions risky?
2. Why are capital budgeting decisions often difficult to make?
3. The predicted net cash flows from an investment may be calculated and expressed directly or indirectly. What is the difference between these two presentations?
4. If depreciation is an expense, why is the amount of net cash flow from an investment calculated by adding depreciation to the net income from the investment?

5. Why is an investment more attractive if it has a short payback period?
6. If two alternate investments have the same payback period, are they equally desirable?
7. What is the average amount invested in a machine during its life if it will cost $132,000 and has a predicted five-year life with a $27,000 salvage value? Assume that the net income is received evenly throughout each year.
8. What is your answer to Question 7, assuming that the net income is received near the end of each year?
9. Is a 15% return on the average investment in a machine a good rate?
10. Why is the present value of $100 that you expect to receive one year from now less than $100? What is the present value of $100 that you expect to receive one year from now, discounted at 12%?
11. Two investment alternatives are expected to generate six years of annual cash flows that have the same net present value when discounted at 11%. Based on this information, can you necessarily conclude that the two alternatives are equally desirable?
12. If the present value of the expected net cash flows from a machine, discounted at 12%, exceeds the amount to be invested, what can you say about the expected rate of return on the investment? What can you say about the expected rate of return if the present value of the net cash flows, discounted at 12%, is less than the amount of the investment?
13. When two investment alternatives have the same total expected cash flows but differ in the timing of those flows, which method of evaluating those investments is superior: (*a*) rate of return on average investment or (*b*) net present value?
14. Why is the value of an investment increased by using accelerated depreciation (instead of straight-line) for income tax reporting?
15. What are the incremental costs of accepting an additional volume of business?
16. A company manufactures and sells 250,000 units of product at $50 per unit in domestic markets. The product costs $30 per unit to manufacture. Can you describe a situation under which the company may be willing to sell an additional 25,000 units of the product in an international market at $24 per unit?
17. Under what conditions is a sunk cost relevant to decision making?
18. What is an out-of-pocket cost? What is an opportunity cost? Are opportunity costs recorded in the accounting records?
19. Any costs that have been incurred in manufacturing a product are sunk costs. Why are sunk costs irrelevant in deciding whether to sell the product in its present condition or to make it into a new product through additional processing?
20. Identify the incremental costs incurred by Federal Express for one additional package that is dropped off by the sender at a local office and delivered as one of a number of other packages to the headquarters of a major corporation. How might the company's pricing policies reflect these incremental costs?

21. Would a net present value analysis be useful to Lands' End in evaluating a proposal for a seasonal catalog that would be sent to a special set of customers? Explain.

LANDS' END DIRECT MERCHANTS

Exercises

Exercise 27–1
Payback period, uniform cash flows
(LO 2)

Calculate the payback periods for these two unrelated investments:

a. A machine costs $100,000, has a $4,000 salvage value, is expected to last five years, and will generate net income of $20,800 per year after straight-line depreciation and after 40% income taxes.

b. A new automatic control system for an existing machine is expected to cost $50,000 and have a useful life of nine years. The system should save $24,000 (after 30% taxes) each year, after deducting straight-line depreciation on the system. The predicted salvage value of the system is $5,000.

Exercise 27–2
Payback period, unequal annual net cash inflows
(LO 1)

The David Company is considering the purchase of an asset for $80,000. The asset is expected to produce the following net cash flows:

Year	Net Cash Inflows
1	$ 20,000
2	25,000
3	30,000
4	40,000
5	6,000
Total	$121,000

The cash flows would occur evenly throughout each year. Calculate the payback period for this investment.

Exercise 27–3
Payback period from income statement data
(LO 2)

A semitrailer rig can be purchased for $120,000 and used for five years to generate these net incomes:

Year 1	$17,000
Year 2	33,600
Year 3	50,200
Year 4	66,800
Year 5	83,400

In projecting the expected net incomes, sum-of-the-years'-digits depreciation was deducted, based on a five-year life and a salvage value of $21,000. Present calculations to show the payback period for the rig. Ignore income taxes.

Exercise 27–4
Calculating average investment
(LO 3)

Asset P is expected to cost $500,000. Management also predicts that it will have a 10-year service life and an $80,000 salvage value. Asset Q is expected to cost $240,000. Management predicts that the asset will have a four-year service life and no salvage value. Straight-line depreciation would be used for these assets.

Calculate the average investment in each asset under the assumptions that the income from using them is to be received (*a*) evenly throughout each year and (*b*) at the end of each year.

Exercise 27–5
Payback and return on average investment
(LO 2, 3)

Kringle Company is considering the purchase of a machine that would allow the company to add a new product to its line. The machine is expected to cost $40,000 with an eight-year life and no salvage value. It will be depreciated on a straight-line basis. The company expects to sell 24,000 units of the machine's product each year. However, the product is very specialized and can be sold only during the holiday season at the end of each year. As a result, all sales and cash flows occur during the last 30 days of the year. Expected annual net income is as follows:

Sales		$31,200
Costs:		
Materials, labor and overhead (except for depreciation on the new machine)	$20,400	
Depreciation on the new machine	5,000	
Selling and administrative expenses	3,000	
Total expenses		$28,400
Operating income		$ 2,800
Income taxes (30%)		840
Net income		$ 1,960

Required

Calculate (*a*) the payback period and (*b*) the return on average investment for this machine.

Exercise 27–6
Net present value of an investment
(LO 3)

After evaluating the risk of the investment described in Exercise 27–5, the Kringle Company concludes that it must earn at least a 4% compounded return on the investment in the machine. Use this rate to determine the net present value of the investment in the machine.

Exercise 27–7
Net present values of investments
(LO 4)

The Amoroso Company can invest in each of three projects, J, K, and L. Each project would require an initial investment of $95,000 and would produce the following annual cash flows:

	J	*K*	*L*
Year 1	$ 10,000	$ 40,000	$ 90,000
Year 2	40,000	40,000	20,000
Year 3	70,000	40,000	10,000
Total	$120,000	$120,000	$120,000

Required

Under the assumption that the company requires a 12% compounded return from its investments, use net present values to determine which project or projects should be acquired.

Exercise 27–8
Analysis of an offer for additional volume
(LO 5)

Charter Company expects to sell 50,000 units of its product during the next period with the following results:

Sales		$750,000
Costs and expenses:		
Direct materials	$ 80,000	
Direct labor	200,000	
Factory overhead	55,000	
Selling expenses	75,000	
Administrative expenses	128,500	
Total costs and expenses		$538,500
Net income		$211,500

The company has an opportunity to sell 15,000 additional units at a price of $10 per unit. The additional sales would not affect the regular sales. Direct material and direct labor unit costs would be the same for the additional units as they are for the regular units. However, the additional volume would create these incremental effects on costs:

- Total factory overhead would increase by 15%.
- Total administrative expenses would increase by $21,500.

Prepare an appropriate analysis to determine whether the company should accept or reject the offer to sell the additional units at the reduced price.

Exercise 27–9
Analysis of a make or buy decision
(LO 5)

Scott Key and Lock Company currently manufactures a part at a cost of $1.65 per unit. This cost is based on a normal production rate of 50,000 units per year. The variable costs are $0.87 per unit, fixed costs related only to the part are $9,000 per year, and allocated fixed costs are $30,000 per year. These allocated costs would continue whether the company makes or buys the part. Scott Key and Lock is considering buying the part from a supplier who has quoted a price of $1.25 per unit. This price would be guaranteed for a three-year period.

Should the company continue to manufacture the part or should it purchase the part from the outside supplier? Support your answer with an analysis.

Exercise 27–10
Analysis of whether to do additional processing on a product
(LO 6)

The McIntyre Company has 5,000 units of a product called Winter that was manufactured for a total cost of $15 per unit. The 5,000 units can be sold at this stage for $162,500. Alternatively, they can receive further processing at a total additional cost of $37,000 and be converted into 1,500 units of Wintergreen and 3,500 units of Wintermint. Wintergreen can be sold for $50 per unit and Wintermint can be sold for $32 per unit.

Required

Prepare an analysis that shows whether the units of Winter should be processed further.

Exercise 27–11
Analysis of best sales mix
(LO 5)

The Knudson Company owns a machine that can produce two different products. Product J can be produced at the rate of 4 units per hour and product K can be produced at the rate of 10 units per hour. The capacity of the machine is 2,000 hours per year. The highly specialized products are sold to a single customer who has agreed to buy all of the company's output up to a maximum of 7,500 units of J and 3,000 units of K. Selling prices and variable costs per unit to produce the products are

	Product J	Product K
Selling price	\$25.00	\$15.00
Variable costs	7.50	9.00

Required

Determine the most profitable sales mix for the company and calculate the contribution margin that results from that sales mix.

Problems

Problem 27–1
Payback, return on investment, and net present value
(LO 2, 3, 4)

The Discenza Company is planning to add a new product to its line. To assemble this product, the company would have to buy a new machine at a cost of \$100,000. The asset is expected to have a four-year life and an \$8,000 salvage value. This additional information is available:

Expected annual sales of new product.	\$475,000
Expected costs:	
Direct materials	125,000
Direct labor	175,000
Factory overhead excluding depreciation on new machine . .	81,000
Selling and administrative expenses.	40,000
State and federal income taxes	40%

All sales are for cash and all costs are out-of-pocket, except the depreciation on the new machine.

Required

1. Calculate the amount of straight-line depreciation that would be taken in each year of the asset's life.
2. Determine the amounts of net income and cash flow expected in each year of the asset's life.
3. Calculate the payback period on the investment in the new machine, assuming that the cash flows occur evenly throughout each year.
4. Calculate the rate of return on the average investment in the new machine, assuming that the net income occurs at the end of each year.
5. Calculate the net present value of the investment with a discount rate of 20%, assuming that all cash flows occur at the end of each year. (Be sure to include the salvage value as a cash flow in the last year of the asset's life.)

Problem 27–2
Payback, return on investment, and net present value
(LO 2, 3, 4)

The Slater Company has the opportunity to invest in one of two projects. Project A requires an investment of $96,000 for new machinery having a four-year life and no salvage value. Project X requires an investment of $96,000 for new machinery having a three-year life and no salvage value. The two projects would produce the following predicted annual results:

	Project A	Project X
Sales	$120,000	$100,000
Expenses:		
Direct materials	$ 16,000	$ 12,000
Direct labor	25,000	18,000
Factory overhead including depreciation	54,000	52,000
Selling and administrative expenses	12,000	12,000
Total expenses	$107,000	$ 94,000
Operating income	$ 13,000	$ 6,000
Income taxes (25%)	3,250	1,500
Net income	$ 9,750	$ 4,500

Assume that the company uses straight-line depreciation and that the cash flows occur at the end of the year.

Required

1. Find the annual cash flows expected for the two projects.
2. Find the payback period expected for the two projects.
3. Find the rate of return on average investment expected for the two projects.
4. Find the net present value of the investment in the two projects, using 8% as the discount rate.
5. Select the project that you would recommend to management, and explain your choice.

Problem 27–3
Income results of added sales
(LO 5)

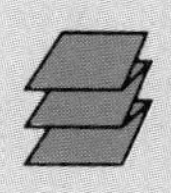

Discorama Company manufactures floppy diskettes that it sells to wholesalers at $1.00 each. The company manufactures and sells approximately 600,000 diskettes each year, and normal costs for the production and sale of this quantity are as follows:

Direct materials	$192,000
Direct labor	48,000
Factory overhead	144,000
Selling expenses	60,000
Administrative expenses	40,000
Total	$484,000

A mail-order retailer has offered to buy 100,000 diskettes for $0.86 each. These diskettes would be marketed under the mail-order company's name and would not affect Discorama's sales through its normal channels.

A study of the costs of the new business reveals the following information:

- Direct material costs are 100% variable.
- The per unit direct labor costs for the additional units would be 50% greater than normal because their production would require overtime pay at one and one-half times the usual labor rate.

- One fourth of the normal annual overhead costs are fixed at any production level from 500,000 to 800,000 units. The remaining three fourths of the annual overhead cost is variable with volume.
- There will be no additional selling costs if the new business is accepted.
- Accepting the new business would increase administrative expenses by a fixed amount of $2,000.

Required

Prepare a three-column comparative income statement that shows

1. The operating income for one year without the special order.
2. The operating income that would be received from the new business.
3. The combined results for one year from normal business and the new business.

Problem 27–4
Calculating cash flows and net present values with alternative tax depreciation methods
(LO 4)

The Couger Corporation is considering a project that would require a $10,000 investment in an asset with no salvage value. The project would produce $4,000 of income before depreciation at the end of each year for six years. The company's income tax rate is 40%. In compiling its tax return and computing its income tax payments, the company can choose between these two alternative depreciation schedules:

	Straight-Line Depreciation Schedule	MACRS Depreciation Schedule
Year 1	$ 1,000	$ 2,000
Year 2	2,000	3,200
Year 3	2,000	1,920
Year 4	2,000	1,152
Year 5	2,000	1,152
Year 6	1,000	576
Total	$10,000	$10,000

Required

1. Produce a five-column table that shows these items for each of the six years: (*a*) income before depreciation, (*b*) straight-line depreciation expense, (*c*) taxable income, (*d*) income taxes, and (*e*) net cash flow. The net cash flow equals the amount of income before depreciation minus the income taxes.
2. Produce a five-column table that shows these items for each of the six years: (*a*) income before depreciation, (*b*) MACRS depreciation expense, (*c*) taxable income, (*d*) income taxes, and (*e*) net cash flow. The net cash flow equals the amount of income before depreciation minus the income taxes.
3. Calculate the net present value of the investment if straight-line depreciation is used. Use 10% as the discount rate.
4. Calculate the net present value of the investment if MACRS depreciation is used. Use 10% as the discount rate.
5. Explain why the MACRS depreciation method increases the net present value of this project.

Problem 27–5
Results of alternative sales mixes
(LO 6)

The Wilcox Company is capable of producing two products, A and B, with the same machine in its factory. These facts are known:

	Product A	Product B
Selling price	$100.00	$200.00
Variable costs	40.00	90.00
Contribution	$ 60.00	$110.00
Machine-hours to produce 1 unit	0.2	0.5
Maximum unit sales per month	1,000	500

The company presently operates the machine for a single eight-hour shift for 22 working days each month. The management is thinking about operating the machine for two shifts, which will increase the machine's availability by another eight hours per day for 22 days per month. This change would require additional fixed costs of $10,000 per month.

Required

1. Determine the contribution margin per machine-hour that each product generates.
2. How many units of A and B should the company produce if it continues to operate with only one shift? How much total contribution margin is produced each month with this mix?
3. If the company adds another shift, how many units of A and B should the company produce? How much total contribution margin would be produced each month with this mix? Should the company add the new shift?
4. Suppose that the company determines it can also increase the maximum sales of product A to 1,500 units per month by spending $20,000 per month in marketing efforts. Should the company pursue this tactic together with the double shift?

Problem 27–6
Analytical essay
(LO 6)

Consider the situation described in Exercise 27–11 for the Knudson Company and the answer prepared for it.

Required

1. How are the most profitable sales mix and contribution margin changed from the given situation if the number of machine-hours is increased to 2,400 hours per year? Explain your findings.
2. How are the most profitable sales mix and contribution margin changed from the given situation if the maximum sales for product J is increased to 9,000 units and the maximum sales for product K is increased to 4,000 units? Explain your findings.

Problem 27–7
Analytical essay
(LO 5)

The Curry Company manufactures widgets by carving them out of solid 100-pound blocks of raw material. Each block costs $60, and the single widget carved from a block can be sold for $100. For many years, the scrap material was simply dumped in a large waste pile and eventually biodegraded harmlessly. This wasted material represents about 20% of the total weight of the block.

Several years ago, another company developed a product that could be made from this waste. At that time, Curry and the other company negotiated an arrangement. Curry would bag the waste in 20-pound sacks, and the other company would pick them up at Curry's factory and pay $20 per bag for them. At the time of entering into the arrangement, the Curry bookkeeper had produced an analysis of the costs and concluded that the price of $1 per pound produced a profit of $0.05 per pound. Although this seemed like a small amount, it was better than nothing, and nothing was all that the company was receiving before. The analysis assigned material cost to the waste as follows:

Item	Selling Price	Percent of Total	Allocated Cost	Cost per Unit
Widget	$100	83.3%	$50.00	$50 per widget
Waste.	20	16.7	10.00	$0.50 per lb.
Total	$120	100.0%	$60.00	

The labor cost of putting the waste into the bags was determined to be $0.20 per pound. Then, overhead was assigned at the normal rate of 125% of the labor cost. As a result, the total cost per pound was determined to be

Material	$0.50
Labor	0.20
Overhead	0.25
Total cost	$0.95

The incremental overhead for the packaging activity was $0.04 per pound, and the remaining $0.21 happened with or without the packaging activity.

A new offer was recently received from a competitor of the company that had been hauling away the bagged waste. This company offered to simply pay $0.60 per pound and pick it up at the plant in bulk. The Curry Company convened a management committee to consider this offer. Sales of widgets had been high and a lot of waste was being produced. Any additional profit from selling it was considered important.

The senior bookkeeper prepared for the meeting by checking the files for the prior analysis. He concluded that the new arrangement would increase the profit to $0.10 per pound, which is the excess of the $0.60 selling price over the raw material cost of $0.50. The junior bookkeeper prepared another analysis, which reallocated the cost of the raw material differently because the selling prices would change. Here are the results of the allocation:

Item	Selling Price	Percent of Total	Allocated Cost	Cost per Unit
Widget	$100	89.3%	$53.58	$53.58 per widget
Waste.	12	10.7	6.42	$0.321 per lb.
Total	$112	100.0%	$60.00	

Thus, this bookkeeper concluded that the new deal would create a profit of nearly $0.28 per pound, which greatly exceeds the present $0.05 per pound.

The marketing manager found the exercise amusing because the waste product used to be simply thrown away. He figured the profit would have to be at least $0.60 per pound anyway it was looked at.

In the meeting, the company's controller and president heard the opinions of the other three. When the president appeared to be leaning toward accepting the new offer, the controller quietly said, "The profit on this new deal doesn't come anywhere near the profit on the old one. We would be making a mistake to change now under these terms." The president quickly regained composure, agreed with the controller, and the meeting adjourned.

Who is right? Was this decision sound? Explain what you think, and support your position with an analysis of the numbers.

Alternate Problems

Problem 27–1A
Payback, return on investment, and net present value
(LO 2, 3, 4)

The Atwater Company is planning to add a new product to its line. To assemble this product, the company would have to buy a new machine at a cost of $75,000. The asset is expected to have a five-year life and a $5,000 salvage value. This additional information is available:

Expected annual sales of new product	$200,000
Expected costs:	
Direct materials	90,000
Direct labor	25,000
Factory overhead excluding depreciation on new machine	50,000
Selling and administrative expenses	11,500
State and federal income taxes	40%

All sales are for cash and all costs are out-of-pocket, except the depreciation on the new machine.

Required

1. Calculate the amount of straight-line depreciation that would be taken in each year of the asset's life.
2. Determine the amounts of net income and cash flow expected in each year of the asset's life.
3. Calculate the payback period on the investment in the new machine, assuming that the cash flows occur evenly throughout each year.
4. Calculate the rate of return on the average investment in the new machine, assuming that the net income occurs at the end of each year.
5. Calculate the net present value of the investment with a discount rate of 20%, assuming that all cash flows occur at the end of each year. (Be sure to include the salvage value as a cash flow in the last year of the asset's life.)

Problem 27–2A
Payback, return on investment, and net present value
(LO 2, 3, 4)

The Reddy Company has the opportunity to invest in one of two projects. Project 42 requires an investment of $120,000 for new machinery having a three-year life and no salvage value. Project 55 also requires an investment of $120,000 for new machinery having a four-year life and no salvage value. The two projects would produce the following predicted annual results:

	Project 42	Project 55
Sales	$282,000	$300,000
Expenses:		
Direct materials	$ 50,000	$110,000
Direct labor	75,000	45,000
Factory overhead including depreciation	110,000	92,000
Selling and administrative expenses	40,000	40,000
Total expenses	$275,000	$287,000
Operating income	$ 7,000	$ 13,000
Income taxes (30%)	2,100	3,900
Net income	$ 4,900	$ 9,100

Assume that the company uses straight-line depreciation and that the cash flows occur at the end of the year.

Required

1. Find the annual cash flows expected for the two projects.
2. Find the payback period expected for the two projects.
3. Find the rate of return on average investment expected for the two projects.
4. Find the net present value of the investment in the two projects, using 10% as the discount rate.
5. Select the project that you would recommend to management, and explain your choice.

Problem 27–3A
Income results of added sales
(LO 5)

SomeKindaCola Company manufactures canned cola drinks that it sells to wholesalers in the local area at $1.50 per six-pack. The company manufactures and sells approximately 100,000 six-packs each month, and normal costs for the production and sale of this quantity are as follows:

Direct materials	$20,000
Direct labor	8,000
Factory overhead	30,000
Selling expenses	5,000
Administrative expenses	21,000
Total	$84,000

An out-of-state distributor has offered to buy 10,000 six-packs next month for $1.20 each. These six-packs would be marketed in other states and would not affect SomeKindaCola's sales through its normal channels.

A study of the costs of the new business reveals the following information:

- Direct material costs are 100% variable.
- The per unit direct labor costs for the additional units would be 100% greater than normal because their production would require special double overtime pay to meet the distributor's deadline.
- Eighty percent of the normal annual overhead costs are fixed at any production level from 60,000 to 150,000 units. The remaining 20% of the annual overhead cost is variable with volume.
- There will be no additional selling costs if the new business is accepted.

- Accepting the new business would increase administrative expenses by a fixed amount of $500.

Required

Prepare a three-column comparative income statement that shows

1. The operating income for one year without the special order.
2. The operating income that would be received from the new business.
3. The combined results for one year from normal business and the new business.

Problem 27–4A
Calculating cash flows and net present values with alternative tax depreciation methods
(LO 4)

The McFadden Corporation is considering a project that would require a $5,000 investment in an asset having no salvage value. The project would produce $3,000 of income before depreciation at the end of each year for six years. The company's income tax rate is 30%. In compiling its tax return and computing its income tax payments, the company can choose between these two alternative depreciation schedules:

	Straight-Line Depreciation Schedule	MACRS Depreciation Schedule
Year 1	$ 500	$1,000
Year 2	1,000	1,600
Year 3	1,000	960
Year 4	1,000	576
Year 5	1,000	576
Year 6	500	288
Total	$5,000	$5,000

Required

1. Produce a five-column table that shows these items for each of the six years: (*a*) income before depreciation, (*b*) straight-line depreciation expense, (*c*) taxable income, (*d*) income taxes, and (*e*) net cash flow. The net cash flow equals the amount of income before depreciation minus the income taxes.
2. Produce a five-column table that shows these items for each of the six years: (*a*) income before depreciation, (*b*) MACRS depreciation expense, (*c*) taxable income, (*d*) income taxes, and (*e*) net cash flow. The net cash flow equals the amount of income before depreciation minus the income taxes.
3. Calculate the net present value of the investment if straight-line depreciation is used. Use 16% as the discount rate.
4. Calculate the net present value of the investment if MACRS depreciation is used. Use 16% as the discount rate.
5. Explain why the MACRS depreciation method increases the net present value of this project.

Problem 27–5A
Results of alternative sales mixes
(LO 6)

The Zawacki Company is capable of producing two products, L and M, with the same machine in its factory. These facts are known:

	Product L	Product M
Selling price	$500.00	$600.00
Variable costs	300.00	350.00
Contribution	$200.00	$250.00
Machine-hours to produce 1 unit	0.4	0.25
Maximum unit sales per month	1,000	800

The company presently operates the machine for a single eight-hour shift for 23 working days each month. The management is thinking about operating the machine for two shifts, which will increase the machine's availability by another eight hours per day for 23 days per month. This change would require additional fixed costs of $15,000 per month.

Required

1. Determine the contribution margin per machine-hour that each product generates.
2. How many units of L and M should the company produce if it continues to operate with only one shift? How much total contribution margin is produced each month with this mix?
3. If the company adds another shift, how many units of L and M should the company produce? How much total contribution margin would be produced each month with this mix? Should the company add the new shift?
4. Suppose that the company determines it can also increase the maximum sales of product M to 1,000 units per month by spending $6,000 per month in marketing efforts. Should the company pursue this tactic together with the double shift?

Problem 27–6A
Analytical essay
(LO 6)

Consider the situation described in Exercise 27–11 for the Knudson Company and the answer prepared for it.

Required

1. How are the most profitable sales mix and contribution margin changed from the given situation if the number of machine-hours is decreased to 1,600 hours per year? Explain your findings.
2. How are the most profitable sales mix and contribution margin changed from the given situation if the maximum sales for product J is decreased to 6,400 units and the maximum sales for product K is increased to 5,000 units? Explain your findings.

Problem 27–7A
Analytical essay
(LO 5)

The Oppermann Company manufactures statues by carving them out of solid 400-pound logs of a special wood. Each log costs $500, and the single statue carved from a log can be sold for $900. For many years, the scrap was simply dumped in a large pile and eventually biodegraded harmlessly. These wood chips represent about 62.5% of the total weight of the log.

Several years ago, another company developed a product that could be made from wood chips. At that time, Oppermann and the other company negotiated an arrangement. Oppermann would package the wood chips in 250 pound boxes, and the other company would pick them up at Oppermann's factory and pay $100 per box for them. At the time of entering into the arrangement, the Oppermann bookkeeper had produced an analysis of the costs and concluded that the price of $0.40 per pound produced a profit of $0.10 per pound. Although this seemed like a small amount, it was better than nothing, and nothing was all that the company was receiving before. The analysis assigned material cost to the wood chips as follows:

Item	Selling Price	Percent of Total	Allocated Cost	Cost per Unit
Statue	$ 900	90.0%	$450.00	$450 per statue
Wood chips	100	10.0	50.00	$0.20 per lb.
Total	$1,000	100.0%	$500.00	

The labor cost of putting the wood chips into the boxes was determined to be $0.05 per pound. Then, overhead was assigned at the normal rate of 100% of the labor cost. As a result, the total cost per pound was determined to be

Material . .	$0.20
Labor. . . .	0.05
Overhead . .	0.05
Total	$0.30

The incremental overhead for the packaging activity was $0.02 per pound, and the remaining $0.03 happened with or without the packaging activity.

A new offer was recently received from a competitor of the company that had been hauling away the boxed wood chips. This company offered to simply pay $0.30 per pound and would pick up the chips at the plant in bulk. The Oppermann Company convened a management committee to consider this offer. Sales of statues had been high and a lot of the wood chips were being produced. Any additional profit from selling them was considered important.

The senior bookkeeper prepared for the meeting by checking the files for the prior analysis. He concluded that the new arrangement would keep the profit of $0.10 per pound, which is the excess of the $0.30 selling price over the raw material cost of $0.20. The junior bookkeeper prepared another analysis, which reallocated the cost of the raw material differently because the selling prices would change. Here are the results of the allocation:

Item	Selling Price	Percent of Total	Allocated Cost	Cost per Unit
Statue	$900	92.3%	$461.50	$461.50 per statue
Wood chips	75	7.7	38.50	$0.154 per lb.
Total	$975	100.0%	$500.00	

Thus, this bookkeeper concluded that the new deal would create a profit of nearly $0.15 per pound, which greatly exceeds the present $0.10 per pound.

The marketing manager found the exercise amusing because the wood chips used to be simply thrown away. He figured the profit would have to be at least $0.30 per pound anyway it was looked at.

In the meeting, the company's controller and president heard the opinions of the other three. When the president appeared to be leaning toward accepting the new offer, the controller quietly said, "The profit on this new deal is below the profit on the old one. We would be making a mistake to change now under these terms." The president quickly regained composure, agreed with the controller, and the meeting adjourned.

Who is right? Was this decision sound? Explain what you think, and support your position with an analysis of the numbers.

Provocative Problems

Provocative Problem 27–1
Nebraska Beef, Inc.
(LO 2, 3, 4, 6)

Nebraska Beef, Inc., operates several feedlots, one of which is located at Calhan. The Calhan feedlot no longer produces a profit because of its distance from sources of feed, relatively high transportation costs, and a lack of modern facilities. As a result, management is considering the possibility of constructing a new feedlot in Trinidad to replace the Calhan lot.

The new feedlot would be close to a feed source and near meat packers. If the Trinidad lot were to be built, the Calhan lot would be closed down. The company president favors making the move for several reasons, but several directors have asked for more detailed information before approving the decision. Their main concern is that abandoning the Calhan lot would create a large loss.

You were asked to analyze the proposal and to provide information to help the directors decide whether to support the president's desire to move to Trinidad. You have developed the data described in the following paragraphs:

Loss from abandoning the Calhan lot. The land and facilities of the Calhan lot have a $1 million book value. Virtually none of the machinery or other assets can be sold, and the land is not suitable for any other use without prohibitive reclamation costs. Based on the price predicted by the company's real estate consultant, only $100,000 cash would be received through the sale of the land and the facilities, after considering income taxes. The $900,000 loss from this sale is standing between the directors and their support for the president.

Investment in the new lot. The new Trinidad feedlot would have an up-front total cost of $5 million. In addition to being closer to feed sources and cattle buyers, this feedlot would double the capacity of the Calhan lot. Management estimates that 100,000 head of cattle could be handled every year.

Comparative costs. At their full capacity volumes of 50,000 and 100,000 head, the costs per head at the old lot and the predicted costs per head at the new lot are

	Calhan Lot	Trinidad Lot
Variable, feed, labor, and operating costs (all are out-of-pocket costs)	$88	$72
Depreciation (fixed cost)	2	5
Total costs per head	$90	$77

The higher per head depreciation cost for the new Trinidad lot arises primarily from the higher total cost, even though it will be able to handle a larger volume.

You should provide a recommendation based on the most complete method of analyzing the data. Present any pertinent schedules needed to produce the data used in your analysis.

To make the problem manageable, assume that both feedlots can operate for 10 years. The revenue per head would be the same at the two feedlots. Despite operating at full capacity, the Calhan lot has only been breaking even, which means that the revenue per head is equal to the cost per head just shown. The corporation is subject to 30% income taxes. It will not be possible to operate both the Calhan and Trinidad lots. As a reflection of the high risk that they perceive, the directors want to have at least a 20% return on any investment that the company would make in the new Trinidad feedlot.

Provocative Problem 27–2
Allsman Corporation
(LO 6)

The Allsman Corporation has operated at less than full capacity for several years. It has been producing and selling around 40,000 units of its product annually at the price of $25 per unit. Costs at this volume are

Direct materials	$ 80,000
Direct labor	200,000
Overhead:	
Variable	320,000
Fixed	50,000
Selling and administrative expenses:	
Variable	50,000
Fixed	100,000
Income taxes	25%

The firm searched unsuccessfully for other ways to use more capacity. Now management is considering processing the product further. Allsman's output is now sold to other manufacturers as their raw material. If the product is processed further, it can be sold for $39 per unit instead of $25. To process the product more completely, the company would incur new annual fixed overhead costs of $30,000. Additional variable manufacturing costs per unit would be

Direct materials	$ 2.50
Direct labor	3.50
Variable manufacturing overhead	5.50
Total	$11.50

Total fixed selling and administrative expenses would be unchanged, but total variable selling and administrative expenses would increase by 40%. The new strategy would not change the number of units sold.

Should the company decide to do this additional processing on the product? Support your conclusion with a cost analysis. Also prepare a comparative income statement that shows the result of the present strategy and the predicted results under the alternative.

Provocative Problem 27–3
Meisinger Corporation
(LO 5)

Every year, the Meisinger Corporation manufactures and sells about 5,000 units of an electronic instrument used in surveying. After 25% income taxes, the company generally earns net income of $800 per unit. Meisinger's main manufacturing process involves assembling several components of the instrument. Some components are also manufactured by the company and others are purchased from outside suppliers.

Among the components that the company has been making is an optical sight that is also available from other suppliers. In making the optical sight, Meisinger uses special equipment that cannot be used for any other purpose. The equipment presently has a $150,000 book value. Five years remain in its life and it is being depreciated at the rate of $30,000 per year. In addition to this depreciation, these per unit costs are incurred in making the optical sight:

Direct materials	$40.00
Direct labor	60.00
Variable overhead	50.00

One of Meisinger's suppliers has just offered to sell optical sights to the company at a delivered price of $162.50 each under a contract that would last five years. If the company accepts this offer, the special equipment can be sold for cash at its book value and the cash can be invested in other projects paying a 20% compounded after-tax return. Because of the risk level in its industry, the company tries to earn at least this rate on all of its investments.

Should the company continue to manufacture optical sights, or should it sell the special equipment and buy them? Support your answer with an analysis.

Provocative Problem 27–4
International Business Machines Corporation

IBM

Find the Management Discussion section of the annual report for International Business Machines Corporation in Appendix J. Within this section, look for the description of the company's asset acquisition program.

1. What amount did IBM invest in assets in the five years prior to the report?
2. What amount did IBM invest in assets in 1990?
3. How does management describe this activity and the company's approach to making the investments?

Provocative Problem 27–5
As a Matter of Ethics: Essay

Ethics

Examine the ethics case on page 1432. What do you think is the right advice to give this manager? Is there anything that might move the proposal through the system more quickly?

Answers to Objective Review Questions

LO 1 (*c*)	LO 4 (*a*)	LO 6 (*d*)
LO 2 (*c*)	LO 5 (*e*)	LO 7 (*e*)
LO 3 (*b*)		

Appendixes

Twelve appendixes supplement the regular topical coverage of *Fundamental Accounting Principles*. Appendixes A through G appear with the specific chapters related to their topics. The other five appendixes are presented in this section of the text. The titles of the 12 appendixes are listed to the right.

APPENDIX

H

Present and Future Values: An Expansion

Because of the time value of money, cash flows occurring at different times are not equivalent. The math techniques described in this appendix allow you to reach more informed decisions about future cash flows or to provide information to others so that they can make more informed decisions.

Topical Coverage

The concept of present value is introduced and applied to accounting problems in Chapters 12 and 16. This appendix is designed to supplement those presentations with additional discussion, more complete tables, and additional homework exercises. In studying this appendix, you will also learn about the concept of future value.

Learning Objectives

After studying Appendix H, you should be able to:

1. Explain what is meant by the present value of a single amount and the present value of an annuity, and be able to use tables to solve present value problems.
2. Explain what is meant by the future value of a single amount and the future value of an annuity, and be able to use tables to solve future value problems.

Present Value of a Single Amount

LO 1 Explain what is meant by the present value of a single amount and the present value of an annuity, and be able to use tables to solve present value problems.

The present value of a single amount to be received or paid at some future date may be expressed as:

$$p = \frac{f}{(1 + i)^n}$$

where

p = Present value
f = Future value
i = Rate of interest per period
n = Number of periods

For example, assume that \$2.20 is to be received one period from now. It would be useful to know how much must be invested now, for one period, at an interest rate of 10% to provide \$2.20. We can calculate that amount with this formula:

$$p = \frac{f}{(1 + i)^n} = \frac{\$2.20}{(1 + .10)^1} = \$2.00$$

Alternatively, we can use the formula to find how much must be invested for two periods at 10% to provide \$2.42:

$$p = \frac{f}{(1 + i)^n} = \frac{\$2.42}{(1 + .10)^2} = \$2.00$$

Note that the number of periods (n) does not have to be expressed in years. Any period of time such as a day, a month, a quarter, or a year may be used.

However, whatever period is used, the interest rate (i) must be compounded for the same period. Thus, if a problem expresses n in months, and i equals 12% per year, then 1% of the amount invested at the beginning of each month is earned that month and added to the investment. Thus, the interest is compounded monthly.

A present value table shows present values for a variety of interest rates (i) and a variety of numbers of periods (n). Each present value is based on the assumption that the future value (f) is 1. The following formula is used to construct a table of present values of a single future amount is:

$$p = \frac{1}{(1 + i)^n}$$

Table H–1 on page H-10 is a table of present values of a single future amount and is often called a *present value of 1* table.

Future Value of a Single Amount

LO 2 Explain what is meant by the future value of a single amount and the future value of an annuity, and be able to use tables to solve future value problems.

The following formula for the present value of a single amount can be modified to become the formula for the future value of a single amount with a simple step:

$$p = \frac{f}{(1 + i)^n}$$

By multiplying both sides of the equation by $(1 + i)^n$, the result is:

$$f = p \times (1 + i)^n$$

For example, we can use this formula to determine that \$2.00 invested for one period at 10% will increase to a future value of \$2.20:

$$\begin{aligned} f &= p \times (1 + i)^n \\ &= \$2.00 \times (1 + .10)^1 \\ &= \$2.20 \end{aligned}$$

Alternatively, assume that \$2.00 will remain invested for three periods at 10%. The \$2.662 amount that will be received after three periods is calculated with the formula as follows:

$$\begin{aligned} f &= p \times (1 + i)^n \\ &= \$2.00 \times (1 + .10)^3 \\ &= \$2.662 \end{aligned}$$

A future value table shows future values for a variety of interest rates (i) and a variety of numbers of periods (n). Each future value is based on the assumption that the present value (p) is 1. Thus the formula used to construct a table of future values of a single amount is

$$f = (1 + i)^n$$

Table H–2 on page H-11 is a table of future values of a single amount and is often called a *future value of 1* table.

In Table H–2, look at the row where $n = 0$ and observe that the future value is 1 for all interest rates because no interest is earned.

Observe that a table showing the present values of 1 and a table showing the future values of 1 contain exactly the same information because both tables are based on the same equation. As you have seen, this equation

$$p = \frac{f}{(1 + i)^n}$$

is nothing more than a reformulation of

$$f = p \times (1 + i)^n$$

Both tables reflect the same four variables p, f, i, and n. Therefore, any problem that can be solved with one of the two tables can also be solved with the other.

For example, suppose that a person invests \$100 for five years and expects to earn 12% per year. How much should the person receive after five years? To solve the problem using Table H–2, find the future value of 1, five periods from now, compounded at 12%. In the table, $f = 1.7623$. Thus, the amount to be accumulated over five years is \$176.23 (\$100 × 1.7623).

Table H–1 shows that the present value of 1, discounted five periods at 12% is 0.5674. Recall that the relationship between present value and future value may be expressed as:

$$p = \frac{f}{(1 + i)^n}$$

This formula can be restated as:

$$p = f \times \frac{1}{(1 + i)^n}$$

In turn, it can be restated as:

$$f = \frac{p}{\frac{1}{(1 + i)^n}}$$

Because we know from Table H–2 that $1/(1 + i)^n$ equals 0.5674, the future value of \$100 invested for five periods at 12% is:

$$f = \frac{\$100}{0.5674} = \$176.24$$

In summary, the future value can be found two ways. First, we can multiply the amount invested by the future value found in Table H–1. Second, we can divide the amount invested by the present value found in Table H–2. As you can see in this problem, immaterial differences can occur between these two methods through rounding.

Present Value of an Annuity

LO 1 Explain what is meant by the present value of a single amount and the present value of an annuity, and be able to use tables to solve present value problems.

An annuity is a series of equal payments occurring at equal intervals, such as three annual payments of $100 each. The present value of an annuity is defined as the present value of the payments one period prior to the first payment. Graphically, this annuity and its present value (p) may be represented as follows:

```
      $100   $100   $100
o------o------o------o
p
```

One way to calculate the present value of this annuity finds the present value of each payment with the formula and adds them together. For this example, assuming an interest rate of 18%, the calculation is

$$p = \frac{\$100}{(1 + .18)^1} + \frac{\$100}{(1 + .18)^2} + \frac{\$100}{(1 + .18)^3} = \$217.43$$

Another way calculates the present value of the annuity by using Table H–1 to compute the present value of each payment and then taking their sum:

First payment:	$p = \$100 \times 0.8475 =$	$ 84.75
Second payment:	$p = \$100 \times 0.7182 =$	71.82
Third payment:	$p = \$100 \times 0.6086 =$	60.86
Total:	$p =$	$217.43

We can also use Table H–1 to solve the problem by first adding the table values for the three payments and then multiplying this sum by the $100 amount of each payment:

From Table H–1:	$i = 18\%, n = 1, p =$	0.8475
	$i = 18\%, n = 2, p =$	0.7182
	$i = 18\%, n = 3, p =$	0.6086
	Sum =	2.1743
	Present value = 2.1743 × $100 =	$217.43

An easier way to solve the problem uses a different table that shows the present values of annuities, like Table H–3 on page H-12, which is often called a *present value of an annuity of 1* table. Look at Table H–3 on the row where $n = 3$ and $i = 18\%$ and observe that the present value is 2.1743. Thus, the present value of an annuity of 1 for three periods, discounted at 18%, is 2.1743.

Although a formula is used to construct a table showing the present values of an annuity, you can construct one by adding the amounts in a present value of 1 table.[1] Examine Table H–1 and Table H–3 to confirm that the following numbers were drawn from those tables:

[1] The formula for the present value of an annuity of 1 is:

$$p = \frac{1 - \dfrac{1}{(1 + i)^n}}{i}$$

From Table H–1		From Table H–3	
$i = 8\%, n = 1$	0.9259		
$i = 8\%, n = 2$	0.8573		
$i = 8\%, n = 3$	0.7938		
$i = 8\%, n = 4$	0.7350		
Total.	3.3120	$i = 8\%, n = 4$	3.3121

The minor difference in the results occurs because the numbers in the tables have been rounded.

In addition to the preceding methods, you can use preprogrammed business calculators and spreadsheet computer programs to find the present value of annuities.

Future Value of an Annuity

LO 2 Explain what is meant by the future value of a single amount and the future value of an annuity, and be able to use tables to solve future value problems.

Just as an annuity has a present value, it also has a future value. The future value of an annuity is the accumulated value of the annuity payments and interest as of the date of the final payment. Consider the earlier annuity of three annual payments of \$100. The points in time at which the present value (p) and the future value (f) occur are shown below:

$100 $100 $100
o——o——o——o
p f

Note that the first payment is made two periods prior to the point at which the future value is determined. Therefore, for the first payment, $n = 2$. For the second payment, $n = 1$. Since the third payment occurs on the future value date, $n = 0$.

One way to calculate the future value of this annuity uses the formula to find the future value of each payment and adds them together. Assuming an interest rate of 18%, the calculation is:

$$f = \$100 \times (1 + .18)^2 + \$100 \times (1 + .18)^1 + \$100 \times (1 + .18)^0 = \$357.24$$

Another way calculates the future value of the annuity by using Table H–2 to find the sum of the future values of each payment:

First payment:	$f = \$100 \times 1.3924 =$	\$139.24
Second payment:	$f = \$100 \times 1.1800 =$	118.00
Third payment:	$f = \$100 \times 1.0000 =$	100.00
Total:	$f =$	\$357.24

A third approach adds the future values of three payments of 1 and multiplies the sum by \$100:

From Table H–2:	$i = 18\%, n = 2, f =$	1.3924
	$i = 18\%, n = 1, f =$	1.1800
	$i = 18\%, n = 0, f =$	1.0000
	Sum =	3.5724

Future value = 3.5724 × \$100 = \$357.24

A fourth and easier way to solve the problem uses a table that shows the future values of annuities, often called a *future value of an annuity of 1* table. Table H–4 on page H-12 is such a table. Note in Table H–4 that when $n = 1$, the future values are equal to 1 ($f = 1$) for all rates of interest because the annuity consists of only one payment and the future value is determined on the date of the payment. Thus, the future value equals the payment.

Although a formula is used to construct a table showing the future values of an annuity of 1, you can construct one by adding the amounts in a future value of 1 table like Table H–2.[2] Examine Table H–2 and Table H–4 to confirm that the following numbers were drawn from those tables:

From Table H–2		**From Table H–4**	
$i = 8\%, n = 0$	1.0000		
$i = 8\%, n = 1$	1.0800		
$i = 8\%, n = 2$	1.1664		
$i = 8\%, n = 3$	1.2597		
Total.	4.5061	$i = 8\%, n = 4$	4.5061

Minor differences may occur because the numbers in the tables have been rounded.

You can also use business calculators and spreadsheet computer programs to find the future values of annuities.

Observe that the future value in Table H–2 is 1.0000 when $n = 0$ but the future value in Table H–4 is 1.0000 when $n = 1$. Why does this apparent contradiction arise? When $n = 0$ in Table H–2, the future value is determined on the date that the single payment occurs. Thus, no interest is earned and the future value equals the payment. However, Table H–4 describes annuities with equal payments occurring each period. When $n = 1$, the annuity has only one payment, and its future value also equals 1 on the date of its final and only payment.

[2] The formula for the future value of an annuity of 1 is:

$$f = \frac{(1 + i)^n - 1}{i}$$

TABLE H–1

Present Value of 1 Due in n *Periods*

Periods	1.0%	1.5%	3.0%	4.0%	8.0%	10.0%	12.0%	14.0%	16.0%	18.0%	20.0%
1	0.9901	0.9852	0.9709	0.9615	0.9259	0.9091	0.8929	0.8772	0.8621	0.8475	0.8333
2	0.9803	0.9707	0.9426	0.9246	0.8573	0.8264	0.7972	0.7695	0.7432	0.7182	0.6944
3	0.9706	0.9563	0.9151	0.8890	0.7938	0.7513	0.7118	0.6750	0.6407	0.6086	0.5787
4	0.9610	0.9422	0.8885	0.8548	0.7350	0.6830	0.6355	0.5921	0.5523	0.5158	0.4823
5	0.9515	0.9283	0.8626	0.8219	0.6806	0.6209	0.5674	0.5194	0.4761	0.4371	0.4019
6	0.9420	0.9145	0.8375	0.7903	0.6302	0.5645	0.5066	0.4556	0.4104	0.3704	0.3349
7	0.9327	0.9010	0.8131	0.7599	0.5835	0.5132	0.4523	0.3996	0.3538	0.3139	0.2791
8	0.9235	0.8877	0.7894	0.7307	0.5403	0.4665	0.4039	0.3506	0.3050	0.2660	0.2326
9	0.9143	0.8746	0.7664	0.7026	0.5002	0.4241	0.3606	0.3075	0.2630	0.2255	0.1938
10	0.9053	0.8617	0.7441	0.6756	0.4632	0.3855	0.3220	0.2697	0.2267	0.1911	0.1615
11	0.8963	0.8489	0.7224	0.6496	0.4289	0.3505	0.2875	0.2366	0.1954	0.1619	0.1346
12	0.8874	0.8364	0.7014	0.6246	0.3971	0.3186	0.2567	0.2076	0.1685	0.1372	0.1122
13	0.8787	0.8240	0.6810	0.6006	0.3677	0.2897	0.2292	0.1821	0.1452	0.1163	0.0935
14	0.8700	0.8118	0.6611	0.5775	0.3405	0.2633	0.2046	0.1597	0.1252	0.0985	0.0779
15	0.8613	0.7999	0.6419	0.5553	0.3152	0.2394	0.1827	0.1401	0.1079	0.0835	0.0649
16	0.8528	0.7880	0.6232	0.5339	0.2919	0.2176	0.1631	0.1229	0.0930	0.0708	0.0541
17	0.8444	0.7764	0.6050	0.5134	0.2703	0.1978	0.1456	0.1078	0.0802	0.0600	0.0451
18	0.8360	0.7649	0.5874	0.4936	0.2502	0.1799	0.1300	0.0946	0.0691	0.0508	0.0376
19	0.8277	0.7536	0.5703	0.4746	0.2317	0.1635	0.1161	0.0829	0.0596	0.0431	0.0313
20	0.8195	0.7425	0.5537	0.4564	0.2145	0.1486	0.1037	0.0728	0.0514	0.0365	0.0261
21	0.8114	0.7315	0.5375	0.4388	0.1987	0.1351	0.0926	0.0638	0.0443	0.0309	0.0217
22	0.8034	0.7207	0.5219	0.4220	0.1839	0.1228	0.0826	0.0560	0.0382	0.0262	0.0181
23	0.7954	0.7100	0.5067	0.4057	0.1703	0.1117	0.0738	0.0491	0.0329	0.0222	0.0151
24	0.7876	0.6995	0.4919	0.3901	0.1577	0.1015	0.0659	0.0431	0.0284	0.0188	0.0126
25	0.7798	0.6892	0.4776	0.3751	0.1460	0.0923	0.0588	0.0378	0.0245	0.0160	0.0105
26	0.7720	0.6790	0.4637	0.3607	0.1352	0.0839	0.0525	0.0331	0.0211	0.0135	0.0087
27	0.7644	0.6690	0.4502	0.3468	0.1252	0.0763	0.0469	0.0291	0.0182	0.0115	0.0073
28	0.7568	0.6591	0.4371	0.3335	0.1159	0.0693	0.0419	0.0255	0.0157	0.0097	0.0061
29	0.7493	0.6494	0.4243	0.3207	0.1073	0.0630	0.0374	0.0224	0.0135	0.0082	0.0051
30	0.7419	0.6398	0.4120	0.3083	0.0994	0.0573	0.0334	0.0196	0.0116	0.0070	0.0042
31	0.7346	0.6303	0.4000	0.2965	0.0920	0.0521	0.0298	0.0172	0.0100	0.0059	0.0035
32	0.7273	0.6210	0.3883	0.2851	0.0852	0.0474	0.0266	0.0151	0.0087	0.0050	0.0029
33	0.7201	0.6118	0.3770	0.2741	0.0789	0.0431	0.0238	0.0132	0.0075	0.0042	0.0024
34	0.7130	0.6028	0.3660	0.2636	0.0730	0.0391	0.0212	0.0116	0.0064	0.0036	0.0020
35	0.7059	0.5939	0.3554	0.2534	0.0676	0.0356	0.0189	0.0102	0.0055	0.0030	0.0017
36	0.6989	0.5851	0.3450	0.2437	0.0626	0.0323	0.0169	0.0089	0.0048	0.0026	0.0014
37	0.6920	0.5764	0.3350	0.2343	0.0580	0.0294	0.0151	0.0078	0.0041	0.0022	0.0012
38	0.6852	0.5679	0.3252	0.2253	0.0537	0.0267	0.0135	0.0069	0.0036	0.0019	0.0010
39	0.6784	0.5595	0.3158	0.2166	0.0497	0.0243	0.0120	0.0060	0.0031	0.0016	0.0008
40	0.6717	0.5513	0.3066	0.2083	0.0460	0.0221	0.0107	0.0053	0.0026	0.0013	0.0007
41	0.6650	0.5431	0.2976	0.2003	0.0426	0.0201	0.0096	0.0046	0.0023	0.0011	0.0006
42	0.6584	0.5351	0.2890	0.1926	0.0395	0.0183	0.0086	0.0041	0.0020	0.0010	0.0005
43	0.6519	0.5272	0.2805	0.1852	0.0365	0.0166	0.0076	0.0036	0.0017	0.0008	0.0004
44	0.6454	0.5194	0.2724	0.1780	0.0338	0.0151	0.0068	0.0031	0.0015	0.0007	0.0003
45	0.6391	0.5117	0.2644	0.1712	0.0313	0.0137	0.0061	0.0027	0.0013	0.0006	0.0003
46	0.6327	0.5042	0.2567	0.1646	0.0290	0.0125	0.0054	0.0024	0.0011	0.0005	0.0002
47	0.6265	0.4967	0.2493	0.1583	0.0269	0.0113	0.0049	0.0021	0.0009	0.0004	0.0002
48	0.6203	0.4894	0.2420	0.1522	0.0249	0.0103	0.0043	0.0019	0.0008	0.0004	0.0002
49	0.6141	0.4821	0.2350	0.1463	0.0230	0.0094	0.0039	0.0016	0.0007	0.0003	0.0001
50	0.6080	0.4750	0.2281	0.1407	0.0213	0.0085	0.0035	0.0014	0.0006	0.0003	0.0001

TABLE H-2

Future Value of 1 Due in n *Periods*

Periods	1.0%	1.5%	3.0%	4.0%	8.0%	10.0%	12.0%	14.0%	16.0%	18.0%	20.0%
0	1.0000	1.0000	1.0000	1.0000	1.0000	1.0000	1.0000	1.0000	1.0000	1.0000	1.0000
1	1.0100	1.0150	1.0300	1.0400	1.0800	1.1000	1.1200	1.1400	1.1600	1.1800	1.2000
2	1.0201	1.0302	1.0609	1.0816	1.1664	1.2100	1.2544	1.2996	1.3456	1.3924	1.4400
3	1.0303	1.0457	1.0927	1.1249	1.2597	1.3310	1.4049	1.4815	1.5609	1.6430	1.7280
4	1.0406	1.0614	1.1255	1.1699	1.3605	1.4641	1.5735	1.6890	1.8106	1.9388	2.0736
5	1.0510	1.0773	1.1593	1.2167	1.4693	1.6105	1.7623	1.9254	2.1003	2.2878	2.4883
6	1.0615	1.0934	1.1941	1.2653	1.5869	1.7716	1.9738	2.1950	2.4364	2.6996	2.9860
7	1.0721	1.1098	1.2299	1.3159	1.7138	1.9487	2.2107	2.5023	2.8262	3.1855	3.5832
8	1.0829	1.1265	1.2668	1.3686	1.8509	2.1436	2.4760	2.8526	3.2784	3.7589	4.2998
9	1.0937	1.1434	1.3048	1.4233	1.9990	2.3579	2.7731	3.2519	3.8030	4.4355	5.1598
10	1.1046	1.1605	1.3439	1.4802	2.1589	2.5937	3.1058	3.7072	4.4114	5.2338	6.1917
11	1.1157	1.1779	1.3842	1.5395	2.3316	2.8531	3.4785	4.2262	5.1173	6.1759	7.4301
12	1.1268	1.1956	1.4258	1.6010	2.5182	3.1384	3.8960	4.8179	5.9360	7.2876	8.9161
13	1.1381	1.2136	1.4685	1.6651	2.7196	3.4523	4.3635	5.4924	6.8858	8.5994	10.6993
14	1.1495	1.2318	1.5126	1.7317	2.9372	3.7975	4.8871	6.2613	7.9875	10.1472	12.8392
15	1.1610	1.2502	1.5580	1.8009	3.1722	4.1772	5.4736	7.1379	9.2655	11.9737	15.4070
16	1.1726	1.2690	1.6047	1.8730	3.4259	4.5950	6.1304	8.1372	10.7480	14.1290	18.4884
17	1.1843	1.2880	1.6528	1.9479	3.7000	5.0545	6.8660	9.2765	12.4677	16.6722	22.1861
18	1.1961	1.3073	1.7024	2.0258	3.9960	5.5599	7.6900	10.5752	14.4625	19.6733	26.6233
19	1.2081	1.3270	1.7535	2.1068	4.3157	6.1159	8.6128	12.0557	16.7765	23.2144	31.9480
20	1.2202	1.3469	1.8061	2.1911	4.6610	6.7275	9.6463	13.7435	19.4608	27.3930	38.3376
21	1.2324	1.3671	1.8603	2.2788	5.0338	7.4002	10.8038	15.6676	22.5745	32.3238	46.0051
22	1.2447	1.3876	1.9161	2.3699	5.4365	8.1403	12.1003	17.8610	26.1864	38.1421	55.2061
23	1.2572	1.4084	1.9736	2.4647	5.8715	8.9543	13.5523	20.3616	30.3762	45.0076	66.2474
24	1.2697	1.4295	2.0328	2.5633	6.3412	9.8497	15.1786	23.2122	35.2364	53.1090	79.4968
25	1.2824	1.4509	2.0938	2.6658	6.8485	10.8347	17.0001	26.4619	40.8742	62.6686	95.3962
26	1.2953	1.4727	2.1566	2.7725	7.3964	11.9182	19.0401	30.1666	47.4141	73.9490	114.4755
27	1.3082	1.4948	2.2213	2.8834	7.9881	13.1100	21.3249	34.3899	55.0004	87.2598	137.3706
28	1.3213	1.5172	2.2879	2.9987	8.6271	14.4210	23.8839	39.2045	63.8004	102.9666	164.8447
29	1.3345	1.5400	2.3566	3.1187	9.3173	15.8631	26.7499	44.6931	74.0085	121.5005	197.8136
30	1.3478	1.5631	2.4273	3.2434	10.0627	17.4494	29.9599	50.9502	85.8499	143.3706	237.3763
31	1.3613	1.5865	2.5001	3.3731	10.8677	19.1943	33.5551	58.0832	99.5859	169.1774	284.8516
32	1.3749	1.6103	2.5751	3.5081	11.7371	21.1138	37.5817	66.2148	115.5196	199.6293	341.8219
33	1.3887	1.6345	2.6523	3.6484	12.6760	23.2252	42.0915	75.4849	134.0027	235.5625	410.1863
34	1.4026	1.6590	2.7319	3.7943	13.6901	25.5477	47.1425	86.0528	155.4432	277.9638	492.2235
35	1.4166	1.6839	2.8139	3.9461	14.7853	28.1024	52.7996	98.1002	180.3141	327.9973	590.6682
36	1.4308	1.7091	2.8983	4.1039	15.9682	30.9127	59.1356	111.8342	209.1643	387.0368	708.8019
37	1.4451	1.7348	2.9852	4.2681	17.2456	34.0039	66.2318	127.4910	242.6306	456.7034	850.5622
38	1.4595	1.7608	3.0748	4.4388	18.6253	37.4043	74.1797	145.3397	281.4515	528.9100	1020.6747
39	1.4741	1.7872	3.1670	4.6164	20.1153	41.1448	83.0812	165.6873	326.4838	635.9139	1224.8096
40	1.4889	1.8140	3.2620	4.8010	21.7245	45.2593	93.0510	188.8835	378.7212	750.3783	1469.7716
41	1.5083	1.8412	3.3599	4.9931	23.4625	49.7852	104.2171	215.3272	439.3165	885.4464	1763.7259
42	1.5188	1.8688	3.4607	5.1928	25.3395	54.7637	116.7231	245.4730	509.6072	1044.8268	2116.4711
43	1.5340	1.8969	3.5645	5.4005	27.3666	60.2401	130.7299	279.8392	591.1443	1232.8956	2539.7653
44	1.5493	1.9253	3.6715	5.6165	29.5560	66.2641	146.4175	319.0167	685.7274	1454.8168	3047.7183
45	1.5648	1.9542	3.7816	5.8412	31.9204	72.8905	163.9876	363.6791	795.4438	1716.6839	3657.2620
46	1.5805	1.9835	3.8950	6.0748	34.4741	80.1795	183.6661	414.5941	922.7148	2025.6870	4388.7144
47	1.5963	2.0133	4.0119	6.3178	37.2320	88.1975	205.7061	472.6373	1070.3492	2390.3106	5266.4573
48	1.6122	2.0435	4.1323	6.5705	40.2106	97.0172	230.3908	538.8065	1241.6051	2820.5665	6319.7487
49	1.6283	2.0741	4.2562	6.8333	43.4274	106.7190	258.0377	614.2395	1440.2619	3328.2685	7583.6985
50	1.6446	2.1052	4.3839	7.1067	46.9016	117.3909	289.0022	700.2330	1670.7038	3927.3569	9100.4382

TABLE H-3

Present Value of an Annuity of 1 per Period

Periods	1.0%	1.5%	3.0%	4.0%	8.0%	10.0%	12.0%	14.0%	16.0%	18.0%	20.0%
1	0.9901	0.9852	0.9709	0.9615	0.9259	0.9091	0.8929	0.8772	0.8621	0.8475	0.8333
2	1.9704	1.9559	1.9135	1.8861	1.7833	1.7355	1.6901	1.6467	1.6052	1.5656	1.5278
3	2.9410	2.9122	2.8286	2.7751	2.5771	2.4869	2.4018	2.3216	2.2459	2.1743	2.1065
4	3.9020	3.8544	3.7171	3.6299	3.3121	3.1699	3.0373	2.9137	2.7982	2.6901	2.5887
5	4.8534	4.7826	4.5797	4.4518	3.9927	3.7908	3.6048	3.4331	3.2743	3.1272	2.9906
6	5.7955	5.6972	5.4172	5.2421	4.6229	4.3553	4.1114	3.8887	3.6847	3.4976	3.3255
7	6.7282	6.5982	6.2303	6.0021	5.2064	4.8684	4.5638	4.2883	4.0386	3.8115	3.6046
8	7.6517	7.4859	7.0197	6.7327	5.7466	5.3349	4.9676	4.6389	4.3436	4.0776	3.8372
9	8.5660	8.3605	7.7861	7.4353	6.2469	5.7590	5.3282	4.9464	4.6065	4.3030	4.0310
10	9.4713	9.2222	8.5302	8.1109	6.7101	6.1446	5.6502	5.2161	4.8332	4.4941	4.1925
11	10.3676	10.0711	9.2526	8.7605	7.1390	6.4951	5.9377	5.4527	5.0286	4.6560	4.3271
12	11.2551	10.9075	9.9540	9.3851	7.5361	6.8137	6.1944	5.6603	5.1971	4.7932	4.4392
13	12.1337	11.7315	10.6350	9.9856	7.9038	7.1034	6.4235	5.8424	5.3423	4.9095	4.5327
14	13.0037	12.5434	11.2961	10.5631	8.2442	7.3667	6.6282	6.0021	5.4675	5.0081	4.6106
15	13.8651	13.3432	11.9379	11.1184	8.5595	7.6061	6.8109	6.1422	5.5755	5.0916	4.6755
16	14.7179	14.1313	12.5611	11.6523	8.8514	7.8237	6.9740	6.2651	5.6685	5.1624	4.7296
17	15.5623	14.9076	13.1661	12.1657	9.1216	8.0216	7.1196	6.3729	5.7487	5.2223	4.7746
18	16.3983	15.6726	13.7535	12.6593	9.3719	8.2014	7.2497	6.4674	5.8178	5.2732	4.8122
19	17.2260	16.4262	14.3238	13.1339	9.6036	8.3649	7.3658	6.5504	5.8775	5.3162	4.8435
20	18.0456	17.1686	14.8775	13.5903	9.8181	8.5136	7.4694	6.6231	5.9288	5.3527	4.8696
21	18.8570	17.9001	15.4150	14.0292	10.0168	8.6487	7.5620	6.6870	5.9731	5.3837	4.8913
22	19.6604	18.6208	15.9369	14.4511	10.2007	8.7715	7.6446	6.7429	6.0113	5.4099	4.9094
23	20.4558	19.3309	16.4436	14.8568	10.3711	8.8832	7.7184	6.7921	6.0442	5.4321	4.9245
24	21.2434	20.0304	16.9355	15.2470	10.5288	8.9847	7.7843	6.8351	6.0726	5.4509	4.9371
25	22.0232	20.7196	17.4131	15.6221	10.6748	9.0770	7.8431	6.8729	6.0971	5.4669	4.9476
26	22.7952	21.3986	17.8768	15.9828	10.8100	9.1609	7.8957	6.9061	6.1182	5.4804	4.9563
27	23.5596	22.0676	18.3270	16.3296	10.9352	9.2372	7.9426	6.9352	6.1364	5.4919	4.9636
28	24.3164	22.7267	18.7641	16.6631	11.0511	9.3066	7.9844	6.9607	6.1520	5.5016	4.9697
29	25.0658	23.3761	19.1885	16.9837	11.1584	9.3696	8.0218	6.9830	6.1656	5.5098	4.9747
30	25.8077	24.0158	19.6004	17.2920	11.2578	9.4269	8.0552	7.0027	6.1772	5.5168	4.9789
31	26.5423	24.6461	20.0004	17.5885	11.3498	9.4790	8.0850	7.0199	6.1872	5.5227	4.9824
32	27.2696	25.2671	20.3888	17.8736	11.4350	9.5264	8.1116	7.0350	6.1959	5.5277	4.9854
33	27.9897	25.8790	20.7658	18.1476	11.5139	9.5694	8.1354	7.0482	6.2034	5.5320	4.9878
34	28.7027	26.4817	21.1318	18.4112	11.5869	9.6086	8.1566	7.0599	6.2098	5.5356	4.9898
35	29.4086	27.0756	21.4872	18.6646	11.6546	9.6442	8.1755	7.0700	6.2153	5.5386	4.9915
36	30.1075	27.6607	21.8323	18.9083	11.7172	9.6765	8.1924	7.0790	6.2201	5.5412	4.9929
37	30.7995	28.2371	22.1672	19.1426	11.7752	9.7059	8.2075	7.0868	6.2242	5.5434	4.9941
38	31.4847	28.8051	22.4925	19.3679	11.8289	9.7327	8.2210	7.0937	6.2278	5.5452	4.9951
39	32.1630	29.3646	22.8082	19.5845	11.8786	9.7570	8.2330	7.0997	6.2309	5.5468	4.9959
40	32.8347	29.9158	23.1148	19.7928	11.9246	9.7791	8.2438	7.1050	6.2335	5.5482	4.9966
41	33.4997	30.4590	23.4124	19.9931	11.9672	9.7991	8.2534	7.1097	6.2358	5.5493	4.9972
42	34.1581	30.9941	23.7014	20.1856	12.0067	9.8174	8.2619	7.1138	6.2377	5.5502	4.9976
43	34.8100	31.5212	23.9819	20.3708	12.0432	9.8340	8.2696	7.1173	6.2394	5.5510	4.9980
44	35.4555	32.0406	24.2543	20.5488	12.0771	9.8491	8.2764	7.1205	6.2409	5.5517	4.9984
45	36.0945	32.5523	24.5187	20.7200	12.1084	9.8628	8.2825	7.1232	6.2421	5.5523	4.9986
46	36.7272	33.0565	24.7754	20.8847	12.1374	9.8753	8.2880	7.1256	6.2432	5.5528	4.9989
47	37.3537	33.5532	25.0247	21.0429	12.1643	9.8866	8.2928	7.1277	6.2442	5.5532	4.9991
48	37.9740	34.0426	25.2667	21.1951	12.1891	9.8969	8.2972	7.1296	6.2450	5.5536	4.9992
49	38.5881	34.5247	25.5017	21.3415	12.2122	9.9063	8.3010	7.1312	6.2457	5.5539	4.9993
50	39.1961	34.9997	25.7298	21.4822	12.2335	9.9148	8.3045	7.1327	6.2463	5.5541	4.9995

TABLE H-4

Future Value of an Annuity of 1 per Period

Periods	1.0%	1.5%	3.0%	4.0%	8.0%	10.0%	12.0%	14.0%	16.0%	18.0%	20.0%
1	1.0000	1.0000	1.0000	1.0000	1.0000	1.0000	1.0000	1.0000	1.0000	1.0000	1.0000
2	2.0100	2.0150	2.0300	2.0400	2.0800	2.1000	2.1200	2.1400	2.1600	2.1800	2.2000
3	3.0301	3.0452	3.0909	3.1216	3.2464	3.3100	3.3744	3.4396	3.5056	3.5724	3.6400
4	4.0604	4.0909	4.1836	4.2465	4.5061	4.6410	4.7793	4.9211	5.0665	5.2154	5.3680
5	5.1010	5.1523	5.3091	5.4163	5.8666	6.1051	6.3528	6.6101	6.8771	7.1542	7.4416
6	6.1520	6.2296	6.4684	6.6330	7.3359	7.7156	8.1152	8.5355	8.9775	9.4420	9.9299
7	7.2135	7.3230	7.6625	7.8983	8.9228	9.4872	10.0890	10.7305	11.4139	12.1415	12.9159
8	8.2857	8.4328	8.8923	9.2142	10.6366	11.4359	12.2997	13.2328	14.2401	15.3270	16.4991
9	9.3685	9.5593	10.1591	10.5828	12.4876	13.5795	14.7757	16.0853	17.5185	19.0859	20.7989
10	10.4622	10.7027	11.4639	12.0061	14.4866	15.9374	17.5487	19.3373	21.3215	23.5213	25.9587
11	11.5668	11.8633	12.8078	13.4864	16.6455	18.5312	20.6546	23.0445	25.7329	28.7551	32.1504
12	12.6825	13.0412	14.1920	15.0258	18.9771	21.3843	24.1331	27.2707	30.8502	34.9311	39.5805
13	13.8093	14.2368	15.6178	16.6268	21.4953	24.5227	28.0291	32.0887	36.7862	42.2187	48.4966
14	14.9474	15.4504	17.0863	18.2919	24.2149	27.9750	32.3926	37.5811	43.6720	50.8180	59.1959
15	16.0969	16.6821	18.5989	20.0236	27.1521	31.7725	37.2797	43.8424	51.6595	60.9653	72.0351
16	17.2579	17.9324	20.1569	21.8245	30.3243	35.9497	42.7533	50.9804	60.9250	72.9390	87.4421
17	18.4304	19.2014	21.7616	23.6975	33.7502	40.5447	48.8837	59.1176	71.6730	87.0680	105.9306
18	19.6147	20.4894	23.4144	25.6454	37.4502	45.5992	55.7497	68.3941	84.1407	103.7403	128.1167
19	20.8109	21.7967	25.1169	27.6712	41.4463	51.1591	63.4397	78.9692	98.6032	123.4135	154.7400
20	22.0190	23.1237	26.8704	29.7781	45.7620	57.2750	72.0524	91.0249	115.3797	146.6280	186.6880
21	23.2392	24.4705	28.6765	31.9692	50.4229	64.0025	81.6987	104.7684	134.8405	174.0210	225.0256
22	24.4716	25.8376	30.5368	34.2480	55.4568	71.4027	92.5026	120.4360	157.4150	206.3448	271.0307
23	25.7163	27.2251	32.4529	36.6179	60.8933	79.5430	104.6029	138.2970	183.6014	244.4868	326.2369
24	26.9735	28.6335	34.4265	39.0826	66.7648	88.4973	118.1552	158.6586	213.9776	289.4945	392.4842
25	28.2432	30.0630	36.4593	41.6459	73.1059	98.3471	133.3339	181.8708	249.2140	342.6035	471.9811
26	29.5256	31.5140	38.5530	44.3117	79.9544	109.1818	150.3339	208.3327	290.0883	405.2721	567.3773
27	30.8209	32.9867	40.7096	47.0842	87.3508	121.0999	169.3740	238.4993	337.5024	479.2211	681.8528
28	32.1291	34.4815	42.9309	49.9676	95.3388	134.2099	190.6989	272.8892	392.5028	566.4809	819.2233
29	33.4504	35.9987	45.2189	52.9663	103.9659	148.6309	214.5828	312.0937	456.3032	669.4475	984.0680
30	34.7849	37.5387	47.5754	56.0849	113.2832	164.4940	241.3327	356.7868	530.3117	790.9480	1181.8816
31	36.1327	39.1018	50.0027	59.3283	123.3459	181.9434	271.2926	407.7370	616.1616	934.3186	1419.2579
32	37.4941	40.6883	52.5028	62.7015	134.2135	201.1378	304.8477	465.8202	715.7475	1103.4960	1704.1095
33	38.8690	42.2986	55.0778	66.2095	145.9506	222.2515	342.4294	532.0350	831.2671	1303.1253	2045.9314
34	40.2577	43.9331	57.7302	69.8579	158.6267	245.4767	384.5210	607.5199	965.2698	1538.6878	2456.1176
35	41.6603	45.5921	60.4621	73.6522	172.3168	271.0244	431.6635	693.5727	1120.7130	1816.6516	2948.3411
36	43.0769	47.2760	63.2759	77.5983	187.1021	299.1268	484.4631	791.6729	1301.0270	2144.6489	3539.0094
37	44.5076	48.9851	66.1742	81.7022	203.0703	330.0395	543.5987	903.5071	1510.1914	2531.6857	4247.8112
38	45.9527	50.7199	69.1594	85.9703	220.3159	364.0434	609.8305	1030.9981	1752.8220	2988.3891	5098.3735
39	47.4123	52.4807	72.2342	90.4091	238.9412	401.4478	684.0102	1176.3378	2034.2735	3527.2992	6119.0482
40	48.8864	54.2679	75.4013	95.0255	259.0565	442.5926	767.0914	1342.0251	2360.7572	4163.2130	7343.8578
41	50.3752	56.0819	78.6633	99.8265	280.7810	487.8518	860.1424	1530.9086	2739.4784	4913.5914	8813.6294
42	51.8790	57.9231	82.0232	104.8196	304.2435	537.6370	964.3595	1746.2358	3178.7949	5799.0378	10577.3553
43	53.3978	59.7920	85.4839	110.0124	329.5830	592.4007	1081.0826	1991.7088	3688.4021	6843.8646	12693.8263
44	54.9318	61.6889	89.0484	115.4129	356.9496	652.6408	1211.8125	2271.5481	4279.5465	8076.7603	15233.5916
45	56.4811	63.6142	92.7199	121.0294	386.5056	718.9048	1358.2300	2590.5648	4965.2739	9531.5771	18281.3099
46	58.0459	65.5684	96.5015	126.8706	418.4261	791.7953	1522.2176	2954.2439	5760.7177	11248.2610	21938.5719
47	59.6263	67.5519	100.3965	132.9454	452.9002	871.9749	1705.8838	3368.8380	6683.4326	13273.9480	26327.2863
48	61.2226	69.5652	104.4084	139.2632	490.1322	960.1723	1911.5898	3841.4753	7753.7818	15664.2586	31593.7436
49	62.8348	71.6087	108.5406	145.8337	530.3427	1057.1896	2141.9806	4380.2819	8995.3869	18484.8251	37913.4923
50	64.4632	73.6828	112.7969	152.6671	573.7702	1163.9085	2400.0182	4994.5213	10435.6488	21813.0937	45497.1908

Summary of the Appendix in Terms of Learning Objectives

LO 1. The present value of a single amount to be received at a future date is the amount that could be invested now at the specified interest rate to yield that future value. The present value of an annuity is the amount that could be invested now at the specified interest rate to yield that series of equal periodic payments. Present value tables and business calculators simplify calculating present values.

LO 2. The future value of a single amount invested at a specified rate of interest is the amount that would accumulate at a future date. The future value of an annuity to be invested at the specified rate of interest is the amount that would accumulate at the date of the final equal periodic payment. Future value tables and business calculators simplify calculating future values.

Objective Review

Answers to the following questions are listed at the end of this appendix. Be sure that you decide which is the one best answer to each question *before* you check the answers.

LO 1 Smith & Company is considering making an investment that would pay $10,000 every six months for three years. The first payment would be received in six months. If Smith & Company requires an annual return of 8%, which of the following statements is true?

a. In determining the future value of the annuity, $n = 6$ and $i = 8\%$.

b. In determining the present value of the annuity, $n = 3$ and $i = 8\%$.

c. Smith & Company should be willing to invest no more than $25,771.

d. Smith & Company should be willing to invest no more than $46,229.

e. Smith & Company should be willing to invest no more than $52,421.

LO 2 On May 9, 1991, Frank and Cindy Huber received news that they had inherited $150,000 from one of Cindy's distant relatives. They decided to deposit the money in a savings account that yields an 8% annual rate of interest. They plan on quitting their jobs to travel around the country when the inheritance equals $299,850. In what year will Frank and Cindy be able to quit working?

a. 1993.

b. 1999.

c. 2000.

d. 2001.

e. 2002.

Exercises

Exercise H–1
Present value of an amount
(LO 1)

Velmar Products, Inc. is considering an investment that is expected to return $345,000 after four years. If the company demands a 10% return, how much will it be willing to pay for this investment?

Exercise H–2
Future value of an amount
(LO 2)

Fairmont Corporation just invested $176,500 in a project expected to earn an 18% annual rate of return. The earnings will be reinvested in the project for 15 years. How much cash will accumulate over that period?

Exercise H–3
Present value of an annuity
(LO 1)

Mantel Manufacturing Company is considering an investment that will return $103,500 at the end of each year for 14 years. If the company demands an annual return of 14%, how much should it be willing to pay?

Exercise H–4
Future value of an annuity
(LO 2)

Diane Belardi is planning to open an individual retirement account in which she will invest $2,100 annually at the end of each year. Belardi plans to retire after making 25 annual investments in a program that earns a return of 12%. How much will be in the account on the date of the final investment?

Exercise H–5
Interest rate on an investment
(LO 1)

Mary Dolan has been offered the possibility of investing $0.3083 for 30 years, after which she will be paid $1. What annual rate of interest will she earn? (Use Table H–1 to find the answer.)

Exercise H–6
Number of periods of an investment
(LO 1)

Conrad Wachs has been offered the possibility of investing $0.0431 at 18% per year. How many years must Wachs wait to receive $1? (Use Table H–1 to find the answer.)

Exercise H–7
Number of periods of an investment
(LO 2)

Bruce Muldoon expects to invest $1 at 20% and hold the investment until it equals $850.5622. How many years will pass before it reaches that amount? (Use Table H–2 to find the answer.)

Exercise H–8
Interest rate on an investment
(LO 2)

Mike Rooney expects to invest $1 and leave it on deposit for 28 years. At that time, he will receive $8.6271. What rate of interest will Rooney earn? (Use Table H–2 to find the answer.)

Exercise H–9
Interest rate on an investment
(LO 1)

Diane Attebury expects an immediate investment of $5.6685 to return $1 annually for 16 years, with the first payment to be received after one year. What rate of interest will Attebury earn? (Use Table H–3 to find the answer.)

Exercise H–10
Number of periods of an investment
(LO 1)

Michael Alper expects an investment of $7.0199 to return $1 annually for several years. If the investment earns a return of 14%, how many annual payments will he receive? (Use Table H–3 to find the answer.)

Exercise H–11
Interest rate on an investment
(LO 2)

Pat Brenner expects to invest $1 annually for 35 years and have an accumulated value of $2,948.3411 on the date of the final payment. If this result occurs, what rate of interest will Brenner earn? (Use Table H–4 to find the answer.)

Exercise H–12
Number of periods of an investment
(LO 2)

Sam Stanfield expects to invest $1 annually in a fund that will earn 12%. How many annual investments must Stanfield make to accumulate $1,911.5898 on the date of the final payment? (Use Table H–4 to find the answer.)

Exercise H–13
Present value of an annuity
(LO 1)

Daphne Rankin financed a new automobile by paying $2,500 cash and agreeing to make 36 monthly payments of $500 each, with the first payment to be made one month after the purchase. The loan bears interest at an annual rate of 18%. What was the cost of the automobile?

Exercise H–14
Future value of an amount
(LO 2)

David Jones deposited $8,500 in a savings account that earns interest at an annual rate of 16%, compounded quarterly. The $8,500 and its earned interest must remain in the account five years before they can be withdrawn. How much money will be in the account at the end of the five years?

Exercise H–15
Future value of an annuity
(LO 2)

Jane Mitchell plans to have $145 withheld from her monthly paycheck and deposited in a savings account that earns 12% annually, compounded monthly. If Mitchell continues with her plan for three years, how much will accumulate in the account on the date of the final deposit?

Exercise H–16
Present value of bonds
(LO 1)

Campton Company plans to issue 18%, 15-year, $500,000 par value, bonds payable that pay interest semiannually on June 30 and December 31. The bonds are dated December 31, 1993, and will be issued on that date. If the market rate of interest for the bonds is 16% on the date of issue, how much cash will the company receive?

Exercise H–17
Future value of a single amount and an annuity
(LO 2)

Medical Equipment Company has decided to establish a fund that will be used after five years to replace a productive facility. The company makes an initial contribution of $230,000 to the fund and plans to make quarterly contributions of $75,000 beginning in three months. The fund is expected to earn 16%, compounded quarterly. How much will be in the fund after five years?

Exercise H–18
Present value of an amount
(LO 1)

Trevor Corporation expects to earn 20% per year on an investment that will pay back $1.2 million after eight years. Use Table H–2 to calculate the present value of the investment.

Exercise H–19
Future value of an amount
(LO 2)

Crawford Company invests $140,000 at 10% per year for 10 years. Use Table H–1 to calculate the future value of the investment after 10 years.

Answers to Objective Review Questions

LO 1 (*e*)

LO 2 (*c*)

APPENDIX

I

Income Taxes

Taxes are as unavoidable as tomorrow's sunrise. Business managers and owners need to know about income taxes so they can avoid paying more than the minimum required by the law without violating its requirements.

Topical Coverage

Perhaps the most common factor affecting businesses in the United States is taxes, especially federal income taxes. Many individual and business decisions are influenced by income tax considerations. In studying this appendix, you will gain an introductory understanding of the rules that govern federal income taxes.

Learning Objectives

After studying Appendix I, you should be able to:

1. List the classes of federal income taxpayers and describe the steps individuals must go through to calculate taxable income.
2. Calculate an individual's gross income tax liability and the net tax payable.
3. Define capital assets and describe the tax treatment for capital losses in comparison with ordinary (noncapital) losses.
4. Describe the differences between the calculations of taxable income and tax liability for corporations and for individuals.
5. Define or explain the terms and phrases listed in the appendix glossary.

History of the Federal Income Tax

Although the federal government first levied an income tax during the Civil War, the history of today's federal income tax dates from the 1913 ratification of the Sixteenth Amendment. Since its ratification, Congress has passed numerous revenue acts and other laws implementing the tax and has placed the responsibility for enforcing income tax laws in the hands of the Treasury Department acting through the Internal Revenue Service. Collectively, the statutes dealing with taxation that have been adopted by Congress are called the **Internal Revenue Code.**

Extensive changes in the tax laws have been enacted more and more frequently in recent years. During the period 1976–1991, major changes were enacted in most years, but especially in 1986.

Despite the fact that tax laws change frequently, the basic concepts of taxation and the tax formula have remained fairly consistent over many decades. While the tax rates and the amount of certain deductions will likely differ in the future, the overall structure of the system is not likely to change greatly. Tax-free treatment for certain types of income and deductibility of certain expenditures will likely continue, although the items eligible for such treatment may vary to some extent over the years.

Synopsis of the Federal Income Tax

Most states and a number of cities levy income taxes, in most cases modeling their laws after the federal laws. However, other than noting the existence of such laws and that they increase the total tax burden and make tax planning even more important, the following discussion is limited to the federal income tax.

ILLUSTRATION I–1

A General Format for Calculating an Individual's Federal Income Tax

Gross income		$xx,xxx
Less: Deductions to arrive at adjusted gross income		(xx,xxx)
Adjusted gross income		$xx,xxx
Less:		
Total itemized deductions or the standard deduction, whichever is larger	$x,xxx	
Deduction for exemptions	x,xxx	xx,xxx
Taxable income		$xx,xxx
Gross tax liability from tax rate schedule		$xx,xxx
Less: Tax credits and prepayments		(xx,xxx)
Net tax payable (or refund)		$ xxx

Classes of Taxpayers

LO 1 List the classes of federal income taxpayers and describe the steps individuals must go through to calculate taxable income.

Federal income tax law recognizes three classes of taxpayers: individuals, corporations, and estates and trusts. Members of each class must file returns and pay taxes on taxable income.

Single proprietorship or partnership businesses are not required to pay federal income taxes. Rather, single proprietors must include the income from their businesses on their individual tax returns. A partnership must file an information return that shows its net income and the distributive shares of the partners. But the partnership is not subject to tax. Instead, the partners must include their shares on their individual returns. In other words, the income of a single proprietorship or partnership, whether withdrawn from the business or not, is taxed as the individual income of the single proprietor or partners.

The treatment given to corporations under the law is different from that of proprietorships or partnerships. A business that is organized as a corporation must file a return and pay taxes on its taxable income. Also, a corporation's stockholders must report dividends as income on their individual returns. Further, when a corporation calculates its taxable income, it cannot deduct dividends it has paid to its stockholders. Thus, the income of a corporation is commonly said to be taxed twice, once as income of the corporation and again as dividend income of its stockholders.

The income tax laws of the federal government also apply to estates and trusts. However, we leave this topic to a more advanced course.

The Individual Income Tax

LO 2 Calculate an individual's gross income tax liability and the net tax payable.

The amount of federal income tax individuals must pay each year depends on their **gross incomes, tax deductions, exemptions,** and **tax credits.** The typical calculation of the tax liability involves the sequence shown in Illustration I–1.

To determine the federal income tax liability of an individual, the amounts of gross income, deductions, exemptions, tax credits (if any), and prepayments are listed on forms supplied by the federal government. Then, the appropriate calculations (additions, subtractions, and so forth) are performed according to the instructions. The listing of the items on the forms is not precisely the same for all classes of taxpayers and does not always follow the general pattern shown in Illustration I–1. However, the illustration shows the relationship of the items and the basic mathematics required in completing the tax forms.

The items that appear on a tax return as gross income, adjusted gross income, deductions, exemptions, tax credits, and prepayments require additional description and explanation.

Gross Income. The income tax law defines gross income as *all income from whatever source derived, unless expressly excluded from taxation by law.* Gross income, therefore, includes income from operating a business; gains from property sales; dividends; interest; rents; royalties; and compensation for services, such as salaries, wages, fees, commissions, bonuses, and tips.

Certain items are specifically excluded from gross income. Examples are gifts; inheritances; scholarships up to the cost of tuition, fees, and course-related materials; social security benefits (unless the taxpayer has a relatively large amount of other income); veterans' benefits; worker's compensation insurance; and, in most cases, the proceeds of life insurance policies paid on the death of the insured. Because these items are excluded from gross income, they are not subject to income tax.

Another item that is generally excluded from gross income is interest on the obligations of the states and their subdivisions. Therefore, states and their subdivisions are able to borrow at a lower rate than would be possible if their bondholders were taxed on the interest they received.

Deductions to Arrive at Adjusted Gross Income. Certain specified items are deducted from gross income to get **adjusted gross income (AGI).** For example, a self-employed person's ordinary and necessary expenses to carry on a business, trade, or profession are deductions to arrive at adjusted gross income. To understand this, recognize that under income tax law, gross profit from sales (sales less cost of goods sold) is gross income to a merchant, and gross legal fees earned are gross income to a lawyer. Therefore, the merchant and the lawyer may deduct all ordinary and necessary expenses of carrying on the business or profession, such as salaries, wages, rent, depreciation, supplies repairs, maintenance, insurance, taxes, and interest.

Expenses of producing rent or royalty income are another category of deductions to arrive at adjusted gross income. Examples of such deductions include depreciation, repairs, real estate taxes, and insurance expense related to the rental property.

Other deductions to arrive at adjusted gross income include certain alimony payments and limited amounts of Individual Retirement Account (IRA) contributions. Also, self-employed persons may deduct limited amounts of contributions to retirement programs (Keogh plans).

Deductions from Adjusted Gross Income. An individual taxpayer is permitted two kinds of deductions from adjusted gross income: (1) the greater of itemized personal expenses or the standard deduction, and (2) the deduction for exemptions.

The Standard Deduction. Individual taxpayers are allowed an automatic deduction of a set amount regardless of how they spend their money. This deduction is known as the **standard deduction.** Taxpayers should elect to deduct the standard deduction if its amount exceeds their itemized deductions (described later). The amounts of the standard deduction for 1992 were

$6,000 on a joint return.

$3,000 on a return for married taxpayers filing separately.

$5,250 for taxpayers classified as heads of households.

$3,600 for other single taxpayers.

However, if the taxpayer can be claimed as a dependent on another person's tax return, the standard deduction is generally limited to the greater of $600 or the taxpayer's **earned income** up to a maximum of $3,600. Earned income includes wages, professional fees, and other forms of compensation for personal services.

In addition to the previous amounts, taxpayers and their spouses filing a joint return are entitled to an additional standard deduction if they are blind or at least age 65. On a joint return the additional deduction is $700 per taxpayer per item. Thus, if both spouses are blind and at least 65, they would receive additional standard deductions of $2,800 (4 × $700) plus the regular standard deduction of $6,000. For single taxpayers, the additional standard deduction is $900 per item instead of $700.

Note that the preceding standard deduction amounts (including the additional $700 or $900) apply to 1992. These items are indexed annually for inflation. As a result, the amounts that can be deducted in future years cannot be stated.

Itemized Personal Expenses. Instead of choosing the standard deduction, taxpayers may itemize and deduct certain personal expenses. Obviously, taxpayers tend to elect the alternative that results in the largest deduction. Itemized deductions commonly consist of certain nonbusiness interest expenses, state and local property and income taxes, charitable contributions, casualty losses, medical expenses, moving expenses, and miscellaneous other deductions.

The rules for interest expense deductions are somewhat detailed, and some interest expense is not fully deductible. Interest classified as *qualified residence interest* is, however, deductible in its entirety. For interest to meet the test of qualified residence interest, the loan must be secured by either the taxpayer's principal or second residence. On such a loan, interest is deductible on a balance of up to $1 million if the purpose of the loan was to acquire, construct, or substantially improve the residence. However, if the loan against the principal or second residence was used for other purposes, the deduction is limited to interest on a balance of $100,000 or less.

Interest on money borrowed for investment purposes is deductible only up to the amount of the taxpayer's net investment income. Also, consumer interest (for example, interest on car loans and credit cards) is not deductible.

Casualty and theft losses are deductible only to the extent that each loss exceeds $100; then the resulting amounts are aggregated and deducted only to the extent they exceed 10% of adjusted gross income. The medical expense deduction is limited to prescription drugs, doctor, dental, hospital, and medical insurance expenses in excess of 7.5% of the taxpayer's adjusted gross income.

Employees may claim itemized deductions for certain unreimbursed expenses they incur in connection with their employment. (The expenses must be paid by the employees and must not be reimbursed by the employer.) These expenses include certain transportation and travel expenses, expenses of an outside salesperson, and moving expenses. Employees who work in more than one place during a day may deduct transportation costs incurred in traveling from one place of employment to another during the day. However, as a general rule, they may not deduct the cost of commuting from home to the first place of employment or from the last place of employment to home.

Travel expenses include, in addition to transportation expenses, the cost of lodging and 80% of the cost of meals while away from home overnight on employment-connected business.[1] Other employee business expenses include such things as long-distance telephone calls, stationery, postage, and moving expenses. Moving expenses are expenses incurred by employees (or self-employed individuals) in moving their place of residence on being transferred by their employers or taking jobs with new employers. Certain minimum requirements as to the distance moved and the length of employment in the new location must be met.

Unreimbursed employee business expenses (other than moving expenses) plus deductions such as tax return preparation fees and safe-deposit box rent are miscellaneous itemized deductions. The total amount of miscellaneous itemized deductions is deductible only to the extent that it exceeds 2% of adjusted gross income. For example, if a taxpayer's adjusted gross income is $30,000 and the sum of the taxpayer's miscellaneous itemized deductions is $1,000, only $400, or $1,000 − $600, can be included in the calculation of total itemized deductions.

Taxpayers with adjusted gross incomes above a certain amount lose a portion of their itemized deductions other than deductions for medical expenses, investment interest, and casualty and theft losses. In 1992, the remaining itemized deductions were reduced by 3% of the excess of the taxpayer's adjusted gross income over $105,250 (or $52,625 if married and filing a separate return).[2] However, the reduction can never be more than 80% of the amount otherwise deductible.

Exemptions. In addition to itemized deductions or the standard deduction, a taxpayer is allowed a second kind of deduction called the deduction for ex-

---

[1] Self-employed taxpayers and corporations are also subject to the rule that limits the deduction for meals to only 80% of the cost.

[2] In future years, these amounts are indexed for inflation.

emptions. The amount of the exemption deduction was $2,300 for 1992 and the amount is adjusted annually for inflation. A taxpayer is allowed one personal exemption. If a husband and wife file a joint return, each is a taxpayer and each is allowed one exemption. Taxpayers are also granted one exemption for each dependent. Persons (such as children) who are claimed as dependents on another taxpayer's return may not claim an exemption deduction for themselves on their own return.[3]

To qualify for an exemption, dependents: (1) must be closely related to the taxpayer or have been a member of the taxpayer's household for the entire year; (2) must have received over half of their support from the taxpayer during the year; (3) must not file a joint return with their spouse unless it is to claim a refund because no tax was owed; and (4) must have had gross income during the year of less than the amount of the personal exemption ($2,300 for 1992). However, you can ignore the gross income test if the person claimed as a dependent is (1) a child of the taxpayer and (2) under 19 years of age at the end of the tax year or under 24 years of age and also a full-time student in an educational institution during each of five months during the year.

Higher income taxpayers also lose a portion of the personal exemption deductions otherwise available. In 1992, the reduction affected taxpayers with adjusted gross incomes of $157,900 if married and filing jointly, $78,950 if married and filing separately, $131,500 if a head of household, and $105,250 if single. In future years, these amounts are indexed for inflation. The reduction of the personal exemptions is 2% for every $2,500 ($1,250 if married filing separately) or fraction thereof by which adjusted gross income exceeds the above cut-off amounts. For example, assume a married couple filing jointly has adjusted gross income of $207,900. Their personal exemptions are reduced by 40%, calculated as follows:

$$\frac{\$207{,}900 - \$157{,}900}{\$2{,}500} = 20 \text{ intervals}$$

$$20 \text{ intervals} \times 2\% = 40\%$$

Recall from the previous discussion that there are deductions to arrive at adjusted gross income and also deductions from adjusted gross income. Each of these two types of deductions must be subtracted at the proper point in the tax calculation because the allowable amounts of some deductions from adjusted gross income are affected by the amount of adjusted gross income.

Federal Income Tax Rates. The tax liability is calculated by applying the appropriate tax rates to taxable income. Illustration I–2 shows the 1992 rates for an unmarried person who does not qualify as a head of household and for married persons who file a joint return or for qualifying widows or widowers. The Tax Rate Schedules in Illustration I–2 are used by taxpayers who do not qualify to use simplified Tax Tables, which are discussed later in this appendix. To use the rate schedules of Illustration I–2, a taxpayer reads down the left column of

[3] In general, the unearned income of children younger than age 14 is taxed at the higher of their tax rate or their parent's top tax rate. In certain circumstances, an election can be made to report the child's unearned income directly on the parent's return.

ILLUSTRATION I–2

Federal Income Tax Rate Schedules

For taxable years beginning in 1992

Schedule X—Single Taxpayers

If taxable income is:	**The tax is:**
Not over $21,450	15% of taxable income
Over $21,450, but not over $51,900	$3,217.50 plus 28% of the excess over $21,450
Over $51,900	$11,743.50 plus 31% of the excess over $51,900

Schedule Y—Married Individuals Filing Joint Returns and Qualifying Widows and Widowers

If taxable income is:	**The tax is:**
Not over $35,800	15% of taxable income
Over $35,800, but not over $86,500	$5,370 plus 28% of the excess over $35,800
Over $86,500	$19,566 plus 31% of the excess over $86,500

the appropriate schedule until arriving at the bracket of his or her taxable income. For example, if an unmarried taxpayer's 1992 taxable income was $28,550, the taxpayer would read down the column of Schedule X to the bracket "over $21,450, but not over $51,900." The right column shows that the tax on $21,450 is $3,217.50, and the excess over $21,450 is taxed at 28%. Thus, the tax on $28,550 is $3,217.50 + (28% × $7,100) = $5,205.50.

Observe in Illustration I–2 that the federal income tax rates are progressive in nature. This means that each additional bracket of taxable income is subject to a higher rate than the preceding bracket. The highest rate specified on the rate schedule is 31%. The **marginal tax rate** is the rate that applies to the next dollar of income to be earned. In the preceding paragraph the taxpayer's marginal tax rate is 28%. By comparison, a single taxpayer with a taxable income above $51,900 has a marginal tax rate of 31%. However, some higher income taxpayers can be subject to a marginal tax rate in excess of 31% because some of their itemized deductions and personal exemption deductions have been phased out.

A husband and wife have a choice concerning rate schedules. They may combine their incomes and use Schedule Y married individuals filing joint returns, or they may each file separate returns using a rate schedule (not shown) that results in a tax for each somewhat in excess of that shown in Illustration I–2 for single taxpayers. The phrase **qualifying widows and widowers** in Schedule Y refers to surviving spouses who (if they have not remarried and have a dependent child) may continue to use Schedule Y for two tax years after the year of their spouse's death.

Also, a person who can qualify as a **head of household** may use a rate schedule (not shown) in which the rates fall between those for unmarried individuals and those for married couples filing jointly. Generally, a head of household is an unmarried or legally separated person who maintains a home in which his or her unmarried child or a qualifying dependent lives for over half the year.

The brackets in the rate schedules shown in Illustration I–2 for 1992 are adjusted each year for changes in the Consumer Price Index. In other words, they are indexed for inflation. As a result, if a person's taxable income increases from year to year but the rate of increase does not exceed the rate of increase in the Consumer Price Index, that person's income is not taxed at a higher rate.

Tax Credits and Prepayments. After an individual's gross income tax liability is computed from the appropriate tax rate schedule, the individual's tax credits and prepayments, if any, are deducted to determine the net tax liability. *Tax credits* represent direct, dollar for dollar, reductions in the amount of tax liability; that is, a $100 tax credit reduces the tax liability by $100. By comparison, deductions reduce the amount of taxable income that is multiplied by the appropriate tax rates to determine the gross tax liability. Thus, a tax credit of $100 is more valuable to the taxpayer than a tax deduction of $100. Assuming a marginal tax rate of 28%, an additional tax deduction of $100 effectively reduces the tax liability by $28 ($100 × 28%), whereas a tax credit of $100 reduces the tax liability by $100.

Various types of tax credits are available. A retired taxpayer with retirement income may receive a *credit for the elderly*. A taxpayer who has paid income taxes to a foreign government may be eligible for a *foreign tax credit*. Also, taxpayers with lower incomes may qualify for an *earned income credit*. The earned income credit, unlike the other tax credits, can generate a tax refund. Thus, it is similar to a negative income tax.

In addition to tax credits, any prepayments of tax are deducted to determine the net tax liability. Most taxpayers have income taxes withheld from their salaries and wages. Other taxpayers are required to estimate the tax and pay the estimated amount in advance installments. Both the income tax withholdings and the estimated tax paid in advance are examples of tax prepayments that are deducted in determining a taxpayer's net tax liability.

LO 3 Define capital assets and describe the tax treatment for capital losses in comparison with ordinary (noncapital) losses.

Special Tax Treatment of Capital Gains and Losses. From a tax planning point of view, an important feature of our federal income tax laws in past years has been the special treatment given to **capital gains and losses**. The precise treatment has varied through the years; at present the favorable treatment for long-term capital gains is a maximum tax rate of 28%. The Internal Revenue Code defines a **capital asset** as any item of property except (1) inventories; (2) trade notes and accounts receivable; (3) real property and depreciable property used in a trade or business; and (4) copyrights, letters, and similar property in the hands of the creator or his or her donee or certain other transferees. Common examples of capital assets held by individuals and subject to sale or exchange are stocks, bonds, and personal residences.

A gain on the sale of a capital asset occurs when the proceeds of the sale exceed the **basis** of the sold asset, and a loss occurs when the asset's basis exceeds the proceeds. The basis of a purchased asset is generally its cost less any depreciation previously allowed or allowable for tax purposes.

Although long-term capital gains are treated favorably, the treatment for long- or short-term capital losses is unfavorable. When an individual's capital losses exceed capital gains, the individual may deduct no more than $3,000 of the excess losses ($1,500 for a married taxpayer filing a separate return) from ordinary income in the year of the loss. A carryover provision allows deductions in subsequent years for losses in excess of the $3,000 or $1,500 limitations.

Remember that real property and depreciable property used in a taxpayer's trade or business are not capital assets. When such properties are sold or exchanged, the excess of losses over gains is fully deductible in arriving at taxable income.

Tax Tables. We previously mentioned that some taxpayers are not required to use the Tax Rate Schedules shown in Illustration I–2. Instead, most individual taxpayers use simplified Tax Tables constructed from the Tax Rate Schedules. Individuals who use the Tax Tables have to calculate their taxable income according to the formula of Illustration I–1 and then search through the appropriate Tax Table to determine their gross income tax liability.

The Corporate Income Tax

LO 4 Describe the differences between the calculations of taxable income and tax liability for corporations and for individuals.

For federal tax purposes, the taxable income of a corporation organized for profit is calculated in much the same way as the taxable income of an individual. However, there are important differences, including these four examples:

1. A corporation (but not an individual) may deduct from gross income the first 70% of dividends received from stock it owns in other domestic corporations. The deduction rises to 80% if the corporation owns at least 20% of the other corporation's stock. In effect, only 30% (or 20%) of such dividends are taxed. However, if two corporations qualify as affiliated corporations, which essentially means that one owns 80% or more of the other's stock, then 100% of the dividends received by the investor corporation from the investee corporation may be deducted. These rules provide relief from the triple taxation of dividends that would otherwise apply.
2. A corporation does not receive preferential treatment for long-term capital gains. A corporation may offset capital losses only against capital gains; and, if the offset results in a net capital loss in any year, the loss may not be deducted from other income. However, it may be carried back to the three preceding years and forward to the next five years and deducted from any capital gains of those years.
3. The standard deduction and the deduction for exemptions do not apply to a corporation. Also, a corporation does not have certain other deductions of an individual, such as that for personal medical expenses.
4. The tax liability of a corporation is calculated using a different rate schedule than those used by individuals. The corporate income tax rates are as follows:

Amount of Taxable Income	Tax rate
Portion from $0 to $50,000	15%
Portion over $50,000 to $75,000 . .	25
Portion in excess of $75,000	34

In addition, if a corporation's taxable income exceeds $100,000, the corporation incurs an additional tax equal to the lesser of 5% of its taxable income in excess of $100,000, or $11,750. This additional tax causes the corporation to lose some, or all, of the tax savings from having income taxed under the rate schedule at rates less than 34%.

To illustrate the use of the corporate rate schedule, assume a corporation has taxable income of $130,000. Its tax liability is calculated as follows:

15% × $50,000	$ 7,500
25% × $25,000	6,250
34% × $55,000	18,700
The lesser of:	
a. 5% × ($130,000 − $100,000), or	
b. $11,750	1,500
	$33,950

Summary of the Appendix in Terms of Learning Objectives

LO 1. The federal income tax is levied on individuals, corporations, and estates and trusts. To calculate an individual's taxable income, first decide whether the income received is excluded (tax free) or included in gross income. Next, subtract deductions to arrive at adjusted gross income. These deductions generally include expenses of a business nature such as the expenses of operating a business as a self-employed person and the expenses of producing rent income. Finally, to arrive at taxable income, you must subtract from adjusted gross income (*a*) the greater of itemized deductions or the standard deduction and (*b*) deductions for exemptions.

LO 2. To calculate an individual's gross tax liability, apply the appropriate tax rate schedule or tax table to taxable income. Thereafter, tax credits and prepayments are subtracted to determine the net tax payable. Unlike deductions, tax credits represent a dollar for dollar reduction in the amount of tax owed.

LO 3. Capital assets include all property except (*a*) inventories; (*b*) trade notes and accounts receivable; (*c*) real and depreciable property used in a trade or business; and (*d*) copyrights, letters, and similar property in the hands of the creator, his or her donee, or certain other transferees. An unlimited amount of ordinary (noncapital) losses may be offset against income. However, the amount of net capital losses that can be used to reduce income in a given year is limited to $3,000 ($1,500 on a separate return) for individuals and $0 for corporate taxpayers. Noncorporate taxpayers pay a maximum tax of 28% on long-term capital gains.

LO 4. Corporations, but not individuals, are entitled to a deduction for dividends received. Individuals receive an exemption deduction and can take a standard deduction if it is greater than their itemized personal deductions; these are not available to corporations. Also, the rate schedules for individuals differ from the corporate rate schedule.

Glossary

LO 5 Define or explain the terms and phrases listed in the appendix glossary.

Adjusted gross income (AGI) gross income minus certain deductions such as business expenses of self-employed persons, expenses to produce rent or royalty income, alimony payments, and limited amounts of contributions to retirement programs for self-employed persons or to Individual Retirement Accounts. p. I-4

Basis In general, the cost of a purchased asset less any depreciation previously allowed or allowable for tax purposes. p. I-9

Capital asset any item of property except (1) inventories, (2) trade notes and accounts receivable, (3) real property and depreciable property used in a trade or business, and (4) copyrights, letters, or similar property. p. I-9

Capital gain or loss the difference between the proceeds from the sale of a capital asset and the basis of the asset. p. I-9

Earned income wages, professional fees, and other forms of compensation for personal services. p. I-5

Exemptions a special deduction that each individual taxpayer is granted for himself or herself and for each dependent, the benefit of which is reduced for high-income taxpayers. p. I-3, I-6, I-7

Gross income all income from whatever source derived, unless expressly excluded from taxation by law. p. I-3, I-4

Head of household an unmarried or legally separated person who maintains for more than half the year a home in which his or her unmarried child or a qualifying dependent lives. p. I-8

Internal Revenue Code collectively, the statutes dealing with taxation that have been adopted by Congress. p. I-2

Marginal tax rate the rate that applies to the next dollar of income to be earned. p. I-8

Qualifying widows and widowers individuals whose spouses are deceased and who remain unmarried and have a dependent child and, therefore, who are allowed to use the income tax rate Schedule Y for two years after their spouses' death. p. I-8

Standard deduction a deduction from adjusted gross income that an individual may claim as an alternative to itemizing his or her personal deductions. p. I-5

Tax credit a dollar amount that can be subtracted from the gross tax liability, thereby providing a dollar for dollar reduction in the liability. p. I-3, I-9

Tax deduction an amount that can be legally subtracted from gross income or from adjusted gross income in the process of determining taxable income. p. I-3, I-4, I-5

Objective Review

Answers to the following questions are listed at the end of this appendix. Be sure that you decide which is the one best answer to each question *before* you check the answers.

LO 1 In calculating the taxable income of an individual, which one of the following statements is not correct?

a. Items such as medical expenses and qualified residence interest are examples of itemized deductions.
b. Tax credits are subtracted after taxable income has been determined (that is, they do not affect the amount of taxable income).
c. Taxpayers who itemize their personal expenses are not entitled to claim any deductions for exemptions.
d. Trade or business expenses of a self-employed person are deductible in arriving at adjusted gross income.
e. A taxpayer can choose to itemize deductions or claim the standard deduction.

LO 2 Which one of the following statements concerning tax liabilities of individuals is not correct?

a. If a taxpayer is in the 28% marginal tax bracket, a $200 tax deduction will reduce taxes by $56 and a $200 tax credit will reduce taxes by $200.
b. According to the rate schedule, the top tax rate is 31%.
c. If married taxpayers filing a joint return have taxable income of $40,800 in 1992, they will have $5,000 of income subject to a 28% tax rate.
d. A single person with taxable income of $25,000 is taxed at a flat rate of 28%.
e. Federal income tax withheld from the taxpayer's salary is an example of a prepayment.

LO 3 An individual taxpayer has taxable income, exclusive of capital gains and losses, of $18,000. In addition, the taxpayer sold a capital asset during the year. The taxpayer will report taxable income of:

a. $18,000 if the taxpayer sold the capital asset for an $8,000 capital loss.
b. $18,000 if the taxpayer sold the capital asset for an $8,000 capital gain.
c. $10,000 if the taxpayer sold the capital asset for an $8,000 capital loss.
d. $21,000 if the taxpayer sold the capital asset for an $8,000 capital gain.
e. $15,000 if the taxpayer sold the capital asset for an $8,000 capital loss.

LO 4 Which one of the following statements is correct?

a. The highest income tax rate applied to corporations is 28%.
b. Both individuals and corporations are allowed to deduct a portion of any dividend income they receive.
c. Married individuals who file a joint return and corporations are subject to a 15% tax rate on the same dollar amount of taxable income.
d. Individuals are entitled to a standard deduction, but corporations are not.
e. The highest tax rates for individuals and corporations are the same.

LO 5 An item that can be subtracted from the gross tax liability, thereby providing a dollar for dollar reduction in the liability is called a(n):

a. Tax deduction.
b. Tax credit.
c. Itemized deduction.
d. Standard deduction.
e. Exemption.

Questions for Class Discussion

1. If an individual taxpayer expects to be in the 28% tax bracket, which should the taxpayer prefer: (*a*) a $150 expenditure that will provide a tax credit of $85 or (*b*) a $150 expenditure that will provide a business expense deduction of $150?
2. What name identifies the body of federal statutes that deal with taxation?
3. What are the classes of taxpayers subject to the federal income tax?
4. Name several items excluded from gross income for tax purposes.
5. What justification might be given for permitting a corporation to claim a tax deduction for a portion of its dividend income?
6. For tax purposes, define a capital asset.
7. What is the significance of defining capital assets differently from other types of assets?
8. An individual had capital asset transactions that resulted in nothing but losses. What tax treatment is given to these losses?
9. What preferential tax treatment, if any, do long-term capital gains receive currently?

Exercises

In some of the exercises and problems that follow, the taxpayers would qualify to use the simplified Tax Tables (not provided in the book) rather than the Tax Rate Schedules. However, you should base all calculations of individual tax liabilities on the Tax Rate Schedules in Illustration I–2.

Exercise I–1
Including or excluding items in gross income (LO 2)

Indicate whether each of the following items should be included in or excluded from gross income for federal income tax purposes.

a. Workers' compensation insurance received as the result of an accident while working on a part-time job.
b. Tips received while working as a waiter.
c. Gain on the sale of a personal automobile bought and rebuilt.
d. Dividends received by an individual.
e. Interest income from state bonds.

f. Gift of stock from an uncle.
g. Cash inherited from a relative.
h. Scholarship received from a state university. The scholarship is for an amount substantially in excess of the cost of the tuition, fees, and course-related materials.

Exercise I–2
Calculating taxable incomes of single individuals
(LO 2)

Karen Stewart, Michael Montgomery, and Jeff Blume are unmarried and have two income tax exemptions each. All are younger than 65 and have good vision. In 1992, their adjusted gross incomes were Stewart, $79,000; Montgomery, $45,000; and Blume, $23,000. Their itemized deductions were Stewart, $13,400; Montgomery, $8,700; and Blume, $3,200. Prepare calculations to show the taxable income of each person.

Exercise I–3
Calculating taxable income on a joint return
(LO 2)

Stanley and Iris Campbell had $74,600 of adjusted gross income in 1992. They are 42 and 41 years old, respectively, and have three children ages 4, 8, and 11. Jewelry with a fair value of $9,200 was stolen during 1992 and their insurance did not cover the loss. They incurred $1,000 in unreimbursed moving expenses as a result of Iris's job transfer. They also incurred the following expenses during the year: local property taxes, $1,720; qualified residence interest on home mortgage, $3,680; hospital insurance, $1,800; and uninsured doctor and dentist bills, $3,900. Prepare a calculation to show their taxable income on a joint return.

Exercise I–4
Individual taxable income
(LO 2)

Morgan Casper, who qualifies as a head of household, had adjusted gross income of $37,800 in 1992 and was entitled to three personal exemption deductions. Her activities and expenditures during the year included the following items. Determine her taxable income.

Qualified interest paid on mortgage on personal residence . . .	$2,100
Medical expenses paid	2,500
Cost of vacation to Washington, D.C..	3,600
Charitable contributions	400
Interest on car loan	1,050
State income taxes paid.	1,360
Flood damage to residence not covered by insurance policy . .	6,800

Exercise I–5
Standard deductions
(LO 2)

Ray and Loretta Palmer file a joint tax return. Ray is age 72, and has no eyesight impairment. Loretta is 62 and legally blind. What is the amount of the standard deduction they may claim on their 1992 joint return?

Exercise I–6
Calculating an individual's income tax liability or refund
(LO 2, 3)

Steve Manchaca earned $39,000 during 1992 as an employee of an engineering firm. He is unmarried and provides one fourth of the support of his 14-year-old sister who lives with him. Manchaca had $7,046 of federal income tax and $3,978 of FICA tax withheld from his paychecks. He received $720 interest on a savings account and inherited $5,000 from his uncle. During the year, he paid $1,480 state income tax, $980 qualified residence interest on the mortgage on his personal residence, and made charitable contributions of $200. Show the calculation of Manchaca's taxable income in the manner outlined in Illustration I–1. Then, using the rate schedule of Illustration I–2, calculate the net federal income tax payable or refund due Manchaca.

Exercise I–7
Individual taxable income and tax liability
(LO 2, 3)

In 1992, Carol had salary income of $61,000 and itemized deductions of $15,790. Carol's brother Phillip had the same amounts of income and itemized deductions. Carol is married and filed a joint return with her husband, Stan, who had no income. Phillip is single. Assume two personal exemption deductions are claimed on the joint return for Carol and Stan and one is claimed on Phillip's return. Calculate the taxable income and gross tax liability to be reported on each return.

Exercise I–8
Capital gains and losses
(LO 4)

The following independent cases involve single individuals who sold some capital assets during 1992. In each case, the person's only other income was a $45,000 salary. For each case, indicate how much each loss will reduce taxable income for 1992.

a. One asset was sold for a $13,600 capital gain and another was sold for a $14,600 capital loss.
b. One asset was sold for a $13,600 capital gain and another was sold for an $11,100 capital loss.
c. One asset was sold for a $13,600 capital gain and another was sold for a $19,400 capital loss.

Exercise I–9
Calculating corporate tax liabilities
(LO 3, 4)

Calculate the 1992 tax liability for each of the following corporations:

a. Gecko Corporation sold three capital assets in 1992. Asset A was sold at a loss of $6,000. Asset B was sold at a gain of $5,500. Asset C was sold at a loss of $3,200. Gecko Corporation's taxable income without the above gains and losses was $275,000.
b. Lightsey Corporation sold three capital assets in 1992. Asset A was sold at a gain of $15,000. Asset B was sold at a gain of $2,300. Asset C was sold at a loss of $12,000. Lightsey Corporation's taxable income without the above gains and losses was $232,000.

Exercise I–10
Analyzing corporate tax rates
(LO 4)

Nilan Corporation reported taxable income for 1992 of $2.5 million. Determine its tax liability. Is the corporation paying tax at a flat rate? Explain.

Problem

Problem I–1
Calculation of individual income tax payable
(LO 2, 3)

George and Jackie Gunn are both 48 years old and file a joint income tax return. They have three children, Ginny, Eva, and Steve. Ginny is a sophomore in high school and earned $2,200 in 1992 from her summer job. Eva, who is 18 years old, graduated from high school in June. She lives at home and attends college part time and works part time. Her income for 1992 was $3,500. Steve is 10 years old. All the children received over half their support from their parents.

George and Jackie Gunn had the following cash receipts and disbursements during 1992:

Cash Receipts

George:	
Salary as administrator of Northwood Community Hospital ($56,000 gross pay less $7,480 federal income taxes and $4,253 FICA taxes)	$44,267
Rent income from duplex purchased in 1991 (cost $126,000, depreciated on a straight-line basis over 31.5 years)	17,400
Inheritance received on the death of father	60,000
Sale of stock (held for five years, at a loss of $2,700)	7,900
Jackie:	
Salary as a lawyer with Harrison, Lockhart, and Smith ($92,000 gross pay less $16,800 federal income taxes, $4,775 FICA taxes, and $2,850 for medical insurance premiums withheld)	67,575
Sale of stock (held for three years, at a gain of $1,300)	12,400

Cash disbursements

Qualified interest on family residence mortgage	8,230
Property taxes on family residence	2,960
Property taxes on rental duplex	2,070
Interest on mortgage on rental duplex	4,890
Electrical repairs at rental duplex	980
Insurance (one year) on rental duplex	460
Prescription drugs	1,700
Charitable contributions	3,970
Tax preparation fee plus other qualified miscellaneous deductions	6,064

Required

Follow the form of Illustration I–1 and use the tax rate schedule of Illustration I–2 to calculate the net federal income tax payable or refund for George and Jackie Gunn.

Alternate Problem

Problem I–1A
Calculation of individual income tax payable
(LO 2, 3)

Robert and Madeline Collins are both 39 years old, have two daughters, and file a joint tax return. The oldest daughter is 23 years old and attended college in both the spring and fall semesters in 1992. During the summer, she earned $4,000. The youngest daughter is a freshman in high school and earned $700 babysitting in 1992. Robert and Madeline Collins provided over half of each daughters' support and had the following cash receipts and disbursements during 1992:

Cash Receipts

Salary to Madeline as principal of Casis High School ($49,000 gross pay less $8,720 federal income taxes and $3,749 FICA taxes)	$36,531
Salary to Robert as engineer at Otec Corporation ($51,000 gross pay less $10,280 federal income taxes and $3,902 FICA taxes)	36,818
Interest on joint savings account	1,200
Interest on bonds issued by the city of Wichita, Kansas	3,900
Proceeds from sale of stock (held for two years, at a gain of $4,500)	18,600
Proceeds from sale of stock (held for five years, at a loss of $9,000)	22,450
Proceeds from insurance received upon death of mother	25,000

Cash Disbursements

Qualified interest on family residence mortgage	6,100
Property taxes on family residence	1,300
Charitable contributions	500
Interest on credit cards	762
Unreimbursed business travel expenses ($1,900 lodging, $960 meals)	2,860
Advance payments of estimated federal income tax	1,200

Required

Follow the form of Illustration I–1 and use the tax rate schedule of Illustration I–2 to calculate the net federal income tax payable or refund for Robert and Madeline Collins.

Answers to Objective Review Questions

LO 1 (*c*)
LO 2 (*d*)
LO 3 (*e*)
LO 4 (*d*)
LO 5 (*b*)

APPENDIX

J

Financial Statements and Related Disclosures from International Business Machines Corporation's 1990 Annual Report

IBM is a huge company that operates literally all over the world. It seems impossible that a person could learn very much about it from only a few pages. But with the accounting knowledge you are learning, you will find a wealth of information in this annual report.

LETTER TO SHAREHOLDERS

NINETEEN NINETY was a good year for IBM. Despite mounting economic and political uncertainties around the world, our performance improved substantially. Worldwide results were encouraging—revenue and earnings increased while our ongoing cost and expense rate declined.

All major geographic areas showed growth, including the best U.S. performance since 1984. With the introductions of the System/390—our most comprehensive product announcement in 25 years—the RISC System/6000 high-performance workstations—already a billion-dollar business—and the well-received PS/1 computer for the home, together with the two most popular computer systems in history—the mid-priced AS/400 and our PS/2 product line, we are offering the strongest line-up of products and services in our history. The breadth of our offerings and our worldwide market presence combined to serve us well in a generally difficult year for the information processing industry.

A CHALLENGING ENVIRONMENT As we begin 1991, weakening economies…high interest rates…events in the Middle East and elsewhere in the world—all are affecting customer buying decisions. There are also tough challenges within our industry—from growing customer requirements for standards and open systems, to the shift in demand from hardware to software and services, to intense pressures from lean and agile competitors.

A STRATEGY FOR GROWTH We believe IBM is well-positioned to prosper in this environment. However, we are managing our business prudently as we pursue our objectives of long-term growth and increased profitability. Our strategy is straightforward and consistent: to provide customers with the best solutions; to strengthen the competitiveness of our products and services; and to improve our efficiency.

We are implementing this strategy through our drive for market-driven quality. Simply stated, this means we are continuously striving to make every IBM offering and every contact with our company perfect in the eyes of our customers.

IBM has long been among the most international of companies, a significant advantage in an increasingly global marketplace. During 1990, we expanded our initiatives in Eastern Europe and moved the headquarters of our Communication Systems line of business from New York to London in order to better respond to customer needs in the fast-growing European telecommunications arena.

IBM PEOPLE—A COMPETITIVE EDGE

IBM's leadership begins with the superior skills and dedication of our people. We are a "learning company" because, increasingly, our ability to create value for customers will depend on specific knowledge and problem-solving skills. That is why we are both educating the men and women of IBM and encouraging them to take risks by advancing new ideas and innovations. Investing in our people is essential because, in the long run, success will accrue to the quickest, smartest and toughest-minded.

IBM Chairman John F. Akers and IBM President Jack D. Kuehler (right).

MORE STREAMLINING As part of our ongoing plan to sharpen IBM's strategic focus, we restructured our typewriter, keyboard and personal printer business in 1990. These operations were consolidated into a wholly owned subsidiary as we worked to form an alliance with Clayton & Dubilier, Inc. to create a new company, LEXMARK International.

In reporting to you last year, we projected a continuing reduction in our work force. Through retirement, attrition and voluntary incentive programs, IBM's worldwide population declined to 373,800 and our U.S. population to 205,500, surpassing the objective we had set for ourselves.

LETTER TO SHAREHOLDERS

MOVING AHEAD During 1991, we will continue to find creative new ways of doing business, expanding our worldwide network of alliances and joint ventures to meet changing customer needs.

With $6.6 billion invested in research, development and engineering in 1990, we are focused on areas with growth potential—with emphasis on software, services, workstations and systems integration—and on areas of strategic importance, such as semiconductor technology.

Our 1990 results were encouraging. We are on the right course, although much remains to be done. The actions we have taken to make IBM a more competitive company are serving us well, and these uncertain times call for continued prudence in managing our business.

Over the longer term, we have confidence in the industry's future and in our ability to deliver greater value for our customers and for our shareholders.

January 29, 1991, by order
of the Board of Directors

John F. Akers
Chairman of the Board

FINANCIAL REPORT

REPORT OF MANAGEMENT

International Business Machines Corporation and Subsidiary Companies

Responsibility for the integrity and objectivity of the financial information presented in this Annual Report rests with IBM management. The accompanying financial statements have been prepared in conformity with generally accepted accounting principles, applying certain estimates and judgments as required.

IBM maintains an effective internal control structure. It consists, in part, of organizational arrangements with clearly defined lines of responsibility and delegation of authority, and comprehensive systems and control procedures. We believe this structure provides reasonable assurance that transactions are executed in accordance with management authorization, and that they are appropriately recorded, in order to permit preparation of financial statements in conformity with generally accepted accounting principles and to adequately safeguard, verify and maintain accountability of assets. An important element of the control environment is an ongoing internal audit program.

To assure the effective administration of internal control, we carefully select and train our employees, develop and disseminate written policies and procedures, provide appropriate communication channels, and foster an environment conducive to the effective functioning of controls. We believe that it is essential for the company to conduct its business affairs in accordance with the highest ethical standards, as set forth in the IBM Business Conduct Guidelines. These guidelines, translated into numerous languages, are distributed to employees throughout the world, and re-emphasized through internal programs to assure that they are understood and followed.

Price Waterhouse, independent accountants, are retained to examine IBM's financial statements. Their accompanying report is based on an examination conducted in accordance with generally accepted auditing standards, including a review of the internal control structure and tests of accounting procedures and records.

The Audit Committee of the Board of Directors is composed solely of outside directors, and is responsible for recommending to the Board the independent accounting firm to be retained for the coming year, subject to stockholder approval. The Audit Committee meets periodically and privately with the independent accountants, with our internal auditors, as well as with IBM management, to review accounting, auditing, internal control structure and financial reporting matters.

John F. Akers — Chairman of the Board

Frank A. Metz, Jr. — Senior Vice President, Finance & Planning

REPORT OF INDEPENDENT ACCOUNTANTS

International Business Machines Corporation and Subsidiary Companies

To the Stockholders and Board of Directors of
International Business Machines Corporation

January 29, 1991

In our opinion, the accompanying consolidated financial statements, appearing on pages 34, 35, 36, 37 and 43 through 58, present fairly in all material respects the financial position of International Business Machines Corporation and its subsidiaries at December 31, 1990 and 1989, and the results of their operations and their cash flows for each of the three years in the period ended December 31, 1990, in conformity with generally accepted accounting principles. These financial statements are the responsibility of the company's management; our responsibility is to express an opinion thereon based on our audits. We conducted our audits in accordance with generally accepted auditing standards which require that we plan and perform the audit to obtain reasonable assurance about whether such statements are free of material misstatement. An audit includes examining, on a test basis, evidence supporting the amounts and disclosures in the financial statements, assessing the accounting principles used and significant estimates made by management, and evaluating the overall financial statement presentation. We believe that our audits provide a reasonable basis for the opinion expressed above.

As discussed in the note regarding Taxes on page 50, the company changed its method of accounting for income taxes in 1988. We concur with this change.

Price Waterhouse

Price Waterhouse
153 East 53rd Street
New York, N.Y. 10022

CONSOLIDATED STATEMENT OF EARNINGS

International Business Machines Corporation and Subsidiary Companies

For the year ended December 31:	1990	1989	1988
(Dollars in millions except per share amounts)			
Revenue:			
Sales	$43,959	$41,586	$39,959
Support services	11,322	9,858	9,285
Software	9,952	8,424	7,927
Rentals and financing	3,785	2,842	2,510
	69,018	62,710	59,681
Cost:			
Sales	19,401	18,001	17,499
Support services	6,617	5,701	4,971
Software	3,126	2,694	2,110
Rentals and financing	1,579	1,305	1,068
	30,723	27,701	25,648
Gross Profit	38,295	35,009	34,033
Operating Expenses:			
Selling, general and administrative	20,709	21,289	19,362
Research, development and engineering	6,554	6,827	5,925
	27,263	28,116	25,287
Operating Income	11,032	6,893	8,746
Other Income, principally interest	495	728	996
Interest Expense	1,324	976	709
Earnings before Income Taxes	10,203	6,645	9,033
Provision for Income Taxes	4,183	2,887	3,542
Net Earnings before Cumulative Effect of Accounting Change	6,020	3,758	5,491
Cumulative Effect of Change in Accounting for Income Taxes	—	—	315
Net Earnings	$ 6,020	$ 3,758	$ 5,806
Per share amounts:			
Before cumulative effect of accounting change	$10.51	$6.47	$9.27
Cumulative effect of change in accounting for income taxes	—	—	.53
Net earnings	$10.51	$6.47	$9.80

Average number of shares outstanding:
1990—572,647,906
1989—581,102,404
1988—592,444,409

The notes on pages 43 through 58 are an integral part of this statement.

CONSOLIDATED STATEMENT OF FINANCIAL POSITION

International Business Machines Corporation and Subsidiary Companies

At December 31:	1990	1989
(Dollars in millions)		
Assets		
Current Assets:		
Cash	$ 1,189	$ 741
Cash equivalents	2,664	2,959
Marketable securities, at cost, which approximates market	698	1,261
Notes and accounts receivable—trade, net of allowances	20,988	18,866
Other accounts receivable	1,656	1,298
Inventories	10,108	9,463
Prepaid expenses and other current assets	1,617	1,287
	38,920	35,875
Plant, Rental Machines and Other Property	53,659	48,410
Less: Accumulated depreciation	26,418	23,467
	27,241	24,943
Investments and Other Assets:		
Software, less accumulated amortization (1990, $5,873; 1989, $4,824)	4,099	3,293
Investments and sundry assets	17,308	13,623
	21,407	16,916
	$87,568	$77,734
Liabilities and Stockholders' Equity		
Current Liabilities:		
Taxes	$ 3,159	$ 2,699
Short-term debt	7,602	5,892
Accounts payable	3,367	3,167
Compensation and benefits	3,014	2,797
Deferred income	2,506	1,365
Other accrued expenses and liabilities	5,628	5,780
	25,276	21,700
Long-Term Debt	11,943	10,825
Other Liabilities	3,656	3,420
Deferred Income Taxes	3,861	3,280
Stockholders' Equity:		
Capital stock, par value $1.25 per share	6,357	6,341
Shares authorized: 750,000,000		
Issued: 1990—571,618,795; 1989—574,775,560		
Retained earnings	33,234	30,477
Translation adjustments	3,266	1,698
	42,857	38,516
Less: Treasury stock, at cost (Shares: 1990—227,604; 1989—75,723)	25	7
	42,832	38,509
	$87,568	$77,734

The notes on pages 43 through 58 are an integral part of this statement.

CONSOLIDATED STATEMENT OF CASH FLOWS

International Business Machines Corporation and Subsidiary Companies

For the year ended December 31:	1990	1989	1988
(Dollars in millions)			
Cash Flow from Operating Activities:			
Net earnings	$ 6,020	$ 3,758	$ 5,806
Adjustments to reconcile net earnings to cash provided from operating activities:			
Depreciation	4,217	4,240	3,871
Amortization of software	1,086	1,185	893
Loss (gain) on disposition of investment assets	32	(74)	(133)
(Increase) in accounts receivable	(2,077)	(2,647)	(2,322)
Decrease (increase) in inventory	17	(29)	(1,232)
(Increase) in other assets	(3,136)	(1,674)	(1,587)
Increase in accounts payable	293	870	265
Increase in other liabilities	1,020	1,743	519
Net cash provided from operating activities	7,472	7,372	6,080
Cash Flow from Investing Activities:			
Payments for plant, rental machines and other property	(6,509)	(6,414)	(5,390)
Proceeds from disposition of plant, rental machines and other property	804	544	409
Investment in software	(1,892)	(1,679)	(1,318)
Purchases of marketable securities and other investments	(1,234)	(1,391)	(2,555)
Proceeds from marketable securities and other investments	1,687	1,860	4,734
Net cash used in investing activities	(7,144)	(7,080)	(4,120)
Cash Flow from Financing Activities:			
Proceeds from new debt	4,676	6,471	4,540
Payments to settle debt	(3,683)	(2,768)	(3,007)
Short-term borrowings less than 90 days—net	1,966	228	1,028
Payments to employee stock plans—net	(76)	(29)	(11)
Payments to purchase and retire capital stock	(415)	(1,759)	(992)
Cash dividends paid	(2,774)	(2,752)	(2,609)
Net cash used in financing activities	(306)	(609)	(1,051)
Effect of Exchange Rate Changes on Cash and Cash Equivalents	131	(158)	(201)
Net Change in Cash and Cash Equivalents	153	(475)	708
Cash and Cash Equivalents at January 1	3,700	4,175	3,467
Cash and Cash Equivalents at December 31	$ 3,853	$ 3,700	$ 4,175
Supplemental Data:			
Cash paid during the year for:			
Income taxes	$ 3,315	$ 3,071	$ 3,405
Interest	$ 2,165	$ 1,605	$ 1,440

The notes on pages 43 through 58 are an integral part of this statement.

CONSOLIDATED STATEMENT OF STOCKHOLDERS' EQUITY

International Business Machines Corporation and Subsidiary Companies

(Dollars in millions)	Capital Stock	Retained Earnings	Translation Adjustments	Treasury Stock	Total
Stockholders' Equity, January 1, 1988	$6,417	$29,016	$2,865	$ (35)	$ 38,263
1988					
Net earnings		5,806			5,806
Cash dividends declared		(2,609)			(2,609)
Capital stock issued under employee plans (1,321,697 shares)	92				92
Purchases (8,140,101 shares) and sales (8,117,596 shares) of treasury stock under employee and stockholder plans—net		(128)		(1)	(129)
Capital stock purchased and retired (8,611,396 shares)	(93)	(899)			(992)
Tax reductions—employee plans	26				26
Translation adjustments			(948)		(948)
Stockholders' Equity, December 31, 1988	6,442	31,186	1,917	(36)	39,509
1989					
Net earnings		3,758			3,758
Cash dividends declared		(2,752)			(2,752)
Capital stock issued under employee plans (824,026 shares)	60				60
Purchases (8,202,058 shares) and sales (8,423,155 shares) of treasury stock under employee and stockholder plans—net		(133)		29	(104)
Capital stock purchased and retired (16,085,900 shares)	(177)	(1,582)			(1,759)
Tax reductions—employee plans	16				16
Translation adjustments			(219)		(219)
Stockholders' Equity, December 31, 1989	6,341	30,477	1,698	(7)	38,509
1990					
Net earnings		6,020			6,020
Cash dividends declared		(2,774)			(2,774)
Capital stock issued under employee plans (686,159 shares)	47				47
Purchases (8,448,626 shares) and sales (8,296,745 shares) of treasury stock under employee and stockholder plans—net		(117)		(18)	(135)
Capital stock purchased and retired (3,842,924 shares)	(43)	(372)			(415)
Tax reductions—employee plans	12				12
Translation adjustments			1,568		1,568
Stockholders' Equity, December 31, 1990	$6,357	$33,234	$3,266	$ (25)	$ 42,832

The notes on pages 43 through 58 are an integral part of this statement.

MANAGEMENT DISCUSSION

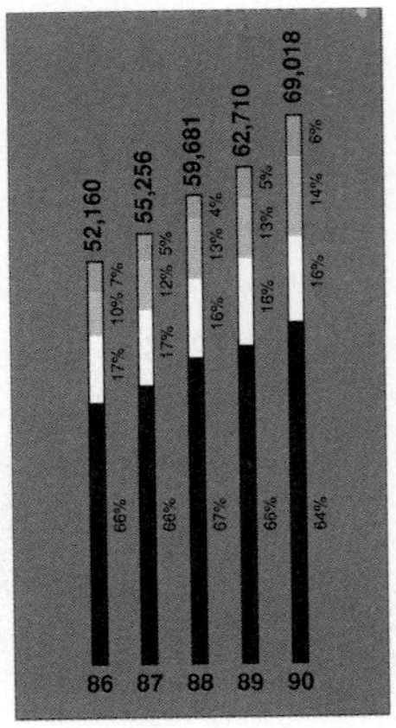

Revenue

(In millions)

- Rentals and Financing
- Software
- Support Services
- Sales

Results of Operations The financial results achieved in 1990 are a substantial improvement over 1989. They reflect the execution of management's strategy to transform the company by increasing emphasis on quality and customer solutions, improving the competitiveness of IBM's products and services, and achieving greater efficiencies from cost and expense management and strategic restructurings.

Worldwide revenue in 1990 totaled $69.0 billion, an increase of 10.1 percent over 1989. The rate of growth continued to be stronger outside the United States, but U.S. operations showed the highest year-to-year revenue growth rate since 1984. Revenue from U.S. operations was $27.1 billion in 1990, an increase of 5.4 percent, following a 1.7 percent increase in 1989 over 1988. Revenue from non-U.S. operations was $41.9 billion, up 13.3 percent from 1989. This was primarily attributable to strong performance in the Europe/Middle East/Africa area, where revenues increased 17.5 percent over 1989. As a percent of total revenue, non-U.S. revenue has grown from 50.3 percent in 1986 to 60.7 percent in 1990.

Net earnings for the year were $6.0 billion compared with $3.8 billion in 1989 and $5.8 billion in 1988. The 1989 earnings were impacted by a $2.4 billion pre-tax charge for actions taken to reduce costs, expenses and structure. Earnings before tax in 1988 were impacted by an $870 million charge related to consolidations of manufacturing and headquarters operations. In addition, a 1988 change in an accounting principle related to income taxes resulted in additional net earnings of $315 million in that year.

Revenue from sales was $44.0 billion, an increase of 5.7 percent compared with a 4.1 percent increase in 1989. Sales revenue from U.S. operations increased slightly in 1990 after a 2.3 percent decline in 1989. While sales revenue remained the largest single category at 63.7 percent of total revenue, the rate of growth in software and services continued to outpace that of hardware. Worldwide revenue from support services increased 14.9 percent in 1990. Maintenance services, the largest component of support services, increased 9.9 percent after declines of 3.8 percent in 1989 and 4.5 percent in 1988. Revenue from maintenance services in the U.S. declined 2.5 percent in 1990 reflecting the transfer in the third quarter of 1989 of IBM's ROLM service operations to a venture owned jointly by IBM and Siemens AG. U.S. maintenance service revenue increased 11.8 percent in the fourth quarter of 1990 compared with the same period in 1989.

Software revenue of $10.0 billion was up 18.1 percent over 1989 with strong growth in both U.S. and non-U.S. operations. In 1989, growth over 1988 was less strong in part because 1988 software revenue included payments made by Fujitsu to IBM as a result of arbitration between the two companies. Revenue from rentals and financing increased more than 30 percent in both the U.S. and non-U.S. areas.

Information on industry segments and classes of similar products or services is presented on page 57.

Revenue from processors increased 1.2 percent in 1990. The extremely well-received midrange models of the new Enterprise System/9000 family and continued strong sales of the Application System/400 more than offset declines in the high-end processors as customers anticipated availability in 1991 of new high-end models of the Enterprise System/9000 family. Processor revenue from U.S. operations declined 3.3 percent.

In workstations, revenue from personal systems increased 14.7 percent worldwide and 6.0 percent

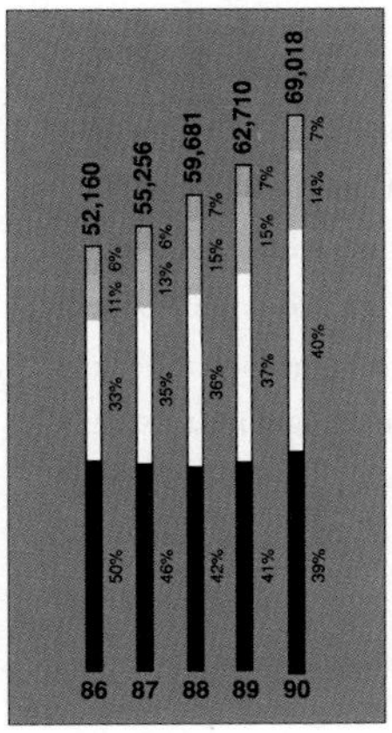

Revenue by Geographic Areas

(In millions)

- ■ Americas
- ■ Asia Pacific
- □ Europe/Middle East/Africa
- ■ United States

in the U.S. Personal systems include the new RISC System/6000 workstation, which has been very well-received in the marketplace, as well as the new Personal System/1 home computer. The increase of 3.4 percent in other workstations revenue is primarily attributable to point-of-sale products.

Revenue from peripherals increased 15.1 percent worldwide and 20.2 percent in the U.S. These increases are due, in large part, to the strong performance of the IBM 3390 Direct Access Storage Device, which the company began to ship in the fourth quarter of 1989.

The gross profit margin of 55.5 percent in 1990 was .7 percentage points below 1989 after adjusting for the restructuring charge recorded in 1989. This decrease is the result of lower gross profit margins on sales, primarily driven by product mix. Revenue from higher margin processors was less in 1990 than in 1989. Profit margins of support services decreased .6 percentage points, primarily due to the continued rapid growth of other support services, whose gross profit margins are lower than those for maintenance. However, gross profit margins of maintenance service increased in 1990 over 1989.

After adjusting for the 1989 restructuring charge, software gross profit margins declined 1.9 percentage points in 1990. This decline is primarily the result of higher service costs associated with the large number of new software products introduced in 1990. Gross profit margins of rentals and financing grew 4.2 percentage points in 1990.

Selling, general and administrative expenses, as reported, showed a decrease of 2.7 percent in 1990 from 1989 and an increase of 10.0 percent in 1989 over 1988. Both 1989 and 1988 were marked by unusual charges which are described in the restructuring note on page 47. If adjusted for these charges, the year-over-year changes would have been a 6.5 percent increase in 1990 and a 5.2 percent increase in 1989. While the effect of currency translation had a favorable impact on overall financial results, it contributed to increased expenses of the non-U.S. operations. In addition, the company incurred somewhat higher than normal expenses for ongoing restructuring actions taken in a number of countries. Expenses in U.S. operations decreased in 1990 as the benefits of past actions to become a more efficient and responsive organization began to show in the financial results.

Expenditures for research, development and engineering amounted to $6.6 billion in 1990, or 9.5 percent of revenue. These expenditures increased 1.6 percent over 1989 after adjusting for the 1989 restructuring charge. These investments are vital for IBM to remain a leader in a highly competitive industry.

Other income decreased 32.0 percent in 1990 to $495 million. This decline is attributable to a 1989 gain on the sale of IBM's interest in Discovision Associates and to lower levels of cash equivalents and marketable securities in 1990.

Interest expense increased 35.7 percent in 1990 to $1.3 billion. The increase is primarily the result of high interest rates on short-term borrowings in subsidiaries whose economic environment is highly inflationary. Exchange gains from currency revaluation on these borrowings largely offset this growth in interest expense. The year-to-year growth rate in interest expense has been abating all year. Interest expense for the fourth quarter was 2.8 percent above the comparable period in 1989.

The effective tax rate of 41.0 percent for 1990 was lower than the 43.4 percent in 1989 primarily as a result of the relative proportion of earnings from

MANAGEMENT DISCUSSION

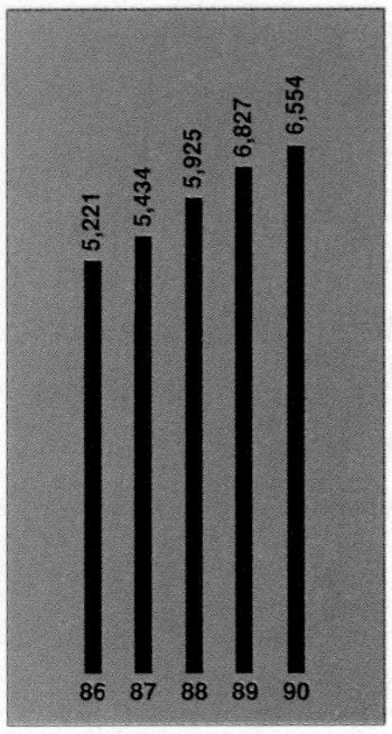

Research, Development and Engineering Expenses

(In millions)

U.S. operations, which are taxed at a lower rate. These earnings were influenced by the restructuring charge taken in the fourth quarter of 1989 and significantly improved earnings from U.S. operations in 1990.

For the quarter ended December 31, 1990, worldwide revenue was $23.1 billion, up 12.7 percent from the prior year's $20.5 billion. Worldwide net earnings for the three months were $2.5 billion in 1990 compared with $.6 billion in 1989. The strong revenue growth in the quarter was in all categories, with growth in the services area especially strong.

In 1990, the company continued its strategy of improving its competitiveness and profitability by streamlining operations and reducing the rate of growth of costs and expenses.

Much of the 1990 activity involved executing initiatives covered by the charge taken against earnings in the fourth quarter of 1989. These included a transition payment program in the U.S. that resulted in a sizable reduction in the U.S. work force. As a result, the company reduced its worldwide population by nearly 9,500 to a year end total of 373,816 people and reduced its U.S. population over 10,000 to 205,533, surpassing the U.S. target it had set for itself. IBM has reduced its worldwide population by more than 33,000 people from its peak in 1986. These reductions were accomplished largely through retirement and incentive programs carried out selectively in countries around the world.

Also in 1990, the company established a wholly owned subsidiary consolidating its typewriter, keyboard, personal printer and related supplies operations. At the same time the company began negotiations with Clayton & Dubilier, Inc., which are expected to lead to the creation of a new information products company in 1991.

The majority of this new company, LEXMARK International, would be owned by Clayton & Dubilier. IBM would have a 10 percent continuing equity interest. This action is consistent with IBM's strategy to concentrate its resources on markets and opportunities where long-term growth prospects are most attractive. The transaction is not expected to have a material effect on the company's financial results. Similar actions in recent years included the sale of IBM's copier sales and service operations, its educational publishing subsidiary and its interest in Discovision Associates.

Management is pleased with the financial results reported in 1990. They represent a continuing pattern of improved financial performance and were achieved under trying economic circumstances.

Growing markets, advancing technologies and expanding uses of computing systems will continue to drive the industry and contribute to IBM's success in the 1990s.

At the same time, uncertainties in the world's economies and intensifying pressures from formidable competitors require that IBM manage its business prudently as it pursues its objective of long-term growth and profitability.

Strengthened ties to customers, geographic diversity, a strong product line and a reduced cost and expense structure provide a healthy financial underpinning and will allow the company to participate fully in the opportunities ahead.

Financial Condition During 1990, IBM continued to make those investments necessary to ensure its success in the information industry in the future. In an increasingly competitive international environment, sustained investments in basic research and applied development are essential to maintain a steady flow of innovative new products that provide

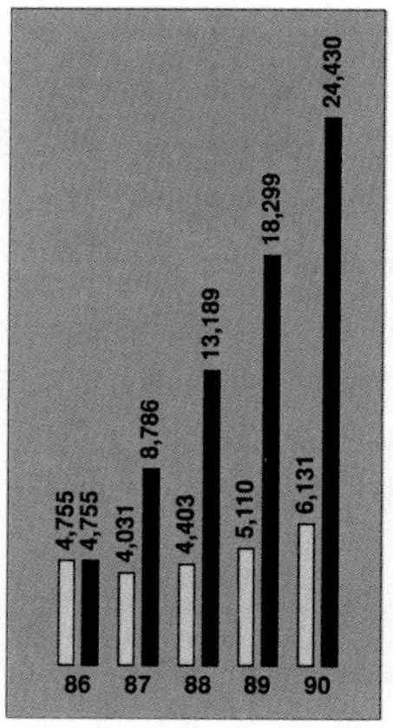

Investment in Plant and Other Property

(In millions)

□ Annual

■ Cumulative for five-year period

the basis for future growth. Adding to an already strong product line in 1990 was the System/390 family, IBM's most comprehensive set of offerings in more than a quarter of a century, the RISC System/6000, a family of high performance workstations well-suited for scientific, engineering, and commercial applications and the PS/1 computer for the home. In addition, new entry-level models of the Application System/400 and high-end models of the Personal System/2, as well as new software products, were introduced in 1990.

Over the past five years, IBM has invested approximately $24 billion in plant and other property, including $6.1 billion in 1990. This continual upgrading of facilities is required to maintain technological leadership, improve productivity and meet customer demand. Management intends to continue prudent investments consistent with these requirements.

In addition to software development costs included in research, development and engineering expense, IBM invested $1.9 billion in capitalized production costs of software products in 1990. Software revenue in 1990 was $10.0 billion, an increase of 18.1 percent over 1989. Increasing investments in software products reflect management's view that this activity will continue to show significant growth. Amortization of capitalized software costs amounted to $1.1 billion in 1990.

Investments and sundry assets increased 27.0 percent in 1990 to $17.3 billion. This increase is primarily due to the success of the financing business which has expanded significantly around the world. The long-term net investment in sales-type leases was $11.2 billion at December 31, 1990, and $8.4 billion at year-end 1989. This represents a 33.8 percent increase following a 29.5 percent increase in 1989 over 1988. Investments and sundry assets also increased as a result of growth in prepaid pension costs of 59.5 percent over the previous year. This increase was primarily due to recognized performance on pension plan assets exceeding the service and interest costs for the year. Prepaid pension cost amounted to $1.0 billion at December 31, 1990.

Working capital was $13.6 billion at December 31, 1990, compared with $14.2 billion at December 31, 1989.

Increased accounts receivable reflects higher levels of sales in December 1990 compared with the same period in 1989, and increased amounts due in 1991 on sales-type lease investments. Inventories increased $645 million, primarily due to currency translation adjustments. Inventories in the United States declined 12.6 percent.

Short-term debt increased $1.7 billion to $7.6 billion at December 31, 1990. In addition to borrowing for normal short-term obligations, the company continued to utilize short-term commercial paper and a money market account for IBM employees as sources of funding to finance customers' leases of IBM equipment. Deferred income increased $1.1 billion in 1990 primarily as a result of increases in unexpired maintenance agreements and new software agreements. These amounts, which are derived primarily from Europe, will be recognized in income over the life of the agreements.

Long-term debt increased $1.1 billion in 1990 to $11.9 billion. This increase is also largely attributable to financing of customers' leasing of IBM equipment.

Deferred income taxes increased 17.7 percent in 1990. This increase is primarily related to the practice in most countries of treating capital leases as operating leases for income tax purposes, as well as the partial reversal of the deferred taxes related to the U.S. restructuring charge recorded in 1989.

MANAGEMENT DISCUSSION

On a consolidated basis, the 1990 and 1989 debt-to-equity ratios were 46 percent and 43 percent, respectively. Consolidated financial statements present important information about the company as a whole. However, management believes that an evaluation of debt/equity relationships requires a separation of the financing and non-financing components of the business, since consolidated statements do not reflect the different leveraging characteristics inherent in these businesses.

The value of assets in finance subsidiaries at December 31, 1990, and December 31, 1989, was $16.0 billion and $12.7 billion, respectively. These amounts are shown in the statement of financial position of finance subsidiaries on page 46. IBM's consolidated balance sheet, however, included another $8.4 billion in 1990 and $6.2 billion in 1989 of financing assets in countries in which the company does not maintain a separate finance subsidiary. Total financing assets, therefore, at year-end 1990 and 1989, were $24.4 billion and $18.9 billion, respectively.

It is industry practice to leverage financing assets with the relationship of debt and equity between 4 and 11 to 1, depending on the nature and quality of the assets. If IBM's debt was allocated to its financing business by applying the more conservative of these relationships, the non-financing component of IBM's business would have a debt-to-equity ratio of 8 percent in 1990 and 11 percent in 1989.

In late 1989, the Board of Directors authorized the company to purchase shares of its capital stock in amounts not to exceed $5,000 million. There is no specific date for completing these purchases. At December 31, 1990, $4,472 million of the authorization remained. Shares purchased under the program have been and will continue to be retired and restored to the status of authorized but unissued shares. Also during 1990, the company continued open-market acquisition of shares to meet most requirements of IBM's stockholder and employee stock plans.

Management expects that the funds required to continue the level of investments necessary to ensure the company's competitiveness, as well as funds used to purchase IBM capital stock from time to time, will be largely generated from normal operations. To the extent that amounts generated from operations need to be supplemented by borrowing, it will be done consistent with management's intent to continue to maintain the highest quality rating of the company's indebtedness.

At December 31, 1990, the company and its subsidiaries had available unused lines of credit with a number of U.S. and non-U.S. banks permitting borrowings, primarily short-term, up to an aggregate of approximately $6,800 million.

Management's confidence in IBM's prospects for growth is founded in the company's worldwide presence, its financial resources, its investments in technology and, above all, the talent, loyalty and energy of the people of IBM.

International Business Machines Corporation and Subsidiary Companies

Significant Accounting Policies

Principles of Consolidation The consolidated financial statements include the accounts of International Business Machines Corporation and its U.S. and non-U.S. subsidiary companies. Investments in joint ventures and other companies in which IBM does not have control, but has the ability to exercise significant influence over operating and financial policies (generally greater than 20% ownership) are accounted for by the equity method. Other investments are accounted for by the cost method.

Translation of Non-U.S. Currency Amounts For non-U.S. subsidiaries which operate in a local currency environment, assets and liabilities are translated to U.S. dollars at year-end exchange rates. Income and expense items are translated at average rates of exchange prevailing during the year. Translation adjustments are accumulated in a separate component of stockholders' equity. For non-U.S. subsidiaries and branches which operate in U.S. dollars or whose economic environment is highly inflationary, inventories and plant, rental machines and other property are translated at approximate rates prevailing when acquired. All other assets and liabilities are translated at year-end exchange rates. Inventories charged to cost of sales and depreciation are remeasured at historical rates. All other income and expense items are translated at average rates of exchange prevailing during the year. Gains and losses which result from remeasurement are included in earnings.

Revenue Revenue is recognized from sales or sales-type leases when the product is shipped, from software when the program is shipped or as monthly license fees accrue, from support services (primarily maintenance services) over the contractual period or as the services are performed, from rentals under operating leases in the month in which they accrue, and from financing at level rates of return over the term of the lease or receivable.

Software Costs related to the conceptual formulation and design of licensed programs are expensed as research and development. Costs incurred subsequent to establishment of technological feasibility to produce the finished product are generally capitalized. The annual amortization of the capitalized amounts is the greater of the amount computed based on the estimated revenue distribution over the products' revenue-producing lives or the straight-line method, but not in excess of six years. Costs to support or service licensed programs are charged against income as incurred or when related revenue is recognized, whichever occurs first.

Depreciation Plant, rental machines and other property are carried at cost and depreciated over their estimated useful lives using the straight-line method.

NOTES TO CONSOLIDATED FINANCIAL STATEMENTS

International Business Machines Corporation and Subsidiary Companies

Significant Accounting Policies (continued)

Goodwill Goodwill is amortized on a straight-line basis over the periods estimated to be benefited, currently not exceeding five years.

Retirement Plans and Other Postretirement Benefits Current service costs of retirement plans are accrued currently. Prior service costs resulting from improvements in the plans are amortized over the average remaining service period of employees expected to receive benefits. Postretirement health care and life insurance benefits are fully accrued, principally at retirement.

Selling Expenses Selling expenses are charged against income as incurred.

Income Taxes Income tax expense is based on reported earnings before income taxes. Deferred income taxes reflect the impact of temporary differences between the amount of assets and liabilities recognized for financial reporting purposes and such amounts recognized for tax purposes. In accordance with Statement of Financial Accounting Standards (SFAS) 96, which the company adopted in 1988, these deferred taxes are measured by applying currently enacted tax laws. Deferred investment tax credits are being amortized as a reduction of income tax expense over the average useful life of the applicable classes of property.

Inventories Raw materials, finished goods and work in process are stated at the lower of average cost or market.

Cash Equivalents All highly liquid investments with a maturity of three months or less at date of purchase are considered to be cash equivalents.

International Business Machines Corporation and Subsidiary Companies

Non-U.S. Operations	1990	1989	1988
(Dollars in millions)			
At end of year:			
Net assets employed:			
Current assets	$24,337	$20,361	$20,005
Current liabilities	15,917	12,124	11,481
Working capital	8,420	8,237	8,524
Plant, rental machines and other property, net	11,628	9,879	9,354
Investments and other assets	9,077	6,822	5,251
	29,125	24,938	23,129
Long-term debt	5,060	3,358	2,340
Other liabilities	2,699	2,607	2,505
Deferred income taxes	2,381	1,814	1,580
	10,140	7,779	6,425
Net assets employed	$18,985	$17,159	$16,704
Number of employees	168,283	167,291	163,904
For the year:			
Revenue	$41,886	$36,965	$34,361
Earnings before income taxes	$ 7,844	$ 7,496	$ 7,088
Provision for income taxes	3,270	3,388	3,009
Net earnings	$ 4,574	$ 4,108	$ 4,079†
Investment in plant, rental machines and other property	$ 3,020	$ 2,514	$ 2,389

† 1988 net earnings before cumulative effect of accounting change for income taxes.

Non-U.S. subsidiaries which operate in a local currency environment account for approximately 90% of the company's non-U.S. revenue. The remaining 10% of the company's non-U.S. revenue is from subsidiaries and branches which operate in U.S. dollars or whose economic environment is highly inflationary.

As the value of the dollar weakens, net assets recorded in local currencies translate into more U.S. dollars than they would have at the previous year's rates. Conversely, as the dollar becomes stronger, net assets recorded in local currencies translate into fewer U.S. dollars than they would have at the previous year's rates. The translation adjustments, resulting from the translation of net assets, amounted to $3,266 million at December 31, 1990, $1,698 million at December 31, 1989, and $1,917 million at December 31, 1988. The changes in translation adjustments since the end of 1988 are a reflection of the strengthening of the dollar in 1989 and the weakening of the dollar in 1990.

Undistributed earnings of non-U.S. subsidiaries included in consolidated retained earnings amounted to $14,388 million at December 31, 1990, $13,207 million at December 31, 1989, and $12,374 million at December 31, 1988. These earnings, which reflect full provision for non-U.S. income taxes, are indefinitely reinvested in non-U.S. operations or will be remitted substantially free of additional tax. Accordingly,

NOTES TO CONSOLIDATED FINANCIAL STATEMENTS

International Business Machines Corporation and Subsidiary Companies

no material provision has been made for taxes that might be payable upon remittance of such earnings. It is extremely improbable that all these earnings would be remitted to the U.S. Nevertheless, SFAS 96, "Accounting for Income Taxes," requires disclosure of the amount of withholding taxes that would be payable were this unlikely event to occur. Therefore, in response to that requirement, it is estimated that such withholding taxes would be as much as $1,200 million.

Finance Subsidiaries

The company's wholly owned finance subsidiaries consist of IBM Credit Corporation and several non-U.S. finance subsidiaries. IBM Credit Corporation offers a wide range of financing services for IBM customers and business partners. Financing products, which are directly related to the sale of IBM products, include leases, installment payment loans and remarketer financing. The non-U.S. finance subsidiaries offer lease financing of selected IBM products and in some cases finance installment receivables.

The following schedule depicts the combined financial information for these finance subsidiaries, of which IBM Credit Corporation accounts for more than 70% of the net earnings. These wholly owned subsidiaries are consolidated in the accompanying financial statements. Financing activity in countries in which the company does not have a finance subsidiary is not included.

Financial position at December 31:	1990	1989
(Dollars in millions)		
Assets:		
Cash and cash equivalents	$ 307	$ 315
Receivables—net	3,421	2,796
Net investment in capital leases	9,702	7,350
Equipment under operating leases—net	2,082	2,030
Other	499	246
Total Assets	$16,011	$12,737

	1990	1989*
(Dollars in millions)		
Liabilities and Stockholder's Equity:		
Short-term debt	$ 4,743	$ 3,482
Deferred taxes and accruals	1,355	1,214
Due to IBM and affiliates	2,641	1,648
Long-term debt	6,006	5,291
Stockholder's equity	1,266	1,102
Total Liabilities and Stockholder's Equity	$16,011	$12,737

Earnings for the years ended December 31:	1990	1989	1988
(Dollars in millions)			
Financing and other income	$1,992	$1,332	$ 914
Interest and other expenses	1,649	1,098	791
Provision for income taxes	112	75	26
Net earnings	$ 231	$ 159	$ 97†

*Reclassified to conform with 1990 presentation.

† 1988 net earnings before cumulative effect of accounting change for income taxes.

International Business Machines Corporation and Subsidiary Companies

Restructuring and Other Actions In December 1989, the company announced a series of actions to reduce costs, expenses and structure.

As a result, the 1989 earnings include a charge, recorded in the fourth quarter, of $2,420 million ($1,500 million after tax or $2.58 per share). $1,335 million of this relates to the costs of facility consolidations and capacity reductions and changes in the valuation and recovery periods of special investments. This amount is included in selling, general and administrative expense. Costs of $500 million associated with employee separations and relocations are also included in selling, general and administrative expense.

Costs of $585 million represent a charge related to the adoption of new guidelines to provide for the earlier recognition of costs in both hardware and software due to the pace of technological change and the company's success in shortening its product cycles. These charges are included in research, development and engineering expenses and in cost of software.

In 1988, $870 million was included in selling, general and administrative expense for manufacturing and headquarters consolidations.

Marketable Securities At December 31:	1990	1989
(Dollars in millions)		
U.S. government securities	$ 92	$ 201
Time deposits and other bank obligations	373	419
Non-U.S. government securities and other fixed-term obligations	233	641
Total	$ 698	$ 1,261
Market value	$ 698	$ 1,263

Inventories At December 31:	1990	1989
(Dollars in millions)		
Current inventories:		
Finished goods	$ 2,851	$ 2,915
Work in process	7,051	6,394
Raw materials	206	154
Total current inventories	10,108	9,463
Work in process included in plant, rental machines and other property	1,498	1,364
Total inventories	$11,606	$10,827

NOTES TO CONSOLIDATED FINANCIAL STATEMENTS

International Business Machines Corporation and Subsidiary Companies

Plant, Rental Machines and Other Property At December 31:

(Dollars in millions)	1990	1989
Land and land improvements	$ 1,645	$ 1,507
Buildings	13,792	12,333
Plant, laboratory and office equipment	35,155	31,064
	50,592	44,904
Less: Accumulated depreciation	24,916	22,017
	25,676	22,887
Rental machines and parts	3,067	3,506
Less: Accumulated depreciation	1,502	1,450
	1,565	2,056
Total	$27,241	$24,943

Investments and Sundry Assets At December 31:

(Dollars in millions)	1990	1989
Net investment in sales-type leases†	$16,914	$12,728
Less: Current portion (net) classified as notes and accounts receivable—trade	5,682	4,332
	11,232	8,396
Prepaid pension cost	1,045	655
Installment payment receivables	896	912
Investments in business alliances	703	660
Mortgage investments	529	509
Goodwill, less accumulated amortization (1990, $406; 1989, $283)	383	392
Other investments and sundry assets*	2,520	2,099
Total	$17,308	$13,623

†These leases relate to IBM equipment and are for terms generally ranging from three to five years. Net investment in sales-type leases includes unguaranteed residual values of approximately $1,350 million and $1,100 million at December 31, 1990 and 1989, and is reflected net of unearned income at these dates of approximately $3,600 million and $2,600 million, respectively.

*Includes, at cost, an investment of $400 million in 7.35% preferred stock of MCI Communications Corporation, which is not convertible, nor is it planned to be publicly traded. MCI has the option to redeem all or part of this issue at any time.

International Business Machines Corporation and Subsidiary Companies

Long-Term Debt At December 31:

(Dollars in millions)

		1990	
Debentures:			
7⅞% convertible, subordinated†	2004	$ 1,254	$ 1,254
8⅜%	2019	750	750
9⅜% (with sinking fund payments to 2003)	2004	238	300
Notes:			
5¾% to 7⅝%	1991-1993	354	854
7¾% to 8⅞%	1991-1995	2,370	2,470
9% to 10¼%	1991-2000	2,300	2,303
Medium-term note program: 7.5% to 15.0%	1991-2008	890	1,057
Other U.S. dollars: 5.0% to 14.7%	1991-2012	508	474
		8,664	9,462
Other currencies (average interest rate at December 31, 1990, in parentheses):			
Swiss francs (6.8%)	1992-1996	1,125	317
French francs (10.1%)	1991-2002	736	486
Canadian dollars (11.4%)	1992-1995	693	443
European currency units (9.0%)	1992-1995	648	599
Australian dollars (14.5%)	1991-1993	580	539
Japanese yen (5.5%)	1991-2019	532	489
Other (10.6%)	1991-2011	684	379
		13,662	12,714
Less: Net unamortized discount		15	6
		13,647	12,708
Less: Current maturities		1,704	1,883
Total		$11,943	$10,825

Annual maturity and sinking fund requirements in millions of dollars on long-term debt outstanding at December 31, 1990, are as follows:
1991, $1,704; 1992, $3,658; 1993, $2,277; 1994, $786; 1995, $1,581; 1996 and beyond, $3,656.

†The 7⅞% convertible subordinated debentures are unsecured subordinated obligations of IBM, which are convertible into IBM capital stock at a conversion price of $153.6563 per share. They are redeemable, at the option of the company, as of November 1990 at a price of 103.150% of the principal amount, and at decreasing prices thereafter. Sinking fund payments starting in 1994 are intended to retire 75% of the debentures prior to maturity. There were no conversions of debentures in 1990.

NOTES TO CONSOLIDATED FINANCIAL STATEMENTS

International Business Machines Corporation and Subsidiary Companies

Taxes	1990	1989	1988
(Dollars in millions)			
Earnings before income taxes:			
U.S. operations	$ 2,359	$ (851)	$1,945
Non-U.S. operations	7,844	7,496	7,088
	$10,203	$6,645	$9,033
Provision for income taxes:			
U.S. operations	$ 913	$ (501)	$ 533
Non-U.S. operations	3,270	3,388	3,009
	4,183	2,887	3,542
Social security, real estate, personal property and other taxes	3,017	2,562	2,528
Total	$ 7,200	$5,449	$6,070
The components of the provision for income taxes are as follows:			
U.S. Federal:			
Current	$ 379	$ 476	$ 79
Deferred	(44)	(1,247)	(86)
Net deferred investment tax credits	(95)	(101)	(125)
	240	(872)	(132)
Non-U.S.:			
Current	3,375	3,025	3,562
Deferred	446	824	87
	3,821	3,849	3,649
U.S. State and local:			
Current	16	107	12
Deferred	106	(197)	13
	122	(90)	25
Total provision	$ 4,183	$2,887	$3,542

In 1988, the company implemented Statement of Financial Accounting Standards (SFAS) 96. This standard calls for adjustment of deferred tax assets and liabilities whenever there is a change in enacted tax rates, with a corresponding adjustment being reflected in income tax expense for that period. Previous rules called for recording these assets and liabilities at the current rate, with no subsequent adjustment for tax rate changes.

The cumulative effect of adopting SFAS 96 for the periods ended prior to January 1, 1988, which amounted to a benefit of $315 million, has been included in 1988 net earnings.

Deferred income taxes reflect the impact of temporary differences between the amount of assets and liabilities recognized for financial reporting purposes and such amounts recognized for tax purposes. The principal items making up the deferred tax provision in 1990 included $573 million related to the partial turnaround of deferred tax assets arising from the 1989 U.S. restructuring charge, $343 million for sales-type leases and installment sales, $276 million for deferred software costs, and $173 million for retirement benefits. These amounts were offset by $205 million of deferred tax benefits associated with the alternative minimum tax and $197 million for depreciation. In 1989, the principal items included $904 million related to the restructuring charge and $159 million for deferred inventory overhead, offset by $339 million for sales-type leases and installment sales and $230 million for deferred software costs. In 1988, the principal items included $283 million for sales-type leases and installment sales and $175 million for deferred software costs, offset by $182 million of deferred tax benefits associated with the alternative minimum tax.

Under the rules of SFAS 96, no financial recognition is allowed for net deferred tax assets in excess of the amount that could be recovered as income tax refunds through existing loss carryback or carryforward provisions. Consequently, at December 31, 1990, the company had unrecognized deferred tax assets of approximately $110 million, most of which have carryforwards for substantial periods. The company is also evaluating the potential realization of other deferred tax assets emanating from the continuing transformation of the company. In addition, the company has approximately $190 million of deferred investment tax credits for financial reporting purposes, which will reduce tax expense in future years. For tax purposes, the company has available tax credit carryforwards of approximately $700 million, the majority of which are available indefinitely and may be used to offset future taxes.

The consolidated effective income tax rate was 41.0% in 1990, 43.4% in 1989, and 39.2% in 1988. In 1990, 1989, and 1988, the higher effective tax rate on earnings of non-U.S. operations accounted for 5.9, 12.6, and 6.6 percentage points, respectively, of the difference between the effective rate and the U.S. federal statutory rate of 34.0%.

NOTES TO CONSOLIDATED FINANCIAL STATEMENTS

International Business Machines Corporation and Subsidiary Companies

Research, Development and Engineering Research, development and engineering expenses amounted to $6,554 million in 1990, $6,827 million in 1989 and $5,925 million in 1988.

Included in these amounts were expenditures of $4,914 million in 1990, $5,201 million in 1989 and $4,419 million in 1988 for a broad program of research and development activities covering basic scientific research in a variety of fields and the application of scientific advances to the development of new and improved products and their uses. The 1989 amount included $375 million associated with the U.S. restructuring. In addition, expenditures for product-related engineering amounted to $1,640 million, $1,626 million and $1,506 million for the same three years.

Interest Cost Interest on borrowings of the company and its subsidiaries amounted to $2,425 million in 1990, $1,853 million in 1989 and $1,321 million in 1988. Of these amounts, $122 million in 1990, $142 million in 1989 and $93 million in 1988 were capitalized. The remainder was charged to cost of rentals and financing and interest expense.

Lines of Credit At December 31, 1990, the company and its subsidiaries had available unused lines of credit with a number of U.S. and non-U.S. banks permitting borrowings, primarily short-term, up to an aggregate of approximately $6,800 million. Interest rates on borrowings would vary from country to country depending on local market conditions.

Rental Expense and Lease Commitments Rental expense, including amounts charged to inventories and fixed assets, amounted to $1,903 million in 1990, $1,765 million in 1989 and $1,566 million in 1988.

Minimum rental commitments, in millions of dollars, under noncancelable leases for 1991 and thereafter are as follows: 1991, $1,558; 1992, $1,342; 1993, $1,161; 1994, $967; 1995, $850; and after 1995, $3,938. These leases are principally for the rental of office premises.

Other Liabilities Other liabilities consist principally of indemnity and retirement plan reserves for non-U.S. employees.

Financial Instruments In March 1990, the Financial Accounting Standards Board issued Statement of Financial Accounting Standards (SFAS) 105. This statement requires disclosure of information about financial instruments with off-balance-sheet risk and about financial instruments with concentrations of credit risk.

As of December 31, 1990, off-balance-sheet risk and concentrations of credit risk were immaterial to the accompanying financial statements. In the normal course of business, the company enters into a variety of forward contracts, options and swaps in order to limit its exposure to loss due to adverse fluctuations in foreign currency exchange and interest rates. These instruments are executed with credit-worthy financial institutions and virtually all foreign currency contracts are denominated in currencies of major industrial countries. As foreign currency exchange rates and interest rates fluctuate, gains and losses on these contracts serve as hedges in that they offset losses and gains that would otherwise impact the company's financial results. Costs associated with entering into such contracts are amortized over the life of the instrument and are not material to the company's financial results.

International Business Machines Corporation and Subsidiary Companies

Retirement Plans The company and its subsidiaries have retirement plans covering substantially all employees. The total cost of all plans for 1990, 1989 and 1988 was $94 million, $328 million and $460 million, respectively.

Pension cost in 1990 was lower than in 1989 principally due to the growth in the expected return on plan assets exceeding the growth in annual interest and service cost. Pension cost in 1989 was lower than in 1988 principally due to changes in actuarial assumptions in the U.S. and several non-U.S. plans, partially offset by amendments to the U.S. plan.

Annual cost is determined using the Projected Unit Credit actuarial method. Prior service cost is amortized on a straight-line basis over the average remaining service period of employees expected to receive benefits. An assumption is made for modified career average plans that the average earnings base period will be updated to the years prior to retirement.

It is the company's practice to fund amounts for pensions sufficient to meet the minimum requirements set forth in applicable employee benefit and tax laws, and such additional amounts the company may determine to be appropriate from time to time. The assets of the various plans include corporate equities, government securities, corporate debt securities and income-producing real estate.

The tables on page 54 provide information on the status of the U.S. retirement plan, and selected non-U.S. plans which represent approximately 98% of the total non-U.S. accumulated benefit obligations.

U.S. Plan: U.S. regular and part-time employees are covered by a noncontributory plan which is funded by company contributions to an irrevocable trust fund, which is held for the sole benefit of employees. Monthly retirement benefits generally represent the greater of a fixed amount per year of service, or a percent of career compensation. For plan purposes, annual compensation before January 1, 1991, is defined as the average annual compensation paid for the years 1981 through 1990. Effective January 1, 1989, benefits become vested upon the completion of five years of service. Prior to January 1, 1989, benefits became vested upon completion of 10 years of service. The number of individuals receiving benefits at December 31, 1990, and December 31, 1989, was 52,895 and 44,701, respectively.

The expected long-term rate of return on plan assets used in the calculation of net periodic pension cost was 9% for 1990, 1989 and 1988. Measurement of the 1990 and 1989 projected benefit obligation was based on an 8½% discount rate and a 5% long-term rate of compensation increase.

Non-U.S. Plans: Most subsidiaries and branches outside the U.S. have retirement plans covering substantially all employees, under which funds are deposited under various fiduciary-type arrangements, annuities are purchased under group contracts, or reserves are provided. Retirement benefits are based on years of service and the employee's compensation, generally during a fixed number of years immediately prior to retirement.

NOTES TO CONSOLIDATED FINANCIAL STATEMENTS

International Business Machines Corporation and Subsidiary Companies

The ranges of assumptions used for the non-U.S. plans reflect the different economic environments within the various countries. The expected long-term rates of return on plan assets used in the calculation of net periodic pension cost ranged from 5% to 12% in both 1990 and 1989 and from 5% to 11% in 1988. Measurement of the 1990 and 1989 projected benefit obligation was based on discount rates ranging from 4½% to 10% and long-term rates of compensation increase ranging from 3% to 8½%.

The funded status at December 31 was as follows:	U.S. Plan		Non-U.S. Plans	
	1990	1989	1990	1989
(Dollars in millions)				
Actuarial present value of benefit obligations:				
Vested benefit obligation	$(13,112)	$(11,642)	$ (9,022)	$ (6,892)
Accumulated benefit obligation	$(13,146)	$(11,708)	$(10,347)	$ (8,056)
Projected benefit obligation	$(17,091)	$(15,451)	$(14,338)	$(11,582)
Plan assets at fair value	22,225	22,867	12,382	11,231
Projected benefit obligation less than (in excess of) plan assets	5,134	7,416	(1,956)	(351)
Unrecognized net (gain) loss	(2,665)	(4,902)	459	(1,108)
Unrecognized prior service cost	1,323	1,092	332	241
Unrecognized net asset established at January 1, 1986	(2,747)	(2,951)	(152)	(163)
Prepaid (accrued) pension cost recognized in the statement of financial position	$ 1,045	$ 655	$ (1,317)	$ (1,381)

Net periodic pension cost for the years ended December 31 included the following components:

	U.S. Plan			Non-U.S. Plans		
	1990	1989	1988	1990	1989	1988
(Dollars in millions)						
Service cost— benefits earned during the period	$ 573	$ 562	$ 579	$ 575	$ 501	$ 482
Interest cost on the projected benefit obligation	1,309	1,194	1,120	837	679	648
Return on plan assets—						
Actual	(160)	(3,950)	(2,058)	665	(1,315)	(1,003)
Deferred	(1,859)	2,214	456	(1,644)	564	340
Net amortizations	(253)	(174)	(152)	(5)	2	5
Net periodic pension cost	$ (390)	$ (154)	$ (55)	$ 428	$ 431	$ 472
Total net periodic pension cost for all non-U.S. plans				$ 484	$ 482	$ 515

International Business Machines Corporation and Subsidiary Companies

Postretirement Benefits The company and its U.S. subsidiaries have medical, dental and life insurance plans for retirees, the estimated cost of which is fully accrued, principally at retirement. This cost amounted to $96 million, $303 million and $105 million in 1990, 1989 and 1988, respectively.

Cost was lower in 1990 primarily because of amounts recorded in 1989 as a result of the announced U.S. restructuring. Cost in 1989 was higher than in 1988 primarily for the same reason.

It is the company's practice to fund amounts for postretirement benefits, with an independent trustee, as deemed appropriate from time to time.

Certain of the company's non-U.S. subsidiaries have similar plans for retirees. However, many retirees outside the U.S. are covered by government-sponsored and administered programs. As a result, the cost of company-sponsored programs outside the U.S. is not significant.

In December 1990, the Financial Accounting Standards Board issued Statement of Financial Accounting Standards (SFAS) No. 106, "Employers' Accounting for Postretirement Benefits Other Than Pensions," which requires that the cost of these benefits be recognized in the financial statements over an employee's active working career. The prevalent practice in industry is to account for these costs on a pay-as-you-go (cash) basis. However, the company's current accounting practice of accruing at retirement, along with its funding policy, will significantly mitigate the financial impact of adopting the new standard.

Adoption is required no later than 1993 for U.S. plans and by 1995 for non-U.S. plans, although earlier adoption is encouraged. Adopting the new standard will create a previously unrecognized obligation covering prior years. This transition obligation may be recognized in future financial statements in one of two ways: (1) by immediate recognition through a cumulative adjustment in the statement of earnings, or (2) on a delayed basis, by amortizing the obligation on a straight-line basis over the average remaining service period of active plan participants.

If the company implements this standard using the delayed recognition basis, the impact on net earnings is expected to be immaterial. If implemented by immediate recognition of the transition obligation, the impact on net earnings will be material in the period adopted.

Stock Purchase Plan In April 1990, stockholders approved the addition of two million shares of capital stock to the 1986 IBM Employees Stock Purchase Plan. Stockholders also approved a new five-year plan, effective July 1, 1990, which authorizes up to fifty million shares of capital stock to be reserved for issuance under the plan. The plan enables employees who are not participants in IBM's stock option programs to purchase IBM's capital stock through payroll deductions of up to 10% of eligible compensation. The price an employee pays for a share of stock is 85% of the average market price on the date the employee has accumulated enough money to buy a share.

During 1990, employees purchased 7,170,973 shares, all of which were treasury shares, for which $679 million was paid to IBM. At December 31, 1990, 47,208,470 shares remain available for purchase.

Stock Repurchase Programs Under programs for purchasing IBM stock, 3,842,924 shares were repurchased during 1990 at a cost of $415 million, 16,085,900 shares were repurchased during 1989 at a cost of $1,759 million and 8,611,396 shares were repurchased during 1988 at a cost of $992 million. The repurchased shares were retired and restored to the status of authorized but unissued shares.

In late 1989, the Board of Directors authorized

NOTES TO CONSOLIDATED FINANCIAL STATEMENTS

International Business Machines Corporation and Subsidiary Companies

the company to purchase from time to time shares of its capital stock not to exceed $5,000 million. At December 31, 1990, $4,472 million of that authorization remained.

Long-Term Performance Plan The IBM 1989 Long-Term Performance Plan provides for incentive awards to be made to officers and other key employees. The plan is administered by the Executive Compensation Committee of the Board of Directors. The Committee determines the type of award to be granted, which may include stock, a stock option, stock appreciation right (SAR), cash or any combination thereof. The number of shares which are available for granting in each year is limited to .85% of IBM's outstanding capital stock as of December 31 of the preceding year. Any unused amount is carried forward and made available for granting in the subsequent year. Prior to 1989, stock options were issued under the IBM 1986 and predecessor Stock Option Plans.

Options allow the purchase of IBM's capital stock at 100% of the market price on the date of grant and have a maximum duration of 10 years. Payment by the optionee upon exercise of an option may be made using IBM stock as well as cash.

SARs offer eligible optionees the alternative of electing not to exercise the related stock option, but to receive payment in cash and/or stock, equivalent to the difference between the option price and the average market price of IBM stock on the date of exercising the right.

The following table summarizes option activity during 1990 and 1989:

Number of Shares Under Option

	1990	1989
Balance at January 1	20,909,547	17,674,645
Options granted	5,309,140	4,629,537
Options exercised	(641,126)	(765,301)
Options terminated	(498,977)	(551,675)
Options cancelled – SARs exercised	(92,765)	(77,659)
Balance at December 31	24,985,819	20,909,547
Exercisable at December 31	14,761,217	12,404,456

The options exercised were at an average option price of $64.02 per share and $64.66 per share in 1990 and 1989, respectively. The shares under option at December 31, 1990, were at option prices ranging from $55.75 to $159.50 per share. The shares under option at December 31, 1989, were at option prices ranging from $55.25 to $159.50 per share.

There were 835,105 and 1,214,110 unused shares carried forward and made available for granting in the subsequent year as of December 31, 1990 and 1989, respectively.

Segment Information

IBM is in the field of advanced information technology. The company operates primarily in the single industry segment which offers customers solutions that incorporate information processing systems, software, communications systems and other products and services. This segment represents more than 90% of consolidated revenue, operating profit and identifiable assets. The schedule on the next page shows revenue by industry segments and by classes of similar products or services within the information technology segment.

Financial information by geographic area is summarized on page 58 to provide a better understanding of IBM's operations. Material interdependencies and overlaps exist among IBM's operating units and, therefore, the information may not be indicative of the financial results of, or investments in, the reported areas were they independent organizations.

International Business Machines Corporation and Subsidiary Companies

Revenue by Industry Segments and Classes of Similar Products or Services

	Consolidated			U.S. Only		
	1990	1989†	1988	1990	1989†	1988
(Dollars in millions)						
Information technology:						
Processors*	$16,433	$16,236	$15,077	$ 5,744	$ 5,941	$ 5,586
Workstations:						
Personal systems*	9,644	8,409	6,934	3,887	3,667	3,004
Other workstations	4,312	4,169	4,550	1,492	1,509	1,745
Peripherals	13,190	11,458	11,280	5,179	4,309	4,764
Software	9,952	8,424	7,927	3,639	3,139	2,925
Maintenance services	7,768	7,070	7,347	2,886	2,959	3,102
Other	5,791	4,938	4,470	2,377	2,215	2,103
	67,090	60,704	57,585	25,204	23,739	23,229
Federal systems	1,928	2,006	2,065	1,928	2,006	2,065
Other business	—	—	31	—	—	26
Total	$69,018	$62,710	$59,681	$27,132	$25,745	$25,320

†Reclassified to conform with 1990 presentation.
*Excludes peripheral functions not embedded, software and maintenance.

While IBM operates primarily in a single industry segment and manages its worldwide business as such, revenue has been categorized into major classes of product.

For purposes of classifying similar information technology products, user programmable equipment having the capability of manipulating data arithmetically or logically and making calculations, in a manner directly addressable by the user through the operation of a stored program, has been classified as processors, except that personal systems are included under workstations. Workstations also include typewriters and other display based terminals. Peripherals include printers, storage and telecommunication devices.

Peripheral functions embedded in processors are classified with processors. Software includes both applications and systems software. Maintenance services consist of separately billed charges for maintenance. Other consists principally of customer solution services, financing revenue and supplies.

Some products logically fit in more than one class and are assigned to a specific class based on a variety of factors. Over time, products tend to overlap, merge into or split from existing classes as a result of changing technologies, market perceptions, and/or customer use. For example, market demand may create requirements for technological enhancements to permit a peripheral product (e.g., printer), to be functionally integrated with a display, a telecommunication device and a processor to form a workstation. Such interchangeability and technological progress tend to make year-to-year comparisons less valid than they would be in an industry less subject to rapid change.

Federal systems consists of specialized information technology products and services primarily for the United States defense, space and other agencies.

Other business consists of training and testing materials for school, home and industrial use offered by Science Research Associates, which was sold by IBM in 1988.

NOTES TO CONSOLIDATED FINANCIAL STATEMENTS

International Business Machines Corporation and Subsidiary Companies

Geographic Areas	1990	1989	1988†
(Dollars in millions)			
United States			
Revenue—Customers	$ 27,132	$25,745	$25,320
Interarea transfers	6,195	5,476	4,951
Total	$ 33,327	$31,221	$30,271
Net earnings	1,459	(325)	1,408
Assets at December 31	43,542	41,635	39,245
Europe/Middle East/Africa			
Revenue—Customers	$ 27,234	$23,170	$21,600
Interarea transfers	976	1,101	955
Total	$ 28,210	$24,271	$22,555
Net earnings	2,977	2,676	2,349
Assets at December 31	30,689	24,732	22,745
Asia Pacific			
Revenue—Customers	$ 9,564	$ 9,202	$ 8,824
Interarea transfers	1,496	1,673	1,837
Total	$ 11,060	$10,875	$10,661
Net earnings	1,151	1,296	1,394
Assets at December 31	8,646	7,666	7,633
Americas			
Revenue—Customers	$ 5,088	$ 4,593	$ 3,937
Interarea transfers	1,615	1,461	1,290
Total	$ 6,703	$ 6,054	$ 5,227
Net earnings	420	173	328
Assets at December 31	6,357	5,395	4,915
Eliminations			
Revenue	$ (10,282)	$ (9,711)	$ (9,033)
Net earnings	13	(62)	12
Assets	(1,666)	(1,694)	(1,501)
Consolidated			
Revenue	$ 69,018	$62,710	$59,681
Net earnings	$ 6,020	$ 3,758	$ 5,491
Assets at December 31	$ 87,568	$77,734	$73,037

†1988 net earnings before cumulative effect of change in accounting for income taxes.

Non-U.S. subsidiaries which operate in a local currency environment account for approximately 90% of the company's non-U. S. revenue. The remaining 10% is from subsidiaries and branches, predominantly in the Americas, which operate in U.S. dollars or whose economic environment is highly inflationary.

In the Europe/Middle East/Africa area, European operations accounted for approximately 95% of revenue in 1990, 1989 and 1988.

Interarea transfers consist principally of completed machines, subassemblies and parts, and software. Machines, subassemblies and parts transfers are generally priced at cost plus an appropriate service charge. Software transfers represent license fees paid by the non-U.S. subsidiaries. The cost and service charges that relate to fixed asset transfers are capitalized and depreciated by the importing area. Interarea accounts receivable, the unamortized portion of service charges, and the net change during the year in unamortized service charges have been eliminated in consolidation.

FIVE-YEAR COMPARISON OF SELECTED FINANCIAL DATA

International Business Machines Corporation and Subsidiary Companies

(Dollars in millions except per share amounts)	1990	1989	1988	1987	1986
For the year					
Revenue	$69,018	$62,710	$59,681	$55,256	$52,160
Net earnings before cumulative effect of accounting change	6,020	3,758	5,491	5,258	4,789
Per share	10.51	6.47	9.27	8.72	7.81
Cumulative effect of change in accounting for income taxes	—	—	315	—	—
Per share	—	—	.53	—	—
Net earnings	6,020	3,758	5,806	5,258	4,789
Per share	10.51	6.47	9.80	8.72	7.81
Cash dividends paid	2,774	2,752	2,609	2,654	2,698
Per share	4.84	4.73	4.40	4.40	4.40
Investment in plant, rental machines and other property	6,548	6,410	5,431	4,312	4,644
Return on stockholders' equity	14.8%	9.6%	14.9%	14.5%	14.4%
At end of year					
Total assets	$87,568	$77,734	$73,037	$70,029	$63,020
Net investment in plant, rental machines and other property	27,241	24,943	23,426	22,967	21,310
Working capital	13,644	14,175	17,956	18,430	15,546
Long-term debt	11,943	10,825	8,518	7,108	6,923
Stockholders' equity	42,832	38,509	39,509	38,263	34,374

SELECTED QUARTERLY DATA

				Per Share		Stock Prices	
(Dollars in millions except per share and stock prices)	Revenue	Gross Profit	Net Earnings	Earnings	Dividends	High	Low
First Quarter	$14,185	$ 7,857	$1,037	$ 1.81	$1.21	$109.38	$ 94.50
Second Quarter	16,495	9,107	1,410	2.45	1.21	122.25	105.00
Third Quarter	15,277	8,600	1,112	1.95	1.21	123.13	96.50
Fourth Quarter	23,061	12,731	2,461	4.30	1.21	116.00	96.25
Total	$69,018	$38,295	$6,020	$10.51	$4.84		
First Quarter	$12,730	$ 7,212	$ 950	$ 1.61	$1.10	$130.88	$107.63
Second Quarter	15,213	8,481	1,340	2.31	1.21	115.75	106.25
Third Quarter	14,305	7,900	877	1.51	1.21	119.38	107.75
Fourth Quarter	20,462	11,416	591	1.04	1.21	109.75	93.38
Total	$62,710	$35,009	$3,758	$ 6.47	$4.73		

There were 789,046 stockholders of record at December 31, 1990. During 1990, stockholders received $2,774 million in cash dividends. The regular quarterly cash dividend payable March 9, 1991 will be at the rate of $1.21 per share. This dividend will be IBM's 304th consecutive quarterly cash dividend.

The stock prices reflect the high and low prices for IBM's capital stock on the New York Stock Exchange composite tape for the last two years.

IBM AND THE COMMUNITY

IBM again led industry in corporate citizenship in 1990, continuing its commitment to affirmative action in the workplace and contributing more than $148 million in cash, equipment and employee expertise in support of educational, social and cultural programs benefiting people around the world.

IBM's affirmative action programs in the United States help ensure minorities, women, persons with disabilities and Vietnam-era and disabled veterans have equal opportunity for employment and advancement within the company. Of the nearly 3,500 employees hired into IBM's operations in the U.S. during 1990, 26.8 percent were minorities and 31.3 percent were women. Minorities and women currently make up 17.6 percent and 29.0 percent, respectively, of the company's U.S. population. In addition, IBM employs about 25,000 Vietnam-era and disabled veterans.

The presence of women and minorities within the company's management structure continued to grow in 1990. At year end, minorities held 12.9 percent of U.S. managerial positions. Women held 20.8 percent. Minorities held 9.8 percent of senior management positions, while women held 13.3 percent.

IBM continued its support of minority owned businesses, purchasing in excess of $195 million in goods and services from more than 950 minority owned firms in 1990. The company also purchased goods and services totaling more than $95 million from more than 1,050 firms owned primarily by women and more than $14 million from 59 organizations with work forces composed predominantly of handicapped workers.

During the year, the company increased its support of programs aimed at enhancing educational achievement of elementary and secondary students, particularly in the fields of language, mathematics, science and computer literacy.

IBM donated more than $22 million to 107 U.S. colleges and universities in all 50 states, Puerto Rico and the District of Columbia to help improve kindergarten-through-12th-grade education through more effective use of technology. A major portion of these grants is aimed at enhancing the training of new and practicing teachers in the use of computer-based coursework, classroom management and networks.

U.S. employees contributed almost $600,000 in the first three months of a new matching grants program, which made possible the purchase of about $3 million in IBM equipment and courseware for K-12 schools.

In Canada, the company committed $2.1 million in cash, equipment and services to support a project to encourage and motivate increased mathematics and science literacy among kindergarten-through-12th-grade students. The project, which involves Canada's provincial ministries of education and several universities, will focus on developing enhanced teacher training programs and establishing model mathematics and science education classrooms.

The company also continued its efforts to support programs that enhance the work skills of unemployed people around the globe. A new job training center in Argentina, in a partnership with the Ministry of Labor, involves considerable IBM employee volunteer effort. In the United Kingdom, IBM is participating in centers in Nottingham and Bristol that also offer training in computer skills to the unemployed.

In partnerships with IBM customers and institutions that care for the blind, IBM Brazil has helped to establish courses that train visually impaired persons to become computer programmers.

In the United States, literacy programs are being

offered at job training centers serving economically disadvantaged persons who need to improve their reading skills. IBM now sponsors 95 such centers in the United States. These centers have graduated more than 40,000 people since the initiative was undertaken in 1968. More than 80 percent of the graduates have been placed in jobs.

IBM demonstrated its continued support for persons with disabilities in 1990 with the announcement that it would make $4.5 million in computer systems available to federally funded disabilities support centers being established throughout the United States. Under this program, personal computers and software will be loaned at no charge to agencies and non-profit organizations designated by states and U.S. territories to operate the centers. The computers will be used to coordinate resources, answer telephone inquiries and demonstrate computer technology solutions that assist people with disabilities.

IBM Mexico signed an agreement with the Health Ministry, the Mexican Foundation for Health and the National Institute for Human Communication to assist the estimated two million Mexicans with hearing and speech problems. Under the agreement, the company will create a laboratory project to support speech therapy with computer-based systems. The project is expected to double the number of patients that can be assisted by professional therapists.

In Japan, IBM employees and their families assist local organizations for the blind to translate books, magazines and newspaper articles into braille using computers and software programs developed by a blind employee of IBM Japan.

IBM Japan recently launched new programs designed to promote company citizenship by offering employees involved in non-profit organizations paid holidays or leaves of absence to pursue their volunteer activities. The company also will consider providing assistance to non-profit organizations in which IBM Japan employees or retirees participate.

IBM maintains its keen interest and commitment to the environment through a variety of projects around the world. IBM France, for example, working in partnership with the Ministry of the Environment, has donated computer equipment and software to seven national parks over the last five years.

In Germany, IBM has provided a computer network to monitor and evaluate water quality data on the 600-mile Elbe River, which is heavily polluted by contaminants that flow into the North Sea. Information from the study will be used to help reduce pollution by 50 percent by 1995. An IBM employee on loan will manage the project for the next five years.

IBM Australia and the Zoological Parks Board of New South Wales have established the IBM Conservation Award to recognize significant achievements in conserving the natural environment. Success in scientific research, application of technology to environmental issues, public education and community programs to encourage care for the environment are eligible for this award.

APPENDIX

K

Financial Statements (excluding footnotes) from the Annual Reports of:

Federal Express Corporation
Lands' End, Inc.
McDonald's Corporation

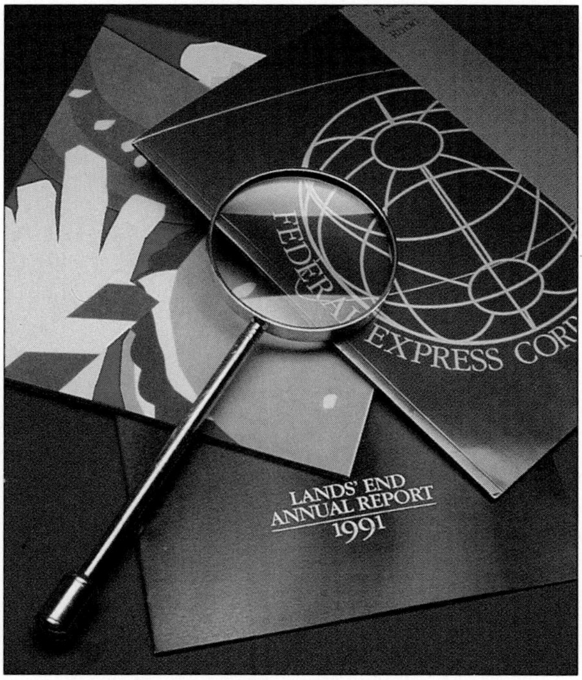

The financial statements in this appendix describe the companies' success in accomplishing what they set out to do. Despite differences between delivering overnight packages, selling mail-order merchandise, and operating fast-food restaurants, many similarities will come clear when you put these reports under the magnifying glass.

Consolidated Statements of Income
Federal Express Corporation and Subsidiaries

Years ended May 31 In thousands, except per share amounts	1991	1990	1989
Revenues	$ 7,688,296	$ 7,015,069	$ 5,166,967
Operating Expenses:			
Salaries and employee benefits (Note 9)	3,438,391	3,045,250	2,308,969
Equipment and facility rentals (Note 5)	755,068	717,443	467,221
Fuel	663,327	521,256	269,803
Depreciation and amortization	534,540	479,188	387,318
Maintenance and repairs	449,394	424,923	279,121
U.K. restructuring charge (Note 13)	121,000	–	–
Other	1,446,783	1,413,430	1,030,100
	7,408,503	6,601,490	4,742,532
Operating Income	279,793	413,579	424,435
Other Income (Expense):			
Interest, net (Note 1)	(181,880)	(188,109)	(115,260)
Gain on disposition of aircraft and related equipment	11,375	13,791	4,709
Payroll tax loss contingency (Note 13)	(32,000)	–	–
Other, net	(36,346)	(20,838)	(15,552)
	(238,851)	(195,156)	(126,103)
Income before Income Taxes and Cumulative Effect of Change in Accounting for Income Taxes	40,942	218,423	298,332
Provision for Income Taxes (Note 8)	35,044	102,659	131,881
Income before Cumulative Effect of Change in Accounting for Income Taxes	5,898	115,764	166,451
Cumulative Effect on Years Prior to 1989 of Change in Accounting for Income Taxes (Notes 1 and 8)	–	–	18,100
Net Income	$ 5,898	$ 115,764	$ 184,551
Earnings per Share (Note 7):			
Before cumulative effect of change in accounting for income taxes	$ .11	$ 2.18	$ 3.18
Cumulative effect on years prior to 1989 of change in accounting for income taxes	–	–	.35
	$ .11	$ 2.18	$ 3.53
Average Shares Outstanding (Note 7)	53,350	53,161	52,272

The accompanying Notes to Consolidated Financial Statements are an integral part of these statements.

Consolidated Balance Sheets
Federal Express Corporation and Subsidiaries

May 31 In thousands	1991	1990
Assets		
Current Assets:		
Cash, including short-term investments of $42,292 and $67,738	$ 117,692	$ 98,499
Receivables, less allowance for doubtful accounts of $37,694 and $31,455	924,773	997,808
Spare parts, supplies and fuel	154,941	110,573
Prepaid expenses and other	85,441	108,523
Total current assets	1,282,847	1,315,403
Property and Equipment, at cost (Notes 4, 5 and 11):		
Flight equipment	2,394,326	2,310,764
Package handling and ground support equipment	1,296,706	1,130,131
Computer and electronic equipment	756,638	671,207
Other	1,447,501	1,356,724
	5,895,171	5,468,826
Less accumulated depreciation and amortization	2,271,145	1,902,505
Net property and equipment	3,624,026	3,566,321
Other Assets:		
Excess of cost over net assets acquired (Notes 1 and 2)	521,079	588,874
Other	244,509	204,475
Total other assets	765,588	793,349
	$ 5,672,461	$ 5,675,073

The accompanying Notes to Consolidated Financial Statements are an integral part of these balance sheets.

In thousands, except common shares	1991	1990
LIABILITIES AND STOCKHOLDERS' INVESTMENT		
CURRENT LIABILITIES:		
Current portion of long-term debt (NOTE 4)	$ 202,653	$ 70,082
Accounts payable	466,621	454,445
Accrued expenses (NOTE 3)	824,498	715,687
Total current liabilities	1,493,772	1,240,214
LONG-TERM DEBT, LESS CURRENT PORTION (NOTE 4)	1,826,781	2,148,142
DEFERRED INCOME TAXES (NOTE 8)	217,436	298,187
OTHER LIABILITIES	465,852	339,343
COMMITMENTS AND CONTINGENCIES (NOTES 4, 5, 9, 11 AND 12)		
COMMON STOCKHOLDERS' INVESTMENT (NOTES 7 AND 9):		
Common Stock, $.10 par value; 100,000,000 shares authorized, 53,632,301 and 53,145,748 shares issued	5,363	5,315
Additional paid-in capital	652,045	639,676
Retained earnings	1,015,205	1,010,090
	1,672,613	1,655,081
Less deferred compensation related to stock plans and treasury stock	3,993	5,894
Total common stockholders' investment	1,668,620	1,649,187
	$ 5,672,461	$ 5,675,073

CONSOLIDATED STATEMENTS OF CASH FLOWS
FEDERAL EXPRESS CORPORATION AND SUBSIDIARIES

Years ended May 31 In thousands	1991	1990	1989
OPERATING ACTIVITIES			
Income before cumulative effect of change in accounting for income taxes	$ 5,898	$ 115,764	$ 166,451
Adjustments to reconcile income to net cash provided by operating activities:			
Depreciation and amortization	534,540	479,188	387,318
Provision for uncollectible accounts	59,721	55,147	31,388
Provision for deferred income taxes and other	64,602	101,057	56,730
Gains from disposals of property and equipment	(1,621)	(8,084)	(4,160)
Changes in operating assets and liabilities, net of effects from purchases of businesses:			
Decrease (increase) in receivables	20,431	(279,596)	(149,531)
Increase in spare parts, supplies and fuel and prepaid expenses	(21,904)	(51,404)	(46,400)
Increase in accounts payable and accrued expenses	110,768	119,838	243,792
Other, net	14,964	(15,580)	(18,839)
Net cash provided by operating activities	787,399	516,330	666,749
INVESTING ACTIVITIES			
Purchases of property and equipment	(1,027,736)	(1,164,061)	(749,099)
Proceeds from disposition of property and equipment:			
Sale-leaseback transactions	275,347	583,744	111,472
Other	5,699	19,722	61,351
Purchases of businesses, net of cash acquired	(24,322)	(30,975)	(625,005)
Other, net	–	(4,568)	(6,219)
Net cash used in investing activities	(771,012)	(596,138)	(1,207,500)
FINANCING ACTIVITIES			
Proceeds from debt issuances	910,703	1,039,568	1,529,611
Principal payments on debt	(916,430)	(1,044,159)	(849,012)
Proceeds from stock issuances (includes treasury)	31,241	44,855	37,916
Purchases of treasury stock	(23,565)	(17,742)	(70,201)
Other, net	857	(1,523)	(5,200)
Net cash provided by financing activities	2,806	20,999	643,114
Net increase (decrease) in cash and cash equivalents	19,193	(58,809)	102,363
Cash and cash equivalents at beginning of period	98,499	157,308	54,945
Cash and cash equivalents at end of period	$ 117,692	$ 98,499	$ 157,308
SUPPLEMENTAL DISCLOSURE OF CASH FLOW INFORMATION			
Cash paid for: Interest (net of capitalized interest)	$ 190,054	$ 195,006	$ 102,676
Income taxes	$ 36,500	$ 130,000	$ 81,058
SUPPLEMENTAL SCHEDULE OF NONCASH INVESTING AND FINANCING ACTIVITIES			
Capital lease obligations and other debt incurred to acquire property and equipment	$ –	$ 2,700	$ 19,010
Exchanges of property and equipment	$ 33,222	$ –	$ –

The accompanying Notes to Consolidated Financial Statements are an integral part of these statements.

CONSOLIDATED STATEMENTS OF CHANGES IN COMMON STOCKHOLDERS' INVESTMENT
FEDERAL EXPRESS CORPORATION AND SUBSIDIARIES

In thousands, except common shares	Common Stock	Additional Paid-in Capital	Retained Earnings	Treasury Stock	Deferred Compen-sation
BALANCE AT MAY 31, 1988	$ 5,286	$ 623,057	$ 726,036	$ –	$ (23,700)
Purchase of treasury stock	–	–	–	(70,201)	–
Issuance of treasury stock under employee incentive plans (1,009,876 shares)	–	2,771	(6,385)	43,582	–
Amortization of deferred compensation	–	–	–	–	11,300
Foreign currency translation adjustment	–	–	(2,773)	–	–
Net income	–	–	184,551	–	–
BALANCE AT MAY 31, 1989	5,286	625,828	901,429	(26,619)	(12,400)
Purchase of treasury stock	–	–	–	(17,742)	–
Issuance of common and treasury stock under employee incentive plans (1,283,493 shares)	29	13,848	(5,270)	44,340	(7,109)
Amortization of deferred compensation	–	–	–	–	13,636
Foreign currency translation adjustment	–	–	(1,833)	–	–
Net income	–	–	115,764	–	–
BALANCE AT MAY 31, 1990	5,315	639,676	1,010,090	(21)	(5,873)
Purchase of treasury stock	–	–	–	(23,565)	–
Issuance of common and treasury stock under employee incentive plans (1,141,283 shares)	48	12,369	(4,483)	23,572	642
Amortization of deferred compensation	–	–	–	–	1,252
Foreign currency translation adjustment	–	–	3,700	–	–
Net income	–	–	5,898	–	–
BALANCE AT MAY 31, 1991	$ 5,363	$ 652,045	$1,015,205	$ (14)	$ (3,979)

The accompanying Notes to Consolidated Financial Statements are an integral part of these statements.

Statements of Operations

Lands' End, Inc.

(Dollars in thousands, except per share data)	For the year ended January 31, 1991	1990	1989
Net sales	$603,975	$545,201	$455,806
Cost of sales	357,307	313,573	261,671
Gross profit	246,668	231,628	194,135
Selling, general and administrative expenses	222,154	184,910	143,486
Income from operations	24,514	46,718	50,649
Other income (expense):			
Interest expense	(1,018)	(1,399)	(1,232)
Interest income	1,187	1,397	1,852
Other	260	554	873
Total other income, net	429	552	1,493
Income before income taxes	24,943	47,270	52,142
Income tax provision	10,200	18,199	19,860
Net income	$ 14,743	$ 29,071	$ 32,282
Net income per share	$0.75	$1.45	$1.61

The accompanying notes are an integral part of these statements.

Balance Sheets

Lands' End, Inc.

(Dollars in thousands)	*January 31,* 1991	1990
Assets		
Current assets:		
Cash and cash equivalents	$ 27,264	$ 8,254
Receivables	1,209	348
Inventory	73,863	85,709
Prepaid expenses	5,488	5,403
Total current assets	107,824	99,714
Property, plant and equipment, at cost:		
Land and buildings	53,127	38,335
Fixtures and equipment	47,646	41,123
Leasehold improvements	1,646	1,512
Construction in progress	—	4,637
Total property, plant and equipment	102,419	85,607
Less - accumulated depreciation and amortization	24,843	18,389
Property, plant and equipment, net	77,576	67,218
Total assets	$185,400	$166,932
Liabilities and shareholders' investment		
Current liabilities:		
Current maturities of long-term debt	$ 1,682	$ 1,775
Accounts payable	37,797	24,415
Advance payment on orders	446	203
Accrued liabilities	13,769	10,568
Accrued profit sharing	—	1,652
Income taxes payable	7,080	5,302
Total current liabilities	60,774	43,915
Long-term debt, less current maturities	3,349	5,031
Deferred income taxes	4,451	3,382
Shareholders' investment:		
Common stock, 20,110,294 and 20,076,294 shares issued, respectively	201	201
Donated capital	8,400	8,400
Paid-in capital	23,782	23,340
Deferred compensation	(1,046)	(959)
Retained earnings	98,381	87,516
Treasury stock, 892,500 and 194,900 shares at cost, respectively	(12,892)	(3,894)
Total shareholders' investment	116,826	114,604
Total liabilities and shareholders' investment	$185,400	$166,932

The accompanying notes are an integral part of these balance sheets.

Statements of Shareholders' Investment

Lands' End, Inc.

(Dollars in thousands)	*Common stock*		Paid-in	Donated	Deferred	Retained	*Treasury stock*		
	Shares	Amount	Capital	Capital	Compensation	Earnings	Shares	Amount	Total
Balance, January 31, 1988	20,040,294	$ 200	$22,308	$ —	$ —	$34,166	—	$ —	$56,674
Donated capital	—	—	—	7,000	—	—	—	—	7,000
Cash dividends paid to common shareholders ($0.20 per share)	—	—	—	—	—	(4,008)	—	—	(4,008)
Net income	—	—	—	—	—	32,282	—	—	32,282
Balance, January 31, 1989	20,040,294	200	22,308	7,000	—	62,440	—	—	91,948
Donated capital	—	—	—	1,400	—	—	—	—	1,400
Cash dividends paid to common shareholders ($0.20 per share)	—	—	—	—	—	(3,995)	—	—	(3,995)
Purchases of treasury stock	—	—	—	—	—	—	194,900	(3,894)	(3,894)
Issuance of additional shares of stock	36,000	1	1,032	—	(1,033)	—	—	—	—
Deferred compensation expense	—	—	—	—	74	—	—	—	74
Net income	—	—	—	—	—	29,071	—	—	29,071
Balance, January 31, 1990	20,076,294	201	23,340	8,400	(959)	87,516	194,900	(3,894)	114,604
Cash dividends paid to common shareholders ($0.20 per share)	—	—	—	—	—	(3,878)	—	—	(3,878)
Purchases of treasury stock	—	—	—	—	267	—	697,600	(8,998)	(8,731)
Issuance of additional shares of stock	34,000	—	442	—	(442)	—	—	—	—
Deferred compensation expense	—	—	—	—	88	—	—	—	88
Net income	—	—	—	—	—	14,743	—	—	14,743
Balance, January 31, 1991	20,110,294	$ 201	$23,782	$8,400	$ (1,046)	$98,381	892,500	$(12,892)	$116,826

The accompanying notes are an integral part of these statements.

Statements of Cash Flows

Lands' End, Inc.

(Dollars in thousands)	*For the year ended January 31,* 1991	1990	1989
Cash flows from operating activities:			
Net income	$14,743	$29,071	$32,282
Adjustments to reconcile net income to net cash –			
Depreciation and amortization	7,041	5,251	3,916
Deferred compensation expense	355	74	—
Deferred income taxes	1,069	2,514	(1,910)
Loss on sales of equipment	142	58	5
Changes in current assets and liabilities:			
Receivables	(861)	407	(481)
Inventory	11,846	(18,889)	(20,376)
Prepaid expenses	(85)	(1,436)	(604)
Accounts payable	13,382	(1,489)	4,681
Advance payment on orders	243	(147)	(103)
Accrued liabilities	3,201	834	2,508
Accrued profit sharing	(1,652)	(1,633)	639
Income taxes payable	1,778	(5,095)	5,003
Net cash flows from operating activities	51,202	9,520	25,560
Cash flows (used for) investing activities:			
Purchases of property, plant and equipment	(17,622)	(24,031)	(15,872)
Construction of activity center (see note – donated capital)	(60)	(1,129)	(7,018)
Proceeds from sales of equipment	141	104	221
Net cash flows (used for) investing activities	(17,541)	(25,056)	(22,669)
Cash flows (used in) from financing activities:			
Proceeds from short-term and long-term debt	5,000	—	—
Payment of short-term and long-term debt	(6,775)	(1,860)	(1,919)
Purchases of treasury stock	(8,998)	(3,894)	—
Donated capital	—	1,400	7,000
Cash dividends paid to common shareholders	(3,878)	(3,995)	(4,008)
Net cash flows (used in) from financing activities	(14,651)	(8,349)	1,073
Net increase (decrease) in cash and cash equivalents	19,010	(23,885)	3,964
Beginning cash and cash equivalents	8,254	32,139	28,175
Ending cash and cash equivalents	$27,264	$8,254	$32,139
Supplemental cash flow disclosures:			
Interest paid	$ 1,066	$ 1,417	$ 1,250
Income taxes paid	9,540	20,780	16,767

The accompanying notes are an integral part of these statements.

McDonald's Corporation CONSOLIDATED STATEMENT OF INCOME

(In millions of dollars, except per common share data) Years ended December 31,	1990	1989	1988
Revenues			
Sales by Company-operated restaurants	$5,018.9	$4,600.9	$4,196.1
Revenues from franchised restaurants	1,620.7	1,464.7	1,324.7
Total revenues	6,639.6	6,065.6	5,520.8
Operating costs and expenses			
Company-operated restaurants			
Food and packaging	1,683.4	1,560.3	1,441.7
Payroll and other employee benefits	1,291.0	1,174.4	1,074.1
Occupancy and other operating expenses	1,161.2	1,043.1	936.7
	4,135.6	3,777.8	3,452.5
Franchised restaurants—occupancy expenses	279.2	240.6	217.5
General, administrative and selling expenses	724.2	656.0	606.3
Other operating (income) expense—net	(95.3)	(46.5)	(43.1)
Total operating costs and expenses	5,043.7	4,627.9	4,233.2
Operating income	1,595.9	1,437.7	1,287.6
Interest expense—net of capitalized interest of $36.0, $29.8, and $29.6	381.2	301.9	237.3
Other nonoperating income (expense)—net	31.6	21.4	(3.8)
Income before provision for income taxes	1,246.3	1,157.2	1,046.5
Provision for income taxes	444.0	430.5	400.6
Net income	$ 802.3	$ 726.7	$ 645.9
Net income per common share	$ 2.20	$ 1.95	$ 1.71
Dividends per common share	$ .33	$ .30	$ .27

The accompanying Financial Comments are an integral part of the consolidated financial statements.

McDonald's Corporation CONSOLIDATED BALANCE SHEET

(In millions of dollars)	December 31, 1990	1989
Assets		
Current assets		
Cash and equivalents	$ 142.8	$ 136.9
Accounts receivable	222.1	207.2
Notes receivable	32.9	27.2
Inventories, at cost, not in excess of market	42.9	46.1
Prepaid expenses and other current assets	108.3	77.3
Total current assets	549.0	494.7
Other assets and deferred charges		
Notes receivable due after one year	102.2	75.8
Investments in and advances to affiliates	335.2	290.5
Miscellaneous	250.0	229.6
Total other assets and deferred charges	687.4	595.9
Property and equipment		
Property and equipment, at cost	11,535.5	9,873.9
Accumulated depreciation and amortization	(2,488.4)	(2,115.6)
Net property and equipment	9,047.1	7,758.3
Intangible assets, net	384.0	326.1
Total assets	$10,667.5	$9,175.0
Liabilities and shareholders' equity		
Current liabilities		
Notes payable	$ 299.0	$ 75.8
Accounts payable	355.7	386.1
Income taxes	82.6	70.7
Other taxes	68.6	66.7
Accrued interest	133.2	134.8
Other accrued liabilities	194.9	173.5
Current maturities of long-term debt	64.7	58.6
Total current liabilities	1,198.7	966.2
Long-term debt	4,428.7	3,902.0
Security deposits by franchisees and other long-term liabilities	162.7	143.3
Deferred income taxes	695.1	613.1
Shareholders' equity		
Preferred stock, no par value; authorized—165.0 million shares; issued—6.9 and 7.0 million	199.7	200.0
Guarantee of ESOP Notes	(196.5)	(199.2)
Common stock, no par value; authorized—1.25 billion shares; issued—415.2 million	46.2	46.2
Additional paid-in capital	173.7	158.9
Retained earnings	5,214.5	4,545.5
Equity adjustment from foreign currency translation	46.7	(29.0)
	5,484.3	4,722.4
Common stock in treasury, at cost; 56.1 and 53.3 million shares	(1,302.0)	(1,172.0)
Total shareholders' equity	4,182.3	3,550.4
Total liabilities and shareholders' equity	$10,667.5	$9,175.0

The accompanying Financial Comments are an integral part of the consolidated financial statements.

McDonald's Corporation CONSOLIDATED STATEMENT OF CASH FLOWS

(In millions of dollars) Years ended December 31,	1990	1989	1988
Operating activities			
Net income	$ 802.3	$ 726.7	$ 645.9
Adjustments to reconcile to cash provided by operations			
Depreciation and amortization	493.3	438.8	383.4
Deferred income taxes	70.8	67.9	66.4
Changes in operating working capital items			
Accounts receivable increase	(26.6)	(15.9)	(22.0)
Inventories, prepaid expenses and other current assets (increase) decrease	(32.1)	.5	(12.5)
Accounts payable increase (decrease)	(14.5)	(32.9)	113.8
Accrued interest increase (decrease)	(1.7)	2.4	(1.8)
Taxes and other liabilities increase	80.5	75.8	15.7
Other—net	(71.0)	(17.1)	(11.8)
Cash provided by operations	1,301.0	1,246.2	1,177.1
Investing activities			
Property and equipment expenditures	(1,570.7)	(1,554.7)	(1,321.3)
Sales of restaurant businesses	130.8	77.3	69.2
Purchases of restaurant businesses	(8[illegible]	(41.1)	(60.1)
Notes receivable additions	(46.2)	(57.3)	(39.2)
Property sales	3[illegible]	83.7	28.0
Notes receivable reductions	61.2	52.3	58.6
Other	(55.2)	(73.5)	(42.5)
Cash used for investing activities	(1,522.5)	(1,513.3)	(1,307.3)
Financing activities			
Notes payable and long-term debt issuances	2,066.6	1,455.8	886.3
Notes payable and long-term debt repayments	(1,569.0)	(855.1)	(540.6)
Treasury stock purchases	(160.3)	(479.2)	(126.0)
Preferred stock issuance		200.0	
Common and preferred stock dividends	(133.3)	(115.2)	(102.5)
Other	23.4	13.3	14.2
Cash provided by financing activities	227.4	219.6	131.4
Cash and equivalents increase (decrease)	5.9	(47.5)	1.2
Cash and equivalents at beginning of year	136.9	184.4	183.2
Cash and equivalents at end of year	$ 142.8	$ 136.9	$ 184.4
Supplemental cash flow disclosures			
Interest paid	$ 370.5	$ 294.0	$ 244.7
Income taxes paid	$ 326.5	$ 306.0	$ 332.1

The accompanying Financial Comments are an integral part of the consolidated financial statements.

McDonald's Corporation CONSOLIDATED STATEMENT OF SHAREHOLDERS' EQUITY

(Dollars and shares in millions, except per share data)	Preferred stock issued		Guarantee of ESOP Notes	Common stock issued		Additional paid-in capital	Retained earnings	Equity adjustment from foreign currency translation	Common stock in treasury	
	Shares	Amount		Shares	Amount				Shares	Amount
Balance at December 31, 1987				415.2	$46.2	$127.7	$3,396.0	$(31.8)	(37.4)	$ (621.4)
Net income							645.9			
Common stock cash dividends ($.27 per share)							(102.5)			
Treasury stock acquisitions									(6.0)	(135.8)
Translation adjustments (net of taxes of $15.5)								35.4		
Stock option exercises and other (including tax benefits of $25.7)						17.6	(4.2)		3.7	39.7
Balance at December 31, 1988				415.2	46.2	145.3	3,935.2	3.6	(39.7)	(717.5)
Net income							726.7			
Common stock cash dividends ($.30 per share)							(112.0)			
Preferred stock cash dividends ($.63 per share)							(4.4)			
Preferred stock issuance	7.0	$200.0	$(200.0)			(.6)				
Treasury stock acquisitions									(16.7)	(497.3)
Translation adjustments (including taxes of $14.6)								(32.6)		
Stock option exercises and other (including tax benefits of $15.1)			.8			14.2			3.1	42.8
Balance at December 31, 1989	7.0	200.0	(199.2)	415.2	46.2	158.9	4,545.5	(29.0)	(53.3)	(1,172.0)
Net income							802.3			
Common stock cash dividends ($.33 per share)							(119.3)			
Preferred stock cash dividends ($2.01 per share)							(14.0)			
ESOP Notes payment			2.7							
Treasury stock acquisitions									(4.9)	(156.5)
Translation adjustments (including tax benefits of $27.4)								75.7		
Stock option exercises and other (including tax benefits of $13.7)	(.1)	(.3)				14.8			2.1	26.5
Balance at December 31, 1990	6.9	$199.7	$(196.5)	415.2	$46.2	$173.7	$5,214.5	$46.7	(56.1)	$(1,302.0)

The accompanying Financial Comments are an integral part of the consolidated financial statements.

APPENDIX

L

AICPA Code of Professional Conduct and IMA Standards of Ethical Conduct for Management Accountants

American Institute of Certified Public Accountants (AICPA) Code of Professional Conduct*

Composition, Applicability, and Compliance

The Code of Professional Conduct of the American Institute of Certified Public Accountants consists of two sections—(1) the Principles and (2) the Rules. The Principles provide the framework for the Rules, which govern the performance of professional services by members. The Council of the American Institute of Certified Public Accountants is authorized to designate bodies to promulgate technical standards under the Rules, and the bylaws require adherence to those Rules and standards.

The Code of Professional Conduct was adopted by the membership to provide guidance and rules to all members—those in public practice, in industry, in government, and in education—in the performance of their professional responsibilities.

Compliance with the Code of Professional Conduct, as with all standards in an open society, depends primarily on members' understanding and voluntary actions, secondarily on reinforcement by peers and public opinion, and ultimately on disciplinary proceedings, when necessary, against members who fail to comply with the Rules.

* As amended January 14, 1992. Reprinted with permission from the Code of Professional Conduct and Bylaws, © 1992 by the American Institute of Certified Public Accountants, Inc.

Section I—Principles

Preamble

Membership in the American Institute of Certified Public Accountants is voluntary. By accepting membership, a certified public accountant assumes an obligation of self-discipline above and beyond the requirements of laws and regulations.

These Principles of the Code of Professional Conduct of the American Institute of Certified Public Accountants express the profession's recognition of its responsibilities to the public, to clients, and to colleagues. They guide members in the performance of their professional responsibilities and express the basic tenets of ethical and professional conduct. The Principles call for an unswerving commitment to honorable behavior, even at the sacrifice of personal advantage.

Article I: Responsibilities

In carrying out their responsibilities as professionals, members should exercise sensitive professional and moral judgments in all their activities.

As professionals, certified public accountants perform an essential role in society. Consistent with that role, members of the American Institute of Certified Public Accountants have responsibilities to all those who use their professional service. Members also have a continuing responsibility to cooperate with each other to improve the art of accounting, maintain the public's confidence, and carry out the profession's special responsibilities for self-governance. The collective efforts of all members are required to maintain and enhance the traditions of the profession.

Article II: The Public Interest

Members should accept the obligation to act in a way that will serve the public interest, honor the public trust, and demonstrate commitment to professionalism.

A distinguishing mark of a profession is acceptance of its responsibility to the public. The accounting profession's public consists of clients, credit grantors, governments, employers, investors, the business and financial community, and others who rely on the objectivity and integrity of certified public accountants to maintain the orderly functioning of commerce. This reliance imposes a public interest responsibility on certified public accountants. The public interest is defined as the collective well-being of the community of people and institutions the profession serves.

In discharging their professional responsibilities, members may encounter conflicting pressures from among each of those groups. In resolving those conflicts, members should act with integrity, guided by the precept that when members fulfill their responsibility to the public, clients' and employers' interest are best served.

Those who rely on certified public accountants expect them to discharge their responsibilities with integrity, objectivity, due professional care, and a genuine interest in serving the public. They are expected to provide quality services, enter into fee arrangements, and offer a range of services—all in a manner that demonstrates a level of professionalism consistent with these Principles of the Code of Professional Conduct.

All who accept membership in the American Institute of Certified Public Accountants commit themselves to honor the public trust. In return for the faith that the public reposes in them, members should seek continually to demonstrate their dedication to professional excellence.

Article III: Integrity

To maintain and broaden public confidence, members should perform all professional responsibilities with the highest sense of integrity.

Integrity is an element of character fundamental to professional recognition. It is the quality from which the public trust derives and the benchmark against which a member must ultimately test all decisions.

Integrity requires a member to be, among other things, honest and candid within the constraints of client confidentiality. Service and the public trust should not be subordinated to personal gain and advantage. Integrity can accommodate the inadvertent error and the honest difference of opinion; it cannot accommodate deceit or subordination of principle.

Integrity is measured in terms of what is right and just. In the absence of specific rules, standards, or guidance, or in the face of conflicting opinions, a member should test decisions and deeds by asking: "Am I doing what a person of integrity would do? Have I retained my integrity?" Integrity requires a member to observe both the form and the spirit of technical and ethical standards; circumvention of those standards constitutes subordination of judgment.

Integrity also requires a member to observe the principles of objectivity and independence and of due care.

Article IV: Objectivity and Independence

A member should maintain objectivity and be freed of conflicts of interest in discharging professional responsibilities. A member in public practice should be independent in fact and appearance when providing auditing and other attestation services.

Objectivity is a state of mind, a quality that lends value to a member's services. It is a distinguishing feature of the profession. The principle of objectivity imposes the obligation to be impartial, intellectually honest, and free of conflicts of interest. Independence precludes relationships that may appear to impair a member's objectivity in rendering attestation services.

Members often serve multiple interests in many different capacities and must demonstrate their objectivity in varying circumstances. Members in public practice render attest, tax, and management advisory services. Other members prepare financial statements in the employment of others, perform internal auditing services, and serve in financial and management capacities in industry, education, and government. They also educate and train those who aspire to admission into the profession. Regardless of service or capacity, members should protect the integrity of their work, maintain objectivity, and avoid any subordination of their judgment.

For a member in public practice, the maintenance of objectivity and independence requires a continuing assessment of client relationships and public responsibility. Such a member who provides auditing and other attestation services should be independent in fact and appearance. In providing all other services, a member should maintain objectivity and avoid conflicts of interest.

Although members not in public practice cannot maintain the appearance of independence, they nevertheless have the responsibility to maintain objectivity in rendering professional services. Members employed by others to prepare financial statements or to perform auditing, tax, or consulting services are charged with the same responsibility for objectivity as members in public practice and must be scrupulous in their application of generally accepted accounting principles and candid in all their dealings with members in public practice.

Article V: Due Care

A member should observe the profession's technical and ethical standards, strive continually to improve competence and the quality of services, and discharge professional responsibility to the best of the member's ability.

The quest for excellence is the essence of due care. Due care requires a member to discharge professional responsibilities with competence and diligence. It imposes the obligation to perform professional services to the best of a member's ability with concern for the best interest of those for whom the services are performed and consistent with the profession's responsibility to the public.

Competence is derived from a synthesis of education and experience. It begins with a mastery of the common body of knowledge required for designation as a certified public accountant. The maintenance of competence requires a commitment to learning and professional improvement that must continue throughout a member's professional life. It is a member's individual responsibility. In all engagements and in all responsibilities, each member should undertake to achieve a level of competence that will assure that the quality of the member's services meets the high level of professionalism required by these Principles.

Competence represents the attainment and maintenance of a level of understanding and knowledge that enables a member to render services with facility and acumen. It also establishes the limitations of a member's capabilities by dictating that consultation or referral may be required when a professional engagement exceeds the personal competence of a member or a member's firm. Each member is responsible for assessing his or her own competence—of evaluating whether education, experience, and judgment are adequate for the responsibility to be assumed.

Members should be diligent in discharging responsibilities to clients, employers, and the public. Diligence imposes the responsibility to render services promptly and carefully, to be thorough, and to observe applicable technical and ethical standards.

Due care requires a member to plan and supervise adequately any professional activity for which he or she is responsible.

Article VI: Scope and Nature of Services

A member in public practice should observe the Principles of the Code of Professional Conduct in determining the scope and nature of services to be provided.

The public interest aspect of certified public accountants' services requires that such services be consistent with acceptable professional behavior for certified public accountants. Integrity requires that service and the public trust not be subordinated to personal gain and advantage. Objectivity and independence require that members be free from conflicts of interest in discharging professional responsibilities. Due care requires that services be provided with competence and diligence.

Each of these Principles should be considered by members in determining whether or not to provide specific services in individual circumstances. In some instances, they may represent an overall constraint on the nonaudit services that might be offered to a specific client. No hard-and-fast rules can be developed to help members reach these judgments, but they must be satisfied that they are meeting the spirit of the Principles in this regard.

In order to accomplish this, members should

- Practice in firms that have in place internal quality-control procedures to ensure that services are competently delivered and adequately supervised.
- Determine, in their individual judgments, whether

the scope and nature of other services provided to an audit client would create a conflict of interest in the performance of the audit function for that client.

- Assess, in their individual judgments, whether an activity is consistent with their role as professionals (for example, Is such activity a reasonable extension or variation of existing services offered by the member or others in the profession?).

Section II—Rules

Applicability

The bylaws of the American Institute of Certified Public Accountants require that members adhere to the Rules of the Code of Professional Conduct. Members must be prepared to justify departures from these Rules.

Definitions

Client. A client is any person or entity, other than the member's employer, that engages a member or a member's firm to perform professional services or a person or entity with respect to which professional services are performed. The term "employer" for these purposes does not include those entities engaged in the practice of public accounting.

Council. The Council of the American Institute of Certified Public Accountants.

Enterprise. For purposes of the Code, the term "enterprise" is synonymous with the term "client."

Financial Statements. Statements and footnotes related thereto that purport to show financial position which relates to a point in time or changes in financial position which relate to a period of time, and statements which use a cash or other incomplete basis of accounting. Balance sheets, statements of income, statements of retained earnings, statements of cash flows, and statements of changes in owners' equity are financial statements.

Incidental financial data included in management advisory services reports to support recommendations to a client and tax returns and supporting schedules do not, for this purpose, constitute financial statements; and the statement, affidavit, or signature of preparers required on tax returns neither constitutes an opinion on financial statements nor requires a disclaimer of such opinion.

Firm. A form of organization permitted by state law or regulation whose characteristics conform to resolutions of Council that is engaged in the practice of public accounting, including the individual owners thereof.

Holding out. In general, any action initiated by a member that informs others of his or her status as a CPA or AICPA-accredited specialist constitutes holding out as a CPA. This would include, for example, any oral or written representation to another regarding CPA status, use of the CPA designation on business cards or letterhead, the display of a certificate evidencing a member's CPA designation, or listing as a CPA in local telephone directories.

Institute. The American Institute of Certified Public Accountants.

Interpretations of Rules of Conduct. Pronouncements issued by the division of professional ethics to provide guidelines concerning the scope and application of the rules of conduct.

Member. A member, associate member, or international associate of the American Institute of Certified Public Accountants.

Practice of Public Accounting. The practice of public accounting consists of the performance for a client, by a member or a member's firm, while holding out as CPA(s), of the professional services of accounting, tax, personal financial planning, litigation support services, and those professional services for which standards are promulgated by bodies designated by Council, such as Statements of Financial Accounting Standards, Statements on Auditing Standards, Statements on Standards for Accounting and Review Services, Statement on Standards for Consulting Services, Statements of Governmental Accounting Standards, Statements on Standards for Attestation Engagements, and Statement on Standards for Accountants' Services on Prospective Financial Information.

However, a member or a member's firm, while holding out as CPA(s), is not considered to be in the practice of public accounting if the member or the member's firm does not perform, for any client, any of the professional services described in the preceding paragraph.

Professional Services. Professional services include all services performed by a member while holding out as a CPA.

Rule 101 Independence

A member in public practice shall be independent in the performance of professional services as required by standards promulgated by bodies designated by Council.

Interpretation of Rule 101. Interpretation 101–1. Independence shall be considered to be impaired if, for example, a member had any of the following transactions, interests, or relationships:

A. During the period of a professional engagement or at the time of expressing an opinion, a member or a member's firm
   1. Had or was committed to acquire any direct or material indirect financial interest in the enterprise.
   2. Was a trustee of any trust or executor or administrator of any estate if such trust or estate had or was committed to acquire any direct or material indirect financial interest in the enterprise.
   3. Had any joint, closely held business investment with the enterprise or with any officer, director, or principal stockholders thereof that was material in relation to the member's net worth or to the net worth of the member's firm.
   4. Had any loan to or from the enterprise or any officer, director, or principal stockholder of the enterprise except as specifically permitted in interpretation 101–5.

B. During the period covered by the financial statements, during the period of the professional engagement, or at the time of expressing an opinion, a member or a member's firm
   1. Was connected with the enterprise as a promoter, underwriter or voting trustee, as a director or officer, or in any capacity equivalent to that of a member of management or of an employee.
   2. Was a trustee for any pension or profit-sharing trust of the enterprise.

The above examples are not intended to be all-inclusive.

Rule 102 Integrity and Objectivity

In the performance of any professional service, a member shall maintain objectivity and integrity, shall be free of conflicts of interest, and shall not knowingly misrepresent facts or subordinate his or her judgment to others.

Rule 201 General Standards

A member shall comply with the following standards and with any interpretations thereof by bodies designated by Council.

A. *Professional Competence.* Undertake only those professional services that the member or the member's firm can reasonably expect to be completed with professional competence.

B. *Due Professional Care.* Exercise due professional care in the performance of professional services.

C. *Planning and Supervision.* Adequately plan and supervise the performance of professional services.

D. *Sufficient Relevant Data.* Obtain sufficient relevant data to afford a reasonable basis for conclusions or recommendations in relation to any professional services performed.

Rule 202 Compliance with Standards

A member who performs auditing, review, compilation, management consulting, tax, or other professional services shall comply with standards promulgated by bodies designated by Council.

Rule 203 Accounting Principles

A member shall not (1) express an opinion or state affirmatively that the financial statements or other financial data of any entity are presented in conformity with generally accepted accounting principles or (2) state that he or she is not aware of any material modifications that should be made to such statements or data in order for them to be in conformity with generally accepted accounting principles, if such statements or data contain any departure from an accounting principle promulgated by bodies designated by Council to establish such principles that has a material effect on the statements or data taken as a whole. If, however, the statements or data contain such a departure and the member can demonstrate that due to unusual circumstances the financial statements or data would otherwise have been misleading, the member can comply with the rule by describing the departure, its approximate effects, if practicable, and the reasons why compliance with the principle would result in a misleading statement.

Rule 301 Confidential Client Information

A member in public practice shall not disclose any confidential client information without the specific consent of the client.

This rule shall not be construed (1) to relieve a member of his or her professional obligations under rules 202 and 203, (2) to affect in any way the member's obligation to comply with a validly issued and enforceable subpoena or summons, or to prohibit a member's compliance with applicable laws and government regulations, (3) to prohibit review of a member's professional practice under AICPA or state CPA society authorization, or (4) to preclude a member from initiating a complaint with, or responding to any inquiry made by, the professional ethics division or trial board of the Institute or a duly constituted investigative or disciplinary body of a state CPA society or Board of Accountancy.

Members of any of the bodies identified in (4) above and members involved with professional practice reviews identified in (3) above shall not use to their own advantage or disclose any member's confidential client information that comes to their attention in carrying out those activities. This prohibition shall not restrict members' exchange of information in connection with the investigative or disciplinary proceedings described in (4) above or the professional practice reviews described in (3) above.

Rule 302 Contingent Fees

A member in public practice shall not:

(1) Perform for a contingent fee any professional services for, or receive such a fee from, a client for whom the member or the member's firm performs:
  - *a.* an audit or review of a financial statement; or,
  - *b.* a compilation of a financial statement when the member expects, or reasonably might expect, that a third party will use the financial statement and the member's compilation report does not disclose a lack of independence; or,
  - *c.* an examination of prospective financial information; or,

(2) Prepare an original or amended tax return or claim for a tax refund for a contingent fee for any client.

The prohibition in (1) above applies during the period in which the member or the member's firm is engaged to perform any of the services listed above and the period covered by any historical financial statements involved in any such listed services.

Except as stated in the next sentence, a contingent fee is a fee established for the performance of any service pursuant to an arrangement in which no fee will be charged unless a specified finding or result is attained, or in which the amount of the fee is otherwise dependent upon the finding or result of such service. Solely for purposes of this rule, fees are not regarded as being contingent if fixed by courts or other public authorities, or, in tax matters, if determined based on the results of judicial proceedings or the findings of governmental agencies.

A member's fees may vary depending, for example, on the complexity of the services rendered.

401 [There are currently no rules in the 400 series.]

Rule 501 Acts Discreditable

A member shall not commit an act discreditable to the profession.

Rule 502 Advertising and Other Forms of Solicitation

A member in public practice shall not seek to obtain clients by advertising or other forms of solicitation in a manner that is false, misleading, or deceptive. Solicitation by the use of coercion, overreaching, or harassing conduct is prohibited.

Rule 503 Commissions and Referral Fees

A. *Prohibited commissions*

A member in public practice shall not for a commission recommend or refer to a client any product or service, or for a commission recommend or refer any product or service to be supplied by a client, or receive a commission, when the member or the member's firm also performs for that client:
  - (*a*) an audit or review of a financial statement; or,
  - (*b*) a compilation of a financial statement when the member expects, or reasonably might expect, that a third party will use the financial statement and the member's compilation report does not disclose a lack of independence; or,
  - (*c*) an examination of prospective financial information.

This prohibition applies during the period in which the member is engaged to perform any of the services listed above and the period covered by any historical financial statements involved in such listed services.

B. *Disclosure of permitted commissions*

A member in public practice who is not prohibited by this rule from performing services for or receiving a commission and who is paid or expects to be paid a commission shall disclose that fact to any person or entity to whom the member recommends or refers a product or service to which the commission relates.

C. *Referral fees*

Any member who accepts a referral fee for recommending or referring any service of a CPA to any person or entity or who pays a referral fee to obtain a client shall disclose such acceptance or payment to the client.

Rule 504 *[There is currently no rule 504.]*

Rule 505 Form of Practice and Name

A member may practice public accounting only in the form of organization permitted by state law or regulation whose characteristics conform to resolutions of Council.

A member shall not practice public accounting under a firm name that is misleading. Names of one or more past partners or shareholders may be included in the firm name of a successor partnership or corporation. Also, a partner or shareholder surviving the death or withdrawal of all other partners or shareholders may continue to practice under a name which includes the name of past partners or shareholders for up to two years after becoming a sole practitioner.

A firm may not designate itself as "Members of the American Institute of Certified Public Accountants" unless all of its owners are members of the Institute.

Appendix A: Council Resolution Designating Bodies to Promulgate Technical Standards

Financial Accounting Standards Board

WHEREAS: In 1959 the Council designated the Accounting Principles Board to establish accounting principles, and

WHEREAS: The Council is advised that the Financial Accounting Standards Board (FASB) has become operational, it is

RESOLVED: That as of the date hereof the FASB, in respect of statements of financial accounting standards finally adopted by such board in accordance with its rule of procedure and the bylaws of the Financial Accounting Foundation, be, and hereby is, designated by this Council as the body to establish accounting principles pursuant to rule 203 and standards on disclosure of financial information for such entities outside financial statements in published financial reports containing financial statements under rule 202 or the Rules of the Code of Professional Conduct of the American Institute of Certified Public Accountants provided, however, any accounting research bulletins, or opinions of the accounting principles board issued or approved for exposure by the accounting principles board prior to April 1, 1973, and finally adopted by such board on or before June 30, 1973, shall constitute statements of accounting principles promulgated by a body designated by Council as contemplated in rule 203 of the Rules of the Code of Professional Conduct unless and until such time as they are expressly superseded by action of the FASB.

Government Accounting Standards Board

WHEREAS: The Government Accounting Standards Board (GASB) has been established by the board of trustees of the Financial Accounting Foundation (FAF) to issue standards of financial accounting and reporting with respect to activities and transactions of state and local government entities, and

WHEREAS: The American Institute of Certified Public Accountants is a signatory to the agreement creating the GASB as an arm of the FAF and has supported the GASB professionally and financially, it is

RESOLVED: That as of the date hereof, the GASB, with respect to statements of governmental accounting standards adopted and issued in July 1984 and subsequently in accordance with its rules of procedure and the bylaws of the FASB, be, and hereby is, designated by the Council of the American Institute of Certified Public Accountants as the body to establish financial accounting principles for state and local governmental entities pursuant to rule 203, and standards on disclosure of financial information for such entities outside financial statements in published financial reports containing financial statements under rule 202.

AICPA Committees and Boards.

WHEREAS: The membership of the Institute has adopted rules 201 and 202 of the Rules of the Code of Professional Conduct, which authorizes the Council to designate bodies to promulgate technical standards with which members must comply, and therefore it is

Accounting and Review Services Committee

RESOLVED: That the AICPA accounting and review services committee is hereby designated to promulgate standards under rules 201 and 202 with respect to unaudited financial statements or other unaudited financial information of an entity that is not required to file financial statements with a regulatory agency in connection with the sale or trading of its securities in a public market.

Auditing Standards Board

RESOLVED: That the AICPA auditing standards board is hereby designated as the body authorized under rules 201 and 202 to promulgate auditing and attest standards and procedures.

RESOLVED: That the auditing standards board shall establish under statements on auditing standards the resp ›nsibilities of members with respect to standards for disclosure of financial information outside financial statements in published financial reports containing financial statements.

Management Consulting Services Executive Committee

RESOLVED: That the AICPA management consulting services executive committee is hereby designated to promulgate standards under rules 201 and 202 with respect to the offering of management consulting services, provided, however, that such standards do not deal with the broad question of what, if any, services should be proscribed.

AND FURTHER RESOLVED: That any Institute committee or board now or in the future authorized by the Council to issue enforceable standards under rules 201 and 202 must observe an exposure process seeking comment from other affected committees and boards, as well as the general membership.

Attestation Standards

RESOLVED: that the AICPA accounting and review services committee, auditing standards board, and management consulting services executive committee are hereby designated as bodies authorized under rules 201 and 202 to promulgate attestation standards in their respective areas of responsibility.

Appendix B: Council Resolution Concerning Form of Organization and Name

RESOLVED: That, under rule 505, a member may practice public accounting in a business form other than a proprietorship or partnership only if such entity has the following characteristics:

1. *Ownership*. All owners shall be persons who hold themselves out to be certified public accountants or public accountants and who perform for clients one or more types of services performed by certified public accountants or public accountants. Owners shall at all times own their equity in their own right and shall be the beneficial owners of the equity capital ascribed to them.
2. *Transfer of Ownership*. Provision shall be made requiring any owner who ceases to be eligible to be an equity owner to dispose of all his or her interest within a reasonable period to a person qualified to be an owner or to the entity.
3. *Directors and Officers*. The principal executive officer shall be an owner and a member of the entity's governing body. Lay governing body members shall not exercise any authority whatsoever over professional matters.
4. *Conduct*. The form of organization shall not change the obligation of its owners, directors, officers, and other employees to comply with the Code of Professional Conduct established by the American Institute of Certified Public Accountants.

Standards of Ethical Conduct for Management Accountants*

Management accountants have an obligation to the organizations they serve, their profession, the public, and themselves to maintain the highest standards of ethical conduct. In recognition of this obligation, the Institute of Management Accountants, formerly the National Association of Accountants, has adopted the following standards of ethical conduct for management accountants. Adherence to these standards is integral to achieving the *Objectives of Management Accounting*. Management accountants shall not commit acts contrary to these standards nor shall they condone the commission of such acts by others within their organizations.

Competence

Management accountants have a responsibility to:

- Maintain an appropriate level of professional competence by ongoing development of their knowledge and skills.

* *Statement of Management Accounting No. 1C*, Institute of Management Accountants (formerly National Association of Accountants), Montvale, N.J. 07645. Reprinted by permission.

- Perform their professional duties in accordance with relevant laws, regulations, and technical standards.
- Prepare complete and clear reports and recommendations after appropriate analyses of relevant and reliable information.

Confidentiality

Management accountants have a responsibility to:

- Refrain from disclosing confidential information acquired in the course of their work except when authorized, unless legally obligated to do so.
- Inform subordinates as appropriate regarding the confidentiality of information acquired in the course of their work and monitor their activities to assure the maintenance of that confidentiality.
- Refrain from using or appearing to use confidential information acquired in the course of their work for unethical or illegal advantage either personally or through third parties.

Integrity

Management accountants have a responsibility to:

- Avoid actual or apparent conflicts of interest and advise all appropriate parties of any potential conflict.
- Refrain from engaging in any activity that would prejudice their ability to carry out their duties ethically.
- Refuse any gift, favor, or hospitality that would influence or would appear to influence their actions.
- Refrain from either actively or passively subverting the attainment of the organization's legitimate and ethical objectives.
- Recognize and communicate professional limitations or other constraints that would preclude responsible judgment or successful performance of an activity.
- Communicate unfavorable as well as favorable information and professional judgments or opinions.
- Refrain from engaging in or supporting any activity that would discredit the profession.

Objectivity

Management accountants have a responsibility to:

- Communicate information fairly and objectively.
- Disclose fully all relevant information that could reasonably be expected to influence an intended user's understanding of the reports, comments, and recommendations presented.

Resolution of Ethical Conflict

In applying the standards of ethical conduct, management accountants may encounter problems in identifying unethical behavior or in resolving an ethical conflict. When faced with significant ethical issues, management accountants should follow the established policies of the organization bearing on the resolution of such conflict. If these policies do not resolve the ethical conflict, management accountants should consider the following course of action:

- Discuss such problems with the immediate superior except when it appears that the superior is involved, in which case the problem should be presented initially to the next higher managerial level. If satisfactory resolution cannot be achieved when the problem is initially presented, submit the issues to the next higher managerial level.

  If the immediate superior is the chief executive officer, or equivalent, the acceptable reviewing authority may be a group such as the audit committee, executive committee, board of directors, board of trustees, or owners. Contact with levels above the immediate superior should be initiated only with the superior's knowledge, assuming the superior is not involved.
- Clarify relevant concepts by confidential discussion with an objective advisor to obtain an understanding of possible courses of action.
- If the ethical conflict still exists after exhausting all levels of internal review, the management accountant may have no other recourse on significant matters than to resign from the organization and to submit an informative memorandum to an appropriate representative of the organization.

Except where legally prescribed, communication of such problems to authorities or individuals not employed or engaged by the organization is not considered appropriate.

User's Guide to GLAS (General Ledger Applications Software)

General Ledger Applications Software was developed by Richard D. Irwin, Inc. to accompany **Fundamental Accounting Principles,** Thirteenth Edition by Kermit D. Larson and Paul B. W. Miller. The software is designed to provide students with experience in using microcomputers in accounting by working selected end-of-chapter problems and practice sets. One master List of Accounts was created incorporating all accounts necessary to complete all problems and practice sets. Students will gain familiarity in working with a general ledger system similar to one they may encounter in a future job situation.

The first screen to appear when you access the system is a title screen. Press <ENTER> at this screen to continue to the data drive designation screen. Enter the full drive path location (A:\ or C:\GLAS) where you want the system to look for problems that have been previously worked. Press <ENTER> to continue to the last of the configuration screens. To continue with **Student Name,** enter your name as you wish for it to appear on all printed reports. This name will be permanently recorded and cannot be changed once it is accepted. Please check it for correctness before pressing <ENTER>.

Throughout the software, the following keys will always produce the following results:

Cursor Movement Keys

ARROW KEYS (left, right, up, down)

PAGE UP and **PAGE DOWN** moves the display up or down through long listings one screen at a time.

HOME and **END** will move the cursor to the beginning or end of a listing.

TAB and **SHIFT TAB** will move the cursor forward and backward between data entry fields.

HOME and **END** will move the cursor to the beginning or end of a data entry fields.

Operating Keys

ENTER accepts data that has been typed on the keyboard or selects menu items.

ESC terminates current operations and returns to the previous menu, for example, leaving the General Journal to return to the Record menu.

Editing Keys

SPACE BAR will advance the cursor one position to the right and will erase characters on the screen as it advances.

BACKSPACE will move the cursor one position to the left and will erase characters on the screen.

DELETE will delete the character located over the cursor.

Loading a Problem

Any time a problem is chosen from the Problem Selection Box a prompt will ask whether you wish to use Original Balances or Current Balances. Original Balances will load only the initial problem data as though no work had been done. Current Balances will load the problem as it was last saved.

Custom Problem

Near the bottom of the Problem Selection Box is the menu choice "Custom". Selecting this choice allows you to set up and work a problem that you or someone else has custom designed. As for all other problems, you will be asked if you wish Original Balances or Current Balances. When setting up a new problem, select Original Balances. You will now notice an additional selection (Edit) on the far right end of the Main Menu. Selecting Edit allows you to Add new accounts, customers, vendors, and employees; Change existing accounts, customers, vendors, and employees; or Delete accounts, customers, vendors, and employees.

Financial Ratios

The problem selection box contains the menu item RATIOS. This option is designed to be used on problems dealing specifically with financial ratios. To use this module, select FINANCIAL RATIOS from the OTHER Main Menu. The ratio module can be used to perform financial ratio calculations for any problem where they would be helpful.

User's Guide to SPATS (Spreadsheet Applications Template Software)

Spreadsheet Applications Template Software was developed by Richard D. Irwin, Inc. to accompany **Fundamental Accounting Principles,** Thirteenth Edition by Kermit D. Larson and Paul B. W. Miller. The software provides students with experience in using microcomputers in accounting by working selected end-of-chapter exercises and problems. SPATS will expose users to the spreadsheets that they will encounter in the future.

The columns of the electronic spreadsheets are identified by letters (A, B, C, etc.). The rows are numbered. A cell is the intersection of a row and a column and is identified with a letter and a number. For example, B6 is the cell located at the intersection of column B and row 6. The position of the cursor, or cell pointer, is called the active cell. The upper left corner of the screen identifies the active cell. The top lines of the spreadsheet are the prompt lines. The menu used to run, print, and save these templates will be located on the prompt lines. When entering labels, formulas, or numbers, your keystrokes are entered on the prompt lines until you press the <ENTER> key to record the data in the active cell. All files on the SPATS disk contain the basic format for solving problems from the text. Most problems have a data section and a solution section. The data section contains the basic facts given in the problem. The solution section requires you to enter the numbers, formulas, and labels to solve the problem. Templates are saved using the same problem or exercise number in the text. For example, E8–6.WK1 contains the template for Exercise 8–6. WK1 is the extension used for LOTUS® 1-2-3® files. WQ1 is the extension used for Quattro Pro files.

To retrieve a file, enter **/FR** (/ File Retrieve) and enter the name of the file. When the file is retrieved, you will see this menu:

Run Print Save What-If Graphics Exit

To select an option, move the menu pointer to the right or left and press <ENTER>. Use the right and left arrow keys to move the menu pointer. The purposes of each menu item are:

RUN: Moves the cursor to the position entering your name and allows you to begin solving the problem.

PRINT: Prints the various steps of the solution.

SAVE: Saves the file to the disk. This option should be selected each time you finish a problem or end the session.

WHAT-IF: Moves you to the what-if question.

GRAPHICS: Moves you to the graphics instructions and question.

EXIT: Erases the current worksheet and leaves you with a blank worksheet. Use this option carefully; if you exit before choosing the save option, you will lose your work.

After you select **Run** from the menu, enter your name. You will be asked to enter three types of data, identified by the words in capital letters, as follows:

LABEL: Used to describe the numbers on the template.

NUMBER: You may need to enter numbers.

FORMULA: Formulas are used on all templates to solve the problem. Formulas should contain cell references whenever possible. If you do not use cell references in developing your formulas, the what-if analyses will be difficult to complete. Entering FORMULAS: (The following conventions should be used in entering formulas):

1. All formulas must begin with a number or mathematical symbol.
2. Mathematical operations are indicated by the following characters:

+Addition −Subtraction *Multiplication \Division ^Exponentiation

3. No spaces should be included in formulas.
4. Parentheses are used to control the order in which the operations are performed.

Saving and Printing a Completed Template

After you have entered all labels, numbers, and formulas, you should save and print the template. Simultaneously press the ALT key and M key to return to the problem menu. Select the save option. Your template will be saved under the same name. For example, Problem 4–24 will be saved as P4–24.WK1. Select the print option from the menu. You will be asked to select the type of printer you are using: DOT Matrix or HP Laser. The final submenu will ask which part of the problem you wish to print, select Solution at this point. If your printout appears to be correct, you should continue to the what-if and graphics parts of the problem. If you detect any errors on the printout, correct the template and print a new solution.

Completing the What-If Analyses

If necessary, press <ALT> <M> to activate the problem menu. Select the What-If option. You will be asked a question that will require to change or interpret data on the original worksheet. Instructions above each what-if question direct your analysis. If you used cell references in developing your formulas, most of the what-if analyses will be relatively easy. If you did not use cell references, you will need to identify all the places in the solution that the changed data will affect. You should print your revised template, but do not save your revisions.

Completing the Graphics Analysis

Many problems have a graphics analysis section. You will be asked to create, modify, or interpret a graph. To move to the graphics section, select Graphics from the problem menu. Follow the instructions to complete the analysis. If you press F10 and do not see a graph, you do not have a monitor capable of displaying graphics. You should either move to a different computer or skip this section.

Index

Check Figures

Problem	Check Figure
1–1	Ending capital, $62,220
1–2	Ending capital, $5,955
1–3	Net income earned in 1993, $65,950
1–4	Ending capital, $6,075
1–5	Part 2. b., owner's equity, $19,400
1–6	No check figure
1–7	No check figure
1–8	No check figure
1–1A	Ending capital, $81,870
1–2A	Ending capital, $10,450
1–3A	Net income earned in 1993, $55,800
1–4A	Ending capital, $15,920
1–5A	Part 2. c., net income, $6,000
1–6A	No check figure
1–7A	No check figure
1–8A	No check figure
2–1	Trial balance totals, $341,000
2–2	Trial balance totals, $92,400
2–3	Trial balance totals, $16,370
2–4	Trial balance totals, $57,400
2–5	Trial balance totals, $51,140
2–6	No check figure
2–7	No check figure
2–1A	Trial balance totals, $188,350
2–2A	Trial balance totals, $73,700
2–3A	Trial balance totals, $11,605
2–4A	Trial balance totals, $25,500
2–5A	Trial balance totals, $24,140
2–6A	No check figure
2–7A	No check figure

Problem	Check Figure
Serial Problem	11/29/93 Cash balance, $3,110
3–1	b. Insurance Expense, $2,620 Dr.
3–2	Adjusted trial balance totals, $133,530
3–3	Adjusted trial balance totals, $272,420
3–4	Adjusted trial balance totals, $279,990
3–5	No check figure
3–6	Net loss, $(3,010)
3–7	a. Store Supplies Expense, $220.00 Dr.
3–8	No check figure
3–9	No check figure
3–1A	b. Insurance Expense, $1,035 Dr.
3–2A	Adjusted trial balance totals, $134,090
3–3A	Adjusted trial balance totals, $276,090
3–4A	Adjusted trial balance totals, $283,990
3–5A	No check figure
3–6A	Net income, $183,270
3–7A	a. Store Supplies Expense, $850 Cr.
3–8A	No check figure
3–9A	No check figure
Serial Problem	Adjusted trial balance totals, $16,196.25
4–1	Adjusted trial balance totals, $88,320
4–2	Adjusted trial balance totals, $149,095
4–3	Adjusted trial balance totals, $79,270
4–4	12/31, Income Summary, $372,145 Cr.
4–5	No check figure
4–6	Adjusted trial balance totals, 6/30/93, $91,225

Problem	Check Figure
4–7	No check figure
4–8	No check figure
4–1A	Adjusted trial balance totals, $186,765
4–2A	Adjusted trial balance totals, $149,910
4–3A	Adjusted trial balance totals, $79,285
4–4A	12/31, Income Summary, $410,450 Cr.
4–5A	No check figure
4–6A	Adjusted trial balance totals, 6/30/93, $61,270
4–7A	No check figure
4–8A	No check figure
Serial Problem	Post-closing trial balance totals, $8,808.25
Comprehensive Problem	Net income, $30,050; Total assets $368,435
5–1	No check figure
5–2	Net income, $41,664
5–3	Net income, $42,366
5–4	Net income, $42,366
5–5	Net income, $50,370
5–6	Net income, $50,370
5–7	Net income, $50,857
5–8	No check figure
5–9	No check figure
5–1A	No check figure
5–2A	Net income, $110,352
5–3A	Net income, $50,592
5–4A	Net income, $50,592
5–5A	Net income, $57,510
5–6A	Net income, $57,510
5–7A	Net income, $56,100
5–8A	No check figure
5–9A	No check figure
Serial Problem	Net income, $7,265.30; Total assets, $18,287.30
6–1	Trial balance totals, $153,830
6–2	Trial balance totals, $153,656
6–3	Trial balance totals, $245,677
6–4	Trial balance totals, $195,118
6–5	Trial balance totals, $312,167
6–6	No check figure
6–7	No check figure
6–1	Trial balance totals, $154,920
6–2A	Trial balance totals, $120,986
6–3	Trial balance totals, $255,491
6–4A	Trial balance totals, $179,363
6–5A	Trial balance totals, $105,915

Problem	Check Figure
6–6A	No check figure
6–7A	No check figure
Comprehensive Problem	Net income, $10,881; Total assets, $300,551
7–1	Sept. 29, Cash, $98.85 Cr.
7–2	Part 3. Cash credits, $178.75, $178.80
7–3	Part 1. Cash credits, $171.00, $87.25
7–4	Reconciled balance, $12,942
7–5	Reconciled balance, $7,946
7–6	Net income both methods, $42,636
7–7	No check figure
7–8	No check figure
7–9	July 31, Vouchers payable balance, $5,833
7–1A	May 31, Cash, $97.45 Cr.
7–2A	Part 3. Cash credits, $147.25, $147.50
7–3A	Part 1. Cash credits, $192.90, $242.40
7–4A	Reconciled balance, $4,317
7–5A	Reconciled balance, $1,828
7–6A	Net loss both methods, $53,155
7–7A	No check figure
7–8A	No check figure
7–9A	Oct. 31, Vouchers payable balance, $3,066
8–1	Part 3. Loss on Market Decline of Short-Term Investments, $1,100 Dr.
8–2	No check figure
8–3	No check figure
8–4	Part 2. Bad Debts Expense, $58,185 Dr.
8–5	1993, Bad Debts Expense, $1,292.40 Dr.
8–6	December 31, Allowance for Doubtful Accounts, $4,908 Dr.
8–7	No check figure
8–8	12/31/94, Allowance to Reduce Short-Term Investments to Market, $5,754 Cr.
8–9	No check figure
8–10	No check figure
8–1A	Part 3. Loss on Market Decline of Short-Term Investments, $3,551.67 Dr.
8–2A	No check figure
8–3A	No check figure
8–4A	Part 2. Bad Debts Expense, $38,600 Dr.
8–5A	1993, Bad Debts Expense, $952.50 Dr.

Problem	Check Figure
8–6A	December 28, Allowance for Doubtful Accounts, $2,555.83 Dr.
8–7A	No check figure
8–8A	12/31/94, Allowance to Reduce Short-Term Investments to Market, $11,576 Cr.
8–9A	No check figure
8–10A	No check figure
9–1	Cost of units sold, $370,000, $391,250, $377,265
9–2	Net income, $42,200, $39,800, $41,261
9–3	Lower of cost or market (inventory as a whole), $48,975, $31,800, $11,850
9–4	No check figure
9–5	Ending FIFO inventory, $210; LIFO, $140
9–6	Inventory shortage at cost, $2,282
9–7	Inventory shortage at cost, $6,960
9–8	Estimated theft loss, $164,954
9–9	Estimated March 31 inventory, $171,720
9–10	No check figure
9–11	No check figure
9–1A	Cost of units sold, $282,000, $319,250, $301,125
9–2A	Net income, $76,900, $62,550, $70,300
9–3A	Lower of cost or market (inventory as a whole), $78,700, $52,960, $39,550
9–4A	No check figure
9–5A	Ending FIFO inventory, $1,140; LIFO, $855
9–6A	Inventory shortage at cost, $5,829
9–7A	Inventory shortage at cost, $13,596
9–8A	Estimated theft loss, $492,247
9–9A	Estimated March 31 inventory, $86,835
9–10A	No check figure
9–11A	No check figure
10–1	Part 2. total accumulated depreciation, $42,500
10–2	Part 3. Depreciation Expense, Land Improvements (Three), $17,718.75
10–3	Part 2. 1994 depreciation expense, $44,841.88
10–4	Depreciation 1992: Machine One, $31,775; Machine Two, $10,250
10–5	Estimated life six years: Double declining balance, $3,330; Sum-of-the-years' digits, $2,860

Problem	Check Figure
10–6	No check figure
10–1A	Part 2. total accumulated depreciation, $69,600
10–2A	Part 3. Depreciation Expense, Land Improvements (B), $7,665
10–3A	Part 2. 1994 depreciation expense, $22,050
10–4A	Depreciation 1992: Machine One, $10,680; Machine Two, $9,160
10–5A	Estimated life eight years: Double-declining balance, $5,000; Sum-of-the-years'-digits, $4,440
10–6A	No check figure
11–1	Ending account balances: Plant Equip., $34,275; Accum. Depr., $6,475
11–2	July 2, 1995, Accum. Depr., Delivery Equip., $17,045.00 Dr.
11–3	Loss on Sale of Machinery (107–25), $7,956.05
11–4	Part 2. Depletion of Mineral Dep., $149,625
11–5	Goodwill, $79,600 or $59,700
11–6	Part 1. June 30, 1994, Loss from Fire, $14,580; Part 2. Dec. 31, 1995, Depr. Expense, Machinery, $10,000
11–7	No check figure
11–8	No check figure
11–1A	Ending account balances: Plant Equip., $66,340; Accum. Depr., $6,880
11–2A	Sept. 29, 1995, Accum. Depr., Delivery Equip., $34,130 Dr.
11–3A	Gain on Sale of Machinery (11–009), $3,927.60
11–4A	Part 2. Depletion of Mineral Dep., $151,200
11–5A	Goodwill, $46,800 or $28,080
11–6A	Part 1. Oct. 1, 1996, Loss from Fire, $19,300; Part 2. Dec. 31, 1994, Depr. Expense, Machinery, $12,400
11–7A	No check figure
11–8A	No check figure
12–1	Part 1. July 31, Warranty Expense, $255; Part 2. Nov. 30, Property Taxes Expense, $1,080
12–2	No check figure
12–3	Payment Plan C, $5,928,120
12–4	Part 4. Long-term notes pay., $355,869 (net)

Problem	Check Figure
12–5	Part 4. Long-term lease liab., $25,350 (net)
12–6	Part 5. Long-term lease liab., $21,406 (net)
12–7	No check figure
12–8	No check figure
12–9	Part 1. Accrued Payroll Payable, $33,368.90
12–10	No check figure
12–11	No check figure
12–1A	Part 1. Mar. 31, Warranty Expense, $1,560; Part 2, Oct. 31, Property Taxes Expense, $660
12–2A	No check figure
12–3A	Payment Plan C, $918,321
12–4A	Part 4. Long-term notes pay., $354,533 (net)
12–5A	Part 4. Long-term lease liab., $421,161 (net)
12–6A	Part 5. Long-term lease liab., $66,961 (net)
12–7A	No check figure
12–8A	No check figure
12–9A	Part 1. Accrued Payroll Payable, $85,377
12–10A	No check figure
12–11A	No check figure
Comprehensive Problem	Net income, $147,954; total assets, $239,780
13–1	(c) Katz, $39,500; Reeves, $36,100; Troy, $48,900
13–2	Year 3—Nuñez, $18,975; Parker, $56,025
13–3	(c) Marshall, $77,541; Spiller, $62,292; Rand, $85,167
13–4	Part 1. (e) Gully, Capital, $69,000 Dr.; Part 2. (c) Speck, Capital, $11,625 Cr.
13–5	(d) Chapel, Capital, $41,516.66 Dr.; Page, Capital, $51,133.34 Dr.
13–6	Part 3—Rohan, Capital, $119,714.80 Dr.; Keene, Capital, $46,507.40 Dr.
13–7	No check figure
13–8	No check figure
13–1A	(c) Jones, $59,400; Rogers, $44,120; Thompson, $31,480
13–2A	Year 2—Jackson, $5,700; Fletcher, $32,300
13–3A	(c) Phillips, $34,040; Fong, $33,360; Campos, $52,600
13–4A	Part 1. (e) Soltani, Capital, $303,000 Dr.; Part 2. (c) Soltani, Capital, $25,200 Cr.

Problem	Check Figure
13–5A	(d) Huggins, Capital, $36,800 Dr.; Hart, Capital, $41,200 Dr.
13–6A	Part 3—Daily, Capital, $148,637.20 Dr.; Murray, Capital, $174,721.50 Dr.; Dryer, Capital, $32,084.30 Dr.
13–7A	No check figure
13–8A	No check figure
V–1	Part 4. Gain on sale of machinery, $22,000
V–2	Net purchasing power loss, $2,741
V–3	Part 1. (c) $1,018,514
V–4	No check figure
V–1A	Part 4. Gain on sale of machinery, $25,000
V–2A	Net purchasing power gain, $1,019
V–3A	Part 1. (c) $239,529
V–4A	No check figure
14–1	Total stockholders' equity, $1,987,000
14–2	Total stockholders' equity, $1,831,550
14–3	Part 1 (c). $129.00 preferred, $13.00 common
14–4	(c) 1996, $15.00 preferred, $1.50 common
14–5	(4) book value per common share, $14.40
14–6	No check figure
14–7	No check figure
14–1A	Total stockholders' equity, $1,998,000
14–2A	Total stockholders' equity, $1,444,000
14–3A	Part 1 (c). $139.00 preferred, $10.70 common
14–4A	(b) 1995, $13.50 preferred, $0.70 common
14–5A	(4) book value per common share, $11.01
14–6A	No check figure
14–7A	No check figure
15–1	Retained earnings, 12/31/93, $200,250
15–2	Total stockholders' equity, Oct. 12, $1,777,095
15–3	Net income, $469,740
15–4	Net income, $34,805
15–5	Cumulative effect of change, $63,194
15–6	1991 net income per share, $10.40
15–7	No check figure
15–8	No check figure
15–1A	Retained earnings, 12/31/93, $671,900
15–2A	Total stockholders' equity, July 28, $8,250,000
15–3A	Net income, $547,420

Problem	Check Figure
15–4A	Net income, $543,230
15–5A	Cumulative effect of change, $(126,000)
15–6A	1991 net income per share, $3.75
15–7A	No check figure
15–8A	No check figure
16–1	Beginning-of-period principal balance, 11/30/95, $124,794
16–2	12/31/93, Ending carrying amount, $1,181,453
16–3	12/31/93, Ending carrying amount, $5,303,756
16–4	12/31/93, Interest Expense, $181,848 Dr.
16–5	12/1/95, Premium on Bonds Payable, $5,161 Dr.
16–6	12/31/93, Interest Expense (interest method), $268,418
16–7	Beginning-of-period fund balance, 12/31/96, $53,625
16–8	No check figure
16–9	No check figure
16–1A	Beginning-of-period principal balance, 12/31/95, $334,053
16–2A	12/31/93, Ending carrying amount, $3,871,856
16–3A	12/31/93, Ending carrying amount, $792,231
16–4A	12/31/93, Interest Expense, $62,491 Dr.
16–5A	10/1/95, Premium on Bonds Payable, $12,423 Dr.
16–6A	12/31/93, Interest Expense (interest method), $431,713
16–7A	Beginning-of-period fund balance, 12/31/96, $125,511
16–8A	No check figure
16–9A	No check figure
17–1	Net cash provided by operating activities, $48,000
17–2	Analysis of Changes column totals, $2,925,000
17–3	Total adjustments, $(19,000)
17–4	Analysis of Changes column totals, $193,000
17–5	Net cash provided by operating activities, $26,700
17–6	Analysis of Changes column totals, $2,025,400
17–7	Total adjustments, $(32,300)
17–8	Analysis of Changes column totals, $412,300

Problem	Check Figure
17–9	No check figure
17–10	No check figure
17–1A	Net cash provided by operating activities, $100,100
17–2A	Analysis of Changes column totals, $3,524,300
17–3A	Total adjustments, $(17,800)
17–4A	Analysis of Changes column totals, $383,300
17–5A	Net cash provided by operating activities, $96,100
17–6A	Analysis of Changes column totals, $3,430,100
17–7A	Total adjustments, plus $58,100
17–8A	Analysis of Changes column totals, $360,200
17–9A	No check figure
17–10A	No check figure
18–1	Carrying value per share: Part 1. $5.20; Part 2. $4.55
18–2	Total consolidated assets, $2,950,350
18–3	Total consolidated assets, $975,980
18–4	Part 2. 1993 total foreign exchange gain, $497.25
18–5	No check figure
18–6	No check figure
18–1A	Carrying value per share: Part 1. $11.91; Part 2. $10.00
18–2A	Total consolidated assets, $1,781,950
18–3A	Total consolidated assets, $2,781,690
18–4A	Part 2. 1993 total foreign exchange gain, $1,212.30
18–5A	No check figure
18–6A	No check figure
19–1	Trend percentage, 1994 total assets, 101.95
19–2	Trend percentage, 1994 total assets, 173.6
19–3	(h) Total asset turnover, 1.7 times
19–4	Part 2. dividend yield: Monarch Co., 7.5%; Command Co., 7.5%
19–5	No check figure
19–6	No check figure
19–7	No check figure
19–1A	Trend percentage, 1994 total assets, 120.51
19–2A	Trend percentage, 1994 total assets, 98.5
19–3A	(h) Total asset turnover, 2.1 times
19–4A	Part 2. dividend yield: Sun Co., 3.0%; Lakeway Co., 3.0%

Problem	Check Figure
19–5A	No check figure
19–6A	No check figure
19–7A	No check figure
20–1	Overhead rate, 130.0%
20–2	Cost of goods manufactured, $618,080
20–3	Overhead rate, 120.0%
20–4	Ending finished goods inventory, $170,000
20–5	Cost of goods manufactured, $450,000
20–6	No check figure
20–7	Turnover ratios: raw materials, 5.3; finished goods, 12.3
20–1A	Overhead rate, 70.0%
20–2A	Cost of goods manufactured, $770,600
20–3A	Overhead rate, 150%
20–4A	Ending finished goods inventory, $126,000
20–5A	Cost of goods manufactured, $669,500
20–6A	No check figure
20–7A	Turnover ratios: raw materials, 5.3; finished goods, 12.3
21–1	Cost of goods manufactured (Jobs 888 and 889), $24,150
21–2	Net income, $9,800
21–3	Finished goods inventory (Job 95), $51,000
21–4	Part 2. Factory Overhead, $800 Cr.
21–5	Balance in Factory Overhead, $384 credit; overapplied
21–6	No check figure
21–7	No check figure
21–1A	Cost of goods manufactured (Jobs 313 and 314), $80,330
21–2A	Net income, $44,050
21–3A	Finished goods inventory (Job 63), $29,800
21–4A	Part 2. Factory Overhead, $2,000 Dr.
21–5A	Balance in Factory Overhead, $800 credit; overapplied
21–6A	No check figure
21–7A	No check figure
22–1	Cost of goods sold, $562,000
22–2	Direct labor cost per equivalent unit, $1.44
22–3	Part 2. costs per equivalent unit: materials, $8.00; labor, $4.00; overhead, $5.00
22–4	Part 2. total costs transferred to finished goods, $340,000

Problem	Check Figure
22–5	Part 2. total costs transferred to finished goods, $862,840
22–6	No check figure
22–7	No check figure
22–1A	Cost of goods sold, $75,000
22–2A	Direct materials cost per equivalent unit, $4.22
22–3A	Part 2. costs per equivalent unit: materials, $1.70; labor, $2.00; overhead, $0.80
22–4A	Part 2. total costs transferred to finished goods, $760,500
22–5A	Part 2. total costs transferred to finished goods, $363,000
22–6A	No check figure
22–7A	No check figure
Comprehensive Problem	Part 5. gross profit, $359,300
23–1	Part 2. Total occupancy cost to Baldwin, $25,140
23–2	Forecasted combined net income, $95,700
23–3	Forecasted net income without Dept. K, $58,220
23–4	Net income from No. 1 tomatoes, $143,820
23–5	Cookware contribution to overhead, $215,600
23–6	Plant controllable costs, $9,000 under budget
23–7	Games revenue over escapable expenses, $375,000
23–8	No check figure
23–1A	Part 2. Total occupancy cost to Amado, $11,440
23–2A	Forecasted combined net income, $161,200
23–3A	Forecasted net income without Dept. 2, $58,350
23–4A	Net income from No. 1 kiwis, $91,800
23–5A	Soccer contribution to overhead, $97,500
23–6A	Plant controllable costs, $10,500 under budget
23–7A	Chocolate revenue over escapable expenses, $75,000
23–8A	No check figure
24–1	Slope of cost line, $0.665 per sales dollar
24–2	Part 5. After-tax income, $210,000
24–3	Part 5. Unit sales, 6,800 units
24–4	Net income under new plan, $191,800

Problem	Check Figure
24–5	Part 4. After-tax income, Product C, $650,000
24–6	New plan break-even point, 350 composite units
24–7	Total cost at 160 units, $4,174
24–8	No check figure
24–1A	Slope of cost line, $0.29 per sales dollar
24–2A	Part 5. After-tax income, $29,250
24–3A	Part 5. Unit sales, 27,200 units
24–4A	Net income under Plan 2, $71,400
24–5A	Part 4. After-tax income, Product L, $114,240
24–6A	New plan break-even point, 950 composite units
24–7A	Total cost at 550 units, $11,112.50
24–8A	No check figure
25–1	Cost of plastic purchases, $612,500
25–2	Product One purchases for June, 62,000 units
25–3	Budgeted total disbursements for July, $314,250
25–4	Budgeted ending cash balance for June, $27,401
25–5	Budgeted net income for May, $36,968
25–6	Budgeted net income for quarter, $153,436
25–7	No check figure
25–8	No check figure
25–1A	Cost of clay purchases, $473,600
25–2A	Product Fifty purchases for October, 9,500 units
25–3A	Budgeted total disbursements for August, $138,550
25–4A	Budgeted ending cash balance for May, $30,000
25–5A	Budgeted net income for February, $73,192
25–6A	Budgeted net income for quarter, $18,645
25–7A	No check figure
25–8A	No check figure
26–1	Budgeted income at 12,000 units, $121,840
26–2	Total variance in income, $26,060 favorable
26–3	Labor price variance, $11,000 favorable
26–4	Total overhead controllable variance, $1,150 favorable

Problem	Check Figure
26–5	Overhead volume variance, $10,000 unfavorable
26–6	Goods in Process Inventory (for overhead variances), $502,400 Dr.
26–7	Total costs at 200,000 units under new plan, $2,250,000
26–8	No check figure
26–1A	Budgeted income at 60,000 units, $101,800
26–2A	Total variance in income, $25,880 unfavorable
26–3A	Labor price variance, $7,750 favorable
26–4A	Total overhead controllable variance, $375 favorable
26–5A	Overhead controllable variance, $790 favorable
26–6A	Goods in Process Inventory (for overhead variances), $219,700 Dr.
26–7A	Total costs at 100,000 units under new plan, $1,000,000
26–8A	No check figure
27–1	Net present value of investment, $11,548
27–2	Return on average investment in Project A, 16.25%
27–3	Combined operating income, $138,000
27–4	Net present value of investment (MACRS), $3,545
27–5	Part 3. Units of B to be produced, 304 units
27–6	Part 1. Units of K to be produced, 3,000 units
27–7	No check figure
27–1A	Net present value of investment, $1,149 (negative)
27–2A	Return on average investment in Project 42, 6.1%
27–3A	Combined operating income, $73,300
27–4A	Net present value of investment (MACRS), $3,750
27–5A	Part 3. Units of L to be produced, 420 units
27–6A	Part 1. Units of J to be produced, 6,400 units
27–7A	No check figure
Appendix H	No check figures
Appendix I	
I–1	Taxable income, $123,299
I–1A	Taxable income, $80,396

413 Sales
414 Sales returns and allowances
415 Sales discounts

Cost of Goods Sold Items

501 Amortization of patents
502 Cost of goods sold
503 Depletion of mine deposit
505 Purchases
506 Purchases returns and allowances
507 Purchases discounts
508 Transportation-in

Manufacturing Accounts

520 Raw materials purchases
521 Freight-in on raw materials
530 Factory payroll
531 Direct labor
540 Factory overhead
541 Indirect materials
542 Indirect labor
543 Factory insurance expired
544 Factory supervision
545 Factory supplies used
546 Factory utilities
547 Miscellaneous production costs
548 Property taxes on factory building
549 Property taxes on factory equipment
550 Rent on factory building
551 Repairs, factory equipment
552 Small tools written off
560 Depreciation of factory equipment
561 Depreciation of factory building

Standard Cost Variance Accounts

580 Direct material quantity variance
581 Direct material price variance
582 Direct labor quantity variance
583 Direct labor price variance
584 Factory overhead volume variance
585 Factory overhead controllable variance

Expenses

Amortization and Depreciation Expenses

601 Amortization expense, ____________
602 Amortization expense, copyrights
604 Depreciation expense, boats
605 Depreciation expense, automobiles
606 Depreciation expense, building ____________
607 Depreciation expense, building ____________
608 Depreciation expense, land improvements ____________
609 Depreciation expense, land improvements ____________
610 Depreciation expense, law library
611 Depreciation expense, trucks
612 Depreciation expense, ____________ equipment
613 Depreciation expense, ____________ equipment
614 Depreciation expense, ____________
615 Depreciation expense, ____________

Employee Related Expenses

620 Office salaries expense
621 Sales salaries expense
622 Salaries expense
623 ____________ wages expense
624 Employees' benefits expense
625 Payroll taxes expense

Financial Expenses

630 Cash over and short
631 Discounts lost
633 Interest expense

Insurance Expenses

635 Insurance expense, delivery equipment
636 Insurance expense, office equipment
637 Insurance expense, ____________

Rental Expenses

640 Rent expense
641 Rent expense, office space
642 Rent expense, selling space
643 Press rental expense
644 Truck rental expense
645 ____________ rental expense

Supplies Expense

650 Office supplies expense
651 Store supplies expense
652 ____________ supplies expense
653 ____________ supplies expense

Miscellaneous Expenses

655 Advertising expense